The World's Great Speeches

Edited by

LEWIS COPELAND,
LAWRENCE W. LAMM

and

STEPHEN J. McKENNA

Fourth Enlarged (1999) Edition

For Reference

Not to be taken from this room

DOVER PUBLICATIONS, INC.
Mineola, New York

Acknowledgment

"Earl of Spencer: Tribute to Diana, Princess of Wales," London, England, 1997, is reprinted with permission of the Author.

Bibliographical Note

This Dover edition, first published in 1999, is a revised and enlarged republication of the third revised and updated edition published by Dover Publications, Inc., in 1973. The book was first published by Doubleday & Co., Inc., in 1942. Part VII, Important Speeches of 1974–1997 has been added in the 1999 edition, as has a new Introduction.

Library of Congress Cataloging-in-Publication Data

The world's great speeches / edited by Lewis Copeland, Lawrence H. Lamm, and Stephen J. McKenna. — 4th enl. 1999 ed.
    p.   cm.
    ISBN 0-486-40903-1
    1. Speeches, addresses, etc. I. Copeland, Lewis. II. Lamm, Lawrence W.
III. McKenna, Stephen J.
PN6121.W66   1999
808.85—dc21
                                           99-32880
                                              CIP

Manufactured in the United States of America
Dover Publications, Inc., 31 East 2nd Street, Mineola, N.Y. 11501

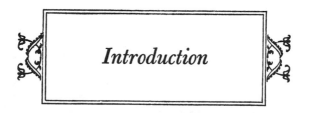

Introduction

TO THE THIRD ENLARGED EDITION

The editors welcome this opportunity to bring *The World's Great Speeches* up to date once more, by the addition of Part V, Important Speeches of the Sixties.

All of the speeches included in the Revised Edition of 1958 are present here in the same sequence and grouping as before. The new material appears in the later pages of the book.

In choosing addresses for Part V, we have sought, as in the earlier Parts, to present material which is significant historically and culturally and which will be welcome both for reading and reference. Although the largest number of addresses is from the fields of statesmanship and political life, other areas of wide interest are also represented.

The new Part is divided into two sections: "XIII. The United States" and "XIV. World Affairs." We commence the Part with President Kennedy's memorable Inaugural Address. The sequence in the Part as a whole is basically chronological, but not rigidly so where enhanced reading interest is gained by placing speeches on related or contrasted subjects next to one another.

As in the earlier Parts, a biographical note precedes each speaker's section, with a second note where there is more than one address by the same speaker. Thus the occasion on which each address was given is clearly indicated.

We are very glad to be able at this time to include a survey of speeches by black Americans as a supplement at the end of the volume. These addresses, which extend from Henry Highland Garnet (1815–1881) to Malcolm X (1925–1965), were selected by Philip S. Foner, professor of history at Lincoln University.

L. W. L.

1972

INTRODUCTION TO THE SECOND EDITION

This revised edition of *The World's Great Speeches* retains all the features which made the first edition a classic in its field, a book popular both for enjoyable reading and as a valuable aid to public speakers.

In preparing this new edition, the publishers have added many outstanding speeches of our own day, speeches delivered during the years since the original edition. Thus, the book is once more a convenient handbook of the best in current spoken thinking on vital national, international, political, economic, and cultural topics, as well as a treasury of the great spoken thoughts of earlier times right through history.

The organization of the book differs somewhat from that of the original edition as described in the Introduction to the First Edition, which we retain as a statement of the philosophy of selection used then and continued in choosing the additions for the Revision.

We wish to point out that the book is now divided into four major sections. Part I, Great Speeches of Earlier Times, remains as it was. Part II, Great Speeches of Recent Times, represents the period following the First World War and the entire period of the Second World War. Part III, Great Speeches of the Modern Period, gives us the years after the Second World War and continues up to the present, covering both domestic and international affairs. Part IV, Informal Speeches, corresponds to the final Part of the original edition. But it is interesting to note that a few of the speeches included in Chapter XI on International Affairs are presented in an informal setting and may therefore be considered examples of informal speeches. This is true of the talks by Dylan Thomas, Frank Lloyd Wright, and Adlai E. Stevenson to the graduating class at Smith.

As in the original edition, at the end of the book the reader will find an Index of Topics, an Index by Nations, and an alphabetical Index of Speakers. The Topical Index will be especially convenient for those who wish to use the book as a guide in the planning of their own public addresses, or for locating quotable passages on specific subjects.

It is the hope of the editors that the Revised Edition will prove in every way as valuable and interesting as the original book and that its welcome will be increased by the inclusion of so many outstanding and varied present-day speeches.

L. W. L.

1958

INTRODUCTION TO THE FIRST EDITION

"Each crisis brings its word and deed," said Whittier.

Human history is primarily a record of important and dramatic events, which have often been profoundly affected by great speeches. From the days of Greece and Rome to our own day, oratory and statesmanship have gone hand in hand. Many men of the sword have been noted also for their stirring eloquence.

Speeches have their origins in antiquity. Perhaps the funeral oration was the first public utterance. As man's progress developed, the need for speech-making increased. The more gifted speakers became the law-makers and leaders. By the time civilization flowered in Athens, oratory became a fine art of government and culture. And so it has continued to our own stormy times.

In making the selection for this volume care has been exercised to include not merely the famous masterpieces of eloquence but also the great historic addresses which are noteworthy for their powerful thought and logical presentation. This collection therefore embraces practically all forms of oratory—fiery and impassioned speeches, learned and philosophic speeches, reflective and poetic speeches, satirical and humorous speeches.

The book has been divided into two major sections. The first section includes the great speeches of earlier times. Here will be found the moving farewell of Socrates, speeches of Demosthenes, Cicero, and other noted orators of Greece and Rome. This section continues with the great orations of the European continent—the religious masterpieces of Luther, Calvin and Pope Leo XIII, the flaming orations of the leaders of the French Revolution, the ennobling utterances of Kossuth, Gambetta, and Zola, and the many others whose speeches are an important part of European history.

This first section also contains the famous speeches of Great Britain and the United States—under separate headings—down to the end of the First World War. In the British chapter will be found the great speeches of Burke, Pitt, Sheridan, Cobden, Bright, Gladstone and Disraeli,.as well as those of the leaders of the First World War.

The American chapter is quite comprehensive. Here may be heard the eloquent voices of Patrick Henry, Samuel Adams and other leaders of the Revolution; the convincing logic of Hamilton, Madison, Marshall and others favoring or opposing the Federal Constitution; the great debates over slavery and secession between Webster, Calhoun, Sumner, Clay, Douglas and Lincoln; the masterpieces of America's later great orators— Ingersoll, Bryan, Beveridge, Debs and many more. The historic Presidential addresses of Washington, Jefferson, Jackson, Lincoln, Cleveland, Wilson are a noteworthy part of this chapter.

One of the outstanding features of this collection is the inclusion of a chapter of rarely printed, significant speeches by such eminent national leaders as Bolivar, Sun Yat-sen, Gandhi and others.

The second section contains the great speeches of our times. The first part of this section includes the speeches of leaders of American industry, labor, and government. This is followed by a number of speeches on international affairs, and by a very full chapter on the Second World War. This chapter includes the important speeches of Chamberlain, Churchill, Hitler, Mussolini, Pétain, Stalin, Konoye, Chiang Kai-shek, and other present-day world figures. Here is history in the making.

In the last part of the second section we have the great speeches of American national defense—those of Franklin Delano Roosevelt, Wendell L. Willkie, Cordell Hull, Henry L. Stimson, Charles A. Lindbergh, Harold L.Ickes, Norman Thomas, and many others who are presenting this fundamental issue to the American people today.

The third section* is composed entirely of informal and after-dinner speeches which are mainly light, witty and humorous. Here will be found the amusing and laugh-provoking speeches of such masters as Depew, Choate, Mark Twain, Barrie, Irvin Cobb, and others.

A fourth section has been added,† which is devoted to addresses dealing with the participation of the United States in the Second World War.

Even though almost all the historic and important addresses are printed in full, it has been possible to include in this volume about 250 speeches delivered by more than 210 speakers. In each case the speaker and speech are preceded by biographical and introductory notes. At the end of the book, the index by topics will aid the reader in quest of certain types of speeches or quotable material; this index covers a wide choice of topics, including Politics, Patriotism, Religion, Fine Arts, Woman, War, Peace, Philosophy, Humor, etc. In the index by nations, all speakers are also classified according to countries of origin. An alphabetical index of speakers concludes the book.

This book should prove a treasure-house for public speakers and those who are studying the art of public speaking. At the same time it is a book for entertaining reading, inspiration and enlightenment. For the world's great speeches are studded with gems of historic fact, profound wisdom, and exalted vision.

LEWIS COPELAND

* PART IV of present edition
† PART II, last section of present edition

Contents

viii   *Contents*

II *The European Continent*

III *Great Britain and Ireland*

IV *The United States*

V *Canada*

PART II

GREAT SPEECHES OF RECENT TIMES

VII *Domestic Affairs in the United States*

VIII *World Affairs and the Second World War*

Contents

IX *The United States and The Second World War*

PART III
GREAT SPEECHES OF THE MODERN PERIOD

X *United States Government*

Contents

XI *International Affairs and the United Nations*

Contents

PART V

IMPORTANT SPEECHES OF THE SIXTIES

XIII *United States*

XIV *World Affairs*

PART VI

SURVEY OF SPEECHES
BY BLACK AMERICANS

Compiled by Philip S. Foner

PART VII

IMPORTANT SPEECHES
OF 1974–1997

Compiled by Stephen J. McKenna

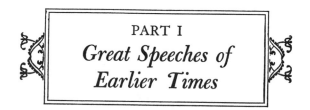

PART I
Great Speeches of
Earlier Times

I. GREECE AND ROME

Pericles

[495? b.c.–429 b.c.]

*The Age of Pericles is famous for the splendid development of the
fine arts. Pericles, the brilliant Athenian statesman, gave mankind one
of the greatest funeral orations ever made. This address was delivered
in 431 b.c., as a memorial to the first Athenian soldiers who fell in
the Peloponnesian War.*

FUNERAL ORATION

Many of those who have spoken before me on these occasions have commended the author of that law which we now are obeying for having
instituted an oration to the honor of those who sacrifice their lives in
fighting for their country. For my part, I think it sufficient for men who
have proved their virtue in action, by action to be honored for it—by
such as you see the public gratitude now performing about this funeral;
and that the virtues of many ought not to be endangered by the management of any one person when their credit must precariously depend on
his oration, which may be good and may be bad. Difficult, indeed, it is,
judiciously to handle a subject where even probable truth will hardly
gain assent. The hearer, enlightened by a long acquaintance, and warm
in his affection, may quickly pronounce everything unfavorably expressed
in respect to what he wishes and what he knows—while the stranger
pronounces all exaggerated through envy of those deeds which he is
conscious are above his own achievement. For the praises bestowed upon
others are then only to be endured, when men imagine they can do those
feats they hear to have been done; they envy what they cannot equal,
and immediately pronounce it false. Yet, as this solemnity hath received its
sanction from the authority of our ancestors, it is my duty also to obey
the law and to endeavor to procure, as far as I am able, the good-will
and approbation of all my audience.

I shall therefore begin first with our forefathers, since both justice and
decency require we should on this occasion bestow on them an honorable
remembrance. In this our country they kept themselves always firmly
settled, and through their valor handed it down free to every since-
succeeding generation. Worthy, indeed, of praise are they, and yet more
worthy are our immediate fathers, since, enlarging their own inheritance
into the extensive empire which we now possess, they bequeathed that,
their work of toil, to us their sons. Yet even these successes we ourselves

here present, we who are yet in the strength and vigor of our days, have nobly improved, and have made such provisions for this our Athens that now it is all-sufficient in itself to answer every exigence of war and of peace. I mean not here to recite those martial exploits by which these ends were accomplished, or the resolute defenses we ourselves and our fathers have made against the formidable invasions of Barbarians and Greeks—your own knowledge of these will excuse the long detail. But by what methods we have risen to this height of glory and power, by what polity and by what conduct we are thus aggrandized, I shall first endeavor to show, and then proceed to the praise of the deceased. These, in my opinion, can be no impertinent topics on this occasion; the discussion of them must be beneficial to this numerous company of Athenians and of strangers.

We are happy in a form of government which cannot envy the laws of our neighbors—for it hath served as a model to others, but is original at Athens. And this our form, as committed not to the few, but to the whole body of the people, is called a democracy. How different soever in a private capacity, we all enjoy the same general equality our laws are fitted to preserve; and superior honors just as we excel. The public administration is not confined to a particular family, but is attainable only by merit. Poverty is not a hindrance, since whoever is able to serve his country meets with no obstacle to preferment from his first obscurity. The offices of the state we go through without obstructions from one another; and live together in the mutual endearments of private life without suspicions; not angry with a neighbor for following the bent of his own humor, nor putting on that countenance of discontent, which pains though it cannot punish—so that in private life we converse without diffidence or damage, while we dare not on any account offend against the public, through the reverence we bear to the magistrates and the laws, chiefly to those enacted for redress of the injured, and to those unwritten, a breach of which is thought a disgrace. Our laws have further provided for the mind most frequent intermissions of care by the appointment of public recreations and sacrifices throughout the year, elegantly performed with a peculiar pomp, the daily delight of which is a charm that puts melancholy to flight. The grandeur of this our Athens causeth the produce of the whole earth to be imported here, by which we reap a familiar enjoyment, not more of the delicacies of our own growth than of those of other nations.

In the affairs of war we excel those of our enemies, who adhere to methods opposite to our own. For we lay open Athens to general resort, nor ever drive any stranger from us whom either improvement or curiosity hath brought amongst us, lest any enemy should hurt us by seeing what is never concealed. We place not so great a confidence in the preparatives and artifices of war as in the native warmth of our souls impelling us to action. In point of education the youth of some peoples are inured, by a course of laborious exercise, to support toil and exercise like men, but we, notwithstanding our easy and elegant way of life, face all the dangers of war as intrepidly as they. This may be proved by facts, since the

Lacedæmonians never invade our territories barely with their own, but with the united strength of all their confederates. But when we invade the dominions of our neighbors, for the most part we conquer without difficulty in an enemy's country those who fight in defense of their own habitations. The strength of our whole force no enemy yet hath ever experienced, because it is divided by our naval expeditions, or engaged in the different quarters of our service by land. But if anywhere they engage and defeat a small party of our forces, they boastingly give it out a total defeat; and if they are beat, they were certainly overpowered by our united strength. What though from a state of inactivity rather than laborious exercise, or with a natural rather than an acquired valor, we learn to encounter danger?—this good, at least, we receive from it, that we never droop under the apprehension of possible misfortunes, and when we hazard the danger, are found no less courageous than those who are continually inured to it. In these respects our whole community deserves justly to be admired, and in many we have yet to mention.

In our manner of living we show an elegance tempered with frugality, and we cultivate philosophy without enervating the mind. We display our wealth in the season of beneficence, and not in the vanity of discourse. A confession of poverty is disgrace to no man, no effort to avoid it is disgrace indeed. There is visible in the same persons an attention to their own private concerns and those of the public; and in others engaged in the labors of life there is a competent skill in the affairs of government. For we are the only people who think him that does not meddle in state affairs—not indolent, but good for nothing. And yet we pass the soundest judgments, and are quick at catching the right apprehensions of things, not thinking that words are prejudicial to actions, but rather the not being duly prepared by previous debate before we are obliged to proceed to execution. Herein consists our distinguishing excellence, that in the hour of action we show the greatest courage, and yet debate beforehand the expediency of our measures. The courage of others is the result of ignorance; deliberation makes them cowards. And those undoubtedly must be owned to have the greatest souls, who, most acutely sensible of the miseries of war and the sweets of peace, are not hence in the least deterred from facing danger.

In acts of beneficence, further, we differ from the many. We preserve friends not by receiving, but by conferring, obligations. For he who does a kindness hath the advantage over him who, by the law of gratitude, becomes a debtor to his benefactor. The person obliged is compelled to act the more insipid part, conscious that a return of kindness is merely a payment and not an obligation. And we alone are splendidly beneficent to others, not so much from interested motives as for the credit of pure liberality. I shall sum up what yet remains by only adding that our Athens in general is the school of Greece; and that every single Athenian amongst us is excellently formed, by his personal qualification, for all the various scenes of active life, acting with a most graceful demeanor and a most ready habit of despatch.

That I have not on this occasion made use of a pomp of words, but the truth of facts, that height to which by such a conduct this state hath risen, is an undeniable proof. For we are now the only people of the world who are found by experience to be greater than in report—the only people who, repelling the attacks of an invading enemy, exempt their defeat from the blush of indignation, and to their tributaries yield no discontent, as if subject to men unworthy to command. That we deserve our power, we need no evidence to manifest. We have great and signal proofs of this, which entitle us to the admiration of the present and future ages. We want no Homer to be the herald of our praise; no poet to deck off a history with the charms of verse, where the opinion of exploits must suffer by a strict relation. Every sea hath been opened by our fleets, and every land hath been penetrated by our armies, which have everywhere left behind them eternal monuments of our enmity and our friendship.

In the just defense of such a state, these victims of their own valor, scorning the ruin threatened to it, have valiantly fought and bravely died. And every one of those who survive is ready, I am persuaded, to sacrifice life in such a cause. And for this reason have I enlarged so much on national points, to give the clearest proof that in the present war we have more at stake than men whose public advantages are not so valuable, and to illustrate, by actual evidence, how great a commendation is due to them who are now my subject, and the greatest part of which they have already received. For the encomiums with which I have celebrated the state have been earned for it by the bravery of these and of men like these. And such compliments might be thought too high and exaggerated if passed on any Greeks but them alone. The fatal period to which these gallant souls are now reduced is the surest evidence of their merit—an evidence begun in their lives and completed in their deaths. For it is a debt of justice to pay superior honors to men who have devoted their lives in fighting for their country, though inferior to others in every virtue but that of valor. Their last service effaceth all former demerits—it extends to the public; their private demeanors reached only to a few. Yet not one of these was at all induced to shrink from danger, through fondness of those delights which the peaceful affluent life bestows—not one was the less lavish of his life, through that flattering hope attendant upon want, that poverty at length might be exchanged for affluence. One passion there was in their minds much stronger than these—the desire of vengeance on their enemies. Regarding this as the most honorable prize of dangers, they boldly rushed towards the mark to glut revenge and then to satisfy those secondary passions. The uncertain event they had already secured in hope; what their eyes showed plainly must be done they trusted their own valor to accomplish, thinking it more glorious to defend themselves and die in the attempt than to yield and live. From the reproach of cowardice, indeed, they fled, but presented their bodies to the shock of battle; when, insensible of fear, but triumphing in hope, in the doubtful charge they instantly dropped—and thus discharged the duty which brave men owed to their country.

As for you, who now survive them, it is your business to pray for a better fate, but to think it your duty also to preserve the same spirit and warmth of courage against your enemies; not judging of the expediency of this from a mere harangue—where any man indulging a flow of words may tell you what you yourselves know as well as he, how many advantages there are in fighting valiantly against your enemies—but, rather, making the daily-increasing grandeur of this community the object of your thoughts and growing quite enamored of it. And when it really appears great to your apprehensions, think again that this grandeur was acquired by brave and valiant men, by men who knew their duty, and in the moments of action were sensible of shame; who, whenever their attempts were unsuccessful, thought it no dishonor for their country to stand in need of anything their valor could do for it, and so made it the most glorious present. Bestowing thus their lives on the public, they have every one received a praise that will never decay, a sepulchre that will always be most illustrious —not that in which their bones lie moldering, but that in which their fame is preserved, to be on every occasion, when honor is the employ of either word or act, eternally remembered. For the whole earth is the sepulchre of illustrious men; nor is it the inscription on the columns in their native land alone that shows their merit, but the memorial of them, better than all inscriptions, in every foreign nation, reposited more durably in universal remembrance than on their own tombs. From this very moment, emulating these noble patterns, placing your happiness in liberty, and liberty in valor, be prepared to encounter all the dangers of war. For to be lavish of life is not so noble in those whom misfortunes have reduced to misery and despair, as in men who hazard the loss of a comfortable subsistence and the enjoyment of all the blessings this world affords by an unsuccessful enterprise. Adversity, after a series of ease and affluence, sinks deeper into the heart of a man of spirit than the stroke of death insensibly received in the vigor of life and public hope.

For this reason, the parents of those who are now gone, whoever of them may be attending here, I do not bewail—I shall rather comfort. It is well known to what unhappy accidents they were liable from the moment of their birth, and that happiness belongs to men who have reached the most glorious period of life, as these now have who are to you the source of sorrow—these whose life hath received its ample measure, happy in its continuance and equally happy in its conclusion. I know it in truth a difficult task to fix comfort in those breasts which will have frequent remembrances, in seeing the happiness of others, of what they once themselves enjoyed. And sorrow flows not from the absence of those good things we have never yet experienced, but from the loss of those to which we have been accustomed. They who are not yet by age past child-bearing should be comforted in the hope of having more. The children yet to be born will be a private benefit to some in causing them to forget such as no longer are, and will be a double benefit to their country in preventing its desolation and providing for its security. For those persons cannot in common justice be regarded as members of equal value to the public who have no children to expose to danger for its safety. But you, whose age is already far advanced, compute the greater share of happiness your longer time hath afforded for so much gain, persuaded in yourselves the remainder will be but short, and enlighten that space by the glory gained by these. It is greatness of soul alone that never grows old, nor is it wealth that delights in the latter stage of life, as some give out, so much as honor.

To you, the sons and brothers of the deceased, whatever number of you are here, a field of hardy contention is opened. For him who no longer is, every one is ready to commend, so that to whatever height you push your deserts, you will scarce ever be thought to equal, but to be somewhat inferior to these. Envy will exert itself against a competitor while life remains; but when death stops the competition, affection will applaud without restraint.

If after this it be expected from me to say anything to you who are now reduced to a state of widowhood, about female virtue, I shall express it all in one short admonition: It is your greatest glory not to be deficient in the virtue peculiar to your sex, and to give men as little handle as possible to talk of your behavior, whether well or ill.

I have now discharged the province allotted me by the laws, and said what I thought most pertinent to this assembly. Our departed friends have by facts been already honored. Their children from this day till they arrive at manhood shall be educated at the public expense of the state which hath appointed so beneficial a meed for these and all future relics of the public contests. For wherever the greatest rewards are proposed for virtue, there the best of patriots are ever to be found. Now let every one respectively indulge in becoming grief for his departed friends, and then retire.

Socrates

[469 B.C.–399 B.C.]

Socrates, the great philosopher, was brought to trial in 399 B.C. on charges that he disbelieved in the accepted gods and that through his heretical teachings he had corrupted the Athenian youth. The following eloquent speech, taken from Plato's Apology, *was made by Socrates when the judges found him guilty and sentenced him to death.*

ON HIS CONDEMNATION TO DEATH

For the sake of no long space of time, O Athenians, you will incur the character and reproach at the hands of those who wish to defame the city, of having put that wise man, Socrates, to death. For those who wish to defame you will assert that I am wise, though I am not. If, then, you had waited for a short time, this would have happened of its own accord; for observe my age, that it is far advanced in life, and near death. But I say this not to you all, but to those only who have condemned me to die. And I say this too to the same persons. Perhaps you think, O Athenians, that I have been convicted through the want of arguments, by which I might have persuaded you, had I thought it right to do and say anything so that I might escape punishment. Far otherwise: I have been convicted through want indeed, yet not of arguments, but of audacity and impudence, and of the inclination to say such things to you as would have been most agreeable for you to hear, had I lamented and bewailed and done and said many other things unworthy of me, as I affirm, but such as you are accustomed to hear from others.

But neither did I then think that I ought, for the sake of avoiding danger, to do anything unworthy of a freeman, nor do I now repent of having so defended myself; but I should much rather choose to die having so defended myself than to live in that way. For neither in a trial nor in battle is it right that I or any one else should employ every possible means whereby he may avoid death; for in battle it is frequently evident that a man might escape death by laying down his arms and throwing himself on the mercy of his pursuers. And there are many other devices in every danger, by which to avoid death, if a man dares to do and say everything.

But this is not difficult, O Athenians, to escape death, but it is much more difficult to avoid depravity, for it runs swifter than death. And now I, being slow and aged, am overtaken by the slower of the two; but my accusers, being strong and active, have been overtaken by the swifter, wickedness. And now I depart, condemned by you to death; but they condemned by truth, as guilty of iniquity and injustice: and I abide my sentence and so do they. These things, perhaps, ought so to be, and I think that they are for the best.

In the next place, I desire to predict to you who have condemned me, what will be your fate: for I am now in that condition in which men most frequently prophesy, namely, when they are about to die. I say then to you, O Athenians, who have condemned me to death, that immediately after my death a punishment will overtake you, far more severe, by Jupiter, than that which you have inflicted on me. For you have done this thinking you should be freed from the necessity of giving an account of your life. The very contrary however, as I affirm, will happen to you. Your accusers will be more numerous, whom I have now restrained, though you did not perceive it; and they will be more severe, inasmuch as they are younger and you will be more indignant. For, if you think that by putting men to death you will restrain any one from upbraiding you because you do not live well, you are much mistaken; for this method of escape is neither possible nor honorable, but that other is most honorable and most easy, not to put a check upon others, but for a man to take heed to himself, how he may be most perfect. Having predicted thus much to those of you who have condemned me, I take my leave of you.

But with you who have voted for my acquittal, I would gladly hold converse on what has now taken place, while the magistrates are busy and I am not yet carried to the place where I must die. Stay with me then, so long, O Athenians, for nothing hinders our conversing with each other, whilst we are permitted to do so; for I wish to make known to you, as being my friends, the meaning of that which has just now befallen me. To me then, O my judges,—and in calling you judges I call you rightly,—a strange thing has happened. For the wonted prophetic voice of my guardian deity, on every former occasion, even in the most trifling affairs, opposed me, if I was about to do anything wrong; but now, that has befallen me which ye yourselves behold, and which any one would think and which is supposed to be the extremity of evil, yet neither when I departed from home in the morning did the warning of the god oppose me, nor when I came up here to the place of trial, nor in my address when I was about to say anything; yet on other occasions it has frequently restrained me in the midst of speaking. But now it has never throughout this proceeding opposed me, either in what I did or said. What then do I suppose to be the cause of this? I will tell you: what has befallen me appears to be a blessing; and it is impossible that we think rightly who suppose that death is an evil. A great proof of this to me is the fact that it is impossible but that the accustomed signal should have opposed me, unless I had been about to meet with some good.

Moreover, we may hence conclude that there is great hope that death is a blessing. For to die is one of two things: for either the dead may be annihilated and have no sensation of anything whatever; or, as it is said, there is a certain change and passage of the soul from one place to another. And if it is a privation of all sensation, as it were, a sleep in which the sleeper has no dream, death would be a wonderful gain. For I think that if anyone, having selected a night in which he slept so soundly as not to have had a dream, and having compared this night with all the other nights and days of his life, should be required on consideration to say how many days and nights he had passed better and more pleasantly than this night throughout his life, I think that not only a private person, but even a great king himself would find them easy to number in comparison with other days and nights. If, therefore, death is a thing of this kind, I say it is a gain; for thus all futurity appears to be nothing more than one night.

But if, on the other hand, death is a removal from hence to another place, and what is said be true, that all the dead are there, what greater blessing can there be than this, my judges? For if, on arriving at Hades, released from these who pretend to be judges, one shall find those who are true judges, and who are said to judge there, Minos and Rhadamanthus, Æacus and Triptolemus, and such others of the demigods as were just during their own life, would this be a sad removal? At what price would you not estimate a conference with Orpheus and Musæus, Hesiod and Homer? I indeed should be willing to die often, if this be true. For to me the sojourn there would be admirable, when I should meet with Palamedes, and Ajax, son of Telamon, and any other of the ancients who has died by an unjust sentence. The comparing my sufferings with theirs would, I think, be no unpleasing occupation.

But the greatest pleasure would be to spend my time in questioning and examining the people there as I have done those here, and discovering who among them is wise, and who fancies himself to be so but is not. At what price, my judges, would not any one estimate the opportunity of questioning him who led that mighty army against Troy, or Ulysses, or Sisyphus, or ten thousand others, whom one might mention, both men and women? with whom to converse and associate, and to question them, would be an inconceivable happiness. Surely for that the judges there do not condemn to death; for in other respects those who live there are more happy than those that are here, and are henceforth immortal, if at least what is said be true.

You, therefore, O my judges, ought to entertain good hopes with respect to death, and to meditate on this one truth, that to a good man nothing is evil, neither while living nor when dead, nor are his concerns neglected by the gods. And what has befallen me is not the effect of chance; but this is clear to me, that now to die, and be freed from my cares, is better for me. On this account the warning in no way turned me aside; and I bear no resentment toward those who condemned me, or against my accusers, although they did not condemn and accuse me with this intention, but thinking to injure me: in this they deserve to be blamed.

Thus much, however, I beg of them. Punish my sons, when they grow up, O judges, paining them as I have pained you, if they appear to you to care for riches or anything else before virtue, and if they think themselves to be something when they are nothing, reproach them as I have done you, for not attending to what they ought, and for conceiving themselves to be something when they are worth nothing. If ye do this, both I and my sons shall have met with just treatment at your hands.

But it is now time to depart,—for me to die, for you to live. But which of us is going to a better state is unknown to every one but God.

Isocrates
[436 B.C.–338 B.C.]

Ranked as one of the most famous orators of Athens, Isocrates is credited with having influenced the oratorical style of Demosthenes, Cicero, and other great orators. His oration "On the Union of Greece to Resist Persia," delivered in 380 B.C., appears here in abridged form.

ON THE UNION OF GREECE TO RESIST PERSIA

IT IS CONFESSED indeed that our state is the most ancient and the greatest, and the most celebrated among all men; and the foundation being thus glorious, on account of what follows these it is still more befitting that we should be honored. For we inhabit this city, not having expelled others, nor having found it deserted, nor collected promiscuously from many nations, but we are of such honorable and genuine birth that we continue for all time possessing this land from which we were born, being sprung from the soil, and being able to call our city by the same names as our nearest relations, for we alone of all the Greeks have a right to call the same—nurse and fatherland and mother. And yet it is right that those who with good reason entertain high thoughts, and who justly dispute the supremacy and who often make mention of their hereditary rights, should prove the origin of their race to be of this nature.

The advantages, then, which we possessed from the beginning, and which were bestowed upon us by fortune, are so great in magnitude; but of how great advantages we have been the cause to the rest we should thus best investigate, if we should go through in detail the time from the commencement, and the exploits of the State in succession; for we shall find that she not only [delivered us] from the dangers in respect of war, but also is the cause of that established order besides in which we dwell and with which we live as free citizens, and by means of which we are able to live.

Of the wars, indeed, the Persian was the most famous; the old achievements, however, are not less strong proofs for those who dispute about hereditary institutions. For when Greece was still in a lowly condition, the Thracians indeed came to our land with Eumolpus the son of Poseidon, and the Scythians with the Amazons the daughters of Mars, not at the same time, but at the time when each of them were rulers of Europe, hating, indeed, the whole race of the Greeks, but making charges against us separately, thinking that by this line of conduct they would incur danger against one state indeed, but would at the same time conquer all.

They did not, however, succeed, but having engaged with our ancestors separately, they were destroyed equally as if they had made war on all together. And the magnitude of the evils which befel them is manifest, for the speeches concerning them would never have lived on for so long a time had not also their achievements far excelled those of other men. It is recorded, then, concerning the Amazons, that not one of those who came went back again, while those who were left at home were driven out of their government on account of their calamity here; and concerning the Thracians, [it is said] that although during the former times they dwelt beside us, on our borders, yet on account of that expedition they left so great an intervening space, that in the district between us, many nations and all kinds of races and great cities have been established.

Glorious indeed, then, are these things, and befitting those who dispute for the supremacy, but akin to what has been said, and such as it is natural that those sprung from such men would perform, were the exploits of those who waged war against Darius and Xerxes.

Always indeed, then, both our ancestors and the Lacedæmonians acted in a spirit of rivalry to each other. Not but what in those times they contended for the most glorious objects, not thinking each other to be enemies, but rivals, not paying court to the foreigner with a view to the slavery of the Greeks, but being of one mind about the common safety, and engaging in a contest as to this, viz., which of the two shall be the authors of it. And they displayed their valor first, indeed, in the case of those sent by Darius. For when these had landed in Attica, the one did not wait for their allies, but making what was a common war a personal one, they went out to meet those who had treated contemptuously the whole of Hellas with their private force, a few against many myriads, as if about to brave the danger in the case of the lives of others, while the others no sooner heard of the war being in Attica than, neglecting everything else they came to assist us, making as great haste as if it was their own country which was being ravaged.

And after these things, when the subsequent expedition took place, which Xerxes led in person, after abandoning his palace and undertaking to become a general, and having collected all the men from Asia; and who, being anxious not to speak in extravagant terms, has spoken about him in language which fell short of the reality?—a man, who reached such a height of arrogance, that considering it to be a trifling achievement to subdue Greece, and wishing to leave behind such a monument as surpasses human nature, ceased not until he had devised and at the same time carried out by compulsion that which all talk of, so that with his armament he sailed through the mainland and marched over the sea, having bridged over the Hellespont and dug a canal through Athos. Against him, indeed, having such high thoughts, and having succeeded in accomplishing such great deeds and having become the lord of so many, they went forth, having divided amongst themselves the danger, the Lacedæmonians indeed to Thermopylæ against the land force, having selected a thousand of themselves, and taking along with them a few of their allies with the intention of preventing them in the narrow pass from advancing farther, while our fathers [went out] to Artemisium, having manned sixty triremes to meet the whole naval force of the enemy. And they had the courage to do these things, not so much through contempt of the enemy as from a spirit of rivalry with each other, the Lacedæmonians indeed envying our state, for the battle at Marathon, and seeking to put themselves on an equality with us, and fearing lest our state should twice in succession become the author of deliverance to the Greeks, and our fathers wishing chiefly indeed to retain their present glory and to make it manifest to all that both in the former case it was through valor and not through fortune that they had conquered; in the next place also to induce the Greeks to maintain a sea-fight by showing to them that valor gets the better of numbers in naval dangers and enterprises equally as in those by land.

And to the king (of Asia), indeed, nothing is more important than to consider by what means we shall never cease warring against one another, while we are so far from bringing any of his interests into collision or causing them to be distracted by factions, that we even endeavor to assist in putting an end to the troubles which have befallen him through fortune; since we also allow him to make use of one of the two armaments in Cyprus, and to blockade the other, though both of them belong to Hellas. For both those who have revolted are friendly disposed towards us and give themselves up to the Lacedæmonians, and the most useful part of those who are serving with Tiribazus and of the land army have been collected from these districts, and the greater part of the navy has sailed along with them from Ionia, who would much more gladly have ravaged Asia in concert than have fought against one another on account of trifles. Of these things we take no thought, but we are disputing about the islands of the Cyclades, and thus heedlessly have we surrendered to the foreign foe cities so many in number and so great in magnitude. Therefore, he is in possession of some, and is on the point of [taking possession of] others, and is plotting against others, having despised all of us, and with good reason. For he has effected what no one of his ancestors ever did; for it has been agreed on, both by us and by the Lacedæmonians, that Asia belongs to the king, and he has taken possession of the Grecian cities with such authority as to raze some of them to the ground, and in others to fortify citadels. And all these things have happened through our folly and not on account of his power.

Our citizens are at this time reconciled with all the others with whom they have been at war, and forget the hostility which has arisen, but to the inhabitants of the continent they do not feel grateful, even when they receive benefits [from them], so undying is the anger they feel toward them. And our fathers condemned many to death for favoring the Medes; and even at the present day, in their public assemblies, they make imprecations, before they transact any other business, on whomsoever of the citizens makes proposals for peace to the Persians. And the Eumolpidæ and the Heralds, in the celebration of the mysteries, on account of their hatred for them, proclaim publicly also to all other foreigners, as they do to homicides, that they are excluded from the sacred rites. And such hostile feelings do we entertain by nature toward them, that even in our legends, we occupy ourselves with most pleasure with those relating to the Trojan and Persian wars, by which it is possible to hear of their calamities. And one might find hymns composed in consequence of the war against the foreigners, but dirges produced for us in consequence of that against the Greeks, and might find the former sung at the festivals, while we call to mind the latter in our calamities. And I think that even the poetry of Homer received greater honors, because he nobly extolled those who made war against the foreign foe; and that for this reason our ancestors wished to make his art honored, both in the contests in poetry and in the education of the younger generation, in order that, hearing frequently his poems, we may learn by heart the enmity which existed toward them, and, emulating the deeds of valor of those who made war upon them, may set our hearts upon the same exploits as they achieved.

Wherefore there appear to me to be very many things which encourage us to make war against them, and especially the present favorable opportunity, than which nothing is more clear. And we must not let it slip. For, in fact, it is disgraceful not to use it when present, but to remember it when it is past. For what additional advantage could we even wish to have, if intending to go to war with the king, beyond what we already possess? Has not Egypt revolted from him, as well as Cyprus; and have not Phœnicia and Syria been devastated owing to the war; and has not

Tyre, on account of which he was greatly elated, been seized by his enemies? And the majority of the cities in Cilicia those on our side possess, and the rest it is not difficult to acquire. But Lycia no one of the Persians ever conquered. And Hecatomnos, the overseer of Caria, in reality indeed has revolted for a long time already, and will confess it whenever we may wish. And from Cnidus to Sinope the Greeks inhabit the coasts of Asia, whom it is not necessary to persuade to go to war, but [only] not to prevent them.

And yet, as we already possess so many bases of operation, and as so great a war encircles Asia, what need is there too accurately to scrutinize what are likely to be the results? For where they are inferior to small portions, it is not uncertain how they would be disposed, if they should be compelled to war with all of us. Now the case stands thus. If, indeed, the king occupy in greater force the cities on the sea-coast, establishing in them greater garrisons than at present, perhaps also those of the islands which are near the mainland, as Rhodes and Samos and Chios, might lean to his fortunes; but if we be the first to seize them, it is probable that those inhabiting Lydia and Phrygia, and the rest of the country which lies above them, would be in the power of those who make these their base of operations. Wherefore it is necessary to hasten and to make no loss of time, that we may not suffer what our fathers did.

And it is fitting to make the expedition in the present age, in order that those who participate in the calamities may also have the enjoyment of the advantages, and may not continue to live unfortunate during all their lifetime. For the time past is sufficient—in which what horror is there which has not happened?—for, though there are many evils already existing in the nature of man, we ourselves have invented in addition more than the necessary evils, having created wars and factions among ourselves, so that some are perishing lawlessly in their own cities, and some are wandering in a foreign land with their children and wives, and many being compelled, through want of the daily necessaries of life, to serve as mercenaries, are dying fighting against their friends on behalf of their enemies. And at this no one has ever been indignant, but they think it becoming to shed tears at the calamities composed by poets, but, though gazing upon many dreadful genuine sufferings happening on account of the war, they are so far from pitying them, that they even take more pleasure in the misfortunes of one another than in their own personal advantages. And perhaps, also, many might laugh at my simplicity, if I were to lament the misfortunes of individuals at such critical times, in which Italy has been devastated, and Sicily reduced to slavery, and so many cities have been surrendered to the foreigners, and the remaining portions of the Greeks are in the greatest dangers.

Now it is necessary to put out of the way these plottings, and to attempt those deeds from which we shall both inhabit our cities in greater security, and be more faithfully disposed to one another, and what is to be said about these matters is simple and easy. For it is neither possible to enjoy a secure peace, unless we make war in concert against the foreign enemy, nor for the Greeks to be of one mind until we consider both our advantages to come from one another, and our dangers to be against the same people.

But when these things have been done, and the embarrassment with regard to our means of living has been taken away, which both dissolves friendships and perverts relationships into enmity, and involves all men in wars and factions, it is not possible that we shall not be of one mind, and entertain toward one another genuine feelings of good will. For which reasons we must esteem it of the greatest importance how we shall, as soon as possible, banish the war from hence to the continent, as this is the only advantage we should reap from the dangers in fighting against one another, namely, if it should seem good to us to employ against the foreign foe the experience which we have derived from them.

And truly we shall not even annoy the cities by enrolling soldiers from them, a thing which is now most troublesome to them in the war against one another; for I think that those who will wish to stay at home will be much fewer in number than those who will desire to follow with us. For who, whether young or old, is so indifferent that he will not wish to have a share in this expedition, commanded indeed by the Athenians and Lacedæmonians, but collected in defense of the liberty of the allies, and sent out by the whole of Hellas, and marching to take vengeance upon the foreign foe? And how great must we consider the fame, and the memory, and the glory which those will either have in their lives, or leave behind them in their deaths, who have been the bravest in such exploits? For where those who made war against Alexander, and captured one city, were deemed worthy of such praises, what panegyrics must we expect that they will obtain who have conquered the whole of Asia? For who, either of those able to write poetry, or of those who understand how to speak, will not labor and study, wishing to leave behind him a memorial for all ages, at the same time of his own intellect and of their valor?

Demosthenes

[384? B.C.–322 B.C.]

Demosthenes is generally acclaimed as one of the greatest orators of all time. His oration "On the Crown," in the opinion of Professor R. C. Jebb, is "the most finished, the most splendid and the most pathetic work of ancient eloquence." It was delivered in Athens in 330 B.C. Portions of this address, as well as his "Second Oration Against Philip," are presented here.

ON THE CROWN

ACCURSED SCRIBBLER! you, to deprive me of the approbation and affection of my countrymen, speak of trophies and battles and ancient deeds, with none of which had this present trial the least concern; but I!—O you third-rate actor!—I, that rose to counsel the state how to maintain her preeminence! in what spirit was I to mount the hustings? In the spirit of one having unworthy counsel to offer?—I should have deserved to perish! You yourselves, men of Athens, may not try private and public causes on the same principles: the compacts of every-day life you are to judge of by particular laws and circumstances; the measures of statesmen, by reference to the dignity of your ancestors. And if you think it your duty to act worthily of them, you should every one of you consider, when you come into court to decide public questions, that together with your staff and ticket the spirit of the commonwealth is delivered to you.

Athenians, you have had many great and renowned orators before me; the famous Callistratus, Aristophon, Cephalus, Thrasybulus, hundreds of others, yet none of them ever thoroughly devoted himself to any measure of state: for instance, the mover of a resolution would not be ambassador; the ambassador would not move a resolution; each one left for himself some relief, and also, should anything happen, an excuse. How then— it may be said—did you so far surpass others in might and boldness as to do everything yourself? I don't say that: but such was my conviction of the danger impending over us, that I considered it left no room or thought for individual security; a man should have been only too happy to perform his duty without neglect. As to myself I was persuaded, perhaps foolishly, yet I was persuaded, that none would move better resolutions than myself, none would execute them better, none as ambassador would show more zeal and honesty. Therefore I undertook every duty myself.

Through my policy, which he arraigns, instead of the Thebans invading this country with Philip, as all expected, they joined our ranks and prevented him;—instead of the war being in Attica, it took place seven hundred furlongs from the city on the confines of Bœotia;—instead of corsairs issuing from Eubœa to plunder us, Attica was in peace on the coast-side during the whole war;—instead of Philip being master of the Hellespont by taking Byzantium, the Byzantines were our auxiliaries against him. Does this computation of services, think you, resemble the casting of accounts? Or should we strike these out on a balance, and not look that they be kept in everlasting remembrance? I will not set down, that of the cruelty, remarkable in cases where Philip got people all at once into his power, others have had the trial; while of the generosity, which, casting about for his future purposes, he assumed toward Athens, you have happily enjoyed the fruits. I pass that by.

If you talk about just conditions with the Thebans, Æschines, or with the Byzantines or Eubœans, or discuss now the question of equal terms, first I say—you are ignorant that of those galleys formerly which defended Greece, being three hundred in number, our commonwealth furnished two hundred, and never (as it seemed) thought herself injured by having done so, never prosecuted those who advised it or expressed any dissatisfaction—shame on her if she had!—but was grateful to the gods, that, when a common danger beset the Greeks, she alone furnished double what the rest did for the preservation of all. Besides, it is but a poor favor you do your countrymen by calumniating me. For what is the use of telling us now what we should have done? Why, being in the city and present, did you not make your proposals then; if indeed they were practicable at a crisis, when we had to accept not what we liked but what the circumstances allowed? Remember, there was one ready to bid against us, to welcome eagerly those that we rejected, and give money into the bargain.

But if I am accused for what I have actually done, how would it have been, if, through my hard bargaining, the states had gone off and attached themselves to Philip, and he had become master at the same time of Eubœa, Thebes, and Byzantium? What, think ye, these impious men would have said or done? Said doubtless, that the states were abandoned —that they wished to join us and were driven away—that he had got command of the Hellespont by the Byzantines, and become master of the corn-trade of Greece—that a heavy neighbor-war had by means of the Thebans been brought into Attica—that the sea had become unnavigable by the excursion of pirates from Eubœa! All this would they have said sure enough, and a great deal besides. A wicked, wicked thing, O Athenians, is a calumniator always, every way spiteful and faultfinding. But this creature is a reptile by nature, that from the beginning never did anything honest or liberal; a very ape of a tragedian, village Œnomaus, counterfeit orator! What advantage has your eloquence been to your country? Now do you speak to us about the past? As if a physician should visit his patients, and not order or prescribe anything to cure the disease, but on the death of any one, when the last ceremonies were performing, should follow him to the grave and expound, how, if the poor fellow had done this and that, he never would have died! Idiot, do you speak now?

Even the defeat—if you exult in that which should make you groan, you accursed one!—by nothing that I have done will it appear to have befallen us. Consider it thus, O Athenians. From no embassy, on which I was commissioned by you, did I ever come away defeated by the ambassadors of Philip—neither from Thessaly, nor from Ambracia, nor from the kings of Thrace, nor from Byzantium, nor from any other place, nor on the last recent occasion from Thebes; but where his ambassadors were vanquished in argument, he came with arms and carried the day. And for this you call me to account; and are not ashamed to jeer the same person for cowardice, whom you require singlehanded to overcome the might of Philip—and that, too, by words! For what else had I at my command? Certainly not the spirit of each individual, nor the fortune of the army, nor the conduct of the war, for which you would make me accountable; such a blunderer are you!

Yet understand me. Of what a statesman may be responsible for I allow the utmost scrutiny; I deprecate it not. What are his functions? To observe things in the beginning, to foresee and foretell them to others, —this I have done: again; wherever he finds delays, backwardness, ignorance, jealousies, vices inherent and unavoidable in all communities, to contract them into the narrowest compass, and on the other hand, to promote unanimity and friendship and zeal in the discharge of duty. All this, too, I have performed; and no one can discover the least neglect on my part. Ask any man, by what means Philip achieved most of his successes, and you will be told, by his army, and by his bribing and corrupting men in power. Well; your forces were not under my command or control; so that I can not be questioned for anything done in that department. But by refusing the price of corruption I have overcome Philip; for as the offer of a bribe, if it be accepted, as vanquished the taker, so the person who refuses it and is not corrupted has vanquished the person offering. Therefore is the commonwealth undefeated as far as I am concerned.

For my part, I regard any one, who reproaches his fellow man with fortune, as devoid of sense. He that is best satisfied with his condition, he that deems his fortune excellent, can not be sure that it will remain so until the evening: how then can it be right to bring it forward, or upbraid another man with it? As Æschines, however, has on this subject (besides many others) expressed himself with insolence, look, men of Athens, and observe how much more truth and humanity there shall be in my discourse upon fortune than in his.

I hold the fortune of our commonwealth to be good, and so I find the oracles of Dodonæan Jupiter and Phythian Apollo declaring to us. The fortune of all mankind, which now prevails, I consider cruel and dreadful: for what Greek, what barbarian, has not in these times experienced a multitude of evils? That Athens chose the noblest policy, that she fares better than those very Greeks who thought, if they abandoned us, they should abide in prosperity, I reckon as part of her good fortune; if she suffered reverses, if all happened not to us as we desired, I conceive she has had that share of the general fortune which fell to our lot. As to my fortune (personally speaking) or that of any individual among us, it should, as I conceive, be judged of in connection with personal matters. Such is my opinion upon the subject of fortune, a right and just one, as it appears to me, and I think you will agree with it. Æschines says that my individual fortune is paramount to that of the commonwealth, the small and mean to the good and great. How can this possibly be?

However, if you are determined, Æschines, to scrutinize my fortune, compare it with your own, and, if you find my fortune better than yours, cease to revile it. Look then from the very beginning. And I pray and entreat that I may not be condemned for bad taste. I don't think any person wise, who insults poverty, or who prides himself on having been bred in affluence: but by the slander and malice of this cruel man I am forced into such a discussion; which I will conduct with all the moderation which circumstances allow.

I had the advantage, Æschines, in my boyhood of going to proper schools, and having such allowance as a boy should have who is to do nothing mean from indigence. Arrived at man's estate, I lived suitably to my breeding; was choirmaster, ship-commander, rate-payer; backward in no acts of liberality public or private, but making myself useful to the commonwealth and to my friends. When I entered upon state affairs,

I chose such a line of politics, that both by my country and many people of Greece I have been crowned many times, and not even you my enemies venture to say that the line I chose was not honorable. Such then has been the fortune of my life: I could enlarge upon it, but I forbear, lest what I pride myself in should give offense.

But you, the man of dignity, who spit upon others, look what sort of fortune is yours compared with mine. As a boy you were reared in abject poverty, waiting with your father in his school, grinding the ink, sponging the benches, sweeping the room, doing the duty of a menial rather than a freeborn man. After you were grown up, you attended your mother in the initiations, reading her books and helping in all the ceremonies; at night wrapping the noviciates in fawn-skin, swilling, purifying, and scouring them with clay and bran, raising them after the lustration, and bidding them say, "Bad I have scaped, and better I have found"; priding yourself that no one ever howled so lustily—and I believe him! for don't suppose that he who speaks so loud is not a splendid howler! In the daytime you led your noble orgiasts, crowned with fennel and poplar, through the highways, squeezing the big-cheeked serpents, and lifting them over your head, and shouting Evœ Saboe, and capering to the words Hyes Attes, Attes Hyes, saluted by the beldames as Leader, Conductor, Chest-bearer, Fan-bearer, and the like, getting as your reward tarts and biscuits and rolls; for which any man might well bless himself and his fortune!

When you were enrolled among your fellow townsmen—by what means I stop not to inquire—when you were enrolled, however, you immediately selected the most honorable of employments, that of clerk and assistant to our petty magistrates. From this you were removed after a while, having done yourself all that you charge others with; and then, sure enough, you disgraced not your antecedents by your subsequent life, but hiring yourself to those ranting players, as they were called, Simylus and Socrates, you acted third parts, collecting figs and grapes and olives like a fruiterer from other men's farms, and getting more from them than from the playing, in which the lives of your whole company were at stake; for there was an implacable and incessant war between them and the audience, from whom you received so many wounds, that no wonder you taunt as cowards people inexperienced in such encounters.

But passing over what may be imputed to poverty, I will come to the direct charges against your character. You espoused such a line of politics (when at last you thought of taking to them) that, if your country prospered, you lived the life of a hare, fearing and trembling and ever expecting to be scourged for the crimes of which your conscience accused you; though all have seen how bold you were during the misfortunes of the rest. A man who took courage at the death of a thousand citizens—what does he deserve at the hands of the living? A great deal more than I could say about him I shall omit; for it is not all I can tell of his turpitude and infamy which I ought to let slip from my tongue, but only what is not disgraceful to myself to mention.

Contrast now the circumstances of your life and mine, gently and with temper, Æschines; and then ask these people whose fortune they would each of them prefer. You taught reading, I went to school; you performed initiations, I received them; you danced in the chorus, I furnished it; you were assembly clerk, I was a speaker; you acted third parts, I heard you; you broke down, and I hissed; you have worked as a statesman for the enemy, I for my country. I pass by the rest; but this very day I am on my probation for a crown, and am acknowledged to be innocent of all offense; while you are already judged to be a pettifogger, and the question is, whether you shall continue that trade, or at once be silenced by not getting a fifth part of the votes. A happy fortune, do you see, you have enjoyed, that you should denounce mine as miserable!

I will have done then with private topics, but say another word or two upon public. If you can mention, Æschines, a single man under the sun, whether Greek or barbarian, who has not suffered by Philip's power formerly and Alexander's now, well and good; I concede to you, that my fortune, or misfortune (if you please), has been the cause of every-thing. But if many that never saw me or heard my voice have been grievously afflicted, not individuals only but whole cities and nations; how much juster and fairer is it to consider, that to the common fortune apparently of all men, to a tide of events overwhelming and lamentable, these disasters are to be attributed. You, disregarding all this, accuse me whose ministry has been among my countrymen, knowing all the while, that a part (if not the whole) of your calumny falls upon the people, and yourself in particular. For if I assumed the sole and absolute direction of our counsels, it was open to you the other speakers to accuse me; but if you were constantly present in all the assemblies, if the state invited public discussion of what was expedient, and if these measures were then believed by all to be the best, and especially by you (for certainly from no good will did you leave me in possession of hopes and admiration and honors, all of which attended on my policy, but doubtless because you were compelled by the truth and had nothing better to advise); is it not iniquitous and monstrous to complain now of measures, than which you could suggest none better at the time?

I should conclude, Æschines, that you undertook this cause to exhibit your eloquence and strength of lungs, not to obtain satisfaction for any wrong. But it is not the language of an orator, Æschines, that has any value, nor yet the tone of his voice, but his adopting the same views with the people, and his hating and loving the same persons that his country does. He that is thus minded will say everything with loyal intention; he that courts persons from whom the commonwealth appre-hends danger to herself, rides not on the same anchorage with the people, and, therefore, has not the same expectation of safety. But—do you see?— I have; for my objects are the same with those of my countrymen; I have no interest separate or distinct. Is that so with you? How can it be—when immediately after the battle you went as ambassador to Philip, who was at that period the author of your country's calamities, notwith-standing that you had before persisted in refusing that office, as all men know?

And who is it that deceives the state? Surely the man who speaks not what he thinks. On whom does the crier pronounce a curse? Surely on such a man. What greater crime can an orator be charged with than that his opinions and his language are not the same? Such is found to be your character. And yet you open your mouth, and dare to look these men in the faces! Do you think they don't know you?—or are sunk in such slumber and oblivion, as not to remember the speeches which you delivered in the assembly, cursing and swearing that you had nothing to do with Philip, and that I brought that charge against you out of personal enmity without foundation? No sooner came the news of the battle, than you forgot all that; you acknowledge and avowed that between Philip and yourself there subsisted a relation of hospitality and friendship—new names these for your contract of hire. For upon what plea of equality or justice could Æschines, son of Glaucothea, the timbrel player, be the friend or acquaintance of Philip? I cannot see. No! You were hired to ruin the interests of your countrymen; and yet, though you have been caught yourself in open treason, and informed against yourself after the fact, you revile and reproach me for things which you will find any man is chargeable with sooner than I.

Many great and glorious enterprises has the commonwealth, Æschines, undertaken and succeeded in through me; and she did not forget them. Here is the proof—On the election of a person to speak the funeral oration immediately after the event, you were proposed, but the people would not have you, notwithstanding your fine voice, nor Demades, though he had just made the peace, nor Hegemon, nor any other of your party—but me. And when you and Pythocles came forward in a brutal and shameful manner (O merciful Heaven!) and urged the same accusations against me which you now do, and abused me, they elected me all the more. The reason—you are not ignorant of it—yet I will tell you. The Athenians knew as well the loyalty and zeal with which I conducted their affairs, as the dishonesty of you and your party; for what you denied upon oath in our prosperity, you confessed in the misfortunes of the republic. They considered, therefore, that men who got security for their politics by the public disasters had been their enemies long before, and were then avowedly such. They thought it right also, that the person who was to speak in honor of the fallen and celebrate their valor should not have sat under the same roof or at the same table with their antagonists; that he should not revel there and sing a pæan over the calamities of Greece in company with their murderers, and then come here and receive distinction; that he should not with his voice act the mourner of their fate, but that he should lament over them with his heart. This they perceived in themselves and in me, but not in any of you; therefore, they elected me, and not you. Nor, while the people felt thus, did the fathers and brothers of the deceased, who were chosen by the people to perform their obsequies, feel differently. For having to order the funeral banquet (according to custom) at the house of the nearest relative to the deceased, they ordered it at mine. And with reason; because, though each to his own was nearer of kin than I was, none was so near to them all collectively. He that had the deepest interest in their safety and success had upon their mournful disaster the largest share of sorrow for them all.

Of this base and infamous conspiracy and profligacy—or rather, O Athenians, if I am to speak in earnest, of this betrayal of Grecian liberty—Athens is by all mankind acquitted, owing to my counsels; and I am acquitted by you. Then do you ask me, Æschines, for what merit I claim to be honored? I will tell you. Because, while all the statesmen in Greece, beginning with yourself, have been corrupted formerly by Philip and now by Alexander, me neither opportunity, nor fair speeches, nor large promises, nor hope, nor fear, nor anything else could tempt or induce to betray aught that I considered just and beneficial to my country. Whatever I have advised my fellow citizens, I have never advised like you men, leaning as in a balance to the side of profit; all my proceedings have been those of a soul upright, honest, and incorrupt; entrusted with affairs of greater magnitude than any of my contemporaries, I have administered them all honestly and faithfully. Therefore do I claim to be honored.

These and the like measures, Æschines, are what become an honorable citizen (by their success—O earth and heaven!—we should have been the greatest of people incontestably, and deserved to be so; even under their failure the result is glory, and no one blames Athens or her policy; all condemn fortune that so ordered things); but never will he desert the interests of the commonwealth, nor hire himself to her adversaries, and study the enemy's advantage instead of his country's; nor on a man who has courage to advise and propose measures worthy of the state, and resolution to persevere in them, will he cast an evil eye, and, if any one privately offends him, remember and treasure it up; no, nor keep himself in a criminal and treacherous retirement, as you so often do. There is indeed a retirement just and beneficial to the state, such as you, the bulk of my countrymen, innocently enjoy; that however is not the retirement of Æschines; far from it. Withdrawing himself from public life when he pleases (and that is often), he watches for the moment when you are tired of a constant speaker, or when some reverse of fortune has befallen you, or anything untoward has happened (and many are the casualties of human life); at such a crisis he springs up an orator, rising from his retreat like a wind; in full voice, with words and phrases collected, he rolls them out audibly and breathlessly, to no advantage or good purpose whatsoever, but to the detriment of some or other of his fellow citizens and to the general disgrace.

Yet from this labor and diligence, Æschines, if it proceeded from an honest heart, solicitous for your country's welfare, the fruits should have been rich and noble and profitable to all—alliances of states, supplies of money, conveniences of commerce, enactment of useful laws, opposition to our declared enemies. All such things were looked for in former times; and many opportunities did the past afford for a good man and true to show himself; during which time you are nowhere to be found, neither first, second, third, fourth, fifth, nor sixth—not in any rank at all—certainly on no service by which your country was exalted. For what alliance has come to the state by your procurement? What succors, what acquisition of good will or credit? What embassy or agency is there of yours, by which the reputation of the country has been increased? What concern domestic, Hellenic, or foreign, of which you have had the management, has improved under it? What galleys? what ammunition? what arsenals? what repair of walls? what cavalry? What in the world are you good for? What assistance in money have you ever given, either to the rich or the poor, out of public spirit or liberality? None. But, good sir, if there is nothing of this, there is at all events zeal and loyalty. Where? when? You infamous fellow! Even at a time when all who ever spoke upon the platform gave something for the public safety, and last Aristonicus gave the sum which he had amassed to retrieve his franchise, you neither came forward nor contributed a mite—not from inability—no, for you have inherited above five talents from Philo, your wife's father, and you had a subscription of two talents from the chairmen of the boards for what you did to cut up the navy law. But, that I may not go from one thing to another and lose sight of the question, I pass this by. That it was not poverty prevented your contributing, already appears; it was, in fact, your anxiety to do nothing against those to whom your political life is subservient. On what occasions then do you show your spirit? When do you shine out? When aught is to be spoken against your countrymen! —then it is you who are splendid in voice, perfect in memory, an admirable actor, a tragic Theocrines.

You mention the good men of olden times; and you are right so to do. Yet it is hardly fair, O Athenians, that he should get the advantage of that respect which you have for the dead, to compare and contrast me with them,—me who am living among you; for what mortal is ignorant, that toward the living there exists always more or less of ill will, whereas the dead are no longer hated even by an enemy? Such being human nature, am I to be tried and judged by the standard of my predecessors? Heaven forbid! It is not just nor equitable, Æschines. Let me be compared with you, or any persons you like of your party who are still alive. And consider this—whether it is more honorable and better for the state, that because of the services of a former age, prodigious though they are beyond all power of expression, those of the present generation should be unrequited and spurned, or that all who give proof of their good intentions should have their share of honor and regard from the people? Yet, indeed—if I must say so much—my politics and principles, if considered fairly, will be found to resemble those of the illustrious ancients, and to have had the same objects in view, while yours resemble those of their calumniators; for it is certain there were persons in those times, who ran down the living, and praised people dead and gone, with a malignant purpose like yourself.

You say that I am nothing like the ancients. Are you like them, Æschines? Is your brother, or any of our speakers? I assert that none is. But pray, my good fellow (that I may give you no other name), try the living with the living and with his competitors, as you would in all cases—poets, dancers, athletes. Philammon did not, because he was inferior to Glaucus of Carystus, and some other champions of a bygone age, depart uncrowned from Olympia, but, because he beat all who entered the ring against him, was crowned and proclaimed conqueror. So I ask you to compare me with the orators of the day, with yourself, with any one you like; I yield to none. When the commonwealth was at liberty to choose for her advantage, and patriotism was a matter of emulation, I showed myself a better counselor than any, and every act of state was pursuant to my decrees and laws and negotiations; none of your party was to be seen, unless you had to do the Athenians a mischief. After that lamentable occurrence, when there was a call no longer for advisers, but for persons obedient to command, persons ready to be hired against their country and willing to flatter strangers, then all of you were in occupation, grand people with splendid equipages; I was powerless, I confess, though more attached to my countrymen than you.

Two things, men of Athens, are characteristic of a well-disposed citizen —so may I speak of myself and give the least offense:—In authority, his constant aim should be the dignity and preeminence of the commonwealth; in all times and circumstances his spirit should be loyal. This depends upon nature; power and might upon other things. Such a spirit, you will find, I have ever sincerely cherished. Only see. When my person was demanded—when they brought Amphictyonic suits against me—when they menaced—when they promised—when they set these miscreants like wild beasts upon me—never in any way have I abandoned my affection for you. From the very beginning I chose an honest and straightforward course in politics, to support the honor, the power, the glory of my fatherland, these to exalt, in these to have been my being. I do not walk about the market-place gay and cheerful because the stranger has prospered, holding out my right hand and congratulating those who I think will report it yonder, and on any news of our own success shudder and groan and stoop to the earth, like these impious men, who rail at Athens, as if in so doing they did not rail at themselves; who look abroad, and if the foreigner thrives by the distresses of Greece, are thankful for it, and say we should keep him so thriving to all time.

Never, O ye gods, may those wishes be confirmed by you! If possible, inspire even in these men a better sense and feeling! But if they are indeed incurable, destroy them by themselves; exterminate them on land and sea; and for the rest of us, grant that we may speedily be released from our present fears, and enjoy a lasting deliverance!

An earlier masterpiece of Demosthenes is his "Second Oration Against Philip," which was delivered in Athens about 344 B.C. The term philippic, *which we apply to any speech of bitter denunciation, is derived from Demosthenes' series of attacks on Philip of Macedon, of which this is perhaps the most famous.*

THE SECOND ORATION AGAINST PHILIP

ATHENIANS! when the hostile attempts of Philip, and those outrageous violations of the peace which he is perpetually committing, are at any time the subject of our debates, the speeches on your side I find humane and just, and that the sentiments of those who inveigh against Philip never fail of approbation; but as to the necessary measures, to speak out plainly, not one has been pursued, nor anything effected even to reward the attention to these harangues. Nay, to such circumstances is our state reduced, that the more fully and evidently a man proves that Philip is acting contrary to his treaty, and harboring designs against Greece, the greater is his difficulty in pointing out your duty.

The reason is this. They who aspire to an extravagant degree of power are to be opposed by force and action, not by speeches; and yet in the first place, we public speakers are unwilling to recommend or to propose anything to this purpose, from the fear of your displeasure; but confine ourselves to general representations of the grievous, of the outrageous nature of his conduct, and the like. Then you who attend are better qualified than Philip, either to plead the justice of your cause or to apprehend it when enforced by others; but as to any effectual opposition to his present designs, in this you are entirely inactive. You see, then, the consequence, the necessary, the natural consequence, each of you excels in that which has engaged your time and application, he in acting, you in speaking. And if, on this occasion, it be sufficient that we speak with a superior force of truth and justice, this may be done with the utmost ease; but if we are to consider how to rectify our present disorders, how to guard against the danger of plunging inadvertently into still greater, against the progress of a power which may at last bear down all opposition—then must our debates proceed in a different manner; and all they who speak, and all you who attend, must prefer the best and most salutary measures to the easiest and most agreeable.

First, then, Athenians, if there be a man who feels no apprehensions at the view of Philip's power, and the extent of his conquests, who imagines that these portend no danger to the state, or that his designs are not all aimed against you, I am amazed! and must entreat the attention of you all while I explain those reasons briefly which induce me to entertain different expectations, and to regard Philip as our real enemy; that if I appear to have looked forward with the more penetrating eye, you may join with me; if they who are thus secure and confident in this man, you may yield to their direction.

In the first place, therefore, I consider the acquisitions made by Philip, when the peace was just concluded, Thermopylæ, and the command of Phocis. What use did he make of these? He chose to serve the interest of Thebes, not that of Athens. And why? As ambition is his great passion, universal empire the sole object of his views; not peace, not tranquillity, not any just purpose: he knew this well, that neither our constitution nor our principles would admit him to prevail on you by anything he could promise, by anything he could do, to sacrifice one state of Greece to your private interest; but that, as you have the due regard to justice, as you have an abhorrence of the least stain on your honor, and as you have that quick discernment which nothing can escape, the moment his attempt was made, you would oppose him with the same vigor as if you yourselves had been immediately attacked. The Thebans, he supposed (and the event confirmed his opinion), would, for the sake of any private advantage, suffer him to act toward others as he pleased; and far from opposing or impeding his designs, would be ready at his command to fight on his side. From the same persuasion he now heaps his favors on the Messenians and Argians. And this reflects the greatest luster on you, my countrymen; for by these proceedings you are declared the only invariable assertors of the rights of Greece—the only persons whom no private attachment, no views of interest, can seduce from their affection to the Greeks.

And that it is with reason he entertains these sentiments of you, and sentiments so different of the Thebans and the Argians, he may be convinced, not from the present only, but from a review of former times; for he must have been informed, I presume he cannot but have heard, that your ancestors, when, by submitting to the king, they might have purchased the sovereignty of Greece, not only scorned to listen when Alexander, this man's ancestor, was made the messenger of such terms, but chose to abandon their city, encountered every possible difficulty, and after all this performed such exploits as men are ever eager to recite, yet with the just force and dignity no man could ever express; and therefore it becomes me to be silent on this subject; for in reality their actions are superior to the power of words. As to the ancestors of the Thebans and the Argians, the one, he knows, fought for the barbarian; the others did not oppose him. He knew, then, that both these people would attend but their private interest, without the least regard to the common cause of Greece. Should he choose you for allies, you would serve him so far only as justice would permit; but if he attached himself to them, he gained assistants in all the schemes of his ambition. This it is that then determined him, this it is that now determines him to their side rather than to yours: not that he sees they have a greater naval force than we; or that, having gained the sovereignty in the inland countries, he declines the command of the seas and the advantages of commerce; or that he has forgotten those pretenses, those promises which obtained him the peace.

But I may be told: It is true, he did act thus; but not from ambition, or from any of those motives of which I accuse him; but as he thought the cause of Thebes more just than ours. This of all pretenses he cannot now allege. Can he, who commands the Lacedæmonians to quit their claim to Messene, pretend that, in giving up Orchomenus and Coronea to the Thebans, he acted from regard to justice? But now comes his last subterfuge. He was compelled, and yielded these places quite against his inclinations, being encompassed by the Thessalian horse and Theban infantry. Fine pretense! Just so, they cry, he is to entertain suspicions of the Thebans; and some spread rumors of their own framing, that he is to fortify Elatea. Yes! these things are yet to be, and so will they remain, in my opinion; but his attack on Lacedæmon, in conjunction with the Thebans and Argians, is not yet to be made. No: he is actually detaching forces, supplying money, and is himself expected at the head of a formidable army. The Lacedæmonians, therefore, the enemies of Thebes, he now infests. And will he then restore the Phocians, whom he has but just now ruined? Who can believe this? I, for my part, can never think, if Philip had been forced into those former measures, or if he had now abandoned the Thebans, that he would make this continued opposition to their enemies. No, his present measures prove that all his past conduct was the effect of choice; and from all his actions, it appears that all his actions are directly leveled against this state; and there is in some sort a necessity for this. Consider, he aims at empire, and from you alone he expects opposition. He has long loaded us with injuries; and of this he himself is most intimately conscious; for those of our possessions which he has reduced to his service he uses as a barrier to his other territories: so that, if he should give up Amphipolis and Potidæa, he would not think himself secure even in Macedon. He is therefore sensible that he entertains designs against you, and that you perceive them. Then, as he thinks highly of your wisdom, he concludes that you must hold him in that abhorrence which he merits; hence is he alarmed, expecting to feel some effects of your resentment (if you have any favorable opportunity) unless he prevent you by his attack. Hence is his vigilance awakened; his arm raised against the state; he courts some of the Thebans, and such of the Peloponnesians as have the same views with him; whom he deems too mercenary to regard anything but present interest, and too perversely stupid to foresee any consequences. And yet persons of but moderate discernment may have some manifest examples to alarm them, which I had occasion to mention to the Messenians and to the Argians. Perhaps it may be proper to repeat them here.

"Messenians!" said I, "how highly, think ye, would the Olynthians have been offended if any man had spoken against Philip at that time when he gave them up Anthemus, a city which the former kings of Macedon had ever claimed? when he drove out the Athenian colony, and gave them Potidæa? when he took all our resentment on himself, and left them to enjoy our dominions? Did they expect to have suffered thus? Had it been foretold, would they have believed it? You cannot think it! Yet, after a short enjoyment of the territories of others, they have been forever despoiled of their own by this man. Inglorious has been their fall, not conquered only, but betrayed and sold by one another; for those intimate correspondences with tyrants ever portend mischief to free states."—"Turn your eyes," said I, "to the Thessalians! think ye, that when he first expelled their tyrants, when he then gave them up Nicæa and Magnesia, that they expected ever to have been subjected to those governors now imposed on them? or that the man who restored them to their seat in the amphictyonic council would have deprived them of their own proper revenues? yet, that such was the event, the world can testify. In like manner, you now behold Philip lavishing his gifts and promises on you. If you are wise, you will pray that he may never appear to have deceived and abused you. Various are the contrivances for the defense and security of cities; as battlements, and walls, and trenches, and every other kind of fortification; all which are the effects of labor, and attended with continual expense. But there is one common bulwark with which men of prudence are naturally provided, the guard and security of all people, particularly of free states, against the assaults of tyrants. What is this? Distrust. Of this be mindful: to this adhere: preserve this carefully, and no calamity can affect you."—"What is it you seek?" said I. "Liberty? And do ye not perceive that nothing can be more adverse to this than the very titles of Philip? Every monarch, every tyrant is an enemy to liberty, and the opposer of laws. Will ye not then be careful lest, while ye seek to be freed from war, you find yourselves his slaves?"

It would be just, Athenians, to call the men before you who gave those promises which induced you to conclude the peace; for neither would I have undertaken the embassy, nor would you, I am convinced, have laid down your arms, had it been suspected that Philip would have acted thus when he had obtained peace. No: the assurances he then gave were quite different from the present actions. There are others also to be summoned. Who are these? The men who, at my return from the second embassy (sent for the ratification of the treaty), when I saw the state abused, and warned you of your danger, and testified the truth, and opposed with all my power the giving up Thermopylæ and Phocis—the men, I say, who then cried out that I, the water-drinker, was morose and peevish; but that Philip, if permitted to pass, would act agreeably to your desires; would fortify Thespia and Platæa; restrain the insolence of Thebes; cut through the Chersonesus at his own expense, and give you up Eubœa and Oropus, as an equivalent for Amphipolis. That all this was positively affirmed you cannot, I am sure, forget, though not remarkable for remembering injuries. And, to complete the disgrace, you have engaged your posterity to the same treaty, in full dependence on those promises; so entirely have you been seduced.

And now, to what purpose do I mention this? and why do I desire that these men should appear? I call the gods to witness, that without the least evasion I shall boldly declare the truth! Not that, by breaking out into invectives, I may expose myself to the like treatment, and once more give my old enemies an opportunity of receiving Philip's gold; nor yet that I may indulge an impertinent vanity of haranguing; but I apprehend the time must come when Philip's actions will give you more concern than at present. His designs, I see, are ripening. I wish my apprehensions may not prove just; but I fear that time is not far off. And when it will no longer be in your power to disregard events; when neither mine nor any other person's information, but your own knowledge, your own senses will assure you of the impending danger, then will your severest resentment break forth. And as your ambassadors have concealed certain things, influenced (as they themselves are conscious) by corruption, I fear that they who endeavor to restore what these men have ruined may feel the weight of your displeasure; for there are some, I find, who generally point their anger, not at the deserving objects, but those most immediately at their mercy.

While our affairs, therefore, remain not absolutely desperate—while it is yet in our power to debate—give me leave to remind you all of one thing, though none can be ignorant of it. Who was the man that persuaded you to give up Phocis and Thermopylæ? which once gained, he also gained free access for his troops to Attica and to Peloponnesus, and obliged us to turn our thoughts from the rights of Greece, from all foreign interests, to a defensive war, in these very territories; whose approach must be severely felt by every one of us; and that very day gave birth to it; for had we not been then deceived, the state could have nothing to apprehend. His naval power could not have been great enough to attempt Attica by sea; nor could he have passed by land through Thermopylæ and Phocis. But he must have either confined himself within the bounds of justice and lived in a due observance of his treaty, or have instantly been involved in a war equal to that which obliged him to sue for peace.

Thus much may be sufficient to recall past actions to your view. May all the gods forbid that the event should confirm my suspicions! for I by no means desire that any man should meet even the deserved punishment of his crimes, when the whole community is in danger of being involved in his destruction.

Cato, the Elder

[234 B.C.–149 B.C.]

Known as the Censor, and as the Elder to distinguish him from his grandson, Marcus Porcius Cato was an implacable enemy of Carthage. He ended many of his speeches before the Roman Forum with the often quoted phrase "Carthage must be destroyed!" Here is part of an address in which he supported a repressive measure against women.

IN SUPPORT OF THE OPPIAN LAW

IF, ROMANS, every individual among us had made it a rule to maintain the prerogative and authority of a husband with respect to his own wife, we should have less trouble with the whole sex. But now our privileges, overpowered at home by female contumacy, are, even here in the Forum, spurned and trodden under foot; and because we are unable to withstand each separately we now dread their collective body. I was accustomed to think it a fabulous and fictitious tale that in a certain island the whole race of males was utterly extirpated by a conspiracy of the women.

But the utmost danger may be apprehended equally from either sex if you suffer cabals and secret consultations to be held: scarcely indeed can I determine, in my own mind, whether the act itself, or the precedent that it affords, is of more pernicious tendency. The latter of these more particularly concerns us consuls and the other magistrates; the former, you, my fellow citizens: for, whether the measure proposed to your consideration be profitable to the state or not, is to be determined by you, who are to vote on the occasion.

As to the outrageous behavior of these women, whether it be merely an act of their own, or owing to your instigations, Marcus Fundanius and Lucius Valerius, it unquestionably implies culpable conduct in magistrates. I know not whether it reflects greater disgrace on you, tribunes, or on the consuls: on you certainly, if you have brought these women hither for the purpose of raising tribunitian seditions; on us, if we suffer laws to be imposed on us by a secession of women, as was done formerly by that of the common people. It was not without painful emotions of shame that I, just now, made my way into the Forum through the midst of a band of women.

Had I not been restrained by respect for the modesty and dignity of some individuals among them, rather than of the whole number, and been unwilling that they should be seen rebuked by a consul, I should not have refrained from saying to them, "What sort of practice is this, of running out into public, besetting the streets, and addressing other women's husbands? Could not each have made the same request to her husband at home? Are your blandishments more seducing in public than in private, and with other women's husbands than with your own? Although if females would let their modesty confine them within the limits of their own rights, it did not become you, even at home, to concern yourselves about any laws that might be passed or repealed here." Our ancestors thought it not proper that women should perform any, even private business, without a director; but that they should be ever under the control of parents, brothers, or husbands. We, it seems, suffer them, now, to interfere in the management of state affairs, and to thrust themselves into the Forum, into general assemblies, and into assemblies of election: for what are they doing at this moment in your streets and lanes? What, but arguing, some in support of the motion of tribunes; others contending for the repeal of the law?

Will you give the reins to their intractable nature, and then expect that themselves should set bounds to their licentiousness, and without your interference? This is the smallest of the injunctions laid on them by usage or the laws, all which women bear with impatience: they long for entire liberty; nay, to speak the truth, not for liberty, but for unbounded freedom in every particular: for what will they not attempt if they now come off victorious? Recollect all the institutions respecting the sex, by which our forefathers restrained their profligacy and subjected them to their husbands; and yet, even with the help of all these restrictions, they can scarcely be kept within bounds. If, then, you suffer them to throw these off one by one, to tear them all asunder, and, at last, to be set on an equal footing with yourselves, can you imagine that they will be any longer tolerable? Suffer them once to arrive at an equality with you, and they will from that moment become your superiors.

But, indeed, they only object to any new law being made against them; they mean to deprecate, not justice, but severity. Nay, their wish is that a law which you have admitted, established by your suffrages, and found in the practice and experience of so many years to be beneficial, should now be repealed; and that by abolishing one law you should weaken all the rest. No law perfectly suits the convenience of every member of the community; the only consideration is, whether, on the whole, it be profitable to the greater part. If, because a law proves obnoxious to a private individual, it must therefore be canceled and annulled, to what purpose is it for the community to enact laws, which those, whom they were particularly intended to comprehend, could presently repeal? Let us, however, inquire what this important affair is which has induced the matrons thus to run out into public in this indecorous manner, scarcely restraining from pushing into the Forum and the assembly of the people.

Is it to solicit that their parents, their husbands, children, and brothers may be ransomed from captivity under Hannibal?

By no means: and far be ever from the commonwealth so unfortunate a situation. Yet, when such was the case, you refused this to the prayers which, on that occasion, their duty dictated. But it is not duty, nor solicitude for their friends; it is religion that has collected them together. They are about to receive the Idæan Mother, coming out of Phrygia from Pessinus.

What motive, that even common decency will not allow to be mentioned, is pretended for this female insurrection? Hear the answer:

That we may shine in gold and purple; that, both on festival and common days, we may ride through the city in our chariots, triumphing over vanquished and abrogated law, after having captured and wrested from you your suffrages; and that there may be no bounds to our expenses and our luxury.

Often have you heard me complain of the profuse expenses of the women—often of those of the men; and that not only of men in private stations, but of the magistrates; and that the state was endangered by two opposite vices, luxury and avarice; those pests which have ever been the ruin of every great state. These I dread the more, as the circumstances of the commonwealth grow daily more prosperous and happy; as the empire increases; as we have passed over into Greece and Asia, places abounding with every kind of temptation that can inflame the passions; and as we have begun to handle even royal treasures: for I greatly fear that these matters will rather bring us into captivity than we them.

Believe me, those statues from Syracuse made their way into this city with hostile effect. I already hear too many commending and admiring the decorations of Athens and Corinth, and ridiculing the earthen images of our Roman gods that stand on the fronts of their temples. For my part, I prefer these gods,—propitious as they are, and I hope will continue, if we allow them to remain in their own mansions.

In the memory of our fathers, Pyrrhus, by his ambassador Cineas, made trial of the dispositions, not only of our men, but of our women also, by offers of presents: at that time the Oppian law, for restraining female luxury, had not been made; and yet not one woman accepted a present. What, think you, was the reason? That for which our ancestors made no provision by law on this subject: there was no luxury existing which might be restrained.

As diseases must necessarily be known before their remedies, so passions come into being before the laws which prescribe limits to them. What called forth the Licinian law, restricting estates to five hundred acres, but the unbounded desire for enlarging estates? What the Cineian law, concerning gifts and presents, but that the plebeians had become vassals and tributaries to the senate? It is not, therefore, in any degree surprising that no want of the Oppian law, or of any other, to limit the expenses of the women, was felt at that time, when they refused to receive gold and purple that was thrown in their way and offered to their acceptance. If Cineas were now to go round the city with his presents, he would find numbers of women standing in the public streets ready to receive them.

There are some passions the causes or motives of which I can no way account for. To be debarred of a liberty in which another is indulged may perhaps naturally excite some degree of shame or indignation; yet, when the dress of all is alike, what inferiority in appearance can any one be ashamed of? Of all kinds of shame, the worst, surely, is the being ashamed of frugality or of poverty; but the law relieves you with regard to both; you want only that which it is unlawful for you to have.

This equalization, says the rich matron, is the very thing that I cannot endure. Why do not I make a figure, distinguished with gold and purple? Why is the poverty of others concealed under this cover of a law, so that it should be thought that, if the law permitted, they would have such things as they are not now able to procure? Romans, do you wish to excite among your wives an emulation of this sort, that the rich should wish to have what no other can have; and that the poor, lest they should be despised as such, should extend their expenses beyond their abilities? Be assured that when a woman once begins to be ashamed of what she ought not to be ashamed of, she will not be ashamed of what she ought. She who can, will purchase out of her own purse; she who cannot, will ask her husband.

Unhappy is the husband, both he who complies with the request, and he who does not; for what he will not give himself, another will. Now they openly solicit favors from other women's husbands; and, what is more, solicit a law and votes. From some they obtain them; although, with regard to you, your property, or your children, you would find it hard to obtain anything from them. If the law ceases to limit the expenses of your wife, you yourself will never be able to limit them. Do not suppose that the matter will hereafter be in the same state in which it was before the law was made on the subject. It is safer that a wicked man should never be accused than that he should be acquitted; and luxury, if it had never been meddled with, would be more tolerable than it will be, now, like a wild beast, irritated by having been chained and then let loose. My opinion is that the Oppian law ought on no account to be repealed. Whatever determination you may come to, I pray all the gods to prosper it.

Hannibal
[247 B.C.–183 B.C.]

Hannibal, the famous Carthaginian general, delivered this speech to his soldiers after his army had crossed the Alps and entered Italy, in 218 B.C.

TO HIS SOLDIERS

IF, SOLDIERS, you shall by and by, in judging of your own fortune, preserve the same feelings which you experienced a little before in the example of the fate of others, we have already conquered; for neither was that merely a spectacle, but, as it were, a certain representation of your condition. And I know not whether fortune has not thrown around you still stronger chains and more urgent necessities than around your captives. On the right and left two seas enclose you, without your possessing even a single ship for escape. The river Po around you, the Po larger and more impetuous than the Rhone; the Alps behind, scarcely passed by you when fresh and vigorous, hem you in.

Here, soldiers, where you have first met the enemy, you must conquer or die; and the same fortune which has imposed the necessity of fighting holds out to you, if victorious, rewards than which men are not wont to desire greater, even from the immortal gods. If we were only about to recover by our valor Sicily and Sardinia, wrested from our fathers, the recompense would be sufficiently ample; but whatever, acquired and amassed by so many triumphs, the Romans possess, all, with its masters themselves, will become yours. To gain this rich reward, hasten, then, and seize your arms, with the favor of the gods.

Long enough, in pursuing cattle among the desert mountains of Lusitania and Celtiberia, you have seen no emolument from so many toils and dangers; it is time to make rich and profitable campaigns, and to gain the great reward of your labors, after having accomplished such a length of journey over so many mountains and rivers, and so many nations in arms. Here fortune has granted you the termination of your labors; here she will bestow a reward worthy of the service you have undergone. Nor, in proportion as the war is great in name, ought you to consider that the victory will be difficult. A despised enemy has often maintained a sanguinary contest, and renowned States and kings have been conquered by a very slight effort.

For, setting aside only the splendor of the Roman name, what remains in which they can be compared to you? To pass over in silence your service for twenty years, distinguished by such valor and success, you have made your way to this place from the pillars of Hercules, from the ocean and the remotest limits of the world, advancing victorious through so many of the fiercest nations of Gaul and Spain; you will fight with a raw army, which this very summer was beaten, conquered, and surrounded by the Gauls, as yet unknown to its general, and ignorant of him. Shall I compare myself—almost born, and certainly bred, in the tent of my father, that most illustrious commander, myself the subjugator of Spain and Gaul, the conqueror too not only of the Alpine nations, but, what is much more, of the Alps themselves—with this six-months' general, the deserter of his army?—to whom, if anyone, having taken away their standards, should to-day show the Carthaginians and Romans, I am sure that he would not know of which army he was consul.

I do not regard it, soldiers, as of small account that there is not a man among you before whose eyes I have not often achieved some military exploit; and to whom, in like manner, I, the spectator and witness of his valor, could not recount his own gallant deeds, particularized by time and place. With soldiers who have a thousand times received my praises and gifts, I, who was the pupil of you all before I became your commander, will march out in battle-array against those who are unknown to and ignorant of each other.

On whatever side I turn my eyes I see nothing but what is full of courage and energy: a veteran infantry; cavalry, both those with and those without the bridle, composed of the most gallant nations,—you, our most faithful and valiant allies, you Carthaginians, who are about to fight as well for the sake of your country as from the justest resentment. We are the assailants in the war, and descend into Italy with hostile standards, about to engage so much more boldly and bravely than the foe, as the confidence and courage of the assailants are greater than those of him who is defensive. Besides, suffering, injury, and indignity inflame and excite our minds: they first demanded me, your leader, for punishment, and then all of you who had laid siege to Saguntum; and had we been given up they would have visited us with the severest tortures.

That most cruel and haughty nation considers everything its own, and at its own disposal; it thinks it right that it should regulate with whom we are to have war, with whom peace; it circumscribes and shuts us up by the boundaries of mountains and rivers which we must not pass, and then does not adhere to those boundaries which it appointed. Pass not the Iberius; have nothing to do with the Saguntines. Saguntum is on the Iberius; you must not move a step in any direction. Is it a small thing that you take away my most ancient provinces—Sicily and Sardinia? Will you take Spain also? And should I withdraw thence, will you cross over into Africa?

Will cross, did I say? They have sent the two consuls of this year, one to Africa, the other to Spain: there is nothing left to us in any quarter, except what we can assert to ourselves by arms. Those may be cowards and dastards who have something to look back upon; whom, flying through safe and unmolested roads, their own lands and their own country will receive: there is a necessity for you to be brave, and, since all between victory and death is broken off from you by inevitable despair, either to conquer, or if fortune should waver, to meet death rather in battle than in flight. If this be well fixed and determined in the minds of you all, I will repeat, you have already conquered; no stronger incentive to victory has been given to man by the immortal gods.

Cicero

[106 B.C.–43 B.C.]

Roman statesman and man of letters, Marcus Tullius Cicero is classed as one of the world's greatest orators of any age. His series of speeches before the Roman senate against Catiline foiled the latter's conspiracies against the state. The first of this series of orations, delivered in 63 B.C., is presented here. Cicero's "Fourth Philippic" is also reproduced.

FIRST ORATION AGAINST CATILINE

WHEN, O Catiline, do you mean to cease abusing our patience? How long is that madness of yours still to mock us? When is there to be an end of that unbridled audacity of yours, swaggering about as it does now? Do not the mighty guards placed on the Palatine Hill—do not the watches posted throughout the city—does not the alarm of the people, and the union of all good men—does not the precaution taken of assembling the senate in this most defensible place—do not the looks and countenances of this venerable body here present, have any effect upon you? Do you not feel that your plans are detected? Do you not see that your conspiracy is already arrested and rendered powerless by the knowledge which everyone here possesses of it? What is there that you did last night, what the night before—where is it that you were—who was there that you summoned to meet you—what design was there which was adopted by you, with which you think that any one of us is unacquainted?

Shame on the age and on its principles! The senate is aware of these things; the consul sees them; and yet this man lives. Lives! aye, he comes even into the senate. He takes a part in the public deliberations; he is watching and marking down and checking off for slaughter every individual among us. And we, gallant men that we are, think that we are doing our duty to the republic if we keep out of the way of his frenzied attacks.

You ought, O Catiline, long ago to have been led to execution by command of the counsel. That destruction which you have been long plotting against us ought to have already fallen on your own head.

What? Did not that most illustrious man, Publius Scipio, the Pontifex Maximus, in his capacity of a private citizen, put to death Tiberius Gracchus, though but slightly undermining the constitution? And shall we, who are the consuls, tolerate Catiline, openly desirous to destroy the whole world with fire and slaughter? For I pass over older instances, such as how Caius Servilius Ahala with his own hand slew Spurius Mælius when plotting a revolution in the state. There was—there was once such virtue in this republic that brave men would repress mischievous citizens with severer chastisement than the most bitter enemy. For we have a resolution of the senate, a formidable and authoritative decree against you, O Catiline; the wisdom of the republic is not at fault, nor the dignity of this senatorial body. We, we alone—I say it openly—we, the consuls, are wanting in our duty.

The senate once passed a decree that Lucius Opimius, the consul, should take care that the republic suffered no injury. Not one night elapsed. There was put to death, on some mere suspicion of disaffection, Caius Gracchus, a man whose family had borne the most unblemished reputation for many generations. There was slain Marcus Fulvius, a man of consular rank, and all of his children. By a like decree of the senate the safety of the republic was intrusted to Caius Marius and Lucius Valerius, the consuls. Did not the vengeance of the republic, did not execution overtake Lucius Saturninus, a tribune of the people, and Caius Servilius, the prætor, without the delay of one single day? But we, for these twenty days, have been allowing the edge of the senate's authority to grow blunt, as it were. For we are in possession of a similar decree of the senate, but we keep it locked up in its parchment—buried, I may say, in the sheath; and according to this decree you ought, O Catiline, to be put to death this instant. You live—and you live, not to lay aside, but to persist in your audacity.

I wish, O conscript fathers, to be merciful; I wish not to appear negligent amid such danger to the state; but I do now accuse myself of remissness and culpable inactivity. A camp is pitched in Italy, at the entrance of Etruria, in hostility to the republic; the number of the enemy increases every day; and yet the general of that camp, the leader of those enemies, we see within the walls—aye, and even in the senate—planning every day some internal injury to the republic. If, O Catiline, I should now order you to be arrested, to be put to death, I should I suppose, have to fear lest all good men should say that I had acted tardily, rather than that any one should affirm that I acted cruelly. But yet this, which ought to have been done long since, I have good reason for not doing as yet; I will put you to death, then, when there shall be not one person possible to be found so wicked, so abandoned, so like yourself, as not to allow that it has been rightly done. As long as one person exists who can dare to defend you, you shall live; but you shall live as you do now, surrounded by my many and trusted guards, so that you shall not be able to stir one finger against the republic; many eyes and ears shall still observe and watch you as they have hitherto done, though you shall not perceive them.

For what is there, O Catiline, that you can still expect, if night is not able to veil your nefarious meetings in darkness, and if private houses cannot conceal the voice of your conspiracy within their walls—if everything is seen and displayed? Change your mind: trust me: forget the slaughter and conflagration you are meditating. You are hemmed in on all sides; all your plans are clearer than the day to us; let me remind you of them. Do you recollect that on the 21st of October I said in the senate, that on a certain day, which was to be the 27th of October, C. Manlius, the satellite and servant of your audacity, would be in arms? Was I mistaken, Catiline, not only in so important, so atrocious, so incredible a fact, but, what is much more remarkable, in the very day? I said also in the senate that you had fixed the massacre of the nobles for the 28th of October, when many chief men of the senate had left Rome, not so much for the sake of saving themselves as of checking your designs. Can you deny that on that very day you were so hemmed in by my guards and my vigilance, that you were unable to stir one finger against the republic; when you said that you would be content with the flight of the rest, and the slaughter of us who remained? What? when you made sure that you would be able to seize Præneste on the 1st of November by a nocturnal attack, did you not find that that colony was fortified by my order, by my garrison, by my watchfulness and care? You do nothing, you plan nothing, think of nothing which I not only do not hear but which I do not see and know every particular of.

Listen while I speak of the night before. You shall now see that I watch far more actively for the safety than you do for the destruction of the republic. I say that you came the night before (I will say nothing obscurely) into the Scythe-dealers' street, to the house of Marcus Lecca; that many of your accomplices in the same insanity and wickedness came there, too. Do you dare to deny it? Why are you silent? I will prove it if you do deny it; for I see here in the senate some men who were there with you.

O ye immortal gods, where on earth are we? in what city are we living? what constitution is ours? There are here—here in our body, O conscript fathers, in this the most holy and dignified assembly of the whole world, men who meditate my death, and the death of all of us, and the destruction of this city, and of the whole world. I, the consul, see them; I ask them their opinion about the republic, and I do not yet attack, even by words, those who ought to be put to death by the sword. You were, then, O Catiline, at Lecca's that night; you divided Italy into sections; you settled where every one was to go; you fixed whom you were to leave at Rome, whom you were to take with you; you portioned out the divisions of the city for conflagration; you undertook that you yourself would at once leave the city, and said that there was then only this to delay you, that I was still alive. Two Roman knights were found to deliver you from this anxiety, and to promise that very night, before daybreak, to slay me in my bed. All this I knew almost before your meeting had broken up. I strengthened and fortified my house with a stronger guard; I refused admittance, when they came, to those whom you sent in the morning to salute me, and of whom I had foretold to many eminent men that they would come to me at that time.

As, then, this is the case, O Catiline, continue as you have begun. Leave the city at last: the gates are open; depart. That Manlian camp of yours has been waiting too long for you as its general. And lead forth with you all your friends, or at least as many as you can; purge the city of your presence; you will deliver me from a great fear, when there is a wall between me and you. Among us you can dwell no longer—I will not bear it, I will not permit it, I will not tolerate it. Great thanks are due to the immortal gods, and to this very Jupiter Stator, in whose temple we are, the most ancient protector of this city, that we have already so often escaped so foul, so horrible, and so deadly an enemy to the republic. But the safety of the commonwealth must not be too often allowed to be risked on one man. As long as you, O Catiline, plotted against me while I was the consul-elect, I defended myself not with a public guard, but by my own private diligence. When, in the next consular comitia, you wished to slay me when I was actually consul, and your competitors also, in the Campus Martius, I checked your nefarious attempt by the assistance and resources of my own friends, without exciting any disturbance publicly. In short, as often as you attacked me, I by myself opposed you, and that, too, though I saw that my ruin was connected with great disaster to the republic. But now you are openly attacking the entire republic.

You are summoning to destruction and devastation the temples of the immortal gods, the houses of the city, the lives of all the citizens; in short, all Italy. Wherefore, since I do not yet venture to do that which is the best thing, and which belongs to my office and to the discipline of our ancestors, I will do that which is more merciful if we regard its rigor, and more expedient for the state. For if I order you to be put to death, the rest of the conspirators will still remain in the republic; if, as I have long been exhorting you, you depart, your companions, these worthless dregs of the republic, will be drawn off from the city too. What is the matter, Catiline? Do you hesitate to do that when I order you which you were already doing of your own accord? The consul orders an enemy to depart from the city. Do you ask me, Are you to go into banishment? I do not order it; but if you consult me, I advise it.

For what is there, O Catiline, that can now afford you any pleasure in this city? for there is no one in it, except that band of profligate conspirators of yours, who does not fear you—no one who does not hate you. What brand of domestic baseness is not stamped upon your life? What disgraceful circumstance is wanting to your infamy in your private affairs? From what licentiousness have your eyes, from what atrocity have your hands, from what iniquity has your whole body ever abstained? Is there one youth, when you have once entangled him in the temptations of your corruption, to whom you have not held out a sword for audacious crime, or a torch for licentious wickedness?

What? when lately by the death of your former wife you had made your house empty and ready for a new bridal, did you not even add another incredible wickedness to this wickedness? But I pass that over, and willingly allow it to be buried in silence, that so horrible a crime may not be seen to have existed in this city, and not to have been chastised. I pass over the ruin of your fortune, which you know is hanging over you against the Ides of the very next month; I come to those things which relate not to the infamy of your private vices, not to your domestic difficulties and baseness, but to the welfare of the republic and to the lives and safety of us all.

Can the light of this life, O Catiline, can the breath of this atmosphere be pleasant to you, when you know that there is not one man of those here present who is ignorant that you, on the last day of the year, when Lepidus and Tullus were consuls, stood in the assembly armed; that you had prepared your hand for the slaughter of the consuls and chief men of the state, and that no reason or fear of yours hindered your crime and madness, but the fortune of the republic? And I say no more of these things, for they are not unknown to every one. How often have you endeavored to slay me, both as consul-elect and as actual consul? how many shots of yours, so aimed that they seemed impossible to be escaped, have I avoided by some slight stooping aside, and some dodging, as it were, of my body? You attempt nothing, you execute nothing, you devise nothing that can be kept hid from me at the proper time; and yet you do not cease to attempt and to contrive. How often already has that dagger of yours been wrested from your hands? how often has it slipped through them by some chance, and dropped down? and yet you cannot any longer do without it; and to what sacred mysteries it is consecrated and devoted by you I know not, that you think it necessary to plunge it in the body of the consul.

But now, what is that life of yours that you are leading? For I will speak to you not so as to seem influenced by the hatred I ought to feel, but by pity, nothing of which is due to you. You came a little while ago into the senate: in so numerous an assembly, who of so many friends and connections of yours saluted you? If this in the memory of man never happened to any one else, are you waiting for insults by word of mouth, when you are overwhelmed by the most irresistible condemnation of silence? Is it nothing that at your arrival all those seats were vacated? that all the men of consular rank, who had often been marked out by you for slaughter, the very moment you sat down, left that part of the benches bare and vacant? With what feelings do you think you ought to bear this? On my honor, if my slaves feared me as all your fellow-citizens fear you, I should think I must leave my house. Do not you think you should leave the city? If I saw that I was even undeservedly so suspected and hated by my fellow-citizens, I would rather flee from their sight than be gazed at by the hostile eyes of every one. And do you, who, from the consciousness of your wickedness, know that the hatred of all men is just and has been long due to you, hesitate to avoid the sight and presence of those men whose minds and senses you offend? If your parents feared and hated you, and if you could by no means pacify them, you would, I think, depart somewhere out of their sight. Now your country, which is the common parent of all of us, hates and fears you, and has no other opinion of you than that you are meditating parricide in her case; and will you neither feel awe of her authority, nor deference for her judgment, nor fear of her power?

And she, O Catiline, thus pleads with you, and after a manner silently speaks to you: There has now for many years been no crime committed but by you; no atrocity has taken place without you; you alone unpunished and unquestioned have murdered the citizens, have harassed and plundered the allies; you alone have had power not only to neglect all laws and investigations, but to overthrow and break through them. Your former actions, though they ought not to have been borne, yet I did bear as well as I could; but now that I should be wholly occupied with fear of you alone, that at every sound I should dread Catiline, that no design should seem possible to be entertained against me which does not proceed from your wickedness, this is no longer endurable. Depart, then, and deliver me from this fear; that, if it be a just one, I may not be destroyed; if an imaginary one, that at least I may at last cease to fear.

If, as I have said, your country were thus to address you, ought she not to obtain her request, even if she were not able to enforce it? What shall I say of your having given yourself into custody? what of your having said, for the sake of avoiding suspicion, that you were willing to dwell in the house of Marcus Lepidus? And when you were not received by him, you dared even to come to me, and begged me to keep you in my house; and when you had received answer from me that I could not possibly be safe in the same house with you, when I considered myself in great danger as long as we were in the same city, you came to Quintus Metellus, the prætor, and being rejected by him, you passed on to your associate, that most excellent man, Marcus Marcellus, who would be, I suppose you thought, most diligent in guarding you, most sagacious in suspecting you, and most bold in punishing you; but how far can we think that man ought to be from bonds and imprisonment who has already judged himself deserving of being given into custody?

Since, then, this is the case, do you hesitate, O Catiline, if you cannot remain here with tranquillity, to depart to some distant land, and to trust your life, saved from just and deserved punishment, to flight and solitude? Make a motion, say you, to the senate (for that is what you demand), and if this body votes that you ought to go into banishment, you say that you will obey. I will not make such a motion, it is contrary to my principles, and yet I will let you see what these men think of you. Begone from the city, O Catiline, deliver the republic from fear; depart into banishment, if that is the word you are waiting for. What now, O Catiline? Do you not perceive, do you not see the silence of these men? They permit it, they say nothing; why wait you for the authority of their words, when you see their wishes in their silence?

But had I said the same to this worthy young man, Publius Sextius, or to that brave man, Marcus Marcellus, before this time the senate would deservedly have laid violent hands on me, consul though I be, in this very temple. But as to you, Catiline, while they are quiet they approve, while they permit me to speak they vote, while they are silent they are loud and eloquent. And not they alone, whose authority forsooth is dear to you, though their lives are unimportant, but the Roman knights, too, those most honorable and excellent men, and the other virtuous citizens who are now surrounding the senate, whose numbers you could see, whose desires you could know, and whose voices you a few minutes ago could hear— aye, whose very hands and weapons I have for some time been scarcely able to keep off from you; but those, too, I will easily bring to attend you to the gates if you leave these places you have been long desiring to lay waste.

And yet, why am I speaking? that anything may change your purpose? that you may ever amend your life? that you may meditate flight or think of voluntary banishment? I wish the gods may give you such a mind; though I see, if alarmed at my words you bring your mind to go into banishment, what a storm of unpopularity hangs over me, if not at present, while the memory of your wickedness is fresh, at all events hereafter. But it is worth while to incur that, as long as that is but a private misfortune of my own, and is unconnected with the dangers of the republic. But we cannot expect that you should be concerned at your own vices, that you should fear the penalties of the laws, or that you should yield to the necessities of the republic, for you are not, O Catiline, one whom either shame can recall from infamy, or fear from danger, or reason from madness.

Wherefore, as I have said before, go forth, and if you wish to make me, your enemy as you call me, unpopular, go straight into banishment. I shall scarcely be able to endure all that will be said if you do so; I shall scarcely be able to support my load of unpopularity if you do go into banishment at the command of the consul; but if you wish to serve my credit and reputation, go forth with your ill-omened band of profligates; betake yourself to Manlius, rouse up the abandoned citizens, separate yourselves from the good ones, wage war against your country, exult in your impious banditti, so that you may not seem to have been driven out by me and gone to strangers, but to have gone invited to your friends.

Though why should I invite you, by whom I know men have been already sent on to wait in arms for you at the Forum Aurelium; who I know has fixed and agreed with Manlius upon a settled day; by whom I know that that silver eagle, which I trust will be ruinous and fatal to you and to all your friends, and to which there was set up in your house a shrine, as it were, of your crimes, has been already sent forward. Need I fear that you can long do without that which you used to worship when going out to murder, and from whose altars you have often transferred your impious hand to the slaughter of citizens?

You will go at last where your unbridled and mad desire has been long hurrying you. And this causes you no grief, but an incredible pleasure.

Nature has formed you, desire has trained you, fortune has preserved you for this insanity. Not only did you never desire quiet, but you never even desired any war but a criminal one; you have collected a band of profligates and worthless men, abandoned not only by all fortune but even by hope.

Then what happiness will you enjoy! with what delight will you exult! in what pleasure will you revel! when in so numerous a body of friends you neither hear nor see one good man. All the toils you have gone through have always pointed to this sort of life; your lying on the ground not merely to lie in wait to gratify your unclean desires, but even to accomplish crimes; your vigilance, not only when plotting against the sleep of husbands, but also against the goods of your murdered victims, have all been preparations for this. Now you have an opportunity of displaying your splendid endurance of hunger, of cold, of want of everything; by which in a short time you will find yourself worn out. All this I effected when I procured your rejection from the consulship, that you should be reduced to make attempts on your country as an exile, instead of being able to distress it as consul, and that that which had been wickedly undertaken by you should be called piracy rather than war.

Now that I may remove and avert, O conscript fathers, any in the least reasonable complaint from myself, listen, I beseech you, carefully to what I say, and lay it up in your inmost hearts and minds. In truth, if my country, which is far dearer to me than my life—if all Italy—if the whole republic were to address me, Marcus Tullius, what are you doing? will you permit that man to depart whom you have ascertained to be an enemy? whom you see ready to become the general of the war? whom you know to be expected in the camp of the enemy as their chief, the author of all this wickedness, the head of the conspiracy, the instigator of the slaves and abandoned citizens, so that he shall seem not driven out of the city by you, but let loose by you against the city? will you not order him to be thrown into prison, to be hurried off to execution, to be put to death with the most prompt severity? What hinders you? is it the customs of our ancestors? But even private men have often in this republic slain mischievous citizens. Is it the laws which have been passed about the punishment of Roman citizens? But in this city those who have rebelled against the republic have never had the rights of citizens. Do you fear odium with posterity? You are showing fine gratitude to the Roman people which has raised you, a man known only by your own actions, of no ancestral renown, through all the degrees of honor at so early an age to the very highest office, if from fear of unpopularity or of any danger you neglect the safety of your fellow-citizens. But if you have a fear of unpopularity, is that arising from the imputation of vigor and boldness, or that arising from that of inactivity and indecision most to be feared? When Italy is laid waste by war, when cities are attacked and houses in flames, do you not think that you will be then consumed by a perfect conflagration of hatred?

To this holy address of the republic, and to the feelings of those men who entertain the same opinion, I will make this short answer: If, O conscript fathers, I thought it best that Catiline should be punished with death, I would not have given the space of one hour to this gladiator to live in. If, forsooth, those excellent men and most illustrious cities not only did not pollute themselves, but even glorified themselves by the blood of Saturninus, and the Gracchi, and Flaccus, and many others of old time, surely I had no cause to fear lest for slaying this parricidal murderer of the citizens any unpopularity should accrue to me with posterity. And if it did threaten me to ever so great a degree, yet I have always been of the disposition to think unpopularity earned by virtue and glory not unpopularity.

Though there are some men in this body who either do not see what threatens, or dissemble what they do see; who have fed the hope of Catiline by mild sentiments, and have strengthened the rising conspiracy by not believing it; influenced by whose authority many, and they not wicked, but only ignorant, if I punished him would say that I had acted cruelly and tyrannically. But I know that if he arrives at the camp of Manlius to which he is going, there will be no one so stupid as not to see that there has been a conspiracy, no one so hardened as not to confess it. But if this man alone were put to death, I know that this disease of the republic would be only checked for a while, not eradicated forever. But if he banishes himself, and takes with him all his friends, and collects at one point all the ruined men from every quarter, then not only will this full-grown plague of the republic be extinguished and eradicated, but also the root and seed of all future evils.

We have now for a long time, O conscript fathers, lived among these dangers and machinations of conspiracy; but somehow or other, the ripeness of all wickedness, and of this long-standing madness and audacity, has come to a head at the time of my consulship. But if this man alone is removed from this piratical crew, we may appear, perhaps, for a short time relieved from fear and anxiety, but the danger will settle down and lie hid in the veins and bowels of the republic. As it often happens that men afflicted with a severe disease, when they are tortured with heat and fever, if they drink cold water seem at first to be relieved, but afterwards suffer more and more severely; so this disease which is in the republic, if relieved by the punishment of this man, will only get worse and worse, as the rest will be still alive.

Wherefore, O conscript fathers, let the worthless begone—let them separate themselves from the good—let them collect in one place—let them, as I have often said before, be separated from us by a wall; let them cease to plot against the consul in his own house—to surround the tribunal of the city prætor—to besiege the senate house with swords—to prepare brands and torches to burn the city; let it, in short, be written on the brow of every citizen what are his sentiments about the republic. I promise you this, O conscript fathers, that there shall be so much diligence in us the consuls, so much authority in you, so much virtue in the Roman knights, so much unanimity in all good men, that you shall see everything made plain and manifest by the departure of Catiline—everything checked and punished.

With these omens, O Catiline, begone to your impious and nefarious war, to the great safety of the republic, to your own misfortune and injury, and to the destruction of those who have joined themselves to you in every wickedness and atrocity. Then do you, O Jupiter, who were consecrated by Romulus with the same auspices as this city, whom we rightly call the stay of this city and empire, repel this man and his companions from your altars and from the other temples—from the houses and walls of the city—from the lives and fortunes of all the citizens; and overwhelm all the enemies of good men, the foes of the republic, the robbers of Italy, men bound together by a treaty and infamous alliance of crimes, dead and alive, with eternal punishments.

The fourth of Cicero's famous Philippics was delivered in Rome in 44 B.C.

THE FOURTH PHILIPPIC

THE GREAT NUMBERS in which you are here met this day, O Romans, and this assembly, greater than, it seems to me, I ever remember, inspires me with both an exceeding eagerness to defend the republic and with a great hope of reestablishing it. Although my courage indeed has never failed, what has been unfavorable is the time; and the moment that has appeared to show any dawn of light, I at once have been the leader in the defense of your liberty. And if I had attempted to have done so before, I should not be able to do so now. For this day, O Romans (that you may not think it is but a trifling business in which we have been engaged), the foundations have been laid for future actions. For the senate has no longer been content with styling Antonius an enemy in words, but it has shown by actions that it thinks him one. And now I am much more elated still, because you too, with such great unanimity and with such a clamor, have sanctioned our declaration that he is an enemy.

And indeed, O Romans, it is impossible but that either the men must be impious who have levied arms against the consul, or else that he must be an enemy against whom they have rightly taken arms. And this doubt the senate has this day removed—not, indeed, that there really was any; but it has prevented the possibility of there being any. Caius Cæsar, who has upheld and who is still upholding the republic and your freedom by his zeal and wisdom, and at the expense of his patrimonial estate, has been complimented with the highest praise of the senate.

I praise you—yes, I praise you greatly, O Romans, when you follow with the most grateful minds the name of that most illustrious youth, or rather boy; for his actions belong to immortality, the name of youth only to his age. I can recollect many things; I have heard of many things; I have read of many things; but in the whole history of the whole world I have never known anything like this. For, when we were weighed down with slavery, when the evil was daily increasing, when we had no defense, while we were in dread of the pernicious and fatal return of Marcus Antonius from Brundusium, this young man adopted the design which none of us had ventured to hope for, which beyond all question none of us were acquainted with, of raising an invincible army of his father's soldiers, and so hindering the frenzy of Antonius, spurred on as it was by the most inhuman counsels, from the power of doing mischief to the republic.

For who is there who does not see clearly that, if Cæsar had not prepared an army, the return of Antonius must have been accompanied by our destruction? For, in truth, he returned in such a state of mind, burning with hatred of you all, stained with the blood of the Roman citizens whom he had murdered at Suessa and at Brundusium, that he thought of nothing but the utter destruction of the republic. And what protection could have been found for your safety and for your liberty if the army of Caius Cæsar had not been composed of the bravest of his father's soldiers? And with respect to his praises and honors—and he is entitled to divine and everlasting honors for his godlike and undying services—the senate has just consented to my proposals, and has decreed that a motion be submitted to it at the very earliest opportunity.

Now, who is there who does not see that by this decree Antonius has been adjudged to be an enemy? For what else can we call him, when the senate decides that extraordinary honors are to be devised for those men who are leading armies against him? What! did not the Martial legion (which appears to me by some divine permission to have derived its name from that god from whom we have heard that the Roman people descended) decide by its resolutions that Antonius was an enemy before the senate had come to any resolution? For if he be not an enemy, we must inevitably decide that those men who have deserted the consul are enemies. Admirably and seasonably, O Romans, have you by your cries sanctioned the noble conduct of the men of the Martial legion, who have come over to the authority of the senate, to your liberty, and to the whole republic, and have abandoned that enemy and robber and parricide of his country. Nor did they display only their spirit and courage in doing this, but their caution and wisdom also. They encamped at Alba, in a city convenient, fortified, near, full of brave men and loyal and virtuous citizens. The fourth legion, imitating the virtue of this Martial legion, under the leadership of Lucius Egnatuleius, whom the senate deservedly praised a little while ago, has also joined the army of Caius Cæsar.

What more adverse decisions, O Marcus Antonius, can you want? Cæsar, who has levied an army against you, is extolled to the skies. The legions are praised in the most complimentary language, which have abandoned you, which were sent for into Italy by you, and which, if you had chosen to be a consul rather than an enemy, were wholly devoted to you. And the fearless and honest decision of those legions is confirmed by the senate, is approved of by the whole Roman people—unless, indeed, you to-day, O Romans, decide that Antonius is a consul and not an enemy. I thought, O Romans, that you did think as you show you do. What! Do you suppose that the municipal towns and the colonies and the prefectures have any other opinion? All men are agreed with one mind; so that every one who wishes the state to be saved must take up every sort of arms against that pestilence. What, I should like to know, does the opinion of Decimus Brutus, O Romans, which you can gather from his edict which has this day reached us, appear to any one deserving of being lightly esteemed? Rightly and truly do you say No, O Romans. For the family and name of Brutus has been by some especial kindness and liberality of the immortal gods given to the republic for the purpose of at one time establishing, and at another of recovering, the liberty of the Roman people. What, then, has been the opinion which Decimus Brutus has formed of Marcus Antonius? He excludes him from his province. He opposes him with his army. He rouses all Gaul to war, which is already roused of its own accord, and in consequence of the judgment which it has itself formed. If Antonius be consul, Brutus is an enemy. Can we then doubt which of these alternatives is the fact?

And just as you now, with one mind and one voice, affirm that you entertain no doubt, so did the senate just now decree that Decimus Brutus deserved excellently well of the republic, inasmuch as he was defending the authority of the senate and the liberty and empire of the Roman people. Defending it against whom? Why, against an enemy. For what other sort of defense deserves praise? In the next place, the province of Gaul is praised, and is deservedly complimented in most honorable language by the senate for resisting Antonius. But if that province considered him the consul, and still refused to receive him, it would be guilty of great wickedness. For all the provinces belong to the consul of right, and are bound to obey him. Decimus Brutus, imperator and consul-elect, a citizen born for the republic, denies that he is consul; Gaul denies it; all Italy denies it; the senate denies it; you deny it. Who, then, thinks that he is consul except a few robbers? Although even they themselves do not believe what they say; nor is it possible that they should differ from the judgment of all men, impious and desperate men though they be. But the hope of plunder and booty blinds their minds: men whom no gifts of money, no allotment of land, nor even that interminable auction has satisfied; who have proposed to themselves the city, the properties, and fortunes of all the citizens as their booty; and who, as long as there is something for them to seize and carry off, think that nothing will be wanting to them; among whom Marcus Antonius (O ye immortal gods! avert, I pray you, and efface this omen) has promised to divide this city. May things rather happen, O Romans, as you pray that they should, and may the chastisement of this frenzy fall on him and on his friend! And, indeed, I feel sure that it will be so. For I think that at present not only men, but the immortal gods, have all united together to preserve this republic. For if the immortal gods foreshow us the future, by means of portents and prodigies, then it has been openly revealed to us that punishment is near at hand to him, and liberty to us. Or if it was impossible for such unanimity on the part of all men to exist without the inspiration of the gods, in either case how can we doubt as to the inclinations of the heavenly deities?

It only remains, O Romans, for you to persevere in the sentiments which you at present display.

I will act, therefore, as commanders are in the habit of doing when their army is ready for battle, who, although they see their soldiers ready to engage, still address an exhortation to them; and in like manner I will exhort you who are already eager and burning to recover your liberty. You have not—you have not indeed, O Romans, to war against an enemy with whom it is possible to make peace on any terms whatever. For he does not now desire your slavery, as he did before, but he is angry now and thirsts for your blood. No sport appears more delightful to him than bloodshed and slaughter, and the massacre of citizens before his eyes. You have not, O Romans, to deal with a wicked and profligate man, but with an unnatural and savage beast. And, since he has fallen into a well, let him be buried in it. For if he escapes out of it, there will be no inhumanity of torture which it will be possible to avoid. But he is at present hemmed in, pressed, and besieged by those troops which we already have, and will soon be still more so by those which in a few days the new consuls will levy. Apply yourselves then to this business, as you are doing. Never have you shown greater unanimity in any cause; never have you been so cordially united with the senate. And no wonder! For the question now is not in what condition we are to live, but whether we are to live at all, or to perish with torture and ignominy.

Although nature, indeed, has appointed death for all men, yet valor is accustomed to ward off any cruelty or disgrace in death. And that is an inalienable possession of the Roman race and name. Preserve, I beseech you, O Romans, this attribute which your ancestors have left you as a sort of inheritance. Although all other things are uncertain, fleeting, transitory, virtue alone is planted firm with very deep roots. It cannot be undermined by any violence; it can never be moved from its position. By it your ancestors first subdued the whole of Italy; then destroyed Carthage, overthrew Numantia, and reduced the most mighty kings and most warlike nations under the dominion of this empire.

And your ancestors, O Romans, had to deal with an enemy who had also a republic, a senate house, a treasury, harmonious and united citizens, and with whom, if fortune had so willed it, there might have been peace and treaties on settled principles. But this enemy of yours is attacking your republic, but has none himself; is eager to destroy the senate, that is to say, the council of the whole world, but has no public council himself; he has exhausted your treasury, and has none of his own. For how can a man be supported by the unanimity of his citizens, who has no city at all? And what principles of peace can there be with that man who is full of incredible cruelty and destitute of faith?

The whole, then, of the contest, O Romans, which is now before the Roman people, the conqueror of all nations, is with an assassin, a robber, a Spartacus. For as to his habitual boast of being like Catiline, he is equal to him in wickedness, but inferior in energy. He, though he had no army, rapidly levied one. This man has lost that very army which he had. As, therefore, by my diligence and the authority of the senate, and your own zeal and valor, you crushed Catiline, so you will very soon hear that this infamous piratical enterprise of Antonius has been put down by your own perfect and unexampled harmony with the senate, and by the good fortune and valor of your armies and generals. I, for my part, as far as I am able to labor and to effect anything by my care and exertions and vigilance and authority and counsel, will omit nothing which I may think serviceable to your liberty. Nor could I omit it without wickedness after all your most ample and honorable kindness to me. However, on this day, encouraged by the motion of a most gallant man, and one most firmly attached to you, Marcus Servilius, whom you see before you, and his colleagues also, most distinguished men and most virtuous citizens; and partly, too, by my advice and my example, we have, for the first time after a long interval, fired up again with a hope of liberty.

Catiline
[108? B.C.–62 B.C.]

Leader of the famous conspiracy against the Roman republic, Lucius Sergius Catiline was a man of unusual ability. The following speech was made by Catiline to his accomplices who had gathered at his house for a general conference.

TO THE CONSPIRATORS

IF YOUR COURAGE and fidelity had not been sufficiently proved by me, this favorable opportunity would have occurred to no purpose; mighty hopes, absolute power, would in vain be within our grasp; nor should I, depending on irresolution or fickle-mindedness, pursue contingencies instead of certainties. But as I have, on many remarkable occasions, experienced your bravery and attachment to me, I have ventured to engage in a most important and glorious enterprise. I am aware, too, that whatever advantages or evils affect you, the same affect me; and to have the same desires and the same aversions is assuredly a firm bond of friendship.

What I have been meditating you have already heard separately. But my ardor for action is daily more and more excited when I consider what our future condition of life must be unless we ourselves assert our claims to liberty. For since the government has fallen under the power and jurisdiction of a few, kings and princes have constantly been their tributaries; nations and states have paid them taxes; but all the rest of us, however brave and worthy, whether noble or plebeian, have been regarded as a mere mob, without interest or authority, and subject to those to whom, if the state were in a sound condition, we should be a terror. Hence all influence, power, honor, and wealth, are in their hands, or where they dispose of them; to us they have left only insults, dangers, persecutions, and poverty. To such indignities, O bravest of men, how long will you submit? Is it not better to die in a glorious attempt, than, after having been the sport of other men's insolence, to resign a wretched and degraded existence with ignominy?

But success (I call gods and men to witness!) is in our own hands. Our years are fresh, our spirit is unbroken; among our oppressors, on the contrary, through age and wealth a general debility has been produced. We have, therefore, only to make a beginning; the course of events will accomplish the rest.

Who in the world, indeed, that has the feelings of a man, can endure that they should have a superfluity of riches, to squander in building over seas and leveling mountains, and that means should be wanting to us even for the necessaries of life; that they should join together two houses or more, and that we should not have a hearth to call our own? They, though they purchase pictures, statues, and embossed plate; though they pull down new buildings and erect others, and lavish and abuse their wealth in every possible method, yet cannot, with the utmost efforts of caprice, exhaust it. But for us there is poverty at home, debts abroad; our present circumstances are bad, our prospects much worse; and what, in a word, have we left, but a miserable existence?

Will you not, then, awake to action? Behold that liberty, that liberty for which you have so often wished, with wealth, honor, and glory, are set before your eyes. All these prizes fortune offers to the victorious. Let the enterprise itself, then, let the opportunity, let your property, your dangers, and the glorious spoils of war, animate you far more than my words. Use me either as your leader or your fellow soldier; neither my heart nor my hand shall be wanting to you. These objects I hope to effect, in concert with you, in the character of consul; unless, indeed, my expectation deceives me, and you prefer to be slaves rather than masters.

The following speech was delivered by Catiline to his soldiers on the eve of the battle which resulted in his defeat and death.

TO HIS TROOPS

I AM well aware, soldiers, that words cannot inspire courage, and that a spiritless army cannot be rendered active, or a timid army valiant, by the speech of its commander. Whatever courage is in the heart of a man, whether from nature or from habit, so much will be shown by him in the field; and on him whom neither glory nor danger can move, exhortation is bestowed in vain; for the terror in his breast stops his ears.

I have called you together, however, to give you a few instructions, and to explain to you, at the same time, my reasons for the course which I have adopted. You all know, soldiers, how severe a penalty the inactivity and cowardice of Lentulus has brought upon himself and us; and how, while waiting for reinforcements from the city, I was unable to march into Gaul. In what situation our affairs now are, you all understand as well as myself. Two armies of the enemy, one on the side of Rome and the other on that of Gaul, oppose our progress; while the want of corn and of other necessaries prevents us from remaining, however strongly we may desire to remain, in our present position. Whithersoever we would go, we must open a passage with our swords. I conjure you, therefore, to maintain a brave and resolute spirit; and to remember, when you advance to battle, that on your own right hands depend riches, honor, and glory, with the enjoyment of your liberty and of your country. If we conquer, all will be safe; we shall have provisions in abundance; and the colonies and corporate towns will open their gates to us. But if we lose the victory through want of courage, those same places will turn against us; for neither place nor friend will protect him whom his arms have not protected. Besides, soldiers, the same exigency does not press upon our adversaries as presses upon us; we fight for our country, for our liberty, for our life; they contend for what but little concerns them, the power of a small party. Attack them, therefore, with so much the greater confidence, and call to mind your achievements of old.

We might, with the utmost ignominy, have passed the rest of our days in exile. Some of you, after losing your property, might have waited at Rome for assistance from others. But because such a life, to men of spirit, was disgusting and unendurable, you resolved upon your present course. If you wish to quit it, you must exert all your resolution, for none but conquerors have exchanged war for peace. To hope for safety in flight when you have turned away from the enemy the arms by which the body is defended is indeed madness. In battle those who are most afraid are always in most danger; but courage is equivalent to a rampart.

When I contemplate you, soldiers, and when I consider your past exploits, a strong hope of victory animates me. Your spirit, your age, your valor, give me confidence; to say nothing of necessity, which makes even cowards brave. To prevent the numbers of the enemy from surrounding us, our confined situation is sufficient. But should Fortune be unjust to your valor, take care not to lose your lives unavenged; take care not to be taken and butchered like cattle, rather than, fighting like men, to leave to your enemies a bloody and mournful victory.

Julius Caesar
[100 B.C.–44 B.C.]

Gaius Julius Caesar, the great Roman general and statesman, took an active part in the senate debates over the treatment to be meted out to the Catilinarian conspirators. He was a shrewd and convincing speaker, although his fame rests mainly upon his amazing military conquests and able civil administration.

ON THE TREATMENT OF THE CONSPIRATORS

IT BECOMES all men, conscript fathers, who deliberate on dubious matters, to be influenced neither by hatred, affection, anger, nor pity. The mind, when such feelings obstruct its view, cannot easily see what is right; nor has any human being consulted, at the same moment, his passions and his interest. When the mind is freely exerted, its reasoning is sound;

but passion, if it gain possession of it, becomes its tyrant, and reason is powerless.

I could easily mention, conscript fathers, numerous examples of kings and nations, who, swayed by resentment or compassion, have adopted injudicious courses of conduct; but I had rather speak of those instances in which our ancestors, in opposition to the impulse of passion, acted with wisdom and sound policy.

In the Macedonian war, which we carried on against King Perses, the great and powerful state of Rhodes, which had risen by the aid of the Roman people, was faithless and hostile to us; yet, when the war was ended, and the conduct of the Rhodians was taken into consideration, our forefathers left them unmolested, lest any should say that war was made upon them for the sake of seizing their wealth, rather than of punishing their faithlessness. Throughout the Punic wars, too, though the Carthaginians, both during peace and in suspensions of arms, were guilty of many acts of injustice, yet our ancestors never took occasion to retaliate, but considered rather what was worthy of themselves than what might justly be inflicted on their enemies.

Similar caution, conscript fathers, is to be observed by yourselves, that the guilt of Lentulus, and the other conspirators, may not have greater weight with you than your own dignity, and that you may not regard your indignation more than your character. If, indeed, a punishment adequate to their crimes be discovered, I consent to extraordinary measures; but if the enormity of their crime exceeds whatever can be devised, I think that we should inflict only such penalties as the laws have provided.

Most of those who have given their opinions before me have deplored, in studied and impressive language, the sad fate that threatens the republic; they have recounted the barbarities of war, and the afflictions that would fall on the vanquished; they have told us that maidens would be dishonored, and youths abused; that children would be torn from the embraces of their parents; that matrons would be subjected to the pleasure of the conquerors; that temples and dwelling-houses would be plundered; that massacres and fires would follow; and that every place would be filled with arms, corpses, blood, and lamentation. But to what end, in the name of the eternal gods! was such eloquence directed? Was it intended to render you indignant at the conspiracy? A speech, no doubt, will inflame him whom so frightful and monstrous a reality has not provoked! Far from it: for to no man does evil, directed against himself, appear a light matter; many, on the contrary, have felt it more seriously than was right.

But to different persons, conscript fathers, different degrees of license are allowed. If those who pass a life sunk in obscurity commit any error, through excessive anger, few become aware of it, for their fame is as limited as their fortune; but of those who live invested with extensive power, and in an exalted station, the whole world knows the proceedings. Thus in the highest position there is the least liberty of action; and it becomes us to indulge neither partiality nor aversion, but least of all animosity; for what in others is called resentment is in the powerful termed violence and cruelty.

I am, indeed, of opinion, conscript fathers, that the utmost degree of torture is inadequate to punish their crime; but the generality of mankind dwell on that which happens last, and, in the case of malefactors, forget their guilt, and talk only of their punishment, should that punishment have been inordinately severe. I feel assured, too, that Decimus Silanus, a man of spirit and resolution, made the suggestions which he offered, from zeal for the state, and that he had no view, in so important a matter, to favor or to enmity; such I know to be his character, and such his discretion. Yet his proposal appears to me, I will not say cruel (for what can be cruel that is directed against such characters?), but foreign to our policy. For, assuredly, Silanus, either your fears, or their treason, must have induced you, a consul-elect, to propose this new kind of punishment. Of fear it is unnecessary to speak, when, by the prompt activity of that distinguished man our consul, such numerous forces are under arms; and as to the punishment, we may say, what is, indeed, the truth, that in trouble and distress death is a relief from suffering, and not a torment; that it puts an end to all human woes; and that, beyond it, there is no place either for sorrow or joy.

But why, in the name of the immortal gods, did you not add to your proposal, Silanus, that, before they were put to death, they should be punished with the scourge? Was it because the Porcian law forbids it? But other laws forbid condemned citizens to be deprived of life, and allow them to go into exile. Or was it because scourging is a severer penalty than death? Yet what can be too severe, or too harsh, toward men convicted of such an offence? But if scourging be a milder punishment than death, how is it consistent to observe the law as to the smaller point, when you disregard it as to the greater?

But who, it may be asked, will blame any severity that shall be decreed against these parricides of their country? I answer that time, the course of events, and fortune, whose caprice governs nations, may blame it. Whatever shall fall on the traitors, will fall on them justly; but it is for you, conscript fathers, to consider well what you resolve to inflict on others. All precedents productive of evil effects have had their origin from what was good; but when a government passes into the hands of the ignorant or unprincipled, any new example of severity, inflicted on deserving and suitable objects, is extended to those that are improper and undeserving of it. The Lacedæmonians, when they had conquered the Athenians, appointed thirty men to govern their state. These thirty began their administration by putting to death, even without a trial, all who were notoriously wicked, or publicly detestable; acts at which the people rejoiced, and extolled their justice. But afterward, when their lawless power gradually increased, they proceeded, at their pleasure, to kill the good and bad indiscriminately, and to strike terror into all; and thus the state, overpowered and enslaved, paid a heavy penalty for its imprudent exultation.

Within our own memory, too, when the victorious Sylla ordered

Damasippus, and others of similar character, who had risen by distressing their country, to be put to death, who did not commend the proceeding? All exclaimed that wicked and factious men, who had troubled the state with their seditious practices, had justly forfeited their lives. Yet this proceeding was the commencement of great bloodshed. For whenever any one coveted the mansion or villa, or even the plate or apparel of another, he exerted his influence to have him numbered among the proscribed. Thus they, to whom the death of Damasippus had been a subject of joy, were soon after dragged to death themselves; nor was there any cessation of slaughter, until Sylla had glutted all his partisans with riches.

Such excesses, indeed, I do not fear from Marcus Tullius, or in these times. But in a large state there arise many men of various dispositions. At some other period, and under another consul, who, like the present, may have an army at his command, some false accusation may be credited as true; and when, with our example for a precedent, the consul shall have drawn the sword on the authority of the senate, who shall stay its progress, or moderate its fury?

Our ancestors, conscript fathers, were never deficient in conduct or courage; nor did pride prevent them from imitating the customs of other nations, if they appeared deserving of regard. Their armor, and weapons of war, they borrowed from the Samnites; their ensigns of authority, for the most part, from the Etrurians; and, in short, whatever appeared eligible to them, whether among allies or among enemies, they adopted at home with the greatest readiness, being more inclined to emulate merit than to be jealous of it. But at the same time, adopting a practice from Greece, they punished their citizens with the scourge, and inflicted capital punishment on such as were condemned. When the republic, however, became powerful, and faction grew strong from the vast number of citizens, men began to involve the innocent in condemnation, and other like abuses were practiced; and it was then that the Porcian and other laws were provided, by which condemned citizens were allowed to go into exile. This lenity of our ancestors, conscript fathers, I regard as a very strong reason why we should not adopt any new measures of severity. For assuredly there was greater merit and wisdom in those, who raised so mighty an empire from humble means, than in us, who can scarcely preserve what they so honorably acquired. Am I of opinion, then, you will ask, that the conspirators should be set free, and that the army of Catiline should thus be increased? Far from it; my recommendation is, that their property be confiscated, and that they themselves be kept in custody in such of the municipal towns as are best able to bear the expense; that no one hereafter bring their case before the senate, or speak on it to the people; and that the senate now give their opinion that he who shall act contrary to this, will act against the republic and the general safety.

Cato, The Younger
[95 B.C.–46 B.C.]

Marcus Porcius Cato, the Younger, was a powerful supporter of Cicero in defeating the conspiracy of Catiline against the Roman government. Grandson of Cato, the Elder, he was an able statesman and brave warrior. The following speech before the Roman senate is abridged.

THE CATILINARIAN CONSPIRATORS

MY FEELINGS, conscript fathers, are extremely different, when I contemplate our circumstances and dangers, and when I revolve in my mind the sentiments of some who have spoken before me. Those speakers, as it seems to me, have considered only how to punish the traitors who have raised war against their country, their parents, their altars, and their homes; but the state of affairs warns us rather to secure ourselves against them, than to take counsel as to what sentence we should pass upon them. Other crimes you may punish after they have been committed; but as to this, unless you prevent its commission, you will, when it has once taken effect, in vain appeal to justice. When the city is taken, no power is left to the vanquished.

But, in the name of the immortal gods, I call upon you, who have always valued your mansions and villas, your statues and pictures, at a higher price than the welfare of your country; if you wish to preserve those possessions, of whatever kind they are, to which you are attached; if you wish to secure quiet for the enjoyment of your pleasures, arouse yourselves, and act in defence of your country. We are not now debating on the revenues, or on injuries done to our allies, but our liberty and our life is at stake.

Often, conscript fathers, have I spoken at great length in this assembly; often have I complained of the luxury and avarice of our citizens, and, by that very means, have incurred the displeasure of many. I, who never excused to myself, or to my own conscience, the commission of any fault, could not easily pardon the misconduct, or indulge the licentiousness, of others. But though you little regarded my remonstrances, yet the republic remained secure; its own strength was proof against your remissness. The question, however, at present under discussion, is not whether we live in a good or bad state of morals; nor how great, or how splendid, the empire of the Roman people is; but whether these things around us, of whatever value they are, are to continue our own, or to fall, with ourselves, into the hands of the enemy.

In such a case, does any one talk to me of gentleness and compassion? For some time past, it is true, we have lost the real names of things; for to lavish the property of others is called generosity, and audacity in wickedness is called heroism; and hence the state is reduced to the brink of ruin. But let those, who thus misname things, be liberal, since such is the practice, out of the property of our allies; let them be merciful to the robbers of the treasury; but let them not lavish our blood, and, while they spare a few criminals, bring destruction on all the guiltless.

Gaius Cæsar, a short time ago, spoke in fair and elegant language, before this assembly, on the subject of life and death; considering as false, I suppose, what is told of the dead; that the bad, going a different way from the good, inhabit places gloomy, desolate, dreary, and full of horror. He accordingly proposed *that the property of the conspirators should be confiscated, and themselves kept in custody in the municipal towns;* fearing, it seems, that, if they remain at Rome, they may be rescued either by their accomplices in the conspiracy, or by a hired mob; as if, forsooth, the mischievous and profligate were to be found only in the city, and not through the whole of Italy, or as if desperate attempts would not be more likely to succeed where there is less power to resist them. His proposal, therefore, if he fears any danger from them, is absurd; but if, amid such universal terror, he alone is free from alarm, it the more concerns me to fear for you and myself.

Be assured, then, that when you decide on the fate of Lentulus and the other prisoners, you at the same time determine that of the army of Catiline and of all the conspirators. The more spirit you display in your decision, the more will their confidence be diminished; but if they shall perceive you in the smallest degree irresolute, they will advance upon you with fury.

Do not suppose that our ancestors, from so small a commencement, raised the republic to greatness merely by force of arms. If such had been the case, we should enjoy it in a most excellent condition; for of allies and citizens, as well as arms and horses, we have a much greater abundance than they had. But there were other things which made them great, but which among us have no existence; such as industry at home, equitable government abroad, and minds impartial in council, uninfluenced by any immoral or improper feeling. Instead of such virtues, we have luxury and avarice; public distress, and private superfluity; we extol wealth, and yield to indolence; no distinction is made between good men and bad; and ambition usurps the honors due to virtue. Nor is this wonderful; since you study each his individual interest, and since at home you are slaves to pleasure, and here to money or favor; and hence it happens that an attack is made on the defenceless state. But on these subjects I shall say no more. Certain citizens, of the highest rank, have conspired to ruin their country; they are engaging the Gauls, the bitterest foes of the Roman name, to join in a war against us; the leader of the enemy is ready to make a descent upon us; and do you hesitate, even in such circumstances, how to treat armed incendiaries arrested within your walls? I advise you to have mercy upon them; they are young men who have been led astray by ambitions; send them away, even with arms in their hands. But such mercy, and such clemency, if they turn those arms against you, will end in misery to yourselves. The case is, assuredly, dangerous, but you do not fear it; yes, you fear it greatly, but you hesitate how to act, through weakness and want of spirit, waiting one for another, and trusting to the immortal gods, who have so often preserved your country in the greatest dangers. But the protection of the gods is not obtained by vows and effeminate supplications; it is by vigilance, activity, and prudent measures, that general welfare is secured. When you are once resigned to sloth and indolence, it is in vain that you implore the gods; for they are then indignant and threaten vengeance.

In the days of our forefathers, Titus Manlius Torquatus, during a war with the Gauls, ordered his own son to be put to death, because he had fought with an enemy contrary to orders. That noble youth suffered for excess of bravery; and do you hesitate what sentence to pass on the most inhuman of traitors? Perhaps their former life is at variance with their present crime. Spare, then, the dignity of Lentulus, if he has ever spared his own honor or character, or had any regard for gods or for men. Pardon the youth of Cethegus, unless this be the second time that he has made war upon his country. As to Gabinius, Statilius, Cœparius, why should I make any remark upon them? Had they ever possessed the smallest share of discretion, they would never have engaged in such a plot against their country.

In conclusion, conscript fathers, if there were time to amend an error, I might easily suffer you, since you disregard words, to be corrected by experience of consequences. But we are beset by dangers on all sides; Catiline, with his army, is ready to devour us; while there are other enemies within the walls, and in the heart of the city; nor can any measures be taken, or any plans arranged, without their knowledge. The more necessary is it, therefore, to act with promptitude. What I advise, then, is this: that since the state, by a treasonable combination of abandoned citizens, has been brought into the greatest peril; and since the conspirators have been convicted on the evidence of Titus Volturcius, and the deputies of the Allobroges, and on their own confession, of having concerted massacres, conflagrations, and other horrible and cruel outrages, against their fellow-citizens and their country, punishment be inflicted, according to the usage of our ancestors, on the prisoners who have confessed their guilt, as on men convicted of capital crimes.

Mark Antony

[83 B.C.–30 B.C.]

The funeral oration of Mark Antony over the dead body of Julius Caesar is accepted as an oratorical masterpiece. Although it was the imaginative creation of Shakespeare for his play, "Julius Caesar," it is based on the historical writings of Dion Cassius and Plutarch.

ORATION ON THE DEAD BODY OF JULIUS CAESAR

ANTONY. Friends, Romans, countrymen, lend me your ears;
I come to bury Caesar, not to praise him.
The evil that men do lives after them;
The good is oft interred with their bones;
So let it be with Caesar. The noble Brutus
Hath told you Caesar was ambitious:
If it were so, it was a grievous fault,
And grievously hath Caesar answer'd it.
Here, under leave of Brutus and the rest,—
For Brutus is an honourable man;
So are they all, all honourable men;
Come I to speak in Caesar's funeral.
He was my friend, faithful and just to me:
But Brutus says he was ambitious;
And Brutus is an honourable man.
He hath brought many captives home to Rome,
Whose ransoms did the general coffers fill:
Did this in Caesar seem ambitious?
When that the poor have cried, Caesar hath wept:
Ambition should be made of sterner stuff:
Yet Brutus says he was ambitious;
And Brutus is an honourable man.
You all did see that on the Lupercal
I thrice presented him a kingly crown,
Which he did thrice refuse: was this ambition?
Yet Brutus says he was ambitious;
And, sure, he is an honourable man.
I speak not to disprove what Brutus spoke,
But here I am to speak what I do know.
You all did love him once, not without cause:
What cause withholds you then to mourn for him?
O judgment; thou are fled to brutish beasts,
And men have lost their reason. Bear with me;
My heart is in the coffin there with Caesar,
And I must pause till it come back to me.

FIRST CITIZEN. Methinks there is much reason in his sayings.
SECOND CITIZEN. If you consider rightly of the matter, Caesar has had
    great wrong.
THIRD CITIZEN. Has he, masters?
    I fear there will a worse come in his place.
FOURTH CITIZEN. Mark'd ye his words? He would not take the crown;
    Therefore 'tis certain he was not ambitious.
FIRST CITIZEN. If it be found so, some will dear abide it.
SECOND CITIZEN. Poor soul! his eyes are red as fire with weeping.
THIRD CITIZEN. There's not a nobler man in Rome than Antony.
FOURTH CITIZEN. Now mark him, he begins again to speak.
ANTONY. But yesterday the word of Caesar might
    Have stood against the world: now lies he there,
    And none so poor to do him reverence.
    O masters, if I were disposed to stir
    Your hearts and minds to mutiny and rage,
    I should do Brutus wrong and Cassius wrong
    Who, you all know, are honourable men.
    I will not do them wrong; I rather choose
    To wrong the dead, to wrong myself and you,
    Than I will wrong such honourable men.
    But here's a parchment with the seal of Caesar;
    I found it in his closet; 'tis his will:
    Let but the commons hear this testament—
    Which pardon me, I do not mean to read—
    And they would go and kiss dead Caesar's wounds
    And dip their napkins in his sacred blood,
    Yea, beg a hair of him for memory,
    And, dying, mention it within their wills,
    Bequeathing it as a rich legacy
    Unto their issue.
FOURTH CITIZEN. We'll hear the will; read it, Mark Antony,
ALL. The will, the will! we will hear Caesar's will.
ANTONY. Have patience, gentle friends, I must not read it;
    It is not meet you know how Caesar loved you.
    You are not wood, you are not stones, but men;
    And, being men, hearing the will of Caesar,
    It will inflame you, it will make you mad:
    'Tis good you know not that you are his heirs;
    For if you should, O, what would come of it.
FOURTH CITIZEN. Read the will; we'll hear it, Antony;
    You shall read us the will, Caesar's will.
ANTONY. Will you be patient? will you stay awhile?
    I have o'ershot myself to tell you of it:
    I fear I wrong the honourable men
    Whose daggers have stabb'd Caesar; I do fear it.
FOURTH CITIZEN. They were traitors: honourable men!
ALL. The will! the testament!

SECOND CITIZEN. They were villains, murderers: the will! read the will.
ANTONY. You will compel me then to read the will?
   Then make a ring about the corpse of Caesar,
   And let me show you him that made the will.
   Shall I descend? and will you give me leave?
ALL. Come down.
SECOND CITIZEN. Descend.   [*He comes down from the pulpit.*]
THIRD CITIZEN. You shall have leave.
FOURTH CITIZEN. A ring; stand round.
FIRST CITIZEN. Stand from the hearse, stand from the body.
SECOND CITIZEN. Room for Antony, most noble Antony.
ANTONY. Nay, press not so upon me; stand far off.
ALL. Stand back. Room. Bear back.
ANTONY. If you have tears, prepare to shed them now.
   You all do know this mantle: I remember
   The first time ever Caesar put it on;
   'Twas on a summer's evening, in his tent,
   That day he overcame the Nervii:
   Look, in this place ran Cassius' dagger through:
   See what a rent the envious Casca made:
   Through this the well-belov'd Brutus stabb'd;
   And as he pluck'd his cursed steel away,
   Mark how the blood of Caesar follow'd it,
   As rushing out of doors, to be resolved
   If Brutus so unkindly knock'd, or no:
   For Brutus, as you know, was Caesar's angel:
   Judge, O you gods, how dearly Caesar loved him.
   This was the most unkindest cut of all;
   For when the noble Caesar saw him stab,
   Ingratitude, more strong than traitors' arms,
   Quite vanquish'd him: then burst his mighty heart;
   And, in his mantle muffling up his face,
   Even at the base of Pompey's statue,
   Which all the while ran blood, great Caesar fell.
   O, what a fall was there, my countrymen!
   Then I, and you, and all of us fell down,
   Whilst bloody treason flourish'd over us.
   O, now you weep, and I perceive you feel
   The dint of pity: these are gracious drops.
   Kind souls, what weep you when you but behold
   Our Caesar's vesture wounded? Look you here,
   Here is himself, marr'd, as you see, with traitors.
FIRST CITIZEN. O piteous spectacle!
SECOND CITIZEN. O noble Caesar!
THIRD CITIZEN. O woful day!
FOURTH CITIZEN. O traitors, villains!
FIRST CITIZEN. O most bloody sight!
SECOND CITIZEN. We will be revenged.

ALL. Revenge! About! Seek! Burn! Fire!
　　Kill! Slay! Let not a traitor live!
ANTONY. Stay, countrymen.
FIRST CITIZEN. Peace there! hear the noble Antony.
SECOND CITIZEN. We'll hear him, we'll follow him, we'll die with him.
ANTONY. Good friends, sweet friends, let me not stir you up
　　To such a sudden flood of mutiny.
　　They that have done this deed are honourable;
　　What private griefs they have, alas, I know not,
　　That made them do it; they are wise and honourable,
　　And will, no doubt, with reasons answer you.
　　I come not, friends, to steal away your hearts: I am no orator, as
　　　　Brutus is;
　　But, as you know me all, a plain blunt man,
　　That love my friend; and that they know full well
　　That gave me public leave to speak of him:
　　For I have neither wit, nor words, nor worth,
　　Action, nor utterance, nor the power of speech,
　　To stir men's blood: I only speak right on;
　　I tell you that which you yourselves do know;
　　Show you sweet Caesar's wounds, poor poor dumb mouths,
　　And bid them speak for me: but were I Brutus,
　　And Brutus Antony, there were an Antony
　　Would ruffle up your spirits, and put a tongue
　　In every wound of Caesar, that should move
　　The stones of Rome to rise and mutiny.
ALL. We'll mutiny.
FIRST CITIZEN. We'll burn the house of Brutus.
THIRD CITIZEN. Away, then! come, seek the conspirators.
ANTONY. Yet hear me, countrymen; yet hear me speak.
ALL. Peace, ho! Hear Antony. Most noble Antony!
ANTONY. Why, friends, you go to do you know not what: wherein hath
　　Caesar thus deserved your loves?
　　Alas, you know not; I must tell you then:
　　You have forgot the will I told you of.
ALL. Most true: the will! Let's stay and hear the will.
ANTONY. Here is the will, and under Caesar's seal.
　　To every Roman citizen he gives,
　　To every several man, seventy-five drachmas.
SECOND CITIZEN. Most noble Caesar! we'll revenge his death.
THIRD CITIZEN. O royal Caesar!
ANTONY. Hear me with patience.
ALL. Peace, ho!
ANTONY. Moreover, he hath left you all his walks,
　　His private arbours and new-planted orchards,
　　On this side Tiber; he hath left them you,
　　And to your heirs for ever; common pleasures,
　　To walk abroad and recreate yourselves.

Here was a Caesar! when comes such another?
FIRST CITIZEN.   Never, never. Come, away, away!
We'll burn his body in the holy place,
And with the brands fire the traitors' houses.
Take up the body.
SECOND CITIZEN.   Go fetch fire.
THIRD CITIZEN.   Pluck down benches.
FOURTH CITIZEN.   Pluck down forms, windows, anything.

                         [*Exeunt Citizens with the body.*]

ANTONY.   Now let it work. Mischief, thou art afoot, take thou what
course thou wilt.

St. Bernard

[1091–1153]

St. Bernard, born in Burgundy, France, and for many years abbot of Clairvaux, was one of the foremost and most eloquent advocates of the Second Crusade (1146), which ended disastrously in Asia Minor.

A SECOND CRUSADE

You CANNOT but know that we live in a period of chastisement and ruin; the enemy of mankind has caused the breath of corruption to fly over all regions; we behold nothing but unpunished wickedness. The laws of men or the laws of religion have no longer sufficient power to check depravity of manners and the triumph of the wicked. The demon of heresy has taken possession of the chair of truth, and God has sent forth His malediction upon His sanctuary.

Oh, ye who listen to me, hasten then to appease the anger of Heaven, but no longer implore His goodness by vain complaints; clothe not yourselves in sackcloth, but cover yourselves with your impenetrable bucklers; the din of arms, the dangers, the labors, the fatigues of war are the penances that God now imposes upon you. Hasten then to expiate your sins by victories over the infidels, and let the deliverance of holy places be the reward of your repentance.

If it were announced to you that the enemy had invaded your cities, your castles, your lands; had ravished your wives and your daughters, and profaned your temples—which among you would not fly to arms? Well, then, all these calamities, and calamities still greater, have fallen upon your brethren, upon the family of Jesus Christ, which is yours. Why do you hesitate to repair so many evils—to revenge so many outrages? Will you allow the infidels to contemplate in peace the ravages they have committed on Christian people? Remembering that their triumph will be a subject for grief to all ages and an eternal opprobrium upon the generation that has endured it. Yes, the living God has charged me to announce to you that He will punish them who shall not have defended Him against His enemies.

Fly then to arms; let a holy rage animate you in the fight, and let the Christian world resound with these words of the prophet, "Cursed be he who does not stain his sword with blood!" If the Lord calls you to the defense of His heritage think not that His hand has lost its power. Could He not send twelve legions of angels or breathe one word and

63

all His enemies would crumble away into dust? But God has considered the sons of men, to open for them the road to His mercy. His goodness has caused to dawn for you a day of safety by calling on you to avenge His glory and His name.

Christian warriors, He who gave His life for you, to-day demands yours in return. These are combats worthy of you, combats in which it is glorious to conquer and advantageous to die. Illustrious knights, generous defenders of the Cross, remember the examples of your fathers who conquered Jerusalem, and whose names are inscribed in Heaven; abandon then the things that perish, to gather unfading palms, and conquer a Kingdom which has no end.

St. Francis
[1182–1226]

St. Francis of Assisi (Italy) renounced all worldliness and led a life of self-denial and religious devotion. Believing in the brotherhood of all men and all nature, he preached the gospel to all—to rich and poor, to criminals and lepers, and even to animals and to birds.

SERMON TO THE BIRDS

MY LITTLE SISTERS, the birds, much bounden are ye unto God, your Creator, and always in every place ought ye to praise Him, for that He hath given you liberty to fly about everywhere, and hath also given you double and triple raiment; moreover He preserved your seed in the ark of Noah, that your race might not perish out of the world; still more are ye beholden to Him for the element of the air which He hath appointed for you; beyond all this, ye sow not, neither do you reap; and God feedeth you, and giveth you the streams and fountains for your drink; the mountains and the valleys for your refuge and the high trees whereon to make your nests; and because ye know not how to spin or sew, God clotheth you, you and your children; wherefore your Creator loveth you much, seeing that He hath bestowed on you so many benefits; and therefore, my little sisters, beware of the sin of ingratitude, and study always to give praises unto God.

Martin Luther
[1483–1546]

*Martin Luther, leader of the Protestant Reformation in Germany,
published his theses against Catholic indulgences in 1517, while he
was still a young priest, and was excommunicated by the Pope in 1520.
At the Diet of Worms, April 1521, summoned by the Emperor Charles
V to try Luther, the founder of Protestantism made his celebrated
speech, reproduced herewith.*

BEFORE THE DIET OF WORMS

MOST SERENE EMPEROR, and You Illustrious Princes and Gracious Lords:—
I this day appear before you in all humility, according to your command,
and I implore your majesty and your august highnesses, by the mercies
of God, to listen with favor to the defense of a cause which I am well
assured is just and right. I ask pardon, if by reason of my ignorance, I
am wanting in the manners that befit a court; for I have not been brought
up in kings' palaces, but in the seclusion of a cloister.

Two questions were yesterday put to me by his imperial majesty; the
first, whether I was the author of the books whose titles were read; the
second, whether I wished to revoke or defend the doctrine I have taught.
I answered the first, and I adhere to that answer.

As to the second, I have composed writings on very different subjects.
In some I have discussed Faith and Good Works, in a spirit at once so
pure, clear, and Christian, that even my adversaries themselves, far from
finding anything to censure, confess that these writings are profitable, and
deserve to be perused by devout persons. The pope's bull, violent as it is,
acknowledges this. What, then, should I be doing if I were now to retract
these writings? Wretched man! I alone, of all men living, should be
abandoning truths approved by the unanimous voice of friends and enemies, and opposing doctrines that the whole world glories in confessing!

I have composed, secondly, certain works against popery, wherein I
have attacked such as by false doctrines, irregular lives, and scandalous
examples, afflict the Christian world, and ruin the bodies and souls of
men. And is not this confirmed by the grief of all who fear God? Is it
not manifest that the laws and human doctrines of the popes entangle,
vex, and distress the consciences of the faithful, while the crying and
endless extortions of Rome engulf the property and wealth of Christendom, and more particularly of this illustrious nation?

If I were to revoke what I have written on that subject, what should
I do . . . but strengthen this tyranny, and open a wider door to so many
and flagrant impieties? Bearing down all resistance with fresh fury, we
should behold these proud men swell, foam, and rage more than ever!
And not merely would the yoke which now weighs down Christians be

made more grinding by my retraction—it would thereby become, so to speak, lawful,—for, by my retraction, it would receive confirmation from your most serene majesty, and all the States of the Empire. Great God! I should thus be like to an infamous cloak, used to hide•and cover over every kind of malice and tyranny.

In the third and last place, I have written some books against private individuals, who had undertaken to defend the tyranny of Rome by destroying faith. I freely confess that I may have attacked such persons with more violence than was consistent with my profession as an ecclesiastic: I do not think of myself as a saint; but neither can I retract these books, because I should, by so doing, sanction the impieties of my opponents, and they would thence take occasion to crush God's people with still more cruelty.

Yet, as I am a mere man, and not God, I will defend myself after the example of Jesus Christ, who said: "If I have spoken evil, bear witness against me" (John xviii, 23). How much more should I, who am but dust and ashes, and so prone to error, desire that every one should bring forward what he can against my doctrine.

Therefore, most serene emperor, and you illustrious princes, and all, whether high or low, who hear me, I implore you by the mercies of God to prove to me by the writings of the prophets and apostles that I am in error. As soon as I shall be convinced, I will instantly retract all my errors, and will myself be the first to seize my writings, and commit them to the flames.

What I have just said I think will clearly show that I have well considered and weighed the dangers to which I am exposing myself; but far from being dismayed by them, I rejoice exceedingly to see the Gospel this day, as of old, a cause of disturbance and disagreement. It is the character and destiny of God's word. "I came not to send peace unto the earth, but a sword," said Jesus Christ. God is wonderful and awful in His counsels. Let us have a care, lest in our endeavors to arrest discords, we be bound to fight against the holy word of God and bring down upon our heads a frightful deluge of inextricable dangers, present disaster, and everlasting desolations. . . . Let us have a care lest the reign of the young and noble prince, the Emperor Charles, on whom, next to God, we build so many hopes, should not only commence, but continue and terminate its course under the most fatal auspices. I might cite examples drawn from the oracles of God. I might speak of Pharaohs, of kings of Babylon, or of Israel, who were never more contributing to their own ruin that when, by measures in appearances most prudent, they thought to establish their authority! "God removeth the mountains and they know not" (Job ix, 5).

In speaking thus, I do not suppose that such noble princes have need of my poor judgment; but I wish to acquit myself of a duty that Germany has a right to expect from her children. And so commending myself to your august majesty, and your most serene highnesses, I beseech you in all humility, not to permit the hatred of my enemies to rain upon me an indignation I have not deserved.

Since your most serene majesty and your high mightinesses require of me a simple, clear and direct answer, I will give one, and it is this: I cannot submit my faith either to the pope or to the council, because it is as clear as noonday that they have fallen into error and even into glaring inconsistency with themselves. If, then, I am not convinced by proof from Holy Scripture, or by cogent reasons, if I am not satisfied by the very text I have cited, and if my judgment is not in this way brought into subjection to God's word, I neither can nor will retract anything; for it cannot be right for a Christian to speak against his conscience. I stand here and can say no more. God help me. Amen.

John Calvin
[1509–1564]

Born in France, John Calvin was a leader of the Protestant Reformation and one of its most eloquent advocates. Because of his religious views, he was banished from Paris in 1533 and from Geneva in 1538. He was allowed to return to Geneva in 1541, from which point he carried on his labors for the spread of his faith. Following is a part of one of his most important sermons.

ON SUFFERING PERSECUTION

THE APOSTLE says, "Let us go forth from the city after the Lord Jesus, bearing His reproach." In the first place he reminds us, altho the swords should not be drawn over us nor the fires kindled to burn us, that we can not be truly united to the Son of God while we are rooted in this world. Wherefore, a Christian, even in repose, must always have one foot lifted to march to battle, and not only so, but he must have his affections withdrawn from the world altho his body is dwelling in it. Grant that this at first sight seems to us hard, still we must be satisfied with the words of St. Paul, "We are called and appointed to suffer." As if he had said, Such is our condition as Christians; this is the road by which we must go if we would follow Christ.

Meanwhile, to solace our infirmity and mitigate the vexation and sorrow which persecution might cause us, a good reward is held forth: In suffering for the cause of God we are walking step by step after the Son of God and have Him for our guide. Were it simply said that to be Christians we must pass through all the insults of the world boldly, to meet death at all times and in whatever way God may be pleased to appoint, we might apparently have some pretext for replying, It is a strange road to go at a peradventure. But when we are commanded to follow the Lord Jesus, His guidance is too good and honorable to be refused.

Are we so delicate as to be unwilling to endure anything? Then we must renounce the grace of God by which He has called us to the hope of salvation. For there are two things which can not be separated—to be members of Christ, and to be tried by many afflictions. We certainly ought to prize such a conformity to the Son of God much more than we do. It is true that in the world's judgment there is disgrace in suffering for the Gospel. But since we know that unbelievers are blind, ought we not to have better eyes than they? It is ignominy to suffer from those who occupy the seat of justice, but St. Paul shows us by his example that we have to glory in scourgings for Jesus Christ, as marks by which God recognizes us and avows us for His own. And we know what St. Luke narrates of Peter and John; namely, that they rejoiced to have been "counted worthy to suffer infamy and reproach for the name of the Lord Jesus."

Ignominy and dignity are two opposites: so says the world which, being infatuated, judges against all reason, and in this way converts the glory of God into dishonor. But, on our part, let us not refuse to be vilified as concerns the world, in order to be honored before God and His angels. We see what pains the ambitious take to receive the commands of a king, and what a boast they make of it. The Son of God presents His commands to us, and every one stands back! Tell me, pray, whether in so doing are we worthy of having anything in common with Him? There is nothing here to attract our sensual nature, but such, notwithstanding, are the true escutcheons of nobility in the heavens. Imprisonment, exile, evil report, imply in men's imagination whatever is to be vituperated; but what hinders us from viewing things as God judges and declares them, save our unbelief? Wherefore let the name of the Son of God have all the weight with us which it deserves, that we may learn to count it honor when He stamps His marks upon us. If we act otherwise our ingratitude is insupportable.

Were God to deal with us according to our deserts, would He not have just cause to chastise us daily in a thousand ways? Nay, more, a hundred thousand deaths would not suffice for a small portion of our misdeeds! Now, if in His infinite goodness He puts all our faults under His foot and abolishes them, and, instead of punishing us according to our demerit, devises an admirable means to convert our afflictions into honor and a special privilege, inasmuch as through them we are taken into partnership with His Son, must it not be said, when we disdain such a happy state, that we have indeed made little progress in Christian doctrine?

It were easy indeed for God to crown us at once without requiring us to sustain any combats; but as it is His pleasure that until the end of the world Christ shall reign in the midst of His enemies, so it is also His pleasure that we, being placed in the midst of them, shall suffer their oppression and violence till He deliver us. I know, indeed, that the flesh kicks when it is to be brought to this point, but still the will of God must have the mastery. If we feel some repugnance in ourselves it need not surprise us; for it is only too natural for us to shun the cross. Still let us not fail to surmount it, knowing that God accepts our obedience, provided we bring all our feelings and wishes into captivity and make them subject to Him.

In ancient times vast numbers of people, to obtain a simple crown of leaves, refused no toil, no pain, no trouble; nay, it even cost them nothing to die, and yet every one of them fought for a peradventure, not knowing whether he was to gain or lose the prize. God holds forth to us the immortal crown by which we may become partakers of His glory. He does not mean us to fight a haphazard, but all of us have a promise of the prize for which we strive. Have we any cause, then, to decline the struggle? Do we think it has been said in vain, "If we die with Jesus Christ we shall also live with him?" Our triumph is prepared, and yet we do all we can to shun the combat.

Frederick The Great
[1712–1786]

Frederick II, King of Prussia, known as Frederick the Great, was a patron of the arts as well as a brilliant military commander. He could discuss philosophy with Voltaire at Sans Souci or spend months on horseback with his soldiers in the field. The following speeches to his generals indicate the mental alertness of this scholar-warrior.

BEFORE INVADING SILESIA, 1740

Gentlemen, I am undertaking a war in which I have no allies but your valor and your good will. My cause is just; my resources are what we ourselves can do; and the issue lies in fortune. Remember continually the glory which your ancestors acquired in the plain of Warsaw, at Fehrbellin and in the expedition to Preussen. Your lot is in your own hands: distinctions and rewards await upon your fine actions which shall merit them.

But what need have I to excite you to glory? It is the one thing you keep before your eyes; the sole object worthy of your labor. We are going to front troops, who, under Prince Eugene, had the highest reputation. Tho Prince Eugene is gone, we shall have to measure our strength against brave soldiers; the greater will be the honor if we can conquer. Adieu. Go forth. I will follow you straightway to the rendezvous of glory which awaits you.

BEFORE THE BATTLE OF LEUTHEN, 1757

It is not unknown to you, gentlemen, what disasters have befallen here while we were busy with the French and Reichs army. Schweidnitz is gone; Duke of Bevern beaten; Breslau gone, and all our war stores there; a good part of Silesia gone; and in fact my embarrassment would be at the impossible pitch, had not I boundless trust in you and your qualities which have been so often manifested as soldiers and sons of your country. Hardly one among you but has distinguished himself by some nobly memorable action: all these services to the State and to me I know well and will never forget.

I flatter myself, therefore, that, in this case, too, nothing will be wanting which the State has a right to expect of your valor. The hour is at hand. I should think I had done nothing if I left the Austrians in possession of Silesia. Let me apprise you, then: I intend, in spite of the rules of art, to attack Prince Karl's army, which is nearly twice our strength, wherever I find it. The question is not of his numbers or the strength of his position; all this by courage, by the skill of our methods, we will try to make good. This step I must risk, or everything is lost. We must beat the enemy, or perish all of us before his batteries. So I read the case; so I will act in it.

Make this, my determination, known to all officers of the army: prepare the men for what work is now to ensue and say that I hold myself entitled to demand exact fulfilment of orders. For you, when I reflect that you are Prussians, can I think that you will act unworthily? But if there should be one or another who dreads to share all dangers with me, he can have his discharge this evening, and shall not suffer the least reproach from me! Hah! I knew it; none of you would desert me. I depend on your help, then, and on victory as sure.

The cavalry regiment that does not on this instant, on orders given, dash full plunge into the enemy, I will, directly after the battle, unhorse and make it a garrison regiment. The infantry battalion which, meet with what it may, shows the least sign of hesitancy, loses its colors and its sabers, and I cut the trimmings from its uniform! Now, good night, gentlemen: shortly we have either beaten the enemy, or we never see one another again.

Desmoulins
[1760–1794]

Camille Benoît Desmoulins was one of the greatest orators of the French Revolution although his speaking was impaired by a painful stammer. His violent speeches inflamed the masses and often influenced the National Convention. Finally he fell into disfavor and was guillotined. Desmoulins delivered the following speech before the National Convention in 1793.

ADVOCATING THE EXECUTION OF LOUIS XVI

IT IS NO USE for Necker to pretend that there is a contract between Louis XVI. and the nation, and to defend it by the principles of civil law. What does he gain by this, and according to these principles in how many ways will this contract not be nullified? Nullified, because it was not ratified by the contracting party; nullified, because Louis XVI. could not release himself without releasing the nation; nullified by the violence, the massacre of the Champ de Mars, and by that death-flag under which the revision was closed; nullified by default of cause and default of bond, in that the obligation rested on the nation, which gave all and received nothing in the way of "consideration," Louis XVI. entering into no obligation on his side, but being left free to commit all crimes with impunity.

But I am ashamed to follow the advocates of Louis XVI. in this discussion of civil law. It is by the law of nations that this trial ought to be regulated. The slavery of nations during ten thousand years has not been able to rescind their indefensible rights. It was these rights that were a standing protest against the reigning of the Charleses, the Henrys, the Frederics, the Edwards, as they were against the despotism of Julius Cæsar. It is a crime to be a king. It was even a crime to be a constitutional king, for the nation had never accepted the constitution. There is only one condition on which it could be legitimate to reign; it is when the whole people formally strips itself of its rights and cedes them to a single man, not only as Denmark did in 1660, but as happens when the entire people has passed or ratified this warrant of its sovereignty. And yet it could not bind the next generation, because death extinguishes all rights. It is the prerogative of those who exist, and who are in possession of this earth, to make the laws for it in their turn. Otherwise, let the dead leave their graves and come to uphold their laws against the living who have repealed them. All other kinds of royalty are imposed upon the people at the risk of their insurrection, just as robbers reign in the forests at the risk of the provost's punishment befalling them. And now after we have risen and recovered our rights, to plead these feudal laws, or even the constitution, in opposition to republican Frenchmen, is to plead the black code to negro conquerors of white men. Our constituents have not sent us here to follow those feudal laws and that pretended constitution, but to abolish it, or rather, to declare that it never existed, and to reinvest the nation with that sovereignty which another had usurped. Either we are truly republicans, giants who rise to the heights of these republican ideas, or we are not giants, but mere pigmies. By the law of nations Louis XVI. as king, even a constitutional king, was a tyrant in a state of revolt against the nation, and a criminal worthy of death. And Frenchmen have no more need to try him than had Hercules to try the boar of Erymanthus, or the Romans to try Tarquin, or Cæsar, who also thought himself a constitutional dictator.

But it is not only a king, it is a criminal accused of crimes that in his person we have to punish.

You must not expect me to indulge in undue exaggeration, and to call him a Nero, as I heard those do who have spoken the most favorably for him. I know that Louis XVI. had the inclinations of a tiger, and if we established courts such as Montesquieu calls the courts of manners and behavior, like that of the Areopagus at Athens, which condemned a child to death for putting out his bird's eyes; if we had an Areopagus, it would have a hundred times condemned this man as dishonoring the human race by the caprices of his wanton cruelties. But as it is not the deeds of his private life, but the crimes of his reign that we are judging, it must be confessed that this long list of accusations against Louis which our committee and our orators have presented to us, while rendering him a thousand times worthy of death, will nevertheless not suggest to posterity the horrors of the reign of Nero, but the crimes of constituents, the crimes of Louis the King, rather than the crimes of Louis Capet.

That which makes the former king justly odious to the people is the four years of perjuries and oaths, incessantly repeated into the nation's ear before the face of heaven, while all the time he was conspiring against the nation. Treason was always with every nation the most abominable of crimes. It has always inspired that horror which is inspired by poison and vipers, because it is impossible to guard against it. So the laws of the Twelve Tables devoted to the Furies the mandatary who betrayed the trust of his constituent, and permitted the latter to kill the former wherever he should find him. So, too, fidelity in fulfilling one's engagements is the only virtue on which those pride themselves who have lost all others. It is the only virtue found among thieves. It is the last bond which holds society—even that of the robbers themselves—together. This comparison, it is, which best paints royalty, by showing how much less villainous is even a robbers' cave than the Louvre, since the maxim of all kings is that of Cæsar: "It is permissible to break one's faith in order to reign." So in his religious idiom, spoke Antoine de Levre to Charles V.: "If you are not willing to be a rascal, if you have a soul to save, renounce the empire." So said Machiavelli in terms very applicable to our situation. For this reason it was, that many years ago in a petition to the National Assembly I quoted this passage: "If sovereignty must be renounced in order to make a people free, he who is clothed with this sovereignty has some excuse in betraying the nation, because it is difficult and against nature to be willing to fall from so high a position." All this proves that the crimes of Louis XVI. are the crimes of the constituents who supported him in his position of king rather than his crimes, that is to say, of those who gave him the right by letters patent to be the "enemy of the nation" and a traitor. But all these considerations, calculated as they may be to soften the horror of his crimes in the eyes of posterity, are useless before the law, in mitigating their punishment. What! Shall the judges forbear to punish a brigand because in his cave he has been brought up to believe that all the possessions of those who pass his cave belong to him? Because his education has so depraved his natural disposition that he could not be anything but a robber? Shall it be alleged as a reason for letting the treason of a king go unpunished, that he could not be anything but a traitor, and as a reason for not giving the nations the example of cutting down this tree, that it can only bear poisons?

In two words, by the declaration of rights, by that code eternal, unchangeable (that provisional code which in all states precedes their complete organization, when special laws shall have modified general laws), the articles of which, effaced by the rust of centuries, the French people adopted with joy, and by the enactment (consecrated as the basis of its constitution) that the law is the same toward all, either for punishment or for protection, reestablished in all their purity, Louis XVI. was divested of his chimerical inviolability.

He can henceforth be regarded only as a conspirator. Followed by the people, he came on the tenth of August,—that famous "Commune"— came to seek an asylum among us, at the foot of the throne of national sovereignty, in the house which was found full of evidences of his plottings and of his crimes. We placed him under arrest and imprisoned him in the Temple, and now it only remains for us to pass sentence upon him.

"But who shall judge this conspirator?" It is astonishing and inconceivable what trouble this question has given to the best heads of the Convention. Removed as we are from Nature and the primitive laws of all society, most of us have not thought that we could judge a conspirator without a jury of accusation, a jury of judgment, and judges who would apply the law, and all have imagined necessary a court more or less extraordinary. So we leave the ancient ruts only to fall into new ones, instead of following the plain road of common sense. Who shall judge Louis XVI.? The whole people, if it can, as the people of Rome judged Manlius and Horatius, nor dreamt of the need of a jury of accusation, to be followed by a jury of judgment, and that in turn by a court which would apply the law to judge a culprit taken in the act. But as we cannot hear the pleas of twenty-five millions of men we must recur to the maxim of Montesquieu: "Let a free people do all that it can by itself and the rest by representatives and commissioners!" And what is the National Convention but the commission selected by the French people to try the last king and to form the constitution of the new republic?

Some claim that such a course would be to unite all the powers—legislative functions and judical functions. Those who have most wearied our ears by reciting the dangers of this cumulation of powers must either deride our simplicity in believing that they respect those limits, or else they do not well understand themselves. For have not constitutional and legislative assemblies assumed a hundred times the functions of judges, whether in annulling the procedure of the Chatelet, and many other tribunals, or in issuing decrees against so many prisoners on suspicion whether there was an accusation or not? To acquit Mirabeau and "P. Equality," or to send Lessart to Orleans, was not that to assume the functions of judges? I conclude from this that those "Balancers," as Mirabeau called them, who continually talk of "equilibrium," and the balance of power, do not themselves believe in what they say. Can it be contested, for example, that the nation which exercises the power of sovereignty does not "cumulate" all the powers? Can it be claimed that the nation cannot delegate, at its will, this or that portion of its powers to whom it pleases? Can any one deny that the nation has cumulatively clothed us here with its powers, both to try Louis XVI. and to construct the constitution? One may well speak of the balance of power and the necessity of maintaining it when the people, as in England, exercises its sovereignty only at the time of elections. But when the nation, the sovereign, is in permanent activity, as formerly at Athens and Rome, and as now in France, when the right of sanctioning the laws is recognized as belonging to it, and when it can assemble every day in its municipalities and sections, and expel the faithless mandataries, the great necessity cannot be seen of maintaining the equilibrium of powers, since it is the people who, with its arm of iron, itself holds the scales ready to drive out the ambitious and the traitorous who wish to make it incline to the side opposite the general interest. It is evident that the people sent us here to judge the king and to give them a constitution. Is the first of these two functions so difficult to fulfill? And have we anything else to do than what Brutus did when the people caused him to judge his two sons himself, and tested him by this, just as the Convention is tested now? He made them come to his tribunal, as you must bring Louis XVI. before you. It produced for him the proofs of their conspiracy as you must present to Louis XVI. that multitude of overwhelming proofs of his plots. They could make no answer to the testimony of a slave, as Louis XVI. will not be able to answer anything to the correspondence of Laporte, and to that mass of written proofs that he paid his body-guard at Coblentz and betrayed the nation. And it only remains for you to prove, as Brutus proved to the Roman people, that you are worthy to begin the Republic and its constitution, and to appease the shades of a hundred thousand citizens whom he caused to perish in pronouncing the same sentence: "Go, lictor, bind him to the stake."

Mirabeau
[1749–1791]

One of the foremost orators of the French Revolution was Gabriel Honoré Victor Riquetti, Comte de Mirabeau. Like the other revolutionary leaders he had to face sooner or later the charge of treason. Here is part of Mirabeau's stirring speech in his own defense, which he delivered before the National Assembly in 1790. His eloquence overcame the opposition, but a year later he died from overwork and dissipation.

AGAINST THE CHARGE OF TREASON

I AM NOT SPEAKING here in order to humor popular malice, to excite bursts of hatred, to bring about fresh divisions. No one knows better than I do that the salvation of everything, and of everybody, lies in harmony and in the destruction of all party spirit; but I cannot help adding that to set on foot infamous arraignments, to change the administration of justice into a weapon of attack which slaves would regard with loathing, is a poor way of effecting that reunion of hearts which alone is wanting for the achievement of our undertaking. I beg permission to resume my argument.

The indictment describes me as an accomplice; there is, then, no charge against me excepting that of complicity. The indictment does not describe me as an accomplice in any specific act of violence, but of a certain person alleged to be the prime mover in such an act. There is, then, no charge against me unless it be proved, first of all, that there was an arch-conspirator; unless it be proved that the charges of complicity implied that I played a secondary part to a principal part; unless it be established that my conduct has been one of the main springs of the act, the movement, the explosion, whose causes are being sought for.

Finally, the indictment does not simply describe me as the accomplice of any specific arch-conspirator, but as the accomplice of Mr. Somebody or other. There is, then, no charge against me unless it be at the same time proved that this prime mover is the chief culprit, and that the charges of which I am the object involve him, and imply a common plot springing from the same causes, and calculated to produce the same effects.

Now, of all that it would thus be indispensable to prove, nothing has been proved.

I forbear to inquire whether the events upon which the evidence is based are to be called calamities or crimes; whether these crimes are the result of conspiracy, a want of caution, or a turn of chance; whether the hypothesis of a single arch-conspirator does not render them a hundred-fold more inexplicable.

I am content to remind you that amongst the acts laid to my charge, some cannot be connected with each other excepting by the logic of tyrants or their tools, because they were committed many months either before or after the insurrection, and others which are contemporaneous with the indictment are evidently neither causes nor effects of it, nor have they had any influence upon it, but are of such a character as quite excludes the idea of their being performed by an agent, a conspirator, or an accomplice, and unless I am supposed to be in the number of those who were culprits in will, though not in deed, and not chargeable with anything beyond that, neither exercise of influence nor incitement, my so-called complicity is a delusion.

I am content to draw your attention to the fact that the charges which are laid against me, so far from proving that I was in collusion with the arch-conspirator concerned, would imply that my relations were of an entirely opposite character; that in denouncing the "fraternal banquet" I was not the only one to style it "an orgy"; that I merely echoed two of my friends, who had adopted the expression before me; that if I had rushed through the ranks of the Flanders regiment I should have done nothing more, according to the indictment itself, than follow the example set by many members of this Assembly; that if the remark, "What does it matter whether it be Louis XVII.?" was made as reported, not only did I have no thought of a change of dynasty, but my ideas, as stated in a letter to a member of this Assembly, did not even turn in the possible contingency of a regent to a brother of a king.

What, then, is the prominent part that I am supposed to have played in the events with which the indictment deals? Where are the proofs of the complicity which is thrown in my teeth? What is the crime concerning which it can possibly be said, "He is either the author or the cause of it"? But I forget that I am adopting the tone of an accused man, when in truth I ought to take that of an accuser.

What is this indictment, supported as it is by evidence which could not be gone through, whose compilation required a whole year for its completion; this indictment which the crime of high treason apparently required, and which fell into the hands of an incompetent tribunal utterly destitute of authority, excepting in the cases of treason against the nation? What sort of an indictment is this, which, threatening in the space of a single year twenty different persons, is now suspended, now resumed, according to the interest and the views, the fears and hopes of its wire-pullers, and has never been anything else during that long period but a weapon of intrigue, a sword suspended over the head of those who are to be ruined or intimidated, cast off or won over; which, finally, after searching heaven and earth for evidence, has not reached any conclusion until one of those who were accused by it either lost faith in or learned to despise the dictatorial power that was keeping him in banishment?

What sort of an indictment is this, which is occupied with individual transgressions concerning which there is no evidence, transgressions whose remote causes are, nevertheless, to be eagerly sought for, without throwing any light upon their proximate causes? What procedure is this, which investigates events easily to be explained without any idea of a conspiracy, and yet has only conspiracy for its basis of investigation—whose first aim has been to conceal real faults, and to replace them by imaginary crimes? It has from the first been guided by vanity, its rage since then has been whetted by hatred, it has been carried by its party spirit, infatuated by its ministerial authority, and, after thus being the slave of many influences in turn, it has ended in an insidious denunciation of your decrees, the king's freedom of choice, his journey to Paris, the wisdom of your deliberation, the nation's love for the monarch.

What sort of an indictment is this, which the most deadly enemies of the Revolution would not have framed in a better way, even if they had been the sole promoters of it, as they have been almost its sole executors; whose tendency has been to set ablaze the most furious party spirit, even in the bosom of this Assembly, and to raise witnesses up in opposition to judges, both throughout the whole kingdom in the provinces, by calumniating the intentions of the capital, and in each town by rendering odious the liberty which was real enough to bring in question the life of the monarch; and in all Europe, by painting the situation of a free king in false colors, as that of a king captive and persecuted; and in depicting this august Assembly as an assembly of factionists? Yes, the secret of this infernal procedure is at last discovered. It is to be found in its full completeness there. It is to be found in the interests of those whose testimony and calumny have woven its tissue; in the weapons it has furnished to the enemies of the republic; this secret lurks, yes, it lurks in the heart of the judges, as it will soon be engraven on the page of history, by the most just and most implacable vengeance.

Danton
[1759–1794]

Probably the greatest orator of the French Revolution—and there were many great ones—was Georges Jacques Danton. It was Danton who inflamed the mob that stormed the Bastille. It was Danton who inspired the National Assembly and the people to fight the enemies of the Revolution who were marching on Paris. A radical advocate of the Reign of Terror, he later became appalled by its ceaseless flow of blood. For this he became suspect, was tried and condemned to the guillotine. The speeches given here were delivered in the National Assembly—the first in 1792, the second in 1793.

"TO DARE AGAIN, EVER TO DARE!"

IT SEEMS a satisfaction for the ministers of a free people to announce to them that their country will be saved. All are stirred, all are enthused, all burn to enter the combat.

You know that Verdun is not yet in the power of our enemies, and that its garrison swears to immolate the first who breathes a proposition of surrender.

One portion of our people will guard our frontiers, another will dig and arm the entrenchments, the third with pikes will defend the interior of our cities. Paris will second these great efforts. The commissioners of the Commune will solemnly proclaim to the citizens the invitation to arm and march to the defense of the country. At such a moment you can proclaim that the capital deserves the esteem of all France. At such a moment this national assembly becomes a veritable committee of war. We ask that you concur with us in directing this sublime movement of the people, by naming commissioners to second and assist all these great measures. We ask that any one refusing to give personal service or to furnish arms shall meet the punishment of death. We ask that proper instructions be given to the citizens to direct their movements. We ask that carriers be sent to all the departments to notify them of the decrees that you proclaim here. The tocsin we shall sound is not the alarm signal of danger, it orders the charge on the enemies of France. [Applause.] To conquer we have need to dare, to dare again, ever to dare! And the safety of France is insured.

"LET FRANCE BE FREE"

The general considerations that have been presented to you are true; but at this moment it is less necessary to examine the causes of the disasters that have struck us than to apply their remedy rapidly. When the edifice is on fire, I do not join the rascals who would steal the furniture; I extinguish the flames. I tell you, therefore, you should be convinced by the despatches of Dumouriez that you have not a moment to spare in saving the republic.

Dumouriez conceived a plan which did honor to his genius. I would render him greater justice and praise than I did recently. But three months ago he announced to the executive power, your general committee of defense, that if we were not audacious enough to invade Holland in the middle of winter, to declare instantly against England the war which actually we had long been making, that we would double the difficulties of our campaign, in giving our enemies the time to deploy their forces. Since we failed to recognize this stroke of his genius, we must now repair our faults.

Dumouriez is not discouraged; he is in the middle of Holland, where he will find munitions of war; to overthrow all our enemies, he wants but Frenchmen, and France is filled with citizens. Would we be free? If we no longer desire it, let us perish, for we have all sworn it. If we wish it, let all march to defend our independence. Your enemies are making their last efforts. Pitt, recognizing he has all to lose, dares spare nothing. Take Holland, and Carthage is destroyed, and England can no longer exist but for liberty! Let Holland be conquered to liberty, and even the commercial aristocracy itself, which at the moment dominates the English people, would rise against the government which had dragged it into despotic war against a free people. They would overthrow this ministry of stupidity, who thought the methods of the *ancien régime* could smother the genius of liberty breathing in France. This ministry once overthrown in the interests of commerce, the party of liberty would show itself; for it is not dead! And if you know your duties, if your commissioners leave at once, if you extend the hand to the strangers aspiring to destroy all forms of tyranny, France is saved and the world is free.

Expedite, then, your commissioners; sustain them with your energy; let them leave this very night, this very evening.

Let them say to the opulent classes, the aristocracy of Europe must succumb to our efforts, and pay our debt, or you will have to pay it! The people have nothing but blood—they lavish it! Go, then, ingrates, and lavish your wealth! [Wild applause.] See, citizens, the fair destinies that await you. What! you have a whole nation as a lever, its reason as your fulcrum, and you have not yet upturned the world! To do this we need firmness and character; and of a truth we lack it. I put to one side all passions. They are all strangers to me save a passion for the public good.

In the most difficult situations, when the enemy was at the gates of Paris, I said to those governing: "Your discussions are shameful; I can see but the enemy. [Fresh applause.] You tire me by squabbling, in place of occupying yourselves with the safety of the republic! I repudiate you all as traitors to our country! I place you all in the same line!" I said to them: "What care I for my reputation? Let France be free, though my name were accursed!" What care I that I am called "a blood-drinker"? Well, let us drink the blood of the enemies of humanity, if needful; but let us struggle, let us achieve freedom. Some fear the departure of the commissioners may weaken one or the other section of this convention. Vain fears! Carry your energy everywhere. The pleasantest declaration will be to announce to the people that the terrible debt weighing upon them will be wrested from their enemies or that the rich will shortly have to pay it. The national situation is cruel. The representatives of value are no longer in equilibrium in the circulation. The day of the working man is lengthened beyond necessity. A great corrective measure is necessary! Conquerors of Holland, reanimate in England the republican party; let us advance France, and we shall go glorified to posterity. Achieve these grand destinies: no more debates, no more quarrels, and the fatherland is saved.

Marat

[1744–1793]

Jean Paul Marat, fiery leader of the French Revolution, saved his head from the guillotine through his great gift of oratory. Arrested in 1793, he delivered the following speech in his defense before the Convention which tried him the same year. He was acquitted in triumph, only to be assassinated a few weeks later by Charlotte Corday, a woman who favored those opposed to him.

DEFENSE AGAINST THE CHARGES

Citizens, Members of the Revolutionary Tribunal: If Roland the patron of the clique of the Girondists had not wasted the public property in misleading the people and perverting the public mind; if the faction of statesmen had not flooded the whole republic with infamous libels of the Commune, the municipality, the sections, the committee of surveillance, and, above all, directed against the deputation of Paris; if they had not so long laid their heads together to defame Danton, Robespierre, and Marat; if they had not ceaselessly represented me as a factionist, an anarchist, a drinker of blood, an ambitious man, who looked for supreme power under the title of tribune, triumvir, and director; if the nation, completely undeceived, had recognized the perfidy of these impostures; if their guilty authors had been branded, I would have resisted the arbitrary acts brought against me under the title of "Decree and Act of Accusation," by a perfidious faction, which I had so often denounced as almost wholly composed of royalists, traitors, and plotters. I would moreover have waited till the constitution had been reinforced by the return of patriotic deputies, before presenting myself at the tribunal, and thus have overwhelmed the vile wretches who are persecuting me to-day with such odious rancor.

If, therefore, I appear before my judges, it is only to rise triumphant and confound imposture; it is to unseal the eyes of that part of the nation which is already led astray on my account; it is to go out a conqueror from this imbroglio, to reassure public opinion, to do a good service to the fatherland, and to strengthen the cause of liberty.

Full of confidence in the enlightenment, the equity, and the civic spirit of this tribunal, I myself urge the most rigorous examination of this affair. Strong in the testimony of my own conscience, in the rectitude of my intentions, in the purity of my civic spirit, I want no indulgence, but I demand strict justice.

I am ready to answer my judges. Nevertheless, before being examined I ought to place before you, citizens, a series of observations, which will put you in a position to judge of the crass ignorance, the absurdity, the iniquity, the perfidy, the implacableness, and the atrocity of my vile accusers.

The decree of accusation brought against me was carried without discussion, in violation of law and in contradiction of all the principles of order, liberty, and justice. For it is a principle of right that no citizen shall be censured without having first been heard. This decree of accusation was brought against me by two hundred and ten members of the faction of statesmen, contrary to the demand of ninety-two members of "the Mountain." That is to say, by two hundred and ten enemies of the country against ninety-two defenders of liberty. It was issued amid the most scandalous uproar, during which the patriots covered the royalists with opprobrium, reproaching them with their lack of civic spirit, their baseness, their machinations. It was issued in spite of the most marked manifestation of public opinion, amid the noise of continuous hootings throughout the tribunes. It was issued in a manner so revolting that twenty members who had been deceived by this faction of statemen refused to vote for it, the decree not having been discussed, and while one of them, yielding to the movement of an honest friend, cried out: "I do not vote, and I greatly fear, after all I have seen, that I have been the dupe of a perfidious cabal."

This decree, far from being the desire of the majority of the convention, as it is the work of a part of the members not making one-third of the assembly, can be regarded only as resulting from the implacable spirit of this faction of the statesmen. You will see that it is the outcome of a criminal plot, for it started after the reading of a certain address to the Jacobins which I had signed as president of the society. This patriotic address, however, was no longer to be attributed to me as a crime, when nearly all my colleagues of "the Mountain" hastened to the desk to sign it. The address was truly republican, and has just been signed by all sections of Paris, and will very soon be signed by all good citizens of France.

Leaving the denunciation of this address which suggested the call for the decree of accusation, the decree naturally came to naught; but it was revived with fury by our enemies when they saw me mount the tribune to renew the proposition to hale Louis Philippe D'Orleans before the Revolutionary Tribunal, and to put a price on the heads of the rebellious and fugitive Capets; a proposition which brought despair to the statesmen, forcing them to place a cord about their own necks if they adopted it, or to confess themselves the partisans of D'Orleans and the Capet rebels, the supporters of royalism, and the accomplices of Dumouriez, if they rejected it. You know with what violence they opposed it. Such a decree, therefore, is only an act of tyranny. It calls for resistance against oppression; and it cannot fail to prove revolting to all good citizens when once it shall be as well known in the departments as it is in Paris.

I pass to the act of accusation. Originating with a committee of legislation almost entirely composed of my most mortal enemies, all members of the faction, it was drawn with such want of reflection that it bears on its face all the characteristics of dense ignorance, falsehood, madness, fury, and atrocity. That act, at a glance, may be seen to be filled with glaring inconsistency, or we should rather say with the spirit of contradiction to the "Decree of Accusation" of which it served as the basis; for it makes no mention of the address drawn up by the Jacobins, the signing of which they attributed to me as a crime; yet this address was what caused the Decree.

When I show how ridiculous and destitute of foundation this act is I feel ashamed of the committee. As the address of the Jacobins contains the sentiments of true republicans, and as it has been signed by nearly all of my colleagues of "the Mountain," the committee, forced to abandon the fundamental count in the accusation, was reduced to the expedient of citing some of my writings which had lain neglected for many months in the dust of their cases, and it stupidly reproduced the denunciation of some others of my writings, a subject which the assembly refused to pursue, passing to the order of the day, as I shall prove in the sequel.

Let us prove now that that act is illegal. It rests wholly, as you have seen, on some of my political opinions. These opinions had almost all been enunciated from the tribune of the convention before being published in my writings. For my writings, whose constant aim is to reveal plots, to unmask traitors, to propose useful measures, are a supplement to what I cannot always explain in the midst of the assembly. Now, article number seven of the fifth section of the "Constitutional Act" states in express terms:—

"The representatives of the nation are inviolable: they cannot be sought, accused, nor judged at any time for what they have said, written, or done in the exercise of their functions as representatives."

The "Act of Accusation" is, therefore, null and void, in that it is diametrically opposed to the fundamental law, which has not been and which cannot be repealed. It is null and void in that it attacks the most sacred right that belongs to a representative of the people.

I am quite aware that this right does not include that of plotting against the state, of attempting any enterprise against the interests of liberty, of attacking the rights of citizens, or of compromising public safety, but it certainly allows a citizen to say, write, or do anything which accords with the sincere purpose of serving the country, of procuring the general welfare, and causing the triumph of liberty. It is so essentially inherent in the functions of the nation's representatives that without it it would be impossible for the faithful to defend the fatherland and themselves against the traitors who would oppress and enslave them.

The patriots of the Constituent Assembly so thoroughly felt the necessity of making the representatives inviolable and unassailable, capable of struggling with impunity against the despot and completing the revolution, that they hastened to consecrate this right by the famous decree of June 23, 1789, before they had even constituted themselves the National Assembly.

They felt so thoroughly that this right was inherent in every public function, that they stretched it to cover every judicial body, every administrative body, and even all citizens united in a primary assembly.

Without this inalienable right could liberty maintain itself a moment against the machinations of its conspiring enemies? Without it, how, in the midst of a corrupt senate, could a small number of deputies, invincibly attached to the fatherland, unmask the traitors who seek to oppress it or put it in fetters?

Without that essential right, how could a small number of far-seeing and determined patriots foil the plots of a numerous faction of schemers? One may judge of this by what happens to us. If the faction of statesmen can under false pretext attack me, expel me from its convention, hale me before a tribunal, hold me in captivity, cause me to perish; to-morrow under other pretexts it will attack Robespierre, Danton, Callot-d'Herbois, Panis, Lindet, Camille, David, Audoin, Laiguelit, Meaulle, Dupuis, Javougues, Granet, and all the other courageous deputies of the convention. It will restrain the others by terror. It will usurp the sovereignty. It will call to its side Dumouriez, Cobourg, Clerfayt, its accomplices. Supported by Prussians, Austrians, and "Emigrants," it will reestablish despotism in the hands of a Capet who will cut the throats of all the known patriots, and it will endow the first employments with the treasures of the state. The decree of accusation issued against me for my political opinions is therefore an attack on national representation, and I do not doubt that the convention, with its quota filled by the return of patriotic commissaries, will soon feel its dangerous consequences, its ill-boding results, and will blush that it should have been decreed in its name, and will hasten to repeal it as destructive of all public liberty.

The act of accusation is not only absurd in that it violates all constitutional liberty and attacks national representations, it is still more so in that the committee, contrary to all principle, turns the convention into a criminal tribunal, for it makes it pronounce without shame an iniquitous judgment, in deciding, without preliminary examination of a single document, without even having placed in question if such writings are mine, that I am found to have provoked murder and pillage, to have called up a power that threatens the sovereignty of the people, dishonored the convention, incited its dissolution, etc.

But what will appear incredible is that the committee calls down, without ceremony, without shame, and without remorse, capital punishment on my head, and cites articles of the penal code, which, according to it, condemned me to death. I doubt not that such is the object they have in view. How many statesmen have been tormented with despair of keeping me in prison, smothering my voice, and restraining my pen? Did not one of them, the atrocious Lacaze, have the impudence to ask the convention, as Dumouriez and Cobourg asked of the faction, that I should be outlawed? So that the act of accusation is a veritable "verdict rendered," which has only now to be executed.

Finally, this act is a tissue of lies and fabrications. It accuses me of having incited to murder and pillage, of setting up a "Chief of State," dishonoring and dissolving a convention, etc. The contrary was proved by the simple reading of my writings. I demand a consecutive reading of the denounced members; for it is not by garbling and mutilating passages that the ideas of an author are to be learnt, it is by reading the context that their meaning may be judged of.

If after the reading any doubts remain, I am here to remove them.

Robespierre
[1758–1794]

Maximilien Marie Isidore Robespierre, one of the leaders and orators of the French Revolution, was one of the strongest advocates of the Reign of Terror which used the guillotine to settle all political differences. In the end Robespierre himself became the victim of this policy when his political enemies gained control. The following speech was made in 1794, shortly before he was condemned and led to the guillotine.

THE FESTIVAL OF THE SUPREME BEING

THE DAY forever fortunate has arrived, which the French people have consecrated to the Supreme Being. Never has the world which He created offered to Him a spectacle so worthy of His notice. He has seen reigning on the earth tyranny, crime, and imposture. He sees at this moment a whole nation, grappling with all the oppressions of the human race, suspend the course of its heroic labors to elevate its thoughts and vows toward the great Being who has given it the mission it has undertaken and the strength to accomplish it.

Is it not He whose immortal hand, engraving on the heart of man the code of justice and equality, has written there the death sentence of tyrants? Is it not He who, from the beginning of time, decreed for all the ages and for all peoples liberty, good faith, and justice?

He did not create kings to devour the human race. He did not create priests to harness us, like vile animals, to the chariots of kings and to give to the world examples of baseness, pride, perfidy, avarice, debauchery, and falsehood. He created the universe to proclaim His power. He created men to help each other, to love each other mutually, and to attain to happiness by the way of virtue.

It is He who implanted in the breast of the triumphant oppressor remorse and terror, and in the heart of the oppressed and innocent calmness and fortitude. It is He who impels the just man to hate the evil one, and the evil man to respect the just one. It is He who adorns with modesty the brow of beauty, to make it yet more beautiful. It is He who makes the mother's heart beat with tenderness and joy. It is He who bathes with delicious tears the eyes of the son pressed to the bosom of his mother. It is He who silences the most imperious and tender passions before the sublime love of the fatherland. It is He who has covered nature with charms, riches, and majesty. All that is good is His work, or is Himself. Evil belongs to the depraved man who oppresses his fellow man or suffers him to be oppressed.

The Author of Nature has bound all mortals by a boundless chain of love and happiness. Perish the tyrants who have dared to break it!

Republican Frenchmen, it is yours to purify the earth which they have soiled, and to recall to it the justice that they have banished! Liberty and virtue together came from the breast of Divinity. Neither can abide with mankind without the other.

O generous People, would you triumph over all your enemies? Practise justice, and render the Divinity the only worship worthy of Him. O People, let us deliver ourselves to-day, under His auspices, to the just transports of a pure festivity. To-morrow we shall return to the combat with vice and tyrants. We shall give to the world the example of republican virtues. And that will be to honor Him still.

The monster which the genius of kings had vomited over France has gone back into nothingness. May all the crimes and all the misfortunes of the world disappear with it! Armed in turn with the daggers of fanaticism and the poisons of atheism, kings have always conspired to assassinate humanity. If they are able no longer to disfigure Divinity by superstition, to associate it with their crimes, they try to banish it from the earth, so that they may reign there alone with crime.

O People, fear no more their sacrilegious plots! They can no more snatch the world from the breast of its Author than remorse from their own hearts. Unfortunate ones, uplift your eyes toward heaven! Heroes of the fatherland, your generous devotion is not a brilliant madness. If the satellites of tyranny can assassinate you, it is not in their power entirely to destroy you. Man, whoever thou mayest be, thou canst still conceive high thoughts for thyself. Thou canst bind thy fleeting life to God, and to immortality. Let nature seize again all her splendor, and wisdom all her empire! The Supreme Being has not been annihilated.

It is wisdom above all that our guilty enemies would drive from the republic. To wisdom alone it is given to strengthen the prosperity of empires. It is for her to guarantee to us the rewards of our courage. Let us associate wisdom, then, with all our enterprises. Let us be grave and discreet in all our deliberations, as men who are providing for the interests of the world. Let us be ardent and obstinate in our anger against conspiring tyrants, imperturbable in dangers, patient in labors, terrible in striking back, modest and vigilant in successes. Let us be generous toward the good, compassionate with the unfortunate, inexorable with the evil, just toward every one. Let us not count on an unmixed prosperity, and on triumphs without attacks, nor on all that depends on fortune or the perversity of others. Sole, but infallible guarantors of our independence, let us crush the impious league of kings by the grandeur of our character, even more than by the strength of our arms.

Frenchmen, you war against kings; you are therefore worthy to honor Divinity. Being of Beings, Author of Nature, the brutalized slave, the vile instrument of despotism, the perfidious and cruel aristocrat, outrages Thee by his very invocation of Thy name. But the defenders of liberty can give themselves up to Thee, and rest with confidence upon Thy paternal bosom. Being of Beings, we need not offer to Thee unjust prayers. Thou knowest Thy creatures, proceeding from Thy hands. Their needs do not escape Thy notice, more than their secret thoughts. Hatred of bad faith and tyranny burns in our hearts, with love of justice and the fatherland. Our blood flows for the cause of humanity. Behold our prayer. Behold our sacrifices. Behold the worship we offer Thee.

Napoleon Bonaparte
[1769–1821]

Napoleon Bonaparte, great military genius and conqueror, knew the value of the spoken word. His addresses to the army illustrate his great gifts of oratory and his ability to select occasions when he could use his gifts most effectively. Here are a few of his more important addresses—important both from historical and oratorical standpoints.

AT THE BEGINNING OF THE ITALIAN CAMPAIGN

SOLDIERS: You are naked and ill-fed! Government owes you much and can give you nothing. The patience and courage you have shown in the midst of this rocky wilderness are admirable; but they gain you no renown; no glory results to you from your endurance. It is my design to lead you into the most fertile plains of the world. Rich provinces and great cities will be in your power; there you will find honor, glory, and wealth. Soldiers of Italy, will you be wanting in courage or perseverance?

ON ENTERING MILAN

Soldiers: You have rushed like a torrent from the top of the Apennines; you have overthrown and scattered all that opposed your march. Piedmont, delivered from Austrian tyranny, indulges her natural sentiments of peace and friendship toward France. Milan is yours, and the republican flag waves throughout Lombardy. The dukes of Parma and Modena owe their political existence to your generosity alone.

The army which so proudly threatened you can find no barrier to protect it against your courage; neither the Po, the Ticino, nor the Adda could stop you for a single day. These vaunted bulwarks of Italy opposed you in vain; you passed them as rapidly as the Apennines.

These great successes have filled the heart of your country with joy. Your representatives have ordered a festival to commemorate your victories, which has been held in every district of the republic. There your fathers, your mothers, your wives, sisters, and mistresses rejoiced in your good fortune and proudly boasted of belonging to you.

Yes, soldiers, you have done much—but remains there nothing more to do? Shall it be said of us that we knew how to conquer, but not how to make use of victory? Shall posterity reproach us with having found Capua in Lombardy?

But I see you already hasten to arms. An effeminate repose is tedious to you; the days which are lost to glory are lost to your happiness. Well, then, let us set forth!

ON BEGINNING THE RUSSIAN CAMPAIGN

Soldiers: The second war of Poland has begun. The first war terminated at Friedland and Tilsit. At Tilsit Russia swore eternal alliance with France and war with England. She has openly violated her oath, and refuses to offer any explanation of her strange conduct till the French eagle shall have passed the Rhine, and consequently shall have left her allies at her discretion. Russia is impelled onward by fatality. Her destiny is about to be accomplished. Does she believe that we have degenerated— that we are no longer the soldiers of Austerlitz? She has placed us between dishonor and war. The choice cannot for an instant be doubtful.

Let us march forward, then, and, crossing the Niemen, carry the war into her territories. The second war of Poland will be to the French army as glorious as the first. But our next peace must carry with it its own guaranty and put an end to that arrogant influence which for the last fifty years Russia has exercised over the affairs of Europe.

FAREWELL TO THE OLD GUARD

Soldiers of my Old Guard: I bid you farewell. For twenty years I have constantly accompanied you on the road to honor and glory. In these latter times, as in the days of our prosperity, you have invariably been models of courage and fidelity. With men such as you our cause could not be lost; but the war would have been interminable; it would have been civil war, and that would have entailed deeper misfortunes on France.

I have sacrificed all my interests to those of the country.

I go, but you, my friends, will continue to serve France. Her happiness was my only thought. It will still be the object of my wishes. Do not regret my fate; if I have consented to survive, it is to serve your glory. I intend to write the history of the great achievements we have performed together. Adieu, my friends. Would I could press you all to my heart.

Carnot

[1753–1823]

Lazare Nicolas Marguerite Carnot was the military genius of the French Revolution, the real organizer of victory for the revolutionary armies. He was a sincere republican and fought vigorously against dictatorship and imperialism. The speech, reproduced in part here, was delivered by Carnot in the National Assembly in 1802.

AGAINST IMPERIALISM

I AM FAR from desiring to diminish the praises accorded the first consul; if we owed him but the code civil, his name would worthily be immortalized to posterity. But whatever the services a citizen has rendered his country, he must expect honors but in the extent of the national recognition of his work. If the citizen has restored public liberty, if he has been a benefactor to his country, would it be a proper recompense to offer him the sacrifice of that liberty? Nay! Would it not be an annulment of his own work to convert that country into his private patrimony?

From the very moment it was proposed to the French people to vote to make the consulate an office for life, each easily judged there was a mental reservation, and saw the ulterior purpose and end of the proposal. In effect, there was seen the rapid succession of a series of institutions evidently monarchical; but at each move anxiety was manifested to reassure disturbed and inquiring spirits on the score of liberty, that these new institutions and arrangements were conceived only to procure the highest protection that could be desired for liberty.

To-day is uncovered and developed in the most positive manner the meaning of so many of these preliminary measures. We are asked to declare ourselves upon a formal proposition to reestablish the monarchical system, and to confer an imperial and hereditary dignity on the first consul.

At that time I voted against a life consulate; I shall vote now against any reestablishment of a monarchy, as I believe it my duty to do. But it was done with no desire to evoke partisanship; without personal feeling; without any sentiment save a passion for the public good, which always impels me to the defense of the popular cause.

I always fully submit to existing laws, even when they are most displeasing. More than once I have been a victim to my devotion to law, and I shall not begin to retrograde to-day. I declare, therefore, that while I combat this proposition, from the moment that a new order of things shall have been established, which shall have received the assent of the mass of our citizens, I shall be first to conform my actions; to give to the supreme authority all the marks of deference commanded by the constitutional oligarchy. Can every member of society record a vow as sincere and disinterested as my own?

I shall not force into the discussion my preference for the general merits of any one system of government over another. On these subjects there are numberless volumes written. I shall charge myself with examining in few words, and in the simplest terms, the particular case in which present circumstances place us. All the arguments thus far made for the reestablishment of monarchy in France are reduced to the statement that it is the only method of assuring the stability of the government and the public tranquillity, the only escape from internal disorder, the sole bond of union against external enemies, that the republican system has been vainly essayed in all possible manners; and that from all these efforts only anarchy has resulted. A prolonged and ceaseless revolution has reawakened a perpetual fear of new disorders, and consequently a deep and universal desire to see reestablished the old hereditary government, changing only the dynasty. To this we must make reply.

I remark here that the government of a single person is no assurance of a stable and tranquil government. The duration of the Roman empire was no longer than that of the Roman republic. Their internecine troubles were greater, their crimes more multiplied. The pride of republicanism, the heroism, and the masculine virtues were replaced by the most ridiculous vanity, the vilest adulation, the boldest cupidity, the most absolute indifference to the national prosperity. Where was any remedy in the heredity of the throne? Was it not regarded as the legitimate heritage of the house of Augustus? Was a Domitian not the son of Vespasian, a Caligula the son of Germanicus, a Commodus the son of Marcus Aurelius? In France, it is true, the last dynasty maintained itself for eight hundred years, but were the people any the less tormented? What have been the internal dissensions? What the foreign wars undertaken for pretensions and rights of succession, which gave birth to the alliances of this dynasty with foreign nations? From the moment that a nation espouses the particular interests of one family, she is compelled to intervene in a multitude of matters which but for this would be to her of uttermost indifference.

We have hardly succeeded in establishing a republic among us, notwith-standing that we have essayed it under various forms, more or less demo-cratic.

After the peace of Amiens, Napoleon had choice between the republican and monarchical systems; he could do as he pleased. He would have met but the slightest opposition. The citadel of liberty was confided to him; he swore to defend it; and, holding his promise, he should have fulfilled the desire of the nation which judged him alone capable of solving the grand problem of public liberty in its vast extent. He might have covered himself with an incomparable glory. Instead of that, what is being done to-day? They propose to make for him an absolute and hereditary property of a great power of which he was made the administrator. Is this the real desire and to the real interest of the first consul himself? I do not believe it.

It is true the state was falling into dissolution, and that absolutism pulled it from the edge of the abyss. But what do we conclude from that? What all the world knows—that political bodies are subject to affections which can be cured but by violent remedies; that sometimes a dictator is necessary for a moment to save liberty. The Romans, who were so jealous of it, never-theless recognized the necessity of this supreme power at intervals. But because a violent remedy has saved a patient, must there be a daily adminis-tration of violent remedies? Fabius, Cincinnatus, Camillus saved Rome by the exercise of absolute power, but they relinquished this power as soon as practicable; they would have killed Rome had they continued to wield it. Cæsar was the first who desired to keep this power: he became its victim, but liberty was lost for futurity. Thus everything that has ever been said up to this date on absolute government proves only the necessity for tem-porary dictatorships in crises of the state, but not the establishment of a permanent and irresponsible power.

It is not from the character of their government that great republics have lacked stability; it is because, having been born in the breasts of storms, it is always in a state of exaltation that they are established. One only was the labor of philosophy, organized calmly. That republic, the United States of America, full of wisdom and of strength, exhibits this phenomenon, and each day their prosperity shows an increase which aston-ishes other nations. Thus it was reserved for the New World to teach the Old that existence is possible and peaceable under the rule of liberty and equality. Yes, I state this proposition, that when a new order of things can be established without fearing partisan influences, as the first consul has done, principally after the peace of Amiens, and as he can still do, it be-comes much easier to form a republic without anarchy than a monarchy without despotism. For how can we conceive a limitation which would not be illusory in a government of which the chief had all the executive power in his hand and all the places to bestow?

They have spoken of institutions to produce all these good effects. But before we propose to establish a monarchy, should we not first assure our-selves and demonstrate to those who are to vote on the question, that these institutions proposed are in the order of possible things, and not meta-physical obstructions, which have been held a reproach to the opposite system? Up to this moment nothing has been successfully invented to curb supreme power but what are called intermediary bodies or privileges. Is it, then, of a new nobility you would speak when you allude to institutions? But such remedies—are they not worse than the disease? For the absolute power of a monarch takes but our liberty, while the institution of privileged classes robs us at the same time of our liberty and our equality. And if even at the commencement dignities and ranks were but personal, we know they would finish always as the fiefs of other times, in becoming hereditary.

To these general principles I shall add a few special observations. I assume that all the French give assent to these proposed changes; but it will be the real free will and wish of Frenchmen which is produced from a register where each is obliged to individually sign his vote. Who does not know what is the influence in similar cases of the presiding authority? From all parties in France, it would be said, springs a universal desire of the citizens for the reestablishment of the hereditary monarchy; but can we not look suspiciously on an opinion, concentrated thus far almost exclusively among public functionaries, when we consider the inconvenience they would have to manifest any contrary opinion; when we know that the liberty of the press is so enfeebled that it is not possible to insert in any journal the most moderate and respectful protests?

Doubtless there will be no making any choice of the hereditary chief, if they declare it necessary to have one.

Is it hoped, in raising this new dynasty, to hasten the period of general peace? Will it not rather be a new obstacle? Are we assured that the other great powers of Europe will assent to this new title? And if they do not, do we take up arms to constrain them? Or after having sunk the title of first consul in that of emperor, will he be content to remain first consul to the rest of Europe while he is emperor only to Frenchmen, or shall we compromise by a vain title the security and the prosperity of the entire nation?

It appears, therefore, infinitely doubtful if the new order of things can give us the stability of the present state. There is for the government one method of consolidation and strength. It is to be just; that no favoritism or bias be of avail to influence its services; that there be a guaranty against robbery and fraud. It is far from me to desire to make any particular application of my language or to criticize the conduct of the government. It is against arbitrary power itself I appeal, and not against those in whose hands this power may reside. Has liberty then been shown to man that he shall never enjoy it? Shall it always be held to his gaze as a fruit, that when he extends the hand to grasp he must be stricken with death? And Nature, which has made liberty such a pressing need to us, does she really desire to betray our confidence? No! I shall never believe this good, so universally preferred to all others—without which all others are nothing—is a simple illusion. My heart tells me that liberty is possible, that its régime is easier and more stable than any arbitrary government, than any oligarchy.

But, nevertheless (I repeat it), I shall be always ready to sacrifice my dearest affections to the interest of our common country; I shall be satisfied to have once more caused to be heard the accents of an independent mind; and my respect for the law will be so much the more sure, as it is the fruit of long misfortunes, and of this reason, which commands us imperiously at this day to reunite as one body against the implacable enemy of one party as well as the other—of this enemy, which is always ready to foment discord, and to whom all means are lawful provided he can attain his end, namely—universal oppression and tyranny over the whole extent of the ocean.

I vote against the proposition.

Victor Hugo
[1802–1885]

On the one hundredth anniversary of Voltaire's death, Victor Marie Hugo, the famous French author and poet, delivered this eloquent tribute in memory of the great French wit, dramatist and philosopher.

VOLTAIRE

A HUNDRED years to-day a man died. He died immortal. He departed laden with years, laden with works, laden with the most illustrious and the most fearful of responsibilities, the responsibility of the human conscience informed and rectified. He went cursed and blessed, cursed by the past, blessed by the future; and these are the two superb forms of glory. On the death-bed he had, on the one hand, the acclaim of contemporaries and of posterity; on the other, that triumph of hooting and of hate which the implacable past bestows upon those who have combated it. He was more than a man; he was an age. He had exercised a function and fulfilled a mission. He had been evidently chosen for the work which he had done by the Supreme Will, which manifests itself as visibly in the laws of destiny as in the laws of nature.

The eighty-four years which this man lived span the interval between the Monarchy at its apogee and the Revolution at its dawn. When he was born, Louis XIV still reigned; when he died, Louis XVI already wore the crown; so that his cradle saw the last rays of the great throne, and his coffin the first gleams from the great abyss.

Before going further, let us come to an understanding upon the word abyss. There are good abysses: such are the abysses in which evil is engulfed.

Since I have interrupted myself, allow me to complete my thought. No word imprudent or unsound will be pronounced here. We are here to perform an act of civilization. We are here to make affirmation of progress, to pay respect to philosophers for the benefits of philosophy, to bring to the Eighteenth century the testimony of the Nineteenth, to honor magnanimous combatants and good servants, to felicitate the noble effort of people, industry, science, the valiant march in advance, the toil to cement human concord; in one word, to glorify peace, that sublime, universal desire. Peace is the virtue of civilization; war is its crime. We are here, at this grand moment, in this solemn hour, to bow religiously before the moral law, and to say to the world, which hears France, this: There is only one power, conscience in the service of justice; and there is only one glory, genius in the service of truth. That said, I continue.

Before the Revolution the social structure was this:—

At the base, the people;

Above the people, religion represented by the clergy;

By the side of religion, justice represented by the magistracy.

And, at that period of human society, what was the people? It was ignorance. What was religion? It was intolerance. And what was justice? It was injustice. Am I going too far in my words? Judge.

I will confine myself to the citation of two facts, but decisive.

At Toulouse, October 13, 1761, there was found in the lower story of a house a young man hanged. The crowd gathered, the clergy fulminated, the magistracy investigated. It was a suicide; they made of it an assassination. In what interest? In the interest of religion. And who was accused? The father. He was a Huguenot, and he wished to hinder his son from becoming a Catholic. There was here a moral monstrosity and a material impossibility; no matter! This father had killed his son; this old man had hanged this young man. Justice travailed, and this was the result. In the month of March, 1762, a man with white hair, Jean Calas, was conducted to a public place, stripped naked, stretched upon a wheel, the members bound upon it, the head hanging. Three men are there upon a scaffold, a magistrate named David, charged to superintend the punishment, a priest to hold the crucifix, and the executioner with a bar of iron in his hand. The patient, stupefied and terrible, regards not the priest, and looks at the executioner. The executioner lifts the bar of iron, and breaks one of his arms. The victim groans and swoons. The magistrate comes forward; they make the condemned inhale salts; he returns to life. Then another stroke of the bar; another groan. Calas loses consciousness; they revive him and the executioner begins again; and, as each limb before being broken in two places receives two blows, that makes eight punishments. After the eighth swooning the priest offers him the crucifix to kiss; Calas turns away his head, and the executioner gives him the *coup de grâce;* that is to say, crushes in his chest with the thick end of the bar of iron. So died Jean Calas.

That lasted two hours. After his death the evidence of the suicide came to light. But an assassination had been committed. By whom? By the judges.

Another fact. After the old man, the young man. Three years later, in 1765, at Abbeville, the day after a night of storm and high wind, there was found upon the pavement of a bridge an old crucifix of worm-eaten wood, which for three centuries had been fastened to the parapet. Who had thrown down this crucifix? Who committed this sacrilege? It is not known. Perhaps a passer-by. Perhaps the wind. Who is the guilty one? The Bishop of Amiens launches a *monitoire*. Not what a *monitoire* was: it was an order to all the faithful, on pain of hell, to declare what they knew or believed they knew of such or such a fact; a murderous injunction, when addressed by fanaticism to ignorance. The *monitoire* of the Bishop of Amiens does its work; the town gossip assumes the character of the crime charged. Justice discovers, or believes it discovers, that on the night when the crucifix was thrown down, two men, two officers, one named La Barre, the other D'Etallonde, passed over the bridge of Abbeville, that they were drunk, and that they sang a guard-room song.

The tribunal was the Seneschalcy of Abbeville. The Seneschalcy of Abbeville was equivalent to the court of the Capitouls of Toulouse. It was not less just. Two orders for arrest were issued. D'Etallonde escaped, La Barre was taken. Him they delivered to judicial examination. He denied having crossed the bridge; he confessed to having sung the song. The Seneschalcy of Abbeville condemned him; he appealed to the Parliament of Paris. He was conducted to Paris; the sentence was found good and confirmed. He was conducted back to Abbeville in chains. I abridge. The monstrous hour arrives. They begin by subjecting the Chevalier de la Barre to the torture ordinary, and extraordinary, to make him reveal his accomplices. Accomplices in what? In having crossed a bridge and sung a song. During the torture one of his knees was broken; his confessor, on hearing the bones crack, fainted away. The next day, June 5, 1766, La Barre was drawn to the great square of Abbeville, where flamed a penitential fire; the sentence was read to La Barre; then they cut off one of his hands, then they tore out his tongue with iron pincers; then, in mercy, his head was cut off and thrown into the fire. So died the Chevalier de la Barre. He was nineteen years of age.

Then, O Voltaire; thou didst utter a cry of horror, and it will be thine eternal glory!

Then didst thou enter upon the appalling trial of the past; thou didst plead, against tyrants and monsters, the cause of the human race, and thou didst gain it. Great man, blessed be thou forever!

The frightful things which I have recalled were accomplished in the midst of a polite society; its life was gay and light; people went and came; they looked neither above nor below themselves; their indifference had become carelessness; graceful poets, Saint Aulaire, Boufflers, Gentil-Bernard, composed pretty verses; the court was all festival; Versailles was brilliant; Paris ignored what was passing; and then it was that, through religious ferocity, the judges made an old man die upon the wheel and the priests tore out a child's tongue for a song.

In the presence of this society, frivolous and dismal, Voltaire alone, having before his eyes those united forces, the court, the nobility, capital; that unconscious power, the blind multitude; that terrible magistracy, so severe to subjects, so docile to the master, crushing and flattering, kneeling upon the people before the king; that clergy, vile *mélange* of hypocrisy and fanaticism; Voltaire alone, I repeat, declared war against that coalition of all the social iniquities, against that enormous and terrible world, and he accepted battle with it. And what was his weapon? That which has the lightness of the wind and the power of the thunderbolt—a pen.

With that weapon he fought; with that weapon he conquered.

Let us salute that memory.

Voltaire conquered; Voltaire waged the splendid kind of warfare, the war of one alone against all; that is to say, the grand warfare. The war of thought against matter, the war of reason against prejudice, the war of the just against the unjust, the war for the oppressed against the oppressor, the war of goodness, the war of kindness. He had the tenderness of a woman and the wrath of a hero. He was a great mind and an immense heart.

He conquered the old code and the old dogma. He conquered the feudal lord, the Gothic judge, the Roman priest. He raised the populace to the dignity of people. He taught, pacificated, and civilized. He fought for Sirven and Montbailly, as for Calas and La Barre; he accepted all the menaces, all the outrages, all the persecutions, calumny, and exile. He was indefatigable and immovable. He conquered violence by a smile, despotism by sarcasm, infallibility by irony, obstinacy by perseverance, ignorance by truth.

I have just pronounced the word *smile.* I pause at it. Smile! It is Voltaire.

Let us say it, pacification is the great side of the philosopher: in Voltaire the equilibrium always reëstablishes itself at last. Whatever may be his just wrath, it passes, and the irritated Voltaire always gives place to the Voltaire calmed. Then in that profound eye the smile appears.

That smile is wisdom. That smile, I repeat, is Voltaire. That smile sometimes becomes laughter, but the philosophic sadness tempers it. Toward the strong it is mockery; toward the weak it is a caress. It disquiets the oppressor, and reassures the oppressed. Against the great it is raillery; for the little it is pity. Ah, let us be moved by that smile! It had in it the rays of the dawn. It illuminated the true, the just, the good, and what there is of worthy in the useful. It lighted up the interior of superstitions. Those ugly things it is salutary to see, he has shown. Luminous, that smile was fruitful also. The new society, the desire for equality and concession and that beginning of fraternity which called itself tolerance, reciprocal good-will, the just accord of men and right, reason recognized as the supreme law, the annihilation of prejudices and prescribed opinions, the serenity of souls, the spirit of indulgence and of pardon, harmony, peace—behold what has come from that great smile!

On the day—very near, without any doubt—when the identity of wisdom and clemency will be recognized, when the amnesty will be proclaimed, I affirm it! up there in the stars Voltaire will smile.

Between two servants of humanity, who appeared eighteen hundred years apart, there is a mysterious relation.

To combat Pharisaism; to unmask imposture; to overthrow tyrannies, usurpations, prejudices, falsehoods, superstitions; to demolish the temple in order to rebuild it, that is to say, to replace the false by the true;

to attack a ferocious magistracy, a sanguinary priesthood; to take a whip and drive the money-changers from the sanctuary; to reclaim the heritage of the disinherited; to protect the weak, the poor, the suffering, the overwhelmed, to struggle for the persecuted and oppressed—that was the war of Jesus Christ! And who waged that war? It was Voltaire.

The completion of the evangelical work is the philosophical work; the spirit of mercy began, the spirit of tolerance continued. Let us say it with a sentiment of profound respect: Jesus wept; Voltaire smiled. Of that divine tear and that human smile is composed the sweetness of the present civilization.

Did Voltaire always smile? No. He was often indignant. You remarked it in my first words.

Certainly measure, reserve, proportion are reason's supreme law. We can say that moderation is the very respiration of the philosopher. That effort of the wise man ought to be to condense into a sort of serene certainty all the approximations of which philosophy is composed. But at certain moments the passion for the true rises powerful and violent, and it is within its right in so doing, like the stormy winds which purify. Never, I insist upon it, will any wise man shake those two august supports of social labor, justice and hope; and all will respect the judge if he is embodied justice, and all will venerate the priest if he represents hope. But if the magistracy calls itself torture, if the Church calls itself Inquisition, then Humanity looks them in the face, and says to the judge: I will none of thy law! and says to the priest: I will none of thy dogma! I will none of thy fire upon the earth and thy hell in the future! Then philosophy rises in wrath, and arraigns the judge before justice, and the priest before God!

That is what Voltaire did. It was grand.

What Voltaire was, I have said; what his age was, I am about to say.

Great men rarely come alone; large trees seem larger when they dominate a forest; there they are at home. There was a forest of minds around Voltaire; that forest was the Eighteenth century. Among those minds there were summits, Montesquieu, Buffon, Beaumarchais, and among others, two the highest after Voltaire—Rousseau and Diderot. Those thinkers taught men to reason; reasoning well leads to acting well; justness in the mind becomes justice in the heart. Those toilers for progress labored usefully. Buffon founded naturalism; Beaumarchais discovered, outside of Molière, a kind of comedy till then almost unknown, the social comedy; Montesquieu made in law some excavations so profound that he succeeded in exhuming the right. As to Rousseau, as to Diderot, let us pronounce those two names apart; Diderot, a vast intelligence, inquisitive, a tender heart, athirst for justice, wished to give certain notions as the foundation of true ideas, and created the encyclopædia. Rousseau rendered to woman an admirable service, completing the mother by the nurse, placing near one another those two majesties of the cradle. Rousseau, a writer, eloquent and pathetic, a profound oratorical dreamer, often divined and proclaimed political truth; his ideal borders upon the real; he had the glory of being the first man in France who called himself citizen. The civic fiber vibrates in Rousseau; that which vibrates in Voltaire is the universal fiber. One can say that in the fruitful Eighteenth century, Rousseau represented the people; Voltaire, still more vast, represented Man. Those powerful writers disappeared, but they left us their soul, the Revolution.

Yes, the French Revolution was their soul. It was their radiant manifestation. It came from them; we find them everywhere in that blest and superb catastrophe, which formed the conclusion of the past and the opening of the future. In that clear light, which is peculiar to revolutions, and which beyond causes permits us to perceive effects, and beyond the first plan the second, we see behind Danton, Diderot, behind Robespierre, Rousseau, and behind Mirabeau, Voltaire. These formed those.

To sum up epochs, by giving them the names of men, to name ages, to make of them in some sort human personages, has only been done by three peoples, Greece, Italy, France. We say, the Age of Pericles, the Age of Augustus, the Age of Leo X, the Age of Louis XIV, the Age of Voltaire. These appellations have a great significance. This privilege of giving names to periods belonging exclusively to Greece, to Italy, and to France, is the highest mark of civilization. Until Voltaire, they were the names of the chiefs of states; Voltaire is more than the chief of a state; he is a chief of ideas; with Voltaire a new cycle begins. We feel that henceforth the supreme governmental power is to be thought. Civilization obeyed force; it will obey the ideal. It was the scepter and the sword broken, to be replaced by the ray of light; that is to say, authority transfigured into liberty. Henceforth, no other sovereignty than the law for the people, and the conscience for the individual. For each of us, the two aspects of progress separate themselves clearly, and they are these: to exercise one's right; that is to say, to be a man; to perform one's duty; that is to say, to be a citizen.

Such is the signification of that word, the Age of Voltaire; such is the meaning of that august event, the French Revolution.

The two memorable centuries which preceded the Eighteenth, prepared for it; Rabelais warned royalty in "Gargantua," and Molière warned the Church in "Tartuffe." Hatred of force and respect for right are visible in those two illustrious spirits.

Whoever says to-day, might makes right, performs an act of the Middle Ages, and speaks to men three hundred years behind their time.

The Nineteenth century glorifies the Eighteenth century. The Eighteenth proposed, the Nineteenth concludes. And my last word will be the declaration, tranquil but inflexible, of progress.

The time has come. The right has found its formula: human federation.

To-day force is called violence, and begins to be judged; war is arraigned. Civilization, upon the complaint of the human race, orders the trial, and draws up the great criminal indictment of conquerors and captains. This witness, History, is summoned. The reality appears. The factitious brilliancy is dissipated. In many cases, the hero is a species of assassin. The peoples begin to comprehend that increasing the magnitude of a crime cannot be its diminution; that, if to kill is a crime, to kill much cannot be an extenuating circumstance; that, if to steal is a shame, to invade cannot be a glory; that *Te Deums* do not count for much in this matter; that homicide is homicide; that bloodshed is bloodshed; that it serves nothing to call one's self Cæsar or Napoleon; and that in the eyes of the eternal God, the figure of a murderer is not changed because, instead of a gallows-cap, there is placed upon his head an emperor's crown.

Ah! let us proclaim absolute truths. Let us dishonor war. No; glorious war does not exist. No; it is not good, and it is not useful, to make corpses. No; it cannot be that life travails for death. No; O mothers who surround me, it cannot be that war, the robber, should continue to take from you your children. No; it cannot be that woman should bear children in pain, that men should be born, that people should plow and sow, that the farmer should fertilize the fields, and the workmen enrich the city, that industry should produce marvels, that genius should produce prodigies, that the vast human activity should in presence of the starry sky, multiply efforts and creations, all to result in that frightful international exposition which is called a field of battle.

The true field of battle, behold it here! It is this rendezvous [at the Exposition, then open] of the masterpieces of human labor which Paris offers the world at this moment. The true victory is the victory of Paris.

Alas! we cannot hide it from ourselves that the present hour, worthy as it is of admiration and respect, has still some mournful aspects; there are still clouds upon the horizon; the tragedy of the peoples is not finished; war, wicked war, is still there, and it has the audacity to lift its head in the midst of this august festival of peace. Princes, for two years past, obstinately adhere to a fatal misunderstanding; their discord forms an obstacle to our concord, and they are ill-inspired to condemn us to the statement of such a contrast.

Let this contrast lead us back to Voltaire. In the presence of menacing possibilities, let us be more pacific than ever. Let us turn toward that great death, toward that great life, toward that great spirit. Let us bend before the venerated sepulcher. Let us take counsel of him whose life, useful to men, was extinguished a hundred years ago, but whose work is immortal. Let us take counsel of the other powerful thinkers, the auxiliaries of this glorious Voltaire—of Jean Jacques, of Diderot, of Montesquieu. Let us give the word to those great voices. Let us stop the shedding of human blood. Enough! enough! despots. Ah! barbarism persists; very well, let civilization be indignant. Let the Eighteenth century come to the help of the Nineteenth. The philosophers, our predecessors, are the apostles of the true; let us invoke those illustrious shades; let them, before monarchies meditating war, proclaim the right of man to life, the right of conscience to liberty, the sovereignty of reason, the holiness of labor, the blessedness of peace; and since night issues from the thrones, let light come from the tombs.

Giuseppe Mazzini
[1805–1872]

One of Italy's greatest sons was Giuseppe Mazzini, who devoted his life to the achievement of the freedom and union of his country under a republican form of government. Here is part of a fervent address made by Mazzini at Milan, in 1848, in memory of two young Italian patriots, executed by the Austrian oppressors.

TO THE YOUNG MEN OF ITALY

WHEN I was commissioned by you, young men, to proffer in this temple a few words sacred to the memory of the brothers Bandiera and their fellow martyrs at Cosenza, I thought that some of those who heard me might exclaim with noble indignation: "Wherefore lament over the dead? The martyrs of liberty are only worthily honored by winning the battle they have begun; Cosenza, the land where they fell, is enslaved; Venice, the city of their birth, is begirt by foreign foes. Let us emancipate them, and until that moment let no words pass our lips save words of war."

But another thought arose: "Why have we not conquered? Why is it that, while we are fighting for independence in the north of Italy, liberty is perishing in the south? Why is it that a war, which should have sprung to the Alps with the bound of a lion, has dragged itself along for four months, with the slow uncertain motion of the scorpion surrounded by a circle of fire? How has the rapid and powerful intuition of a people newly arisen to life been converted into the weary, helpless effort of the sick man turning from side to side? Ah! had we all arisen in the sanctity of the idea for which our martyrs died; had the holy standard of their faith preceded our youth to battle; had we reached that unity of life which was in them so powerful, and made of our every action a thought, and of our every thought an action; had we devoutly gathered up their last words in our hearts, and learned from them that liberty and independence are one; that God and the people, the fatherland and humanity, are the two inseparable terms of the device of every people striving to become a nation; that Italy can have no true life till she be one, holy in the equality and love of all her children, great in the worship of eternal truth, and consecrated to a lofty mission, a moral priesthood among the peoples of Europe—we should now have had, not war, but victory; Cosenza would not be compelled to venerate the memory of her martyrs in secret, nor Venice be restrained from honoring them with a monument; and we, gathered here together, might gladly invoke their sacred names, without uncertainty as to our future destiny, or a cloud of sadness on our brows, and say to those precursor souls: 'Rejoice! for your spirit is incarnate in your brethren, and they are worthy of you.'"

The idea which they worshiped, young men, does not as yet shine forth in its full purity and integrity upon your banner. The sublime program which they, dying, bequeathed to the rising Italian generation, is yours; but mutilated, broken up into fragments by the false doctrines, which, elsewhere overthrown, have taken refuge amongst us. I look around, and I see the struggles of desperate populations, an alternation of generous rage and of unworthy repose; of shouts for freedom and of formulæ of servitude, throughout all parts of our peninsula; but the soul of the country, where is it? What unity is there in this unequal and manifold movement—where is the word that should dominate the hundred diverse and opposing counsels which mislead or seduce the multitude? I hear phrases usurping the national omnipotence—"the Italy of the north—the league of the states—federative compacts between princes,"—but Italy, where is it? Where is the common country, the country which the Bandiera hailed as thrice initiatrix of a new era of European civilization?

Intoxicated with our first victories, improvident for the future, we forgot the idea revealed by God to those who suffered; and God has punished our forgetfulness by deferring our triumph. The Italian movement, my countrymen, is, by decree of Providence, that of Europe. We arise to give a pledge of moral progress to the European world. But neither political fictions, nor dynastic aggrandizements, nor theories of expediency, can transform or renovate the life of the peoples. Humanity lives and moves through faith; great principles are the guiding stars that lead Europe towards the future. Let us turn to the graves of our martyrs, and ask inspiration of those who died for us all, and we shall find the secret of victory in the adoration of a faith. The angel of martyrdom and the angel of victory are brothers; but the one looks up to heaven, and the other looks down to earth; and it is when, from epoch to epoch, their glances meet between earth and heaven, that creation is embellished with a new life, and a people arises from the cradle or the tomb, evangelist or prophet.

I will sum up for you in a few words this faith of our martyrs; their external life is known to you all; it is now a matter of history and I need not recall it to you.

The faith of the brothers Bandiera, which was and is our own, was based upon a few simple uncontrovertible truths, which few, indeed, venture to declare false, but which are nevertheless forgotten or betrayed by most:—

God and the People.

God at the summit of the social edifice; the people, the universality of our brethren, at the base. God, the Father and Educator; the people, the progressive interpreter of his law.

No true society can exist without a common belief and a common aim. Religion declares the belief and the aim. Politics regulate society in the practical realization of that belief, and prepare the means of attaining that aim. Religion represents the principle, politics the application. There is but one sun in heaven for all the earth. There is one law for all those who people the earth. It is alike the law of the human being and of collective humanity. We are placed here below, not for the capricious exercise of our own individual faculties,—our faculties and liberty are the means, not the end,—not to work out our own happiness upon earth; happiness can only be reached elsewhere, and there God works for us; but to consecrate our existence to the discovery of a portion of the Divine law; to practice it as far as our individual circumstances and powers allow, and to diffuse the knowledge and love of it among our brethren.

We are here below to labor fraternally to build up the unity of the human family, so that the day may come when it shall represent a single sheepfold with a single shepherd,—the spirit of God, the Law.

To aid our search after truth, God has given to us tradition and the voice of our own conscience. Wherever they are opposed, is error. To attain harmony and consistence between the conscience of the individual and the conscience of humanity, no sacrifice is too great. The family, the city, the fatherland, and humanity, are but different spheres in which to exercise our activity and our power of sacrifice towards this great aim. God watches from above the inevitable progress of humanity, and from time to time he raises up the great in genius, in love, in thought, or in action, as priests of His truth, and guides to the multitude on their way.

These principles,—indicated in their letters, in their proclamations, and in their conversation,—with a profound sense of the mission intrusted by God to the individual and to humanity, were to Attilio and Emilio Bandiera and their fellow martyrs the guide and comfort of a weary life; and, when men and circumstances had alike betrayed them, these principles sustained them in death, in religious serenity and calm certainty of the realization of their immortal hopes for the future of Italy. The immense energy of their souls arose from the intense love which informed their faith. And could they now arise from the grave and speak to you, they would, believe me, address you, though with a power very different from that which is given to me, in counsel not unlike this which I now offer to you.

Love! love is the flight of the soul towards God; towards the great, the sublime, and the beautiful, which are the shadow of God upon earth. Love your family, the partner of your life, those around you ready to share your joys and sorrows; love the dead who were dear to you and to whom you were dear. But let your love be the love taught you by Dante and by us—the love of souls that aspire together; do not grovel on the earth in search of a felicity which it is not the destiny of the creature to reach here below; do not yield to a delusion which inevitably would degrade you into egotism. To love is to give and take a promise for the future. God has given us love, that the weary soul may give and receive support upon the way of life. It is a flower springing up on the path of duty; but it cannot change its course. Purify, strengthen, and improve yourselves by loving. Act always—even at the price of increasing her earthly trials—so that the sister soul united to your own may never need, here or elsewhere, to blush through you or for you. The time will come when, from the height of a new life, embracing the whole past and comprehending its secret, you will smile together at the sorrows you have endured, the trials you have overcome.

Love your country. Your country is the land where your parents sleep, where is spoken that language in which the chosen of your heart, blushing, whispered the first word of love; it is the home that God has given you, that by striving to perfect yourselves therein, you may prepare to ascend to Him. It is your name, your glory, your sign among the people. Give to it your thoughts, your counsels, your blood. Raise it up, great and beautiful as it was foretold by our great men, and see that you leave it uncontaminated by any trace of falsehood or of servitude; unprofaned by dismemberment. Let it be one, as the thought of God. You are twenty-five millions of men, endowed with active, splendid faculties; possessing a tradition of glory the envy of the nations of Europe. An immense future is before you; you lift your eyes to the loveliest heaven, and around you smiles the loveliest land in Europe; you are encircled by the Alps and the sea, boundaries traced out by the finger of God for a people of giants—you are bound to be such, or nothing. Let not a man of that twenty-five millions remain excluded from the fraternal bond destined to join you together; let not a glance be raised to that heaven which is not the glance of a free man. Let Rome be the ark of your redemption, the temple of your nation. Has she not twice been the temple of the destinies of Europe? In Rome two extinct worlds, the Pagan and the Papal, are superposed like the double jewels of a diadem; draw from these a third world greater than the two. From Rome, the holy city, the city of love (Amor), the purest and wisest among you, elected by the vote and fortified by the inspiration of a whole people, shall dictate the pact that shall make us one, and represent us in the future alliance of the peoples. Until then you will either have no country or have her contaminated or profaned.

Love humanity. You can only ascertain your own mission from the aim set by God before humanity at large. God has given you your country as cradle, and humanity as mother; you cannot rightly love your brethren of the cradle if you love not the common mother. Beyond the Alps, beyond the sea, are other peoples now fighting or preparing to fight the holy fight of independence, of nationality, of liberty; other peoples striving by different routes to reach the same goal—improvement, association, and the foundation of an authority which shall put an end to moral anarchy and re-link earth to heaven; an authority which mankind may love and obey without remorse or shame. Unite with them; they will unite with you. Do not invoke their aid where your single arm will suffice to conquer; but say to them that the hour will shortly sound for a terrible struggle between right and blind force, and that in that hour you will ever be found with those who have raised the same banner as yourselves.

And love, young men, love and venerate the ideal. The ideal is the word of God. High above every country, high above humanity, is the country of the spirit, the city of the soul, in which all are brethren who believe in the inviolability of thought and in the dignity of our immortal soul; and the baptism of this fraternity is martyrdom. From that high sphere spring the principles which alone can redeem the peoples. Arise for the sake of these, and not from impatience of suffering or dread of evil. Anger, pride, ambition, and the desire of material prosperity are arms common alike to the peoples and their oppressors, and even should you conquer with these to-day, you would fall again to-morrow; but principles belong to the peoples alone, and their oppressors can find no arms to oppose them. Adore enthusiasm, the dreams of the virgin soul, and the visions of early youth, for they are a perfume of paradise which the soul retains in issuing from the hands of its Creator. Respect above all things your conscience; have upon your lips the truth implanted by God in your hearts, and, while laboring in harmony, even with those who differ from you, in all that tends to the emancipation of our soil, yet ever bear your own banner erect and boldly promulgate your own faith.

Such words, young men, would the martyrs of Cosenza have spoken, had they been living amongst you; and here, where it may be that, invoked by our love, their holy spirits hover near us, I call upon you to gather them up in your hearts and to make of them a treasure amid the storms that yet threaten you; storms which, with the name of our martyrs on your lips and their faith in your hearts, you will overcome.

God be with you, and bless Italy!

Giuseppe Garibaldi
[1807–1882]

This eloquent appeal to his soldiers was made, in 1860, by Giuseppe Garibaldi, celebrated Italian patriot, who fought the Austrians for the liberation and unification of Italy.

TO HIS SOLDIERS

We must now consider the period which is just drawing to a close as almost the last stage of our national resurrection, and prepare ourselves to finish worthily the marvelous design of the elect of twenty generations, the completion of which Providence has reserved for this fortunate age.

Yes, young men, Italy owes to you an undertaking which has merited the applause of the universe. You have conquered and you will conquer still, because you are prepared for the tactics that decide the fate of battles. You are not unworthy the men who entered the ranks of a Macedonian phalanx, and who contended not in vain with the proud conquerors of Asia. To this wonderful page in our country's history another more glorious still will be added, and the slave shall show at last to his free brothers a sharpened sword forged from the links of his fetters.

To arms, then, all of you! all of you! And the oppressors and the mighty shall disappear like dust. You, too, women, cast away all the cowards from your embraces; they will give you only cowards for children, and you who are the daughters of the land of beauty must bear children who are noble and brave. Let timid doctrinaires depart from among us to carry their servility and their miserable fears elsewhere. This people is its own master. It wishes to be the brother of other peoples, but to look on the insolent with a proud glance, not to grovel before them imploring its own freedom. It will no longer follow in the trail of men whose hearts are foul. No! No! No!

Providence has presented Italy with Victor Emmanuel. Every Italian should rally round him. By the side of Victor Emmanuel every quarrel should be forgotten, all rancor depart. Once more I repeat my battle-cry: "To arms, all—all of you!" If March, 1861, does not find one million of Italians in arms, then alas for liberty, alas for the life of Italy. Ah, no, far be from me a thought which I loathe like poison. March of 1861, or if need be February, will find us all at our post—Italians of Calatafimi, Palermo, Ancona, the Volturno, Castelfidardo, and Isernia, and with us every man of this land who is not a coward or a slave. Let all of us rally round the glorious hero of Palestro and give the last blow to the crumbling edifice of tyranny. Receive, then, my gallant young volunteers, at the honored conclusion of ten battles, one word of farewell from me.

I utter this word with deepest affection and from the very bottom of my heart. To-day I am obliged to retire, but for a few days only. The hour of battle will find me with you again, by the side of the champions of Italian liberty. Let those only return to their homes who are called by the imperative duties which they owe to their families, and those who by their glorious wounds have deserved the credit of their country. These, indeed, will serve Italy in their homes by their counsel, by the very aspect of the scars which adorn their youthful brows. Apart from these, let all others remain to guard our glorious banners. We shall meet again before long to march together to the redemption of our brothers who are still slaves of the stranger. We shall meet again before long to march to new triumphs.

Cavour
[1810–1861]

Count Camillo Benso di Cavour, "the regenerator of Italy," was for many years Premier of his country. Under his leadership the cause of Italian unity was greatly advanced, the clerical question was settled and the first Italian parliament established. The following speech was made in 1861, and appears here in abridged form.

ROME AND ITALY

ROME should be the capital of Italy. There can be no solution of the Roman question without the acceptance of this premise by Italy and by all Europe. If any one could conceive of a united Italy with any degree of stability, and without Rome for its capital, I would declare the Roman question difficult, if not impossible, of solution. And why have we the right, the duty, of insisting that Rome shall be united to Italy? Because without Rome as the capital of Italy, Italy cannot exist.

But here begin the difficulties of the problem. We must go to Rome, but there are two conditions: We must go there in concert with France, otherwise the union of Rome with the rest of Italy will be interpreted by the great mass of Catholics, within Italy and without, as the signal of the slavery of the church. We must go, therefore, to Rome in such a way that the true independence of the pontiff will not be diminished. We must go to Rome, but the civil power must not extend to spiritual things. These are the two conditions that must be fulfilled if this united Italy is to exist.

As to the first, it would be folly, in the present condition of affairs in Europe, to think of going to Rome in the face of the opposition of France. Yet more: even if, through events which I believe improbable and impossible, France were reduced to a condition which forbade material interference with our actions, we should none the less avoid uniting Rome to the rest of Italy, if, by so doing, we caused loss to our allies.

We have contracted a great debt toward France. I do not claim that the narrow moral code which affects individual actions should be applied *ad literam* to international relations. Still there are certain moral principles which even nations may not violate with impunity.

I know that many diplomats profess contrary views. I remember hearing a famous Austrian statesman applauded a few years ago when he laughingly declared that in a short time Austria would astound Europe by her ingratitude to Russia. As a matter of fact, Austria kept her word; you already know, and if you do not I can testify to the fact, that at the Congress of Paris no power showed more hostility to Russia or tried harder to aggravate the conditions of peace than Austria, whose sword had done nothing toward imposing peace upon her old ally. But, gentlemen, the violation of that great moral principle did not go unpunished. After a few years Russia had her revenge; and we should be glad of it, for I do not hesitate to attribute to the unforgotten ingratitude of Austria the facility with which friendly relations were established between Russia and ourselves, relations now unfortunately interrupted, but, I hope, without changing the feelings of Russia for Italy, and without any alteration of the sympathy for us which has always dwelt in the bosom of the Czar.

Gentlemen, we have an even graver motive for cooperating with France. When, in 1859, we invoked French aid, when the emperor consented to descend into Italy at the head of his legions, he made no secret of his pledges to the court of Rome. We accepted his aid without protest against those pledges. Now, after reaping such advantages from that alliance, we can protest against the pledges only to a certain point. But then, you will object, the solution of the Roman question is impossible!

I answer: If the second of our conditions is fulfilled, the first will offer few obstacles. That is, if we can so act that the reunion of Rome to Italy does not cause alarm to Catholic society. By Catholic society I mean the great mass of people who profess religious belief from conviction and not for political ends, and who are free from vulgar prejudices. If, I say, we can persuade the great mass of Catholics that the uniting of Rome to Italy can be accomplished without sacrificing the liberty of the church, the problem will, I think, be solved.

We must not deceive ourselves; there are many who, while not prejudiced against Italy nor against liberal ideas, yet fear that, if Rome were united to Italy, the seat of Italian government established there and the king seated in the Quirinal, the pontiff would lose both dignity and independence; they fear that the pope, instead of being the head of Catholicism, would be reduced to the rank of grand almoner or head chaplain.

If these fears were well founded, if the fall of the temporal power would really have this consequence, I would not hesitate to say that the union of Rome to the Italian state would be fatal not only to Catholicism, but to the existence of Italy itself. Yet further, I can imagine no greater misfortune for a cultured people than to see in the hands of its rulers not only the civil, but also the religious power.

The history of centuries proves to us that wherever this union was consummated civilization immediately ceased to advance and, therefore, necessarily began to retrograde; the most detestable of despotisms followed, and this whether a caste of priests usurped the temporal power, or a caliph or sultan seized control of things spiritual. Everywhere this fatal union has produced the same result; God forbid that it should ever be so here! . . .

When these doctrines have received the solemn sanction of the national parliament, when it will be no longer lawful to doubt the feelings of Italians, when it is clear to the world that they are not hostile to the religion of their fathers, but wish to preserve this religion in their country, when it is no longer necessary to show them how to prosper and to develop their resources by combating a power which was an obstacle, not only to the reorganization of Italy but also to the spread of Catholicity, I believe that the greater part of Catholic society will absolve the Italians, and will place where it belongs the responsibility of the fatal struggle which the pope insists upon waging against the country in whose midst he lives.

But God avert this fatal chance! At the risk of being considered utopian, I believe that when the proclamation of the principles which I have just declared, and when the indorsement of them that you will give, are known and considered at Rome and in the Vatican, I believe, I say, that those Italian fibers which the reactionary party has, as yet, been unable to remove from the heart of Pius IX. will again vibrate, and there will be accomplished the greatest act that any people have yet performed. And so it will be given to the same generation to have restored a nation, and to have done what is yet greater, yet more sublime, an act of which the influence is incalculable, that is, to have reconciled the papacy with the civil power, to have made peace between church and state, between the spirit of religion and the great principles of liberty. Yes, I hope that it will be given us to compass these two great acts, which will most assuredly carry to the most distant posterity the worthiness of the present generation of Italians.

Louis Kossuth
[1802–1894]

On his arrival in New York City in 1851 as a political exile, Louis Kossuth, Hungarian patriot and revolutionary leader, delivered this fervent and eloquent tribute to the people of the United States.

AMERICA'S WELCOME

LET ME, before I go to work, have some hours of rest upon this soil of freedom, your happy home. Freedom and home; what heavenly music in those two words! Alas! I have no home, and the freedom of my people is downtrodden. Young Giant of free America, do not tell me that thy shores are an asylum to the oppressed and a home to the homeless exile. An asylum it is; but all the blessings of your glorious country, can they drown into oblivion the longing of the heart and the fond desires for our native land? My beloved native land! thy very sufferings make thee but dearer to my heart; thy bleeding image dwells with me when I wake, as it rests with me in the short moments of my restless sleep. It has accompanied me over the waves. It will accompany me when I go back to fight over again the battle of thy freedom once more. I have no idea but thee; I have no feeling but thee.

Even here, with this prodigious view of greatness, freedom, and happiness which spreads before my astonished eyes, my thoughts are wandering toward home; and when I look over these thousands of thousands before me, the happy inheritance of yonder freedom for which your fathers fought and bled—and when I turn to you, citizens, to bow before the majesty of the United States, and to thank the people of New York for their generous share in my liberation, and for the unparalleled honor of this reception—I see, out of the very midst of this great assemblage, rise the bleeding image of Hungary, looking to you with anxiety, whether there be in the luster of your eyes a ray of hope for her; whether there be in the thunder of your huzzas a trumpet-call of resurrection. If there were no such ray of hope in your eyes, and no such trumpet-call in your cheers, then woe to Europe's oppressed nations. They will stand alone in the hour of need. Less fortunate than you were, they will meet no brother's hand to help them in the approaching giant struggle against the leagued despots of the world; and woe, also, to me. I will feel no joy even here; and the days of my stay here will turn out to be lost to my fatherland—lost at the very time when every moment is teeming in the decision of Europe's destiny.

Gentlemen, I have to thank the people, Congress, and government of the United States for my liberation from captivity. Human tongue has no words to express the bliss which I felt, when I—the downtrodden Hungary's wandering chief—saw the glorious flag of the Stripes and Stars fluttering over my head—when I first bowed before it with deep respect—when I saw around me the gallant officers and the crew of the *Mississippi* frigate—the most of them the worthiest representatives of true American principles, American greatness, American generosity—and to think that it was not a mere chance which cast the Star-spangled Banner around me, but that it was your protecting will—to know that the United States of America, conscious of their glorious calling, as well as of their power, declared, by this unparalleled act, to be resolved to become the protectors of human rights—to see a powerful vessel of America coming to far Asia to break the chains by which the mightiest despots of Europe fettered the activity of an exiled Magyar, whose very name disturbed the proud security of their sleep—to feel restored by such a protection, and, in such a way, to freedom, and by freedom to activity; you may be well aware of what I have felt, and still feel, at the remembrance of this proud moment of my life. Others spoke—you acted; and I was free! You acted; and at this act of yours, tyrants trembled; humanity shouted out with joy; the downtrodden people of Magyars—the downtrodden, but not broken—raised their heads with resolution and with hope, and the brilliancy of your Stars was greeted by Europe's oppressed nations as the morning star of rising liberty. Now, gentlemen, you must be aware how boundless the gratitude must be which I feel for you.

Humble as I am, God, the Almighty, has selected me to represent the cause of humanity before you. My warrant to this capacity is written in the sympathy and confidence of all who are oppressed, and of all who, as your elder brother, the people of Britain, sympathize with the oppressed—my warrant to this capacity is written in the hopes and expectations you have entitled the world to entertain, by liberating me out of my prison, and by restoring me to activity. But it has pleased the Almighty to make out of my humble self yet another opportunity for a thing which may prove a happy turning-point in the destinies of the world. I bring you a brotherly greeting from the people of Great Britain. I speak not in official character, imparted by diplomacy, whose secrecy is the curse of the world, but I am the harbinger of the public spirit of the people, which has the right to impart a direction to its government, and which I witnessed, pronouncing itself in the most decided manner, openly—that the people of England, united to you with enlightened brotherly love, as it is united in blood—conscious of your strength, as it is conscious of its own, has forever abandoned every sentiment of irritation and rivalry, and desires the brotherly alliance of the United States to secure to every nation the sovereign right to dispose of itself, and to protect the sovereign right of nations against the encroaching arrogance of despots; and leagued to you against the league of despots, to stand together, with you, godfather to the approaching baptism of European liberty.

I came not to your glorious shores to enjoy a happy rest—I came not with the intention to gather triumphs of personal distinction, but because a humble petitioner, in my country's name, as its freely chosen constitutional chief, humbly to entreat your generous aid; and then it is to this aim that I will devote every moment of my time, with the more assiduity, with the more restlessness, as every moment may bring a report of events which may call me to hasten to my place on the battle-field, where the great, and I hope, the last battle will be fought between liberty and despotism—a moment marked by the finger of God to be so near that every hour of delay of your generous aid may prove fatally disastrous to oppressed humanity. And, thus having stated my position to be that of a humble petitioner in the name of my oppressed country, let me respectfully ask: Do you not regret to have bestowed upon me the high honor of this glorious reception, unparalleled in history?

I say unparalleled in history, though I know that your fathers have welcomed Lafayette in a similar way; but Lafayette had mighty claims to your country's gratitude. He had fought in your ranks for your freedom and independence; and, what was still more, in the hour of your need he was the link of your friendly connection with France—a connection the results of which were two French fleets of more than thirty-eight men-of-war and three thousand gallant men, who fought side by side with you against Cornwallis, before Yorktown; the precious gift of twenty-four thousand muskets; a loan of nineteen millions of dollars; and even the preliminary treaties of your glorious peace negotiated at Paris by your immortal Franklin. I hope the people of the United States, now itself in the happy condition to aid those who are in need of aid, as itself was once in need, will kindly remember these facts; and you, citizens of New York, you will yourselves become the Lafayettes of Hungary. Lafayette had great claims to your love and sympathy, but I have none. I came a humble petitioner, with no other claims than those which the oppressed have to the sympathy of freemen who have the power to help, with the claim which the unfortunate has to the happy, and the downtrodden has to the protection of eternal justice and of human rights. In a word, I have no other claims than those which the oppressed principle of freedom has to the aid of victorious liberty.

Leon Gambetta
[1838–1882]

Leon Gambetta, French lawyer and statesman, was a man of un-
usual ability and eloquence. His brilliant defense of a political prisoner
of Napoleon III made him famous. He was elected deputy; and when
the empire fell, it was Gambetta who proclaimed the third French
republic. When the Germans surrounded Paris in 1870, Gambetta
escaped in a balloon—a dramatic feat in those days. When peace and
order came, he turned over his powers to the new republic. This
speech was delivered in 1873.

TO THE DELEGATES FROM ALSACE

ON RECEIVING from your hands this testimonial of the indissoluble bonds
of solidarity which unite to each other the various members of the great
French family—for the moment, alas, separated as you say—I know not
which feeling touches me more poignantly, the sentiment of gratitude or
that of grief.

It is truly terrible to think that it is on the day on which we are
negotiating, for a golden price,—hard and necessary results of our defeats
the evacuation of our departments,—to think that this lesson, this last
exhortation, are given us by you. I feel all the grief which you experience
in being obliged to count, to weigh, to postpone your hopes. I realize
that you have need, as we have, to tell yourselves that you will not give
way to it. I well know that you are right in repeating to yourselves that
constancy is one of the qualities of your race. Ah! it is from that very
circumstance that our dear Alsace was particularly necessary to French
unity. She represented among us, by the side of that mobility and lightness, which, unfortunately, at certain moments mar our national character,
she represented, I say, an invincible energy. And on this great pathway
of invasion she was always found the first and the last to defend the
fatherland!

It is for that reason, that as long as she returns not to the family, we
may justly say there is neither a France nor a Europe.

But the hour is serious and full of difficulties, and it is greatly to be
feared that if we give ear only to things which excite our patriotism and
to bitter remembrances which recall us to impossible struggles, to the
sentiment of our isolation in the world, to the memory of the weaknesses
which have overwhelmed us—we shall go to some extreme, and compromise a cause which we might better serve.

Yes, in our present meeting, what ought to be reported and repeated
to the constituents who have chosen me—who have saluted in me, the
last one to protest, and to defend their rights and their honor,—is by no

means a word of excitement or enthusiasm, but rather a message of resignation, albeit of active resignation.

We must take account of the state of France, we must look it squarely in the face. At the present hour the Republic, which you associate and always have associated not only with the defense of the fatherland, but also with her upraising and regeneration, the Republic, I say, claims the allegiance of some from necessity, of others from interest, and, of the generality of sensible people, from sentiments of patriotism.

To-day, under the stress of events and the great struggles of which we have been the victims, France has learned—so, at least, we may believe from recent and decisive manifestations—that the Republic is henceforward to be regarded as the common pledge of the rebirth of our nation's material and moral forces.

This great result could only have been obtained by means of reserve and prudence. The Republic could gain intellectual assent, conciliate interests, make progress in the general conscience, only by means of moderation among republicans, by proving to the majority of the indifferent, that only in this way is the spirit of order, of civil peace, and of progress peacefully and rationally to be obtained.

This demonstration is now merely commencing. We must follow it up, continue it. Especially must tardy convictions be made absolute. These have assisted us for some time, but in their turn may confirm the convictions of others, on which we have not counted, and which, gradually, under the influence of a continuous republican agitation, are transformed and enlarged, and become the general convictions of all.

We are favored by the circumstances of the hour. I do not mean that we ought to count on this to do everything, but we must take account of the fact and use it to solicit from all the spirit of concord, the spirit of union, and above all, the spirit of resignation and sacrifice. Ah! it is indeed cruel to ask of these brothers, harshly abandoned, the spirit of sacrifice and resignation, and yet it is of these that we make the supreme demand that they will not harass the country in her travail of reconstruction. And just as yours has been the section in which the greatest numbers have taken arms for the national defense, just as you have given your children and your gold, just as you have borne for the longest period, bullets, fire, bombs, and the exactions of the enemy, so during this unhappy peace you must give to France the example of a population able to preserve its sentiments without rushing to extremes, without provoking an intervention.

Ah! how strongly those who struggled felt that there was no other resource, and no other honor for France, than to make the flag of the Republic the flag of the nation. There was something in this spectacle to urge us to retire within ourselves and to seek by starting fresh, by yielding to a new impulse, to impress the French mind, whatever the true means of restoring our moral and scientific greatness, financial probity, and military strength. And when we have in all the work-yards of construction rebuilt France piece by piece, do you believe that this will be ignored by Europe, and that nations will fail to think twice before approving and ratifying the outrageous gospel of force? Do you believe that that barbarous and Gothic axiom that might makes right will remain inscribed in the annals of international law? No! No!

If an ill-omened silence has greeted such a theory, it is because France was cast down. But there is not another country in Europe that does not think France should renew herself. They are not thinking of assisting her—they have not arrived at that—to that position our best wishers and those who sympathize with us the most desire for her. We have not received, and we shall not for a long time receive, either aid or cooperation, but the sentiment of the neighboring nations is plainly seen. They feel that the storm may not have spent all its strength on us, and that it may visit other countries and strike other peoples. The sentiment of general self-preservation is springing up. They are looking from France, and they see the occidental world empty.

Let us show our strength to those who are examining our morality, our internal power, and avoid displaying, as we have till now too often done, the spectacle of dynastic quarrels or dissension about chimeras.

Let us give this pledge to Europe, that we have no other aim than to take all the time necessary to arrive at that moral and material position where there is no need of drawing the sword, where people yield to right all that is her due, because they feel that there is force behind.

But let us neither be unduly elated, nor depressed by discouragement.

Let us take to the letter—and this is a reflection that you will permit me to make in the presence of this bronze group which you have been so good as to offer me—let us take to the letter the thought which has animated the artist and the patriot. As this mother, who, extending her hand over the body of her fallen son, and feeling her bosom pressed by her babe, as yet too feeble to bear arms, counts only on the future, let us take the only course worthy of people truly animated by a wise and steadfast purpose. Let us not talk of revenge or speak rash words. Let us collect ourselves. Let us ever work to acquire that quality which we lack, that quality of which you have so admirably spoken—patience that nothing discourages, tenacity which wears out even time itself.

Then, gentlemen, when we have undergone this necessary renovation, time enough will have passed to bring about changes in the world around us. For this world which surrounds us is not, even now, in a very enviable situation. The din of arms, because it has ceased in France, has not ceased elsewhere.

One need not travel very far among his neighbors to perceive that on all sides preparations are being made, that the match is lighted. The only activity that prevails amid the operations of governments is military activity.

I do not say that from this we should draw delusive inferences. We should simply understand that the true program for every good Frenchman is, above all, to discipline himself at home, to devote himself to making of each citizen a soldier, and, if it be possible, an educated man, and leaving the rest to come to us in the process of our national growth.

Our enemies have given us examples on this point, which you know better than we do. For you, dwelling just on the frontiers, between them and us, have derived from intercourse with them a greater intellectual culture, have learnt the application of scientific ideas to promote the interests of practical life, at the same time that you still possess that fire, that energy, that vigor, which are characteristic of the French race.

It is with you and like you that we wish to labor, without letting ourselves be turned from our end by monarchical conspiracies. You can repeat to your brothers of Alsace that there is nothing to be feared from that quarter. That fear would be of a nature singularly alarming to your patriotic hopes. And again I say, gentlemen, now that sophists on all sides are declaring that if we remain a Republic we shall lack alliances outside and that we shall find no cooperation nor aid in the governments of Europe, again I say that if there be a *régime,* a system of government which has above all a horror of the spirit of conquest and annexation, it is the Republican. Any other political combination than the Republic would lead to civil war and foreign occupation. And we should have but one passion, one aim—to get rid of that. We ought to repeat the cry of Italy, "Out with the foreigners!"

Be persuaded, be sure, that under a government which is resolved to follow a truly national policy you can wait and need never despair.

As for me, you know the sentiments I have avowed to you; you know how completely I am yours. I have no other ambition than to remain faithful to the charge you have given me, and which I shall consider as the law and honor of my life.

Let those among you, gentlemen, who have the sorrowful honor of rejoining your compatriots of Alsace, say that after I had seen you I could not find in my heart a single word which would express, as I would have it do, the profound gratitude that I feel toward you.

Emile Zola
[1840–1902]

When Captain Alfred Dreyfus, a French Jew, was falsely accused by army corruptionists and anti-Semites of having sold military secrets to Germany, Emile Zola, liberal French novelist, championed his cause. Zola's vigorous defense of Dreyfus brought a charge of libel against the writer. Following is Zola's speech at his trial, which was in fact an appeal for justice for Dreyfus.

APPEAL FOR DREYFUS

In the chamber at the sitting of January 22, M. Meline, the Prime Minister, declared, amid the frantic applause of his complaisant majority, that he had confidence in the twelve citizens to whose hands he intrusted the defense of the army. It was of you, gentlemen, that he spoke. And just as General Billot dictated its decision to the court martial intrusted with the acquittal of Major Esterhazy, by appealing from the tribune for respect for the *chose jugée,* so likewise M. Meline wished to give you the order to condemn me out of respect for the army which he accuses me of having insulted!

I denounce to the conscience of honest men this pressure brought to bear by the constituted authorities upon the justice of the country. These are abominable political maneuvers, which dishonor a free nation. We shall see, gentlemen, whether you will obey.

But it is not true that I am here in your presence by the will of M. Meline. He yielded to the necessity of prosecuting me only in great trouble, in terror of the new step which the advancing truth was about to take. This everybody knew. If I am before you, it is because I wished it. I alone decided that this obscure, this abominable affair, should be brought before your jurisdiction, and it is I alone of my free will who chose you,—you, the loftiest, the most direct emanation of French justice, —in order that France might at last know all, and give her opinion. My act had no other object, and my person is of no account. I have sacrificed it, in order to place in your hands not only the honor of the army, but the imperiled honor of the nation.

It appears that I was cherishing a dream in wishing to offer you all the proofs: considering you to be the sole worthy, the sole competent judge. They have begun by depriving you with the left hand of what they seemed to give you with the right. They pretended, indeed, to accept your jurisdiction, but if they had confidence in you to avenge the members of the court martial, there were still other officers who remained superior even to your jurisdiction. Let who can, understand. It is absurdity doubled with hypocrisy, and it is abundantly clear that they dreaded your good sense,—that they dared not run the risk of letting us tell all and of letting you judge the whole matter. They pretend that they wished to limit the scandal. What do you think of this scandal? Of my act, which consisted in bringing the matter before you,—in wishing the people, incarnate in you, to be the judge? They pretend also that they could not accept a revision in disguise, thus confessing that in reality they have but one dread, that of your sovereign control. The law has in you its entire representation, and it is this law of the people elect that I have wished for,—this law which, as a good citizen, I hold in profound respect, and not the suspicious procedure whereby they hoped to make you a derision.

I am thus excused, gentlemen, for having brought you here from your private affairs without being able to inundate you with the full flood of light of which I dreamed. The light, the whole light,—this was my sole, my passionate desire! And this trial has just proved it. We have had to fight—step by step—against an extraordinarily obstinate desire for darkness. A battle has been necessary to obtain every atom of truth. Everything has been refused us. Our witnesses have been terrorized in the hope of preventing us from proving our point. And it is on your behalf alone that we have fought, that this proof might be put before you in its entirety, so that you might give your opinion without remorse in your consciences. I am certain, therefore, that you will give us credit for our efforts, and that, moreover, sufficient light has been thrown upon the affair.

You have heard the witnesses; you are about to hear my counsel, who will tell you the true story: the story that maddens everybody and which no one knows. I am, therefore, at my ease. You have the truth at last, and it will do its work. M. Meline thought to dictate your decision by intrusting to you the honor of the army. And it is in the name of the honor of the army that I too appeal to your justice.

I give M. Meline the most direct contradiction. Never have I insulted the army. I spoke, on the contrary, of my sympathy, my respect for the nation in arms, for our dear soldiers of France, who would rise at the first menace to defend the soil of France. And it is just as false that I attacked the chiefs, the generals who would lead them to victory. If certain persons at the War Office have compromised the army itself by their acts, is it to insult the whole army to say so? Is it not rather to act as a good citizen to separate it from all that compromises it, to give the alarm, so that the blunders which alone have been the cause of our defeat shall not occur again, and shall not lead us to fresh disaster?

I am not defending myself, moreover. I leave history to judge my act, which was a necessary one; but I affirm that the army is dishonored when gendarmes are allowed to embrace Major Esterhazy after the abominable letters written by him. I affirm that that valiant army is insulted daily by the bandits who, on the plea of defending it, sully it by their degrading championship,—who trail in the mud all that France still honors as good and great. I affirm that those who dishonor that great national army are those who mingle cries of "Vive l'armée!" with those of "A bas les juifs!" and "Vive Esterhazy!" Grand Dieu! the people of St. Louis, of Bayard, of Condé, and of Hoche: the people which counts a hundred great victories, the people of the great wars of the Republic and the Empire, the people whose power, grace, and generosity have dazzled the world, crying "Vive Esterhazy!" It is a shame the stain of which our efforts on behalf of truth and justice can alone wash off!

You know the legend which has grown up: Dreyfus was condemned justly and legally by seven infallible officers, whom it is impossible even to suspect of a blunder without insulting the whole army. Dreyfus expiates in merited torments his abominable crime. And as he is a Jew, a Jewish syndicate is formed, an international *sans patrie* syndicate, disposing of hundreds of millions, the object of which is to save the traitor at any price, even by the most shameless intrigues. And thereupon this syndicate began to heap crime on crime: buying consciences, casting France into a disastrous agitation, resolved on selling her to the enemy, willing even to drive all Europe into a general war rather than renounce its terrible plan.

It is very simple, nay childish, if not imbecile. But it is with this poisoned bread that the unclean Press has been nourishing our people now for some months. And it is not surprising if we are witnessing a dangerous crisis; for when folly and lies are thus sown broadcast you necessarily reap insanity.

Gentlemen, I would not insult you by supposing that you have yourselves been duped by this nursery tale. I know you; I know who you are. You are the heart and the reason of Paris, of my great Paris; where I was born, which I love with an infinite tenderness, which I have been studying and writing of now for forty years. And I know likewise what is now passing in your brains; for, before coming to sit here as defendant, I sat here on the bench where you are now. You represent there the average opinion; you try to illustrate prudence and justice in the mass. Soon I shall be in thought with you in the room where you deliberate, and I am convinced that your effort will be to safeguard your interests as citizens, which are, of course, the interests of the whole nation. You may make a mistake, but you will do so in the thought that while securing your own weal you are securing the weal of all.

I see you at your homes at evening under the lamp; I hear you talk with your friends; I accompany you into your factories and shops. You are all workers—some tradesmen, others manufacturers, some exercising liberal professions. And your very legitimate anxiety is the deplorable state into which business has fallen. Everywhere the present crisis threatens to become a disaster. The receipts fall off; transactions become more and more difficult. So that the idea which you have brought here, the thought which I read in your countenances, is that there has been enough of this and that it must be ended. You have not gone the length of saying, like many: "What matters it that an innocent man is at the Ile du Diable? Is the interest of a single man worth this disturbing a great country?" But you say, nevertheless, that the agitation which we are raising, we who hunger for truth and justice, costs too dear! And if you condemn me, gentlemen, it is that thought which will be at the bottom of your verdict. You desire tranquillity for your homes, you wish for the revival of business, and you may think that by punishing me you will stop a campaign which is injurious to the interests of France.

Well, gentlemen, if that is your idea, you are entirely mistaken. Do me the honor of believing that I am not defending my liberty. By punishing me you would only magnify me. Whoever suffers for truth and justice becomes august and sacred. Look at me. Have I the look of a hireling, of a liar, and a traitor? Why should I be playing a part? I have behind me neither political ambition nor sectarian passion. I am a free writer, who has given his life to labor; who to-morrow will reenter the ranks and resume his suspended task. And how stupid are those who call me an Italian;—me, born of a French mother, brought up by grandparents in the Beauce, peasants of that vigorous soil; me, who lost my father at seven years of age, who did not go to Italy till I was fifty-four. And yet, I am proud that my father was from Venice,—the resplendent city whose ancient glory sings in all memories. And even if I were not French, would not the forty volumes in the French language, which I have sent by millions of copies throughout the world, suffice to make me a Frenchman?

So I do not defend myself. But what a blunder would be yours if you were convinced that by striking me you would reestablish order in our unfortunate country. Do you not understand now that what the nation is dying of is the obscurity in which there is such an obstinate determination to leave it? The blunders of those in authority are being heaped upon those of others; one lie necessitates another, so that the mass is becoming formidable. A judicial blunder was committed, and then to hide it a fresh crime against good sense and equity has had daily to be committed! The condemnation of an innocent man has involved the acquittal of a guilty man, and now to-day you are asked in turn to condemn me because I gave utterance to my pain beholding our country embarked on this terrible course. Condemn me, then! But it will be one more fault added to the others—a fault the burden of which you will bear in history. And my condemnation, instead of restoring the peace for which you long, and which we all of us desire, will be only a fresh seed of passion and disorder. The cup, I tell you, is full; do not make it run over!

Why do you not exactly estimate the terrible crisis through which the country is passing? They say that we are the authors of the scandal, that it is lovers of truth and justice who are leading the nation astray, and urging it to riot. Really this is a mockery! To speak only of General Gillot—was he not warned eighteen months ago? Did not Colonel Picquart insist that he should take in hand the matter of revision, if he did not wish the storm to burst and overturn everything! Did not M. Scheurer-Kestner, with tears in his eyes, beg him to think of France, and save her from such a catastrophe? No! our desire has been to facilitate everything, to allay everything; and if the country is now in trouble, the responsibility lies with the power which, to cover the guilty, and in the furtherance of political interests, has denied everything, hoping to be strong enough to prevent the truth from being shed. It has maneuvered in behalf of darkness, and it alone is responsible for the present distraction of conscience!

The Dreyfus case! ah, gentlemen, that has now become a very small affair. It is lost and far-away in view of the terrifying questions to which it has given rise. There is no longer any Dreyfus case. The question now is whether France is still the France of the rights of man, the France that gave freedom to the world, and that ought to give it justice. Are we still the most noble, the most fraternal, the most generous nation? Shall we preserve our reputation in Europe for equity and humanity? Are not all the victories that we have won called in question? Open your eyes, and understand that, to be in such confusion, the French soul must have been stirred to its depths in face of a terrible danger. A nation cannot be thus upset without imperiling its moral existence. This is an exceptionally serious hour; the safety of the nation is at stake.

And when you shall have understood that, gentlemen, you will feel that but one remedy is possible,—to tell the truth, to do justice. Anything that keeps back the light, anything that adds darkness to darkness, will only prolong and aggravate the crisis. The rôle of good citizens, of those who feel it to be imperatively necessary to put an end to this matter, is to demand broad daylight. There are already many who think so. The men of literature, philosophy, and science are rising on every hand in the name of intelligence and reason. And I do not speak of the foreigner, of the shudder that has run through all Europe. Yet the foreigner is not necessarily the enemy. Let us not speak of the nations that may be our adversaries to-morrow. Great Russia, our ally, little and generous Holland; all the sympathetic peoples of the north; those lands of the French tongue, Switzerland and Belgium,—why are men's hearts so full, so overflowing with fraternal suffering? Do you dream then of a France isolated in the world? When you cross the frontier, do you wish them to forget your traditional renown for equity and humanity?

Dreyfus is innocent. I swear it! I stake my life on it—my honor! At this solemn moment, in the presence of this tribunal, which is the representative of human justice: before you, gentlemen, who are the very incarnation of the country, before the whole of France, before the whole world, I swear that Dreyfus is innocent. By my forty years of work, by the authority that this toil may have given me, I swear that Dreyfus is innocent. By the name I have made for myself, by my works which have helped for the expansion of French literature, I swear that Dreyfus is innocent. May all that melt away, may my works perish, if Dreyfus be not innocent! He is innocent. All seems against me—the two Chambers, the civil authority, the most widely-circulated journals, the public opinion which they have poisoned. And I have for me only the ideal,—an ideal of truth and justice. But I am quite calm; I shall conquer. I was determined that my country should not remain the victim of lies and injustice. I may be condemned here. The day will come when France will thank me for having helped to save her honor.

Leo XIII

[1810–1903]

*One of the most influential addresses on social and economic sub-
jects ever delivered in the Vatican was the one made by Pope Leo
XIII in 1901. A part of this address, widely circulated and often
quoted, is given here.*

CHRISTIAN DEMOCRACY

THE grave discussions on economical questions which for some time past have disturbed the peace of several countries of the world are growing in frequency and intensity to such a degree that the minds of thoughtful men are filled, and rightly so, with worry and alarm. These discussions take their rise in the bad philosophical and ethical teaching which is now widespread among the people. The changes also which the mechanical inventions of the age have introduced, the rapidity of communication between places and the devices of every kind for diminishing labor and increasing gain, all add bitterness to the strife; and lastly, matters have been brought to such a pass by the struggle between capital and labor, fomented as it is by professional agitators, that the countries where these disturbances most frequently occur find themselves confronted with ruin and disaster.

At the very beginning of Our Pontificate We clearly pointed out what the peril was which confronted Society on this head, and We deemed it Our duty to warn Catholics, in unmistakable language, how great the error was which was lurking in the utterances of Socialism, and how great the danger was that threatened not only their temporal possessions, but also their morality and religion. That was the purpose of Our Encyclical Letter "Quod Apostolici Muneris" which We published on the eighteenth of December in the year 1878; but as these dangers day by day threatened still greater disaster, both to individuals and the commonwealth, We strove with all the more energy to avert them. This was the object of Our Encyclical "Rerum Novarum" of the fifteenth May, 1891, in which We dwelt at length on the rights and duties which both classes of Society—those, namely, who control capital, and those who contribute labor—are bound in relation to each other; and at the same time, We made it evident that the remedies which are most useful to protect the cause of Religion, and to terminate the contest between the different classes of Society, were to be found in the precepts of the Gospel.

Nor, with God's grace, were Our hopes entirely frustrated. Even those who are not Catholics, moved by the power of truth, avowed that the Church must be credited with a watchful care over all classes of Society, and especially those whom fortune had least favored. Catholics, of course, profited abundantly by these Letters, for they not only received encouragement and strength for the admirable enterprises in which they were engaged, but also obtained the light which they desired, by the help of which they were able with greater safety and with more plentiful blessings to continue the efforts which they had been making in the matter of which We are now speaking. Hence it happened that the differences of opinion which prevailed among them were either removed or their acrimony diminished and the discussion laid aside. In the work which they had undertaken this was effected, viz.: that in their efforts for the elevation of the poorer classes, especially in those places where the trouble is greatest, many new enterprises were set on foot; those which were already established were increased, and all reaped the blessing of a greater stability imparted to them. Some of these works were called "Bureaus of the People," their object being to supply information. Rural Savings Banks had been established, and various Associations, some for mutual aid, others of relief, were organized. There were Working Men's Societies and other enterprises for work or beneficence. Thus under the auspices of the Church united action of Catholics was secured as well as wise discrimination exercised in the distribution of help for the poor who are often as badly dealt with by chicanery and exploitation of their necessities, as they are oppressed by indigence and toil. These schemes of popular benevolence were, at first, distinguished by no particular appellation. The name of "Christian Socialism" with its derivatives which was adopted by some was very properly allowed to fall into disuse. Afterwards some asked to have it called "The Popular Christian Movement." In the countries most concerned with this matter, there are some who are known as "Christian Socialists." Elsewhere the movement is described as "Christian Democracy," and its partisans "Christian Democrats," in contradistinction to those who are designated as "Socialists," and whose system is known as "Social Democracy." Not much exception is taken to the former, i.e., "Christian Socialism," but many excellent men find the term "Christian Democracy" objectionable. They hold it to be very ambiguous and for this reason open to two objections. It seems by implication to covertly favor popular government, and to disparage other methods of political administration. Secondly, it appears to belittle religion by restricting its scope to the care of the poor, as if the other sections of Society were not of its concern. More than that, under the shadow of its name there might easily lurk a design to attack all legitimate power either civil or sacred. Wherefore, since this discussion is now so widespread, so exaggerated, and so bitter, the consciousness of duty warns Us to put a check on this controversy and to define what Catholics are to think on this matter. We also propose to describe how the movement may extend its scope and be made more useful to the commonwealth.

What "Social Democracy" is and what "Christian Democracy" ought to be, assuredly no one can doubt. The first, with due consideration to the greater or less intemperance of its utterance, is carried to such an excess by many as to maintain that there is really nothing existing above the natural order of things, and that the acquirement and enjoyment of corporal and external goods constitute man's happiness. It aims at putting all government in the hands of the people, reducing all ranks to the same level, abolishing all distinction of class, and finally introducing community of goods. Hence the right of ownership is to be abrogated, and whatever property a man possesses, or whatever means of livelihood he has, is to be common to all.

As against this, "Christian Democracy," by the fact that it is Christian, is built, and necessarily so, on the basic principles of Divine Faith, and provides for the betterment of the masses, with the ulterior object of availing itself of the occasion to fashion their minds for things which are everlasting. Hence, for "Christian Democracy" justice is sacred; it must maintain that the right of acquiring and possessing property cannot be impugned, and it must safeguard the various distinctions and degrees which are indispensable in every well-ordered commonwealth. Finally it must endeavor to preserve in every human society the form and the character which God ever impresses on it. It is clear, therefore, that there is nothing in common between "Social" and "Christian Democracy." They differ from each other as much as the sect of Socialism differs from the profession of Christianity.

Moreover, it would be a crime to distort this name of "Christian De-mocracy" to politics, for although democracy, both in its philological and philosophical significations, implies popular government, yet in its present application it is so to be employed that, removing from it all political sig-nificance, it is to mean nothing else than a benevolent and Christian move-ment in behalf of the people. For the laws of nature and of the Gospel, which by right are superior to all human contingencies, are necessarily in-dependent of all modifications of civil government, while at the same time they are in concord with everything that is not repugnant to morality and justice. They are, therefore, and they must remain absolutely free from political parties, and have nothing to do with the various changes of ad-ministration which may occur in a nation; so that Catholics may and ought to be citizens according to the constitution of any state, guided as they are by those laws which command them to love God above all things, and their neighbors as themselves. This has always been the discipline of the Church. The Roman Pontiffs acted upon this principle whenever they dealt with different countries, no matter what might be the character of their governments. Hence, the mind and the action of Catholics who are devoted to the amelioration of the working classes can never be actuated with the purpose of favoring and introducing one government in place of another.

In the same manner, from "Christian Democracy" We must remove another possible subject of reproach, namely, that while looking after the advantage of the working people they should act in such a manner as to forget the upper classes of Society; for they also are of the greatest use in preserving and perfecting the commonwealth. As We have explained, the Christian law of charity will prevent Us from so doing. For it extends to all classes of Society, and all should be treated as members of the same family, as children of the same Heavenly Father, as redeemed by the same Saviour, and called to the same eternal heritage. Hence the doctrine of the Apostle who warns us that "we are one body and one spirit called to the one hope in our vocation; one Lord, one Faith, and one Baptism; one God and the Father of all who is above all, and through all, and in us all." Wherefore on account of the nature of the union which exists between the different classes of Society and which Christian brotherhood makes still closer, it follows that no matter how great Our devotion may be in helping the people, We should all the more keep Our hold upon the upper classes, because association with them is proper and necessary, as We shall explain later on, for the happy issue of the work in which We are engaged.

Let there be no question of fostering under this name of "Christian Democracy" any intention of diminishing the spirit of obedience, or of withdrawing people from their lawful rulers. Both the natural and the Christian law command us to revere those who, in their various grades, are above us in the State, and to submit ourselves to their just commands. It is quite in keeping with our dignity as men and Christians to obey, not only exteriorly but from the heart, as the Apostle expresses it, *for con-science sake,* when he commands us to keep our soul subject to the higher powers. It is abhorrent to the profession of a Christian for any one to be unwilling to be subject and obedient to those who rule in the Church, and first of all to the bishops whom (without prejudice to the universal power of the Roman Pontiff) "the Holy Ghost has placed to rule the Church of God which Christ has purchased by His blood" (Acts xx. 28). He who thinks or acts otherwise is guilty of ignoring the grave precept of the Apostle who bids us to obey our rulers and to be subject to them, for they watch, having to give an account of our souls. Let the faithful everywhere implant these principles deep in their souls, and put them in practice in their daily life, and let the ministers of the Gospel meditate them profoundly, and incessantly labor not merely by exhortation but especially by example to make them enter into the souls of others.

Otto von Bismarck
[1815–1898]

War and armaments were the main weapons of the "Iron Chancellor," Otto von Bismarck, in his energetic and successful efforts to unify the German states and to make Prussia dominant in Europe. It is part of an address on war and armaments made by Bismarck before the German Reichstag in 1888 that we reproduce here.

WAR AND ARMAMENTS IN EUROPE

I DO NOT speak willingly, for under existing conditions a word unfortunately spoken may be ruinous, and the multiplication of words can do little to explain the situation, either to our own people or to foreigners. I speak unwillingly, but I fear that if I kept silent there would be an increase rather than a diminution of the expectations which have attached themselves to this debate, of unrest in the public mind, of the disposition to nervousness at home and abroad. The public might believe the question to be so difficult and critical that a minister for foreign affairs would not dare to touch upon it. I speak, therefore, but I can say truly that I speak with reluctance. I might limit myself to recalling expressions to which I gave utterance from this same place a year and a day ago. Little change has taken place in the situation since then.

The fears which have been excited during the year have been occasioned more by Russia than by France, or I may say that the occasion was rather the exchange of mutual threats, excitements, reproaches, and provocations which have taken place during the summer between the Russian and the French press. But I do not believe that the situation in Russia is materially different now from what it was a year ago.

Since the great war of 1870 was concluded, has there been any year, I ask you, without its alarm of war? Just as we were returning, at the beginning of the seventies, they said: When will we have the next war?

When will the "revanche" be fought? In five years at latest. They said to us then: "The question of whether we will have war, and of the success with which we shall have it (it was a representative of the center who upbraided me with it in the Reichstag), depends today only on Russia. Russia alone has the decision in her hands."

In these days we must be as strong as we can; and if we will, we can be stronger than any other country of equal resources in the world. And it would be a crime not to use our resources. If we do not need an army prepared for war, we do not need to call for it. It depends merely on the not very important question of the cost—and it is not very important, though I mention it incidentally. When I say that we must strive continually to be ready for all emergencies, I advance the proposition that, on account of our geographical position, we must make greater efforts than other powers would be obliged to make in view of the same ends. We lie in the middle of Europe. We have at least three fronts on which we can be attacked. France has only an eastern boundary; Russia only its western, exposed to assault. We are, moreover, more exposed than any other people to the danger of hostile coalition because of our geographical position, and because, perhaps, of the feeble power of cohesion which, until now, the German people has exhibited when compared with others. At any rate, God has placed us in a position where our neighbors will prevent us from falling into a condition of sloth—of wallowing in the mire of mere existence.

The bill will bring us an increase of troops capable of bearing arms—a possible increase, which, if we do not need it, we need not call out, but can leave the men at home. But we will have it ready for service if we have arms for it. And that is a matter of primary importance. I remember the carbine which was furnished by England to our landwehr in 1813, and with which I had some practise as a hunter—that was no weapon for a soldier. We can get arms suddenly for an emergency, but if we have them ready for it, then this bill will count for a strengthening of our peace forces and a reenforcement of the peace league as great as if a fourth great power had joined the alliance with an army of seven hundred thousand men—the greatest yet put in the field.

I think, too, that this powerful reenforcement of the army will have a quieting effect on our own people, and will in some measure relieve the nervousness of our exchanges, of our press, and of our public opinion. I hope they all will be comforted if they make it clear to themselves that after this reenforcement, and from the moment of the signature and publication of the bill, the soldiers are there. But arms are necessary, and we must provide better ones if we wish to have an army of triarians—of the best manhood that we have among our people; of fathers of family over thirty years old. And we must give them the best arms that can be had.

I am never for an offensive war, and if war can come only through our initiative, it will not begin. Fire must be kindled by some one before it can burn, and we will not kindle it. Neither the consciousness of our strength, as I have just represented it, nor the trust in our alliances, will prevent us from continuing with our accustomed zeal our accustomed efforts to keep the peace. We will not allow ourselves to be led by bad temper; we will not yield to prejudice. It is undoubtedly true that the threats, the insults, the provocations which have been directed against us have aroused great and natural animosities on our side. And it is hard to rouse such feelings in the Germans, for they are less sensitive to the dislike of others toward them than any other nation. We are taking pains, however, to soften these animosities, and in the future, as in the past, we will strive to keep the peace with our neighbors—especially with Russia. When I say "especially with Russia," I mean that France offers us no security for the success of our efforts, though I will not say that it does not help. We will never seek occasion to quarrel. We will never attack France. I do not believe that a disturbance of the peace is imminent, and I beg that you will consider the pending measure without regard to that thought or that apprehension, looking on it rather as a full restoration of the mighty power which God has created in the German people—a power to be used if we need it. If we do not need it we will not use it, and we will seek to avoid the necessity for its use. This attempt is made somewhat more difficult by threatening articles in foreign newspapers, and I may give special admonition to the outside world against the continuance of such articles. They lead to nothing. The threats made against us—not by the government, but in the newspapers—are incredibly stupid, when it is remembered that they assume that a great and proud power such as the German empire is capable of being intimidated by an array of black spots made by a printer on paper, a mere marshaling of words. If they would give up that idea, we could reach a better understanding with both our neighbors. Every country is finally answerable for the wanton mischief done by its newspapers, and the reckoning is liable to be presented some day in the shape of a final decision from some other country. We can be bribed very easily—perhaps too easily—with love and good-will. But with threats, never!

We Germans fear God, and nothing else in the world.

It is the fear of God which makes us love peace and keep it. He who breaks it against us ruthlessly will learn the meaning of the warlike love of the Fatherland which in 1813 rallied to the standard the entire population of the then small and weak kingdom of Prussia; he will learn, too, that this patriotism is now the common property of the entire German nation, so that whoever attacks Germany will find it unified in arms, every warrior having in his heart the steadfast faith that God will be with us.

Bethmann-Hollweg
[1856–1921]

On August 4, 1914, Theobald von Bethmann-Hollweg, Chancellor of Germany, made a vigorous address before the Reichstag, in which he attempted to justify the loosing of the great war on the world. This historic address follows.

GERMANY AND THE WAR

A TREMENDOUS CRISIS threatens Europe. Since we won for ourselves the German Empire and earned the respect of the world for forty-four years we have lived in peace and have protected the peace of Europe. By peaceful labor we waxed strong and mighty and consequently aroused envy. With firm endurance we have seen how, under the pretext that Germany was eager for war, enmity was fostered in the East and West and chains were forged against us. The wind thus sown now rises in storm. We wished to live on in peaceful labor and from the Kaiser to the youngest soldier went the unexpressed vow: Only in defense of a just cause shall our sword fly from its scabbard. [Applause.] The day when we must draw it has come upon us against our will, against our honest efforts. Russia has set the torch to the house. [Stormy shouts of "Quite right!"] We are forced to war against Russia and France.

Gentlemen, a series of documents put together in the stress of events which are crowding upon one another, has been placed before you. Allow me to bring out the facts which characterize our attitude.

From the first moment of the Austro-Serbian crisis we declared that this affair must be restricted to Austria-Hungary and Serbia and we worked to that end. All the cabinets, especially that of England, represent the same point of view. Russia alone declared that she must have a word in the settlement of this dispute. With this the danger of European entanglements raised its threatening head. ["Very true!"] As soon as the first definite reports of military preparations in Russia were received, we stated to St. Petersburg in a friendly but emphatic way that warlike measures against Austria would find us on the side of our ally [Stormy applause] and that military preparations against ourselves would compel us to take counter measures [Renewed applause]; but mobilization is very near war. Russia gave us solemn assurances of her desire for peace. [Stormy cries "Hear, hear!"] And that she was making no military preparations against us. [Excitement.] In the meantime England sought to mediate between St. Petersburg and Vienna, in which she was warmly supported by us. ["Hear, hear!"] On July 28th the Kaiser besought the Czar by telegram to bear in mind that it was the right and duty of Austria-Hungary to defend herself against the Pan-Serbian agitation, which threatened to undermine Austria-Hungary's existence. [Hearty assent.] The

Kaiser drew the attention of the Czar to the fact that the solidarity of monarchical interests was threatened by the crime of Sarajevo. ["Hear, hear!"] He begged him to give his personal support in clearing away the differences. At about the same time, and before the receipt of this telegram, the Czar on his side begged the Kaiser for his help, and asked him to advise moderation in Vienna. The Kaiser undertook the rôle of mediator. But scarcely had the action ordered by him been started, when Russia mobilized all her forces directed against Austria-Hungary. ["Hear, hear!"] Austria-Hungary, however, had only mobilized those army corps which were directly aimed at Serbia ["Hear, hear!"]; only two army corps toward the North, far away from the Russian frontier. [Renewed cries of "Hear! Hear!"]

The Kaiser immediately called the Czar's attention to the fact that by reason of this mobilization of the Russian forces against Austria, his rôle of mediator, undertaken at the Czar's request, was rendered more difficult if not impossible. Nevertheless, we continued our work of mediation in Vienna, going to the utmost bounds—permitted by our treaty relations. ["Hear! Hear!"] During this time Russia, of her own accord, renewed her assurances that she was not taking any military measures against us. [Great excitement.]

July 31st arrived. In Vienna the decision was to be made. By our efforts up to that time we had succeeded in bringing it about that Vienna again took up the discussion with St. Petersburg through direct conversations which had ceased for some time. ["Hear, hear!"] But even before the final decision had been reached in Vienna, came the news that Russia had mobilized her entire military force against us as well. ["Hear, hear!"] The Russian government, which knew from our repeated representations what mobilization on our frontier meant, did not notify us of this mobilization, nor did it give us any explanation of it. ["Hear, hear!"] Not before the afternoon of the 31st did a telegram come from the Czar to the Kaiser, in which he guaranteed that his army would take up no provocative attitude against us. ["Hear, hear!" and laughter.] But mobilization on our frontier had been in full progress since the night between July 30th and 31st. ["Hear, hear!"] While we, at the request of Russia, were meditating in Vienna, the Russian forces drew up along our long and almost entirely open frontier; and France while not yet mobilizing nevertheless admits that she was taking military measures.

And we—up to that moment—we purposely had not called a single reserve, for the sake of European peace. [Energetic applause.] Were we still to wait patiently until perhaps the powers between whom we are wedged chose the time to strike? [Many cries of "No, no!"] To subject Germany to this danger would have been a crime! [Stormy, long-continued assent.] For that reason, still on the 31st we demanded Russian demobilization as the only measure which could still preserve the peace of Europe. ["Quite right!"] The Imperial Ambassador in St. Petersburg was furthermore instructed to declare to the Russian government that, in case of a rejection of our demand, we should have to consider that a state of war existed.

The Imperial Ambassador carried out these instructions. How Russia has replied to our demand for demobilization, we still do not know to-day. [Cries of "Hear, hear!"] No telegraphic communications in regard to this have reached us ["Hear, hear!"] although the telegraph has delivered many less important messages. [Renewed cries of "Hear, hear!"]

Thus, when the time limit expired, the Kaiser saw himself forced on August 1st, at 5 o'clock in the afternoon, to order the mobilization of our forces. [Energetic applause.]

At the same time we had to assure ourselves as to what France's position would be. To our definite question as to whether she would remain neutral in case of a German-Russian war, France replied that she would do as her interests demanded. [Laughter.] This was an evasive reply to our question, if not a refusal. ["Quite true."]

The Kaiser nevertheless gave the order to respect the French frontier absolutely. This order was strictly carried out with a single exception. France, who mobilized at the same time that we did, declared that she would respect a zone of 10 kilometres from the frontier. ["Hear, hear!"] And what actually occurred? Aviators throwing bombs, cavalry patrols, French companies breaking into our territory! ["Hear, hear!"] In this manner France, although no state of war had yet been declared, had violated the peace, and actually attacked us. ["Quite true."]

In regard to the one exception mentioned I have the following report from the Chief of the General Staff: "Of the French complaints in regard to the violation of the frontier from our side, we admit only one. Against express command, a patrol of the 14th Army Corps, apparently led by an officer, crossed the frontier on August 2nd. This patrol was apparently shot down—only one man has returned. But long before this single case of frontier infringement, French aviators penetrated into Southern Germany and threw bombs on our railways and at the 'Schlucht Pass' French troops have attacked our frontier patrols. Up to now our troops, according to order, have confined themselves entirely to defensive action." This is the report of the General Staff.

Gentlemen, we are now in a state of necessity [Energetic assent], and necessity knows no law. [Stormy agreement.] Our troops have occupied Luxemburg [Applause]; perhaps they have already entered Belgian territory. [Renewed applause.] Gentlemen, this violates the rules of international law. The French government declared in Brussels that it was willing to respect the neutrality of Belgium as long as the enemy respected it. But we knew that France stood ready to invade. ["Hear, hear."] France could wait, we could not. A French attack on our flank on the lower Rhine might have been fatal to us. [Applause.] We were thus forced to ignore the just protests of the Luxemburg and Belgian governments. ["Quite right."] The wrong—I speak openly—the wrong that we do now, we will try to make good again, as soon as our military ends have been reached. [Applause.] Whoever is threatened as we are, and battles for all that is sacred, dares think only of how he can hack his way out! [Long, stormy applause and clapping from all sides of the house.]

Gentlemen, we stand shoulder to shoulder with Austria-Hungary.

As to England's attitude, the declarations which Sir Edward Grey made yesterday in the House of Commons make clear the standpoint adopted by the English government. We have declared to the English government that, as long as England remains neutral our fleet will not attack the north coast of France and that we will not injure the territorial integrity and independence of Belgium. This declaration I now repeat before the whole world. ["Hear, hear!"] And I may add that as long as England remains neutral we shall be ready, if equal assurances are given, to take no hostile measures against French merchant vessels. [Applause.]

Gentlemen, this is what has happened. I repeat the words of the Kaiser, "Germany enters the fight with a clear conscience!" [Applause.] We battle for the fruits of our peaceful labors, for the inheritance of a great past and for our future. The fifty years have not yet passed in which Moltke said we should have to stand armed, ready to defend our inheritance, and the conquest of 1870. Now the great hour of trial has struck for our people. But we meet it with a clear confidence. [Stormy applause.] Our army stands in the field, our fleet is ready for battle backed by the entire German people. [Long enthusiastic applause. All the members rise.] The entire German people to the last man! [Renewed applause.]

You, gentlemen, know the full extent of your duty. The bills before you need no further explanation. I beg you to pass them speedily. [Stormy applause.]

Kaiser Wilhelm II

[1859–1941]

This was the call to arms which developed into the First World War (1914–18). It was made by Kaiser Wilhelm II of Germany on August 6, 1914.

ADDRESS TO THE GERMAN PEOPLE

SINCE the founding of the Empire, during a period of forty-three years, it has been my zealous endeavor and the endeavor of my ancestors to preserve peace to the world and in peace to promote our vigorous development. But our enemies envy us the success of our toil. All professed and secret hostility from East and West and from beyond the sea, we have till now borne in the consciousness of our responsibility and power. Now, however, our opponents desire to humble us. They demand that we look on with folded arms while our enemies gird themselves for treacherous attack. They will not tolerate that we support our ally with unshaken loyalty, who fights for its prestige as a great power, and with whose abasement our power and honor are likewise lost. Therefore the sword must decide. In the midst of peace the world attacks us. Therefore up! To arms! All hesitation, all delay were treachery to the Fatherland. It is a question of the existence or non-existence of the Empire which our fathers founded anew. It is the question of the existence or the non-existence of German might and German culture. We shall defend ourselves to the last breath of man and beast. And we shall survive this fight, even though it were against a world of enemies. Never yet was Germany conquered when she was united. Then forward march with God! He will be with us as He was with our fathers.

Jean Jaurès
[1859–1914]

The great French Socialist leader and orator, Jean Jaurès, fought to his last breath in an heroic effort for peace when the first dark clouds of the World War began to settle over Europe in 1914. On July 29 he addressed a meeting of many thousands at Brussels, called by the International Socialist Bureau. This speech, given here, was his last; for two days later he was assassinated in Paris by a pro-war fanatic.

LAST SPEECH

THE diplomats negotiate. It seems that they will be satisfied to take from Serbia a little of its blood. We have, therefore, a little rest to insure peace. But to what lessons is Europe submitted? After twenty centuries of Christianity, after one hundred years of the triumph of the rights of men, how is it possible that millions of persons, without knowing why, can kill each other?

And Germany? If she knew of the Austrian note it is inexcusable to have allowed such a step. And if official Germany did not know of the Austrian note what is her governmental wisdom? You have a contract which binds you and drags you into war and you don't know why you have been dragged? I ask, what people have given such an example of anarchy? [Applause.]

Nevertheless the authorities hesitate. Let us profit thereby and organize. For us, socialists, our duty is simple. We do not need to impose upon our government a policy of peace; our government is practising it. I, who have never hesitated to bring upon my head the hatred of our patriots by my obstinate will and by my desire to bring about a Franco-German understanding, have the right to say that the French government desires peace. [Applause.]

The French government is the best ally for peace of the English government which has taken the initiative in conciliation and gives Russia advice of prudence and patience. As for us, it is our duty to insist that the government shall speak to Russia with force so that she will refrain. If unfortunately Russia pays no heed, it is our duty to say, "We know of but one treaty; the treaty which binds us to the human race." [Applause.]

This is our duty, and in expressing it we find ourselves in accord with our German comrades who demand that their government see to it that Austria moderates her acts. It is possible that the telegram of which I spoke is due partly to that desire of the German workers. One cannot go against the wish of four millions of enlightened consciences.

Do you know what the proletarians are? They are the men who have collectively an affection for peace and a horror of war. The chauvinists, the nationalists, are men who have collectively a love for war and slaughter. When, however, they feel over their heads the menace of conflicts and wars which may put an end to their capitalistic existence, then they remind themselves that they have friends who seek to reduce the storm. But for the supreme masters, the ground is mined. In the drunkenness of the first battles they will succeed in pulling along the masses. But gradually as disease completes the work of the shells, as death and misery strike, these men will turn to German, French, Russian, Austrian and Italian authorities and demand what reasons they can give for all the corpses. And then revolution let loose will say, "Go and beg grace from God and man."

René Viviani
[1863–1925]

One of the most stirring speeches of the First World War was the address of René Viviani, Premier of France, before the Chamber of Deputies on December 22, 1914. It follows.

THE SPIRIT OF FRANCE

THIS communication is not the customary declaration in which a Government, presenting itself to Parliament for the first time, defines its policy. For the moment there is but one policy—a relentless fight until Europe attains definite liberation guaranteed by a completely victorious peace. That was the cry uttered by all when, in the sitting of August 4, a sacred union arose, as the President of the Republic has so well said, which will throughout history remain an honor to the country. It is the cry which all Frenchmen repeat after having put an end to the disagreements which have so often embittered our hearts and which a blind enemy took for irremediable division. It is the cry that rises from the glorious trenches into which France has thrown all her youth, all her manhood.

Before this unexpected uprising of national feeling, Germany has been troubled in the intoxication of her dream of victory. On the first day of the conflict she denied right, appealed to force, flouted history, and in order to violate the neutrality of Belgium and to invade France, invoked the law of self-interest alone. Since then her Government, learning that it had to reckon with the opinion of the world, has recently attempted to put her conduct in a better light by trying to throw the responsibility for the war upon the Allies. But through all the gross falsehoods, which fail to deceive even the most credulous, the truth has become apparent. All the documents published by the nations interested and the remarkable speech made the other day at Rome by one of the most illustrious representatives of the noble Italian nation, demonstrate that for a long time our enemy has intended a *coup de force*. If it were necessary, a single one of these documents would suffice to enlighten the world. When, at the suggestion of the English Government, all the nations concerned were asked to suspend their military preparations and enter into negotiations in London, France and Russia on July 31, 1914, adhered to this proposal. Peace would have been saved even at this last moment, if Germany had conformed to this proposal. But Germany precipitated matters. She declared war on Russia on August 1 and made an appeal to arms inevitable. And if Germany, by her diplomacy, killed the germ of peace, it is because for more than forty years she had untiringly pursued her aim, which was to crush France in order to achieve the enslavement of the world.

Since, in spite of their attachment to peace, France and her Allies have been obliged to endure war, they will wage it to the end. Faithful to the signature which she set to the treaty of September 4 last, in which she engaged her honor—that is to say, her life—France, in accord with her Allies, will not lay down her arms until she has avenged outraged right, regained forever the provinces torn from her by force, restored to heroic Belgium the fullness of her material prosperity and her political independence, and broken Prussian militarism, so that on the basis of justice she may rebuild a regenerated Europe.

This plan of war and this plan of peace are not inspired by any presumptuous hope. We have the certainty of success. We owe this certainty to the whole army, to the navy which, in conjunction with the English Navy, gives us the mastery of the sea, to the troops which have repulsed in Morocco attacks that will not be repeated. We owe it to the soldiers who are defending our flag in those distant colonies of France, who, on the first day that war broke out, turned with patriotic affection towards the mother country; we owe it to our army, whose heroism in numerous combats has been guided by their incomparable chiefs, from the victory on the Marne to the victory in Flanders; we owe it to the nation, which has equaled that heroism with union in silence and quiet trust in critical hours.

Thus we have shown to the world that an organized democracy can serve by its vigorous action the ideal of liberty and equality which constitutes its greatness. Thus we have shown to the world, to use the words of our Commander-in-Chief, who is both a great soldier and a noble citizen—that "the Republic may well be proud of the army that she has prepared." And thus this impious war has brought out all the virtues of our race, both those with which we were credited, of initiative, *élan,* bravery and fearlessness, and those which we were not supposed to possess —endurance, patience, and stoicism. Let us do honor to all these heroes. Glory to those who have fallen before the victory, and to those also who through it will avenge them to-morrow. A nation which can arouse such enthusiasm can never perish.

Everything serves to demonstrate the vitality of France, the security of her credit, the confidence which she inspires in all, despite the war which is shaking and impoverishing the world. The state of her finances is such that she can continue the war until the day when the necessary reparation has been obtained.

We should honor also those innocent civilian victims who hitherto had been safe from the ravages of war, and whom the enemy, in the effort to terrify the nation which remains and will continue immovable, has captured or massacred. The Government hereby takes a solemn engagement, which it has already partly discharged, in asking you to open a credit of three hundred million francs ($60,000,000). France will rebuild the ruins, anticipating the indemnities that we shall exact and the help of a contribution which the entire nation will pay, proud to fulfill its duty of national solidarity, in the hour of distress for a portion of its sons.

Gentlemen, the day of final victory has not yet come. Till that day our task will be a severe one, and it may be long drawn out. Let us stiffen our will and courage. Destined to uphold the heaviest burden of glory that a people can carry this country is prepared for every sacrifice.

Our Allies know it. Those nations who have no immediate interest in the fight know it too, and it is in vain that an unbridled campaign of false news has attempted to rouse in them the sympathy which has been won by us. If Germany, at the beginning of the war, made pretense to doubt it, she doubts no longer. Let her recognize once more that on this day the French Parliament, after more than four months of battle, has renewed before the world the spectacle that it gave on the day on which our nation took up the challenge.

In order to conquer, heroism on the frontier does not suffice. There must be union within. Let us continue to preserve this sacred union intact from every attempt made upon it. To-day, as it was yesterday, and as it will be to-morrow, let us have only one cry—Victory; only one vision before our eyes—"La Patrie"; only one ideal—Right. It is for Right that we are striving, for which Belgium has poured out her blood, for which unshakable England, faithful Russia, intrepid Serbia, and the gallant Japanese Navy are still striving.

If this is the most gigantic war that history has ever known, it is not because nations are in arms to conquer new lands, to obtain material advantage or political and economic rights; it is because they are fighting to settle the fate of the world. Nothing more grand has ever appeared before the eyes of men. Against barbarism and despotism, against a system of provocation and methodical menace which Germany called peace, against the system of murder and universal pillage which Germany calls war, against the insolent military caste which has unchained this scourge, France, the liberator and avenger, with her Allies, has raised herself at one bound.

The stakes are more than our own lives. Let us continue, then, to work with a single mind, and to-morrow, in the peace of victory, when politics have been freed from the restraints which we have voluntarily placed upon them, we shall recall with pride these tragic days, for they will have made us more valiant and better.

Cardinal Mercier
[1851–1926]

Here is the celebrated sermon of Cardinal Mercier on the day of the National Fête, July 21, 1916, at Brussels, delivered in defiance of the German Governor of Belgium. At the close of the service the crowds, unable to control their emotion, cried "Long live Belgium," "Long live Liberty." The sermon and the demonstration that followed cost the city 1,000,000 marks—this was the fine collected by the German authorities.

CORONATION DAY SERMON

Jerusalem was made an habitation of strangers;
Her festival days were turned into mourning.
*1st Book of Maccabees,
Chapter 1, verses 40, 41.*

BELOVED BRETHREN: We ought to have met together here to celebrate the 86th anniversary of our national independence.

To-day, in fourteen years' time, our restored cathedrals and our rebuilt churches will be thrown widely open; the crowds will surge in; our King Albert, standing on his throne, will bow his unconquered head before the King of Kings; the Queen and the Royal Princes will surround him; we shall hear again the joyous peals of our bells, and throughout the whole country, under the vaulted arches of our churches, the Belgians, hand in hand, will renew their vows to their God, their Sovereign, and their liberty, while the bishops and the priests, interpreters of the soul of the nation, will intone a triumphant Te Deum in a common transport of joyous thanksgiving.

To-day the hymn of joy dies on our lips.

The Jewish people in captivity at Babylon, sitting in tears on the banks of the Euphrates, watched the waters of the river flow by. Their dumb harps were hung on the willows by the bank. Who amongst them would have the courage to sing the song of Jehovah in a strange land? "O Jerusalem," cried the Psalmist, "if ever I forget thee, let my right hand wither, let my tongue cleave to the roof of my mouth if I do not remember thee; if thou art no longer the beginning of my joys."

The Psalm ends in imprecations: but we do not allow ourselves to repeat them: we are not of the Old Testament, tolerating the laws of retaliation: "An eye for an eye, and a tooth for a tooth." Our lips, purified by the fire of Christian charity, utter no words of hate. To hate is to make it one's object to do harm to others and to delight in so doing. Whatever may be our sufferings, we must not wish to show hatred towards those who have inflicted them. Our national unity is joined with a feeling of universal brotherhood. But even this feeling of universal brotherhood is dominated by our respect for the unconditional justice, without which no relationship is possible, either between individuals or between nations.

And that is why, with St. Thomas Aquinas, the most authoritative teacher of Christian Theology, we proclaim that public retribution is commendable.

Crimes, violation of justice, outrage on the public peace whether enacted by an individual or by a group must be repressed. Men's minds are stirred up, tortured, uneasy, as long as the guilty one is not put back in his place, as the strong, healthy, colloquial expression has it. To put men and things back in their places is to reëstablish order, readjust the balance and restore peace on a just basis.

Public retribution in this sense may distress the affected sentimentality of a weak nature; all the same, it is, says St. Thomas, the expression and the decree of the highest, the purest form of charity, and of the zeal which is its flame. It does not make a target of suffering, but a weapon wherewith to avenge outraged justice.

How can one love order without hating disorder; intelligently wish for peace without expelling that which is destroying it; love a brother, that is to say wish him well, without desiring that willingly, or by force, his will shall bend before the unalterable edicts of justice and truth?

It is from these heights that one must view the war in order to understand the greatness of its extent.

Once more, perhaps, you will find yourself face to face with effeminate natures for whom the war means nothing beyond explosions of mines, bursting of shells, massacres of men, spilling of blood, piling up of corpses. You will meet politicians of narrow vision who see no further stake in a battle beyond the interest of one day, the taking of so much ground, of a stretch of country, or of a province.

But no! If, in spite of its horrors, war, I mean a just war, has so much austere beauty, it is because war brings out the disinterested enthusiasm of a whole people, which gives, or is prepared to give, its most precious possession, even life itself for the defense and the vindication of things which cannot be weighed, which cannot be calculated, but which can never be swallowed up: Justice, Honor, Peace, Liberty!

Do you not feel that, in these two years, the war, the ardent unflagging interest which you give to it, purifies you, separates your higher nature from the dross, draws you away to uplift you towards something nobler and better than yourselves?

You are rising towards the ideals of justice and honor. They support you and draw you upwards.

And, because this ideal, if it is not a vain abstraction, which evaporates like the phantasies of a dream, must have its foundation in a living subject, I am never tired of maintaining this truth, which holds us all under its yoke. God reveals Himself as the Master, the Director of events, and of our wills, the holy Master of the universal conscience.

Ah, if we could clasp in our arms our heroes who are fighting for us over there, or are awaiting anxiously in the trenches their turn to go under fire; if we could take them by surprise, and feel the beating of their hearts, would not each one of them say to us: I am doing my duty, I am sacrificing myself on the altar of justice?

And you, wives and mothers, tell us in your turn of the beauty of these tragic years; wives, whose every thought goes, sad, but resigned, towards the absent one, bringing him your hopes, your long expectation, your prayers. Mothers, whose divided existence is consumed in unceasing anguish, you have given your sons, and you will not take them back; we stand breathless with unceasing admiration before you.

The head of one of our noblest families wrote to me: "Our son in the 7th Line Regiment has fallen; my wife and I are broken-hearted; and yet, if it had to be, we would give him again."

One of the curates of the capital has been condemned to twelve years penal servitude. I was allowed to go into his cell to embrace and to bless him. "I have three brothers at the front," he said, "and I think I am here chiefly because I helped the youngest, he is only seventeen—to rejoin the elder ones; one of my sisters is in a neighbouring cell, but, thank God, my mother is not left alone; indeed she has sent us a message to say so; she does not weep."

Is it not true that our mothers make us think of the mother of the Maccabees?

What lessons of moral greatness there are to be learnt here around us, and in exile and in the prisons, and in the concentration camps, in Holland and in Germany!

Do we think enough of what those brave men must be suffering, who since the beginning of the war, from the morrow of the defense of Liège and Namur, or the retreat from Antwerp, saw their military career shattered, and now chafe and fret under their inability to bear arms; these guardians of our rights, and of our communal liberties, whose valor has reduced them to inaction?

It needs courage to throw oneself forward, but it needs no less to hold oneself back. Sometimes it is more noble to suffer in silence than to act.

And what of these two years of calm submission by the Belgian people before the inevitable; this unshakable tenacity, which moved a humble woman, before whom the possibilities of an approaching conclusion of peace were being discussed, to say: "Oh, as for us, we must not worry; we can go on waiting." How beautiful is all this, and how full of instruction for the generations to come.

This is what you must look at, my brothers, the greatness of the nation in her sacrifice; our universal and enduring brotherhood in anguish and in mourning, and in the same unconquerable hope; this is what you must look at to appraise your Belgian fatherland at its true value.

Now the first exponents of this moral greatness are our soldiers.

Until that day when they return to us, and when grateful Belgium acclaims the living, and places a halo of glory about the memory of her dead, let us build up for them in our hearts a permanent monument of sacred gratitude.

Let us pray for those who are no more. Let us exclude no one from our commiseration; the blood of Christ was shed for all. Some of them are atoning in Purgatory for the last remnants of their human weakness. It is for you to hasten their entry into Paradise. Succor the poor in distress, both the poor who are known to you and those who are ashamed to beg. Give of your abundance to those who are in need of the necessities of life. Be present at the Mass, which is celebrated every week in your parish churches for our dead soldiers; take your children with you, encourage them to communicate, and communicate with them.

Let us also pray for those who are still holding the firing line on the field of battle. Remember that, even at this moment, while I am speaking to you, some of them are in the agony of death. The prospect of eternity stretches out before them. Let us think of them, let us mortify ourselves for them, resign ourselves to God for them, and obtain for them a holy death.

"Our soldiers are our masters," wrote a French Academician yesterday; "they are our leaders, our teachers, our judges, our supporters, our true friends; let us be worthy of them, let us imitate them, so that we may not do less than our duty; they are always ready to do more than their own."

The hour of deliverance approaches, but it has not yet struck. Let us be patient. Let us not suffer our courage to waver. Let us surrender to Divine Providence the work of making perfect our national probation.

Young women, young girls, let me ask if you are thinking seriously enough about the gravity of this present time? I entreat you not to turn aside from the mourning of your country. There are attitudes, there are ways of behaving which are an insult to grief.

For your modesty is at all times a virtue and a halo of glory; but to-day it is in addition a patriotic duty.

You, also, must think of the privations and of the endurance of our soldiers.

Let us all try to adopt the great principle of austerity in our lives.

"How much," continues the patriot whom I have just quoted, "how much ought we, in the relatively easy conditions and the less exposed districts, which are ours, and which do not deserve the name of fire zones, to endeavor to reduce and simplify our needs, and like the soldiers, though in our own sphere, to show more concentrated energy. Let us not allow ourselves a moment's distraction or relaxation. Let us devote every minute in our lives to the magnificent cause for which our brothers are so devoutly sacrificing theirs.

"And, just as our heroes at the front show us a wonderful and consoling spectacle of indissoluble unity, of a brotherhood in arms which nothing can destroy, even so, in our ranks, less compact and well-disciplined though they may be, we shall earnestly strive to maintain the same patriotic sense of union. We will respect the truce imposed on our quarrels by the one great Cause which alone ought to use and absorb all our powers of attack and combat; and if there are any godless or unfortunate people, who fail to understand the urgency and the beauty of this national precept, and insist, in spite of all, on keeping alive and fomenting the passions which divide us when other matters are concerned, we will turn aside our heads, and continue without answering them, to remain faithful to the pact of fellowship, of friendship, of loyal and true confidence which we have concluded with them, even in spite of themselves, under the great inspiration of the war."

The approaching date of the first centenary of our independence ought to find us stronger, more intrepid, more united than ever. Let us prepare ourselves for it with work, with patience and in true brotherhood.

When, in 1930, we recall the dark years of 1915–1916, they will appear to us as the brightest, the most majestic and, if, from to-day we resolve that they shall be so, the happiest and the most fruitful in our.national history. *Per crucem ad lucem*—from the sacrifice flashes forth the light!

Georges Clemenceau
[1841–1929]

"The Tiger," as Georges Clemenceau was known, was made Premier of France when the fortunes of the World War were going against the republic. His will and energy helped to turn the tide against the Germans. This militant speech was delivered by Clemenceau in the Chamber of Deputies on June 4, 1918, in reply to opposition socialists.

ONE AIM: VICTORY

WHEN I ACCEPTED the premiership offered to me by the President of the Republic I could not ignore the fact that we were at the most critical period of the war. I remember that I told you we should pass together through difficult and exacting times; I remember I spoke of "cruel hours." No one protested when I announced that they would come. They are coming and the only question is whether we can stand them. [Applause and interruptions.]

When Russia's desertion occurred, when men who believed that it was only necessary to will a democratic peace to obtain it from William II, had given up their country, unwittingly I prefer to think, to the army of the invader, what one of you here could believe that the million German soldiers who were thus liberated would not be turned against us? This and more is what happened. For four years our forces have been wearing themselves out. Our front was guarded by a line of soldiers which was becoming thinner and thinner, with our allies who had themselves suffered enormous losses. And at that moment you saw arrive against you a fresh mass of German divisions in good condition when you were far from your best strength.

Is there any one of you who did not realize that under the shock of this enormous mass our lines had to give way at some points? Certainly not, for in all the conversations which I had with members of this assembly, the question asked me was, how much we had to give way.

The recoil was very serious for the English army, which had suffered formidable losses. It was grave and dangerous for the French army. I said dangerous, serious, but nothing more, and there is nothing in that to shake the confidence we should have in our soldiers. [Applause and interruptions.]

Our men are engaged in the battle, a terrible one. They fought one against five without sleep for three and four days together. [Applause and interruptions.] These soldiers, these great soldiers, have good and great leaders: worthy of them in every way. [Applause and interruptions.] I have seen these leaders at work and some of them against whom I will not deny that I was prejudiced, struck me with admiration. [Applause.]

Is that saying that there are nowhere mistakes? I cannot maintain that. I know it too well; my duty is to discover these mistakes and correct them. In this I am supported by two great soldiers,—General Foch and General Petain. [Applause.] General Foch enjoys the confidence of our allies to such a degree that yesterday at the conference of Versailles they wished to have their unanimous confidence in him expressed in the communiqué given to the press. [Applause and interruptions.]

These men are at this moment fighting in the hardest battle of the war, fighting it with a heroism which I can find no phrase worthy to express. [Applause.] And it is we who for a mistake made in such and such a place, or which may not even have been made, demand explanations, on the field of battle of a man worn with fatigue. It is of this man that we demand to know whether on such and such a day he did such and such a thing! Drive me from this place if that is what you ask, for I will not do it. [Applause.]

I came here with the desire to find simple, brief and measured words to express the sentiment of the French people at the front and at the rear, to show the world a state of mind which cannot be analyzed, but which at this moment is the admiration of all civilized people. [Applause.]

I accuse no one. I am the leader of these men and it is my duty to punish them if I consider it of general benefit to do so; but it is also my greater duty to protect them if they have been unjustly attacked. [Applause.]

The army is better than we could ever have expected and when I say "the army" I mean men of all ranks who are under fire. That is one of the elements of our confidence, the main element. Although faith in a cause is an admirable thing, it will not bring victory; men must die for their faith to assure victory and our men are dying. We have an army made up of our children and our brothers—what can we say against it? Their leaders too have come from among us; they too are our brothers, they too are good soldiers. They come back covered with wounds when they are not left on the field of battle. What can you say against them? [Applause.]

We have yielded ground, much more ground than either you or I should have wished. There are men without number who have paid for this with their blood, without reproach. I know of the deeds of a group of lost men, Bretons, surrounded in a wood all night. The next day, still resisting, they sent a carrier pigeon to their corps to say "We are here. We have promised not to yield. We shall fight to the end. If you can come to find us, come; we can hold out half a day longer." [Applause.]

Those men make and safeguard the country of which you are so proud. They die for the greatest and most noble ideal—to continue a history which shall be the foremost among all the histories of civilized peoples.

Our own duty is very simple, very tame. We run no danger. We are at our posts, you here, I with my cabinet—posts which are not dangerous as are those of the soldiers, but which are nevertheless where the capital interests of the country are decided.

As long as you remain calm, confident in yourself, determined to hold out to the end of this hard struggle, victory is yours. It is yours because our enemies, who are not as intelligent as they are said to be, have only one method—to throw their whole force into the venture and risk everything. They tried it at Verdun and on the Yser, at Dunkirk and at Calais. They were checked—by whom? First by the English and then by the French. After that they appeared in Champagne; they advanced. Do you think it possible to make a war in which you never have to retreat? There is only one thing that matters, the victorious issue, the final success. Our men can only give their lives; but you through patience, firmness and determination can give them what they deserve—victory. [Applause.]

You have before you a government, which, as it told you at the very beginning, never conceived of the possibility of negotiating without victory. [Applause.] You know what you are doing. You can keep us in power or send us away; but as long as you keep us, whatever may happen, you can be sure that the country will be defended to the death and that no force will be spared to obtain success. [Applause.] We will never consent to anything but peace with victory. That is the watchword of our government. [Applause and interruptions.]

The Germans are once more staking all. The "coup" which they are attempting is to terrorize you, to frighten you so that you will abandon the struggle. [Applause.] One must be ignorant of German tactics to doubt this. Why did they suddenly throw all their forces on the Yser? It was to gain Calais, to separate us from England and force us to surrender. For what was the dreadful march on Paris? To take Paris and through terror force us to surrender. Why are they beginning again to-day? To secure this effect of terror which they have never yet achieved.

The decision is in your hands for the simple reason that it is not a matter of mere reasoning but a question of action. The Americans are coming. The forces of the English and the French, as well as of our enemies, are worn out; but we have allies who are coming as a decisive factor. I have said from the beginning that American coöperation would decide the issue of the war. The point is this: events in Russia have allowed a million of the enemy's men to appear on the Franco-British front. We have allies, whom we did not have in 1870, when we yielded because we were alone. We have allies, who represent the foremost nations of the world, who have pledged themselves to continue the war to the end, to the success which we hold in our grasp, which we are on the point of achieving if we have the necessary tenacity. [Applause.]

I declare, and it must be my last word, that victory depends upon us. The civil forces must rise to the height of their duty; it is not necessary to make this demand of the soldiers. Send me away if I have been an unworthy servant; drive me out, condemn me, but at least take the trouble to formulate criticisms. As for me, I assert that the French people have in all ways done their full duty. Those who have fallen have not fallen in vain, for they have made French history great. It remains for the living to complete the magnificent work of the dead. [Applause.]

Alexander Kerensky

[1881–1970]

Alexander Kerensky was one of the foremost leaders in the move-
ment that overthrew Czarism in Russia. He ruled that country for a
short time—until the new Russian Republic was displaced by the Bol-
shevist dictatorship. Here is an example of Kerensky's oratory—a rous-
ing call to the Russian people, made in March 1917.

TO WORKINGMEN AND SOLDIERS

COMRADES! In entering the Provisional Government I remain a republican. In my work I must depend for help on the will of the people. I must have in the people my powerful support. May I trust you as I trust myself? [Tremendous cheers.]

I cannot live without the people, and if ever you begin to doubt me, kill me! I declare to the Provisional Government that I am a representative of democracy and that the government must take especially into account the views I shall uphold as a representative of the people, by whose efforts the old government was overthrown.

Comrades! Time does not wait, I call you to organization and discipline. I ask you to support us, your representatives, who are prepared to die for the people and have given the people their whole life.

Comrades! In my jurisdiction are all the premiers and ministers of the old régime. They will answer before the law for all crimes against the people. [Cries of "No mercy for them."]

Comrades! Regenerated Russia will not resort to the shameful means utilized by the old régime; without trial nobody will be condemned. All prisoners will be tried in the open court of the people.

Comrades, soldiers and citizens! All measures taken by the new government will be published.

Soldiers! I ask your coöperation. Free Russia is born and none will succeed in wresting liberty from the hands of the people. Do not listen to the promptings of the agents of the old régime. Listen to your officers. Long live free Russia!

Leon Trotzky
[1877–1940]

*Leon Trotzky, associated with Lenin in establishing the Communist
government, was a leading figure in Soviet Russia until shortly after
Lenin's death in 1924. He took an active part in organizing the Red
Army. The following speech was made by Trotzky to the Red Army
in April 1919, when it was engaged in fighting the White Guard led
by Kolchak. Trotzky was exiled by Stalin in 1929, and slain by an
assassin in Mexico City in 1940.*

TO THE RED ARMY

THESE SPRING MONTHS become the decisive months in the history of
Europe. At the same time this spring will decide definitely the fate of the
bourgeois and rich peasant, anti-Soviet Russia.

In the east, Kolchak has mobilized all his forces, has thrown in all his
reserves, for he knows definitely that if he does not win immediately then
he will never win. Spring has come, the spring that decides. Of course the
partial victories of Kolchak are insignificant in comparison with the
general conquests of Soviet authority in Russia and in the whole world.
What does the temporary loss of Ufa mean in the face of the occupation
of Odessa, the movement into the Crimea and especially the establishment
of the Bavarian Soviet Republic? What does the evacuation of Belebey,
caused by military considerations, mean in the face of the powerful
growth of the proletarian revolution in Poland and in Italy? Nevertheless,
it would be criminal frivolity on our part to disregard the danger represented by the White Guardist bands of Kolchak on the east. Only stubbornness, steadfastness, watchfulness, and courage in the military struggle
have guaranteed till now to the Russian Soviet Republic its international
success. The victorious struggle of the Red Army on all fronts aroused the
spirit of the European working class, and has made possible the establishment and strengthening first of the Hungarian and then of the Bavarian
Republic. Our work has not yet been completed. The bands of Denikin
have not been definitely defeated. The bands of Kolchak continue to move
toward the Volga.

Spring has come; the spring that decides; our strength is increased ten-
fold by the consciousness of the fact that the wireless stations of Moscow,
Kiev, Budapest, and Munich not only exchange brotherly greetings but
business agreements respecting common defensive struggle. But at home,
on our own territory, we must direct the main portion of our increased
strength against the most dangerous enemy—against the Kolchak bands.
Our comrades of the Volga district are well aware of this. In the province
of Samara all Soviet institutions have been put on a war footing, and the
best forces have been diverted to support the army, to form reserve regi-

ments to carry on agitation of an educational character in the ranks of the Red Army. Party, Soviet, and trade union organizations in Syzran have unanimously responded to the appeal of the central authority to support the eastern front. A special shock regiment is being organized from the workmen and popular elements, which only recently were groaning under the heel of the White Guardist. The Volga district is becoming the center of attention of all Soviet Russia. To carry out our international duty we must first of all break up the bands of Kolchak in order to support the victorious workmen of Hungary and Bavaria. In order to assist the uprising of workmen in Poland, Germany, and all Europe, we must establish definitely and irrefutably the Soviet authority over the whole extent of Russia.

To the Urals: This is the slogan of the Red Army and of the whole Soviet country.

The Urals will be the last stage in this bitter struggle. Victory in the Urals not only will give grain to the famished country and cotton to the textile industries, but will secure finally the well-earned rest of our heroic Red Army.

Nikolai Lenin
[1870–1924]

Leader of the Bolshevist party and first dictator of Soviet Russia, Nikolai Lenin was also a great orator. The following defense of proletarian dictatorship was made by Lenin before the Communist International Congress in 1919.

THE DICTATORSHIP OF THE PROLETARIAT

THE GROWTH of the revolutionary movement of the proletariat in all countries has called forth convulsive efforts of the bourgeoisie and its agents in workmen's organizations, to find ideal political arguments in defense of the rule of the exploiters. Among these arguments stands out particularly condemnation of dictatorship and defense of democracy. The falseness and hypocrisy of such an argument, which has been repeated in thousands of forms in the capitalist press and at the conference of the yellow International in February, 1919, Berne, are evident to all who have not wished to betray the fundamental principle of socialism.

First of all, this argument is used with certain interpretations of "democracy in general" and "dictatorship in general" without raising the point as to which class one has in mind. Such a statement of the question, leaving out of consideration the question of class as though it were a general national matter, is direct mockery of the fundamental doctrine of socialism, namely, the doctrine of class struggle, which the socialists who have gone over to the side of the bourgeoisie recognize when they talk, but forget when they act. For in no civilized capitalist country does there exist "democracy in general," but there exists only bourgeois democracy, and one is speaking not of "dictatorship in general" but of dictatorship of the oppressed classes, that is, of the proletariat with respect to the oppressors and exploiters, that is, the bourgeoisie, in order to overcome the resistance which the exploiters make in their struggle to preserve their rule.

History teaches that no oppressed class has ever come into power and cannot come into power, without passing through a period of dictatorship, that is, the conquest of power and the forcible suppression of the most desperate and mad resistance which does not hesitate to resort to any crimes, such has always been shown by the exploiters. The bourgeoisie, whose rule is now defended by the socialists who speak against "dictatorship in general" and who espouse the cause of "democracy in general," has won power in the progressive countries at the price of a series of uprisings, civil wars, forcible suppression of kings, feudal lords, and slave owners, and of their attempts at restoration. The socialists of all countries in their books and pamphlets, in the resolutions of their congresses, in their propaganda speeches, have explained to the people thousands and millions of times the class character of these bourgeois revolutions, and of this bourgeois dictatorship. Therefore the present defense of bourgeois democracy in the form of speeches about "democracy in general," and the present wails and shouts against the dictatorship of the proletariat in the form of wails about "dictatorship in general," are a direct mockery of socialism, and represent in fact going over to the bourgeoisie and denying the right of the proletariat to its own proletariat revolution, and a defense of bourgeois reformism, precisely at the historic moment when bourgeois reformism is collapsing the world over, and when the war has created a revolutionary situation.

All socialists who explain the class character of bourgeois civilization, or bourgeois democracy, of bourgeois parliamentarism, express the thought which Marx and Engels expressed with the most scientific exactness when they said that the most democratic bourgeois republic is nothing more than a machine for the suppression of the working class by the bourgeoisie, for the suppression of the mass of the toilers by a handful of capitalists. There is not a single revolutionist, not a single Marxist of all those who are now shouting against dictatorship and for democracy, who would not have sworn before the workmen that he recognizes this fundamental truth of socialism. And now, when the revolutionary proletariat begins to act and move for the destruction of this machinery of oppression, and to win the proletarian dictatorship, these traitors to socialism report the situation as though the bourgeoisie were giving the laborers pure democracy, as though the bourgeoisie were abandoning resistance and were ready to submit to the majority of the toilers, as though there were no state machinery for the suppression of labor by capital in a democratic republic.

Workmen know very well that "freedom of meetings," even in the most democratic bourgeois republic is an empty phrase, for the rich have all the best public and private buildings at their disposal, and also sufficient leisure time for meetings and for protection of these meetings by the bourgeois apparatus of authority. The proletarians of the city and of the village, and the poor peasants, that is, the overwhelming majority of the population, have none of these three things. So long as the situation is such, "equality," that is, "pure democracy," is sheer fraud.

The capitalists have always called "freedom" the freedom to make money for the rich, and the freedom to die of hunger for workmen. The capitalists call "freedom" the freedom of the rich, freedom to buy up the press, to use wealth, to manufacture and support so-called public opinion. The defenders of "pure democracy" again in actual fact turn out to be the defenders of the most dirty and corrupt system of the rule of the rich over the means of education of the masses. They deceive the people by attractive, fine-sounding, beautiful but absolutely false phrases, trying to dissuade the masses from the concrete historic task of freeing the press from the capitalists who have gotten control of it. Actual freedom and equality will exist only in the order established by the Communists, in which it will be impossible to become rich at the expense of another, where it will be impossible either directly or indirectly to subject the press to the power of money, where there will be no obstacle to prevent any toiler from enjoying and actually realizing the equal right to the use of public printing presses and of the public fund of paper.

Dictatorship of the proletariat resembles dictatorship of other classes in that it was called forth by the need to suppress the forcible resistance of a class that was losing its political rulership. But that which definitely distinguishes a dictatorship of the proletariat from a dictatorship of other classes, from a dictatorship of the bourgeoisie in all the civilized capitalist countries, is that the dictatorship of the landlords and of the bourgeoisie was the forcible suppression of the resistance of the overwhelming majority of the population, namely, the toilers. On the other hand, the dictatorship of the proletariat is the forcible suppression of the resistance of the exploiters, that is, of an insignificant minority of the population— of landlords and capitalists.

It therefore follows that a dictatorship of the proletariat must necessarily carry with it not only changes in the form and institutions of democracy, speaking in general terms, but specifically such a change as would secure an extension such as has never been seen in the history of the world of the actual use of democratism by the toiling classes.

Marshal Ferdinand Foch
[1851–1929]

This is the closing part of a tribute from one great French soldier to another. The address was delivered before the tomb of Napoleon in Paris, on the one hundredth anniversary of his death, by Marshal Ferdinand Foch, on May 5, 1921.

NAPOLEON

IF ONE CONSIDERS that Napoleon revealed his powers in 1796 at the age of twenty-seven, it is plain that nature endowed him extraordinarily. These talents he applied unceasingly through the whole length of his prodigious career.

Through them he marks out his way along a resplendent path in the military annals of humanity. He carries his victorious eagles from the Alps to the Pyramids, and from the banks of the Tagus to those of the Moskova, surpassing in their flight the conquests of Alexander, of Hannibal and of Cæsar. Thus he remains the great leader, superior to all others in his prodigious genius, his need of activity, his nature, ardent to excess, which is always favorable to the profits of war but dangerous to the equilibrium of peace.

Thus he lifts the art of war far above all known heights, but this carries him to regions of dizziness. Identifying the greatness of the country with his own, he would rule the destinies of nations with arms, as if one could bring about the prosperity of the people from a succession of victories at grievous sacrifices. As if this people could live by glory instead of by labor. As if the conquered nations, deprived of their independence, would not rise some day to reconquer it, putting an end to a régime of force and presenting armies strong in numbers and invincible in the ardor of outraged justice. As if in a civilized world, moral right should not be greater than a power created entirely by force, however talented that force might be. In attempting this Napoleon himself goes down, not for lack of genius, but because he attempted the impossible, because he undertook with a France exhausted in every way, to bend to his laws a Europe already instructed by its misfortunes, and soon entirely in arms.

Decidedly, duty is common to all. Higher than commanding armies victoriously, there is our country to be served for her good as she understands it; there is justice to be respected everywhere. Above war there is peace.

Assuredly, the most gifted man errs who, in dealing with humanity, depends upon his own insight and intelligence and discards the moral law of society, created by respect for the individual, and those principles of liberty, equality and fraternity, the basis of our civilization, and the essence of Christianity.

Sire, sleep in peace; from the tomb itself you labor continually for France. At every danger to the country, our flags quiver at the passage of the Eagle. If our legions have returned victorious through the triumphal arch which you built, it is because the sword of Austerlitz marked out their direction, showing how to unite and lead the army that won the victory. Your masterly lessons, your determined labors, remain indefeasible examples. In studying them and meditating on them the art of war grows daily greater. It is only in the reverently and thoughtfully gathered rays of your immortal glory that generations of the distant future shall succeed in grasping the science of combat and the management of armies for the sacred cause of the defense of the country.

Aristide Briand
[1862–1932]

Many times Premier of France, Briand was noted for his strong advocacy of international peace and disarmament. He was a vigorous supporter of the League of Nations and took a leading part in its sessions. We give here part of his address delivered on November 21, 1921, at the Washington Conference on Naval Disarmament, which he attended as the French representative.

NAVAL DISARMAMENT

WE KNOW there is one part of Germany that is for peace. There are many people, especially among the working classes, who want to work, who have had enough of this war, who have had enough of war altogether, and are most anxious to settle down in peace, and also to set to work. We shall do everything to help that Germany, and if she wants to restore her balance in the bosom of a pacific republic and democratic institutions, then we can help her, and we shall be able to contemplate the future with feelings of security.

But, gentlemen, there is another Germany, a Germany which has not changed her mind and to which the last war has taught no lesson. That Germany keeps thoughts in the back of her mind; she has the same designs which she entertained before the war; she has kept the same preoccupations and she cherishes the same ambitions as the Hohenzollerns did. And how can we close our eyes to this? How can we ignore this state of things?

This, gentlemen, is happening at our very doors; we have only got to look. This is happening but a few miles from us, and we follow the thoughts of the Germans, or certain Germans, and the evolution which is taking place. And more than that, we have witnessed certain attempts to return to the former state of things.

What is Germany but a vast country of industry—industrially organized? Germany always had two aims. The first was trade, commerce. And that is only natural. The second was war. All her industries, all her manufactures, have been working to the full during the war, and they have developed since.

Everything is ready in Germany, the plans, the designs and calibers. Everything is there ready to insure a steady manufacturing of guns, machine guns and rifles. Suppose that during a period of diplomatic tension, purposely protracted for a number of weeks, certain of the manufactures, certain of the works, begin to fabricate, just at the beginning, just to start the war, just to set the war going, and then go on manufacturing guns and rifles and artillery; what would happen? It is not only in Germany that industry can work to the full. You can make preparations outside. In fact, preparations have actually taken place. In fact, great captains of industry or great industrial magnates have bought important firms in Scandinavia and in other parts of Europe.

It is easy enough to fabricate these guns without our seeing it, outside of our supervision. You know very well that it is possible to build great railroads. You know very well that it is impossible to bring here the proof that Germany is not actually making or purchasing war materials.

It is different from the navy. It is rather difficult to lay the keel of a ship in the stocks, to prepare the dockyards without the world knowing it. But suppose that was possible, do you think you could launch a capital ship without somebody being on the spot and knowing what was happening? But the guns, the rifles, the machine guns—any instruments used on the field of battle—they can be manufactured and cannot be controlled with any measure of certainty.

Ah, gentlemen, this is not the first time in history that France has had to face a situation of this kind. We have known Prussia disarmed. And disarmed by whom? By Napoleon. Well, that Prussia, which seemed practically disarmed, which was harmless to all intents and purposes, we found her again on the battlefield and we were nearly bled white. How can we forget that?

Of course, we know what is often said of the French people. It is often said that we are a frivolous nation and that naturally, when the danger is past, we turn our minds to other things—just as befits a frivolous people. Evidently, gentlemen, we are not the sort of men to keep our eyes steadily fixed on whatever is sad and depressing.

We have not been doing that since the war, but we have been too deeply wounded, I might almost say murdered, to forget the direful lesson which has just been taught us. Gentlemen, there are too many homes in mourning in the country, there are too many men in the streets that are disabled and maimed. Even if we wanted to forget, we could not.

Therefore, we have not the right and we do not intend to leave France defenseless. France must, to all intents and purposes, protect herself.

III. GREAT BRITAIN AND IRELAND

Oliver Cromwell
[1599-1658]

In the struggle between parliament and king, Oliver Cromwell, son of a farmer and brewer, emerged as the brilliant commander of the rebellious forces. Cromwell decisively defeated the armies of Charles I, and personally signed the warrant for his execution. After conquering Scotland and Ireland, Cromwell dissolved parliament, formed a new parliament entirely under his control, and then made himself Lord Protector of England. Following are parts of his famous speech on the dissolution of parliament, which he delivered on January 22, 1655.

ON THE DISSOLUTION OF PARLIAMENT

THIS GOVERNMENT called you hither; the constitution thereof being limited so—a single person and a Parliament. And this was thought most agreeable to the general sense of the nation;—having had experience enough, by trial, of other conclusions; judging this most likely to avoid the extremes of monarchy on the one hand, and of democracy on the other;—and yet not to found *dominium in gratia* "either." And if so, then certainly to make the authority more than a mere notion, it was requisite that it should be as it is in this "frame of" government; which puts it upon a true and equal balance. It has been already submitted to the judicious, true and honest people of this nation, whether the balance be not equal? And what their judgment is, is visible—by submission to it; by acting upon it; by restraining their trustees from meddling with it. And it neither asks nor needs any better ratification? But when trustees in Parliament shall, by experience, find any evil in any parts of this "frame of" government, "a question" referred by the government itself to the consideration of the Protector and Parliament—of which evil or evils time itself will be the best discoverer:—how can it be reasonably imagined that a person or persons, coming in by election, and standing under such obligations, and so limited, and so necessitated by oath to govern for the people's good, and to make their love, under God, the best under-propping and only safe footing:—how can it, I say, be imagined that the present or succeeding Protectors will refuse to agree to alter any such thing in the government as may be found to be for the good of the people? Or to recede from anything which he might be convinced casts the balance too much to the single person? And although, for the present, the keeping up

147

and having in his power the militia seems the hardest "condition," yet if the power of the militia should be yielded up at such a time as this, when there is as much need of it to keep this cause (now most evidently impugned by all enemies), as there was to get it "for the sake of this cause":—what would become of us all! Or if it should not be equally placed in him and the Parliament, but yielded up at any time—it determines his power either for doing the good he ought, or hindering Parliaments from perpetuating themselves; from imposing what religion they please on the consciences of men, or what government they please upon the nation. Thereby subjecting us to dissettlement in every Parliament, and to the desperate consequences thereof. And if the nation shall happen to fall into a blessed peace, how easily and certainly will their charge be taken off, and their forces be disbanded! And then where will the danger be to have the militia thus stated? What if I should say: If there be a disproportion, or disequality as to the power, it is on the other hand!

And if this be so, wherein have you had cause to quarrel? What demonstrations have you held forth to settle me to your opinion? I would you had made me so happy as to have let me know your grounds! I have made a free and ingenuous confession of my faith to you. And I could have wished it had been in your hearts to have agreed that some friendly and cordial debates might have been toward mutual conviction. Was there none amongst you to move such a thing? No fitness to listen to it? No desire of a right understanding? If it be not folly in me to listen to town talk, such things have been proposed; and rejected, with stiffness and severity, once and again. Was it not likely to have been more advantageous to the good of this nation? I will say this to you for myself; and to that I have my conscience as a thousand witnesses, and I have my comfort and contentment in it; and I have the witness too of divers here, who I think truly would scorn to own me in a lie: That I would not have been averse to any alteration, of the good of which I might have been convinced. Although I could not have agreed to the taking it off the foundation on which it stands; namely, the acceptance and consent of the people.

I will not presage what you have been about, or doing, in all this time. Nor do I love to make conjectures. But I must tell you this: That as I undertook this government in the simplicity of my heart and as before God, and to do the part of an honest man, and to be true to the interest— which in my conscience "I think" is dear to many of you; though it is not always understood what God in His wisdom may hide from us, as to peace and settlement:—so I can say that no particular interest, either of myself, estate, honor, or family, are, or have been, prevalent with me to this undertaking. For if you had, upon the old government, offered me this one, this one thing—I speak as thus advised, and before God; as having been to this day of this opinion; and this hath been my constant judgment, well known to many who hear me speak:—if, "I say," this one thing had been inserted, this one thing, that the government should have been placed in my family hereditary, I would have rejected it. And I could have done no other according to my present conscience and light.

I will tell you my reason;—though I cannot tell what God will do with me, nor with you, nor with the nation, for throwing away precious opportunities committed to us.

Now to speak a word or two to you. Of that, I must profess in the name of the same Lord, and wish there had been no cause that I should have thus spoken to you! I told you that I came with joy the first time; with some regret the second; yet now I speak with most regret of all! I look upon you as having among you many persons that I could lay down my life individually for. I could, through the grace of God, desire to lay down my life for you. So far am I from having an unkind or unchristian heart towards you in your particular capacities! I have this indeed as a work most incumbent upon me; this of speaking these things to you. I consulted what might be my duty in such a day as this; casting up all considerations. I must confess, as I told you, that I did think occasionally, this nation had suffered extremely in the respects mentioned; as also in the disappointment of their expectations of that justice which was due to them by your sitting thus long. "Sitting thus long;" and what have you brought forth? I did not nor cannot comprehend what it is. I would be loath to call it a fate; that were too paganish a word. But there hath been something in it that we had not in our expectations.

I did think also, for myself, that I am like to meet with difficulties; and that this nation will not, as it is fit it should not, be deluded with pretexts of necessity in that great business of raising of money. And were it not that I can make some dilemmas upon which to resolve some things of my conscience, judgment and actions, I should shrink at the very prospect of my encounters. Some of them are general, some are more special. Supposing this cause or this business must be carried on, it is either of God or of man. If it be of man, I would I had never touched it with a finger. If I had not had a hope fixed in me that this cause and this business was of God, I would many years ago have run from it. If it be of God, He will bear it up. If it be of man, it will tumble; as everything that hath been of man since the world began hath done. And what are all our histories, and other traditions of actions in former times, but God manifesting Himself, that He hath shaken, and tumbled down and trampled upon, everything that He had not planted? And as this is, so let the All-wise God deal with it. If this be of human structure and invention, and if it be an old plotting and contriving to bring things to this issue, and that they are not the births of Providence—then they will tumble. But if the Lord take pleasure in England, and if He will do us good—He is very able to bear us up! Let the difficulties be whatsoever they will, we shall in His strength be able to encounter with them. And I bless God I have been inured to difficulties; and I never found God failing when I trusted in Him. I can laugh and sing, in my heart, when I speak of these things to you or elsewhere. And though some may think it is a hard thing to raise money without Parliamentary authority upon this nation; yet I have another argument to the good people of this nation, if they would be safe, and yet have no better principle: Whether they prefer the having of their will though it be their destruction, rather than comply with things of necessity? That will excuse me. But I should wrong my native country to suppose this.

For I look at the people of these nations as the blessing of the Lord: and they are a people blessed by God. They have been so; and they will be so, by reason of that immortal seed which hath been, and is, among them: those regenerated ones in the land, of several judgments; who are all the flock of Christ, and lambs of Christ.

We know the Lord hath poured this nation from vessel to vessel till He poured it into your lap, when you came first together. I am confident that it came so into your hands; and was not judged by you to be from counterfeited or feigned necessity, but by Divine providence and dispensation. And this I speak with more earnestness, because I speak for God and not for men. I would have any man to come and tell of the transactions that have been, and of those periods of time wherein God hath made these revolutions; and find where he can fix a feigned necessity! I could recite particulars, if either my strength would serve me to speak, or yours to hear. If you would consider the great hand of God in His great dispensations, you would find that there is scarce a man who fell off, at any period of time when God had any work to do, who can give God or His work at this day a good word.

"It was," say some, "the cunning of the Lord Protector"—I take it to myself—"it was the craft of such a man, and his plot, that hath brought it about!" And, as they say in other countries, "There are five or six cunning men in England that have skill; they do all these things." Oh, what blasphemy is this! Because men that are without God in the world, and walk not with Him, know not what it is to pray or believe, and to receive returns from God, and to be spoken unto by the Spirit of God—who speaks without a Written Word sometimes, yet according to it! God hath spoken heretofore in divers manners. Let Him speak as He pleaseth. Hath He not given us liberty, nay, is it not our duty to go to the law and the testimony? And there we shall find that there have been impressions, in extraordinary cases, as well without the Written Word as with it. And therefore there is no difference in the thing thus asserted from truths generally received—except we will exclude the Spirit; without whose concurrence all other teachings are ineffectual. He doth speak to the hearts and consciences of men; and leadeth them to His law and testimony.

There is another necessity, which you have put upon us, and we have not sought. I appeal to God, angels and men—if I shall "now" raise money according to the article in the government, whether I am not compelled to do it! Which "government" had power to call you hither; and did;—and instead of seasonably providing for the army, you have labored to overthrow the government, and the army is now upon free-quarter! And you would never so much as let me hear a tittle from you concerning it. Where is the fault? Has it not been as if you had a purpose to put this extremity upon us and the nation? I hope this was not in your minds. I am not willing to judge so:—but such is the state into which we are reduced. By the designs of some in the army who are now in custody it was designed to get as many of them as possible—through discontent for want of money, the army being in a barren country, near thirty weeks behind in pay, and upon other specious pretences—to march for England out of Scotland; and, in discontent, to seize their General there [General Monk], a faithful and honest man, that so another [Colonel Overton] might head the army. And all this opportunity taken from your delays. Whether will this be a thing of feigned necessity? What could it signify, but "The army are in discontent already; and we will make them live upon stones; we will make them cast off their governors and discipline?" What can be said to this? I list not to unsaddle myself, and put the fault upon your backs. Whether it hath been for the good of England, whilst men have been talking of this thing or the other, and pretending liberty and many good words—whether it has been as it should have been? I am confident you cannot think it has. The nation will not think so. And if the worst should be made of things, I know not what the Cornish men nor the Lincolnshire men may think, or other counties; but I believe they will all think they are not safe. A temporary suspension of "caring for the greatest liberties and privileges" (if it were so, which is denied) would not have been of such damage as the not providing against free-quarter hath run the nation upon. And if it be my "liberty" to walk abroad in the fields, or to take a journey, yet it is not my wisdom to do so when my house is on fire!

I have troubled you with a long speech; and I believe it may not have the same resentment with all that it hath with some. But because that is unknown to me, I shall leave it to God;—and conclude with this: That I think myself bound, as in my duty to God, and to the people of these nations for their safety and good in every respect—I think it my duty to tell you that it is not for the profit of these nations, nor for common and public good, for you to continue here any longer. And therefore I do declare unto you, that I do dissolve this Parliament.

Sir Robert Walpole
[1676–1745]

Sir Robert Walpole, Earl of Oxford, had a spectacular career, ranging from being convicted of bribery to being twice Prime Minister. Here are parts of his speech of defense against a motion for his removal from Parliament, delivered in 1741.

ON A MOTION FOR HIS REMOVAL

It has been observed by several gentlemen, in vindication of this motion, that if it should be carried, neither my life, liberty, nor estate will be affected. But do the honorable gentlemen consider my character and reputation as of no moment? Is it no imputation to be arraigned before this House, in which I have sat forty years, and to have my name transmitted to posterity with disgrace and infamy? I will not conceal my sentiments, that to be named in Parliament as a subject of inquiry is to me a matter of great concern. But I have the satisfaction, at the same time, to reflect, that the impression to be made depends upon the consistency of the charge and the motives of the prosecutors.

If my whole administration is to be scrutinized and arraigned, why are the most favorable parts to be omitted? If facts are to be accumulated on one side, why not on the other? And why may not I be permitted to speak in my own favor? Was I not called by the voice of the King and the nation to remedy the fatal effects of the South Sea project, and to support declining credit? Was I not placed at the head of the treasury when the revenues were in the greatest confusion? Is credit revived, and does it now flourish? Is it not at an incredible height? and if so, to whom must that circumstance be attributed? Has not tranquillity been preserved both at home and abroad, notwithstanding a most unreasonable and violent opposition? Has the true interest of the nation been pursued, or has trade flourished? Have gentlemen produced one instance of this exorbitant power; of the influence which I extend to all parts of the nation; of the tyranny with which I oppress those who oppose, and the liberality with which I reward those who support me? But having first invested me with a kind of mock dignity, and styled me a prime minister, they impute to me an unpardonable abuse of that chimerical authority which they only have created and conferred. If they are really persuaded that the army is annually established by me, that I will have the sole disposal of posts and honors, that I employ this power in the destruction of liberty and the diminution of commerce, let me awaken them from their delusion. Let me expose to their view the real condition of the public weal. Let me show them that the Crown has made no encroachments, that all supplies have been granted by Parliament, that all questions have been debated with the same freedom as before the fatal period in which my counsels are said to have gained the ascendancy—an ascendancy from which they deduce the loss of trade, the approach of slavery, the preponderance of prerogative, and the extension of influence. But I am far from believing that they feel those apprehensions which they so earnestly labor to communicate to others; and I have too high an opinion of their sagacity not to conclude that, even in their own judgment, they are complaining of grievances that they do not suffer, and promoting rather their private interest than that of the public.

What is this unbounded sole power which is imputed to me? How has it discovered itself, or how has it been proved?

What have been the effects of the corruption, ambition, and avarice with which I am so abundantly charged?

Have I ever been suspected of being corrupted? A strange phenomenon, a corrupter himself not corrupt! Is ambition imputed to me? Why then do I still continue a commoner? I, who refused a white staff and a peerage? I had, indeed, like to have forgotten the little ornament about my shoulders [the garter], which gentlemen have so repeatedly mentioned in terms of sarcastic obloquy. But surely, though this may be regarded with envy or indignation in another place, it cannot be supposed to raise any resentment in this House, where many may be pleased to see those honors which their ancestors have worn, restored again to the Commons.

Have I given any symptoms of an avaricious disposition? Have I obtained any grants from the Crown since I have been placed at the head of the treasury? Has my conduct been different from that which others in the same station would have followed? Have I acted wrong in giving the place of auditor to my son, and in providing for my own family? I trust that their advancement will not be imputed to me as a crime, unless it shall be proved that I placed them in offices of trust and responsibility for which they were unfit.

But while I unequivocally deny that I am sole and prime minister, and that to my influence and direction all the measures of the Government must be attributed, yet I will not shrink from the responsibility which attaches to the post I have the honor to hold; and should, during the long period in which I have sat upon this bench, any one step taken by Government be proved to be either disgraceful or disadvantageous to the nation, I am ready to hold myself accountable.

To conclude, sir, though I shall always be proud of the honor of any trust or confidence from His Majesty, yet I shall always be ready to remove from his councils and presence when he thinks fit; and therefore I should think myself very little concerned in the event of the present question, if it were not for the encroachment that will thereby be made upon the prerogatives of the Crown. But I must think that an address to His Majesty to remove one of his servants, without so much as alleging any particular crime against him, is one of the greatest encroachments that was ever made upon the prerogatives of the Crown. And therefore, for the sake of my master, without any regard for my own, I hope all those who have a due regard for our constitution, and for the rights and prerogatives of the Crown, without which our constitution cannot be preserved, will be against this motion.

John Wesley
[1703–1791]

The following portions of a sermon by John Wesley indicate the power and appeal of simple and direct language so characteristic of this great English divine.

GOD'S LOVE TO FALLEN MAN

How INNUMERABLE are the benefits which God conveys to the children of men through the channel of sufferings, so that it might well be said,

"What are termed afflictions in the language of men are in the language of God styled blessings." Indeed, had there been no suffering in the world, a considerable part of religion, yea, and in some respects, the most excellent part, could have had no place therein: since the very existence of it depends on our suffering: so that had there been no pain it could have had no being. Upon this foundation, even our suffering, it is evident all our passive graces are built; yea, the noblest of all Christian graces, love enduring all things. Here is the ground for resignation to God, enabling us to say from the heart, in every trying hour, "It is the Lord: let Him do what seemeth Him good." "Shall we receive good at the hand of the Lord, and shall we not receive evil?" And what a glorious spectacle is this! Did it not constrain even a heathen to cry out, *"Ecce spectaculum Deo dignum!"* See a sight worthy of God: a good man struggling with adversity, and superior to it. Here is the ground for confidence in God, both with regard to what we feel and with regard to what we should fear, were it not that our soul is calmly stayed on him. What room could there be for trust in God if there was no such thing as pain or danger? Who might not say then, "The cup which my Father had given me, shall I not drink it?" It is by sufferings that our faith is tried, and, therefore, made more acceptable to God. It is in the day of trouble that we have occasion to say, "Though he slay me, yet will I trust in him." And this is well pleasing to God, that we should own him in the face of danger; in defiance of sorrow, sickness, pain, or death.

Again: Had there been neither natural nor moral evil in the world, what must have become of patience, meekness, gentleness, long-suffering? It is manifest they could have had no being: seeing all these have evil for their object. If, therefore, evil had never entered into the world, neither could these have had any place in it. For who could have returned good for evil, had there been no evil-doer in the universe? How had it been possible, on that supposition, to overcome evil with good?

Will you say, "But all of these graces might have been divinely infused into the hearts of men." Undoubtedly they might: but if they had, there would have been no use or exercise for them. Whereas in the present state of things we can never long want occasion to exercise them. And the more they are exercised, the more all our graces are strengthened and increased. And in the same proportion as our resignation, our confidence in God, our patience and fortitude, our meekness, gentleness, and long-suffering, together with our faith and love of God and man increase, must our happiness increase, even in the present world.

Yet again: As God's permission of Adam's fall gave all his posterity a thousand opportunities of suffering, and thereby of exercising all those passive graces which increase both their holiness and happiness: so it gives them opportunities of doing good in numberless instances, of exercising themselves in various good works, which otherwise could have had no being. And what exertions of benevolence, of compassion, of godlike mercy, had been totally prevented! Who could then have said to the lover of men—

> Thy mind throughout my life be shown,
>   While listening to the wretches' cry,
> The widow's or the orphan's groan;
>   On mercy's wings I swiftly fly,
> The poor and needy to relieve;
> Myself, my all for them to give?

It is the just observation of a benevolent man—

> All worldly joys are less,
> Than that one joy of doing kindnesses.

Surely in keeping this commandment, if no other, there is great reward. "As we have time, let us do good unto all men"; good of every kind and in every degree. Accordingly the more good we do (other circumstances being equal), the happier we shall be. The more we deal our bread to the hungry, and cover the naked with garments; the more we relieve the stranger, and visit them that are sick or in prison: the more kind offices we do to those that groan under the various evils of human life,—the more comfort we receive even in the present world; the greater the recompense we have in our own bosom.

To sum up: As the more holy we are upon earth, the more happy we must be (seeing there is an inseparable connection between holiness and happiness); as the more good we do to others, the more of present reward redounds into our own bosom: even as our sufferings for God lead us to rejoice in him "with joy unspeakable and full of glory"; therefore the fall of Adam first, by giving us an opportunity of being far more holy; secondly, by giving us the occasions of doing innumerable good works which otherwise could not have been done; and, thirdly, by putting it into our power to suffer for God, whereby "the Spirit of glory and of God rests upon us"; may be of such advantage to the children of men even in the present life, as they will not thoroughly comprehend till they attain life everlasting.

William Pitt, Earl of Chatham
[1708–1778]

The course of history would have been profoundly affected if George III had listened to the advice of William Pitt, Earl of Chatham, leading British statesman of his day. The American revolution might not have taken place, for Pitt was a friend of the colonists, as the eloquent speech partly reproduced here shows. Pitt delivered this speech in the House of Commons, on January 14, 1766.

ON THE RIGHT OF TAXING AMERICA

IT IS MY OPINION that this kingdom has no right to lay a tax upon the colonies. At the same time, I assert the authority of this kingdom over the colonies to be sovereign and supreme, in every circumstance of government and legislation whatsoever. They are the subjects of this kingdom; equally entitled with yourselves to all the natural rights of mankind and the peculiar privileges of Englishmen; equally bound by its laws, and equally participating in the constitution of this free country. The Americans are the sons, not the bastards of England! Taxation is no part of the governing or legislative power. The taxes are a voluntary gift and grant of the Commons alone. In legislation the three estates of the realm are alike concerned; but the concurrence of the peers and the Crown to a tax is only necessary to clothe it with the form of a law. The gift and grant is of the Commons alone. In ancient days, the Crown, the barons, and the clergy possessed the lands. In those days, the barons and the clergy gave and granted to the Crown. They gave and granted what was their own! At present, since the discovery of America, and other circumstances permitting, the Commons are become the proprietors of the land. The Church (God bless it!) has but a pittance. The property of the lords, compared with that of the Commons, is as a drop of water in the ocean; and this House represents those Commons, the proprietors of the lands; and those proprietors virtually represent the rest of the inhabitants. When, therefore, in this House, we give and grant, we give and grant what is our own. But in an American tax, what do we do? "We, your Majesty's Commons for Great Britain, give and grant to your Majesty"—what? Our own property! No! "We give and grant to your Majesty" the property of your Majesty's Commons of America! It is an absurdity in terms.

The distinction between legislation and taxation is essentially necessary to liberty. The Crown and the peers are equally legislative powers with the Commons. If taxation be a part of simple legislation, the Crown and the peers have rights in taxation as well as yourselves; rights which they will claim, which they will exercise, whenever the principle can be supported by power.

There is an idea in some that the colonies are virtually represented in the House. I would fain know by whom an American is represented here. Is he represented by any knight of the shire, in any county in this kingdom? Would to God that respectable representation was augmented to a greater number! Or will you tell him that he is represented by any representative of a borough? a borough which, perhaps, its own representatives never saw! This is what is called the rotten part of the constitution. It cannot continue a century. If it does not drop, it must be amputated. The idea of a virtual representation of America in this House is the most contemptible idea that ever entered into the head of a man. It does not deserve a serious refutation.

The Commons of America, represented in their several assemblies, have ever been in possession of the exercise of this, their constitutional right, of giving and granting their own money. They would have been slaves if they had not enjoyed it! At the same time, this kingdom, as the supreme governing and legislative power, has always bound the colonies by her laws, by her regulations, and restrictions in trade, in navigation, in manufactures, in everything, except that of taking their money out of their pockets without their consent.

Gentlemen, sir, have been charged with giving birth to sedition in America. They have spoken their sentiments with freedom against this unhappy act, and that freedom has become their crime. Sorry I am to hear the liberty of speech in this House imputed as a crime. But the imputation shall not discourage me. It is a liberty I mean to exercise. No gentleman ought to be afraid to exercise it. It is a liberty by which the gentleman who calumniates it might have profited. He ought to have desisted from his project. The gentleman tells us America is obstinate; America is almost in open rebellion. I rejoice that America has resisted. Three millions of people, so dead to all the feelings of liberty as voluntarily to submit to be slaves, would have been fit instruments to make slaves of the rest.

Edmund Burke
[1729–1797]

Edmund Burke, British statesman and distinguished orator, fought for liberal and progressive policies during his thirty years of public life. He favored the abolition of the slave trade, opposed the ruthless exploitation of India, and urged a policy of conciliation towards the American colonies. Here are portions of his famous speech on Conciliation with America, delivered in the House of Commons in 1775, and his speech against Warren Hastings during the trial before the House of Lords in 1788.

CONCILIATION WITH AMERICA

AMERICA, gentlemen say, is a noble object. It is an object well worth fighting for. Certainly it is, if fighting a people be the best way of gaining them. Gentlemen in this respect will be led to their choice of means by their complexions and their habits. Those who understand the military art will, of course, have some predilection for it. Those who wield the thunder of the state may have more confidence in the efficacy of arms. But I confess, possibly for want of this knowledge, my opinion is much more in favor of prudent management than of force; considering force not as an odious, but a feeble instrument for preserving a people so numerous, so active, so growing, so spirited as this, in a profitable and subordinate connection with us.

First, sir, permit me to observe, that the use of force alone is but temporary. It may subdue for a moment, but it does not remove the necessity of subduing again; and a nation is not governed which is perpetually to be conquered.

My next objection is its uncertainty. Terror is not always the effect of force; and an armament is not a victory. If you do not succeed, you are without resource; for, conciliation failing, force remains; but, force failing, no further hope of reconciliation is left. Power and authority are sometimes bought by kindness, but they can never be begged as alms by an impoverished and defeated violence.

A further objection to force is that you impair the object by your very endeavors to preserve it. The thing you fought for is not the thing which you recover; but depreciated, sunk, wasted, and consumed in the cóntest. Nothing less will content me than *whole* America. I do not choose to consume its strength along with our own, because in all parts it is the British strength that I consume. I do not choose to be caught by a foreign enemy at the end of this exhausting conflict, and still less in the midst of it. I may escape; but I can make no insurance against such an event. Let me add, that I do not choose wholly to break the American spirit, because it is the spirit that has made the country.

Lastly, we have no sort of experience in favor of force as an instrument in the rule of our colonies. Their growth and their utility have been owing to methods altogether different. Our ancient indulgence has been said to be pursued to a fault. It may be so; but we know, if feeling is evidence, that our fault was more tolerable than our attempt to mend it; and our sin far more salutary than our penitence.

These, sir, are my reasons for not entertaining that high opinion of untried force, by which many gentlemen, for whose sentiments in other particulars I have great respect, seem to be so greatly captivated.

But there is still behind a third consideration concerning this object, which serves to determine my opinion on the sort of policy which ought to be pursued in the management of America, even more than its population and its commerce—I mean its temper and character. In this character of the Americans a love of freedom is the predominating feature which marks and distinguishes the whole; and, as an ardent is always a jealous affection, your colonies become suspicious, restive, and untractable, whenever they see the least attempt to wrest from them by force, or shuffle from them by chicane, what they think the only advantage worth living for. This fierce spirit of liberty is stronger in the English colonies, probably, than in any other people of the earth, and this from a variety of powerful causes, which, to understand the true temper of their minds, and the direction which this spirit takes, it will not be amiss to lay open somewhat more largely.

The people of the colonies are descendants of Englishmen. England, sir, is a nation which still, I hope, respects, and formerly adored, her freedom. The colonists emigrated from you when this part of your character was most predominant; and they took this bias and direction the moment they parted from your hands. They are, therefore, not only devoted to liberty, but to liberty according to English ideas and on English principles. Abstract liberty, like other mere abstractions, is not to be found. Liberty inheres in some sensible object; and every nation has formed to itself some favorite point which, by way of eminence, becomes the criterion of their happiness. It happened, you know, sir, that the great contests for freedom in this country were, from the earliest times, chiefly upon the question of taxing. Most of the contests in the ancient common-wealths turned primarily on the right of election of magistrates, or on the balance among the several orders of the state. The question of money was not with them so immediate. But in England it was otherwise. On this point of taxes the ablest pens and most eloquent tongues have been exercised; the greatest spirits have acted and suffered.

Permit me, sir, to add another circumstance in our colonies, which contributes no mean part toward the growth and effect of this untractable spirit—I mean their education. In no other country, perhaps, in the world is the law so general a study. The profession itself is numerous and powerful, and in most provinces it takes the lead. The greater number of the deputies sent to Congress were lawyers. But all who read, and most do read, endeavor to obtain some smattering in that science. I have been told by an eminent bookseller that in no branch of his business, after tracts of popular devotion, were so many books as those on the law exported to the plantations. The colonists have now fallen into the way of printing them for their own use. I hear that they have sold nearly as many of "Blackstone's Commentaries" in America as in England.

The last cause of this disobedient spirit in the colonies is hardly less powerful than the rest, as it is not merely moral, but laid deep in the natural constitution of things. Three thousand miles of ocean lie between you and them. No contrivance can prevent the effect of this distance in weakening government. Seas roll and months pass between the order and the execution; and the want of a speedy explanation of a single point is enough to defeat the whole system. You have, indeed, "winged ministers" of vengeance, who carry your bolts in their pouches to the remotest verge of the sea. But there a power steps in that limits the arrogance of raging passion and furious elements, and says: "So far shalt though go, and no farther."

I do not mean to commend either the spirit in this excess, or the moral causes which produce it. Perhaps a more smooth and accom-modating spirit of freedom in them would be more acceptable to us. Perhaps ideas of liberty· might be desired, more reconcilable with an arbitrary and boundless authority. Perhaps we might wish the colonists to be persuaded that their liberty is more secure when held in trust for them by us, as guardians during a perpetual minority, than with any part of it in their own hands. But the question is not whether their spirit deserves praise or blame. What, in the name of God, shall we do with it? You have before you the object, such as it is, with all its glories, with all its imperfections on its head. You see the magnitude, the importance, the temper, the habits, the disorders. By all these considerations we are strongly urged to determine something concerning it. We are called upon to fix some rule and line for our future conduct which may give a little stability to our politics, and prevent the return of such unhappy delibera-tions as the present. Every such return will bring the matter before us in a still more untractable form. For, what astonishing and incredible things have we not seen already? What monsters have not been generated from this unnatural contention?

We are indeed, in all disputes with the colonies, by the necessity of things, the judge. It is true, sir; but I confess that the character of judge in my own cause is a thing that frightens me. Instead of filling me with pride, I am exceedingly humbled by it. I cannot proceed with a stern, assured, judical confidence, until I find myself in something more like a judicial character. Sir, these considerations have great weight with me, when I find things so circumstanced that I see the same party at once a civil litigant against me in point of right and a culprit before me; while I sit as criminal judge on acts of his whose moral quality is to be decided on upon the merits of that very litigation. Men are every now and then put, by the complexity of human affairs, into strange situations; but justice is the same, let the judge be in what situation he will.

In this situation, let us seriously and cooly ponder, what is it we have got by all our menaces, which have been many and ferocious. What advantage have we derived from the penal laws we have passed, and which, for the time, have been severe and numerous? What advances have we made toward our object by the sending of a force which, by land and sea, is no contemptible strength? Has the disorder abated? Nothing less. When I see things in this situation, after such confident hopes, bold promises, and active exertions, I cannot, for my life, avoid a suspicion that the plan itself is not correctly right.

If, then, the removal of the causes of this spirit of American liberty be, for the greater part, or rather entirely, impracticable; if the ideas of criminal process be inapplicable, or, if applicable, are in the highest degree inexpedient, what way yet remains? No way is open but the third and last—to comply with the American spirit as necessary, or, if you please, to submit to it as a necessary evil.

If we adopt this mode, if we mean to conciliate and concede, let us see of what nature the concessions ought to be. To ascertain the nature of our concessions, we must look at their complaint. The colonies complain that they have not the characteristic mark and seal of British freedom. They complain that they are taxed in parliament in which they are not represented. If you mean to satisfy them at all, you must satisfy them with regard to this complaint. If you mean to please any people, you must give them the boon which they ask; not what you may think better for them, but of a kind totally different.

Such is steadfastly my opinion of the absolute necessity of keeping up the concord of this empire by a unity of spirit, though in a diversity of operations, that, if I were sure the colonists had, at their leaving this country, sealed a regular compact of servitude; that they had solemnly abjured all the rights of citizens; that they had made a vow to renounce all ideas of liberty for them and their posterity to all generations, yet I should hold myself obliged to conform to the temper I found universally prevalent in my own day, and to govern two millions of men, impatient of servitude, on the principles of freedom. I am not determining a point of law. I am restoring tranquillity, and the general character and situation of a people must determine what sort of government is fitted for them. That point nothing else can or ought to determine.

My idea, therefore, without considering whether we yield as matter of right, or grant as matter of favor, is *to admit the people of our colonies into an interest in the Constitution,* and, by recording that admission in the journals of parliament, to give them as strong an assurance as the nature of the thing will admit, that we mean forever to adhere to that solemn declaration of systematic indulgence.

The Americans will have no interest contrary to the grandeur and glory of England, when they are not oppressed by the weight of it; and they will rather be inclined to respect the acts of a superintending legislature, when they see them the acts of that power which is itself the security, not the rival, of their secondary importance. In this assurance my mind most perfectly acquiesces, and I confess I feel not the least alarm from the discontents which are to arise from putting people at their ease; nor do I apprehend the destruction of this empire from giving, by an act of free grace and indulgence, to two millions of my fellow citizens, some share of those rights upon which I have always been taught to value myself.

A revenue from America transmitted hither—do not delude yourselves —you never can receive it—no, not a shilling. We have experienced that from remote countries it is not to be expected. If, when you attempted to extract revenue from Bengal, you were obliged to return in loan what you had taken in imposition, what can you expect from North America? for certainly, if ever there was a country qualified to produce wealth, it is India; or an institution fit for the transmission, it is the East India Company. America has none of these aptitudes. If America gives you taxable objects on which you lay your duties here, and gives you, at the same time, a surplus by a foreign sale of her commodities to pay the duties on these objects which you tax at home, she has performed her part to the British revenue. But with regard to her own internal establishments, she may, I doubt not she will, contribute in moderation; I say in moderation, for she ought not to be permitted to exhaust herself. She ought to be reserved to a war, the weight of which, with the enemies that we are most likely to have, must be considerable in her quarter of the globe. There she may serve you, and serve you essentially.

For that service, for all service, whether of revenue, trade, or empire, my trust is in her interest in the British Constitution. My hold of the colonies is in the close affection which grows from common names, from kindred blood, from similar privileges, and equal protection. These are ties which, though light as air, are as strong as links of iron. Let the colonies always keep the idea of their civil rights associated with your government; they will cling and grapple to you, and no force under heaven will be of power to tear them from their allegiance. But let it be once understood that your government may be one thing, and their privileges another; that these two things may exist without any mutual relation; the cement is gone; the cohesion is loosened; and everything hastens to decay and dissolution. As long as you have the wisdom to keep the sovereign authority of this country as the sanctuary of liberty, the sacred temple consecrated to our common faith, wherever the chosen race and sons of England worship freedom, they will turn their faces toward you. The more they multiply, the more friends you will have. The more ardently they love liberty, the more perfect will be their obedience. Slavery they can have anywhere. It is a weed that grows in every soil. They may have it from Spain; they may have it from Prussia; but, until you become lost to all feeling of your true interest and your natural dignity, freedom they can have from none but you. This is the commodity of price, of which you have the monopoly. This is the true Act of Navigation, which binds to you the commerce of the colonies, and through them secures to you the wealth of the world. Deny them this participation of freedom, and you break that sole bond which originally made, and must still preserve, the unity of the empire. Do not entertain so weak an imagination as that your registers and your bonds, your affidavits and your sufferances, your cockets and your clearances, are what form the great securities of your commerce. Do not dream that your letters of office, and your instructions, and your suspending clauses, are the things that hold together the great contexture of this mysterious whole. These things do not make your government. Dead instruments, passive tools as they are, it is the spirit of the English communion that gives all their life and efficacy to them. It is the spirit of the English Constitution which, infused through the mighty mass, pervades, feeds, unites, invigorates, vivifies every part of the empire, even down to the minutest member.

Is it not the same virtue which does everything for us here in England?

Do you imagine, then, that it is the land tax which raises your revenue, that it is the annual vote in the committee of supply which gives you your army? or that it is the mutiny bill which inspires it with bravery and discipline? No! surely no! It is the love of the people; it is their attachment to their government, from the sense of the deep stake they have in such a glorious institution, which gives you your army and your navy, and infuses into both that liberal obedience, without which your army would be a base rabble, and your navy nothing but rotten timber.

All this, I know well enough, will sound wild and chimerical to the profane herd of those vulgar and mechanical politicians, who have no place among us; a sort of people who think that nothing exists but what is gross and material, and who, therefore, far from being qualified to be directors of the great movement of empire, are not fit to turn a wheel in the machine. But to men truly initiated and rightly taught, these ruling and master principles, which, in the opinion of such men as I have mentioned, have no substantial existence, are in truth everything and all in all. Magnanimity in politics is not seldom the truest wisdom; and a great empire and little minds go ill together. If we are conscious of our situation, and glow with zeal to fill our place as becomes our station and ourselves, we ought to auspicate all our public proceeding on America with the old warning of the church, *sursum corda!* We ought to elevate our minds to the greatness of that trust to which the order of Providence has called us. By adverting to the dignity of this high calling, our ancestors have turned a savage wilderness into a glorious empire, and have made the most extensive and the only honorable conquests, not by destroying, but by promoting, the wealth, the number, the happiness of the human race. Let us get an American revenue as we have got an American empire. English privileges have made it all that it is; English privileges alone will make it all it can be.

In full confidence of this unalterable truth, I now, *quod felix faustumque sit,* lay the first stone in the temple of peace; and I move you, "That the colonies and plantations of Great Britain in North America, consisting of fourteen separate governments, and containing two millions and upwards of free inhabitants, have not had the liberty and privilege of electing and sending any knights and burgesses, or others, to represent them in the high court of parliament."

INDICTMENT OF WARREN HASTINGS

My lords, I do not mean now to go farther than just to remind your lordships of this—that Mr. Hastings' government was one whole system of oppression, of robbery of individuals, of spoliation of the public, and of supersession of the whole system of the English government, in order to vest in the worst of the natives all the power that could possibly exist in any government; in order to defeat the ends which all governments ought, in common, to have in view. In the name of the Commons of England, I charge all this villainy upon Warren Hastings, in this last moment of my application to you.

My lords, what is it that we want here, to a great act of national justice? Do we want a cause, my lords? You have the cause of oppressed princes, of undone women of the first rank, of desolated provinces and of wasted kingdoms.

Do you want a criminal, my lords? When was there so much iniquity ever laid to the charge of any one? No, my lords, you must not look to punish any other such delinquent from India. Warren Hastings has not left substance enough in India to nourish such another delinquent.

My lords, is it a prosecutor you want? You have before you the Commons of Great Britain as prosecutors; and I believe, my lords, that the sun, in his beneficent progress round the world, does not behold a more glorious sight than that of men, separated from a remote people by the material bounds and barriers of nature, united by the bond of a social and moral community—all the Commons of England resenting, as their own, the indignities and cruelties that we offered to all the people of India.

Do we want a tribunal? My lords, no example of antiquity, nothing in the modern world, nothing in the range of human imagination, can supply us with a tribunal like this. We commit safely the interests of India and humanity into your hands. Therefore, it is with confidence that, ordered by the Commons,

I impeach Warren Hastings, Esquire, of high crimes and misdemeanors.

I impeach him in the name of the Commons of Great Britain in Parliament assembled, whose parliamentary trust he has betrayed.

I impeach him in the name of all the Commons of Great Britain, whose national character he has dishonored.

I impeach him in the name of the people of India, whose laws, rights and liberties he has subverted; whose properties he has destroyed; whose country he has laid waste and desolate.

I impeach him in the name and by virtue of those eternal laws of justice which he has violated.

I impeach him in the name of human nature itself, which he has cruelly outraged, injured and oppressed, in both sexes, in every age, rank, situation, and condition of life.

My lords, at this awful close, in the name of the Commons and sur-rounded by them, I attest the retiring, I attest the advancing generations, between which, as a link in the great chain of eternal order, we stand. We call this nation, we call the world to witness, that the Commons have shrunk from no labor; that we have been guilty of no prevarication; that we have made no compromise with crime; that we have not feared any odium whatsoever, in the long warfare which we have carried on with the crimes, with the vices, with the exorbitant wealth, with the enormous and overpowering influence of Eastern corruption.

My lords, it has pleased Providence to place us in such a state that we appear every moment to be upon the verge of some great mutations. There is one thing, and one thing only, which defies all mutation: that which existed before the world, and will survive the fabric of the world itself—I mean justice; that justice which, emanating from the Divinity, has a place in the breast of every one of us, given us for our guide with regard to ourselves and with regard to others, and which will stand, after this globe is burned to ashes, our advocate or our accuser, before the great Judge, when He comes to call upon us for the tenor of a well-spent life.

My lords, the Commons will share in every fate with your lordships; there is nothing sinister which can happen to you, in which we shall not all be involved; and, if it should so happen that we shall be subjected to some of those frightful changes which we have seen—if it should happen that your lordships, stripped of all the decorous distinctions of human society, should, by hands at once base and cruel, be led to those scaffolds and machines of murder upon which great kings and glorious queens have shed their blood, amidst the prelates, amidst the nobles, amidst the magistrates, who supported their thrones—may you in those moments feel that consolation which I am persuaded they felt in the critical moments of their dreadful agony!

My lords, if you must fall, may you so fall! but, if you stand—and stand I trust you will—together with the fortune of this ancient monarchy, together with the ancient laws and liberties of this great and illustrious kingdom, may you stand as unimpeached in honor as in power; may you stand, not as a substitute for virtue, but as an ornament of virtue, as a security for virtue; may you stand long, and long stand the terror of tyrants; may you stand the refuge of afflicted nations; may you stand a sacred temple, for the perpetual residence of an inviolable justice!

Richard Brinsley Sheridan
[1751–1816]

When only thirty-six years old, Richard Brinsley Sheridan was con-
queror of two worlds. He was one of the greatest dramatists of his
period and one of the greatest orators in Parliament. His magnificent
speech at the trial of Warren Hastings, parts of which are reproduced
here, was praised by Edmund Burke as "the most astonishing effort
of eloquence of which there is any record or tradition." Hastings,
British governor of India, had been charged with the brutal treatment
of the people of India and was being tried before the House of Lords
in 1788.

AT THE TRIAL OF WARREN HASTINGS

INSINUATIONS have been thrown out that my honorable colleagues and myself are actuated by motives of malignity against the unfortunate prisoner at the bar. An imputation of so serious a nature cannot be permitted to pass altogether without comment; though it comes in so loose a shape, in such whispers and oblique hints as to prove to a certainty that it was made in the consciousness, and, therefore, with the circumspection of falsehood.

I can, my lords, most confidently aver, that a prosecution more disinterested in all its motives and ends; more free from personal malice or personal interest; more perfectly public, and more purely animated by the simple and unmixed spirit of justice, never was brought in any country, at any time, by any body of men, against any individual. What possible resentment can we entertain against the unfortunate prisoner? What possible interest can we have in his conviction? What possible object of a personal nature can we accomplish by his ruin? For myself, my lords, I make this solemn asseveration, that I discharge my breast of all malice, hatred, and ill-will against the prisoner, if at any time indignation at his crimes has planted in it these passions; and I believe, my lords, that I may with equal truth answer for every one of my colleagues.

We are, my lords, anxious, in stating the crimes with which he is charged, to keep out of recollection the person of the unfortunate prisoner. In prosecuting him to conviction, we are impelled only by a sincere abhorrence of his guilt, and a sanguine hope of remedying future delinquency. We can have no private incentive to the part we have taken. We are actuated singly by the zeal we feel for the public welfare, and by an honest solicitude for the honor of our country, and the happiness of those who are under its dominion and protection.

With such views, we really, my lords, lose sight of Mr. Hastings, who, however great in some other respects, is too insignificant to be blended with these important circumstances. The unfortunate prisoner is, at best, to my mind, no mighty object. Amid the series of mischiefs and enormities to my sense seeming to surround him, what is he but a petty nucleus, involved in its laminæ, scarcely seen or heard of?

This prosecution, my lords, was not, as is alleged, "begot in prejudice, and nursed in error." It originated in the clearest conviction of the wrongs which the natives of Hindostan have endured by the maladministration of those in whose hands this country had placed extensive powers; which ought to have been exercised for the benefit of the governed, but which was used by the prisoner for the shameful purpose of oppression. I repeat with emphasis, my lords, that nothing personal or malicious has induced us to institute this prosecution. It is absurd to suppose it.

You see, my lords, that the British government, which ought to have been a blessing to the powers in India connected with it, has proved a scourge to the natives, and the cause of desolation to their most flourishing provinces.

Behold, my lords, this frightful picture of the consequences of a government of violence and oppression! Surely the condition of wretchedness to which this once happy and independent prince is reduced by our cruelty, and the ruin which in some way has been brought up on his country, call loudly upon your lordships to interpose, and to rescue the national honor and reputation from the infamy to which both will be exposed if no investigation be made into the causes of their calamities, and no punishment inflicted on the authors of them. By policy as well as justice you are vehemently urged to vindicate the English character in the East; for, my lords, it is manifest that the native powers have so little reliance on our faith, that the preservation of our possessions in that division of the world can only be effected by convincing the princes that a religious adherence to its engagements with them shall hereafter distinguish our India government.

It will not, I trust, be concluded that because Mr. Hastings has not marked every passing shade of guilt, and because he has only given the bold outline of cruelty, he is therefore to be acquitted. It is laid down by the law of England, that law which is the perfection of reason, that a person ordering an act to be done by his agent is answerable for that act with all its consequences. *"Quod facit per alium, facit per se."* Middleton was appointed, in 1777, the confidential agent, the second self, of Mr. Hastings. The Governor-General ordered the measure. Even if he never saw nor heard afterwards of its consequences, he was therefore answerable for every pang that was inflicted, and for all the blood that was shed. But he did hear, and that instantly, of the whole. He wrote to accuse Middleton of forbearance and of neglect! He commanded him to work upon the hopes and fears of the princesses, and to leave no means untried, until, to speak his own language, which was better suited to the banditti of a cavern, "he obtained possession of the secret hoards of the old ladies." He would not allow even of a delay of two days to smooth the compelled approaches of a son to his mother, on this occasion! His orders were peremptory. After this, my lords, can it be said that the prisoner was ignorant of the acts, or not culpable for their consequences? It is true he did not direct the guards, the famine, and the bludgeons; he did not weigh the fetters, nor number the lashes to be inflicted on his victims; but yet he is just as guilty as if he had borne an active and personal share in each transaction. It is as if he had commanded that the heart should be torn from the bosom, and enjoined that no blood should follow. He is in the same degree accountable to the law, to his country, to his conscience, and to his God!

The prisoner has endeavored also to get rid of a part of his guilt by observing that he was but one of the supreme council, and that all the rest had sanctioned those transactions with their approbation. Even if it were true that others did participate in the guilt, it cannot tend to diminish his criminality. But the fact is, that the council erred in nothing so much as in a reprehensible credulity given to the declarations of the Governor-General. They knew not a word of those transactions until they were finally concluded. It was not until the January following that they saw the mass of falsehood which had been published under the title of "Mr. Hastings' Narrative." They were, then, unaccountably duped to permit a letter to pass, dated the twenty-ninth of November, intended to seduce the directors into a belief that they had received intelligence at that time, which was not the fact. These observations, my lords, are not meant to cast any obloquy on the council; they undoubtedly were deceived; and the deceit practised on them is a decided proof of his consciousness of guilt. When tired of corporeal infliction Mr. Hastings was gratified by insulting the understanding. The coolness and reflection with which this act was managed and concerted raises its enormity and blackens its turpitude. It proves the prisoner to be that monster in nature, a deliberate and reasoning tyrant! Other tyrants of whom we read, such as a Nero, or a Caligula, were urged to their crimes by the impetuosity of passion. High rank disqualified them from advice, and perhaps equally prevented reflection. But in the prisoner we have a man born in a state of mediocrity; bred to mercantile life; used to system; and accustomed to regularity; who was accountable to his masters, and therefore was compelled to think and to deliberate on every part of his conduct. It is this cool deliberation, I say, which renders his crimes more horrible, and his character more atrocious.

When, my lords, the Board of Directors received the advices which Mr. Hastings thought proper to transmit, though unfurnished with any other materials to form their judgment, they expressed very strongly their doubts, and properly ordered an inquiry into the circumstances of the alleged disaffection of the begums, declaring it, at the same time, to be a debt which was due to the honor and justice of the British nation. This inquiry, however, Mr. Hastings thought it absolutely necessary to elude. He stated to the council, in answer, "that it would revive those animosities that subsisted between the begums and the nabob [Asoph Dowlah], which had then subsided. If the former were inclined to appeal to a foreign jurisdiction, they were the best judges of their own feeling, and should be left to make their own complaint." All this, however, my lords, is nothing to the magnificent paragraph which concludes this communication. "Besides," says he, "I hope it will not be a departure from official language to say that the majesty of justice ought not to be approached without solicitation. She ought not to descend to inflame or provoke, but to withhold her judgment until she is called on to determine." What is still more astonishing is that Sir John Macpherson, who, though a man of sense and honor, is rather Oriental in his imagination, and not learned in the sublime and beautiful from the immortal leader of this prosecution, was caught by this bold, bombastic quibble, and joined in the same words, "That the majesty of justice ought not to be approached without solicitation." But, my lords, do you, the judges of this land, and the expounders of its rightful laws—do you approve of this mockery and call it the character of justice, which takes the form of right to excite wrong? No, my lords, justice is not this halt and miserable object; it is not the ineffective bauble of an Indian pagod; it is not the portentous phantom of despair; it is not like any fabled monster, formed in the eclipse of reason, and found in some unhallowed grove of superstitious darkness and political dismay! No, my lords. In the happy reverse of all this, I turn from the disgusting caricature to the real image! Justice I have now before me august and pure! The abstract idea of all that would be perfect in the spirits and the aspirings of men!—where the mind rises; where the heart expands; where the countenance is ever placid and benign; where her favorite attitude is to stoop to the unfortunate; to hear their cry and to help them; to rescue and relieve, to succor and save; majestic, from its mercy; venerable, from its utility; uplifted, without pride; firm, without obduracy; beneficent in each preference; lovely, though in her frown!

On that justice I rely—deliberate and sure, abstracted from all party purpose and political speculation; not on words, but on facts. You, my lords, will hear me, I conjure, by those rights which it is your best privilege to preserve; by that fame which it is your best pleasure to inherit; by all those feelings which refer to the first term in the series of existence, the original compact of our nature, our controlling rank in the creation. This is the call on all to administer to truth and equity, as they would satisfy the laws and satisfy themselves, with the most exalted bliss possible or conceivable for our nature; the self-approving consciousness of virtue, when the condemnation we look for will be one of the most ample mercies accomplished for mankind since the creation of the world! My lords, I have done.

William Pitt
[1759–1806]

William Pitt (the younger) was the son of William Pitt, Earl of Chatham. For about half of his comparatively short life he was practically the ruler of England, serving as Prime Minister most of this time. His greatest task, of course, was to lead England in its struggle with Napoleon, and it is part of an address on this subject, delivered in the House of Commons, on February 3, 1800, that is presented here.

ON HIS REFUSAL TO NEGOTIATE WITH BONAPARTE

THAT BONAPARTE has an interest in making peace is at best but a doubtful proposition, and that he has an interest in preserving it is still more uncertain. That it is his interest to negotiate, I do not indeed deny. It is his interest, above all, to engage this country in separate negotiation, in order to loosen and dissolve the whole system of the confederacy on the Continent, to palsy at once the arms of Russia, or of Austria, or of any other country that might look to you for support; and then either to break off his separate treaty, or, if he should have concluded it, to apply the lesson which is taught in his school of policy in Egypt, and to revive at his pleasure those claims of indemnification which may have been reserved to some happier period.

This is precisely the interest which he has in negotiation. But on what grounds are we to be convinced that he has an interest in concluding and observing a solid and permanent pacification? Under all the circumstances of his personal character, and his newly acquired power, what other security has he for retaining that power but the sword? His hold upon France is the sword, and he has no other. Is he connected with the soil, or with the habits, the affections, or the prejudices of the country? He is a stranger, a foreigner, and a usurper. He unites in his own person everything that a pure republican must detest; everything that an enraged Jacobin has abjured; everything that a sincere and faithful royalist must feel as an insult. If he is opposed at any time in his career, what is his appeal? He appeals to his fortune; in other words, to his army and his sword. Placing, then, his whole reliance upon military support, can he afford to let his military renown pass away, to let his laurels wither, to let the memory of his trophies sink in obscurity? Is it certain that with his army confined within France, and restrained from inroads upon her neighbors, that he can maintain, at his devotion, a force sufficiently numerous to support his power? Having no object but the possession of absolute dominion, no passion but military glory, is it to be reckoned as certain that he can feel such an interest in permanent peace as would justify us in laying down our arms, reducing our expense, and relinquishing our means of security, on the faith of his engagements? Do we believe that, after the conclusion of peace, he would not still sigh over the lost trophies of Egypt, wrested from him by the celebrated victory of Aboukir, and the brilliant exertions of that heroic band of British seamen, whose influence and example rendered the Turkish troops invincible at Acre? Can he forget that the effect of these exploits enabled Austria and Prussia, in one campaign, to recover from France all which she had acquired by his victories, to dissolve the charm which for a time fascinated Europe, and to show that their generals, contending in a just cause, could efface, even by their success and their military glory, the most dazzling triumphs of his victorious and desolating ambition?

Can we believe, with these impressions on his mind, that if, after a year, eighteen months, or two years of peace had elapsed, he should be tempted by the appearance of fresh insurrection in Ireland, encouraged by renewed and unrestrained communication with France, and fomented by the fresh infusion of Jacobin principles; if we were at such a moment without a fleet to watch the ports of France, or to guard the coasts of Ireland, without a disposable army, or an embodied militia capable of supplying a speedy and adequate reënforcement, and that he had suddenly the means of transporting thither a body of twenty or thirty thousand French troops; can we believe that, at such a moment, his ambition and vindictive spirit would be restrained by the recollection of engagements or the obligation of treaty? Or if, in some new crisis of difficulty and danger to the Ottoman Empire, with no British navy in the Mediterranean, no confederacy formed, no force collected to support it, an opportunity should present itself for resuming the abandoned expedition to Egypt, for renewing the avowed and favorite project of conquering and colonizing that rich and fertile country, and of opening the way to wound some of the vital interests of England, and to plunder the treasures of the East, in order to fill the bankrupt coffers of France—would it be the interest of Bonaparte, under such circumstances, or his principles, his moderation, his love of peace, his aversion to conquest, and his regard for the independence of other nations—would it be all or any of these that would secure us against an attempt which would leave us only the option of submitting without a struggle to certain loss and disgrace, or of renewing the contest which we had prematurely terminated, without allies, without preparation, with diminished means, and with increased difficulty and hazard?

Hitherto I have spoken only of the reliance which we can place on the professions, the character, and the conduct of the present First Consul; but it remains to consider the stability of his power. The Revolution has been marked throughout by a rapid succession of new depositaries of public authority, each supplanting its predecessor. What grounds have we to believe that this new usurpation, more odious and more undisguised than all that preceded it, will be more durable? Is it that we rely on the particular provisions contained in the code of the pretended constitution, which was proclaimed as accepted by the French people as soon as the garrison of Paris declared their determination to exterminate all its enemies, and before any of its articles could even be known to half the country, whose consent was required for its establishment?

I will not pretend to inquire deeply into the nature and effects of a constitution which can hardly be regarded but as a farce and a mockery. If, however, it could be supposed that its provisions were to have any effect, it seems equally adapted to two purposes: that of giving to its founder, for a time, an absolute and uncontrolled authority; and that of laying the certain foundation of disunion and discord, which, if they once prevail, must render the exercise of all the authority under the constitution impossible, and leave no appeal but to the sword.

Is, then, military despotism that which we are accustomed to consider as a stable form of government? In all ages of the world it has been attended with the least stability to the persons who exercised it, and with the most rapid succession of changes and revolution. In the outset of the French Revolution its advocates boasted that it furnished a security forever, not to France only, but to all countries in the world, against military despotism; that the force of standing armies was vain and delusive; that no artificial power could resist public opinion; and that it was upon the foundation of public opinion alone that any government could stand. I believe that in this instance, as in every other, the progress of the French Revolution has belied its professions; but, so far from its being a proof of the prevalence of public opinion against military force, it is instead of the proof, the strongest exception from that doctrine which appears in the history of the world. Through all the stages of the Revolution military force has governed, and public opinion has scarcely been heard. But still I consider this as only an exception from a general truth. I still believe that in every civilized country, not enslaved by a Jacobin faction, public opinion is the only sure support of any government. I believe this with the more satisfaction, from a conviction that, if this contest is happily terminated, the established governments of Europe will stand upon that rock firmer than ever; and, whatever may be the defects of any particular constitution, those who live under it will prefer its continuance to the experiment of changes which may plunge them in the unfathomable abyss of revolution, or extricate them from it only to expose them to the terrors of military despotism. And to apply this to France, I see no reason to believe that the present usurpation will be more permanent than any other military despotism which has been established by the same means, and with the same defiance of public opinion.

What, then, is the inference I draw from all that I have now stated? Is it that we will in no case treat with Bonaparte? I say no such thing. But I say, as has been said in the answer returned to the French note, that we ought to wait for "experience and the evidence of facts" before we are convinced that such a treaty is admissible. The circumstances I have stated would well justify us if we should be slow in being convinced; but on a question of peace and war, everything depends upon degree and upon comparison. If, on the one hand, there should be an appearance that the policy of France is at length guided by different maxims from those which have hitherto prevailed; if we should hereafter see signs of stability in the government which are not now to be traced; if the progress of the allied army should not call forth such a spirit in France as to make it probable that the act of the country itself will destroy the system now prevailing; if the danger, the difficulty, the risk of continuing the contest should increase, while the hope of complete ultimate success should be diminished; all these, in their due place, are considerations which, with myself and, I can answer for it, with every one of my colleagues, will have their just weight. But at present these considerations all operate one way; at present there is nothing from which we can presage a favorable disposition to change in the French councils. There is the greatest reason to rely on powerful cooperation from our allies; there are the strongest marks of a disposition in the interior of France to active resistance against this new tyranny; and there is every ground to believe, on reviewing our situation and that of the enemy, that, if we are ultimately disappointed of that complete success which we are at present entitled to hope, the continuance of the contest, instead of making our situation comparatively worse, will have made it comparatively better.

Charles James Fox
[1749–1806]

Charles James Fox was unique among great British statesmen in that practically his entire career was passed in parliamentary opposition. He denounced the repressive policies of the British government in dealing with the American colonists and championed the cause of the colonies. He took issue with Pitt on his refusal to negotiate with Napoleon, who had made overtures for peace. Fox, who was a great orator, made an eloquent plea for the end of the Napoleonic War in the House of Commons on February 3, 1800, a part of which follows.

ON REFUSAL TO NEGOTIATE WITH BONAPARTE

Sir, we have heard to-night a great many most acrimonious invectives against Bonaparte, against all the course of his conduct, and against the unprincipled manner in which he seized upon the reins of government. I will not make his defense. I think all this sort of invective, which is used only to inflame the passions of this House and of the country, exceedingly ill-timed, and very impolitic. But I say I will not make his defense. I am not sufficiently in possession of materials upon which to form an opinion on the character and conduct of this extraordinary man.

On his arrival in France, he found the government in a very unsettled state, and the whole affairs of the Republic deranged, crippled, and involved. He thought it necessary to reform the government; and he did reform it, just in the way in which a military man may be expected to carry on a reform. He seized on the whole authority for himself. It will not be expected from me that I should either approve or apologize for such an act. I am certainly not for reforming governments by such expedients; but how this House can be so violently indignant at the idea of military despotism, is, I own, a little singular, when I see the composure with which they can observe it nearer home—nay, when I see them regard it as a frame of government most peculiarly suited to the exercise of free opinion, on a subject the most important of any that can engage the attention of a people. Was it not the system which was so *happily* and so *advantageously* established of late, all over Ireland, and which even now the government may, at its pleasure, proclaim over the whole of that kingdom? Are not the persons and property of the people left, in many districts, at this moment, to the entire will of military commanders?

"It is not the interest of Bonaparte," it seems, "sincerely to enter into a negotiation, or if he should even make peace, sincerely to keep it." But how are we to decide upon his sincerity? By refusing to treat with him? Surely, if we mean to discover his sincerity, we ought to hear the propositions which he desires to make. "But peace would be unfriendly to his system of military despotism." Sir, I hear a great deal about the short-lived nature of military despotism. I wish the history of the world would bear gentlemen out in this description of it. Was not the government erected by Augustus Cæsar a military despotism? and yet it endured for six or seven hundred years. Military despotism, unfortunately, is too likely in its nature to be permanent, and it is not true that it depends on the life of the first usurper. Though half of the Roman emperors were murdered, yet the military despotism went on; and so it would be, I fear, in France. If Bonaparte should disappear from the scene, to make room perhaps, for Berthier, or any other general, what difference would that make in the quality of French despotism, or in our relation to the country? We may as safely treat with a Bonaparte, or with any of his successors, be they who they may, as we could with a Louis XVI., a Louis XVII., or a Louis XVIII. There is no difference but in the name. Where the power essentially resides, thither we ought to go for peace.

But, sir, if we are to reason on the fact, I should think that it is the interest of Bonaparte to make peace. A lover of military glory, as that general must necessarily be, may he not think that his measure of glory is full; that it may be tarnished by a reverse of fortune, and can hardly be increased by any new laurels? He must feel that, in the situation to which he is now raised, he can no longer depend on his own fortune, his own genius, and his own talents, for a continuance of his success. He must be under the necessity of employing other generals, whose misconduct or incapacity might endanger his power, or whose triumphs even might affect the interest which he holds in the opinion of the French. Peace, then, would secure to him what he has achieved, and fix the inconstancy of fortune.

But this will not be his only motive. He must see that France also requires a respite—a breathing interval, to recruit her wasted strength. To procure her this respite, would be, perhaps, the attainment of more solid glory, as well as the means of acquiring more solid power, than anything which he can hope to gain from arms, and from the proudest triumphs. May he not, then, be zealous to secure this fame, the only species of fame, perhaps, that is worth acquiring? Nay, granting that his soul may still burn with the thirst of military exploits, is it not likely that he is disposed to yield to the feelings of the French people, and to consolidate his power by consulting their interests? I have a right to argue in this way when suppositions of his insincerity are reasoned upon on the other side. Sir, these aspersions are, in truth, always idle, and even mischievous. I have been too long accustomed to hear imputations and calumnies thrown out upon great and honorable characters, to be much influenced by them.

My honorable and learned friend [Mr. Erskine] has paid this night a most just, deserved, and eloquent tribute of applause to the memory of that great and unparalleled character, who is so recently lost to the world. I must, like him, beg leave to dwell a moment on the venerable George Washington, though I know that it is impossible for me to bestow anything like adequate praise on a character which gave us, more than any other human being, the example of a perfect man; yet, good, great, and unexampled as General Washington was, I can remember the time when he was not better spoken of in this House than Bonaparte is at present. The right honorable gentleman who opened this debate [Mr. Dundas] may remember in what terms of disdain, or virulence, even of contempt, General Washington was spoken of by gentlemen on that side of the House. Does he not recollect with what marks of indignation any member was stigmatized as an enemy to this country who mentioned with common respect the name of General Washington? If a negotiation had then been proposed to be opened with that great man, what would have been said? Would you treat with a rebel, a traitor! What an example would you not give by such an act! I do not know whether the right honorable gentleman may not yet possess some of his old prejudices on the subject. I hope not: I hope by this time we are all convinced that a republican government, like that of America, may exist without danger or injury to social order, or to established monarchies. They have happily shown that they can maintain the relations of peace and amity with other states. They have shown, too, that they are alive to the feelings of honor; but they do not lose sight of plain good sense and discretion. They have not refused to negotiate with the French, and they have accordingly the hopes of a speedy termination of every difference. We cry up their conduct, but we do not imitate it.

Where, then, sir, is this war, which on every side is pregnant with such horrors, to be carried? Where is it to stop? Not till we establish the House of Bourbon! And this you cherish the hope of doing, because you have had a successful campaign. So that we are called upon to go on merely as a speculation. We must keep Bonaparte for some time longer at war, as a state of probation. Gracious God, sir! is war a state of probation? Is peace a rash system? Is it dangerous for nations to live in amity with each other? Are your vigilance, your policy, your common powers of observation, to be extinguished by putting an end to the horrors of war?

Can not this state of probation be as well undergone without adding to the catalog of human sufferings? "But we must *pause!*" What! must the bowels of Great Britain be torn out—her best blood be spilled—her treasures wasted—that you may make an experiment? Put yourselves—oh! that you would put yourselves in the field of battle, and learn to judge of the sort of horrors that you excite! In former wars a man might, at least, have some feeling, some interest, that served to balance in his mind the impressions which a scene of carnage and of death must inflict.

If a man had been present at the Battle of Blenheim, for instance, and had inquired the motive of the battle, there was not a soldier engaged who could not have satisfied his curiosity, and even, perhaps, allayed his feelings. They were fighting, they knew, to repress the uncontrolled ambition of the Grand Monarch. But if a man were present now at a field of slaughter, and were to inquire for what they were fighting—"Fighting!" would be the answer; "they are not fighting; they are *pausing.*" "Why is that man expiring? Why is that other writhing with agony? What means this implacable fury?" The answer must be: "You are quite wrong, sir; you deceive yourself—they are not fighting—do not disturb them—they are merely *pausing!* This man is not expiring with agony—that man is not dead—he is only pausing! Lord help you, sir! they are not angry with one another; they have no cause of quarrel; but their country thinks that there should be a *pause.* All that you see, sir, is nothing like fighting—there is no harm, nor cruelty, nor bloodshed in it whatever; it is nothing more than a *political pause!* It is merely to try an experiment—to see whether Bonaparte will not behave himself better than heretofore; and in the meantime we have agreed to a *pause,* in pure friendship!" And is this the way, sir, that you are to show yourselves the advocates of order? You take up a system calculated to uncivilize the world—to destroy order—to trample on religion—to stifle in the heart, not merely the generosity of noble sentiment, but the affections of social nature; and in the prosecution of this system, you spread terror and devastation all around you.

Sir, I have done. I have told you my opinion. I think you ought to have given a civil, clear, and explicit answer to the overture which was fairly and handsomely made you. If you were desirous that the negotiation should have included all your allies, as the means of bringing about a general peace, you should have told Bonaparte so. But I believe you were afraid of his agreeing to the proposal.

George Canning
[1770–1827]

The fame of George Canning, statesman and orator, is based mainly on the liberal policies he pursued as head of the Foreign Office. He supported non-intervention and national and liberal movements in Europe. He recognized on behalf of his country the independence of the republics of South America, and thus paved the way for the establishment of the Monroe Doctrine as an international principle. In a speech at Liverpool in 1814, parts of which follow, Canning expresses the feelings of the British people at the victory over Napoleon.

THE FALL OF NAPOLEON

CAN ANY MAN now look back upon the trial which we have gone through, and maintain that, at any period during the last twenty years, the plan of insulated policy could have been adopted, without having in the event, at this day, prostrated England at the foot of a conqueror? Great, indeed, has been the call upon our exertions; great, indeed, has been the drain upon our resources; long and wearisome has the struggle been; and late is the moment at which peace is brought within our reach. But even though the difficulties of the contest may have been enhanced, and its duration protracted by it, yet is there any man who seriously doubts whether the having associated our destinies with the destinies of other nations be or be not that which, under the blessing of Providence, has eventually secured the safety of all?

It is at the moment when such a trial has come to its issue, that it is fair to ask of those who have suffered under the pressure of protracted exertion (and of whom rather than of those who are assembled around me— for by whom have such privations been felt more sensibly?)—it is now, I say, the time to ask whether, at any former period of the contest, such a peace could have been made as would at once have guarded the national interests and corresponded with the national character. I address myself now to such persons only as think the character of a nation an essential part of its strength, and consequently of its safety. But if, among persons of that description, there be one who, with all his zeal for the glory of his country, has yet at times been willing to abandon the contest in mere weariness and despair, of such a man I would ask, whether he can indicate the period at which he now wishes such an abandonment had been consented to by the Government of Great Britain.

Is there any man that has a heart in his bosom who does not find, in the contemplation of this contrast alone, a recompense for the struggles and the sufferings of years?

But, gentlemen, the doing right is not only the most honorable course of action—it is also the most profitable in its results. At any former period of the war, the independence of almost all the other countries, our allies, would have to be purchased with sacrifices profusely poured out from the lap of British victory. Not a throne to be reëstablished, not a province to be evacuated, not a garrison to be withdrawn, but this country would have had to make compensation out of her conquests for the concessions obtained from the enemy. Now, happily, this work is already done, either by our efforts or to our hands. The peninsula free—the lawful commonwealth of European states already, in a great measure, restored, Great Britain may now appear in the congress of the world, rich in conquests, nobly and rightfully won, with little claim upon her faith or her justice, whatever may be the spontaneous impulse of her generosity or her moderation.

Such, gentlemen, is the situation and prospect of affairs at the moment at which I have the honor to address you. That you, gentlemen, may have your full share in the prosperity of your country is my sincere and earnest wish. The courage with which you bore up in adverse circumstances eminently entitles you to this reward.

Thomas Babington Macaulay
[1800–1859]

Lord Macaulay, historian and poet, was also active in affairs of state, administrative as well as legislative. Following is part of an address he delivered in the House of Commons on March 1, 1831.

ON THE REFORM BILL

MY HONORABLE FRIEND, the member for the University of Oxford [Sir Robert Inglis] tells us that if we pass this law [extension of suffrage] England will soon be a republic. The reformed House of Commons will, according to him, before it has sat ten years, depose the king and expel the lords from their House. Sir, if my honorable friend could prove this, he would have succeeded in bringing an argument for democracy infinitely stronger than any that is to be found in the works of Paine. My honorable friend's proposition is in fact this: that our monarchical and aristocratical institutions have no hold on the public mind of England; that these institutions are regarded with aversion by a decided majority of the middle class. This, sir, I say, is plainly deducible from his proposition; for he tells us that the representatives of the middle class will inevitably abolish royalty and nobility within ten years; and there is surely no reason to think that the representatives of the middle class will be more inclined to a democratic revolution than their constituents. Now, sir, if I were convinced that the great body of the middle class in England look with aversion on monarchy and aristocracy, I should be forced, much against my will, to come to this conclusion that monarchical and aristocratical institutions are unsuited to my country. Monarchy and aristocracy, valuable and useful as I think them, are still valuable and useful as means and not as ends. The end of government is the happiness of the people, and I do not conceive that, in a country like this, the happiness of the people can be promoted by a form of government in which the middle classes place no confidence, and which exists only because the middle classes have no organ by which to make their sentiments known. But, sir, I am fully convinced that the middle classes sincerely wish to uphold the royal prerogatives and the constitutional rights of the peers.

The question of parliamentary reform is still behind. But signs, of which it is impossible to misconceive the import, do most clearly indicate that, unless that question also be speedily settled, property, and order, and all the institutions of this great monarchy, will be exposed to fearful peril. Is it possible that gentlemen long versed in high political affairs can not read these signs? Is it possible that they can really believe that the representative system of England, such as it now is, will last till the year 1860? If not, for what would they have us wait? Would they have us wait merely that we may show to all the world how little we have profited by our own recent experience?

Would they have us wait, that we may once again hit the exact point where we can neither refuse with authority nor concede with grace? Would they have us wait, that the numbers of the discontented party may become larger, its demands higher, its feelings more acrimonious, its organization more complete? Would they have us wait till the whole tragicomedy of 1827 has been acted over again; till they have been brought into office by a cry of "No Reform," to be reformers, as they were once before brought into office by a cry of "No Popery," to be emancipators? Have they obliterated from their minds—gladly, perhaps, would some among them obliterate from their minds—the transactions of that year? And have they forgotten all the transactions of the succeeding year? Have they forgotten how the spirit of liberty in Ireland, debarred from its natural outlet, found a vent by forbidden passages? Have they forgotten how we were forced to indulge the Catholics in all the license of rebels, merely because we chose to withhold from them the liberties of subjects? Do they wait for associations more formidable than that of the Corn Exchange, for contributions larger than the Rent, for agitators more violent than those who, three years ago, divided with the king and the Parliament the sovereignty of Ireland? Do they wait for that last and most dreadful paroxysm of popular rage, for that last and most cruel test of military fidelity?

Let them wait, if their past experience shall induce them to think that any high honor or any exquisite pleasure is to be obtained by a policy like this. Let them wait, if this strange and fearful infatuation be indeed upon them, that they should not see with their eyes, or hear with their ears, or understand with their heart. But let us know our interest and our duty better. Turn where we may, within, around, the voice of great events is proclaiming to us: Reform, that you may preserve. Now, therefore, while everything at home and abroad forebodes ruin to those who persist in a hopeless struggle against the spirit of the age; now, while the crash of the proudest throne of the continent is still resounding in our ears; now, while the roof of a British palace affords an ignominious shelter to the exiled heir of forty kings; now, while we see on every side ancient institutions subverted, and great societies dissolved; now, while the heart of England is still sound; now, while old feelings and old associations retain a power and a charm which may too soon pass away; now, in this your accepted time, now, in this your day of salvation, take counsel, not of prejudice, not of party spirit, not of the ignominious pride of a fatal consistency, but of history, of reason, of the ages which are past, of the signs of this most portentous time.

Pronounce in a manner worthy of the expectation with which this great debate has been anticipated, and of the long remembrance which it will leave behind. Renew the youth of the State. Save property, divided against itself. Save the multitude, endangered by its own ungovernable passions. Save the aristocracy, endangered by its own unpopular power. Save the greatest, and fairest, and most highly civilized community that ever existed, from calamities which may in a few days sweep away all the rich heritage of so many ages of wisdom and glory. The danger is terrible. The time is short. If this bill should be rejected, I pray to God that none of those who concur in rejecting it may ever remember their votes with unavailing remorse, amid the wreck of laws, the confusion of ranks, the spoliation of property, and the dissolution of social order.

Richard Cobden
[1804–1865]

Richard Cobden, statesman and economist, has won world fame as a powerful advocate of free trade, but he was also a consistent liberal in all domestic and foreign questions. He supported the Union cause in England and opposed British expansionist policies. His greatest oratorical triumph was his speech in the House of Commons on March 13, 1845, favoring the repeal of the "protective" Corn Law. When he had finished, Prime Minister Peel, who was expected to reply, is said to have crumpled up his notes and said to a colleague, "You may answer this; I cannot." Parts of this speech follow.

THE EFFECTS OF PROTECTION ON AGRICULTURE

I HOLD that the landed proprietors are the parties who are responsible if the laborers have not employment. You have absolute power; there is no doubt about that. You can, if you please, legislate for the laborers, or yourselves. Whatever you may have done besides, your legislation has been adverse to the laborer, and you have no right to call upon the farmers to remedy the evils which you have caused. Will not this evil—if evil you call it—press on you more and more every year? What can you do to remedy the mischief? I only appear here now because you have proposed nothing. We all know your system of allotments, and we are all aware of its failure. What other remedy have you? For, mark you, that is worse than a plaything, if you were allowed to carry out your own views. [Hear!] Aye, it is well enough for some of you that there are wiser heads than your own to lead you, or you would be conducting yourselves into precisely the same condition in which they are in Ireland, but with this difference—this increased difficulty— that there they do manage to maintain the rights of property by the aid of the English Exchequer and 20,000 bayonets; but divide your own country into small allotments, and where would be the rights of property? What do you propose to do now? That is the question. Nothing has been brought forward this year, which I have heard, having for its object to benefit the great mass of the English population; nothing I have heard suggested which has at all tended to alleviate their condition.

You admit that the farmer's capital is sinking from under him, and that he is in a worse state than ever. Have you distinctly provided some plan to give confidence to the farmer, to cause an influx of capital to be expended upon his land, and so bring increased employment to the laborer? How is this to be met? I can not believe you are going to make this a political game. You must set up some specific object to benefit the agricultural interest. It is well said that the last election was an agricultural triumph. There are two hundred county members sitting behind the prime minister who prove that it was so.

What, then, is your plan for this distressing state of things? That is what I want to ask you. Do not, as you have done before, quarrel with me because I have imperfectly stated my case; I have done my best, and I again ask you what you have to propose? I tell you that this "Protection," as it has been called, is a failure. It was so when you had the prohibition up to 80s. You know the state of your farming tenantry in 1821. It was a failure when you had a protection price of 60s., for you know what was the condition of your farm tenantry in 1835. It is a failure now with your last amendment, for you have admitted and proclaimed it to us; and what is the condition of your agricultural population at this time?

I ask, what is your plan? I hope it is not a pretense—a mere political game that has been played throughout the last election, and that you have not all come up here as mere politicians. There are politicians in the House—men who look with an ambition—probably a justifiable one—to the honors of office. There may be men who—with thirty years of continuous service, having been pressed into a groove from which they can neither escape nor retreat—may be holding office, high office, maintained there probably at the expense of their present convictions which do not harmonize very well with their early opinions. I make allowances for them; but the great body of the honorable gentlemen opposite came up to this House, not as politicians, but as the farmers' friends, and protectors of the agricultural interests. Well, what do you propose to do? You have heard the prime minister declare that,

if he could restore all the protection which you have had, that protection would not benefit agriculturists. Is that your belief? If so, why
not proclaim it? And if it is not your conviction, you will have falsified
your mission in this House by following the right honorable baronet
out into the lobby, and opposing inquiry into the condition of the
very men who sent you here.

With mere politicians I have no right to expect to succeed in this
motion. But I have no hesitation in telling you that, if you give me a
committee of this House, I will explode the delusion of agricultural
protection! I will bring forward such a mass of evidence, and give you
such a preponderance of talent and of authority, that when the blue
book is published and sent forth to the world, as we can now send it,
by our vehicles of information, your system of protection shall not
live in public opinion for two years afterward. Politicians do not want
that. This cry of protection has been a very convenient handle for
politicians. The cry of protection carried the counties at the last election,
and politicians gained honors, emoluments, and place by it. But is that
old tattered flag of protection, tarnished and torn as it is already, to
be kept hoisted still in the counties for the benefit of politicians; or will
you come forward honestly and fairly to inquire into this question?
I can not believe that the gentry of England will be made mere drum-
heads to be sounded upon by a prime minister to give forth unmeaning
and empty sounds, and to have no articulate voice of their own. No!
You are the gentry of England who represent the counties. You are
the aristocracy of England. Your fathers led our fathers; you may lead
us if you will go the right way. But, although you have retained your influence with this country longer than any other aristocracy, it has not
been by opposing popular opinion, or by setting yourselves against the
spirit of the age.

In other days, when the battle and the hunting-fields were the tests
of manly vigor, your fathers were first and foremost there. The aristocracy of England were not like the noblesse of France, the mere
minions of a court; nor were they like the hidalgos of Madrid, who
dwindled into pigmies. You have been Englishmen. You have not shown
a want of courage and firmness when any call has been made upon you.
This is a new era. It is the age of improvement; it is the age of social
advancement, not the age for war or for feudal sports. You live in a
mercantile age, when the whole wealth of the world is poured into
your lap. You can not have the advantages of commercial rents and
feudal privileges; but you may be what you always have been, if you
will identify yourselves with the spirit of the age. The English people
look to the gentry and aristocracy of their country as their leaders. I,
who am not one of you, have no hesitation in telling you that there
is a deep-rooted, an hereditary prejudice, if I may so call it, in your
favor in this country. But you never got it, and you will not keep it,
by obstructing the spirit of the age. If you are indifferent to enlightened
means of finding employment for your own peasantry; if you are found
obstructing that advance which is calculated to knit nations more

together in the bonds of peace by means of commercial intercourse; if you are found fighting against the discoveries which have almost given breath and life to material nature, and setting up yourselves as obstructives of that which destiny has decreed shall go on,—why, then, you will be the gentry of England no longer, and others will be found to take your place.

And I have no hesitation in saying that you stand just now in a very critical position. There is a wide-spread suspicion that you have been tampering with the best feelings and with the honest confidence of your constituents in this cause. Everywhere you are doubted and suspected. Read your own organs, and you will see that this is the case. Well, then, this is the time to show that you are not the mere party politicians which you are said to be. I have said that we shall be opposed in this measure by politicians; they do not want inquiry. But I ask you to go into this committee with me. I will give you a majority of county members. You shall have a majority of the Central Society in that committee. I ask you only to go into a fair inquiry as to the causes of the distress of your own population. I only ask that this matter may be fairly examined. Whether you establish my principle or yours, good will come out of the inquiry; and I do, therefore, beg and entreat the honorable independent country gentlemen of this House that they will not refuse, on this occasion, to go into a fair, a full, and an impartial inquiry.

John Bright
[1811–1889]

John Bright was one of the greatest liberal statesmen and one of the greatest orators in English history. He championed ably and eloquently nearly every reform measure of his day, and it was due mainly to his stand that the "Trent" affair did not bring on war between England and the United States. This affair was the forcible seizure and removal of the Confederate commissioners from the Trent, a British ship in the Bahama channel, by a United States naval vessel. Following is an abridgment of Bright's speech on the "Trent" affair, delivered in Rochdale on December 4, 1861.

THE "TRENT" AFFAIR

I AM OBLIGED to say—and I say it with the utmost pain—that if we have not done things that are plainly hostile to the North, and if we have not expressed affection for slavery, and, outwardly and openly, hatred for the Union—I say that there has not been that friendly and cordial neutrality, which, if I had been a citizen of the United States, I should have expected; and I say further, that, if there has existed considerable irritation at that, it must be taken as a measure of the high appreciation which the people of those States place upon the opinion of the people of England.

But there has occurred an event which was announced to us only a week ago, which is one of great importance, and it may be one of some peril. It is asserted that what is called "international law" has been broken by the seizure of the Southern commissioners on board an English trading steamer by a steamer of war of the United' States. Now, what is international law? You have heard that the opinions of the law officers of the crown are in favor of this view of the case—that the law has been broken. I am not at all going to say that it has not. It would be imprudent in me to set my opinion on a legal question which I have only partially examined, against their opinion on the same question, which I presume they have carefully examined. But this I say, that international law is not to be found in an act of Parliament—it is not in so many clauses. You know that it is difficult to find the law. I can ask the mayor, or any magistrate around me, whether it is not very difficult to find the law, even when you have found the Act of Parliament, and found the clause. But when you have no Act of Parliament, and no clause, you may imagine that the case is still more difficult.

Now, maritime law, or international law, consists of opinions and precedents for the most part, and it is very unsettled. The opinions are the opinions of men of different countries, given at different times; and the precedents are not always like each other. The law is very unsettled, and, for the most part, I believe it to be exceedingly bad. In past times, as you know from the histories you read, this country has been a fighting country; we have been belligerents, and as belligerents, we have carried maritime law by your own powerful hand, to a pitch that has been very oppressive to foreign, and especially so to neutral, nations. Well, now, for the first time, unhappily—almost for the first time in our history for the last two hundred years—we are not belligerents, but neutrals; and we are disposed to take, perhaps, rather a different view of maritime and international law.

Now, the act which has been committed by the American steamer, in my opinion, whether it was legal or not, was both impolitic and bad. That is my opinion. I think it may turn out, almost certainly, that, so far as the taking of those men from that ship was concerned, it was an act wholly unknown to, and unauthorized by, the American government. And if the American government believe, on the opinion of their law officers, that the act is illegal, I have no doubt they will make fitting reparation; for there is no government in the world that has so strenuously insisted upon modifications of international law, and been so anxious to be guided always by the most moderate and merciful interpretation of that law.

Now, our great advisers of the *Times* newspaper have been persuading people that this is merely one of a series of acts which denote the determination of the Washington government to pick a quarrel with the people of England. Did you ever know anybody who was not very nearly dead drunk, who, having as much upon his hands as he could manage, would offer to fight everybody about him? Do you believe that the United States government, presided over by President Lincoln, so constitutional in all his acts, so moderate as he has been—representing at this moment that great party in the United States, happily now in the ascendency, which has always been especially in favor of peace, and especially friendly to England—do you believe that such a government, having now upon its hands an insurrection of the most formidable character in the South, would invite the armies and the fleets of England to combine with that insurrection, and, it might be, to render it impossible that the Union should ever again be restored? I say, that single statement, whether it came from a public writer or a public speaker, is enough to stamp him forever with the character of being an insidious enemy of both countries.

What can be more monstrous than that we, as we call ourselves, to some extent, an educated, a moral, and a Christian nation—at a moment when an accident of this kind occurs, before we have made a representation to the American government, before we have heard a word from it in reply—should be all up in arms, every sword leaping from its scabbard, and every man looking about for his pistols and his blunder-busses? I think the conduct pursued—and I have no doubt just the same is pursued by a certain class in America—is much more the conduct of savages than of Christian and civilized men. No, let us be calm. You recollect how we were dragged into the Russian war—how we "drifted" into it. You know that I, at least, have not upon my head any of the guilt of that fearful war. You know that it cost one hundred millions of money to this country; that it cost at least the lives of forty thousand Englishmen; that it disturbed your trade; that it nearly doubled the armies of Europe; that it placed the relations of Europe on a much less peaceful footing than before; and that it did not effect one single thing of all those that it was promised to effect.

Now, then, before I sit down, let me ask you what is this people, about which so many men in England at this moment are writing, and speaking, and thinking, with harshness, I think with injustice, if not with great bitterness? Two centuries ago, multitudes of the people of this country found a refuge on the North American continent, escaping from the tyranny of the Stuarts and from the bigotry of Laud. Many noble spirits from our country made great experiments in favor of human freedom on that continent. Bancroft, the great historian of his own country, has said, in his own graphic and emphatic language, "The history of the colonization of America is the history of the crimes of Europe."

At this very moment, then, there are millions in the United States who personally, or whose immediate parents have at one time been citizens of this country. They found a home in the Far West; they subdued the wilderness; they met with plenty there, which was not afforded them in their native country; and they have become a great people. There may be persons in England who are jealous of those States. There may be men who dislike democracy, and who hate a republic; there may be even those whose sympathies warm toward the slave oligarchy of the South. But of this I am certain, that only misrepresentation the most gross, or calumny the most wicked can sever the tie which unites the great mass of the people of this country with their friends and brethren beyond the Atlantic.

Now, whether the Union will be restored or not, or the South achieve an unhonored independence or not, I know not, and I predict not. But this I think I know—that in a few years, a very few years, the twenty millions of freemen in the North will be thirty millions, or even fifty millions—a population equal to or exceeding that of this kingdom. When that time comes, I pray that it may not be said among them, that in the darkest hour of their country's trials, England, the land of their fathers, looked on with icy coldness and saw unmoved the perils and calamities of their children. As for me, I have but this to say: I am but one in this audience, and but one in the citizenship of this country; but if all other tongues are silent, mine shall speak for that policy which gives hope to the bondmen of the South, and which tends to generous thoughts, and generous words, and generous deeds, between the two great nations who speak the English language, and from their origin are alike entitled to the English name.

Benjamin Disraeli
[1804–1881]

Benjamin Disraeli, Lord Baeconsfield, statesman and novelist, played a dazzling role in British history. As Tory leader and Prime Minister he was the embodiment of British imperialism. Favorite of Queen Victoria and idol of the conservatives, he led the fight against liberal policies and reforms with great skill and strategy. Probably his greatest triumph was his diplomatic victory at the Congress of Berlin. Here are parts of Disraeli's speech at a magnificent banquet given in his honor in London on July 27, 1878, where he was introduced as "the greatest conqueror, who has vanquished war and brought us back peace."

PEACE WITH HONOR

WHEN I STUDY the catalogue of congratulatory regrets with attention, the Convention of Constantinople appears to be the ground on which a great assault is to be made on the Government. It is said that we have increased, and dangerously increased, our responsibilities as a nation by that Convention. In the first place, I deny that we have increased our responsibilities by that Convention. I maintain that by that Convention we have lessened our responsibilities. Suppose now, for example, the settlement of Europe had not included the Convention of Constantinople and the occupation of the isle of Cyprus; suppose it had been limited to the mere Treaty of Berlin; what, under all probable circumstances, might then have occurred? In ten, fifteen, it might be in twenty, years, the power and resources of Russia having revived, some quarrel would again have occurred, Bulgarian or otherwise [cheers], and in all probability the armies of Russia would have been assailing the Ottoman dominions both in Europe and Asia, and enveloping and enclosing the city of Constantinople and its all-powerful position. [Cheers.]

Now, what would be the probable conduct, under these circumstances, of the Government of this country, whoever the ministers might be, whatever party might be in power? I fear there might be hesitation for a time—a want of decision—a want of firmness; but no one doubts that ultimately England would have said: "This will never do; we must prevent the conquest of Asia Minor [cheers]; we must interfere in this matter, and arrest the course of Russia." [Cheers.] No one, I am sure, in this country who impartially considers this question can for a moment doubt what, under any circumstances, would have been the course of this country. [Cheers.]

Well, then, that being the case, I say it is extremely important that this country should take a step beforehand [cheers] which should indicate what the policy of England would be; that you should not have your Ministers meeting in a Council Chamber, hesitating and doubting and considering contingencies, and then acting at last, but acting perhaps too late. [Cheers.] I say, therefore, that the responsibilities of this country have not been increased [cheers]; the responsibilities already existed, though I for one would never shrink from increasing the responsibilities of this country, if they are responsibilities which ought to be undertaken. [Cheers.] The responsibilities of this country are practically diminished by the course we have taken.

My lords and gentlemen, one of the results of my attending the Congress of Berlin has been to prove, what I always suspected to be the absolute fact, that neither the Crimean war, nor this horrible devastating war which has just terminated, would have taken place, if England had spoken with the necessary firmness. [Loud cheers.]

Russia has complaints to make against this country that neither in the case of the Crimean war nor on this occasion—and I do not shrink from my share of the responsibility in this matter—was the voice of England so clear and decided as to exercise a due share in the guidance of European opinion. [Cheers.]

Suppose, gentlemen, that my noble friend and I had come back with the Treaty of Berlin, and had not taken the step which is to be questioned within the next eight-and-forty hours, could we, with any self-respect, have met our countrymen when they asked, what securities have you made for the peace of Europe? How far have you diminished the chance of perpetually recurring war on this question of the East by the Treaty of Berlin? Why, they could say, all we have gained by the Treaty of Berlin is probably the peace of a few years, and at the end of that time the same phenomenon will arise and the Ministers of England must patch up the affair as well as they could.

That was not the idea of public duty entertained by my noble friend and myself. [Cheers.] We thought the time had come when we ought to take steps which would produce some order out of the anarchy and chaos that had so long prevailed. [Cheers.] We asked ourselves, was it absolutely a necessity that the fairest provinces of the world should be the most devastated and most ill-used, and for this reason that there is no security for life or property so long as that country is in perpetual fear of invasion and aggression? [Cheers.]

It was under these circumstances that we recommended the course we have taken; and I believe that the consequences of that policy will tend to and even secure peace and order in a portion of the globe which hitherto has seldom been blessed by these celestial visitants. [Cheers.]

I hold that we have laid the foundation of a state of affairs which may open a new continent to the civilization of Europe [cheers], and that the welfare of the world and the wealth of the world may be increased by availing ourselves of that tranquillity and order which the more intimate connection of England with that country will now produce. [Cheers.]

But I am sorry to say that though we taxed our brains and our thought to establish a policy which might be beneficial to the country, we have not satisfied those who are our critics. [Cheers.]

I was astonished to learn that the Convention of the fourth of June has been described as "an insane convention." It is a strong epithet. I do not myself pretend to be as competent a judge of insanity as my right honorable opponent. [Gladstone.] I will not say to the right honorable gentleman, *naviget Anticyram,* but I would put this issue to an English jury—Which do you believe the most likely to enter into an insane convention—a body of English gentlemen honored by the favor of their Sovereign and the confidence of their fellow-subjects, managing your affairs for five years, I hope with prudence, and not altogether without success [cheers], or a sophisticated rhetorician, inebriated with the exuberance of his own verbosity [loud cheers and laughter], and gifted with an egotistical imagination that can at all times command an interminable and inconsistent series of arguments to malign an opponent and to glorify himself? [Continued cheers and laughter.]

My lords and gentlemen, I leave the decision upon that Convention to the Parliament and people of England. [Loud cheers.] I believe that in that policy are deeply laid the seeds of future welfare, not merely to England, but to Europe and Asia; and confident that the policy we have recommended is one that will be supported by the country, I and those that act with me can endure these attacks. [Loud cheers.]

William Ewart Gladstone
[1809–1898]

The two outstanding British statesmen and orators of the nine-teenth century were William Ewart Gladstone and Benjamin Disraeli. Gladstone, the Liberal, fought the policies of Disraeli when the latter was Prime Minister, and likewise defended his reform measures against all opposition when he himself held that high office. Here are portions of a speech made by Gladstone at West Calder on November 7, 1879, typical of the many he delivered in and out of Parliament.

ON DOMESTIC AND FOREIGN AFFAIRS

Today, gentlemen, as I know that many among you are interested in the land, and as I feel that what is termed "agricultural distress" is at the present moment a topic too serious to be omitted from our consideration, I shall say some words upon the subject of that agricultural distress, and particularly, because in connection with it there have arisen in some quarters of the country proposals, which have received a countenance far beyond their deserts, to reverse or to compromise the work which it took us one whole generation to achieve, and to revert to the mischievous, obstructive, and impoverishing system of protection.

But are we such children that, after spending twenty years—as I may say from 1840 to 1860—in breaking down the huge fabric of protection, in 1879 we are seriously to set about building it up again? If that be right, gentlemen, let it be done, but it will involve on our part a most humiliating confession. In my opinion it is not right. Protection, however, let me point out, now is asked for in two forms, and I am next going to quote Lord Beaconsfield for the purpose of expressing my concurrence with him.

Mostly, I am bound to say, as far as my knowledge goes, protection has not been asked for by the agricultural interest, certainly not by the farmers of Scotland.

It has been asked for by certain injudicious cliques and classes of persons connected with other industries—connected with some manu-facturing industries. They want to have duties laid upon manufactures.

But here Lord Beaconsfield said—and I cordially agree with him—that he would be no party to the institution of a system in which protection was to be given to manufactures, and to be refused to agriculture.

That one-sided protection I deem to be totally intolerable, and I reject it even at the threshold as unworthy of a word of examination or discussion.

But let us go on to two-sided protection, and see whether that is any better—that is to say, protection in the shape of duties on manufactures, and protection in the shape of duties upon corn, duties upon meat, duties upon butter and cheese and eggs, and everything that can be produced from the land. Now, gentlemen, in order to see whether we can here find a remedy for our difficulties, I prefer to speculation and mere abstract argument the method of reverting to experience. Experience will give us very distinct lessons upon this matter. We have the power, gentlemen, of going back to the time when protection was in full and unchecked force, and of examining the effect which it produced upon the wealth of the country. How, will you say, do I mean to test that wealth? I mean to test that wealth by the exports of the country, and I will tell you why, because your prosperity depends upon the wealth of your customers—that is to say, upon their capacity to buy what you produce. And who are your customers? Your customers are the industrial population of the country, who produce what we export and send all over the world. Consequently, when exports increase, your customers are doing a large business, are growing wealthy, are putting money in their pockets, and are able to take that money out of their pockets in order to fill their stomachs with what you produce. When, on the contrary, exports do not increase, your customers are poor, your prices go down, as you have felt within the last few years, in the price of meat, for example, and in other things, and your condition is proportionally depressed.

What has been the case, gentlemen, since we cast off the superstition of protection, since we discarded the imposture of protection? From 1842, gentlemen, onward, the successive stages of free trade began; in 1842, in 1845, in 1846, in 1853, and again in 1860, the large measures were carried which have completely reformed your customs tariff, and reduced it from a taxation of twelve hundred articles to a taxation of, I think, less than twelve.

Now, under the system of protection, the export trade of the country, the wealth and the power of the manufacturing and producing classes to purchase your agricultural products, did not increase at all.

But since 1842, and down to the present time, we have had the successive adoption of free-trade measures; and what has been the state of the export business of the country? It has risen in this degree, that that which from 1840 to 1842 averaged £50,000,000, from 1873 to 1878 averaged £218,000,000. You know very well, that while restriction was in force, you did not get the prices that you have been getting for the last twenty years. The price of wheat has been much the same as it had been before. The price of oats is a better price than was to be had on the average of protective times. But the price, with the exception of wheat, of almost every agricultural commodity, the price of wool, the price of meat, the price of cheese, the price of everything that the soil produces, has been largely increased in a market free and open to the world; because, while the artificial advantage which you got through protection, as it was supposed to be an advantage, was removed, you were brought into that free and open market, and the energy of free trade so enlarged the buying capacity of your customers that they were willing and able to give you, and did give you, a great deal more for your meat, your wool, and your products in general, than you would ever have got under the system of protection.

Pericles, the great Athenian statesman, said with regard to women, their greatest merit was to be never heard of.

Now, what Pericles untruly said of women, I am very much disposed to say of foreign affairs—their great merit would be to be never heard of. Unfortunately, instead of being never heard of, they are always heard of, and you hear almost of nothing else; and I can't promise you, gentlemen, that you will be relieved from this everlasting din, because the consequences of an unwise meddling with foreign affairs are consequences that will for some time necessarily continue to trouble you, and that will find their way to your pockets in the shape of increased taxation.

The first thing is to foster the strength of the empire by just legislation and economy at home, thereby producing two of the great elements of national power—namely, wealth, which is a physical element, and union and contentment, which are moral elements—and to reserve the strength of the empire, to reserve the expenditure of that strength for great and worthy occasions abroad. Here is my first principle of foreign policy: good government at home.

My second principle of foreign policy is this, that its aim ought to be to preserve to the nations of the world—and especially, were it but for shame, when we recollect the sacred name we bear as Christians, especially to the Christian nations of the world—the blessings of peace. That is my second principle.

In my opinion the third sound principle is this: to strive to cultivate and maintain, aye, to the very uttermost, what is called the concert of Europe; to keep the powers of Europe in union together. And why? Because by keeping all in union together you neutralize, and fetter, and bind up the selfish aims of each.

My fourth principle is: That you should avoid needless and entangling engagements. You may boast about them, you may brag about them, you may say you are procuring consideration for the country. You may say that an Englishman can now hold up his head among the nations. But what does all this come to, gentlemen? It comes to this, that you are increasing your engagements without increasing your strength; and if you increase engagements without increasing strength, you diminish strength, you abolish strength; you really reduce the empire and do not increase it. You render it less capable of performing its duties; you render it an inheritance less precious to hand on to future generations.

My fifth principle is this, gentlemen: To acknowledge the equal rights of all nations. You may sympathize with one nation more than another. Nay, you must sympathize in certain circumstances with one nation more than another. You sympathize most with those nations, as a rule, with which you have the closest connection in language, in blood, and in religion, or whose circumstances at the time seem to give the strongest claim to sympathy. But in point of right all are equal, and you have no right to set up a system under which one of them is to be placed under moral suspicion or espionage, or to be made the constant subject of invective.

And that sixth is: That in my opinion foreign policy, subject to all the limitations that I have described, the foreign policy of England should always be inspired by the love of freedom. There should be a sympathy with freedom, a desire to give it scope, founded not upon visionary ideas, but upon the long experience of many generations within the shores of this happy isle, that in freedom you lay the firmest foundations both of loyalty and order; the firmest foundations for the development of individual character, and the best provision for the happiness of the nation at large.

Cardinal Manning
[1808–1892]

Henry Edward, Cardinal Manning, Roman Catholic prelate, delivered a notable address on anti-Semitism at a meeting held in London on February 1, 1882, called by the Lord Mayor to protest against the persecution of Jews in Russia.

ANTI-SEMITISM

My Lord Mayor, Ladies and Gentlemen:—It has often fallen to my lot to move a resolution in meetings such as this, but never in my memory have I moved one with more perfect conviction of my reason or more entire concurrence of my heart. Before I use any further words, it will, perhaps, be better that I should read what that resolution is. It is, "That this meeting, while disclaiming any right or desire to interfere in the internal affairs of another country, and desiring that the most amicable relations between England and Russia should be preserved, feels it a duty to express its opinion that the laws of Russia relating to the Jews tend to degrade them in the eyes of the Christian population, and to expose Russian Jewish subjects to the outbreaks of fanatical ignorance."

I need not disclaim, for I accept the eloquent disclaimer of the noble lord, that we are not met here for a political purpose. If there were a suspicion of any party politics, I should not be standing here. It is because I believe that we are highly above all the tumults of party politics, that we are in the serene region of human sympathy and human justice, that I am here to-day.

Further, I may say that while we do not pretend to touch upon any question in the internal legislation of Russia, there are laws larger than any Russian legislation—the laws of humanity and of God, which are the foundation of all other laws, and if in any legislation they be violated, all the nations of Christian Europe, the whole commonwealth of civilized and Christian men would instantly acquire a right to speak out aloud.

And now I must touch upon one point, which I acknowledge has been very painful to me. We have all watched for the last twelve months the anti-Semitic movement in Germany. I look upon it with a twofold feeling—in the first place with horror as tending to disintegrate the foundations of social life, and, secondly, with great fear lest it may light up an animosity, which has already taken flame in Russia and may spread elsewhere. I have read with great regret an elaborate article, full, no doubt, of minute observations, written from Prussia and published in the *Nineteenth Century,* giving a description of the class animosities, jealousies, and rivalries which are at present so rife in that country. When I read that article, my first feeling was one of infinite sorrow that the power and energy of the Old Testament should be so much greater in Brandenburg than those of the New. I am sorry to see that a society penetrated with rationalism has not so much Christian knowledge, Christian power, Christian character, and Christian virtue as to render it impossible that, cultivated, refined, industrious, and energetic as they are, they should endanger the Christian society of that great kingdom. I have also read with pain accounts of the condition of the Russian Jews, bringing against them accusations which, if I touch upon them, I must ask my Jewish friends near me to believe I reject with incredulity and horror. Nevertheless, I have read that the cause of what has happened in Russia is that the Jews have been pliers of infamous trades—usurers, immoral, demoralizing, and I know not what. When I read these accusations, I ask, Will they be cured by crime, murder, outrage, abominations of every sort? Are they not learning the lesson from those who ought to teach a higher?

Again, if it be true, which I do not believe, that they are in the condition described are they not under penal laws? Is there anything that can degrade men more than to close against intelligence, energy, and industry all the honorable careers of public life? Is there anything that can debase and irritate the soul of man more than to be told, "You must not pass beyond that boundary; you must not go within eighteen miles of that frontier; you must not dwell in that town; you must live only in that province"? I do not know how anyone can believe that the whole population can fail to be affected in its inmost soul by such laws; and if it be possible to make it worse, this is the mode and the discipline to make it so.

They bring these accusations against the Russian Jews; why do they not bring them against the Jews of Germany? By the acknowledgment of the anti-Semitic movement, the Jews in Germany rise head and shoulders above their fellows. Why do they not bring these accusations against the Jews of France? Is there any career of public utility, any path of honor, civil or military, in which the Jews have not stood side by side with their countrymen? If the charge is brought against the Jews of Russia, who will bring it against the Jews of England? For uprightness, for refinement, for generosity, for charity, for all the graces and virtues that adorn humanity, where will be found examples brighter or more true of human excellence than in this Hebrew race? And when we are told that the accounts of those atrocities are not to be trusted, I ask if there were to appear in the newspapers long and minute narratives of murder, rapine, and other atrocities round about the Egyptian hall, in Old Jewry, in Houndsditch, in Shoreditch, if it were alleged that the Lord Mayor was looking on, that the metropolitan police did nothing, that the guards at the Tower were seen mingled with the mob, I believe you would thank any man who gave you an opportunity of exposing and contradicting the statement.

There is a book, my lord, which is common to the race of Israel and to us Christians. That book is a bond between us, and in that book I read that the people of Israel are the eldest people upon the earth. Russia, and Austria, and England of yesterday compared with the imperishable people which, with an inextinguishable life and immutable traditions, and faith in God and in the laws of God, scattered as it is all over the world, passing through the fires unscathed, trampled into the dust, and yet never combining with the dust into which it is trampled, lives still a witness and a warning to us. We are in the bonds of brotherhood with it. The New Testament rests upon the Old. They believe in half of that for which we would give our lives. Let us then acknowledge that we unite in a common sympathy. I read in that book these words, "I am angry with a great anger with the wealthy nations that are at ease, because I was a little angry with Israel, and they helped forward the affliction." That is, my people were scattered; they suffered unknown and unimaginable sufferings, and the nations of the world that dwell at ease and were wealthy, and had power in their hands, helped forward a very weighty affliction which was upon them all.

My lord, I only hope this—that not one man in England who calls himself a civilized or Christian man will have it in his heart to add by a single word to that which this great and ancient and noble people suffer; but that we shall do all we can by labor, by speech, and by prayer to lessen if it be possible, or at least to keep ourselves from sharing in sympathy with these atrocious deeds.

Joseph Chamberlain
[1836–1914]

*Joseph Chamberlain (father of Austen and Neville Chamberlain)
was a militant advocate of conservative policies at home and abroad.
He was an outspoken imperialist and vigorously pursued the expansion
of the British empire while colonial secretary and prominent member
of various Tory governments. Here are some of his views expressed
as principal guest at a dinner given in London on November 6, 1895,
to celebrate the completion of the Natal-Transvaal Railway.*

THE BRITISH EMPIRE

THIS OCCASION has been honored by the presence of the representatives of
sister colonies, who are here to offer words of sympathy and encouragement; and, in view of the representative character of the gathering, I
think, perhaps, I may be permitted, especially as this is the first occasion
upon which I have publicly appeared in my capacity as Minister for the
colonies [cheers] to offer a few words of general application. ["Hear!
Hear!"]

I think it will not be disputed that we are approaching a critical
stage in the history of the relations between ourselves and the self-
governing colonies. We are entering upon a chapter of our colonial
history, the whole of which will probably be written in the next few
years, certainly in the lifetime of the next generation, and which will be
one of the most important in our colonial annals, since upon the events
and policy which it describes will depend the future of the British
Empire. That Empire, gentlemen, that world-wide dominion to which
no Englishman can allude without a thrill of enthusiasm and patriotism,
which has been the admiration, and perhaps the envy, of foreign
nations, hangs together by a thread so slender that it may well seem
that even a breath would sever it.

There have been periods in our history, not so very far distant, when
leading statesmen, despairing of the possibility of maintaining anything
in the nature of a permanent union, have looked forward to the time
when the vigorous communities to which they rightly intrusted the
control of their own destinies would grow strong and independent,
would assert their independence, and would claim entire separation from
the parent stem. The time to which they looked forward has arrived
sooner than they expected. The conditions to which they referred have
been more than fulfilled; and now these great communities, which have
within them every element of national life, have taken their rank amongst
the nations of the world; and I do not suppose that any one would
consider the idea of compelling them to remain within the Empire as
within the region of intelligent speculation. Yet, although, as I have

said, the time has come, and the conditions have been fulfilled, the results which these statesmen anticipated have not followed. [Cheers.] They felt, perhaps, overwhelmed by the growing burdens of the vast dominions of the British Crown. They may well have shrunk from the responsibilities and the obligations which they involve; and so it happened that some of them looked forward not only without alarm, but with hopeful expectation, to a severance of the union which now exists.

But if such feelings were ever entertained they are entertained no longer. [Cheers.] As the possibility of separation has become greater, the desire for separation has become less. [Renewed cheers.] While we on our part are prepared to take our share of responsibility, and to do all that may fairly be expected from the mother country, and while we should look upon a separation as the greatest calamity that could befall us ["Hear! Hear!"] our fellow subjects on their part see to what a great inheritance they have come by mere virtue of their citizenship; and they must feel that no separate existence, however splendid, could compare with that which they enjoy equally with ourselves as joint heirs of all the traditions of the past, and as joint partakers of all the influence, resources and power of the British Empire. [Cheers.]

I rejoice at the change that has taken place. I rejoice at the wider patriotism, no longer confined to this small island, which embraces the whole of Greater Britain and which has carried to every clime British institutions and the best characteristics of the British race. [Renewed cheering.] How could it be otherwise? We have a common origin, we have a common history, a common language, a common literature, and a common love of liberty and law. We have common principles to assert, we have common interests to maintain. ["Hear! Hear!"] I said it was a slender thread that binds us together. I remember on one occasion having been shown a wire so fine and delicate that a blow might break it; yet I was told that it was capable of transmitting an electrical energy that would set powerful machinery in motion. May it not be the same with the relations which exist between the colonies and ourselves; and may not that thread of union be capable of carrying a force of sentiment and of sympathy which will yet be a potent factor in the history of the world? ["Hear! Hear!"]

There is a word which I am almost afraid to mention, lest at the very outset of my career I should lose my character as a practical statesman. I am told on every hand that Imperial Federation is a vain and empty dream. [Cries of "No! No!"] I will not contest that judgment, but I will say this: that that man must be blind, indeed, who does not see that it is a dream which has vividly impressed itself on the mind of the English-speaking race, and who does not admit that dreams of that kind, which have so powerful an influence upon the imagination of men, have somehow or another an unaccountable way of being realized in their own time. ["Hear! Hear!"] If it be a dream, it is a dream that appeals to the highest sentiments of patriotism, as well as to our material interests. It is a dream which is calculated to stimulate and to inspire every one who cares for the future of the Anglo-Saxon people. [Cheers.] I think myself that the spirit of the time is, at all events, in the direction of such a movement. How far it will carry us no man can tell; but, believe me, upon the temper and the tone in which we approach the solution of the problems which are now coming upon us depend the security and the maintenance of that world-wide dominion, that edifice of imperial rule, which has been so ably built for us by those who have gone before. [Cheers.]

Emmeline Pankhurst
[1858–1928]

One of the most eloquent and energetic leaders of the woman suffrage movement during the early part of this century was Emmeline Pankhurst. She was head of the "militants" of England and often braved arrest and prosecution in furthering the right of women to vote. The following is part of an address which she delivered in Hartford, Connecticut, on November 13, 1913.

MILITANT SUFFRAGISTS

I DO NOT COME here as an advocate, because whatever position the suffrage movement may occupy in the United States of America, in England it has passed beyond the realm of advocacy and it has entered into the sphere of practical politics. It has become the subject of revolution and civil war, and so to-night I am not here to advocate woman suffrage. American suffragists can do that very well for themselves. I am here as a soldier who has temporarily left the field of battle in order to explain—it seems strange it should have to be explained—what civil war is like when civil war is waged by women. I am not only here as a soldier temporarily absent from the field of battle; I am here—and that, I think, is the strangest part of my coming—I am here as a person who, according to the law courts of my country, it has been decided, is of no value to the community at all; and I am adjudged because of my life to be a dangerous person, under sentence of penal servitude in a convict prison. So you see there is some special interest in hearing so unusual a person address you. I dare say, in the minds of many of you —you will perphaps forgive me this personal touch—that I do not look either very like a soldier or very like a convict, and yet I am both.

It would take too long to trace the course of militant methods as adopted by women, because it is about eight years since the word militant was first used to describe what we were doing; it is about eight years since the first militant action was taken by women. It was not militant at all, except that it provoked militancy on the part of those who were opposed to it. When women asked questions in political meetings and failed to get answers, they were not doing anything militant. To ask questions at political meetings is an acknowledged right of all people who attend public meetings; certainly in my country, men have always done it, and I hope they do it in America, because it seems to me that if you allow people to enter your legislatures without asking them any questions as to what they are going to do when they get there you are not exercising your citizen rights and your citizen duties as you ought. At any rate in Great Britain it is a custom, a time-honored one, to ask questions of candidates for Parliament and ask questions of members of the government. No man was ever put out of a public meeting for asking a question until Votes for Women came onto the political horizon. The first people who were put out of a political meeting for asking questions, were women; they were brutally ill-used; they found themselves in jail before twenty-four hours had expired. But instead of the newspapers, which are largely inspired by the politicians, putting militancy and the reproach of militancy, if reproach there is, on the people who had assaulted the women, they actually said it was the women who were militant and very much to blame.

It was not the speakers on the platform who would not answer them, who were to blame, or the ushers at the meeting; it was the poor women who had had their bruises and their knocks and scratches, and who were put into prison for doing precisely nothing but holding a protest meeting in the street after it was all over. However, we were called militant for doing that, and we were quite willing to accept the name, because militancy for us is time-honored; you have the church militant and in the sense of spiritual militancy we were very militant indeed. We were determined to press this question of the enfranchise-ment of the women to the point where we were no longer to be ignored by the politicians as had been the case for about fifty years, during which time women had patiently used every means open to them to win their political enfranchisement.

Experience will show you that if you really want to get anything done, it is not so much a matter of whether you alienate sympathy; sympathy is a very unsatisfactory thing if it is not practical sympathy. It does not matter to the practical suffragist whether she alienates sym-pathy that was never of any use to her. What she wants is to get something practical done, and whether it is done out of sympathy or whether it is done out of fear, or whether it is done because you want to be comfortable again and not be worried in this way, doesn't par-ticularly matter so long as you get it. We had enough of sympathy for fifty years; it never brought us anything; and we would rather have an angry man going to the government and saying, my business is interfered with and I won't submit to its being interfered with any longer because you won't give women the vote, than to have a gentleman come onto our platforms year in and year out and talk about his ardent sympathy with woman suffrage.

"Put them in prison," they said; "that will stop it." But it didn't stop it. They put women in prison for long terms of imprisonment, for making a nuisance of themselves—that was the expression when they took petitions in their hands to the door of the House of Commons; and they thought that by sending them to prison, giving them a day's imprisonment, would cause them to all settle down again and there would be no further trouble. But it didn't happen so at all: instead of the women giving it up, more women did it, and more and more and more women did it until there were three hundred women at a time, who had not broken a single law, only "made a nuisance of themselves" as the politicians say.

The whole argument with the anti-suffragists, or even the critical suffragist man, is this: that you can govern human beings without their consent. They have said to us, "Government rests upon force; the women haven't force, so they must submit." Well, we are showing them that government does not rest upon force at all; it rests upon consent. As long as women consent to be unjustly governed, they can be; but directly women say: "We withhold our consent, we will not be governed any longer so long as that government is unjust," not by the forces of civil war can you govern the very weakest woman. You can kill that woman, but she escapes you then; you cannot govern her. And that is, I think, a most valuable demonstration we have been making to the world.

Now, I want to say to you who think women cannot succeed, we have brought the government of England to this position, that it has to face this alternative; either women are to be killed or women are to have the vote. I ask American men in this meeting, what would you say if in your State you were faced with that alternative, that you must either kill them or give them their citizenship,—women, many of whom you respect, women whom you know have lived useful lives, women whom you know, even if you do not know them personally, are animated with the highest motives, women who are in pursuit of liberty and the power to do useful public service? Well, there is only one answer to that alternative; there is only one way out of it, unless you are prepared to put back civilization two or three generations; you must give those women the vote. Now that is the outcome of our civil war.

You won your freedom in America when you had the Revolution, by bloodshed, by sacrificing human life. You won the Civil War by the sacrifice of human life when you decided to emancipate the negro. You have left it to the women in your land, the men of all civilized countries have left it to women, to work out their own salvation. That is the way in which we women of England are doing. Human life for us is sacred, but we say if any life is to be sacrificed it shall be ours; we won't do it ourselves, but we will put the enemy in the position where they will have to choose between giving us freedom or giving us death.

Sir Edward Grey
[1862–1933]

England's dramatic efforts for peace just before the outbreak of the First World War were revealed in an historic address before the House of Commons on August 3, 1914, by Sir Edward Grey, Secretary of State for Foreign Affairs. Parts of this address follow.

ENGLAND'S POSITION

IN THE PRESENT CRISIS, it has not been possible to secure the peace of Europe; because there has been little time, and there has been a disposition—at any rate in some quarters on which I will not dwell—to force things rapidly to an issue, at any rate, to the great risk of peace, and, as we now know, the result of that is that the policy of peace, as far as the Great Powers are concerned, is in danger. I do not want to dwell on that, and to comment on it, and to say where the blame seems to lie, which Powers were most in favor of peace, which were most disposed to risk or endanger peace, because I would like the House to approach this crisis in which we are now, from the point of view of British interests, British honor, and British obligations, free from all passion as to why peace has not been preserved.

It now appears from the news I have received to-day—which has come quite recently, and I am not yet quite sure how far it has reached me in an accurate form—that an ultimatum has been given to Belgium by Germany, the object of which was to offer Belgium friendly relations with Germany on condition that she would facilitate the passage of German troops through Belgium. Well, Sir, until one has these things absolutely definitely, up to the last moment, I do not wish to say all that one would say if one were in a position to give the House full, complete, and absolute information upon the point. We were sounded in the course of last week as to whether if a guarantee were given that, after the war, Belgian integrity would be preserved that would content us. We replied that we could not bargain away whatever interests or obligations we had in Belgian neutrality.

We have great and vital interests in the independence—and integrity is the least part—of Belgium. If Belgium is compelled to submit to allow her neutrality to be violated, of course the situation is clear. Even if by agreement she admitted the violation of her neutrality, it is clear she could only do so under duress. The smaller states in that region of Europe ask but one thing. Their one desire is that they should be left alone and independent. The one thing they fear is, I think, not so much that their integrity but that their independence should be interfered with. If in this war which is before Europe the neutrality of one of those countries is violated, if the troops of one of the combatants violate its neutrality and no action can be taken to resent it, at the end of the war, whatever the integrity may be, the independence will be gone.

Sir, if it be the case that there has been anything in the nature of an ultimatum to Belgium, asking her to compromise or violate her neutrality, whatever may have been offered to her in return, her independence is gone if that holds. If her independence goes, the independence of Holland will follow. I ask the House from the point of view of British interests, to consider what may be at stake. If France is beaten in a struggle of life and death, beaten to her knees, loses her position as a great Power, becomes subordinate to the will and power of one greater than herself—consequences which I do not anticipate, because I am sure that France has the power to defend herself with all the energy and ability and patriotism which she has shown so often—still, if that were to happen, and if Belgium fell under the same dominating influence, and then Holland, and then Denmark, then would not Mr. Gladstone's words come true, that just opposite to us there would be a common interest against the unmeasured aggrandizement of any Power.

It may be said, I suppose, that we might stand aside, husband our strength, and whatever happened in the course of this war, at the end of it intervene with effect to put things right, and to adjust them to our own point of view. If, in a crisis like this, we run away from those obligations of honor and interest as regards the Belgian Treaty, I doubt whether, whatever material force we might have at the end, it would be of very much value in face of the respect that we should have lost. And I do not believe, whether a great Power stands outside this war or not, it is going to be in a position at the end of it to exert its superior strength. For us, with a powerful fleet, which we believe able to protect our commerce, to protect our shores, and to protect our interests, if we are engaged in war, we shall suffer but little more than we shall suffer even if we stand aside.

There is but one way in which the Government could make certain at the present moment of keeping outside this war, and that would be that it should immediately issue a proclamation of unconditional neutrality. We cannot do that. We have made the commitment to France that I have read to the House which prevents us from doing that. We have got the consideration of Belgium which prevents us also from any unconditional neutrality, and, without those conditions absolutely satisfied and satisfactory, we are bound not to shrink from proceeding to the use of all the forces in our power. If we did take that line by saying, "We will have nothing whatever to do with this matter under any conditions"—the Belgian treaty obligations, the possible position in the Mediterranean, with damage to British interests, and what may happen to France from our failure to support France—if we were to say that all these things mattered nothing, were as nothing, and to say we would stand aside, we should, I believe, sacrifice our respect and good name and reputation before the world, and should not escape the most serious and grave economic consequences.

The most awful responsibility is resting upon the Government in deciding what to advise the House of Commons to do. We have disclosed our mind to the House of Commons. We have disclosed the issue, the information which we have, and made clear to the House, I trust, that we are prepared to face that situation, and that should it develop, as probably it may develop, we will face it. We worked for peace up to the last moment, and beyond the last moment. How hard, how persistently, and how earnestly we strove for peace last week, the House will see from the Papers that will be before it.

But that is over, as far as the peace of Europe is concerned. We are now face to face with a situation and all the consequences which it may yet have to unfold. We believe we shall have the support of the House at large in proceeding to whatever the consequence may be and whatever measures may be forced upon us by the development of facts or action taken by others.

I have put the vital facts before the House, and if, as seems not improbable, we are forced, and rapidly forced, to take our stand upon those issues, then I believe, when the country realizes what is at stake, what the real issues are, the magnitude of the impending dangers in the West of Europe, which I have endeavored to describe to the House, we shall be supported throughout, not only by the House of Commons, but by the determination, the resolution, the courage, and the endurance of the whole country.

David Lloyd George
[1863–1945]

David Lloyd George, who became Prime Minister during the First World War, was noted for his rough-and-tumble oratory which won him many triumphs in Parliament and in public meetings. Here are portions of his famous "Appeal to the Nation," probably the greatest speech of his career. He delivered it at Queen's Hall, on September 19, 1914, while he was Commissioner of Munitions.

AN APPEAL TO THE NATION

THERE IS NO MAN in this room who has always regarded the prospect of engaging in a great war with greater reluctance and with greater repugnance than I have done throughout the whole of my political life. ["Hear, hear!"] There is no man either inside or outside this room more convinced that we could not have avoided it without national dishonor. [Great applause.] I am fully alive to the fact that every nation that has ever engaged in war has always invoked the sacred name of honor. Many a crime has been committed in its name; there are some being committed now. All the same, national honor is a reality, and any nation that disregards it is doomed. ["Hear, hear!"] Why is our honor as a country involved in this war? Because, in the first instance, we are bound by honorable obligations to defend the independence, the liberty, the integrity, of a small neighbor that has always lived peaceably. [Applause.] She could not have compelled us; she was weak; but the man who declines to discharge his duty because his creditor is too poor to enforce it is a blackguard. [Loud applause.] We entered into a treaty—a solemn treaty—two treaties—to defend Belgium and her integrity. Our signatures are attached to the documents. Our signatures do not stand there alone; this country was not the only country that undertook to defend the integrity of Belgium. Russia, France, Austria, Prussia—they are all there. Why are Austria and Prussia not performing the obligations of their bond? It is suggested that when we quote this treaty it is purely an excuse on our part—it is our low craft and cunning to cloak our jealousy of a superior civilization—[Laughter]—that we are attempting to destroy.

It is the interest of Prussia to break the treaty, and she has done it. [Hisses.] She avows it with cynical contempt for every principle of justice. She says "Treaties only bind you when your interest is to keep them." [Laughter.] "What is a treaty?" says the German Chancellor; "A scrap of paper." Have you any £5 notes about you? [Laughter and applause.] I am not calling for them. [Laughter.] Have you any of those neat little Treasury £1 notes? [Laughter.] If you have, burn them; they are only scraps of paper. [Laughter and applause.] What are they made of? Rags. [Laughter.] What are they worth? The whole credit of the British Empire. [Loud applause.] Scraps of paper! I have been dealing with scraps of paper within the last month. One suddenly found the commerce of the world coming to a standstill. The machine had stopped. Why? I will tell you. We discovered—many of us for the first time, for I do not pretend that I do not know much more about the machinery of commerce to-day than I did six weeks ago, and there are many others like me—we discovered that the machinery of commerce was moved by bills of exchange. I have seen some of them— [Laughter]—wretched, crinkled, scrawled over, blotched, frowsy, and yet those wretched little scraps of paper move great ships laden with thousands of tons of precious cargo from one end of the world to the other. [Applause.] What is the motive power behind them? The honor of commercial men. [Applause.] Treaties are the currency of International statesmanship. [Applause.] Let us be fair: German merchants, German traders, have the reputation of being as upright and straightforward as any traders in the world—["Hear, hear!"]—but if the currency of German commerce is to be debased to the level of that of her statesmanship, no trader from Shanghai to Valparaiso will ever look at a German signature again. [Loud applause.] This doctrine of the scrap of paper, this doctrine which is proclaimed by Bernhardi, that treaties only bind a nation as long as it is to its interest, goes under the root of all public law. It is the straight road to barbarism. ["Hear, hear!"] It is as if you were to remove the Magnetic Pole because it was in the way of a German cruiser. [Laughter.] The whole navigation of the seas would become dangerous, difficult, and impossible; and the whole machinery of civilization will break down if this doctrine wins in this way. ["Hear, hear!"] We are fighting against barbarism [Applause] and there is one way of putting it right. If there are nations that say they will only respect treaties when it is to their interest to do so, we must make it to their interest to do so for the future. [Applause.]

What is their defense? Consider the interview which took place between our Ambassador and the great German officials. When their attention was called to this treaty to which they were parties, they said, "We cannot help that. Rapidity of action is the great German asset." There is a greater asset for a nation than rapidity of action and that is honest dealing. [Loud applause.] What are Germany's excuses? She says Belgium was plotting against her; Belgium was engaged in a great conspiracy with Britain and France to attack her. Not merely is it not true, but Germany knows it is not true. ["Hear, hear!"] France offered Belgium five army corps to defend her if she was attacked. Belgium said, "I do not require them; I have the word of the Kaiser. Shall Cæsar send a lie?" [Laughter and applause.] All these tales about conspiracy have been vamped up since. A great nation ought to be ashamed to behave like a fraudulent bankrupt, perjuring its way through its obligations. ["Hear, hear!"] What she says is not true. She has deliberately broken this treaty, and we are in honor bound to stand by it. [Applause.]

Belgium has been treated brutally. ["Hear, hear!"] How brutally we shall not yet know. We already know too much. What had she done? Had she sent an ultimatum to Germany? Had she challenged Germany? Was she preparing to make war on Germany? Had she inflicted any wrong upon Germany which the Kaiser was bound to redress? She was one of the most unoffending little countries in Europe. ["Hear, hear!"] There she was—peaceable, industrious, thrifty, hard-working, giving offense to no one. And her cornfields have been trampled, her villages have been burnt, her art treasures have been destroyed, her men have been slaughtered—yea, and her women and children too. [Cries of "Shame."] Hundreds and thousands of her people, their neat comfortable little homes burnt to the dust, are wandering homeless in their own land. What was their crime? Their crime was that they trusted to the word of a Prussian King. [Applause.]

Have you read the Kaiser's speeches? If you have not a copy I advise you to buy one; they will soon be out of print, and you will not have many more of the same sort. [Laughter and applause.] They are full of the glitter and bluster of German militarism—"mailed fist," and "shining armor." Poor old mailed fist. Its knuckles are getting a little bruised. Poor shining armor! The shine is being knocked out of it. [Applause.] There is the same swagger and boastfulness running through the whole of the speeches.

Treaties? They tangle the feet of Germany in her advance. Cut them with the sword. Little nations? They hinder the advance of Germany. Trample them in the mire under the German heel! The Russian Slav? He challenges the supremacy of Germany in Europe. Hurl your legions at him and massacre him! Christianity? Sickly sentimentalism about sacrifice for others! Poor pap for German digestion! We will have a new diet. We will force it upon the world. It will be made in Germany [Laughter and applause]—a diet of blood and iron. What remains? Treaties have gone. The honor of nations has gone. Liberty has gone. What is left? Germany! Germany is left!—*"Deutschland über Alles!"*

They think we cannot beat them. It will not be easy. It will be a long job; it will be a terrible war; but in the end we shall march through terror to triumph. [Applause.] We shall need all our qualities —every quality that Britain and its people possess—prudence in counsel, daring in action, tenacity in purpose, courage in defeat, moderation in victory; in all things faith. [Loud applause.]

Arthur James Balfour
[1848–1930]

Noted as a great scholar and statesman, Arthur James Balfour was also a brilliant speaker and debater. He held many high offices, and was Prime Minister from 1902 to 1905. This tribute to the United States was delivered in a Fourth of July celebration in London in 1917.

THE FOURTH OF JULY

ON THIS ANNIVERSARY in every part of the world American citizens meet together and renew, as it were, their vows of devotion to the great ideals which have animated them. All the world admires, and all the world sympathizes with the vast work of the great American Republic. All the world looks back upon the one hundred forty-one years which have elapsed since the Declaration of Independence and sees in that one hundred forty-one years an expansion in the way of population,. in the way of wealth and of power, material and spiritual, which is unexampled in that period, and, as far as I know, in the history of the world.

We of the British race, who do not fall short of the rest of the world in our admiration in this mighty work, look at it in some respects in a different way, and must look at it in a different way, from that of other people. From one point of view we have surely a right to look at it with a special satisfaction, a satisfaction born of the fact that, after all, the thirteen colonies were British colonies; that the thirteen colonies, in spite of small controversies, grew up broadly speaking, under the protection of England; that it was our wars, the English wars with Spain in the sixteenth century, with Holland in the seventeenth century, and with France in the eighteenth century, which gave that security from external European attack which enabled those thirteen colonies to develop into the nucleus of the great community of which they were the origin.

We British may also surely, without undue vanity, pride ourselves on the fact that the men who founded the great American Republic, the men whose genius contrived its constitution, their forefathers who, struggling in the wilderness, gradually developed the basis of all that has happened since, were men speaking the English language, obeying and believing in English laws, and nourished upon English literature; and although we may say that the originality and power and endurance were theirs, they were men of our own race, born of the same stock, and to that extent as least we may feel that we have some small and not insignificant part in the great development which the world owes to their genius, courage, and love of liberty.

In that sense we may well look with peculiar pride and satisfaction upon this great anniversary. There is, of course, another side to the question. The Fourth of July is the anniversary of the separation, the final political separation—not, thank God, the final separation in sentiment, in emotion, or in ideal—but the final separation between the thirteen colonies and the Mother Country. We of the Mother Country cannot look back on that event as representing one of our successes. No doubt there was something to be said, though perhaps it is not often said, for those on this side of the Atlantic who fought for unity, who desired to preserve the unity of the Empire. Unity is a cause for which the American people have sacrificed rivers of blood and infinite treasure.

I am not going into ancient history, but the mistake we made, an almost inevitable mistake at that particular period of the development of the history of the world, was in supposing that unity was possible so long as one part of the Empire which you tried to unite, speaking the same language, having the same traditions and laws, having the same love of liberty and the same ideals, would consent to remain a part of the Empire except on absolutely equal terms. That was a profound mistake, a mistake which produced a great schism and produced all the collateral, though I am glad to think subordinate, evils which followed on that great schism.

All I can say in excuse for my forefathers is that, utterly defective as the colonial policy of Great Britain in the middle of the eighteenth century undoubtedly was, it was far better than the colonial policy of any other country. Imperfectly as we conceived the kind of relations that might, or could, bind the colonies to their Mother Country, thoroughly as we misconceived them, we misconceived them less than most of our neighbors.

If I rightly read the signs of the times, a truer perspective and a more charitable perspective is now recognized and felt by all the heirs of these sad and ancient glories. Heaven knows I do not grudge the glories of Washington and his brother soldiers. I do not shed tears over the British defeat which ended in the triumphant establishment of the American Republic. I do not express any regrets on that subject. My only regrets are that the memories of it should carry with them the smallest trace of bitterness on our side. I do not know why there should be. I think it may properly carry memories of triumph on your side, but it should be a triumph seen in its true perspective, and by this true perspective seen in such a way that it does not interfere with the continuity of history in the development of free institutions, and with the consciousness of common kinship and common ideals, and the considerations which ought to bind us together, and which have bound us together, and which year by year, generation by generation, and century by century are going to bind us still closer in the future.

James Ramsay MacDonald
[1866–1937]

England's participation in the First World War was vigorously opposed by James Ramsay MacDonald, labor parliamentarian who later became Prime Minister. He favored a negotiated peace, and when peace came through victory he favored a generous and lasting peace. Here are his views as expressed in 1919 before the Labor Party Conference.

PEACE

TODAY, as I read about the Peace, as I hoped and prayed about the Peace, I thought of the almost countless graves scattered in the centre of Europe. Many of our children are lying there. It must be in the hearts of all of us to build a fair monument to those men who will never come back to bless us with their smiles. Do they not want a grand and magnificent monument built for them so that the next generations, even if they forget their names, shall never forget their sacrifice? That is what I want. I almost felt I heard the grass growing over them in a magnificent, soothing harmony, and that simple soothing peace of the growing grass seemed to grow louder and more magnificent until the riot and distractive sound of the guns were stifled and stilled by it. Can we not have that sentiment today, that feeling in our hearts? Can we not go in imagination to where our children lie, and feel that, in Europe, in our own hearts, that same peace shall rule, and through sorrow and through sacrifice we shall obtain that wisdom and light which will enable Europe to possess peace for ever?

Lady Astor
[1879–1964]

Lady Astor, American born (Nancy Langhorne), was the first woman to be elected to the British House of Commons. She was known as a keen debater and forceful speaker. Parts of an address which she delivered at Town Hall, New York City, on April 9, 1922, follow.

WOMEN IN POLITICS

My entrance into the House of Commons was not, as some thought, in the nature of a revolution. It was an evolution. My husband was the one who started me off on this downward path—from the fireside to public life. If I have helped the cause of women he is the one to thank, not me.

A woman in the House of Commons! It was almost enough to have broken up the House. I don't blame them—it was equally hard on the woman as it was on them. A pioneer may be a picturesque figure, but they are often rather lonely ones. I must say for the House of Commons, they bore their shock with dauntless decency. No body of men could have been kinder and fairer to a "pirate" than they were. When you hear people over here trying to run down England, please remember that England was the first large country to give the vote to women and that the men of England welcomed an American born woman in the House with a fairness and a justice which, at least, this woman never will forget.

Women and politics—some women have always been in politics, and have not done badly, either. It was when we had the Lancastrian Kings that it was said that the Kings were made Kings by act of Parliament— they did rule by means of Parliament. Then Henry VIII., that old scalawag, accepted the principles of the Lancastrians to rule by Parliament, but he wanted the principle in an entirely different way. He made Parliament the engine of his will: he pressed or frightened it into doing anything he wished. Under his guidance Parliament defied and crushed all other powers, spiritually and temporally, and he did things which no King or Parliament ever attempted to do—things unheard of and terrible.

Then Elizabeth came along. It is true she scolded her Parliament for meddling with matters with which, in her opinion, they had no concern, and more than once soundly rated the Speaker of her Commons, but she never carried her quarrels too far, and was able to end her disputes by some clever compromise; in other words, she never let Parliament down, and that is what I don't believe any wise woman will do in spite of the fears of some of the men.

Now, why are we in politics? What is it all about? Something much bigger than ourselves. Schopenhauer was wrong in nearly everything he wrote about women—and he wrote a lot, but he was right in one thing. He said, in speaking of women, "the race is to her more than the individual," and I believe that it is true. I feel somehow we do care about the race as a whole, our very nature makes us take a forward vision; there is no reason why women should look back—mercifully we have no political past; we have all the mistakes of sex legislation with its appalling failures to guide us.

We should know what to avoid, it is no use blaming the men—we made them what they are—and now it is up to us to try and make ourselves—the makers of men—a little more responsible in the future. We realize that no one sex can govern alone. I believe that one of the reasons why civilization has failed so lamentably is that it has had a one-sided government. Don't let us make the mistake of ever allowing that to happen again.

I can conceive of nothing worse than a man-governed world except a woman-governed world—but I can see the combination of the two going forward and making civilization more worthy of the name of civilization based on Christianity, not force. A civilization based on justice and mercy. I feel men have a greater sense of justice and we of mercy. They must borrow our mercy and we must use their justice. We are new brooms; let us see that we sweep the right rooms.

George Bernard Shaw

[1856-1950]

When George Bernard Shaw, the noted playwright and man of letters, was seventy years old on July 26, 1926, the Parliamentary Labor Party gave a dinner in his honor, James Ramsay MacDonald presiding. The government had prohibited the broadcasting of Mr. Shaw's speech on this occasion because it might be "partisan." This gave the Irish wit a fine opportunity to lambaste the government and censorship, which he did in his inimitable style.

ON HIS SEVENTIETH BIRTHDAY

OF LATE YEARS the public have been trying to tackle me in every way they possibly can, and failing to make anything of it they have turned to treating me as a great man. This is a dreadful fate to overtake anybody. There has been a distinct attempt to do it again now, and for that reason I absolutely decline to say anything about the celebration of my seventieth birthday. But when the Labor Party, my old friends the Labor Party, invited me here I knew that I should be all right. We have discovered the secret that there are no great men, and we have discovered the secret that there are no great nations or great States.

We leave that kind of thing to the nineteenth century, where they properly belong. Here you all know that I am an extraordinarily clever fellow at my job. But I have not got the "great-man feeling." You have not got it either. My predecessor in my professional business, Shakespeare, lived in a middle-class set, but there was one person in that set who was not a middle-class man. He was a bricklayer, and when, after Shakespeare's death, the middle class generally started to celebrate Shakespeare by issuing a folio edition of his works (I haven't come to that yet, but I have no doubt some one will do it), all the middle class generally wrote magnificent songs about the greatness of Shakespeare. Curiously enough, the only tribute ever quoted or remembered to-day is the tribute of the bricklayer, who said: "I liked the man as well as anybody did this side of idolatry."

When I began as a young man Labor was attached to Liberalism and to Radicalism. Now Liberalism had its traditions, the traditions of 1649, of 1798, of 1848, and those traditions are still rampant in what is called the Communist Party. What were those traditions? Those traditions were barricades, civil war and regicide. Those are the genuine Liberal traditions [laughter], and the only reason that we can't say they exist to-day is that the Liberal Party itself has ceased to exist.

The Radical Party was publican and atheist, and its great principle was in the great historical phrase, that the world would never be at peace until the last king was strangled in the entrails of the last priest. When asked to put it a little more explicitly, and to put it into practical politics, they said that the world was full of tribulation and injustice because the Archbishop of Canterbury got fifteen thousand a year and because perpetual pensions were enjoyed by the descendants of Charles II's mistresses.

Now, however, we have built up a Constitutional Party. We have built it up on a socialistic basis. My friend, Mr. Sidney Webb, Mr. MacDonald and myself said definitely at the beginning that what we had got to do was to make the Socialist Party a constitutional party to which any respectable God-fearing man could belong without the slightest compromise of his respectability. We got rid of all those traditions; that is why Governments in the present day are more afraid of us than they were of any of the Radical people.

Our position is a perfectly simple one and we have the great advantage of understanding our position. We oppose socialism to capitalism, and our great difficulty is that capitalists have not the slightest notion of what capitalism means. Yet it is a very simple thing. It is a theory of the Socialist Party that if you will take care of private property and if you will make all the sources of production as private property and maintain them as private property, in so far as that is a contract made between persons on that basis, then production will take care of itself and distribution will take care of itself.

According to the capitalists, there will be a guarantee to the world that every man in the country would get a job. They didn't contend it would be a well-paid job, because if it was well paid a man would save up enough one week to stop working the next week, and they were determined to keep a man working the whole time on a bare subsistence wage—and, on the other hand, divide an accumulation of capital.

They said capitalism not only secured this for the working man, but, by insuring fabulous wealth in the hands of a small class of people, they would save money whether they liked it or not and would have to invest it. That is capitalism, and this Government is always interfering with capitalism. Instead of giving a man a job or letting him starve they are giving him doles—after making sure he has paid for them first. They are giving capitalists subsidies and making all sorts of regulations that are breaking up their own system. All the time they are doing it, and we are telling them it is breaking up, they don't understand.

We say in criticism of capitalism: Your system has never kept its promises for one single day since it was promulgated. Our production is ridiculous. We are producing eighty horsepower motor cars when many more houses should be built. We are producing most extravagant luxuries while children starve. You have stood production on its head. Instead of beginning with the things the nation needs most, you are beginning at just the opposite end. We say distribution has become so glaringly ridiculous that there are only two people out of the 47,000,000 people in this country who approve of the present system of distribution—one is the Duke of Northumberland and the other is Lord Banbury.

We are opposed to that theory. Socialism, which is perfectly clear and unmistakable, says the thing you have got to take care of is your distribution. We have to begin with that, and private property, if it stands in the way of good distribution, has got to go.

A man who holds public property must hold it on the public condition on which, for instance, I carry my walking stick. I am not allowed to do what I like with it. I must not knock you on the head with it. We say that if distribution goes wrong, everything else goes wrong—religion, morals, government. And we say, therefore (this is the whole meaning of our socialism), we must begin with distribution and take all the necessary steps.

I think we are keeping it in our minds because our business is to take care of the distribution of wealth in the world; and I tell you, as I have told you before, that I don't think there are two men, or perhaps one man, in our 47,000,000 who approves of the existing distribution of wealth. I will go even further and say that you will not find a single person in the whole of the civilized world who agrees with the existing system of the distribution of wealth. It has been reduced to a blank absurdity. You can prove that by asking any intelligent middle-class man if he thinks it right that he should go begging for a civil list pension while a baby in its cradle is being fought over in the law courts because it has only got six millions to be brought up on.

The first problem of distribution is distribution to the baby. It must have a food income and a better income than anybody else's income if the new generation is to be a first-class generation. Yet a baby has no morals, no character, no industry, and it hasn't even common decency. [Laughter.] And it is to that abandoned person that the first duty of the Government is due. That is a telling example of this question of distribution. It reaches our question, which really is a question which is going to carry us to triumph.

I think the day will come when we will be able to make the distinction between us and the capitalists. We must get certain leading ideas before the people. We should announce that we are not going in for what was the old-fashioned idea of redistribution, but the redistribution of income. Let it always be a question of income.

I have been very happy here to-night. I entirely understand the distinction made by our chairman to-night when he said you hold me in social esteem and a certain amount of personal affection. I am not a sentimental man, but I am not insensible to all that. I know the value of all that, and it gives me, now that I have come to the age of seventy (it will not occur again and I am saying it for the last time), a great feeling of pleasure that I can say what a good many people can't say.

I know now that when I was a young man and took the turning that led me into the Labor Party, I took the right turning in every sense.

Daniel O'Connell
[1755-1847]

Daniel O'Connell, the great Irish statesman, was known as the Liberator of Ireland. Largely through his efforts the right of Catholics to equal treatment with Protestants was recognized. As leader of The Catholic Association and eloquent spokesman for his people in parliament, O'Connell succeeded in causing the enactment of several reforms in the treatment of Ireland by the British. O'Connell delivered the following speech in the House of Commons on February 4, 1836.

JUSTICE FOR IRELAND

IT APPEARS to me impossible to suppose that the House will consider me presumptuous in wishing to be heard for a short time on this question, especially after the distinct manner in which I have been alluded to in the course of the debate. If I had no other excuse, that would be sufficient; but I do not want it; I have another and a better—the question is one in the highest degree interesting to the people of Ireland. It is, whether we mean to do justice to that country—whether we mean to continue the injustice which has been already done to it, or to hold out the hope that it will be treated in the same manner as England and Scotland. That is the question. We know what "lip service" is; we do not want that. There are some men who will even declare that they are willing to refuse justice to Ireland; while there are others who, though they are ashamed to say so, are ready to consummate the iniquity, and they do so.

England never did do justice to Ireland—she never did. What we have got of it we have extorted from men opposed to us on principle —against which principle they have made us such concessions as we have obtained from them. The right honorable baronet opposite [Sir Robert Peel] says he does not distinctly understand what is meant by a principle. I believe him. He advocated religious exclusion on religious motives; he yielded that point at length, when we were strong enough to make it prudent for him to do so.

Here am I calling for justice to Ireland; but there is a coalition to-night—not a base unprincipled one—God forbid!—it is an extremely natural one; I mean that between the right honorable baronet and the noble lord the member for North Lancashire [Lord Stanley]. It is a natural coalition, and it is impromptu; for the noble lord informs us he had not even a notion of taking the part he has until the moment at which he seated himself where he now is. I know his candor; he told us it was a sudden inspiration which induced him to take part against Ireland. I believe it with the most potent faith, because I know that he requires no preparation for voting against the interests of the Irish people. [Groans.] I thank you for that groan—it is just of a piece with the rest. I regret much that I have been thrown upon arguing this particular question, because I should have liked to have dwelt upon the speech which has been so graciously delivered from the throne to-day—to have gone into its details, and to have pointed out the many great and beneficial alterations and amendments in our existing institutions which it hints at and recommends to the House. The speech of last year was full of reforms in words, and in words only; but this speech contains the great leading features of all the salutary reforms the country wants; and if they are worked out fairly and honestly in detail, I am convinced the country will require no further amelioration of its institutions, and that it will become the envy and admiration of the world. I, therefore, hail the speech with great satisfaction.

It has been observed that the object of a king's speech is to say as little in as many words as possible; but this speech contains more things than words—it contains those great principles which, adopted in practice, will be most salutary not only to the British Empire, but to the world. When speaking of our foreign policy, it rejoices in the coöperation between France and this country; but it abstains from conveying any ministerial approbation of alterations in the domestic laws of that country which aim at the suppression of public liberty, and the checking of public discussion, such as call for individual reprobation, and which I reprobate as much as any one. I should like to know whether there is a statesman in the country who will get up in this House and avow his approval of such proceedings on the part of the French government. I know it may be done out of the House amid the cheers of an assembly of friends; but the government have, in my opinion, wisely abstained from reprobating such measures in the speech, while they have properly exulted in such a union of the two countries as will contribute to the national independence and the public liberty of Europe.

Years are coming over me, but my heart is as young and as ready as ever in the service of my country, of which I glory in being the pensionary and the hired advocate. I stand in a situation in which no man ever stood yet—the faithful friend of my country—its servant— its slave, if you will—I speak its sentiments by turns to you and to itself. I require no £20,000,000 on behalf of Ireland—I ask you only for justice: will you—can you—I will not say dare you refuse, because that would make you turn the other way. I implore you, as English gentlemen, to take this matter into consideration now, because you never had such an opportunity of conciliating. Experience makes fools wise; you are not fools, but you have yet to be convinced. I cannot forget the year 1825. We begged then as we would for a beggar's boon; we asked for emancipation by all that is sacred amongst us, and I remember how my speech and person were treated on the Treasury Bench, when I had no opportunity of reply. The other place turned us out and sent us back again, but we showed that justice was with us. The noble lord says the other place has declared the same sentiments with himself; but he could not use a worse argument. It is the very reason why we should acquiesce in the measure of reform, for we have no hope from that House—all our hopes are centered in this; and I am the living representative of those hopes. I have no other reason for adhering to the ministry than because they, the chosen representatives of the people of England, are anxiously determined to give the same measure of reform to Ireland as that which England has received. I have not fatigued myself, but the House, in coming forward upon this occasion. I may be laughed and sneered at by those who talk of my power; but what has created it but the injustice that has been done in Ireland? That is the end and the means of the magic, if you please—the groundwork of my influence in Ireland. If you refuse justice to that country, it is a melancholy consideration to me to think that you are adding substantially to that power and in-fluence, while you are wounding my country to its very heart's core; weakening that throne, the monarch who sits upon which, you say you respect; severing that union which, you say, is bound together by the tightest links, and withholding that justice from Ireland which she will not cease to seek till it is obtained; every man must admit that the course I am taking is the legitimate and proper course—I defy any man to say it is not. Condemn me elsewhere as much as you please, but this you must admit. You may taunt the ministry with having coalesced me, you may raise the vulgar cry of "Irishman and Papist" against me, you may send out men called ministers of

God to slander and calumniate me; they may assume whatever garb they please, but the question comes into this narrow compass. I demand, I respectfully insist on equal justice for Ireland, on the same principle by which it has been administered to Scotland and England. I will not take less. Refuse me that if you can.

Robert Emmet
[1778–1803]

Robert Emmet, Irish patriot, at an early age became the militant and eloquent leader of the United Irishmen. In 1803 he led an unsuccessful uprising in Dublin. His followers dispersed, but he was caught while trying to see and bid farewell to Sarah Curran, the girl he was engaged to marry. He was only twenty-five years old when the court convicted him of high treason and sentenced him to death. The following speech was an impromptu one, and was delivered on September 19, 1803.

PROTEST AGAINST SENTENCE AS TRAITOR

MY LORDS:—What have I to say why sentence of death should not be pronounced on me according to law? I have nothing to say that can alter your predetermination, nor that it will become me to say with any view to the mitigation of that sentence which you are here to pronounce, and I must abide by. But I have that to say which interests me more than life, and which you have labored (as was necessarily your office in the present circumstances of this oppressed country) to destroy. I have much to say why my reputation should be rescued from the load of false accusation and calumny which has been heaped upon it. I do not imagine that, seated where you are, your minds can be so free from impurity as to receive the least impression from what I am going to utter—I have no hopes that I can anchor my character in the breast of a court constituted and trammeled as this is—I only wish, and it is the utmost I expect, that your lordships may suffer it to float down your memories untainted by the foul breath of prejudice, until it finds some more hospitable harbor to shelter it from the storm by which it is at present buffeted.

Was I only to suffer death after being adjudged guilty by *your* tribunal, I should bow in silence, and meet the fate that awaits me without a murmur; but the sentence of law which delivers my body to the executioner, will, through the ministry of that law, labor in its own vindication to consign my character to obloquy—for there must be guilt somewhere: whether in the sentence of the court or in the catastrophe, posterity must determine. A man in my situation, my lords, has not only to encounter the difficulties of fortune, and the force of power over minds which it has corrupted or subjugated, but the difficulties of established prejudice: the man dies, but his memory lives. That mine may not perish, that it may live in the respect of my countrymen, I seize upon this opportunity to vindicate myself from some of the charges alleged against me. When my spirit shall be wafted to a more friendly port; when my shade shall have joined the bands of those martyred heroes who have shed their blood on the scaffold and in the field, in defense of their country and of virtue, this is my hope: I wish that my memory and name may animate those who survive me, while I look down with complacency on the destruction of that perfidious government which upholds its domination by blasphemy of the Most High—which displays its power over man as over the beasts of the forest—which sets man upon his brother, and lifts his hand in the name of God against the throat of his fellow who believes or doubts a little more or a little less than the government standard—a government which is steeled to barbarity by the cries of the orphans and the tears of the widows which it has made. [Interruption by the court.]

I appeal to the immaculate God—I swear by the throne of Heaven, before which I must shortly appear—by the blood of the murdered patriots who have gone before me—that my conduct has been through all this peril and all my purposes, governed only by the convictions which I have uttered, and by no other view, than that of their cure, and the emancipation of my country from the superinhuman oppression under which she has so long and too patiently travailed; and that I confidently and assuredly hope that, wild an chimerical as it may appear, there is still union and strength in Ireland to accomplish this noble enterprise. Of this I speak with the confidence of intimate knowledge, and with the consolation that appertains to that confidence. Think not, my lords, I say this for the petty gratification of giving you a transitory uneasiness; a man who never yet raised his voice to assert a lie, will not hazard his character with posterity by asserting a falsehood on a subject so important to his country, and on an occasion like this. Yes, my lords, a man who does not wish to have his epitaph written until his country is liberated, will not leave a weapon in the power of envy; nor a pretense to impeach the probity which he means to preserve even in the grave to which tyranny consigns him. [Interruption by the court.]

Again I say, that what I have spoken, was not intended for your lordship, whose situation I commiserate rather than envy—my expressions were for my countrymen; if there is a true Irishman present, let my last words cheer him in the hour of his affliction. [Interruption by the court.]

I have always understood it to be the duty of a judge when a prisoner has been convicted, to pronounce the sentence of the law; I have also understood that judges sometimes think it their duty to hear with patience, and to speak with humanity; to exhort the victim of the laws, and to offer with tender benignity his opinions of the motives by which he was actuated in the crime, of which he had been adjudged guilty: that a judge has thought it his duty so to have done, I have no doubt—but where is the boasted freedom of your institutions, where is the vaunted impartiality, clemency, and mildness of your courts of justice, if an unfortunate prisoner, whom your policy, and not pure justice, is about to deliver into the hands of the executioner, is not suffered to explain his motives sincerely and truly, and to vindicate the principles by which he was actuated?

My lords, it may be a part of the system of angry justice, to bow a man's mind by humiliation to the purposed ignominy of the scaffold; but worse to me than the purposed shame, or the scaffold's terrors, would be the shame of such unfounded imputations as have been laid against me in this court: you, my lord [Lord Norbury], are a judge, I am the supposed culprit; I am a man, you are a man also; by a revolution of power, we might change places, though we never could change characters; if I stand at the bar of this court, and dare not vindicate my character, what a farce is your justice? If I stand at this bar and dare not vindicate my character, how dare you calumniate it? Does the sentence of death which your unhallowed policy inflicts on my body, also condemn my tongue to silence and my reputation to reproach? Your executioner may abridge the period of my existence, but while I exist I shall not forbear to vindicate my character and motives from your aspersions; and as a man to whom fame is dearer than life, I will make the last use of that life in doing justice to that reputation which is to live after me, and which is the only legacy I can leave to those I honor and love, and for whom I am proud to perish. As men, my lord, we must appear at the great day at one common tribunal, and it will then remain for the searcher of all hearts to show a collective universe who was engaged in the most virtuous actions, or actuated by the purest motives—my country's oppressors or—— [Interruption by the court.]

My lord, will a dying man be denied the legal privilege of ex-culpating himself, in the eyes of the community, of an undeserved reproach thrown upon him during his trial, by charging him with ambition, and attempting to cast away, for a paltry consideration, the liberties of his country? Why did your lordship insult me? or rather why insult justice, in demanding of me why sentence of death should not be pronounced? I know, my lord, that form prescribes that you should ask the question; the form also presumes a right of answering. This no doubt may be dispensed with—and so might the whole ceremony of trial, since sentence was already pronounced at the castle, before your jury was impaneled; your lordships are but the priests of the oracle, and I submit; but I insist on the whole of the forms.

I am charged with being an emissary of France! An emissary of France! And for what end? It is alleged that I wished to sell the independence of my country! And for what end? Was this the object of my ambition? And is this the mode by which a tribunal of justice reconciles contradictions? No, I am no emissary; and my ambition was to hold a place among the deliverers of my country—not in power, nor in profit, but in the glory of the achievement! Sell my country's independence to France! And for what? Was it for a change of masters? No! But for ambition! O my country, was it personal ambition that could influence me? Had it been the soul of my actions, could I not by my education and fortune, by the rank and consideration of my family, have placed myself among the proudest of my oppressors? My country was my idol; to it I sacrificed every selfish, every endearing sentiment; and for it, I now offer up my life. O God! No, my lord; I acted as an Irishman, determined on delivering my country from the yoke of a foreign and unrelenting tyranny, and from the more galling yoke of a domestic faction, which is its joint partner and perpetrator in the parricide, for the ignominy of existing with an exterior of splendor and of conscious depravity. It was the wish of my heart to extricate my country from this doubly riveted despotism.

I wished to place her independence beyond the reach of any power on earth; I wished to exalt you to that proud station in the world.

Connection with France was indeed intended, but only as far as mutual interest would sanction or require. Were they to assume any authority inconsistent with the purest independence, it would be the signal for their destruction; we sought aid, and we sought it, as we had assurances we should obtain it—as auxiliaries in war and allies in peace.

Were the French to come as invaders or enemies, uninvited by the wishes of the people, I should oppose them to the utmost of my strength. Yes, my countrymen, I should advise you to meet them on the beach, with a sword in one hand, and a torch in the other; I would meet them with all the destructive fury of war; and I would animate my countrymen to immolate them in their boats, before they had contaminated the soil of my country. If they succeeded in landing, and if forced to retire before superior discipline, I would dispute every inch of ground, burn every blade of grass, and the last intrenchment of liberty should be my grave. What I could not do myself, if I should fall, I should leave as a last charge to my countrymen to accomplish; because I should feel conscious that life, any more than death, is unprofitable, when a foreign nation holds my country in subjection.

But it was not as an enemy that the succors of France were to land. I looked indeed for the assistance of France; but I wished to prove to France and to the world that Irishmen deserved to be assisted!—that they were indignant at slavery, and ready to assert the independence and liberty of their country.

I wished to procure for my country the guarantee which Washington procured for America. To procure an aid, which, by its example, would be as important as its valor, disciplined, gallant, pregnant with science and experience; which would perceive the good, and polish the rough points of our character. They would come to us as strangers, and leave us as friends, after sharing in our perils and elevating our destiny. These were my objects—not to receive new taskmasters, but to expel old tyrants; these were my views, and these only became Irishmen. It was for these ends I sought aid from France; because France, even as an enemy, could not be more implacable than the enemy already in the bosom of my country. [Interruption by the court.]

I have been charged with that importance in the efforts to emancipate my country, as to be considered the *keystone* of the combination of Irishmen; or, as your lordship expressed it, "the life and blood of conspiracy." You do me honor overmuch. You have given to the subaltern all the credit of a superior. There are men engaged in this *conspiracy,* who are not only superior to me, but even to your own conceptions of yourself, my lord; men, before the splendor of whose genius and virtues, I should bow with respectful deference, and who would think themselves dishonored to be called your friend— who would not disgrace themselves by shaking your bloodstained hand—— [Interruption by the court.]

What, my lord, shall you tell me, on the passage to that scaffold, which that tyranny, of which you are only the intermediary executioner, has erected for my murder, that I am accountable for all the blood that has and will be shed in this struggle of the oppressed against the oppressor?—shall you tell me this—and must I be so very a slave as not to repel it?

I do not fear to approach the omnipotent Judge, to answer for the conduct of my whole life; and am I to be appalled and falsified by a mere remnant of mortality here? By you, too, who, if it were possible to collect all the innocent blood that you have shed in your unhallowed ministry, in one great reservoir, your lordship might swim in it. [Interruption by the court.]

Let no man dare, when I am dead, to charge me with dishonor; let no man attaint my memory by believing that I could have engaged in any cause but that of my country's liberty and independence; or that I could have become the pliant minion of power in the oppression or the miseries of my countrymen. The proclamation of the provisional government speaks for our views; no inference can be tortured from it to countenance barbarity or debasement at home, or subjection, humiliation, or treachery from abroad; I would not have submitted to a foreign oppressor for the same reason that I would resist the foreign and domestic oppressor; in the dignity of freedom I would have fought upon the threshold of my country, and its enemy should enter only by passing over my lifeless corpse. Am I, who lived but for my country, and who have subjected myself to the dangers of the jealous and watchful oppressor, and the bondage of the grave, only to give my countrymen their rights, and my country her independence, and am I to be loaded with calumny, and not suffered to resent or repel it —no, God forbid!

If the spirits of the illustrious dead participate in the concerns and cares of those who are dear to them in this transitory life—oh, ever dear and venerated shade of my departed father, look down with scrutiny upon the conduct of your suffering son; and see if I have even for a moment deviated from those principles of morality and patriotism which it was your care to instil into my youthful mind, and for which I am now to offer up my life!

My lords, you are impatient for the sacrifice—the blood which you seek is not congealed by the artificial terrors which surround your victim; it circulates warmly and unruffled, through the channels which God created for noble purposes, but which you are bent to destroy, for purposes so grievous, that they cry to heaven. Be yet patient! I have but a few words more to say. I am going to my cold and silent grave: my lamp of life is nearly extinguished: my race is run: the grave opens to receive me, and I sink into its bosom! I have but one request to ask at my departure from this world—it is the charity of its silence! Let no man write my epitaph: for as no man who knows my motives dare now vindicate them, let not prejudice or ignorance asperse them. Let them and me repose in obscurity and peace, and my tomb remain uninscribed, until other times, and other men, can do justice to my character; when my country takes her place among the nations of the earth, then, and not till then, let my epitaph be written. I have done.

Charles Stewart Parnell
[1846–1891]

Charles Stewart Parnell, famous Irish Nationalist leader, devoted his life to the cause of Ireland. He was jailed under the Coercion Act in 1881, which made him more powerful in prison than he ever had been outside. His constant agitation for the rights of Ireland led to the introduction of the Home Rule Bill in 1886 by the Gladstone government. Following are parts of Parnell's speech in support of this bill, delivered in the House of Commons on June 7, 1886.

THE HOME RULE BILL

WE FEEL that under this Bill this Imperial Parliament will have the ultimate supremacy and the ultimate sovereignty. I think the most useful part of the Bill is that in which the prime minister throws the responsibility upon the new Legislature of maintaining that order in Ireland without which no state and no society can exist. I understand the supremacy of the Imperial Parliament to be this—that they can interfere in the event of the powers which are conferred by this Bill being abused under certain circumstances. But the Nationalists in accepting this Bill go, as I think, under an honorable understanding not to abuse those powers; and we pledge ourselves in that respect for the Irish people, as far as we can pledge ourselves, not to abuse those powers, and to devote our energies and our influence which we may have with the Irish people to prevent those powers from being abused. But, if those powers should be abused, the Imperial Parliament will have at its command the force which it reserves to itself, and it will be ready to intervene, but only in the case of grave necessity arising.

I believe this is by far the best mode in which we can hope to settle this question. You will have real power of force in your hands, and you ought to have it; and if abuses are committed and injustice be perpetrated you will always be able to use that force to put a stop to them. You will have the power and the supremacy of Parliament untouched and unimpaired, just as though this Bill had never been brought forward. We fully recognize this to be the effect of the Bill. I now repeat what I have already said on the first reading of the measure that we look upon the provisions of the Bill as a final settlement of this question, and that I believe that the Irish people have accepted it as such a settlement. We have had this measure accepted in the sense I have indicated by all the leaders of every section of national opinion both in Ireland and outside Ireland. It has been so accepted in the United States of America, and by the Irish population in that country with whose vengeance some honorable members are so fond of threatening us. Not a single dissentient voice has been raised against this Bill by any Irishman—not by any Irishman holding national opinions —and I need scarcely remind the House that there are sections among Irish Nationalists just as much as there are even among the great Conservative party. I say that as far as it is possible for a nation to accept a measure cheerfully, freely, gladly, and without reservation as a final settlement,—I say that the Irish people have shown that they have accepted this measure in that sense.

I will now leave this question of the supremacy of the Imperial Parliament, and I will turn to one that was strongly dwelt upon by the right honorable gentleman the member for East Edinburgh. I mean the influence which he fears the Irish priesthood will seek to exercise upon the future education of the Irish people. I may say at once that I am quite sure that the right honorable gentleman's apprehensions upon this subject are genuine, so far as they go, and that at the same time he has no desire to fan the flame of religious discord. On the whole, I think that the right honorable gentleman has spoken very fairly in reference to this part of the question; and I will not say that, perhaps as a Protestant, had I not had, as I have had, abundant experience of Ireland, I might not have been inclined to share his fears myself. Certainly, I have no such fears; but it is rather remarkable that this question of education is the only matter the right honorable gentleman has any fears about in dealing with the question of Protestant and Catholic in Ireland. I can, however, assure the right honorable gentleman that we Irishmen shall be able to settle this question of Irish education very well among ourselves. There are many Liberal Nationalists in Ireland—I call them Liberal Nationalists, because I take the phrase in reference to this question of education—there are many Liberal Nationalists who do not altogether share the views of the Roman Catholic Church upon the subject of education, and they are anxious that Ulster should remain an integral part of Ireland in order that they may share the responsibility of government and may influence that government by the feelings which they have with regard to this question of education. You may depend upon it that in an Irish Legislature Ulster, with such representatives as she now has in the Imperial Parliament, would be able to successfully resist the realization of any idea which the Roman Catholic hierarchy might entertain with regard to obtaining an undue control of Irish education. But I repeat that we shall be able to settle this question and others very satisfactorily to all the parties concerned among ourselves.

I come next to the question of the protection of the minority. I have incidentally dwelt on this point in respect to the matter of education; but I should like, with the permission of the House, to say a few words more about it, because it is one on which great attention has been bestowed. One would think from what we hear that the Protestants of Ireland were going to be handed over to the tender mercies of a set of thugs and bandits. The honorable and gallant member for North Armagh [Major Saunderson] cheers that. I only wish that I was as safe in the North of Ireland when I go there as the honorable and gallant member would be in the South. What do honorable gentlemen mean by the protection of the loyal minority? In the first place, I ask them what they mean by the loyal minority. The right honorable member for East Edinburgh [Mr. Goschen] does not seem to have made up his mind, even at this late stage of the discussion, as to what loyal Ulster he means. When asked the question, he said he meant the same loyal Ulster as was referred to by the prime minister in his speech; but he would not commit himself by telling us what signification he attributed to the prime minister's expression. Well, I have examined the prime minister's reference since then, and I find that he referred to the whole province of Ulster. He did not select a little bit of the province, because the opposition had not discovered this point at that time; and consequently I suppose I may assume that the right honorable member for East Edinburgh also referred to the whole province of Ulster when he asked for special protection for it. He has not, however, told us how he would specially protect it.

You must give up the idea of protecting the Protestants either as a body or as a majority by the establishment of a separate legislature either in Ulster or in any portion of Ulster. No, sir, we can not give up a single Irishman. We want the energy, the patriotism, the talents, and the work of every Irishman to insure that this great experiment shall be a successful one. We want, sir, all creeds and all classes in Ireland. We can not consent to look upon a single Irishman as not belonging to us.

We do not blame the small proportion of the Protestants of Ireland who feel any real fear. I admit, sir, that there is a small proportion of them who do feel this fear. We do not blame them; we have been doing our best to allay that fear, and we shall continue to do so. Theirs is not the shame and disgrace of this fear. That shame and disgrace belong to right honorable gentlemen and noble lords of English political parties who, for selfish interests, have sought to rekindle the embers—the almost expiring embers—of religious bigotry. Ireland has never injured the right honorable gentleman, the member for West Birmingham. I do not know why he should have added the strength of his powerful arm; why he should, like another Brennus —let us hope not with the same result—why he should have thrown his sword into the scale against Ireland. I am not aware that we have either personally or politically attempted to injure the right honorable gentleman, yet he and his kind seek to dash this cup from the lips of the Irish people—the first cup of cold water that has been offered to our nation since the recall of Lord Fitzwilliam.

Now, sir, what does it all come to? It comes to two alternatives when everything has been said and everything has been done. One alternative is the coercion which Lord Salisbury put before the country, and the other is the alternative offered by the prime minister, carrying with it the lasting settlement of a treaty of peace. If you reject this bill, Lord Salisbury was quite right in what he said as to coercion. With great respect to the cries of "No" by honorable members above the gangway, I beg to say, you will have to resort to coercion. That is not a threat on my part—I would do much to prevent the necessity for resorting to coercion; but I say it will be inevitable, and the best-intentioned Radical who sits on those benches, and who thinks that he "never, never will be a party to coercion," will be found very soon walking into the division lobby in favor of the strongest and most drastic coercion bill, or, at the very outside, pitifully abstaining. We have gone through it all before. During the last five years I know, sir, there have been very severe and drastic coercion bills; but it will require an even severer and more drastic measure of coercion now. You will require all that you have had during the last five years, and more besides.

What, sir, has that coercion been? You have had, sir, during those five years—I do not say this to influence passion or awaken bitter memories—you have had during those five years the suspension of the Habeas Corpus Act; you have had a thousand of your Irish fellow subjects held in prison without specific charge, many of them for long periods of time, some of them for twenty months, without trial and without any intention of placing them on trial—I think of all these thousand persons arrested under the Coercion Act of the late Mr. Forster scarcely a dozen were put on their trial; you have had the Arms Acts; you have had the suspension of trial by jury—all during the last five years. You have authorized your police to enter the domicile of a citizen, of your fellow subject in Ireland, at any hour of the day or night, and to search every part of this domicile, even the beds of the women, without warrant. You have fined the innocent for offenses committed by the guilty; you have taken power to expel aliens from this country; you have revived the Curfew Law and the blood-money of your Norman conquerors; you have gagged the Press and seized and suppressed newspapers; you have manufactured new crimes and offenses, and applied fresh penalties unknown to your laws for these crimes and offenses. All this you have done for five years, and all this and much more you will have to do again. The provision in the bill for terminating the representation of Irish members has been very vehemently objected to, and the right honorable gentleman, the member for the Border Burghs [Mr. Trevelyan], has said that there is no half-way house between separation and the maintenance of law and order in Ireland by imperial authority. I say, with just as much sincerity of belief, and just as much experience as the right honorable gentleman that, in my judgment, there is no half-way house between the concession of legislative autonomy to Ireland and the disfranchisement of the country and her government as a crown colony. But, sir, I refuse to believe that these evil days must come. I am convinced there are a sufficient number of wise and just members in this House to cause it to disregard appeals made to passion and to pocket, and to choose the better way of the prime minister—the way of founding peace and good will among nations; and when the numbers in the division lobby come to be told, it will also be told, for the admiration of all future generations, that England and her Parliament, in this nineteenth century, was wise enough, brave enough, and generous enough to close the strife of centuries, and to give peace, prosperity, and happiness to suffering Ireland.

Arthur Griffith
[1872–1922]

Arthur Griffith was the leader of the militant Sinn Fein movement. His efforts for Irish independence frequently resulted in his imprisonment until the British government finally granted Ireland the rights of a free state, although it was still short of the republic for which Griffith and the other leaders strove. However, Griffith favored the acceptance of the free state status and the approval of the treaty establishing it, as his speech before the Dail Eireann in Dublin on January 7, 1922, parts of which are given below, shows.

THE IRISH FREE STATE

I WILL not accept the invitation of the Minister of Defense to dishonor my signature and thereby become immortalized in Irish history. I have signed the Treaty, and the man or the nation that dishonors its signature is dishonored forever. No man can dishonor his signature without dishonoring the nation. [Hear, Hear.]

We went to London as plenipotentiaries and we came back with a treaty. We thought that we had done something for the good of the Irish nation, but we were indicted in Dublin from the day we came back. We were told that we had let down the Republic, and the Irish people were led to believe that we were sent to London with a mandate to get a republic and that we had violated the mandate. Before I went to London I said at a Cabinet meeting that if I went to London I would try for a republic, and if I could get it I would bring it back. We did try for a republic. One of the Deputies said that we were guilty of treason against the Republic. If we are guilty of treason against the Republic, let the Irish people try us for that treason. I have nothing on my conscience. What I did I did for the best interests of Ireland. I believed I was doing right, and I would do the same again. [Cheers.]

I have listened for days to discussions of the oath. If we are going to have a form of association with the British Empire we must have an oath, and such an oath was put before us when we were going back to London, and the differences between the oaths is just a difference in terms.

The Treaty has been called names which have not been paralleled since the days of Biddy Moriarty. When the delegates came back there was at least one thing that might have been done. Our colleagues might have discussed the Treaty on its merits and without reference to whether the men who brought it back were honorable or dishonorable. The Treaty has faults. We can call spirits from the vasty deep, but will they come? I could draw up a much more satisfactory Treaty, but it would not be adopted. Does the Treaty give away the honor of Ireland? "No." It is not dishonorable to Ireland. It is not an ideal one. It could be better. It is no more finality than we are the final generation on the earth. [Cheers.] No man can set bounds to the march of a nation, but we can accept this Treaty and deal with it in good faith with the English people and through the evolution of events reach the common goal. Who is going to say what the world is going to be in ten years hence? It does not mean that we cannot go beyond this Treaty, but we can move on towards an ultimate goal. This Treaty gives the Irish people what they have not had for centuries—a foothold in their own country. It gives Ireland solid ground on which she can stand, and Ireland has been for one hundred years a quagmire and bog where there was no foothold.

Reject the Treaty, and you throw Ireland back into what she was before this Treaty came. I am not a prophet—I cannot argue with prophets [laughter]—but I know where Ireland was twenty or thirty years ago. I know where Ireland was when there were only half a dozen of us in Dublin to keep the national ideal alive. We never deserted the national ideal. Are you going to go back on the few who had faith in their people and faith in their country? You can accept this Treaty and make it the basis of an Irish Ireland. You can reject the Treaty, and you can throw Ireland into what it was years ago.

When we agreed to enter into these negotiations with England we were bound to respect whatever the Irish people thought of the Treaty.

I have heard gentlemen sitting here say that it does not matter what their constituents said. I tell you that it does. If Democratic Government is going to remain on the earth, then the representative must voice the opinion of his constituents. If his conscience will not let him do that, he has only one way out and that is to resign. It is a negation of democratic right to vote against the will of the constituents. You are doing here what Castlereagh and Pitt did in 1800 when they refused to let the Irish Parliament be dissolved on the question of the Union so that the people might be consulted. You are now trying to reject that Treaty without allowing the Irish people to say whether they want it or do not want it. ["No, no."] You are trying to do that. What you will do is kill democracy. You will remove from the Dail every vestige of authority to speak for the people of Ireland. It will be a Junta attempting to dictate to the people of Ireland, and the people of Ireland, I think, will deal with that. There is no man here who would stand on a platform in his constituency and say that he was against the Treaty. [Cries of "Yes."] [Interruptions.] The people of Ireland are ninety-eight per cent for this Treaty. [Cries of "No" and "Yes."] Everyone of you knows it. [Interruptions.]

The Irish people will not be deceived. You may try to muzzle its voice, but it will pierce through. [Cheers.]

You have heard all that might be said against us here. You have been spoken to as if you had a republic governing and functioning all through Ireland, and that you were going to give up this governing and functioning republic for the Treaty. You know well that instead of governing and functioning through Ireland the utmost we could do was to hold, and barely hold the position we were in. The British Army is in occupation of the country, and it can be got out of the country by the ratification of the Treaty. Those who vote against the Treaty are those who vote to keep the British Army in Ireland. Under the Treaty the British Army will march out of Ireland. Is the Dail going to keep that Army in the country? Some members here have the idea that the people of the present generation are going to die that the next generation may get something. That is not sanity, it is not politics or statesmanship. Those who say that this generation should immolate themselves for the sake of the next are not talking sanely. This generation is Ireland, and it has got the right to live, as past generations had and future generations will have. We have been put into the position of making this Treaty appear as if it were a bigger thing than it is. It is the utmost that Ireland can get, and it is a Treaty that Ireland can honorably accept. Some of us have spoken here as if there were no Irish people outside these doors, as if there were no economic question, as if there were not tens of thousands of unemployed and thousands of struggling farmers who want to live. If you reject this Treaty, the Irish people will kick you out.

I want to see this country placed on its feet. We want the British taxgatherers out of the country. We want to hold our trade, our harbors, and our commerce, and we want to have the right and the power of educating our people and building up the nation. Reject the Treaty and what will happen? Years ago when I saw the poverty, misery, and degradation of the people, and the name of Ireland forgotten in Europe, I found that the cause of her misfortunes was the infamous Act of Union. From the passing of that Act chaos reigned in Ireland, and she has lost twelve millions of her population. The country has been ravaged by famine, the emigrant ship, the prison cell, and the scaffold. The cause of those evils is the presence of the English Army of Occupation. [Cheers.] Are you then, by vote this evening, going to keep the English Army here? Do you know what it means? Are you going to accept this Treaty, which gives you power to stand on an equality with the nations of the world, or are you going back, without hope, in this generation at least, of success, to the position in which you were?

I will not sacrifice the Irish nation on the altar of a false unity. I will not agree to preserve the semblance of unity if it means plunging the country into war. I will not agree that the people of Ireland shall be crucified on a formula. You have heard much about principles and honor, and those virtues are all on the other side. My principle is "Ireland for the Irish." [Hear, hear.] If I could get a republic I would have it, but I would not sacrifice my people for the sake of a form of government. The Treaty gives the Irish people the means of working out their own destiny, and there are no other means open to you of doing it. I say to the people of Ireland that it is their duty to see that this Treaty is carried into operation, for it gives them for the first time in a century the chance of taking their place amongst the nations of the world. [Loud cheers.]

IV. THE UNITED STATES

Jonathan Edwards
[1703–1758]

Jonathan Edwards, Puritan theologian, was famous for his sermons on sin, hell and punishment, themes that were dwelt upon so frequently in Colonial times. Following are portions of a sermon which he delivered in Enfield, Conn., on July 8, 1741.

SINNERS IN THE HANDS OF AN ANGRY GOD

THE wrath of God is like great waters that are dammed for the present; they increase more and more, and rise higher and higher, till an outlet is given; and the longer the stream is stopped, the more rapid and mighty is its course, when once it is let loose. 'Tis true, that judgment against your evil work has not been executed hitherto; the floods of God's vengeance have been withheld; but your guilt in the meantime is constantly increasing, and you are every day treasuring up more wrath; the waters are continually rising, and waxing more and more mighty; and there is nothing but the mere pleasure of God that holds the waters back, that are unwilling to be stopped, and press hard to go forward. If God should only withdraw his hand from the floodgate, it would immediately fly open, and the fiery floods of the fierceness and wrath of God would rush forth with inconceivable fury, and would come upon you with omnipotent power; and if your strength were ten thousand times greater than it is, yea, ten thousand times greater than the strength of the stoutest, sturdiest devil in hell, it would be nothing to withstand or endure it.

The bow of God's wrath is bent, and the arrow made ready on the string, and justice bends the arrow at your heart, and strains the bow, and it is nothing but the mere pleasure of God, and that of an angry God, without any promise or obligation at all, that keeps the arrow one moment from being made drunk with your blood.

Thus are all you that never passed under a great change of heart by the mighty power of the Spirit of God upon your souls; all that were never born again, and made new creatures, and raised from being dead in sin to a state of new and before altogether unexperienced light and life (however you may have reformed your life in many things, and may have had religious affections, and may keep up a form of religion in your families and closets, and in the house of God, and may be strict in it), you are thus in the hands of an angry God; 'tis nothing but his mere pleasure that keeps you from being this moment swallowed up in everlasting destruction.

The God that holds you over the pit of hell, much as one holds a spider or some loathsome insect over the fire, abhors you, and is dreadfully provoked; his wrath towards you burns like fire; he looks upon you as worthy of nothing else, but to be cast into the fire; he is of purer eyes than to bear to have you in his sight; you are ten thousand times so abominable in his eyes, as the most hateful and venomous serpent is in ours. You have offended him infinitely more than ever a stubborn rebel did his prince: and yet it is nothing but his hand that holds you from falling into the fire every moment. 'Tis ascribed to nothing else, that you did not go to hell the last night; that you were suffered to awake again in this world after you closed your eyes to sleep; and there is no other reason to be given why you have not dropped into hell since you arose in the morning, but that God's hand has held you up. There is no other reason to be given why you haven't gone to hell since you have sat here in the house of God, provoking his pure eyes by your sinful wicked manner of attending his solemn worship. Yea, there is nothing else that is to be given as a reason why you don't this very moment drop down into hell.

O sinner! consider the fearful danger you are in. 'Tis a great furnace of wrath, a wide and bottomless pit, full of the fire of wrath, that you are held over in the hand of that God whose wrath is provoked and incensed as much against you as against many of the damned in hell. You hang by a slender thread, with the flames of divine wrath flashing about it, and ready every moment to singe it and burn it asunder; and you have no interest in any Mediator, and nothing to lay hold of to save yourself, nothing to keep off the flames of wrath, nothing of your own, nothing that you ever have done, nothing that you can do, to induce God to spare you one moment.

And let every one that is yet out of Christ and hanging over the pit of hell, whether they be old men and women or middle-aged or young people or little children, now hearken to the loud calls of God's word and providence. This acceptable year of the Lord that is a day of such great favor to some will doubtless be a day of as remarkable vengeance to others. Now undoubtedly it is as it was in the days of John the Baptist, the ax is in an extraordinary manner laid at the root of the trees, that every tree that bringeth not forth good fruit may be hewn down and cast into the fire.

Therefore let every one that is out of Christ now awake and fly from the wrath to come. The wrath of Almighty God is now undoubtedly hanging over a great part of his congregation. Let every one fly out of Sodom. *"Haste and escape for your lives, look not behind you, escape to the mountain, lest ye be consumed."*

John Hancock

[1737–1793]

John Hancock, of Massachusetts, was a fearless and eloquent champion of the American colonists in their struggle against British oppression. He was president of the Continental Congress and the first to sign the revolutionary Declaration of Independence. Here are parts of his oration in memory of those who died in the Boston massacre of 1770, which he delivered in Boston on March 5, 1774.

THE BOSTON MASSACRE

LET NOT the history of the illustrious House of Brunswick inform posterity that a king, descended from that glorious monarch, George II., once sent his British subjects to conquer and enslave his subjects in America. But be perpetual infamy entailed upon that villain who dared to advise his master to such execrable measures; for it was easy to foresee the consequences which so naturally followed upon sending troops into America, to enforce obedience to acts of the British Parliament, which neither God nor man ever empowered them to make. It was reasonable to expect that troops, who knew the errand they were sent upon, would treat the people whom they were to subjugate, with a cruelty and haughtiness which too often buried the honorable character of a soldier in the disgraceful name of an unfeeling ruffian. The troops, upon their first arrival, took possession of our senate house, and pointed their cannon against the judgment hall, and even continued them there whilst the supreme court of judicature for this province was actually sitting to decide upon the lives and fortunes of the king's subjects. Our streets nightly resounded with the noise of riot and debauchery; our peaceful citizens were hourly exposed to shameful insults, and often felt the effects of their violence and outrage. But this was not all: as though they thought it not enough to violate our civil rights, they endeavored to deprive us of the enjoyment of our religious privileges, to vitiate our morals, and thereby render us deserving of destruction. Did not a reverence for religion sensibly decay? Did not our infants almost learn to lisp out curses before they knew their horrid import? Did not our youth forget they were Americans, and regardless of the admonitions of the wise and aged, servilely copy from their tyrants those vices which finally must overthrow the empire of Great Britain? And must I be compelled to acknowledge that even the noblest, fairest part of all the lower creation did not entirely escape the cursed snare? When virtue has once erected her throne within the female breast, it is upon so solid a basis that nothing is able to expel the heavenly inhabitant. But have there not been some, few, indeed, I hope, whose youth and inexperience have rendered them a prey to wretches, whom, upon the least reflection, they would have despised and hated as foes to God and their country? I fear there have been some such unhappy instances, or why have I seen an honest father clothed with shame? or why a virtuous mother drowned in tears?

But I forbear, and come reluctantly to the transactions of that dismal night, when in such quick succession we felt the extremes of grief, astonishment, and rage; when Heaven in anger, for a dreadful moment, suffered hell to take the reins; when Satan with his chosen band opened the sluices of New England's blood, and sacrilegiously polluted our land with the dead bodies of her guiltless sons! Let this sad tale of death never be told without a tear; let not the heaving bosom cease to burn with a manly indignation at the barbarous story through the long tracts of future time; let every parent tell the shameful story to his listening children until tears of pity glisten in their eyes, and boiling passions shake their tender frames; and whilst the anniversary of that ill-fated night is kept a jubilee in the grim court of pandemonium, let all America join in one common prayer to Heaven, that the inhuman, unprovoked murders of the fifth of March, 1770, planned by Hillsborough, and a knot of treacherous knaves in Boston, and executed by the cruel hand of Preston and his sanguinary coadjutors, may ever stand in history without a parallel. But what, my countrymen, withheld the ready arm of vengeance from executing instant justice on the vile assassins? Perhaps you feared promiscuous carnage might ensue, and that the innocent might share the fate of those who had performed the infernal deed. But were not all guilty? Were you not too tender of the lives of those who came to fix a yoke on your necks? But I must not too severely blame a fault, which great souls only can commit. May that magnificence of spirit which scorns the low pursuits of malice, may that generous compassion which often preserves from ruin, even a guilty villain, forever actuate the noble bosoms of Americans! But let not the miscreant host vainly imagine that we feared their arms. No, them we despised; we dread nothing but slavery. Death is the creature of a poltroon's brains; 'tis immortality to sacrifice ourselves for the salvation of our country. We fear not death. That gloomy night, the pale-faced moon, and the affrighted stars that hurried through the sky, can witness that we fear not death. Our hearts which, at the recollection, glow with rage that four revolving years have scarcely taught us to restrain, can witness that we fear not death; and happy it is for those who dared to insult us, that their naked bones are not now piled up an everlasting monument of Massachusetts' bravery. But they retired, they fled, and in that flight they found their only safety. We then expected that the hand of public justice would soon inflict that punishment upon the murderers which, by the laws of God and man, they had incurred. But let the unbiased pen of a Robertson, or perhaps of some equally famed American, conduct this trial before the great tribunal of succeeding generations. And though the murderers may escape the just resentment of an enraged people; though drowsy justice, intoxicated by the poisonous draught prepared for her cup, still nods upon her rotten seat, yet be assured, such complicated crimes will meet their due reward. Tell me, ye bloody butchers! ye villains high and low! ye wretches who contrived, as well as you who executed the inhuman deed! do you not feel the goads and stings of conscious guilt pierce through your savage bosoms? Though some of you may think yourselves exalted to a height that bids defiance to human justice; and others shroud yourselves beneath the mask of hypocrisy, and build your hopes of safety on the low arts of cunning, chicanery, and falsehood; yet do you not sometimes feel the gnawings of that worm which never dies? Do not the injured shades of Maverick, Gray, Caldwell, Attucks, and Carr, attend you in your solitary walks; arrest you even in the midst of your debaucheries, and fill even your dreams with terror? But if the unappeased manes of the dead should not disturb their murderers, yet surely even your obdurate hearts must shrink, and your guilty blood must chill within your rigid veins, when you behold the miserable Monk, the wretched victim of your savage cruelty. Observe his tottering knees, which scarce sustain his wasted body; look on his haggard eyes; mark well the death-like paleness on his fallen cheek, and tell me, does not the sight plant daggers in your souls? Unhappy Monk! cut off, in the gay morn of manhood, from all the joys which sweeten life, doomed to drag on a pitiful existence, without even a hope to taste the pleasures of returning health! Yet, Monk, thou livest not in vain; thou livest a warning to thy country, which sympathizes with thee in thy sufferings; thou livest an affecting, an alarming instance of the unbounded violence which lust of power, assisted by a standing army, can lead a traitor to commit.

Ye dark designing knaves, ye murderers, parricides! how dare you tread upon the earth, which has drunk in the blood of slaughtered innocents, shed by your wicked hands? How dare you breathe that air which wafted to the ear of Heaven the groans of those who fell a sacrifice to your accursed ambition? But if the laboring earth doth not expand her jaws; if the air you breathe is not commissioned to be the minister of death; yet, hear it and tremble! The eye of Heaven penetrates the darkest chambers of the soul, traces the leading clue through all the labyrinths which your industrious folly has devised; and you, however you may have screened yourselves from human eyes, must be arraigned, must lift your hands, red with the blood of those whose death you have procured, at the tremendous bar of God!

Surely you never will tamely suffer this country to be a den of thieves. Remember, my friends, from whom you sprang. Let not a meanness of spirit, unknown to those whom you boast of as your fathers, excite a thought to the dishonor of your mothers. I conjure you, by all that is dear, by all that is honorable, by all that is sacred, not only that ye pray, but that ye act; that, if necessary, ye fight, and even die, for the prosperity of our Jerusalem. Break in sunder, with noble disdain, the bonds with which the Philistines have bound you.

I have the most animating confidence that the present noble struggle for liberty will terminate gloriously for America. And let us play the man for our God, and for the cities of our God; while we are using the means in our power, let us humbly commit our righteous cause to the great Lord of the universe, who loveth righteousness and hateth iniquity.

Patrick Henry
[1736-1799]

With very little schooling Patrick Henry developed into one of the greatest natural orators of the Revolution. He was only 29 years old when he was elected to the Virginia House of Burgesses. Later he became governor of the state. It was on March 28, 1775, that he delivered his impassioned speech before the Virginia Convention of Delegates, ending with the immortal words, "Give me liberty, or give me death!" This speech follows.

"GIVE ME LIBERTY, OR GIVE ME DEATH!"

MR. PRESIDENT: No man thinks more highly than I do of the patriotism, as well as abilities, of the very worthy gentlemen who have just addressed the House. But different men often see the same subject in different lights; and, therefore, I hope that it will not be thought disrespectful to those gentlemen, if, entertaining as I do, opinions of a character very opposite to theirs, I shall speak forth my sentiments freely and without reserve. This is no time for ceremony. The question before the House is one of awful moment to this country. For my own part I consider it as nothing less than a question of freedom or slavery; and in proportion to the magnitude of the subject ought to be the freedom of the debate. It is only in this way that we can hope to arrive at truth, and fulfil the great responsibility which we hold to God and our country. Should I keep back my opinions at such a time, through fear of giving offence, I should consider myself as guilty of treason towards my country, and of an act of disloyalty towards the majesty of heaven, which I revere above all earthly kings.

Mr. President, it is natural to man to indulge in the illusions of hope. We are apt to shut our eyes against a painful truth, and listen to the song of that siren, till she transforms us into beasts. Is this the part of wise men, engaged in a great and arduous struggle for liberty? Are we disposed to be of the number of those who, having eyes, see not, and having ears, hear not, the things which so nearly concern their temporal salvation? For my part, whatever anguish of spirit it may cost, I am willing to know the whole truth; to know the worst and to provide for it.

I have but one lamp by which my feet are guided; and that is the lamp of experience. I know of no way of judging of the future but by the past. And judging by the past, I wish to know what there has been in the conduct of the British ministry for the last ten years, to justify those hopes with which gentlemen have been pleased to solace themselves and the House? Is it that insidious smile with which our petition has been lately received? Trust it not, sir; it will prove a snare to your feet. Suffer not yourselves to be betrayed with a kiss. Ask yourselves how this gracious reception of our petition comports with these war-like preparations which cover our waters and darken our land. Are fleets and armies necessary to a work of love and reconciliation? Have we shown ourselves so unwilling to be reconciled, that force must be called in to win back our love? Let us not deceive ourselves, sir. These are the implements of war and subjugation; the last arguments to which kings resort. I ask gentlemen, sir, what means this martial array, if its purpose be not to force us to submission? Can gentlemen assign any other possible motives for it? Has Great Britain any enemy, in this quarter of the world, to call for all this accumulation of navies and armies? No, sir, she has none. They are meant for us; they can be meant for no other. They are sent over to bind and rivet upon us those chains which the British ministry have been so long forging. And what have we to oppose to them? Shall we try argument? Sir, we have been trying that for the last ten years. Have we anything new to offer on the subject? Nothing. We have held the subject up in every light of which it is capable; but it has been all in vain. Shall we resort to entreaty and humble supplication? What terms shall we find which have not been already exhausted? Let us not, I beseech you, sir, deceive ourselves longer. Sir, we have done everything that could be done, to avert the storm which is now coming on. We have petitioned; we have remonstrated; we have supplicated; we have prostrated ourselves before the throne, and have implored its interposition to arrest the tyrannical hands of the ministry and Parliament. Our petitions have been slighted; our remonstrances have produced additional violence and insult; our supplications have been disregarded; and we have been spurned, with contempt, from the foot of the throne. In vain, after these things, may we indulge the fond hope of peace and reconciliation. There is no longer any room for hope. If we wish to be free—if we mean to preserve inviolate those inestimable privileges for which we have been so long contending—if we mean not basely to abandon the noble struggle in which we have been so long engaged, and which we have pledged ourselves never to abandon until the glorious object of our contest shall be obtained, we must fight! I repeat it, sir, we must fight! An appeal to arms and to the God of Hosts is all that is left us!

They tell us, sir, that we are weak; unable to cope with so formidable an adversary. But when shall we be stronger? Will it be the next week, or the next year? Will it be when we are totally disarmed, and when a British guard shall be stationed in every house? Shall we gather strength by irresolution and inaction? Shall we acquire the means of effectual resistance, by lying supinely on our backs, and hugging the delusive phantom of hope, until our enemies shall have bound us hand and foot? Sir, we are not weak, if we make a proper use of the means which the God of nature hath placed in our power. Three millions of people, armed in the holy cause of liberty, and in such a country as that which we possess, are invincible by any force which our enemy can send against us. Besides, sir, we shall not fight our battles alone. There is a just God who presides over the destinies of nations; and who will raise up friends to fight our battles for us. The battle, sir, is not to the strong alone; it is to the vigilant, the active, the brave. Besides, sir, we have no election. If we were base enough to desire it, it is now too late to retire from the contest. There is no retreat, but in submission and slavery! Our chains are forged! Their clanking may be heard on the plains of Boston! The war is inevitable—and let it come! I repeat it, sir, let it come!

It is in vain, sir, to extenuate the matter. Gentlemen may cry peace, peace—but there is no peace. The war is actually begun! The next gale that sweeps from the north will bring to our ears the clash of resounding arms! Our brethren are already in the field! Why stand we here idle? What is it that gentlemen wish? What would they have? Is life so dear, or peace so sweet, as to be purchased at the price of chains and slavery? Forbid it, Almighty God! I know not what course others may take; but as for me, give me liberty, or give me death!

Samuel Adams
[1722-1803]

Samuel Adams, great American patriot, was one of the ablest leaders of the revolutionaries of Massachusetts and later of the Continental Congress. Here are portions of an eloquent address on American independence which he delivered at the State House in Philadelphia, on August 1, 1776, a month after the signing of the Declaration of Independence.

AMERICAN INDEPENDENCE

WE ARE NOW on this continent, to the astonishment of the world, three millions of souls united in one cause. We have large armies, well disciplined and appointed, with commanders inferior to none in military skill, and superior in activity and zeal. We are furnished with arsenals and stores beyond our most sanguine expectations, and foreign nations are waiting to crown our success by their alliances. There are instances of, I would say, an almost astonishing Providence in our favor; our success has staggered our enemies, and almost given faith to infidels; so we may truly say it is not our own arm which has saved us.

The hand of Heaven appears to have led us on to be, perhaps, humble instruments and means in the great providential dispensation which is completing. We have fled from the political Sodom; let us not look back, lest we perish and become a monument of infamy and derision to the world. For can we ever expect more unanimity and a better preparation for defense; more infatuation of counsel among our enemies, and more valor and zeal among ourselves? The same force and resistance which are sufficient to procure us our liberties will secure us a glorious independence and support us in the dignity of free, imperial states. We cannot suppose that our opposition has made a corrupt and dissipated nation more friendly to America, or created in them a greater respect for the rights of mankind. We can therefore expect a restoration and establishment of our privileges, and a compensation for the injuries we have received, from their want of power, from their fears, and not from their virtues. The unanimity and valor which will effect an honorable peace can render a future contest for our liberties unnecessary. He who has strength to chain down the wolf is a madman if he let him loose without drawing his teeth and paring his nails.

We have no other alternative than independence, or the most ignominious and galling servitude. The legions of our enemies thicken on our plains; desolation and death mark their bloody career; whilst the mangled corpses of our countrymen seem to cry out to us as a voice from Heaven.

Our union is now complete; our constitution composed, established, and approved. You are now the guardians of your own liberties. We may justly address you, as the *decemviri* did the Romans, and say: "Nothing that we propose can pass into a law without your consent. Be yourselves, O Americans, the authors of those laws on which your happiness depends."

You have now in the field armies sufficient to repel the whole force of your enemies and their base and mercenary auxiliaries. The hearts of your soldiers beat high with the spirit of freedom; they are animated with the justice of their cause, and while they grasp their swords can look up to Heaven for assistance. Your adversaries are composed of wretches who laugh at the rights of humanity, who turn religion into derision, and would, for higher wages, direct their swords against their leaders or their country. Go on, then, in your generous enterprise, with gratitude to Heaven for past success, and confidence of it in the future. For my own part, I ask no greater blessing than to share with you the common danger and common glory. If I have a wish dearer to my soul than that my ashes may be mingled with those of a Warren and a Montgomery, it is that these American States may never cease to be free and independent.

Benjamin Franklin
[1706–1790]

Benjamin Franklin, philosopher, diplomat, and statesman, was one of the outstanding patriots of the Revolution. His range of knowledge was remarkably great and his abilities in different fields were extraordinary, all of which he put at the service of his country. The following is taken from a speech he delivered before the Constitutional Convention of 1787.

ON THE FAULTS OF THE CONSTITUTION

I CONFESS that I do not entirely approve of this Constitution at present; but, sir, I am not sure I shall never approve of it, for, having lived long, I have experienced many instances of being obliged, by better information or fuller consideration, to change opinions even on important subjects, which I once thought right, but found to be otherwise. It is therefore that, the older I grow, the more apt I am to doubt my own judgment of others. Most men, indeed, as well as most sects in religion, think themselves in possession of all truth, and that wherever others differ from them, it is so far error. Steele, a Protestant, in a dedication, tells the pope that the only difference between our two churches in their opinions of the certainty of their doctrine is, the Romish Church is infallible, and the Church of England is never in the wrong. But, though many private persons think almost as highly of their own infallibility as of that of their sect, few express it so naturally as a certain French lady, who, in a little dispute with her sister, said: "But I meet with nobody but myself that is always in the right."

In these sentiments, sir, I agree to this Constitution with all its faults—if they are such—because I think a general government necessary for us, and there is no form of government but what may be a blessing to the people if well administered; and I believe, further, that this is likely to be well administered for a course of years, and can only end in despotism, as other forms have done before it, when the people shall become so corrupted as to need despotic government, being incapable of any other. I doubt, too, whether any other convention we can obtain may be able to make a better Constitution; for, when you assemble a number of men, to have the advantage of their joint wisdom, you inevitably assemble with those men all their prejudices, their passions, their errors of opinion, their local interests, and their selfish views. From such an assembly can a perfect production be expected?

It therefore astonishes me, sir, to find this system approaching so near to perfection as it does; and I think it will astonish our enemies, who are waiting with confidence to hear that our counsels are confounded like those of the builders of Babel, and that our States are on the point

of separation, only to meet hereafter for the purpose of cutting one another's throats. Thus I consent, sir, to this Constitution, because I expect
no better, and because I am not sure that it is not the best. The opinions
I have had of its errors I sacrifice to the public good. I have never
whispered a syllable of them abroad. Within these walls they were
born, and here they shall die. If every one of us, in returning to our
constituents, were to report the objections he has had to it, and endeavor
to gain partizans in support of them, we might prevent its being
generally received, and thereby lose all the salutary effects and great
advantages resulting naturally in our favor among foreign nations, as
well as among ourselves, from our real or apparent unanimity. Much
of the strength and efficiency of any government, in procuring and
securing happiness to the people, depends on opinion, on the general
opinion of the goodness of that government, as well as of the wisdom
and integrity of its governors. I hope, therefore, for our own sakes,
as a part of the people, and for the sake of our posterity, that we shall
act heartily and unanimously in recommending this Constitution wherever our influence may extend, and turn our future thoughts and endeavors to the means of having it well administered.

On the whole, sir, I can not help expressing a wish that every member of the convention who may still have objections to it, would, with
me, on this occasion, doubt a little of his own infallibility, and, to make
manifest our unanimity, put his name to this instrument.

James Madison
[1751–1836]

*James Madison, fourth President of the United States, played a
powerful role in the framing of the Federal Constitution of the
United States. He was an advocate of a strong central government,
and through his skill in debate and in harmonizing conflicting interests succeeded in having most of his views approved by the
Constitutional Convention of 1787. Following are parts of an address
he delivered before the Convention of Virginia, his native state,
on June 6, 1788, urging the adoption of the Federal Constitution.*

THE STATES AND THE FEDERAL GOVERNMENT

GIVE me leave to say something of the nature of the government, and
to show that it is perfectly safe and just to vest it with the power
of taxation. There are a number of opinions; but the principal question
is, whether it be a federal or a consolidated government. In order to
judge properly of the question before us, we must consider it minutely,
in its principal parts. I myself conceive that it is of a mixed nature; it
is, in a manner, unprecedented. We cannot find one express prototype

in the experience of the world: it stands by itself. In some respects, it is a government of a federal nature; in others, it is of a consolidated nature. Even if we attend to the manner in which the Constitution is investigated, ratified, and made the act of the people of America, I can say, notwithstanding what the honorable gentleman has alleged, that this government is not completely consolidated; nor is it entirely federal. Who are the parties to it? The people—not the people as composing one great body, but the people as composing thirteen sovereignties. Were it, as the gentleman asserts, a consolidated government, the assent of a majority of the people would be sufficient for its establishment, and as a majority have adopted it already, the remaining States would be bound by the act of the majority, even if they unanimously reprobated it. Were it such a government as is suggested, it would be now binding on the people of this State, without having had the privilege of deliberating upon it; but, sir, no State is bound by it, as it is, without its own consent. Should all the States adopt it, it will be then a government established by the thirteen States of America, not through the intervention of the Legislatures, but by the people at large. In this particular respect, the distinction between the existing and proposed governments is very material. The existing system has been derived from the dependent, derivative authority of the Legislatures of the States; whereas this is derived from the superior power of the people. If we look at the manner in which alterations are to be made in it, the same idea is in some degree attended to. By the new system, a majority of the States cannot introduce amendments; nor are all the States required for that purpose; three-fourths of them must concur in alterations; in this there is a departure from the federal idea. The members to the national House of Representatives are to be chosen by the people at large, in proportion to the numbers in the respective districts. When we come to the Senate, its members are elected by the States in their equal and political capacity; but had the government been completely consolidated, the Senate would have been chosen by the people, in their individual capacity, in the same manner as the members of the other House. Thus it is of complicated nature, and this complication, I trust, will be found to exclude the evils of absolute consolidation, as well as of a mere confederacy. If Virginia were separated from all the States, her power and authority would extend to all cases; in like manner, were all powers vested in the general government, it would be a consolidated government; but the powers of the Federal government are enumerated; it can only operate in certain cases: it has legislative powers on defined and limited objects, beyond which it cannot extend its jurisdiction.

But the honorable member has satirized, with peculiar acrimony, the power given to the general government by this Constitution. I conceive that the first question on this subject is, whether these powers be necessary; if they be, we are reduced to the dilemma of either submitting to the inconvenience, or losing the Union. Let us consider the most important of these reprobated powers; that of direct taxation is most generally objected to. With respect to the exigencies of government, there is no question but the most easy mode of providing for them will be adopted. When, therefore, direct taxes are not necessary, they will not be recurred to. It can be of little advantage to those in power to raise money in a manner oppressive to the people. To consult the conveniences of the people will cost them nothing, and in many respects will be advantageous to them. Direct taxes will only be recurred to for great purposes. What has brought on other nations those immense debts, under the pressure of which many of them labor? Not the expenses of their governments, but war. If this country should be engaged in war (and I conceive we ought to provide for the possibility of such a case), how would it be carried on? By the usual means provided from year to year? As our imports will be necessary for the expenses of government, and other common exigencies, how are we to carry on the means of defence? How is it possible a war could be supported without money or credit? And would it be possible for government to have credit, without having the power of raising money? No, it would be impossible for any government, in such a case, to defend itself. Then, I say, sir, that it is necessary to establish funds for extraordinary exigencies, and give this power to the general government; for the utter inutility of previous requisitions on the States is too well known. Would it be possible for those countries, whose finances and revenues are carried to the highest perfection, to carry on the operations of government on great emergencies, such as the maintenance of a war, without an uncontrolled power of raising money? Has it not been necessary for Great Britain, notwithstanding the facility of the collection of her taxes, to have recourse very often to this and other extraordinary methods of procuring money? Would not her public credit have been ruined, if it was known that her power to raise money was limited? Has not France been obliged, on great occasions, to recur to unusual means, in order to raise funds? It has been the case in many countries, and no government can exist unless its powers extend to make provisions for every contingency. If we were actually attacked by a powerful nation, and our general government had not the power of raising money, but depended solely on requisitions, our condition would be truly deplorable: if the revenues of this commonwealth were to depend on twenty distinct authorities, it would be impossible for it to carry on its operations. This must be obvious to every member here: I think, therefore, that it is necessary for the preservation of the Union that this power should be given to the general government.

John Marshall
[1755–1835]

John Marshall, celebrated American jurist, was chief justice of the Supreme Court of the United States for nearly thirty-five years. He served in the War of Independence, rising to the rank of captain. Following are parts of an address he delivered before the Virginia Convention on June 10, 1788, in which he urged the ratification of the new Constitution.

JUSTICE AND THE FEDERAL CONSTITUTION

PERMIT me to attend to what the honorable gentleman, Mr. Henry, has said. He has expatiated on the necessity of a due attention to certain maxims—to certain fundamental principles, from which a free people ought never to depart. I concur with him in the propriety of the observance of such maxims. They are necessary in any government, but more essential to a democracy than to any other. What are the favorite maxims of democracy? A strict observance of justice and public faith, and a steady adherence to virtue. These, sir, are the principles of a good government. No mischief, no misfortune, ought to deter us from a strict observance of justice and public faith. Would to Heaven that these principles had been observed under the present government! Had this been the case,. the friends of liberty would not be so willing now to part with it. Can we boast that our government is founded on these maxims? Can we pretend to the enjoyment of political freedom or security, when we are told that a man has been, by an act of Assembly, struck out of existence without a trial by jury, without examination, without being confronted with his accusers and witnesses, without the benefits of the law of the land? Where is our safety, when we are told that this act was justifiable, because the person was not a Socrates? What has become of the worthy member's maxims? Is this one of them? Shall it be a maxim that a man shall be deprived of his life without the benefit of law? Shall such a deprivation of life be justified by answering, that the man's life was not taken *secundum artem,* because he was a bad man? Shall it be a maxim that government ought not to be empowered to protect virtue?

The honorable member, after attempting to vindicate that tyrannical legislative act to which I have been alluding, proceeded to take a view of the dangers to which this country is exposed. He told us that the principal danger arose from a government which, if adopted, would give away the Mississippi. I intended to proceed regularly, by attending to the clause under debate; but I must reply to some observations which were dwelt upon to make impressions on our minds unfavorable to the plan upon the table. Have we no navigation in, or do we derive no benefit from, the Mississippi? How shall we retain it? By retaining that weak government which has hitherto kept it from us? Is it thus that we shall secure that navigation? Give the government the power of retaining it, and then we may hope to derive actual advantages from it. Till we do this, we cannot expect that a government which hitherto has not been able to protect it, will have the power to do it hereafter. Have we attended too long to consider whether this government would be able to protect us? Shall we wait for further proofs of its inefficacy? If on mature consideration, the constitution will be found to be perfectly right on the subject of treaties, and containing no danger of losing that navigation, will he still object? Will he object because eight States are unwilling to part with it? This is no good ground of objection.

He then stated the necessity and probability of obtaining amendments. This we ought to postpone until we come to that clause, and make up our minds whether there be anything unsafe in this system. He conceived it impossible to obtain amendments after adopting it. If he was right, does not his own argument prove that in his own conception, previous amendments cannot be had? for, sir, if subsequent amendments cannot be obtained, shall we get amendments before we ratify? The reasons against the latter do not apply against the former. There are in this State, and in every State in the Union, many who are decided enemies of the Union. Reflect on the probable conduct of such men. What will they do? They will bring amendments which are local in their nature, and which they know will not be accepted. What security have we that other States will not do the same? We are told that many in the States were violently opposed to it. They are more mindful of local interests. They will never propose such amendments as they think would be obtained. Disunion will be their object. This will be attained by the proposal of unreasonable amendments. This, sir, though a strong cause, is not the only one that will militate against previous amendments. Look at the comparative temper of this country now, and when the late Federal Convention met. We had no idea then of any particular system. The formation of the most perfect plan was our object and wish. It was imagined that the States would accede to, and be pleased with, the proposition that would be made them. Consider the violence of opinions, the prejudices and animosities which have been since imbibed. Will not these operate greatly against mutual concessions, or a friendly concurrence? This will, however, be taken up more properly another time. He says, we wish to have a strong, energetic, powerful government. We contend for a well-regulated democracy. He insinuates that the power of the government has been enlarged by the convention, and that we may apprehend it will be enlarged by others. The convention did not, in fact, assume any power.

They have proposed to our consideration, a scheme of government which they thought advisable. We are not bound to adopt it, if we disapprove of it. Had not every individual in this community a right to tender that scheme which he thought most conducive to the welfare of his country? Have not several gentlemen already demonstrated that the convention did not exceed their powers? But the Congress have the power of making bad laws, it seems. The Senate, with the President, he informs us, may make a treaty which shall be disadvantageous to us; and that, if they be not good men, it will not be a good constitution. I shall ask the worthy member only, if the people at large, and they alone, ought to make laws and treaties. Has any man this in contemplation? You cannot exercise the powers of government personally yourselves. You must trust to agents. If so, will you dispute giving them the power of acting for you, from an existing possibility that they may abuse it? As long as it is impossible for you to transact your business in person, if you repose no confidence in delegates, because there is a possibility of their abusing it, you can have no government; for the power of doing good is inseparable from that of doing some evil.

Alexander Hamilton
[1757–1804]

Alexander Hamilton's name is associated with two great contributions to his country. Largely through his skill and efforts the Constitutional Convention of 1787 framed the finely balanced document that has proved so successful over the years. The other contribution was his putting the finances of the government on a practical basis as the first Secretary of the Treasury of the United States. Hamilton was killed in a duel with Aaron Burr. The following is part of an address he delivered before the Constitutional Convention of New York, his state, urging the ratification of the Federal Constitution.

THE FEDERAL CONSTITUTION

GENTLEMEN indulge too many unreasonable apprehensions of danger to the state governments; they seem to suppose that the moment you put men into a national council they become corrupt and tyrannical, and lose all their affection for their fellow citizens. But can we imagine that the senators will ever be so insensible of their own advantage as to sacrifice the genuine interest of their constituents? The state governments are essentially necessary to the form and spirit of the general system. As long, therefore, as Congress has a full conviction of this necessity, they must, even upon principles purely national, have as firm an attachment to the one as to the other. This conviction can never leave them, unless they become madmen. While the Constitution continues to be read and its principle known, the states must, by every rational man, be considered as essential, component parts of the Union; and therefore the idea of sacrificing the former to the latter is wholly inadmissible.

The objectors do not advert to the natural strength and resources of state governments, which will ever give them an important superiority over the general government. If we compare the nature of their different powers, or the means of popular influence which each possesses, we shall find the advantage entirely on the side of the states. This consideration, important as it is, seems to have been little attended to. The aggregate number of representatives throughout the states may be two thousand. Their personal influence will, therefore, be proportionably more extensive than that of one or two hundred men in Congress. The state establishments of civil and military officers of every description, infinitely surpassing in number any possible correspondent establishments in the general government,. will create such an extent and complication of attachments as will ever secure the predilection and support of the people. Whenever, therefore, Congress shall meditate any infringement of the state constitutions, the great body of the people will naturally take part with their domestic representatives. Can the general government withstand such a united opposition? Will the people suffer themselves to be stripped of their privileges? Will they suffer their legislatures to be reduced to a shadow and a name? The idea is shocking to common sense.

From the circumstances already explained, and many others which might be mentioned, results a complicated, irresistible check, which must ever support the existence and importance of the state governments. The danger, if any exists, flows from an opposite source. The probable evil is, that the general government will be too dependent on the state legislatures, too much governed by their prejudices, and too obsequious to their humors; that the states, with every power in their hands, will make encroachments on the national authority, till the Union is weakened and dissolved.

There are certain social principles in human nature from which we may draw the most solid conclusions with respect to the conduct of individuals and of communities. We love our families more than our neighbors; we love our neighbors more than our countrymen in general. The human affections, like the solar heat, lose their intensity as they depart from the center, and become languid in proportion to the expansion of the circle on which they act. On these principles, the attachment of the individual will be first and forever secured by the state governments; they will be a mutual protection and support. Another source of influence, which has already been pointed out, is the various official connections in the states. Gentlemen endeavor to evade the force of this by saying that these offices will be insignificant. This is by no means true. The state officers will ever be important, because they are necessary and useful. Their powers are such as are extremely interesting to the people; such as affect their property, their liberty, and life.

What is more important than the administration of justice and the execution of the civil and criminal laws? Can the state governments become insignificant while they have the power of raising money independently and without control? If they are really useful, if they are calculated to promote the essential interests of the people, they must have their confidence and support. The states can never lose their powers till the whole people of America are robbed of their liberties. These must go together; they must support each other, or meet one common fate. On the gentleman's principle, we may safely trust the state governments, though we have no means of resisting them; but we cannot confide in the national government, though we have an effectual constitutional guard against every encroachment. This is the essence of their argument, and it is false and fallacious beyond conception.

With regard to the jurisdiction of the two governments, I shall certainly admit that the Constitution ought to be so formed as not to prevent the states from providing for their own existence; and I maintain that it is so formed, and that their power of providing for themselves is sufficiently established. This is conceded by one gentleman, and in the next breath the concession is retracted. He says Congress has but one exclusive right in taxation—that of duties on imports; certainly, then, their other powers are only concurrent. But to take off the force of this obvious conclusion he immediately says that the laws of the United States are supreme; and that where there is one supreme there cannot be a concurrent authority; and further, that where the laws of the Union are supreme, those of the states must be subordinate; because there cannot be two supremes. This is curious sophistry. That two supreme powers cannot act together is false. They are inconsistent only when they are aimed at each other or at one indivisible object. The laws of the United States are supreme as to all their proper, constitutional objects; the laws of the states are supreme in the same way. These supreme laws may act on different objects without clashing; or they may operate on different parts of the same common object with perfect harmony. Suppose both governments should lay a tax of a penny on a certain article; has not each an independent and uncontrollable power to collect its own tax? The meaning of the maxim, there cannot be two supremes, is simply this—two powers cannot be supreme over each other. This meaning is entirely perverted by the gentlemen. But, it is said, disputes between collectors are to be referred to the federal courts. This is again wandering in the field of conjecture. But suppose the fact is certain; is it not to be presumed that they will express the true meaning of the Constitution and the laws? Will they not be bound to consider the concurrent jurisdiction; to declare that both the taxes shall have equal operation; that both the powers, in that respect, are sovereign and co-extensive? If they transgress their duty, we are to hope that they will be punished. Sir, we cannot reason from probabilities alone. When we leave common sense, and give ourselves up to conjecture, there can be no certainty, no security in our reasonings.

George Washington
[1732–1799]

Victorious commander-in-chief of the colonial forces and honored first President of the United States, George Washington is the author of two notable addresses, often quoted for their wise and patriotic sentiments. They are presented here in full. The Inaugural Address was delivered before the Senate on April 30, 1789, and the Farewell Address was made public on September 19, 1796.

INAUGURAL ADDRESS

FELLOW-CITIZENS of the Senate, and of the House of Representatives: Among the vicissitudes incident to life, no event could have filled me with greater anxieties, than that of which the notification was transmitted by your order, and received on the fourteenth day of the present month. On the one hand, I was summoned by my country, whose voice I can never hear but with veneration and love, from a retreat which I had chosen with the fondest predilection, and in my flattering hopes with an immutable decision as the asylum of my declining years; a retreat which was rendered every day more necessary, as well as more dear to me, by the addition of habit to inclination, and of frequent interruptions in my health to the gradual waste committed on it by time. On the other hand, the magnitude and difficulty of the trust, to which the voice of my country called me, being sufficient to awaken in the wisest and most experienced of her citizens a distrustful scrutiny into his qualifications, could not but overwhelm with despondence, one, who inheriting inferior endowments from nature, and unpractised in the duties of civil administration, ought to be peculiarly conscious of his own deficiencies. In this conflict of emotions, all I dare aver, is, that it has been my faithful study to collect my duty from a just appreciation of every circumstance by which it might be affected. All I dare hope is, that if in executing this task, I have been too much swayed by a grateful remembrance of former instances, or by an affectionate sensibility to this transcendent proof of the confidence of my fellow-citizens, and have thence too little consulted my incapacity as well as disinclination for the weighty and untried cares before me, my error will be palliated by the motives which misled me, and its consequences be judged by my country, with some share of the partiality in which they originated.

Such being the impressions under which I have, in obedience to the public summons, repaired to the present station, it would be peculiarly improper to omit in this first official act, my fervent supplications to that Almighty Being who rules over the universe—who presides in the councils of nations—and whose providential aids can supply every human defect, that his benediction may consecrate to the liberties and happiness of the people of the United States, a government instituted by themselves for these essential purposes; and may enable every instrument, employed in its administration, to execute with success the functions allotted to his charge. In tendering this homage to the great author of every public and private good, I assure myself that it expresses your sentiments not less than my own, nor those of my fellow-citizens at large, less than either. No people can be bound to acknowledge and adore the invisible hand, which conducts the affairs of men, more than the people of the United States. Every step, by which they have advanced to the character of an independent nation, seems to have been distinguished by some token of providential agency; and in the important revolution just accomplished in the system of their united government, the tranquil deliberations and voluntary consent of so many distinct communities, from which the event has resulted, cannot be compared with the means by which most governments have been established, without some return of pious gratitude along with a humble anticipation of the future blessings which the past seem to presage. These reflections, arising out of the present crisis, have forced themselves too strongly on my mind to be suppressed. You will join with me, I trust, in thinking that there are none under the influence of which the proceedings of a new and free government can more auspiciously commence.

By the article establishing the executive department, it is made the duty of the President, "to recommend to your consideration such measures as he shall judge necessary and expedient." The circumstances under which I now meet you will acquit me from entering into that subject, farther than to refer to the great constitutional charter under which you are assembled; and which, in defining your powers, designates the objects to which your attention is to be given. It will be more consistent with those circumstances, and far more congenial with the feelings which actuate me, to substitute, in place of a recommendation of particular measures, the tribute that is due to the talents, the rectitude, and the patriotism which adorn the characters selected to devise and adopt them. In these honorable qualifications, I behold the surest pledges, that as, on one side, no local prejudices or attachments, no separate views, nor party animosities, will misdirect the comprehensive and equal eye which ought to watch over this great assemblage of communities and interests; so on another, that the foundations of our national policy will be laid in the pure and immutable principles of private morality; and the pre-eminence of free government be exemplified by all the attributes which can win the affections of its citizens, and command the respect of the world. I dwell on this prospect with every satisfaction which an ardent love for my country can inspire: since there is no truth more thoroughly established, than that there exists in the economy and course of nature, an indissoluble union between virtue and happiness, between duty and advantage, between the genuine maxims of an honest and magnanimous policy and the solid rewards of public prosperity and felicity: since we ought to be no less persuaded, that the propitious smiles of heaven can never be expected on a nation that disregards the eternal rules of order and right, which heaven itself has ordained: and since the preservation of the sacred fire of liberty, and the destiny of the republican model of government, are justly considered as deeply, perhaps as finally staked, on the experiment entrusted to the hands of the American people.

Besides the ordinary objects submitted to your care, it will remain with your judgment to decide, how far an exercise of the occasional power delegated by the fifth article of the constitution is rendered expedient at the present juncture by the nature of objections which have been urged against the system, or by the degree of inquietude which has given birth to them. Instead of undertaking particular recommendations on this subject, in which I could be guided by no lights derived from official opportunities, I shall again give way to my entire confidence in your discernment and pursuit of the public good; for I assure myself that whilst you carefully avoid every alteration which might endanger the benefits of an united and effective government, or which ought to await the future lessons of experience; a reverence for the characteristic rights of freemen, and a regard for the public harmony, will sufficiently influence your deliberations on the question how far the former can be more impregnably fortified, or the latter be safely and advantageously promoted.

To the preceding observations I have one to add, which will be most properly addressed to the House of Representatives. It concerns myself, and will therefore be as brief as possible. When I was first honored with a call into the service of my country, then on the eve of an arduous struggle for its liberties, the light in which I contemplated my duty required that I should renounce every pecuniary compensation. From this resolution I have in no instance departed. And being still under the impressions which produced it, I must decline, as inapplicable to myself, any share in the personal emoluments, which may be indispensably included in a permanent provision for the executive department; and must accordingly pray that the pecuniary estimates for the station in which I am placed, may, during my continuance in it, be limited to such actual expenditures as the public good may be thought to require.

Having thus imparted to you my sentiments, as they have been awakened by the occasion which brings us together, I shall take my present leave; but not without resorting once more to the benign Parent of the human race, in humble supplication, that since He has been pleased to favor the American people, with opportunities for deliberating in perfect tranquillity, and dispositions for deciding with unparalleled unanimity on a form of government, for the security of their union, and the advancement of their happiness; so His divine blessing may be equally conspicuous in the enlarged views, the temperate consultations, and the wise measures on which the success of this government must depend.

FAREWELL ADDRESS

FRIENDS AND FELLOW-CITIZENS: The period for a new election of a citizen, to administer the executive government of the United States, being not far distant, and the time actually arrived when your thoughts must be employed in designating the person who is to be clothed with that important trust, it appears to me proper, especially as it may conduce to a more distinct expression of the public voice, that I should now apprise you of the resolution I have formed, to decline being considered among the number of those out of whom a choice is to be made.

I beg you, at the same time, to do me the justice to be assured that this resolution has not been taken without a strict regard to all the considerations appertaining to the relation which binds a dutiful citizen to his country; and that in withdrawing the tender of service which silence, in my situation, might imply, I am influenced by no diminution of zeal for your future interest, no deficiency of grateful respect for your past kindness, but am supported by a full conviction that the step is compatible with both.

The acceptance of, and continuance hitherto, in the office to which your suffrages have twice called me, have been a uniform sacrifice of inclination to the opinion of duty, and to a deference for what appeared to be your desire. I constantly hoped that it would have been much earlier in my power, consistently with motives which I was not at liberty to disregard, to return to that retirement from which I had been reluctantly drawn. The strength of my inclination to do this, previous to the last election, had even led to the preparation of an address, to declare it to you; but mature reflection on the then perplexed and critical posture of our affairs with foreign nations, and the unanimous advice of persons entitled to my confidence, impelled me to abandon the idea.

I rejoice that the state of your concerns, external as well as internal, no longer renders the pursuit of inclination incompatible with the sentiment of duty or propriety, and am persuaded, whatever partiality may be retained for my services, that in the present circumstances of our country, you will not disapprove of my determination to retire.

The impressions with which I first undertook the arduous trust were explained on the proper occasion. In the discharge of this trust I will only say, that I have with good intentions contributed towards the organization and administration of the government, the best exertions of which a very fallible judgment was capable. Not unconscious, in the outset, of the inferiority of my qualifications, experience, in my own eyes, perhaps still more in the eyes of others, has strengthened the motives to diffidence of myself; and every day the increasing weight of years admonishes me more and more that the shade of retirement is as necessary to me as it will be welcome. Satisfied that if any circumstances have given peculiar value to my services they were temporary, I have the consolation to believe, that while choice and prudence invite me to quit the political scene, patriotism does not forbid it.

In looking forward to the moment which is intended to terminate the career of my public life, my feelings do not permit me to suspend the deep acknowledgment of that debt of gratitude which I owe to my beloved country for the many honors it has conferred upon me; still more for the steadfast confidence with which it has supported me; and for the opportunities I have thence enjoyed of manifesting my inviolable attachment, by services, faithful and persevering, though in usefulness unequal to my zeal. If benefits have resulted to our country from these services, let it always be remembered to your praise, and as an instructive example in our annals, that under circumstances in which the passions, agitated in every direction, were liable to mislead, amidst appearances sometimes dubious, vicissitudes of fortune often discouraging, in situations in which not unfrequently want of success has countenanced the spirit of criticism, the constancy of your support was the essential prop of the efforts, and the guarantee of the plans by which they were effected. Profoundly penetrated with this idea, I shall carry it with me to my grave, as a strong incitement to unceasing wishes that heaven may continue to you the choicest tokens of its beneficence; that your union and brotherly affection may be perpetual; that the free constitution, which is the work of your hands, may be sacredly maintained; that its administration, in every department, may be stamped with wisdom and virtue; that, in fine, the happiness of the people of these States, under the auspices of liberty, may be made complete by so careful a preservation and so prudent a use of this blessing as will acquire to them the glory of recommending it to the applause, the affection, and adoption of every nation which is yet a stranger to it.

Here, perhaps, I ought to stop. But a solicitude for your welfare, which cannot end but with my life, and the apprehension of danger, natural to that solicitude, urge me, on an occasion like the present, to offer to your solemn contemplation, and to recommend to your frequent review, some sentiments, which are the result of much reflection, of no inconsiderable observation, and which appear to me all-important to the permanency of your felicity as a people. These will be offered to you with the more freedom, as you can only see in them the disinterested warnings of a parting friend, who can possibly have no personal motive to bias his counsel. Nor can I forget, as an encouragement to it, your indulgent reception of my sentiments on a former and not dissimilar occasion.

Interwoven as is the love of liberty with every ligament of your hearts, no recommendation of mine is necessary to fortify or confirm the attachment.

The unity of government which constitutes you one people is also now dear to you. It is justly so, for it is a main pillar in the edifice of your real independence, the support of your tranquillity at home, your peace abroad, of your safety, of your prosperity, of that very liberty which you so highly prize. But as it is easy to foresee, that from different causes and from different quarters, much pains will be taken, many artifices employed, to weaken in your minds the conviction of this truth; as this is the point in your political fortress against which the batteries of internal and external enemies will be most constantly and actively (though often covertly and insidiously) directed, it is of infinite moment that you should properly estimate the immense value of your national union, to your collective and individual happiness; that you should cherish a cordial, habitual, and immovable attachment to it; accustoming yourselves to think and speak of it as of the palladium of your political safety and prosperity, watching for its preservation with jealous anxiety; discountenancing whatever may suggest even a suspicion that it can in any event be abandoned; and indignantly frowning upon the first dawning of every attempt to alienate any portion of our country from the rest, or to enfeeble the sacred ties which now link together the various parts.

For this you have every inducement of sympathy and interest. Citizens, by birth or choice, of a common country, that country has a right to concentrate your affections. The name of American, which belongs to you in your national capacity, must always exalt the just pride of patriotism more than any appellation derived from local discriminations. With slight shades of difference, you have the same religion, manners, habits, and political principles. You have, in a common cause, fought and triumphed together; the independence and liberty you possess are the work of joint councils and joint efforts, of common dangers, sufferings, and successes.

But these considerations, however powerfully they address themselves to your sensibility, are greatly outweighed by those which apply more immediately to your interest. Here every portion of our country finds the most commanding motives for carefully guarding and preserving the union of the whole.

The North, in an unrestrained intercourse with the South, protected by the equal laws of a common government, finds, in the productions of the latter, great additional resources of maritime and commercial enterprise, and precious materials of manufacturing industry. The South, in the same intercourse, benefiting by the agency of the North, sees its agriculture grow and its commerce expand. Turning partly into its own channels the seamen of the North, it finds its particular navigation invigorated; and while it contributes, in different ways, to nourish and increase the general mass of the national navigation, it looks forward to the protection of a maritime strength, to which itself is unequally adapted. The East, in like intercourse with the West, already finds, and in the progressive improvement of interior communications, by land and water, will more and more find a valuable vent for the commodities which it brings from abroad or manufactures at home. The West derives from the East supplies requisite to its growth and comfort, and what is perhaps of still greater consequence, it must of necessity owe the secure enjoyment of indispensable outlets for its own productions to the weight, influence, and the future maritime strength of the Atlantic side of the Union, directed by an indissoluble community of interest as one nation. Any other tenure, by which the West can hold this essential advantage, whether derived from its own separate strength, or from an apostate and unnatural connection with any foreign power, must be intrinsically precarious.

While, then, every part of our country thus feels an immediate and particular interest in union, all the parts combined cannot fail to find, in the united mass of means and efforts, greater strength, greater resource, proportionably greater security, from external danger, a less frequent interruption of their peace by foreign nations; and what is of inestimable value, they must derive from union an exemption from those broils and wars between themselves which so frequently afflict neighboring countries, not tied together by the same government, which their own rivalships alone would be sufficient to produce, but which opposite foreign alliances, attachments, and intrigues, would stimulate and embitter. Hence, likewise, they will avoid the necessity of those overgrown military establishments, which, under any form of government, are inauspicious to liberty, and which are to be regarded as particularly hostile to republican liberty. In this sense it is that your union ought to be considered as a main prop of your liberty, and that the love of the one ought to endear to you the preservation of the other.

These considerations speak a persuasive language to every reflecting and virtuous mind, and exhibit the continuance of the union as a primary object of patriotic desire. Is there a doubt whether a common government can embrace so large a sphere? Let experience solve it. To listen to mere speculation, in such a case, were criminal. We are authorized to hope that a proper organization of the whole, with the auxiliary agency of governments for the respective subdivisions, will afford a happy issue to the experiment. 'Tis well worth a fair and full experiment. With such powerful and obvious motives to union, affecting all parts of our country, while experience shall not have demonstrated its impracticability, there will always be reason to distrust the patriotism of those who, in any quarter, may endeavor to weaken its bands.

In contemplating the causes which may disturb our union, it occurs, as a matter of serious concern, that any ground should have been furnished for characterizing parties by geographical discriminations—Northern and Southern, Atlantic and Western—whence designing men may endeavor to excite a belief that there is a real difference of local interests and views. One of the expedients of party to acquire influence within particular districts is to misrepresent the opinions and aims of other districts. You cannot shield yourselves too much against the jealousies and heart-burnings which spring from these misrepresentations; they tend to render alien to each other those who ought to be bound together by fraternal affection. The inhabitants of our western country have lately had a useful lesson on this head. They have seen, in the negotiation by the executive, and in the unanimous ratification by the Senate, of the treaty with Spain, and in the universal satisfaction of that event throughout the United States, a decisive proof how unfounded were the suspicions propagated among them of a policy in the general government and in the Atlantic States, unfriendly to their interests in regard to the Mississippi; they have been witnesses to the formation of two treaties—that with Great Britain and that with Spain—which secure to them everything they could desire, in respect to our foreign relations, towards confirming their prosperity. Will it not be their wisdom to rely, for the preservation of these advantages, on the union by which they were procured? Will they not henceforth be deaf to those advisers, if such there are, who would sever them from their brethren, and connect them with aliens?

To the efficacy and permanency of your union, a government for the whole is indispensable. No alliances, however strict, between the parts, can be an adequate substitute; they must inevitably experience the infractions and interruptions, which alliances, in all times, have experienced. Sensible of this momentous truth, you have improved upon your first essay by the adoption of a constitution of government better calculated than your former for an intimate union, and for the efficacious management of your common concerns. This government, the offspring of our own choice, uninfluenced and unawed, adopted upon full investigation and mature deliberation, completely free in its principles, in the distribution of its powers, uniting security with energy, and containing within itself a provision for its own amendment, has a just claim to your confidence and your support. Respect for its authority, compliance with its laws, acquiescence in its measures, are duties enjoined by the fundamental maxims of true liberty. The basis of our political systems is the right of the people to make and to alter the constitutions of government. But the constitution, which at any time exists, until changed by an explicit and authentic act of the whole people, is sacredly obligatory upon all. The very idea of the power and the right of the people to establish a government presupposes the duty of every individual to obey the established government.

All obstructions to the execution of the laws, all combinations and associations, under whatever plausible character, with the real design to direct, control, counteract, or awe the regular deliberation and action of the constituted authorities, are destructive of this fundamental principle, and of fatal tendency. They serve to organize faction, to give it an artificial and extraordinary force, to put in the place of the delegated will of the nation, the will of a party, often a small, but artful and enterprising minority of the community; and according to the alternate triumphs of different parties, to make the public administration the mirror of the ill-concerted and incongruous projects of faction, rather than the organ of consistent and wholesome plans, digested by common councils, and modified by mutual interests.

However combinations or associations of the above description may now and then answer popular ends, they are likely, in the course of time and things, to become potent engines, by which cunning, ambitious, and unprincipled men will be enabled to subvert the power of the people, and to usurp for themselves the reins of government; destroying afterward the very engines which have lifted them to unjust dominion.

Toward the preservation of your government and the permanency of your present happy state, it is requisite, not only that you speedily discountenance irregular opposition to its acknowledged authority, but also that you resist with care the spirit of innovation upon its principles, however specious the pretexts. One method of assault may be to effect, in the forms of the constitution, alterations which will impair the energy of the system, and thus to undermine what cannot be directly overthrown. In all the changes to which you may be invited, remember that time and habit are at least as necessary to fix the true character of governments as of other human institutions; that experience is the surest standard by which to test the real tendency of the existing constitution of a country; that facility in changes, upon the credit of mere hypothesis and opinion, exposes to perpetual change, from the endless variety of hypothesis and opinion. And remember especially, that for the efficient management of your common interests, in a country so extensive as ours, a government of as much vigor as is consistent with the perfect security of liberty, is indispensable. Liberty itself will find in such a government, with powers properly distributed and adjusted, its surest guardian. It is, indeed, little else than a name, where the government is too feeble to withstand the enterprises of faction; to confine each member of society within the limits prescribed by the laws, and to maintain all in the secure and tranquil enjoyment of the rights of person and property.

I have already intimated to you the danger of parties in the State, with particular reference to the founding of them on geographical discrimination. Let me now take a more comprehensive view, and warn you, in the most solemn manner, against the baneful effects of the spirit of party, generally.

This spirit, unfortunately, is inseparable from our nature, having its root in the strongest passions of the human mind. It exists under different shapes, in all governments, more or less stifled, controlled, or repressed. But in those of the popular form, it is seen in its greatest rankness, and is truly their worst enemy.

The alternate domination of one faction over another, sharpened by the spirit of revenge, natural to party dissensions, which, in different ages and countries, has perpetrated the most horrid enormities, is itself a frightful despotism. But this leads, at length, to a more formal and permanent despotism. The disorders and miseries, which result, gradually incline the minds of men to seek security and repose in the absolute power of an individual; and sooner or later, the chief of some prevailing faction, more able or more fortunate than his competitors, turns this disposition to the purposes of his own elevation on the ruins of public liberty.

Without looking forward to an extremity of this kind, (which, nevertheless, ought not to be entirely out of sight,) the common and continual mischiefs of the spirit of party are sufficient to make it the interest and duty of a wise people to discourage and restrain it.

It serves always to distract the public councils, and enfeeble the public administration. It agitates the community with ill-founded jealousies and false alarms; kindles the animosity of one part against another; foments occasionally riot and insurrection. It opens the door to foreign influence and corruption, which find a facilitated access to the government itself, through the channels of party passion. Thus the policy and the will of one country are subjected to the policy and will of another.

There is an opinion, that parties, in free countries, are useful checks upon the administration of the government, and serve to keep alive the spirit of liberty. This, within certain limits, is probably true; and, in governments of a monarchical cast, patriotism may look with indulgence, if not with favor, upon the spirit of party. But in those of popular character, in governments purely elective, it is a spirit not to be encouraged. From their natural tendency, it is certain there will always be enough of that spirit for every salutary purpose. And there being constant danger of excess, the effort ought to be, by force of public opinion, to mitigate and assuage it. A fire not to be quenched, it demands a uniform vigilance to prevent its bursting into a flame, lest, instead of warming, it should consume.

It is important, likewise, that the habits of thinking, in a free country, should inspire caution in those entrusted with its administration, to confine themselves within their respective constitutional spheres, avoiding, in the exercise of the powers of one department, to encroach upon another. The spirit of encroachment tends to consolidate the powers of all the departments in one, and thus to create, whatever the form of government, a real despotism. A just estimate of that love of power, and proneness to abuse it, which predominate in the human heart, is sufficient to satisfy us of the truth of this position. The necessity of reciprocal checks in the exercise of political power, by dividing and distributing it into different depositaries, and constituting each the guardian of the public weal against invasion by the other, has been evinced by experiments ancient and modern: some of them in our country, and under our own eyes. To preserve them must be as necessary as to institute them. If, in the opinion of the people, the distribution or modification of the constitutional powers, be, in any particular, wrong, let it be corrected by an amendment in the way which the constitution designates. But let there be no change by usurpation; for though this, in one instance, may be the instrument of good, it is the customary weapon by which free governments are destroyed. The precedent must always greatly overbalance, in permanent evil, any partial or transient benefit which the use can at any time yield.

Of all the dispositions and habits, which lead to political prosperity, religion and morality are indispensable supports. In vain would that man claim the tribute of patriotism, who should labor to subvert these great pillars of human happiness, these firmest props of the destinies of men and citizens. The mere politician, equally with the pious man, ought to respect and to cherish them. A volume could not trace all their connection with private and public felicity. Let it simply be asked, where is the security for property, for reputation, for life, if the sense of religious obligation desert the oaths, which are the instruments of investigation in courts of justice? And let us with caution indulge the supposition that morality can be maintained without religion. Whatever may be conceded to the influence of refined education on minds of peculiar structure, reason and experience both forbid us to expect, that national morality can prevail in exclusion of religious principles.

It is substantially true, that virtue or morality is a necessary spring of popular government. The rule, indeed, extends with more or less force to every species of free government. Who, that is a sincere friend to it, can look with indifference upon attempts to shake the foundation of the fabric?

Promote, then, as an object of primary importance, institutions for the general diffusion of knowledge. In proportion as the structure of a government gives force to public opinion, it is essential that public opinion should be enlightened.

As a very important source of strength and security, cherish public credit. One method of preserving it is to use it as sparingly as possible; avoiding occasions of expense by cultivating peace, but remembering also that timely disbursements to prepare for danger frequently prevent much greater disbursements to repel it; avoiding likewise the accumulation of debt, not only by shunning occasions of expense, but by vigorous exertions in time of peace to discharge the debts which unavoidable wars may have occasioned, not ungenerously throwing upon posterity the burden which we ourselves ought to bear. The execution of these maxims belongs to your representatives, but it is necessary that public opinion should co-operate. To facilitate to them the performance of their duty, it is essential that you should practically bear in mind, that towards the payment of debts there must be revenue; that to have revenue there must be taxes; that no taxes can be devised which are not more or less inconvenient and unpleasant; that the intrinsic embarrassment, inseparable from the selection of the proper objects (which is always the choice of difficulties) ought to be a decisive motive for a candid construction of the conduct of the government in making it,.and for a spirit of acquiescence in the measures for obtaining revenue which the public exigencies may at any time dictate.

Observe good faith and justice towards all nations; cultivate peace and harmony with all; religion and morality enjoin this conduct; and can it be that good policy does not equally enjoin it? It will be worthy of a free, enlightened, and, at no distant period, a great nation, to give to mankind the magnanimous and too novel example of a people always guided by an exalted justice and benevolence. Who can doubt that, in the course of time and things, the fruits of such a plan would richly repay any temporary advantages that might be lost by a steady adherence to it? Can it be, that Providence has not connected the permanent felicity of a nation with its virtue? The experiment, at least, is recommended by every sentiment which ennobles human nature. Alas! is it rendered impossible by its vices?

In the execution of such a plan, nothing is more essential than that permanent, inveterate antipathies against particular nations, and passionate attachments for others, should be excluded; and that in place of them, just and amicable feelings towards all should be cultivated. The nation, which indulges towards another an habitual hatred, or an habitual fondness, is in some degree a slave. It is a slave to its animosity or to its affection, either of which is sufficient to lead it astray from its duty and its interest. Antipathy in one nation against another, disposes each more readily to offer insult and injury, to lay hold of slight causes of umbrage, and to be haughty and intractable, when accidental or trifling occasions of dispute occur.

Hence frequent collisions, obstinate, envenomed, and bloody contests. The nation, prompted by ill-will and resentment, sometimes impels to war the government, contrary to the best calculations of policy. The government sometimes participates in the national propensity, and adopts through passion what reason would reject; at other times, it makes the animosity of the nation subservient to projects of hostility instigated by pride, ambition and other sinister and pernicious motives. The peace often, and sometimes, perhaps, the liberty of nations, has been the victim.

So, likewise, a passionate attachment of one nation for another produces a variety of evils. Sympathy for the favorite nation facilitating the illusion of an imaginary common interest in cases where no real common interest exists, and infusing into one the enmities of the other, betrays the former into a participation in the quarrels and wars of the latter, without adequate inducement or justification. It leads also to concessions to the favorite nation of privileges denied to others, which is apt doubly to injure the nation making the concessions; by unnecessarily parting with what ought to have been retained; and by exciting jealousy, ill-will, and a disposition to retaliate, in the parties from whom equal privileges are withheld; and it gives to ambitious, corrupted, or deluded citizens (who devote themselves to the favorite nation) facility to betray, or sacrifice the interests of their own country, without odium, sometimes even with popularity; gilding, with the appearances of a virtuous sense of obligation, a commendable deference for public opinion, or laudable zeal for public good, the base or foolish compliances of ambition, corruption, or infatuation.

As avenues to foreign influence, in innumerable ways, such attachments are particularly alarming to the truly enlightened and independent patriot. How many opportunities do they afford to tamper with domestic factions; to practise the arts of seduction; to mislead public opinion; to influence or awe the public councils! Such an attachment of a small or weak nation, toward a great and powerful one, dooms the former to be the satellite of the latter.

Against the insidious wiles of foreign influence (I conjure you to believe me, fellow-citizens), the jealousy of a free people ought to be constantly awake; since history and experience prove, that foreign influence is one of the most baneful foes of republican government. But that jealousy, to be useful, must be impartial; else it becomes the instrument of the very influence to be avoided, instead of a defence against it. Excessive partiality for one foreign nation, and excessive dislike of another, cause those whom they actuate, to see danger only on one side; and serve to veil and even second the arts of influence on the other. Real patriots, who may resist the intrigues of the favorite, are liable to become suspected and odious; while its tools and dupes usurp the applause and confidence of the people, to surrender their interests.

The great rule of conduct for us, in regard to foreign nations is, in extending our commercial relations, to have with them as little political connection as possible. So far as we have already formed engagements, let them be fulfilled with perfect good faith. Here let us stop.

Europe has a set of primary interests, which to us have none, or a very remote relation. Hence she must be engaged in frequent controversies, the causes of which are essentially foreign to our concerns. Hence, therefore, it must be unwise in us to implicate ourselves, by artificial ties, in the ordinary vicissitudes of her politics, or the ordinary combinations and collisions of her friendships and enmities.

Our detached and distant situation invites and enables us to pursue a different course. If we remain one people, under an efficient government, the period is not far off when we may defy material injury from external annoyance; when we may take such an attitude as will cause the neutrality we may at any time resolve upon, to be scrupulously respected; when belligerent nations, under the impossibility of making acquisitions upon us, will not lightly hazard the giving us provocation; when we may choose peace or war, as our interest, guided by justice, shall counsel.

Why forego the advantages of so peculiar a situation? Why quit our own, to stand upon foreign ground? Why, by interweaving our destiny with that of any part of Europe, entangle our peace and prosperity in the toils of European ambition, rivalship, interest, humor, or caprice?

'Tis our true policy to steer clear of permanent alliances with any portion of the foreign world; so far, I mean, as we are now at liberty to do it; for let me not be understood as capable of patronizing infidelity to existing engagements. I hold the maximum no less applicable to public than to private affairs, that honesty is always the best policy. I repeat it, therefore, let those engagements be observed in their genuine sense. But, in my opinion, it is unnecessary, and would be unwise, to extend them.

Taking care always to keep ourselves, by suitable establishments, in a respectable defensive posture, we may safely trust to temporary alliances for extraordinary emergencies.

Harmony, and a liberal intercourse with all nations, are recommended by policy, humanity, and interest. But even our commercial policy should hold an equal and impartial hand; neither seeking nor granting exclusive favors or preferences; consulting the natural course of things; diffusing and diversifying, by gentle means, the streams of commerce, but forcing nothing; establishing, with powers so disposed, in order to give trade a stable course, to define the rights of our merchants, and to enable the government to support them, conventional rules of intercourse, the best that present circumstances and mutual opinion will permit, but temporary, and liable to be, from time to time, abandoned or varied, as experience and circumstances shall dictate; constantly keeping in view, that it is folly in one nation to look for disinterested favors from another; that it must pay, with a portion of its independence, for whatever it may accept under that character; that, by such acceptance, it may place itself in the condition of having given equivalents for nominal favors, and yet of being reproached with ingratitude for not giving more. There can be no greater error than to expect to calculate upon real favors from nation to nation. It is an illusion, which experience must cure, which a just pride ought to discard.

In offering to you, my countrymen, these counsels of an old and affectionate friend, I dare not hope they will make the strong and lasting impression I could wish; that they will control the usual current of the passions, or prevent our nation from running the course which has hitherto marked the destiny of nations! But, if I may even flatter myself, that they may be productive of some partial benefit, some occasional good; that they may now and then recur to moderate the fury of party spirit; to warn against the mischiefs of foreign intrigues; to guard against the impostures of pretended patriotism; this hope will be a full recompense for the solicitude for your welfare, by which they have been dictated.

How far, in the discharge of my official duties, I have been guided by the principles which have been delineated, the public records and other evidences of my conduct must witness to you and to the world. To myself the assurance of my own conscience is, that I have at least believed myself to be guided by them.

In relation to the still subsisting war in Europe, my proclamation of April 22, 1793, is the index to my plan. Sanctioned by your approving voice, and by that of your representatives in both Houses of Congress, the spirit of that measure has continually governed me, uninfluenced by any attempts to deter or divert me from it.

After deliberate examination, with the aid of the best lights I could obtain, I was well satisfied that our country, under all the circumstances of the case, had a right to take, and was bound in duty and interest to take, a neutral position. Having taken it, I determined, as far as should depend upon me, to maintain it with moderation, perseverance, and firmness.

The considerations which respect the right to hold this conduct, it is not necessary, on this occasion, to detail. I will only observe, that, according to my understanding of the matter, that right, so far from being denied by any of the belligerent powers, has been virtually admitted by all.

The duty of holding a neutral conduct may be inferred, without anything more, from the obligation which justice and humanity impose on every nation, in cases in which it is free to act, to maintain inviolate the relations of peace and amity towards other nations.

The inducements of interest for observing that conduct will best be referred to your own reflection and experience. With me, a predominant motive has been to endeavor to gain time to our country to settle and mature its yet recent institutions, and to progress, without interruption, to that degree of strength and consistency which is necessary to give it, humanly speaking, the command of its own fortunes.

Though, in reviewing the incidents of my administration, I am unconscious of intentional error, I am, nevertheless, too sensible of my defects, not to think it probable that I may have committed many errors. Whatever they may be, I fervently beseech the Almighty to avert or mitigate the evils to which they may tend. I shall also carry with me the hope that my country will never cease to view them with indulgence, and that after forty-five years of my life dedicated to its service, with an upright zeal, the faults of incompetent abilities will be consigned to oblivion, as myself must soon be to the mansions of rest.

Relying on its kindness in this, as in other things, and actuated by that fervent love towards it, which is so natural to a man who views in it the native soil of himself and his progenitors for several generations, I anticipate, with pleasing expectations, that retreat in which I promise myself to realize, without alloy, the sweet enjoyment of partaking, in the midst of my fellow-citizens, the benign influence of good laws under a free government—the ever favorite object of my heart, and the happy reward, as I trust, of our mutual cares, labors, and dangers.

Thomas Jefferson
[1743–1826]

Thomas Jefferson, third President of the United States, was one of the great leaders of the American Revolution. He drafted the Declaration of Independence and championed the Bill of Rights in the Federal Constitution. A man of many gifts and liberal views he took an active part in the affairs of the young republic. He was minister to France and Washington's Secretary of State. He was elected President in 1800.

FIRST INAUGURAL ADDRESS

FRIENDS AND FELLOW-CITIZENS: Called upon to undertake the duties of the first executive office of our country, I avail myself of the presence of that portion of my fellow-citizens which is here assembled, to express my grateful thanks for the favor with which they have been pleased to look toward me, to declare a sincere consciousness, that the task is above my talents, and that I approach it with those anxious and awful presentiments, which the greatness of the charge, and the weakness of my powers, so justly inspire. A rising nation, spread over a wide and fruitful land, traversing all the seas with the rich productions of their industry, engaged in commerce with nations who feel power and forget right, advancing rapidly to destinies beyond the reach of mortal eye; when I contemplate these transcendent objects, and see the honor, the happiness, and the hopes of this beloved country committed to the issue and the auspices of this day, I shrink from the contemplation, and humble myself before the magnitude of the undertaking. Utterly, indeed, should I despair, did not the presence of many, whom I see here, remind me, that, in the other high authorities provided by our constitution, I shall find resources of wisdom, of virtue, and of zeal, on which to rely under all difficulties. To you, then, gentlemen, who are charged with the sovereign functions of legislation, and to those associated with you, I look with encouragement for that guidance and support which may enable us to steer with safety the vessel in which we are all embarked, amidst the conflicting elements of a troubled world.

During the contest of opinion through which we have passed, the animation of discussions and of exertions has sometimes worn an aspect which might impose on strangers unused to think freely, and to speak and to write what they think; but this being now decided by the voice of the nation, announced according to the rules of the constitution, all will of course arrange themselves under the will of the law, and unite in common efforts for the common good. All too will bear in mind this sacred principle, that though the will of the majority is in all cases to prevail, that will, to be rightful, must be reasonable; that the minority possess their equal rights, which equal laws must protect, and to violate which would be oppression. Let us then, fellow-citizens, unite with one heart and one mind, let us restore to social intercourse that harmony and affection without which liberty and even life itself are but dreary things. And let us reflect, that having banished from our land that religious intolerance under which mankind so long bled and suffered, we have yet gained little, if we countenance a political intolerance, as despotic, as wicked, and as capable of as bitter and bloody persecutions. During the throes and convulsions of the ancient world, during the agonizing spasms of infuriated man, seeking through blood and slaughter his long-lost liberty, it was not wonderful that the agitation of the billows should reach even this distant and peaceful shore; that this should be more felt and feared by some, and less by others, and should divide opinions as to measures of safety; but every difference of opinion is not a difference of principle. We have called by different names brethren of the same principle. We are all Republicans; we are all Federalists. If there be any among us who wish to dissolve this Union, or to change its republican form, let them stand undisturbed as monuments of the safety with which error of opinion may be tolerated, where reason is left free to combat it. I know, indeed, that some honest men fear that a republican government cannot be strong; that this government is not strong enough. But would the honest patriot, in the full tide of successful experiment, abandon a government which has so far kept us free and firm, on the theoretic and visionary fear, that this government, the world's best hope, may, by possibility, want energy to preserve itself? I trust not. I believe this, on the contrary, the strongest government on earth. I believe it the only one where every man, at the call of the law, would fly to the standard of the law, and would meet invasions of the public order as his own personal concern. Sometimes it is said that man cannot be trusted with the government of himself. Can he then be trusted with the government of others? Or, have we found angels in the form of kings, to govern him? Let history answer this question.

Let us then, with courage and confidence, pursue our own federal and republican principles; our attachment to union and representative government. Kindly separated by nature and a wide ocean from the exterminating havoc of one quarter of the globe; too high-minded to endure the degradation of the others, possessing a chosen country, with room enough for our descendants to the thousandth and thousandth generation, entertaining a due sense of our equal right to the use of our own faculties, to the acquisition of our own industry, to honor and confidence from our fellow-citizens, resulting not from birth, but from our actions and their sense of them, enlightened by a benign religion, professed in deed and practised in various forms, yet all of them inculcating honesty, truth, temperance, gratitude, and the love of man, acknowledging and adoring an overruling Providence, which, by all its dispensations, proves that it delights in the happiness of man here, and his greater happiness hereafter; with all these blessings, what more is necessary to make us a happy and prosperous people? Still one thing more, fellow-citizens, a wise and frugal government, which shall restrain men from injuring one another, shall leave them otherwise free to regulate their own pursuits of industry and improvement, and shall not take from the mouth of labor the bread it has earned. This is the sum of good government; and this is necessary to close the circle of our felicities.

About to enter, fellow-citizens, upon the exercise of duties which comprehend everything dear and valuable to you, it is proper you should understand what I deem the essential principles of our government, and consequently, those which ought to shape its administration. I will compress them within the narrowest compass they will bear, stating the general principle, but not all its limitations. Equal and exact justice to all men, of whatever state or persuasion, religious or political; peace, commerce, and honest friendship with all nations, entangling alliances with none; the support of the State governments in all their rights, as the most competent administrations for our domestic concerns, and the surest bulwarks against anti-republican tendencies; the preservation of the general government in its whole constitutional vigor, as the sheet-anchor of our peace at home and safety abroad; a jealous care of the right of election by the people, a mild and safe corrective of abuses which are lopped by the sword of revolution where peaceable remedies are unprovided; absolute acquiescence in the decisions of the majority, the vital principle of republics, from which there is no appeal but to force, the vital principle and immediate parent of despotism; a well-disciplined militia, our best reliance in peace, and for the first moments of war, till regulars may relieve them; the supremacy of the civil over the military authority; economy in the public expense, that labor may be lightly burdened; the honest payment of our debts, and sacred preservation of the public faith; encouragement of agriculture, and of commerce as its handmaid; the diffusion of information, and arraignment of all abuses at the bar of the public reason; freedom of religion, freedom of the press, and freedom of person, under the protection of the *habeas corpus,* and trial by juries impartially selected. These principles form the bright constellation, which has gone before us, and guided our steps through an age of revolution and reformation. The wisdom of our sages, and blood of our heroes, have been devoted to their attainment; they should be the creed of our political faith, the text of civic instruction, the touchstone by which to try the services of those we trust; and should we wander from them in moments of error or of alarm, let us hasten to retrace our steps, and to regain the road which alone leads to peace, liberty, and safety.

I repair, then, fellow-citizens, to the post you have assigned me. With experience enough in subordinate offices to have seen the difficulties of this, the greatest of all, I have learned to expect that it will rarely fall to the lot of imperfect man, to retire from this station with the reputation and the favor which bring him into it. Without pretensions to that high confidence you reposed in our first and greatest revolutionary character, whose pre-eminent services had entitled him to the first place in his country's love, and destined for him the fairest page in the volume of faithful history, I ask so much confidence only as may give firmness and effect to the legal administration of your affairs. I shall often go wrong through defect of judgment. When right, I shall often be thought wrong by those whose positions will not command a view of the whole ground. I ask your indulgence for my own errors, which will never be intentional; and your support against the errors of others, who may condemn what they would not, if seen in all its parts. The approbation implied by your suffrage, is a great consolation to me for the past; and my future solicitude will be, to retain the good opinion of those who have bestowed it in advance, to conciliate that of others, by doing them all the good in my power, and to be instrumental to the happiness and freedom of all.

Relying then on the patronage of your good-will, I advance with obedience to the work, ready to retire from it whenever you become sensible how much better choices it is in your power to make. And may that infinite power which rules the destinies of the universe, lead our councils to what is best, and give them a favorable issue for your peace and prosperity.

Gouverneur Morris
[1752–1816]

Gouverneur Morris, of New York, was a member of the Continental Congress and of the Committee that drafted the Federal Constitution. He was minister to France in 1792–94. He delivered this eloquent funeral oration over the body of Alexander Hamilton at Trinity Church, New York City, on July 14, 1804.

ALEXANDER HAMILTON

IF ON THIS SAD, this solemn occasion, I should endeavor to move your commiseration, it would be doing injustice to that sensibility which has been so generally and so justly manifested. Far from attempting to excite your emotions, I must try to repress my own; and yet, I fear, that, instead of the language of a public speaker, you will hear only the lamentations of a wailing friend. But I will struggle with my bursting heart, to portray that heroic spirit, which has flown to the mansions of bliss.

Students of Columbia—he was in the ardent pursuit of knowledge in your academic shades when the first sound of the American war called him to the field. A young and unprotected volunteer, such was his zeal, and so brilliant his service, that we heard his name before we knew his person. It seemed as if God had called him suddenly into existence, that he might assist to save a world! The penetrating eye of Washington soon perceived the manly spirit which animated his youthful bosom. By this excellent judge of men he was selected as an aid, and thus he became early acquainted with, and was a principal actor in the more important scenes of our Revolution. At the siege of York, he pertinaciously insisted on and he obtained the command of a Forlorn Hope. He stormed the redoubt; but let it be recorded that not one single man of the enemy perished. His gallant troops, emulating the heroism of their chief, checked the uplifted arm, and spared a foe no longer resisting. Here closed his military career.

Shortly after the war, your favor—no, your discernment, called him to public office. You sent him to the convention at Philadelphia; he there assisted in forming that constitution which is now the bond of our union, the shield of our defense, and the source of our prosperity. In signing the compact, he expressed his apprehension that it did not contain sufficient means of strength for its own preservation; and that in consequence we should share the fate of many other republics, and pass through anarchy to despotism. We hoped better things. We confided in the good sense of the American people; and, above all, we trusted in the protecting providence of the Almighty. On this important subject he never concealed his opinion. He disdained concealment.

Knowing the purity of his heart, he bore it as it were in his hand, exposing to every passenger its inmost recesses. This generous indiscretion subjected him to censure from misrepresentation. His speculative opinions were treated as deliberate designs; and yet you all know how strenuous, how unremitting were his efforts to establish and to preserve the Constitution. If, then, his opinion was wrong, pardon, O pardon! that single error, in a life devoted to your service.

At the time when our government was organized, we were without funds, though not without resources. To call them into action, and establish order in the finances, Washington sought for splendid talents, for extensive information, and above all, he sought for sterling, incorruptible integrity. All these he found in Hamilton. The system then adopted, has been the subject of much animadversion. If it be not without a fault, let it be remembered that nothing human is perfect. Recollect the circumstances of the moment—recollect the conflict of .opinion— and, above all, remember that a minister of a republic must bend to the will of the people. The administration which Washington formed was one of the most efficient, one of the best that any country was ever blessed with. And the result was a rapid advance in power and prosperity, of which there is no example in any other age or nation. The part which Hamilton bore is universally known.

His unsuspecting confidence in professions, which he believed to be sincere, led him to trust too much to the undeserving. This exposed him to misrepresentation. He felt himself obliged to resign. The care of a rising family, and the narrowness of his fortune, made it a duty to return to his profession for their support. But though he was compelled to abandon public life, never, no, never for a moment did he abandon the public service. He never lost sight of your interests. I declare to you, before that God, in whose presence we are now especially assembled, that in his most private and confidential conversations, the single objects of discussion and consideration were your freedom and happiness. You well remember the state of things which again called forth Washington from his retreat to lead your armies. You know that he asked for Hamilton to be his second in command. That venerable sage well knew the dangerous incidents of a military profession, and he felt the hand of time pinching life at its source. It was probable that he would soon be removed from the scene, and that his second would succeed to the command. He knew by experience the importance of that place—and he thought the sword of America might safely be confided to the hand which now lies cold in that coffin. Oh! my fellow citizens, remember this solemn testimonial that he was not ambitious. Yet he was charged with ambition, and, wounded by the imputation, when he laid down his command he declared, in the proud independence of his soul, that he never would accept of any office, unless in a foreign war he should be called on to expose his life in defense of his country. This determination was immovable. It was his fault that his opinions and his resolutions could not be changed. Knowing his own firm purpose, he was indignant at the charge that he sought for place or power. He was ambitious only for glory, but he was deeply solicitous for you. For himself he feared nothing; but he feared that bad men might, by false professions, acquire your confidence, and abuse it to your ruin.

Brethren of the Cincinnati—there lies our chief! Let him still be our model. Like him, after long and faithful public services, let us cheerfully perform the social duties of private life. Oh! he was mild and gentle. In him there was no offense; no guile. His generous hand and heart were open to all.

Gentlemen of the bar—you have lost your brightest ornament. Cherish and imitate his example. While, like him, with justifiable and with laudable zeal, you pursue the interests of your clients, remember, like him, the eternal principle of justice.

Fellow citizens—you have long witnessed his professional conduct, and felt his unrivaled eloquence. You know how well he performed the duties of a citizen—you know that he never courted your favor by adulation or the sacrifice of his own judgment. You have seen him contending against you, and saving your dearest interests, as it were, in spite of yourselves. And you now feel and enjoy the benefits resulting from the firm energy of his conduct. Bear this testimony to the memory of my departed friend. I charge you to protect his fame. It is all he has left—all that these poor orphan children will inherit from their father. But, my countrymen, that fame may be a rich treasure to you also. Let it be the test by which to examine those who solicit your favor. Disregarding professions, view their conduct, and on a doubtful occasion ask, Would Hamilton have done this thing?

You all know how he perished. On this last scene I cannot, I must not dwell. It might excite emotions too strong for your better judgment. Suffer not your indignation to lead to an act which might again offend the insulted majesty of the laws. On his part, as from his lips, though with my voice—for his voice you will hear no more—let me entreat you to respect yourselves.

And now, ye ministers of the everlasting God, perform your holy office, and commit these ashes of our departed brother to the bosom of the grave.

American Indians

Following are two forceful speeches made by Indian warriors. The first was delivered by Red Jacket in 1805 at a council of chiefs of the Six Nations after a white missionary had addressed them. The second was delivered by Tecumseh in 1810 at Vincennes, Ind., in council with Governor Harrison.

RED JACKET

FRIEND AND BROTHER:—It was the will of the Great Spirit that we should meet together this day. He orders all things and has given us a fine day for our council. He has taken His garment from before the sun and caused it to shine with brightness upon us. Our eyes are opened that we see clearly; our ears are unstopped that we have been able to hear distinctly the words you have spoken. For all these favors we thank the Great Spirit, and Him only.

Brother, this council fire was kindled by you. It was at your request that we came together at this time. We have listened with attention to what you have said. You requested us to speak our minds freely. This gives us great joy; for we now consider that we stand upright before you and can speak what we think. All have heard your voice and all speak to you now as one man. Our minds are agreed.

Brother, you say you want an answer to your talk before you leave this place. It is right you should have one, as you are a great distance from home and we do not wish to detain you. But first we will look back a little and tell you what our fathers have told us and what we have heard from the white people.

Brother, listen to what we say. There was a time when our forefathers owned this great island. Their seats extended from the rising to the setting sun. The Great Spirit had made it for the use of Indians. He had created the buffalo, the deer, and other animals for food. He had made the bear and the beaver. Their skins served us for clothing. He had scattered them over the country and taught us how to take them. He had caused the earth to produce corn for bread. All this He had done for His red children because He loved them. If we had some disputes about our hunting-ground they were generally settled without the shedding of much blood.

But an evil day came upon us. Your forefathers crossed the great water and landed on this island. Their numbers were small. They found friends and not enemies. They told us they had fled from their own country for fear of wicked men and had come here to enjoy their religion. They asked for a small seat. We took pity on them, granted their request, and they sat down among us. We gave them corn and meat; they gave us poison in return.

The white people, brother, had now found our country. Tidings were carried back and more came among us. Yet we did not fear them. We took them to be friends. They called us brothers. We believed them and gave them a larger seat. At length their numbers had greatly increased. They wanted more land; they wanted our country. Our eyes were opened and our minds became uneasy. Wars took place. Indians were hired to fight against Indians, and many of our people were destroyed. They also brought strong liquor among us. It was strong and powerful, and has slain thousands.

Brother, our seats were once large and yours were small. You have now become a great people, and we have scarcely a place left to spread our blankets. You have got our country, but are not satisfied; you want to force your religion upon us.

Brother, continue to listen. You say that you are sent to instruct us how to worship the Great Spirit agreeably to His mind; and, if we do not take hold of the religion which you white people teach we shall be unhappy hereafter. You say that you are right and we are lost. How do we know this to be true? We understand that your religion is written in a Book. If it was intended for us, as well as you, why has not the Great Spirit given to us, and not only to us, but why did He not give to our forefathers the knowledge of that Book, with the means of understanding it rightly. We only know what you tell us about it. How shall we know when to believe, being so often deceived by the white people?

Brother, you say there is but one way to worship and serve the Great Spirit. If there is but one religion, why do you white people differ so much about it? Why not all agreed, as you can all read the Book?

Brother, we do not understand these things. We are told that your religion was given to your forefathers and has been handed down from father to son. We also have a religion which was given to our forefathers and has been handed down to us, their children. We worship in that way. It teaches us to be thankful for all the favors we receive, to love each other, and to be united. We never quarrel about religion.

Brother, the Great Spirit has made us all, but He has made a great difference between His white and His red children. He has given us different complexions and different customs. To you He has given the arts. To these He has not opened our eyes. We know these things to be true. Since He has made so great a difference between us in other things, why may we not conclude that He has given us a different religion according to our understanding? The Great Spirit does right. He knows what is best for His children; we are satisfied.

Brother, we do not wish to destroy your religion or take it from you. We only want to enjoy our own.

Brother, you say you have not come to get our land or our money, but to enlighten our minds. I will now tell you that I have been at your meetings and saw you collect money from the meeting. I can not tell what this money was intended for, but suppose that it was for your minister; and, if we should conform to your way of thinking, perhaps you may want some from us.

Brother, we are told that you have been preaching to the white people in this place. These people are our neighbors. We are acquainted with them. We will wait a little while and see what effect your preaching has upon them. If we find it does them good, makes them honest, and less disposed to cheat Indians, we will then consider again of what you have said.

Brother, you have now heard our answer to your talk, and this is all we have to say at present. As we are going to part, we will come and take you by the hand, and hope the Great Spirit will protect you on your journey and return you safe to your friends.

TECUMSEH

It is true I am a Shawanee. My forefathers were warriors. Their son is a warrior. From them I only take my existence; from my tribe I take nothing. I am the maker of my own fortune; and oh! that I could make that of my red people, and of my country, as great as the conceptions of my mind, when I think of the Spirit that rules the universe. I would not then come to Governor Harrison, to ask him to tear the treaty and to obliterate the landmark; but I would say to him: Sir, you have liberty to return to your own country. The being within, communing with past ages, tells me that once, nor until lately, there was no white man on this continent. That it then all belonged to red men, children of the same parents, placed on it by the Great Spirit that made them, to keep it, to traverse it, to enjoy its productions, and to fill it with the same race. Once a happy race. Since made miserable by the white people, who are never contented, but always encroaching. The way, and the only way, to check and to stop this evil, is for all the red men to unite in claiming a common and equal right in the land, as it was at first, and should be yet; for it never was divided, but belongs to all for the use of each. That no part has a right to sell, even to each other, much less to strangers; those who want all, and will not do with less.

The white people have no right to take the land from the Indians, because they had it first; it is theirs. They may sell, but all must join. Any sale not made by all is not valid. The late sale is bad. It was made by a part only. Part do not know how to sell. It requires all to make a bargain for all. All red men have equal rights to the unoccupied land. The right of occupancy is as good in one place as in another. There cannot be two occupations in the same place. The first excludes all others. It is not so in hunting or traveling; for there the same ground will serve many, as they may follow each other all day; but the camp is stationary, and that is occupancy. It belongs to the first who sits down on his blanket or skins which he has thrown upon the ground; and till he leaves it no other has a right.

Edward Everett
[1794–1865]

Edward Everett, of Massachusetts, was an outstanding orator of his day. He was president of Harvard, United States Senator, Secretary of State, and prominent in the affairs of state and nation. On August 1, 1826, Everett delivered, at Charlestown, Mass., an eloquent tribute to John Adams and Thomas Jefferson, who had both died on the preceding Fourth of July. Part of this address follows.

ADAMS AND JEFFERSON

THE JUBILEE of America is turned into mourning. Its joy is mingled with sadness; its silver trumpet breathes a mingled strain. Henceforward, while America exists among the nations of the earth, the first emotion of the fourth of July will be of joy and triumph in the great event which immortalizes the day; the second will be one of chastened and tender recollection of the venerable men who departed on the morning of the jubilee. This mingled emotion of triumph and sadness has sealed the beauty and sublimity of our great anniversary. In the simple commemoration of a victorious political achievement there seems not enough to occupy our purest and best feelings. The fourth of July was before a day of triumph, exultation, and national pride; but the angel of death has mingled in the glorious pageant to teach us we are men. Had our venerated fathers left us on any other day, it would have been henceforward a day of mournful recollection. But now, the whole nation feels, as with one heart, that since it must sooner or later have been bereaved of its revered fathers, it could not have wished that any other had been the day of their decease. Our anniversary festival was before triumphant; it is now triumphant and sacred. It before called out the young and ardent to join in the public rejoicing; it now also speaks, in a touching voice, to the retired, to the gray-headed, to the mild and peaceful spirits, to the whole family of sober freemen. It is henceforward, what the dying Adams pronounced it, "a great and a good day." It is full of greatness, and full of goodness. It is absolute and complete. The death of the men who declared our independence—their death on the day of the jubilee—was all that was wanting to the fourth of July. To die on that day, and to die together, was all that was wanting to Jefferson and Adams.

Friends, fellow citizens, free, prosperous, happy Americans! The men who did so much to make you so are no more. The men who gave nothing to pleasure in youth, nothing to repose in age, but all to that country, whose beloved name filled their hearts, as it does ours, with joy, can now do no more for us; nor we for them. But their memory remains, we will cherish it; their bright example remains, we will strive to imitate it; the fruit of their wise counsels and noble acts remains, we will gratefully enjoy it.

They have gone to the companions of their cares, of their dangers, and their toils. It is well with them. The treasures of America are now in heaven. How long the list of our good, and wise, and brave, assembled there! How few remain with us! There is our Washington; and those who followed him in their country's confidence are now met together with him, and all their illustrious company.

The faithful marble may preserve their image; the engraven brass may proclaim their worth; but the humblest sod of Independent America, with nothing but the dew-drops of the morning to gild it, is a prouder mausoleum than kings or conquerors can boast. The country is their monument. Its independence is their epitaph. But not to their country is their praise limited. The whole earth is the monument of illustrious men. Wherever an agonizing people shall perish, in a generous convulsion, for want of a valiant arm and a fearless heart, they will cry, in the last accents of despair, O for a Washington, an Adams, a Jefferson! Wherever a regenerated nation, starting up in its might, shall burst the links of steel that enchain it, the praise of our venerated fathers shall be remembered in their triumphal song!

The contemporary and successive generations of men will disappear, and in the long lapse of ages, the races of America, like those of Greece and Rome, may pass away. The fabric of American freedom, like all things human, however firm and fair, may crumble into dust. But the cause in which these our fathers shone is immortal. They did that to which no age, no people of civilized men, can be indifferent. Their eulogy will be uttered in other languages, when those we speak, like us who speak them, shall be all forgotten. And when the great account of humanity shall be closed, in the bright list of those who have best adorned and served it, shall be found the names of our Adams and our Jefferson!

Daniel Webster
[1782–1852]

Daniel Webster, United States Senator from Massachusetts, is ranked among the world's great orators. His historic reply to Senator Robert Young Hayne, of South Carolina, dealing with issues that were then beginning to divide the North and the South, is generally considered a masterpiece of debate and eloquence. Parts of this speech, delivered in the Senate on January 26, 1830, follow.

REPLY TO HAYNE

MR. PRESIDENT: When the mariner has been tossed for many days, in thick weather, and on an unknown sea, he naturally avails himself of the first pause in the storm, the earliest glance of the sun, to take his latitude, and ascertain how far the elements have driven him from his true course. Let us imitate this prudence, and, before we float farther on the waves of this debate, refer to the point from which we departed, that we may at least be able to conjecture where we now are. I ask for the reading of the resolution.

[The secretary read the resolution.]

We have thus heard, sir, what the resolution is, which is actually before us for consideration; and it will readily occur to everyone that it is almost the only subject about which something has not been said in the speech, running through two days, by which the Senate has been now entertained by the gentleman from South Carolina. Every topic in the wide range of our public affairs, whether past or present—everything, general or local, whether belonging to national politics, or party politics, seems to have attracted more or less of the honorable member's attention, save only the resolution before the Senate. He has spoken of everything but the public lands. They have escaped his notice. To that subject, in all his excursions, he has not paid even the cold respect of a passing glance.

When this debate, sir, was to be resumed on Thursday morning, it so happened that it would have been convenient for me to be elsewhere. The honorable member, however, did not incline to put off the discussion to another day. He had a shot, he said, to return, and he wished to discharge it. That shot, sir, which it was kind thus to inform us was coming, that we might stand out of the way, or prepare ourselves to fall before it, and die with decency, has now been received. Under all advantages, and with expectation awakened by the tone which preceded it, it has been discharged, and has spent its force. It may become me to say no more of its effect, than that, if nobody is found, after all, either killed or wounded by it, it is not the first time, in the history of human affairs, that the vigor and success of the war have not quite come up to the lofty and sounding phrase of the manifesto.

The people, sir, erected this government. They gave it a constitution, and in that constitution they have enumerated the powers which they bestow on it. They have made it a limited government. They have defined its authority. They have restrained it to the exercise of such powers as are granted; and all others, they declare, are reserved to the States, or the people. But, sir, they have not stopped here. If they had, they would have accomplished but half their work. No definition can be so clear as to avoid possibility of doubt; no limitation so precise, as to exclude all uncertainty. Who, then, shall construe this grant of the people? Who shall interpret their will, where it may be supposed they have left it doubtful? With whom do they repose this ultimate right of deciding on the powers of the government? Sir, they have settled all this in the fullest manner. They have left it, with the government itself, in its appropriate branches. Sir, the very chief end, the main design, for which the whole constitution was framed and adopted, was to establish a government that should not be obliged to act through State agency, or depend on State opinion and State discretion. The people had had quite enough of that kind of government, under the confederacy. Under that system, the legal action—the application of law to individuals—belonged exclusively to the States. Congress could only recommend—their acts were not of binding force, till the States had adopted and sanctioned them. Are we in that condition still? Are we yet at the mercy of State discretion, and State construction? Sir, if we are, then vain will be our attempt to maintain the constitution under which we sit.

But, sir, the people have wisely provided, in the constitution itself, a proper, suitable mode and tribunal for settling questions of constitutional law. There are in the constitution, grants of powers to Congress; and restrictions on these powers. There are, also, prohibitions on the States. Some authority must, therefore, necessarily exist, having the ultimate jurisdiction to fix and ascertain the interpretation of these grants, restrictions, and prohibitions. The constitution has itself pointed out, ordained, and established that authority. How has it accomplished this great and essential end? By declaring, sir, that "the constitution and the laws of the United States, made in pursuance thereof, shall be the supreme law of the land, anything in the constitution or laws of any State to the contrary notwithstanding."

This, sir, was the first great step. By this the supremacy of the constitution and laws of the United States is declared. The people so will it. No State law is to be valid which comes in conflict with the constitution, or any law of the United States passed in pursuance of it. But who shall decide this question of interference? To whom lies the last appeal? This, sir, the constitution itself decides, also, by declaring, "that the judicial power shall extend to all cases arising under the constitution and laws of the United States." These two provisions, sir, cover the whole ground. They are in truth, the keystone of the arch. With these, it is a constitution; without them, it is a confederacy. In pursuance of these clear and express provisions, Congress established, at its very first session, in the judicial act, a mode for carrying them into full effect, and for bringing all questions of constitutional power to the final decision of the supreme court. It then, sir, became a government. It then had the means of self-protection; and, but for this, it would, in all probability, have been now among things which are past. Having constituted the government, and declared its powers, the people have further said, that since somebody must decide on the extent of these powers, the government shall itself decide; subject, always, like other popular governments, to its responsibility to the people. And now, sir, I repeat, how is it that a State legislature acquires any power to interfere? Who, or what, gives them the right to say to the people, "We, who are your agents and servants for one purpose, will undertake to decide that your other agents and servants, appointed by you for another purpose, have transcended the authority you gave them!" The reply would be, I think, not impertinent—"Who made you a judge over another's servants? To their own masters they stand or fall."

Sir, I deny this power of State legislatures altogether. It cannot stand the test of examination. Gentlemen may say, that in an extreme case, a State government might protect the people from intolerable oppression. Sir, in such a case, the people might protect themselves, without the aid of the State governments. Such a case warrants revolution. It must make, when it comes, a law for itself. A nullifying act of a State legislature cannot alter the case, nor make resistance any more lawful. In maintaining these sentiments, sir, I am but asserting the rights of the people. I state what they have declared, and insist on their right to declare it. They have chosen to repose this power in the general government, and I think it my duty to support it, like other constitutional powers.

For myself, sir, I do not admit the jurisdiction of South Carolina, or any other State, to prescribe my constitutional duty; or to settle, between me and the people, the validity of laws of Congress, for which I have voted. I decline her umpirage. I have not sworn to support the constitution according to her construction of its clauses. I have not stipulated, by my oath of office, or otherwise, to come under any responsibility, except to the people, and those whom they have appointed to pass upon the question, whether laws, supported by my votes, conform to the constitution of the country. And, sir, if we look to the general nature of the case, could anything have been more preposterous, than to make a government for the whole Union, and yet leave its powers subject, not to one interpretation, but to thirteen, or twenty-four, interpretations? Instead of one tribunal, established by all, responsible to all, with power to decide for all—shall constitutional questions be left to four-and-twenty popular bodies, each at liberty to decide for itself, and none bound to respect the decisions of others; and each at liberty, too, to give a new construction on every new election of its own members? Would anything, with such a principle in it, or rather with such a destitution of all principle, be fit to be called a government? No, sir. It should not be denominated a constitution. It should be called, rather, a collection of topics, for everlasting controversy; heads of debate for a disputatious people. It would not be a government. It would not be adequate to any practical good, nor fit for any country to live under. To avoid all possibility of being misunderstood, allow me to repeat again, in the fullest manner, that I claim no powers for the government by forced or unfair construction. I admit that it is a government of strictly limited powers; of enumerated, specified, and particularized powers; and that whatsoever is not granted, is withheld. But notwithstanding all this, and however the grant of powers may be expressed, its limit and extent may yet, in some cases, admit of doubt; and the general government would be good for nothing, it would be incapable of long existing, if some mode had not been provided, in which those doubts, as they should arise, might be peaceably, but authoritatively, solved.

And now, Mr. President, let me run the honorable gentleman's doctrine a little into its practical application. Let us look at his probable *modus operandi.* If a thing can be done, an ingenious man can tell how it is to be done. Now, I wish to be informed, how this State interference is to be put in practice without violence, bloodshed, and rebellion. We will take the existing case of the tariff law. South Carolina is said to have made up her opinion upon it. If we do not repeal it (as we probably shall not) she will then apply to the case the remedy of her doctrine. She will, we must suppose, pass a law of her legislature, declaring the several acts of Congress, usually called the tariff laws, null and void, so far as they respect South Carolina, or the citizens thereof. So far, all is a paper transaction, and easy enough. But the collector at Charleston is collecting the duties imposed by these tariff laws—he therefore must be stopped. The collector will seize the goods if the tariff duties are not paid. The State authorities will undertake their rescue; the marshal, with his posse, will come to the collector's aid, and here the contest begins. The militia of the State will be called out to sustain the nullifying act. They will march, sir, under a very gallant leader: for I believe the honorable member himself commands the militia of that part of the State. He will raise the nullifying act on his standard, and spread it out as his banner! It will have a preamble, bearing, That the tariff laws are palpable, deliberate, and dangerous violations of the constitution! He will proceed, with this banner flying, to the custom-house in Charleston:

"All the while,
Sonorous metal, blowing martial sounds."

Arrived at the custom-house, he will tell the collector that he must collect no more duties under any of the tariff laws. This he will be somewhat puzzled to say, by the way, with a grave countenance, considering what hand South Carolina, herself, had in that of 1816. But, sir, the collector would, probably, not desist at his bidding. He would show him the law of Congress, the treasury instruction, and his own oath of office. He would say, he should perform his duty, come what might. Here would ensue a pause: for they say that a certain stillness precedes the tempest. The trumpeter would hold his breath awhile, and before all this military array should fall on the custom-house, collector, clerks, and all, it is very probable some of those composing it, would request of their gallant commander-in-chief, to be informed a little upon the point of law; for they have, doubtless, a just respect for his opinions as a lawyer, as well as for his bravery as a soldier. They know he has read Blackstone and the constitution, as well as Turenne and Vauban. They would ask him, therefore, something concerning their rights in this matter. They would inquire whether it was not somewhat dangerous to resist a law of the United States. What would be the nature of their offence, they would wish to learn, if they, by military force and array, resisted the execution in Carolina of a law of the United States, and it should turn out, after all, that the law was constitutional? He would answer, of course, treason. No lawyer could give any other answer. John Fries, he would tell them, had learned that some years ago. How, then, they would ask, do you propose to defend us? We are not afraid of bullets, but treason has a way of taking people off, that we do not much relish. How do you propose to defend us? "Look at my floating banner," he would reply; "see there the nullifying law!" Is it your opinion, gallant commander, they would then say, that if we should be indicted for treason, that same floating banner of yours would make a good plea in bar? "South Carolina is a sovereign State," he would reply. That is true—but would the judge admit our plea? "These tariff laws," he would repeat, "are unconstitutional, palpably, deliberately, dangerously." That all may be so; but if the tribunal should not happen to be of that opinion, shall we swing for it? We are ready to die for our country, but it is rather an awkward business, this dying without touching the ground! After all, that is a sort of hemp tax, worse than any part of the tariff.

Mr. President, the honorable gentleman would be in a dilemma, like that of another great general. He would have a knot before him which he could not untie. He must cut it with his sword. He must say to his followers, defend yourselves with your bayonets; and this is war—civil war.

Direct collision, therefore, between force and force, is the unavoidable result of that remedy for the revision of unconstitutional laws which the gentleman contends for. It must happen in the very first case to which it is applied. Is not this the plain result? To resist, by force, the execution of a law, generally, is treason. Can the courts of the United States take notice of the indulgence of a State to commit treason? The common saying, that a State cannot commit treason herself, is nothing to the purpose. Can she authorize others to do it? If John Fries had produced an act of Pennsylvania, annulling the law of Congress, would it have helped his case? Talk about it as we will, these doctrines go the length of revolution. They are incompatible with any peaceable administration of the government. They lead directly to disunion and civil commotion; and, therefore, it is, that at their commencement, when they are first found to be maintained by respectable men, and in a tangible form, I enter my public protest against them all.

The honorable gentleman argues, that if this government be the sole judge of the extent of its own powers, whether that right of judging be in Congress, or the Supreme Court, it equally subverts State sovereignty. This the gentleman sees, or thinks he sees, although he cannot perceive how the right of judging, in this matter, if left to the exercise of State legislatures, has any tendency to subvert the government of the Union. The gentleman's opinion may be, that the right ought not to have been lodged with the general government; he may like better such a constitution, as we should have under the right of State interference; but I ask him to meet me on the plain matter of fact; I ask him to meet me on the constitution itself; I ask him if the power is not found there—clear and visibly found there?

But, sir, what is this danger, and what the grounds of it? Let it be remembered, that the constitution of the United States is not unalterable. It is to continue in its present form no longer than the people who established it shall choose to continue it. If they shall become convinced that they have made an injudicious or inexpedient partition and distribution of power, between the State governments and the general government, they can alter that distribution at will.

If anything be found in the national constitution, either by original provision, or subsequent interpretation, which ought not to be in it, the people know how to get rid of it. If any construction be established, unacceptable to them, so as to become, practically, a part of the constitution, they will amend it, at their own sovereign pleasure: but while the people choose to maintain it, as it is; while they are satisfied with it, and refuse to change it, who has given, or who can give, to the State legislatures a right to alter it, either by interference, construction, or otherwise? Gentlemen do not seem to recollect that the people have any power to do anything for themselves; they imagine there is no safety for them, any longer than they are under the close guardianship of the State legislatures. Sir, the people have not trusted their safety, in regard to the general constitution, to these hands. They have required other security, and taken other bonds. They have chosen to trust themselves, first, to the plain words of the instrument, and to such construction as the government itself, in doubtful cases, should put on its own powers, under their oaths of office, and subject to their responsibility to them: just as the people of a State trust their own State governments with a similar power. Secondly, they have reposed their trust in the efficacy of frequent elections, and in their own power to remove their own servants and agents, whenever they see cause. Thirdly, they have reposed trust in the judicial power, which, in order that it might be trustworthy, they have made as respectable, as disinterested, and as independent as was practicable. Fourthly, they have seen fit to rely, in case of necessity, or high expediency, on their known and admitted power, to alter or amend the constitution, peaceably and quietly, whenever experience shall point out defects or imperfections. And, finally, the people of the United States have, at no time, in no way, directly or indirectly, authorized any State legislature to construe or interpret their high instrument of government; much less to interfere, by their own power, to arrest its course and operation.

If, sir, the people in these respects, had done otherwise than they have done, their constitution could neither have been preserved, nor would it have been worth preserving. And, if its plain provisions shall now be disregarded, and these new doctrines interpolated in it, it will become as feeble and helpless a being, as its enemies, whether early or more recent, could possibly desire. It will exist in every State, but as a poor dependent on State permission. It must borrow leave to be; and will be, no longer than State pleasure, or State discretion, sees fit to grant the indulgence, and to prolong its poor existence.

But, sir, although there are fears, there are hopes also. The people have preserved this, their own chosen constitution, for forty years, and have seen their happiness, prosperity, and renown, grow with its growth, and strengthen with its strength. They are now, generally, strongly attached to it. Overthrown by direct assault, it cannot be; evaded, undermined, nullified, it will not be, if we, and those who shall succeed us here, as agents and representatives of the people, shall conscientiously and vigilantly discharge the two great branches of our public trust—faithfully to preserve, and wisely to administer it.

Mr. President, I have thus stated the reasons of my dissent to the doctrines which have been advanced and maintained. I am conscious of having detained you and the Senate much too long. I was drawn into the debate with no previous deliberation such as is suited to the discussion of so grave and important a subject. But it is a subject of which my heart is full, and I have not been willing to suppress the utterance of its spontaneous sentiments. I cannot, even now, persuade myself to relinquish it, without expressing, once more, my deep conviction, that, since it respects nothing less than the union of the States, it is of most vital and essential importance to the public happiness. I profess, sir, in my career, hitherto, to have kept steadily in view the prosperity and honor of the whole country, and the preservation of our federal Union. It is to that Union we owe our safety at home, and our consideration and dignity abroad. It is to that Union that we are chiefly indebted for whatever makes us most proud of our country. That Union we reached only by the discipline of our virtues in the severe school of adversity. It had its origin in the necessities of disordered finance, prostrate commerce, and ruined credit. Under its benign influences, these great interests immediately awoke, as from the dead, and sprang forth with newness of life. Every year of its duration has teemed with fresh proofs of its utility and its blessings; and, although our territory has stretched out wider and wider, and our population spread farther and farther, they have not outrun its protection or its benefits. It has been to us all a copious fountain of national, social, and personal happiness. I have not allowed myself, sir, to look beyond the Union, to see what might lie hidden in the dark recess behind. I have not coolly weighed the chances of preserving liberty when the bonds that unite us together shall be broken asunder. I have not accustomed myself to hang over the precipice of disunion, to see whether, with my short sight, I can fathom the depth of the abyss below; nor could I regard him as a safe counsellor in the affairs of this government, whose thoughts should be mainly bent on considering, not how the Union shall be best preserved, but how tolerable might be the condition of the people when it shall be broken up and destroyed. While the Union lasts, we have high, exciting, gratifying prospects spread out before us, for us and our children. Beyond that I seek not to penetrate the veil. God grant that, in my day, at least, that curtain may not rise. God grant, that on my vision never may be opened what lies behind. When my eyes shall be turned to behold, for the last time, the sun in heaven, may I not see him shining on the broken and dishonored fragments of a once glorious Union; on States dissevered, discordant, belligerent; on a land rent with civil feuds, or drenched, it may be, in fraternal blood! Let their last feeble and lingering glance, rather behold the gorgeous ensign of the republic, now known and honored throughout the earth, still full high advanced, its arms and trophies streaming in their original lustre, not a stripe erased or polluted, nor a single star obscured—bearing for its motto, no such miserable interrogatory, as What is all this worth? Nor those other words of delusion and folly, liberty first, and union afterwards—but everywhere, spread all over in characters of living light, blazing on all its ample folds, as they float over the sea and over the land, and in every wind under the whole heavens, that other sentiment, dear to every true American heart—liberty and union, now and forever, one and inseparable.

Andrew Jackson
[1767–1845]

Andrew Jackson, Tennessean, hero of the Battle of New Orleans in 1815, was the seventh President of the United States. Jackson's administration was a stormy one, especially noted for its strong opposition to the rechartering of the Bank of the United States. Following is his second inaugural address, delivered on March 4, 1833.

SECOND INAUGURAL ADDRESS

THE WILL of the American people, expressed through their unsolicited suffrages, calls me before you to pass through the solemnities preparatory to taking upon myself the duties of president of the United States for another term. For their approbation of my public conduct through a period which has not been without its difficulties, and for this renewed expression of their confidence in my good intentions, I am at a loss for terms adequate to the expression of my gratitude.

It shall be displayed to the extent of my humble abilities in continued efforts so to administer the government as to preserve their liberty and promote their happiness.

So many events have occurred within the last four years which have necessarily called forth—sometimes under circumstances the most delicate and painful—my views of the principles and policy which ought to be pursued by the general government, that I need on this occasion but allude to a few leading considerations connected with some of them.

The foreign policy adopted by our government soon after the formation of our present Constitution, and very generally pursued by successive administrations, has been crowned with almost complete success, and has elevated our character among the nations of the earth. To do justice to all and to submit to wrong from none has been during my administration its growing maxim, and so happy have been its results that we are not only at peace with all the world, but have few causes of controversy, and those of minor importance, remaining unadjusted.

In the domestic policy of this government, there are two objects which especially deserve the attention of the people and their representatives, and which have been and will continue to be the subjects of my increasing solicitude. They are the preservation of the rights of the several States and the integrity of the Union.

These great objects are necessarily connected, and can only be attained by an enlightened exercise of the powers of each within its appropriate sphere, in conformity with the public will constitutionally expressed. To this end it becomes the duty of all to yield a ready and patriotic submission to the laws constitutionally enacted, and thereby promote and strengthen a proper confidence in those institutions of the several States and of the United States which the people themselves have ordained for their own government.

My experience in public concerns and the observation of a life somewhat advanced confirm the opinions long since imbibed by me, that the destruction of our State governments or the annihilation of their control over the local concerns of the people would lead directly to revolution and anarchy, and finally to despotism and military domination. In proportion, therefore, as the general government encroaches upon the rights of the States, in the same proportion does it impair its own power and detract from its ability to fulfil the purposes of its creation. Solemnly impressed with these considerations, my countrymen will ever find me ready to exercise my constitutional powers in arresting measures which may directly or indirectly encroach upon the rights of the States or tend to consolidate all political power in the general government. But of equal, and, indeed, of incalculable importance is the union of these States, and the sacred duty of all to contribute to its preservation by a liberal support of the general government in the exercise of its just powers. You have been wisely admonished to "accustom yourselves to think and speak of the Union as the palladium of your political safety and prosperity, watching for its preservation with jealous anxiety, discountenancing whatever may suggest even a suspicion that it can, in any event, be abandoned, and indignantly frowning upon the first dawning of any attempt to alienate any portion of our country from the rest, or to enfeeble the sacred ties which now link together the various parts." Without union our independence and liberty would never have been achieved; without union they never can be maintained. Divided into twenty-four, or even a smaller number, of separate communities, we shall see our internal trade burdened with numberless restraints and exactions; communication between distant points and sections obstructed or cut off; our sons made soldiers to deluge with blood the fields they now till in peace; the mass of our people borne down and impoverished by taxes to support armies and navies, and military leaders at the head of their victorious legions becoming our lawgivers and judges. The loss of liberty, of all good government, of peace, plenty, and happiness, must inevitably follow a dissolution of the Union. In supporting it, therefore, we support all that is dear to the freeman and the philanthropist.

The time at which I stand before you is full of interest. The eyes of all nations are fixed on our Republic. The event of the existing crisis will be decisive in the opinion of mankind of the practicability of our federal system of government. Great is the stake placed in our hands; great is the responsibility which must rest upon the people of the United States. Let us realize the importance of the attitude in which we stand before the world. Let us exercise forbearance and firmness. Let us extricate our country from the dangers which surround it, and learn wisdom from the lessons they inculcate.

Deeply impressed with the truth of these observations, and under the obligation of that solemn oath which I am about to take, I shall continue to exert all my faculties to maintain the just powers of the Constitution and to transmit unimpaired to posterity the blessings of our federal Union. At the same time it will be my aim to inculcate by my official acts the necessity of exercising by the general government those powers only that are clearly delegated; to encourage simplicity and economy in the expenditures of the government; to raise no more money from the people than may be requisite for these objects, and in a manner that will best promote the interests of all classes of the community and of all portions of the Union. Constantly bearing in mind that in entering into society "individuals must give up a share of liberty to preserve the rest," it will be my desire so to discharge my duties as to foster with our brethren in all parts of the country a spirit of liberal concession and compromise, and, by reconciling our fellow citizens to those partial sacrifices which they must unavoidably make for the preservation of a greater good, to recommend our invaluable government and Union to the confidence and affections of the American people.

Finally, it is my most fervent prayer to that Almighty Being before whom I now stand, and who has kept us in His hands from the infancy of our Republic to the present day, that He will so overrule all my intentions and actions and inspire the hearts of my fellow citizens that we may be preserved from dangers of all kinds and continue for ever a united and happy people.

Wendell Phillips
[1811–1884]

Wendell Phillips, of Massachusetts, was one of the greatest orators of the abolitionist movement. He also championed woman suffrage, penal reform and other progressive causes. Following is part of a stirring speech, which Phillips delivered in Faneuil Hall, Boston, December 8, 1837, in protest against the murder of Elijah Lovejoy, the abolitionist editor.

THE MURDER OF LOVEJOY

ELIJAH LOVEJOY was not only defending the freedom of the press, but he was under his own roof, in arms with the sanction of the civil authority. The men who assailed him went against and over the laws. The *mob,* as the gentleman (a previous speaker) terms it—mob, forsooth! certainly we sons of the tea-spillers are a marvelously patient generation!—the "orderly mob" which assembled in the Old South to destroy the tea, were met to resist, not the laws, but illegal enactions. Shame on the American who calls the tea tax and stamp act *laws!* Our fathers resisted, not the King's prerogative, but the King's usurpation. To find any other account, you must read our Revolutionary history upside down. Our State archives are loaded with arguments of John Adams to prove the taxes laid by the British Parliament unconstitutional —beyond its power. It was not until this was made out that the men of New England rushed to arms. The arguments of the Council Chamber and the House of Representatives preceded and sanctioned the contest. To draw the conduct of our ancestors into a precedent for mobs, for a right to resist laws we ourselves have enacted, is an insult to their memory. The difference between the excitements of those days and our own, which the gentleman in kindness to the latter has overlooked, is simply this: the men of that day went for the right, as secured by the laws. They were the people rising to sustain the laws and Constitution of the province. The rioters of our days go for their own wills, right or wrong. Sir, when I heard the gentleman lay down principles which place the murderers of Alton side by side with Otis and Hancock, with Quincy and Adams, I thought those pictured lips [pointing to the portraits in the hall] would have broken into voice to rebuke the recreant American—the slanderer of the dead. The gentleman said that he should sink into insignificance if he dared to gainsay the principles of these resolutions. Sir, for the sentiments he has uttered, on soil consecrated by the prayers of Puritans and the blood of patriots, the earth should have yawned and swallowed him up.

Some persons seem to imagine that anarchy existed at Alton from the commencement of these disputes. Not at all. "No one of us," says an eye-witness and a comrade of Lovejoy, "has taken up arms during these disturbances but at the command of the mayor." Anarchy did not settle down on that devoted city till Lovejoy breathed his last. Till then the law, represented in his person, sustained itself against its foes. When he fell, civil authority was trampled under foot. He had "planted himself on his constitutional rights,—appealed to the laws,—claimed the protection of the civil authority,—taken refuge under the broad shield of the Constitution. When through that he was pierced and fell, he fell but one sufferer in a common catastrophe." He took refuge under the banner of liberty—amid its folds; and when he fell, its glorious stars and stripes, the emblem of free institutions, around which cluster so many heart-stirring memories, were blotted out in the martyr's blood.

It has been stated, perhaps inadvertently, that Lovejoy or his comrades fired first. This is denied by those who have the best means of knowing. Guns were first fired by the mob. After being twice fired on, those within the building consulted together and deliberately returned the fire. But suppose they did fire first. They had a right so to do; not only the right which every citizen has to defend himself, but the further right which every civil officer has to resist violence. Even if Lovejoy fired the first gun, it would not lessen his claim to our sympathy, or destroy his title to be considered a martyr in defense of a free press. The question now is, Did he act within the Constitution and the laws? The men who fell in State street, on the 5th of March, 1770, did more than Lovejoy is charged with. They were the *first* assailants upon some slight quarrel, they pelted the troops with every missile within reach. Did this bate one jot of the eulogy with which Hancock and Warren hallowed their memory, hailing them as the first martyrs in the cause of American liberty? If, sir, I had adopted what are called peace principles, I might lament the circumstances of this case. But all you who believe as I do, in the right and duty of magistrates to execute the laws, join with me and brand as base hypocrisy the conduct of those who assemble year after year on the 4th of July to fight over the battles of the Revolution, and yet "damn with faint praise" or load with obloquy, the memory of this man who shed his blood in defense of life, liberty, property, and the freedom of the press!

Throughout that terrible night I find nothing to regret but this, that, within the limits of our country, civil authority should have been so prostrated as to oblige a citizen to arm in his own defense, and to arm in vain. The gentleman says Lovejoy was presumptuous and imprudent— he "died as the fool dieth." And a reverend clergyman of the city tells us that no citizen has a right to publish opinions disagreeable to the community! If any mob follows such publication, on him rests its guilt. He must wait, forsooth, till the people come up to it and agree with him! This libel on liberty goes on to say that the want of right to speak as we think is an evil inseparable from republican institutions! If this be so, what are they worth? Welcome the despotism of the Sultan, where one knows what he may publish and what he may not, rather than the tyranny of this many-headed monster, the mob, where we know not what we may do or say, till some fellow citizen has tried it, and paid for the lesson with his life. This clerical absurdity chooses as a check for the abuses of the press, not the law, but the dread of a mob. By so doing, it deprives not only the individual and the minority of their rights, but the majority also, since the expression of their opinion may sometime provoke disturbances from the minority. A few men may make a mob as well as many. The majority, then, have no right, as Christian men, to utter their sentiments, if by any possibility it may lead to a mob! Shades of Hugh Peters and John Cotton, save us from such pulpits!

Imagine yourself present when the first news of Bunker Hill battle reached a New England town. The tale would have run thus: "The patriots are routed,—the redcoats victorious,—Warren lies dead upon the field." With what scorn would that Tory have been received, who should have charged Warren with imprudence! who should have said that, bred a physician, he was "out of place" in that battle, and "died as the fool dieth." How would the intimation have been received, that Warren and his associates should have merited a better time? But if success be, indeed, the only criterion of prudence, *Respice finem,*— wait till the end!

Presumptuous to assert the freedom of the press on American ground! Is the assertion of such freedom before the age? So much before the age as to leave one no right to make it because it displeases the community? Who invents this libel on his country? It is this very thing which entitles Lovejoy to greater praise. The disputed right which provoked the Revolution—taxation without representation—is far beneath that for which he died. One word, gentlemen. As much as thought is better than money, so much is better the cause in which Lovejoy died nobler than a mere question of taxes. James Otis thundered in this hall when the King did but touch his pocket. Imagine, if you can, his indignant eloquence had England offered to put a gag upon his lips. The question that stirred the Revolution touched our civil interests. This concerns us not only as citizens, but as immortal beings. Wrapped up in its fate, saved or lost with it, are not only the voice of the statesman, but the instructions of the pulpit and the progress of our faith.

Mr. Chairman, from the bottom of my heart I thank that brave little band at Alton for resisting. We must remember that Lovejoy had fled from city to city,—suffered the destruction of three presses patiently. At length he took counsel with friends, men of character, of tried integrity, of wide views, of Christian principle. They thought the crisis had come; it was full time to assert the laws. They saw around them, not a community like our own, of fixed habits, of character moulded and settled, but one "in the gristle, not yet hardened into the bone of manhood." The people there, children of our older States, seem to have forgotten the blood-tried principles of their fathers the moment they lost sight of our New England hills. Something was to be done to show them the priceless value of the freedom of the press, to bring back and set right their wandering and confused ideas. He and his advisers looked out on a community, staggering like a drunken man, indifferent to their rights and confused in their feelings. Deaf to argument, haply they might be stunned into sobriety. They saw that of which we cannot judge, the *necessity* of resistance. Insulted law called for it. Public opinion, fast hastening on the downward course, must be arrested.

Does not the event show they judged rightly? Absorbed in a thousand trifles, how has the nation all at once come to a stand? Men begin, as in 1776 and 1640, to discuss principles, to weigh characters, to find out where they are. Haply, we may awake before we are borne over the precipice.

Rufus Choate
[1799–1859]

Rufus Choate, of Massachusetts, one of the country's foremost lawyers and orators, was also active in politics. He was a member of both branches of Congress, becoming Senator when Daniel Webster retired. Here are parts of Choate's address, delivered at Fanueil Hall, Boston, in 1850.

THE PRESERVATION OF THE UNION

I KNOW very well that to sound a false alarm is a shallow and contemptible thing. But I know, also, that too much precaution is safer than too little, and I believe that less than the utmost is too little now. Better, it is said, to be ridiculed for too much care than to be ruined by too confident a security. I have, then, a profound conviction that the Union is in danger. I will tell you where I think the danger lies. It is, that while the people sleep, politicians and philanthropists of the legislative hall, the stump, and the press, will talk and write us out of our Union. Yes, while you sleep, while the merchant is loading his ships, and the farmer is gathering his harvests, and the music of the hammer and shuttle wake around, and we are all steeped in the enjoyment of that vast and various good which a common government places within our reach. There are influences that never sleep, and which are creating and diffusing a PUBLIC OPINION in whose hot and poisoned breath, before we yet perceive our evil plight, this Union may melt as frostwork in the sun. Do we sufficiently appreciate how omnipotent is opinion in the matter of all government? Do we consider especially in how true a sense it is the creator, must be the upholder, and may be the destroyer of our united government? Do we often enough advert to the distinction, that while our state governments must exist almost of necessity, and with no effort from within or without, the UNION of the states is a totally different creation—more delicate, more artificial, more recent, far more truly a mere production of the reason and the will—standing in far more need of an ever-surrounding care to preserve and repair it and urge it along its highway?

And now, charged with the trust of holding together such a nation as this, what have we seen? What do we see to-day? Exactly this. It has been for many months—years, I may say, but assuredly for a long season—the peculiar infelicity, say, rather, terrible misfortune of this country, that the attention of the people has been fixed, without the respite of a moment, exclusively on one of those subjects—the only one on which we disagree precisely according to geographical lines. And not so only, but this subject has been one—unlike tariff, or internal improvements, or the disbursement of the public money, on which the dispute cannot be maintained for an hour without heat of blood, mutual loss of respect, alienation of regard—menacing to end in hate strong and cruel as the grave.

I call this only a terrible misfortune. I blame here and now no man and no policy for it. Circumstances have forced it upon us all; and down to the hour that the series of compromise measures was completed and presented to the country, or certainly to Congress, I will not here and now say that it was the fault of one man, or one region of country, or one party more than another.

They tell us that slavery is so wicked a thing that they must pursue it, by agitation, to its home in the states; and that if there is an implied engagement to abstain from doing so, it is an engagement to neglect an opportunity of doing good, and void in the forum of conscience. But was it ever heard of that one may not formally bind himself to abstain from what he thinks a particular opportunity of doing good? A contract in general restraint of philanthropy or any other useful calling is void; but a contract to abstain from a specific sphere of exertion is not void, and may be wise and right. To entitle himself to instruct heathen children on week days, might not a pious missionary engage not to attempt to preach to their parents on Sunday? To win the opportunity of achieving the mighty good summed up in the pregnant language of the preamble to the Constitution, such good as man has not on this earth been many times permitted to do or dream of, we might well surrender the privilege of reviling the masters of slaves, with whom we must "either live or bear no life."

Fellow citizens, the first of men are the builders of empires. Here is, my friends, here, right here—in doing something in our day and generation toward "forming a more perfect union"; in doing something by literature, by public speech, by sound industrial policy, by the careful culture of fraternal love and regard, by the intercourse of business and friendship, by all the means within our command, in doing something to leave the Union, when we die, stronger than we found it—here, here is the field of our grandest duties and highest rewards. Let the grandeur of such duties, let the splendor of such rewards, suffice us. Let them reconcile and constrain us to turn from that equivocal philanthropy which violates contracts, which tramples on law, which confounds the whole subordination of virtues, which counts it a light thing that a nation is rent asunder, and the swords of brothers sheathed in the bosoms of brothers, if thus the chains of one slave may be violently and prematurely broken.

John Caldwell Calhoun
[1782-1850]

Champion of the South in the great Senatorial battles over the issues of slavery and secession, John Caldwell Calhoun, of South Carolina, was admired and respected for his abilities and eloquence by his opponents in Congress and throughout the country. He was Secretary of War in President Monroe's cabinet and was elected Vice President, with John Quincy Adams. Here are parts of his last speech in the Senate, delivered in 1850.

SLAVERY

I HAVE, senators, believed from the first that the agitation of the subject of slavery would, if not prevented by some timely and effective measure, end in disunion. Entertaining this opinion, I have, on all proper occasions, endeavored to call the attention of both the two great parties which divide the country, to adopt some such measure to prevent so great a disaster, but without success. The agitation has been permitted to proceed, with almost no attempt to resist it, until it has reached a period when it can no longer be disguised or denied that the Union is in danger. You have thus forced upon you the greatest and the gravest question that ever can come under your consideration: How can the Union be preserved?

To this question there can be but one answer: that the immediate cause is, the almost universal discontent which pervades all the states composing the southern section of the Union. This widely extended discontent is not of recent origin. It commenced with the agitation of the slavery question, and has been increasing ever since.

One of the causes is, undoubtedly, to be traced to the long-continued agitation of the slave question on the part of the North, and the many aggressions which they have made on the rights of the South, during that time.

There is another, lying back of it, but with which this is intimately connected, that may be regarded as the great and primary cause. It is to be found in the fact that the equilibrium between the two sections in the government, as it stood when the Constitution was ratified, and the government put in action, has been destroyed. At that time there was nearly a perfect equilibrium between the two, which afforded ample means to each to protect itself against the aggression of the other;

but as it now stands, one section has exclusive power of controlling the government, which leaves the other without any adequate means of protecting itself against its encroachment and oppression.

The cry of Union! Union! the glorious Union! can no more prevent disunion, than the cry of Health! health! glorious health! on the part of the physician can save a patient lying dangerously ill. So long as the Union, instead of being regarded as a protector, is regarded in the opposite character by not much less than a majority of the states, it will be in vain to attempt to concentrate them by pronouncing eulogies on it.

Besides, this cry of Union comes commonly from those whom we cannot believe to be sincere. It usually comes from our assailants; but we cannot believe them to be sincere, for if they loved the Union, they would necessarily be devoted to the Constitution. It made the Union, and to destroy the Constitution would be to destroy the Union. But the only reliable and certain evidence of devotion to the Constitution is, to abstain, on the one hand, from violating it, and to repel, on the other, all attempts to violate it. It is only by faithfully performing those high duties that the Constitution can be preserved, and with it the Union.

Nor can we regard the profession of devotion to the Union, on the part of those who are not our assailants, as sincere, when they pronounce eulogies upon the Union evidently with the intent of charging us with disunion, without uttering one word of denunciation against our assailants. If friends of the Union, their course should be to unite with us in repelling these assaults, and denouncing the authors as enemies of the Union. Why they avoid this and pursue the course they obviously do, it is for them to explain.

Nor can the Union be saved by invoking the name of the illustrious Southerner, whose mortal remains repose on the western bank of the Potomac. He was one of us—a slave-holder and a planter. We have studied his history, and find nothing in it to justify submission to wrong. On the contrary, his great fame rests on the solid foundation that, while he was careful to avoid doing wrong to others, he was prompt and decided in repelling wrong. I trust that, in this respect, we profited by his example.

Nor can we find anything in his history to deter us from seceding from the Union, should it fail to fulfill the objects for which it was instituted, by being permanently and hopelessly converted into the means of oppression instead of protection. On the contrary, we find much in his example to encourage us, should we be forced to the extremity of deciding between submission and disunion.

I have now, senators, done my duty, in expressing my opinions fully, freely, and candidly on this solemn occasion. In doing so, I have been governed by the motives which have governed me in all the stages of the agitation of the slavery question since its commencement, and exerted myself to arrest it, with the intention of saving the Union, if it could be done, and, if it cannot, to save the section where it has pleased Providence to cast my lot, and which, I sincerely believe, has justice and the Constitution on its side. Having faithfully done my duty to the best of my ability, both to the Union and my section, throughout the whole of this agitation, I shall have the consolation, let what will come, that I am free from all responsibility.

Henry Clay
[1777-1852]

Known as the "Great Pacificator" and "Great Compromiser," Henry Clay of Kentucky was one of the famous orators of Congress during the historic debates dealing with the differences of the North and South. He was Speaker of the House and later became United States Senator. Following is part of a speech he delivered in the Senate in 1850.

ON THE COMPROMISE OF 1850

IT HAS been objected against this measure that it is a compromise. It has been said that it is a compromise of principle, or of a principle. Mr. President, what is a compromise? It is a work of mutual concession —an agreement in which there are reciprocal stipulations—a work in which, for the sake of peace and concord, one party abates his extreme demands in consideration of an abatement of extreme demands by the other party: it is a measure of mutual concession—a measure of mutual sacrifice. Undoubtedly, Mr. President, in all such measures of compromise, one party would be very glad to get what he wants, and reject what he does not desire but which the other party wants. But when he comes to reflect that, from the nature of the government and its operations, and from those with whom he is dealing, it is necessary upon his part, in order to secure what he wants, to grant something to the other side, he should be reconciled to the concession which he has made in consequence of the concession which he is to receive, if there is no great principle involved, such as a violation of the Constitution of the United States. I admit that such a compromise as that ought never to be sanctioned or adopted. But I now call upon any senator in his place to point out from the beginning to the end, from California to New Mexico, a solitary provision in this bill which is violative of the Constitution of the United States.

The responsibility of this great measure passes from the hands of the committee, and from my hands. They know, and I know, that it is an awful and tremendous responsibility. I hope that you will meet it with a just conception and a true appreciation of its magnitude, and the magnitude of the consequences that may ensue from your decision one way or the other. The alternatives, I fear, which the measure presents, are concord and increased discord; a servile civil war, originating in its causes on the lower Rio Grande, and terminating possibly in its consequences on the upper Rio Grande in the Santa Fé country, or the restoration of harmony and fraternal kindness. I believe from the bottom of my soul that the measure is the reunion of this Union. I believe it is the dove of peace, which, taking its aerial flight from the dome of the capitol, carries the glad tidings of assured peace and restored harmony to all the remotest extremities of this distracted land. I believe that it will be attended with all these beneficent effects. And now let us discard all resentment, all passions, all petty jealousies, all personal desires, all love of place, all hankerings after the gilded crumbs which fall from the table of power. Let us forget popular fears, from whatever quarter they may spring. Let us go to the limpid fountain of unadulterated patriotism, and, performing a solemn lustration, return divested of all selfish, sinister, and sordid impurities, and think alone of our God, our country, our consciences, and our glorious Union—that Union without which we shall be torn into hostile fragments, and sooner or later become the victims of military despotism or foreign domination.

Mr. President, what is an individual man? An atom, almost invisible without a magnifying glass—a mere speck upon the surface of the immense universe; not a second in time, compared to immeasurable, never-beginning, and never-ending eternity; a drop of water in the great deep, which evaporates and is borne off by the winds; a grain of sand, which is soon gathered to the dust from which it sprung. Shall a being so small, so petty, so fleeting, so evanescent, oppose itself to the onward march of a great nation which is to subsist for ages and ages to come; oppose itself to that long line of posterity which, issuing from our loins, will endure during the existence of the world? Forbid it, God. Let us look to our country and our cause, elevate ourselves to the dignity of pure and disinterested patriots, and save our country from all impending dangers. What if, in the march of this nation to greatness and power, we should be buried beneath the wheels that propel it onward! What are we—what is any man—worth who is not ready and willing to sacrifice himself for the benefit of his country when it is necessary?

I call upon all the South. Sir, we have had hard words, bitter words, bitter thoughts, unpleasant feelings toward each other in the progress of this great measure. Let us forget them. Let us sacrifice these feelings. Let us go to the altar of our country and swear, as the oath was taken of old, that we will stand by her; that we will support her; that we will uphold her Constitution; that we will preserve her union; and that we will pass this great, comprehensive, and healing system of measures, which will hush all the jarring elements and bring peace and tranquillity to our homes.

Let me, Mr. President, in conclusion, say that the most disastrous consequences would occur, in my opinion, were we to go home, doing nothing to satisfy and tranquillize the country upon these great questions. What will be the judgment of mankind, what the judgment of that portion of mankind who are looking upon the progress of this scheme of self-government as being that which holds the highest hopes and expectations of ameliorating the condition of mankind—what will their judgment be? Will not all the monarchs of the Old World pronounce our glorious republic a disgraceful failure? Will you go home and leave all in disorder and confusion—all unsettled—all open? The contentions and agitations of the past will be increased and augmented by the agitations resulting from our neglect to decide them. Sir, we shall stand condemned by all human judgment below, and of that above it is not for me to speak. We shall stand condemned in our own consciences, by our own constituents, and by our own country. The measure may be defeated. I have been aware that its passage for many days was not absolutely certain. From the first to the last, I hoped and believed it would pass, because from the first to the last I believed it was founded on the principles of just and righteous concession, of mutual conciliation. I believe that it deals unjustly by no part of the Republic; that it saves their honor, and, as far as it is dependent upon Congress, saves the interests of all quarters of the country. But, sir, I have known that the decision of its fate depended upon four or five votes in the Senate of the United States, whose ultimate judgment we could not count upon the one side or the other with absolute certainty. Its fate is now committed to the Senate, and to those five or six votes to which I have referred. It may be defeated. It is possible that, for the chastisement of our sins and transgressions, the rod of Providence may be still applied to us, may be still suspended over us. But, if defeated, it will be a triumph of ultraism and impracticability—a triumph of a most extraordinary conjunction of extremes; a victory won by abolitionism; a victory achieved by free-soilism; a victory of discord and agitation over peace and tranquillity; and I pray to Almighty God that it may not, in consequence of the inauspicious result, lead to the most unhappy and disastrous consequences to our beloved country.

Charles Sumner
[1811–1874]

Charles Sumner, Senator from Massachusetts, was probably the most militant advocate of the abolition of slavery, in the United States Congress. His energy and eloquence won for him the enmity of extremists from the South. As a result of the speech, reproduced here in part, which he delivered in the Senate on May 19–20, 1856, Sumner was assaulted, in the Senate chamber, by a nephew of one of the opposing Senators. Sumner never fully recovered from this attack.

THE CRIME AGAINST KANSAS

THE WICKEDNESS which I now begin to expose is immeasurably aggravated by the motive which prompted it. Not in any common lust for power did this uncommon tragedy have its origin. It is the rape of a virgin Territory, compelling it to the hateful embrace of slavery; and it may be clearly traced to a depraved longing for a new slave State, the hideous offspring of such a crime, in the hope of adding to the power of slavery in the National Government. Yes, sir; when the whole world, alike Christian and Turk, is rising up to condemn this wrong, and to make it a hissing to the nations, here in our Republic, *force*—ay, sir, FORCE—has been openly employed in compelling Kansas to this pollution, and all for the sake of political power. There is the simple fact, which you will in vain attempt to deny, but which in itself presents an essential wickedness that makes other public crimes seem like public virtues.

But this enormity, vast beyond comparison, swells to dimensions of wickedness which the imagination toils in vain to grasp, when it is understood that for this purpose are hazarded the horrors of intestine feud not only in this distant Territory, but everywhere throughout the country. Already the muster has begun. The strife is no longer local, but national. Even now, while I speak, portents hang on all the arches of the horizon threatening to darken the broad land, which already yawns with the mutterings of civil war. The fury of the propagandists of slavery, and the calm determination of their opponents, are now diffused from the distant Territory over widespread communities, and the whole country, in all its extent—marshaling hostile divisions, and foreshadowing a strife which, unless happily averted by the triumph of freedom, will become war—fratricidal, parricidal war—with an accumulated wickedness beyond the wickedness of any war in human annals; justly provoking the avenging judgment of Providence and the avenging pen of history, and constituting a strife, in the language of the ancient writer, more than *foreign*, more than *social*, more than *civil;*

but something compounded of all these strifes, and in itself more than war; *sed potius commune quoddam ex omnibus, et plus quam bellum.*

Such is the crime which you are to judge. But the criminal also must be dragged into day, that you may see and measure the power by which all this wrong is sustained. From no common source could it proceed. In its perpetration was needed a spirit of vaulting ambition which would hesitate at nothing; a hardihood of purpose which was insensible to the judgment of mankind; a madness for slavery which would disregard the Constitution, the laws, and all the great examples of our history; also a consciousness of power such as comes from the habit of power; a combination of energies found only in a hundred arms directed by a hundred eyes; a control of public opinion through venal pens and a prostituted press; an ability to subsidize crowds in every vocation of life—the politician with his local importance, the lawyer with his subtle tongue, and even the authority of the judge on the bench; and a familiar use of men in places high and low, so that none, from the President to the lowest border postmaster, should decline to be its tool; all these things and more were needed, and they were found in the slave power of our Republic. There, sir, stands the criminal, all unmasked before you—heartless, grasping, and tyrannical—with an audacity beyond that of Verres, a subtlety beyond that of Machiavel, a meanness beyond that of Bacon, and an ability beyond that of Hastings. Justice to Kansas can be secured only by the prostration of this influence; for this the power behind—greater than any President—which succors and sustains the crime. Nay, the proceedings I now arraign derive their fearful consequences only from this connection.

In now opening this great matter, I am not insensible to the austere demands of the occasion; but the dependence of the crime against Kansas upon the slave power is so peculiar and important that I trust to be pardoned while I impress it with an illustration, which to some may seem trivial. It is related in Northern mythology that the god of Force, visiting an enchanted region, was challenged by his royal entertainer to what seemed an humble feat of strength—merely, sir, to lift a cat from the ground. The god smiled at the challenge, and, calmly placing his hand under the belly of the animal, with superhuman strength strove, while the back of the feline monster arched far upward, even beyond reach, and one paw actually forsook the earth, until at last the discomfited divinity desisted; but he was little surprised at his defeat when he learned that this creature, which seemed to be a cat, and nothing more, was not merely a cat, but that it belonged to and was a part of the great terrestrial serpent, which, in its innumerable folds, encircled the whole globe. Even so the creature, whose paws are now fastened upon Kansas, whatever it may seem to be, constitutes in reality a part of the slave power, which, in its loathsome folds, is now coiled about the whole land. Thus do I expose the extent of the present contest, where we encounter not merely local resistance, but also the unconquered sustaining arm behind. But out of the vastness of the crime attempted, with all its woe and shame, I derive a well-founded assurance of a commensurate vastness of effort against it by the aroused masses of the country, determined not only to vindicate right against wrong, but to redeem the Republic from the thraldom of that oligarchy which prompts, directs, and concentrates the distant wrong.

But, before entering upon the argument, I must say something of a general character, particularly in response to what has fallen from Senators who have raised themselves to eminence on this floor in championship of human wrongs. I mean the Senator from South Carolina (Mr. Butler), and the Senator from Illinois (Mr. Douglas), who, though unlike as Don Quixote and Sancho Panza, yet, like this couple, sally forth together in the same adventure. I regret much to miss the elder Senator from his seat; but the cause, against which he has run a tilt, with such activity of animosity, demands that the opportunity of exposing him should not be lost; and it is for the cause that I speak. The Senator from South Carolina has read many books of chivalry, and believes himself a chivalrous knight, with sentiments of honor and courage. Of course he has chosen a mistress to whom he has made his vows, and who, though ugly to others, is always lovely to him; though polluted in the sight of the world, is chaste in his sight— I mean the harlot, Slavery. For her, his tongue is always profuse in words. Let her be impeached in character, or any proposition made to shut her out from the extension of her wantonness, and no extravagance of manner or hardihood of assertion is then too great for this Senator. The frenzy of Don Quixote, in behalf of his wench, Dulcinea del Toboso, is all surpassed. The asserted rights of slavery, which shock equality of all kinds, are cloaked by a fantastic claim of equality. If the slave States cannot enjoy what, in mockery of the great fathers of the Republic, he misnames equality under the Constitution—in other words, the full power in the national territories to compel fellow-men to unpaid toil, to separate husband and wife, and to sell little children at the auction block—then, sir, the chivalric Senator will conduct the State of South Carolina out of the Union! Heroic knight! Exalted Senator! A second Moses come for a second exodus!

But not content with this poor menace, which we have been twice told was "measured," the Senator in the unrestrained chivalry of his nature, has undertaken to apply opprobrious words to those who differ from him on this floor. He calls them "sectional and fanatical;" and opposition to the usurpation in Kansas he denounces as "an uncalculating fanaticism." To be sure these charges lack all grace of originality, and all sentiment of truth; but the adventurous Senator does not hesitate. He is the uncompromising, unblushing representative on this floor of a flagrant *sectionalism,* which now domineers over the Republic, and yet with a ludicrous ignorance of his own position—unable to see himself as others see him—or with an effrontery which even his white head ought not to protect from rebuke, he applies to those here who resist his *sectionalism* the very epithet which designates himself. The men who strive to bring back the Government to its original policy, when freedom and not slavery was sectional, he arraigns as *sectional*. This will not do. It involves too great a perversion of terms. I tell that Senator that it is to himself, and to the "organization" of which he is the "committed advocate," that this epithet belongs. I now fasten it upon them. For myself, I care little for names; but since the question has been raised here, I affirm that the Republican party of the Union is in no just sense *sectional,* but, more than any other party, *national;* and that it now goes forth to dislodge from the high places of the Government the tyrannical sectionalism of which the Senator from South Carolina is one of the maddest zealots.

As the Senator from South Carolina is the Don Quixote, the Senator from Illinois (Mr. Douglas) is the squire of slavery, its very Sancho Panza, ready to do all its humiliating offices. This Senator, in his labored address, vindicating his labored report—piling one mass of elaborate error upon another mass—constrained himself, as you will remember, to unfamiliar decencies of speech. Of that address I have nothing to say at this moment, though before I sit down I shall show something of its fallacies. But I go back now to an earlier occasion, when, true to his native impulses, he threw into this discussion, "for a charm of powerful trouble," personalities most discreditable to this body. I will not stop to repel the imputations which he cast upon myself; but I mention them to remind you of the "sweltered venom sleeping got," which, with other poisoned ingredients, he cast into the cauldron of this debate. Of other things I speak. Standing on this floor, the Senator issued his rescript, requiring submission to the usurped power of Kansas; and this was accompanied by a manner—all his own—such as befits the tyrannical threat. Very well. Let the Senator try. I tell him now that he cannot enforce any such submission. The Senator, with the slave power at his back, is strong; but he is not strong enough for this purpose. He is bold. He shrinks from nothing. Like Danton, he may cry, *"l'audace! l'audace! toujours l'audace!"* but even his audacity cannot compass this work. The Senator copies the British officer who, with boastful swagger, said that with the hilt of his sword he would cram the "stamps" down the throats of the American people, and he will meet with a similar failure. He may convulse this country with a civil feud. Like the ancient madman, he may set fire to this temple of constitutional liberty, grander than the Ephesian dome; but he cannot enforce obedience to that tyrannical usurpation.

The Senator dreams that he can subdue the North. He disclaims the open threat, but his conduct still implies it. How little that Senator knows himself or the strength of the cause which he persecutes! He is but a mortal man; against him is an immortal principle. With finite power he wrestles with the infinite, and he must fall. Against him are stronger battalions than any marshaled by mortal arm—the inborn, ineradicable, invincible sentiments of the human heart; against him is nature in all her subtle forces; against him is God. Let him try to subdue these.

William Henry Seward
[1801–1872]

William Henry Seward, famed Secretary of State in President Lincoln's cabinet, was elected governor of New York in 1838. In 1849 he entered the United States Senate, representing New York for twelve years. In 1860 he lost the Republican Presidential nomination to Lincoln after a close contest. The following speech, parts of which are reproduced here, was delivered in Rochester, N.Y., on October 25, 1858.

THE IRREPRESSIBLE CONFLICT

THE HISTORY OF the Democratic party commits it to the policy of slavery. It has been the Democratic party, and no other agency, which has carried that policy up to its present alarming culmination. Without stopping to ascertain, critically, the origin of the present Democratic party, we may concede its claim to date from the era of good feeling which occurred under the administration of President Monroe. At that time, in this State, and about that time in many others of the free States, the Democratic party deliberately disfranchised the free colored or African citizen, and it has pertinaciously continued this disfranchisement ever since. This was an effective aid to slavery; for, while the slaveholder votes for his slaves against freedom, the freed slave in the free States is prohibited from voting against slavery.

In 1824 the democracy resisted the election of John Quincy Adams—himself before that time an acceptable Democrat—and in 1828 it expelled him from the presidency and put a slaveholder in his place, although the office had been filled by slaveholders thirty-two out of forty years.

In 1836, Martin Van Buren—the first non-slaveholding citizen of a free State to whose election the Democratic party ever consented—signalized his inauguration into the presidency by a gratuitous announcement that under no circumstances would he ever approve a bill for the abolition of slavery in the District of Columbia. From 1838 to 1844 the subject of abolishing slavery in the District of Columbia and in the national dockyards and arsenals, was brought before Congress by repeated popular appeals. The Democratic party thereupon promptly denied the right of petition, and effectually suppressed the freedom of speech in Congress, so far as the institution of slavery was concerned.

From 1840 to 1843 good and wise men counselled that Texas should remain outside the Union until she should consent to relinquish her self-instituted slavery; but the Democratic party precipitated her admission into the Union, not only without that condition, but even with a covenant that the State might be divided and reorganized so as to constitute four slave States instead of one.

In 1846, when the United States became involved in a war with Mexico, and it was apparent that the struggle would end in the dismemberment of that republic, which was a non-slaveholding power, the Democratic party rejected a declaration that slavery should not be established within the territory to be acquired. When, in 1850, governments were to be instituted in the territories of California and New Mexico, the fruits of that war, the Democratic party refused to admit New Mexico as a free State, and only consented to admit California as a free State on the condition, as it has since explained the transaction, of leaving all of New Mexico and Utah open to slavery, to which was also added the concession of perpetual slavery in the District of Columbia, and the passage of an unconstitutional, cruel, and humiliating law, for the recapture of fugitive slaves, with a further stipulation that the subject of slavery should never again be agitated in either chamber of Congress. When, in 1854, the slaveholders were contentedly reposing on these great advantages, then so recently won, the Democratic party unnecessarily, officiously, and with super-serviceable liberality, awakened them from their slumber, to offer and force on their acceptance the abrogation of the law which declared that neither slavery nor involuntary servitude should ever exist within that part of the ancient territory of Louisiana which lay outside of the State of Missouri, and north of the parallel of 36° 30′ of north latitude— a law which, with the exception of one other, was the only statute of freedom then remaining in the federal code.

In 1856, when the people of Kansas had organized a new State within the region thus abandoned to slavery, and applied to be admitted as a free State into the Union, the Democratic party contemptuously rejected their petition, and drove them with menaces and intimidations from the halls of Congress, and armed the President with military power to enforce their submission to a slave code, established over them by fraud and usurpation. At every subsequent stage of a long contest which has since raged in Kansas, the Democratic party has lent its sympathies, its aid, and all the powers of the government which it controlled, to enforce slavery upon that unwilling and injured people. And now, even at this day, while it mocks us with the assurance that Kansas is free, the Democratic party keeps the State excluded from her just and proper place in the Union, under the hope that she may be dragooned into the acceptance of slavery.

The Democratic party, finally, has procured from a supreme judiciary, fixed in its interest, a decree that slavery exists by force of the constitution in every territory of the United States, paramount to all legislative authority, either within the territory or residing in Congress.

Such is the Democratic party. It has no policy, state or federal, for finance, or trade, or manufacture, or commerce, or education, or internal improvements, or for the protection or even the security of civil or religious liberty. It is positive and uncompromising in the interest of slavery—negative, compromising, and vacillating, in regard to everything else. It boasts its love of equality, and wastes its strength, and even its life, in fortifying the only aristocracy known in the land. It professes fraternity, and, so often as slavery requires, allies itself with proscription. It magnifies itself for conquests in foreign lands, but it sends the national eagle forth always with chains, and not the olive branch, in his fangs.

This dark record shows you, fellow-citizens, what I was unwilling to announce at an earlier stage of this argument, that of the whole nefarious schedule of slaveholding designs which I have submitted to you, the Democratic party has left only one yet to be consummated— the abrogation of the law which forbids the African slave-trade.

I know—few, I think, know better than I—the resources and energies of the Democratic party, which is identical with the slave power. I do ample justice to its traditional popularity. I know further—few, I think, know better than I—the difficulties and disadvantages of organizing a new political force, like the Republican party, and the obstacles it must encounter in laboring without prestige and without patronage. But, understanding all this, I know that the Democratic party must go down, and that the Republican party must rise into its place. The Democratic party derived its strength, originally, from its adoption of the principles of equal and exact justice to all men. So long as it practised this principle faithfully it was invulnerable. It became vulnerable when it renounced the principle, and since that time it has maintained itself, not by virtue of its own strength, or even of its traditional merits, but because there as yet had appeared in the political field no other party that had the conscience and the courage to take up, and avow, and practise the life-inspiring principle which the Democratic party had surrendered. At last, the Republican party has appeared. It avows, now, as the Republican party of 1800 did, in one word, its faith and its works, "Equal and exact justice to all men." Even when it first entered the field, only half organized, it struck a blow which only just failed to secure complete and triumphant victory. In this, its second campaign, it has already won advantages which render that triumph now both easy and certain.

The secret of its assured success lies in that very characteristic which, in the mouth of scoffers, constitutes its great and lasting imbecility and reproach. It lies in the fact that it is a party of one idea; but that is a noble one—an idea that fills and expands all generous souls; the idea of equality—the equality of all men before human tribunals and human laws, as they all are equal before the divine tribunal and divine laws.

I know, and you know, that a revolution has begun. I know, and all the world knows, that revolutions never go backward. Twenty senators and a hundred representatives proclaim boldly in Congress to-day sentiments and opinions and principles of freedom which hardly so many men, even in this free State, dared to utter in their own homes twenty years ago. While the government of the United

States, under the conduct of the Democratic party, has been all that
time surrendering one plain and castle after another to slavery, the
people of the United States have been no less steadily and perseveringly
gathering together the forces with which to recover back again all
the fields and all the castles which have been lost, and to confound
and overthrow, by one decisive blow, the betrayers of the constitution
and freedom forever.

John Brown
[1800–1859]

*John Brown, of Ossawatomie, Kansas, became one of the most
famous figures in the fight against slavery during the years preceding the Civil War. His methods were militant. He was for the
immediate liberation of slaves. On the night of October 16, 1859,
leading a small band of supporters, Brown seized the arsenal at
Harpers Ferry, now in West Virginia. He was captured, tried and
convicted. On being sentenced to death, on November 2, 1859,
Brown made this extemporaneous speech to the court.*

ON BEING SENTENCED TO DEATH

I HAVE, may it please the Court, a few words to say.

In the first place, I deny everything but what I have all along admitted:
of a design on my part to free slaves. I intended certainly to have
made a clean thing of that matter, as I did last winter, when I went
into Missouri and there took slaves without the snapping of a gun
on either side, moving them through the country, and finally leaving
them in Canada. I designed to have done the same thing again on
a larger scale. That was all I intended. I never did intend murder,
or treason, or the destruction of property, or to excite or incite slaves to
rebellion, or to make insurrection.

I have another objection, and that is that it is unjust that I should
suffer such a penalty. Had I interfered in the manner which I admit,
and which I admit has been fairly proved—for I admire the truthfulness
and candor of the greater portion of the witnesses who have testified
in this case—had I so interfered in behalf of the rich, the powerful,
the intelligent, the so-called great, or in behalf of any of their friends,
either father, mother, brother, sister, wife or children, or any of that
class, and suffered and sacrificed what I have in this interference,
it would have been all right. Every man in this Court would have
deemed it an act worthy of reward rather than punishment.

This Court acknowledges, too, as I suppose, the validity of the law
of God. I see a book kissed, which I suppose to be the Bible, or at
least the New Testament, which teaches me that all things whatsoever

I would that men should do to me, I should do even so to them. It teaches me, further, to remember them that are in bonds as bound with them. I endeavored to act up to that instruction. I say I am yet too young to understand that God is any respecter of persons. I believe that to have interfered as I have done, as I have always freely admitted I have done, in behalf of His despised poor, I did no wrong, but right. Now, if it is deemed necessary that I should forfeit my life for the furtherance of the ends of justice, and mingle my blood further with the blood of my children and with the blood of millions in this slave country whose rights are disregarded by wicked, cruel, and unjust enactments, I say, let it be done.

Let me say one word further. I feel entirely satisfied with the treatment I have received on my trial. Considering all the circumstances, it has been more generous than I expected. But I feel no consciousness of guilt. I have stated from the first what was my intention, and what was not. I never had any design against the liberty of any person, nor any disposition to commit treason or incite slaves to rebel or make any general insurrection. I never encouraged any man to do so, but always discouraged any idea of that kind.

Let me say, also, in regard to the statements made by some of those who were connected with me, I hear it has been stated by some of them that I have induced them to join me. But the contrary is true. I do not say this to injure them, but as regretting their weakness. Not one but joined me of his own accord, and the greater part at their own expense. A number of them I never saw, and never had a word of conversation with, till the day they came to me, and that was for the purpose I have stated.

Now, I have done.

William Lloyd Garrison
[1805–1879]

William Lloyd Garrison, of Massachusetts, was probably the outstanding leader of the abolitionist movement. He was editor of the "Liberator," president of the American Anti-Slavery Society, and one of the most popular and forceful abolitionist speakers. Here is Garrison's eloquent tribute to John Brown, delivered in Boston, December 2, 1859.

ON THE DEATH OF JOHN BROWN

GOD FORBID that we should any longer continue the accomplices of thieves and robbers, of men-stealers and women-whippers! We must join together in the name of freedom. As for the Union—where is it and what is it? In one-half of it no man can exercise freedom of speech or the press—no man can utter the words of Washington, ot Jefferson, of Patrick Henry—except at the peril of his life; and Northern men are everywhere hunted and driven from the South if they are supposed to cherish the sentiment of freedom in their bosoms. We are living under an awful despotism—that of a brutal slave oligarchy. And they threaten to leave us if we do not continue to do their evil work, as we have hitherto done it, and go down in the dust before them! Would to heaven they would go! It would only be the paupers clearing out from the town, would it not? But, no, they do not mean to go; they mean to cling to you, and they mean to subdue you. But will you be subdued? I tell you our work is the dissolution of this slavery-cursed Union, if we would have a fragment of our liberties left to us! Surely between freemen, who believe in exact justice and impartial liberty, and slaveholders, who are for cleaning down all human rights at a blow, it is not possible there should be any Union whatever. "How can two walk together except they be agreed?" The slaveholder with his hands dripping in blood—will I make a compact with him? The man who plunders cradles—will I say to him, "Brother, let us walk together in unity"? The man who, to gratify his lust or his anger, scourges woman with the lash till the soil is red with her blood—will I say to him: "Give me your hand; let us form a glorious Union"? No, never—never! There can be no union between us: "What concord hath Christ with Belial?" What union has freedom with slavery? Let us tell the inexorable and remorseless tyrants of the South that their conditions hitherto imposed upon us, whereby we are morally responsible for the existence of slavery, are horribly inhuman and wicked, and we cannot carry them out for the sake of their evil company.

By the dissolution of the Union we shall give the finishing blow to the slave system; and then God will make it possible for us to form a true, vital, enduring, all-embracing Union, from the Atlantic to the Pacific—one God to be worshipped, one Saviour to be revered, one policy to be carried out—freedom everywhere to all the people, without regard to complexion or race—and the blessing of God resting upon us all! I want to see that glorious day! Now the South is full of tribulation and terror and despair, going down to irretrievable bankruptcy, and fearing each bush an officer! Would to God it might all pass away like a hideous dream! and how easily it might be! What is it that God requires of the South to remove every root of bitterness, to allay every fear, to fill her borders with prosperity? But one simple act of justice, without violence and convulsion, without danger and hazard. It is this: "Undo the heavy burdens, break every yoke, and let the oppressed go free!" Then shall thy light break forth as the morning, and thy darkness shall be as the noonday. Then shalt thou call and the Lord shall answer; thou shalt cry, and he shall say: "Here I am." "And they that shall be of thee shall build the old waste places; thou shalt raise up the foundations of many generations; and thou shalt be called the repairer of the breach, the restorer of paths to dwell in."

How simple and how glorious! It is the complete solution of all the difficulties in the case. Oh, that the South may be wise before it is too late, and give heed to the word of the Lord! But, whether she will hear or forbear, let us renew our pledges to the cause of bleeding humanity, and spare no effort to make this truly the land of the free and the refuge of the oppressed!

> "Onward, then, ye fearless band,
> Heart to heart, and hand to hand;
> Yours shall be the Christian's stand,
> Or the martyr's grave."

Stephen Arnold Douglas
[1813–1861]

Stephen Arnold Douglas, a lawyer by profession, held public office to the end of his life from the time he was elected to the Illinois legislature at the age of twenty-three. He was a member of both branches of Congress and a leader of the Democratic party. Although he was a strong opponent of Abraham Lincoln on the slavery question, Douglas sided with the North when secession became a reality. Below are parts of his speech delivered in a joint debate with Lincoln at Freeport, Ill., in the campaign of 1858.

REPLY TO LINCOLN

Ladies and gentlemen: I am glad that at last I have brought Mr. Lincoln to the conclusion that he had better define his position on certain political questions to which I called his attention at Ottawa. He there showed no disposition, no inclination, to answer them. I did not present idle questions for him to answer merely for my gratification. I laid the foundation for those interrogatories by showing that they constituted the platform of the party whose nominee he is for the Senate. I did not presume that I had the right to catechise him as I saw proper, unless I showed that his party, or a majority of it, stood upon the platform and were in favor of the propositions upon which my questions were based. I desired simply to know, inasmuch as he had been nominated as the first, last, and only choice of his party, whether he concurred in the platform which that party had adopted for its government. In a few moments I will proceed to review the answers which he has given to these interrogatories; but in order to relieve his anxiety, I will first respond to these which he has presented to me. Mark you, he has not presented interrogatories which have ever received the sanction of the party with which I am acting, and hence he has no other foundation for them than his own curiosity.

First, he desires to know if the people of Kansas shall form a constitution by means entirely proper and unobjectionable, and ask admission into the Union as a State, before they have the requisite population for a member of Congress, whether I will vote for that admission. Well, now, I regret exceedingly that he did not answer that interrogatory himself before he put it to me, in order that we might understand, and not be left to infer on which side he is. Mr. Trumbull, during the last session of Congress, voted from the beginning to the end against the admission of Oregon, although a free State, because she had not the requisite population for a member of Congress. Mr. Trumbull would not consent, under any circumstances, to let a State, free or slave, come into the Union until it had the requisite population. As Mr. Trumbull is in the field fighting for Mr. Lincoln, I would like to have Mr. Lincoln answer his own question, and tell me whether he is fighting Trumbull on that issue or not. But I will answer his question. In reference to Kansas, it is my opinion that as she has population enough to constitute a slave State, she has people enough for a free State. I will not make Kansas an exceptional case to the other States of the Union. I hold it to be a sound rule of universal application to require a territory to contain the requisite population for a member of Congress before it is admitted as a State into the Union. I made that proposition in the Senate in 1856, and I renewed it during the last session in a bill providing that no territory of the United States should form ‧a constitution and apply for admission, until it had the requisite population. On another occasion, I proposed, that neither Kansas nor any other territory should be admitted until it had the requisite population. Congress did not adopt any of my propositions containing this general rule, but did make an exception of Kansas. I will stand by that exception. Either Kansas must come in as a free State, with whatever population she may have, or the rule must be applied to all the other territories alike.

The next question propounded to me by Mr. Lincoln is: Can the people of the territory in any lawful way, against the wishes of any citizen of the United States, exclude slavery from their limits prior to the formation of a State constitution? I answer emphatically, as Mr. Lincoln has heard me answer a hundred times from every stump in Illinois, that in my opinion the people of a territory can, by lawful means, exclude slavery from their limits prior to the formation of a State constitution. Mr. Lincoln knew that I had answered that question over and over again. He heard me argue the Nebraska Bill on that principle all over the State in 1854, in 1855, and in 1856, and he has no excuse for pretending to be in doubt as to my position on that question. It matters not what way the Supreme Court may hereafter decide as to the abstract question whether slavery may or may not go into a territory under the constitution; the people have the lawful means to introduce it or exclude it as they please, for the reason that slavery cannot exist a day or an hour anywhere, unless it is supported by local police regulations. Those police regulations can only be established by the local legislature; and if the people are opposed to slavery, they will elect representatives to that body who will, by unfriendly legislation, effectually prevent the introduction of it into their midst. If, on the contrary, they are for it, their legislation will favor its extension. Hence, no matter what the decision of the Supreme Court may be on that abstract question, still the right of the people to make a slave territory or a free territory is perfect and complete under the Nebraska Bill. I hope Mr. Lincoln deems my answer satisfactory on that point.

The third question which Mr. Lincoln presented is: "If the Supreme Court of the United States shall decide that a State of this Union cannot exclude slavery from its own limits, will I submit to it?" I am amazed that Lincoln should ask such a question. "A schoolboy knows better." Yes, a schoolboy does know better. Mr. Lincoln's object is to cast an imputation upon the Supreme Court. He knows that there never was but one man in America, claiming any degree of intelligence or decency, who ever for a moment pretended such a thing. It is true that the Washington "Union," in an article published on the seventeenth of last December, did put forth that doctrine, and I denounced the article on the floor of the Senate in a speech which Mr. Lincoln now pretends was against the President. The Union had claimed that slavery had a right to go into the free States, and that any provisions in the constitution or laws of the free States to the contrary was null and void. I denounced it in the Senate, as I said before, and I was the first man who did. Lincoln's friends, Trumbull and Seward and Hale and Wilson, and the whole black Republican side of the Senate, were silent. They left it to me to denounce it. And what was the reply made to me on that occasion? Mr. Toombs, of Georgia, got up and undertook to lecture me on the ground that I ought not to have deemed the article worthy of notice and ought not to have replied to it; that there was not one man, woman, or child south of the Potomac, in any slave State, who did not repudiate any such pretension. Mr. Lincoln knows that that reply was made on the spot, and yet now he asks this question. He might as well ask me: "Suppose Mr. Lincoln should steal a horse, would you sanction it?" and it would be as genteel in me to ask him, in the event he stole a horse, what ought to be done with him. He casts an imputation upon the Supreme Court of the United States by supposing that they would violate the constitution of the United States. I tell him that such a thing is not possible. It would be an act of moral treason that no man on the bench could ever descend to. Mr. Lincoln himself would never in his partisan feelings so far forget what was right as to be guilty of such an act.

The fourth question of Mr. Lincoln is: "Are you in favor of acquiring additional territory, in disregard as to how such acquisition may affect the Union on the slavery question?" This question is very ingeniously and cunningly put.

The Black Republican creed lays it down expressly, that under no circumstances shall we acquire any more territory unless slavery is first prohibited in the country. I ask Mr. Lincoln whether he is in favor of that proposition. Are you [addressing Mr. Lincoln] opposed to the acquisition of any more territory, under any circumstances, unless slavery is prohibited in it? That he does not like to answer. When I ask him whether he stands up to that article in the platform of his party he turns, Yankee fashion, and, without answering it, asks me whether I am in favor of acquiring territory without regard to how it may affect the Union on the slavery question. I answer that whenever it becomes necessary, in our growth and progress, to acquire more territory, that I am in favor of it, without reference to the question of slavery; and when we have acquired it, I will leave the people free to do as they please, either to make it slave or free territory, as they prefer. It is idle to tell me or you that we have territory enough. Our fathers supposed that we had enough when our territory extended to the Mississippi River, but a few years' growth and expansion satisfied them that we needed more, and the Louisiana Territory, from the west branch of the Mississippi to the British possessions, was acquired. Then we acquired Oregon, then California and New Mexico. We have enough now for the present, but this is a young and a growing nation. It swarms as often as a hive of bees; and as new swarms are turned out each year, there must be hives in which they can gather and make their honey. In less than fifteen years, if the same progress that has distinguished this country for the last fifteen years continue, every foot of vacant land between this and the Pacific Ocean owned by the United States will be occupied. Will you not continue to increase at the end of fifteen years as well as now? I tell you, increase and multiply and expand is the law of this nation's existence. You cannot limit this great republic by mere boundary lines, saying: "thus far shalt thou go, and no further." Any one of you gentlemen might as well say to a son twelve years old that he is big enough, and must not grow any larger, and in order to prevent his growth, put a hoop around him to keep him to his present size. What would be the result? Either the hoop must burst and be rent asunder, or the child must die. So it would be with this great nation. With our natural increase, growing with a rapidity unknown in any other part of the globe, with the tide of emigration that is fleeing from despotism in the Old World to seek refuge in our own, there is a constant torrent pouring into this country that requires more land, more territory upon which to settle; and just as fast as our interests and our destiny require additional territory in the North, in the South, or on the islands of the ocean, I am for it, and when we acquire it, will leave the people, according to the Nebraska Bill, free to do as they please on the subject of slavery and every other question.

I trust now that Mr. Lincoln will deem himself answered on his four points.

Jefferson Davis
[1808–1889]

Jefferson Davis, president of the Confederate States of America, was for many years United States Senator from Mississippi. When his state declared her intention to secede from the Union, Davis delivered the following historic farewell address in the Senate. This was on January 21, 1861.

ON WITHDRAWAL FROM THE UNION

I RISE, Mr. President, for the purpose of announcing to the Senate that I have satisfactory evidence that the State of Mississippi, by a solemn ordinance of her people in convention assembled, has declared her separation from the United States. Under these circumstances, of course my functions are terminated here. It has seemed to me proper, however, that I should appear in the Senate to announce that fact to my associates, and I will say but very little more. The occasion does not invite me to go into argument, and my physical condition would not permit me to do so if it were otherwise; and yet it seems to become me to say something on the part of the state I here represent, on an occasion so solemn as this.

It is known to senators who have served with me here that I have for many years advocated, as an essential attribute of state sovereignty, the right of a state to secede from the Union. Therefore, if I had not believed there was justifiable cause; if I had thought that Mississippi was acting without sufficient provocation, or without an existing necessity, I should still, under my theory of the government, because of my allegiance to the state of which I am a citizen, have been bound by her action. I, however, may be permitted to say that I do think that she has justifiable cause, and I approve of her act. I conferred with her people before that act was taken, counseled them then that, if the state of things which they apprehended should exist when the convention met, they should take the action which they have now adopted.

I hope none who hear me will confound this expression of mine with the advocacy of the right of a state to remain in the Union, and to disregard its constitutional obligations by the nullification of the law. Such is not my theory. Nullification and secession, so often confounded, are indeed antagonistic principles. Nullification is a remedy which it is sought to apply within the Union, and against the agent of the states. It is only to be justified when the agent has violated his constitutional obligation, and a state, assuming to judge for itself, denies the right of the agent thus to act, and appeals to the other states of the Union for a decision; but when the states themselves, and when the people of the states, have so acted as to convince us that they will not regard our constitutional rights, then, and then for the first time, arises the doctrine of secession in its practical application.

A great man who now reposes with his fathers, and who has been often arraigned for a want of fealty to the Union, advocated the doctrine of nullification, because it preserved the Union. It was because of his deep-seated attachment to the Union, his determination to find some remedy for existing ills short of a severance of the ties which bound South Carolina to the other states, that Mr. Calhoun advocated the doctrine of nullification, which he proclaimed to be peaceful, to be within the limits of state power, not to disturb the Union, but only to be a means of bringing the agent before the tribunal of the states for their judgment.

Secession belongs to a different class of remedies. It is to be justified upon the basis that the states are sovereign. There was a time when none denied it. I hope the time may come again, when a better comprehension of the theory of our government, and the inalienable rights of the people of the states, will prevent any one from denying that each state is a sovereign, and thus may reclaim the grants which it has made to any agent whomsoever.

I therefore say I concur in the action of the people of Mississippi, believing it to be necessary and proper, and should have been bound by their action if my belief had been otherwise; and this brings me to the important point which I wish on this last occasion to present to the Senate. It is by this confounding of nullification and secession that the name of the great man whose ashes now mingle with his mother earth has been invoked to justify coercion against a seceded state. The phrase "to execute the laws" was an expression which General Jackson applied to the case of a state refusing to obey the laws while yet a member of the Union. That is not the case which is now presented. The laws are to be executed over the United States, and upon the people of the United States. They have no relation to any foreign country. It is a perversion of terms, at least it is a great misapprehension of the case, which cites that expression for application to a state which has withdrawn from the Union. You may make war on a foreign state. If it be the purpose of gentlemen, they may make war against a state which has withdrawn from the Union; but there are no laws of the United States to be executed within the limits of a seceded state. A state finding herself in the condition in which Mississippi has judged she is, in which her safety requires that she should provide for the maintenance of her rights out of the Union, surrenders all the benefits (and they are known to be many), deprives herself of the advantages (they are known to be great), severs all the ties of affection (and they are close and enduring), which have bound her to the Union; and thus divesting herself of every benefit, taking upon herself every burden, she claims to be exempt from any power to execute the laws of the United States within her limits.

I well remember an occasion when Massachusetts was arraigned before the bar of the Senate, and when then the doctrine of coercion was rife and to be applied against her because of the rescue of a fugitive slave in Boston. My opinion then was the same that it is now. Not in a spirit of egotism, but to show that I am not influenced in my opinion because the case is my own, I refer to that time and that occasion as containing the opinion which I then entertained, and on which my present conduct is based. I then said, if Massachusetts, following her through a stated line of conduct, chooses to take the last step which separates her from the Union, it is her right to go, and I will neither vote one dollar nor one man to coerce her back, but will say to her, God speed, in memory of the kind associations which once existed between her and the other states.

It has been a conviction of pressing necessity, it has been a belief that we are to be deprived in the Union of the rights which our fathers bequeathed to us, which has brought Mississippi into her present decision. She has heard proclaimed the theory that all men are created free and equal, and this made the basis of an attack upon her social institutions; and the sacred Declaration of Independence has been invoked to maintain the position of the equality of the races. That Declaration of Independence is to be construed by the circumstances and purposes for which it was made. The communities were declaring their independence; the people of those communities were asserting that no man was born—to use the language of Mr. Jefferson—booted and spurred to ride over the rest of mankind; that men were created equal—meaning the men of the political community; that there was no divine right to rule; that no man inherited the right to govern; that there were no classes by which power and place descended to families, but that all stations were equally within the grasp of each member of the body politic. These were the great principles they announced; these were the purposes for which they made their declaration; these were the end to which their enunciation was directed. They have no reference to the slave; else, how happened it that among the items of arraignment made against George III. was that he endeavored to do just what the North had been endeavoring of late to do—to stir up insurrection among our slaves? Had the Declaration announced that the negroes were free and equal, how was the prince to be arraigned for stirring up insurrection among them? And how was this to be enumerated among the high crimes which caused the colonies to sever their connection with the mother country? When our Constitution was formed, the same idea was rendered more palpable, for there we find provision made for that very class of persons as property; they were not put upon the footing of equality with white men—not even upon that of paupers and convicts; but, so far as representation was concerned, were discriminated against as a lower caste, only to be represented in the numerical proportion of three-fifths.

Then, senators, we recur to the compact which binds us together; we recur to the principles upon which our government was founded;

and when you deny them, and when you deny to us the right to withdraw from a government which, thus perverted, threatens to be destructive of our rights, we but tread in the path of our fathers when we proclaim our independence, and take the hazard. This is done not in hostility to others, not to injure any section of the country, not even for our own pecuniary benefit; but from the high and solemn motive of defending and protecting the rights we inherited, and which it is our sacred duty to transmit unshorn to our children.

I find in myself, perhaps, a type of the general feeling of my constituents toward yours. I am sure I feel no hostility to you, senators from the North. I am sure there is not one of you, whatever sharp discussion there may have been between us, to whom I cannot now say, in the presence of my God, I wish you well; and such, I am sure, is the feeling of the people whom I represent toward those whom you represent. I therefore feel that I but express their desire when I say I hope, and they hope, for peaceful relations with you, though we must part. They may be mutually beneficial to us in the future, as they have been in the past, if you so will it. The reverse may bring disaster on every portion of the country; and if you will have it thus, we will invoke the God of our fathers, who delivered them from the power of the lion, to protect us from the ravages of the bear; and thus, putting our trust in God, and in our own firm hearts and strong arms, we will vindicate the right as best we may.

In the course of my service here, associated at different times with a great variety of senators, I see now around me some with whom I have served long; there have been points of collision; but whatever of offense there has been to me, I leave here; I carry with me no hostile remembrance. Whatever offense I have given which has not been redressed, or for which satisfaction has not been demanded, I have, senators, in this hour of our parting, to offer you my apology for any pain which, in heat of discussion, I have inflicted. I go hence unencumbered of the remembrance of any injury received, and having discharged the duty of making the only reparation in my power for any injury offered.

Mr. President and senators, having made the announcement which the occasion seemed to me to require, it only remains for me to bid you a final adieu.

Abraham Lincoln
[1809-1865]

The life story of the "Great Emancipator" is known to every American. Of a poor family and with no formal education, Abraham Lincoln became a popular country lawyer, member of the Illinois Legislature and finally of Congress. In 1858 he ran for the Senate, debating with Stephen A. Douglas, his opponent for the office. Lincoln's forceful denunciation of slavery in this campaign attracted the attention of the North, which resulted in his selection as the Presidential nominee of the new Republican party in 1860. His election to the Presidency, his conduct of the war against the rebellious South, his freeing of the slaves, and his assassination following the victory of the Union armies, are an immortal story. Following are Lincoln's famous "A House Divided Against Itself" speech, which was delivered at the Republican State Convention at Springfield, Ill., June 16, 1858, on his nomination to the Senate; the touching "Farewell Address at Springfield," delivered on February 11, 1861; the oratorical gem, "Address at Gettysburg," delivered at Gettysburg, Pa., November 19, 1863, and the Second Inaugural Address delivered at Washington, March 4, 1865.

ON HIS NOMINATION TO THE SENATE

MR. PRESIDENT AND GENTLEMEN OF THE CONVENTION: If we could first know where we are, and whither we are tending, we could better judge what to do, and how to do it. We are now far into the fifth year since a policy was initiated with the avowed object, and confident promise, of putting an end to slavery agitation. Under the operation of that policy, that agitation not only has not ceased, but has constantly augmented. In my opinion, it will not cease until a crisis shall have been reached and passed. "A house divided against itself cannot stand." I believe this government cannot endure permanently half slave and half free. I do not expect the Union to be dissolved; I do not expect the house to fall; but I do expect that it will cease to be divided. It will become all one thing, or all the other. Either the opponents of slavery will arrest the further spread of it, and place it where the public mind shall rest in the belief that it is in the course of ultimate extinction; or its advocates will push it forward till it shall become alike lawful in all the States, old as well as new, North as well as South. Have we no tendency to the latter condition? Let anyone who doubts carefully contemplate that now almost complete legal combination-piece of machinery, so to speak—compounded of the Nebraska doctrine and the Dred Scott decision. Let him consider not only what work the machinery is adapted to do, and how well adapted, but also let him study the history of its construction, and trace, if he can, or rather fail, if he can, to trace the evidences of design and concert of action among its chief architects from the beginning.

The new year of 1854 found slavery excluded from more than half the States by State constitutions, and from most of the national territory by Congressional prohibition. Four days later commenced the struggle which ended in repealing that Congressional prohibition. This opened all the national territory to slavery, and was the first point gained. But, so far, Congress only had acted, and an indorsement, by the people, real or apparent, was indispensable, to save the point already gained and give chance for more. This necessity had not been overlooked, but had been provided for, as well as might be, in the notable argument of "squatter sovereignty," otherwise called "sacred right of self-government"; which latter phrase though expressive of the only rightful basis of any government, was so perverted in this attempted use of it as to amount to just this: That, if any one man choose to enslave another, no third man shall be allowed to object. That argument was incorporated with the Nebraska bill itself, in the language which follows: "It being the true intent and meaning of this act, not to legislate slavery into any territory or State, nor to exclude it therefrom; but to leave the people thereof perfectly free to form and regulate their domestic institutions in their own way, subject only to the constitution of the United States." Then opened the roar of loose declamation in favor of "squatter sovereignty," and "sacred right of self-government." "But," said opposition members, "let us amend the bill so as to expressly declare that the people of the territory may exclude slavery." "Not we," said the friends of the measure; and down they voted the amendment.

While the Nebraska bill was passing through Congress, a law-case, involving the question of a negro's freedom, by reason of his owner having voluntarily taken him first into a free State, and then into a territory covered by the Congressional prohibition, and held him as a slave for a long time in each, was passing through the United States Circuit Court for the District of Missouri; and both Nebraska bill and lawsuit were brought to a decision in the same month of May, 1854. The negro's name was Dred Scott, which name now designates the decision finally made in the case. Before the then next Presidential election, the law-case came to, and was argued in, the Supreme Court of the United States; but the decision of it was deferred until after the election. Still, before the election, Senator Trumbull, on the floor of the Senate, requested the leading advocate of the Nebraska bill to state his opinion whether the people of a territory can constitutionally exclude slavery from their limits; and the latter answers: "That is a question for the Supreme Court."

The election came, Mr. Buchanan was elected, and the indorsement, such as it was, secured. That was the second point gained. The indorsement, however, fell short of a clear popular majority by nearly four hundred thousand votes, and so, perhaps, was not overwhelmingly reliable and satisfactory. The outgoing President, in his last annual message, as impressively as possible, echoed back upon the people the weight and authority of the indorsement. The Supreme Court met again, did not announce their decision, but ordered a reargument. The presidential inauguration came, and still no decision of the court; but the incoming President, in his inaugural address, fervently exhorted the people to abide by the forthcoming decision, whatever it might be. Then, in a few days, came the decision. The reputed author of the Nebraska bill finds an early occasion to make a speech at this capital, indorsing the Dred Scott decision, and vehemently denouncing all opposition to it. The new President, too, seizes the early occasion of the Silliman letter to indorse and strongly construe that decision, and to express his astonishment that any different view had ever been entertained.

At length a squabble springs up between the President and the author of the Nebraska bill, on the mere question of fact, whether the Lecompton constitution was, or was not, in any just sense, made by the people of Kansas; and in that quarrel the latter declares that all he wants is a fair vote for the people, and that he cares not whether slavery be voted down or voted up. I do not understand his declaration, that he cares not whether slavery be voted down or voted up, to be intended by him other than as an apt definition of the policy he would impress upon the public mind—the principle for which he declares he has suffered so much, and is ready to suffer to the end. And well may he cling to that principle. If he has any parental feeling, well may he cling to it. That principle is the only shred left of his original Nebraska doctrine. Under the Dred Scott decision squatter sovereignty squattered out of existence—tumbled down like temporary scaffolding —like the mould at the foundry, served through one blast, and fell back into loose sand—helped to carry an election, and then was kicked to the winds. His late joint struggle with the Republicans against the Lecompton constitution involves nothing of the original Nebraska doctrine. That struggle was made on a point—the right of a people to make their own constitution—upon which he and the Republicans have never differed.

The several points of the Dred Scott decision, in connection with Senator Douglas's "care-not" policy, constitute the piece of machinery in its present state of advancement. This was the third point gained. The working points of that machinery are: (1) That no negro slave, imported as such from Africa, and no descendant of such slave, can ever be a citizen of any State, in the sense of that term as used in the constitution of the United States. This point is made in order to deprive the negro, in every possible event, of the benefit of that provision of the United States constitution, which declares that "the citizens of each State shall be entitled to all privileges and immunities of citizens in the several States." (2) That, "subject to the constitution of the United States," neither Congress nor a territorial legislature can exclude slavery from any United States territory. This point is made in order that individual men may fill up the territories with slaves, without danger of losing them as property, and thus to enhance the chances of permanency to the institution through all the future. (3) That whether the holding a negro in actual slavery in a free State makes him free, as against the holder, the United States courts will not decide, but will leave to be decided by the courts of any slave State the negro may be forced into by the master. This point is made, not to be pressed immediately; but, if acquiesced in for a while, and apparently indorsed by the people at an election, then to sustain the logical conclusion that what Dred Scott's master might lawfully do with Dred Scott, in the State of Illinois, every other master may lawfully do with any other one or one thousand slaves, in Illinois, or in any other free State.

Auxiliary to all this, and working hand in hand with it, the Nebraska doctrine, or what is left of it, is to educate and mould public opinion, at least Northern public opinion, not to care whether slavery is voted down or voted up. This shows exactly where we now are, and partially, also, whither we are tending.

It will throw additional light on the latter to go back, and run the mind over the string of historical facts already stated. Several things will now appear less dark and mysterious than they did when they were transpiring. The people were to be left "perfectly free," "subject only to the constitution." What the constitution had to do with it, outsiders could not then see. Plainly enough now, it was an exactly fitted niche for the Dred Scott decision to come in afterward, and declare the perfect freedom of the people to be just no freedom at all. Why was the amendment expressly declaring the right of the people voted down? Plainly enough now, the adoption of it would have spoiled the niche for the Dred Scott decision. Why was the court decision held up? Why even a senator's individual opinion withheld till after the presidential election? Plainly enough now: the speaking out then would have damaged the "perfectly free" argument upon which the election was to be carried. Why the outgoing President's felicitation on the indorsement? Why the delay of a reargument? Why the incoming President's advance exhortation in favor of the decision? These things look like the cautious patting and petting of a spirited horse preparatory to mounting him, when it is dreaded that he may give the rider a fall. And why the hasty after-indorsement of the decision by the President and others?

We cannot absolutely know that all these exact adaptations are the result of preconcert. But when we see a lot of framed timbers, different portions of which we know have been gotten out at different times and places, and by different workmen—Stephen, Franklin, Roger, and James, for instance—and when we see these timbers joined together, and see that they exactly make the frame of a house or a mill, all the tenons and mortices exactly fitting, and all the lengths and proportions of the different pieces exactly adapted to their respective places, and not a piece too many or too few—not omitting even scaffolding—or, if a single piece be lacking, we see the place in the frame exactly fitted and prepared yet to bring such piece in—in such a case, we find it impossible not to believe that Stephen, Franklin and Roger and James all understood one another from the beginning, and all worked upon a common plan or draft drawn up before the first blow was struck.

It should not be overlooked that, by the Nebraska bill, the people of a State, as well as territory, were to be left "perfectly free," "subject only to the constitution." Why mention a State? They were legislating for territories, and not for or about States. Certainly, the people of a State are and ought to be subject to the constitution of the United States; but why is mention of this lugged into this merely territorial law? Why are the people of a territory and the people of a State therein lumped together, and their relation to the constitution therein treated as being precisely the same? While the opinion of the court, by Chief Justice Taney, in the Dred Scott case, and the separate opinions of all the concurring judges, expressly declare that the constitution of the United States permits neither Congress nor a territorial legislature to exclude slavery from any United States territory, they all omit to declare whether or not the same Constitution permits a State, or the people of a State, to exclude it. Possibly, this is a mere omission; but who can be quite sure, if McLean or Curtis had sought to get into the opinion a declaration of unlimited power in the people of a State to exclude slavery from their limits, just as Chase and Mace sought to get such declaration, in behalf of the people of a territory, into the Nebraska bill—I ask, who can be quite sure that it would not have been voted down in the one case as it had been in the other? The nearest approach to the point of declaring the power of a State over slavery is made by Judge Nelson. He approaches it more than once, using the precise idea, and almost the language, too, of the Nebraska act. On one occasion, his exact language is: "Except in cases when the power is restrained by the constitution of the United States, the law of the State is supreme over the subjects of slavery within its jurisdiction." In what cases the power of the States is so restrained by the United States Constitution is left an open question, precisely as the same question, as to the restraint on the power of the territories, was left open in the Nebraska act. Put this and that together, and we have another nice little niche, which we may, ere long, see filled with another Supreme Court decision, declaring that the constitution of the United States does not permit a State to exclude slavery from its limits. And this may especially be expected if the doctrine of "care not whether slavery be voted down or voted up," shall gain upon the public mind sufficiently to give promise that such a decision can be maintained when made.

Such a decision is all that slavery now lacks of being alike lawful in all the States. Welcome or unwelcome, such decision is probably coming, and will soon be upon us, unless the power of the present political dynasty shall be met and overthrown. We shall lie down pleasantly dreaming that the people of Missouri are on the verge of making their State free, and we shall awake to the reality, instead, that the Supreme Court has made Illinois a slave State. To meet and overthrow that dynasty is the work before all those who would prevent that consummation. That is what we have to do. How can we best do it?

There are those who denounce us openly to their own friends, and yet whisper us softly that Senator Douglas is the aptest instrument there is with which to effect that object. They wish us to infer all, from the fact that he now has a little quarrel with the present head of the dynasty; and that he has regularly voted with us on a single point, upon which he and we have never differed. They remind us that he is a great man, and that the largest of us are very small ones. Let this be granted. "But a living dog is better than a dead lion." Judge Douglas, if not a dead lion, for this work, is at least a caged and toothless one. How can he oppose the advances of slavery? He doesn't care anything about it. His avowed mission is impressing the "public heart" to care nothing about it. A leading Douglas Democratic newspaper thinks Douglas's superior talent will be needed to resist the revival of the African slave-trade. Does Douglas believe an effort to revive that trade is approaching? He has not said so. Does he really think so? But if it is, how can he resist it? For years he has labored to prove it a sacred right of white men to take negro slaves into the new territories. Can he possibly show that it is less a sacred right to buy them where they can be bought cheapest? And unquestionably they can be bought cheaper in Africa than in Virginia. He has done all in his power to reduce the whole question of slavery to one of a mere right of property; and as such, how can he oppose the foreign slave-trade? How can he refuse that trade in that "property" shall be "perfectly free," unless he does it as a protection to the home production? And as the home producers will probably ask the protection, he will be wholly without a ground of opposition. Senator Douglas holds, we know, that a man may rightfully be wiser to-day than he was yesterday—that he may rightfully change when he finds himself wrong. But can we, for that reason, run ahead, and infer that he will make any particular change, of which he himself has given no intimation? Can we safely base our action upon any such vague inference? Now, as ever, I wish not to misrepresent Judge Douglas's position, question his motives, or do aught that can be personally offensive to him. Whenever, if ever, he and we can come together on principle, so that our cause may have assistance from his great ability, I hope to have interposed no adventitious obstacle. But, clearly, he is not now with us—he does not pretend to be, he does not promise ever to be.

Our cause, then, must be intrusted to, and conducted by its own undoubted friends—those whose hands are free, whose hearts are in the work—who do care for the result. Two years ago the Republicans of the nation mustered over thirteen hundred thousand strong. We did this under the single impulse of resistance to a common danger. With every external circumstance against us, of strange, discordant, and even hostile elements, we gathered from the four winds, and formed and fought the battle through, under the constant hot fire of a disciplined, proud, and pampered enemy. Did we brave all then, to falter now?—now, when that same enemy is wavering, dissevered, and belligerent! The result is not doubtful. We shall not fail—if we stand firm, we shall not fail. Wise counsels may accelerate, or mistakes delay it; but, sooner or later, the victory is sure to come.

FAREWELL ADDRESS AT SPRINGFIELD

My friends:—No one not in my position can appreciate the sadness I feel at this parting. To this people I owe all that I am. Here I have lived more than a quarter of a century; here my children were born, and here one of them lies buried. I know not how soon I shall see you again. A duty devolves upon me which is, perhaps, greater than that which has devolved upon any other man since the days of Washington. He never could have succeeded except for the aid of Divine Providence, upon which he at all times relied. I feel that I cannot succeed without the same Divine Aid which sustained him; and in the same Almighty Being I place my reliance for support; and I hope you, my friends, will all pray that I may receive that Divine Assistance, without which I cannot succeed, but with which success is certain. Again I bid you all an affectionate farewell.

ADDRESS AT GETTYSBURG

Fourscore and seven years ago our fathers brought forth on this continent a new nation, conceived in liberty and dedicated to the proposition that all men are created equal. Now we are engaged in a great civil war, testing whether that nation, or any nation so conceived and so dedicated, can long endure. We are met on a great battlefield of that war. We have come to dedicate a portion of that field as a final resting place for those who here gave their lives that that nation might live. It is altogether fitting and proper that we should do this. But, in a larger sense, we cannot dedicate—we cannot consecrate—we cannot hallow—this ground. The brave men, living and dead, who struggled here have consecrated it far above our poor power to add or to detract. The world will little note nor long remember what we say here, but it can never forget what they did here. It is for us, the living, rather to be dedicated here to the unfinished work which they who fought here have thus far so nobly advanced. It is rather for us to be here dedicated to the great task remaining before us—that from these honored dead we take increased devotion to that cause for which they gave the last full measure of devotion; that we here highly resolve that these dead shall not have died in vain; that this nation, under God, shall have a new birth of freedom; and that government of the people, by the people, for the people, shall not perish from the earth.

SECOND INAUGURAL ADDRESS

Fellow-countrymen: At this second appearing to take the oath of the presidential office, there is less occasion for an extended address than there was at first. Then a statement, somewhat in detail, of a course to be pursued seemed very fitting and proper. Now, at the expiration of four years, during which public declarations have been constantly called forth on every point and phase of the great contest which still absorbs the attention and engrosses the energies of the nation, little that is new could be presented.

The progress of our arms, upon which all else chiefly depends, is as well known to the public as to myself, and it is, I trust, reasonably satisfactory and encouraging to all. With high hope for the future, no prediction in regard to it is ventured.

On the occasion corresponding to this four years ago, all thoughts were anxiously directed to an impending civil war. All dreaded it, all sought to avoid it. While the inaugural address was being delivered from this place, devoted altogether to saving the Union without war, insurgent agents were in the city seeking to destroy it with war—seeking to dissolve the Union and divide the effects by negotiation. Both parties deprecated war, but one of them would make war rather than let the nation survive, and the other would accept war rather than let it perish, and the war came. One-eighth of the whole population were colored slaves, not distributed generally over the Union, but localized in the Southern part of it. These slaves constituted a peculiar and powerful interest. All knew that this interest was somehow the cause of the war. To strengthen, perpetuate, and extend this interest was the object for which the insurgents would rend the Union by war, while the government claimed no right to do more than to restrict the territorial enlargement of it.

Neither party expected for the war the magnitude or the duration which it has already attained. Neither anticipated that the cause of the conflict might cease when, or even before the conflict itself should cease. Each looked for an easier triumph, and a result less fundamental and astounding. Both read the same Bible and pray to the same God, and each invokes His aid against the other. It may seem strange that any men should dare to ask a just God's assistance in wringing their bread from the sweat of other men's faces, but let us judge not that we be not judged. The prayer of both could not be answered. That of neither has been answered fully. The Almighty has His own purposes. Woe unto the world because of offences, for it must needs be that offences come, but woe to that man by whom the offence cometh. If we shall suppose that American slavery is one of those offences which, in the providence of God, must needs come, but which having continued through His appointed time, He now wills to remove, and that He gives to both North and South this terrible war as the woe due to those by whom the offence came, shall we discern there any departure from those divine attributes which the believers in a living God always ascribe to Him? Fondly do we hope, fervently do we pray, that this mighty scourge of war may speedily pass away. Yet if God wills that it continue until all the wealth piled by the bondsman's two hundred and fifty years of unrequited toil shall be sunk, and until every drop of blood drawn with the lash shall be paid by another drawn with the sword, as was said three thousand years ago, so still it must be said, that the judgments of the Lord are true and righteous altogether.

With malice toward none, with charity for all, with firmness in the right as God gives us to see the right, let us finish the work we are in, to bind up the nation's wounds, to care for him who shall have borne the battle, and for his widow and his orphans, to do all which may achieve and cherish a just and a lasting peace among ourselves and with all nations.

Henry Ward Beecher
[1813–1887]

Henry Ward Beecher, famous pastor of Plymouth Church, Brooklyn, N.Y., was one of the great orators of his day, being especially gifted as a fluent extemporaneous speaker. Here are parts of a speech he delivered at Liverpool, England, on October 16, 1863.

THE SYSTEM OF SLAVERY

For MORE than twenty-five years I have been made perfectly familiar with popular assemblies in all parts of my country, except the extreme South. There has not, for the whole of that time, been a single day of my life when it would have been safe for me to go south of Mason and Dixon's line in my own country, and all for one reason: my solemn, earnest, persistent testimony against that which I consider to be the most atrocious thing under the sun—the system of American slavery in a great, free republic. (Cheers.) I have passed through that early period when right of free speech was denied to me. Again and again I have attempted to address audiences that, for no other crime than that of free speech, visited me with all manner of contumelious epithets; and now since I have been in England, although I have met with greater kindness and courtesy on the part of most than I deserved, yet, on the other hand, I perceive that the Southern influence prevails to some extent in England. (Applause and uproar.) It is my old acquaintance; I understand it perfectly (laughter) and I have always held it to be an unfailing truth that where a man had a cause that would bear· examination he was perfectly willing to have it spoken about. (Applause.) And when in Manchester I saw those huge placards: "Who is Henry Ward Beecher?" (Laughter, cries of "quite right," and applause.) And when in Liverpool I was told that there were those blood-red placards, purporting to say what Henry Ward Beecher had said, and calling upon Englishmen to suppress free speech—I tell you what I thought. I thought simply this: "I am glad of it." (Laughter.) Why? Because if they had felt perfectly secure, that *you* are the minions of the South and the slaves of slavery, they would have been perfectly still. (Applause and uproar.) And, therefore, when I saw so much nervous apprehension that, if I were permitted to speak —(hisses and applause)—when I found they were afraid to have me speak—(hisses, laughter and "No, no!")—when I found that they considered my speaking damaging to their cause—(applause)—when I found that they appealed from facts and reasonings to mob law (applause and uproar), I said, no man need tell me what the heart and secret counsel of these men are. They tremble and are afraid. (Applause, laughter, hisses, "No, no!" and a voice: "New York mob.") Now, personally, it is a matter of very little consequence to me whether I speak here to-night or not. (Laughter and cheers.) But, one thing is very certain, if you do permit me to speak here to-night you will hear very plain talking. (Applause and hisses.) You will not find a man—(interruption)—you will not find me to be a man that dared to speak about Great Britain three thousand miles off, and then is afraid to speak to Great Britain when he stands on her shores. (Immense applause and hisses.) And if I do not mistake the tone and temper of Englishmen, they had rather have a man who opposes them in a manly way (applause from all parts of the hall) than a sneak that agrees with them in an unmanly way. (Applause and "Bravo!") Now, if I can carry you with me by sound convictions, I shall be immensely glad (applause); but if I cannot carry you with me by facts and sound arguments, I do not wish you to go with me at all; and all that I ask is simply fair play. (Applause, and a voice: "You shall have it too.")

It is said that the North is fighting for Union, and not for emancipation. The North is fighting for Union, for that insures emancipation. (Loud cheers, "Oh, oh!" "No, no!" and cheers.) A great many men say to ministers of the Gospel: "You pretend to be preaching and working for the love of the people. Why, you are all the time preaching for the sake of the Church." What does the minister say? "It is by means of the Church that we help the people," and when men say that we are fighting for the Union, I too say we are fighting for the Union. ("Hear, hear!" and a voice: "That's right.") But the motive determines the value; and why are we fighting for the Union? Because we never shall forget the testimony of our enemies. They have gone off declaring that the Union in the hands of the North was fatal to slavery. (Loud applause.) There is testimony in court for you. (A voice: "See that," and laughter.)

In the first place I am ashamed to confess that such was the thoughtlessness—(interruption)—such was the stupor of the North—(renewed interruption)—you will get a word at a time; to-morrow will let folks see what it is you don't want to hear—that for a period of twenty-five years she went to sleep, and permitted herself to be drugged and poisoned with the Southern prejudice against black men. (Applause and uproar.) The evil was made worse, because, when any object whatever has caused anger between political parties, a political animosity arises against that object, no matter how innocent in itself; no matter what were the original influences which excited the quarrel. Thus the colored man has been the football between the two parties in the North, and has suffered accordingly. I confess it to my shame. But I am speaking now on my own ground, for I began twenty-five years ago, with a small party, to combat the unjust dislike of the colored man. (Loud applause, dissension, and uproar. The interruption at this point became so violent that the friends of Mr. Beecher throughout the hall rose to their feet, waving hats and handkerchiefs, and renewing their shouts of applause. The interruption lasted some minutes.) Well, I have lived to see a total revolution in the Northern feeling—I stand here to bear solemn witness of that. It is not my opinion; it is my knowledge. (Great uproar.) Those men who undertook to stand up for the rights of all men —black as well as white—have increased in number; and now what party in the North represents those men that resist the evil prejudices of past years? The Republicans are that party. (Loud applause.) And who are those men in the North that have oppressed the negro? They are the *Peace Democrats;* and the prejudice for which in England you are attempting to punish me, is a prejudice raised by the men who have opposed me all my life. These pro-slavery Democrats abused the negro. I defended him, and they mobbed me for doing it. Oh, justice! (Loud laughter, applause, and hisses.)

There is another fact that I wish to allude to—not for the sake of reproach or blame, but by way of claiming your more lenient consideration—and that is, that slavery was entailed upon us by your action. ("Hear, hear!") Against the earnest protests of the Colonists the then Government of Great Britain—I will concede not knowing what were the mischiefs—ignorantly, but in point of fact, forced slave traffic on the unwilling Colonists. (Great uproar, in the midst of which one individual was lifted up and carried out of the room amidst cheers and hisses.)

I was going to ask you, suppose each child is born with hereditary disease; suppose this disease was entailed upon him by parents who had contracted it by their own misconduct, would it be fair that those parents that had brought into the world the diseased child, should rail at that child because it was diseased? ("No, no!") Would not the child have a right to turn 'round and say: "Father, it was your fault that I had it, and you ought to be pleased to be patient with my deficiencies." (Applause and hisses, and cries of "Order!" Great interruption and great disturbance here took place on the right of the platform; and the chairman said that if the persons around the unfortunate individual who had caused the disturbance would allow him to speak alone, but not assist him in making the disturbance, it might soon be put an end to. The interruption continued until another person was carried out of the hall. Mr. Beecher continued.) I do not ask that you should justify slavery in us, because it was wrong in you two hundred years ago; but having ignorantly been the means of fixing it upon us, now that we are struggling with mortal struggles to free ourselves from it, we have a right to your tolerance, your patience, and charitable constructions.

No man can unveil the future; no man can tell what revolutions are about to break upon the world; no man can tell what destiny belongs to France, nor to any of the European powers; but one thing is certain, that in the exigencies of the future there will be combinations and recombinations, and that those nations that are of the same faith, the same blood, and the same substantial interests ought not to be alienated from each other, but ought to stand together. (Immense cheering and hisses.) I do not say that you ought not to be in the most friendly alliance with France or with Germany; but I do say that your own children, the offspring of England, ought to be nearer to you than any people of strange tongue. (A voice: "Degenerate sons," applause and hisses; another voice: "What about the Trent?") If there had been any feelings of bitterness in America, let me tell you that they had been excited, rightly or wrongly, under the impression that Great Britain was going to intervene between us and our own lawful struggle. (A voice: "No!" and applause.) With the evidence that there is no such intention, all bitter feelings will pass away. (Applause.) We do not agree with the recent doctrine of neutrality as a question of law. But it is past, and we are not disposed to raise that question. We accept it now as a fact, and we say that the utterance of Lord Russell at Blairgowrie —(Applause, hisses, and a voice: "What about Lord Brougham?")—together with the declaration of the Government in stopping war-steamers here—(great uproar, and applause)—has gone far toward quieting every fear and removing every apprehension from our minds. (Uproar and shouts of applause.) And now in the future it is the work of every good man and patriot not to create divisions, but to do the things that will make for peace. ("Oh, oh," and laughter.) On our part it shall be done. (Applause and hisses, and "No, no.") On your part it ought to be done; and when in any of the convulsions that come upon the world, Great Britain finds herself struggling single-handed against the gigantic powers that spread oppression and darkness—(applause, hisses, and uproar)—there ought to be such cordiality that she can turn and say to her first-born and most illustrious child, "Come!" ("Hear, hear!" applause, tremendous cheers, and uproar.) I will not say that England cannot again, as hitherto, single-handed manage any power—(applause and uproar)—but I will say that England and America together for religion and liberty—(A voice: "Soap, soap," uproar, and great applause) —are a match for the world. (Applause; a voice: "They don't want any more soft soap.") Now, gentlemen and ladies—(A voice: "Sam Slick;" and another voice: "Ladies and gentlemen, if you please,")—when I came I was asked whether I would answer questions, and I very readily consented to do so, as I had in other places; but I will tell you it was because I expected to have the opportunity of speaking with some sort of ease and quiet. (A voice: "So you have.") I have for an hour and a half spoken against a storm—("Hear, hear!")—and you yourselves are witnesses that, by the interruption, I have been obliged to strive with my voice, so that I no longer have the power to control this assembly. (Applause.) And although I am in spirit perfectly willing to answer any question, and more than glad of the chance, yet I am by this very unnecessary opposition to-night incapacitated physically from doing it. Ladies and gentlemen, I bid you good evening.

Susan B. Anthony
[1820–1906]

Susan B. Anthony, of New York, noted advocate of temperance, anti-slavery and woman suffrage, was arrested in 1872 for casting a vote in the Presidential election. She was fined $100, refused to pay the fine, and never did pay it. The following speech was delivered in 1873.

ON WOMAN'S RIGHT TO SUFFRAGE

FRIENDS AND FELLOW CITIZENS:—I stand before you to-night under indictment for the alleged crime of having voted at the last presidential election, without having a lawful right to vote. It shall be my work this evening to prove to you that in thus voting, I not only committed no crime, but, instead, simply exercised my *citizen's rights,* guaranteed to me and all United States citizens by the National Constitution, beyond the power of any State to deny.

The preamble of the Federal Constitution says:

"We, the people of the United States, in order to form a more perfect union, establish justice, insure *domestic* tranquillity, provide for the common defense, promote the general welfare, and secure the blessings of liberty to ourselves and our posterity, do ordain and establish this Constitution for the United States of America."

It was we, the people; not we, the white male citizens; nor yet we, the male citizens; but we, the whole people, who formed the Union. And we formed it, not to give the blessings of liberty, but to secure them; not to the half of ourselves and the half of our posterity, but to the whole people—women as well as men. And it is a downright mockery to talk to women of their enjoyment of the blessings of liberty while they are denied the use of the only means of securing them provided by this democratic-republican government—the ballot.

For any State to make sex a qualification that must ever result in the disfranchisement of one entire half of the people is to pass a bill of attainder, or an *ex post facto* law, and is therefore a violation of the supreme law of the land. By it the blessings of liberty are for ever withheld from women and their female posterity. To them this government has no just powers derived from the consent of the governed. To them this government is not a democracy. It is not a republic. It is an odious aristocracy; a hateful oligarchy of sex; the most hateful aristocracy ever established on the face of the globe; an oligarchy of wealth, where the rich govern the poor. An oligarchy of learning, where the educated govern the ignorant, or even an oligarchy of race, where the Saxon rules the African, might be endured; but this oligarchy of sex, which makes father, brothers, husband, sons, the oligarchs over the mother and sisters, the wife and daughters of every household—which ordains all men sovereigns, all women subjects, carries dissension, discord and rebellion into every home of the nation.

Webster, Worcester and Bouvier all define a citizen to be a person in the United States, entitled to vote and hold office.

The only question left to be settled now is: Are women persons? And I hardly believe any of our opponents will have the hardihood to say they are not. Being persons, then, women are citizens; and no State has a right to make any law, or to enforce any old law, that shall abridge their privileges or immunities. Hence, every discrimination against women in the constitutions and laws of the several States is to-day null and void, precisely as in every one against negroes.

Robert Green Ingersoll
[1833-1899]

Recognized as a great orator of unusual power, Robert Green Ingersoll devoted his talents to the legal profession and to lecturing against orthodox religion. His eloquent speech nominating James G. Blaine for president at the Republican National Convention, in Cincinnati, on June 15, 1876, made Ingersoll nationally famous. The oration at the grave of his. brother, Ebon C. Ingersoll, was delivered at Washington, D.C., on June 3, 1879.

BLAINE—THE PLUMED KNIGHT

Massachusetts may be satisfied with the loyalty of Benjamin H. Bristow; so am I; but if any man nominated by this convention cannot carry the state of Massachusetts, I am not satisfied with the loyalty of that state. If the nominee of this convention cannot carry the grand old Commonwealth of Massachusetts by seventy-five thousand majority, I would advise them to sell out Faneuil Hall as a Democratic headquarters. I would advise them to take from Bunker Hill that old monument of glory.

The Republicans of the United States demand as their leader in the great contest of 1876 a man of intelligence, a man of integrity, a man of well-known and approved political opinions. They demand a statesman; they demand a reformer after, as well as before, the election. They demand a politician in the highest, the broadest, and best sense —a man of superb moral courage. They demand a man acquainted with public affairs—with the wants of the people—with not only the requirements of the hour, but with the demands of the future. They demand a man broad enough to comprehend the relations of this government to the other nations of the earth. They demand a man well versed in the powers, duties, and prerogatives of each and every department of this government. They demand a man who will sacredly preserve the financial honor of the United States—one who knows enough to know that the national debt must be paid through the prosperity of this people; one who knows enough to know that all the financial theories in the world cannot redeem a single dollar; one who knows enough to know that all the money must be made, not by law, but by labor; one who knows enough to know that the people of the United States have the industry to make the money and the honor to pay it over just as fast as they make it.

The Republicans of the United States demand a man who knows that prosperity and resumption, when they come, must come together; that when they come they will come hand in hand through the golden harvest fields; hand in hand by the whirling spindles and turning wheels; hand in hand past the open furnace doors; hand in hand by the flaming forges; hand in hand by the chimneys filled with eager fire—greeted and grasped by the countless sons of toil.

This money has to be dug out of the earth. You cannot make it by passing resolutions in a political convention.

The Republicans of the United States want a man who knows that this government should protect every citizen at home and abroad; who knows that any government that will not defend its defenders and protect its protectors is a disgrace to the map of the world. They demand a man who believes in the eternal separation and divorcement of church and school. They demand a man whose political reputation is spotless as a star; but they do not demand that their candidate shall have a certificate of moral character signed by a Confederate Congress. The man who has in full, heaped and rounded measure, all these splendid qualifications is the present grand and gallant leader of the Republican party—James G. Blaine.

Our country, crowned with the vast and marvelous achievements of its first century, asks for a man worthy of the past and prophetic of her future; asks for a man who has the audacity of genius; asks for a man who is the grandest combination of heart, conscience, and brain beneath her flag. Such a man is James G. Blaine.

For the Republican host, led by this intrepid man, there can be no defeat.

This is a grand year; a year filled with the recollections of the Revolution, filled with proud and tender memories of the past, with the sacred legends of liberty; a year in which the sons of freedom will drink from the fountains of enthusiasm; a year in which the people call for a man who has preserved in Congress what our soldiers won upon the field; a year in which we call for the man who has torn from the throat of treason the tongue of slander—for the man who has snatched the mask of Democracy from the hideous face of Rebellion—for the man who, like an intellectual athlete, has stood in the arena of debate and challenged all comers, and who, up to the present moment, is a total stranger to defeat.

Like an armed warrior, like a plumed knight, James G. Blaine marched down the halls of the American Congress and threw his shining lance full and fair against the brazen foreheads of the defamers of his country and the maligners of his honor. For the Republicans to desert this gallant leader now is as though an army should desert their general upon the field of battle.

James G. Blaine is now, and has been for years, the bearer of the sacred standard of the Republican party. I call it sacred, because no human being can stand beneath its folds without becoming and without remaining free.

Gentlemen of the convention, in the name of the great Republic, the only republic that ever existed upon this earth; in the name of all her defenders and of all her supporters; in the name of all her soldiers living; in the name of all her soldiers dead upon the field of battle; and in the name of those who perished in the skeleton clutch of famine at Andersonville and Libby, whose sufferings he so vividly remembers, Illinois— Illinois nominates for the next President of this country that prince of parliamentarians, that leader of leaders, James G. Blaine.

ORATION AT HIS BROTHER'S GRAVE

My friends:—I am going to do that which the dead oft promised he would do for me.

The loved and loving brother, husband, father, friend died where manhood's morning almost touches noon, and while the shadows still were falling toward the west.

He had not passed on life's highway the stone that marks the highest point, but, being weary for a moment, he lay down by the wayside, and, using his burden for a pillow, fell into that dreamless sleep that kisses down his eyelids still. While yet in love with life and raptured with the world he passed to silence and pathetic dust.

Yet, after all, it may be best, just in the happiest, sunniest hour of all the voyage, while eager winds are kissing every sail, to dash against the unseen rock, and in an instant hear the billows roar above a sunken ship. For, whether in midsea or 'mong the breakers of the farther shore, a wreck at last must mark the end of each and all. And every life, no matter if its hour is rich with love and every moment jeweled with joy, will, at its close, become a tragedy as sad and deep and dark as can be woven of the warp and woof of mystery and death.

This brave and tender man in every storm of life was oak and rock, but in the sunshine he was vine and flower. He was the friend of all heroic souls. He climbed the heights and left all superstitions far below, while on his forehead fell the golden dawning of the grander day.

He loved the beautiful, and was with color, form, and music touched to tears. He sided with the weak, and with a willing hand gave alms;

with loyal heart and with purest hands he faithfully discharged all public trusts.

He was a worshiper of liberty, a friend of the oppressed. A thousand times I have heard him quote these words: "For justice all places, a temple, and all seasons, summer." He believed that happiness was the only good, reason the only torch, justice the only worship, humanity the only religion, and love the only priest. He added to the sum of human joy; and were every one to whom he did some loving service to bring a blossom to his grave, he would sleep to-night beneath a wilderness of flowers.

Life is a narrow vale between the cold and barren peaks of two eternities. We strive in vain to look beyond the heights. We cry aloud, and the only answer is the echo of our wailing cry. From the voiceless lips of the unreplying dead there comes no word; but in the night of death hope sees a star, and listening love can hear the rustle of a wing.

He who sleeps here, when dying, mistaking the approach of death for the return of health, whispered with his latest breath: "I am better now." Let us believe, in spite of doubts and dogmas, and tears and fears, that these dear words are true of all the countless dead.

And now to you who have been chosen, from among the many men he loved, to do the last sad office for the dead, we give this sacred dust. Speech cannot contain our love. There was, there is, no greater, stronger, manlier man.

James Gillespie Blaine
[1830–1893]

Following is the closing part of an address on the death of President Garfield, victim of an assassin, delivered by James G. Blaine, in the House of Representatives on February 27, 1882.

ON THE DEATH OF GARFIELD

For the second time in this generation the great departments of the government of the United States are assembled in the Hall of Representatives, to do honor to the memory of a murdered president. Lincoln fell at the close of a mighty struggle, in which the passions of men had been deeply stirred. The tragical termination of his great life added but another to the lengthened succession of horrors which had marked so many lintels with the blood of the firstborn. Garfield was slain in a day of peace, when brother had been reconciled to brother, and when anger and hate had been banished from the land.

Great in life, he was surpassingly great in death. For no cause, in the very frenzy of wantonness and wickedness, by the red hand of murder, he was thrust from the full tide of this world's interest, from its hopes, its aspirations, its victories, into the visible presence of death—and he did not quail. Not alone for one short moment in which, stunned and dazed, he could give up life, hardly aware of its relinquishment, but through days of deadly languor, through weeks of agony, that was not less agony because silently borne, with clear sight and calm courage he looked into his open grave. What blight and ruin met his anguished eyes, whose lips may tell—what brilliant, broken plans, what baffled, high ambitions, what sundering of strong, warm, manhood's friendship, what bitter rending of sweet household ties! Behind him a proud, expectant nation, a great host of sustaining friends, a cherished and happy mother, wearing the full, rich honors of her early toil and tears; the wife of his youth, whose whole life lay in his; the little boys not yet emerged from childhood's day of frolic; the fair young daughter; the sturdy sons just springing into closest companionship, claiming every day and every day rewarding a father's love and care; and in his heart the eager, rejoicing power to meet all demands. And his soul was not shaken. His countrymen were thrilled with instant, profound, and universal sympathy. Masterful in his mortal weakness, he became the center of a nation's love, enshrined in the prayers of a world. But all the love and all the sympathy could not share with him his suffering. He trod the wine-press alone. With unfaltering front he faced death. With unfailing tenderness he took leave of life. Above the demoniac hiss of the assassin's bullet he heard the voice of God. With simple resignation he bowed to the Divine decree.

As the end drew near his early craving for the sea returned. The stately mansion of power had been to him the wearisome hospital of pain, and he begged to be taken from his prison walls, from its oppressive, stifling air, from its homelessness and its hopelessness. Gently, silently, the love of a great people bore the pale sufferer to the longed-for healing of the sea, to live or to die, as God should will, within sight of the heaving billows, within sound of its manifold voices. With a wan, fevered face, tenderly lifted to the cooling breeze, he looked out wistfully upon the ocean's changing wonders; on its far sails; on its restless waves, rolling shoreward to break and die beneath the noonday sun; on the red clouds of evening, arching low to the horizon; on the serene and shining pathway of the star. Let us think that his dying eyes read a mystic meaning which only the rapt and parting soul may know. Let us believe that in the silence of the receding world he heard the great waves breaking on a further shore and felt already upon his wasted brow the breath of the eternal morning.

Grover Cleveland
[1837–1908]

Grover Cleveland, of New York, was elected President of the United States in 1884, was defeated by Benjamin Harrison in 1888, and was elected for a second time in 1892. Cleveland is noted for his firm adherence to conservative policies and honest administration, including his many vetoes of wasteful bills passed by Congress. He was also a strong advocate of "sound money." Here is his first inaugural address, delivered on March 4, 1885.

FIRST INAUGURAL ADDRESS

FELLOW-CITIZENS: In the presence of this vast assemblage of my countrymen I am about to supplement and seal by the oath which I shall take the manifestation of the will of a great and free people. In the exercise of their power and right of self-government they have committed to one of their fellow-citizens a supreme and sacred trust, and he here consecrates himself to their service.

This impressive ceremony adds little to the solemn sense of responsibility with which I contemplate the duty I owe to all the people of the land. Nothing can relieve me from anxiety lest by any act of mine their interests may suffer, and nothing is needed to strengthen my resolution to engage every faculty and effort in the promotion of their welfare.

Amid the din of party strife the people's choice was made, but its attendant circumstances have demonstrated anew the strength and safety of a government by the people. In each succeeding year it more clearly appears that our democratic principle needs no apology, and that in its fearless and faithful application is to be found the surest guaranty of good government.

But the best results in the operation of a government wherein every citizen has a share largely depend upon a proper limitation of purely partisan zeal and effort and a correct appreciation of the time when the heat of the partisan should be merged in the patriotism of the citizen.

To-day the executive branch of the government is transferred to new keeping. But this is still the government of all the people, and it should be none the less an object of their affectionate solicitude. At this hour the animosities of political strife, the bitterness of partisan defeat, and the exultation of partisan triumph should be supplanted by an ungrudging acquiescence in the popular will and a sober, conscientious concern for the general weal. Moreover, if from this hour we cheerfully and honestly abandon all sectional prejudice and distrust, and determine, with manly confidence in one another, to work out harmoniously the achievement of our national destiny, we shall deserve to realize all the benefits which our happy form of government can bestow.

On this auspicious occasion we may well renew the pledge of our devotion to the constitution, which, launched by the founders of the republic and consecrated by their prayers and patriotic devotion, has for almost a century borne the hopes and the aspirations of a great people through prosperity and peace and through the shock of foreign conflicts and the perils of domestic strife and vicissitudes.

By the father of his country our constitution was commended for adoption as "the result of a spirit of amity and mutual concession." In that same spirit it should be administered, in order to promote the lasting welfare of the country and to secure the full measure of its priceless benefits to us and to those who will succeed to the blessings of our national life. The large variety of diverse and competing interests subject to federal control persistently seeking the recognition of their claims, need give us no fear that "the greatest good to the greatest number" will fail to be accomplished if in the halls of national legislation that spirit of amity and mutual concession shall prevail in which the constitution had its birth. If this involves the surrender or postponement of private interests and the abandonment of local advantages, compensation will be found in the assurance that the common interest is subserved and the general welfare advanced.

In the discharge of my official duty I shall endeavor to be guided by a just and unstrained construction of the constitution, a careful observance of the distinction between the powers granted to the federal government and those reserved to the States or to the people, and by a cautious appreciation of those functions which by the constitution and laws have been assigned to the executive branch of the government.

But he who takes the oath to-day to preserve, protect, and defend the constitution of the United States only assumes the solemn obligation which every patriotic citizen—on the farm, in the workshop, in the busy marts of trade, and everywhere—should share with him. The constitution which prescribes his oath, my countrymen, is yours; the government you have chosen him to administer for a time is yours; the suffrage which executes the will of freemen is yours; the laws and the entire scheme of our civil rule, from the town meeting to the State capitals and the national capital, is yours. Your every voter, as surely as your chief magistrate, under the same high sanction, though in a different sphere, exercises a public trust. Nor is this all. Every citizen owes to the country a vigilant watch and close scrutiny of its public servants and a fair and reasonable estimate of their fidelity and usefulness. Thus is the people's will impressed upon the whole framework of our civil polity—municipal, State, and federal; and this is the price of our liberty and the inspiration of our faith in the republic.

It is the duty of those serving the people in public place to closely limit public expenditures to the actual needs of the government economically administered, because this bounds the right of the government to exact tribute from the earnings of labor or the property of the citizen, and because public extravagance begets extravagance among the people. We should never be ashamed of the simplicity and prudential economies which are best suited to the operation of a republican form of government and most compatible with the mission of the American people. Those who are selected for a limited time to manage public affairs are still of the people, and may do much by their example to encourage, consistently with the dignity of their official functions, that plain way of life which among their fellow-citizens aids integrity and promotes thrift and prosperity.

The genius of our institutions, the needs of our people in their home life, and the attention which is demanded for the settlement and development of the resources of our vast territory, dictate the scrupulous avoidance of any departure from that foreign policy commended by the history, the traditions, and the prosperity of our republic. It is the policy of independence, favored by our position and defended by our known love of justice and by our own power. It is the policy of peace suitable to our interests. It is the policy of neutrality, rejecting any share in foreign broils and ambitions upon other continents and repelling their intrusion here. It is the policy of Monroe, and of Washington, and of Jefferson—"Peace, commerce, and honest friendship with all nations; entangling alliance with none."

A due regard for the interests and prosperity of all the people demands that our finances shall be established upon such a sound and sensible basis as shall secure the safety and confidence of business interests and make the wages of labor sure and steady, and that our system of revenue shall be so adjusted as to relieve the people of unnecessary taxation, having a due regard to the interests of capital invested and workingmen employed in American industries, and preventing the accumulation of a surplus in the treasury to tempt extravagance and waste.

Care for the property of the nation and for the needs of future settlers requires that the public domain should be protected from purloining schemes and unlawful occupation.

The conscience of the people demands that the Indians within our boundaries shall be fairly and honestly treated as wards of the government and their education and civilization promoted with a view to their ultimate citizenship, and that polygamy in the Territories, destructive of the family relation and offensive to the moral sense of the civilized world, shall be repressed.

The laws should be rigidly enforced which prohibit the immigration of a servile class to compete with American labor, with no intention of acquiring citizenship, and bringing with them and retaining habits and customs repugnant to our civilization.

The people demand reform in the administration of the government and the application of business principles to public affairs. As a means to this end, civil service reform should be in good faith enforced. Our citizens have the right to protection from the incompetency of public employés who hold their places solely as the reward of partisan service, and from the corrupting influence of those who promise and the vicious methods of those who expect such rewards; and those who worthily seek public employment have the right to insist that merit and competency shall be recognized instead of party subserviency or the surrender of honest political belief.

In the administration of a government pledged to do equal and exact justice to all men, there should be no pretext for anxiety touching the protection of the freedmen in their rights or their security in the enjoyment of their privileges under the constitution and its amendments. All discussion as to their fitness for the place accorded to them as American citizens is idle and unprofitable except as it suggests the necessity for their improvement. The fact that they are citizens entitles them to all the rights due to that relation and charges them with all its duties, obligations and responsibilities.

These topics and the constant and ever-varying wants of an active and enterprising population may well receive the attention and the patriotic endeavor of all who make and execute the federal law. Our duties are practical and call for industrious application, an intelligent perception of the claims of public office, and above all, a firm determination, by united action, to secure to all the people of the land the full benefits of the best form of government ever vouchsafed to man. And let us not trust to human effort alone, but humbly acknowledging the power and goodness of Almighty God, who presides over the destiny of nations and who has at all times been revealed in our country's history, let us invoke his aid and his blessing upon our labors.

Chauncey Mitchell Depew

[1834–1928]

The name of Chauncey Mitchell Depew ranks high in any list of American orators. He was successful in law, politics and business. For many years he was president of the New York Central Railroad. Depew delivered an oration at the opening of the World's Fair in Chicago, in 1892. Parts of this address follow.

THE COLUMBIAN ORATION

THIS DAY belongs not to America, but to the world. The results of the event it commemorates are the heritage of the peoples of every race and clime. We celebrate the emancipation of man. The preparation was the work of almost countless centuries; the realization was the revelation of one. The Cross on Calvary was hope; the cross raised on San Salvador was opportunity. But for the first, Columbus would never have sailed; but for the second, there would have been no place for the planting, the nurture, and the expansion of civil and religious liberty.

The spirit of Columbus hovers over us to-day. Only by celestial intelligence can it grasp the full significance of this spectacle and ceremonial.

From the first century to the fifteenth counts for little in the history of progress, but in the period between the fifteenth and the twentieth is crowded the romance and reality of human development. Life has been prolonged, and its enjoyment intensified. The powers of the air and the water, the resistless forces of the elements, which in the time of the discoverer were the visible terrors of the wrath of God, have been subdued to the service of man. Art and luxuries which could be possessed and enjoyed only by the rich and noble, the works of genius which were read and understood only by the learned few, domestic comforts and surroundings beyond the reach of lord or bishop, now adorn and illumine the homes of our citizens. Serfs are sovereigns and the people are kings. The trophies and splendors of their reign are commonwealths, rich in every attribute of great states, and united in a Republic whose power and prosperity and liberty and enlightenment are the wonder and admiration of the world.

All hail, Columbus, discoverer, dreamer, hero, and apostle! We, here, of every race and country, recognize the horizon which bounded his vision and the infinite scope of his genius. The voice of gratitude and praise for all the blessings which have been showered upon mankind by his adventure is limited to no language, but is uttered in every tongue. Neither marble nor brass can fitly form his statue. Continents are his monument, and unnumbered millions present and to come, who enjoy in their liberties and their happiness the fruits of his faith, will reverently guard and preserve, from century to century, his name and fame.

Booker T. Washington
[1859?–1915]

Booker T. Washington, Negro educator and leader, was born on a plantation in Virginia. He was founder of the Tuskegee Institute in Alabama, an educational organization for Negroes which grew under his administration from a little shanty to more than 40 buildings. The following speech was delivered by Washington before the Harvard Alumni in 1896, after he received an honorary degree of Master of Arts from Harvard University. Another speech is included in the Supplement: Survey of Speeches by Black Americans, at the end of this book.

THE AMERICAN STANDARD

MR. PRESIDENT AND GENTLEMEN:—It would in some measure relieve my embarrassment if I could, even in a slight degree, feel myself worthy of the great honor which you do me to-day. Why you have called me from the Black Belt of the South, from among my humble people, to share in the honors of this occasion, is not for me to explain; and yet it may not be inappropriate for me to suggest that it seems to me that one of the most vital questions that touch our American life, is how to bring the strong, wealthy, and learned into helpful touch with the poorest, most ignorant, and humble, and at the same time make the one appreciate the vitalizing, strengthening influence of the other. How shall we make the mansions on yon Beacon Street feel and see the need of the spirits in the lowliest cabin in Alabama cotton fields or Louisiana sugar bottoms? This problem Harvard University is solving, not by bringing itself down, but by bringing the masses up.

If through me, a humble representative, seven millions of my people in the South might be permitted to send a message to Harvard—Harvard that offered up on death's altar, young Shaw, and Russell, and Lowell and scores of others, that we might have a free and united country—that message would be, "Tell them that the sacrifice was not in vain. Tell them that by the way of the shop, the field, the skilled hand, habits of thrift and economy, by way of industrial school and college, we are coming. We are crawling up, working up, yea, bursting up. Often through oppression, unjust discrimination, and prejudice, but through them we are coming up, and with proper habits, intelligence, and property, there is no power on earth that can permanently stay our progress."

If my life in the past has meant anything in the lifting up of my people and the bringing about of better relations between your race and mine, I assure you from this day it will mean doubly more. In the economy of God, there is but one standard by which an individual can succeed—there is but one for a race. This country demands that every race measure itself by the American standard. By it a race must rise or fall, succeed or fail, and in the last analysis mere sentiment counts for little. During the next half century and more, my race must continue passing through the severe American crucible. We are to be tested in our patience, our forbearance, our perseverance, our power to endure wrong, to withstand temptations, to economize, to acquire and use skill; our ability to compete, to succeed in commerce, to disregard the superficial for the real, the appearance for the substance, to be great and yet small, learned and yet simple, high and yet the servant of all. This, this is the passport to all that is best in the life of our Republic, and the Negro must possess it, or be debarred.

While we are thus being tested, I beg of you to remember that wherever our life touches yours, we help or hinder. Wherever your life touches ours, you make us stronger or weaker. No member of your race in any part of our country can harm the meanest member of mine, without the proudest and bluest blood in Massachusetts being degraded. When Mississippi commits crime, New England commits crime, and in so much lowers the standard of your civilization. There is no escape—man drags man down, or man lifts man up.

In working out our destiny, while the main burden and center of activity must be with us, we shall need in a large measure in the years that are to come as we have in the past, the help, the encouragement, the guidance that the strong can give the weak. Thus helped, we of both races in the South soon shall throw off the shackles of racial and sectional prejudices and rise as Harvard University has risen and as we all should rise, above the clouds of ignorance, narrowness, and selfishness, into that atmosphere, that pure sunshine, where it will be our highest ambition to serve man, our brother, regardless of race or previous condition.

William Jennings Bryan
[1860–1925]

William Jennings Bryan, of Nebraska, was made nationally famous by his speech favoring free coinage of silver at the ratio of 16 to 1, which he delivered before the Democratic National Convention in Chicago in 1896. This speech, known as "The Cross of Gold," is reproduced in part here. Bryan was the unsuccessful Democratic candidate for President in 1896, 1900 and 1908. For about two years (1913–1915) he was Secretary of State in President Wilson's cabinet. Bryan was an ardent Prohibitionist, and a fundamentalist in religion.

THE CROSS OF GOLD

They say that we are opposing national bank currency; it is true. If you will read what Thomas Benton said, you will find he said that, in searching history, he could find but one parallel to Andrew Jackson; that was Cicero, who destroyed the conspiracy of Catiline and saved Rome. Benton said that Cicero only did for Rome what Jackson did for us when he destroyed the bank conspiracy and saved America. We say in our platform we believe that the right to coin and issue money is a function of government. We believe it. We believe that it is a part of sovereignty, and can no more with safety be delegated to private individuals than we could afford to delegate to private individuals the power to make penal statutes or levy taxes. Mr. Jefferson, who was once regarded as good Democratic authority, seems to have differed in opinion from the gentleman who has addressed us on the part of the minority. Those who are opposed to this proposition tell us that the issue of paper money is a function of the bank, and that the government ought to go out of the banking business. I stand with Jefferson rather than with them, and tell them, as he did, that the issue of money is a function of government, and that the banks ought to go out of the governing business.

They complain about the plank which declares against life tenure in office. They have tried to strain it to mean that which it does not mean. What we propose by that plank is the life tenure which is being built up in Washington, and which excludes from participation in official benefits the humbler members of society.

Let me call your attention to two or three important things. The gentleman from New York says that he will propose an amendment to the platform providing that the proposed change in our monetary system shall not affect contracts already made. Let me remind you that there is no intention of affecting those contracts which, according to present laws, are made payable in gold; but if he means to say that we cannot change our monetary system without protecting those who have loaned money before the change was made, I desire to ask him where, in law or in morals, he can find justification for not protecting the debtors when the act of 1873 was passed, if he now insists that we must protect the creditors.

He says he will also propose an amendment which will provide for the suspension of free coinage if we fail to maintain a parity within a year. We reply that when we advocate a policy which we believe will be successful, we are not compelled to raise a doubt as to our own sincerity by suggesting what we shall do if we fail. I ask him, if he would apply his logic to us, why he does not apply it to himself. He says he wants this country to try to secure an international agreement. Why does he not tell us what he is going to do if he fails to secure an international agreement? There is more reason for him to do that than there is for us to provide against the failure to maintain the parity. Our opponents have tried for twenty years to secure an international agreement, and those are waiting for it most patiently who do not want it at all.

And now, my friends, let me come to the paramount issue. If they ask us why it is that we say more on the money question than we say upon the tariff question, I reply that, if protection has slain its thousands, the gold standard has slain its tens of thousands. If they ask us why we do not embody in our platforms all the things that we believe in, we reply that when we have restored the money of the Constitution all other necessary reforms will be possible; but that until this is done there is no other reform that can be accomplished.

Why is it that within three months such a change has come over the country? Three months ago when it was confidently asserted that those who believe in the gold standard would frame our platform and nominate our candidates, even the advocates of the gold standard did not think that we could elect a President. And they had good reason for their doubt, because there is scarcely a State here to-day asking for the gold standard which is not in the absolute control of the Republican party. But note the change. Mr. McKinley was nominated at St. Louis upon a platform which declared for the maintenance of the gold standard until it can be changed into bimetallism by international government. Mr. McKinley was the most popular man among the Republicans, and three months ago everybody in the Republican party' prophesied his election. How is it to-day? Why, the man who was once pleased to think that he looked like Napoleon—that man shudders to-day when he remembers that he was nominated on the anniversary of the battle of Waterloo. Not only that, but as he listens he can hear with ever-increasing distinctness the sound of the waves as they beat upon the lonely shores of St. Helena.

Henry Cabot Lodge
[1850–1924]

*Henry Cabot Lodge, of Massachusetts, was a member of the House
of Representatives before he became a member of the Senate.
Lodge was one of the Senators who opposed President Wilson on
the issue of the League of Nations. In 1900 he supported President
McKinley on the issue of the Philippines. Here is part of a speech he
delivered on March 7, 1900.*

THE RETENTION OF THE PHILIPPINES

THE POLICY we offer is simple and straightforward. We believe in the
frank acceptance of existing facts, and in dealing with them as they are
and not on a theory of what they might or ought to be. We accept the
fact that the Philippine Islands are ours to-day, and that we are responsible
for them before the world. The next fact is that there is a war in those
islands, which, with its chief in hiding, and no semblance of a government, has now degenerated into mere guerilla fighting and brigandage,
with a precarious existence predicated on the November elections. Our
immediate duty, therefore, is to suppress this disorder, put an end to
fighting, and restore peace and order. That is what we are doing. That
is all we are called upon to do in order to meet the demands of the living
present. Beyond this we ought not to go by a legislative act, except to
make such provision that there may be no delay in re-establishing civil
government when the war ends. The question of our constitutional
right and power to govern those islands in any way we please I shall not
discuss. Not only is it still in the future, but if authority is lacking, the
Constitution gives full right and authority to hold and govern the
Philippines without making them either economically or politically part
of our system, neither of which they should ever be. When our great
Chief Justice, John Marshall—*"magnum et venerabile nomen"*—declared
in the Cherokee case that the United States could have under its control,
exercised by treaty or the laws of Congress, a "domestic and dependent
nation," I think he solved the question of our constitutional relations to
the Philippines. Further than the acts and the policy, which I have just
stated, I can only give my own opinion and belief as to the future, and as
to the course to be pursued in the Philippines. I hope and believe that we
shall retain the islands, and that, peace and order once restored, we shall
and should re-establish civil government, beginning with the towns and
villages, where the inhabitants are able to manage their own affairs. We
should give them honest administration, and prompt and efficient courts.
We should see to it there is entire protection to persons and property, in
order to encourage the development of the islands by the assurance of
safety to investors of capital. All men should be protected in the free

exercise of their religion, and the doors thrown open to missionaries of all Christian sects. The land, which belongs to the people, and of which they have been robbed in the past, should be returned to them and their titles made secure. We should inaugurate and carry forward, in the most earnest and liberal way, a comprehensive system of popular education. Finally, while we bring prosperity to the islands by developing their resources, we should, as rapidly as conditions will permit, bestow upon them self-government and home rule. Such, in outline, is the policy which I believe can be and will be pursued toward the Philippines. It will require time, patience, honesty, and ability for its completion, but it is thoroughly practicable and reasonable.

The foundation of it all is the retention of the islands by the United States, and it is to that question that I desire to address myself. I shall not argue our title to the islands by the law of nations, for it is perfect. No other nation has ever questioned it. It is too plain a proposition to warrant the waste of time and words upon it. Equally plain is our right under the Constitution, by a treaty which is the supreme law of the land, to hold those islands. I will not argue this point nor the entire legality of all that the President has done in accordance with his constitutional power and with the law passed by Congress at the last session which recognized the necessity of an increased army in order to cope with the existing insurrection. The opposition rests its weight on grounds widely different from these. They assert that on moral grounds we have no right to take or retain the Philippines, and that as a matter of expediency our whole Eastern policy was a costly mistake. I traverse both assertions. I deny both propositions. I believe we are in the Philippines as righteously as we are there rightfully and legally. I believe that to abandon the islands, or to leave them now, would be a wrong to humanity, a dereliction of duty, a base betrayal of the Filipinos who have supported us, led by the best men of Luzon, and in the highest degree contrary to sound morals. As to expediency, the arguments in favor of the retention of the Philippines seem to me so overwhelming that I should regard their loss as a calamity to our trade and commerce, and to all our business interests so great that no man can measure it.

William McKinley
[1843–1901]

William McKinley, of Ohio, was President of the United States during the Spanish-American War. He was reelected in 1900, and had completed about six months of his second administration when he was assassinated during a visit to the Pan-American Exposition in Buffalo. Here follows part of the address he delivered on the day he was fatally shot—September 5, 1901.

ADDRESS AT BUFFALO

EXPOSITIONS are the timekeepers of progress. They record the world's advancement. They stimulate the energy, enterprise, and intellect of the people, and quicken human genius. They go into the home. They broaden and brighten the daily life of the people. They open mighty storehouses of information of the student. Every exposition, great or small, has helped to some onward step. Comparison of ideas is always educational, and as such instructs the brain and hand of man. Friendly rivalry follows, which is the spur to industrial improvement, the inspiration to useful invention and to high endeavor in all departments of human activity. It exacts a study of the wants, comforts, and even the whims of the people, and recognizes the efficacy of high quality and new prices to win their favor. The quest for trade is an incentive to men of business to devise, invent, improve, and economize in the cost of production. Business life, whether among ourselves or with other people, is ever a sharp struggle for success. It will be none the less so in the future. Without competition we would be clinging to the clumsy and antiquated processes of farming and manufacture and the methods of business of long ago, and the twentieth would be no further advanced than the eighteenth century. But though commercial competitors we are, commercial enemies we must not be.

The Pan-American Exposition has done its work thoroughly, presenting in its exhibits evidences of the highest skill, and illustrating the progress of the human family in the western hemisphere. This portion of the earth has no cause for humiliation for the part it has performed in the march of civilization. It has not accomplished everything; far from it. It has simply done its best; and without vanity or boastfulness, and recognizing the manifold achievements of others, it invites the friendly rivalry of all the powers in the peaceful pursuits of trade and commerce, and will coöperate with all in advancing the highest and best interests of humanity. The wisdom and energy of all the nations are none too great for the world's work. The success of art, science, industry, and invention is an international asset and a common glory.

After all, how near, one to the other, is every part of the world!

Modern inventions have brought into close relation widely separated peoples and made them better acquainted. Geographic and political divisions will continue to exist, but distances have been effaced. Swift ships and fast trains are becoming cosmopolitan. They invade fields which a few years ago were impenetrable. The world's products are exchanged as never before, and with increasing transportation facilities come increasing knowledge and larger trade. Prices are fixed with mathematical precision by supply and demand. The world's selling prices are regulated by market and crop reports. We travel greater distances in a shorter space of time and with more ease than was ever dreamed of by the fathers. Isolation is no longer possible or desirable. The same important news is read, though in different languages, the same day in all Christendom. The telegraph keeps us advised of what is occurring everywhere, and the press foreshadows, with more or less accuracy, the plans and purposes of the nations. Market prices of products and of securities are hourly known in every commercial mart, and the investments of the people extend beyond their own national boundaries into the remotest parts of the earth. Vast transactions are conducted, and international exchanges are made, by the tick of the cable. Every event of interest is immediately bulletined. The quick gathering and transmission of news, like rapid transit, are of recent origin, and are made possible by the genius of the inventor and the courage of the investor. It took a special messenger of the government, with every facility known at the time for rapid travel, nineteen days to go from the city of Washington to New Orleans with a message to General Jackson that the war with England had ceased, and a treaty of peace had been signed. How different now!

These buildings will disappear, this creation of art and beauty and industry will perish from sight, but their influence will remain to

> Make it live beyond its too short living,
> With praises and thanksgiving.

Who can tell the new thoughts that have been awakened, the ambitions fired, and the high achievements that will be wrought through this exposition? Gentlemen, let us ever remember that our interest is in concord, not conflict; and that our real eminence rests in the victories of peace, not those of war. We hope that all who are represented here may be moved to higher and nobler effort for their own and the world's good, and that out of this city may come, not only greater commerce and trade for us all, but, more essential than these, relations of mutual respect, confidence, and friendship which will deepen and endure.

Our earnest prayer is that God will graciously vouchsafe prosperity, happiness, and peace to all our neighbors, and like blessings to all the peoples and powers of earth.

Robert Marion La Follette
[1855–1925]

One of the foremost liberal United States Senators of the early part of this century was Robert Marion La Follette, of Wisconsin. He championed many progressive causes and ran unsuccessfully for President on an independent ticket in 1924. Here are parts of a speech he delivered in Milwaukee in 1902.

MANHOOD OR MONEY

WE BELIEVE with the President, as recognized by him in daily speech, that these great monopolies constitute the foremost of national questions. We uphold his hands in his effort to curb these trusts by the enforcement of laws now upon the Statute books. There is probably not an important trust in the United States which does not have the assistance of railroads in destroying its competitors in business. The limitation and control of these public-service corporations in the legitimate field, as common carriers, are an important element in the practical solution of the problem with which we have to deal.

In accepting renomination for the office of governor at the hands of the Republican party, I said:

"The greatest danger menacing public institutions to-day is the overbalancing control of city, state, and national legislatures by the wealth and power of public-service corporations."

I made this statement advisedly then. I repeat it now. Not in a spirit of hostility to any interest, but deeply impressed with its profound significance to republican institutions and its ultimate influence upon all citizens and all citizenship.

The idea is not new. It is not peculiar to Wisconsin.

The responsibility it brings cannot be shirked or pushed aside or postponed. The national government, every state government—particularly that of every rich and prosperous state—every city government—particularly that of every large city—has this problem to solve; not at some other time, but now.

The question of primary elections is one of government for the people and by the people. Under our system of government by political parties, two elements, equal in importance, are involved in the exercise of suffrage; one, the making of the ballot; the other, the casting of the ballot. The right to cast the ballot is regarded as sacred. The right to make the ballot is equally sacred. No man would be willing to delegate his power to vote the ballot at general elections. No man shall be compelled to delegate his power to make his ballot. Boss Tweed said: "You may elect whichever candidates you please to office, if you will allow me to select the candidates." The boss can always afford to say, "You may vote any ticket you please so long as I make all the tickets." The character of the men nominated and the influences to which they owe their nomination determine the character of government.

The result and the only result sought by a primary election is to give to every man an equal voice in the selection of all candidates; to lodge in the people the absolute right to say who their candidates for office shall be; to root out forever the power of the political boss to control the selection of officials through the manipulation of caucuses and conventions. A primary election should provide the same safeguards for nominating candidates as for electing them. It should fix the day, name the hour, use the same polling places, have the same election officers, provide the Australian ballot, containing the names of all the candidates to be voted upon at the election. It should be an election, possessing all the legal sanctions of an election.

It is needless to trace the evolution of the political machine, its combination with aggregate wealth and corporate power, making the interests of the citizen and the state subservient to their selfish ends. The names of the great bosses to-day are better known than the great statesmen. The tendency to monopolization of political control by a few men in each party, county, city, state, and community has operated, except in cases of profound interest, excitement, and tremendous effort, to disfranchise the great majority of citizens in so far as participating in the caucus and convention is concerned.

The day that Chief Justice Ryan prophesied would come is here. The issue he said would arise is pending.

"Which shall rule—wealth or man; which shall lead—money or intellect; who shall fill public stations—educated and patriotic freemen, or the feudal servants of corporate power?"

If the chosen representative does not represent the citizen, his voice is stifled; is denied any part in government. If majority decision as determined by the law of the land is ignored and reversed, if the expressed will of the people is scorned and scorned again—then the popular government of the people, by the people, and for the people is at an end. Its forms may be observed—you may have the mockery of "elections," and the force of "representation," but a government based upon the will of the people has perished from the earth.

Theodore Roosevelt
[1858–1919]

Theodore Roosevelt was Governor of New York before being elected Vice-President of the United States. He became President when Mc-Kinley was assassinated. He was reelected in 1904. He left the Republican party in 1912, when its convention refused him another nomination. He ran that year for President on the independent Progressive or "Bull Moose" ticket, but lost. Roosevelt was an ardent advocate of many social reforms and "the strenuous life." Here is part of a speech on the latter subject, which he delivered in Chicago in 1899.

THE STRENUOUS LIFE

GENTLEMEN:—In speaking to you, men of the greatest city of the West, men of the State which gave to the country Lincoln and Grant, men who preëminently and distinctly embody all that is most American in the American character, I wish to preach not the doctrine of ignoble ease but the doctrine of the strenuous life; the life of toil and effort; of labor and strife; to preach that highest form of success which comes not to the man who desires mere easy peace but to the man who does not shrink from danger, from hardship, or from bitter toil, and who out of these wins the splendid ultimate triumph.

The timid man, the lazy man, the man who distrusts his country, the overcivilized man, who has lost the great fighting, masterful virtues, the ignorant man and the man of dull mind, whose soul is incapable of feeling the mighty lift that thrills "stern men with empires in their brains"—all these, of course, shrink from seeing the nation undertake its new duties; shrink from seeing us build a navy and army adequate to our needs; shrink from seeing us do our share of the world's work by bringing order out of chaos in the great, fair tropic islands from which the valor of our soldiers and sailors has driven the Spanish flag. These are the men who fear the strenuous life, who fear the only national life which is really worth leading. They believe in that cloistered life which saps the hardy virtues in a nation, as it saps them in the individual; or else they are wedded to that base spirit of gain and greed which recognizes in commercialism the be-all and end-all of national life, instead of realizing that, though an indispensable element, it is after all but one of the many elements that go to make up true national greatness. No country can long endure if its foundations are not laid deep in the material prosperity which comes from thrift, from business energy and enterprise, from hard unsparing effort in the fields of industrial activity; but neither was any nation ever yet truly great if it relied upon material prosperity alone. All honor must be paid to the architects of our material prosperity; to the great captains of industry who have built our factories and our railroads; to the strong men who toil for wealth with brain or hand; for great is the debt of the nation to these and their kind. But our debt is yet greater to the men whose highest type is to be found in a statesman like Lincoln, a soldier like Grant. They showed by their lives that they recognized the law of work, the law of strife; they toiled to win a competence for themselves and those dependent upon them; but they recognized that there were yet other and even loftier duties— duties to the nation and duties to the race.

I preach to you, then, my countrymen, that our country calls not for the life of ease, but for the life of strenuous endeavor. The twentieth century looms before us big with the fate of many nations. If we stand idly by, if we seek merely swollen, slothful ease, and ignoble peace, if we shrink from the hard contests where men must win at hazard of their lives and at the risk of all they hold dear, then the bolder and stronger peoples will pass us by and will win for themselves the domination of the world. Let us therefore boldly face the life of strife, resolute to do our duty well and manfully; resolute to uphold righteousness by deed and by word; resolute to be both honest and brave, to serve high ideals, yet to use practical methods. Above all, let us shrink from no strife, moral or physical, within or without the nation, provided we are certain that the strife is justified; for it is only through strife, through hard and dangerous endeavor, that we shall ultimately win the goal of true national greatness.

Jane Addams
[1860–1935]

Jane Addams, of Illinois, was widely known and highly regarded for her active interest in many progressive causes. She devoted her wealth and life to Hull House, a famous settlement for social service in Chicago. Miss Addams delivered the following address at the Union League Club, Chicago, on February 23, 1903.

WASHINGTON'S BIRTHDAY

We meet together upon these birthdays of our great men, not only to review their lives, but to revive and cherish our own patriotism. This matter is a difficult task. In the first place, we are prone to think that by merely reciting these great deeds we get a reflected glory, and that the future is secure to us because the past has been so fine.

In the second place, we are apt to think that we inherit the fine qualities of those great men, simply because we have had a common descent and are living in the same territory.

As for the latter, we know full well that the patriotism of common descent is the mere patriotism of the clan—the early patriotism of the tribe. We know that the possession of a like territory is merely an advance upon that, and that both of them are unworthy to be the patriotism of a great cosmopolitan nation whose patriotism must be large enough to obliterate racial distinction and to forget that there are such things as surveyor's lines. Then when we come to the study of great men it is easy to think only of their great deeds, and not to think enough of their spirit. What is a great man who has made his mark upon history? Every time, if we think far enough, he is a man who has looked through the confusion of the moment and has seen the moral issue involved; he is a man who has refused to have his sense of justice distorted; he has listened to his conscience until conscience becomes a trumpet call to like-minded men, so that they gather about him and together, with mutual purpose and mutual aid, they make a new period in history.

Let us assume for a moment that if we are going to make this day of advantage to us, we will have to take this definition of a great man. We will have to appeal to the present as well as to the past. We will have to rouse our national consciences as well as our national pride, and we will all have to remember that it lies with the young people of this nation whether or not it is going to go on to a finish in any wise worthy of its beginning.

If we go back to George Washington, and ask what he would be doing were he bearing our burdens now, and facing our problems at this moment, we would, of course, have to study his life bit by bit; his life as a soldier, as a statesman, and as a simple Virginia planter.

First, as a soldier. What is it that we admire about the soldier? It certainly is not that he goes into battle; what we admire about the soldier is that he has the power of losing his own life for the life of a larger cause; that he holds his personal suffering of no account; that he flings down in the gage of battle his all, and says, "I will stand or fall with this cause." That, it seems to me, is the glorious thing we most admire, and if we are going to preserve that same spirit of the soldier, we will have to found a similar spirit in the civil life of the people, the same pride in civil warfare, the spirit of courage, and the spirit of self-surrender which lies back of this.

If we look out upon our national perspective, do we not see certainly one great menace which calls for patriotism? We see all around us a spirit of materialism—an undue emphasis put upon material possessions; an inordinate desire to win wealth; an inordinate fear of losing wealth; an inordinate desire to please those who are the possessors of wealth. Now, let us say, if we feel that this is a menace, that with all our power, with all the spirit of a soldier, we will arouse high-minded youth of this country against this spirit of materialism. We will say to-day that we will not count the opening of markets the one great field which our nation is concerned in, but that when our flag flies anywhere it shall fly for righteousness as well as for increased commercial prosperity; that we will see to it that no sin of commercial robbery shall be committed where it floats; that we shall see to it that nothing in our commercial history will not bear the most careful scrutiny and investigation; that we will restore commercial life, however complicated, to such honor and simple honesty as George Washington expressed in his business dealings.

Let us take, for a moment, George Washington as a statesman. What was it he did, during those days when they were framing a constitution, when they were meeting together night after night, and trying to adjust the rights and privileges of every class in the community? What was it that sustained him during all those days, all those weeks, during all those months and years? It was the belief that they were founding a nation on the axiom that all men are created free and equal. What would George Washington say if he found that among us there were causes constantly operating against that equality? If he knew that any child which is thrust prematurely into industry has no chance in life with children who are preserved from that pain and sorrow; if he knew that every insanitary street, and every insanitary house, cripples a man so that he has no health and no vigor with which to carry on his life labor; if he knew that all about us are forces making against skill, making against the best manhood and womanhood, what would he say? He would say that if the spirit of equality means anything, it means like opportunity, and if we once lose like opportunity we lose the only chance we have toward equality throughout the nation.

Let us take George Washington as a citizen. What did he do when he retired from office, because he was afraid holding office any longer might bring a wrong to himself and harm to his beloved nation? We say that he went back to his plantation on the Potomac. What were his thoughts during the all too short days that he lived there? He thought of many possibilities, but, looking out over his country, did he fear that there should rise up a crowd of men who held office, not for their country's good, but for their own good? Would he not have foreboded evil if he had known that among us were groups and hordes of professional politicians, who, without any blinking or without any pretense that they did otherwise, apportioned the spoils of office, and considered an independent man as a mere intruder, as a mere outsider; if he had seen that the original meaning of office-holding and the function of government had become indifferent to us, that we were not using our foresight and our conscience in order to find out this great wrong which was sapping the foundations of self-government? He would tell us that anything which makes for better civic service, which makes for a merit system, which makes for fitness for office, is the only thing which will tell against this wrong, and that this course is the wisest patriotism. What did he write in his last correspondence? He wrote that he felt very unhappy on the subject of slavery, that there was, to his mind, a great menace in the holding of slaves. We know that he neither bought nor sold slaves himself, and that he freed his own slaves in his will. That was a century ago. A man who a century ago could do that, would he, do you think, be indifferent now to the great questions of social maladjustment which we feel all around us? His letters breathe a yearning for a better condition for the slaves as the letters of all great men among us breathe a yearning for the better condition of the unskilled and underpaid. A wise patriotism, which will take hold of these questions by careful legal enactment, by constant and vigorous enforcement, because of the belief that if the meanest man in the republic is deprived of his rights, then every man in the republic is deprived of his rights, is the only patriotism by which public-spirited men and women, with a thoroughly aroused conscience, can worthily serve this republic. Let us say again that the lessons of great men are lost unless they reënforce upon our minds the highest demands which we make upon ourselves; that they are lost unless they drive our sluggish wills forward in the direction of their highest ideals.

Stephen S. Wise

[1874-1949]

Stephen Samuel Wise, founder and rabbi of the Free Synagogue of New York City and a founder of the Zionist Organization of America, was widely known as a great orator. Here is part of an address which he delivered at Springfield, Illinois, under the auspices of the Lincoln Centennial Association, February 12, 1914.

LINCOLN, MAN AND AMERICAN

WE DWELL in times of great perplexity and are beset by far-reaching problems of social, industrial and political import. We shall not greatly err if upon every occasion we consult the genius of Abraham Lincoln. We shall not falter nor swerve from the path of national righteousness if we live by the moral genius of the great American commoner.

Instead of following Lincoln, we too often strive to make it appear that he is following us. Instead of emulating him we too often venture to appropriate him. Instead of sitting at his feet as his disciples, and humbly heeding the echoes of his lips, we attribute to him our own petty slogans. The truth is that Lincoln belongs to no party to-day, though in his time he stood well and firmly within party ranks. His spirit ought to-day to inform all parties. He was a partisan second, an American first, as he is the first of Americans. Men and measures must not claim him for their own. He remains the standard by which to measure men. His views are not binding upon us, but his point of view will always be our inspiration. He would not be blindly followed who was open-minded and open-visioned. He did not solve all the problems of the future, but he did solve the problem of his own age. Ours is not to claim his name for our standards but his aim as our standard.

Lincoln is become for us the test of human worth, and we honor men in the measure in which they approach the absolute standard of Abraham Lincoln. Other men may resemble and approach him; he remains the standard whereby all other men are measured and appraised. Gibbon tells us that two hundred and fifty years after the death of Trajan, the Senate, in calling out the customary acclamation on the accession of an Emperor, wished that he might surpass the felicity of Augustus and the virtue of Trajan. Melior Trajano—better than Trajan! Such a standard is Lincoln become for us, save that we dare not hope that any American may serve his country better than did Lincoln. However covetous of honor for our country we may be, we cherish no higher hope for the land we love than that the servants of the Republic in all time may rise to the stature of Abraham Lincoln.

In his lifetime Lincoln was maligned and traduced, but detraction during a man's lifetime affords no test of his life's value nor offers any forecast of history's verdict. It would almost seem as if the glory of immortality were anticipated in the life of the great by detraction and denial whilst yet they lived. When a Lincoln-like man arises, let us recognize and fitly honor him. There could be no poorer way of honoring the memory of Lincoln than to assume, as we sometimes do, that the race of Lincolns has perished from the earth, and that we shall never look upon his like again. One way to ensure the passing of the Lincolns is to assume that another Lincoln can nevermore arise. Would we find Lincoln to-day, we must not seek him in the guise of a rail-splitter, nor as a wielder of the backwoodsman's axe, but as a mighty smiter of wrong in high places and low.

Not very long ago I chanced upon a rarely beautiful custom in the city of Florence. It was the day of the martyrdom "of a prophet sent by God." A multitude stood before the spot where he was done to death —his hands miraculously uplifted in blessing in the very moment of torture and death—and every man brought a rose petal in token of reverence and gratitude to the martyred soul. This day every American citizen, every American man and woman and child has in spirit brought a petal to the grave of Lincoln, who sleeps to-night beneath a wilderness of love-tokens from men of all faiths and tongues and races and backgrounds—who are become one and indivisible in their love and honor for the memory of Abraham Lincoln.

I have sometimes thought that the noblest tribute paid to the memory of Lincoln was the word of Phillips Brooks in Westminster Abbey when, pointing out that the test of the world to every nation was—Show us your man—he declared that America names Lincoln. But the first word spoken after the death of Lincoln is truest and best—the word of Secretary of War Stanton, standing by the side of that scene of peace— "Now he belongs to the ages." It was verdict and prophecy alike, for Lincoln is not America's, he is the world's; he belongs not to our age, but to the ages; and yet, though he belongs to all time and to all peoples, he is our own, for he was an American.

Woodrow Wilson
[1856–1924]

Woodrow Wilson, born in Virginia, was an American scholar-statesman. From professor and president of Princeton University he went to the Governorship of New Jersey. In 1912 he was the successful Democratic candidate for President. Reforms in the tariff and national banking marked the early part of his administration, but after August, 1914, serious problems of the spreading World War began to overshadow domestic issues. Reelected in 1916, he faced the menace of unrestricted submarine warfare with militant diplomacy until war with Germany became inevitable in April 1917. Wilson's speeches played an important part in the prosecution of the war. They solidified the Allies and demoralized the Central Powers. When victory came, Wilson proposed to the Peace Conference the League of Nations as an instrument for the preservation of world peace. The Peace Conference included the League proposal in the peace treaty but the United States Senate, influenced by isolationists, rejected the treaty. Several important addresses of Wilson are given here. Wilson delivered the following speech before the Senate on January 21, 1917.

PEACE WITHOUT VICTORY

GENTLEMEN OF THE SENATE: On the 18th of December last I addressed an identic note to the Governments of the nations now at war requesting them to state, more definitely than they had yet been stated by either group of belligerents, the terms upon which they would deem it possible to make peace. I spoke on behalf of humanity and of the rights of all neutral nations like our own, many of whose most vital interests the war puts in constant jeopardy.

The Central Powers united in a reply which stated merely that they were ready to meet their antagonists in conference to discuss terms of peace.

The Entente Powers have replied much more definitely, and have stated, in general terms, indeed, but with sufficient definiteness to imply details, the arrangements, guarantees, and acts of reparation which they deem to be the indispensable conditions of a satisfactory settlement.

We are that much nearer a definite discussion of the peace which shall end the present war.

I have sought this opportunity to address you because I thought that I owed it to you, as the council associated with me in the final determination of our international obligations, to disclose to you without reserve the thought and purpose that have been taking form in my mind in regard to the duty of our Government in those days to come when it will be necessary to lay afresh and upon a new plan the foundations of peace among the nations.

It is inconceivable that the people of the United States should play no part in that great enterprise. To take part in such a service will be the opportunity for which they have sought to prepare themselves by the very principles and purposes of their polity and the approved practices of their Government, ever since the days when they set up a new nation in the high and honorable hope that it might in all that it was and did show mankind the way to liberty. They cannot, in honor, withhold the service to which they are now about to be challenged. They do not wish to withhold it. But they owe it to themselves and to the other nations of the world to state the conditions under which they will feel free to render it.

That service is nothing less than this—to add their authority and their power to the authority and force of other nations to guarantee peace and justice throughout the world.

Is the present war a struggle for a just and secure peace or only for a new balance of power? If it be only a struggle for a new balance of power, who will guarantee, who can guarantee, the stable equilibrium of the new arrangement? Only a tranquil Europe can be a stable Europe. There must be not only a balance of power, but a community of power; not organized rivalries, but an organized common peace.

Fortunately, we have received very explicit assurances on this point. The statesmen of both of the groups of nations, now arrayed against one another, have said, in terms that could not be misinterpreted, that it was no part of the purpose they had in mind to crush their antagonists. But the implications of these assurances may not be equally clear to all, may not be the same on both sides of the water. I think it will be serviceable if I attempt to set forth what we understand them to be.

They imply first of all that it must be a peace without victory. It is not pleasant to say this. I beg that I may be permitted to put my own interpretation upon it and that it may be understood that no other interpretation was in my thought. I am seeking only to face realities and to face them without soft concealments. Victory would mean peace forced upon the loser, a victor's terms imposed upon the vanquished. It would be accepted in humiliation, under duress, at an intolerable sacrifice, and would leave a sting, a resentment, a bitter memory, upon which terms of peace would rest, not permanently, but only as upon quicksand.

Only a peace between equals can last; only a peace the very principle of which is equality and a common participation in a common benefit.

I have spoken upon these great matters without reserve, and with the utmost explicitness because it has seemed to me to be necessary if the world's yearning desire for peace was anywhere to find free voice and utterance. Perhaps I am the only person in high authority among all the peoples of the world who is at liberty to speak and hold nothing back. I am speaking as an individual, and yet I am speaking also, of course, as the responsible head of a great Government, and I feel confident that I have said what the people of the United States would wish me to say.

May I not add that I hope and believe that I am, in effect, speaking for liberals and friends of humanity in every nation and of every program of liberty? I would fain believe that I am speaking for the silent mass of mankind everywhere who have as yet had no place or opportunity to speak their real hearts out concerning the death and ruin they see to have come already upon the persons and the homes they hold most dear.

And in holding out the expectation that the people and the Government of the United States will join the other civilized nations of the world in guaranteeing the permanence of peace upon such terms as I have named, I speak with the greater boldness and confidence because it is clear to every man who can think that there is in this promise no breach in either our traditions or our policy as a nation, but a fulfillment rather of all that we have professed or striven for.

I am proposing, as it were, that the nations should with one accord adopt the doctrine of President Monroe as the doctrine of the world: That no nation should seek to extend its policy over any other nation or people, but that every people should be left free to determine its own policy, its own way of development, unhindered, unthreatened, unafraid, the little along with the great and powerful.

I am proposing that all nations henceforth avoid entangling alliances which would draw them into competition of power, catch them in a net of intrigue and selfish rivalry, and disturb their own affairs with influences intruded from without. There is no entangling alliance in a concert of power. When all unite to act in the same sense and with the same purpose, all act in the common interest and are free to live their own lives under a common protection.

I am proposing government by the consent of the governed; that freedom of the seas which in international conference after conference representatives of the United States have urged with the eloquence of those who are the convinced disciples of liberty; and that moderation of armaments which makes of armies and navies a power for order merely, not an instrument of aggression or of selfish violence.

These are American principles, American policies. We can stand for no others. And they are also the principles and policies of forward-looking men and women everywhere, of every modern nation, of every enlightened community. They are the principles of mankind, and must prevail.

President Wilson delivered the following address before a joint session of Congress on April 2, 1917.

DECLARATION OF WAR

GENTLEMEN OF THE CONGRESS: I have called the Congress into extraordinary session because there are serious, very serious choices of policy to be made, and made immediately, which it was neither right nor constitutionally permissible that I should assume the responsibility of making.

On the third of February last I officially laid before you the extraordinary announcement of the Imperial German Government that on and after the first day of February it was its purpose to put aside all restraints of law or of humanity and use its submarines to sink every vessel that sought to approach either the ports of Great Britain and Ireland or the western coasts of Europe or any of the ports controlled by the enemies of Germany within the Mediterranean. That had seemed to be the object of the German submarine warfare earlier in the war, but since April of last year the Imperial Government had somewhat restrained the commanders of its undersea craft in conformity with its promise then given to us that passenger boats should not be sunk and that due warning would be given to all other vessels which its submarines might seek to destroy, when no resistance was offered or escape attempted, and care taken that their crews were given at least a fair chance to save their lives in their open boats. The precautions taken were meager and haphazard enough, as was proved in distressing instance after instance in the progress of the cruel and unmanly business, but a certain degree of restraint was observed. The new policy has swept every restriction aside. Vessels of every kind, whatever their flag, their character, their cargo, their destination, their errand, have been ruthlessly sent to the bottom without warning and without thought of help or mercy for those on board, the vessels of friendly neutrals along with those of belligerents. Even hospital ships and ships carrying relief to the sorely bereaved and stricken people of Belgium, though the latter were provided with safe conduct through the proscribed areas by the German Government itself and were distinguished by unmistakable marks of identity, have been sunk with the same reckless lack of compassion or of principle.

I was for a little while unable to believe that such things would in fact be done by any government that had hitherto subscribed to humane practices of civilized nations. International law had its origin in the attempt to set up some law which would be respected and observed upon the seas, where no nation had right of dominion and where lay the free highways of the world. By painful stage after stage has that law been built up, with meager enough results, indeed, after all was accomplished that could be accomplished, but always with a clear view, at least, of what the heart and conscience of mankind demanded. This minimum of right the German Government has swept aside, under the plea of retaliation and necessity and because it had no weapons which it could use at sea except these which it is impossible to employ as it is employing them without throwing to the wind all scruples of humanity or of respect for the understandings that were supposed to underlie the intercourse of the world. I am not now thinking of the loss of property involved, immense and serious as that is, but only of the wanton and wholesale destruction of the lives of non-combatants, men, women, and children, engaged in pursuits which have always, even in the darkest periods of modern history, been deemed innocent and legitimate. Property can be paid for; the lives of peaceful and innocent people cannot be. The present German submarine warfare against commerce is a warfare against mankind.

It is a war against all nations. American ships have been sunk, American lives taken, in ways which it has stirred us very deeply to learn of, but the ships and people of other neutral and friendly nations have been sunk and overwhelmed in the waters in the same way. There has been no discrimination. The challenge is to all mankind. Each nation must decide for itself how it will meet it. The choice we make for ourselves must be made with a moderation of counsel and a temperateness of judgment befitting our character and our motives as a nation. We must put excited feeling away. Our motive will not be revenge or the victorious assertion of the physical might of the nation, but only the vindication of right, of human right, of which we are only a single champion.

When I addressed the Congress on the twenty-sixth of February last I thought that it would suffice to assert our neutral rights with arms, our right to use the seas against unlawful interference, our right to keep our people safe against unlawful violence. But armed neutrality, it now appears, is impracticable. Because submarines are in effect outlaws when used as the German submarines have been used against merchant shipping, it is impossible to defend ships against their attacks as the law of nations has assumed that merchantmen would defend themselves against privateers or cruisers, visible craft giving chase upon the open sea. It is common prudence in such circumstances, grim necessity indeed, to endeavor to destroy them before they have shown their own intention. They must be dealt with upon sight, if dealt with at all. The German Government denies the right of neutrals to use arms at all within the areas of the sea which it has proscribed, even in the defense of rights which no modern publicist has ever before questioned their right to defend. The intimation is conveyed that the armed guards which we have placed on our merchant ships will be treated as beyond the pale of law and subject to be dealt with as pirates would be. Armed neutrality is ineffectual enough at best; in such circumstances and in the face of such pretensions it is worse than ineffectual; it is likely only to produce what it was meant to prevent; it is practically certain to draw us into the war without either the rights or the effectiveness of belligerents. There is one choice we cannot make, we are incapable of making; we will not choose the path of submission and suffer the most sacred rights of our nation and our people to be ignored or violated. The wrongs against which we now array ourselves are no common wrongs; they cut to the very roots of human life.

With a profound sense of the solemn and even tragical character of the step I am taking and of the grave responsibilities which it involves, but in unhesitating obedience to what I deem my constitutional duty, I advise that the Congress declare the recent course of the Imperial German Government to be in fact nothing less than war against the Government and people of the United States; that it formally accept the status of belligerent which has thus been thrust upon it; and that it take immediate steps not only to put the country in a more thorough state of defense, but also to exert all its power and employ all its resources to bring the Government of the German Empire to terms and end the war.

What this will involve is clear. It will involve the utmost practicable coöperation in counsel and action with the governments now at war with Germany, and, as incident to that, the extension to those governments of the most liberal financial credits, in order that our resources may so far as possible be added to theirs. It will involve the organization and mobilization of all the material resources of the country to supply the materials of war and serve the incidental needs of the nation in the most abundant and yet the most economical and efficient way possible. It will involve the immediate full equipment of the navy in all respects but particularly in supplying it with the best means of dealing with the enemy's submarines. It will involve the immediate addition to the armed forces of the United States already provided for by law in case of war of at least five hundred thousand men, who should, in my opinion, be chosen upon the principle of universal liability to service, and also the authorization of subsequent additional increments of equal force so soon as they may be needed and can be handled in training. It will involve also, of course, the granting of adequate credits to the Government, sustained, I hope, so far as they can equitably be sustained by the present generation, by well-conceived taxation.

I say sustained so far as may be equitable by taxation because it seems to me that it would be most unwise to base the credits which will now be necessary entirely on money borrowed. It is our duty, I most respectfully urge, to protect our people so far as we may against the very serious hardships and evils which would be likely to arise out of the inflation which would be produced by vast loans.

In carrying out the measures by which these things are to be accomplished we should keep constantly in mind the wisdom of interfering as little as possible in our own preparation and in the equipment of our own military forces with the duty—for it will be a very practical duty—of supplying the nations already at war with Germany with the materials which they can obtain only from us or by our assistance. They are in the field and we should help them in every way to be effective there.

I shall take the liberty of suggesting, through the several executive departments of the Government, for the consideration of your committees, measures for the accomplishment of the several objects I have mentioned. I hope that it will be your pleasure to deal with them as having been framed after very careful thought by the branch of the Government upon whom the responsibility of conducting the war and safeguarding the nation will most directly fall.

While we do these things, these deeply momentous things, let us be very clear, and make very clear to all the world, what our motives and our objects are. My own thought has not been driven from its habitual and normal course by the unhappy events of the last two months, and I do not believe that the thought of the nation has been altered or clouded by them. I have exactly the same things in mind now that I had in mind when I addressed the Senate on the twenty-second of January last; the same that I had in mind when I addressed the Congress on the third of February and on the twenty-sixth of February. Our object now, as then, is to vindicate the principles of peace and justice in the life of the world as against selfish and autocratic power, and to set up among the really free and self-governed peoples of the world such a concert of purpose and of action as will henceforth ensure the observance of those principles. Neutrality is no longer feasible or desirable where the peace of the world is involved and the freedom of its peoples, and the menace to that peace and freedom lies in the existence of autocratic governments, backed by organized force which is controlled wholly by their will, not by the will of their people. We have seen the last of neutrality in such circumstances. We are at the beginning of an age in which it will be insisted that the same standards of conduct and of responsibility for wrong done shall be observed among nations and their governments that are observed among the individual citizens of civilized States.

We have no quarrel with the German people. We have no feeling towards them but one of sympathy and friendship. It was not upon their impulse that their government acted in entering this war. It was not with their previous knowledge or approval. It was a war determined upon as wars used to be determined upon in the old, unhappy days when peoples were nowhere consulted by their rulers and wars were provoked and waged in the interest of dynasties or of little groups of ambitious men who were accustomed to use their fellow-men as pawns and tools. Self-governed nations do not fill their neighbor states with spies or set the course of intrigue to bring about some critical posture of affairs which will give them an opportunity to strike and make conquest. Such designs can be successfully worked out only under cover and where no one has the right to ask questions. Cunningly contrived plans of deception or aggression, carried, it may be, from generation to generation, can be worked out and kept from the light only within the privacy of courts or behind the carefully guarded confidences of a narrow and privileged class. They are happily impossible where public opinion commands and insists upon full information concerning all the nation's affairs.

A steadfast concert for peace can never be maintained except by a partnership of democratic nations. No autocratic government could be trusted to keep faith within it or observe its covenants. It must be a league of honor, a partnership of opinion. Intrigue would eat its vitals away; the plottings of inner circles who could plan what they would and render account to no one would be a corruption seated at its very heart. Only free peoples can hold their purpose and their honor steady to a common end and prefer the interests of mankind to any narrow interest of their own.

Does not every American feel that assurance has been added to our hope for the future peace of the world by the wonderful and heartening things that have been happening within the last few weeks in Russia? Russia was known by those who knew her best to have been always in fact democratic at heart in all the vital habits of her thought, in all the intimate relationships of her people that spoke their natural instinct, their habitual attitude towards life. The autocracy that crowned the summit of her political structure, long as it had stood and terrible as was the reality of its power, was not in fact Russian in origin, character, or purpose; and now it has been shaken off and the great, generous Russian people have been added, in all their naïve majesty and might, to the forces that are fighting for freedom in the world, for justice, and for peace. Here is a fit partner for a League of Honor.

One of the things that has served to convince us that the Prussian autocracy was not and could never be our friend is that from the very outset of the present war it has filled our unsuspecting communities, and even our offices of government, with spies and set criminal intrigues everywhere afoot against our national unity of counsel, our peace within and without, our industries and our commerce. Indeed, it is now evident that its spies were here even before the war began; and it is unhappily not a matter of conjecture but a fact proved in our courts of justice that the intrigues which have more than once come perilously near to disturbing the peace and dislocating the industries of the country have been carried on at the instigation, with the support, and even under the personal direction of official agents of the Imperial Government accredited to the Government of the United States. Even in checking these things and trying to extirpate them we have sought to put the most generous interpretation possible upon them because we knew that their source lay, not in any hostile feeling of the German people toward us (who were, no doubt, as ignorant of them as we ourselves were), but only in the selfish designs of a government that did what it pleased and told its people nothing. But they have played their part in serving to convince us at last that that government entertains no real friendship for us, and means to act against our peace and security at its convenience. That it means to stir up enemies against us at our very doors the intercepted note to the German Minister at Mexico City is eloquent evidence.

We are accepting this challenge of hostile purpose because we know that in such a government, following such methods, we can never have a friend; and that in the presence of its organized power, always lying in wait to accomplish we know not what purpose, there can be no assured security for the democratic governments of the world. We are now about to accept the gauge of battle with this natural foe to liberty and shall, if necessary, spend the whole force of the nation to check and nullify its pretensions and its power. We are glad, now that we see the facts with no veil of false pretense about them, to fight thus for the ultimate peace of the world and for the liberation of its peoples, the German peoples included; for the rights of nations, great and small, and the privilege of men everywhere to choose their way of life and of obedience. The world must be made safe for democracy. Its peace must be planted upon the tested foundations of political liberty. We have no selfish ends to serve. We desire no conquest, no dominion. We seek no indemnities for ourselves, no material compensation for the sacrifices we shall freely make. We are but one of the champions of the rights of mankind. We shall be satisfied when those rights have been made as secure as the faith and the freedom of nations can make them.

Just because we fight without rancor and without selfish object, seeking nothing for ourselves but what we shall wish to share with all free peoples, we shall, I feel confident, conduct our operations as belligerents without passion and ourselves observe with proud punctilio the principles of right and of fair play we profess to be fighting for.

I have said nothing of the government allied with the Imperial Government of Germany because they have not made war upon us or challenged us to defend our right and our honor. The Austro-Hungarian Government has, indeed, avowed its unqualified endorsement and acceptance of the reckless and lawless submarine warfare adopted now without disguise by the Imperial German Government, and it has therefore not been possible for this Government to receive Count Tarnowski, the Ambassador recently accredited to this Government by the Imperial and Royal Government of Austria-Hungary; but that Government has not actually engaged in warfare against citizens of the United States on the seas, and I take the liberty, for the present at least, of postponing a discussion of our relations with the authorities at Vienna. We enter this war only where we are clearly forced into it because there are no other means of defending our rights.

It will be all the easier for us to conduct ourselves as belligerents in a high spirit of right and fairness because we act without animus, not with enmity toward a people or with the desire to bring any injury or disadvantage upon them, but only in armed opposition to an irresponsible government which has thrown aside all considerations of humanity and of right and is running amuck. We are, let me say again, the sincere friends of the German people, and shall desire nothing so much as the early reëstablishment of intimate relations of mutual advantage between us,—however hard it may be for them, for the time being, to believe that this is spoken from our hearts. We have borne with their present government through all these bitter months because of that friendship, exercising a patience and forbearance which would otherwise have been impossible. We shall, happily, still have an opportunity to prove that friendship in our daily attitude and actions toward the millions of men and women of German birth and native sympathy who live among us and share our life, and we shall be proud to prove it towards all who are in fact loyal to their neighbors and to the Government in the hour of test. They are, most of them, as true and loyal Americans as if they had never known any other fealty or allegiance. They will be prompt to stand with us in rebuking and restraining the few who may be of a different mind and purpose. If there should be disloyalty, it will be dealt with with a firm hand of stern repression; but, if it lifts its head at all, it will lift it only here and there and without countenance except from a lawless and malignant few.

It is a distressing and oppressive duty, Gentlemen of the Congress, which I have performed in thus addressing you. There are, it may be, many months of fiery trial and sacrifice ahead of us. It is a fearful thing to lead this great peaceful people into war, into the most terrible and disastrous of all wars, civilization itself seeming to be in the balance. But the right is more precious than peace, and we shall fight for the things which we have always carried nearest our hearts—for democracy, for the right of those who submit to authority to have a voice in their own governments, for the rights and liberties of small nations, for a universal dominion of right by such a concert of free peoples as shall bring peace and safety to all nations and make the world itself at last free. To such a task we can dedicate our lives and our fortunes, everything that we are and everything that we have, with the pride of those who know that the day has come when America is privileged to spend her blood and her might for the principles that gave her birth and happiness and the peace which she has treasured. God helping her, she can do no other.

The following historic address was delivered by President Wilson before a joint session of Congress on January 8, 1918.

THE FOURTEEN POINTS

GENTLEMEN OF THE CONGRESS: Once more, as repeatedly before, the spokesmen of the Central Empires have indicated their desire to discuss the objects of the war and the possible basis of a general peace. Parleys have been in progress at Brest-Litovsk between Russian representatives and representatives of the Central Powers to which the attention of all the belligerents has been invited for the purpose of ascertaining whether it may be possible to extend these parleys into a general conference with regard to terms of peace and settlement. The Russian representatives presented not only a perfectly definite statement of the principles upon which they would be willing to conclude peace, but also an equally definite program of the concrete application of those principles. The representatives of the Central Powers, on their part, presented an outline of settlement which, if much less definite, seemed susceptible of liberal interpretation until their specific program of practical terms was added. That program proposed no concessions at all, either to the sovereignty of Russia or to the preferences of the population with whose fortunes it dealt, but meant, in a word, that the Central Empires were to keep every foot of territory their armed forces had occupied—every province, every city, every point of vantage—as a permanent addition to their territories and their power. It is a reasonable conjecture that the general principles of settlement which they at first suggested originated with the more liberal statesmen of Germany and Austria, the men who have begun to feel the force of their own peoples' thought and purpose, while the concrete terms of actual settlement came from the military leaders who have no thought but to keep what they have got. The negotiations have been broken off. The Russian representatives were sincere and in earnest. They cannot entertain such proposals of conquest and domination.

The whole incident is full of significance. It is also full of perplexity. With whom are the Russian representatives dealing? For whom are the representatives of the Central Empires speaking? Are they speaking for the majorities of their respective Parliaments or for the minority parties, that military and imperialistic minority which has so far dominated their whole policy and controlled the affairs of Turkey and of the Balkan States, which have felt obliged to become their associates in this war? The Russian representatives have insisted, very justly, very wisely, and in the true spirit of modern democracy that the conferences they have been holding with the Teutonic and Turkish statesmen should be held within open, not closed, doors, and all the world has been audience, as was desired. To whom have we been listening, then? To those who speak the spirit and intention of the resolutions of the German Reichstag of the 9th of July last, the spirit and intention of the liberal leaders and parties of Germany, or to those who resist and defy that spirit and intention and insist upon conquest and subjugation? Or are we listening in fact, to both, unreconciled and in open and hopeless contradiction? These are very serious and pregnant questions. Upon the answer to them depends the peace of the world.

But whatever the results of the parleys at Brest-Litovsk, whatever the confusions of counsel and of purpose in the utterances of the spokesmen of the Central Empires, they have again attempted to acquaint the world with their objects in the war and have again challenged their adversaries to say what their objects are and what sort of settlement they would deem just and satisfactory. There is no good reason why that challenge should not be responded to, and responded to with the utmost candor. We did not wait for it. Not once, but again and again we have laid our whole thought and purpose before the world, not in general terms only, but each time with sufficient definition to make it clear what sort of definite terms of settlement must necessarily spring out of them. Within the last week Mr. Lloyd George has spoken with admirable candor and in admirable spirit for the people and Government of Great Britain. There is no confusion of counsel among the adversaries of the Central Powers, no uncertainty of principle, no vagueness of detail. The only secrecy of counsel, the only lack of fearless frankness, the only failure to make definite statement of the objects of the war, lies with Germany and her allies. The issues of life and death hang upon these definitions. No statesman who has the least conception of his responsibility ought for a moment to permit himself to continue this tragical and appalling outpouring of blood and treasure unless he is sure beyond a peradventure that the objects of the vital sacrifice are part and parcel of the very life of society and that the people for whom he speaks think them right and imperative as he does.

There is, moreover, a voice calling for these definitions of principle and of purpose which is, it seems to me, more thrilling and more compelling than any of the many moving voices with which the troubled air of the world is filled. It is the voice of the Russian people. They are prostrate and all but helpless, it would seem, before the grim power of Germany, which has hitherto known no relenting and no pity. Their power apparently is shattered. And yet their soul is not subservient. They will not yield either in principle or in action. Their conception of what is right, of what is humane and honorable for them to accept, has been stated with a frankness, a largeness of view, a generosity of spirit, and a universal human sympathy which must challenge the admiration of every friend of mankind; and they have refused to compound their ideals or desert others that they themselves may be safe. They call to us to say what it is that we desire, in what, if in anything our purpose and our spirit differ from theirs; and I believe that the people of the United States would wish me to respond with utter simplicity and frankness. Whether their present leaders believe it or not, it is our heartfelt desire and hope that some way may be opened whereby we may be privileged to assist the people of Russia to attain their utmost hope of liberty and ordered peace.

It will be our wish and purpose that the processes of peace, when they are begun, shall be absolutely open, and that they shall involve and permit henceforth no secret understandings of any kind. The day of conquest and aggrandizement is gone by; so is also the day of secret covenants entered into in the interest of particular Governments and likely at some unlooked-for moment to upset the peace of the world. It is this happy fact, now clear to the view of every public man whose thoughts do not still linger in an age that is dead and gone, which makes it possible for every nation whose purposes are consistent with justice and the peace of the world to avow now or at any other time the objects it has in view.

We entered this war because violations of right had occurred which touched us to the quick and made the life of our own people impossible unless they were corrected and the world secured once for all against their recurrence. What we demand in this war, therefore, is nothing peculiar to ourselves. It is that the world be made fit and safe to live in; and particularly that it be made safe for every peace-loving nation which, like our own, wishes to live its own life, determine its own institutions, be assured of justice and fair dealings by the other peoples of the world, as against force and selfish aggression. All of the peoples of the world are in effect partners in this interest and for our own part we see very clearly that unless justice be done to others it will not be done to us.

The program of the world's peace, therefore, is our program, and that program, the only possible program, as we see it, is this:

I. Open covenants of peace must be arrived at, after which there will surely be no private international action or rulings of any kind, but diplomacy shall proceed always frankly and in the public view.

II. Absolute freedom of navigation upon the seas, outside territorial waters, alike in peace and in war, except as the seas may be closed in whole or in part by international action for the enforcement of international covenants.

III. The removal, so far as possible, of all economic barriers and the establishment of an equality of trade conditions among all the nations consenting to the peace and associating themselves for its maintenance.

IV. Adequate guaranties given and taken that national armaments will reduce to the lowest point consistent with domestic safety.

V. Free, open-minded, and absolutely impartial adjustment of all colonial claims, based upon a strict observance of the principle that in determining all such questions of sovereignty the interests of the population concerned must have equal weight with the equitable claims of the government whose title is to be determined.

VI. The evacuation of all Russian territory and such a settlement of all questions affecting Russia as will secure the best and freest coöperation of the other nations of the world in obtaining for her an unhampered and unembarrassed opportunity for the independent determination of her own political development and national policy, and assure her of a sincere welcome into the society of free nations under institutions of her own choosing; and, more than a welcome, assistance also of every kind that she may need and may herself desire. The treatment accorded Russia by her sister nations in the months to come will be the acid test of their good-will, of their comprehension of her needs as distinguished from their own interests, and of their intelligent and unselfish sympathy.

VII. Belgium, the whole world will agree, must be evacuated and restored, without any attempt to limit the sovereignty which she enjoys in common with all other free nations. No other single act will serve as this will serve to restore confidence among the nations in the laws which they have themselves set and determined for the government of their relations with one another. Without this healing act the whole structure and validity of international law is forever impaired.

VIII. All French territory should be freed and the invaded portions restored, and the wrong done to France by Prussia in 1871 in the matter of Alsace-Lorraine, which has unsettled the peace of the world for nearly fifty years, should be righted, in order that peace may once more be made secure in the interest of all.

IX. A readjustment of the frontiers of Italy should be effected along clearly recognizable lines of nationality.

X. The peoples of Austria-Hungary, whose place among the nations we wish to see safeguarded and assured, should be accorded the freest opportunity of autonomous development.

XI. Roumania, Serbia, and Montenegro should be evacuated; occupied territories restored; Serbia accorded free and secure access to the sea; and the relations of the several Balkan States to one another determined by friendly counsel along historically established lines of allegiance and nationality; and international guaranties of the political and economic independence and territorial integrity of the several Balkan States should be entered into.

XII. The Turkish portions of the present Ottoman Empire should be assured a secure sovereignty, but the other nationalities which are now under Turkish rule should be assured an undoubted security of life and an absolutely unmolested opportunity of autonomous development, and the Dardanelles should be permanently opened as a free passage to the ships and commerce of all nations under international guaranties.

XIII. An independent Polish state should be erected which should include the territories inhabited by indisputably Polish populations, which should be assured a free and secure access to the sea, and whose political and economic independence and territorial integrity should, be guaranteed by international covenant.

XIV. A general association of nations must be formed under specific covenants for the purpose of affording mutual guaranties of political independence and territorial integrity to great and small states alike.

In regard to these essential rectifications of wrong and assertions of right, we feel ourselves to be intimate partners of all the Governments and peoples associated together against the imperialists. We cannot be separated in interest or divided in purpose. We stand together until the end.

For such arrangements and covenants we are willing to fight and to continue to fight until they are achieved; but only because we wish the right to prevail and desire a just and stable peace, such as can be secured only by removing the chief provocations to war, which this program does remove. We have no jealousy of German greatness, and there is nothing in this program that impairs it. We grudge her no achievement or distinction of learning or of pacific enterprise such as have made her record very bright and very enviable. We do not wish to injure her or to block in any way her legitimate influence or power. We do not wish to fight her either with arms or with hostile arrangements of trade, if she is willing to associate herself with us and the other peace-loving nations of the world in covenants of justice and law and fair dealing. We wish her only to accept a place of equality among the peoples of the world—the new world in which we now live—instead of a place of mastery.

Neither do we presume to suggest to her any alteration or modification of her institutions. But it is necessary, we must frankly say, and necessary as a preliminary to any intelligent dealings with her on our part, that we should know whom her spokesmen speak for when they speak to us, whether for the Reichstag majority or for the military party and the men whose creed is imperial domination.

We have spoken now, surely, in terms too concrete to admit of any further doubt or question. An evident principle runs through the whole program I have outlined. It is the principle of justice to all peoples and nationalities, and their right to live on equal terms of liberty and safety with one another, whether they be strong or weak. Unless this principle be made its foundation, no part of the structure of international justice can stand. The people of the United States could act upon no other principle, and to the vindication of this principle they are ready to devote their lives, their honor, and everything that they possess. The moral climax of this, the culminating and final war for human liberty, has come, and they are ready to put their own strength, their own highest purpose, their own integrity and devotion to the test.

President Wilson opened the discussion on the League of Nations before the Peace Conference, in Paris, on January 25, 1919, as follows.

THE LEAGUE OF NATIONS

MR. CHAIRMAN:—I consider it a distinguished privilege to be permitted to open the discussion in this Conference on the League of Nations. We have assembled for two purposes: to make the present settlements which have been rendered necessary by this war, and also to secure the peace of the world, not only by the present settlements, but by the arrangements we shall make at this Conference for its maintenance. The League of Nations seems to me to be necessary for both of these purposes. There are many complicated questions connected with the present settlements which perhaps cannot be successfully worked out to an ultimate issue by the decisions we shall arrive at here. I can easily conceive that many of these settlements will need subsequent consideration, that many of the decisions we make shall need subsequent alteration in some degree; for, if I may judge by my own study of some of these questions, they are not susceptible of confident judgments at present.

It is, therefore, necessary that we should set up some machinery by which the work of this Conference should be rendered complete. We have assembled here for the purpose of doing very much more than making the present settlements that are necessary. We are assembled under very peculiar conditions of world opinion. I may say, without straining the point, that we are not representatives of governments, but representatives of peoples. It will not suffice to satisfy governmental circles anywhere. It is necessary that we should satisfy the opinion of mankind. The burdens of this war have fallen in an unusual degree upon the whole population of the countries involved. I do not need to draw for you the picture of how the burden has been thrown back from the front upon the older men, upon the women, upon the children, upon the homes of the civilized world, and how the real strain of the war has come where the eye of government could not reach, but where the heart of humanity beat. We are bidden by these people to make a peace which will make them secure. We are bidden by these people to see to it that this strain does not come upon them, and I venture to say that it has been possible for them to bear this strain because they hoped that those who represented them could get together after this war and make such another sacrifice unnecessary.

It is a solemn obligation on our part, therefore, to make permanent arrangements that justice shall be rendered and peace maintained. This is the central object of our meeting. Settlements may be temporary, but the action of the nations in the interest of peace and justice must be permanent. We can set up permanent processes. We may not be able to set up permanent decisions. Therefore, it seems to me that we must take, so far as we can, a picture of the world into our minds.

Is it not a startling circumstance, for one thing, that the great discoveries of science, that the quiet studies of men in laboratories, that the thoughtful developments which have taken place in quiet lecture-rooms, have now been turned to the destruction of civilization? The powers of destruction have not so much multiplied as gained facility. The enemy whom we have just overcome had at his seats of learning some of the principal centers of scientific study and discovery, and he used them in order to make destruction sudden and complete; and only the watchful, continuous coöperation of men can see to it that science, as well as armed men, is kept within the harness of civilization.

In a sense, the United States is less interested in this subject than the other nations here assembled. With her great territory and her extensive sea borders, it is less likely that the United States should suffer from the attack of enemies than that many of the other nations here should suffer; and the ardor of the United States—for it is a very deep and genuine ardor—for the society of nations is not an ardor springing out of fear or apprehension, but an ardor springing out of the ideals which have come to consciousness in this war. In coming into this war the United States never for a moment thought that she was intervening in the politics of Europe, or the politics of Asia, or the politics of any part of the world. Her thought was that all the world had now become conscious that there was a single cause which turned upon the issues of this war. That was the cause of justice and of liberty for men of every kind and place. Therefore, the United States would feel that her part in this war had been played in vain if there ensued upon it a body of European settlements. She would feel that she could not take part in guaranteeing those European settlements unless that guaranty involved the continuous superintendence of the peace of the world by the associated nations of the world.

Therefore, it seems to me that we must concert our best judgment in order to make this League of Nations a vital thing—not merely a formal thing, not an occasional thing, not a thing sometimes called into life to meet an exigency, but always functioning in watchful attendance upon the interests of the nations, and that its continuity should be a vital continuity; that it should have functions that are continuing functions, and that do not permit an intermission of its watchfulness and of its labor; that it should be the eye of the nations to keep watch upon the common interest, an eye that did not slumber, an eye that was everywhere watchful and attentive.

And if we do not make it vital, what shall we do? We shall disappoint the expectations of the peoples. This is what their thought centers upon. I have had the very delightful experience of visiting several nations since I came to this side of the water, and every time the voice of the body of the people reached me through any representative, at the front of the plea stood the hope for the League of Nations. Gentlemen, the select classes of mankind are no longer the governors of mankind. The fortunes of mankind are now in the hands of the plain people of the whole world. Satisfy them, and you have not only justified their confidence, but established peace. Fail to satisfy them, and no arrangement that you can make will either set up or steady the peace of the world.

You can imagine, gentlemen, I dare say, the sentiments and the purpose with which representatives of the United States support this great project for a League of Nations. We regard it as the keystone of the whole program which expressed our purposes and ideals in this war and which the associated nations accepted as the basis of the settlement. If we return to the United States without having made every effort in our power to realize this program, we should return to meet the merited scorn of our fellow-citizens. For they are a body that constitutes a great democracy. They expect their leaders to speak their thoughts and no private purpose of their own. They expect their representatives to be their servants. We have no choice but to obey their mandate. But it is with the greatest enthusiasm and pleasure that we accept that mandate; and because this is the keystone of the whole fabric, we have pledged our every purpose to it, as we have to every item of the fabric. We would not dare abate a single item of the program which constitutes our instruction. We would not dare compromise upon any matter as the champion of this thing—this peace of the world, this attitude of justice, this principle that we are the masters of no people, but are here to see that every people in the world shall choose its own masters and govern its own destinies, not as we wish but as it wishes. We are here to see, in short, that the very foundations of this war are swept away.

Those foundations were the private choice of small coteries of civil rulers and military staffs. Those foundations were the aggression of great powers upon small. Those foundations were the holding together of empires of unwilling subjects by the duress of arms. Those foundations were the power of small bodies of men to work their will and use mankind as pawns in a game. And nothing less than the emancipation of the world from these things will accomplish peace. You can see that the representatives of the United States are, therefore, never put to the embarrassment of choosing a way of expediency, because they have laid down for them the unalterable lines of principle. And, thank God, those lines have been accepted as the lines of settlement by all the high-minded men who have had to do with the beginnings of this great business.

I hope, Mr. Chairman, that when it is known, as I feel confident it will be known, that we have adopted the principles of the League of Nations and mean to work out that principle in effective action, we shall by that single thing have lifted a great part of the load of anxiety from the hearts of men everywhere. We stand in a peculiar case. As I go about the streets here I see everywhere the American uniform. Those men came into the war after they had uttered our purposes. They came as crusaders, not merely to win a war, but to win a cause; and I am responsible to them, for it fell to me to formulate the purposes for which I asked them to fight, and I, like them, must be a crusader for these things, whatever it costs and whatever it may be necessary to do, in honor, to accomplish the object for which they fought.

I have been glad to find from day to day that there is no question of our standing alone in this matter, for there are champions of this cause upon every hand. I am merely avowing this in order that you may understand why, perhaps, it fell to us, who are disengaged from the politics of this great continent and of the Orient, to suggest that this was the keystone of the arch, and why it occurred to the generous mind of our President to call upon me to open this debate. It is not because we alone represent this idea, but because it is our privilege to associate ourselves with you in representing it.

I have only tried in what I have said to give you the fountains of the enthusiasm which is within us for this thing, for those fountains spring, it seems to me, from all the ancient wrongs and sympathies of mankind, and the very pulse of the world seems to beat to the surface in this enterprise.

William Edgar Borah
[1865–1940]

A member of the United States Senate from Idaho, from 1907 to the day of his death, William Edgar Borah became one of the fore-most speakers and debaters of that body. He was considered a great authority on the Constitution and international affairs. Borah was a leading opponent of President Wilson on the issue of the League of Nations. Here are parts of the speech which Borah delivered in the Senate on November 19, 1919, when the peace treaty was under consideration.

THE LEAGUE OF NATIONS

IF THE LEAGUE includes the affairs of the world, does it not include the affairs of all the world? Is there any limitation of the jurisdiction of the council or of the assembly upon the question of peace or war? Does it not have now, under the reservations, the same as it had before, the power to deal with all matters of peace or war throughout the entire world? How shall you keep from meddling in the affairs of Europe or keep Europe from meddling in the affairs of America?

Mr. President, there is another and even more commanding reason why I shall record my vote against this treaty. It imperils what I conceive to be the underlying, the very first principles of this Republic. It is in conflict with the right of our people to govern themselves free from all restraint, legal or moral, of foreign powers. It challenges every tenet of my political faith. If this faith were one of my contriving, if I stood here to assert principles of government of my own evolving, I might well be charged with intolerable presumption, for we all recognize the ability of those who urge a different course. But I offer in justification of my course nothing of my own—save the deep and abiding reverence I have for those whose policies I humbly but most ardently support. I claim no merit save fidelity to American principles and devotion to American ideals as they were wrought out from time to time by those who built the Republic and as they have extended and maintained throughout these years. In opposing the treaty I do nothing more than decline to renounce and tear out of my life the sacred traditions which throughout fifty years have been translated into my whole intellectual and moral being. I will not, I cannot, give up my belief that America must, not alone for the happiness of her own people, but for the moral guidance and greater contentment of the world, be permitted to live her own life. Next to the tie which binds a man to his God is the tie which binds a man to his country, and all schemes, all plans, however ambitious and fascinating they seem in their proposal, but which would embarrass or entangle and impede or shackle her sovereign will, which would compromise her freedom of action I unhesitatingly put behind me.

Sir, we are told that this treaty means peace. Even so, I would not pay the price. Would you purchase peace at the cost of any part of our independence? We could have had peace in 1776—the price was high, but we could have had it. James Otis, Sam Adams, Hancock, and Warren were surrounded by those who urged peace and British rule. All through that long and trying struggle, particularly when the clouds of adversity lowered upon the cause there was a cry of peace—let us have peace. We could have had peace in 1860; Lincoln was counseled by men of great influence and accredited wisdom to let our brothers—and, thank heaven, they are brothers—depart in peace. But the tender, loving Lincoln, bending under the fearful weight of impending civil war, an apostle of peace, refused to pay the price, and a reunited country will praise his name forevermore—bless it because he refused peace at the price of national honor and national integrity. Peace upon any other basis than national independence, peace purchased at the cost of any part of our national integrity, is fit only for slaves, and even when purchased at such a price it is a delusion, for it cannot last.

But your treaty does not mean peace—far, very far, from it. If we are to judge the future by the past it means war. Is there any guaranty of peace other than the guaranty which comes of the control of the war-making power by the people? Yet what great rule of democracy does the treaty leave unassailed? The people in whose keeping alone you can safely lodge the power of peace or war nowhere, at no time and in no place, have any voice in this scheme for world peace. Autocracy which has bathed the world in blood for centuries reigns supreme. Democracy is everywhere excluded. This, you say, means peace.

Can you hope for peace when love of country is disregarded in your scheme, when the spirit of nationality is rejected, scoffed at? Yet what law of that moving and mysterious force does your treaty not deny? With a ruthlessness unparalleled your treaty in a dozen instances runs counter to the divine law of nationality. Peoples who speak the same language, kneel at the same ancestral tombs, moved by the same traditions, animated by a common hope, are torn asunder, broken in pieces, divided, and parceled out to antagonistic nations. And this you call justice. This, you cry, means peace. Peoples who have dreamed of independence, struggled and been patient, sacrificed and been hopeful, peoples who were told that through this Peace Conference they should realize the aspirations of centuries, have again had their hopes dashed to earth. One of the most striking and commanding figures in this war, soldier and statesman, turned away from the peace table at Versailles declaring to the world, "The promise of the new life, the victory of the great humane ideals, for which the peoples have shed their blood and given their treasure without stint, the fulfillment of their aspirations toward a new international order and a fairer and better world are not written into the treaty." No; your treaty means injustice. It means slavery. It means war. And to all this you ask this Republic to become a party. You ask it to abandon the creed under which it has grown to power and accept the creed of autocracy, the creed of repression and force.

Mr. President, I turn from this scheme based upon force to another scheme, planned one hundred and forty-three years ago in old Independence Hall, in the city of Philadelphia, based upon liberty. I like it better. I have become so accustomed to believe in it that it is difficult for me to reject it out of hand. I have difficulty in subscribing to the new creed of oppression, the creed of dominant and subject peoples. I feel a reluctance to give up the belief that all men are created equal—the eternal principle in government that all governments derive their just powers from the consent of the governed. I cannot get my consent to exchange the doctrine of George Washington for the doctrine of Frederick the Great translated into mendacious phrases of peace. I go back to that serene and masterful soul who pointed the way to power and glory for the new and then weak Republic, and whose teachings and admonitions even in our majesty and dominance we dare not disregard.

I know well the answer to my contention. It has been piped about of late from a thousand sources—venal sources, disloyal sources, sinister sources—that Washington's wisdom was of his day only and that his teachings are out of fashion—things long since sent to the scrap heap of history—that while he was great in character and noble in soul he was untrained in the arts of statescraft and unlearned in the science of government. The puny demagogue, the barren editor, the sterile professor now vie with each other in apologizing for the temporary and commonplace expedients which the Father of our Country felt constrained to adopt in building a republic!

What is the test of statesmanship? Is it the formation of theories, the utterance of abstract and incontrovertible truths, or is it the capacity and the power to give to a people that concrete thing called liberty, that vital and indispensable thing in human happiness called free institutions and to establish over all and above all the blessed and eternal reign of order and law? If this be the test, where shall we find another whose name is entitled to be written beside the name of Washington? His judgment and poise in the hour of turmoil and peril, his courage and vision in times of adversity, his firm grasp of fundamental principles, his almost inspired power to penetrate the future and read there the result, the effect of policies, have never been excelled, if equaled, by any of the world's commonwealth builders. Peter the Great, William the Silent, and Cromwell the Protector, these and these alone perhaps are to be associated with his name as the builders of States and the founders of governments. But in exaltation of moral purpose, in the unselfish character of his work, in the durability of his policies, in the permanency of the institutions which he more than any one else called into effect, his service to mankind stands out separate and apart in a class by itself. The works of these other great builders, where are they now? But the work of Washington is still the most potent influence for the advancement of civilization and the freedom of the race.

Reflect for a moment over his achievements. He led the Revolutionary Army to victory. He was the very first to suggest a union instead of a confederacy. He presided over and counseled with great wisdom the convention which framed the Constitution. He guided the Government through its first perilous years. He gave dignity and stability and honor to that which was looked upon by the world as a passing experiment, and finally, my friends, as his own peculiar and particular contribution to the happiness of his countrymen and to the cause of the Republic, he gave us his great foreign policy under which we have lived and prospered and strengthened for nearly a century and a half. This policy is the most sublime confirmation of his genius as a statesman. It was then, and it now is, an indispensable part of our whole scheme of government. It is to-day a vital, indispensable element in our entire plan, purpose, and mission as a nation. To abandon it is nothing less than a betrayal of the American people. I say betrayal deliberately, in view of the suffering and the sacrifice which will follow in the wake of such a course.

But under the stress and strain of these extraordinary days, when strong men are being swept down by the onrushing forces of disorder and change, when the most sacred things of life, the most cherished hopes of a Christian world seem to yield to the mad forces of discontent—just such days as Washington passed through when the mobs of Paris, wild with new liberty and drunk with power, challenged the established institutions of all the world, but his steadfast soul was unshaken—under these conditions come again we are about to abandon this policy so essential to our happiness and tranquillity as a people and our stability as a Government. No leader with his commanding influence and his unquailing courage stands forth to stem the current. But what no leader can or will do, experience, bitter experience, and the people of this country in whose keeping, after all, thank God, is the Republic, will ultimately do. If we abandon his leadership and teachings, we will go back. We will return to this policy. Americanism shall not, cannot die. We may go back in sackcloth and ashes, but we will return to the faith of the fathers. America will live her own life. The independence of this Republic will have its defenders. Thousands have suffered and died for it, and their sons and daughters are not of the breed who will be betrayed into the hands of foreigners. The noble face of the Father of his Country, so familiar to every boy and girl, looking out from the walls of the Capitol in stern reproach, will call those who come here for public service to a reckoning. The people of our beloved country will finally speak, and we will return to the policy which we now abandon. America, disenthralled and free, in spite of all these things, will continue her mission in the cause of peace, of freedom, and of civilization.

Eugene Victor Debs
[1855–1926]

Eugene Victor Debs, of Indiana, was prominently identified with the labor and Socialist movement of the country throughout his entire life. He led the famous Pullman strike of 1894 and was one of the organizers of the Socialist party. Debs was frequently the Socialist candidate for President and its greatest orator. He opposed the American entry into the World War and was sentenced to prison after being convicted on the charge of obstructing the draft. Here is part of his speech delivered before the court, on receiving sentence in September, 1918.

ON RECEIVING SENTENCE

YOUR HONOR, years ago I recognized my kinship with all living beings, and I made up my mind that I was not one bit better than the meanest of earth. I said then, I say now, that while there is a lower class, I am in it; while there is a criminal element, I am of it; while there is a soul in prison, I am not free.

If the law under which I have been convicted is a good law, then there is no reason why sentence should not be pronounced upon me. I listened to all that was said in this court in support and justification of this law, but my mind remains unchanged. I look upon it as a despotic enactment in flagrant conflict with democratic principles and with the spirit of free institutions.

Your Honor, I have stated in this court that I am opposed to the form of our present Government; that I am opposed to the social system in which we live; that I believed in the change of both—but by perfectly peaceable and orderly means.

I believe, Your Honor, in common with all Socialists, that this nation ought to own and control its industries. I believe, as all Socialists do, that all things that are jointly needed and used ought to be jointly owned—that industry, the basis of life, instead of being the private property of the few and operated for their enrichment, ought to be the common property of all, democratically administered in the interest of all.

I have been accused, Your Honor, of being an enemy of the soldier. I hope I am laying no flattering unction to my soul when I say that I don't believe the soldier has a more sympathetic friend than I am. If I had my way there would be no soldiers. But I realize the sacrifice they are making, Your Honor. I can think of them. I can feel for them. I can sympathize with them. That is one of the reasons why I have been doing what little has been in my power to bring about a condition of affairs in this country worthy of the sacrifices they have made and that they are now making in its behalf.

Your Honor, I wish to make acknowledgment of my thanks to the counsel for the defense. They have not only defended me with exceptional legal ability, but with a personal attachment and devotion of which I am deeply sensible, and which I can never forget.

Your Honor, I ask no mercy. I plead for no immunity. I realize that finally the right must prevail. I never more clearly comprehended than now the great struggle between the powers of greed on the one hand and upon the other the rising hosts of freedom.

I can see the dawn of a better day of humanity. The people are awakening. In due course of time they will come to their own.

When the mariner, sailing over tropic seas, looks for relief from his weary watch, he turns his eyes toward the Southern Cross, burning luridly above the tempest-tossed ocean. As the midnight approaches, the Southern Cross begins to bend, and the whirling worlds change their places, and with starry finger-points the Almighty marks the passage of time upon the dial of the universe, and though no bell may beat the glad tidings, the lookout knows that the midnight is passing—that relief and rest are close at hand.

Let the people take heart and hope everywhere, for the cross is bending, the midnight is passing, and joy cometh with the morning.

Your Honor, I thank you, and I thank all of this court for their courtesy, for their kindness, which I shall remember always.

I am prepared to receive your sentence.

Elihu Root

[1845–1937]

Elihu Root, of New York, was one of the foremost lawyers of the country and one of the most prominent leaders of the Republican party. He was Secretary of State under Presidents Theodore Roosevelt and William Howard Taft, and a member of the United States Senate for many years. Root was one of the few Republican leaders who favored the League of Nations. Following is the speech he made at a dinner of the Woodrow Wilson Foundation on December 27, 1926, on being honored with its award for that year.

A PLEA FOR THE LEAGUE OF NATIONS

MR. CHAIRMAN, Mrs. Wilson, Ladies and Gentlemen: I beg you to believe that I deeply appreciate the honor that you do me. The finest thing about it is the spirit in which it was done, which was able to brush aside as incidental long political opposition, and not a few differences of opinion publicly avowed and to rest upon fundamental identity of purpose with fitting proportion, proportion suitable to the high distinction of the great President whose memory you celebrate, and suitable to the deep and permanent purpose of your organization. In foreign affairs it is peculiarly true that the spirit in which work is done is everything.

M. Briand in the Washington Conference five years ago said, very wisely as well as very eloquently, that in Europe there must be moral disarmament before there could be physical disarmament, and ever since he has been applying to the disturbed conditions of Europe that sage philosophy, to his own immortal glory and to the great benefit of all mankind.

Nations always will differ. They differ in inherited characteristics and predilections and traditions and modes of thought and feeling, but there never is a difference so great that it cannot be peaceably settled if approached in the right spirit. And there never can be a difference so trifling that it may not be made the occasion of war if it is approached in the wrong spirit.

We are confronted by some difficulties in this regard in this country. We have long been a member of the community of nations and adjusting with our sister nations the rights and obligations and duties of members of that community arising from the necessity of neighborhood by means of the modes of diplomatic procedure which had been built up in the course of centuries—foreign officers and ambassadors and ministers and diplomatic notes and diplomatic memoranda and treaties and mediation and conciliation and so forth—but at the close of the Great War, when the greater part of the nations of the world united in the League of Nations, they entered upon a new mode of regulating their conduct with regard to each other and adjusting the differences that arise in the ordinary course of international affairs.

Instead of the old method, they proceed by formal conference of Council and Assembly and a large part of the business which foreign officers and ambassadors used to do in the old methods are now done through the machinery of the League. We have stood out of the League and we are going on in the old ways, by the old methods, and the utmost friendly consideration is needed to reconcile the conduct of international affairs in the new way by our sister nations across the Atlantic, and the old way by ourselves.

It is a very difficult thing to make a horse that trots and a horse that gallops pull evenly in the same team. If the League of Nations had been formed against the United States, the matter would be simple, but it was not formed against the United States, it was formed in friendship to the United States. It was formed in the acceptation that we would be a member, and it was formed with the understanding, based upon the judgment of our representative, our negotiator, our agent in the Conference at Paris, that it would be acceptable to the people of the United States.

We had a perfect right to refuse to enter into the treaty. Fair notice of that was given by the provisions of our Constitution. Nevertheless, President Wilson, when he went to Paris, was our representative; he was our negotiator; he was our agent; he was the only one to whom the nations of Europe could look to ascertain what would be satisfactory to the people of the United States. When the League was completed, when we refused to become a member of it, and Europe was left with an incomplete organization, left without the support of the most populous and richest and most potentially powerful nation whose name was written into the covenant; when Europe was left with that incomplete organization to deal with the world parties that were set loose by the adjustment of territory and of sovereignty under the Treaty of Versailles, what would we naturally have said, what would any gentleman have said to another who had been brought into such an untoward condition by his representatives and agent? Mistaken, but in good faith, what but an expression of the most sincere regret; what but an expression of a confirmed intention and a strong desire to do everything possible to prevent our abstaining from the League from being injurious to our old friends.

What did we do? Has there ever been an exhibition by America of friendship or sympathy with the League and its work? Unfortunately, the controversy which resulted in our determining not to enter the League was violent and bitter feelings were aroused, and those feelings came to be carried over to the League itself, and it came to be a common thing that we would read in the newspapers and hear in speech and conversation expressions of expectation that the League would fail, and evident pleasure when it seemed that it might fail. Those feelings were extended to the Court which was presently created to cover another part of the field in the same effort to bring about permanent peace. Reprisals began to come from the other side. Unkind expressions never can be confined to one side. Reprisals began to come, disagreeable things were said upon the other side, and a period of pin pricks has proceeded for years. It has colored and conditioned the consideration of the debts between the foreign nations and ourselves.

That is not all. Not only did we forget the demands of honorable obligation resting upon old associations and fellowship and the expectations raised by our own representative, but consider the service that was rendered by the League and by the Court. For these years the League in the political field and the Court in the judicial field have been rendering the best service in the cause of peace known to the history of civilization; incomparably the best.

War results from a state of mind. These institutions have been teaching the people of Europe to think in terms of peace rather than in terms of war. They have been teaching them by actual practice, by things done; to think of conference instead of war, about policies; to think of argument and proof and judicial judgment, instead of war, about rights; teaching them to acquire habits of thinking and of acting that way. The question of war or peace for the next generation is being settled now, to-day, by the character and habits of thought and feeling, the standards of conduct which the people of the world are learning to guide them in the exigencies of the future.

We, the great peace-loving people, what have we done to help in this wonderful new work? No sympathy, no moral support, no brotherhood—No! Our Executive Department has done the best it could, for Governments can do but little. It is the people, the power of the people behind the Government that means everything.

We have allowed insensate prejudice, camouflaged but futile phrases to appear, but falsely appear, to represent the true heart of the American people, with all its idealism, with its breadth of human sympathy, with its strong desire that our country should do its share for peace and happiness and noble life in all the world.

Are the qualities which saved the soul of a nation worth that wealth and prosperity? But these qualities do not long survive disuse. The repercussions of our domestic strife seem to have prevented the effectiveness of our noblest impulses.

These, my friends, are some of the evils visited upon us by a hateful and contentious spirit from which may the good Lord deliver us.

Oliver Wendell Holmes
[1841–1935]

Oliver Wendell Holmes, distinguished member of the Supreme Court for over half a century, delivered the following gem over the radio on March 7, 1931, on the occasion of the celebration of his ninetieth birthday.

"LIVE—I AM COMING!"

IN THIS SYMPOSIUM my part is only to sit in silence. To express one's feelings as the end draws near is too intimate a task.

But I may mention one thought that comes to me as a listener in. The riders in a race do not stop short when they reach the goal. There is a little finishing canter before coming to a standstill. There is time to hear the kind voices of friends and to say to oneself: The work is done. But just as one says that, the answer comes: "The race is over, but the work never is done while the power to work remains. The canter that brings you to a standstill need not be only coming to rest. It cannot be, while you still live. For to live is to function. That is all there is to living."

And so I end with a line from a Latin poet who uttered the message more than fifteen hundred years ago, "Death plucks my ear and says: Live—I am coming."

Sir John A. Macdonald

[1815–1891]

Sir John A. Macdonald was the first premier of Canada, holding that post from 1867 until his death, with the exception of five years, 1873-78. A leader of the Conservative party, he was highly respected for his efforts towards Canadian unity and prestige. He was a leader in the movement for Canadian federation as the speech, reproduced in part here, shows. Sir John delivered this speech before the Canadian parliament in 1865.

ON CANADIAN FEDERATION

MR. SPEAKER: In fulfillment of the promise made by the government to Parliament at its last session, I have moved this resolution. I have had the honor of being charged, on behalf of the government, to submit a scheme for the confederation of all the British North American Provinces—a scheme which has been received, I am glad to say, with general if not universal approbation in Canada. The scheme, as propounded through the press, has received almost no opposition. While there may be occasionally, here and there, expressions of dissent from some of the details, yet the scheme as a whole has met with almost universal approval, and the government has the greatest satisfaction in presenting it to this House.

Although we have nominally a legislative union in Canada; although we sit in one Parliament, supposed constitutionally to represent the people without regard to sections or localities—yet we know, as a matter of fact, that since the union in 1841 we have had a federal union, that, in matters affecting Upper Canada solely, members from that section claimed and generally exercised the right of exclusive legislation, while members from Lower Canada legislated in matters affecting only their own section. We have had a federal union in fact, though a legislative union in name; and in the hot contests of late years, if on any occasion a measure affecting any one section were interfered with by the members from the other—if, for instance, a measure locally affecting Upper Canada were carried or defeated, against the wishes of its majority, by one from Lower Canada—my honorable friend, the president of the Council, and his friends denounced with all their energy and ability such legislation as an infringement of the rights of the Upper Province. Just in the same way, if any act concerning Lower Canada were pressed into law, against the wishes of the majority of her representatives, by those from Upper Canada, the Lower Canadians would rise as one man and protest against such a violation of their peculiar rights.

The whole scheme of confederation as propounded by the conference as agreed to and sanctioned by the Canadian government, and as now presented for the consideration of the people and the legislature, bears upon its face the marks of compromise. Of necessity there must have been a great deal of mutual discussion. When we think of the representatives of five colonies, all supposed to have different interests, meeting together, charged with the duty of protecting those interests and of pressing the views of their own localities and sections, it must be admitted that had we not met in a spirit of conciliation and with an anxious desire to promote this union; if we had not been impressed with the idea contained in the words of the resolution—"that the best interests and present and future prosperity of British North America would be promoted by a federal union under the crown of Great Britain"—all our efforts might have proved to be of no avail. If we had not felt that, after coming to this conclusion, we were bound to set aside our private opinions on matters of detail; if we had not felt ourselves bound to look at what was practicable—not obstinately rejecting the opinions of others nor adhering to our own; if we had not met, I say, in a spirit of conciliation, and with an anxious, overruling desire to form one people under one government, we never would have succeeded.

In the constitution we propose to continue the system of responsible government which has existed in this Province since 1841, and which has long obtained in the mother country. This is a feature of our constitution as we have it now, and as we shall have it in the federation in which, I think, we avoid one of the great defects in the constitution of the United States. There the President, during his term of office, is in a great measure a despot, a one-man power, with the command of the naval and military forces; with an immense amount of patronage as head of the executive, and with the veto power as a branch of the legislature; perfectly uncontrolled by responsible advisers, his Cabinet being departmental officers merely, whom he is not obliged by the Constitution to consult with unless he chooses to do so.

With us the sovereign, or in this country the representative of the sovereign, can act only on the advice of his ministers, those ministers being responsible to the people through Parliament. Prior to the formation of the American Union, as we all know, the different states which entered into it were separate colonies. They had no connection with each other further than that of having a common sovereign, just as with us at present. Their constitutions and their laws were different. They might and did legislate against each other, and when they revolted against the mother country they acted as separate sovereignties and carried on the war by a kind of treaty of alliance against the common enemy. Ever since the Union was formed, the difficulty of what is called "state rights" has existed, and this had much to do in bringing on the present unhappy war in the United States. They commenced, in fact, at the wrong end. They declared by their Constitution that each state was a sovereignty in itself, and that all the powers incident to a sovereignty belonged to each state, except those powers which by the Constitution were conferred upon the general government and Congress.

Here we have adopted a different system. We have strengthened the general government. We have given the general legislature all the great subjects of legislation. We have conferred on them, not only specifically and in detail, all the powers which are incident to sovereignty, but we have expressly declared that all subjects of general interest not distinctly and exclusively conferred upon the local governments and local legislatures shall be conferred upon the general government and legislature. We have thus avoided that great source of weakness which has been the cause of the disruption of the United States. We have avoided all conflict of jurisdiction and authority, and if this constitution is carried out, as it will be in full detail in the imperial act to be passed if the colonies adopt the scheme, we will have in fact, as I said before, all the advantages of a legislative union under one administration, with at the same time the guaranties for local institutions and for local laws which are insisted upon by so many in the Provinces now, I hope, to be united.

I think it is well that in framing our constitution our first act should have been to recognize the sovereignty of her Majesty. I believe that while England has no desire to lose her colonies, but wishes to retain them; while I am satisfied that the public mind of England would deeply regret the loss of these Provinces—yet, if the people of British North America, after full deliberation, had stated that they considered it was for their interest, for the advantage of the future British North America, to sever the tie, such is the generosity of the people of England that, whatever their desire to keep these colonies, they would not seek to compel us to remain unwilling subjects of the British crown. If, therefore, at the conference, we had arrived at the conclusion that it was for the interest of these Provinces that a severance should take place, I am sure that her Majesty and the imperial Parliament would have sanctioned that severance. We accordingly felt that there was a propriety in giving a distinct declaration of opinion on that point, and that in framing the constitution its first sentence should declare that "The executive authority or government shall be vested in the sovereign of the United Kingdom of Great Britain and Ireland, and be administered according to the well-understood principles of the British constitution, by the sovereign personally, or by the representative of the sovereign duly authorized."

We provide that "the executive authority shall be administered by the sovereign personally, or by the representative of the sovereign duly authorized." It is too much to expect that the queen should vouchsafe us her personal governance or presence except to pay us—as the heir-apparent to the throne, our future sovereign, has already paid us—the graceful compliment of a visit. The executive authority must therefore be administered by her Majesty's representative. We place no restriction on her Majesty's prerogative in the selection of her representative. As it is now, so it will be if this constitution is adopted. The sovereign has unrestricted freedom of choice. Whether in making her selection, she may send us one of her own family, a royal prince, as a viceroy to rule over us, or one of the great statesmen of England to represent her, we know not. We leave that to her Majesty in all confidence. But we may be permitted to hope that when the union takes place, and we become the great country which British North America is certain to be, it will be an object worthy the ambition of the statesmen of England to be charged with presiding over our destinies.

Sir Wilfrid Laurier
[1841–1919]

Sir Wilfrid Laurier, of French-Canadian origin, became Liberal leader in 1887 and Premier of Canada in 1896. He held that office for fourteen years. When the World War began in 1914, Laurier defended Great Britain's cause and supported all measures to aid it in the prosecution of war, excepting conscription. Here are parts of an address which Sir Wilfrid delivered in Chicago on October 9, 1899.

CANADA, ENGLAND, AND THE UNITED STATES

I FEEL that though the relations between Canada and the United States are good, though they are brotherly, though they are satisfactory, in my judgment they are not as good, as brotherly, as satisfactory as they ought to be. We are of the same stock. We spring from the same races on one side of the line as on the other. We speak the same language. We have the same literature, and for more than a thousand years we have had a common history.

Let me recall to you the lines which, in the darkest days of the Civil War, the Puritan poet of America issued to England:—

> "O Englishmen! O Englishmen!
> In hope and creed,
> In blood and tongue, are brothers,
> We all are heirs of Runnymede."

Brothers we are, in the language of your own poet. May I not say that, while our relations are not always as brotherly as they ought to have been? May I not ask, Mr. President, on the part of Canada and on the part of the United States, if we are sometimes too prone to stand by the full conceptions of our rights, and exact all our rights to the last pound of flesh? May I not ask if there have not been too often between us petty quarrels, which happily do not wound the heart of the nation?

Sir, I am proud to say, in the presence of the Chief Executive of the United States, that it is the belief of the Canadian government that we should make the government of President McKinley and the present government of Canada, with the assent of Great Britain, so to work together to remove all causes of dissension between us. And whether the commission which sat first in the old city of Quebec and sat next in the city of Washington—but whether sitting in Quebec or sitting in Washington, I am sorry to say the result has not been commensurate with our expectations.

Shall I speak my mind? (Cries of "Yes!") We met a stumbling block in the question of the Alaskan frontier. Well, let me say here and now the commission would not settle that question, and referred it to their particular governments, and they are now dealing with it. May I be permitted to say here and now that we do not desire one inch of your land?

But if I state, however, that we want to hold our own land, will not that be an American sentiment, I want to know? However, though that would be a British sentiment or Canadian, I am here to say, above all, my fellow countrymen, that we do not want to stand upon the extreme limits of our rights. We are ready to give and to take. We can afford to be just; we can afford to be generous, because we are strong. We have a population of seventy-seven millions—I beg pardon, I am mistaken, it is the reverse of that. But pardon my mistake, although it is the reverse, I am sure the sentiment is the same.

But though we may have many little bickerings of that kind, I speak my whole mind, and I believe I speak the mind of all you gentlemen when I say that, after all, when we go down to the bottom of our hearts we will find that there is between us a true, genuine affection. There are no two nations to-day on the face of the globe so united as Great Britain and the United States of America.

The secretary of state told us some few months ago that there was no treaty of alliance between Great Britain and the United States of America. It is very true there is between the United States of America and Great Britain to-day no treaty of alliance which the pen can write and which the pen can unmake, but there is between Great Britain and the United States of America a unity of blood which is thicker than water, and I appeal to recent history when I say that whenever one nation has to face an emergency—a greater emergency than usual— forthwith the sympathies of the other nation go to her sister.

Sir, an incident took place in the month of June last which showed to me at all events conclusively that there is between us a very deep and sincere affection. I may be pardoned if I recall that instance, because I have to speak of myself.

In the month of June last I spoke on the floor of the House of Commons of Canada on the question of Alaska, and I enunciated the very obvious truism that international problems can be settled in one of two ways only: either by arbitration or war. And although I proceeded to say immediately that war between Great Britain and the United States would be criminal and would not be thought of for a moment, still the very word "war" created quite an excitement in this country. With that causeless excitement, though I was indirectly the cause of it, I do not at this moment find any fault, because it convinced me, to an absolute certainty, that between your country and my country the relations have reached a degree of dignity and respect and affection that even the word "war" is never to be mentioned in a British Assembly or in an American Assembly. The word is not to be pronounced, not even to be predicated. It is not to be pronounced at all. The very idea is abhorrent to us.

There was a civil war in the last century. There was a civil war between England and her American colonies, and their relations were severed. If they were severed, American citizens, as you know they were, through no fault of your fathers, the fault was altogether the fault of the British government of that day. If the British government of that day had treated the American colonies as the British government for the last twenty or fifty years has treated its colonies; if Great Britain had given you then the same degree of liberty which it gives to Canada, my country; if it had given you, as it has given us, legislative independence absolute, the result would have been different—the course of victory, the course of history, would have been different.

But what has been done cannot be undone. You cannot expect that the union which has been severed shall ever be restored; but can we not escape—can we not hope that if the union cannot be restored under the law, at least there can be a union of hearts? Can we not hope that the banners of England and the banners of the United States shall never, never again meet in conflict, except in those conflicts provided by the arts of peace, such as we see to-day in the harbor of New York, in the contest between the "Shamrock" and the "Columbia" for the supremacy of naval architecture and naval prowess? Can we not hope that if ever the banners of England and the banners of the United States are again to meet on the battlefield, they shall meet entwined together in the defense of the oppressed, for the enfranchisement of the downtrodden, and for the advancement of liberty, progress, and civilization?

Sir Robert Laird Borden
[1854–1937]

Sir Robert Laird Borden became leader of the Conservative opposi-
tion in 1901 and Premier of Canada in 1912. He opposed the re-
ciprocity treaty offered Canada by President Taft of the United States.
Sir Robert was a strong supporter of the cause of the Allies during
the World War. He retired in 1919. Following is part of an address
he delivered at a patriotic meeting in London on August 4, 1915.

THE VOICE OF THE EMPIRE

FOR A HUNDRED YEARS we have not had any wars which threatened the existence of our Empire, and for more than fifty years we have not been involved in any war which might perhaps be called a great one. Under the conditions of modern democracies here and elsewhere in the Empire considerations of material prosperity have been urged, and this is especially a danger in a new country like Australia or Canada. The call of the market-place has been sometimes clamorous and insistent, and in days such as these the soul of a nation is more truly tried than it is in war days, for the highest character of an Empire is sometimes formed then and not in the days of stress and trial, through the consequences of duty and self-sacrifice.

I rejoice greatly that in these islands and in the Overseas Dominions men have realized most fully that there is something greater than material prosperity, something greater than life itself. This war cannot fail to influence most profoundly the whole future of the world and of civilization. It has already most profoundly influenced the people of this Empire. There were great strivings for wealth everywhere, but no one could deny that the material advancement and prosperity of the Empire has not in itself been a good thing. The standards of life for the people have been raised and comfort increased. It is not the wealth we should rail at. Rome fell, I know, at a time of wealth, but it was because she made wealth her god.

In the early days of the war we were much comforted by the fact that men and women were ready to make sacrifices for this, the greatest cause of all. In Canada, and I am sure elsewhere throughout the Empire, there has been manifest a spirit of coöperation, of mutual helpfulness, of a desire to assist, of self-sacrifice which is most comforting to those who have at heart the welfare of our Empire in years to come. So I am sure it will be in the future. The influence of a spirit of helpfulness and self-sacrifice which we see everywhere throughout the world and within our Empire is one for which I give thanks and am most grateful.

I have come far across this ocean to see our men within these islands and at the front, and our men in hospitals who are wounded. To see them, whether at the front, where they stand almost within the valley of the shadow of death, or wounded in the hospitals, is an inspiration in itself. I am glad to say that in visiting the hospitals I have had the opportunity of speaking to many soldiers, officers and men, from these islands, and with them I have found, as among our Canadians, just one spirit, a wonderful spirit of heroism and of patience, a spirit of consecration to the cause we all have at heart. We who come from overseas are touched by all this, perhaps more than you can imagine.

Last night I walked down the Embankment. At my right was the great Abbey, at my left the great Cathedral. The historic river was at my feet. Here came in bygone centuries the Celt, the Saxon, the Dane, the Norman, each in turn, finally all in coöperation, lending their influence to our national life. And how splendid a structure they built; what an influence for good it has carried throughout the world!

Standing thus on what seems to us hallowed ground, we of the Overseas Dominions meditate perhaps more than you do on the wonderful memories of the past and the great events to which the life of our Empire has moved. Let us never for one moment forget that of all the mighty events in our history none are greater than those through which we are passing to-day. Is an Empire like ours worth living for? Yes, and worth dying for, too. And it is something greater than it was a year ago. Indeed, it can never be quite the same again. The old order has in some measure passed away. Once for all it has been borne in upon the minds and souls of all of us that the great policies which touch and control the issues of peace and war concern more than the peoples of these islands.

And more than that, we shall so bear ourselves in this war and in the mighty events to which it must lead, that whether in these islands or in the Overseas Dominions citizenship of this Empire shall be a still greater and more noble possession in the years to come than it has been even in the glorious past. I have spoken to you frankly on some matters of great moment. If I had not done so I should have been unworthy of my position. And now before I close let me bring to you this latest message from Canada:

For those who have fallen in this struggle we shall not cease to strive. We are supremely confident that that cause will assuredly triumph and for that great purpose we are inspired with an inflexible determination to do our part.

Simon Bolivar
[1783–1830]

Simon Bolivar, the Liberator of South America, was born in Venezuela. He led the revolutions which won from Spain the national independence of the countries now known as Venezuela, Colombia, Ecuador, Panama, Peru and Bolivia. He was a brilliant military leader and a great statesman. Here are parts of an eloquent address delivered by Bolivar in Angostura on February 15, 1819, at the opening of the Second National Congress of Venezuela.

ADDRESS AT ANGOSTURA

LEGISLATORS! I deposit in your hands the supreme command of Venezuela. Yours is now the august duty of devoting yourselves to achieving the happiness of the Republic; you hold in your hands the scales of our destinies, the measure of our glory; your hands will seal the decrees insuring our Liberty. At this moment the Supreme Chief of the Republic is nothing but a plain citizen, and such he wishes to remain until death. I will serve, however, in the career of a soldier while there are enemies in Venezuela. The country has a multitude of most worthy sons capable of guiding her; talents, virtues, experience, and all that is required to direct free men, are the patrimony of many of those who are representing the people here; and outside of this Sovereign Body, there are citizens, who at all times have shown their courage in facing danger, prudence in avoiding it, and the art, in short, to govern themselves and of governing others. These illustrious men undoubtedly merit the vote of Congress, and they will be entrusted with the Government that I have just resigned so cordially and sincerely and forever.

The continuation of authority in the same person has frequently proved the undoing of democratic governments. Repeated elections are essential to the system of popular government, because there is nothing so dangerous as to suffer Power to be vested for a long time in one citizen. The people become accustomed to obeying him, and he becomes accustomed to commanding, hence the origin of usurpation and tyranny. A proper zeal is the guarantee of republican liberty, and our citizens must very justly fear that the same Magistrate who has governed them for a long time, may continue to rule them forever.

And, now that by this act of adherence to the Liberty of Venezuela, I can aspire to the glory of being counted among her most faithful lovers, permit me, Sirs, to state with the frankness of a true republican, my respectful opinion regarding the scope of this *Project of a Constitution,* which I take the liberty to submit, as a token of the sincerity and candor of my sentiments. As this is a question involving the welfare of all, I venture to believe that I have the right to be heard by the Representatives of the People. Well I know that in your wisdom you have no need of counsel; I am also aware that my *project* may perhaps appear to you erroneous and impracticable. But, Sirs, receive with benevolence this work which is a tribute of my sincere submission to Congress rather than the outcome of a presumptuous levity. On the other hand, your functions being the creation of a body politic, and, one might say, the creation of an entire community surrounded by all the difficulties offered by a situation—a most peculiar and difficult one— the voice of a citizen may perhaps point out a hidden or unknown danger.

By casting a glance over the past, we shall see what is the basic element of the Republic of Venezuela.

America, on becoming separated from the Spanish monarchy, found itself like the Roman Empire, when that enormous mass fell to pieces in the midst of the ancient world. Each dismembered portion formed then an independent nation in accordance with its situation or its interests, the difference being that those members established anew their former associations. We do not even preserve the vestiges of what once we were; we are not Europeans, we are not Indians, but an intermediate species between the aborigines and the Spaniards—Americans by birth and Europeans in right, we are placed in the dilemma of disputing with the natives our titles of possession and maintaining ourselves in the country where we were born, against the opposition of the invaders. Thus, ours is a most extraordinary and complicated case. Moreover, our part has always been a purely passive one; our political existence has always been null, and we find ourselves in greater difficulties in attaining our liberty than we ever had when we lived on a plane lower than servitude, because we had been robbed not only of liberty but also of active and domestic tyranny. Allow me to explain this paradox.

In an absolute régime, authorized power does not admit any limits. The will of the despot is the supreme law, arbitrarily executed by the subordinates who participate in the organized oppression according to the measure of the authority they enjoy.

They are intrusted with civil, political, military and religious functions; but in the last analysis, the Satraps of Persia are Persians, the Pashas of the Great Master are Turks, the Sultans of Tartary are Tartars. China does not send for her Mandarins to the land of Genghis-khan, her conqueror. America, on the contrary, received all from Spain, which had really deprived her of true enjoyment and exercise of active tyranny, by not permitting us to share in our own domestic affairs and interior administration. This deprivation had made it impossible for us to become acquainted with the course of public affairs; neither did we enjoy that personal consideration which the glamour of power inspires in the eyes of the multitude, so important in the great revolutions. I will say, in short, we were kept in estrangement, absent from the universe and all that relates to the science of government.

The people of America having been held under the triple yoke of ignorance, tyranny and vice, have not been in a position to acquire either knowledge, power or virtue. Disciples of such pernicious masters, the lessons we have received and the examples we have studied, are most destructive. We have been governed more by deception than by force, and we have been degraded more by vice than by superstition. Slavery is the offspring of Darkness; an ignorant people is a blind tool, turned to its own destruction; ambition and intrigue exploit the credulity and inexperience of men foreign to all political, economical or civil knowledge; mere illusions are accepted as reality, license is taken for liberty, treachery for patriotism, revenge for justice. Even as a sturdy blind man who, relying on the feeling of his own strength, walks along with the assurance of the most wideawake man and, striking against all kinds of obstacles, can not steady his steps.

A perverted people, should it attain its liberty, is bound to lose this very soon, because it would be useless to try to impress upon such people that happiness lies in the practice of righteousness; that the reign of law is more powerful than the reign of tyrants, who are more inflexible, and all ought to submit to the wholesome severity of the law; that good morals, and not force, are the pillars of the law and that the exercise of justice is the exercise of liberty. Thus, Legislators, your task is the more laborious because you are to deal with men misled by the illusions of error, and by civil incentives. Liberty, says Rousseau, is a succulent food, but difficult to digest. Our feeble fellow-citizens will have to strengthen their mind much before they will be ready to assimilate such wholesome nourishment. Their limbs made numb by their fetters, their eyesight weakened in the darkness of their dungeons and their forces wasted away through their foul servitude, will they be capable of marching with a firm step towards the august temple of Liberty? Will they be capable of coming close to it, and admiring the light it sheds, and of breathing freely its pure air?

Consider well your decision, Legislators. Do not forget that you are about to lay the foundations of a new people, which may some day rise to the heights that Nature has marked out for it, provided you make those foundations proportionate to the lofty place which that people is to fill. If your selection be not made under the guidance of the Guardian Angel of Venezuela, who must inspire you with wisdom to choose the nature and form of government that you are to adopt for the welfare of the people; if you should fail in this, I warn you, the end of our venture would be slavery.

The annals of past ages display before you thousands of governments. Recall to mind the nations which have shone most highly on the earth and you will be grieved to see that almost the entire world has been, and still is, a victim of bad government. You will find many systems of governing men, but all are calculated to oppress them, and if the habit of seeing the human race, led by shepherds of peoples, did not dull the horror of such a revolting sight, we would be astonished to see our social species grazing on the surface of the globe, even as lowly herds destined to feed their cruel drivers.

Nature, in truth, endows us at birth with the instinctive desire for liberty; but whether because of negligence, or because of an inclination inherent in humanity, it remains still under the bonds imposed on it. And as we see it in such a state of debasement we seem to have reason to be persuaded that the majority of men hold as a truth the humiliating principle that it is harder to maintain the balance of liberty than to endure the weight of tyranny. Would to God that this principle, contrary to the morals of Nature, were false! Would to God that this principle were not sanctioned by the indolence of man as regards his most sacred rights!

Many ancient and modern nations have cast off oppression; but those which have been able to enjoy a few precious moments of liberty are most rare, as they soon relapsed into their old political vices; because it is the people more often than the government, that bring on tyranny. The habit of suffering domination makes them insensible to the charms of honor and national prosperity, and leads them to look with indolence upon the bliss of living in the midst of liberty, under the protection of laws framed by their own free will. The history of the world proclaims this awful truth!

Only democracy, in my opinion, is susceptible of absolute freedom. But where is there a democratic government that has united at the same time power, prosperity and permanence? Have we not seen, on the contrary, aristocracy, monarchy rearing great and powerful empires for centuries and centuries? What government is there older than that of China? What republic has exceeded in duration that of Sparta, that of Venice? The Roman Empire, did it not conquer the world? Does not France count fourteen centuries of monarchy? Who is greater than England? These nations, however, have been, or still are, aristocracies and monarchies.

Notwithstanding such bitter reflections, I am filled with unbounded joy because of the great strides made by our republic since entering upon its noble career. Loving that which is most useful, animated by what is most just and aspiring to what is most perfect, Venezuela in separating from the Spanish Nation has recovered her independence, her freedom, her equality, her national sovereignty. In becoming a democratic republic, she proscribed monarchy, distinctions, nobility, franchises and privileges; she declared the rights of man, the liberty of action, of thought, of speech, of writing. These preeminently liberal acts will never be sufficiently admired for the sincerity by which they are inspired. The first Congress of Venezuela has impressed upon the annals of our legislation with indelible characters the majesty of the people, so fittingly expressed in the consummation of the social act best calculated to develop the happiness of a Nation.

Now that after infinite victories we have succeeded in annihilating the Spanish hosts, the Court of Madrid in desperation has vainly endeavored to impose upon the mind of the magnanimous sovereigns who have just destroyed usurpation and tyranny in Europe, and must be the protectors of the legality and justice of the American cause. Being incapable of attaining our submission by force of arms, Spain has recourse to her insidious policy; being unable to conquer us, she has brought into play her devious artfulness. Ferdinand has humbled himself to the extent of confessing that he needs foreign protection to bring us back to his ignominious yoke, a yoke that there is no power which could impose on us! Venezuela, fully convinced of possessing sufficient strength to repel her oppressors, has made known by the voice of the government her final determination to fight to the death in defense of her political life, not only against Spain, but against all men, if all men had degraded themselves to the extent of espousing the defense of a devouring government whose only incentives are a death dealing sword and the flames of the inquisition. A government that wants not domains, but deserts, not cities but ruins, not vassals but graves. The Declaration of the Republic of Venezuela is the most glorious, most heroic, most worthy Act of a free people; it is the one that with the greatest satisfaction I have the honor to offer Congress, being already sanctioned by the unanimous will of the free people of Venezuela.

Since the second epoch of our Republic our army has lacked military elements; it has always lacked arms, it has always lacked ammunitions, has always been poorly equipped. Now the soldiers, defenders of our independence, are not only armed with justice, but also with force. Our troops can cope with the most select of Europe, since there is no inequality in the weapons of destruction. Such great advantages are due to the boundless liberality of some generous foreigners who have heard the groans of humanity, and have seen the Cause of Right yield. But they have not been mere spectators, they have rushed with their generous help and have loaned the Republic everything that was needed for the triumph of its philanthropical principles. These friends of humanity are the guardian angels of America and to them we owe eternal gratitude, and the religious fulfillment of the sacred obligations we have contracted with them. The national debt, Legislators, is a sacred trust in the faith, the honor and the gratitude of Venezuela. Let it be respected like the Holy Ark, holding not only the rights of our benefactors, but the glory of our faithfulness. May we perish before we break a pledge which has saved the country and the life of her children.

The merging of New Granada and Venezuela into one Great State, has been the unanimous wish of the peoples and the government of both republics. The fortunes of war have effected this union so earnestly desired by all Colombians; in fact, we are incorporated. These sister countries have already entrusted to you their interests, their rights and their destinies. In contemplating the union of these countries my soul rises to the heights demanded by the colossal perspective of such a wonderful picture. Soaring among the coming ages my imagination rests on the future centuries, and seeing from afar with admiration and amazement the prosperity, the splendor and the life which have come to this vast region, I feel myself carried away, and I see her in the very heart of the universe, stretching along her lengthy shores between two oceans which Nature has separated, but which our country unites through long wide channels. I can see her as the bond, as the center, as the emporium of the human family. I can see her sending to all the corners of the globe the treasure hidden in her mountains of silver and gold; I see her sending broadcast, by means of her divine plants, health and life to the sufferers of the old world; I see her confiding her precious secrets to the learned who do not know how much her store of knowledge is superior to the store of wealth bestowed by Nature upon her; I can see her sitting on the throne of liberty, the scepter of justice in her hand, crowned by glory, showing the old world the majesty of the modern world.

Deign, Legislators, to accept with indulgence the profession of my political faith, the highest wishes of my heart and the fervent prayer which on behalf of the people I dare address you: Deign to grant to Venezuela a government preeminently popular, preeminently just, preeminently moral, which will hold in chains oppression, anarchy and guilt. A government which will allow righteousness, tolerance, peace to reign; a government which will cause equality and liberty to triumph under the protection of inexorable laws.

Gentlemen, commence your duties; I have finished mine.

Jan C. Smuts

[1870-1950]

General Jan C. Smuts, who fought the English in the Boer War, became Prime Minister (1919-24, 1939-48) of the Union of South Africa. He was an important figure in the British Empire and League of Nations. The following is part of a speech delivered by General Smuts before the Conference of Prime Ministers in London, 1921.

PEACE AND EMPIRE

PEACE is wanted by the world. Peace is wanted especially by the peoples of the British Empire. We are a peaceful Empire, our very nature is such that peace is necessary for us. We have no military aims to serve, we have no militaristic ideals, and it is only in a peaceful world that our ideals can be realized. It should, therefore, be the main, in fact, the only object of British policy to secure real peace for the Empire and the world generally. Now the Prime Minister stated in his speech what progress has been made toward the attainment of this ideal. He pointed out that some of the matters which gave us the greatest trouble in Paris had been settled. The question of reparations, which was, perhaps, the most difficult and intricate with which we had to deal in Paris, has finally, after some years of debate and trouble, been eliminated, in a settlement which, I venture to hope, will prove final and workable. That is a very great advance. The other great advance that· has been made—and it is an enormous advance—is the final disarmament of Germany. That the greatest military Empire that has ever existed in history should be reduced to a peace establishment of 100,000 men is something which I considered practically impossible. It is a great achievement, so far-reaching, indeed, that it ought to become the basis of a new departure in world policy. We cannot stop with Germany, we cannot stop with the disarmament of Germany. It is impossible for us to continue to envisage the future of the world from the point of view of war. I believe it is impossible for us to contemplate the piling up of armaments in the future of the world and the exhaustion of our very limited remaining resources in order to carry out a policy of that kind.

Such a policy would be criminal, it would be the betrayal of the causes for which we fought during the War, and if we embarked on such a policy it would be our undoing. If we were to go forward into the future staggering under the load of military and naval armaments whilst our competitors in Central Europe were free from the incubus of great armies, we should be severely handicapped, and in the end we should have the fruits of victory lost to us by our post-war policy. Already circumstances are developing on those lines. Already under the operation of inexorable economic factors we find that the position is developing to the advantage of Central Europe. The depreciation of their currencies, the universal depreciation of currencies, and the unsettlement of the exchanges are having the effect of practical repudiation of liabilities on the part of a large part of the Continent. If we add to our financial responsibilities and have, in addition· to pile on the fresh burdens of new armies and navies I am afraid the future for us is very dark indeed, and we shall in the long run lose all we have won on the field of battle.

Armaments depend upon policy, and therefore I press very strongly that our policy should be such as to make the race for armaments impossible. That should be the cardinal feature of our foreign policy. We should not go into the future under this awful handicap of having to support great armaments, build new fleets, raise new armies, whilst our economic competitors are free of that liability under the Peace Treaty. The most fatal mistake of all, in my humble opinion, would be a race of armaments against America. America is the nation that is closest to us in all the human ties. The Dominions look upon her as the oldest of them. She is the relation with whom we most closely agree, and with whom we can most cordially work together. She left our circle a long time ago because of a great historic mistake. I am not sure that a wise policy after the great events through which we have recently passed might not repair the effects of that great historic error, and once more bring America on to lines of general coöperation with the British Empire. America, after all, has proved a stanch and tried friend during the War. She came in late because she did not realize what was at stake. In the very darkest hour of the War she came in and ranged herself on our side. That was, I believe, the determining factor in the victory of our great cause.

You spoke yesterday most eloquently on the Peace Treaty, the sacredness of the Peace Treaty, and the obligation to carry out the Peace Treaty. There is one chapter in that Treaty which, to my mind, should be especially sacred to the British Empire. That is the first chapter on the League of Nations. The Covenant may be faulty, it may need amendment in order to make it more workable and more generally acceptable, but let us never forget that the Covenant embodies the most deeply felt longings of the human race for a better life. There, more than anywhere else, do we find a serious effort made to translate into practical reality the great ideals that actuated us during the War. The method of understanding instead of violence, of free coöperation, of consultation and conference in all great difficulties which we have found so fruitful in our Empire system, is the method which the League attempts to apply to the affairs of the world. Let us, in the British Empire, back it for all it is worth. It may well prove, for international relations, the way out of the present morass. It may become the foundation of a new international system which will render armaments unnecessary, and give the world at large the blessings which we enjoy in our lesser League of Nations in the Empire.

Rabindranath Tagore
[1861–1941]

Rabindranath Tagore, Hindu poet and author, was also interested in politics, but unlike the militant nationalists of his country, he placed social reforms before political independence. His ideas are expressed in a speech on nationalism in India, which he delivered in America in 1925. Parts of this speech follow.

NATIONALISM IN INDIA

INDIA has never had a real sense of nationalism. Even though from childhood I had been taught that idolatry of the Nation is almost better than reverence for God and humanity, I believe I have outgrown that teaching, and it is my conviction that my countrymen will truly gain their India by fighting against the education which teaches them that a country is greater than the ideals of humanity.

The educated Indian at present is trying to absorb some lessons from history contrary to the lessons of our ancestors. The East, in fact, is attempting to take unto itself a history which is not the outcome of its own living. Japan, for example, thinks she is getting powerful through adopting Western methods, but, after she has exhausted her inheritance, only the borrowed weapons of civilization will remain to her. She will not have developed herself from within.

Europe has her past. Europe's strength therefore lies in her history. We, in India, must make up our minds that we cannot borrow other people's history, and that if we stifle our own we are committing suicide. When you borrow things that do not belong to your life, they only serve to crush your life.

And therefore I believe that it does India no good to compete with Western civilization in its own field. But we shall be more than compensated if, in spite of the insults heaped upon us, we follow our own destiny.

We must know for certain that there is a future before us and that future is waiting for those who are rich in moral ideals and not in mere things. And it is the privilege of man to work for fruits that are beyond his immediate reach, and to adjust his life, not in slavish conformity to the examples of some present success or even to his own prudent past, limited in its aspiration, but to an indefinite future bearing in its heart the ideals of our highest expectations.

We must recognize that it is providential that the West has come to India. And yet some one must show the East to the West, and convince the West that the East has her contribution to make to the history of civilization. India is no beggar of the West. And yet even though the West may think she is, I am not for thrusting off Western civilization and becoming segregated in our independence. Let us have a deep association. If Providence wants England to be the channel of that communication, of that deeper association, I am willing to accept it with all humility. I have great faith in human nature, and I think the West will find its true mission. I speak bitterly of Western civilization when I am conscious that it is betraying its trust and thwarting its own purpose. The West must not make herself a curse to the world by using her power for her own selfish needs, but, by teaching the ignorant and helping the weak, she should save herself from the worst danger that the strong is liable to incur by making the feeble acquire power enough to resist her intrusion. And also she must not make her materialism to be the final thing, but must realize that she is doing a service in freeing the spiritual being from the tyranny of matter.

I am not against one nation in particular, but against the general idea of all nations. What is the Nation?

It is the aspect of a whole people as an organized power. This organization incessantly keeps up the insistence of the population on becoming strong and efficient. But this strenuous effort after strength and efficiency drains man's energy from his higher nature where he is self-sacrificing and creative. For thereby man's power of sacrifice is diverted from his ultimate object, which is moral, to the maintenance of this organization, which is mechanical. Yet in this he feels all the satisfaction of moral exaltation and therefore becomes supremely dangerous to humanity. He feels relieved of the urging of his conscience when he can transfer his responsibility to this machine which is the creation of his intellect and not of his complete moral personality. By this device the people which loves freedom perpetuates slavery in a large portion of the world with the comfortable feeling of pride of having done its duty; men who are naturally just can be cruelly unjust both in their act and their thought, accompanied by a feeling that they are helping the world to receive its deserts; men who are honest can blindly go on robbing others of their human rights for self-aggrandizement, all the while abusing the deprived for not deserving better treatment. We have seen in our everyday life even small organizations of business and profession produce callousness of feeling in men who are not naturally bad, and we can well imagine what a moral havoc it is causing in a world where whole peoples are furiously organizing themselves for gaining wealth and power.

Nationalism is a great menace. It is the particular thing which for years has been at the bottom of India's troubles. And inasmuch as we have been ruled and dominated by a nation that is strictly political in its attitude, we have tried to develop within ourselves, despite our inheritance from the past, a belief in our eventual political destiny.

It was my conviction that what India most needed was constructive work coming from within herself. In this work we must take all risks and go on doing the duties which by right are ours, though in the teeth of persecution; winning moral victory at every step, by our failure and suffering. We must show those who are over us that we have in ourselves the strength of moral power, the power to suffer for truth.

Mohandas K. Gandhi
[1869–1948]

Mohandas K. Gandhi, the great Hindu nationalist leader, addressed over 50,000 of his followers in Madras, India, on August 12, 1920, on non-cooperation with England. Here are parts of this speech.

NON-COOPERATION

WHAT is this non-cooperation, about which you have heard much, and why do we want to offer this non-cooperation? I wish to go for the time being into the way. There are two things before this country: the first and the foremost is the Khilafat question. On this the heart of the Mussalmans of India has become lascerated. British pledges given after the greatest deliberation by the Prime Minister of England in the name of the English nation, have been dragged into the mire. The promises given to Moslem India on the strength of which, the consideration that was expected by the British nation was exacted, have been broken, and the great religion of Islam has been placed in danger. The Mussalmans hold—and I venture to think they rightly hold—that, so long as British promises remain unfulfilled, so long is it impossible for them to tender whole-hearted fealty and loyalty to the British connection; and if it is to be a choice for a devout Mussalman between loyalty to the British connection and loyalty to his Code and Prophet, he will not require a second to make his choice,—and he has declared his choice. The Mussalmans say frankly, openly, and honourably to the whole world that if the British Ministers and the British nation do not fulfil the pledges given to them and do not wish to regard with respect the sentiments of the 70 millions of the inhabitants of India who profess the faith of Islam, it will be impossible for them to retain Islamic loyalty. It is a question, then, for the rest of the Indian population to consider whether they want to perform a neighbourly duty by their Mussalman countrymen, and if they do, they have an opportunity of a life time which will not occur for another hundred years, to show their good-will, fellowship and friendship and to prove what they have been saying for all these long years that the Mussalman is the brother of the Hindu. If the Hindu regards that before the connection with the British nation comes his natural connection with his Moslem brother, then I say to you that if you find that the Moslem claim is just, that it is based upon real sentiment, and that its back ground is this great religious feeling, you cannot do otherwise than help the Mussalman through and through, so long as their cause remains just, and the means for attaining the end remains equally just, honourable and free from harm to India. These are the plain conditions which the Indian Mussalmans have accepted; and it was when they saw that they could accept the proffered aid of the Hindus, that they could always justify the cause and the means before the whole world, that they decided to accept the proffered hand of fellowship. It is then for the Hindus and Mohammedans to offer a united front to the whole of the Christian powers of Europe and tell them that weak as India is, India has still got the capacity of preserving her self-respect, she still knows how to die for her religion and for her self-respect.

That is the Khilafat in a nut-shell; but you have also got the Punjab. The Punjab has wounded the heart of India as no other question has for the past century. I do not exclude from my calculation the Mutiny of 1857. Whatever hardships India had to suffer during the Mutiny, the insult that was attempted to be offered to her during the passage of the Rowlatt legislation and that which was offered after its passage were unparalleled in Indian history. It is because you want justice from the British nation in connection with the Punjab atrocities you have to devise ways and means as to how you can get this justice. The House of Commons, the House of Lords, Mr. Montagu, the Viceroy of India, every one of them know what the feeling of India is on this Khilafat question and on that of the Punjab; the debates in both the Houses of Parliament, the action of Mr. Montagu and that of the Viceroy have demonstrated to you completely that they are not willing to give the justice which is India's due and which she demands. I suggest that our leaders have got to find a way out of this great difficulty and unless we have made ourselves even with the British rulers in India and unless we have gained a measure of self-respect at the hands of the British rulers in India, no connection, and no friendly intercourse is possible between them and ourselves. I, therefore, venture to suggest this beautiful and unanswerable method of non-cooperation.

I have been told that non-cooperation is unconstitutional. I venture to deny that it is unconstitutional. On the contrary, I hold that non-co-operation is a just and religious doctrine; it is the inherent right of every human being and it is perfectly constitutional. A great lover of the British Empire has said that under the British constitution even a successful rebellion is perfectly constitutional and he quotes historical instances, which I cannot deny, in support of his claim. I do not claim any constitutionality for a rebellion successful or otherwise, so long as that rebellion means in the ordinary sense of the term, what it does mean, namely, wresting justice by violent means. On the contrary, I have said it repeatedly to my countrymen that violence, whatever end it may serve in Europe, will never serve us in India.

My brother and friend Shaukat Ali believes in methods of violence; and if it was in his power to draw the sword against the British Empire, I know that he has got the courage of a man and he has got also the wisdom to see that he should offer that battle to the British Empire. But because he recognises as a true soldier that means of violence are not open to India, he sides with me accepting my humble assistance and pledges his word that so long as I am with him and so long as he believes in the doctrine, so long will he not harbour even the idea of violence against any single Englishman or any single man on earth. I am here to tell you that he has been as true as his word and has kept it religiously. I am here to bear witness that he has been following out this plan of non-violent Non-cooperation to the very letter and I am asking India to follow this non-violent non-cooperation. I tell you that there is not a better soldier living in our ranks in British India than Shaukat Ali. When the time for the drawing of the sword comes, if it ever comes, you will find him drawing that sword and you will find me retiring to the jungles of Hindustan. As soon as India accepts the doctrine of the sword, my life as an Indian is finished. It is because I believe in a mission special to India and it is because I believe that the ancients of India after centuries of experience have found out that the true thing for any human being on earth is not justice based on violence but justice based on sacrifice of self, justice based on Yagna and Kurbani,—I cling to that doctrine and I shall cling to it for ever,—it is for that reason I tell you that whilst my friend believes also in the doctrine of violence and has adopted the doctrine of non-violence as a weapon of the weak, I believe in the doctrine of non-violence as a weapon of the strongest. I believe that a man is the strongest soldier for daring to die unarmed with his breast bare before the enemy. So much for the non-violent part of non-cooperation. I therefore, venture to suggest to my learned countrymen that so long as the doctrine of non-cooperation remains non-violent, so long there is nothing unconstitutional in that doctrine.

I ask further, is it unconstitutional for me to say to the British Government 'I refuse to serve you?' Is it unconstitutional for our worthy Chairman to return with every respect all the titles that he has ever held from the Government? Is it unconstitutional for any parent to withdraw his children from a Government or aided school? Is it unconstitutional for a lawyer to say 'I shall no longer support the arm of the law so long as that arm of law is used not to raise me but to debase me'? Is it unconstitutional for a civil servant or for a judge to say, 'I refuse to serve a Government which does not wish to respect the wishes of the whole people?' I ask, is it unconstitutional for a policeman or for a soldier to tender his resignation when he knows that he is called to serve a Government which traduces his own countrymen? Is it unconstitutional for me to go to the 'krishan,' to the agriculturist, and say to him 'it is not wise for you to pay any taxes, if these taxes are used by the Government not to raise you but to weaken you?' I hold and I venture to submit, that there is nothing unconstitutional in it. What is more, I have done every one of these things in my life and nobody has questioned the constitutional character of it. I was in Kaira working in the midst of 7 lakhs of agriculturists. They had all suspended the payment of taxes and the whole of India was at one with me. Nobody considered that it was unconstitutional. I submit that in the whole plan of non-cooperation, there is nothing unconstitutional. But I do venture to suggest that it will be highly unconstitutional in the midst of this unconstitutional Government,—in the midst of a nation which has built up its magnificent constitution, —for the people of India to become weak and to crawl on their belly —it will be highly unconstitutional for the people of India to pocket every insult that is offered to them; it is highly unconstitutional for the 70 millions of Mohammedans of India to submit to a violent wrong done to their religion; it is highly unconstitutional for the whole of India to sit still and cooperate with an unjust Government which has trodden under its feet the honour of the Punjab. I say to my countrymen so long as you have a sense of honour and so long as you wish to remain the descendants and defenders of the noble traditions that have been handed to you for generations after generations, it is unconstitutional for you not to non-cooperate and unconstitutional for you to cooperate with a Government which has become so unjust as our Government has become. I am not anti-English; I am not anti-British; I am not anti any Government; but I am anti-untruth—anti-humbug and anti-injustice. So long as the Government spells injustice, it may regard me as its enemy, implacable enemy. I had hoped at the

Congress at Amritsar—I am speaking God's truth before you—when I pleaded on bended knees before some of you for cooperation with the Government. I had full hope that the British ministers who are wise, as a rule, would placate the Mussalman sentiment that they would do full justice in the matter of the Punjab atrocities; and therefore, I said:—let us return good-will to the hand of fellowship that has been extended to us, which I then believed was extended to us through the Royal Proclamation. It was on that account that I pleaded for cooperation. But to-day that faith having gone and obliterated by the acts of the British ministers, I am here to plead not for futile obstruction in the Legislative council but for real substantial non-cooperation which would paralyse the mightiest Government on earth. That is what I stand for to-day. Until we have wrung justice, and until we have wrung our self-respect from unwilling hands and from unwilling pens there can be no cooperation. Our Shastras say and I say so with the greatest deference to all the greatest religious preceptors of India but without fear of contradiction, that our Shastras teach us that there shall be no cooperation between injustice and justice, between an unjust man and a justice-loving man, between truth and untruth. Cooperation is a duty only so long as Government protects your honour, and non-cooperation is an equal duty when the Government instead of protecting robs you of your honour. That is the doctrine of non-cooperation.

Sun Yat-sen
[1866–1925]

Sun Yat-sen was the Father of the Chinese republic. In 1895 he was involved in a revolutionary plot. He escaped and thereafter for many years worked outside of China for the overthrow of the Chinese monarchy. His ideas on nationalism, democracy and socialism were furthered by Chinese revolutionaries in and out of China until success met their persistent efforts in 1912, when the Emperor abdicated, and Sun Yat-sen was made provisional president. From 1912 to 1925 Sun Yat-sen held various high posts, including the presidency, of the various republican regimes that came and went in turbulent China. The following are parts of an address which he delivered on March 2, 1924.

NATIONAL MORALE AND WORLD TRANQUILLITY

ALTHOUGH we are behind the foreigners in scientific achievement, our native ability is adequate to the construction of a great material civilization, which is proved by the concrete evidence of past achievements. We invented the compass, printing, porcelain, gunpowder, and the curing of tea and weaving of silk. Foreigners have made good use of these inventions. For example, modern ocean transportation would be impossible if there were no compass. The fast printing machine, which turns out tens of thousands of copies per hour, had its origin in China. Foreign military greatness comes from gunpowder, which was first used by the Chinese. Furthermore, many of the latest inventions in architecture in the West have been practiced in the East for thousands of years. This genius of our race for material inventions seems now to be lost; and so our greatness has become but the history of bygone glories.

I believe that we have many things to learn from the West, and that we can learn them. Many Westerners maintain that the hardest thing to learn is aerial science; already many Chinese have become skillful aviators. If aeronautics can be learned, I believe everything can be learned by our people. Science is only three hundred years old, and it was not highly developed until fifty years ago. Formerly coal was used as the source of energy; now the age of coal has given place to the age of electricity.

Recently America had a plan for nationalizing the water-power of the country. America has hundreds of thousands of factories. Each big factory has to have a power-house which consumes a tremendous amount of coal. The railroads in the country are busily engaged in transporting coal, and have little time for transporting agricultural products. As a means of economizing coal and lessening transportation, a national central power-house is suggested. When such a house is built, the entire nation will receive energy from one central station. The result will be the elimination of enormous waste and the increase of efficiency.

When we learn from the West, it is evident that we should learn the latest inventions instead of repeating the different steps of development. In the case of the power-house, we may well learn to adopt the centralized plan of producing electricity, and need not follow the old plan of using coal to produce energy. In this way we can easily within ten years catch up with the West in material achievement.

The time is critical. We have no time to waste, and we ought to take the latest and the best that the West can offer. Our intelligence is by no means inferior to that of the Japanese. With our historical background and our natural and human resources, it should be easier for us than it was for Japan to rise to the place of a first class Power by a partial adaptation of Western civilization. We ought to be ten times stronger than Japan because our country is more than ten times bigger and richer than Japan. China is potentially equal to ten Powers. At present England, America, France, Italy, and Japan constitute the so-called "Big Five." Even with the rise of Germany and Soviet Russia, the world has only seven Powers. When China becomes strong, she can easily win first place in the Council of Nations.

Now the question is: How can we become a first class Power? Our ancestors adopted a policy of "helping the weak and curbing the strong": a policy of international justice resting upon a sound moral foundation. As a result, the small nations in Asia, including Annam, Burmah, Korea, and Siam enjoyed peace, freedom, and independence for thousands of years. As soon as China became weak, these small nations were annexed by the Powers, and so they lost their liberty and independence. When China becomes strong again, it will be our duty to help these nations win back their freedom. This is a great responsibility! If we cannot fulfill this great responsibility, what is the use of China being strong and powerful?

Again, if China follows at the heels of the imperialistic and militaristic nations, China's ascendency to power, would not only be useless, but harmful to humanity. The only glorious and honorable path for us to pursue is to maintain in full force the old policy of "helping the weak and curbing the strong."

Gentlemen, we ought to decide at this hour what is to be the fundamental policy for which the nation is to stand, and where our hope and our greatness lie. When the days of our prosperity come, we must not forget the pain and misery which we are now suffering from the pressure of economic and political forces of the Powers. When our country becomes powerful, we should assume the responsibility of delivering those nations which suffer in the same way as we do now. This is what the *Ta Hsueh* means by "securing world tranquillity" (*p'ing t'ien hsia*). The way to proceed is to revive our spirit of nationalism and to restore our country to its original position of a "Single Power." We should use our old moral values and our love of peace as the foundation of national reconstruction; and look forward to the day when we shall become leaders in world reconstruction upon lines of international justice and good will. This is the mission of our 400,000,000. Gentlemen, each one of you is one of the 400,000,000; and you personally should assume this responsibility. But your first step is to revive your spirit of nationalism!

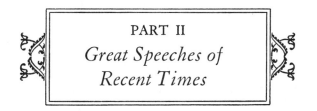

PART II

*Great Speeches of
Recent Times*

William Green

[1873-1952]

In 1924 William Green succeeded Samuel Gompers as President of the American Federation of Labor. Following are parts of an address delivered by Mr. Green in 1925 before the Harvard Union.

MODERN TRADE UNIONISM

WE ALL KNOW from a study of history the progress of the working people from the stage of barbarism to that of slavery, serfdom and later individual freedom. In the early days of human history the wants of the masses were few and simple. Acquisition of food and shelter satisfied the human instinct and practically all personal needs. Each community depended upon its productive ability to supply the meager demand for the necessaries of life. There was very little transportation of foodstuffs and manufacturing was practically unknown. Through conquest and acquisition the strong overpowered the weak and made slaves of the people. Those who were made slaves and serfs were compelled, through forced labor, to work for their masters and lords upon such terms and conditions as the owners and lords fixed for them.

In the development of civilization the use of tools grew and multiplied. Later the use of steam power revolutionized the whole industrial organization and transportation. Manufacturing enterprises were formed and undertaken in all civilized countries. With these changes in civilization came a change in the mode of living. Towns and cities were built and this necessitated the building of highways and railroads so that foodstuffs could be brought from the agricultural sections to the cities, travel could be facilitated and manufactured products carried into the fields of commerce. All of these changes took place with surprising rapidity, practically revolutionizing the existing social and industrial order.

The human element played a very important part in the transition. The workers were brought together in groups upon the railroads, in the manufacturing plants and in the mines. They became the users of the tools, the operators of the engines and machines. Naturally, the question of wages and conditions of employment became a subject of vital interest to both employers and employees. Differences of opinion arose as to what the wage schedule should be and what constituted tolerable conditions of employment. Out of the differences which arose between employers and employees grew the organization of workers. In the beginning it was crude, simple and of little influence. These organizations we called unions, and were different from the medieval organizations which included all in the industry, called guilds, and their members were both skilled and semi-skilled artisans of master and journeymen workmen. As this form of organization increased both in numbers and influence much opposition was encountered. This opposition became so great that they were classed as revolutionary and against the public interest. Legislation was passed making strikes illegal and the relationship between the employer and employee that of master and servant. From that day to this the struggle for human liberty and industrial freedom has been directed against the legislative restraints and limitations which have been imposed upon the activities of the workers in the formation and growth of their trade unions. The whole process has been slow and tedious. Whatever success has come in the work of organization and in the benefits and blessings which have come through organization to the men and women who toil has all been achieved as a result of the exercise of great effort, intense suffering, much sacrificing and the expenditure of huge sums of money.

It is clear to all who have studied the history of this great social and economic development that trade unionism is not a discovery or a formula. It grew and evolved slowly out of the needs of human experience. In the beginning when unions were first formed their primary purpose was to defend the workers against wage reductions and unfair treatment. They were regarded almost solely as defensive measures for defensive purposes only. It seemed that the thought uppermost in the minds of the workers was the maintenance of what had been secured by them in the way of wages and working conditions. The methods employed in those days could be characterized as dominantly militant. The rule of force and might seemed to guide and influence the thoughts and actions of the workers. Concessions granted to workers by employers were usually forced through the medium of industrial warfare. There was little attention given to the thought or suggestion of conference, understanding and reasoning between employers and employees. The thought of fight to win, of force and brutality seemed to inspire both employers and employees in their industrial relationships.

From such crude and primitive beginnings trade unionism, or organized labor, has grown into the place which, with increasing influence, it occupies in our social and industrial life today. During the formative period organized labor relied almost solely upon its economic strength while today it places immeasurable value upon the convincing power of logic, facts and the righteousness of its cause. More and more organized labor is coming to believe that its best interests are promoted through concord rather than by conflict. It prefers the conference table to the strike field.

Trade unionism has kept pace with the progress which has been made in industry. It has emerged from its primitive state into a modern institution, grappling with modern problems in a modern way. It is resolutely facing the task of seeking and finding a remedy for existing industrial ills. In doing so organized labor is not committed to any dogma or to any inflexible rule. It shapes its policies in accordance with experience and the circumstances which it is called upon to meet. While the exercise of the right to bargain collectively, to use its economic strength, when such action is justifiable, is considered to be fundamental it follows a policy of elasticity in its executive and administrative work.

Organized labor recognizes and appreciates the value and importance of education. It believes that the workers can advance their economic and social interests through education and knowledge. The workers believe fully that the future of the trade union movement is very largely conditioned upon the effectiveness with which we link up educational opportunities with trade union undertakings. The trade unions were truly pioneers in demanding free public schools so that there might be equal educational opportunities. Along with the adoption of the free public school institution labor is advocating a constant widening of the service rendered by the public schools. Culture should not be the heritage of any limited group. All should be enabled to make their life experiences opportunities for culture. The statement made by Lord Haldane that "class division in knowledge goes deeper than any other class division" is profoundly significant.

We believe that the only way to assure our civilization a culture instinct with life is to make the work process an agency for educating the worker. Whether that work process be making pottery, managing a steel plant, or operating a power loom, it is in the day's work that the human agent shows most clearly what manner of man he is and finds opportunity for growth. If he brings to his work an attitude of mind that is inquiring, resourceful, constructive, he increases his service many fold. When trade unions have established certain fundamental rights which assure industrial justice, and the channels through which mutual problems may be discussed and considered, there is created an opportunity for this higher kind of workmanship. If the whole industrial situation stimulates initiative and therefore workmanship, educational possibilities are quickened. Industrial development of that character will purge our civilization of the blight of commercialism and low ideals. The trade union movement is making its contribution to that end and can accomplish much more when management offers understanding cooperation.

The trade union movement has been passing through that period when physical controversies and the tactics of force were most effective; it is now in a period when its leaders must seek the conference room, and there, by exposition and demonstration, convince conferees of the justice and wisdom of Labor's position. In such service Labor is finding a special need for trained representatives and effective information.

The organizations of labor are adjusting themselves to the marked changes which have come through education and the modernization of industry. The union of the workers is not standing still. It is consolidating the gains of the past and pressing courageously along the highway of progress. The union itself is an elemental response to the human instinct for group action in dealing with group problems. Daily work in industry is now a collective undertaking. The union expresses the workmen's unsatisfied desire for self-betterment in all of the phases that desire may find expression. No substitute can hope to replace the union for it has the intrinsic right to existence which comes from service rendered to fit changing stages of development. Many wage earners have had dreams of ownership of industry but we all know that whatever the ownership, private, governmental or employee, the vital problem for us is the terms and relations we have with management. To deal with this problem, labor must always have its voluntary organizations directed and managed by itself.

Alfred E. Smith

[1873–1944]

Alfred E. Smith, former Governor of New York, attacked religious prejudice in American politics, in a speech at Oklahoma City, on September 20, 1928. This speech was delivered during his campaign as Democratic candidate for President. Parts of this speech follow.

RELIGIOUS PREJUDICE AND POLITICS

"I FEEL that I owe it to the Democratic party to talk out plainly. If I had listened to the counselors that advised political expediency I would probably keep quiet, but I'm not by nature a quiet man. (Laughter and applause.)

"I never keep anything to myself. I talk it out. And I feel I owe it, not only to the party, but I sincerely believe that I owe it to the country itself to drag this un-American propaganda out into the open.

"Because this country, to my way of thinking, cannot be successful if it ever divides on sectarian lines. (Applause.) If there are any considerable number of our people that are going to listen to appeals to their passion and to their prejudice, if bigotry and intolerance and their sister vices are going to succeed, it is dangerous for the future life of the Republic, and the best way to kill anything un-American is to drag it out into the open; because anything un-American cannot live in the sunlight. (Applause.)

"Where does all this propaganda come from? Who is paying for its distribution? One of the women leaders of North Carolina was talking to me in the executive chamber in Albany about two weeks ago, and she said: 'Governor, I have some notion about the cost of distributing election material. The amount of it that has come into our state could not be printed and distributed for less than $1,000,000.'

"Where is the money coming from? I think we got the answer the other day when a woman went into the national committee in Washington and meekly walked up to the man in charge and said: 'I want some literature on Governor Smith; I want the non-political kind.' And he brought her down stairs, put her in an automobile and took her over to an office where a paper is published called 'The Fellowship Forum,' which, for a number of years, has been engaged in this senseless, foolish, stupid attack upon the Catholic Church and the members of the faith. (Applause.)

"Prior to the convention the grand dragon of the Realm of Arkansas wrote to one of the delegates from Arkansas, and in the letter he advised the delegate that he not vote for me in the national convention, and he put it on the ground of upholding American ideals against institutions as established by our forefathers. Now, can you think of any man or any group of men banded together in what they call the Ku-Klux Klan, who profess to be 100 per cent Americans, and forget the great principle that Jefferson stood for, the equality of man, and forget that our forefathers in their wisdom, foreseeing probably such a sight as we look at to-day, wrote into the fundamental law of the country that at no time was religion to be regarded as a qualification for public office.

"Just think of a man breathing the spirit of hatred against millions of his fellow citizens, proclaiming and subscribing at the same time to the doctrine of Jefferson, of Lincoln, of Roosevelt and of Wilson. Why, there is no greater mockery in this world to-day than the burning of the Cross, the emblem of faith, the emblem of salvation, the place upon which Christ Himself made the great sacrifice for all of mankind, by these people who are spreading this propaganda, while the Christ they are supposed to adore, love and venerate, during all of His lifetime on earth, taught the holy, sacred writ of brotherly love.

"So much for him. (A voice: "That is plenty.")

"Now we know there is another lie, or series of lies, being carefully put out around the country, and it is surprising to find the number of people who seem to believe it. I would have refrained from talking about this if it were not for the avalanche of letters that have poured into the national committee and have poured into my own office in the executive department at Albany asking for the facts. And that is the lie that has been spread around: that since I have been Governor of the State of New York nobody has ever been appointed to office but Catholics. (Loud noises.)

"We are losing time on the radio. Please wait.

"The cabinet of the governorship is made up of fourteen men. Three of them are Catholics, ten of them are Protestants and one of them is a Jew. (Applause.) Outside of the cabinet members, the Governor appoints two boards and commissions under the cabinet of twenty-six people. Twelve of them are Catholics, fourteen of them are Protestants. Aside from that of his boards and commissions, the Governor appoints 157. Thirty-five of them are Catholics, 106 of them are Protestants, twelve of them are Jews, and four I was unable to find out anything about. (Laughter and applause.)

"Judicial appointments, county appointments, and all positions in the various judicial and county districts of the state not directly related to the Executive Department, although appointed by the Governor to fill vacancies: Total number of appointments, 175; 64 Catholics, 90 Protestants, and 12 that we don't know anything about. (Laughter and applause.)

"Now just another word and I am going to finish. Here is the meanest thing that I have seen in the whole campaign. This is the product of the lowest and most cunning mind that could train itself to do something mean and dirty. This was sent to me by a member of the Masonic order, a personal friend of mine. It purports to be a circular sent out under Catholic auspices to Catholic voters and tells how 'We have control in New York, stick together and we'll get control of the country.' And designedly it said to the roster of the Masonic order in my state, because so many of that order are friends of mine and have been voting for me for the last ten years, 'Stand together.'

"Now, I disown that circular, the Democratic party disowns it, and I have no right to talk for the Catholic Church, but I'll take a chance and say that nobody inside of the Catholic Church has been stupid enough to do a thing like that. (Applause.)

"Let me make myself perfectly clear. I do not want any Catholic in the United States of America to vote for me on the 6th of November because I am a Catholic (applause). If any Catholic in this country believes that the welfare, the well-being, the prosperity, the growth and the expansion of the United States is best conserved and best promoted by the election of Hoover, I want him to vote for Hoover and not for me (applause).

"But, on the other hand, I have the right to say that any citizen of this country that believes I can promote its welfare, that I am capable of steering the ship of state safely through the next four years and then votes against me because of my religion, he is not a real, pure, genuine American. (Applause.)

Fiorello H. LaGuardia
[1882-1947]

Fiorello H. LaGuardia, popular reform Mayor of New York City, was an outstanding civic leader, who had also served in Congress. Reproduced here are parts of an address delivered by him in 1934 at the Labor Day celebration of the Chicago World's Fair.

AMERICAN LABOR

TODAY is Labor Day. It is America's Day. It is typically American because American labor, whenever it gathers, does so with love for its flag and country and loyalty to its government. Labor in the United States is not and never has been antagonistic to its form of government. In every crisis labor has stood steadfastly and loyally in support of constituted government and in upholding the Constitution of the Republic. Even in periods darkest for organized labor, when it was forced to undergo the greatest degree of exploitation, it fought for its rights and the protection of its members without seeking the destruction of our form of government.

So it is fitting and proper on this day, when American labor meets in all parts of the country, that Federal, state and local officials join in expressing a debt of gratitude to American labor for that constant and consistent loyalty and to join with you in your efforts to give to the working man and woman that economic security that is an essential factor in the full enjoyment of the liberties guaranteed by the Constitution as written by the Fathers.

Our purpose today is not to review and reiterate the mistakes of the past. American labor is generous. It will forgive. It cannot forget. It will learn. It refuses to permit a repetition of the mistakes of the past. It can no longer be ignored and it must take its rightful place in the nation's council adjusting existing inequalities and providing the stability of the future.

There is a definite school of thought in the country which believes that an industrial financial crisis is a blessing. They call it an inevitable economic cycle. Fortunately this school of thought has not a large following. But part of the following is found in high financial, industrial and political circles. General unemployment they hail as part of a so-called law of supply and demand that will create a highly competitive labor market, that will bring down wages, so that factories, to use their own language, "will be able to start again at low production costs and thereby meet the competition of the Chinese coolie, of Japanese industry and of other low-wage countries." Such an economic philosophy is contrary to the fundamental principles of American life. In addition, it is economically fallacious, unsound and impossible.

We have learned that unless there is employment for all there will be profits for none.

The best market for American agriculture is American labor and the best market for the products of American labor is the American farmer. Cut down the purchasing power of the one and it is immediately reflected in the other, and the entire economic structure of the country is disrupted. The trouble is that many who should have known are only opening their eyes today. They are seeking to protect themselves after their own factory doors have been locked. Industrial leadership is still uncertain and timid. Financial leadership seems to have entirely disappeared. This is no time for labor to become panicky. It must use its head. It must supply its share of leadership in solving the nation's problems and in bringing our country back on its feet.

American labor always has problems which must be solved with American employers and American capital. It is fair to speak frankly on that point too. A strike is the last means of solution, and not the first; it is justifiable only after every resource of discussion and negotiation has been tried and has failed. During strikes it must always be remembered that the public interest is paramount. The safety of great masses of people not parties to the discussion, and the functioning of government, can never be at stake in government, can never be at stake in any bargaining process. Starvation is not a legitimate weapon for capital to use against labor. It is no more legitimate for labor to use it against the public.

Labor should not permit itself to be ensnared in a mesh of cross-politics. It has no need to be. When American labor adopts a definite program, and that program is sound, based on American fundamentals, no party can ignore that program.

Clarence S. Darrow
[1857-1938]

Clarence S. Darrow was an outstanding lawyer and orator. He was identified with the defense of prominent labor leaders, including Debs, Haywood and the McNamara brothers. He was also a successful criminal lawyer. Following is the closing part of his eloquent address as Attorney for the Defense in the Loeb and Leopold case, delivered in Chicago in 1924, in which he pleaded against capital punishment and succeeded in obtaining the lesser penalty of life imprisonment for both of the defendants.

A PLEA FOR MERCY

THERE are causes for this terrible crime. There are causes, as I have said, for everthing that happens in the world. War is a part of it; education is a part of it; birth is a part of it; money is a part of it—all these conspired to compass the destruction of these two poor boys.

Has the court any right to consider anything but these two boys? The State says that your Honor has a right to consider the welfare of the community, as you have. If the welfare of the community would be benefited by taking these lives, well and good. I think it would work evil that no one could measure. Has your Honor a right to consider the families of these two defendants? I have been sorry, and I am sorry for the bereavement of Mr. and Mrs. Frank, for those broken ties that cannot be healed. All I can hope and wish is that some good may come from it all. But as compared with the families of Leopold and Loeb, the Franks are to be envied—and everyone knows it.

I do not know how much salvage there is in these two boys. I hate to say it in their presence, but what is there to look forward to? I do not know but what your Honor would be merciful if you tied a rope around their necks and let them die; merciful to them, but not merciful to civilization, and not merciful to those who would be left behind. To spend the balance of their days in prison is mighty little to look forward to, if anything. Is it anything? They may have the hope that as the years roll around they might be released. I do not know. I do not know. I will be honest with this court as I have tried to be from the beginning. I know that these boys are not fit to be at large. I believe they will not be until they pass through the next stage of life, at forty-five or fifty. Whether they will then, I cannot tell. I am sure of this; that I will not be here to help them. So far as I am concerned, it is over.

I would not tell this court that I do not hope that some time, when life and age have changed their bodies, as they do, and have changed their emotions, as they do—that they may once more return to life. I would be the last person on earth to close the door of hope to any human being that lives, and least of all to my clients. But what have they to look forward to? Nothing. And I think here of the stanza of Housman:

> Now hollow fires burn out to black,
>   And lights are fluttering low:
> Square your shoulders, lift your pack
>   And leave your friends and go.
> O never fear, lads, naught's to dread,
>   Look not left nor right:
> In all the endless road you tread
>   There's nothing but the night.

I care not, your Honor, whether the march begins at the gallows or when the gates of Joliet close upon them, there is nothing but the night, and that is little for any human being to expect.

But there are others to consider. Here are these two families, who have led honest lives, who will bear the name that they bear, and future generations must carry it on.

Here is Leopold's father—and this boy was the pride of his life. He watched him, he cared for him, he worked for him; the boy was brilliant and accomplished, he educated him, and he thought that fame and position awaited him, as it should have awaited. It is a hard thing for a father to see his life's hopes crumble into dust.

Should he be considered? Should his brothers be considered? Will it do society any good or make your life safer, or any human being's life safer, if it should be handed down from generation to generation, that this boy, their kin, died upon the scaffold?

And Loeb's, the same. Here are the faithful uncle and brother, who have watched here day by day, while Dickie's father and his mother are too ill to stand this terrific strain, and shall be waiting for a message which means more to them than it can mean to you or me. Shall these be taken into account in this general bereavement?

Have they any rights? Is there any reason, your Honor, why their proud names and all the future generations that bear them shall have this bar sinister written across them? How many boys and girls, how many unborn children will feel it? It is bad enough as it is, God knows. It is bad enough, however it is. But it's not yet death on the scaffold. It's not that. And I ask your Honor, in addition to all that I have said, to save two honorable families from a disgrace that never ends, and which could be of no avail to help any human being that lives.

Now, I must say a word more and then I will leave this with you where I should have left it long ago. None of us are unmindful of the public; courts are not, and juries are not. We placed our fate in the hands of a trained court, thinking that he would be more mindful and considerate than a jury. I cannot say how people feel. I have stood here for three months as one might stand at the ocean trying to sweep back the tide. I hope the seas are subsiding and the wind is falling, and I believe they are, but I wish to make no false pretense to this court. The easy thing and the popular thing to do is to hang my clients. I know it. Men and women who do not think will applaud. The cruel and thoughtless will approve. It will be easy to-day; but in Chicago, and reaching out over the length and breadth of the land, more and more fathers and mothers, the humane, the kind and the hopeful, who are gaining an understanding and asking questions not only about these poor boys, but about their own— these will join in no acclaim at the death of my clients. These would ask that the shedding of blood be stopped, and that the normal feelings of man resume their sway. And as the days and the months and the years go on, they will ask it more and more. But, your Honor, what they shall ask may not count. I know the easy way. I know your Honor stands between the future and the past. I know the future is with me, and what I stand for here; not merely for the lives of these two unfortunate lads, but for all boys and all girls; for all of the young, and as far as possible, for all of the old. I am pleading for life, understanding, charity, kindness, and the infinite mercy that considers all. I am pleading that we overcome cruelty with kindness and hatred with love. I know the future is on my side. Your Honor stands between the past and the future. You may hang these boys; you may hang them by the neck until they are dead. But in doing it you will turn your face toward the past. In doing it you are making it harder for every other boy who in ignorance and darkness must grope his way through the mazes which only childhood knows. In doing it you will make it harder for unborn children. You may save them and make it easier for every child that sometime may stand where these boys stand. You will make it easier for every human being with an aspiration and a vision and a hope and a fate. I am pleading for the future; I am pleading for a time when hatred and cruelty will not control the hearts of men. When we can learn by reason and judgment and understanding and faith that all life is worth saving, and that mercy is the highest attribute of man.

I feel that I should apologize for the length of time I have taken. This case may not be as important as I think it is, and I am sure I do not need to tell this court, or to tell my friends that I would fight just as hard for the poor as for the rich. If I should succeed in saving these boys' lives and do nothing for the progress of the law, I should feel sad, indeed. If I can succeed, my greatest reward and my greatest hope will be that I have done something for the tens of thousands of other boys, for the countless unfortunates who must tread the same road in blind childhood that these poor boys have trod—that I have done something to help human understanding, to temper justice with mercy, to overcome hate with love.

John L. Lewis
[1880–1969]

The 1937 organizing campaign of the C.I.O. (Congress of Industrial Organizations) resulted in many bitterly fought strikes. In defense of the C.I.O., John L. Lewis, its president, delivered a radio address on September 3, 1937, parts of which follow.

THE RIGHTS OF LABOR

THE United States Chamber of Commerce, the National Association of Manufacturers and similar groups representing industry and financial interests are rendering a disservice to the American people in their attempts to frustrate the organization of labor and in their refusal to accept collective bargaining as one of our economic institutions.

These groups are encouraging a systematic organization under the sham pretext of local interests. They equip these vigilantes with tin hats, wooden clubs, gas masks and lethal weapons and train them in the arts of brutality and oppression.

No tin hat brigade of goose-stepping vigilantes or bibble-babbling mob of blackguarding and corporation-paid scoundrels will prevent the onward march of labor, or divert its purpose to play its natural and rational part in the development of the economic, political and social life of our nation.

Unionization, as opposed to communism, presupposes the relation of employment; it is based upon the wage system and it recognizes fully and unreservedly the institution of private property and the right to investment profit. It is upon the fuller development of collective bargaining, the wider expansion of the labor movement, the increased influence of labor in our national councils, that the perpetuity of our democratic institutions must largely depend.

The organized workers of America, free in their industrial life, conscious partners in production, secure in their homes and enjoying a decent standard of living, will prove the finest bulwark against the intrusion of alien doctrines of government.

Do those who have hatched this foolish cry of communism in the C.I.O. fear the increased influence of labor in our democracy? Do they fear its influence will be cast on the side of shorter hours, a better system of distributed employment, better homes for the underprivileged, social security for the aged, a fairer distribution of the national income?

Certainly the workers that are being organized want a voice in the determination of these objectives of social justice.

Certainly labor wants a fairer share in the national income. Assuredly labor wants a larger participation in increased productive efficiency. Obviously the population is entitled to participate in the fruits of the genius of our men of achievement in the field of the material sciences.

Labor has suffered just as our farm population has suffered from a viciously unequal distribution of the national income. In the exploitation of both classes of workers has been the source of panic and depression, and upon the economic welfare of both rests the best assurance of a sound and permanent prosperity.

Under the banner of the Committee for Industrial Organization American labor is on the march. Its objectives today are those it had in the beginning: to strive for the unionization of our unorganized millions of workers and for the acceptance of collective bargaining as a recognized American institution.

It seeks peace with the industrial world. It seeks cooperation and mutuality of effort with the agricultural population. It would avoid strikes. It would have its rights determined under the law by the peaceful negotiations and contract relationships that are supposed to characterize American commercial life.

Until an aroused public opinion demands that employers accept that rule, labor has no recourse but to surrender its rights or struggle for their realization with its own economic power.

The objectives of this movement are not political in a partisan sense. Yet it is true that a political party which seeks the support of labor and makes pledges of good faith to labor must, in equity and good conscience, keep that faith and redeem those pledges.

The spectacle of august and dignified members of Congress, servants of the people and agents of the Republic, skulking in hallways and closets, hiding their faces in a party caucus to prevent a quorum from acting upon a larger measure, is one that emphasizes the perfidy of politicians and blasts the confidence of labor's millions in politicians' promises and statesmen's vows.

Labor next year cannot avoid the necessity of a political assay of the work and deeds of its so-called friends and its political beneficiaries. It must determine who are its friends in the arena of politics as elsewhere. It feels that its cause is just and that its friends should not view its struggle with neutral detachment or intone constant criticism of its activities.

Those who chant their praises of democracy, but who lose no chance to drive their knives into labor's defenseless back, must feel the weight of labor's woe, even as its open adversaries must ever feel the thrust of labor's power.

Labor, like Israel, has many sorrows. Its women weep for their fallen and they lament for the future of the children of the race. It ill behooves one who has supped at labor's table and who has been sheltered in labor's

house to curse with equal fervor and fine impartiality both labor and its
adversaries when they become locked in deadly embrace.

I repeat that labor seeks peace and guarantees its own loyalty, but the
voice of labor, insistent upon its rights, should not be annoying to the
ears of justice nor offensive to the conscience of the American people.

William Allen White

[1868–1944]

William Allen White, editor of the Emporia Gazette, won the
Pulitzer Prize in 1947 for The Autobiography of William Allen
White. *He spoke before the International Management Congress*
in Washington, D. C. on September 20, 1937. Parts of this address
follow.

SPEAKING FOR THE CONSUMER

IN THIS DISCUSSION I am supposed to represent the public—the American
consumer. He is a mythical character who never lived on land or sea,
but for that matter, the capitalist is a myth and the worker's status is an
economic hypothesis. It is trite to say that in America we are all more or
less owners, all workers of high or low degrees, and certainly we are all
consumers. We are all the children of John Q. Public, and our interests as
members of the consuming public are after all our chief end and objective as citizens of our democracy.

Let me begin by telling you both, laborer and capitalist, that you
have got us citizen consumers in a pretty sad mess. Every time we
consumers think of what one of you has done we are dead sore at
each of you until we begin to think of what the other has done.
Let me start on capital, the employer. Not that he is more to blame
than labor. But he is more responsible. He enjoys more freedom. He
could have done better. You employers have wasted twenty years
since the end of the World War. In those twenty years, a little intelligent
self-interest, a little foresight—not much—would have solved equitably
the problems that are now pressing upon us, problems that have been
adjusted in haste and in the emergency of calamity. Take the eight-
hour day. You knew that it was coming. Why didn't you men willingly,
sensibly grant it? But no. You had to fight it, every inch, and make
the consuming public think you were greedy—when you were not.
You were just dumb—dumb to give labor a sense of deep antagonism.
Take the old age pension and job insurance to cover seasonal and
technological unemployment. A thousand voices rose across the land,
telling you of the trouble ahead. What did you do? You put cotton
in your ears, and if you could hear through the cotton you began
yelling "Communism!" at the academician and the liberal politician
and spokesmen of the consuming public. Everyone realized 20 years

ago and more that sooner or later, with the pensions of the Civil War gone which took care of the aged until the World War, we should have old age pensions as a federal problem. Yet you employers let a generation of old people, unprovided for, begin to clamor for old age pensions and begin to listen to demagogues with silly panaceas. Then, having squandered your substance, you turned your men on the street in the days of the locust, and put into the hands of the most adroit politician America ever has seen the votes of ten million men whom your slipshod social viewpoint rendered jobless. If a dozen or twenty years ago you, Mr. Capitalist, had used the social sense of the average man in the street, this problem of unemployment and old age pensions would not be handing to your arch-enemies an organized subsidized class-conscious proletariat which can be voted to your destruction. By your sloth you created the particular head devil who is mocking you. He is your baby. You begot him two decades ago in the days of your youth when you were going to handle your business in your own way and no man could come into your shop and tell you how to run it!

But labor has been no Solomon. The proper business of a labor union is to get higher wages, better hours and good shop conditions for the workmen. But when labor en masse plunks its vote for its own party, then the spirit of party loyalty begins to obscure labor's objectives—high wages, short hours, decent shop conditions. Thus class-conscious labor leaders become more interested in their party welfare than in the fundamental objectives of labor unions. So we shall have the class-conscious political worker trading his vote not for the immediate objective of wages, hours and shop conditions, but for power for his political labor boss. The political labor boss will ask the workers to swallow a whole ticket in order to dominate a whole government. He would turn a democracy into a contest between two class-conscious parties, a class-conscious proletariat and a class-conscious plutocracy. In that setup where is the Consumer; where indeed is the compromise between labor and capital under the supervision of a middle class? In short with only two class-conscious political parties what becomes of democracy? The labor union militant and undefiled—yes; the vertical union and the closed shop? Yes. But a class-conscious labor party in a democracy—no! If labor insists upon maintaining its class lines of bitter intransigent hostility to all capital, the American middle class—old John Q. Public and his heirs and assigns will not support labor.

This is a middle-class country and the middle class will have its will and way. For the middle class is the real owner of American industry. The middle class is also 80% worker and the consumer of 80% of American industrial production in the home market. The middle class thinks and feels chiefly as The Consumer. And before the middle class demands an increase in either interest for investors or higher wages for the worker, the middle class will demand fair prices and a stable industry. That means industrial peace. No peace is lasting until it is founded upon that essential equitable compromise between the contending forces—capital and labor—known as justice.

Thomas E. Dewey
[1902–1971]

Thomas E. Dewey, Governor of New York from 1942 to 1954,
who was the Republican candidate for the Presidency in 1944 and
1948, had made an earlier bid for the nomination. The following
speech, of which we give the closing part, was made at the launch-
ing of this first try, at Minneapolis on December 6, 1939, while he
was District Attorney of New York.

RENDEZVOUS WITH DESPAIR

THE PRESIDENT has said we have a rendezvous with destiny. We seem
to be on our way toward a rendezvous with despair.

Fellow-Republicans, as a party, let us turn away from that rendezvous
and let us start going in the other direction and start now.

The one ultimate unforgivable crime is to despair of the republic.
The one essential to the survival of the republic is to know it will
survive and will survive into a future that is always larger, always better.
In every era for a century and a half it has been doomed to death
by gloomy young theorists and by tired and hopeless elders. And history
laughs at them as each time the dynamic forces of a free republic
led by free men have given the lie to the defeatists while the system
of free economic enterprise has marched onward, sweeping the nation's
increased population to full employment and ever higher living standards.

Nor is history the only answer to these gloomy predictions. For we
have about us in every state, in every city, on every farm, the answer.
Here in our own America we have the man-power, the wealth, the
natural resources, the genius to invent and create. We have the industrial skill to release that ever-flowing stream of new inventions and
greater productivity wherein lies the future of our own America. I
don't say to you, close your eyes and have faith—I say to you, open your
eyes, look around you and be convinced.

Here is the final answer to the defeatism of the new deal.

All history proves it is wrong. Our own eyes and our own brains tell
us it is wrong. And because its basic theory is wrong, it has done only
half its job. It is a duty of national government to perform its social
obligations. I believe this administration has sincerely attempted to
fulfill those obligations. But that is only half the job. The other half
is to maintain, to encourage the economic system which supports the
government and makes performance of social obligations possible.

Society has a permanent, deep-rooted obligation to its aged, its
blind, its sick, its unemployed. But it is not enough to say no one shall
starve. It is a cruel illusion to pass laws which are a mere promise
without also taking measures necessary to fulfillment of that promise.
The present administration has thought it well enough to make the
promise, leaving the performance to come from the savings of the last

generation, achieved under Republican administrations, and mortgaging the earnings of the next generation, which will also be under Republican administrations. Our obligation—and I say ours because the Democratic administration has failed—is to start producing the goods and earning the money so that those promises can be fulfilled.

Our first task is to sweep away the obstacles to that fulfillment. There is only one source of real money in any free country and that is private enterprise, the enterprise of the farmer, the worker, and the business man. It is our first, our primary task, to create the conditions under which this enterprise can go to work.

Until we first make up our minds that this is our purpose, there is no use discussing particular problems.

Do we believe in the continued growth of this country or do we believe we have reached our economic limit? All history and every observation of your own eyes proves that America is not finished. It need never be finished. There is no limit to America.

There is a force in America that has been held in check which once released can give us the employment that we need. It has nothing to do with slick monetary schemes. It has nothing to do with slick economic panaceas. This force is the energy of American enterprise, great and small. Given a chance, it can produce employment, can generate new purchasing power and set in motion once more the surging flow of commercial venture.

Government hostility, repressive taxation and economic quackery have kept this force from going to work. Our firm resolve must be to give it a chance and to encourage enterprise.

Nor does this involve tolerance of abuses in business or in any other element of society, civil or criminal. Where there are abuses in business, it is the function of government to correct them as they arise. But we can cure abuses in business without creating abuses by government.

Tonight I propose that we Americans, of whatever party, make up our minds that we do believe in the continued growth of this country.

Let us know the truth that the frontiers of social and economic expansion of America have not yet been discovered; that there is room and plenty in all this land for all the young men and women who are growing up in it; that there is work to do for them and all that follow.

Is it true that America is matured and completed and overbuilt and incapable of further expansion and new achievements? Is it true that all we can do from now on is to administer the achievements we already have? I do not say no temperately. I say no with resentment and anger.

Let us again learn to believe in the ability of a free people to solve its problems if given a chance. We can and we will again go forward. The one thing I want to do in whatever way I can is to help make the courage of eternal youth run once more in the veins of my party and of my country.

Herbert Hoover
[1874–1964]

Herbert Hoover, thirty-first President of the United States, delivered a Constitution Day address, September 17, 1935, at San Diego, California. Here is the address.

THE BILL OF RIGHTS

IN THE twelve minutes which I occupy in this discussion I shall refer to but one phase of the Constitution in its many bearings upon national life—that is the Bill of Rights.

Today the Constitution is indeed under more vivid discussion than at any time since the years before the Civil War. The background of that issue was Negro slavery, but in the foreground was the Constitutional question of States' rights and in the final determination was the fate of the Union. The aroused interest of today is again the rights of men. Today the issue is the rights of the individual in relation to the government; this too involves the fate of the nation. If for no other reason, this discussion has been forced upon us because new philosophies and new theories of government have arisen in the world which militantly deny the validity of our principles.

Our Constitution is not alone the working plan of a great Federation of States under representative government. There is embedded in it also the vital principles of the American system of liberty. That system is based upon certain inalienable freedoms and protections which not even the government may infringe and which we call the Bill of Rights. It does not require a lawyer to interpret those provisions. They are as clear as the Ten Commandments. Among others the freedom of worship, freedom of speech and of the press, the right of peaceable assembly, equality before the law, just trial for crime, freedom from unreasonable search, and security from being deprived of life, liberty, or property without due process of law, are the principles which distinguish our civilization. Herein are the invisible sentinels which guard the door of every home from invasion of coercion, of intimidation and fear. Herein is the expression of the spirit of men who would be forever free.

These rights were no sudden discovery, no over-night inspiration. They were established by centuries of struggle in which men died fighting bitterly for their recognition. Their beginnings lie in the Magna Charta at Runnymede five hundred and seventy years before the Constitution was written. Down through the centuries the Habeas Corpus, the "Petition of Rights," the "Declaration of Rights," the growth of the fundamental maxims of the Common Law, marked their expansion and security. Our forefathers migrated to America that they might attain them more fully. When they wrote the Declaration of Independence they boldly extended these rights. Before the Constitution could be ratified patriotic men who feared a return to tyranny, whose chains had been thrown off only after years of toil and bloody war, insisted that these hard-won rights should be incorporated in black and white within the Constitution—and so came the American Bill of Rights.

In the hurricane of revolutions which have swept the world since the Great War, men, struggling with the wreckage and poverty of that great catastrophe and the complications of the machine age, are in despair surrendering their freedom for false promises of economic security. Whether it be Fascist Italy, Nazi Germany, Communist Russia, or their lesser followers, the result is the same. Every day they repudiate every principle of the Bill of Rights. Freedom of worship is denied. Freedom of speech is suppressed. The press is censored and distorted with propaganda. The right of criticism is denied. Men go to jail or the gallows for honest opinion. They may not assemble for discussion. They speak of public affairs only in whispers. They are subject to search and seizure by spies and inquisitors who haunt the land. The safeguards of justice in trial or imprisonment are set aside. There is no right in one's savings or one's own home which the government need respect.

Here is a form of servitude, of slavery—a slipping back toward the Middle Ages. Whatever these governments are, they have one common denominator—the citizen has no assured rights. He is submerged into the State. Here is the most fundamental clash known to mankind—that is, free men and women, co-operating under orderly liberty, as contrasted with human beings made pawns of dictatorial government; men who are slaves of despotism, as against free men who are the masters of the State.

Even in America, where liberty blazed brightest and by its glow shed light on all the others, it is besieged from without and challenged from within. Many, in honest belief, hold that we cannot longer accommodate the growth of science, technology and mechanical power to the Bill of Rights and our form of government. With that I do not agree. Men's inventions cannot be of more value than men themselves. But it would be better that we sacrifice something of economic efficiency than to surrender these primary liberties. In them lies a spiritual right of men. Behind them is the conception which is the highest development of the Christian faith—the conception of individual freedom with brotherhood. From them is the fullest flowering of individual human personality.

Those who proclaim that by the Machine Age there is created an irreconcilable conflict in which Liberty must be sacrificed should not forget the battles for these rights over the centuries, for let it be remembered that in the end these are undying principles which spring from the souls of men. We imagine conflict not because the principles of Liberty are unworkable in a machine age, but because we have not worked them conscientiously or have forgotten their true meaning.

Nor do I admit that sacrifice of these rights would add to economic efficiency or would gain in economic security, or would find a single job or would give a single assurance in old age. The dynamic forces which sustain economic security and progress in human comfort lie deep below the surface. They reach to those human impulses which are watered alone by freedom. The initiative of men, their enterprise, the inspiration of thought, flower in full only in the security of these rights.

And by practical experience under the American system we have tested this truth. And here I may repeat what I have said elsewhere. Down through a century and a half this American concept of human freedom has enriched the whole world. From the release of the spirit, the initiative, the co-operation, and the courage of men, which alone comes of these freedoms, has been builded this very machine age with all its additions of comfort, its reductions of sweat. Wherever in the world the system of individual liberty has been sustained, mankind has been better clothed, better fed, better housed, has had more leisure. Above all, men and women have had more self-respect. They have been more generous and of finer spirit. Those who scoff that liberty is of no consequence to the underprivileged and the unemployed are grossly ignorant of the primary fact that it is through the creative and the productive impulses of free men that the redemption of those sufferers and their economic security must come. Any system which curtails these freedoms and stimulants to men destroys the possibility of the full production from which economic security can alone come.

These rights and protections of the Bill of Rights are safeguarded in the Constitution through a delicate balance and separation of powers in the framework of our government. That has been founded on the experience over centuries including our own day.

Liberty is safe only by a division of powers and upon local self-government. We know full well that power feeds upon itself—partly from the greed of power and partly from the innocent belief that utopia can be attained by dictation or coercion.

Nor is respect for the Bill of Rights a fetter upon progress. It has been no dead hand that has carried the living principles of liberty over these centuries. Without violation of these principles and their safeguards we have amended the Constitution many times in the past century to meet the problems of growing civilization. We will no doubt do so many times again. Always groups of audacious men in government or out will attempt to consolidate privilege against their fellows. New invention and new ideas require the constant remolding of our civilization. The functions of government must be readjusted from time to time to restrain the strong and protect the weak. That is the preservation of liberty itself. We ofttimes interpret some provisions of the Bill of Rights so that they override others. They indeed jostle each other in course of changing national life—but their respective domains can be defined by virtue, by reason, and by law. And the freedom of men is not possible without virtue, reason, and law.

Liberty comes alone and lives alone where the hard-won rights of men are held inalienable, where governments themselves may not infringe, where governments are indeed but the mechanisms to protect and sustain these principles. It was this concept for which America's sons have died on a hundred battlefields.

The nation seeks for solution of many difficulties. These solutions can come alone through the constructive forces which arise from the spirit of free men and women. The purification of Liberty from abuses, the restoration of confidence in the rights of men, from which come the release of the dynamic forces of initiative and enterprise, are alone the methods through which these solutions can be found and the purpose of American life assured.

Charles Evans Hughes

[1862–1948]

The following address was delivered at the One Hundred and Fiftieth Anniversary of the meeting of the First Congress of the United States, March 4, 1939, by Chief Justice Charles Evans Hughes.

OUR GOVERNMENT

MR. PRESIDENT, Mr. Vice President, Mr. Speaker, Members of the Senate and House of Representatives, members of the Diplomatic Corps, ladies and gentlemen:

I thank Senator Barkley from the depths of my heart for his very generous words.

Gentlemen of the Senate and House of Representatives, the most significant fact in connection with this anniversary is that after 150 years, notwithstanding expansion of territory, enormous increase in population, and profound economic changes, despite direct attack and subversive influences, there is every indication that the vastly preponderant sentiment of the American people is that our form of government shall be preserved.

We come from our distinct departments of governmental activity to testify to our unity of aim in maintaining that form of government in accordance with our common pledge. We are here not as masters but as servants, not to glory in power but to attest our loyalty to the commands and restrictions laid down by our sovereign, the people of the United States, in whose name and by whose will we exercise our brief authority. If as such representatives we have, as Benjamin Franklin said, "no more durable preeminence than the different grains in an hour glass," we serve our hour by unremitting devotion to the principles which have given our Government both stability and capacity for orderly progress in a world of turmoil and revolutionary upheavals. Gratifying as is the record of achievement, it would be extreme folly to engage in mere laudation or to surrender to the enticing delusions of a thoughtless optimism. Forms of government, however well contrived, cannot assure their own permanence. If we owe to the wisdom and restraint of the fathers a system of government which has thus far stood the test, we all recognize that it is only by wisdom and restraint in our own day that we can make that system last. If today we find ground for confidence that our institutions which have made for liberty and strength will be maintained, it will not be due to abundance of physical resources or to productive capacity, but because these are at the command of a people who still cherish the principles which underlie our system and because of the general appreciation of what is essentially sound in our governmental structure.

With respect to the influences which shape public opinion, we live in a new world. Never have these influences operated more directly, or with such variety of facile instruments, or with such overwhelming force. We have mass production in opinion as well as in goods. The grasp of tradition and of sectional prejudgment is loosened. Postulates of the past must show cause. Our institutions will not be preserved by veneration of what is old, if that is simply expressed in the formal ritual of a shrine. The American people are eager and responsive. They listen attentively to a vast multitude of appeals and, with this receptivity, it is only upon their sound judgment that we can base our hope for a wise conservatism with continued progress and appropriate adaptation to new needs.

We shall do well on this anniversary if the thought of the people is directed to the essentials of our democracy. Here in this body we find the living exponents of the principle of representative government—not government by direct mass action but by representation which means leadership as well as responsiveness and accountability.

Here the ground swells of autocracy, destructive of parliamentary independence, have not yet upset or even disturbed the authority and responsibility of the essential legislative branch of democratic institutions. We have a National Government equipped with vast powers which have proved to be adequate to the development of a great nation, and at the same time maintaining the balance between centralized authority and local autonomy. It has been said that to preserve that balance, if we did not have States we should have to create them. In our 48 States we have the separate sources of power necessary to protect local interests and thus also to preserve the central authority, in the vast variety of our concerns, from breaking down under its own weight. Our States, each with her historic background and supported by the loyal sentiment of her citizens, afford opportunity for the essential activity of political units, the advantages of which no artificial territorial arrangement could secure. If our checks and balances sometimes prevent the speedy action which is thought desirable, they also assure in the long run a more deliberate judgment. And what the people really want, they generally get. With the ultimate power of change through amendment in their hands they are always able to obtain whatever a preponderant and abiding sentiment demands.

We not only praise individual liberty but our constitutional system has the unique distinction of insuring it. Our guaranties of fair trials, of due process in the protection of life, liberty, and property—which stands between the citizen and arbitrary power—of religious freedom, of free speech, free press and free assembly, are the safeguards which have been erected against the abuses threatened by gusts of passion and prejudice which in misguided zeal would destroy the basic interests of democracy. We protect the fundamental right of minorities, in order to save democratic government from destroying itself by the excesses of its own power. The firmest ground for confidence in the future is that more than ever we realize that, while democracy must have its organization and controls, its vital breath is individual liberty.

I am happy to be here as the representative of the tribunal which is charged with the duty of maintaining, through the decision of controversies, these constitutional guaranties. We are a separate but not an independent arm of government. You, not we, have the purse and the sword. You, not we, determine the establishment and the jurisdiction of the lower Federal courts and the bounds of the appellate jurisdiction of the Supreme Court. The Congress first assembled on March 4, 1789, and on September 24, 1789, as its twentieth enactment, passed the Judiciary Act—to establish the judicial courts of the United States—a statute which is a monument of wisdom, one of the most satisfactory acts in the long history of notable congressional legislation. It may be said to take rank in our annals as next in importance to the Constitution itself.

In thus providing the judicial establishment, and in equipping and sustaining it, you have made possible the effective functioning of the department of government which is designed to safeguard with judicial impartiality and independence the interests of liberty. But in the great enterprise of making democracy workable we are all partners. One member of our body politic cannot say to another: "I have no need of thee." We work in successful cooperation by being true, each department to its own functions, and all to the spirit which pervades our institutions, exalting the processes of reason, seeking through the very limitations of power the promotion of the wise use of power, and finding the ultimate security of life, liberty, and the pursuit of happiness, and the promise of continued stability and a rational progress in the good sense of the American people.

Anthony Eden

[1897–1977]

Anthony Eden, Prime Minister of Great Britain from 1955 to 1957, first became Secretary of State of Foreign Affairs in 1935. As an advocate of a firm policy in dealing with the increasing aggression of the German and Italian dictators, Eden resigned his office in 1938 when Prime Minister Neville Chamberlain decided upon an opposite course. When Winston Churchill succeeded Chamberlain as Prime Minister in 1940, Eden returned to the cabinet, first as Secretary of War and then again as Secretary of State for Foreign Affairs. Following is Eden's speech, explaining his resignation from the Chamberlain cabinet, delivered before the House of Commons on February 21, 1938.

A FIRM POLICY

THERE are occasions when strong political convictions must override all other considerations. Of such an occasion, only the individual himself can be the judge.

The objective of foreign policy in this country is and must always be the maintenance of peace. If, however, peace is to be enduring, it must rest on foundations of frank reciprocity and of mutual respect. It follows that we must be ready to negotiate with all countries, whatever their forms of government, in order to promote international understanding. But we must also be watchful that, in our conception of such negotiations and in the method by which we seek to further them, we are, in fact, strengthening, not undermining, the foundations on which international confidence rests.

The immediate issue is whether such official conversations (between the British and Italian governments) should be opened in Rome now. In my conviction, the attitude of the Italian government to international problems in general, and this country in particular, is not yet such as to justify this course. The ground has been in no respect prepared. Propaganda against this country by the Italian government is rife throughout the world. I am myself pledged to this House not to open conversations with Italy until this hostile propaganda ceases. Moreover, little progress in fact, though much in promise, has been made with the solution of the Spanish problem. Let me make it plain that I do not suggest and would not advocate that the government should refuse conversations with the Italian government, or indeed with any other government which shows any disposition to conversation with us for betterment of international understanding. Yet we must see that the conditions in which these conversations take place are such as to make for the likelihood, if not for the certainty, of their success. In my view, those conditions do not exist today.

In January of last year, after difficult negotiations, we signed an Anglo-Italian agreement. Within a very few days—indeed, almost simultaneously—a considerable consignment of Italians left for Spain. It may be said that this was not a breach of our understanding; but no one, I think, will contend that it did not run counter to its spirit. The same agreement contained a specific clause dealing with the cessation of propaganda, yet propaganda was scarcely diminished for an instant.

Then last summer the Prime Minister and Signor Mussolini exchanged letters, and after that for a few days relations between our two countries took a marked turn for the better. There ensued the incidents in the Mediterranean, with which the House is familiar.

My submission is that we cannot run the risk of further repetition of these experiences.

We must agree not only on the need for withdrawal (of the foreign fighters now in Spain), but on the conditions of withdrawal. We have had assurances enough of that in the past. We must go farther, and show the world not only promises but achievement.

We cannot consider this problem except in relation to the international situation as a whole. We are in the presence of progressive deterioration of respect for international obligations. It is quite impossible to judge these things in a vacuum. This is the moment for this country to stand firm, not to plunge into negotiations unprepared, with foreknowledge that the obstacle to their success has not been resolved.

Agreements that are worth while are never made on the basis of threats, nor, in the past, has this country been willing to negotiate in such conditions.

It has never entered into my conception to suggest that the Italian forces alone should be withdrawn from Spain, but only that the Italian government should agree to, and carry out with others, a fair scheme for the proposed withdrawal of all forces from Spain.

I am conscious why I stand here, and why my colleagues take another view. If they are right, their chances for success will certainly be enhanced if their policy is pursued through another Foreign Secretary.

I should not be frank with the House if I pretended it is an isolated issue between the Prime Minister and myself. It is not. Within the last few weeks, upon one of the most important decisions of foreign policy, which did not concern Italy at all, the difference was fundamental. Moreover, it recently has become clear to me, and, I think to him, that there is between us a real difference in the outlook and method.

Of late the conviction has steadily grown upon me that there has been too keen a desire on our part to make terms with others, rather than that others should make terms with us. This has never been the attitude of this country in the past. It should not, in the interests of peace, be our attitude today.

I do not believe we can make progress in European appeasement— more particularly in the light of the events of the last few days—if we allow the impression to gain currency abroad that we yield to constant pressure.

I am certain in my own mind that progress depends, above all, on the temper of the nation, and that temper must find expression in a firm spirit. That spirit, I am confident, is there. Not to give voice to it is, I believe, fair neither to this country nor to the world.

Neville Chamberlain
[1869–1940]

*Neville Chamberlain, a business man by training and a conserva-
tive in politics, succeeded Stanley Baldwin as Prime Minister of Great
Britain, in 1937. Working, as he said, for "peace in our time," he endeavored to reach an agreement with Hitlerite Germany, the Munich
Pact being the culmination of his appeasement policy. Following are
parts of his speech defending the Munich agreement which he delivered in the House of Commons on October 3, 1938. The Munich
Pact failed to stop Nazi aggression. Within a year England was at
war with Germany, and in 1940 Chamberlain's ministry was overthrown in Parliament.*

THE MUNICH AGREEMENT

WHEN the House met last Wednesday we were all under the shadow of an imminent menace. A war more stark and terrible than had ever taken place before seemed to be staring us in the face. Before I had sat down, a message had come which gave us new hope that peace might yet be saved. That day, or a few days later, we joined in joy and thankfulness that the prayers of millions had been answered.

Our anxiety has been lifted from our hearts. On the members of the Cabinet the strain of responsibility has been for weeks almost over-whelming. Some of us, I have no doubt, will carry the marks of it for the rest of our days.

Hard things have been said about the German Chancellor today and in the past, but I do feel that the House ought to recognize the difficulty for a man in that position to take back such an emphatic declaration as he had already made and to recognize that in consenting, even though it were only at the last minute, to discuss with the representa-tives of other powers those things which he had declared he had already decided once and for all, was a real contribution on his part.

As regards Signor Mussolini, his contribution was certainly notable, and perhaps decisive. It was on his suggestion that the final stages of mobilization were postponed for twenty-four hours, to give us an opportunity of discussing the situation, and I wish to say that at the conference itself both he and the Italian Foreign Secretary, Count Ciano, were most helpful in the discussion.

It was they who, very early in the proceeding, produced a memorandum which Daladier and I were able to accept as a basis of discussion.

I think Europe and the world have reason to be grateful to the head of the Italian government for contributing to a peaceful solution.

Mr. Duff Cooper has alluded in somewhat bitter terms to my conversation last Friday morning with Herr Hitler. I do not know why that conversation should give rise to suspicion, still less to criticism.

I ended it with no pact. I made no new commitments. There is no secret understanding. Our conversation was hostile to no other nations.

The object of that conversation for which I asked was to try to extend a little further the personal contact which I had established with Herr Hitler, which I believed to be essential to modern diplomacy.

Finally, there are the noncommittal conversations carried on on my part with a view to seeing whether there could be points in common between the head of a democratic government and the ruler of a totalitarian state. You see the result.

A declaration has been published, in which Mr. Duff Cooper finds so much ground for suspicion. What does it say?

The first paragraph says, "That we agree in recognizing that the question of Anglo-German relations is of first importance to the two countries and to Europe."

Will any one deny that?

The second is an expression of opinion only. It says we regard the agreement signed and the Anglo-German naval agreement as symbolic of the desire of our two peoples never to go to war with one another again.

Does any one doubt that that is the desire of the people?

(The Prime Minister then read the last paragraph of the declaration suggesting that Germany and Britain might continue their efforts to remove all possible sources of differences.)

Is there any one who will stand up and condemn that sentence? I believe there are many who will feel with me that in this declaration signed by the German Chancellor and myself there is something more than a pious expression of opinion.

In our relations with other countries everything depends upon there being sincerity and goodwill on both sides. I believe there is sincerity and goodwill on both sides. That is why the significance goes far beyond its actual words.

Ever since I assumed my present office my main purpose has been to work for the pacification of Europe, for the removal of those suspicions and animosities which have so long poisoned the air.

The path that leads to peace is a long one and bristles with obstacles. This question of Czechoslovakia is the latest and perhaps the most dangerous. Now that we have got past it I feel that it may be possible to make further progress along the road to sanity.

If there is one lesson which I think we have to learn from the events of this last week, it is this: Peace is not to be obtained by sitting still and waiting for it to come: It requires active and positive effort.

I know I shall have plenty of critics who will say I have been guilty of facile optimism and that the better plan would have been to disbelieve every word by rulers of other great states of Europe.

I am too much of a realist to believe that we are going to achieve our purpose in a day. We have only laid the foundations of peace. The superstructure is not even begun.

Winston Churchill
[1874–1965]

Winston Churchill, Prime Minister of Great Britain from 1940 to 1945, and from 1951 to 1955, was recognized as one of the great orators of our time. His speeches before Parliament and over the radio during the Second World War were widely quoted, and not only heartened his people but electrified liberty-loving peoples of the entire world. At an early age Churchill fought in India and Egypt. He was a correspondent in the South African War, was captured by the Boers and escaped. In 1911 he was made First Lord of the Admiralty, and when the First World War began, Churchill had the fleet ready. He directed and took part in several spectacular expeditions. When Hitler was preparing for aggression, Churchill's eloquent voice was heard in Parliament and on the rostrum warning England and urging her to prepare for defense. Not much attention was paid to him at that time, but when England was faced with grave danger in 1939 and 1940, Churchill was called upon to succeed, as Prime Minister, Neville Chamberlain, whose policy of appeasement Churchill had fought. Churchill's Conservative Party was defeated in 1945, and Clement Attlee of the Labor Party succeeded as Prime Minister. The Conservatives returned to power in 1951, and Churchill was Prime Minister from that time until his retirement in April, 1955. He became Sir Winston Churchill in 1953. This great orator is represented here by five speeches; and a sixth—a major later speech—will be found in Chapter XI. The following address, Churchill's first speech before Parliament after his appointment as Prime Minister, was delivered on May 13, 1940.

"BLOOD, SWEAT AND TEARS"

ON FRIDAY EVENING last I received from His Majesty the mission to form a new administration.

It was the evident will of Parliament and the nation that this should be conceived on the broadest possible basis and that it should include all parties.

I have already completed the most important part of this task. A war cabinet has been formed of five members, representing, with the Labor, Opposition and Liberals, the unity of the nation.

It was necessary that this should be done in one single day on account of the extreme urgency and rigor of events. Other key positions were filled yesterday. I am submitting a further list to the King tonight. I hope to complete the appointment of principal Ministers during tomorrow.

The appointment of other Ministers usually takes a little longer. I trust when Parliament meets again this part of my task will be completed and that the administration will be complete in all respects.

I considered it in the public interest to suggest to the Speaker that the House should be summoned today. At the end of today's proceedings, the adjournment of the House will be proposed until May 21 with provision for earlier meeting if need be. Business for that will be notified to M. P.'s at the earliest opportunity.

I now invite the House by a resolution to record its approval of the steps taken and declare its confidence in the new government. The resolution:

"That this House welcomes the formation of a government representing the united and inflexible resolve of the nation to prosecute the war with Germany to a victorious conclusion."

To form an administration of this scale and complexity is a serious undertaking in itself. But we are in the preliminary phase of one of the greatest battles in history. We are in action at many other points —in Norway and in Holland—and we have to be prepared in the Mediterranean. The air battle is continuing, and many preparations have to be made here at home.

In this crisis I think I may be pardoned if I do not address the House at any length today, and I hope that any of my friends and colleagues or former colleagues who are affected by the political reconstruction will make all allowances for any lack of ceremony with which it has been necessary to act.

I say to the House as I said to Ministers who have joined this government, I have nothing to offer but blood, toil, tears and sweat. We have before us an ordeal of the most grievous kind. We have before us many, many months of struggle and suffering.

You ask, what is our policy? I say it is to wage war by land, sea and air. War with all our might and with all the strength God has given us, and to wage war against a monstrous tyranny never surpassed in the dark and lamentable catalogue of human crime. That is our policy.

You ask, what is our aim? I can answer in one word. It is victory. Victory at all costs—victory in spite of all terrors—victory, however long and hard the road may be, for without victory there is no survival.

Let that be realized. No survival for the British Empire, no survival for all that the British Empire has stood for, no survival for the urge, the impulse of the ages, that mankind shall move forward toward his goal.

I take up my task in buoyancy and hope. I feel sure that our cause will not be suffered to fail among men.

I feel entitled at this juncture, at this time, to claim the aid of all and to say, "Come then, let us go forward together with our united strength."

The epic story of the defense of Dunkirk and the evacuation of the British Expeditionary Force was dramatically told by Churchill before the House of Commons on June 4, 1940.

DUNKIRK

From the moment when the defenses at Sedan on the Meuse were broken at the end of the second week in May only a rapid retreat to Amiens and the south could have saved the British-French armies who had entered Belgium at the appeal of the Belgian King.

This strategic fact was not immediately realized. The French High Command hoped it would be able to close the gap. The armies of the north were under their orders. Moreover, a retirement of that kind would have involved almost certainly the destruction of a fine Belgian Army of twenty divisions and abandonment of the Whole of Belgium.

Therefore, when the force and scope of the German penetration was realized and when the new French Generalissimo, General [Maxime] Weygand, assumed command in place of General Gamelin, an effort was made by the French and British Armies in Belgium to keep holding the right hand of the Belgians and give their own right hand to the newly created French Army which was to advance across the Somme in great strength.

However, the German eruption swept like a sharp scythe south of Amiens to the rear of the armies in the north—eight or nine armored divisions, each with about 400 armored vehicles of different kinds divisible into small self-contained units.

This force cut off all communications between us and the main French Army. It severed our communications for food and ammunition. It ran first through Amiens, afterward through Abbeville, and it shore its way up the coast to Boulogne and Calais, almost to Dunkirk.

Behind this armored and mechanized onslaught came a number of German divisions in lorries, and behind them, again, plodded comparatively slowly the dull, brute mass of the ordinary German Army and German people, always ready to be led to the trampling down in other lands of liberties and comforts they never have known in their own.

I said this armored scythe stroke almost reached Dunkirk—almost but not quite. Boulogne and Calais were scenes of desperate fighting. The guards defended Boulogne for a while and were then withdrawn by orders from this country.

The rifle brigade of the Sixtieth Rifles (Queen Victoria's Rifles), with a battalion of British tanks and 1,000 Frenchmen, in all about 4,000 strong, defended Calais to the last. The British brigadier was given an hour to surrender. He spurned the offer. Four days of intense street fighting passed before the silence reigned in Calais which marked the end of a memorable resistance.

Only thirty unwounded survivors were brought off by the navy, and we do not know the fate of their comrades. Their sacrifice was not, however, in vain. At least two armored divisions which otherwise would have been turned against the B. E. F. had to be sent to overcome them. They have added another page to the glories of the light division.

The time gained enabled the Gravelines water line to be flooded and held by French troops. Thus the port of Dunkirk was held open. When it was found impossible for the armies of the north to reopen their communications through Amiens with the main French armies, only one choice remained. It seemed, indeed, a forlorn hope. The Belgian and French armies were almost surrounded. Their sole line of retreat was to a single port and its neighboring beaches. They were pressed on every side by heavy attacks and were far outnumbered in the air.

When a week ago today I asked the House to fix this afternoon for the occasion of a statement, I feared it would be my hard lot to announce from this box the greatest military disaster of our long history.

I thought, and there were good judges who agreed with me, that perhaps 20,000 or 30,000 men might be re-embarked, but it certainly seemed that the whole French First Army and the whole B. E. F., north of the Amiens-Abbeville gap would be broken up in open field or else have to capitulate for lack of food and ammunition.

These were the hard and heavy tidings I called on the House and nation to prepare themselves for.

The whole root and core and brain of the British Army, around which and upon which we were building and are able to build the great British armies of later years, seemed due to perish upon the field. That was the prospect a week ago, but another blow which might have proved final was still to fall upon us.

The King of the Belgians called upon us to come to his aid. Had not this ruler and his government severed themselves from the Allies who rescued their country from extinction in the late war, and had they not sought refuge in what has been proved to be fatal neutrality, then the French and British armies at the outset might well have saved not only Belgium but perhaps even Holland.

At the last moment, when Belgium was already invaded, King Leopold called upon us to come to his aid, and even at the last moment we came. He and his brave and efficient army of nearly half a million strong guarded our eastern flank; this kept open our only retreat to the sea.

Suddenly, without any prior consultation and with the least possible notice, without the advice of his ministers and on his own personal act, he sent a plenipotentiary to the German Command surrendering his army and exposing our flank and the means of retreat.

I asked the House a week ago to suspend its judgment because the facts were not clear. I do not think there is now any reason why we should not form our own opinions upon this pitiful episode. The surrender of the Belgian Army compelled the British Army at the shortest notice to cover a flank to the sea of more than thirty miles' length which otherwise would have been cut off.

In doing this and closing this flank, contact was lost inevitably between the British and two of three corps forming the First French Army who were then further from the coast than we were. It seemed impossible that large numbers of Allied troops could reach the coast. The enemy attacked on all sides in great strength and fierceness, and their main power, air force, was thrown into the battle.

The enemy began to fire cannon along the beaches by which alone shipping could approach or depart. They sowed magnetic mines in the channels and seas and sent repeated waves of hostile aircraft, sometimes more than 100 strong, to cast bombs on a single pier that remained and on the sand dunes.

Their U-boats, one of which was sunk, and motor launches took their toll of the vast traffic which now began. For four or five days the intense struggle raged. All armored divisions, or what was left of them, together with great masses of German infantry and artillery, hurled themselves on the ever narrowing and contracting appendix within which the British and French armies fought.

Meanwhile the Royal Navy, with the willing help of countless merchant seamen and a host of volunteers, strained every nerve and every effort and every craft to embark the British and Allied troops.

Over 220 light warships and more than 650 other vessels were engaged. They had to approach this difficult coast, often in adverse weather, under an almost ceaseless hail of bombs and increasing concentration of artillery fire. Nor were the seas themselves free from mines and torpedoes.

It was in conditions such as these that our men carried on with little or no rest for days and nights, moving troops across dangerous waters and bringing with them always the men whom they had rescued. The numbers they brought back are the measure of their devotion and their courage.

Hospital ships, which were plainly marked, were the special target for Nazi bombs, but the men and women aboard them never faltered in their duty.

Meanwhile the R. A. F., who already had been intervening in the battle so far as its range would allow it to go from home bases, now used a part of its main metropolitan fighter strength to strike at German bombers.

The struggle was protracted and fierce. Suddenly the scene has cleared. The crash and thunder has momentarily, but only for the moment, died away. The miracle of deliverance achieved by the valor and perseverance, perfect discipline, faultless service, skill and unconquerable vitality is a manifesto to us all.

The enemy was hurled back by the British and French troops. He was so roughly handled that he dare not molest their departure seriously. The air force decisively defeated the main strength of the German Air Force and inflicted on them a loss of at least four to one.

The navy, using nearly 1,000 ships of all kinds, carried over 335,000 men, French and British, from the jaws of death back to their native land and to the tasks which lie immediately before them.

We must be very careful not to assign to this deliverance attributes of a victory. Wars are not won by evacuations, but there was a victory inside this deliverance which must be noted.

Many of our soldiers coming back have not seen the air force at work. They only saw the bombers which escaped their protective attack. This was a great trial of strength between the British and German Air Forces.

Can you conceive of a greater objective for the power of Germany in the air than to make all evacuations from these beaches impossible and to sink all of the ships, numbering almost 1,000? Could there have been an incentive of greater military importance and significance to the whole purpose of the war?

They tried hard and were beaten back. They were frustrated in their task; we have got the armies away and they have paid fourfold for any losses sustained. Very large formations of German airplanes were turned on several occasions from the attack by a quarter their number of R. A. F. planes and dispersed in different directions. Twelve airplanes have been hunted by two. One airplane was driven into the water and cast away by the charge of a British airplane which had no more ammunition.

All of our types and our pilots have been vindicated. The Hurricane, Spitfires and Defiance have been vindicated. When I consider how much greater would be our advantage in defending the air above this island against overseas attacks, I find in these facts a sure basis on which practical and reassuring thoughts may rest, and I will pay my tribute to these young airmen.

May it not be that the cause of civilization itself will be defended by the skill and devotion of a few thousand airmen? There never has been, I suppose, in all the history of the world such opportunity for youth.

The Knights of the Round Table and the Crusaders have fallen back into distant days, not only distant but prosaic; but these young men are going forth every morning, going forth holding in their hands an instrument of colossal shattering power, of whom it may be said that every morn brought forth a noble chance and every chance brought forth a noble deed. These young men deserve our gratitude, as all brave men who in so many ways and so many occasions are ready and will continue to be ready to give their life and their all to their native land.

I return to the army. In a long series of very fierce battles, now on this front, now on that, fighting on three fronts at once, battles fought by two or three divisions against an equal or sometimes larger number of the enemy, and fought very fiercely on old ground so many of us knew so well, our losses in men exceed 30,000 in killed, wounded and missing. I take this occasion for expressing the sympathy of the House with those who have suffered bereavement or are still anxious.

The President of the Board of Trade (Sir Andrew Duncan) is not here today. His son has been killed, and many here have felt private affliction of the sharpest form, but I would say about the missing—we have had a large number of wounded come home safely to this country—there may be very many reported missing who will come back home some day.

In the confusion of departure it is inevitable that many should be cut off. Against this loss of over 30,000 men we may set the far heavier loss certainly inflicted on the enemy, but our losses in material are enormous. We have perhaps lost one-third of the men we lost in the opening days of the battle on March 21, 1918, but we have lost nearly as many guns—nearly 1,000—and all our transport and all the armored vehicles that were with the army of the north.

These losses will impose further delay on the expansion of our military strength. That expansion has not been proceeding as fast as we had hoped. The best of all we had to give has been given to the B. E. F., and although they had not the number of tanks and some articles of equipment which were desirable they were a very well and finely equipped army. They had the first fruits of all our industry had to give. That has gone and now here is further delay.

How long it will be, how long it will last depends upon the exertions which we make on this island. An effort, the like of which has never been seen in our records, is now being made. Work is proceeding night and day, Sundays and week days. Capital and labor have cast aside their interests, rights and customs and put everything into the common stock. Already the flow of munitions has leaped forward. There is no reason why we should not in a few months overtake the sudden and serious loss that has come upon us without retarding the development of our general program.

Nevertheless, our thankfulness at the escape of our army with so many men, and the thankfulness of their loved ones, who passed through an agonizing week, must not blind us to the fact that what happened in France and Belgium is a colossal military disaster.

The French Army has been weakened, the Belgian Army has been lost and a large part of those fortified lines upon which so much faith was reposed has gone, and many valuable mining districts and factories have passed into the enemy's possession.

The whole of the channel ports are in his hands, with all the strategic consequences that follow from that, and we must expect another blow to be struck almost immediately at us or at France.

We were told that Hitler has plans for invading the British Isles.

This has often been thought of before. When Napoleon lay at Boulogne for a year with his flat-bottomed boats and his Grand Army, some one told him there were bitter weeds in England. There certainly were and a good many more of them have since been returned. The whole question of defense against invasion is powerfully affected by the fact that we have for the time being in this island incomparably more military forces than we had in the last war. But this will not continue. We shall not be content with a defensive war. We have our duty to our Allies.

We have to reconstitute and build up the B. E. F. once again under its gallant Commander in Chief, Lord Gort. All this is en train. But now I feel we must put our defense in this island into such a high state of organization that the fewest possible numbers will be required to give effectual security and that the largest possible potential offensive effort may be released.

On this we are now engaged. It would be very convenient to enter upon this subject in secret sessions. The government would not necessarily be able to reveal any great military secrets, but we should like to have our discussions free and without the restraint imposed by the fact that they would be read the next day by the enemy.

The government would benefit by the views expressed by the House. I understand that some request is to be made on this subject, which will be readily acceded to by the government. We have found it necessary to take measures of increasing stringency, not only against enemy aliens and suspicious characters of other nationalities but also against British subjects who may become a danger or a nuisance should the war be transported to the United Kingdom.

I know there are a great many people affected by the orders which we have made who are passionate enemies of Nazi Germany. I am very sorry for them, but we cannot, under the present circumstances, draw all the distinctions we should like to do. If parachute landings were attempted and fierce fights followed, those unfortunate people would be far better out of the way for their own sake as well as ours.

There is, however, another class for which I feel not the slightest sympathy. Parliament has given us powers to put down fifth column activities with the strongest hand, and we shall use those powers subject to the supervision and correction of the House without hesitation until we are satisfied and more than satisfied that this malignancy in our midst has been effectually stamped out.

Turning once again to the question of invasion, there has, I will observe, never been a period in all those long centuries of which we boast when an absolute guarantee against invasion, still less against serious raids, could have been given to our people. In the days of Napoleon the same wind which might have carried his transports across the Channel might have driven away a blockading fleet. There is always the chance, and it is that chance which has excited and befooled the imaginations of many continental tyrants.

We are assured that novel methods will be adopted, and when we see the originality, malice and ingenuity of aggression which our enemy displays we may certainly prepare ourselves for every kind of novel stratagem and every kind of brutal and treacherous manoeuvre. I think no idea is so outlandish that it should not be considered and viewed with a watchful, but at the same time steady, eye.

We must never forget the solid assurances of sea power and those which belong to air power if they can be locally exercised. I have myself full confidence that if all do their duty and if the best arrangements are made, as they are being made, we shall prove ourselves once again able to defend our island home, ride out the storms of war and outlive the menace of tyranny, if necessary, for years, if necessary, alone.

At any rate, that is what we are going to try to do. That is the resolve of His Majesty's Government, every man of them. That is the will of Parliament and the nation. The British Empire and the French Republic, linked together in their cause and their need, will defend to the death their native soils, aiding each other like good comrades to the utmost of their strength, even though a large tract of Europe and many old and famous States have fallen or may fall into the grip of the Gestapo and all the odious apparatus of Nazi rule.

We shall not flag nor fail. We shall go on to the end. We shall fight in France and on the seas and oceans; we shall fight with growing confidence and growing strength in the air.

We shall defend our island whatever the cost may be; we shall fight on beaches, landing grounds, in fields, in streets and on the hills. We shall never surrender and even if, which I do not for the moment believe, this island or a large part of it were subjugated and starving, then our empire beyond the seas, armed and guarded by the British Fleet, will carry on the struggle until in God's good time the New World, with all its power and might, sets forth to the liberation and rescue of the Old.

In telling the story of the fall of France and presenting the grim outlook for Britain, Churchill delivered one of his greatest speeches. The date of this speech is June 18, 1940, and the place is the House of Commons.

"THEIR FINEST HOUR"

I SPOKE the other day of the colossal military disaster which occurred when the French High Command failed to withdraw the northern armies from Belgium at a moment when they knew that the French front was decisively broken at Sedan and on the Meuse.

This delay entailed the loss of fifteen or sixteen French divisions and threw out of action the whole of the British Expeditionary Force.

Our army were indeed rescued by the British Navy from Dunkirk, but only with the loss of all their cannon, vehicles and modern equipment. This loss inevitably took some weeks to repair, and in the first two of these weeks the Battle of France had been lost.

When we consider the heroic resistance made by the French Army against heavy odds in this battle, and the enormous loss inflicted upon the enemy and the evident exhaustion of the enemy, it might well be thought that these twenty-five divisions of the best troops—best trained and equipped—might have turned the scales. However, General Weygand had to fight without them.

Only three British divisions or their equivalent were able to stand in the line with their French comrades. They have suffered severely, but they have fought well. We sent every man we could to France, as fast as we could re-equip and transport their formations.

I am not reciting these facts for the purpose of recrimination. That I judge to be utterly futile and even harmful. We cannot afford it. I recite them in order to explain why it was we did not have, as we could have had, between twelve and fourteen British divisions fighting in the line in this battle instead of only three.

Now I put all this aside. I put it on the shelf from which the historians may select their documents in order to tell their story. We have to think of the future and not of the past. This also applies in a small way to our own affairs at home.

There are many who wish to hold an inquest upon the conduct of the government and of Parliament during the years which led up to this catastrophe. They wish to indict those who were responsible for the guidance of our affairs.

This also would be a foolish and pernicious process. There are too many in it. Let each man search his conscience and search his speeches, as I frequently search mine. Of this I am quite sure, that if we open a quarrel between the past and the present we shall find that we have lost the future.

Therefore I cannot accept the drawing of any distinctions between members of the present government which was formed in a moment of crisis in order to unite members of all parties and all sections of opinion. It has received the almost unanimous support of both Houses of Parliament and its members are going to stand together and, subject to the authority of the House of Commons, we are going to govern the country and fight the war.

It is absolutely necessary at a time like this that every Minister who tries each day to do his duty shall be respected and their subordinates must know that their chiefs are not threatened men who are here today and gone tomorrow.

Their directions must be punctually and effectively given. Without this concentrated power we cannot do what lies before us. I do not think it would be very advantageous for the House to prolong this debate this afternoon under the conditions of a public sitting. We are to have a secret session on Thursday that would be a better opportunity for many earnest expressions of opinion which may be desired for the House to discuss our vital matters without having everything read the next morning by our dangerous foe.

The military events which have happened in France during the last fortnight have not come to me with any sense of surprise; indeed, I indicated a fortnight ago as clearly as I could to the House, that the worst possibilities were open and I made it perfectly clear that whatever happened in France, it would make no difference to the resolve of Britain and the British Empire to fight on, if necessary for years, and if necessary alone.

During the last few days we have successfully brought off the great majority of troops which were on the lines of communication in France. A very large number, scores of thousands, and seven-eighths of all the troops we have sent to France since the beginning of the war. About 350,010 out of 400,000 men are safely back in this country. Others are still fighting with the French and fighting with considerable success.

We have also brought back a great mass of stores, rifles and munitions of all kinds which have accumulated in France during the last nine months. We have therefore in this island today a very large and powerful military force. This includes all our best trained and finest troops, including scores of thousands of those who have already measured their quality against the Germans and found themselves at no disadvantage.

We have under arms at the present time in this island over 1,250,000 men. Behind these we have the local defense volunteers, numbering 500,000, only a portion of whom, however, are armed with rifles or other firearms.

We have incorporated into our defense force a mass of weapons and we expect very large additions to these weapons in the near future. In preparation, we intend to call up, drill and train, further large numbers at once.

Those who are not called up or who are employed upon the vast business of munitions production in all its branches serve their country best by remaining at their ordinary work until they are required.

We also have the Dominion armies here. The Canadians had actually landed in France, but have now been safely withdrawn much disappointed and are here with all their artillery and equipment. These very high-class forces from the dominions will now take part in the defense of their mother country.

Lest the account which I have given of these large forces should raise the question why they did not take part in the great battle in France, I must make it clear that apart from the divisions training at home, only twelve divisions were equipped to fight on a scale which justified their being sent abroad. This was fully up to the number that the French had been led to expect would be available in France at the ninth month of the war. The rest of our forces at home will steadily increase.

Thus, the invasion of Great Britain at this time would require the transport across the seas of hostile armies on a very large scale and after they had been so transported, they would have to be continually maintained with all the immense mass of munitions and supplies which are required for continuous battle, as continuous battle it would be.

Now here is where we come to the navy. After all, we have a navy; some people seem to forget it. We must remind them. For more than thirty years I have been concerned in discussions about the possibility of an overseas invasion and I took the responsibility on behalf of the Admiralty at the beginning of the last war of allowing all the regular troops to be sent out of the country although our Territorials had only just been called up and were quite untried.

Therefore, these islands for several months were denuded of fighting forces, but the Admiralty had confidence in the defense by the navy, although at that time the Germans had a magnificent battle fleet in the proportion of 10 to 16 and even though they were capable of fighting a general engagement any day. Now they have only a couple of heavy ships worth speaking of.

We are also told that the Italian Navy is coming to gain sea superiority in these waters. If that is seriously intended, I can only say we shall be delighted to offer Mussolini free safeguarded passage through the Straits of Gibraltar in order that he may play the part which he aspires to do. There is general curiosity in the British Fleet to find out whether the Italians are up to the level they were in the last war or whether they have fallen off.

Therefore, it seems to me that as far as sea-borne invasion on a great scale is concerned, we are far more capable of meeting it than we were at many periods in the last war and during the early months of this war before our troops were trained and while the British Expeditionary Force was abroad.

The navy was never intended to prevent the raids of bodies of five or ten thousand men flung across and thrown suddenly ashore at several points on the coast some dark night or foggy morning. The efficacy of sea power, especially under modern conditions, depends upon the invading force being of a large size and, if it is of a large size, the navy has something they can find and, as it were, bite on.

Now we must remember that even five divisions, even lightly equipped, would require 200 to 250 ships, and with modern air reconnaissance and photography it would not be easy to collect such an armada and marshal it across the seas with any powerful naval force to escort it with any possibility that it would not be intercepted long before it reached the coast and the men all drowned in the sea, or, at the worst, blown to pieces with their equipment when they were trying to land.

We have also a great system of mine fields, recently reinforced, through which we alone know the channel. If the enemy tries to sweep a channel through these mine fields it will be the task of the navy to destroy these mine-sweepers and any other force employed to protect them. There ought to be no difficulty about this, owing to our superiority at sea.

These are the well-tested and well-proved arguments on which we have relied for many years, but the question is whether there are any new methods by which they can be circumvented. Odd as it may seem, some attention has been given to this by the Admiralty whose prime duty and responsibility it is to destroy any large sea-borne expedition before it reaches or at the moment when it reaches these shores. It would not be useful to go into details and it might even suggest ideas to other people that they have not got and who would not be likely to give us any of their ideas in exchange.

All I would say is that untiring vigilance and mind-searching must be devoted to the subject, because. the enemy is crafty, cunning and full of novel treacheries and strategies.

The House may be assured that the utmost ingenuity is being displayed by competent officers, well trained in planning and thoroughly up to date, to measure and to counterwork the novel possibilities which many suggest are absurd but seem not utterly rash.

Some people will ask why it was that the British Navy was not able to prevent the movement of a large army from Germany into Norway across the Skagerrak. But conditions in the Channel and in the North Sea are in no way like those which prevail in the Skagerrak. In the Skagerrak, because of the distance, we could give no air support to our surface ships and consequently, lying as we did close to the enemy's main air power in Norwegian waters, we were compelled to use only our submarines.

We could not enforce a decisive blockade or interruption of the enemy's surface vessels. Our vessels took a heavy toll but could not prevent the invasion. But in the Channel and in the North Sea, on the other hand, our forces, aided by submarines, will operate with close and effective air assistance.

This brings me naturally to the great question of invasion from the air and the impending struggle between the British and German Air Forces.

It seems quite clear that no invasion on a scale beyond the capacity of our ground forces to crush speedily is likely to take place from the air until our air force has been definitely overpowered. In the meantime, there may be raids by parachute troops and attempted descents by air-borne soldiers. We ought to be able to give those gentry a warm reception, both in the air and if they reach the ground in any condition to continue their dispute. The great question is, can we break Hitler's air weapon?

Now, of course, it is a very great pity that we have not got an air force at least equal to that of the most powerful enemy within reach of our shores, but we have a very powerful air force, which has proved itself far superior in quality both in men and in many types of machines to what we have met so far in the numerous fierce air battles which have been fought.

In France, where we were at a considerable disadvantage and lost many machines on the ground in the airdromes, we were accustomed to inflict upon the enemy a loss of two to two-and-a-half to one. In the fighting over Dunkirk, which was a sort of No Man's Land, we undoubtedly gained a local mastery of the air and inflicted on the German Air Force losses on the scale of three or four to one.

Any one looking at the photographs of the re-embarkation, showing the masses of troops assembled on the beaches, affording an ideal target for hours at a time, must realize that this embarkation would not have been possible unless the enemy had resigned all hope of recovery of air superiority at that point.

In these islands the advantage to the defenders will be very great. We ought to improve upon that rate of three or four to one, which was realized at Dunkirk.

In addition, there are, of course, a great many injured machines and men who get down safely after an air fight. But all those who fall in an attack upon this island would land on friendly soil and live to fight another day, whereas all the injured enemy machines and their complements will be total losses, as far as the Germans are concerned.

During the great battle in France we gave very great and continuous aid to the French, both by fighters and bombers, but in spite of all pressure, we never allowed the entire metropolitan strength of our air force in fighters to be consumed. This decision was painful, but it was also right.

The battle was, however, lost by the unfortunate strategic opening and by the extraordinary unforeseen power of the armored columns and by the very great preponderance of the German Army in numbers.

Our fighter air force might easily have been exhausted as a mere incident in that struggle and we should have found ourselves at the present time in a very unhappy plight. I am happy to inform the House that our fighter air strength is stronger at the present time relatively to the German, which has suffered terrible losses, than it has ever been. Consequently we believe ourselves to possess the capacity to continue the war in the air under better conditions than we have ever experienced before.

I look forward confidently to the exploits of our fighter pilots, who will have the glory of saving their native land and our island home from the most deadly of all attacks.

There remains the danger of the bombing attacks, which will certainly be made very soon upon us by the bomber forces of the enemy. It is quite true that these forces are superior in number to ours, but we have a very large bombing force also which we shall use to strike at the military targets in Germany without intermission.

I do not at all underrate the severity of the ordeal which lies before us, but I believe that our countrymen will show themselves capable of standing up to it and carrying on in spite of it at least as well as any other people in the world.

It will depend upon themselves, and every man and woman will have the chance of showing the finest qualities of their race and of rendering the highest service to their cause.

For all of us, whatever our sphere or station, it will be a help to remember the famous lines:

> He nothing common did, or mean
> Upon that memorable scene.

I have thought it right on this occasion to give the House and the country some indication of the solid, practical grounds upon which we are basing our invincible resolve to continue the war, and I can assure them that our professional advisers of the three services unitedly advise that we should do it, and that there are good and reasonable hopes of final victory.

We have fully informed all the self-governing dominions and we have received from all Prime Ministers messages couched in the most moving terms, in which they endorse our decision and declare themselves ready to share our fortunes and persevere to the end.

We may now ask ourselves in what way has our position worsened since the beginning of the war. It is worsened by the fact that the Germans have conquered a large part of the coast of the Allies in Western Europe, and many small countries have been overrun by them. This aggravates the possibility of air attack and adds to our naval preoccupation, but it in no way diminishes, but on the contrary definitely increases, the power of our long-distance blockade.

Should military resistance come to an end in France—which is not yet, though it will in any case be greatly diminished—the Germans can concentrate their forces both military and industrial upon us. But for the reason given to the House this will not be easy to apply.

If invasion becomes more imminent, we have been relieved from the task of maintaining a large army in France and we have a far larger and more efficient force here to meet it.

If Hitler can bring under despotic control the industries of the countries he has conquered, this will add greatly to his already vast armament output. On the other hand, this will not happen immediately and we are now assured of immense continued and increasing support in munitions of all kinds from the United States, and especially of airplanes and pilots from across the ocean. They will come from regions beyond the reach of enemy bombers.

I do not see how any of these factors can operate to our detriment, on balance, before the Winter comes, and the Winter will impose a strain upon the Nazi regime, with half Europe writhing and starving under its heel, which, for all their ruthlessness, will run them very hard.

We must not forget that from the moment we declared war on Sept. 3, it was always possible for Germany to turn all her air force on this country. There would also be other devices of invasion, and France could do little or nothing to prevent her. We have therefore lived under this danger during all these months.

In the meanwhile, however, we have enormously improved our methods of defense and we have learned what we had no right to assume at the beginning, of the individual superiority of our aircraft and pilots.

Therefore in casting up this dread balance sheet and contemplating our dangers with a disillusioned eye, I see great reasons for intense exertion and vigilance, but none whatever for panic or despair. During the first four months of the last war the Allies experienced nothing but disaster and disappointment, and yet at the end their morale was higher than that of the Germans, who had moved from one aggressive triumph to another.

During that war we repeatedly asked ourselves the question, "How are we going to win?" and no one was ever able to answer it with much precision, until at the end, quite suddenly and unexpectedly, our terrible foe collapsed before us and we were so glutted with victory that in our folly we cast it away.

We do not yet know what will happen in France or whether the French resistance will be prolonged both in France and in the French Empire overseas. The French Government will be throwing away great opportunities and casting away their future if they do not continue the war in accordance with their treaty obligations, from which we have not felt able to release them.

The House will have read the historic declaration in which, at the desire of many Frenchmen and of our own hearts, we have proclaimed our willingness to conclude at the darkest hour in French history a union of common citizenship in their struggle.

However matters may go in France or with the French Government, or another French Government, we in this island and in the British Empire will never lose our sense of comradeship with the French people.

If we are now called upon to endure what they have suffered, we shall emulate their courage, and if final victory rewards our toils they shall share the gain—aye, freedom shall be restored to all. We abate nothing of our just demands. Czechs, Poles, Norwegians, Dutch and Belgians, who have joined their causes with our own, all shall be restored.

What General Weygand called the Battle of France is over. The Battle of Britain is about to begin. On this battle depends the survival of Christian civilization.

Upon it depends our own British life and the long continuity of our institutions and our empire. The whole fury and might of the enemy must very soon be turned upon us. Hitler knows he will have to break us in this island or lose the war.

If we can stand up to him all Europe may be freed and the life of the world may move forward into broad sunlit uplands; but if we fail, the whole world, including the United States and all that we have known and cared for, will sink into the abyss of a new dark age made more sinister and perhaps more prolonged by the lights of a perverted science.

Let us therefore brace ourselves to our duty and so bear ourselves that if the British Commonwealth and Empire last for a thousand years, men will still say "This was their finest hour."

On the morning of June 22, 1941, Hitler ordered his armies to invade Russia. The evening of the same day, Churchill broadcast to the world the British position on this development in the Second World War. This speech follows.

THE WAR ON RUSSIA

I HAVE TAKEN occasion to speak to you tonight because we have reached one of the climacterics of the war. In the first of these intense turning points, a year ago, France fell prostrate under the German hammer and we had to face the storm alone.

The second was when the Royal Air Force beat the Hun raiders out of the daylight air and thus warded off the Nazi invasion of our islands while we were still ill-armed and ill-prepared.

The third turning point was when the President and Congress of the United States passed the lease and lend enactment, devoting nearly 2,000,-000,000 sterling of the wealth of the New World to help us defend our liberties and their own.

Those were the three climacterics.

The fourth is now upon us.

At 4 o'clock this morning Hitler attacked and invaded Russia. All his usual formalities of perfidy were observed with scrupulous technique. A nonaggression treaty had been solemnly signed and was in force between the two countries. No complaint had been made by Germany of its nonfulfillment. Under its cloak of false confidence the German armies drew up in immense strength along a line which stretched from the White Sea to the Black Sea and their air fleets and armored divisions slowly and methodically took up their stations.

Then, suddenly, without declaration of war, without even an ultimatum, the German bombs rained down from the sky upon the Russian cities; the German troops violated the Russian frontiers and an hour later the German Ambassador, who till the night before was lavishing his assurances of friendship, almost of alliance, upon the Russians, called upon the Russian Foreign Minister to tell him that a state of war existed between Germany and Russia.

Thus was repeated on a far larger scale the same kind of outrage against every form of signed compact and international faith which we have witnessed in Norway, in Denmark, in Holland, in Belgium and which Hitler's accomplice and jackal, Mussolini, so faithfully imitated in the case of Greece.

All this was no surprise to me. In fact I gave clear and precise warnings to Stalin of what was coming. I gave him warnings as I have given warnings to others before. I can only hope that these warnings did not fall unheeded.

All we know at present is that the Russian people are defending their native soil and that their leaders have called upon them to resist to the utmost.

Hitler is a monster of wickedness, insatiable in his lust for blood and plunder. Not content with having all Europe under his heel or else terrorized into various forms of abject submission, he must now carry his work of butchery and desolation among the vast multitudes of Russia and of Asia. The terrible military machine which we and the rest of the civilized world so foolishly, so supinely, so insensately allowed the Nazi gangsters to build up year by year from almost nothing; this machine cannot stand idle, lest it rust or fall to pieces. It must be in continual motion, grinding up human lives and trampling down the homes and the rights of hundreds of millions of men.

Moreover, it must be fed not only with flesh but with oil. So now this bloodthirsty guttersnipe must launch his mechanized armies upon new fields of slaughter, pillage and devastation. Poor as are the Russian peasants, workmen and soldiers, he must steal from them their daily bread. He must devour their harvests. He must rob them of the oil which drives their plows and thus produce a famine without example in human history.

And even the carnage and ruin which his victory, should he gain it—though he's not gained it yet—will bring upon the Russian people, will itself be only a stepping stone to the attempt to plunge the four or five hundred millions who live in China and the 350,000,000 who live in India into that bottomless pit of human degradation over which the diabolic emblem of the swastika flaunts itself.

It is not too much to say here this pleasant Summer evening that the lives and happiness of a thousand million additional human beings are now menaced with brutal Nazi violence. That is enough to make us hold our breath.

But presently I shall show you something else that lies behind and something that touches very nearly the life of Britain and of the United States.

The Nazi regime is indistinguishable from the worst features of Communism. It is devoid of all theme and principle except appetite and racial domination. It excels in all forms of human wickedness, in the efficiency of its cruelty and ferocious aggression. No one has been a more consistent opponent of Communism than I have for the last twenty-five years. I will unsay no words that I've spoken about it. But all this fades away before the spectacle which is now unfolding.

The past, with its crimes, its follies and its tragedies, flashes away. I see the Russian soldiers standing on the threshold of their native land, guarding the fields which their fathers have tilled from time immemorial. I see them guarding their homes, their mothers and wives pray, ah, yes, for there are times when all pray for the safety of their loved ones, for the return of the breadwinner, of the champion, of their protectors.

I see the 10,000 villages of Russia, where the means of existence was wrung so hardly from the soil, but where there are still primordial human joys, where maidens laugh and children play. I see advancing upon all this, in hideous onslaught, the Nazi war machine, with its clanking, heel-clicking, dandified Prussian officers, its crafty expert agents, fresh from the cowing and tying down of a dozen countries. I see also the dull, drilled, docile, brutish masses of the Hun soldiery, plodding on like a swarm of crawling locusts. I see the German bombers and fighters in the sky, still smarting from many a British whipping, so delightful to find what they believe is an easier and a safer prey. And behind all this glare, behind all this storm, I see that small group of villainous men who planned, organized and launched this cataract of horrors upon mankind.

And then my mind goes back across the years to the days when the Russian armies were our Allies against the same deadly foe, when they fought with so much valor and constancy and helped to gain a victory, from all share in which, alas, they were, through no fault of ours, utterly cut off.

I have lived through all this and you will pardon me if I express my feelings and the stir of old memories. But now I have to declare the decision of His Majesty's Government, and I feel sure it is a decision in which the great Dominions will, in due course, concur. And that we must speak of now, at once, without a day's delay. I have to make the declaration but, can you doubt what our policy will be?

We have but one aim and one single irrevocable purpose. We are resolved to destroy Hitler and every vestige of the Nazi regime. From this nothing will turn us. Nothing. We will never parley; we will never negotiate with Hitler or any of his gang. We shall fight him by land; we shall fight him by sea; we shall fight him in the air, until, with God's help we have rid the earth of his shadow and liberated its people from his yoke.

Any man or State who fights against Nazism will have our aid. Any man or State who marches with Hitler is our foe. This applies not only to organized States but to all representatives of that vile race of Quislings who make themselves the tools and agents of the Nazi regime against their fellow countrymen and against the lands of their births. These Quislings, like the Nazi leaders themselves, if not disposed of by their fellow countrymen, which would save trouble, will be delivered by us on the morrow of victory to the justice of the Allied tribunals. That is our policy and that is our declaration.

It follows, therefore, that we shall give whatever help we can to Russia and to the Russian people. We shall appeal to all our friends and Allies in every part of the world to take the same course and pursue it as we shall, faithfully and steadfastly to the end.

We have offered to the Government of Soviet Russia any technical or economic assistance which is in our power and which is likely to be of service to them. We shall bomb Germany by day as well as by night in ever-increasing measure, casting upon them month by month a heavier discharge of bombs and making the German people taste and gulp each month a sharper dose of the miseries they have showered upon mankind.

It is noteworthy that only yesterday the Royal Air Force, striking inland over France, cut down with very small loss to themselves twenty-eight of the Hun fighting machines in the air above the French soil they have invaded, defiled and profess to hold.

But this is only a beginning. From now henceforward the main expansion of our air force proceeds with gathering speed. In another six months the weight of the help we are receiving from the United States in war materials of all kinds, especially in heavy bombers, will begin to tell. This is no class war. It is a war in which the whole British Empire and Commonwealth of Nations is engaged without distinction of race, creed or party.

It is not for me to speak of the action of the United States, but this I will say: If Hitler imagines that his attack on Soviet Russia will cause the slightest division of aims or slackening of effort in the great democracies, who are resolved upon his doom, he is woefully mistaken. On the contrary, we shall be fortified and encouraged in our efforts to rescue mankind from his tyranny. We shall be strengthened and not weakened in our determination and in our resources.

This is no time to moralize upon the follies of countries and governments which have allowed themselves to be struck down one by one when by united action they could so easily have saved themselves and saved the world from this catastrophe.

But, when I spoke a few minutes ago of Hitler's bloodlust and the hateful appetites which have impelled or lured him on his Russian adventure, I said there was one deeper motive behind his outrage. He wishes to destroy the Russian power because he hopes that if he succeeds in this he will be able to bring back the main strength of his army and air force from the east and hurl it upon this island, which he knows he must conquer or suffer the penalty of his crimes.

His invasion of Russia is no more than a prelude to an attempted invasion of the British Isles. He hopes, no doubt, that all this may be accomplished before the Winter comes and that he can overwhelm Great Britain before the fleets and air power of the United States will intervene. He hopes that he may once again repeat upon a greater scale than ever before that process of destroying his enemies one by one, by which he has so long thrived and prospered, and that then the scene will be clear for the final act, without which all his conquests would be in vain, namely, the subjugation of the Western Hemisphere to his will and to his system.

The Russian danger is therefore our danger and the danger of the United States just as the cause of any Russian fighting for his hearth and home is the cause of free men and free peoples in every quarter of the globe.

Let us learn the lessons already taught by such cruel experience. Let us redouble our exertions and strike with united strength while life and power remain.

Shortly after America's entry in the Second World War, Winston Churchill, the British Prime Minister, arrived in Washington to confer with President Roosevelt on unified military effort and strategy. On December 26, 1941, Mr. Churchill delivered the following address in the Senate chamber to members of both houses of Congress, the Cabinet and the United States Supreme Court. He was enthusiastically applauded throughout his speech, and at its end he received an ovation that lasted several minutes.

ADDRESS BEFORE UNITED STATES CONGRESS

MEMBERS of the Senate and of the House of Representatives of the United States, I feel gratefully honored that you should have thus invited me to enter the United States Senate chamber and address the Representatives of both branches of Congress.

The fact that my American forebears have for so many generations played their part in the life of the United States and that here I am, an Englishman, welcomed in your midst makes this experience one of the most moving and thrilling in my life, which is already long and has not been entirely uneventful.

I wish indeed that my mother, whose memory I cherish across the veil of years, could have been here to see me. By the way, I cannot help reflecting that if my father had been American and my mother British, instead of the other way around, I might have got here on my own.

In that case, this would not have been the first time you would have heard my voice. In that case I would not have needed any invitation, but if I had it is hardly likely that it would have been unanimous. So, perhaps, things are better as they are. I may confess, however, that I do not feel quite like a fish out of water in a legislative assembly where English is spoken.

I am a child of the House of Commons. I was brought up in my father's house to believe in democracy; trust the people, that was his message. I used to see him cheered at meetings and in the streets by crowds of working men way back in those aristocratic Victorian days when Disraeli said, "The world was for the few and for the very few." Therefore, I have been in full harmony with the tides which have flowed on both sides of the Atlantic against privileges and monopoly and I have steered confidently towards the Gettysburg ideal of government of the people, by the people, for the people.

I owe my advancement entirely to the House of Commons, whose servant I am. In my country, as in yours, public men are proud to be the servants of the State and would be ashamed to be its masters. On any day, if they thought the people wanted it, the House of Commons could, by a simple vote, remove me from my offce. But I am not worrying about it at all.

As a matter of fact, I am sure they will approve very highly of my journey here, for which I obtained the King's permission, in order to meet the President of the United States, and to arrange with him for all that mapping of our military plans and for all those intimate meetings of the high officers of both countries, which are indispensable for the successful prosecution of the war.

I should like to say, first of all, how much I have been impressed and encouraged by the breadth of view and sense of proportion which I have found in all quarters over here to which I have had access. Any one who did not understand the size and solidarity of the foundation of the United States might easily have expected to find an excited, disturbed, self-centered atmosphere, with all minds fixed upon the novel, startling and painful episodes of sudden war as it hit America.

After all, the United States has been attacked and set upon by three most powerfully armed dictator States, the greatest military power in Europe, the greatest military power in Asia—Japan, Germany and Italy have all declared and are making war upon you, and the quarrel is opened, which can only end in their overthrow or yours.

But, here in Washington in these memorable days, I have found an Olympian fortitude which, far from being based upon complacency, is only the mask of an inflexible purpose and the proof of a sure, well-grounded confidence in the final outcome.

We in Britain had the same feeling in our darkest days. We, too, were sure that in the end all would be well. You do not, I am certain, underrate the severity of the ordeal to which you and we have still to be subjected. The forces ranged against us are enormous. They are bitter. They are ruthless. The wicked men and their factions, who have launched their peoples on the path of war and conquest, know that they will be called to terrible account if they cannot beat down by force of arms the peoples they have assailed.

They will stop at nothing. They have a vast accumulation of war weapons of all kinds. They have highly trained and disciplined armies, navies and air services. They have plans and designs which have long been contrived and matured. They will stop at nothing that violence or treachery can suggest. It is quite true that on our side our resources in man power and materials are far greater than theirs. But only a portion of your resources are as yet mobilized and developed, and we both of us have much to learn in the cruel art of war.

We have, therefore, without doubt, a time of tribulation before us. In this same time some ground will be lost which it will be hard and costly to regain. Many disappointments and unpleasant surprises await us. Many of them will afflict us before the full marshaling of our latent and total power can be accomplished.

For the best part of twenty years the youth of Britain and America have been taught that war was evil, which is true, and that it would never come again, which has been proved false. For the best part of twenty years the youth of Germany, of Japan and Italy have been taught that aggressive war is the noblest duty of the citizen and that it should be begun as soon as the necessary weapons and organization have been made. We have performed the duties and tasks of peace. They have plotted and planned for war. This naturally has placed us, in Britain, and now places you, in the United States, at a disadvantage which only time, courage and untiring exertion can correct.

We have indeed to be thankful that so much time has been granted to us. If Germany had tried to invade the British Isles after the French collapse in June, 1940, and if Japan had declared war on the British Empire and the United States at about the same date, no one can say what disasters and agonies might not have been our lot. But now at the end of December, 1941, our transformation from easygoing peace to total war efficiency has made very great progress.

The broad flow of munitions in Great Britain has already begun. Immense strides have been made in the conversion of American industry to military purposes, and now that the United States is at war, it is possible for orders to be given every day which in a year or eighteen months hence will produce results in war power beyond anything which has been seen or foreseen in the dictator States.

Provided that every effort is made, that nothing is kept back, that the whole man power, brain power, virility, valor and civic virtue of the English-speaking world, with all its galaxy of loyal, friendly or associated communities and States, provided that it is bent unremittingly to the simple but supreme task, I think it would be reasonable to hope that the end of 1942 will see us quite definitely in a better position than we are now. And that the year 1943 will enable us to assume the initiative upon an ample scale. Some people may be startled or momentarily depressed when, like your President, I speak of a long and a hard war.

Our peoples would rather know the truth, somber though it be. And after all, when we are doing the noblest work in the world, not only defending our hearths and homes but the cause of freedom in every land, the question of whether deliverance comes in 1942 or 1943 or 1944 falls into its proper place in the grand proportions in human history.

Sure I am that this day now we are the masters of our fate, that the task which has been set us is not above our strength, that its pangs and toils are not beyond our endurance. As long as we have faith in our cause and unconquerable will power, salvation will not be denied us.

In the words of the Psalmist: "He shall not be afraid of evil tidings, his heart is fixed, trusting in the Lord."

Not all the tidings will be evil. On the contrary, mighty strokes of war have already been dealt against the enemy—the glorious defense of their native soil by the Russian armies and people. Wounds have been inflicted upon the Nazi tyranny and system which have bitten deep and will fester and inflame not only in the Nazi body but in the Nazi mind.

The boastful Mussolini has crumpled already. He is now but a lackey and a serf, the merest utensil of his master's will. He has inflicted great suffering and wrong upon his own industrious people. He has been stripped of all his African empire, Abysinnia has been liberated. Our armies of the East, which were so weak and ill-equipped at the moment of French desertion, now control all the regions from Teheran to Bengazi and from Aleppo and Cyprus to the sources of the Nile.

For many months we devoted ourselves to preparing to take the offensive in Libya. The very considerable battle which has been proceeding there for the last six weeks in the desert has been most fiercely fought on both sides. Owing to the difficulties of supply upon the desert flank we were never able to bring numerically equal forces to bear upon the enemy. Therefore we had to rely upon a superiority in the numbers and qualities of tanks and aircraft, British and American.

For the first time, aided by these—for the first time we have fought the enemy with equal weapons. For the first time we have made the Hun feel the sharp edge of those tools with which he has enslaved Europe. The armed forces of the enemy in Cyrenaica amounted to about 150,000 men, of whom a third were Germans. General Auchinleck set out to destroy totally that armed force, and I have every reason to believe that his aim will be fully accomplished.

I am so glad to be able to place before you, members of the Senate and of the House of Representatives, at this moment when you are entering the war, the proof that, with proper weapons and proper organization, we are able to beat the life out of the savage Nazi. What Hitlerism is suffering in Libya is only a sample and a foretaste of what we have got to give him and his accomplices wherever this war should lead us in every quarter of the globe.

There are good tidings also from blue water. The lifeline of supplies which joins our two nations across the ocean, without which all would fail—that lifeline is flowing steadily and freely in spite of all that the enemy can do. It is a fact that the British Empire, which many thought eighteen months ago was broken and ruined, is now incomparably stronger and is growing stronger with every month.

Lastly, if you will forgive me for saying it, to me the best tidings of all, the United States, united as never before, has drawn the sword for freedom and cast away the scabbard.

All these tremendous steps have led the subjugated peoples of Europe to lift up their heads again in hope. They have put aside forever the shameful temptation of resigning themselves to the conqueror's will. Hope has returned to the hearts of scores of millions of men and women, and with that hope there burns a flame of anger against the brutal, corrupt invader. And still more fiercely burn the fires of hatred and contempt for the filthy Quislings whom he has suborned.

In a dozen famous ancient States, now prostrate under the Nazi yoke, the masses of the people—all classes and creeds—await the hour of liberation when they, too, will once again be able to play their part and strike their blows like men. That hour will strike and its solemn peal will proclaim that night is past and that the dawn has come.

The onslaught upon us, so long and so secretly planned by Japan, has presented both our countries with grievous problems for which we could not be fully prepared. If people ask me, as they have a right to ask me in England, "Why is it that you have not got an ample equipment of modern aircraft and army weapons of all kinds in Malaya and in the East Indies?"

I can only point to the victory General Auchinleck has gained in the Libyan campaign. Had we diverted and dispersed our gradually growing resources between Libya and Malaya, we should have been found wanting in both theatres.

If the United States has been found at a disadvantage at various points in the Pacific Ocean, we know well that that is to no small extent because of the aid which you have been giving to us in munitions for the defense of the British Isles, and for the Libyan campaign, and above all, because of your help in the Battle of the Atlantic, upon which all depends and which has in consequence been successfully and prosperously maintained.

Of course, it would have been much better, I freely admit, if we had had enough resources of all kinds to be at full strength at all threatened points, but considering how slowly and reluctantly we brought ourselves to large-scale preparations, and how long these preparations take, we had no right to expect to be in such a fortunate position.

The choice of how to dispose of our hitherto limited resources had to be made by Britain in time of war and by the United States in time of peace. And I believe that history will pronounce that upon the whole, and it is upon the whole that these matters must be judged, that the choice made was right.

Now that we are together, now that we are linked in a righteous comradeship of arms, now that our two considerable nations, each in perfect unity, have joined all their life energies in a common resolve, a new scene opens upon which a steady light will glow and brighten.

Many people have been astonished that Japan should, in an single day, have plunged into war against the United States and the British Empire. We all wonder why, if this dark design, with its laborious and intricate preparations, had been so long filling their secret minds, they did not choose our moment of weakness eighteen months ago.

Viewed quite dispassionately, in spite of the losses we have suffered and the further punishment we shall have to take, it certainly appears an irrational act. It is, of course, only prudent to assume that they have made very careful calculations, and think they see their way through.

Nevertheless, there may be another explanation. We know that for many years past the policy of Japan has been dominated by secret societies of subalterns and junior officers of the army and navy who have enforced their will upon successive Japanese cabinets and parliaments by the assassination of any Japanese statesman who opposed or who did not sufficiently further their aggressive policies. It may be that these societies, dazzled and dizzy with their own schemes of aggression and the prospect of early victory, have forced their country against its better judgment into war. They have certainly embarked upon a very considerable undertaking.

After the outrages they have committed upon us at Pearl Harbor, in the Pacific Islands, in the Philippines, in Malaya and the Dutch East Indies they must now know that the stakes for which they have decided to play are mortal. When we look at the resources of the United States and the British Empire, compared to those of Japan, when we remember those of

China, which have so long valiantly withstood invasion and tyranny, and when also we observe the Russian menace which hangs over Japan, it becomes still more difficult to reconcile Japanese action with prudence or even with sanity.

What kind of a people do they think we are? Is it possible that they do not realize that we shall never cease to persevere against them until they have been taught a lesson which they and the world will never forget?

Members of the Senate and members of the House of Representatives, I will turn for one moment more from the turmoil and convulsions of the present to the broader spaces of the future.

Here we are together facing a group of mighty foes who seek our ruin. Here we are together defending all that to free men is dear.

Twice in a single generation the catastrophe of world war has fallen upon us. Twice in our lifetime has the long arm of fate reached out across the oceans to bring the United States into the forefront of the battle. If we had kept together after the last war, if we had taken common measures for our safety, this renewal of the curse need never have fallen upon us.

Do we not owe it, to ourselves, to our children, to tormented mankind, to make sure that these catastrophes do not engulf us for the third time? It has been proved that pestilences may break out in the Old World which carry their destructive ravages into the New World from which, once they are afoot, the New World cannot escape.

Duty and prudence alike command, first, that the germ centers of hatred and revenge should be constantly and vigilantly curbed and treated in good time and that an adequate organization should be set up to make sure that the pestilence can be controlled at its earliest beginning before it spreads and rages throughout the entire earth.

Five or six years ago it would have been easy without shedding a drop of blood for the United States and Great Britain to have insisted on the fulfillment of the disarmament clauses of the treaties which Germany signed after the Great War.

And that also would have been the opportunity for assuring to the Germans those materials, those raw materials, which we declared in the Atlantic Charter should not be denied to any nation, victor or vanquished.

The chance has passed. It is gone. Prodigious hammer strokes have been needed to bring us together today.

If you will allow me to use other language I will say that he must indeed have a blind soul who cannot see that some great purpose and design is being worked out here below, of which we have the honor to be the faithful servants.

It is not given to us to peer into the mysteries of the future. Still I avow my hope and faith, sure and inviolate, that in the days to come the British and American people will for their own safety and for the good of all walk together in majesty, in justice and in peace.

Clement R. Attlee

[1883–1967]

Clement R. Attlee, Prime Minister of Great Britain from 1945 to 1951, was for many years leader of the Labor Party in the House of Commons. He represented the British government at the 1941 conference of the International Labor Organization, held in New York City. Following is part of the speech delivered by Attlee on October 29, 1941.

THE ATLANTIC CHARTER

WE DO not envisage an end to this war save victory. We are determined not only to win the war but to win the peace. Plans must be prepared in advance. Action must be taken now if the end of the war is not to find us unprepared. But the problems of the peace cannot be solved by one nation in isolation. The plans of a post-war Britain must be fitted into the plans of a post-war world, for this fight is not just a fight between nations. It is a fight for the future of civilization. Its result will affect the lives of all men and women—not only those now engaged in the struggle.

It is certain that until the crushing burden of armaments throughout the world is lifted from the backs of the people, they cannot enjoy the maximum social well-being which is possible. We cannot build the city of our desire under the constant menace of aggression. Freedom from fear and freedom from want must be sought together.

The joint expression of aims common to the United States and the British Commonwealth of Nations known as the Atlantic Charter includes not only purposes covering war but outlines of more distant objectives.

It binds us to endeavor with due respect to our existing obligations to further the enjoyment by all States, great and small, victors and vanquished, of access on equal terms to trade and raw materials which are needed for their economic prosperity. In addition it records our desire to bring about the fullest collaboration between all nations in the economic field with the object of securing for all labor standards, economic advancement and social security. But it is not enough to applaud these objectives. They must be attained. And if mistakes are to be avoided, there must be the closest international collaboration in which we in the United Kingdom will gladly play our part.

We are determined that economic questions and questions of the universal improvement of standards of living and nutrition shall not be neglected as they were after the last war owing to the preoccupation with political problems. The fact is that wars do not enrich but impoverish the world and bold statesmanship will be needed if we are to repair the ravages of war and to insure to all the highest possible measure of labor standards, economic advancement and social security to which the Atlantic Charter looks forward.

W. L. Mackenzie King

[1874-1950]

William Lyon Mackenzie King was Canadian Prime Minister from 1921 to 1930, and from 1935 to 1948. He was elected to the House of Commons in 1908 as a Liberal, and a year later became the first Minister of Labor. He was defeated in the 1911 elections and was out of politics until he became leader of the Party in 1921, when the Liberals returned to power. Following are parts of an address Prime Minister King delivered before the Associated Canadian Organizations of New York City, on June 17, 1941.

CANADA AND THE WAR

I SPEAK to you tonight as the head of the government of a country which, for almost two years, has been actively and unitedly at war. In accepting your invitation, I have not been unmindful that, though it was extended by Canadian friends, I, nevertheless, would be speaking in a country other than my own, and to citizens or residents of a nation which is at peace—or at least, officially at peace.

You have asked me to tell you something of the causes and ideals which led us to take up arms; something of what Canada is doing, and has been doing, as a nation at war; something, too, of our hopes for the world which will rise when peace comes again to bless mankind.

The Canadian people entered this war of their own free will. As one people, we made the momentous decision by the free vote of a free Parliament. Our declaration of war was signed by the King upon the recommendation of His Majesty's Canadian Ministers. The King's proclamation was in the name of Canada. We, in Canada, were as free to make war or to abstain from making war, as the people of the United States are free to make war or to abstain from making war.

The decision of the Canadian Parliament was given as soon after the outbreak of war as Parliament could be called together. It was a prompt and united decision. There was no hesitation. There was no compulsion. We knew humanity's cry was upon us all. We took our stand as a free and independent people who wished to do their utmost to thwart aggression, to maintain freedom, to crush the cursed creed of Nazism, to preclude world domination by any power, and to end forever, if that were possible, the substitution of force for reason as an instrument of national policy.

Our people went to war for the sake of Canada, but not for Canada alone. We went to war as well for the sake of Britain, for North American civilization which we are proud to defend, and for the sake of that humanity which is above all nations. We saw clearly that Canadian freedom, that North American freedom, was one with British freedom.

We went to war at Britain's side because we believed hers to be the right side. I do not hesitate to say that Britain or no Britain, Canada would never have entered the war if, at the outset, our country had not seen the issue clearly for itself and believed it to be what all free peoples know it to be today.

In our unhesitating decision, and our action which followed, we were true to ourselves. For if any nation was ever inspired by high ideals, unselfish motives and a passion for human freedom and social and national justice, that land was and is Canada. We have a national history without stain of aggression, exploitation, or territorial greed. We have worked always in patience for peace.

In our dealings with other nations, we have been amongst the foremost exponents of conciliation, mediation and arbitration; and the most consistent advocates of international good-will and understanding.

We are nationally minded because, as Canadians, we are free and independent. But we see no escape, no safety, no refuge in national isolation. We are internationally minded because our people know that a threat to freedom anywhere is a threat to freedom everywhere. We know that there are no longer any geographical defenses strong enough in themselves to prevent the onset of aggression. We know that tyrannical ambition, once it overleaps itself, will overleap every boundary whether it be mountain or sea.

Knowing these things, and realizing the strength of the enemy, we entered the conflict—English-speaking Canadians, French-speaking Canadians—as a united nation.

Don't let any one dare to tell you that French-speaking Canada is not on the side of freedom in this war. The union of the children of New France and their English-speaking brothers which fashioned the Canadian nation remains unbroken and will always so remain.

The generosity of our citizenship into which men of many races have been freely welcomed, has been repaid by unquestioned loyalty to our institutions and our cause.

As soon as the cloud on the horizon, no larger than Hitler's hand, resolved itself into the storm of conflict, we determined that we would not wait until the enemy was at our gates. We went to meet him at sea, in the air and on land. Against total war, we have brought and shall continue to bring total effort.

For nearly two years we have been at war. In the war we have had from the beginning two major tasks. We continue to play two major parts. Like Britain, we are a nation at war with all the power of our resources and all the strength of our will. For nearly two years we have gathered our strength as we have taken our allotted place in the conflict. Our soldiers, our sailors and our airmen are with Britain and her other allies in the front line of battle. Our forces on land, at sea and in the air have been and are being equipped and maintained at our own expense. In addition, like the United States, we are helping Britain by sending to her, to the limit of our capacity, the products of our factories, our farms, our forests and our mines.

The task of arming and fighting as a nation is our own free contribution to the cause of freedom. The task of aiding Britain with munitions and money is an additional effort which Canada is also making for the common cause.

With the United States, and like the United States, we are helping to provide the tools. With Britain and like Britain, we are doing our utmost to help finish the job.

I have tried to tell you why. We believe that everything which free men value and cherish, on this side of the grave, is in peril in this war. The right of men, rich and poor, to be treated as men; the right of men to make the laws by which they shall be governed; the right of men to work where they will, at what they will; the right of womankind to the serenity and sanctity of the home; the right of children to play in safety under peaceful heavens; the right of old men and women to the tranquillity of their sunset; the right to speak the truth in our hearts; the right to worship in our own way the God in whom we believe.

We know that if we lose this fight, all fruits will wither and fall from the tree of liberty. But we shall not lose it. We shall not lose it because the people of Britain stand and will stand in undaunted fortitude and magnificent resistance. We shall not lose it because, although some nations may lie crushed today, their souls can never be destroyed. We shall not lose it because we, on this continent of North America, who have been the pioneers of the frontiers of freedom, have already begun to stamp out the prairie fire of tyranny, anarchy and barbarism which every day draws closer to our homes.

For today, whether we will it or not, we are all roof watchers and fire fighters. As Canadians, we are proud to fight the flames with the people of Britain who have maintained for free men their faith in freedom, and kept inviolate the majesty of the human spirit.

As Canadians, we are proud of our great and good neighbor, and grateful to know, as all the world knows, that she is with us heart and soul; that her genius, her skill and her strength work against time for those who fight for freedom.

Some day peace will crown the sacrifices of all. When that day comes the peoples of the British Commonwealth and the peoples of the United States will be found at each other's side, united more closely than ever in one great endeavor to undo the wrongs that have been done mankind. For it is, I believe, the unshaken and unshakable purpose of both that there shall be established upon this earth, now so rapidly becoming hideous with the blackened ruins of civilization itself, a freedom wider, and more deeply founded, than ever before in human history.

Surely we have all come to see that the present conflict is something more than a war between Germany and other powers; that it is "a struggle between permanent and irreconcilable claimants for the soul of man." On the one side stands spiritual freedom with its high regard for human values, the dignity of manhood, the worth of honest toil and the sacredness of human personality. On the other side is the spirit of Nazism and Fascism with their "coarse material standards," their "cult of power as an end in itself," their "subordination of personality to mechanism" and their "worship of an elaborate and soul-destroying organization." This false and evil spirit has, in our own day, in our own and other lands, permeated all too deeply many phases of social and industrial life. It must be the purpose of our high endeavor to destroy it for all time.

While that work is being done, it will be ours, as well, to do all that lies within us to make supreme upon the earth that friendship among men and nations which has ever lain hidden in the heart of mankind.

Edouard Daladier

[1884-1970]

Edouard Daladier first became Premier of France in 1933. After his ministry was overthrown, he returned to the government in 1936 as Secretary of War. In 1938 he was again chosen Premier and was the head of the French government throughout the Munich negotiations and the early part of the Second World War. On March 19, 1940, he was succeeded by Paul Reynaud. The following is a radio address to the people of France, which was delivered by Premier Daladier, on January 29, 1940.

NAZIS' AIM IS SLAVERY

AT THE end of five months of war one thing has become more and more clear. It is that Germany seeks to establish a domination over the world completely different from any known in history.

The domination at which the Nazis aim is not limited to the displacement of the balance of power and the imposition of supremacy of one nation. It seeks the systematic and total destruction of those conquered by Hitler, and it does not treat with the nations which he has subdued. He destroys them. He takes from them their whole political and economic existence and seeks even to deprive them of their history and their culture. He wishes to consider them only as vital space and a vacant territory over which he has every right.

The human beings who constitute these nations are for him only cattle. He orders their massacre or their migration. He compels them to make room for their conquerors. He does not even take the trouble to impose any war tribute on them. He just takes all their wealth, and, to prevent any revolt, he wipes out their leaders and scientifically seeks the physical and moral degradation of those whose independence he has taken away.

Under this domination, in thousands of towns and villages in Europe there are millions of human beings now living in misery which, some months ago, they could never have imagined. Austria, Bohemia, Slovakia and Poland are only lands of despair. Their whole peoples have been deprived of the means of moral and material happiness. Subdued by treachery or brutal violence, they have no other recourse than to work for their executioners who grant them scarcely enough to assure the most miserable existence.

There is being created a world of masters and slaves made in the image of Germany herself. For, while Germany is crushing beneath her tyranny the men of every race and language she is herself being crushed beneath her own servitude and her domination mania. The German worker and peasant are the slaves of their Nazi masters while the worker and peasant of Bohemia and Poland have become in turn slaves of these slaves. Before this first realization of a mad dream the whole world might well shudder.

Nazi propaganda is entirely founded on the exploitation of the weaknesses of the human heart. It does not address itself to the strong or the heroic. It tells the rich they are going to lose their money. It tells the worker this is a rich man's war. It tells the intellectual and the artist that all he cherished is being destroyed by war. It tells the lover of good things that soon he would have none of them. It says to the Christian believer: "How can you accept this massacre?" It tells the adventurer—"a man like you should profit by the misfortunes of your country."

It is those who speak this way who have destroyed or confiscated all the wealth they could lay their hands on, who have reduced their workers to slavery, who have ruined all intellectual liberty, who have imposed terrible privations on millions of men and women and who have made murder their law. What do contradictions matter to them if they can lower the resistance of those who wish to bar the path of their ambition to be masters of the world?

For us there is more to do than merely win the war. We shall win it, but we must also win a victory far greater than that of arms. In this world of masters and slaves, which those madmen who rule at Berlin are seeking to forge, we must also save liberty and human dignity.

Paul Reynaud
[1878–1966]

Paul Reynaud was the heroic Premier of France during those tragic weeks when the Nazi hordes with their overwhelming superiority in airplanes and tanks crushed and conquered the republic. He fought to the last, as his radio broadcast of June 13, 1940, reproduced here, shows.

FRANCE WILL LIVE AGAIN!

IN THE DISTRESS fallen upon the fatherland one thing above all should be said. At the moment when fortune overwhelms them, I wish to cry out to the world the heroism of the French Armies, the heroism of our soldiers, the heroism of our chiefs.

I have seen arrive from the battle, men who had not slept in five days, harassed by airplanes, fatigued by long marches and heavy combats.

These men, whose nerves the enemy had thought broken, had no doubt about the final issue of the war. They had no doubt about the future of the fatherland.

The heroism of the armies of Dunkirk has been exceeded in the fighting from the sea to the Argonne. The soul of France is not broken.

Our race does not allow itself to be beaten down by invasion. How many of these [invasions] the soil on which we live has gone through in the course of the centuries; our race has always thrown back or dominated the invaders.

The world must know of the sufferings of France. The world must know of what they owe her. The hour has come for them to pay their debt.

The French Army has been the vanguard of the army of the democracies. It has sacrificed itself, but in losing this battle it has dealt telling blows to the common enemy. The hundreds of tanks destroyed, airplanes shot down, losses in men, the synthetic gasoline factories and planes— all that explains the present state of morale of the German people despite their victories.

France, wounded, has the right to turn to other democracies and to say: "We have claims on you." None of these with a sense of justice can deny this.

But it is one thing to approve and another thing to act. We know what a high place ideals hold in the life of the great American people. Will they hesitate still to declare themselves against Nazi Germany?

You know that I have demanded it [help] of President Roosevelt. I have sent him tonight a new and final appeal.

Each time that I have asked the President of the United States to increase in all forms the assistance permitted by American law, he has generously complied, and it has been approved by his people.

But today we are at a more advanced point. Today, the life of France is at stake, at least France's essence of life. Our fight, each day more painful, has no further sense if in continuing we do not see even far away the hope of a common victory growing.

The superiority and quality of British aviation increases. It is necessary that clouds of war planes from across the Atlantic come to crush the evil force that dominates Europe.

Despite our reverses the power of the democracies remains immense. We have the right to hope that the day is coming when all that power will be placed in force. That is why we maintain hope in our hearts. That is also why we have wished France to keep a free government and have left Paris.

It was necessary to prevent Hitler from suppressing the legal government and declaring to the world that France had only a puppet government, in his pay, like those he has attempted to constitute here, there and everywhere.

In the great trials of their history our people have known days when they were troubled by defeatist counsel. It is because they never abdicated that they were great.

No matter what happens in the coming days, the French are going to suffer. May they be worthy of the past of their nation. May they become brothers. May they unite about their wounded fatherland.

The day of resurrection will come!

Henri Philippe Pétain
[1856-1951]

Marshal Henri Philippe Pétain was noted as the defender of Verdun in World War I. When Hitler's armies conquered most of France in 1940, the aged marshal succeeded Paul Reynaud as head of government. His first act was to ask for an armistice. Pétain abolished democratic institutions in France and made himself a totalitarian chief. Outlining the new dictatorship, Pétain broadcast to the French people, on July 11, 1940, the speech which follows. At the end of the war, in 1945, Marshal Pétain was convicted of high treason, and was imprisoned on the island of Yeu, off the coast of Brittany.

"I NEED YOUR CONFIDENCE!"

IMMENSE tasks face France. One has only to stop and think of the refugees and the supply problem to estimate their gravity and scope. The nation's communications must be restored. Each man must be returned to his hearth and his job.

In these dark days, after France has been forced to the ground militarily, new trials have been inflicted upon her.

England, after a long alliance, has in a most opportunistic manner attacked our partially disarmed and immobilized warships in our ports. Nothing could justify that aggression. If England thought we would give our fleet to Germany, she was wrong.

The fleet received orders to defend itself and did so valiantly, despite the inequality of the battle. [At Oran, Algeria.]

France stands alone, attacked today by England for whom she consented to many severe sacrifices.

We have a most difficult task to accomplish for which I need your confidence.

I have formed a new government composed of twelve Ministers who will be assisted by general secretaries taken from the principal services of the State. Governors will be in charge of the twelve large Provinces.

Power will thus find itself centralized and decentralized simultaneously. Officials will not be subjected to too much supervision. They will be free to operate and quicker to have more responsibility for their acts.

In order to regulate certain questions in a better manner, the government is preparing a seat for itself in the occupied territories. For that reason we have requested that Versailles and the ministerial quarters in Paris be vacated for us.

We must apply ourselves to create an elite corps without any other consideration than their capacity to command.

Labor is France's supreme resource.

International capitalism and socialism exploited and degraded France. Both participated in preliminaries of the war. We must create a new order in which we no longer admit them.

We shall renounce neither profit, which is a powerful inducement, nor savings. Gains will remain as recompense for both labor and investment.

Your work will be defended, your families will have the respect and protection of the nation.

We must recreate lost confidence. The French family will remain the depositary for France's long and honorable history.

We know that youth must live and draw its strength from the open air which will prepare it for life's battles. We must see to that.

Let us give ourselves to France; she always has led her people to greatness.

Eamon de Valera
[1882–1975]

Eamon de Valera, Prime Minister of Eire (Ireland) 1932-1948, 1951-1954, and again commencing 1957, was born in New York of an Irish mother and a Spanish father. He had early become identified with the Irish republican movement and fought any compromise with England after the Irish Free State was established. In 1927 he and his followers decided to participate in parliamentary elections, and in 1932 they secured control of the government. Following are parts of an address celebrating the opening of the Athlone Broadcasting Station, delivered on February 6, 1933.

IRELAND AMONG THE NATIONS

IRELAND has much to seek from the rest of the world, and much to give back in return, much that she alone can give. Her gifts are the fruit of special qualities of mind and heart, developed by centuries of eventful history. Alone among the countries of Western Europe, she never came under the sway of Imperial Rome. When all her neighbours were in tutelage, she was independent, building up her own civilisation undisturbed. When Christianity was brought to her shores it was received with a joy and eagerness, and held with a tenacity of which there is hardly such another example.

Since the period of her missionary greatness, Ireland has suffered a persecution to which for cruelty, ingenuity and persistence there is no parallel. It did not break—it strengthened—the spirit and devotion of her people and prepared them for the renewal of their mission at a time when it is of no less vital importance to the world than was the mission of the Irish saints of the seventh and eighth centuries to the world of their day.

Next to her services to religion, Ireland's greatest contribution to the welfare of humanity has been the example of devotion to freedom which she has given throughout seven hundred years. The invaders who came to Ireland in the twelfth century belonged to a race that had already subjugated England and a great part of Western Europe. Like the Norsemen before them, it was in Ireland that they met the most serious resistance—a resistance which was continued generation after generation against the successors of the first invaders until our own time, a resistance which will inevitably continue until the last sod of Irish soil is finally freed.

The Irish language is one of the oldest, and, from the point of view of the philologist, one of the most interesting in Europe. It is a member of the Indo-European family, principal of the Celtic group, of which the other two dialects are ancient Gaulish, which has come down to us only in inscriptions, and Brythonic, represented to-day by Welsh and Breton. Irish is closely related to Greek and Sanscrit, and still more closely to Latin.

The tradition of Irish learning—the creation of the monastic and bardic schools—was not wholly lost even during the darkest period of the English occupation. So far as the law could do it, education was made impossible for the Catholic population at home, but Irish scholarship was kept alive in the colleges for Irish ecclesiastics in Louvain, Rome, Salamanca, Paris and elsewhere on the Continent. In Ireland itself the schools of poetry survived in some places until the beginning of the eighteenth century, maintaining to the end their rigorous discipline. The "hedge schools," taught by wandering scholars, frustrated in a measure the design to reduce the people to illiteracy, and kept the flame of knowledge alight, however feebly, throughout the island.

Anglo-Irish literature, though far less characteristic of the nation than that produced in the Irish language, includes much that is of lasting worth. Ireland has produced in Dean Swift perhaps the greatest satirist in the English language; in Edmund Burke probably the greatest writer on politics; in William Carleton a novelist of the first rank; in Oliver Goldsmith a poet of rare merit. Henry Grattan was one of the most eloquent orators of his time—the golden age of oratory in the English language. Theobald Wolfe Tone has left us one of the most delightful autobiographies in literature. Several recent or still living Irish novelists and poets have produced work which is likely to stand the test of time. The Irish theatre movement has given us the finest school of acting of the present day, and some plays of high quality.

Ireland's music is of a singular beauty. Based on pentatonic scale its melodies reach back to a period anterior to the dawn of musical history. It stands pre-eminent amongst the music of the Celtic nations. It is characterised by perfection of form and variety of melodic content. It is particularly rich in tunes that imply exquisite sensitiveness. The strange fitfulness of the lamentations and love songs, the transition from gladness to pathos, have thrilled the experts, and made them proclaim our music the most varied and the most poetical in the world. Equal in rhythmic variety are our dance tunes—spirited and energetic in keeping with the temperament of our people.

I have spoken at some length of Ireland's history and her contributions to European culture, because I wish to emphasise that what Ireland has done in the past she can do in the future. The Irish genius has always stressed spiritual and intellectual rather than material values. That is the characteristic that fits the Irish people in a special manner for the task, now a vital one, of helping to save Western civilisation. The great material progress of recent times, coming in a world where false philosophies already reigned, has distorted men's sense of proportion; the material has usurped the sovereignty that is the right of the spiritual. Everywhere to-day the consequences of this perversion of the natural order are to be seen. Spirit and mind have ceased to rule. The riches which the world sought, and to which it sacrificed all else, have become a curse by their very abundance.

In this day, if Ireland is faithful to her mission, and, please God, she will be, if as of old she recalls men to forgotten truths, if she places before them the ideals of justice, of order, of freedom rightly used, of Christian brotherhood—then, indeed, she can do the world a service as great as that which she rendered in the time of Columcille and Columbanus, because the need of our time is in no wise less.

You sometimes hear Ireland charged with a narrow and intolerant Nationalism, but Ireland to-day has no dearer hope than this: that, true to her own holiest traditions, she may humbly serve the truth and help by truth to save the world.

Maxim Litvinov

| 1876-1952 |

Maxim Litvinov was Commissar of Foreign Affairs of Soviet Russia from 1930 to 1939. He promoted friendly relations between Soviet Russia and the democracies and championed collective security through the League of Nations. He resigned when Stalin found it expedient to sign a non-aggression treaty with Hitler in 1939. Following are parts of an address he delivered before the League of Nations at Geneva, when he appeared as the first delegate of Soviet Russia to the League.

THE LEAGUE OF NATIONS

THE organization of peace! Could there be a loftier and at the same time more practical and urgent task for the coöperation of all nations? The words used in political slogans have their youth and their age. If they are used too often without being applied they wear themselves out and end by losing potency. Then they have to be revived and instilled with new meaning. The sound and the meaning of the words "organization of peace" ought now to be different from their sound and meaning twelve or fifteen years ago. Then to many members of the League of Nations war seemed to be a remote theoretical danger, and there seemed to be no hurry as to its prevention. Now, war must appear to all as the threatening danger of tomorrow. Now, the organization of peace for which so far very little has been done, must be set against the extremely active organization of war. Then many believed that the spirit of war might be exorcised by adjurations—by resolutions and declarations. Now, everybody knows that the exponents of the idea of war, the open promulgators of the refashioning of the map of Europe and Asia by the sword, are not to be intimidated by paper obstacles. Members of the League know this by experience.

We are now confronted with the task of averting war by more effective means. The failure of the Disarmament Conference, on which formerly such high hopes were placed, in its turn compels us to seek more effective means. We must accept the incontestable fact that in the present complicated state of political and economic interests, no war of any serious dimensions can be localized and any war, whatever its issue, will turn out to have been but the first of a series. We must also tell ourselves that sooner or later any war will bring misfortune to all countries, whether belligerents or neutrals. The lesson of the World War, the results of which both belligerents and neutrals are suffering from to this day, must not be forgotten. The impoverishment of the whole world, the lowering of living standards for both manual and brain workers, unemployment, the robbing of all-and-sundry of their confidence in the morrow, not to speak of the fall in cultural values, the return of some countries to medieval ideology—such are the consequences of the World War, even now, sixteen years after its cessation, making themselves acutely felt.

Finally, we must realize once and for all that no war with political or economic aims is capable of restoring so-called historical justice and that all it could do would be to substitute new and perhaps still more glaring injustices for old ones, and that every new peace treaty bears within it the seeds of fresh warfare. Further we must not lose sight of the new increase in armaments going on under our very eyes, the chief danger of which consists in its qualitative still more than in its quantitative increase, in the vast increase of potential destruction. The fact that aerial warfare has with such lightning speed won itself an equal place with land and naval warfare is sufficient corroboration of this argument.

I do not consider it the moment to speak in detail about effective means for the prevention of impending and openly promulgated war. One thing is quite clear for me and that is that peace and security cannot be organized on the shifting sands of verbal promises and declarations. The nations are not to be soothed into a feeling of security by assurances of peaceful intentions, however often they are repeated, especially in those places where there are grounds for expecting aggression or where, only the day before, there have been talk and publications about wars of conquest in all directions, for which both ideological and material preparations are being made. We should establish that any State is entitled to demand from its neighbors, near and remote, guarantees for its security, and that such a demand is not to be considered as an expression of mistrust. Governments with a clear conscience and really free from all aggressive intentions, cannot refuse to give, in place of declarations, more effective guarantees which would be extended to themselves and give them also a feeling of complete security.

I am by no means overrating the opportunities and means of the League of Nations for the organization of peace. I realize, better perhaps than any of you, how limited these means are. I am aware that the League does not possess the means for the complete abolition of war. I am, however, convinced that with the firm will and close coöperation of all its members a great deal could be done at any given moment for the utmost diminution of the danger of war, and this is a sufficiently honorable and lofty task whose fulfilment would be of incalculable advantage to humanity.

Haile Selassie
[1890–1975]

When Ethiopia, first victim of the dictators, was threatened by the vastly superior armies of Fascist Italy, Haile Selassie I, ruler of this ancient land, broadcast an appeal to the democracies. This was on September 13, 1935. Following is part of his address.

THE POSITION OF ETHIOPIA

FIVE months before the pretext found in December in the Ualual incident, Italy had begun the armament of her colonies, armament which since has been intensified and increased by the continuous sending of troops, mechanized equipment and ammunition during the entire duration of the work of the Council of the League of Nations and the work of the arbitration board.

Now that the pretext on which they planned to make war upon us has vanished, Italy, after having obtained from the powers their refusal to permit us to purchase armaments and ammunition which we do not manufacture and which are necessary to our defense, seeks to discredit the Ethiopian people and their government before world opinion.

They characterize us as a barbarous people whom it is necessary to civilize. The attitude of Italy will be judged by history. We will see whether it is the act of a nation that prides herself as being the epitome of civilization to make an unjust attack on a pacific people, recently disarmed and which placed all their confidence in her promise of peace and friendship which the civilized nation had previously given in a treaty made on her own initiative seven years before, to be exact, August 2, 1928.

Italy seeks to justify the unworthy act which she prepares to commit against our people. To this end, instead of replying to the legal argument which we have presented to demonstrate the violation of our territory, and the armed and illegal occupation of our territory by Italian troops, her government presents at the last moment a documentation against our people patiently and slyly assembled by numerous paid agents distributed throughout our territory under the guise of diplomatic representatives.

It is not the place or the moment here to reply legally or quarrel with Italy on their accusation, which as yet is known to us only by hearsay. To this memorandum, presented on September 4 to the League of Nations, which as yet has not had time to reach us, our government is able to reply point by point and to answer the league on all these accusations formulated at the last hour against us and to sustain the court of world opinion which now ought to judge.

Our delegation at Geneva has received our formal instructions to demand of the Council of the League of Nations the institution of an international commission of inquiry, the only organ competent to decide such a question after having heard both parties to the dispute.

The Ethiopian people are firmly attached to peace, but they are at the same time animated by a deep love of country. Whatever may be the state of disarmament in which they unjustly find themselves through the diplomatic manoeuvres of Italy, our people are jealous of their independence and know how and will use even swords and spears in defense of the acres they have cultivated and which they love.

We do not want war. Ethiopia puts her confidence in God, and she knows His justice transcends that of man. She knows that the modern methods of war invented by men to dispose of others have never been a true symbol of civilization.

She gives thanks to those statesmen who, in spite of the immensity of their problems, have given months of their efforts to assure the maintenance of a peace which the demands of Italy disturb.

The Ethiopian Government, the Ethiopian church and all her people pray to God that he may assist and direct them in their efforts for the maintenance of peace. Ethiopia is conscious of having always fulfilled all her international obligations and having until now made all the sacrifices compatible with her honor and dignity to assure a peaceful solution of the present conflict.

She wishes and hopes with all her heart that an amicable and peaceful settlement, in accordance with right and justice, will intervene, and the officers of the Council of the League of Nations, in conformity with the pact, will compel all the nations of the world, great and small, who hold peace as their ideal to halt this crisis which threatens to stop all civilization.

Frederico Laredo Bru

[1885-1946]

Frederico Laredo Bru, President of Cuba from 1936 to 1940, opened the second meeting of the Foreign Ministers of the 21 American republics, which convened at Havana, Cuba, on July 21, 1940. Following is the speech he delivered on this occasion.

UNITED HEMISPHERE DEFENSE

EXCELLENCIES:

For the second time the unusual responsibility that places in your worthy hands the destiny of twenty-one nations entreats you urgently to put solemnly into words the anxious but firm will of free America.

The first [Pan-American consultative] meeting, held in Panama following the agreements of Buenos Aires and Lima, was an important landmark in inter-American relations. The records of that conference bear witness that the momentous agreements, strengthened by continental friendship, binding us to each other and maintaining our countries in their traditional adherence to laws and rules, have given life and success to their democratic institutions, and, even now in the midst of disconcerting events, make our relations with other countries peaceful, decent and respectable.

This time you have elected to meet in Havana, capital of one of the last republics to constitute itself in this hemisphere, but one which never was remiss in asserting characteristically American ideals, based on liberty, peace and international justice. These very same ideals inspired the heroic decisions and immortal exploits of our illustrious men—companions of Washington, Bolivar, Hidalgo, San Martín, Sucre, Artigas, Petio and Duarte among others—who fought indefatigably to the end for the independence of the Cuban people.

Certainly, this great assembly does not evoke the historical memories lent to your first meeting in Panama by the fact that that occurred in the legendary city where was held the very first conference of American countries, called by Simon Bolivar to resist the designs of foreign regimes anxious to re-establish their lordship over these lands, where, eventually, right would triumph.

But if in Havana you do not find an opportunity for such prestigious recollection, you will find at least a people the apostles of whose political faith exerted themselves to stress the necessity of promoting international common feeling; a people whose independence was kneaded not only by the blood of its sons but also by the blood and the encouragements of other continental peoples.

Marti was one of the forerunners of this movement, and this sentence of his was fittingly selected by his countrymen to be engraved on the bronze fence encircling the Tree of American Fraternity: "It is the hour of recounting and the united march and we must go forward in closed formation, like the silver ore in the base of the Andes."

America is constituted by States of similar political organization hatched in the warmth of the same afflictions. Its analogous enthusiasms had created, by living together in a sympathetic neighborhood, an atmosphere of fraternal regionalisms which would have permitted our hemisphere to keep itself within its geographical unity and its peaceful traditions, away from conflicts not directly affecting it. We lived decorously in peace, and aimed at keeping that peace. Our aspirations could not have been nobler nor our behavior more specifically transparent.

We envied nobody anything; our sole preoccupation was thriving on our democratic institutions, which we considered good enough to consolidate our well-being in safety. We endeavored to succeed in our own behalf and also to become serviceable to others. We proclaimed the worthiness of lawful acquisitions over brittle conquests by force and violence.

Unfortunately, this regime of quiescence and confidence does not seem assured of further continuance. Nobody with an honorable conscience can deny that the Western Hemisphere is entering a new life of alarms and threats. From October of last year—the date of your former meeting—to the present time, humanity has gone through on its march, gradually becoming dizzy and senseless, toward the destruction of whatever constituted the highest aims of civilized man.

It seems as if divine predestination forces us Americans, the heirs of Western culture, to be definitely the sole custodians of an international morale which becomes dim and deteriorates with the ruin of great peoples and the dramatic, contemptuous silence of the highest virtues, of which yesterday mankind was proud.

This sacred mission that the American continent assumes through setting itself up as trustee for the remainder of betrayed civilization—civilization pushed to the edge of the precipice—is the aim that reunites you today in order to defend and harbor it, relieving it from the utter rejection that might harass it to its last corners in the New World.

The dangers, you know well, Excellencies, increase day by day, and our America will be lucky if, due to its miraculous isolation, it can continue to avoid profound reactions to the distressing events we are living through. The fiendish fate which has befallen scientific instruments created by human wisdom for friendlier, more effective intercourse between individuals and peoples turns them into a tragic admonition for our countries, which trusted that their remoteness and manifest lack of interest in illegitimate ambitions would keep them out of the roving conflict that respects no right which is weakly claimed, nor forgives the justified abstentions of those who have not made out of covetousness for another's possessions their ideals for national aggrandizement.

Upon this bleak present reality, that nevertheless cannot, withal, cloud the hopes of daybreak in the hearts of its men of good will, America has made itself ready for a protective preparedness and for a progressive defense of its common rights, which is the only policy proper to maintain it in its own peaceful life and insure it permanent enjoyment of its own felicity.

Men from the north, the south and the center, solidly joined together and consecrated every one by the blessed equalizing religion of America, welcome! The government and people of Cuba, in stretching toward you sincerely hospitable arms, earnestly hope for the success of your difficult task.

So, while other countries may vegetate around the margins of the law of nations, trusting only in force, we Americans proceed perfectly renewed within our traditional concepts of regional independence, reciprocal consideration and fraternal solidarity: the indestructible bases of the relations of this hemisphere.

Excellencies, I have the honor to proclaim inaugurated the second meeting of the Ministers of Foreign Affairs of the American Republics.

Adolf Hitler

[1889-1945]

Born in Austria, Adolf Hitler served in World War I as a corporal. After the war, he joined the German Workers Party which soon became the National Socialist Party. In 1923 he led the abortive Munich beer hall putsch, and while in prison wrote "Mein Kampf." Released from prison a year later, he then devoted himself to the building up of the Nazi (National Socialist) movement. Their power grew until, in 1932, Hitler was appointed Reich Chancellor by President Von Hindenburg. On the death of the latter in 1934, Hitler seized all power and declared himself "Fuehrer." In 1937, with Dictator Mussolini, he established the Rome-Berlin Axis. In 1938 he annexed Austria and the Sudeten part of Czechoslovakia and invaded Poland, which resulted in war with Great Britain and France. He entered into a non-aggression treaty with Stalin. Within two years Hitler's armies invaded, conquered, and occupied practically all of Western Europe. On June 22, 1941, Hitler broke his treaty with Stalin and began an invasion of Russia. From this time his almost unimpeded advance began to be frustrated. Hitler declared war on the United States, and the events which followed led finally to the collapse of the Third Reich in 1945.

Hitler's oratorical powers over the masses played a great part in his spectacular rise. His speeches were rambling and repetitious but contain forceful and satirical passages. Following are parts of the speech which first disclosed his menacing intentions against Europe, delivered before the Reichstag on February 20, 1938.

GERMANY'S CLAIMS

DESPITE the really exemplary discipline, strength and restraint which National Socialists preserved in their revolution, we have seen that a certain portion of the foreign press inundated the new Reich with a virtual flood of lies and calumnies. It was a remarkable mixture of arrogance and deplorable ignorance which led them to act as the judges of a people who should be presented as models to these democratic apostles.

The best proof for showing up these lies is success. For if we had acted during these five years like the democratic world citizens of Soviet Russia, that is, like those of the Jewish race, we would not have succeeded in making out of a Germany, which was in the deepest material collapse, a country of material order. For this very reason we claim the right to surround our work with that protection which renders it impossible for criminal elements or for the insane to disturb it.

Whoever disturbs this mission is the enemy of the people, whether he pursues his aim as a bolshevist democrat, a revolutionary terrorist or a reactionary dreamer. In such a time of necessity those who act in the name of God are not those who, citing Bible quotations, wander idly about the country and spend the day partly doing nothing and partly criticizing the work of others; but those whose prayers take the highest form of uniting man with his God, that is the form of work.

I had a right to turn against every one who, instead of helping, thought his mission was to criticize our work. Foreign nations contributed nothing apart from this spirit, for their rejection was tinged by hate or a spirit of knowing better than we know.

It was the A B C of our creed to find help in our own strength. The standard of living of the nation is the outcome of its total production; in other words, the value of every wage and salary corresponds to the volume of goods produced as a result of the work performed. This is a very unpopular doctrine in a time resounding with cries such as "higher wages and less work."

Next to the United States, Germany today has become the greatest steel country in the world. I could give many more examples. They are documentary proof of the work such as our people never before achieved. To these successes will be added in a few years the gigantic results of the Four-Year Plan. Is it not a joke of history when those very countries which themselves have only crises think they can criticize us and give us advice?

We have given the German nation that weapon of steel which presents a wall at our frontiers against the intentions of the malicious international press campaign.

At the conclusion of the next decade the German people will bear in mind the success of their efficiency and will be filled with a supreme pride. One of these achievements is the construction of a national leadership which is far removed from parliamentary democracy as it is from military dictatorship.

If ever international agitation or poisoning of opinion should attempt to rupture the peace of the Reich, then steel and iron would take the German people and German homesteads under their protection. The world would then see, as quick as lightning, to what extent this Reich, people, party and these armed forces are fanatically inspired with one spirit, one will.

If Great Britain should suddenly dissolve today and England become dependent solely on her own territory, then the people there would, perhaps, have more understanding of the seriousness of the economic tasks which confront us. If a nation which commands no gold reserves. no foreign exchange—not because National Socialism reigns but because a parliamentary, democratic State was exploited for fifteen years by a world hungry after loot; in other words, if a nation which must feed 140 people to the square kilometer and has no colonies, if a nation which lacks numerous raw materials and is not willing to live an illusory life through credits, reduces the number of its unemployed in five years to nil and improves its standard of living, then all those should remain silent who, despite great economic advantages, scarcely succeed in solving their own unemployment problems.

The claim for German colonial possessions, therefore, will be voiced from year to year with increasing vigor. These possessions, which Germany did not take away from other countries and which today are practically of no value to these powers, are indispensable for our own people.

I should like to refute here the hope that such claims can be averted by granting credits. Above all, we do not wish for naïve assurances that we shall be permitted to buy what we need. We reject such statements once and for all.

You will not expect me to discuss in detail the individual international plans which appear to arouse the varied interests of the various governments. They are too uncertain and they lack the clarity necessary for me to be able to express myself on these questions. Above all, however, take note of my deep-seated distrust of all so-called conferences which may provide interesting hours of conversation for those taking part in them, but generally lead to the disappointment of hopeful mankind.

I cannot allow our natural claims to be coupled with political business. Recently rumors have been cropping up, rumors that Germany was about to revise her opinion concerning her return to the League of Nations. I should like again to declare that in 1919 the peace treaty was forced upon some countries. This treaty brought in its train far-reaching inroads upon the lives of the peoples involved. The rape of national and economic destinies and of the communal lives of the nations took place under a cloud of moralizing phrases which, perhaps, tended to salve the uneasy conscience of those who instituted the affair.

After the revision of the map of the world and of territorial and racial spheres, which was as thorough as it was fundamental, had been effected by means of force, a League of Nations was founded whose task it was to crystallize these crazy, unreasonable proceedings and to coordinate its results into an everlasting and unalterable basis of life.

I notice very often that English politicians would be glad to give back to us our colonies if they were not so disturbed by the thought of the wrong and violence which would thus be done to the native inhabitants.

All those colonial empires have not come into being through plebiscites. They are today naturally integral parts of the States in question and form, as such, part of that world order which always has been designated to us, especially by democratic policies, as the "world order of right."

That right the League of Nations now has been ordered to protect. I cannot understand why a nation which itself has been robbed by force should join such illustrious company and I cannot permit the conclusion to be drawn that we should not be prepared to fight for the principles of justice just because we are not in the League of Nations. On the contrary, we do not belong to the League of Nations because we believe that it is not an institution of justice but an institution for defending the interests of Versailles.

A number of material considerations must, however, be added.

First, we left the League of Nations because—loyal to its origin and obligations—it refused us the right to equal armament and just as equal security.

Second, we will never re-enter it because we do not intend to allow ourselves to be used anywhere in the world by a majority vote of the League of Nations for the defense of an injustice.

Third, we believe we will please all those nations who are misled by misfortune to rely on and trust the League of Nations as a factor of genuine help. We should have regarded it as more correct, for instance, in the case of the Ethiopian war, for the League to have shown more understanding for vital Italian needs and less disposition to help the Ethiopians with promises. This would, perhaps, have enabled a more simple and reasonable solution for the whole problem.

Fourth, on no account will we allow the German nation to become entangled in conflicts in which the nation itself is not interested. We are not willing to stand up for the territorial or economic interests of others without the slightest benefits to Germans being visible. Moreover, we ourselves do not expect such support from others. Germany is determined to impose upon herself wise moderation in her interests and demands. But if German interests should be seriously at stake we shall not expect to receive support from the League of Nations but we shall assume the right from the beginning to shoulder our task ourselves.

Fifth, we do not intend to allow our attitude to be determined in the future by any international institution which, while excluding official recognition of indisputable facts, resembles less the acts of a man of considered judgment than the habits of a certain type of large bird [evidently the ostrich]. The interests of nations in so far as their existence or non-existence are ultimately concerned are stronger than formalistic considerations. For in the year 2038 it is possible that new States may have arisen or others disappeared without this new state of affairs having been registered at Geneva.

Germany will not take part in such unreasonable proceedings by being a member of the League of Nations.

With one country alone have we scorned to enter into relations. That State is Soviet Russia. We see in bolshevism more now than before the incarnation of human destructive forces. We do not blame the Russian people as such for this gruesome ideology of destruction. We know it is a small Jewish intellectual group which led a great nation into this position of madness. If this doctrine would confine itself territorially to Russia maybe one could put up with it. Alas, Jewish international bolshevism attempts to hollow out the nations of the world from its Soviet center.

As I have more than once stated Germany has in Europe no more territorial demands to make of France. With the return of the Saar we trust the period of Franco-German territorial differences is finally closed.

Germany also has no quarrel with England apart from her colonial wishes. However, there is no cause for any conceivable conflict. The only thing that has poisoned and thus injured the common life of these two countries is the utterly unendurable press campaign which in these two countries has existed under the motto "freedom of personal opinion."

The British Government desires the limitation of armaments or the prohibition of bombing. I myself proposed this some time ago. However, I also suggested at the time that the most important thing was to prevent the poisoning of the world's public opinion by infamous press articles. That which strengthened our sympathy with Italy, if this were possible, is the fact that in that country State policy and press policy tread the same road.

There are more than 10,000,000 Germans in States adjoining Germany which before 1866 were joined to the bulk of the German nation by a national link. Until 1918 they fought in the great war shoulder to shoulder with the German soldiers of the Reich. Against their own free will they were prevented by peace treaties from uniting with the Reich.

This was painful enough, but there must be no doubt about one thing: Political separation from the Reich may not lead to deprivation of rights, that is the general rights of racial self-determination which were solemnly promised to us in Wilson's fourteen points as a condition for the armistice. We cannot disregard it just because this is a case concerning Germans.

In the long run it is unbearable for a world power, conscious of herself, to know there are citizens at her side who are constantly being inflicted with the severest sufferings for their sympathy or unity with the total nation, its faith and philosophy.

We well know there can scarcely be a frontier line in Europe which satisfies all. It should be all the more important to avoid the torture of national minorities in order not to add to the suffering of political separation, the suffering of persecution on account of their belonging to a certain people.

That it is possible to find ways leading to the lessening of tension has been proved. But he who tries to prevent by force such lessening of tension through creating an equilibrium in Europe will some day inevitably conjure up force among the nations themselves. It cannot be denied that Germany herself, as long as she was powerless and defenseless, was compelled to tolerate many of these continual persecutions of the German people on our frontier.

But just as England stands up for her interests all over the globe, present-day Germany will know how to guard its more restricted interests. To these interests of the German Reich belong also the protection of those German peoples who are not in a position to secure along our frontiers their political and philosophical freedom by their own efforts.

I may say that since the League of Nations has abandoned its continuous attempts at disturbance in Danzig and since the advent of the new commissioner this most dangerous place for European peace has entirely lost its menace.

Poland respects the national conditions in the Free City of Danzig and Germany respects Polish rights.

Now. I turn to Austria. It is not only the same people but above all a long communal history and culture which bind together the Reich and Austria.

Difficulties which emerged in the carrying out of the agreement of July 11, 1936, made essential an attempt to remove misunderstandings and obstacles to final reconciliation. It is clear that whether we wished it or not an intolerable position might have developed that would have contained the seeds of catastrophe. It does not lie in the power of man to stop the rolling stone of fate which through neglect or lack of wisdom has been set moving.

I am happy to say that these ideas correspond with the viewpoint of the Austrian Chancellor, whom I invited to visit me. The underlying intention was to bring about a détente in our relations which would guarantee to National Socialist sympathizers in Austria within the limits of the law the same rights enjoyed by other citizens.

In connection with it there was to be an act of conciliation in the form of a general amnesty and better understanding between the two States through closer and friendlier relations in the various spheres of cultural, political and economic cooperation. All this is a development within the framework of the treaty of July 11.

I wish to pay tribute to the Austrian Chancellor for his efforts to find together with me a way which is just as much in the interests of both countries as in that of the entire German people whose sons we all are regardless of where we came from. I believe we have thus made a contribution to European peace.

Our satisfactory relations with other countries are known to all. Above all it is to be mentioned our cooperation with those two great powers which, like Germany, have recognized bolshevism as a world danger and are therefore determined to resist the Comintern with a common defense. It is my earnest wish to see this cooperation with Italy and Japan more and more extended.

The German people is no warlike nation. It is a soldierly one which means it does not want a war but does not fear it. It loves peace but it also loves its honor and freedom.

The new Reich shall belong to no class, no profession but to the German people. It shall help the people find an easier road in this world. It shall help them in making their lot a happier one. Party, State, armed forces, economics are institutions and functions which can only be estimated as a means toward an end. They will be judged by history according to the services they render toward this goal. Their purpose, however, is to serve the people.

I now pray to God that He will bless in the years to come our work, our deeds, our foresight, our resolve; that the Almighty may protect us from both arrogance and cowardly servility, that He may help us find the right way which He has laid down for the German people and that He may always give us courage to do the right thing and never to falter or weaken before any power or any danger.

Long live Germany and the German people.

Hitler's speech of September 26, 1938, which he delivered before 15,000 fanatical followers at the Sportspalast, Berlin, was made while the Munich agreement was being negotiated. It is historic because in this speech he twice asserted that if the Sudeten territories were ceded by Czechoslovakia this would be the last territorial demand Germany would make. How this promise was kept is now history.
Parts of Hitler's speech follow.

NO MORE TERRITORIAL DEMANDS

I HAVE ATTACKED all seemingly impossible problems with a firm will to solve them peaceably if at all feasible even at the risk of more or less important German sacrifices.

I am a front soldier myself and I know how terrible war is.

I wanted to spare the German nation this experience and therefore I took up problem after problem with a firm resolve to attempt everything to make an amicable solution possible.

The hardest problem I found, my fellow citizens, was Polish-German relations. We faced the danger here of steering ourselves into, let us say, fanatical hysteria. The danger existed that in this case a conception like inherited enmity would gain possession of our peoples as well as the Polish people.

This I wanted to forestall. I know perfectly well that I would not have succeeded alone if at that time there had been a democracy of western construction in Poland.

For these democracies running over with peace phrases are the most bloodthirsty war instigators.

There was no democracy in Poland but there was a man. With him we succeeded in less than a year in arriving at an agreement which for the duration of ten years basically removes the danger of any clash.

We all are determined, and also convinced, that this agreement will bring about lasting and continuous pacification, because problems in eight years are no different from those today.

We do not have to expect anything from each other. We recognize this. We are two peoples. They shall live. One cannot annihilate the other. I recognize this and we must see it: A State of 33,000,000 people will always strive for an outlet to the sea.

Here the road to understanding had to be found, and it was found. And it is being widened and expanded.

Of course, down there realities are often grim. Nationalities and little racial groups often fight with each other.

But the decisive thing is: The two administrations and all sensible and reasonable people in both countries have a firm will and a firm resolve continually to improve relations.

That was a great deed of mine, and a real act of peace which weighs more than all the jabbering in the Geneva League of Nations palace.

Now I have tried during this time also gradually to bring about good and enduring relations with other nations.

We have given guarantees for the States in the West. We have guaranteed to all contiguous neighbors the inviolability of their territory so far as Germany is concerned.

That is not a phrase—that is our sacred will.

We are not interested in breaking peace. We do not want anything from these peoples. It is a fact that these our offers were meeting with increasing acceptance and also growing understanding.

Slowly, more and more nations are departing from the idiotic delusion of Geneva; I should like to say, departing not from collective peace obligations but from collective war obligations.

They are withdrawing from them and they begin to see problems soberly and are ready for understanding and peace.

I have gone farther.

I extended a hand to England. I renounced voluntarily ever again joining any naval conference so as to give the British Empire a feeling of security, not because I could not build more—and there should be no illusion about that—but exclusively for this reason: to safeguard permanent peace between both nations.

To be sure, there is here one pre-condition—it cannot be admitted that one party should say: I do not want to fight you any more and therefore I offer to cut my armaments down to 35 per cent, and that the other party should say from time to time: We will fight again when it suits us.

That won't do. Such an agreement is morally justified only when both peoples shake hands on an honest promise never to wage war upon each other again.

Germany has this will. We all hope that among the English people those will prevail who are of the same mind. I have gone further. Immediately after the Saar had been returned to the Reich by plebiscite, I told France there were no more differences between France and us.

I said: Alsace-Lorraine does not exist any more for us.

These people really have not been asked their opinion in the last few decades. We believe that the inhabitants of those parts are happiest when they are not being fought over.

And we all do not want any more war with France. We want nothing of France, absolutely nothing.

And when the Saar territory was returned to the Reich, thanks to—I will say so right here—thanks to France's loyal execution of the treaties, I immediately gave this frank assurance: Now all the territorial differences between France and Germany are settled.

I no longer see any differences at all. There are two nations. They can live best if they work together.

After this renunciation, irrevocable once and forever, I turned to another problem, solvable more easily than others because a mutual philosophic basis served as a prerequisite for an easier mutual understanding: Germany's relations to Italy.

Certainly the solution of this problem is my work only partially. The other part is due to the rare great man (Premier Mussolini) whom the Italian people is fortunate to possess as its leader.

This relation has long left a sphere of clear economic and political expediency and over treaties and alliances has turned into a real strong union of hearts.

Here an axis was formed represented by two peoples, both of whom in their philosophical and political ideas found themselves in close indissoluble friendship.

Here, too, I cut the cloth finally and definitely, convinced of my responsibility toward my countrymen.

I have relieved the world of a problem that from now on no longer exists for us.

Bitter as it may be for a few, in the last analysis the interest of the German nation stands above all.

This interest, however, is: To be able to work in peace.

This whole activity, my fellow citizens, is not a phrase that cannot be proved, but instead this activity is demonstrated by facts which no political liar can remove.

Two problems remained.

Here I had to make a reservation.

Ten million Germans found themselves outside the Reich's confines in two large contiguous regions—Germans who desired to come back into their homeland. This number of 10,000,000 is not a trifle. It is a question of one-fourth of the number of inhabitants France has.

And if France during forty years did not renounce its claim to a few million French in Alsace-Lorraine, certainly we have a right before God and man to keep up our claim to these 10,000,000 Germans.

Somewhere, my fellow countrymen, there is a limit—a limit where yielding must cease, because it would otherwise become a harmful weakness and I would have no right to maintain a place in German history if I were simply to renounce 10,000,000 without caring about them. I would then have no moral right to be Fuehrer of the German people.

I have taken upon myself sufficient sacrifices in the way of renunciations. Here was a limit beyond which I could not go. How right this was has been proven, first by the plebiscite in Austria; in fact, by the entire history of the reunion of Austria with the Reich. A glowing confession of faith was pronounced at that time—a confession such as others certainly had not hoped for.

A flaming testimony was given at that time, a declaration such as others surely had not hoped would be given.

It was then we saw that for democracies a plebiscite becomes superfluous or even obnoxious as soon as it does not produce results democracies hoped for.

Nevertheless this problem was solved to the happiness of the great German people, and now we confront the last problem that must and shall be solved.

This is the last territorial demand I have to make in Europe, but it is a demand on which I will not yield.

Its history is as follows: In 1918 Central Europe was torn up and reshaped by some foolish or crazy so-called statesmen under the slogan "self-determination and the right of nations."

Without regard to history, origin of peoples, their national wishes, their economic necessities, they smashed up Europe and arbitrarily set up new States.

To this, Czechoslovakia owed its existence.

This Czech State began with one big lie and its father's name was Benes. (Cries of hang him.)

This Herr Benes at that time turned up at Versailles and told them that there was the Czechoslovak nation. (Loud laughter.)

He had to invent this lie to bolster up an insignificant number of his own nationals so as to make them seem more important.

I said in the Reichstag on Feb. 20, that this (meaning the Czechoslovak situation) must be changed. Only Herr Benes changed it differently. He started a more radical system of oppression, greater terror, a period of dissolutions, bans, confiscations, etc.

This went on until May 21, and you cannot deny, my friends, that it was truly endless German patience that we practiced.

This May 21 was unbearable enough. I have told the story of this month already at the Reich's party convention.

There at last were to be elections in Czechoslovakia. They could no longer be postponed.

So Herr Benes thinks out a way to intimidate Germans there—military occupation of those sections. (Shouts of bloodhound.)

He still keeps up this military occupation in the expectation that so long as his hirelings are there nobody will dare raise a hand against him.

It was an impudent lie that Germany had mobilized. That had to be used in order to cloak the Czech mobilization, excuse it and explain it.

What happened then, you know. The infamous international world set at Germany. Germany had not called upon one man. It never thought of solving this problem militarily.

I still had hopes that the Czechs would recognize at the last minute that this tyrannic regime could not keep up.

But Herr Benes believed Germany was fair game. Of course, he thought he was covered by France and England and nothing could possibly happen to him.

And if everything failed there still was Soviet Russia to fall back on.

Thus the answer of that man was: No, more than ever, shoot down, arrest and incarcerate all those whom he did not like for some reason. Then, finally, my demands came from Nuremberg.

The demands now were quite clear. Now, for the first time, I said, that at last nearly twenty years after Mr. Wilson's right of self-determination for the 3,500,000 must be enforced and we shall not just look on any longer.

And again Herr Benes replied: New victims, new incarcerations, new arrests. The German element gradually began to flee.

Then came England. I informed Mr. Chamberlain unequivocally of what we regard as the only possibility of solution.

It is the most natural solution possible.

I know that all these nationalities no longer want to remain with this Herr Benes.

In the first place, however, I speak of Germans. For these Germans I have now spoken and now given assurances that I am no longer willing to look on quietly and passively as this lunatic believes he can simply mishandle 3,500,000 human beings.

I left no doubt that German patience at last was exhausted. I left no doubt it was the way of our German mentality to take things long and patiently, that, however, the moment comes once when this must be ended.

And now, in fact, England and France agreed to dispatch the only possible demand to Czechoslovakia, namely to free the German region and cede it to the Reich.

I am thankful to Mr. Chamberlain for all his trouble and I assured him that the German people wants nothing but peace, but I also declared that I cannot go beyond the limits of our patience.

I further assured him and I repeat here that if this problem is solved, there will be no further territorial problems in Europe for Germany.

And I further assured him that at the moment that Czechoslovakia has solved her other problems, that is, when the Czechs have reconciled themselves with their other minorities, the Czech State no longer interests me and that, if you please, I give him the guarantee: We do not want any Czechs.

But equally I want now to declare before the German people that as regards the Sudeten German problem, my patience is now exhausted.

I now head the procession of my people as first soldier and behind me —may the world know this—there now marches a people and a different one than that of 1918.

Errant mentors of those times succeeded in infiltrating the poison of democratic phrases into our people, but the German people of today is not the German people of 1918.

In these hours we will take one holy common resolve. It shall be stronger than any pressure, any peril. And when this will is stronger than pressure and peril, it will break the pressure and peril.

Hitler's boasting of his conquest of nearly all of Europe and his hatred of Churchill form the theme of a speech that he delivered before the Reichstag on May 4, 1941. Here are parts of this speech.

GERMAN CONQUESTS

On MAY 10 of last year perhaps the most memorable struggle in all German history commenced. The enemy front was broken up in a few days and the stage was then set for the operation that culminated in the greatest battle of annihilation in the history of the world. Thus France collapsed, Belgium and Holland were already occupied, and the battered remnants of the British expeditionary force were driven from the European Continent, leaving their arms behind.

On July 19, 1940, I then convened the German Reichstag for the third time in order to render that great account which you all still remember. The meeting provided me with the opportunity of expressing the thanks of the nation to its soldiers in a form suited to the uniqueness of the event.

Once again I seized the opportunity of urging the world to make peace. And what I foresaw and prophesied at that time happened. My offer of peace was misconstrued as a symptom of fear and cowardice.

The European and American warmongers succeeded once again in befogging the sound common sense of the masses, who can never hope to profit from this war, by conjuring up false pictures of new hope. Thus, finally, under pressure of public opinion, as formed by their press, they once more managed to induce the nation to continue this struggle.

Even my warnings against night bombings of the civilian population, as advocated by Mr. Churchill, were interpreted as a sign of German impotence. He, the most bloodthirsty or amateurish strategist that history has ever known, actually saw fit to believe that the reserve displayed for months by the German Air Force could be looked upon only as proof of their incapacity to fly by night.

So this man for months ordered his paid scribblers to deceive the British people into believing that the Royal Air Force alone—and no others—was in a position to wage war in this way, and that thus ways and means had been found to force the Reich to its knees by the ruthless onslaught of the British Air Force on the German civilian population in conjunction with the starvation blockade.

Again and again I uttered these warnings against this specific type of aerial warfare and I did so for over three and a half months. That these warnings failed to impress Mr. Churchill does not surprise me in the least. For what does this man care for the lives of others? What does he care for culture or for architecture?

When war broke out he stated clearly that he wanted to have his war, even though the cities of England might be reduced to ruins. So now he has got his war.

My assurances that from a given moment every one of his bombs would be returned if necessary a hundredfold failed to induce this man to consider even for an instant the criminal nature of his action. He professes not to be in the least depressed and he even assures us that the British people, too, after such bombing raids, greeted him with a joyous serenity, causing him to return to London refreshed by his visits to the stricken areas.

It is possible that this sight strengthened Mr. Churchill in his firm determination to continue the war in this way, and we are no less determined to continue to retaliate, if necessary, a hundred bombs for every one of his and to go on doing so until the British nation at last gets rid of this criminal and his methods.

The appeal to forsake me, made to the German nation by this fool and his satellites on May Day, of all days, is only to be explained either as symptomatic of a paralytic disease or of a drunkard's ravings. His abnormal state of mind also gave birth to a decision to transform the Balkans into a theatre of war.

For over five years this man has been chasing around Europe like a madman in search of something that he could set on fire. Unfortunately, he again and again finds hirelings who open the gates of their country to this international incendiary.

After he had succeeded in the course of the past Winter in persuading the British people by a wave of false assertions and pretensions that the German Reich, exhausted by the campaign in the preceding months, was completely spent, he saw himself obliged, in order to prevent an awakening of the truth, to create a fresh conflagration in Europe.

In so doing he returned to the project that had been in his mind as early as the Autumn of 1939 and the Spring of 1940. It was thought possible at the time to mobilize about 100 divisions in Britain's interest.

The sudden collapse which we witnessed in May and June of the past year forced these plans to be abandoned for the moment. But by the Autumn of last year Mr. Churchill began to tackle this problem once again.

The reverses suffered by the Italian Army in North Africa, owing to a certain material inferiority of their tanks and anti-tank guns, finally led Mr. Churchill to believe that the time was ripe to transfer the theatre of war from Libya to Greece. He ordered the transport of the remaining tanks and of the infantry division, composed mainly of Anzacs, and was convinced that he could now complete his scheme, which was to set the Balkans aflame.

Thus did Mr. Churchill commit one of the greatest strategic blunders of this war. As soon as there could be no further doubt regarding Britain's intentions of gaining a foothold in the Balkans, I took the necessary steps.

Germany, by keeping pace with these moves, assembled the necessary forces for the purpose of counteracting any possible tricks of that gentleman.

Germany had no intention of starting a war in the Balkans. On the contrary, it was our honest intention as far as possible to contribute to a settlement of the conflict with Greece by means that would be tolerable to the legitimate wishes of Italy.

The Duce not only consented to but lent his full support to our efforts to bring Yugoslavia into a close community of interests with our peace aims. Thus it finally became possible to induce the Yugoslav Government to join the Three-power Pact, which made no demands whatever on Yugoslavia but only offered that country advantages.

Thus on March 26 of this year a pact was signed in Vienna that offered the Yugoslav State the greatest future conceivable and could have assured peace for the Balkans. Believe me, gentlemen, on that day I left the beautiful city of the Danube truly happy not only because it seemed as though almost eight years of foreign policies had received their reward but also because I believed that perhaps at the last moment German intervention in the Balkans might not be necessary.

We were all stunned by the news of that coup, carried through by a handful of bribed conspirators who had brought about the event that caused the British Prime Minister to declare in joyous words that at last he had something good to report.

You will surely understand, gentlemen, that when I heard this I at once gave orders to attack Yugoslavia. To treat the German Reich in this way is impossible. One cannot spend years in concluding a treaty that is in the interest of the other party merely to discover that this treaty has not only been broken overnight but also that it had been answered by the insulting of the representative of the German Reich, by the threatening of his military attaché, by the injuring of the aide de camp of this attaché, by the maltreating of numerous other Germans, by demolishing property, by laying waste the homes of German citizens and by terrorizing.

God knows that I wanted peace. But I can do nothing but protect the interests of the Reich with those means which, thank God, are at our disposal. I made my decision at that moment all the more calmly because I knew that I was in accord with Bulgaria, who had always remained unshaken in her loyalty to the German Reich, and with the equally justified indignation of Hungary.

The consequences of this campaign are extraordinary. In view of the fact that a small set of conspirators in Belgrade again were able to foment trouble in the service of extracontinental interests, the radical elimination of this danger means the removal of an element of tension for the whole of Europe.

The Danube as an important waterway is thus safeguarded against any further act of sabotage. Traffic has been resumed in full.

Apart from the modest correction of its frontiers, which were infringed as a result of the outcome of the World War, the Reich has no special territorial interests in these parts. As far as politics are concerned we are merely interested in safeguarding peace in this region, while in the realm of economics we wish to see an order that will allow the production of goods to be developed and the exchange of products to be resumed in the interests of all.

It is, however, only in accordance with supreme justice if those interests are also taken into account that are founded upon ethnographical, historical or economic conditions.

I can assure you that I look into the future with perfect tranquillity and great confidence. The German Reich and its allies represent power, military, economic and, above all, in moral respects, which is superior to any possible coalition in the world. The German armed forces will always do their part whenever it may be necessary. The confidence of the German people will always accompany their soldiers.

Benito Mussolini
[1883–1945]

Benito Mussolini was an active agitator and editor before World War I and fought in that war. At the end of the war he organized the "Fascisti." In 1922 he became Premier of Italy after the Fascist "March on Rome," adopting the title "Il Duce." In 1924 the murder of Matteotti, leading opponent of the Fascists, was followed by wide extension of Mussolini's dictatorship. In 1935 he invaded and conquered Ethiopia. In 1937 he established with Hitler the Rome-Berlin Axis, and gave military aid to the Spanish rebels. In 1939 he conquered Albania. In 1940 he declared war against France and England, and attempted an invasion of Greece. In 1941, as a junior partner of Hitler, Mussolini declared war against Russia and later the United States. He lost Ethiopia after defeat by the British in East Africa. Sicily and then Italy were successfully invaded by the Allies, and Mussolini was deposed by his country in 1943. He attempted to reinstate his government in 1945, but was again ousted. He was shot trying to leave his country in disguise.

Two speeches by Mussolini are presented here. The first was broadcast October 2, 1933, on the eve of his invasion of Ethiopia. The second speech, "Anniversary of Italy's Entry in the War," was delivered before the Chamber of Fasces and Corporations on June 11, 1941.

A CALL TO ARMS

BLACK SHIRTS of revolution, men and women of all Italy, Italians all over the world, beyond the mountains, beyond the seas, listen. A solemn hour is about to strike in the history of the country. Twenty million Italians are at this moment gathered in the squares of all Italy. It is the greatest demonstration that human history records. Twenty millions, one heart alone, one will alone, one decision.

This manifestation signifies that the tie between Italy and Fascism is perfect, absolute, unalterable. Only brains softened by puerile illusions, by sheer ignorance, can think differently, because they do not know what exactly is the Fascist Italy of 1935.

For many months the wheel of destiny and of the impulse of our calm determination moves toward the goal. In these last hours the rhythm has increased and nothing can stop it now.

It is not only an army marching towards its goal, but it is forty-four million Italians marching in unity behind this army. Because the blackest of injustices is being attempted against them, that of taking from them their place in the sun. When in 1915 Italy threw in her fate with that of the Allies, how many cries of admiration, how many promises were heard? But after the common victory, which cost Italy six hundred thousand dead, four hundred thousand lost, one million wounded, when peace was being discussed around the table only the crumbs of a rich colonial booty were left for us to pick up. For thirteen years we have been patient while the circle tightened around us at the hands of those who wish to suffocate us.

We have been patient with Ethiopia for forty years. It is enough now.

The League of Nations instead of recognizing the rights of Italy dares talk of sanctions, but until there is proof to the contrary I refuse to believe that the authentic people of France will join in supporting sanctions against Italy. Six hundred thousand dead whose devotion was so heroic that the enemy commander justly admired them—those fallen would now turn in their graves.

And until there is proof to the contrary, I refuse to believe that the authentic people of Britain will want to spill blood and send Europe into a catastrophe for the sake of a barbarian country, unworthy of ranking among civilized nations. Nevertheless, we cannot afford to overlook the possible developments of tomorrow.

To economic sanctions, we shall answer with our discipline, our spirit of sacrifice, our obedience. To military sanctions, we shall answer with military measures. To acts of war, we shall answer with acts of war.

A people worthy of their past and their name cannot and never will take a different stand. Let me repeat, in the most categorical manner, that the sacred pledge which I make at this moment before all the Italians gathered together today, is that I shall do everything in my power to prevent a colonial conflict from taking on the aspect and weight of a European war.

This conflict may be attractive to certain minds which hope to avenge their disintegrated temples through this new catastrophe. Never, as at this historical hour, have the people of Italy revealed such force of character, and it is against this people to which mankind owes its greatest conquest, this people of heroes, of poets and saints, of navigators, of colonizers, that the world dares threaten sanctions.

Italy! Italy! entirely and universally Fascist! The Italy of the black shirt revolution, rise to your feet, let the cry of your determination rise to the skies and reach our soldiers in East Africa. Let it be a comfort to those who are about to fight. Let it be an encouragement to our friends and a warning to our enemies. It is the cry of Italy which goes beyond the mountains and the seas out into the great world. It is the cry of justice and of victory.

ANNIVERSARY OF ITALY'S ENTRY IN THE WAR

COMRADES, this is a memorable, solemn day. It is just a year since our entrance into the war. A year filled with events, giddy, historical developments. A year during which Italian soldiers on land, sea and in the sky fought heroically, mostly on the fronts of Europe and Africa.

No one doubts any longer, in the light of unquestionable published documents, that between Italy and Greece there should be a rendering of accounts. At Athens, newspapers begin finally to disclose the criminal backstage of Greek policy. Since August, 1940, I had proof that Greece no longer was keeping even the appearance of neutrality. In the same months there was a period of tension which was followed by a few weeks of calm.

Thus, on Oct. 15, it was unanimously decided to break hesitancies and take to the field at the end of the month.

It was absolutely mathematical that in April, even if nothing happened to change the Balkan situation, the Italian Army would have broken through and annihilated the Greek Army.

It is necessary to state honestly that many Greek detachments fought courageously. It is sad to affirm, furthermore, that the Greek Army would not have held for six months without the aid of England. The Greek Army was fed, supplied and armed by the English. Aviation was English. Anti-aircraft and artillery also was English. Not less than 60,000 English were in services and special groups flanked the Greek Army.

Material aid furnished by Turkey was modest. Its value did not amount to 2,000,000 Turkish pounds.

While Italian troops were pushing to liquidate the Greek Army Yugoslavia revealed through a coup d'état its real sentiments. The Axis war against Yugoslavia, therefore, was rendered inevitable. Axis armies acted together with lightning rapidity. While the second Army of the Alps was moving down along the Dalmatian Coast with forced marches which tried the resistance of our soldiers, the Greeks retired fighting to the rearguard and tried a last moment trick in genuine Ulysses style to hold us at the border of Albania, offering an armistice to the Germans and not to us.

They were called energetically to reason by me and finally surrendered unconditionally.

Regarding Yugoslavia, it revealed almost immediately the inconsistency and, it may be said "falsity" of its state organism in the third mosaic State artificially created at Versailles. With exclusively anti-Italian function it falls into pieces at the first shock.

The Yugoslav Army for which Paris and the Little Entente circle had created a reputation of "invincibility" was put out of action with the first blows. The English still made a few appearances on battlefields, but found Hellenic soil also burned under their feet and they abandoned —fleeing by the usual sea route—dying Greece.

Political and military consequences which sprang up by the elimination of England from her last European bases have profoundly changed the map of that region—changed for the better, especially if every one will keep a sense of proportion—that is to say, change toward a more reasonable arrangement according to justice, taking into account all elements which go to make them up and frequently snarl problems.

Here also it has not been possible to reach an arrangement perfect in every way, but one must not hope for the absolute in such matters.

Bulgaria annexes Macedonia, which is prevalently Bulgarian, and Western Thrace.

Hungary has enlarged her confines and Germany has carried hers to the left bank of the Sava. The rest of Slovenia has become an Italian province with a special regime. The most important fact is resurrection, after two centuries, of the Croat State.

With the annexation of almost all of the islands of the Dalmatian Peninsula, with the creation of two provinces of Split and Kotor and the enlarging of old, extremely faithful Zara, the Dalmatian problem may be considered solved, especially taking into account relations between the Kingdoms of Italy and Croatia, whose crown has been offered to a Savoy-Aosta.

If we wished we could have pushed our borders from Velebiti to the Albanian Alps but we would, in my opinion, have made a mistake. Without counting others, we would have brought within our borders several hundred thousand foreign elements naturally hostile.

The conquest of Crete places at the disposition of the Axis air and naval bases very close for mass attacks on the Egyptian coast. Life will become ever more difficult for the English naval forces stationed at the bases of Egypt and Palestine. The objective, which consists of expelling Britain from the Eastern Mediterranean, will be reached and with it a gigantic step will be taken toward a victorious epilogue of war.

Collaboration between the powers of the Tripartite Pact is under way. But above all, collaboration between Germany and Italy is under way.

Ridiculous rumors which were speculating on eventual frictions or dissensions, come of the feeble minded who worked even further like the English Prime Minister in his useless Christmas Eve speech, are reduced to silence.

Added to this Japan is in perfect line with the Tripartite Pact. The Japanese are a proud, loyal people which would not remain indifferent in the face of American aggression against the Axis powers.

With the other powers adhering to the Tripartite Pact, namely, Hungary, Slovakia, Rumania and Bulgaria, relations are more than cordial even where special political accords do not exist.

Regarding Turkey, that country has until now refused all English solicitations. President Inonu has seen the tragic fate that awaits all nations which in any way trust themselves to Britain. But I wish to take this occasion to say to President Inonu that Italy intends to follow toward Turkey that policy of comprehension and collaboration which was inaugurated in 1928 and which for us is still in effect.

If Spain and Turkey are out of the fighting there is one trans-oceanic State which seems likely to enter it. It is well that it be known that American intervention does not bother us excessively. Specific declaration of war would not change the present situation, which is one of de facto war, if not de jure. American intervention, when employed completely, would be late, and if it were not later would not remove the terms of the problem. American intervention will not give victory to Britain but will prolong the war; will not limit the area of war but will extend it to other oceans; will change the United States regime into an authoritarian, totalitarian one in comparison with which the European forerunners—fascist and nazi—will feel themselves far surpassed and perfected.

When it is desired to be called a dictator in the pure classical meaning of the word, Sulla is cited. Sulla appears to us a modest amateur compared with Delano Roosevelt.

By agreement with the German command, almost all of Greece, including Athens, will be occupied by Italian troops. This lays a very serious problem before us, especially from the point of view of food, but we shall face it seeking to alleviate as far as possible miseries inflicted upon the Greek people by their governors subordinated to London and having in mind that Greece re-enters into Italy's vital Mediterranean space.

Many times after Cheren the English have announced the campaign in Italian Africa might be considered more or less virtually concluded. But after Cheren they had to go up against Amba Alagi, where for the second time Italian resistance reached epic proportion. After the fall of Amba Alagi the English again proclaimed that all was now finished. Instead, they are still fighting. There are three zones where our barricaded troops are still giving the English plenty of wool to twist—Tankali, Gimma and Gondar.

How long it may last cannot be known, but it is certain that resistance will be protracted to the limits of human possibility.

Even the whole conquest of the empire by the English has no decisive importance toward the ending of the war. This is a vendetta of strictly personal character which could have no influence on the results of a war which has dug even deeper chasms between Italy and Britain I cannot tell you today when or how, but I affirm in the most categoric manner that we shall return to that land bathed by our blood and——

Our dead shall not go unavenged.

Vyacheslav M. Molotov
[1889–1986]

Vyacheslav M. Molotov, Foreign Minister of the U.S.S.R., was prominent in the Bolshevist revolution of 1917 and closely associated with Lenin and later Stalin. In 1930 he became Premier; in 1939 was also Foreign Minister. In 1940 Molotov was Vice-Premier under Stalin. After Stalin's death in 1953, Molotov was among the most powerful men in Soviet Russia, and continued as Foreign Minister under Bulganin and Krushchev.

On the outbreak of war with Germany, June 22, 1941, Molotov broadcast the following address.

THE NAZI WAR ON RUSSIA

CITIZENS of the Soviet Union:

The Soviet Government and its head, Comrade Stalin, have authorized me to make the following statement:

Today at 4 o'clock A.M., without any claims having been presented to the Soviet Union, without a declaration of war, German troops attacked our country, attacked our borders at many points and bombed from their airplanes our cities Zhitomir, Kiev, Sevastopol, Kaunas and some others, killing and wounding over 200 persons.

There were also enemy air raids and artillery shelling from Rumanian and Finnish territory.

This unheard of attack upon our country is perfidy unparalleled in the history of civilized nations. The attack on our country was perpetrated despite the fact that a treaty of non-aggression had been signed between the U. S. S. R. and Germany and that the Soviet Government most faithfully abided by all provisions of this treaty.

The attack upon our country was perpetrated despite the fact that during the entire period of operation of this treaty the German Government could not find grounds for a single complaint against the U. S. S. R. as regards observance of this treaty.

Entire responsibility for this predatory attack upon the Soviet Union falls fully and completely upon the German Fascist rulers.

At 5:30 A.M.—that is, after the attack had already been perpetrated, Von der Schulenburg, the German Ambassador in Moscow, on behalf of his government made the statement to me as People's Commissar of Foreign Affairs to the effect that the German Government had decided to launch war against the U. S. S. R. in connection with the concentration of Red Army units near the eastern German frontier.

In reply to this I stated on behalf of the Soviet Government that, until the very last moment, the German Government had not presented any claims to the Soviet Government, that Germany attacked the U. S. S. R. despite the peaceable position of the Soviet Union, and that for this reason Fascist Germany is the aggressor.

On instruction of the government of the Soviet Union I also stated that at no point had our troops or our air force committed a violation of the frontier and therefore the statement made this morning by the Rumanian radio to the effect that Soviet aircraft allegedly had fired on Rumanian airdromes is a sheer lie and provocation.

Likewise a lie and provocation is the whole declaration made today by Hitler, who is trying belatedly to concoct accusations charging the Soviet Union with failure to observe the Soviet-German pact.

Now that the attack on the Soviet Union has already been committed, the Soviet Government has ordered our troops to repulse the predatory assault and to drive German troops from the territory of our country.

This war has been forced upon us, not by the German people, not by German workers, peasants and intellectuals, whose sufferings we well understand, but by the clique of bloodthirsty Fascist rulers of Germany who have enslaved Frenchmen, Czechs, Poles, Serbians, Norway, Belgium, Denmark, Holland, Greece and other nations.

The government of the Soviet Union expresses its unshakable confidence that our valiant army and navy and brave falcons of the Soviet Air Force will acquit themselves with honor in performing their duty to the fatherland and to the Soviet people, and will inflict a crushing blow upon the aggressor.

This is not the first time that our people have had to deal with an attack of an arrogant foe. At the time of Napoleon's invasion of Russia our people's reply was war for the fatherland, and Napoleon suffered defeat and met his doom.

It will be the same with Hitler, who in his arrogance has proclaimed a new crusade against our country. The Red Army and our whole people will again wage victorious war for the fatherland, for our country, for honor, for liberty.

The government of the Soviet Union expresses the firm conviction that the whole population of our country, all workers, peasants and intellectuals, men and women, will conscientiously perform their duties and do their work. Our entire people must now stand solid and united as never before.

Each one of us must demand of himself and of others discipline, organization and self-denial worthy of real Soviet patriots, in order to provide for all the needs of the Red Army, Navy and Air Force, to insure victory over the enemy.

The government calls upon you, citizens of the Soviet Union, to rally still more closely around our glorious Bolshevist party, around our Soviet Government, around our great leader and comrade, Stalin. Ours is a righteous cause. The enemy shall be defeated. Victory will be ours.

Joseph Stalin

[1879-1953]

Joseph Stalin as a young revolutionary in the days of Czarism was several times arrested and exiled to Siberia—and each time escaped. He became a Bolshevist editor and in 1917 participated in the revolution which resulted in the establishment of the Soviet form of government in Russia, with Lenin at its head. In 1922 Stalin was appointed general secretary of the Communist party, and two years later he succeeded Lenin as the virtual ruler of Russia. In 1928 he exiled Trotzky, his chief opponent, and in 1938 his regime "liquidated" many leading Bolshevists after spectacular trials on charges of treason. In 1939 Stalin entered into a non-aggression treaty with Hitler and invaded Finland. In 1941 Hitler broke the treaty and invaded Russia. Stalin continued as dictator until his death in 1953.

Following is Stalin's historic "scorched earth" speech, which Stalin, as the new Premier and chairman of the State Committee of Defense, broadcast to the Russian people and military forces on July 3, 1941.

"DEFEND EVERY INCH OF SOVIET SOIL!"

COMRADES! Citizens! Brothers and Sisters! Men of our Army and Navy! I am addressing you, my friends!

The perfidious military attack on our fatherland, begun on June 22 by Hitler Germany, is continuing.

In spite of heroic resistance of the Red Army, and although the enemy's finest divisions and finest air force units have already been smashed and have met their doom on the field of battle, the enemy continues to push forward, hurling fresh forces into the attack.

Hitler's troops have succeeded in capturing Lithuania, a considerable part of Latvia, the western part of Byelo-Russia [White Russia] and a part of the Western Ukraine.

The Fascist air force is extending the range of operations of its bombers and is bombing Murmansk, Orsha, Mogilev, Smolensk, Kiev, Odessa and Sevastopol.

A grave danger hangs over our country.

How could it have happened that our glorious Red Army surrendered a number of our cities and districts to the Fascist armies?

Is it really true that German Fascist troops are invincible, as is ceaselessly trumpeted by boastful Fascist propagandists? Of course not!

History shows that there are no invincible armies, and never have been. Napoleon's Army was considered invincible, but it was beaten successively by Russian, English and German Armies. Kaiser Wilhelm's German Army in the period of the first imperialist war was also considered invincible, but it was beaten several times by Russian and Anglo-French forces, and was finally smashed by Anglo-French forces.

The same must be said of Hitler's German Fascist Army today. This army has not yet met with serious resistance on the Continent of Europe. Only on our territory has it met serious resistance, and if as a result of this resistance the finest divisions of Hitler's German Fascist Army have been defeated by our Red Army, it means that this army, too, can be smashed and will be smashed as were the armies of Napoleon and Wilhelm.

As to part of our territory having nevertheless been seized by German Fascist troops, this is chiefly due to the fact that the war of Fascist Germany on the U. S. S. R. began under conditions favorable for German forces and unfavorable for Soviet forces.

The fact of the matter is that troops of Germany, as a country at war, were already fully mobilized, and 170 divisions hurled by Germany against the U. S. S. R. and brought up to the Soviet frontiers were in a state of complete readiness, only awaiting the signal to move into action, whereas Soviet troops had little time to effect mobilization and move up to the frontiers.

Of no little importance in this respect is the fact that Fascist Germany suddenly and treacherously violated the non-aggression pact she concluded in 1939 with the U. S. S. R., disregarding the fact that she would be regarded as an aggressor by the whole world. Naturally, our peace-loving country, not wishing to take the initiative of breaking the pact, could not resort to perfidy.

It may be asked: How could the Soviet Government have consented to conclude a non-aggression pact with such treacherous fiends as Hitler and Ribbentrop? Was not this an error on the part of the Soviet Government? Of course not!

Non-aggression pacts are pacts of peace between two States. It was such a pact that Germany proposed to us in 1939. Could the Soviet Government have declined such a proposal? I think that not a single peace-loving State could decline a peace treaty with a neighboring State even though the latter was headed by such fiends and cannibals as Hitler and Ribbentrop.

But that, of course, only on one indispensable condition—namely, that this peace treaty does not infringe either directly or indirectly on the territorial integrity, independence and honor of a peace-loving State.

As is well known, the non-aggression pact between Germany and the U. S. S. R. is precisely such a pact.

What did we gain by concluding a non-aggression pact with Germany? We secured for our country peace for a year and a half and the opportunity of preparing its forces to repulse Fascist Germany should she risk an attack on our country despite the pact.

This was a definite advantage for us and a disadvantage for Fascist Germany.

What has Fascist Germany gained and what has she lost by treacherously tearing up the pact and attacking the U. S. S. R.?

She gained a certain advantageous position for her troops for a short period, but she has lost politically by exposing herself in the eyes of the entire world as a bloodthirsty aggressor.

There can be no doubt that this short-lived military gain for Germany is only an episode, while the tremendous political gain of the U. S. S. R. is a serious and lasting factor that is bound to form the basis for development of decisive military successes of the Red Army in the war with Fascist Germany.

That is why our whole valiant Red Army, our whole valiant Navy, all our falcons of the air, all peoples of our country, all the finest men and women of Europe, America and Asia, and, finally, all the finest men and women of Germany, condemn the treacherous acts of the German Fascists and sympathize with the Soviet Government, approve the conduct of the Soviet Government and see that ours is a just cause, that the enemy will be defeated, that we are bound to win.

By virtue of this war which has been forced upon us our country has come to death grips with its most malicious and most perfidious enemy—German fascism.

Our troops are fighting heroically against an enemy armed to the teeth with tanks and aircraft. Overcoming innumerable difficulties the Red Army and Navy are self-sacrificingly disputing every inch of Soviet soil.

The main forces of the Red Army are coming into action armed with thousands of tanks and airplanes. Men of the Red Army are displaying unexampled valor. Our resistance to the enemy is growing in strength and power. Side by side with the Red Army the entire Soviet people is rising in defense of our native land.

What is required to put an end to the danger hovering over our country, and what measures must be taken to smash the enemy?

Above all, it is essential that our people, the Soviet people, should understand the full immensity of the danger that threatens our country and abandon all complacency, all heedlessness, all those moods of peaceful, constructive work which were so natural before the war but which are fatal today when war has fundamentally changed everything.

The enemy is cruel and implacable. He is out to seize our lands watered with our sweat, to seize our grain and soil secured by our labor.

He is out to restore the rule of landlords, to restore Czarism, to destroy national culture and the national State existence of Russians, Ukrainians, Byelo-Russians, Lithuanians, Letts, Estonians, Uzbeks, Tartars, Moldavians, Georgians, Armenians, Azerbaijanians, and the other free peoples of the Soviet Union, to Germanize them, to convert them into slaves of German princes and barons.

Thus the issue is one of life or death for the Soviet State, for the peoples of the U. S. S. R.: the issue is whether peoples of the Soviet Union shall remain free or fall into slavery.

The Soviet people must realize this and abandon all heedlessness, they must mobilize themselves and reorganize all their work on new, wartime lines, when there can be no mercy to the enemy.

Further, there must be no room in our ranks for whimperers and cowards, for panic-mongers and deserters; our people must know no fear in the fight and must selflessly join our patriotic war of liberation, our war against the Fascist enslavers.

Lenin, the great founder of our State, used to say that the chief virtue of the Soviet people must be courage, valor, fearlessness in struggle, readiness to fight together with the people against the enemies of our country.

This splendid virtue of the Bolshevik must become the virtue of millions and millions of the Red Army, of the Red Navy, of all peoples of the Soviet Union.

All our work must be immediately reconstructed on a war footing, everything must be subordinated to the interests of the front and the task of organizing demolition of the enemy.

The peoples of the Soviet Union now see that there is no taming of German fascism in its savage fury and hatred of our country which has insured all working people labor in freedom and prosperity.

The peoples of the Soviet Union must rise against the enemy and defend their rights and their land. The Red Army, Red Navy and all citizens of the Soviet Union must defend every inch of Soviet soil, must fight to the last drop of blood for our towns and villages, must display the daring initiative and intelligence that are inherent in our people.

We must organize all-round assistance to the Red Army, insure powerful reinforcements for its ranks and supply of everything it requires, we must organize rapid transport of troops and military freight and extensive aid to the wounded.

We must strengthen the Red Army's rear, subordinating all our work to this cause, all our industries must be got to work with greater intensity to produce more rifles, machine guns, artillery, bullets, shells, airplanes; we must organize the guarding of factories, power stations, telephonic and telegraphic communications, and arrange effective air raid precautions in all localities.

We must wage a ruthless fight against all disorganizers of the rear, deserters, panic-mongers, rumor-mongers, exterminate spies, diversionists, enemy parachutists, rendering rapid aid in all this to our destroyer battalions. We must bear in mind that the enemy is crafty, unscrupulous, experienced in deception and dissemination of false rumors.

We must reckon with all this and not fall victim to provocation. All who by their panic-mongering and cowardice hinder the work of defense, no matter who they are, must be immediately haled before a military tribunal.

In case of a forced retreat of Red Army units, all rolling stock must be evacuated; to the enemy must not be left a single engine, a single railway car, not a single pound or grain or a gallon of fuel.

Collective farmers must drive off all their cattle and turn over their grain to the safekeeping of State authorities for transportation to the rear. All valuable property including non-ferrous metals, grain and fuel which cannot be withdrawn must without fail be destroyed.

In areas occupied by the enemy, guerrilla units, mounted and foot, must be formed, diversionist groups must be organized to combat enemy troops, to foment guerrilla warfare everywhere, to blow up bridges, roads, damage telephone and telegraph lines and to set fire to forests, stores and transports.

In occupied regions conditions must be made unbearable for the enemy and all his accomplices. They must be hounded and annihilated at every step and all their measures frustrated.

This war with Fascist Germany cannot be considered an ordinary war. It is not only a war between two armies, it is also a great war of the entire Soviet people against the German fascist forces.

The aim of this national war in defense of our country against the fascist oppressors is not only elimination of the danger hanging over our country, but also aid to all European peoples groaning under the yoke of German fascism.

In this war of liberation we shall not be alone.

In this great war we shall have loyal allies in the peoples of Europe and America, including German people who are enslaved by Hitlerite despots.

Our war for the freedom of our country will merge with the struggle of the peoples of Europe and America for their independence, for democratic liberties. It will be a united front of peoples standing for freedom and against enslavement and threats of enslavement by Hitler's Fascist armies.

In this connection the historic utterance of British Prime Minister Churchill regarding aid to the Soviet Union and the declaration of the U. S. A. Government signifying readiness to render aid to our country, which can only evoke a feeling of gratitude in the hearts of the peoples of the Soviet Union, are fully comprehensible and symptomatic.

Comrades, our forces are numberless. The overweening enemy will soon learn this to his cost. Side by side with the Red Army and Navy thousands of workers, collective farmers and intellectuals are rising to fight the enemy aggressor. The masses of our people will rise up in their millions. The working people of Moscow and Leningrad already have commenced to form vast popular levies in support of the Red Army.

Such popular levies must be raised in every city which is in danger of an enemy invasion, all working people must be roused to defend our freedom, our honor, our country—in our patriotic war against German fascism.

In order to insure a rapid mobilization of all forces of the peoples of the U. S. S. R., and to repulse the enemy who treacherously attacked our country, a State Committee of Defense has been formed in whose hands the entire power of the State has been vested.

The State Committee of Defense has entered into its functions and calls upon all our people to rally around the party of Lenin-Stalin and around the Soviet Government so as self-denyingly to support the Red Army and Navy, demolish the enemy and secure victory.

All our forces for the support of our heroic Red Army and our glorious Red Navy!

All the forces of the people—for the demolition of the enemy!

Forward, to our victory!

Fumimaro Konoye

[1891-1945]

Prince Fumimaro Konoye was one of the most powerful men behind the Japanese throne. He was Premier from 1937 to 1941, the period of Japanese aggression against China and Indo-China and Japan's military alliance with Germany and Italy. He committed suicide on learning that he would be tried as a war criminal. Following are parts of a broadcast by Premier Konoye, September 28, 1940, the day after Japan joined the Rome-Berlin axis.

THE TRIPLE ALLIANCE

WORLD HISTORY is at a turning point. The Japanese Government has entered into the triple alliance for peace and for development of the world. We are aware of our heavy responsibility. I shall tell you the true state of affairs and ask you to awaken to our position.

Affairs in East Asia have gradually deteriorated, and settlement of the China affair has been difficult, so the government has decided radical measures were needed to settle what is really a civil war.

It is natural that Germany and Italy, who were making a new order in Europe, should make common cause with Japan. The division of the world into several spheres of co-existence and mutual prosperity would benefit all nations. The European war has been caused by efforts to suppress this desire.

We face an emergency unprecedented in our history. Enforcement of the treaty of alliance may become necessary. However difficult the position may become, the government is determined to face its responsibilities.

During the past three years Japan has made tremendous sacrifices and has lost many loyal soldiers. Prolongation of the China war on one hand and establishment of the new order and armament replenishment on the other have exacted heavy sacrifices and have made life difficult.

Taking internal conditions and the international outlook into consideration, the government decided the triple alliance was Japan's best way. Our efforts will decide our fate. No effort will be too great. I ask the people to rise to overcome the nation's difficulties.

Chiang Kai-shek
[1886–1975]

Generalissimo Chiang Kai-shek, leader of the Chinese Nation-
alists and formerly head of the Chinese government, delivered an
address at the weekly memorial meeting of the Central Kuoming-
tang Headquarters, at Chunking on December 26, 1938, in which
he answered a statement made shortly before by Prince Konoye,
Premier of Japan. The closing part of this address is given here.

WAR BETWEEN JUSTICE AND FORCE

THE year and a half's war has laid for us a solid foundation for national
regeneration. We fear no problems, nor are we concerned over impending dangers. We merely lament the fate of Japan, the present status
of which was brought about by the hard efforts and sacrifices of her
reformist patriots. Today, her people are powerless, her throne without
prerogative, and her politicians without integrity and knowledge, thus
allowing a few hot-headed young militarists to do as they please. They
are sapping Japan's national strength, shaking her national foundations
and advancing savagely on the infamous road of self-seeking at the
expense of others. In the eyes of these young Japanese militarists, China
does not exist, nor do the other countries of the world. They have regard
neither for discipline, nor for law, nor yet for their own government.
Guided by their greed, cruelty, and violence, they do as they please. If
such conduct be allowed to continue, the future of Japan is indeed full
of danger. Although we are sworn enemies of the Japanese militarists,
yet we are still neighbours to the Japanese people, who share with us a
language of a common origin. Reviewing Japan's history and looking
forward to her future, we not only see danger in her path but lament
her lot.

Comrades, you should realize that the Japanese militarists are now
heading blindly into a maze. They have forgotten their own history, their
own position, and can neither see the outside world and their own
crisis, nor recognize their neighbour, a revolutionary China. There are
but two aspects to their thought. On the one hand they are so blind
to facts as vainly to hope that China might accept their outrageous
terms, and on the other hand they rely on their cunning to achieve
some tour-de-force and to benefit by hoodwinking the world. Because
they themselves are stupid, they believe the peoples of the world are
to be befooled. Because they themselves are violent, they believe that
force can dominate this world.

As borne out by the terms embodied in his statement, Konoye wants
to close China's Open Door and break the Nine-Power Treaty by
establishing a so-called "new order in East Asia," and to expel European

and American influence from China by creating a so-called "unity of East Asia" and "economic bloc," and to revive the Twenty-one Demands presented to Yuan Shih-kai by "stationing troops in China" and setting aside "Inner Mongolia as a Special Area." Summing up, Japan intends to force China to destroy by her own hand the principles of Open Door and Equal Opportunity, the League of Nations Covenant, the Nine-Power Treaty, the Sino-Soviet Non-Aggression Pact and other international treaties, by resorting to such terms as "creating a new order in East Asia." They wish to bind our hands, squeeze our arteries, yet they expect us to follow in their footsteps by breaking faith and despising loyalty to hasten the realization of their domination in East Asia, after which they might direct the world. Throughout five thousand years, China has always been guided by good faith and sincerity, in her statecraft. How can we be made to yield by threats and abandon our stand?

China as a state is founded on the principles not to oppress the undefended, nor fear the aggressive. More particularly, she is not willing to violate pacts or break faith and thus destroy the righteous principles governing the relations of mankind. I remember the meeting of Tanaka and our late Tsungli (Dr. Sun Yat-sen) in Shanghai in the third year of the Republic which coincided with the outbreak of the Great War in Europe. Tanaka proposed that East Asiatics should at that time denounce all ratified relations with foreign countries and erect a new order in East Asia. Dr. Sun queried: "Would it not involve the breaking of international treaties?" To which Tanaka answered: "Is not the denunciation of treaties and termination of unequal obligations advantageous to China?" "Unequal treaties should be terminated by straightforward and legitimate procedure," solemnly declared Dr. Sun, "and China is not prepared to become a party to the illegal denunciation of treaties even though advantageous to our country." Comrades, such is China's spirit. It is also the spirit of the Three People's Principles. We have relied on this spirit to resist invasion; we have depended on this spirit to resist all forms of domination, force and violence. We should be sustained by this spirit to restore order in East Asia and offer it as a contribution towards enduring world peace.

To conclude, this war on the part of Japan is violent banditry brought about by the total collapse of morals and sound principles in that country. Insofar as China is concerned, we have courageously taken upon our shoulders the world responsibility of fighting for justice and righteousness. Of late, the Japanese militarists have lost their senses, and prompted by sheer inertia, are rapidly going the way to exceed all bounds and damage the civilization and happiness of mankind. Nations of the world which are bound by treaty obligations should have acted to maintain the sanctity of treaties and apply punitive measures against the aggressor so that light might have been restored to the present scene of impenetrable darkness. But the nations hesitated and looked on. China, unmindful of any sacrifice, however, took upon herself the immense responsibility at the time when the fate of righteousness and justice was in the balance.

Our object in prosecuting this war of Resistance, is to complete the task of national revolution and secure for China independence, liberty and equality. Internationally, our object is to support righteousness and justice, restore the prestige of treaties, and re-establish peace and order. This is a war between good and evil, between right and wrong. It is a war between justice and force, and a war between an abider by the law and a breaker of it. It is also a war between righteousness and brute-force.

A Chinese proverb says: "Virtue never lacks company; it will ever find support." The force of world justice will rise, and men of goodwill ultimately co-operate in the interests of rectitude. On our part, we should hold fast to our stand and fix our eyes steadfastly on our goal, and be firm in our determination. Our firmness should increase with greater difficulties, and our courage should rise with prolonged Resistance. The entire nation should carry on with oneness of heart. The final victory will be ours. I urge my comrades, our army, and our people to redouble their efforts in order to attain success.

Pius XII

[1876–1958]

When Pius XI died in 1939, his Papal Secretary of State, Eugenio Cardinal Pacelli, was elected Pope. He took the name of his predecessor, becoming Pius XII. On Easter Sunday, April 13, 1941, His Holiness broadcast from the Vatican the following address to the world.

APPEAL FOR PEACE

WE MOST cordially greet you all, beloved sons and daughters of Rome and of the entire world, in the spirit of alleluia of Easter morn, in the joyful spirit of the resurrection and peace of Christ, after the desolation of His divine passion: but, unfortunately, there has been no resurrection, no restoration, of peace among nations and in our joyful greeting to you there must be intermingled that note of distress which was the cause of great sadness and continual sorrow to the heart of Paul the Apostle while he was preoccupied about his brethren who were his kinsmen according to the flesh (Romans 9:2).

In the lamentable spectacle of human conflict which we are now witnessing we acknowledge the valor and loyalty of all those who with a deep sense of duty are fighting for the defense and posterity of their fatherland; we recognize, too, the prodigious and in itself efficacious development made in industrial and technical fields; nor do we overlook the many generous and praiseworthy gestures of magnanimity which have been made toward the enemy: but while we acknowledge, we feel obliged none the less to state that the ruthless struggle has at times assumed forms which can be described only as atrocious.

May all belligerents, who also have human hearts molded by mothers' love, show some feeling of charity for the sufferings of civilian populations, for defenseless women and children, for the sick and aged, all of whom are often exposed to greater and more widespread perils of war than those faced by soldiers at the front.

We beseech the belligerent powers to abstain until the very end from the use of still more homicidal instruments of warfare; for the introduction of such weapons inevitably results in their retaliatory use, often with greater violence and cruelty by the enemy. If already we must lament the fact that the limits of legitimate warfare have been repeatedly exceeded, would not a more widespread use of increasingly barbarous offensive weapons soon transform the war into an unspeakable horror?

In this tempest of misfortunes and perils, of afflictions and fears, our most powerful and safest haven of trust and peace is found in prayer to God, in whose hands rests not only the destiny of men but also the outcome of their most obdurate dissensions; wherefore we express our gratitude to Catholics of the entire world for the fervor with which they responded to our call to prayer and sacrifice for peace on Nov. 24.

Today we repeat that invitation to you and to all those who raise their minds and hearts to God and we beseech you not to relax your prayerful vigilance but rather to reanimate and redouble it.

Yes, let us pray for early peace. Let us pray for universal peace; not for peace based upon the oppression and destruction of peoples but peace which, while guaranteeing the honor of all nations, will satisfy their vital needs and insure the legitimate rights of all.

We have constantly accompanied prayer with our own endeavors. To the very limit of our power and with a vigilant consciousness of impartiality in spirit and in our apostolic office, we have left nothing undone or untried in order to forestall or shorten the conflict, to humanize the methods of war, to alleviate suffering and to bring assistance and comfort to the victims of war.

We have not hesitated to indicate in unmistakably clear terms the necessary principles and sentiments which must constitute the determining basis of a future peace that will assure the sincere and loyal consent of all peoples. But we are saddened to note that there seems to be as yet little likelihood of an approximate realization of peace that will be just, in accordance with human and Christian norms.

Thus our supplications to Heaven must be raised with ever increasing meaning and fervor, that a new spirit may take root and develop in all peoples and especially among those whose greater power gives them wider influence and imposes upon them additional responsibility; the spirit of willingness, devoid of sham and artifice, that is ready to make mutual sacrifices in order to build, upon the accumulated ruins of war, a new edifice of fraternal solidarity among the nations of the world, an edifice built upon new and stronger foundations, with fixed and stable guarantees, and with a high sense of moral sincerity which would repudiate every double standard of morality and justice for the great and small or for the strong and the weak.

Truth, like man, has but a single face: and truth is our weapon, just as prayer is our defense and strength, and the living, sincere and disinterested apostolic word, inspired by fraternal affection, our entree to the hearts of men.

These are not offensive and bloody weapons but the arms of spirit, arms of our mind and heart. Nothing can impede or restrain us from using them to secure and safeguard just rights, true human brotherhood and genuine peace, wherever the sacred duty of our office prompts us and compassion for the multitude rekindles our love.

Nothing can restrain us from repeatedly calling to the observance of the precept of love those who are children of the church of Christ, those who, because of their faith in the Divine Saviour, or at least in our Father who is in Heaven, are very near to us.

Nothing can impede or restrain us from doing all in our power in order that, in the tempest of surging waves of enmity among the peoples of the earth, the divine ark of the church of Christ may be held firmly by the anchor of hope under the golden rays of peace—that blessed vision of peace which, in the midst of worldly conflicts, is the refuge and abode and sustenance of that fraternal spirit, founded in God and ennobled in the shadow of the cross, with which the course must be set if we are to escape from the present tempest and reach the shore of a happier and more deserving future.

However, under the vigilant providence of God and armed only with prayer, exhortation and consolation, we shall persevere in our battle for peace in behalf of suffering humanity. May the blessings and comforts of heaven descend on all victims of this war: upon you who are prisoners and upon your family from whom you are separated and who are anxious about you, and upon you refugees and dispossessed who have lost your homes and land, your life's support.

We share with you your anguish and suffering. If it is not allowed us—as we would honestly desire—to take upon ourselves the burden of your sorrows, may our paternal and cordial sympathy serve as the balm which will temper the bitterness of your misfortune with today's greeting of the alleluia, the hymn of Christ's triumph over earthly martyrdom, the blossom of the olive tree of Gethsemane flourishing in the precious hope of resurrection and of the new and eternal life in which there will be neither sorrows nor struggles. In His vale of tears there is no lasting city (Hebrews, xiii, 14), no eternal fatherland.

Here below we are all exiles and wanderers; our true citizenship, which is limitless, is in heaven, in eternity, in God. If worldly hopes have bitterly deluded you, remember that hope in God never fails or deceives. You must make one resolve, not to allow yourselves to be induced either by your sad lot or by the malice of men to waver in your allegiance to Christ.

Prosperity and adversity are part and parcel of man's earthly existence; but what is of the utmost importance, and we say it with St. Augustine, is the use that is made of what is called prosperity or adversity. For the virtuous man is neither exalted by worldly well-being nor humbled by temporal misfortune; the evil man, on the other hand, being corrupted in prosperity, is made to suffer in adversity.

To the powers occupying territories during the war, we say, with all due consideration: Let your conscience guide you in dealing justly, humanely and providently with the peoples of occupied territories. Do not impose upon them burdens which you in similar circumstances have felt or would feel to be unjust.

Prudent and helpful humanitarianism is the commendation and boast of wise generals; and the treatment of prisoners and civilians in occupied areas is the surest indication and proof of the civilization of individuals and nations. But, above all, remember that upon the manner in which you deal with those whom the fortunes of war put in your hands may depend the blessing or curse of God on your own fatherland.

Contemplation of a war that is so cruel in all its aspects and the thought of the suffering children of the church inspires in the heart of the common Father and forms upon our lips words of comfort and encouragement for the pastors and faithful of those places where the church, the spouse of Christ, is suffering most; where fidelity to her, the public profession of her doctrines, the conscientious and practical observance of her laws, moral resistance to atheism and to de-Christianizing influences deliberately favored or tolerated, are being openly or insidiously opposed and daily in various ways made increasingly difficult.

The records and artifices of this generally secret and at times even public martyrdom, which insidious or open impiety makes followers of the crucified suffer, are multiplying daily and constitute as it were in an encyclopedia of many volumes, annals of heroic sacrifices, and furnish moving verification of the words of our divine Saviour: "The servant is not greater than his master. If they have persecuted me, they will also persecute you." (John 15:20.)

Is this divine warning not a source of tender comfort on that sorrowful and bitter way of the cross which you are following because of your fidelity to Christ? To all of you who are walking so sadly along this way, priests and religious, men and women and particularly you young men, pride and joy of your families, who are called upon to bear the burden of these merciless and bitter days—whatever be your origin, language, race, social condition or profession—all you upon whom the seal of suffering for Christ is stamped so clearly, a sign no less of suffering than of glory, as it was to the great Apostle Paul, you are numbered among those privileged intimates who are nearest to the cross of Calvary and by this very fact nearest also to the pierced heart of Christ and to our own.

On that we were able to make you appreciate how profoundly our heart has been pierced by the cry of the Apostle of the Gentiles, "Who is weak, and I am not weak?" (Second Corinthians, 11:29.) The sacrifices you are called upon to make, your suffering in mind and body, your concern for your own faith and still more for the faith of your children, we are aware of them, we share them with you, we lament them before God.

And yet withal, on this day we greet you with joyful alleluia; for it is the day of Christ's triumph over his crucifiers, open and secret, ancient and modern. We convey that greeting to you with the voice and confidence with which, even in the days of the persecution, the early Christians exultantly sang that alleluia.

Perhaps you do not recall the words of our Lord to Martha: "I am the resurrection and the life: he that believeth in Me shall not die for ever." (John, xi, 25-26.) The certainty that through sacrifice for their faith, even to the sacrifice of their life, they were assuring themselves of resurrection made of the martyrs heroes of Christ, faithful unto death.

You enjoy that same certainty. Imitate them and with the greatest prophet of the new and eternal testament raise your eyes to that heavenly Jerusalem where Christ gloriously reigns and rules and, while rewarding His good and faithful servants, proclaims the mystery and splendor of their triumph in the shining whiteness of their garments, in the indelible inscription of their names in the book of life and in decreeing that they be exalted before His Father and the heavenly court, with admirable words which you in your perilous trials must never forget: "He that shall overcome, shall thus be clothed in white garments, and I will not blot out his name out of the book of life, and I will confess his name before My Father, and before His angels." (Apocalypse, iii:5.)

Beloved sons and daughters! To Jesus Christ, "Prince of Kings of the earth, who hath washed us from our sins in His own blood" (Apocalypse, i:5), raise your eyes while, as pledge of that heavenly peace which He alone can give to us and which we implore of Him in superabundant measure for all humanity, we impart to you, to pastors and faithful, to your families, to your children, that Christ may protect and keep you in His grace and love; to those who in the fulfillment of duty are fighting on land and sea and in the sky and especially to all those who have been so severely lashed by the scourge of war, with heart overflowing with love, our paternal apostolic benediction.

May the blessings of Almighty God, Father, Son and Holy Ghost, descend upon you and remain forever, amen.

Franklin Delano Roosevelt
[1882–1945]

Franklin Delano Roosevelt, thirty-second President of the United States, was Assistant Secretary of the Navy under President Wilson, and was Governor of New York from 1929 to 1931. In 1932 he was elected President on the Democratic ticket. He entered the White House when the country was in the depths of an unprecedented depression. His New Deal program, aimed at recovery, included many social and economic measures directly controlled by the federal government. He was reelected in 1936. The popularity of the New Deal, and Roosevelt's vigorous national defense policy aided him in being reelected in 1940, becoming the first "third term" President in American history. He was elected to a fourth term, but the strain of his struggle through the years of economic disaster and war undoubtedly contributed to his death, two months after his inauguration.

President Roosevelt was one of the most forceful speakers of the time. His "fireside chats" were the first radio broadcasts ever made by a President directly to the people. The addresses by President Roosevelt given here cover the period of his inauguration through the early part of the Second World War.

Following is his First Inaugural Address, delivered at Washington, March 4, 1933.

FIRST INAUGURAL ADDRESS

Present hoover, Mr. Chief Justice, my friends:

This is a day of national consecration, and I am certain that my fellow-Americans expect that on my induction into the Presidency I will address them with a candor and a decision which the present situation of our nation impels.

This is preëminently the time to speak the truth, the whole truth, frankly and boldly. Nor need we shrink from honestly facing conditions in our country today. This great nation will endure as it has endured, will revive and will prosper.

So first of all let me assert my firm belief that the only thing we have to fear is fear itself—nameless, unreasoning, unjustified terror which paralyzes needed efforts to convert retreat into advance.

In every dark hour of our national life a leadership of frankness and vigor has met with that understanding and support of the people themselves which is essential to victory. I am convinced that you will again give that support to leadership in these critical days.

In such a spirit on my part and on yours we face our common difficulties. They concern, thank God, only material things. Values have shrunken to fantastic levels; taxes have risen; our ability to pay has fallen; government of all kinds is faced by serious curtailment of income; the means of exchange are frozen in the currents of trade; the withered leaves of industrial enterprise lie on every side; farmers find no markets for their produce; the savings of many years in thousands of families are gone.

More important, a host of unemployed citizens face the grim problem of existence, and an equally great number toil with little return. Only a foolish optimist can deny the dark realities of the moment.

Yet our distress comes from no failure of substance. We are stricken by no plague of locusts. Compared with the perils which our forefathers conquered because they believed and were not afraid, we have still much to be thankful for. Nature still offers her bounty and human efforts have multiplied it. Plenty is at our doorstep, but a generous use of it languishes in the very sight of the supply.

Primarily, this is because the rulers of the exchange of mankind's goods have failed through their own stubbornness and their own incompetence, have admitted their failure and abdicated. Practices of the unscrupulous money changers stand indicted in the court of public opinion, rejected by the hearts and minds of men.

True, they have tried, but their efforts have been cast in the pattern of an outworn tradition. Faced by failure of credit, they have proposed only the lending of more money.

Stripped of the lure of profit by which to induce our people to follow their false leadership, they have resorted to exhortations, pleading tearfully for restored confidence. They know only the rules of a generation of self-seekers.

They have no vision, and when there is no vision the people perish.

The money changers have fled from their high seats in the temple of our civilization. We may now restore that temple to the ancient truths.

The measure of the restoration lies in the extent to which we apply social values more noble than mere monetary profit.

Happiness lies not in the mere possession of money; it lies in the joy of achievement, in the thrill of creative effort.

The joy and moral stimulation of work no longer must be forgotten in the mad chase of evanescent profits. These dark days will be worth all they cost us if they teach us that our true destiny is not to be ministered unto but to minister to ourselves and to our fellow-men.

Recognition of the falsity of material wealth as the standard of success goes hand in hand with the abandonment of the false belief that public office and high political position are to be valued only by the standards of pride of place and personal profit; and there must be an end to a conduct in banking and in business which too often has given to a sacred trust the likeness of callous and selfish wrongdoing.

Small wonder that confidence languishes, for it thrives only on honesty, on honor, on the sacredness of obligations, on faithful protection, on unselfish performance. Without them it cannot live.

Restoration calls, however, not for changes in ethics alone. This nation asks for action, and action now.

Our greatest primary task is to put people to work. This is no unsolvable problem if we face it wisely and courageously.

It can be accomplished in part by direct recruiting by the government itself, treating the task as we would treat the emergency of a war, but at the same time, through this employment, accomplishing greatly needed projects to stimulate and reorganize the use of our natural resources.

Hand in hand with this, we must frankly recognize the overbalance of population in our industrial centers and, by engaging on a national scale in a redistribution, endeavor to provide a better use of the land for those best fitted for the land.

The task can be helped by definite efforts to raise the values of agricultural products and with this the power to purchase the output of our cities.

It can be helped by preventing realistically the tragedy of the growing loss, through foreclosure, of our small homes and our farms.

It can be helped by insistence that the Federal, State and local governments act forthwith on the demand that their cost be drastically reduced.

It can be helped by the unifying of relief activities which today are often scattered, uneconomical and unequal. It can be helped by national planning for and supervision of all forms of transportation and of communications and other utilities which have a definitely public character.

There are many ways in which it can be helped, but it can never be helped merely by talking about it. We must act, and act quickly.

Finally, in our progress toward a resumption of work we require two safeguards against a return of the evils of the old order; there must be a strict supervision of all banking and credits and investments; there must be an end to speculation with other people's money, and there must be provision for an adequate but sound currency.

These are the lines of attack. I shall presently urge upon a new Congress in special session detailed measures for their fulfillment, and I shall seek the immediate assistance of the several States.

Through this program of action we address ourselves to putting our own national house in order and making income balance outgo.

Our international trade relations, though vastly important, are, in point of time and necessity, secondary to the establishment of a sound national economy.

I favor as a practical policy the putting of first things first. I shall spare no effort to restore world trade by international economic readjustment, but the emergency at home cannot wait on that accomplishment.

The basic thought that guides these specific means of national recovery is not narrowly nationalistic.

It is the insistence, as a first consideration, upon the interdependence of the various elements in and parts of the United States—a recognition of the old and permanently important manifestation of the American spirit of the pioneer.

It is the way to recovery. It is the immediate way. It is the strongest assurance that the recovery will endure.

In the field of world policy I would dedicate this nation to the policy of the good neighbor—the neighbor who resolutely respects himself and, because he does so, respects the rights of others—the neighbor who respects his obligations and respects the sanctity of his agreements in and with a world of neighbors.

If I read the temper of our people correctly, we now realize, as we have never realized before, our interdependence on each other; that we cannot merely take, but we must give as well; that if we are to go forward we must move as a trained and loyal army willing to sacrifice for the good of a common discipline, because, without such discipline, no progress is made, no leadership becomes effective.

We are, I know, ready and willing to submit our lives and property to such discipline because it makes possible a leadership which aims at a larger good.

This I propose to offer, pledging that the larger purposes will bind upon us all as a sacred obligation with a unity of duty hitherto evoked only in time of armed strife.

With this pledge taken, I assume unhesitatingly the leadership of this great army of our people, dedicated to a disciplined attack upon our common problems.

Action in this image and to this end is feasible under the form of government which we have inherited from our ancestors.

Our Constitution is so simple and practical that it is possible always to meet extraordinary needs by changes in emphasis and arrangement without loss of essential form.

That is why our constitutional system has proved itself the most superbly enduring political mechanism the modern world has produced. It has met every stress of vast expansion of territory, of foreign wars, of bitter internal strife, of world relations.

It is to be hoped that the normal balance of executive and legislative authority may be wholly adequate to meet the unprecedented task before us. But it may be that an unprecedented demand and need for undelayed action may call for temporary departure from that normal balance of public procedure.

I am prepared under my constitutional duty to recommend the measures that a stricken nation in the midst of a stricken world may require.

These measures, or such other measures as the Congress may build out of its experience and wisdom, I shall seek, within my constitutional authority, to bring to speedy adoption.

But in the event that the Congress shall fail to take one of these two courses, and in the event that the national emergency is still critical, I shall not evade the clear course of duty that will then confront me.

I shall ask the Congress for the one remaining instrument to meet the crisis—broad executive power to wage a war against the emergency as great as the power that would be given to me if we were in fact invaded by a foreign foe.

For the trust reposed in me I will return the courage and the devotion that befit the time. I can do no less.

We face the arduous days that lie before us in the warm courage of national unity; with the clear consciousness of seeking old and precious moral values; with the clean satisfaction that comes from the stern performance of duty by old and young alike.

We aim at the assurance of a rounded and permanent national life.

We do not distrust the future of essential democracy. The people of the United States have not failed. In their need they have registered a mandate that they want direct, vigorous action.

They have asked for discipline and direction under leadership. They have made me the present instrument of their wishes. In the spirit of the gift I take it.

In this dedication of a nation we humbly ask the blessing of God. May He protect each and every one of us! May He guide me in the days to come!

President Roosevelt delivered the following address at Buenos Aires, Argentina, on December 1, 1936, in opening the Inter-American Conference for the Maintenance of Peace.

HEMISPHERE DEFENSE FOR DEMOCRACY

MEMBERS of the American Family of Nations; my friends:

On the happy occasion of the convening of this conference I address you thus, because members of a family need no introduction or formalities when, in pursuance of excellent custom, they meet together for their common good.

As a family we appreciate the hospitality of our host, President Justo, and the government and people of Argentina; and all of us are happy that to our friend, Dr.' Saavedra Lamas, has come the well deserved award of the Nobel Prize for great service in the cause of world peace.

Three years ago the American family met in near-by Montevideo, the great capital of the Republic of Uruguay. They were dark days. A shattering depression, unparalleled in its intensity, held us with the rest of the world in its grasp. And on our own continent a tragic war was raging between two of our sister republics.

And yet, at that conference there was born not only hope for our common future but a greater measure of mutual trust between the

American democracies than had ever existed before. In this Western Hemisphere the night of fear has been dispelled. Many of the intolerable burdens of economic depression have been lightened and, due in no small part to our common efforts, every nation of this hemisphere is today at peace with its neighbors.

This is no conference to form alliances, to divide the spoils of war, to partition countries, to deal with human beings as though they were pawns in a game of chance. Our purpose, under happy auspices, is to secure the continuance of the blessing of peace.

Three years ago, recognizing that a crisis was being thrust upon the New World, with splendid unanimity our twenty-one republics set an example to the whole world by proclaiming a new spirit, a new day in the affairs of this hemisphere.

And while the succeeding period has justified in full measure all that was said and done at Montevideo, it has unfortunately emphasized the seriousness of threats to peace among other nations. Events elsewhere have served only to strengthen our horror of war and all that war means. The men and women and children of the Americas know that warfare in this day and age, warfare means more than the mere clash of armies; they see the destruction of cities and of farms—they foresee that children and grandchildren, if they survive, will stagger for long years not only under the burden of poverty but also amid the threat of broken society and the destruction of constitutional government.

And I am profoundly convinced that the plain people everywhere in the civilized world, not only here in the Americas but everywhere else, wish to live in peace one with another. And still leaders and governments resort to war. Truly, if the genius of mankind that has invented the weapons of death cannot discover the means of preserving peace, civilization as we know it lives in an evil day.

But we cannot now, especially in view of our common purpose, accept any defeatist attitude. We have learned by hard experience that peace is not to be had for the mere asking; that peace, like other great privileges, can be obtained only by hard and consistent effort. And we are here to dedicate ourselves and our countries to that work.

You who assemble today carry with you in your deliberations the hopes of millions of human beings in other less fortunate lands. Beyond the ocean we see continents rent asunder by old hatreds and new fanaticism. We hear the demand that injustice and inequality be corrected by resorting to the sword and not by resorting to reason and peaceful justice. We hear the cry that new markets can be achieved only through conquest. We read that the sanctity of treaties between nations is disregarded.

We know, too, that vast armaments are rising on every side and that the work of creating them employs men and women by the millions. It is natural, however, for us to conclude that such employment is false employment; that it builds no permanent structures, creates no consumers' goods for the maintenance of a lasting prosperity. We know that nations guilty of these follies inevitably face the day either when their weapons of destruction must be used against their neighbors or when an unsound economy, like a house of cards, will fall apart.

In either case, even though the Americas become involved in no war, we must suffer too. The madness of a great war in other parts of the world would affect us and threaten our good in a hundred ways. And the economic collapse of any nation or nations must of necessity harm our own prosperity.

Can we, the republics of the New World, help the Old World to avert the catastrophe that impends? Yes, I am confident that we can.

First, it is our duty by every honorable means to prevent any future war among ourselves. This can best be done through the strengthening of the processes of constitutional democratic government—to make these processes conform to the modern need for unity and efficiency and, at the same time, preserve the individual liberties of our citizens. By so doing, the people of our nations, unlike the people of many nations who live under other forms of government, can and will insist on their intention to live in peace. Thus will democratic government be justified throughout the world.

In the determination to live at peace among ourselves we in the Americas make it at the same time clear that we stand shoulder to shoulder in our final deliberations that others who, driven by war madness or land hunger, might seek to commit acts of aggression against us will find a hemisphere wholly prepared to consult together for our mutual safety and our mutual good.

And I repeat what I said in speaking before the Congress and the Supreme Court of Brazil, "Each one of us has learned the glories of independence. Let each one of us learn the glories of interdependence."

Secondly, and in addition to the perfecting of the mechanism of peace, we can strive even more strongly than in the past to prevent the creation of those conditions which give rise to war. Lack of social or political justice within the borders of any nation is always cause for concern. Through democratic processes we can strive to achieve for the Americas the highest possible standard of living conditions for all our people. Men and women blessed with political freedom, willing to work, able to find work, rich enough to maintain their families and to educate their children, contented with their lot in life and on terms of friendship with their neighbors, they will defend themselves to the utmost but will never consent to take up arms for a war of conquest.

Interwoven with these problems is the further self-evident fact that the welfare and the prosperity of each of our nations depends in large part on the benefits derived from commerce among ourselves and with other nations, for our present civilization rests on the basis of an international exchange of commodities. Every nation of the world has felt the evil effects of recent efforts to erect trade barriers of every known kind. Every individual citizen has suffered from them.

And it is no accident that the nations which have carried this process farthest are those which proclaim most loudly that they require war as an instrument of their policy. It is no accident that attempts to be self-sufficient have led to falling standards for their people and to ever-increasing loss of the democratic ideals in a mad race to pile armament upon armament. And it is no accident that, because of these suicidal policies and the suffering attending them, many of their people have come, unfortunately, to believe with despair that the price of war seems less than the price of peace.

This state of affairs, my friends, we must refuse to accept with every instinct of defense, with every exhortation of enthusiastic hope, with every use of mind and skill.

I cannot refrain here from reiterating my gratification that in this, as in so many other achievements, the American republics have given a salutary example to the world. The resolution adopted at the Inter-American Conference at Montevideo indorsing the principles of liberal trade policies has shone forth like a beacon in the storm of economic madness which has been sweeping over the entire world during these later years. Truly, if the principles there embodied find still wider applications in your deliberations it will be a notable contribution to the cause of peace. For my own part, I have done all in my power to sustain the consistent efforts of my Secretary of State in negotiating agreements for reciprocal trade, and even though the individual results may seem small, the total of them is significant. These policies in recent weeks have received the approval of the people of the United States, and they have, I am sure, the sympathy of the other nations here assembled.

There are many other causes for war—among them long-festering feuds, unsettled frontiers, territorial rivalries; but these sources of danger which still exist in the Americas, I am thankful to say, are not only few in number but already on the way to peaceful adjudication. While the settlement of such controversies may necessarily involve adjustments at home or in our relations with our neighbors which may appear to involve material sacrifice, let no man or woman forget that there is no profit in war. Sacrifices in the cause of peace are infinitesimal compared with the holocaust of war.

Peace comes from the spirit and must be grounded in faith. In seeking peace, perhaps we can best begin by proudly affirming the faith of the Americas; the faith in freedom and its fulfillment which has proved a mighty fortress beyond reach of successful attack in half of the world.

That faith arises from a common hope and a common design given us by our fathers in differing form but with a single aim—freedom and security of the individual, which has become the foundation of our peace.

If, then, by making war in our midst impossible, and if within our-selves and among ourselves we can give greater freedom and fulfillment to the individual lives of our citizens, the democratic form of repre-sentative government will have justified the high hopes of the liberating fathers. Democracy is still the hope of the world. If we in our generation can continue its successful applications in the Americas it will spread and supersede other methods by which men are governed and which seem to most of us to run counter to our ideals of human liberty and human progress.

Three centuries of history, three centuries sowed the seeds which grew into our nations; the fourth century saw those nations become equal and free and brought us to a common system of constitutional government; the fifth century is giving to us a common meeting ground of mutual help and understanding. Our hemisphere has at last come of age. We are here assembled to show its unity to the world. We took from our ancestors a great dream. We here offer it back as a great unified reality.

And finally, in expressing our faith of the Western World, let us affirm:

That we maintain and defend the democratic form of constitutional representative government.

That through such government we can more greatly provide a wider distribution of culture, of education, of thought and of free expression.

That through it we can obtain a greater security of life for our citizens and a more equal opportunity for them to prosper.

That through it we can best foster commerce and the exchange of art and science between nations; that through it we can avoid the rivalry of armament, avert hatred and encourage good will and true justice.

And that through it we offer hope for peace and a more abundant life to the peoples of the whole world.

But this faith, this faith of the Western World will not be complete if we fail to affirm our faith in God. In the whole history of mankind, far back into the dim past before man knew how to record thoughts or events, the human race has been distinguished from other forms of life by the existence—the fact—of religion. Periodic attempts to deny God have always come and will always come to naught.

In the constitutions and in the practice of our nations is the right of freedom of religion. But this ideal, these words presuppose a belief and a trust in God.

The faith of the Americas, therefore, lies in the spirit. The system, the sisterhood of the Americas is impregnable so long as her nations maintain that spirit.

In that faith and spirit we will have peace over the Western World. In that faith and spirit we will all watch and guard our hemisphere. In that faith and spirit may we also, with God's help, offer hope to our brethren overseas.

This speech, a stirring appeal for all-out aid to the democracies fighting Nazi aggression, is often referred to as the "Arsenal of Democracy" speech. President Roosevelt broadcast it from the White House on December 29, 1940.

"THE ARSENAL OF DEMOCRACY"

MY FRIENDS:

This is not a fireside chat on war. It is a talk on national security; because the nub of the whole purpose of your President is to keep you now, and your children later, and your grandchildren much later, out of a last-ditch war for the preservation of American independence and all of the things that American independence means to you and to me and to ours.

Tonight, in the presence of a world crisis, my mind goes back eight years to a night in the midst of a domestic crisis. It was a time when the wheels of American industry were grinding to a full stop, when the whole banking system of our country had ceased to function.

I well remember that while I sat in my study in the White House, preparing to talk with the people of the United States, I had before my eyes the picture of all those Americans with whom I was talking. I saw the workmen in the mills, the mines, the factories; the girl behind the counter; the small shopkeeper; the farmer doing his Spring plowing; the widows and the old men wondering about their life's savings.

I tried to convey to the great mass of American people what the banking crisis meant to them in their daily lives.

Tonight I want to do the same thing, with the same people, in this new crisis which faces America.

We met the issue of 1933 with courage and realism. We face this new crisis—this new threat to the security of our nation—with the same courage and realism.

Never before since Jamestown and Plymouth Rock has our American civilization been in such danger as now.

For on Sept. 27, 1940—this year—by an agreement signed in Berlin, three powerful nations, two in Europe and one in Asia, joined themselves together in the threat that if the United States of America interfered with or blocked the expansion program of these three nations —a program aimed at world control—they would unite in ultimate action against the United States.

The Nazi masters of Germany have made it clear that they intend not only to dominate all life and thought in their own country, but also to enslave the whole of Europe, and then to use the resources of Europe to dominate the rest of the world.

It was only three weeks ago that their leader stated this: "There are two worlds that stand opposed to each other." And then in defiant reply to his opponents he said this: "Others are correct when they say: 'With this world we cannot ever reconcile ourselves.' * * * I can beat any other power in the world." So said the leader of the Nazis.

In other words, the Axis not merely admits but the Axis proclaims that there can be no ultimate peace between their philosophy—their philosophy of government—and our philosophy of government.

In view of the nature of this undeniable threat, it can be asserted, properly and categorically, that the United States has no right or reason to encourage talk of peace until the day shall come when there is a clear intention on the part of the aggressor nations to abandon all thought of dominating or conquering the world.

At this moment the forces of the States that are leagued against all peoples who live in freedom are being held away from our shores. The Germans and the Italians are being blocked on the other side of the Atlantic by the British and by the Greeks, and by thousands of soldiers and sailors who were able to escape from subjugated countries. In Asia the Japanese are being engaged by the Chinese nation in another great defense.

In the Pacific Ocean is our fleet.

Some of our people like to believe that wars in Europe and in Asia are of no concern to us. But it is a matter of most vital concern to us that European and Asiatic war-makers should not gain control of the oceans which lead to this hemisphere.

One hundred and seventeen years ago the Monroe Doctrine was conceived by our government as a measure of defense in the face of a threat against this hemisphere by an alliance in Continental Europe. Thereafter, we stood guard in the Atlantic, with the British as neighbors. There was no treaty. There was no "unwritten agreement."

And yet there was the feeling, proven correct by history, that we as neighbors could settle any disputes in peaceful fashion. And the fact is that during the whole of this time the Western Hemisphere has remained free from aggression from Europe or from Asia.

Does any one seriously believe that we need to fear attack anywhere in the Americas while a free Britain remains our most powerful naval neighbor in the Atlantic? And does any one seriously believe, on the other hand, that we could rest easy if the Axis powers were our neighbors there?

If Great Britain goes down, the Axis powers will control the Continents of Europe, Asia, Africa, Australasia, and the high seas—and they will be in a position to bring enormous military and naval resources against this hemisphere. It is no exaggeration to say that all of us in all the Americas would be living at the point of a gun—a gun loaded with explosive bullets, economic as well as military.

We should enter upon a new and terrible era in which the whole world, our hemisphere included, would be run by threats of brute force. And to survive in such a world, we would have to convert ourselves permanently into a militaristic power on the basis of war economy.

Some of us like to believe that even if Britain falls, we are still safe, because of the broad expanse of the Atlantic and of the Pacific.

But the width of those oceans is not what it was in the days of clipper ships. At one point between Africa and Brazil the distance is less than it is from Washington to Denver, Colo., five hours for the latest type of bomber. And at the north end of the Pacific Ocean, America and Asia almost touch each other.

Why, even today we have planes that could fly from the British Isles to New England and back again without refueling. And remember that the range of the modern bomber is ever being increased.

During the past week many people in all parts of the nation have told me what they wanted me to say tonight. Almost all of them expressed a courageous desire to hear the plain truth about the gravity of the situation. One telegram, however, expressed the attitude of the small minority who want to see no evil and hear no evil, even though they know in their hearts that evil exists. That telegram begged me not to tell again of the ease with which our American cities could be bombed by any hostile power which had gained bases in this Western Hemisphere. The gist of that telegram was: "Please, Mr. President, don't frighten us by telling us the facts."

Frankly and definitely there is danger ahead—danger against which we must prepare. But we well know that we cannot escape danger, or the fear of danger, by crawling into bed and pulling the covers over our heads.

Some nations of Europe were bound by solemn non-intervention pacts with Germany. Other nations were assured by Germany that they need never fear invasion. Non-intervention pact or not, the fact remains that they were attacked, overrun, thrown into modern slavery at an hour's notice or even without any notice at all.

As an exiled leader of one of these nations said to me the other day, "The notice was a minus quantity. It was given to my government two hours after German troops had poured into my country in a hundred places." The fate of these nations tells us what it means to live at the point of a Nazi gun.

The Nazis have justified such actions by various pious frauds. One of these frauds is the claim that they are occupying a nation for the purpose of "restoring order." Another is that they are occupying or controlling a nation on the excuse that they are "protecting it" against the aggression of somebody else.

For example, Germany has said that she was occupying Belgium to save the Belgians from the British. Would she then hesitate to say to any South American country: "We are occupying you to protect you from aggression by the United States"?

Belgium today is being used as an invasion base against Britain, now fighting for its life. And any South American country, in Nazi hands, would always constitute a jumping off place for German attack on any one of the other republics of this hemisphere.

Analyze for yourselves the future of two other places even nearer to Germany if the Nazis won. Could Ireland hold out? Would Irish freedom be permitted as an amazing pet exception in an unfree world? Or the islands of the Azores, which still fly the flag of Portugal after five centuries? You and I think of Hawaii as an outpost of defense in the Pacific. And yet the Azores are closer to our shores in the Atlantic than Hawaii is on the other side.

There are those who say that the Axis powers would never have any desire to attack the Western Hemisphere. That is the same dangerous form of wishful thinking which has destroyed the powers of resistance of so many conquered peoples. The plain facts are that the Nazis have proclaimed, time and again, that all other races are their inferiors and therefore subject to their orders. And most important of all, the vast resources and wealth of this American hemisphere constitute the most tempting loot in all of the round world.

Let us no longer blind ourselves to the undeniable fact that the evil forces which have crushed and undermined and corrupted so many others are already within our own gates. Your government knows much about them and every day is ferreting them out.

Their secret emissaries are active in our own and in neighboring countries. They seek to stir up suspicion and dissension, to cause internal strife. They try to turn capital against labor, and vice versa. They try to reawaken long slumbering racial and religious enmities which should have no place in this country. They are active in every group that promotes intolerance. They exploit for their own ends our own natural abhorrence of war.

These trouble-breeders have but one purpose. It is to divide our people, to divide them into hostile groups and to destroy our unity and shatter our will to defend ourselves.

There are also American citizens, many of them in high places, who, unwittingly in most cases, are aiding and abetting the work of these agents. I do not charge these American citizens with being foreign agents. But I do charge them with doing exactly the kind of work that the dictators want done in the United States.

These people not only believe that we can save our own skins by shutting our eyes to the fate of other nations. Some of them go much further than that. They say that we can and should become the friends and even the partners of the Axis powers. Some of them even suggest that we should imitate the methods of the dictatorships. But Americans never can and never will do that.

The experience of the past two years has proven beyond doubt that no nation can appease the Nazis. No man can tame a tiger into a kitten by stroking it. There can be no appeasement with ruthlessness. There can be no reasoning with an incendiary bomb. We know now that a nation can have peace with the Nazis only at the price of total surrender.

Even the people of Italy have been forced to become accomplices of the Nazis; but at this moment they do not know how soon they will be embraced to death by their allies.

The American appeasers ignore the warning to be found in the fate of Austria, Czecho-Slovakia, Poland, Norway, Belgium, the Netherlands, Denmark and France. They tell you that the Axis powers are going to win anyway; that all of this bloodshed in the world could be saved, that the United States might just as well throw its influence into the scale of a dictated peace and get the best out of it that we can.

They call it a "negotiated peace." Nonsense! Is it a negotiated peace if a gang of outlaws surrounds your community and on threat of extermination makes you pay tribute to save your own skins?

Such a dictated peace would be no peace at all. It would be only another armistice, leading to the most gigantic armament race and the most devastating trade wars in all history. And in these contests the Americas would offer the only real resistance to the Axis powers. With all their vaunted efficiency, with all their parade of pious purpose in this war, there are still in their background the concentration camp and the servants of God in chains.

The history of recent years proves that the shootings and the chains and the concentration camps are not simply the transient tools but the very altars of modern dictatorships. They may talk of a "new order" in the world, but what they have in mind is only a revival of the oldest and worst tyranny. In that there is no liberty, no religion, no hope.

The proposed "new order" is the very opposite of a United States of Europe or a United States of Asia. It is not a government based upon the consent of the governed. It is not a union of ordinary, self-respecting men and women to protect themselves and their freedom and their dignity from oppression. It is an unholy alliance of power and pelf to dominate and to enslave the human race.

The British people and their allies today are conducting an active war against this unholy alliance. Our own future security is greatly dependent on the outcome of that fight. Our ability to "keep out of war" is going to be affected by that outcome.

Thinking in terms of today and tomorrow, I make the direct statement to the American people that there is far less chance of the United States getting into war if we do all we can now to support the nations defending themselves against attack by the Axis than if we acquiesce in their defeat, submit tamely to an Axis victory, and wait our turn to be the object of attack in another war later on.

If we are to be completely honest with ourselves, we must admit that there is risk in any course we may take. But I deeply believe that the great majority of our people agree that the course that I advocate involves the least risk now and the greatest hope for world peace in the future.

The people of Europe who are defending themselves do not ask us to do their fighting. They ask us for the implements of war, the planes, the tanks, the guns, the freighters which will enable them to fight for their liberty and for our security. Emphatically we must get these weapons to them, get them to them in sufficient volume and quickly enough so that we and our children will be saved the agony and suffering of war which others have had to endure.

Let not the defeatists tell us that it is too late. It will never be earlier. Tomorrow will be later than today.

Certain facts are self-evident.

In a military sense Great Britain and the British Empire are today the spearhead of resistance to world conquest. And they are putting up a fight which will live forever in the story of human gallantry.

There is no demand for sending an American expeditionary force outside our own borders. There is no intention by any member of your government to send such a force. You can, therefore, nail, nail any talk about sending armies to Europe as deliberate untruth.

Our national policy is not directed toward war. Its sole purpose is to keep war away from our country and away from our people.

Democracy's fight against world conquest is being greatly aided, and must be more greatly aided, by the rearmament of the United States and by sending every ounce and every ton of munitions and supplies that we can possibly spare to help the defenders who are in the front lines. And it is no more unneutral for us to do that than it is for Sweden, Russia and other nations near Germany to send steel and ore and oil and other war materials into Germany every day in the week.

We are planning our own defense with the utmost urgency, and in its vast scale we must integrate the war needs of Britain and the other free nations which are resisting aggression.

This is not a matter of sentiment or of controversial personal opinion. It is a matter of realistic, practical military policy, based on the advice of our military experts who are in close touch with existing warfare. These military and naval experts and the members of the Congress and the Administration have a single-minded purpose—the defense of the United States.

This nation is making a great effort to produce everything that is necessary in this emergency—and with all possible speed. And this great effort requires great sacrifice.

I would ask no one to defend a democracy which in turn would not defend every one in the nation against want and privation. The strength of this nation shall not be diluted by the failure of the government to protect the economic well-being of its citizens.

If our capacity to produce is limited by machines, it must ever be remembered that these machines are operated by the skill and the stamina of the workers. As the government is determined to protect the rights of the workers, so the nation has a right to expect that the men who man the machines will discharge their full responsibilities to the urgent needs of defense.

The worker possesses the same human dignity and is entitled to the same security of position as the engineer or the manager or the owner. For the workers provide the human power that turns out the destroyers, and the planes and the tanks.

The nation expects our defense industries to continue operation without interruption by strikes or lockouts. It expects and insists that management and workers will reconcile their differences by voluntary or legal means, to continue to produce the supplies that are so sorely needed.

And on the economic side of our great defense program, we are, as you know, bending every effort to maintain stability of prices and with that the stability of the cost of living.

Nine days ago I announced the setting up of a more effective organization to direct our gigantic efforts to increase the production of munitions. The appropriation of vast sums of money and a well-coordinated executive direction of our defense efforts are not in themselves enough. Guns, planes, ships and many other things have to be built in the factories and the arsenals of America. They have to be produced by workers and managers and engineers with the aid of machines which in turn have to be built by hundreds of thousands of workers throughout the land.

In this great work there has been splendid cooperation between the government and industry and labor. And I am very thankful.

American industrial genius, unmatched throughout all the world in the solution of production problems, has been called upon to bring its resources and its talents into action. Manufacturers of watches, of farm implements, of linotypes and cash registers and automobiles, and sewing machines and lawn mowers and locomotives, are now making fuses and bomb packing crates and telescope mounts and shells and pistols and tanks.

But all of our present efforts are not enough. We must have more ships, more guns, more planes—more of everything. And this can be accomplished only if we discard the notion of "business as usual." This job cannot be done merely by superimposing on the existing productive facilities the added requirements of the nation for defense.

Our defense efforts must not be blocked by those who fear the future consequences of surplus plant capacity. The possible consequences of failure of our defense efforts now are much more to be feared.

And after the present needs of our defense are past, a proper handling of the country's peacetime needs will require all of the new productive capacity, if not still more.

No pessimistic policy about the future of America shall delay the immediate expansion of those industries essential to defense. We need them.

I want to make it clear that it is the purpose of the nation to build now with all possible speed every machine, every arsenal, every factory that we need to manufacture our defense material. We have the men—the skill—the wealth—and above all, the will.

I am confident that if and when production of consumer or luxury goods in certain industries requires the use of machines and raw materials that are essential for defense purposes, then such production must yield, and will gladly yield, to our primary and compelling purpose.

So I appeal to the owners of plants—to the managers—to the workers —to our own government employees—to put every ounce of effort into producing these munitions swiftly and without stint. With this appeal I give you the pledge that all of us who are officers of your government will devote ourselves to the same whole-hearted extent to the great task that lies ahead.

As planes and ships and guns and shells are produced, your government, with its defense experts, can then determine how best to use them to defend this hemisphere. The decision as to how much shall be sent abroad and how much shall remain at home must be made on the basis of our over-all military necessities.

We must be the great arsenal of democracy. For us this is an emergency as serious as war itself. We must apply ourselves to our task with the same resolution, the same sense of urgency, the same spirit of patriotism and sacrifice as we would show were we at war.

We have furnished the British great material support and we will furnish far more in the future.

There will be no "bottlenecks" in our determination to aid Great Britain. No dictator, no combination of dictators, will weaken that determination by threats of how they will construe that determination.

The British have received invaluable military support from the heroic Greek Army and from the forces of all the governments in exile. Their strength is growing. It is the strength of men and women who value their freedom more highly than they value their lives.

I believe that the Axis powers are not going to win this war. I base that belief on the latest and best of information.

We have no excuse for defeatism. We have every good reason for hope—hope for peace, yes, and hope for the defense of our civilization and for the building of a better civilization in the future.

I have the profound conviction that the American people are now determined to put forth a mightier effort than they have ever yet made to increase our production of all the implements of defense, to meet the threat to our democratic faith.

As President of the United States, I call for that national effort. I call for it in the name of this nation which we love and honor and which we are privileged and proud to serve. I call upon our people with absolute confidence that our common cause will greatly succeed.

An historic step in the defense of the United States was taken by President Roosevelt on September 11, 1941, in proclaiming the government's determination to maintain the freedom of the seas by shooting first, if necessary, any Nazi warships and submarines in the lanes of American shipping. The President's speech, broadcast from the White House, follows.

FREEDOM OF THE SEAS

My fellow americans:

The Navy Department of the United States has reported to me that on the morning of Sept. 4 the United States destroyer Greer, proceeding in full daylight toward Iceland, had reached a point southeast of Greenland. She was carrying American mail to Iceland. She was flying the American flag. Her identity as an American ship was unmistakable.

She was then and there attacked by a submarine. Germany admits that it was a German submarine. The submarine deliberately fired a torpedo at the Greer, followed later by another torpedo attack. In spite of what Hitler's propaganda bureau has invented, and in spite of what any American obstructionist organization may prefer to believe, I tell you the blunt fact that the German submarine fired first upon this American destroyer without warning, and with deliberate design to sink her.

Our destroyer, at the time, was in waters which the Government of the United States had declared to be waters of self-defense, surrounding outposts of American protection in the Atlantic.

In the north of the Atlantic, outposts have been established by us in Iceland, in Greenland, in Labrador and in Newfoundland. Through these waters there pass many ships of many flags. They bear food and other supplies to civilians; and they bear matériel of war, for which the people of the United States are spending billions of dollars, and which, by Congressional action, they have declared to be essential for the defense of our own land.

The United States destroyer, when attacked, was proceeding on a legitimate mission.

If the destroyer was visible to the submarine when the torpedo was fired, then the attack was a deliberate attempt by the Nazis to sink a clearly identified American warship.

On the other hand, if the submarine was beneath the surface of the sea and, with the aid of its listening devices, fired in the direction of the sound of the American destroyer without even taking the trouble to learn its identity, as the official German communiqué would indicate, then the attack was even more outrageous. For it indicates a policy of indiscriminate violence against any vessel sailing the seas, belligerent or non-belligerent.

This was piracy, piracy legally and morally. It was not the first nor the last act of piracy which the Nazi government has committed against the American flag in this war, for attack has followed attack.

A few months ago an American flag merchant ship, the Robin Moor, was sunk by a Nazi submarine in the middle of the South Atlantic, under circumstances violating long-established international law and violating every principle of humanity. The passengers and the crew were forced into open boats hundreds of miles from land, in direct violation of international agreements signed by nearly all nations, including the government of Germany. No apology, no allegation of mistake, no offer of reparations has come from the Nazi government.

In July, 1941, nearly two months ago, an American battleship in North American waters was followed by a submarine which for a long time sought to manoeuvre itself into a position of attack upon the battleship. The periscope of the submarine was clearly seen. No British or American submarines were within hundreds of miles of this spot at the time, so the nationality of the submarine is clear.

Five days ago a United States Navy ship on patrol picked up three survivors of an American-owned ship operating under the flag of our sister republic of Panama, the S.S. Sessa.

On Aug. 17 she had been first torpedoed without warning, and then shelled, near Greenland, while carrying civilian supplies to Iceland. It is feared that the other members of her crew have been drowned. In view of the established presence of German submarines in this vicinity, there can be no reasonable doubt as to the identity of the flag of the attacker.

Five days ago another United States merchant ship, the Steel Seafarer, was sunk by a German aircraft in the Red Sea 220 miles south of Suez. She was bound for an Egyptian port.

So four of the vessels sunk or attacked flew the American flag and were clearly identifiable. Two of these ships were warships of the American Navy. In the fifth case the vessel sunk clearly carried the flag of our sister republic of Panama.

In the face of all this we Americans are keeping our feet on the ground. Our type of democratic civilization has outgrown the thought of feeling compelled to fight some other nation by reason of any single piratical attack on one of our ships. We are not becoming hysterical or losing our sense of proportion. Therefore, what I am thinking and saying tonight does not relate to any isolated episode.

Instead, we Americans are taking a long-range point of view in regard to certain fundamentals, a point of view in regard to a series of events on land and on sea which must be considered as a whole, as a part of a world pattern.

It would be unworthy of a great nation to exaggerate an isolated incident, or to become inflamed by some one act of violence. But it would be inexcusable folly to minimize such incidents in the face of evidence which makes it clear that the incident is not isolated, but part of a general plan.

The important truth is that these acts of international lawlessness are a manifestation of a design, a design that has been made clear to the American people for a long time. It is the Nazi design to abolish the freedom of the seas and to acquire absolute control and domination of these seas for themselves.

For with control of the seas in their own hands, the way can become obviously clear for their next step, domination of the United States, domination of the Western Hemisphere by force of arms. Under Nazi control of the seas no merchant ship of the United States or of any other American republic would be free to carry on any peaceful commerce, except by the condescending grace of this foreign and tyrannical power.

The Atlantic Ocean, which has been and which should always be a free and friendly highway for us, would then become a deadly menace to the commerce of the United States, to the coasts of the United States and even to the inland cities of the United States.

The Hitler government, in defiance of the laws of the sea, in defiance of the recognized rights of all other nations, has presumed to declare, on paper, that great areas of the seas, even including a vast expanse lying in the Western Hemisphere, are to be closed and that no ships may enter them for any purpose, except at peril of being sunk. Actually they are sinking ships at will and without warning in widely separated areas both within and far outside of these far-flung pretended zones.

This Nazi attempt to seize control of the oceans is but a counterpart of the Nazi plots now being carried on throughout the Western Hemisphere, all designed toward the same end. For Hitler's advance guards, not only his avowed agents but also his dupes among us, have sought to make ready for him footholds and bridgeheads in the New World, to be used as soon as he has gained control of the oceans.

His intrigues, his plots, his machinations, his sabotage in this New World are all known to the Government of the United States. Conspiracy has followed conspiracy.

For example, last year a plot to seize the government of Uruguay was smashed by the prompt action of that country, which was supported in full by her American neighbors. A like plot was then hatching in Argentina, and that government has carefully and wisely blocked it at every point. More recently an endeavor was made to subvert the government of Bolivia and within the past few weeks the discovery was made of secret air landing fields in Colombia within easy range of the Panama Canal. I could multiply instance upon instance.

To be ultimately successful in world mastery, Hitler knows that he must get control of the seas. He must first destroy the bridge of ships which we are building across the Atlantic and over which we shall continue to roll the implements of war to help destroy him, to destroy all his works in the end. He must wipe out our patrol on sea and in the air if he is to do it. He must silence the British Navy.

I think it must be explained over and over again to people who like to think of the United States Navy as an invincible protection that this can be true only if the British Navy survives. And that, my friends, is simple arithmetic.

For if the world outside of the Americas falls under Axis domination, the shipbuilding facilities which the Axis powers would then possess in all of Europe, in the British Isles and in the Far East would be much greater than all the shipbuilding facilities and potentialities of all of the Americas, not only greater, but two or three times greater —enough to win.

Even if the United States threw all its resources into such a situation, seeking to double and even redouble the size of our Navy, the Axis powers, in control of the rest of the world, would have the man power and the physical resources to outbuild us several times over.

It is time for all Americans of all the Americas to stop being deluded by the romantic notion that the Americas can go on living happily and peacefully in a Nazi-dominated world.

Generation after generation, America has battled for the general policy of the freedom of the seas. And that policy is a very simple one —but a basic, a fundamental one. It means that no nation has the right to make the broad oceans of the world at great distances from the actual theatre of land war unsafe for the commerce of others.

That has been our policy, proved time and time again, in all our history.

Our policy has applied from the earliest days of the republic and still applies, not merely to the Atlantic but to the Pacific and to all other oceans as well.

Unrestricted submarine warfare in 1941 constitutes a defiance—an act of aggression—against that historic American policy.

It is now clear that Hitler has begun his campaign to control the seas by ruthless force and by wiping out every vestige of international law, every vestige of humanity.

His intention has been made clear. The American people can have no further illusions about it.

No tender whisperings of appeasers that Hitler is not interested in the Western Hemisphere, no soporific lullabies that a wide ocean protects us from him can long have any effect on the hard-headed, far-sighted and realistic American people.

Because of these episodes, because of the movements and operations of German warships, and because of the clear, repeated proof that the present government of Germany has no respect for treaties or for international law, that it has no decent attitude toward neutral nations or human life—we Americans are now face to face not with abstract theories but with cruel, relentless facts.

This attack on the Greer was no localized military operation in the North Atlantic. This was no mere episode in a struggle between two nations. This was one determined step toward creating a permanent world system based on force, on terror and on murder.

And I am sure that even now the Nazis are waiting, waiting to see whether the United States will by silence give them the green light to go ahead on this path to destruction.

The Nazi danger to our Western World has long ceased to be a mere possibility. The danger is here now—not only from a military enemy but from an enemy of all law, all liberty, all morality, all religion.

There has now come a time when you and I must see the cold inexorable necessity of saying to these inhuman, unrestrained seekers of world conquest and permanent world domination by the sword—"You seek to throw our children and our children's children into your form of terrorism and slavery. You have now attacked our own safety. You shall go no further."

Normal practices of diplomacy—note writing—are of no possible use in dealing with international outlaws who sink our ships and kill our citizens.

One peaceful nation after another has met disaster because each refused to look the Nazi danger squarely in the eye, until it actually had them by the throat.

The United States will not make that fatal mistake.

No act of violence, no act of intimidation will keep us from maintaining intact two bulwarks of defense: First, our line of supply of matériel to the enemies of Hitler, and second, the freedom of our shipping on the high seas.

No matter what it takes, no matter what it costs, we will keep open the line of legitimate commerce in these defensive waters of ours.

We have sought no shooting war with Hitler. We do not seek it now. But· neither do we want peace so much that we are willing to pay for it by permitting him to attack our naval and merchant ships while they are on legitimate business.

I assume that the German leaders are not deeply concerned tonight, or any other time, by what the real Americans or the American Government says or publishes about them. We cannot bring about the downfall of nazism by the use of long-range invective.

But when you see a rattlesnake poised to strike, you do not wait until he has struck before you crush him.

These Nazi submarines and raiders are the rattlesnakes of the Atlantic. They are a menace to the free pathways of the high seas. They are a challenge to our own sovereignty. They hammer at our most precious rights when they attack ships of the American flag—symbols of our independence, our freedom, our very life.

It is clear to all Americans that the time has come when the Americas themselves must now be defended. A continuation of attacks in our own waters, or in waters which could be used for further and greater attacks on us, will inevitably weaken American ability to repel Hitlerism.

Do not let us be hair-splitters. Let us not ask ourselves whether the Americas should begin to defend themselves after the first attack, or the fifth attack, or the tenth attack, or the twentieth attack.

The time for active defense is now.

Do not let us split hairs. Let us not say, "We will only defend ourselves if the torpedo succeeds in getting home, or if the crew and the passengers are drowned."

This is the time for prevention of attack.

If submarines or raiders attack in distant waters, they can attack equally well within sight of our own shores. Their very presence in any waters which America deems vital to its defense constitutes an attack.

In the waters which we deem necessary for our defense American naval vessels and American planes will no longer wait until Axis submarines lurking under the water, or Axis raiders on the surface of the sea, strike their deadly blow—first.

Upon our naval and air patrol—now operating in large number over a vast expanse of the Atlantic Ocean—falls the duty of maintaining the American policy of freedom of the seas—now. That means, very simply, very clearly, that our patrolling vessels and planes will protect all merchant ships—not only American ships but ships of any flag—engaged in commerce in our defensive waters. They will protect them from submarines; they will protect them from surface raiders.

This situation is not new. The second President of the United States, John Adams, ordered the United States Navy to clean out European privateers and European ships of war which were infesting the Caribbean and South American waters, destroying American commerce.

The third President of the United States, Thomas Jefferson, ordered the United States Navy to end the attacks being made upon American and other ships by the corsairs of the nations of North Africa.

My obligation as President is historic; it is clear; yes, it is inescapable.

It is no act of war on our part when we decide to protect the seas that are vital to American defense. The aggression is not ours. Ours is solely defense.

But let this warning be clear. From now on, if German or Italian vessels of war enter the waters the protection of which is necessary for American defense, they do so at their own peril.

The orders which I have given as Commander in Chief of the United States Army and Navy are to carry out that policy—at once.

The sole responsibility rests upon Germany. There will be no shooting unless Germany continues to seek it.

That is my obvious duty in this crisis. That is the clear right of this sovereign nation. This is the only step possible, if we would keep tight the wall of defense which we are pledged to maintain around this Western Hemisphere.

I have no illusions about the gravity of this step. I have not taken it hurriedly or lightly. It is the result of months and months of constant thought and anxiety and prayer. In the protection of your nation and mine it cannot be avoided.

The American people have faced other grave crises in their history—with American courage, with American resolution. They will do no less today.

They know the actualities of the attacks upon us. They know the necessities of a bold defense against these attacks. They know that the times call for clear heads and fearless hearts.

And with that inner strength that comes to a free people conscious of their duty, conscious of the righteousness of what they do, they will—with divine help and guidance—stand their ground against this latest assault upon their democracy, their sovereignty and their freedom.

On December 7, 1941, Japanese bombers attacked American territory in the Pacific at the very moment when negotiations for a peaceful settlement of all issues between the United States and Japan were under way. The following day President Roosevelt addressed a joint session of Congress requesting a declaration of the existence of a state of war between Japan and the United States. Congress immediately voted in favor of such a declaration. The President's message is reproduced here.

FOR A DECLARATION OF WAR AGAINST JAPAN

Mr. vice president, Mr. Speaker, members of the Senate and the House of Representatives:

Yesterday, Dec. 7, 1941—a date which will live in infamy—the United States of America was suddenly and deliberately attacked by naval and air forces of the empire of Japan.

The United States was at peace with that nation, and, at the solicitation of Japan, was still in conversation with its government and its Emperor looking toward the maintenance of peace in the Pacific.

Indeed, one hour after Japanese air squadrons had commenced bombing in the American island of Oahu the Japanese Ambassador to the United States and his colleague delivered to our Secretary of State a formal reply to a recent American message. And, while this reply stated that it seemed useless to continue the existing diplomatic negotiations, it contained no threat or hint of war or of armed attack.

It will be recorded that the distance of Hawaii from Japan makes it obvious that the attack was deliberately planned many days or even weeks ago. During the intervening time the Japanese Government has deliberately sought to deceive the United States by false statements and expressions of hope for continued peace.

The attack yesterday on the Hawaiian Islands has caused severe damage to American naval and military forces. I regret to tell you that very many American lives have been lost. In addition, American ships have been reported torpedoed on the high seas between San Francisco and Honolulu.

Yesterday the Japanese Government also launched an attack against Malaya.

Last night Japanese forces attacked Hong Kong.

Last night Japanese forces attacked Guam.

Last night Japanese forces attacked the Philippine Islands.

Last night the Japanese attacked Wake Island.

And this morning the Japanese attacked Midway Island.

Japan has therefore undertaken a surprise offensive extending through out the Pacific area. The facts of yesterday and today speak for themselves. The people of the United States have already formed their opinions and well understand the implications to the very life and safety of our nation.

As Commander in Chief of the Army and Navy I have directed that all measures be taken for our defense, that always will our whole nation remember the character of the onslaught against us.

No matter how long it may take us to overcome this premeditated invasion, the American people, in their righteous might, will win through to absolute victory.

I believe that I interpret the will of the Congress and of the people when I assert that we will not only defend ourselves to the uttermost but will make it very certain that this form of treachery shall never again endanger us.

Hostilities exist. There is no blinking at the fact that our people, our territory and our interests are in grave danger.

With confidence in our armed forces, with the unbounding determination of our people, we will gain the inevitable triumph. So help us God.

I ask that the Congress declare that since the unprovoked and dastardly attack by Japan on Sunday, Dec. 7, 1941, a state of war has existed between the United States and the Japanese Empire.

On the evening of December 8, 1941, President Roosevelt addressed the American people over the radio concerning Japan's attack on the United States and America's answer to the challenge. At the time that this address was made, there was no indication of any change in the relations between the United States and Germany and Italy; but on the morning of December 11, 1941, Germany and Italy both declared war on the United States. President Roosevelt at once sent a message to Congress requesting that the existence of a state of war between the United States and Germany, and the United States and Italy be declared. Congress immediately voted in favor of both declarations. The President did not address Congress at this time, nor did he make an address to the people, as he had already fully discussed America's entrance into the war in the speech which follows.

AMERICA'S ANSWER TO JAPAN'S CHALLENGE

The sudden criminal attacks perpetrated by the Japanese in the Pacific provide the climax of a decade of international immorality.

Powerful and resourceful gangsters have banded together to make war upon the whole human race. Their challenge has now been flung at the United States of America. The Japanese have treacherously violated the long-standing peace between us. Many American soldiers and sailors have been killed by enemy action. American ships have been sunk; American airplanes have been destroyed.

The Congress and the people of the United States have accepted that challenge.

Together with other free peoples, we are now fighting to maintain our right to live among our world neighbors in freedom and in common decency, without fear of assault.

I have prepared the full record of our past relations with Japan, and it will be submitted to the Congress. It begins with the visit of Commodore

Perry to Japan eighty-eight years ago. It ends with the visit of two Japanese emissaries to the Secretary of State last Sunday, an hour after Japanese forces had loosed their bombs and machine guns against our flag, our forces and our citizens.

I can say with utmost confidence that no Americans today or a thousand years hence need feel anything but pride in our patience and in our efforts through all the years toward achieving a peace in the Pacific which would be fair and honorable to every nation, large or small. And no honest person, today or a thousand years hence, will be able to suppress a sense of indignation and horror at the treachery committed by the military dictators of Japan under the very shadow of the flag of peace borne by their special envoys in our midst.

The course that Japan has followed for the past ten years in Asia has paralleled the course of Hitler and Mussolini in Europe and in Africa. Today, it has become far more than a parallel. It is collaboration, actual collaboration, so well calculated that all the continents of the world, and all the oceans, are now considered by the Axis strategists as one gigantic battlefield.

In 1931, ten years ago, Japan invaded Manchukuo—without warning.

In 1935, Italy invaded Ethiopia—without warning.

In 1938, Hitler occupied Austria—without warning.

In 1939, Hitler invaded Czecho-Slovakia—without warning.

Later in 1939, Hitler invaded Poland—without warning.

In 1940, Hitler invaded Norway, Denmark, the Netherlands, Belgium and Luxembourg—without warning.

In 1940, Italy attacked France and later Greece—without warning.

And in this year, 1941, the Axis Powers attacked Yugoslavia and Greece and they dominated the Balkans—without warning.

In 1941 also, Hitler invaded Russia—without warning.

And now Japan has attacked Malaya and Thailand—and the United States—without warning.

It is all of one pattern.

We are now in this war. We are all in it—all the way. Every single man, woman and child is a partner in the most tremendous undertaking of our American history. We must share together the bad news and the good news, the defeats and the victories—the changing fortunes of war.

So far, the news has been all bad. We have suffered a serious set-back in Hawaii. Our forces in the Philippines, which include the brave people of that commonwealth, are taking punishment, but are defending themselves vigorously. The reports from Guam and Wake and Midway Islands are still confused, but we must be prepared for the announcement that all these three outposts have been seized.

The casualty lists of these first few days will undoubtedly be large. I deeply feel the anxiety of all families of the men in our armed forces and the relatives of people in cities which have been bombed. I can only give them my solemn promise that they will get news just as quickly as possible.

This government will put its trust in the stamina of the American people and will give the facts to the public as soon as two conditions have been fulfilled; first, that the information has been definitely and officially confirmed; and, second, that the release of the information at the time it is received will not prove valuable to the enemy directly or indirectly.

Most earnestly I urge my countrymen to reject all rumors. These ugly little hints of complete disaster fly thick and fast in wartime. They have to be examined and appraised.

As an example, I can tell you frankly that until further surveys are made, I have not sufficient information to state the exact damage which has been done to our naval vessels at Pearl Harbor. Admittedly the damage is serious. But no one can say how serious until we know how much of this damage can be repaired and how quickly the necessary repairs can be made.

I cite as another example a statement made on Sunday night that a Japanese carrier had been located and sunk off the Canal Zone. And when you hear statements that are attributed to what they call "an authoritative source," you can be reasonably sure that under these war circumstances the "authoritative source" was not any person in authority.

Many rumors and reports which we now hear originate with enemy sources. For instance, today the Japanese are claiming that as a result of their one action against Hawaii they have gained naval supremacy in the Pacific. This is an old trick of propaganda which has been used innumerable times by the Nazis. The purposes of such fantastic claims are, of course, to spread fear and confusion among us, and to goad us into revealing military information which our enemies are desperately anxious to obtain.

Our government will not be caught in this obvious trap—and neither will our people.

It must be remembered by each and every one of us that our free and rapid communication must be greatly restricted in wartime. It is not possible to receive full, speedy, accurate reports from distant areas of combat. This is particularly true where naval operations are concerned. For in these days of the marvels of radio it is often impossible for the commanders of various units to report their activities by radio, for the very simple reason that this information would become available to the enemy, and would disclose their position and their plan of defense or attack.

Of necessity there will be delays in officially confirming or denying reports of operations, but we will not hide facts from the country if we know the facts and if the enemy will not be aided by their disclosure.

To all newspapers and radio stations—all those who reach the eyes and ears of the American people—I say this: You have a most grave responsibility to the nation now and for the duration of this war.

If you feel that our government is not disclosing enough of the truth, you have every right to say so. But—in the absence of all the facts, as revealed by official sources—you have no right to deal out unconfirmed reports in such a way as to make people believe they are gospel truth.

Every citizen, in every walk of life, shares this same responsibility. The lives of our soldiers and sailors—the whole future of this nation—depend upon the manner in which each and every one of us fulfills his obligation to our country.

Now a word about the recent past—and the future. A year and a half has elapsed since the fall of France, when the whole world first realized the mechanized might which the Axis nations had been building for so many years. America has used that year and a half to great advantage. Knowing that the attack might reach us in all too short a time, we immediately began greatly to increase our industrial strength and our capacity to meet the demands of modern warfare.

Precious months were gained by sending vast quantities of our war matériel to the nations of the world still able to resist Axis aggression. Our policy rested on the fundamental truth that the defense of any country resisting Hitler or Japan was in the long run the defense of our own country. That policy has been justified. It has given us time, invaluable time, to build our American assembly lines of production.

Assembly lines are now in operation. Others are being rushed to completion. A steady stream of tanks and planes, of guns and ships, of shells and equipment—that is what these eighteen months have given us.

But it is all only a beginning of what has to be done. We must be set to face a long war against crafty and powerful bandits. The attack at Pearl Harbor can be repeated at any one of many points in both oceans and along both our coast lines and against all the rest of the hemisphere.

It will not only be a long war, it will be a hard war. That is the basis on which we now lay all our plans. That is the yardstick by which we measure what we shall need and demand; money, materials, doubled and quadrupled production—ever increasing. The production must be not only for our own Army and Navy and air forces. It must reinforce the other armies and navies and air forces fighting the Nazis and the war lords of Japan throughout the Americas and the world.

I have been working today on the subject of production. Your government has decided on two broad policies.

The first is to speed up all existing production by working on a seven-day-week basis in every war industry, including the production of essential raw materials.

The second policy, now being put into form, is to rush additions to the capacity of production by building more new plants, by adding to old plants, and by using the many smaller plants for war needs.

Over the hard road of the past months we have at times met obstacles and difficulties, divisions and disputes, indifference and callousness. That is now all past—and, I am sure, forgotten.

The fact is that the country now has an organization in Washington built around men and women who are recognized experts in their own fields. I think the country knows that the people who are actually responsible in each and every one of these many fields are pulling together with a teamwork that has never before been excelled.

On the road ahead there lies hard work—gruelling work—day and night, every hour and every minute.

I was about to add that ahead there lies sacrifice for all of us.

But it is not correct to use that word. The United States does not consider it a sacrifice to do all one can, to give one's best to our nation, when the nation is fighting for its existence and its future life.

It is not a sacrifice for any man, old or young, to be in the Army or the Navy of the United States. Rather is it a privilege.

It is not a sacrifice for the industrialist or the wage-earner, the farmer or the shopkeeper, the trainman or the doctor, to pay more taxes, to buy more bonds, to forego extra profits, to work longer or harder at the task for which he is best fitted. Rather, it is a privilege.

It is not a sacrifice to do without many things to which we are accustomed if the national defense calls for doing without.

A review this morning leads me to the conclusion that at present we shall not have to curtail the normal articles of food. There is enough food for all of us and enough left over to send to those who are fighting on the same side with us.

There will be a clear and definite shortage of metals of many kinds for civilian use for the very good reason that in our increased program we shall need for war purposes more than half of that portion of the principal metals which during the past year have gone into articles for civilian use. We shall have to give up many things entirely.

I am sure that the people in every part of the nation are prepared in their individual living to win this war. I am sure they will cheerfully help to pay a large part of its financial cost while it goes on. I am sure they will cheerfully give up those material things they are asked to give up.

I am sure that they will retain all those great spiritual things without which we cannot win through.

I repeat that the United States can accept no result save victory, final and complete. Not only must the shame of Japanese treachery be wiped out, but the sources of international brutality, wherever they exist, must be absolutely and finally broken.

In my message to the Congress yesterday I said that we "will make very certain that this form of treachery shall never endanger us again." In order to achieve that certainty, we must begin the great task that is before us by abandoning once and for all the illusion that we can ever again isolate ourselves from the rest of humanity.

In these past few years—and, most violently, in the past few days—we have learned a terrible lesson.

It is our obligation to our dead—it is our sacred obligation to their children and our children—that we must never forget what we have learned.

And what we all have learned is this:

There is no such thing as security for any nation—or any individual—in a world ruled by the principles of gangsterism.

There is no such thing as impregnable defense against powerful aggressors who sneak up in the dark and strike without warning.

We have learned that our ocean-girt hemisphere is not immune from severe attack—that we cannot measure our safety in terms of miles on any map.

We may acknowledge that our enemies have performed a brilliant feat of deception, perfectly timed and executed with great skill. It was a thoroughly dishonorable deed, but we must face the fact that modern warfare as conducted in the Nazi manner is a dirty business. We don't like it—we didn't want to get in it—but we are in it and we're going to fight it with everything we've got.

I do not think any American has any doubt of our ability to administer proper punishment to the perpetrators of these crimes.

Your government knows that for weeks Germany has been telling Japan that if Japan did not attack the United States, Japan would not share in dividing the spoils with Germany when peace came. She was promised by Germany that if she came in she would receive the complete and perpetual control of the whole of the Pacific area—and that means not only the Far East, not only all of the islands in the Pacific, but also a stranglehold on the west coast of North, Central and South America.

We also know that Germany and Japan are conducting their military and naval operations in accordance with a joint plan. That plan considers all peoples and nations which are not helping the Axis powers as common enemies of each and every one of the Axis powers.

That is their simple and obvious grand strategy. That is why the American people must realize that it can be matched only with similar grand strategy.

We must realize, for example, that Japanese successes against the United States in the Pacific are helpful to German operations in Libya; that any German success against the Caucasus is inevitably an assistance to Japan in her operations against the Dutch East Indies; that a German attack against Algiers or Morocco opens the way to a German attack against South America.

On the other side of the picture, we must learn to know that guerrilla warfare against the Germans in Serbia helps us; that a successful Russian offensive against the Germans helps us; and that British successes on land or sea in any part of the world strengthen our hands.

Remember always that Germany and Italy, regardless of any formal declaration of war, consider themselves at war with the United States at this moment just as much as they consider themselves at war with Britain and Russia. And Germany puts all the other republics of the Americas into the category of enemies. The people of the hemisphere can be honored by that.

The true goal we seek is far above and beyond the ugly field of battle. When we resort to force, as now we must, we are determined that this force shall be directed toward ultimate good as well as against immediate evil. We Americans are not destroyers—we are builders.

We are now in the midst of a war, not for conquest, not for vengeance, but for a world in which this nation, and all that this nation represents, will be safe for our children. We expect to eliminate the danger from Japan, but it would serve us ill if we accomplished that and found that the rest of the world was dominated by Hitler and Mussolini.

We are going to win the war and we are going to win the peace that follows.

And in the dark hours of this day—and through dark days that may be yet to come—we will know that the vast majority of the members of the human race are on our side. Many of them are fighting with us. All of them are praying for us. For, in representing our cause, we represent theirs as well—our hope and their hope for liberty under God.

Calling for total war effort—"our task is hard . . . the time is short"—President Roosevelt delivered in person the following message on the state of the Union before the reassembled Seventy-seventh Congress, on January 6, 1942.

FIRST WAR ADDRESS BEFORE CONGRESS

Mr. Vice President, Mr. Speaker, members of the Senate and the House of Representatives of the United States:

In fulfilling my duty to report on the state of the Union, I am proud to say to you that the spirit of the American people was never higher than it is today. The Union was never more closely knit together and this country was never more deeply determined to face the solemn tasks before it.

The response of the American people has been instantaneous, and it will be sustained until our security is assured.

Exactly one year ago today I said to this Congress: "When the dictators are ready to make war upon us they will not wait for an act of war on our part. They, not we, will choose the time and the place and the method of their attack."

We now know their choice of the time, a peaceful December morning, Dec. 7, 1941.

We know their choice of the place, an outpost, an American outpost, in the Pacific.

We know their choice of the method, the method of Hitler himself.

Japan's scheme of conquest goes back half a century. It is not merely a policy of seeking living room, it was a plan which included the subjugation of all the peoples in the Far East and in the islands of the Pacific, and the domination of that ocean by Japanese military and naval control of the western coasts of North, Central and South America.

The development of this ambitious conspiracy was marked by the war against China in 1894; the subsequent occupation of Korea; the war against Russia in 1904; the illegal fortification of the mandated Pacific islands following 1920; the seizure of Manchuria in 1931 and the invasion of China in 1935.

A similar policy of criminal conquest was adopted by Italy. The Fascists first revealed their imperial designs in Libya and Tripoli. In 1935, they seized Abyssinia. Their goal was the domination of all North Africa, Egypt, part of France and the entire Mediterranean world.

But, the dreams of empire of the Japanese and Fascist leaders were modest in comparison with the gargantuan aspirations of Hitler and his Nazis. Even before they came to power in 1933, their plans for that conquest had been drawn. They provided for ultimate domination, not of any one section of the world but of the whole earth and all the oceans on it.

When Hitler organized his Berlin-Rome-Tokyo alliance, all these plans of conquest became a single plan. Under this, in addition to her own schemes of conquest, Japan's role was obviously to cut off our supply of weapons of war to Britain and Russia and China, weapons which increasingly were speeding the day of Hitler's doom. The act of Japan at Pearl Harbor was intended to stun us, to terrify us to such an extent that we would divert our industrial and military strength to the Pacific area or even to our own continental defense.

The plan has failed in its purpose. We have not been stunned. We have not been terrified or confused. This very reassembling of the Seventy-seventh Congress today is proof of that. For the mood of quiet grim resolution which here prevails bodes ill for those who conspired and collaborated to murder world peace.

And that mood is stronger than any mere desire for revenge. It expresses the will of the American people to make very certain that the world will never so suffer again.

Admittedly, we have been faced with hard choices. It was bitter, for example, not to relieve the heroic and historic defenders of Wake Island. It was bitter for us not to be able to land a million men from a thousand ships in the Philippine Islands.

But this adds only to our determination to see to it that the Stars and Stripes will fly again over Wake and Guam, and that the brave people of the Philippines will be rid of Japanese imperialism and will live in freedom and security and independence.

Powerful and offensive actions must and will be taken in proper time. The consolidation of the United Nations' total war effort against our common enemy is being achieved.

That was and is the purpose of conferences which have been held during the past two weeks in Washington and Moscow and Chungking. This is the primary objective of the declaration of solidarity signed in Washington on Jan. 1, 1942, by twenty-six nations against the Axis powers.

Difficult choices may have to be made in the months to come. We do not shrink from such decisions. We and those united with us will make those decisions with courage and determination.

Plans have been laid here and in the other capitals for co-ordinated and co-operative action by all the United Nations, military action and economic action. Already we have established, as you know, unified command of land, sea and air forces in the Southwestern Pacific theatre of war.

There will be a continuation of conferences and consultations among military staffs, so that the plans and operations of each will fit into the general strategy designed to crush the enemy. We shall not fight isolated wars, each nation going its own way. These twenty-six nations are united not in spirit and determination alone but in the broad conduct of the war in all its phases.

For the first time since the Japanese and the Fascists and the Nazis started along that blood-stained course of conquest, they now face the fact that superior forces are assembling against them. Gone forever are the days when the aggressors could attack and destroy their victims one by one, destroy them without unity of resistance. We of the United Nations will so dispose our forces that we can strike at the common enemy wherever the greatest damage can be done.

The militarists of Berlin and Tokyo started this war, but the massed, angered forces of common humanity will finish it.

Destruction of the material and spiritual centers of civilization, this has been and still is the purpose of Hitler and his Italian and Japanese chessmen. They would wreck the power of the British Commonwealth and of Russia and of China and of the Netherlands and then combine their forces to achieve their ultimate goal, the conquest of the United States.

They know that victory for us means victory for freedom.

They know that victory for us means victory for the institution of democracy, the ideal of the family, the simple principles of common decency and humanity.

They know that victory for us means victory for religion. And they could not tolerate that. The world is too small to provide adequate living room for both Hitler and God. In proof of that, the Nazis have now announced their plan for enforcing their new German pagan religion all over the world, the plan by which the Holy Bible and the Cross of Mercy would be displaced by Mein Kampf and the swastika and the naked sword.

Our own objectives are clear; the objective of smashing the militarism imposed by war lords upon their enslaved peoples; the objective of liberating the subjugated nations; the objective of establishing and securing freedom of speech, freedom of religion, freedom from want and freedom from fear everywhere in the world.

We shall not stop short of these objectives. Nor shall we be satisfied merely to gain them and then call it a day. I know that I speak for the American people and I have good reason to believe that I speak also for all the other peoples that fight with us when I say that this time we are determined not only to win the war but also to maintain the security of the peace that will follow.

But we know that modern methods of warfare make it a task not only of shooting and fighting but an even more urgent one of working and producing.

Victory requires the actual weapons of war and the means of transporting them to a dozen points of combat.

It will not be sufficient for us and the other United Nations to produce a slightly superior supply of munitions to that of Germany and Japan and Italy and the stolen industries in the countries which they have overrun.

The superiority of the United Nations in munitions and ships must be overwhelming, so overwhelming that the Axis nations can never hope to catch up with it.

And so in order to attain this overwhelming superiority the United States must build planes and tanks' and guns and ships to the utmost limit of our national capacity. We have the ability and capacity to produce arms not only for our own forces but also for the armies, navies and air forces fighting on our side.

And our overwhelming superiority of armament must be adequate to put weapons of war at the proper time into the hands of those men in the conquered nations, who stand ready to seize the first opportunity to revolt against their German and Japanese oppressors, and against the traitors in their own ranks, known by the already infamous name of "Quislings." And I think that it is a sad prophecy to say that as we get guns to the patriots in those lands they too will fire shots heard round the world.

This production of ours in the United States must be raised far above present levels, even though it will mean the dislocation of the lives and occupations of millions of our own peoples. We must raise our sights all along the production line. Let no man say it cannot be done. It must be done and we have undertaken to do it.

I have just sent a letter of directive to the appropriate departments and agencies of our government, ordering that immediate steps be taken:

First, to increase our production rate of airplanes so rapidly that in this year, 1942, we shall produce 60,000 planes, 10,000, by the way, more than the goal that we set a year and a half ago. This includes 45,000 combat planes, bombers, dive bombers, pursuit planes. The rate of increase will be maintained, continued, so that next year, 1943, we shall produce 125,000 planes, including 100,000 combat planes.

Second, to increase our production rate of tanks so rapidly that in this year, 1942, we shall produce 45,000 tanks, and to continue that increase so that next year, 1943, we shall produce 75,000 tanks.

Third, to increase our production rate of anti-aircraft guns so rapidly that in this year, 1942, we shall produce 20,000 of them, and to continue that increase so that next year, 1943, we shall produce 35,000 anti-aircraft guns.

And fourth, to increase our production rate of merchant ships so rapidly that in this year, 1942, we shall build 8,000,000 deadweight tons, as compared with a 1941 completed production of 1,100,000. And finally, we shall continue that increase so that next year, 1943, we shall build 10,000,000 tons of shipping.

These figures and similar figures for a multitude of other implements of war will give the Japanese and the Nazis a little idea of just what they accomplished in the attack at Pearl Harbor.

And I rather hope that all these figures which I have given will become common knowledge in Germany and Japan.

Our task is hard. Our task is unprecedented and the time is short. We must strain every existing armament producing facility to the utmost. We must convert every available plant and tool to war production. That goes all the way from the greatest plants to the smallest, from the huge automobile industry to the village machine shop.

Production for war is based on men and women, the human hands and brains which collectively we call labor. Our workers stand ready to work long hours. To turn out more in a day's work. To keep the wheels turning and the fires burning twenty-four hours a day and seven days a week. They realize well that on the speed and efficiency of their work depend the lives of their sons and brothers on the fighting front.

Production for war is based on metals and raw materials, steel, copper, rubber, aluminum, zinc, tin. Greater and greater quantities of them will have to be diverted to war purposes. Civilian use of them will have to be cut further and still further and in many cases completely eliminated.

War costs money. So far we have hardly even begun to pay for it. We devoted only 15 per cent of our national income to national defense. As will appear in my budget message tomorrow, our war program for the coming fiscal year will cost $56,000,000,000, or in other words more than half of the estimated annual national income. That means taxes and bonds, and bonds and taxes. It means cutting luxuries and other nonessentials. In a word, it means an all-out war by individual effort and family effort in a united country.

Only this all-out scale of production will hasten the ultimate all-out victory. Speed will count. Lost ground can always be regained, lost time never. Speed will save lives, speed will save this nation, which is in peril, speed will save our freedom and our civilization, and slowness has never been an American characteristic.

As the United States goes into its full stride, we must always be on guard, on guard against misconception that will arise naturally or which will be planted among us by our enemies.

We must guard against complacency. We must not underrate the enemy. He is powerful and cunning, cruel and ruthless. He will stop at nothing that gives him a chance to kill and to destroy. He has trained his people to believe that their highest perfection is achieved by waging war. For many years he has prepared for this very conflict, planning and plotting and training and arming and fighting. We have already tasted defeat. We may suffer further setbacks. We must face that fact of a hard war, a long war, a bloody war, a costly war.

We must, on the other hand, guard against defeatism. That has been one of the chief weapons of Hitler's propaganda machine, used time and again with deadly results. It will not be used successfully on the American people.

We must guard against divisions among ourselves and among all the other United Nations. We must be particularly vigilant against racial discrimination in any of its ugly forms. Hitler will try again to breed mistrust and suspicion between one individual and another, one group and another, one race and another, one government and another. He will try to use the same technique of falsehood and rumor-mongering with which he divided France from Britain. He is trying to do this even now; but he will find a unity, a unity of will and purpose against him which will persevere until the destruction of all his black designs upon the freedom and people of the world.

We cannot wage this war in a defensive spirit. As our power and resources are fully mobilized we shall carry the attack against the enemy. We shall hit him, and hit him again, wherever and whenever we can reach him.

We must keep him far from our shores, for we intend to bring this battle to him on his own home grounds.

American armed forces must be used in any place in all the world where it seems advisable to engage the forces of the enemy. In some cases these operations will be defensive in order to protect key positions. In other cases these operations will be offensive in order to strike at the common enemy with a view to his complete encirclement and eventual total defeat. American armed forces will operate at many points in the Far East. American armed forces will be on all the oceans, helping to guard the essential communications which are vital to the United Nations.

American land and air and sea forces will take positions in the British Isles, which constitute an essential fortress in this great world struggle.

American armed forces will help to protect this hemisphere, and help also to protect bases outside of this hemisphere which could be used for an attack on the Americas.

If any of our enemies from Europe or from Asia attempt long range raids by suicide squadrons of bombing planes, they will do so only in the hope of terrorizing our people and disrupting our morale. Our people are not afraid of that. We know that we may have to pay a heavy price for freedom. We will pay this price with a will. Whatever the price, it is a thousand times worth it. No matter what our enemies, in their desperation, may attempt to do to us, we will say, as the people of London have said, "We can take it." And what's more, we can give it back, and we will give it back, with compound interest.

When our enemies challenged our country to stand up and fight, they challenged each and every one of us, and each and every one of us has accepted the challenge for himself and his nation.

There were only some four hundred United States Marines who in the heroic and historic defense of Wake Island inflicted such great losses on the enemy. Some of those men were killed in action and others are now prisoners of war. When the survivors of that great fight are liberated and restored to their homes, they will learn that a hundred and thirty million of their fellow citizens have been inspired to render their own full share of service and sacrifice.

We can well say that our men on the fighting fronts have already proved that Americans today are just as rugged and just as tough as any of the heroes whose exploits we celebrate on the Fourth of July.

Many people ask, "When will this war end?" There is only one answer to that. It will end just as soon as we make it end by our combined efforts, our combined strength, our combined determination to fight through and work through until the end, the end of militarism in Germany and Italy and Japan. Most certainly we shall not settle for less.

That is the spirit in which discussions have been conducted during the visit of the British Prime Minister to Washington. Mr. Churchill and

I understand each other, our motives and our purposes. Together during the past two weeks we have faced squarely the major military and economic problems of this greatest world war.

All in our nations have been cheered by Mr. Churchill's visit. We have been deeply stirred by his great message to us. He is welcome in our midst now and in days to come. And we unite in wishing him a safe return to his home. For we are fighting on the same side with the British people who fought alone the long terrible months and withstood the enemy with fortitude and tenacity and skill.

We are fighting on the same side with the Russian people who have seen the Nazi hordes swarm up to the very gates of Moscow and who with almost superhuman will and courage have forced the invaders back into retreat.

We are fighting on the same side as the brave people of China, those millions who for four and a half long years have withstood bombs and starvation and have whipped the invaders time and again in spite of the superior Japanese equipment and arms.

Yes, we are fighting on the same side with the indomitable Dutch.

We are fighting on the same side as all the other governments in exile whom Hitler and all his armies and all his Gestapo have not been able to conquer.

But we of the United Nations are not making all this sacrifice of human effort and human lives to return to the kind of world we had after the last World War. We are fighting today for security and progress and for peace, not only for ourselves but for all men, not only for one generation but for all generations. We are fighting to cleanse the world of ancient evils, ancient ills.

Our enemies are guided by brutal cynicism, by unholy contempt for the human race. We are inspired by a faith which goes back through all the years to the first chapter of the Book of Genesis—"God created man in His own image."

We on our side are striving to be true to that divine heritage. We are fighting, as our fathers have fought, to uphold the doctrine that all men are equal in the sight of God. Those on the other side are striving to destroy this deep belief and to create a world in their own image, a world of tyranny and cruelty and serfdom.

That is the conflict that day and night now pervades our lives. No compromise can end that conflict. There never has been and never can be successful compromise between good and evil. Only total victory can reward the champions of tolerance and decency and freedom and faith.

Wendell L. Willkie
| 1892-1944 |

Here follow two addresses by Wendell L. Willkie, Republican can-
didate for President in 1940. The first is his "Loyal Opposition"
speech, delivered over the radio on November 11, 1940, shortly after
the Presidential election. This speech is reproduced in part. The second,
"American Liberty," is also a radio address, which Mr. Willkie de-
livered on the Fourth of July, 1941. The latter speech is given here
in full.

"LOYAL OPPOSITION"

PEOPLE OF AMERICA:

Twenty-two years ago today, a great conflict raging on the battlefields of Europe came to an end. The guns were silent. A new era of peace began and for that era the people of our Western World—our democratic world—held the highest hopes.

Those hopes have not been fulfilled. The democratic way of life did not become stronger—it became weaker. The spirit of constitutional government flickered like a dying lamp. And within the last year or so the light from that lamp has disappeared entirely upon the continent of Europe.

We in America watched darkness fall upon Europe. And as we watched, there approached an important time for us—the national election of 1940.

In that election, and in our attitudes after that election, the rest of the world would see an example of democracy in action, an example of a great people faithful to their Constitution and to their elected representatives.

The campaign preceding this election stirred us deeply. Millions upon millions of us who had never been active in politics took part in it. The people flocked to the polling places in greater numbers than ever before in history.

Nearly 50,000,000 people exercised on November 5 the right of the franchise—the precious right which we inherited from our forefathers and which we must cherish and pass on to future generations.

Thus it came about that although constitutional government had been blotted out elsewhere, here in America men and women kept it triumphantly alive.

No matter which side you were on, on that day, remember that this great, free expression of our faith in the free system of government must have given hope to millions upon millions of others—on the heroic island of Britain—in the ruined cities of France and Belgium—yes, perhaps even to people in Germany and in Italy. It has given hope wherever man hopes to be free.

In the campaign preceding this election, serious issues were at stake. People became bitter. Many things were said which in calmer moments might have been left unsaid or might have been worded more thoughtfully.

But we Americans know that the bitterness is a distortion, not a true reflection of what is in our hearts. I can truthfully say that there is no bitterness in mine. I hope there is none in yours.

We have elected Franklin Roosevelt President. He is your President. He is my President. We all of us owe him the respect due to his high office. We give him that respect. We will support him with our best efforts for our country. And we pray that God may guide his hand during the next four years in the supreme task of administering the affairs of the people.

It is a fundamental principle of the democratic system that the majority rules. The function of the minority, however, is equally fundamental. It is about the function of that minority—22,000,000 people, nearly half of our electorate, that I wish to talk to you tonight.

A vital element in the balanced operation of democracy is a strong, alert and watchful opposition. That is our task for the next four years. We must constitute ourselves a vigorous, loyal and public-spirited opposition party.

It has been suggested that in order to present a united front to a threatening world, the minority should now surrender its convictions and join the majority. This would mean that in the United States of America there would be only one dominant party—only one economic philosophy—only one political philosophy of life. This is a totalitarian idea—it is a slave idea—it must be rejected utterly.

The British people are unified with a unity almost unexampled in history for its endurance and its valor. Yet that unity co-exists with an unimpaired freedom of criticism and of suggestion.

In the continual debates of the House of Commons and the House of Lords, all of the government's policies, its taxation, its expenditures, its military and naval policies, its basic economic policies, are brought under steady, friendly, loyal, critical review. Britain survives free. Let us Americans choose no lesser freedom.

In Britain some opposition party leaders are members of the government and some say that a similar device should be adopted here. That is a false conception of our government. When a leader of the British Liberal party or a member of the British Labor party becomes a member of the Churchill Cabinet he becomes—from the British parliamentary point of view—an equal of Mr. Churchill's.

This is because the British Cabinet is a committee of the Houses of Parliament. It is a committee of equals, wherein the Prime Minister is chairman, a lofty chairman, indeed, and yet but a chairman. The other members are his colleagues.

With us the situation as you well know is different. Our executive branch is not a committee of our legislative branch. Our President is independent of our Congress. The members of his Cabinet are not his colleagues. They are his administrative subordinates. They are subject to his orders.

An American President could fill his whole Cabinet with leaders of the opposition party and still our Administration would not be a two-party administration. It would be an administration of a majority President giving orders to minority representatives of his own choosing. These representatives must concur in the President's convictions. If they do not they have no alternative except to resign.

Clearly no such device as this can give us in this country any self-respecting agreement between majority and minority for concerted effort toward the national welfare. Such a plan for us would be but the shadow— not the substance of unity.

Our American unity cannot be made with words or with gestures. It must be forged between the ideas of the opposition and the practices and the policies of the administration. Ours is a government of principles and not one merely of. men. Any member of the minority party, though willing to die for his country, still retains the right to criticize the policies of the government. This right is imbedded in our constitutional system.

We, who stand ready to serve our country behind our Commander in Chief, nevertheless retain the right, and I will say the duty, to debate the course of our government. Ours is a two-party system. Should we ever permit one party to dominate our lives entirely, democracy would collapse and we would have dictatorship.

Therefore, to you who have so sincerely given yourselves to this cause, which you chose me to lead, I say: "Your function during the next four years is that of the loyal opposition." You believe deeply in the principles that we stood for in the recent election. And principles are not like a football suit to be put on in order to play a game and then taken off when the game is over.

It is your constitutional duty to debate the policies of this or any other Administration and to express yourselves freely and openly to those who represent you in your state and national government.

Now let me, however, raise a single warning. Ours is a very powerful opposition—On November 5 ·we were a minority by only a few million votes. Let us not, therefore, fall into the partisan error of opposing things just for the sake of opposition. Ours must not be an opposition against— it must be an opposition for—an opposition for a strong America; a productive America. ·For only the productive can be strong and only the strong can be free.

AMERICAN LIBERTY

Men and women, I want to talk to you today very simply and very sincerely about the things that are in my heart and in my mind. All over America people are gathered in city, in village and in town, celebrating the Fourth of July, which is America's patriotic holiday. Speakers are telling of our heroic past, reciting the deeds, the gallant deeds, of our soldiers, recalling to our people our long struggle for liberty and the developments of our free system.

Songs are being sung, songs that move the hearts of men. Prayers are being offered all over America. Men are rededicating themselves to the principles of human freedom. But there is not a thoughtful person in all our broad land but understands that this Fourth of July celebration is in many ways more significant than any one of the celebrations we have had in the last one hundred and fifty years.

We understand, we appreciate and try to realize that as we celebrate liberty in America we must also celebrate the hope that liberty will return to many peoples who have been deprived of it in other countries.

Since the last celebration of this holiday in America millions of people, just like us, who lived peaceful, contented lives, lived free lives, with the right to go about their way of life as they pleased, have been deprived of their liberty. And we also know that unless their liberty is restored liberty cannot remain a permanent possession of America.

Liberty, like all doctrines, must be an expanding doctrine. It must be constantly searching out for new areas, or else it will die. We understand that if we permit the last stronghold of liberty in Europe to fall before the onslaught of totalitarianism the opportunity to save liberty in America will be lessened and, therefore, the overwhelming percentage of the American people are resolved that at whatever hazard or cost we will sustain the fighting men of Britain.

Every minute more and more people in America are coming to realize that the hope of Britain standing up depends upon our seeing to it that the products of our factories and our farms are delivered to her, and I am quite sure that before long now the great force of the American Navy will be brought into play to insure the delivery of those products to the fighting men of Britain.

American liberty means, of course, certain governmental processes. It means the right of men to vote in free election for public officials of their own choice, responsive to their will; it means, of course, the right of men to have their differences determined in courts undominated by government and the powerful.

It means, of course, the right of freedom of religion and freedom of speech and freedom from another thing that has come into the world with the cruelty of totalitarianism—the freedom from espionage, the freedom from interference with one's private life and one's daily doings and one's daily habits.

But American liberty means much more than that. American liberty is a religion. It is a thing of the spirit. It is an aspiration on the part of people for not alone a free life but a better life; and so I say to you people of the world, I think I know the heart of the American people. I have lived among them; I know them well. And despite the occasional hesitation and doubts, the American people will reach out, will give their utmost to see that this precious thing we call liberty shall not disappear from the world, either in Europe or in Asia or in America.

Yet none of us underestimates either the cost or the effort that will be required to do this. The forces of totalitarianism have harnessed and directed this mechanical age for the creation of the greatest military machine that the world has ever seen. It has directed the energies of 80,000,000 people toward one end—toward aggression, toward the destruction of other people; and we with our free way of life, with our individual desires and opinions, did not learn until lately how to meet such a menace.

But I am proud to say of my fellow-citizens in the United States that they are beginning to realize it now and that the vast industrial and agricultural resources of our nation are being brought into a firm and cohesive force. The spirit of our people is arising to direct that force so that totalitarianism will disappear from this world.

I was talking recently to some of my fellow-soldiers of the World War of 1917 to 1919, and I told them how proud I was that it is the soldiers of that war who are the leaders in the movement in America today against isolationism and defeatism. It is the soldiers of 1917 to 1919 that are calling America to a rededication to the spirit of liberty.

Many people preached for many years to those soldiers that all they did in the last war was futile and to no avail. As I told them, they did not make a mistake in fighting that first World War—as a matter of fact, if they had not, perhaps today there would be no liberty to fight for. Their mistake was in not fighting after the war as citizens to see that the kind of world was brought into being in which there could exist no such force as totalitarianism today.

When we have triumphed in this war, all men who fought in the last war must see to it that there is a peace drawn not in bitterness and in hatred, not of unpayable indemnities, not of the kind that produces inevitably another war, but that we must draw a peace in which the defeated people have the same right to the aspiration of liberty and of a full life as the conquered.

We must see to it that the trade areas of the world are enlarged, that artificial barriers between men are removed, so that there will be a constantly rising standard of living for all men who work, in which men of all races and creeds and religions and nations can live in peace and harmony, in which the just fruits of enterprise will find their just fulfillment, in which children may look forward to a constantly better world, free of hatred and bitterness and narrow isolationism and of economic degradation.

I speak tonight not alone to my fellow-citizens of America: I speak to the citizens of the remaining free country of Europe. I speak to the people of the enslaved countries of Europe. I speak to the people of Germany, where my forebears came from, and I say to all of you, American liberty is a generous thing. We reach out to all of you and only hope and pray that every one of you may have liberty.

We want to share it with you all. All we seek to do is to remove from the world the menace of a doctrine of government and a system of economics that lives by the enslavement of men, lives by the enslavement of men under its own rule, lives by the enslavement of men that it conquers.

Surely before another Fourth of July celebration comes about all the world will join with America in celebrating the principles of human freedom.

Cordell Hull

[1871-1955]

Hemisphere defense became a vital issue in 1936 when the stormy clouds of the approaching Second World War began to darken the horizon. An Inter-American Conference for the Maintenance of Peace was held that year at Buenos Aires, Argentina, which was attended by representatives of the 21 American republics. Cordell Hull, Secretary of State of the United States, was chairman of the American delegation, and delivered the opening address on December 5, 1936. This address follows.

THE PILLARS OF ENDURING PEACE

THE PRIMARY purpose of this Conference is to banish war from the Western Hemisphere. In its earnest pursuit of this great undertaking, it is necessary at the outset to visualize numerous dangerous conditions and practices in general international affairs to the extent that they bear upon and affect the work of this Conference. It is manifest that every country today is faced with a supreme alternative. Each must play its part in determining whether the world will slip backward toward war and savagery, or whether it can maintain and will advance the level of civilization and peace. None can escape its responsibility.

The 21 American republics cannot remain unconcerned by the grave and threatening conditions in many parts of the world. Our convocation here in Buenos Aires utters this hemisphere's common voice of its interest, nay, its intense concern, over the determination of this momentous question. The repercussions of wars and preparations for wars have been so universally disastrous that it is now as plain as mathematical truth that each nation in any part of the world is concerned in peace in every part of the world. The nations of all the Americas, through their chosen delegates, have assembled to make careful survey and analysis of all aspects of their responsibilities; to take account of their common duties; and to plan accordingly for the safety and welfare of their peoples.

The Western Hemisphere must now face squarely certain hard realities. For the purpose of our undertaking, we must frankly recognize that for some time the forces of militarism have been in the ascendant in a large part of the word; those of peace have been correspondingly on the decline. We should be lacking in common sense if we ignored the plain fact that the effects of these forces will unavoidably have direct impact upon all of us. We should be lacking in ordinary caution if we fail to counsel together for our common safety and welfare.

It is bad enough when many statesmen and peoples close their minds and memories to the awful lesson taught by the millions of soldiers sacrificed in the World War; the shattered cities, the desolated fields, and all the other material, moral, and spiritual ravages of that conflict. Still worse, that war has brought in its train wounds to man's heart and spirit, national hatreds and fears, the dislocation or destruction of indispensable political and governmental structures, and the collapse or cool abandonment of former high standards of national conduct. The supreme tragedy is completed by the breakdown of the commerce of mind and culture, the attempt to isolate the nations of the earth into sealed compartments, all of which have made war a burden not to be endured by mankind.

The delegates of the American nations, meeting here in the face of these grave and threatening world conditions, must realize that mere words will not suffice. From every wise and practical viewpoint, concrete peace planning, peace views, and peace objectives are imperative. We must quicken our words and our hopes into a specific, embracing program to maintain peace. Such a program, adequately implemented, should constitute an armory of peace. It should comprise a structure affording all practical means for safeguarding peace. At a time when many other governments or peoples fail or fear to proclaim and embrace a broad or definite peace plan or movement, while their statesmen are shouting threats of war, it is all the more necessary that we of the Americas must cry out for peace, keep alive the spirit of peace, live by the rules of peace, and forthwith perfect the machinery for its maintenance. Should we fail to make this outstanding contribution, it would be a practical desertion of the cause of peace and a tragic blow to the hopes of humanity.

In meeting this problem, the American republics are in a peculiarly advantageous situation. There are among us no radical differences, no profound mistrusts or deep hatreds. On the contrary we are inspired by the impulse to be constant friends and the determination to be peaceful neighbors.

We recognize the right of all nations to handle their affairs in any way they choose, and this quite irrespective of the fact that their way may be different from our way or even repugnant to our ideas. But we cannot fail to take cognizance of the international aspect of their policies when and to the extent that they may react upon us. I, myself, am unalterably of the view that a policy leading to war may react upon us. In the face of any situation directly leading to war, can we therefore be other than apprehensive?

In sustaining the firm determination that peace must be maintained and that any country whose policies make war likely is threatening injury to all, I believe that the nations of this hemisphere would find themselves in accord with governments elsewhere. I strongly entertain the hope that a united group of American nations may take common action at this Conference further to assure peace among themselves and define their attitude toward war; and that this action may not only demonstrate the happy position of the New World, but, though designed primarily for our own benefit, embody policies of world application and correspond to the views and interests of nations outside this hemisphere.

There is no need for war. There is a practical alternative policy at hand, complete and adequate. It is no exclusive policy aimed at the safety or supremacy of a few, leaving others to struggle with distressful situations. It demands no sacrifices comparable to the advantages which will result to each nation and to each individual.

In these circumstances the representatives of the 21 American republics should frankly call the attention of the people of this hemisphere to the possibilities of danger to their future peace and progress and at the same time set forth the numerous steps that can well be undertaken as the most effective means of improving and safeguarding the conditions of permanent peace.

While carefully avoiding any political entanglements, my Government strives at all times to cooperate with other nations to every practical extent in support of peace objectives, including reduction or limitation of armaments, the control of traffic in arms, taking the profits out of war, and the restoration of fair and friendly economic relationships. We reject war as a method of settling international disputes and favor such methods as conference, conciliation, and arbitration.

Peace can be partially safeguarded through international agreements. Such agreements, however, must reflect the utmost good faith; this alone can be the guaranty of their significance and usefulness. Contemporary events clearly show that, where mutual trust, good will, and sincerity of purpose are lacking, pacts or agreements fail; and the world is seized by fear and left to the mercy of the wreckers.

The Conference has the duty of considering all peace proposals of merit. Let me enumerate and briefly discuss eight separate and vitally important principles and proposals for a comprehensive peace program and peace structure. They are not designed to be all-inclusive. In considering them, we should be guided by the knowledge that other forces and agencies of peace exist besides those made and to be made on our continents; what we do contemplates no conflict with sincere efforts the world over.

First. I would emphasize the local and unilateral responsibility of each nation carefully to educate and organize its people in opposition to war and its underlying causes. Support must be given to peace, to the most effective policies for its preservation; and, finally, each nation must maintain conditions within its own borders which will permit it to adopt national policies that can be peacefully pursued. More than any other factor, a thoroughly informed and alert public opinion in each country as to the suitable and desirable relationships with other nations and the principles underlying them, enables a government in time of crisis to act promptly and effectively for peace.

The forces of peace everywhere are entitled to function both through governments and through public opinion. The peoples of the world would be far wiser if they expended more of their hard-earned money in organizing the forces of peace and fewer of the present 5 billion dollars in educating and training their military forces.

Since the time when Thomas Jefferson insisted upon a "decent respect to the opinions of mankind", public opinion has controlled foreign policy in all democracies. It is, therefore, all important that every platform, every pulpit, and every forum should become constant and active agencies in the great work of education and organization. The limited extent of such highly organized and intelligent public opinion in support of peace is by far the largest drawback to any plan to prevent war. Truly the first step is that each nation must thus make itself safe for peace. This, too, develops a common will for freedom, the soil from which peace springs.

People everywhere should be made to know of the peace mechanisms. Even more, there should be brought home to them the knowledge that trade, commerce, finance, debts, communications, have a bearing on peace. The workman at his bench, the farmer on his land, the shopkeeper by his shelves, the clerk at his books, the laborer in factory, plantation, mine, or construction camp, must realize that his work is the work of peace; that to interrupt it for ends of national or personal rapacity is to drive him toward quick death by bayonets, or to slower, but not less grievous suffering, through economic distress.

In all our countries we have scholars who can demonstrate these facts; let them not be silent. Our churches have direct contact with all groups; may they remember that the peacemakers are the children of God. We have artists and poets who can distill their needed knowledge into trenchant phrase and line; they have work to do. Our great journals on both continents cover the world. Our women are awake; our youth sentient; our clubs and organizations make opinion everywhere. There is a strength here available greater than that of armies. We have but to ask its aid; it will be swift to answer, not only here, but in continents beyond the seas.

Second. Indispensable in their influence for peace and well-being are frequent conferences between representatives of the nations and intercourse between their peoples. Collaboration and the exchange of views, ideas, and information are the most effective means of establishing understanding, friendship, and trust. I would again emphasize that any written pacts or agreements not based upon such relationships as these too often exist on paper only. Development of the atmosphere of peace, understanding, and good will during our sessions here will alone constitute a vast accomplishment.

Third. Any complete program would include safeguarding the nations of this hemisphere from using force, one against the other, through the consummation of all of the five well-known peace agreements, produced in chief part by previous conferences, as well as through the Draft Convention Coordinating the Existing Treaties between the American States and Extending Them in Certain Respects, which the Delegation of the United States is presenting for the consideration of this Conference.

In these, virtually all of the essentials of adequate machinery are present. If their operation is somewhat implemented by provisions in the draft proposal I have just mentioned to be considered by this Conference, such machinery would be complete.

The first of these is the Treaty to Avoid and Prevent Conflicts between the American States, which was signed in Santiago in 1923.

The second is the Treaty for the Renunciation of War, known as the Kellogg-Briand Pact, or the Pact of Paris, signed at Paris in 1928.

The third is the General Convention of Inter-American Conciliation, signed at Washington in 1929.

The fourth is the General Treaty of Inter-American Arbitration, signed at Washington in 1929.

The fifth is the Anti-War Treaty of Nonaggression and Conciliation, signed at Rio de Janeiro in 1933.

While the Montevideo Conference in 1933 went on record in favor of the valid execution of these five agreements by each of the 21 governments represented, several have not yet completed this ratification. These agreements provide a many-sided and flexible functioning machinery for the adjustment of difficulties that may arise in this hemisphere. A government could not give more tangible proof of its readiness to translate into practicable form its desire to promote and to maintain peace. Swift action by all of us to ratify these agreements should be the natural assertion of our intentions.

Fourth. If war should occur, any peace program must provide for the problem then presented. For the belligerent, there is the ruin and suffering of war. For the neutrals, there is the task of remaining neutral, of not being too disturbed in their own affairs, of not having their own peace imperiled, of working in common to restrict the war and bring it to an end. Can we in this Conference work out for ourselves a common line of policy that might be pursued during a period of neutrality? Some first broad approaches toward that end are, I think, possible. If these are to be sound they must be inspired by the determination to stay at peace. When interests are challenged, when minds are stirred, when entry into war in some particular juncture may appear to offer to some country the chance of national advantage, then determination is needed to retain neutrality. The maintenance of neutrality is an achievement to be attained more readily if undertaken jointly. Such agreement would be a tremendous safeguard for each of us. It might be a powerful means of ending war.

When we have done all that seems to be possible in extending and perfecting an integrated and permanent mechanism for preserving peaceful relations among ourselves, and when we have placed in operation these various instruments, the 21 republics of this hemisphere will have given overt expression to the most determined will for peace to be found in the world today. In the face of a weakening elsewhere in the world of reliance on and observance of international agreements, we shall have proclaimed our firm intention that these peaceful instruments shall be the foundation of relations between nations throughout this whole region.

If we can endow peace with certainty, if we can make it glow in our part of the world, then we may indulge the hope that our example will not be in vain.

Fifth. The peoples of this region have a further opportunity. They must make headway with a liberal policy of commerce, which would lower excessive barriers to trade and lessen injurious discriminations as between the trade of different countries. This means the substitution of a policy of economic benefit, good will, and fair dealing for one stimulated by greedy and short-sighted calculations of momentary advantage in an impractical isolation. It would have most beneficial effects, both direct and indirect, upon political difficulties and antagonisms.

A thriving international commerce, well adjusted to the resources and talents of each country, brings benefit to all. It keeps men employed, active and usefully supplying the wants of others. It leads each country to look upon others as helpful counterparts to itself rather than as antagonists. It opens up to each country, to the extent mutually profitable and desirable, the resources and the organized productive power of other countries; by its benefits small nations with limited territory or resources can have a varied, secure, and prosperous life; it can bring improvement to those who feel their toil too hard and their reward too meager.

Prosperity and peace are not separate entities. To promote one is to promote the other. The economic well-being of peoples is the greatest single protection against civil strife, large armaments, war. Economic isolation and military force go hand in hand; when nations cannot get what they need by the normal processes of trade, they will continue to resort to the use of force. A people employed and in a state of reasonable comfort is not a people among whom class struggles, militarism, and war can thrive. But a people driven to desperation by want and misery is at all times a threat to peace, their conditions an invitation to disorder and chaos, both internal and external.

The intervening years have given added significance to the economic program adopted at the Conference at Montevideo 3 years ago. That program is today the greatest potential force both for peace and prosperity. Our present Conference should reaffirm and secure action upon this program of economic intelligence.

One feature of the resolutions adopted at Montevideo was the support for the principle of equality of treatment as the basis of acceptable commercial policy. This rule has been followed in a number of commercial agreements that have already been concluded between American nations. Their benefits are already becoming manifest and will continue to grow. We cannot blind ourselves to the fact, however, that at the same time there has taken place an extension of discriminatory practices; these have tended to counteract the advantages resulting from the liberalizing terms embodied in other agreements.

I would urge again the wisdom of avoiding discrimination in our commercial policy. The practice of discrimination prevents trade from following the lines which would produce the greatest economic benefits—it inevitably in the long run must provoke retaliation from those who suffer from discrimination; makes it more difficult for countries eager to pursue a liberal trade policy to secure the fair gains from this policy, and thereby checks the lowering of restrictions. It will not serve our broad and deep aims; on the contrary, if steadily extended will lead us into new controversies and difficulties. The Montevideo program offers the only alternative to the present short-sighted, war-breeding bilateral bargaining method of trade, to the exclusion of triangular and multilateral trade, which is being employed in many parts of the world with sterile results.

The ends we seek can best be achieved by the concurrent or concerted action of many countries. Each can exert itself steadfastly amidst the particular circumstances of its economic situation to make its contribution toward the rebuilding of trade. Each can grant new opportunities to others as it receives new opportunities for itself. All are called upon to share in the concurrent or concerted action which is required. Any country which seeks the benefits of the program while avoiding its responsibilities, will in time shut itself off from the benefits. Any country which is tempted or forced by some special calculation to depart from these lines of action and which conveys and seeks special advantage jeopardizes the progress, and perhaps the very existence, of the program. Faithful dealing, without favor, between equal partners will be required to readjust trade along the lines of growth, which is our goal.

Sixth. The Conference must recognize the all-important principle of practical international cooperation to restore many indispensable relationships between nations; for international relationships, in many vital respects, are at a low ebb. The entire international order is severely dislocated. Chaotic conditions in the relations between nations have appeared. Human progress already has slowed down.

Nations in recent years have sought to live a hermit existence by isolating themselves from each other in suspicion and fear. The inevitable result is not unlike that experienced by a community where individuals undertake to live a hermit existence, with the resultant decline and decay of the spiritual, the moral, the educational, and the material benefits and blessings which spring from community organization and effort. The difference, when nations live apart, is that the entire human race in countless instances suffers irreparable injury—political, moral, material, spiritual, and social. Today, for illustration, through lack of comprehension, understanding, and confidence, we see many nations exhausting their material substance and the vitality of their people by piling up huge armaments. We behold others, in their attempted isolation, becoming more indifferent and less considerate toward the rights, privileges, and honest opinions of others. National character and conduct are threatened with utter demoralization. At no distant time we shall see a state of moral and spiritual isolation, bringing with it the condemnation of the world, covering great parts of the earth, unless peoples halt and turn toward a sane course.

Seventh. International law has been in large measure flouted. It should be reestablished, revitalized, and strengthened by general demand. International law protects the peace and security of nations and so safeguards them against maintaining great armaments and wasting their substance in continual readiness for war. Founded upon justice and humanity, the great principles of international law are the source and fountain of the equality, the security, and the very existence of nations. Armies and navies are no permanent substitute. Abandonment of the rule of law would not only leave small or unarmed states at the mercy of the reckless and powerful but would hopelessly undermine all international order. It is inconceivable that the civilized nations would long delay a supreme effort to reestablish that rule of law.

Eighth. Observance of understandings, agreements, and treaties between nations constitutes the foundation of international order. May I say here that this is not a time for crimination or recrimination, nor is such in my mind during this discussion. There must be the fullest patience and forbearance, one country with another, as the nations endeavor to climb back to that high ground of wholesome and elevating relationship of loyalty to the given word and faithful fair dealing.

International agreements have lost their force and reliability as a basis of relations between nations. This extremely ominous and fateful development constitutes the most dangerous single phenomenon in the world of today; not international law merely, but that which is higher—moral law—and the whole integrity and honor of governments are in danger of being ruthlessly trampled upon. There has been a failure of the spirit. There is no task more urgent than that of remaking the basis of trusted agreement between nations. They must ardently seek the terms of new agreements and stand behind them with unfailing will. The vitality of international agreements must be restored.

If the solemn rights and obligations between nations are to be treated lightly or brushed aside, the nations of the world will head straight toward international anarchy and chaos. And soon, too, the citizen begins to lower his individual standards of personal, moral, and business conduct to those of his government. Trust in each nation's honor and faith in its given word must be restored by the concerted resolve of all governments.

It is to the interest of everyone that there be an end of treaties broken by arbitrary unilateral action. Peaceful procedure, agreements between the signatories, and mutual understanding must be restored as the means of modifying or ending international agreements.

It would be a frightful commentary on the human race if, with the awful lesson of its disastrous experience, responsible and civilized governments should now fail.

The nations of this continent should omit no word or act in their attempt to meet the dangerous conditions which endanger peace. Let our actions here at Buenos Aires constitute the most potent possible appeal to peacemakers and war makers throughout the world.

So only does civilization become real. So only can we rightly ask that universal support which entitles governments to speak for their peoples to the world not with the voice of propaganda but with that of truth. Having affirmed our faith, we should be remiss if we were to leave anything undone which will tend to assure our peace here and make us powerful for peace elsewhere. In a very real sense, let this continent set the high example of championing the forces of peace, democracy, and civilization.

James Bryant Conant
[1893–1978]

Following are parts of an address by James Bryant Conant, president of Harvard University from 1933 to 1953, before the Southern College Conference in Memphis, Tennessee, on October 21, 1940.

WHAT ARE WE ARMING TO DEFEND?

WHAT are we arming to defend?

We are arming, I take it, to prevent such a change in the political and economic situation in this country as would make us a subservient people to a foreign master state. We are arming to prevent such a revolution in our way of life as would make this land for everyone who values liberty a prison-house. But we are not arming to defend an invariant type of political system. I should be unwilling personally to declare even that we are arming to defend democracy, for the word democracy has suffered grievously in this last decade. Democracy can mean anything from a dictatorship of the proletariat to a preservation of the *status quo*. It can mean a belief in the divine right of fifty-one per cent of the voters to alter in any way at any moment all laws and customs. Or it can mean the continuation in power in some locality of a privileged class.

We are not arming to defend a particular form of representative government. We may at some later time wish to modify and simplify our highly complex governmental pattern. But most of us would believe we were arming to defend certain principles embodied in our constitutional form of government. First, the civil liberties of the individual, summed up in the Bill of Rights. Second, the political machinery which enables the mass of the people to decide through elected representatives on major issues. Third, the written laws and constitutions which, together with tradition, protect the rights of the minority on the one hand, and on the other prevent sudden gusts of popular opinion from altering the structure of society.

Democracy interpreted by some of those who love to mouth this word has been at times a false shield to cover the aims of revolutionists. The Constitution, let us admit, has also been used as a false shield for others. It has been too often proclaimed as all but divine by those who seek under its protection only to hold a personal and privileged position. Between the disgruntled who would be revolutionists and the complacent privileged who would be Bourbons, a true democracy must steer a middle course.

The history of this republic has been unique. And the uniqueness of our way of life rests not so much on constitutional democracy as on our social system—a system which is the embodiment of the golden mean of which I speak. I believe that fundamentally it is this unique form of society that we are really arming to defend. I believe that the ambition of every thoughtful citizen of this republic is to assist in keeping inviolate the free way of life which has developed on this continent in the last two hundred years.

I have ventured on other occasions to speak of the American ideal as that of a free and classless, or casteless, society—a society made classless through the maximum of social mobility. Let me examine for a moment the phrase "social mobility," for this is the heart of my argument. If large numbers of young people can develop their own capacities irrespective of the economic status of their parents, then social mobility is high. If, on the other hand, the future of a young man or woman is determined almost entirely by inherited privilege or the lack of it, social mobility is nonexistent. You are all familiar with the old American adage, "Three generations from shirt sleeves to shirt sleeves." This implies a high degree of social mobility, both up and down. It implies that sons and daughters must and can seek their own level, obtain their own economic rewards, engage in any occupation irrespective of what their parents might have done.

Such is the American ideal. But I gravely fear that social and economic changes during the last forty years have whittled away much of the reality on which the ideal is founded. To be sure, we are all willing still to pay lip service to such phrases as "there are no classes in America." But mere lip service does not meet the altered conditions of modern times. We must endeavor in every way possible to reëstablish the validity of our ideal

There are many citizens of this nation who are less concerned than I am with the immediate danger to our integrity stated in terms of force. They worry rather lest the internal seeds of dissension, some poison indigenous to democracy shall destroy our soul. I recognize the causes of their apprehension, but these causes are not new. May I remind you of the famous pessimistic letter of Lord Macaulay? In this letter, written in 1857, Macaulay predicted the eventual collapse of any nation which had universal suffrage. England he felt was safe, for he boasted that in England, to use his own words, "The supreme power is in the hands of a class, numerous indeed, but select, of an educated class, of a class which is, and knows itself to be, deeply interested in the security of property and the maintenance of order."

On the other hand, prophesied Macaulay, when the United States comes to a period of depression and unemployment, this nation will be unable to ride the storm. Through such evil times the Whig historian wished us a good deliverance. "But," he said, "my reason and my wishes are at war; and I cannot help foreboding the worst. It is quite plain that your government will never be able to restrain a distressed and discontented majority, for with you the majority is the government, and has the rich, who are always a minority, absolutely at its mercy. . . . I seriously apprehend that you will, in some such season of adversity as I have described, do things which will prevent prosperity from returning."

Some of you may have heard this pessimistic letter repeated very often in the last half dozen years. Some of you may feel that the crisis which

Macaulay predicted is close at hand. If so, an answer given nearly seventy years ago by a future president of the United States, General James A. Garfield, may be both relevant and heartening. Personally I may say it is the only answer to Macaulay's letter that I have seen which will stand up against thoughtful analysis rather than wishful thinking. It speaks in terms of the characteristic American spirit—speaks with calm optimism of the unique nature of our institutions.

In an address in 1873 on "The Future of the Republic; its Dangers and its Hopes," Garfield referred to Macaulay's letter with these words: "I venture the declaration," he said, "that this opinion of Macaulay's is vulnerable on several grounds. It leaves out the great counterbalancing force of universal education. But furthermore, it is based upon a belief from which few if any British writers have been able to emancipate themselves; namely, the belief that mankind are born into permanent classes, and that in the main they must live, work, and die in the fixed class or condition in which they are born. It is hardly possible for a man reared in an aristocracy like that of England to eliminate this conviction from his mind. . . . The English theory of national stability is, that there must be a permanent class who shall hold in their own hands so much of the wealth, the privilege, and the political power of the kingdom, that they can compel the admiration and obedience of all other classes. . . . Where such permanent classes exist, the conflict of which Macaulay speaks is inevitable."

Mark these words carefully, gentlemen, for I believe they entitle General Garfield to high credit for political foresight. To my mind, the inevitable conflict of which he speaks, a conflict which is sure to come when permanent classes and universal suffrage exist in one nation, has been in progress in Great Britain during the past few years. It seems to me that in the last decade the political forces in England have been paralyzed by a deep cleavage between the two major parties, a cleavage reflecting the struggle of which Garfield spoke.

But whether I am right or not in my interpretation of current history, let me finish Garfield's statement: "We point to the fact," said the future President, "that in this country there are no classes in the British sense of the word—no impassable barriers of caste. In our political society there run no fixed horizontal strata above which none can pass. Our society resembles rather the waves of the ocean, whose every drop may move freely among its fellows, and may rise toward the light until it flashes on the crest of the highest wave."

"Our society resembles rather the waves of the ocean, whose every drop may move freely among its fellows. . . ."

These magnificent, brave words, gentlemen, summarize for me the unique ideal of American life. As long as they express the fundamentals of our social philosophy—the vision towards which we as a people strive—we still have a firm basis on which the citizens of this country may stand united. Through the willingness of all contending groups to labor devoutly for this unique American ideal, a true national loyalty can be securely anchored, the militant faith of all can be pledged to a unifying tradition and a common cause. As long as we as a democratic free people are willing to make every needed sacrifice to preserve this cause, we can face the future with real confidence. Then, and only then, may we hope to weather the tempests of our time.

Charles A. Lindbergh
[1902–1974]

Charles A. Lindbergh, who was first to fly alone across the Atlantic, delivered the following address at a rally of the America First Committee held at Manhattan Center, New York City, on April 23, 1941.

AN INDEPENDENT POLICY

THERE are many viewpoints from which the issues of this war can be argued. Some are primarily idealistic. Some are primarily practical. One should, I believe, strive for a balance of both. But, since the subjects that can be covered in a single address are limited, tonight I shall discuss the war from a viewpoint which is primarily practical. It is not that I believe ideals are unimportant, even among the realities of war; but if a nation is to survive in a hostile world its ideals must be backed by the hard logic of military practicability. If the outcome of war depended upon ideals alone, this would be a different world than it is today.

I know I will be severely criticized by the interventionists in America when I say we should not enter a war unless we have a reasonable chance of winning. That, they will claim, is far too materialistic a viewpoint. They will advance again the same arguments that were used to persuade France to declare war against Germany in 1939. But I do not believe that our American ideals and our way of life will gain through an unsuccessful war. And I know that the United States is not prepared to wage war in Europe successfully at this time. We are no better prepared today than France was when the interventionists in Europe persuaded her to attack the Siegfried Line.

I have said before, and I will say again, that I believe it will be a tragedy to the entire world if the British empire collapses. That is one of the main reasons why I opposed this war before it was declared, and why I have constantly advocated a negotiated peace. I did not feel that England and France had a reasonable chance of winning. France has now been defeated and despite the propaganda and confusion of recent months it is now obvious that England is losing the war. I believe this is realized even by the British government. But they have one last desperate plan remaining. They hope that they may be able to persuade us to send another American Expeditionary Force to Europe and to share with England militarily, as well as financially, the fiasco of this war.

I do not blame England for this hope, or for asking for our assistance.

But we now know that she declared a war under circumstances which led to the defeat of every nation that sided with her from Poland to Greece. We know that in the desperation of war England promised to all these nations armed assistance that she could not send. We know that she misinformed them, as she has misinformed us, concerning her state of preparation, her military strength and the progress of the war.

In time of war, truth is always replaced by propaganda. I do not believe we should be too quick to criticize the actions of a belligerent nation. There is always the question whether we, ourselves, would do better under similar circumstances. But we in this country have a right to think of the welfare of America first, just as the people in England thought first of their own country when they encouraged the smaller nations of Europe to fight against hopeless odds. When England asks us to enter this war she is considering her own future and that of her empire. In making our reply, I believe we should consider the future of the United States and that of the Western Hemisphere.

It is not only our right, but it is our obligation as American citizens to look at this war objectively, and to weigh our chances for success if we should enter it. I have attempted to do this, especially from the standpoint of aviation, and I have been forced to the conclusion that we cannot win this war for England, regardless of how much assistance we extend.

I ask you to look at the map of Europe today and see if you can suggest any way in which we could win this war if we entered it. Suppose we had a large army in America, trained and equipped. Where would we send it to fight? The campaigns of the war show only too clearly how difficult it is to force a landing, or to maintain an army, on a hostile coast. Suppose we took our Navy from the Pacific and used it to convoy British shipping. That would not win the war for England. It would, at best, permit her to exist under the constant bombing of the German air fleet. Suppose we had an air force that we could send to Europe. Where could it operate? Some of our squadrons might be based in the British Isles, but it is physically impossible to base enough aircraft in the British Isles alone to equal in strength the aircraft that can be based on the continent of Europe.

I have asked these questions on the supposition that we had in existence an army and an air force large enough and well enough equipped to send to Europe; and that we would dare to remove our Navy from the Pacific. Even on the basis, I do not see how we could invade the continent of Europe successfully as long as all of that continent and most of Asia is under Axis domination. But the fact is that none of these suppositions are correct. We have only a one-ocean Navy. Our Army is still untrained and inadequately equipped for foreign war. Our air force is deplorably lacking in modern fighting planes because most of them have already been sent to Europe.

When these facts are cited, the interventionists shout that we are defeatists, that we are undermining the principles of democracy, and that we are giving comfort to Germany by talking about our military weakness. But every thing I mention here has been published in our newspapers, and in the reports of Congressional hearings in Washington. Our military position is well known to the governments of Europe and Asia. Why, then, should it not be brought to the attention of our own people?

I say it is the interventionist in America, as it was in England and in France, who gives comfort to the enemy. I say it is they who are undermining the principles of democracy when they demand that we take a course to which more than 80 per cent of our citizens are opposed. I charge them with being the real defeatists, for their policy has led to the defeat of every country that followed their advice since this war began. There is no better way to give comfort to an enemy than to divide the people of a nation over the issue of foreign war. There is no shorter road to defeat than by entering a war with inadequate preparation. Every nation that has adopted the interventionist policy of depending on some one else for its own defense has met with nothing but defeat and failure.

When history is written, the responsibility for the downfall of the democracies of Europe will rest squarely upon the shoulders of the interventionists who led their nations into war uninformed and unprepared. With their shouts of defeatism, and their disdain of reality, they have already sent countless thousands of young men to death in Europe. From the campaign of Poland to that of Greece, their prophecies have been false and their policies have failed. Yet these are the people who are calling us defeatists in America today. And they have led this country, too, to the verge of war.

There are many such interventionists in America, but there are more people among us of a different type. That is why you and I are assembled here tonight. There is a policy open to this nation that will lead to success—a policy that will leave us free to follow our own way of life, and to develop our own civilization. It is not a new and untried idea. It was advocated by Washington. It was incorporated in the Monroe Doctrine. Under its guidance, the United States became the greatest nation in the world. It is based upon the belief that the security of a nation lies in the strength and character of its own people. It recommends the maintenance of armed forces sufficient to defend this hemisphere from attack by any combination of foreign powers. It demands faith in an independent American destiny. This is a policy of the America First Committee today. It is a policy not of isolation, but of independence; not of defeat, but of courage. It is a policy that led this nation to success during the most trying years of our history, and it is a policy that will lead us to success again.

We have weakened ourselves for many months, and still worse, we have divided our own people by this dabbling in Europe's wars. While we should have been concentrating on American defense, we have been forced to argue over foreign quarrels. We must turn our eyes and our faith back to our own country before it is too late. And when we do this, a different vista opens before us. Practically every difficulty we would face in invading Europe becomes an asset to us in defending America. Our enemy, and not we, would then have the problem of transporting millions of troops across the ocean and landing them on a hostile shore. They, and not we, would have to furnish the convoys to transport guns and trucks and munitions and fuel across 3,000 miles of water. Our battleships and submarines would then be fighting close to their home bases. We would then do the bombing from the air, and the torpedoing at sea. And if any part of an enemy convoy should ever pass our Navy and air force, they would still be faced with the guns of our Coast Artillery, and behind them, the divisions of our Army.

The United States is better situated from a military standpoint than any other nation in the world. Even in our present condition of unpreparedness, no foreign power is in a position to invade us today. If we concentrate on our own defenses, and build the strength that this nation should maintain, no foreign army will ever attempt to land on American shores.

Was it not inevitable for this country? Such a claim is defeatism in the true sense. No one can make us fight abroad unless we ourselves are willing to do so. No one will attempt to fight us here if we arm ourselves as a great nation should be armed. Over 100,000,000 people in this nation are opposed to entering the war. If the principles of democracy mean anything at all, that is reason enough for us to stay out. If we are forced into a war against the wishes of an overwhelming majority of our people, we will have proved democracy such a failure at home that there will be little use fighting for it abroad.

The time has come when those of us who believe in an independent American destiny must band together and organize for strength. We have been led toward war by a minority of our people. This minority has power. It has influence. It has a loud voice. But it does not represent the American people. During the last several years I have traveled over this country, from one end to the other. I have talked to many hundreds of men and women, and I have had letters from tens of thousands more, who feel the same way as you and I.   These people—the majority of hard-working American citizens—are with us. They are the true strength of our country. And they are beginning to realize, as you and I, that there are times when we must sacrifice our normal interests in life in order to insure the safety and the welfare of our nation.

Such a time has come. Such a crisis is here. That is why the America First Committee has been formed—to give voice to the people who have no newspaper, or news reel, or radio station at their command; to the people who must do the paying and the fighting and the dying, if this country enters the war.

Whether or not we do enter the war rests upon the shoulders of you in this audience, upon us here on this platform, upon meetings of this kind that are being held by Americans in every section of the United States today. It depends upon the action we take and the courage we show at this time. If you believe in an independent destiny for America, if you believe that this country should not enter the war in Europe, we ask you to join the America First Committee in its stand. We ask you to share our faith in the ability of this nation to defend itself, to develop its own civilization, and to contribute to the progress of mankind in a more constructive and intelligent way than has yet been found by the warring nations of Europe. We need your support, and we need it now. The time to act is here.

Henry L. Stimson

[1867-1950]

Henry L. Stimson served as Secretary of War under President Taft and Secretary of State under President Hoover. In 1940 he became Secretary of War in the cabinet of President Franklin D. Roosevelt. Here are parts of a radio address which Mr. Stimson delivered on May 6, 1941.

A GRAVE SITUATION

THE PEOPLE of the United States have been greatly blessed by the geographical conditions of their homeland. Two broad oceans lie to the east and west of us, while north and south of us are only friendly nations of whose intentions and power we have no fear. Thus the instinct of our people in regard to their ocean defense is a sound instinct. There is great possibility of protection in the fact that we have the Atlantic Ocean between us and Europe, and the Pacific Ocean between us and Asia. So long as those oceans are under our own or of friendly control, their broad waters constitute an insuperable barrier to any armies which may be built up by would-be aggressor governments. But that condition of friendly control is imperative. If it should be lost, the oceans over night would become easy channels for the path of attack against us.

The development of modern air power greatly intensifies this necessity of friendly control of the oceans. It now makes it necessary for us to command not only the reaches of ocean adjacent to our own shores but the entire reach of the oceans surrounding the western continent; for, if hostile nations possessing powerful armies and air power can once make a landing on the shores of our weaker neighbor nations either north or south of us, our immunity is gone. It would then become a comparatively simple matter for them to establish air bases within striking distance of the great industrial cities which now fill our country. And the only way in which we could prevent this would be the intolerable method of ourselves maintaining armies large enough to command the areas of our continent for thousands of miles beyond our own borders. Such a condition would transform the good neighbor relations which now prevail throughout the American republics, into the same abhorrent system of forceful domination which we are seeking to keep out of the hemisphere. In short, to the nations of America, friendly control of the surrounding oceans is a condition of the reign of freedom and mutual independence which now prevails in that continent.

For over one hundred years the control of the Atlantic Ocean has been exercised by the British fleet. By the Washington Treaty of 1922 Great Britain voluntarily consented to parity between her fleet and ours and thus admitted us to an equal share in that control. The significant feature to us of this century-old condition has been that a country speaking our language, possessing our traditions of individual and legal freedom, and inhabited by a population from which considerably more than fifty per cent of our own population is descended, has been accepted by us as a dominant factor in the ocean defense upon which our safety and mode of life depend. During that century we have accommodated our whole method of life to that situation. We have maintained no large standing armies. We have built populous cities upon our seacoast which are easily vulnerable to attack from the Atlantic Ocean. We have in short adopted a mode of national life which is dependent upon the continuance of a sea power of which we ourselves feel in no apprehension.

Today that situation is gravely threatened. The British Isles, which have been a fortress against any despotic approach to our shores through the northern reaches of the Atlantic, are threatened both by attacks from the air and blockade from the sea. If their government should fall either from starvation or from attack, the British fleet, if it survived at all, would have no adequate base for its continued operations. If the British Isles should fall, all of the great shipyards of Britain would pass into the hands of the aggressor nations and their maritime shipbuilding capacity, thus augmented, would become six or seven times as large as our own. Under such conditions our own fleet would be quite unable to protect the western hemisphere from the overwhelming sea power which would then confront it. Even today its tonnage is exceeded by the combined tonnage of the Axis powers and, with the enormous preponderance in building capacity which they would then have, command of the entire seas surrounding us would in time inevitably pass into their hands.

The unrestricted submarine warfare which Germany is carrying on in the North Atlantic, sinking ships without warning and without the possibility of saving the lives of their crews, is not a legal blockade under the rules of marine warfare. It has never been recognized as lawful by the United States. America's spokesmen at international conferences have again and again condemned it as a form of piracy. It was expressly the violation of law and humanity involved in unrestricted submarine warfare which in 1917 caused the President and Congress to take up arms in defense of the freedom of the seas. Today Germany by these same illegal means is not only seeking to frighten our commerce and our vessels from the Atlantic; she has extended even into the western hemisphere a zone into which she has forbidden us to enter. Hitler has not only torn up all the rules of international law but he is expanding his lawless activities into our hemisphere.

Our government is acting with care and prudence. But our own self defense requires that limits should be put to lawless aggression on the ocean.

I am not one of those who think that the priceless freedom of our country can be saved without sacrifice. It can not. That has not been the way by which during millions of years humanity has slowly and painfully toiled upwards towards a better and more humane civilization.

The men who suffered at Valley Forge and won at Yorktown gave more than money to the cause of freedom.

Today a small group of evil leaders have taught the young men of Germany that the freedom of other men and nations must be destroyed. Today these young men are ready to die for that perverted conviction. Unless we on our side are ready to sacrifice and, if need be, die for the conviction that the freedom of America must be saved, it will not be saved. Only by a readiness for the same sacrifice can that freedom be preserved.

Harold L. Ickes

[1874-1952]

Harold L. Ickes, Secretary of the Interior under President Franklin D. Roosevelt, addressed the following to an "I am an American" Day meeting on Central Park Mall, New York, May 18, 1941.

WHAT CONSTITUTES AN AMERICAN

I WANT to ask a few simple questions. And then I shall answer them.

What has happened to our vaunted idealism? Why have some of us been behaving like scared chickens? Where is the million-throated, democratic voice of America?

For years it has been dinned into us that we are a weak nation; that we are an inefficient people; that we are simple-minded. For years we have been told that we are beaten, decayed, and that no part of the world belongs to us any longer.

Some amongst us have fallen for this carefully pickled tripe. Some amongst us have fallen for this calculated poison. Some amongst us have begun to preach that the "wave of the future" has passed over us and left us a wet, dead fish.

They shout—from public platforms, in printed pages, through the microphones—that it is futile to oppose the "wave of the future." They cry that we Americans, we free Americans nourished on Magna Carta and the Declaration of Independence, hold moth-eaten ideas. They exclaim that there is no room for free men in the world any more and that only the slaves will inherit the earth. America—the America of Washington and Jefferson and Lincoln and Walt Whitman—, they say, is waiting for the undertaker and all the hopes and aspirations that have gone into the making of America are dead too.

However, my fellow citizens, this is not the real point of the story. The real point—the shameful point—is that many of us are listening to them and some of us almost believe them.

I say that it is time for the great American people to raise its voice and cry out in mighty triumph what it is to be an American. And why it is that only Americans, with the aid of our brave allies—yes, let's call them "allies"—the British, can and will build the only future worth having. I mean a future, not of concentration camps, not of physical torture and mental straitjackets, not of sawdust bread or of sawdust Caesars—I mean a future when free men will live free lives in dignity and in security.

This tide of the future, the democratic future, is ours. It is ours if we show ourselves worthy of our culture and of our heritage.

But make no mistake about it; the tide of the democratic future is not like the ocean tide—regular, relentless, and inevitable. Nothing in human affairs is mechanical or inevitable. Nor are Americans mechanical. They are very human indeed.

What constitutes an American? Not color nor race nor religion. Not the pedigree of his family nor the place of his birth. Not the coincidence of his citizenship. Not his social status nor his bank account. Not his trade nor his profession. An American is one who loves justice and believes in the dignity of man. An American is one who will fight for his freedom and that of his neighbor. An American is one who will sacrifice property, ease and security in order that he and his children may retain the rights of free men. An American is one in whose heart is engraved the immortal second sentence of the Declaration of Independence.

Americans have always known how to fight for their rights and their way of life. Americans are not afraid to fight. They fight joyously in a just cause.

We Americans know that freedom, like peace, is indivisible. We cannot retain our liberty if three-fourths of the world is enslaved. Brutality, injustice and slavery, if practiced as dictators would have them, universally and systematically, in the long run would destroy us as surely as a fire raging in our nearby neighbor's house would burn ours if we didn't help to put out his.

If we are to retain our own freedom, we must do everything within our power to aid Britain. We must also do everything to restore to the conquered peoples their freedom. This means the Germans too.

Such a program, if you stop to think, is selfishness on our part. It is the sort of enlightened selfishness that makes the wheels of history go around. It is the sort of enlightened selfishness that wins victories.

Do you know why? Because we cannot live in the world alone, without friends and without allies. If Britain should be defeated, then the totalitarian undertaker will prepare to hang crepe on the door of our own independence.

Perhaps you wonder how this could come about? Perhaps you have heard "them"—the wavers of the future—cry, with calculated malice, that even if Britain were defeated we could live alone and defend ourselves single handed, even against the whole world.

I tell you that this is a cold blooded lie.

We would be alone in the world, facing an unscrupulous military-economic bloc that would dominate all of Europe, all of Africa, most of Asia, and perhaps even Russia and South America. Even to do that, we would have to spend most of our national income on tanks and guns and planes and ships. Nor would this be all. We would have to live perpetually as an armed camp, maintaining a huge standing army, a gigantic air force, two vast navies. And we could not do this without endangering our freedom, our democracy, our way of life.

Perhaps such is the America "they"—the wavers of the future—foresee. Perhaps such is the America that a certain aviator, with his contempt for democracy, would prefer. Perhaps such is the America that a certain Senator desires. Perhaps such is the America that a certain mail-order executive longs for.

But a perpetually militarized, isolated and impoverished America is not the America that our fathers came here to build.

It is not the America that has been the dream and the hope of countless generations in all parts of the world.

It is not the America that one hundred and thirty million of us would care to live in.

The continued security of our country demands that we aid the enslaved millions of Europe—yes, even of Germany—to win back their liberty and independence. I am convinced that if we do not embark upon such a program we will lose our own freedom.

We should be clear on this point. What is convulsing the world today is not merely another old-fashioned war. It is a counter revolution against our ideas and ideals, against our sense of justice and our human values.

Three systems today compete for world domination. Communism, fascism, and democracy are struggling for social-economic-political world control. As the conflict sharpens, it becomes clear that the other two, fascism and communism, are merging into one. They have one common enemy, democracy. They have one common goal, the destruction of democracy.

This is why this war is not an ordinary war. It is not a conflict for markets or territories. It is a desperate struggle for the possession of the souls of men.

This is why the British are not fighting for themselves alone. They are fighting to preserve freedom for mankind. For the moment, the battleground is the British Isles. But they are fighting our war; they are the first soldiers in trenches that are also our front-line trenches.

In this world war of ideas and of loyalties we believers in democracy must do two things. We must unite our forces to form one great democratic international. We must offer a clear program to freedom-loving peoples throughout the world.

Freedom-loving men and women in every land must organize and tighten their ranks. The masses everywhere must be helped to fight their oppressors and conquerors.

We, free, democratic Americans are in a position to help. We know that the spirit of freedom never dies. We know that men have fought and bled for freedom since time immemorial. We realize that the liberty-loving German people are only temporarily enslaved. We do not doubt that the Italian people are looking forward to the appearance of another Garibaldi. We know how the Poles have for centuries maintained a heroic resistance against tyranny. We remember the brave struggle of the Hungarians under Kossuth and other leaders. We recall the heroic figure of Masaryk and the gallant fight for freedom of the Czech people. The story of the Yugoslavs', especially the Serbs', blows for liberty and independence is a saga of extraordinary heroism. The Greeks will stand again at Thermopylae, as they have in the past. The annals of our American sister-republics, too, are glorious with freedom-inspiring exploits. The noble figure of Simon Bolivar, the great South American liberator, has naturally been compared with that of George Washington.

No, liberty never dies. The Genghis Khans come and go. The Attilas come and go. The Hitlers flash and sputter out. But freedom endures.

Destroy a whole generation of those who have known how to walk with heads erect in God's free air, and the next generation will rise against the oppressors and restore freedom. Today in Europe, the Nazi Attila may gloat that he has destroyed democracy. He is wrong. In small farmhouses all over Central Europe, in the shops of Germany and Italy, on the docks of Holland and Belgium, freedom still lives in the hearts of men. It will endure like a hardy tree gone into the wintertime, awaiting the spring.

And, like spring, spreading from the South into Scandinavia, the democratic revolution will come. And men with democratic hearts will experience comradeship across artificial boundaries.

These men and women, hundreds of millions of them, now in bondage or threatened with slavery, are our comrades and our allies. They are only waiting for our leadership and our encouragement, for the spark that we can supply.

These hundreds of millions of liberty-loving people, now oppressed, constitute the greatest sixth column in history. They have the will to destroy the Nazi gangsters.

We have always helped in struggles for human freedom. And we will help again. But our hundreds of millions of liberty-loving allies would despair if we did not provide aid and encouragement. The quicker we help them the sooner this dreadful revolution will be over. We cannot, we must not, we dare not delay much longer.

The fight for Britain is in its crucial stages. We must give the British *everything* we have. And by everything, I mean everything needed to beat the life out of our common enemy.

The second step must be to aid and encourage our friends and allies *everywhere*. And by everywhere I mean Europe and Asia and Africa and America.

And finally, the most important of all, we Americans must gird spiritually for the battle. We must dispel the fog of uncertainty and vacillation. We must greet with raucous laughter the corroding arguments of our appeasers and fascists. They doubt democracy. We affirm it triumphantly so that all the world may hear:

Here in America we have something so worth living for that it is worth dying for! The so-called "wave of the future" is but the slimy backwash of the past. We have not heaved from our necks the tyrant's crushing heel, only to stretch our necks out again for its weight. Not only will we fight for democracy, we will make it more worth fighting for. Under our free institutions, we will work for the good of mankind, including Hitler's victims in Germany, so that all may have plenty and security.

We American democrats know that when good will prevails among men there will be a world of plenty and a world of security.

In the words of Winston Churchill, "Are we downhearted? ' No, we are not! But someone is downhearted! Witness the terrified flight of Hess, Hitler's Number Three Man. And listen to this—listen carefully:

"The British nation can be counted upon to carry through to victory any struggle that it once enters upon no matter how long such a struggle may last or however great the sacrifices that may be necessary or whatever the means that have to be employed; and all this even though the actual military equipment at hand may be utterly inadequate when compared with that of other nations."

Do you know who wrote that? Adolf Hitler in *Mein Kampf*. And do you know who took down that dictation? Rudolf Hess.

We will help to make Hitler's prophecy come true. We will help brave England drive back the hordes from Hell who besiege her and then we will join for the destruction of savage and blood-thirsty dictators everywhere. But we must be firm and decisive. We must know our will and make it felt. And we must hurry.

Frank Knox

[1874–1944]

Frank Knox was the Republican Vice-Presidential candidate in 1936. He entered the cabinet of President Franklin D. Roosevelt in 1940, becoming Secretary of the Navy. Here are parts of an address he delivered before the convention of the American Legion in Milwaukee on September 15, 1941.

WE MUST FIGHT FOR OUR LIBERTIES

WE NOW know how futile it is to place our trust in written promises to forsake war as an instrument of national policy. Promises to keep the peace are just so much worthless paper to be scrapped when some ruthless, acquisitive leaders of greedy and warlike people feel so disposed.

The only peace in which the world can put any confidence, for at least one hundred years to come, is the kind of peace that can be enforced by the peace-loving nations of the world. It will not be sufficient just to love peace if these nations are to support the cause of peace effectively.

It is imperatively necessary to have not only the will to peace but the power to enforce it!

In such a world as that of today, sea power for America is more vital, more essential, than ever before in its history. We are on the way to achieve that power! We shall soon have the fleet that will make us the greatest maritime power the world has ever known, and we have the materials, the skills and the capacity to maintain that leadership indefinitely!

This will only be achieved, however, if the American people learn, in these crucial years, how needful for their own security and welfare is sea power, and if they determine out of a love for peace, not for war, to maintain that sea power in the years that lie ahead.

We hear a great deal these days concerning the attitude of the American people toward war. There has never been any secret nor any division in this matter. The American people are not war-like. They are peace-minded. They have no national objectives, or policies, which must be promoted by war.

In any choice between war and peace, all but a lunatic few would, of course, vote for peace. It is utterly foolish to talk about a plebiscite on war. It is never true that a people may choose between peace and war, unless they are satisfied with a peace on terms dictated by an aggression.

If we want an honest test of sentiment and really desire to know the mind of the American people with respect to their own defense, and the defense of their rights, the questions we should ask them in the light of the present war situation might be broached in this fashion:

Do you want to lose your liberties?

Do you want security for your family and for your property?

Are the vital interests of this country in peril?

If your liberties are in danger, if your family and its security are in peril, if the vital interests of the United States are threatened, will you surrender them or will you fight for them?

If you put the question that way, and that is the way it is being put, what percentage of the American people, think you, would answer negatively?

The answer would be in an affirmative that would shock the confidence even of a dictator like Hitler. You could expect no other answer from Americans. If the time ever comes when such a question is not answered affirmatively, if under such circumstances the American people do not oppose war, rather than surrender, then this country of ours would cease to be the country we have always known and will become a land occupied by cowardly vassals, abject subjects of a more virile race of men.

You cannot preserve liberties such as we enjoy, save by willingness to fight for them if need be.

A worthy, righteous peace is the fruit of effort. You don't get peace, you don't retain peace just by being peaceable. You get it, if it is worth having, by a constant willingness to work and sacrifice and risk for it.

You have it now. The people in the United States have it now because other men of other generations have been willing, when necessary, to fight for the conditions that make peace possible. If you think by just keeping peaceable and never going to war that you can get a just peace in this world, you are wrong.

That is the one way in which to surely lose peace.

The currency with which you pay for peace is made up of manly courage, fearless virility, readiness to serve justice and honor at any cost, and a mind and a heart attuned to sacrifice.

A peace temporarily enjoyed by a people without these qualities is but a prelude to certain disaster. That nation that regards the avoidance of war as the highest good regardless of the price exacted for peace in its honor, its rights, its vital interests, is a nation both wretched and contemptible and cannot long endure.

This does not mean that we must not exhaust every honorable means to foster and promote peace, but we must be sure that we seek and enjoy a righteous peace, for those who put peace before righteousness, and justice, and liberty do infinite harm and always fail of their purpose ultimately.

We must also remember that it is only the strong who can promote and preserve a righteous peace. When war threatens and human liberties are at stake, when attempts at world-wide dominion are to the fore, we must be sure that the world understands that we do not withhold our hand through weakness or timidity.

Idle and futile is the voice of the weak nation, or the craven nation, when it clamors for peace.

At this point I should like to quote from a former President, Theodore Roosevelt, who, like Franklin D. Roosevelt, was a courageous, virile champion of just and righteous peace, and a foe of those who put peace before righteousness. Theodore Roosevelt once said:

"Peace is a great good, and doubly harmful, therefore, is the attitude of those who advocate it in terms that would make it synonymous with selfish and cowardly shrinking from warring against the existence of evil. The wisest and most far-seeing champions of peace will ever remember that, in the first place, to be good it must be righteous, for an unrighteous and cowardly peace may be worse than any war; and in the second place, that it can often be obtained only at the cost of war."

A powerful national defense, especially on the high seas, is a prerequisite of a peace-promoting, justice-loving America. During the last half dozen years it has been clear to almost any man that a powerful fleet and a powerful air force, neither of which can be extemporized, are vital essentials to our national security in a time of great world turbulence.

Fulton J. Sheen

[1895–1979]

The Reverend Fulton J. Sheen, Auxiliary Bishop of New York, at the time that he was associated with the Catholic University of America, spoke on the radio program, the Catholic Hour. Parts of an address delivered on that program, April 6, 1941, are reproduced here.

THE CROSS AND THE DOUBLE CROSS

THERE is no such thing as living without a cross. We are free only to choose between crosses. Will it be the Cross of Christ which redeems us from our sins, or will it be the Double Cross, the Swastika, the hammer and sickle, the fasces?

Why are we a troubled nation today? Why do we live in fear—we who define freedom as the right to do whatever we pleased; we who have no altars in our churches, no discipline in our schools, and no sacrifices in our lives? We fear because our false freedom and license and apostasy from God have caught up with us, as they did with the Prodigal. We would not accept the yoke of Christ; so now we must tremble at the yoke of Caesar. We willed to be free from God; now we must face the danger of being enslaved to a citizen of the foreign country. In seeking to live without the Cross, we got a cross—not one of Christ's making or our own, but the devil's!

The basic spirit of the modern world for the last century has been a determination to escape the Cross. But has the world escaped Calvary? What did Finland, Estonia, Latvia, Poland, China, Czecho-Slovakia, Albania, Austria, France and other nations get within the past two years but a cross? What is England fearing today but a cross? What do we fear today, but a cross? What does the world fear, but a diabolically cruel, tortured cross made of guns, hammers, sickles, and bombs—the thing that started out to be a cross and then double-crossed itself because it has double-crossed the world?

And that threat throws us into a terrific dilemma. Can we meet that double cross without the Cross? Can a democracy of ease and comfort overcome a system built on sacrifices? Can a nation which permits the break-up of the family by divorce, defeat a nation which forcefully bends the family to the nation? Can they, who for seven years tightened their belts, gave up butter for guns, endured every conceivable limitation, be conquered by ease and comfort? Dr. Alexis Carrel was right in saying that in America: "A good time has been our national cry. The perfect life as viewed by the average youth or adult is a round of ease or entertainment; of motion pictures, radio programs, parties, alcohol, and sexual excesses. This indolent and undisciplined way of life has sapped our individual vigor and imperilled our democratic form of government. Our race pitifully needs new supplies of discipline, morality and intelligence."

The rise of militarism and the Gospel of Force in the modern world is a result of the vacuum created by the abandonment of the Cross. Europe was nourished on Christian virtues; it knew obedience to authority, self-discipline, penance, and the need of redemption. But when it began to starve through the abandonment of the Bread of the Father's House, it seized, like the Prodigal, on the fodder of militarism and the glorification of fame. Like the empty house of the Gospel, the modern world swept itself clean of the Cross of Christ, but only to be possessed by the devils of the double cross. As Voltaire said: "If man had no God, he would make himself one!" So too, we might add, if man had no Cross, he would make himself one. And he has. Apostate from Calvary, the glorification of military virtues in these states is the feeble compensation for a yoke that is sweet and a burden that is light. As Mussolini said on August 24, 1934, "We are becoming a warlike nation—that is to say, one endowed to a higher degree with virtues of obedience, sacrifice, and dedication to country." This so-called heroic attitude toward life is being invoked in deadly earnest by millions in Germany and Russia, and by all who espouse their cause in other nations. In the days when the Cross lived in the hearts of men, war was considered a calamity, a scourge sent by God; but now in the days of the double cross, it is justified as the noblest of virtues for the sake of the nation as in Italy, the race as in Germany, and the class as in Russia. They believe what Van Moltke wrote in 1880: "Without War the world would become swamped in materialism." Imagine! To save us from materialism, we must have war! He is right in saying that to save us from materialism we must have sacrifice. He is wrong in saying it must come from war. But if there is no Cross to inspire it, whence shall it come but from the double cross?

We in America are now faced with the threat of that double cross. To revert to our theme. Our choice is not: Will we or will we not have more discipline, more respect for law, more order, more sacrifice; but, where will we get it? Will we get it from without, or from within, Will it be inspired by Sparta or Calvary? By Valhalla or Gethsemane? By Militarism or Religion?- By the double cross or the Cross? By Caesar or by God?

That is the choice facing America today. The hour of false freedom is past. No longer can we have education without discipline, family life without sacrifice, individual existence without moral responsibility, economics and politics without subservience to the common good. We are now only free to say whence it shall come. We will have a sword. Shall it be only the sword that thrusts outward to cut off the ears of our enemies, or the sword that pierces inward to cut out our own selfish pride? May heaven grant that, unlike the centurion, we pierce not the heart of Christ before we discover His Divinity and Salvation.

Away with those educators and propagandists who, by telling us we need no Cross, make possible having one forged for us abroad. Away with those who, as we gird ourselves for sacrifice based on love of God and Calvary, sneer: "Come down from the Cross" (*Matthew* 27:40).

That cry has been uttered before on Calvary, as His enemies shouted: "He saved others, himself he cannot save" (*Mark* 15:31). They were now willing to admit he had saved others; they could well afford to do it for now He apparently could not save Himself.

Of course, He could not save Himself. No man can save himself who saves another. The rain cannot save itself, if it is to bud the greenery; the sun cannot save itself if it is to light the world; the seed cannot save itself if it is to make the harvest; a mother cannot save herself if she is to save her child; a soldier cannot save himself if he is to save his country. It was not weakness which made Christ hang on the Cross; it was obedience to the law of sacrifice, of love. For how could He save us if He ever saved Himself? Peace He craved; but as St. Paul says, there is no peace but through the blood of the Cross. Peace we want; but there is none apart from sacrifice. Peace is not a passive, but an active virtue. Our Lord never said: "Blessed are the peaceful," but "Blessed are the Peacemakers." The Beatitude rests only on those who *make it* out of trial, out of suffering, out of cruelty, even out of sin. God hates peace in those who are destined for war. And we are destined for war—a war against a false freedom which endangered our freedom; a war for the Cross against the double cross; a war to make America once more what it was intended to be from the beginning—a country dedicated to liberty under God; a war of the *militia Christi:* "Having our loins girt about with truth and having on the breastplate of justice . . . the shield of faith . . . the helmet of salvation (*Ephesians* 6:10–17). For only those who carry the Sword of the Spirit have the right and have the power to say to the enemies of the Cross, "Put thy sword back into its scabbard."

The great tragedy is that the torch of sacrifice and truth has been snatched from the hands of those who should hold it, and is borne aloft by the enemies of the Cross. The Pentecostal fires have been stolen from the altar of God and now burn as tongues of fire in those who grind the altars into dust. The fearlessness born of love of God which once challenged the armies of Caesar is now espoused to Caesar. We live in an age of saints in reverse, when apostles who are breathed on by the evil spirit outdare those animated by the Holy Spirit of God. The fires for causes like Communism, Nazism, and Fascism, that burn downwards, are more intense than the fires that burn upwards in the hearts of those who pay only lip service to God. But this passion by which men deliver themselves over to half-truths and idiocies should make us realize what a force would enter history again if there were but a few saints in every nation who could help the world, because they were not enmeshed in it; who would, like their Master on the Cross, not seek to save the world as it is, but to be saved from it; who would demonstrate to those who still have decent hearts, as we believe we have in America, that it is possible to practice sacrifice without turning the world into a vast slaughterhouse. There is no escaping the Cross!

That is why the hope, the real hope of the world, is not in those politicians who, indifferent to Divinity, offer Christ and Barabbas to the mob to save their tumbling suffrage. It is not in those economists who would drive Christ from their shores like the Gerasenes, because they feared loss of profit on their swine. It is not in those educators who, like other Pilates, sneer: "What is Truth"—then Crucify it. The hope of the world is in the crucified in every land; in those bearing the Cross of Christ; in the mothers of Poland who, like other Rachels, mourn for their children; in the wives weeping for their husbands stolen into the servitude of war; in the sons and daughters kissing the cold earth of Siberia as the only one of the things God made that they are left to see; in bleeding feet and toil-worn hands; in persecuted Jews, blood-brothers of Christ, of whom God said: "He who curses you, I shall curse"; in the priests in concentration camps who, like Christ, in other Gethsemanes, find a way to offer their own blood in the chalice of their own body.

The hope of the world is in the Cross of Christ borne down the ages in the hearts of suffering men, women, and children, who, if we only knew it, are saving us from the double cross more than our guns and ships.

We in America are now brought face to face with the heritage of a freedom derived from God. The hour has struck when we have to take up a Cross. There is no escaping the Cross. Who shall give it to us? Shall it be imposed by chastisement, or shall it be freely accepted by penance? I believe in America's power of regeneration. I believe we can remake ourselves from within in order that we be not remade from without. I believe in the future of America; but I believe in it only as I believe in Easter—after it has passed through Good Friday.

Dorothy Thompson
[1894–1961]

Following are parts of an address delivered by Dorothy Thompson, American journalist and author, before a convention of the International Affiliation of Sales and Advertising Clubs at Toronto, Canada, on May 2, 1941.

HITLER'S PLANS FOR CANADA AND THE UNITED STATES

EVERY NATION on this globe and every individual on this globe will presently learn what a few have always known: that there are times in history when the business of one is the business of all, when life or death is a matter of choice, and when no one alive can avoid making that choice. These times occur seldom in history, these times of inevitable decisions. But this is one of those times.

Before this epoch is over, every living human being will have chosen, every living human being will have lined up with Hitler or against him, every living human being will either have opposed this onslaught or supported it. For if he tries to make no choice that in itself will be a choice. If he takes no side, he is on Hitler's side; if he does not act that is an act—for Hitler.

The Japan Times Advertiser, which is a controlled organ of the Japanese Foreign Office, has set them forth. They have appeared along with the suggestion that Mr. Matsuoka come to America and induce President Roosevelt to join Japan in an attempt to mediate the war. The proposed terms affect Canada, no less than any other part of the British Empire, and affect us as intimately as though we were already an active belligerent. They reveal with complete clarity what is in the minds of the Axis powers. They reveal what they consider to be the New Order of a Thousand Years.

Let us take a look at them; let us see what is the price for peace.

The British Empire and Commonwealth will be utterly destroyed. India and South Africa are to be given independence. I leave out of account the fact that South Africa already has independence. She is to be made more independent by depriving her of the protection of the rest of the English-speaking world. She is to be made independent, as Slovakia was made independent in order to compel her dependence, her total dependence upon the Axis powers.

Thus also the freedom of India. She is to be made free between the nut-cracker of Russia and Japan. Australia is to be opened to Japanese emigration. She would be colonized by the Japanese, and being colonized, claimed as an integral part of the Japanese Empire.

All Western and all Eastern bases of the British Empire—Gibraltar, Malta, Aden, the Red Sea, Singapore, Hong Kong—are to be demilitarized in a world bristling with Axis weapons. The Dutch East Indies and French Indo-China are to be liberated from oppressive rule and put under Japanese economic control.

The seat of authority of the British Empire is to remain, for the time being, on the British Isles. But these islands will be able to exercise no authority over themselves or over any part of the world. For across from them will be the mightiest, consolidated, regimented and enslaved block of human beings ever gathered together under one despot in the history of the human race.

Nazi Germany is to organize the entire continent as one corporate State, with its capital in Berlin. This means that nationality in Europe, except for minor matters of local administration, is to be abolished. The whole of Western Europe is to be organized as a huge vertical trust, in which the executives, directors, and majority stockholders will be the German Nazi Party.

The Japanese peace terms, of course, do not say this, but that is what a corporate State is, and that is what the German procedure in Holland, Norway, and France, in Poland and Czecho-Slovakia already show the plan to be. And to this corporation is to be attached the whole of Africa.

This means the end of the British Isles.

Canada may say to herself, "Thank God we are in North America." But under the terms of the Axis plan, though we seek to fly to the uttermost part of the earth, behold they are there! Some of my fellow-countrymen still think this is just another European war, but the trouble is that Hitler and Matsuoka happen to disagree with them. We are not yet in the war, but we are included in the peace.

The seat of authority of the British Empire is gradually to be transferred to Canada. There will be no British Empire, according to the peace terms; and what this means, my friends, is that the British Isles are going to be evacuated. Over a year ago I received the information that this was Hitler's plan for Britain. He intends to remove from those islands as he has removed from Poland all those persons who, whether by virtue of superior intelligence, or popular leadership, or executive ability, or ardent patriotism are capable of keeping alive in masses of people of the memory of a great past and the hope of a future.

He intends to reduce the population of those isles, first to reduce the leadership, then to reduce the actual numbers and send them to Canada. What happened to the Jews, and then happened to the Czechs and the Poles, is proposed for the English, the greatest Diaspora in the human history.

Canada and the United States are to cease building more ships. In the Japanese peace terms, the Anglo-American navy is treated as one. There are still people in my country who do not wish to keep it as one, but Hitler and Matsuoka are already doing so. We are to agree to build no more naval vessels until the Axis powers have caught up with us in the one field in which we are superior. After that we shall have a naval holiday—provided we behave ourselves. We people of the United States are to relinquish all naval bases west of Hawaii and to reduce that stronghold in importance. That means that we are to have naval parity and no bases from which to operate our vessels except our own ports.

The United States are to agree not to form a hegemony in South America and to accord the fullest freedom of equality and opportunity to Germany and her allies in that continental brotherhood. I pass over the fact that we have never had a hegemony over Latin America nor ever desired one, that we have never claimed over South America an exclusive sphere of influence. The so-called peace terms mean that from Cape Horn to the Panama Canal we are freely to permit the economic, political, propaganda and military penetration of the Axis powers and that to oppose will constitute a breach of the peace.

You men and women of Canada are tied up inescapably in the destiny first of the British Empire and, should that fail, in the destiny of the United States. And the destiny of one is the destiny of the other. It is no longer a question of our will. We, who did not early enough make the choice for ourselves, have now had it made for us.

Should Britain fall, all that is left of it would be penned up together with the United States on the North American continent, completely encircled and utterly powerless to take an offensive. East and west, north and south, occupying all the strategic bases in the Atlantic and the Pacific commanding all the rest of the economic power of the globe, directing the lives of over two billion men and women of all races and colors, would be two master-races: the German and the Japanese. This is not what I say, this is what Mr. Matsuoka says.

In this world people get what they passionately desire, and woe unto them if they desire the wrong thing. If we desire isolation, we shall have it—the isolation of a prison camp in a hostile community. We shall be penned up on this Continent, while hostile nations east of us, and west of us, and north of us, and south of us, do their level best, their vicious scheming, organized, subsidized, ruthless best to destroy us from inside; to set Canadians against the people of the States; to set labor against capital and capital against labor; the masses against the intelligentsia, and the intelligentsia against the masses; the Irish against the English; the Catholics against the Protestants, the Negroes against the whites, the whites against the Negroes, and everybody against the Jews, in order that the war which we sought to avoid elsewhere may occur here in an internecine fight, the running amok and berserk of an imprisoned colony.

This is their plan. This has always been their plan, to stir nationality against nationality, race against race, class against class, creed against creed, that their mutual destruction of each other may work out for the glory of Hitler and the grandeur of Japan. They count on our freedom— our individual freedom, our individual interests, our individual pursuit of pleasure and happiness—as the means of our destruction of ourselves.

And good men, honest men, unwitting men, work together with the frustrated, the fanatic, the sick, the bitter, the cowardly, the corrupt, the greedy, the selfish, for the end that this civilization may perish from this earth. And democracy and freedom face the bitterest of all tests. It is not the test of arms, it is truly the test of whether they are worthy to survive.

Henry A. Wallace
[1888–1965]

Henry A. Wallace was Vice-President of the United States from 1941 to 1945 and presidential candidate in 1948. Following are parts of an address delivered to the Foreign Policy Association, New York, April 8, 1941.

AMERICA'S SECOND CHANCE

THE UNITED STATES now has her second opportunity to make the world safe for democracy. During World War No. 1 and the fifteen years which followed, our intentions were of the highest, but our judgment was not good. From the depths of our hearts we responded to the idealism of Woodrow Wilson. Our boys enlisted to save the democracy of Western Europe and the New World from encroachment by the imperialism of a militaristic Prussia. Our boys thought they knew what they were fighting for. That is why they fought so well.

In World War No. 1 we fought well, believed profoundly and produced tremendously. Aside from that, our record was not so good. When the peace came we refused to accept responsibility for the world we had helped to create. We turned our back on Europe and said we were isolationists. During the war, prices, taxes and wages had doubled. When the war ended, consumers wanted lower prices, employers wanted lower wages, and everybody wanted lower taxes. Therefore, everyone talked about getting back to normalcy.

The desire of the American millions for normalcy and for isolation caused our people to refuse to accept the world responsibility which had been brought to them by World War No. 1. The United States of the 1920's thought that we, a creditor nation, could create prosperity by exporting more goods than we imported. Laboring under that illusion, we raised our tariff in 1922 and again in 1930. The destructive effect of these high tariffs on our exports did not come home to us until we stopped loaning money to foreign countries. We learned by hard experience that a creditor nation which cultivates a high-tariff policy and an isolationist psychology is certain to bring disaster on itself and the rest of the world as well. Yes, after World War No. 1 we were offered responsibility but instead of accepting it we gave to the world high tariffs and isolation. We thought by employing high tariffs and isolation we could protect ourselves and avoid the responsibility which our creditor position, our geographical situation, our vast natural resources and our trained population have so clearly marked out for us at this stage of world history.

Those who preached isolation and normalcy were skilled in their political insight. They appealed successfully to the blind prejudices of the people who were disillusioned when the war excitement stopped, when taxes went higher and prices fell and unemployment increased. The people were hungry for isolation, high tariffs and normalcy—the very things which would make our problem worse. Looking backward, we can afford to be charitable toward the isolationists and high-tariff men of the nineteen twenties but we cannot feel so kindly toward those mistaken men as to encourage others in the future to repeat their mistakes.

As we have pondered on the lessons of World War No. 1, our desire to remain at peace has increased. But at the same time, our study of the aggressor nations has led us to realize that the greatest likelihood of remaining at peace is to make these ruthless, treaty-breaking nations understand that the American people are ready to go to war if their rights are transgressed at any vital point. It is one of the rights of the American people to defend democracy by helping the nations resisting aggression to the limit with planes, ships, munitions, and food.

A second right of the American people is to defend the multi-lateral revision of the Monroe Doctrine as defined at the Havana Conference. Bismarck called the Monroe Doctrine an impudence and the Nazis use stronger language. The Germans look on Latin America as their eventual happy hunting ground, and, therefore, we may be sure that as soon as they have the power they will so push us around politically and economically as to force us into war.

Properly equipped with a Bill of Duties, the United States can shoulder her responsibility to the world in the peace that is to come. Without such a Bill of Duties, I fear peace will mean world chaos. With such a Bill we can help build a Pax Democratica which will bless us and the whole world for a century to come.

We can not, once the present menace is overcome, trust again to the blind forces of chance, to the oceans that have shrunk, to wishful thinking and illusions based on a false reading of history to escape our responsibility.

Norman Thomas
[1884–1970]

Norman Thomas, leader and Presidential candidate of the Socialist party for many years, delivered a radio address on June 29, 1941, parts of which follow.

AMERICA AND THE WAR

I INSIST that if once we let ourselves be plunged into this war, our liberties will be gone. The same oceans which are so mighty a barrier for our own defense will prove an insuperable obstacle to our conquest of distant continents by any price we can afford to pay. The probable cost of this war in the lives of our sons staggers the imagination. Its cost in money means bankruptcy something close to a subsistence level of life during the war, and a post-war economic crisis besides which 1932 will be remembered as a year of prosperity. To make the people maintain so insensate a conflict, propaganda, censorship, and conscription, raised to the highest degree, will become necessary. Every bitterness of division among us will be increased. The last chance for the orderly development of a nobler democracy on the face of the earth will have gone. It will not come again with the signing of some sort of peace. Instead there will be a bitter and confused reaction; dictatorship, either of the government in office or some stronger, more demagogic rival, will appear the only alternative to chaos. The idealists who will have helped put us into another war for democracy or the survivors among them will live to see democracy slain in America by the war they sought.

No sincerity of their intentions can alter this fact, for it is not they who will rule the storms of war. War has its own logic, which is the logic of despotism, of the complete subordination of the individual and of groups of individuals, farmers and workers, to the needs and the will of the military state.

Even today the sincere idealists are a small minority among the war makers. Far more powerful are the banking and other business interests who hold the opinion so often voiced by Wendell Willkie that in some mysterious way another military victory by the British Empire, with our aid, in a world caught in the throes of revolution as well as war, will save the old system of private capitalism, the old gold standard, and the types of international trade. Still worse are the imperialists like Henry Luce, Dorothy Thompson in some of her moods, and the extraordinary Senator Pepper, who preach the glories of American imperialism as if that were the American destiny, and bid us grow great by joining the British in exploiting in the name of God and our own profit, the wretched poverty of the natives of Asia and Africa. Nothing alarms me more than the growth of imperialism in the last few months in America.

I have said that the most powerful of the men and forces making for war are capitalist and imperialist. The historian of the future may well record that war came to America because an economic system which could not expand to meet human needs turned like a moth to the flame —and as fatally—to the expansion of armament economics and war.

But the most numerous of the war makers are neither idealists on the one hand, nor supporters of capitalism on the other. They are plain people who are being panicked into war by the propaganda of hysteria. They are told that because we cannot defend Omaha from bombers traveling from Berlin by way of Africa, Brazil, Yucatan and the Mississippi valley tomorrow—which is false—they must seize Dakar today. Which is insane.

They are told that American economy on this great continent with neighbors whom we can draw to us with ties of friendly cooperation cannot be democratic, humane or successful if a dictator temporarily achieves power over Europe. If this is true it is only because American economy and American idealism are already defeated.

I believe in world trade. I believe that Americans may be wise enough to enjoy some world trade on fairly decent terms despite the dictators of Europe and Asia. But I do not believe in world war to save a world trade that normally runs only to 5, 6, or 7 percent of our total business. We can, if we will, on this continent, with the cooperation of friendly nations on this hemisphere, conquer poverty for our people, whatever the temporary fate of Europe. But only if we will keep out of war.

I do not say this because I am indifferent to Europe's fate. I would go far to cooperate with the whole world to make peace more lasting and glorious. Only recently I have denounced the Administration for imposing new, shocking, and unnecessary restrictions on our already limited offer of asylum to the victims of war and fascism in Europe.

I am not affirming that we can ignore the dangers of the world in which we live, or that a Hitler victory far more complete than he has yet won will not add to those dangers. I am denouncing the hysteria which grossly exaggerates those dangers and even more dangerously minimizes the perils of our involvement in war. I am insisting that a determined America which will keep its sons out of war, can, if it will, make its own democracy work, and by the contagion of its example in a world where alleged democracy has failed, do far more for mankind than by involving itself in a war for which neither Churchill nor Roosevelt has dared to state specific aims.

America's noblest destiny is not empire. It is to demonstrate the possibility of conquering poverty and keeping freedom in a land at peace. We have better work for our sons to do than to have them die to see which of two cruel and treacherous dictators shall master the European continent or what empire shall rob the peoples of Africa, Asia and the islands of the sea.

I am against our participation in this war not only because I hate war, but because I hate fascism and all totalitarianism, and love democracy. I speak not only for myself, but for my Party in summoning my fellow countrymen to demand that our country be kept out of war, not as an end in itself, but as a condition to the fulfillment of all our hopes and dreams for a better life for ourselves and our children, yes, and all the children of this great land. The extraordinary shifts and changes in European alliances should but confirm our resolution to stay out of Europe's war, and, ourselves at peace, to seek as occasion permits, the peace of the world.

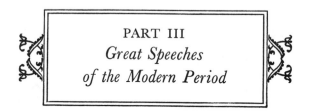

PART III
*Great Speeches
of the Modern Period*

X. UNITED STATES GOVERNMENT

Bernard Mannes Baruch

[1870–1965]

Bernard M. Baruch, American elder statesman, was a valued adviser to presidents from Wilson to Eisenhower. In 1946 and 1947, he was United States representative to the United Nations Atomic Energy Commission, and the American program at that time for the control of atomic weapons came to be called the "Baruch plan." The plan was enthusiastically received, but later became subject to much debate. Following are portions of Mr. Baruch's speech at the opening session of the Atomic Energy Commission of the United Nations, in New York City, on June 14, 1946.

CONTROL OF ATOMIC WEAPONS

We ARE HERE to make a choice between the quick and the dead.

That is our business.

Behind the black portent of the new atomic age lies a hope which, seized upon with faith, can work our salvation. If we fail, then we have damned every man to be the slave of fear. Let us not deceive ourselves: We must elect world peace or world destruction.

Science has torn from nature a secret so vast in its potentialities that our minds cower from the terror it creates. Yet terror is not enough to inhibit the use of the atomic bomb. The terror created by weapons has never stopped man from employing them. For each new weapon a defense has been produced, in time. But now we face a condition in which adequate defense does not exist.

Science, which gave us this dread power, shows that it can be made a giant help to humanity, but science does not show us how to prevent its baleful use. So we have been appointed to obviate that peril by finding a meeting of the minds and the hearts of our peoples. Only in the will of mankind lies the answer.

In this crisis we represent not only our governments but, in a larger way, we represent the peoples of the world. We must remember that the peoples do not belong to the governments, but that the governments belong to the peoples. We must answer their demands; we must answer the world's longing for peace and security.

In that desire the United States shares ardently and hopefully. The search of science for the absolute weapon has reached fruition in this country. But

587

she stands ready to proscribe and destroy this instrument—to lift its use from death to life—if the world will join in a pact to that end.

In our success lies the promise of a new life, freed from the heart-stopping fears that now beset the world. The beginning of victory for the great ideals for which millions have bled and died lies in building a workable plan. Now we approach the fulfillment of the aspirations of mankind. At the end of the road lies the fairer, better, surer life we crave and mean to have.

Only by a lasting peace are liberties and democracies strengthened and deepened. War is their enemy. And it will not do to believe that any of us can escape war's devastation. Victor, vanquished and neutrals alike are affected physically, economically and morally.

Against the degradation of war we can erect a safeguard. That is the guerdon for which we reach. Within the scope of the formula we outline here, there will be found, to those who seek it, the essential elements of our purpose. Others will see only emptiness. Each of us carries his own mirror in which is reflected hope—or determined desperation—courage or cowardice.

There is famine throughout the world today. It starves men's bodies. But there is a greater famine—the hunger of men's spirit. That starvation can be cured by the conquest of fear, and the substitution of hope, from which springs faith—faith in each other; faith that we want to work together toward salvation; and determination that those who threaten the peace and safety shall be punished.

The peoples of these democracies gathered here have a particular concern with our answer, for their peoples hate war. They will have a heavy exaction to make of those who fail to provide an escape. They are not afraid of an internationalism that protects; they are unwilling to be fobbed off by mouthings about narrow sovereignty, which is today's phrase for yesterday's isolationism.

The basis of a sound foreign policy, in this new age, for all the nations here gathered, is that: anything that happens, no matter where or how, which menaces the peace of the world, or the economic stability, concerns each and all of us.

That, roughly, may be said to be the central theme of the United Nations. It is with that thought we gain consideration of the most important subject than can engage mankind—life itself.

Now, if ever, is the time to act for the common good. Public opinion supports a world movement toward security. If I read the signs aright, the peoples want a program, not composed merely of pious thoughts, but of enforceable sanctions—an international law with teeth in it.

We of this nation, desirous of helping to bring peace to the world and realizing the heavy obligations upon us, arising from our possession of the means for producing the bomb and from the fact that it is part of our armament, are prepared to make our full contribution toward effective control of atomic energy.

But before a country is ready to relinquish any winning weapons, it must have more than words to reassure it. It must have a guarantee of safety, not only against the offenders in the atomic area, but against the illegal users of other weapons—bacteriological, biological, gas—perhaps—why not?—against war itself.

In the elimination of war lies our solution, for only then will nations cease to compete with one another in the production and use of dread "secret" weapons which are evaluated solely by their capacity to kill. This devilish program takes us back not merely to the Dark Ages, but from cosmos to chaos. If we succeed in finding a suitable way to control atomic weapons, it is reasonable to hope that we may also preclude the use of other weapons adaptable to mass destruction. When a man learns to say "A" he can, if he chooses, learn the rest of the alphabet, too.

Let this be anchored in our minds:

Peace is never long preserved by weight of metal or by an armament race. Peace can be made tranquil and secure only by understanding and agreement fortified by sanctions. We must embrace international co-operation or international disintegration.

Science has taught us how to put the atom to work. But to make it work for good instead of for evil lies in the domain dealing with the principles of human duty. We are now facing a problem more of ethics than of physics.

The solution will require apparent sacrifice in pride and in position, but better pain as the price of peace than death as the price of war.

Harry S. Truman

[1884-1972]

The thirty-third President of the United States, Harry S. Truman, whose home was in Independence, Missouri, operated the family farm near there from 1906 to 1917. He served in World War I, later became a judge in Missouri, and was elected United States Senator from Missouri in 1934, and reelected in 1940. In 1944, he was elected Vice-President, and on the death of President Roosevelt, April 12, 1945, acceded to the Presidency. He was elected President in 1948.

Two addresses by Mr. Truman are presented here: the first, his inaugural speech, was delivered January 20, 1949; the second, a speech on the office of the president, delivered some time after his term of office, when he had returned to private life.

INAUGURAL ADDRESS

I ACCEPT with humility the honor which the American people have conferred upon me. I accept it with a deep resolve to do all that I can for the welfare of this nation and for the peace of the world.

In performing the duties of my office, I need the help and the prayers of every one of you. I ask for your encouragement and for your support. The tasks we face are difficult, and we can accomplish them only if we work together.

Each period of our national history has had its special challenges. Those that confront us now are as momentous as any in the past. Today marks the beginning not only of a new Administration, but of a period that will be eventful, perhaps decisive, for us and for the world.

It may be our lot to experience, and in a large measure to bring about, a major turning point in the long history of the human race. The first half of this century has been marked by unprecedented and brutal attacks on the rights of man, and by the two most frightful wars in history. The supreme need of our time is for men to learn to live together in peace and harmony.

The peoples of the earth face the future with grave uncertainty, composed almost equally of great hopes and great fears. In this time of doubt, they will look to the United States as never before for good will, strength, and wise leadership.

It is fitting, therefore, that we take this occasion to proclaim to the world the essential principles of faith by which we live, and to declare our aims to all peoples.

The American people stand firm in the faith which has inspired this nation from the beginning. We believe that all men have a right to freedom of thought and expression. We believe that all men are created equal because they are created in the image of God.

From this faith we will not be moved.

The American people desire, and are determined to work for, a world in which all nations and all peoples are free to govern themselves as they see fit and to achieve a decent and satisfying life. Above all else, our people desire, and are determined to work for, peace on earth—a just and lasting peace—based on genuine agreement freely arrived at by equals.

In the pursuit of these aims, the United States and other like-minded nations find themselves directly opposed by a regime with contrary aims and a totally different concept of life. That regime adheres to a false philosophy which purports to offer freedom, security, and greater opportunity to mankind. Misled by that philosophy, many peoples have sacrificed their liberties only to learn to their sorrow that deceit and mockery, poverty and tyranny, are their reward. That false philosophy is communism.

These differences between communism and democracy do not concern the United States alone. People everywhere are coming to realize that what is involved is material well-being, human dignity, and the right to believe in and worship God.

Since the end of hostilities, the United States has invested its substance and its energy in a great constructive effort to restore peace, stability, and freedom to the world. In the coming years, our program for peace and freedom will emphasize four major courses of action.

First, we will continue to give unfaltering support to the United Nations and related agencies, and we will continue to search for ways to strengthen their authority and increase their effectiveness. We believe that the United

Nations will be strengthened by the new nations which are being formed in lands now advancing toward self-government under democratic principles.

Second, we will continue our programs for world economic recovery. This means that we must keep our full weight behind the European Recovery Program. We are confident of the success of this major venture in world recovery. We believe that our partners in this effort will achieve the status of self-supporting nations once again. In addition, we must carry out our plans for reducing the barriers to world trade and increasing its volume. Economic recovery and peace itself depend on increasing world trade.

Third, we will strengthen freedom-loving nations against the dangers of aggression. We are working out with a number of countries a joint agreement designed to strengthen the security of the North Atlantic area. If we can make it sufficiently clear, in advance, that any armed attack affecting our national security would be met with overwhelming force, the armed attack might never occur.

Fourth, we must embark on a bold new program for making the benefits of our scientific advances and industrial progress available for the improvement and growth of underdeveloped areas. Our aim should be to help the free peoples of the world through their own efforts, to produce more food, more clothing, more materials for housing, and more mechanical power to lighten their burdens. We invite other countries to pool their technological resources in this undertaking. Their contributions will be warmly welcomed. This should be a cooperative enterprise in which all nations work together through the United Nations and its specialized agencies whenever practicable. It must be a world-wide effort for the achievement of peace, plenty, and freedom.

Our allies are the millions who hunger and thirst after righteousness.

In due time, as our stability becomes manifest, as more and more nations come to know the benefits of democracy and to participate in growing abundance, I believe that those countries which now oppose us will abandon their delusions and join with the free nations of the world in a just settlement of international differences.

Events have brought our American democracy to new influence and new responsibilities. They will test our courage, our devotion to duty, and our concept of liberty. But I say to all men, what we have achieved in liberty, we will surpass in greater liberty.

Steadfast in our faith in the Almighty, we will advance toward a world where man's freedom is secure. To that end we will devote our strength, our resources, and our firmness of resolve. With God's help, the future of mankind will be assured in a world of justice, harmony, and peace.

Mr. Truman continued his long-time interest in the historical aspects of government after retiring from public office. In this speech at the Truman Birthday Dinner in New York City, May 8, 1954, he discusses the development of the presidential powers to the present time, stressing the present need for a strong executive branch.

POWERS OF THE PRESIDENT

There's never been an office—an executive office—in all the history of the world with the responsibility and the power of the Presidency of the United States. That is the reason in this day and age that it must be run and respected as at no other time in the history of the world because it can mean the welfare of the world or its destruction.

When the founding fathers outlined the Presidency in Article II of the Constitution, they left a great many details out and vague. I think they relied on the experience of the nation to fill in the outlines. The office of the chief executive has grown with the progress of this great republic. It has responded to the many demands that our complex society has made upon the Government. It has given our nation a means of meeting our greatest emergencies. Today, it is one of the most important factors in our leadership of the free world.

Many diverse elements entered into the creation of the office, springing, as it did, from the parent idea of the separation of powers.

In the first place, the President became the leader of a political party. The party under his leadership had to be dominant enough to put him in office. This political party leadership was the last thing the Constitution contemplated. The President's election was not intended to be mixed up in the hurly-burly of partisan politics.

I wish some of those old gentlemen could come back and see how it worked. The people were to choose wise and respected men who would meet in calm seclusion and choose a President and the runner-up would be Vice President.

All of this went by the board—thought most of the original language remains in the Constitution. Out of the struggle and tumult of the political arena a new and different President emerged—the man who led a political party to victory and retained in his hand the power of party leadership. That is, he retained it, like the sword Excalibur, if he could wrest it from the scabbard and wield it.

Another development was connected with the first. As the President came to be elected by the whole people, he became responsible to the whole people. I used to say the only lobbyist the whole people had in Washington was the President of the United States. Our whole people looked to him for leadership, and not confined within the limits of a written document. Every hope and every fear of his fellow citizens, almost every aspect of their welfare and activity, falls within the scope of his concern—indeed, it falls within the scope of his duty. Only one who has held that office can really appreciate that. It is the President's responsibility to look at all questions from the point of view of the whole people. His written and spoken word commands national and often international attention.

These powers which are not explicitly written into the Constitution are the powers which no President can pass on to his successor. They go only to him who can take and use them. However, it is these powers, quite as much as those enumerated in Article II of the Constitution, which make the Presidential system unique and which give the papers of Presidents their peculiarly revealing importance.

For it is through the use of these great powers that leadership arises, events are molded and administrations take on their character.

And so a successful administration is one of strong Presidential leadership. Weak leadership—or no leadership—produces failure and often disaster.

This does not come from the inherent incapacity of the people of the nation. It is inherent in the legislative government where there is no executive strong and able enough to rally the people to a sustained effort of will and prepared to use its power of party control to the fullest extent.

Again, we see today history repeating itself as the legislative branch of the Government, under the overshadowing fear of communism, expands its functions and activities into the very center of the power of the executive branch.

The President is responsible for the administration of his office. And that means for the administration of the entire executive branch. It is not the business of Congress to run the agencies of government for the President.

Unless this principle is observed, it is impossible to have orderly government. The legislative power will ooze into the executive offices. It will influence and corrupt the decisions of the executive branch. It will affect promotions and transfers. It will warp and twist policies.

Not only does the President cease to be a master in his own house, but the whole house of government becomes one which has no master. The power of decision then rests only in the legislative branch, and the legislative branch by its very nature is not equipped to perform these executive functions.

To this kind of encroachment it is the duty of the President to say firmly and flatly "No, you can't do it." The investigative power of Congress is not limitless. It extends only so far as to permit the Congress to acquire the information that it honestly needs to exercise its legislative functions. Exercised beyond these limits, it becomes a manifestation of unconstitutional power. It raises the threat of a legislative dictatorship and that's the worst dictatorship in the world.

Today the tasks of leadership falling upon the President spring not only from our national problems but from those of the whole world. Today that leadership will determine whether our Government will function effectively, and upon its functioning depends the survival of each of us and also on that depends the survival of the free world, if I may be so bold as to say that.

And today our Government cannot function properly unless it follows the provisions of the Constitution. Our Government cannot function properly unless the President is master in his own house and unless the executive departments and agencies of the Government, including the armed forces, are responsible only to the President.

I hope and believe that we will pass through this present crisis successfully. I do not believe that the Congress will succeed in taking over the functions of the executive if the President presents the problem in its constitutional light. I have always maintained that the internal security of the executive branch was a matter for the President himself to handle. President Eisenhower in his first State of the Union Message announced the same principle. If this Administration under his leadership will act upon this principle, we can look forward to the continuation of constitutional government as our founding fathers intended it to be.

Douglas MacArthur
[1880–1964]

General Douglas MacArthur, Supreme Commander of Allied Forces in the Southwest Pacific during World War II, accepted the Japanese surrender in 1945, and commanded occupation forces in Japan. With the outbreak of war in Korea in June, 1950, General MacArthur became Commander of United Nations Forces supporting the Republic of Korea against North Korean and later Chinese Communist troops. Relieved of his post of command in Korea as a result of his criticism of government policy and his use of military tactics not approved by the government, General MacArthur defended his conduct in an address to the joint houses of Congress, heard by broadcast across the nation. Following is part of this speech of April 19, 1951.

OLD SOLDIERS NEVER DIE

I STAND on this rostrum with a sense of deep humility and great pride— humility in the wake of those great architects of our history who have stood here before me, pride in the reflection that this home of legislative debate represents human liberty in the purest form yet devised.

Here are centered the hopes and aspirations and faith of the entire human race.

I do not stand here as advocate for any partisan cause, for the issues are fundamental and reach quite beyond the realm of partisan considerations. They must be resolved on the highest plane of national interest if our course is to prove sound and our future protected.

I trust, therefore, that you will do me the justice of receiving that which I have to say as solely expressing the considered viewpoint of a fellow American.

I address you with neither rancor nor bitterness in the fading twilight of life, with but one purpose in mind: to serve my country.

The issues are global, and so interlocked that to consider the problems of one sector oblivious to those of another is to court disaster for the whole. While Asia is commonly referred to as the gateway to Europe, it is no less true that Europe is the gateway to Asia, and the broad influence of the one cannot fail to have its impact upon the other.

There are those who claim our strength is inadequate to protect on both fronts, that we cannot divide our effort. I can think of no greater expression of defeatism.

If a potential enemy can divide his strength on two fronts, it is for us to counter his efforts. The Communist threat is a global one. Its successful advance in one sector threatens the destruction of every other sector. You cannot appease or otherwise surrender to communism in Asia without simultaneously undermining our efforts to halt its advance in Europe.

I have from the beginning believed that the Chinese Communists' support of the North Koreans was the dominant one. Their interests are at present parallel with those recently displayed not only in Korea but also in Indo-China and Tibet and pointing potentially toward the South, reflects predominantly the same lust for expansion of power which has animated every would-be conqueror since the beginning of time.

While I was not consulted prior to the President's decision to intervene in support of the republic of Korea, that decision, from a military standpoint, proved a sound one. As I say, it proved a sound one, as we hurled back the invader and decimated his forces. Our victory was complete, and our objectives within reach, when Red China intervened with numerically superior ground forces.

This created a new war and an entirely new situation, a situation not contemplated when our forces were committed against the North Korean invaders; a situation which called for new decisions in the diplomatic sphere to permit the realistic adjustment of military strategy. Such decisions have not been forthcoming.

While no man in his right mind would advocate sending our ground forces into continental China, and such was never given a thought, the new situation did urgently demand a drastic revision of strategic planning if our political aim was to defeat this new enemy as we had defeated the old.

Apart from the military need, as I saw it, to neutralize the sanctuary protection given the enemy north of the Yalu, I felt that military necessity in the conduct of the war made necessary—

(1) The intensification of our economic blockade against China.

(2) The imposition of a naval blockade against the China coast.

(3) Removal of restrictions on air reconnaissance of China's coastal area and of Manchuria.

(4) Removal of restrictions on the forces of the republic of China on Formosa, with logistical support to contribute to their effective operations against the Chinese mainland.

For entertaining these views, all professionally designed to support our forces committed to Korea and bring hostilities to an end with the least possible delay and at a saving of countless American and Allied lives, I have been severely criticized in lay circles, principally abroad, despite my understanding that from a military standpoint the above views have been fully shared in the past by practically every military leader concerned with the Korean campaign, including our own Joint Chiefs of Staff.

I called for reinforcements, but was informed that reinforcements were not available. I made clear that if not permitted to destroy the enemy built-up bases north of the Yalu, if not permitted to utilize the friendly Chinese force of some six hundred thousand men on Formosa, if not permitted to blockade the China coast to prevent the Chinese Reds from getting succor from without, and if there were to be no hope of major reinforcements, the position of the command from the military standpoint forbade victory.

We could hold in Korea by constant maneuver and at an appropriate area where our supply-line advantages were in balance with the supply-line disadvantages of the enemy, but we could hope at best for only an indecisive campaign with its terrible and constant attrition upon our forces if the enemy utilized his full military potential.

I have constantly called for the new political decisions essential to a solution.

Efforts have been made to distort my position. It has been said in effect that I was a warmonger. Nothing could be further from the truth.

I know war as few other men now living know it, and nothing to me is more revolting. I have long advocated its complete abolition, as its very destructiveness on both friend and foe has rendered it useless as a means of settling international disputes.

Indeed, on the second day of September, 1945, just following the surrender of the Japanese nation on the battleship *Missouri,* I formally cautioned as follows:

"Men since the beginning of time have sought peace. Various methods through the ages have been attempted to devise an international process to prevent or settle disputes between nations. From the very start workable methods were found in so far as individual citizens were concerned, but the mechanics of an instrumentality of larger international scope have never been successful.

"Military alliances, balances of powers, leagues of nations, all in turn failed, leaving the only path to be by way of the crucible of war. The utter destructiveness of war now blocks out this alternative. We have had our last chance. If we will not devise some greater and more equitable system, our Armageddon will be at our door. The problem basically is theological and involves a spiritual recrudescence, an improvement of human character that will synchronize with our almost matchless advances in science, art, literature, and all material and cultural developments of the past two thousand years. It must be of the spirit if we are to save the flesh."

But once war is forced upon us, there is no other alternative than to apply every available means to bring it to a swift end. War's very object is victory, not prolonged indecision.

In war, there is no substitute for victory.

The tragedy of Korea is further heightened by the fact that its military action is confined to its territorial limits: It condemns that nation, which it is our purpose to save, to suffer the devastating impact of full naval and air bombardment while the enemy's sanctuaries are fully protected from such attack and devastation.

Of the nations of the world, Korea alone, up to now, is the sole one which has risked its all against communism. The magnificence of the courage and fortitude of the Korean people defies description. They have chosen to risk death rather than slavery. Their last words to me were: "Don't scuttle the Pacific."

I am closing my fifty-two years of military service. When I joined the army, even before the turn of the century, it was the fulfillment of all my boyish hopes and dreams.

The world has turned over many times since I took the oath on the plain at West Point, and the hopes and dreams have long since vanished, but I still remember the refrain of one of the most popular barracks ballads of that day which proclaimed most proudly that old soldiers never die; they just fade away.

And like the old soldier of that ballad, I now close my military career and just fade away, an old soldier who tried to do his duty as God gave him the light to see that duty. Good-by.

Adlai Ewing Stevenson

[1900–1965]

Adlai E. Stevenson was Democratic candidate for President in 1952 and 1956. He had been Governor of Illinois from 1948 to 1953. Upon his nomination, he was recognized as a statesman of exceptional distinction and a speaker of unusual ability. His addresses reached a large audience, not only during the campaigns but also in later years. In 1961 President Kennedy appointed him United States ambassador to the United Nations, where he served until 1965.

Three of his speeches are included in this book, one on page 647 and two here: his acceptance of the nomination as Democratic candidate for President on July 26, 1952; and a speech on United States policy in the Far East delivered in 1955.

ACCEPTANCE OF NOMINATION

I ACCEPT your nomination—and your program.

I should have preferred to hear those words uttered by a stronger, a wiser, a better man than myself. But after listening to the President's speech, I even feel better about myself.

None of you, my friends, can wholly appreciate what is in my heart. I can only hope that you understand my words. They will be few.

I have not sought the honor you have done me. I could not seek it because I aspired to another office, which was the full measure of my ambition. And one does not treat the highest office within the gift of the people of Illinois as an alternative or as a consolation prize.

I would not seek your nomination for the presidency because the burdens of that office stagger the imagination. Its potential for good or evil now and in the years of our lives smothers exultation and converts vanity to prayers.

Now that you have made your decision I will fight to win that office with all my heart and my soul. And with your help, I have no doubt that we will win.

You have summoned me to the highest mission within the gift of any people. I could not be more proud. Better men than I were at hand for this mighty task, and I owe to you and to them every resource of mind and of strength that I possess to make your deed today a good one for our country and for our party. I am confident, too, that your selection of a candidate for Vice-President will strengthen me and our party immeasurably in the hard, the implacable work that now lies ahead of all of us.

I know that you join me in gratitude and in respect for the great Democrats and the leaders of our generation whose names you have considered here in this convention, whose vigor, whose character, and devotion to the Republic we love so well have won the respect of countless Americans and enriched our party.

I shall need them, we shall need them, because I have not changed in any respect since yesterday. Your nomination, awesome as I find it, has not enlarged my capacities. So I am profoundly grateful and emboldened by their comradeship and their fealty. And I have been deeply moved by their expressions of good will and support. And I cannot, my friends, resist the urge to take the one opportunity that has been afforded me to pay my humble respects to a very great and good American whom I am proud to call my kinsman—Alben Barkley of Kentucky.

I hope and pray that we Democrats, win or lose, can campaign not as a crusade to exterminate the opposing party, as our opponents seem to prefer, but as an opportunity to educate and elevate a people whose destiny is leadership, not alone of a rich and prosperous, contented country as in the past, but of a world in ferment.

And, my friends, even more important than winning the election is governing the nation. That is the test of a political party—the acid, final test. When the tumult and the shouting die, when the bands are gone and the lights are dimmed, there is the stark reality of responsibility in an hour of history haunted with those gaunt, grim specters of strife, dissension, and ruthless, inscrutable, and hostile power abroad.

The ordeal of the twentieth century—the bloodiest, most turbulent era of the Christian age—is far from over. Sacrifice, patience, understanding, and implacable purpose may be our lot for years to come.

Let's face it. Let's talk sense to the American people. Let's tell them the truth, that there are no gains without pains, that we are now on the eve of great decisions, not easy decisions, like resistance when you're attacked, but a long, patient, costly struggle which alone can assure triumph over the great enemies of man—war, poverty, and tyranny—and the assaults upon human dignity which are the most grievous consequences of each.

Let's tell them that the victory to be won in the twentieth century, this portal to the golden age, mocks the pretensions of individual acumen and ingenuity. For it is a citadel guarded by· thick walls of ignorance and mistrust which do not fall before the trumpets' blast or the politicians' imprecations or even the generals' baton. They are, my friends, walls that must be directly stormed by the hosts of courage, morality, and of vision, standing shoulder to shoulder, unafraid of ugly truth, contemptuous of lies, half-truths, circuses, and demagoguery.

Help me to do the job this autumn of conflict and campaign; help me to do the job in these years of darkness, of doubt, and of crisis which stretch beyond the horizon of tonight's happy vision, and we will justify our glorious past and the loyalty of silent millions who look to us for compassion, for understanding, and for honest purpose. Thus we will serve our great tradition greatly.

I ask of you all you have; I will give to you all I have, even as he who came here tonight and honored me, as he has honored you—the Democratic party—by a lifetime of service and bravery that will find him an imperishable page in the history of the Republic and of the Democratic party—President Harry S. Truman.

And finally, my friends, in the staggering task that you have assigned me, I shall always try "to do justly, to love mercy, and walk humbly with God."

Following are parts of a speech by Adlai E. Stevenson, in a radio broadcast April 11, 1955, giving his view of America's position during the crisis concerning Formosa and the smaller islands off the Chinese mainland.

UNITED STATES FAR EASTERN POLICY

MY FELLOW COUNTRYMEN:—I have not spoken to you for more than four months and I do so tonight only because I have been deeply disturbed by the recent course of events in the Far East and because many of you have asked me for my views. I have waited until the first excitement about the islands of Quemoy and Matsu has subsided and we can more calmly examine our situation in the Straits of Formosa and in Asia. In matters of national security emotion is no substitute for intelligence, nor rigidity for prudence. To act coolly, intelligently and prudently in perilous circumstances is the test of a man—and also a nation.

Our common determination, Republicans and Democrats alike, is to avoid atomic war and to achieve a just and lasting peace. We all agree on that, I think, but not on the ways and means to that end. And that's what I want to talk about—war and ways and means to a peaceful solution of the present crisis in the Straits of Formosa.

On this April evening I remember vividly that it was in April just ten years ago that the largest conference in all diplomatic history met at San Francisco to write the Charter of the United Nations—a charter of liberation for the peoples of the earth from the scourge of war and of want.

The spirit of San Francisco was one of optimism and of boundless hope. The long night was lifting; Hitler's armies were on the eve of collapse; the war lords of Japan were tottering. Our hearts were high in that bright blue dawn of a new day—just ten years ago.

But tonight, despite the uneasy truces in Korea and Indochina, our country once again confronts the iron face of war—war that may be unlike anything that man has seen since the creation of the world, for the weapons man has created can destroy not only his present but his future as well. With the invention of the hydrogen bomb and all of the frightful spawn of fission and of fusion the human race has crossed one of the great watersheds of history, and mankind stands in a new territory in uncharted lands.

The tragedy is that the possibility of war just now seems to hinge upon Quemoy and Matsu, small islands that lie almost as close to the coast of China as Staten Island does to New York; islands that presumably have been fortified by the Chinese Nationalists with our approval and assistance.

Should we be plunged into another great war, the maintenance of our alliances and the respect and goodwill of the uncommitted nations of Asia will be far more important to us than the possession of these offshore islands by General Chiang Kai-shek ever could be. Moreover, the maintenance of a united front is of vital importance to the defense of Formosa itself, since, in addition to the material and military support our friends might contribute, their moral support and the knowledge by the Communist leaders that they would be facing a united free world would be a much more effective deterrent to an assault on Formosa than is our present lonely and irresolute position on the offshore islands.

One of the weaknesses of our position is that we have been making Formosa policy as we thought best regardless of others.

We have not made it clear that we are helping to hold Formosa, not as an offensive but as a purely defensive measure. We have not made it clear because the Administration has not been clear itself. But we can't expect other nations to support policies they disagree with, let alone ambiguous and dangerous policies.

Joint action along the lines I've indicated would put Formosa policy on a much broader and a more comprehensive basis. In the eyes of the Asian nations, we would thereby achieve a consistent and morally unquestionable position in providing for the protection of the Formosans according to the principles and ideals of international law.

In the eyes of our European friends and allies we would once more have asserted our full belief in the value, indeed in the indispensability, of maintaining the alliance of the free world against the slave world. And in the eyes of our Nationalist friends on Formosa, surely the understanding and the support of the bulk of the non-Communist world is a much stronger defense of Formosa than these islands can possibly be.

But if the Chinese Communists refuse; if they insist on force and reject any peaceful solution, then at least it would be clear to everyone who the aggressors were. And, clearly, if the Chinese are so bent on violence, so intoxicated by their success, so indifferent to the grisly realities of modern war, then we have no alternative but to meet force with force. But let us at least meet it with our allies beside us and the blame placed squarely where it belongs—not on America's fantasies and inflexibility, but on the unteachable 'and unquenchable ambition and indifference to human life of China's Communist regime.

I think we must renounce go-it-alone-ism.

We shall have to face the fact that General Chiang's army cannot invade the mainland unless we are prepared to accept enormous burdens and risks —alone.

The world will respect us for recognizing mistakes and correcting them. But if our present posture in the offshore islands, for example, is a wrong one, who will respect us for stubbornly persisting in it?

If we cease to deceive ourselves over the hard realities of power in the Formosa situation we shall have taken the first step towards our first essential—restoration of unity of purpose and action between ourselves and our allies in the free world. But our friends have made it clear that so long as fantasy, rigidity and domestic politics seem to stand in the way of peaceful Formosa settlement, they will not support us if in spite of our endeavors a conflict should break out.

So, finally, let us face the fact that keeping friends these days calls for more statesmanship than challenging enemies, and the cause of world peace transcends any domestic political considerations.

But, preoccupied as we all are these days with the immediate problem of these islands, we must try to keep things in perspective somehow and not lose sight of our main objectives. For beyond Quemoy and Matsu, and even Formosa, lie the urgent and larger problems of Asia—the growing attraction of enormous, reawakened China, the struggle of the underdeveloped countries to improve their condition and keep their independence, and the grave misgivings about America.

If the best hope for today's world is a kind of atomic balance, the decisive battle in the struggle against aggression may be fought out not on battlefields but in the minds of men, and the area of decision may well be out there among the uncommitted peoples of Asia and of Africa who look and listen and who must, in the main, judge us by what we say and do.

It is not only over the defense of the offshore islands that we need a new sense of direction and to mend our fences. Too often of late we have turned to the world a face of stern military power. Too often the sound we hear from Washington is the call to arms, the rattling of the saber. Too often our constructive, helpful economic programs have been obscured, our good done by stealth. Thus have we Americans, the most peaceful and generous people on earth, been made to appear hard, belligerent, careless of those very qualities of humanity which, in fact, we value most. The picture of America—the kindly, generous, deeply pacific people who are really America —has been clouded in the world, to the comfort of the aggressors and to the dismay of our friends.

As best we can, let us then correct this distorted impression, for we will win no hearts and minds in the new Asia by uttering louder threats and brandishing bigger swords. The fact is we have not created excess military strength. The fact is that compared to freedom's enemies we have created if anything too little; the trouble is that we have tried to cover our deficiencies with bold words and have thus obscured our peaceful purposes and our ultimate reliance on quiet firmness rather than bluster and vacillation, on wisdom rather than warnings, on forbearance rather than dictation.

We will be welcome to the sensitive people of Asia, more as engineers and doctors and agricultural experts, coming to build, to help, to heal, than as soldiers. Point Four was an idea far more stirring, far more powerful, than all of the empty slogans about "liberation" and "retaliation" and "unleashing" rolled together.

So I say, let us present once more the true face of America—warm and modest and friendly, dedicated to the welfare of all mankind, and demanding nothing except a chance for all to live and let live, to grow and govern as they wish, free from interference, free from intimidation, free from fear.

Let this be the American mission in the hydrogen age. Let us stop slandering ourselves and appear before the world once more as we really are— as friends, not as masters; as apostles of principle, not of power; in humility, not arrogance; as champions of peace, not as harbingers of war. For our strength lies, not alone in our proving grounds and our stockpiles, but in our ideals, our goals, and their universal appeal to all men who are struggling to breathe free.

Dwight David Eisenhower
[1890–1969]

Dwight D. Eisenhower, thirty-fourth President of the United States, was Supreme Commander of Allied Forces in Western Europe in the Second World War. After the war, he was for a short time president of Columbia University. In 1952, on the Republican ticket, he won the largest popular vote ever cast for a United States President.

President Eisenhower, called "Ike" by millions of Americans, is represented here by three speeches: the speech made at his Inauguration, January 20, 1953; his proposal for the peacetime use of atomic energy; and a speech at the opening of the Geneva Conference of 1955. A fourth speech, his Farewell Address, will be found in Part V.

INAUGURAL ADDRESS

THE WORLD and we have passed the midway point of a century of continuing challenge. We sense with all our faculties that forces of good and evil are massed and armed and opposed as rarely before in history.

This fact defines the meaning of this day. We are summoned, by this honored and historic ceremony, to witness more than the act of one citizen swearing his oath of service, in the presence of his God, We are called as a people, to give testimony, in the sight of the world, to our faith that the future shall be long to the free.

Since this century's beginning, a time of tempest has seemed to come upon the continents of the earth. Masses of Asia have wakened to strike off shackles of the past. Great nations of Europe have waged their bloodiest wars. Thrones have toppled and their vast empires have disappeared. New nations have been born.

For our own country, it has been a time of recurring trial. We have grown in power and in responsibility. We have passed through the anxieties of depression and of war to a summit unmatched in man's history. Seeking to secure peace in the world, we have had to fight through the forests of the Argonne to the shores of Iwo Jima, and to the cold mountains of Korea.

In the swift rush of great events, we find ourselves groping to know the full sense and meaning of the times in which we live. In our quest of understanding, we beseech God's guidance. We summon all our knowledge of the past and we scan all signs of the future. We bring all our wit and will to meet the question: how far have we come in man's long pilgrimage from darkness toward light? Are we nearing the light—a day of freedom and of peace for all mankind? Or are the shadows of another night closing in upon us?

Great as are the preoccupations absorbing us at home, concerned as we are with matters that deeply affect our livelihood today and our vision of the future, each of these domestic problems is dwarfed by, and often even created by, this question that involves all human kind.

This trial comes at a moment when man's power to achieve good or to inflict evil surpasses the brightest hopes and the sharpest fears of all ages. We can turn rivers in their courses, level mountains to the plains. Ocean and land and sky are avenues for our colossal commerce. Disease diminishes and life lengthens.

Yet the promise of this life is imperiled by the very genius that has made it possible. Nations amass wealth. Labor sweats to create—and turns out devices to level not only mountains but also cities. Science seems ready to confer upon us, as its final gift, the power to erase human life from this planet.

At such a time in history, we, who are free, must proclaim anew our faith.

This faith is the abiding creed of our fathers. It is our faith in the deathless dignity of man, governed by eternal moral and natural laws.

This faith defines our full view of life. It establishes, beyond debate, those gifts of the Creator that are man's inalienable rights, and that make all men equal in his sight!

In the light of this equality, we know that the virtues most cherished by free peoples—love of truth, pride of work, devotion to country—all are treasures equally precious in the lives of the most humble and of the most exalted. The men who mine coal and fire furnaces and balance ledgers and turn lathes and pick cotton and heal the sick and plant corn—all serve as proudly, and as profitably, for America as the statesmen who draft treaties or the legislators who enact laws.

This faith rules our whole way of life. It decrees that we, the people, elect leaders not to rule but to serve. It asserts that we have the right to choice of our own work and to the reward of our own toil. It inspires the initiative that makes our productivity the wonder of the world. And it warns that any man who seeks to deny equality in all his brothers betrays the spirit of the free and invites the mockery of the tyrant.

It is because we, all of us, hold to these principles that the political changes accomplished this day do not imply turbulence, upheaval or disorder. Rather this change expresses a purpose of strengthening our dedication and devotion to the precepts of our founding documents, a conscious renewal of faith in our country and in the watchfulness of a divine Providence.

The enemies of this faith know no god but force, no devotion but its use. They tutor men in treason. They feed upon the hunger of others. Whatever defies them, they torture, especially the truth.

Here, then, is joined no pallid argument between slightly differing philosophies. This conflict strikes directly at the faith of our fathers and the lives of our sons. No principle or treasure that we hold, from the spiritual knowledge of our free schools and churches to the creative magic of free labor and capital, nothing lies safely beyond the reach of the struggle.

Freedom is pitted against slavery; light against dark.

The faith we hold belongs not to us alone but to the free of all the world. This common bond binds the grower of rice in Burma and the planter of wheat in Iowa, the shepherd in southern Italy and the mountaineer in the Andes. It confers a common dignity upon the French soldier who dies in Indo-China, the British soldier killed in Malaya, the American life given in Korea.

We know, beyond this, that we are linked to all free peoples not merely by a noble idea but by a simple need. No free people can for long cling to any privilege or enjoy any safety in economic solitude. For all our own material might, even we need markets in the world for the surpluses of our farms and of our factories. Equally, we need for these same farms and factories vital materials and products of distant lands. This basic law of interdependence, so manifest in the commerce of peace, applies with thousand-fold intensity in the event of war.

So are we persuaded by necessity and by belief that the strength of all free peoples lies in unity, their danger in discord.

To produce this unity, to meet the challenge of our time, destiny has laid upon our country the responsibility of the free world's leadership. So it is proper that we assure our friends once again that, in the discharge of this responsibility, we Americans know and observe the difference between world leadership and imperialism; between firmness and truculence; between a thoughtfully calculated goal and spasmodic reaction to the stimulus of emergencies.

We wish our friends the world over to know this above all: we face the threat—not with dread and confusion—but with confidence and conviction.

We feel this moral strength because we know that we are not helpless prisoners of history. We are free men. We shall remain free, never to be proven guilty of the one capital offense against freedom, a lack of staunch faith.

In pleading our just cause before the bar of history and in pressing our labor for world peace, we shall be guided by certain fixed principles.

These principles are:

(1) Abhorring war as a chosen way to balk the purposes of those who threaten us, we hold it to be the first task of statesmanship to develop the strength that will deter the forces of aggression and promote the conditions of peace. For, as it must be the supreme purpose of all free men, so it must be the dedication of their leaders, to save humanity from preying upon itself.

In the light of this principle, we stand ready to engage with any and all others in joint effort to remove the causes of mutual fear and distrust among nations, and so to make possible drastic reductions of armaments. The sole requisites for undertaking such effort are that—in their purpose —they be aimed logically and honestly toward secure peace for all; and that—in their result—they provide methods by which every participating nation will prove good faith in carrying out its pledge.

(2) Realizing that common sense and common decency alike dictate

the futility of appeasement, we shall never try to placate an aggressor by the false and wicked bargain of trading honor for security. For in the final choice a soldier's pack is not so heavy a burden as a prisoner's chains.

(3) Knowing that only a United States that is strong and immensely productive can help defend freedom in our world, we view our nation's strength and security as a trust upon which rests the hope of free men everywhere. It is the firm duty of each of our free citizens and of every free citizen everywhere to place the cause of his country before the comfort and convenience of himself.

(4) Honoring the identity and heritage of each nation of the world, we shall never use our strength to try to impress upon another people our own cherished political and economic institutions.

(5) Assessing realistically the needs and capacities of proven friends of freedom, we shall strive to help them to achieve their own security and well-being. Likewise, we shall count upon them to assume, within the limits of their resources, their full and just burdens in the common defense of freedom.

(6) Recognizing economic health as an indispensable basis of military strength and the free world's peace, we shall strive to foster everywhere, and to practice ourselves, policies that encourage productivity and profitable trade. For the impoverishment of any single people in the world means danger to the well-being of all other peoples.

(7) Appreciating that economic need, military security, and political wisdom combine to suggest regional groupings of free peoples, we hope, within the framework of the United Nations, to help strengthen such special bonds the world over. The nature of these ties must vary with the different problems of different areas.

In the Western Hemisphere, we enthusiastically join with all our neighbors in the work of perfecting a community of fraternal trust and common purpose.

In Europe, we ask that enlightened and inspired leaders of the Western nations strive with renewed vigor to make the unity of their peoples a reality. Only as free Europe unitedly marshals its strength can it effectively safeguard, even with our help, its spiritual and cultural heritages.

(8) Conceiving the defense of freedom, like freedom itself, to be one and indivisible, we hold all continents and peoples in equal regard and honor. We reject any insinuation that one race or another, one people or another, is in any sense inferior or expendable.

(9) Respecting the United Nations as the living sign of all people's hope for peace, we shall strive to make it not merely an eloquent symbol but an effective force. And in our quest of honorable peace, we shall neither compromise, nor tire, nor ever cease.

By these rules of conduct, we hope to be known to all peoples.

By their observance, an earth of peace may become not a vision but a fact.

This hope—this supreme aspiration—must rule the way we live.

We must be ready to dare all for our country. For history does not long entrust the care of freedom to the weak or the timid. We must acquire proficiency in defense and display stamina in purpose.

We must be willing, individually and as a nation, to accept whatever sacrifices may be required of us. A people that values its privileges above its principles soon loses both.

These basic precepts are not lofty abstractions, far removed from matters of daily living. They are laws of spiritual strength that generate and define our material strength. Patriotism means equipped forces and prepared citizenry. Moral stamina means more energy and more productivity, on the farm and in the factory. Love of liberty means the guarding of every resource that makes freedom possible—from the sanctity of our families and the wealth of our soil to the genius of our scientists.

So each citizen plays an indispensable role. The productivity of our heads, our hands, and our hearts is the source of all the strength we can command for both the enrichment of our lives and the winning of peace.

No person, no home, no community can be beyond the reach of this call. We are summoned to act in wisdom and in conscience, to work with industry, to teach with persuasion, to preach with conviction, to weigh our every deed with care and with compassion. For this truth must be clear before us: whatever America hopes to bring to pass in the world must first come to pass in the heart of America.

The peace we seek, then, is nothing less than the practice and the fulfillment of our whole faith, among ourselves and in our dealings with others. It signifies more than stilling the guns, easing the sorrow of war.

More than an escape from death, it is a way of life.

More than a haven for the weary, it is a hope for the brave.

This is the hope that beckons us onward in this century of trial. This is the work that awaits us all, to be done with bravery, with charity—and with prayer to Almighty God.

President Eisenhower spoke before the General Assembly of the United Nations, December 8, 1953, proposing the pooling of atomic materials for peaceful use. The President was widely acclaimed for this speech, which is given here in part.

PEACEFUL USE OF ATOMIC ENERGY

I KNOW that the American people share my deep belief that if a danger exists in the world, it is a danger shared by all—and equally, that if a hope exists in the mind of one nation, that hope should be shared by all.

I feel impelled to speak today in a language that in a sense is new—which I, who have spent so much of my life in the military profession, would have preferred never to use.

That new language is the language of atomic warfare.

Occasional pages of history do record the faces of the "Great Destroyers" but the whole book of history reveals mankind's never-ending quest for peace and mankind's God-given capacity to build.

It is with the book of history, and not with isolated pages, that the United States will ever wish to be identified. My country wants to be constructive, not destructive. It wants agreements, not wars, among nations. It wants itself to live in freedom and in the confidence that the people of every other nation enjoy equally the right of choosing their own way of life.

So my country's purpose is to help us move out of this dark chamber of horrors into the light, to find a way by which the minds of men, the hopes of men, the souls of men everywhere, can move forward toward peace and happiness and well-being.

In this quest I know that we must not lack patience.

I know that in a world divided, such as ours today, salvation cannot be attained by one dramatic act.

I know that many steps will have to be taken over many months before the world can look at itself one day and truly realize that a new climate of mutually peaceful confidence is abroad in the world.

But I know, above all else, that we must start to take these steps —now.

The gravity of the time is such that every new avenue of peace, no matter how dimly discernible, should be explored.

There is at least one new avenue of peace which has not yet been well explored—an avenue now laid out by the General Assembly of the United Nations.

The United States, heeding the suggestion of the General Assembly of the United Nations, is instantly prepared to meet privately with such other countries as may be "principally involved," to seek "an acceptable solution" to the atomic armament race which overshadows not only the peace, but the very life, of the world.

We shall carry into these private or diplomatic talks a new conception.

The United States would seek more than the mere reduction or elimination of atomic materials available for military purposes.

It is not enough just to take this weapon out of the hands of the soldiers. It must be put into the hands of those who will know how to strip its military casing and adapt it to the arts of peace.

The United States knows that if the fearful trend of atomic military build-up can be reversed, this greatest of destructive forces can be developed into a great boon, for the benefit of all mankind.

The United States knows that peaceful power from atomic energy is no dream of the future. That capability, already proved, is here—now— today. Who can doubt, if the entire body of the world's scientists and engineers had adequate amounts of fissionable material with which to test and develop their ideas, that this capability would rapidly be transformed into universal, efficient, and economic usage?

To hasten the day when fear of the atom will begin to disappear from the minds of the people and the governments of the East and West, there are certain steps that can be taken now.

I therefore make the following proposal:

The Governments principally involved, to the extent permitted by elementary prudence, to begin now and continue to make joint contributions from their stockpiles of normal uranium and fissionable materials to an International Atomic Energy Agency. We would expect that such an agency would be set up under the aegis of the United Nations.

The ratios of contributions, the procedures and other details would properly be within the scope of the "private conversations" I gave referred to earlier.

The United States is prepared to undertake these explorations in good faith. Any partner of the United States acting in the same good faith will find the United States a not unreasonable or ungenerous associate.

Undoubtedly initial and early contributions to this plan would be small in quantity. However, the proposal has the great virtue that it can be undertaken without irritations and mutual suspicions incident to any attempt to set up a completely acceptable system of world-wide inspection and control.

The Atomic Energy Agency could be made responsible for the impounding, storage and protection of the contributed fissionable and other materials. The ingenuity of our scientists will provide special safe conditions under which such a bank of fissionable material can be made essentially immune to surprise seizure.

The more important responsibility of this Atomic Energy Agency would be to devise methods whereby this fissionable material would be allocated to serve the peaceful pursuits of mankind. Experts would be mobilized to apply atomic energy to the needs of agriculture, medicine, and other peaceful activities. A special purpose would be to provide abundant electrical energy in the power starved areas of the world. Thus the contributing powers would be dedicating some of their strength to serve the needs rather than the fears of mankind.

The United States would be more than willing—it would be proud— to take up with others "principally involved" the development of plans whereby such peaceful use of atomic energy would be expedited.

Of those "principally involved" the Soviet Union must, of course, be one.

I would be prepared to submit to the Congress of the United States, and with every expectation of approval, any such plan that would:

First—encourage world-wide investigation into the most effective peacetime uses of fissionable material, and with the certainty that the scientists had all the material needed for conducting all experiments that were appropriate;

Second—begin to diminish the potential destructive power of the world's atomic stockpiles;

Third—allow all peoples of all nations to see that, in this enlightened age, the great powers of the earth, both of the East and the West, are interested in human aspirations first rather than in building up the armaments of war;

Fourth—open up a new channel for peaceful discussion and initiate at least a new approach to the many difficult problems that must be solved in both private and public conversations if the world is to shake off the inertia imposed by fear and make positive progress toward peace.

Against the dark background of the atomic bomb, the United States does not wish merely to present strength, but also the desire and hope for peace.

The coming months will be fraught with fateful decisions. In this Assembly; in the capitals and military headquarters of the world; in the hearts of men everywhere, be they governed or governors—may they be the decisions which will lead this world out of fear into peace.

The heads of government of the Big Four—Britain, France, Soviet Russia, and the United States—met at Geneva, Switzerland, to discuss world problems "at the summit." Parts of President Eisenhower's speech at the opening session, July 18, 1955, are given here; and part of the address at the same session by Premier Bulganin of the U.S.S.R. will be found later in the book.

THE SPIRIT OF GENEVA

We meet here for a simple purpose. We have come to find a basis for accommodation which will make life safer and happier not only for the nations we represent but for people elsewhere.

We are here in response to a universal urge, recognized by Premier Bulganin in his speech of July 15, that the political leaders of our great countries find a path to peace.

We cannot expect here, in the few hours of a few days, to solve all the problems of all the world that need to be solved. Indeed, the four of us meeting here have no authority from others that could justify us even in attempting that.

The roots of many of these problems are buried deep in wars, conflict and history.

They are made even more difficult by the differences in governmental ideologies and ambitions. Manifestly it is out of the question in the short time available to the heads of government meeting here to trace out the causes and origins of these problems and to devise agreements that could with complete fairness to all eliminate them.

Nevertheless, we can, perhaps, create a new spirit that will make possible future solutions of problems which are within our responsibilities. And, equally important, we can try to take here and now at Geneva the first steps on a new road to a just and durable peace.

No doubt there are among our nations philosophical convictions which are in many respects irreconcilable. Nothing that we can say or do here will change that fact. However, it is not always necessary that people should think alike and believe alike before they can work together. The essential thing is that none should attempt by force or trickery to make his beliefs prevail and thus impose his system on the unwilling.

There is the problem of communication and human contacts among our peoples. We frankly fear the consequences of a situation where whole peoples are isolated from the outside world. The American people want to be friends with the Soviet peoples. There are no natural differences between our peoples or our nations. There are no territorial conflicts or commercial rivalries. Historically, our two countries have always been at peace.

But friendly understanding between peoples does not readily develop when there are artificial barriers such as now interfere with communication. It is time that all curtains, whether of guns or laws or regulations, should begin to come down. But this can only be done in an atmosphere of mutual respect and confidence.

I trust that we are not here merely to catalogue our differences. We are not here to repeat the same dreary exercises that have characterized most of our negotiations of the past ten years. We are here in response to the peaceful aspirations of mankind to start with the kind of discussions which will inject a new spirit into our diplomacy: and to launch fresh negotiations under conditions of good augury.

In that way, and perhaps only in that way, can our meeting, necessarily brief, serve to generate and put in motion the new forces needed to set us truly on the path to peace. For this I am sure all humanity will devoutly pray.

Earl Warren

[1891-1974]

Earl Warren was Chief Justice of the U.S. Supreme Court from 1953 to 1969 and Governor of California from 1943 to 1953.
The following is an address delivered on August 19, 1954, by Justice Warren at the dedication of the American Bar Center in Chicago.

A HOME FOR AMERICAN JURISPRUDENCE

UNTIL TODAY, the buildings which we are here dedicating were mere walls and ceilings, composites of mortar, bricks and steel. Like other structures they could have been adapted to a variety of uses and to purposes either high or low.

Today in the presence of each other and standing before the world, we of the American Bar Association testify to the high purpose which brought them into being and to the fond hopes for their usefulness to mankind.

From this day forward we shall call 'them home, with all that word implies, not only for the organized bar of the nation, but also for the abiding spirit of American jurisprudence. Not merely a home for lawyers, but also for the law.

Pilgrims of freedom will beat a path to our shrine, and after being refreshed here, will return to the four corners of the country, equipped with knowledge and strengthened in spirit. Perhaps even pilgrims from other lands will come bringing us knowledge of how freedom fares in their particular sections of the globe, prepared to exchange ideas and learn with us how we can apply to ever-changing conditions the never-changing principles of freedom. It is from a wonderful vantage point that we will be privileged to thus commune.

Our home looks out upon beautiful Lake Michigan, whose friendly waters alone separate this part of the country from that of our incomparable Canadian neighbors to the north.

It is part of the invisible boundary line from ocean to ocean that only a surveyor could define; the most secure boundary line on earth because it is guarded zealously on both sides solely by friendship. To strangers it should be an inspiration to see those two great countries existing side by side in harmony with each other merely because both are dedicated to freedom, to justice and to peace.

It should also be evidence, if evidence is needed, to prove that if we are to achieve a peaceful world, it will be accomplished through ideas rather than armaments, through a sense of justice and mutual friendships rather than with guns and bombs and guided missiles. We are living in a world of ideas and going through a world war of ideas. Everywhere there is a contest for the hearts and minds of people.

Every political concept is under scrutiny. Our American system like all others is on trial both at home and abroad. The way it works; the manner in which it solves the problems of our day; the extent to which we maintain the spirit of our Constitution with its "Bill of Rights," will in the long run do more to make it both secure and the object of adulation than the number of hydrogen bombs we stockpile.

We believe that so long as human nature is such as it is, there must be a constant struggle to preserve our freedoms. We do not propose to let nature take its course.

On the contrary, we are determined here to create the climate essential to the constant improvement of both the text of our law and its application to the affairs of people. We earnestly hope this center will be the catalyst for our entire profession. Here every lawyer from city, town or country, as an individual or through his local or state bar association, could make his presence felt to remedy the defects we have inherited as well as those that continually creep into human institutions.

As lawyers we know better than most other people that there are defects in our administration of justice. With adequate research we can strengthen our leadership in remedying them. Some of these defects we know now.

We are sensitive to the fact that technicalities, anachronisms and lack of uniformity in the law still beset us in the ascertainment of facts and that haphazard methods of appointing judges, inadequate court organization and loose courtroom practices too often cause delay, confusion, inefficiency and consequent unjustifiable expense.

Here in our new home, we will honestly face all of our family problems as an integral part of greater problems of justice. We will maintain the

American concept of freedom and justice for all. We will rededicate ourselves to constitutional principles. We will urge others to do likewise.

The genius of our American institutions is the spirit that has been breathed into them—the spirit of a free, just and friendly people. As that spirit is strengthened or weakened so is our government strengthened or weakened.

We of the American Bar Association would not only maintain that spirit, we would fortify it to meet every emergency that could confront our nation in the confused and turbulent world in which we are living.

To that cause we dedicate our American Bar Center. In that cause we dedicate ourselves to "do justly and love mercy and walk humbly with God."

Winston Churchill

[1874–1965]

Winston Churchill was leader of the opposition in the House of Commons from 1945 to 1951, when the Labor Party was in power. In a speech delivered at Westminster College in Fulton, Missouri, on March 5, 1946, Churchill again proved his extraordinary gift for creating a phrase that will never be forgotten. That phrase, in this case, described the closely guarded Soviet bloc, the "iron curtain." Parts of this speech follow.

AN IRON CURTAIN HAS DESCENDED

It is an honor, ladies and gentlemen, perhaps almost unique, for a private visitor to be introduced to an academic audience by the President of the United States. Amid his heavy burdens, duties and responsibilities—unsought but not recoiled from—the President has traveled a thousand miles to dignify and magnify our meeting here today and to give me an opportunity of addressing this kindred nation, as well as my own countrymen across the ocean and perhaps some other countries, too.

The President has told you that it is his wish, as I am sure it is yours. that I should have full liberty to give my true and faithful counsel in these anxious and baffling times. I shall certainly avail myself of this freedom.

Let me, however, make it clear that I have no official mission or status of any kind and that I speak only for myself. There is nothing here but what you see. I can, therefore, allow my mind, with the experience of a lifetime, to play over the problems which beset us on the morrow of our absolute victory in arms, and to try to make sure, with what strength I have, that what has been gained with so much sacrifice and suffering shall be preserved for the future glory and safety of mankind.

The United States stands at this time at the pinnacle of world power. It is a solemn moment for the American democracy. For with this primacy in power is also joined an awe-inspiring accountability to the future. As you look around you, you must feel not only the sense of duty done but also you must feel anxiety lest you fall below the level of achievement. Opportunity is here now, clear and shining, for both our countries. To reject it or ignore it or fritter it away will bring upon us the long reproaches of the after-time.

It is necessary that constancy of mind, persistency of purpose and the grand simplicity of decision shall rule and guide the conduct of the

English-speaking peoples in peace as they did in war. We must and I believe we shall prove ourselves equal to this severe requirement.

A shadow has fallen upon the scenes so lately lightened, lighted by the Allied victory. Nobody knows what Soviet Russia and its Communist international organization intends to do in the immediate future, or what are the limits, if any, to their expansive and proselytizing tendencies.

I have a strong admiration and regard for the valiant Russian people and for my wartime comrade, Marshal Stalin. There is deep sympathy and good-will in Britain—and I doubt not here also—toward the peoples of all the Russias and a resolve to persevere through many differences and rebuffs in establishing lasting friendships.

It is my duty, however, and I am sure you would not wish me not to state the facts as I see them to you, it is my duty to place before you certain facts about the present position in Europe.

From Stettin in the Baltic to Trieste in the Adriatic, an iron curtain has descended across the Continent. Behind that line lie all the capitals of the ancient states and central and eastern Europe. Warsaw, Berlin, Prague, Vienna, Budapest, Belgrade, Bucharest and Sofia, all these famous cities and the populations around them lie in what I might call the Soviet sphere, and all are subject, in one form or another, not only to Soviet influence but to a very high and in some cases increasing measure of control from Moscow.

Police governments are pervading from Moscow. But Athens alone, with its immortal glories, is free to decide its future at an election under British, American and French observation.

The safety of the world, ladies and gentlemen, requires a unity in Europe from which no nation should be permanently outcast. It is from the strong parent races in Europe that the world wars we have witnessed, or which occurred in former times, have sprung.

Twice in our own lifetime we have—the United States against her wishes and her traditions, against arguments the force of which it is impossible not to comprehend—twice we have seen them drawn by irresistible forces into these wars in time to secure the victory of the good cause, but only after frightful slaughter and devastation have occurred.

Twice the United States has had to send several millions of its young men across the Atlantic to fight the wars. But now we all can find any nation, wherever it may dwell, between dusk and dawn. Surely we should work with conscious purpose for a grand pacification of Europe within the structure of the United Nations and in accordance with our charter.

However, in a great number of countries, far from the Russian frontiers and throughout the world, Communist fifth columns are established and work in complete unity and absolute obedience to directions they receive from the Communist center.

The outlook is also anxious in the Far East and especially in Manchuria. The agreement which was made at Yalta, to which I was party, was extremely favorable to Soviet Russia, but it was made at a time when no one could say that the German war might not extend all through the summer and autumn of 1945 and when the Japanese war was expected by the best judges to last for a further eighteen months from the end of the German war.

I had, however, felt bound to portray the shadow which, alike in the West and in the East, falls upon the world. I was a Minister at the time of the Versailles treaty and a close friend of Mr. Lloyd George, who was the head of the British delegation at that time. I did not myself agree with many things that were done, but I have a very vague impression in my mind of that situation, and I find it painful to contrast it with what prevails now. In those days there were high hopes and unbounded confidence that the wars were over, and that the League of Nations would become all-powerful. I do not see or feel that same confidence or even the same hopes in the haggard world at the present time.

On the other hand, ladies and gentlemen, I repulse the idea that a new war is inevitable; still more that it is imminent. It is because I am sure that our fortunes are still in our hands, in our own hands, and that we hold the power to save the future, that I feel the duty to speak out now that I have the occasion and opportunity to do so.

I do not believe that Soviet Russia desires war. What they desire is the fruits of war and the indefinite expansion of their power and doctrines.

But what we have to consider here today while time remains, is the permanent prevention of war and the establishment of conditions of freedom and democracy as rapidly as possible in all countries. Our difficulties and dangers will not be removed by closing our eyes to them. They will not be removed by mere waiting to see what happens; nor will they be removed by a policy of appeasement.

What is needed is a settlement, and the longer that is delayed, the more difficult it will be and the greater our dangers will become.

If the population of the English-speaking Commonwealth be added to that of the United States, with all such coöperation implies in the air, on the sea, all over the globe, and in science and in industry, and in moral force, there will be no quivering, precarious balance of power to offer its temptation to ambition or adventure. On the contrary, there will be an overwhelming assurance of security.

If we adhere faithfully to the charter of the United Nations and walk forward in sedate and sober strength, seeking no one's land or treasure, seeking to lay no arbitrary control upon the thoughts of men, if all British moral and material forces and convictions are joined with your own fraternal association, the high roads of the future will be clear, not only for us but for all.

Jawaharlal Nehru
[1889–1964]

Jawaharlal Nehru, Prime Minister of India, was an associate of Gandhi and was prominent in Indian nationalist movements. He was imprisoned during the Second World War for his firm stand against India's participation in the war without guarantee of independence. In 1947, Nehru became the first Prime Minister of independent India.

Presented here are parts of two speeches by Nehru. The first was delivered March 23, 1947, inaugurating the Asian conference at New Delhi. The second speech was delivered February 2, 1948, before the Constituent Assembly at New Delhi, three days after the assassination of Gandhi. The death of their revered leader was a shock to all of India, and Nehru well expressed their great sense of loss.

ASIA FINDS HERSELF AGAIN

FRIENDS AND fellow Asians, what has brought you here, men and women of Asia? Why have you come from the various countries of this mother continent of ours and gathered together in the ancient city of Delhi? Some of us, greatly daring, sent you invitations for this Conference and you gave a warm welcome to that invitation. And yet it was not merely the call from us, but some deeper urge that brought you here.

We stand at the end of an era and on the threshold of a new period of history. Standing on this watershed which divides two epochs of human history and endeavour, we can look back on our long past and look forward to the future that is taking shape before our eyes. Asia, after a long period of quiescence, has suddenly become important again in world affairs. It we view the millenia of history, this content of Asia, with which Egypt has been so intimately connected in cultural fellowship, has played a mighty role in the evolution of humanity. It was here that civilization began and man started on his unending adventure of life. Here the mind of man searched unceasingly for truth and the spirit of man shone out like a beacon which lighted up the whole world.

This dynamic Asia from which great streams of culture flowed in all directions gradually became static and unchanging. Other peoples and other continents came to the fore and with their new dynamism spread out and took possession of great parts of the world. This mighty continent became just a field for the rival imperialisms of Europe, and Europe became the centre of history and progress in human affairs.

A change is coming over the scene now and Asia is again finding herself. We live in a tremendous age of transition and already the next stage takes shape when Asia takes her rightful place with the other continents.

It is at this great moment that we meet here and it is the pride and privilege of the people of India to welcome their fellow Asians from other countries, to confer with them about the present and the future, and lay the foundation of our mutual progress, well-being and friendship.

In this Conference and in this work there are no leaders and no followers. All countries of Asia have to meet together on an equal basis in a common task and endeavor. It is fitting that India should play her part in this new phase of Asian development. Apart from the fact that India herself is emerging into freedom and independence, she is the natural centre and focal point of the many forces at work in Asia. Geography is a compelling factor, and geographically she is so situated as to be the meeting point of Western and Northern and Eastern and South-East Asia. Because of this, the history of India is a long history of her relations with the other countries of Asia. Streams of culture have come to India from the west and the east and been absorbed in India, producing the rich and variegated culture which is India today. At the same time, streams of culture have flowed from India to distant parts of Asia. If you would know India you have to go to Afghanistan and Western Asia, to Central Asia, to China and Japan and to the countries of South-East Asia. There you will find magnificent evidence of the vitality of India's culture which spread out and influenced vast numbers of people.

I do not wish to speak to you of the past, but rather of the present.

In this crisis in world history Asia will necessarily play a vital role. The countries of Asia can no longer be used as pawns by others; they are bound to have their own policies in world affairs. Europe and America have contributed very greatly to human progress and for that we must yield them praise and honour, and learn from them the many lessons they have to teach. But the West has also driven us into wars and conflicts without number and even now, the day after a terrible war, there is talk of further wars in the atomic age that is upon us In this atomic age Asia will have to function effectively in the maintenance of peace. Indeed, there can be no peace unless Asia plays her part. There is today conflict in many countries, and all of us in Asia are full of our own troubles. Nevertheless, the whole spirit and outlook of Asia are peaceful, and the emergence of Asia in world affairs will be a powerful influence for world peace.

We have arrived at a stage in human affairs when the ideal of One World and some kind of a World Federation seem to be essential, though there are many dangers and obstacles in the way. We should work for that ideal and not for any grouping which comes in the way of this larger world group. We, therefore, support the United Nations structure which is painfully emerging from its infancy. But in order to have One World, we must also, in Asia, think of the countries of Asia co-operating together for that larger ideal.

This Conference, in a small measure, represents this bringing together of the countries of Asia. Whatever it may achieve, the mere fact of its taking place is itself of historic significance. Indeed, this occasion is unique in history, for never before has such a gathering met together at any place. So even in meeting we have achieved much and I have no doubt that out of this meeting greater things will come. When the history of our present times is written, this event may well stand out as a land-mark which divides the past of Asia from the future. And because we are participating in this making of history, something of the greatness of historic events comes to us all.

All over Asia we are passing through trials and tribulations. In India also you will see conflict and trouble. Let us not be disheartened by this; this is inevitable in an age of mighty transition. There are a new vitality and powerful creative impulses in all the peoples of Asia. The masses are awake and they demand their heritage. Strong winds are blowing all over Asia. Let us not be afraid of them, but rather welcome them for only with their help can we build the new Asia of our dreams. Let us have faith in these great new forces and the dream which is taking shape. Let us, above all, have faith in the human spirit which Asia has symbolized for those long ages past.

A GLORY HAS DEPARTED

WE PRAISE people in well-chosen words and we have some kind of a measure for greatness. How shall we praise him and how shall we measure him, because he was not of the common clay that all of us are made of? He came, lived a fairly long span of life and has passed away. No words of praise of ours in this House are needed, for he has had greater praise in his life than any living man in history. And during these two or three days since his death he has had the homage of the world; what can we add to that? How can we praise him, how can we who have been children of his, and perhaps more intimately his children than the children of his body, for we have all been in some greater or smaller measure the children of his spirit, unworthy as we were?

A glory has departed and the sun that warmed and brightened our lives has set and we shiver in the cold and dark. Yet, he would not have us feel this way. After all, that glory that we saw for all these years, that man with the divine fire, changed us also—and such as we are, we have been moulded by him during these years; and out of that divine fire many of us also took a small spark which strengthened and made us work to some extent on the lines that he fashioned. And so if we praise him, our words seem rather small and if we praise him, to some extent we also praise ourselves. Great men and eminent men have monuments in bronze and marble set up for them, but this man of divine fire managed in his life-time to become enshrined in millions and millions of hearts so that all of us became somewhat of the stuff that he was made of, though to an infinitely lesser degree. He spread out in this way all over India not in palaces only, or in select places or in assemblies but in every hamlet and hut of the lowly and those who suffer. He lives in the hearts of millions and he will live for immemorial ages.

What then can we say about him except to feel humble on this occasion? To praise him we are not worthy—to praise him whom we could not follow adequately and sufficiently. It is almost doing him an injustice just to pass him by with words when he demanded work and labour and sacrifice from us; in a large measure he made this country, during the last thirty years or more, attain to heights of sacrifice which in that particular domain have never been equalled elsewhere. He succeeded in that. Yet ultimately things happened which no doubt made him suffer tremendously though his tender face never lost its smile and he never spoke a harsh word to anyone. Yet, he must have suffered—suffered for the failing of this generation whom he had trained, suffered because we went away from the path that he had shown us. And ultimately the hand of a child of his—for he after all is as much a child of his as any other Indian—a hand of the child of his struck him down.

Long ages afterwards history will judge of this period that we have passed through. It will judge of the successes and the failures—we are too near it to be proper judges and to understand what has happened and what has not happened. All we know is that there was a glory and that it is no more; all we know is that for the moment there is darkness, not so dark certainly because when we look into our hearts we still find the living flame which he lighted there. And if those living flames exist, there will not be darkness in this land and we shall be able, with our effort, remembering him and following his path, to illumine this land again, small as we are, but still with the fire that he instilled into us.

He was perhaps the greatest symbol of the India of the past, and may I say, of the India of the future, that we could have had. We stand on this perilous edge of the present between that past and the future to be and we face all manner of perils and the greatest peril is sometimes the lack of faith which comes to us, the sense of frustration that comes to us, the sinking of the heart and of the spirit that comes to us when we see ideals go overboard, when we see the great things that we talked about somehow pass into empty words and life taking a different course. Yet, I do believe that perhaps this period will pass soon enough.

He has gone, and all over India there is a feeling of having been left desolate and forlorn. All of us sense that feeling, and I do not know when we shall be able to get rid of it, and yet together with that feeling there is also a feeling of proud thankfulness that it has been given to us of this generation to be associated with this mighty person. In ages to come, centuries and maybe millenia after us, people will think of this generation when this man of God trod on earth and will think of us who, however small, could also follow his path and tread the holy ground where his feet had been. Let us be worthy of him.

Oswaldo Aranha

[1894–1960]

Oswaldo Aranha, Brazilian lawyer and diplomat, was a leader during the Vargas revolution in 1930, and after that time served his government in various capacities. He was Ambassador to the United States, and Brazilian representative to the United Nations.

Presented here are parts of the speech delivered by Dr. Aranha as President of the United Nations General Assembly, at the closing session of that body on November 29, 1947, in New York.

A NEW ORDER THROUGH THE UNITED NATIONS

THIS ASSEMBLY, even more than the preceding ones, had the merit of exposing world problems and of compelling their definition. It was featured by frankness, by explicitness, by a necessary and courageous approach to realities formerly kept under diplomatic wraps and shrouded by political conveniences.

Such is the principal mission of the United Nations — to unveil truth and to face reality, that its action be properly guided in the maintenance of peace and of the security of peoples.

Those who do not as yet believe in the work of our organization or who doubt the immediate and future results of the action of our Assembly are victims of self-deceit, for the United Nations and the principles embodied in its Charter admit of no denial. This organization can only be a meeting point for men of good will and nations of good faith. We have no room for those who refuse to believe, to hope and to understand.

This Assembly had laid bare the struggles, the divergencies, the misgivings, the rivalries that beset the world today. But these were not created by the United Nations. On the contrary, this organization was created to seek a better solution for such conflicts and maladjustments in international life.

This Assembly was, therefore, a searching of world conscience through the conscience of each and all of the members of the United Nations.

We were not daunted by reality despite its often menacing aspects. There was freedom of speech here and recrimination marred, at times, the debates.

But he who resorts to words hardly ever resorts to force. Strong language has been used here, but this very fact lent us the authority to condemn a proposal which aimed at penalizing freedom of thought, of speech and of writing, which is inherent to human civilization. It did not preclude, however, the adoption of a resolution of "spiritual disarmament" capable of aiding and expediting that of material disarmament, which was adopted at the last session and which was so long desired and so necessary to the peaceful communion of peoples.

It is beyond doubt, also, that the comprehension of "democracy" itself, through our debates and these resolutions, acquired clearer and better defined aspects, capable of favoring a conciliatory conception half way between the extremes in which contemporary political thought is struggling.

The establishment of the headquarters committee, at whose opening session I had the honor to preside, is worthy of special mention. As President, it is my duty and my pleasure to extend congratulations to Ambassador Warren Austin and to Mr. Trygve Lie on the success of their efforts toward securing, under very satisfactory conditions, the loan which has made it possible for the committee to begin its task of constructing our future headquarters.

Another aspect of our resolutions which, in my opinion, was highly significant was that of the growing tendency of the Assembly to resort to the International Court of Justice for clarification of the legal aspects of many doubts which still exist in our interpretation of the Charter and even in its application. It would be absurd to deny the court the right to interpret the Charter within the limits of its competence, but the Assembly must play its part in meeting the requirements of political situations.

Among the outstanding gains of this Assembly was that of the growing influence of the opinion of the small states. The freedom and equal standing of nations was, in this session, one of the milestones of our progress. Another noted feature was the concessions made by the great powers to the tendency of the small nations in favor of an ever greater extension of the trusteeship system.

One cannot attempt in our organization to accomplish too much in too short a time. In my opinion we have advanced too fast and endeavored to embrace too many problems. Many of our resolutions suffer from these mistakes with all their negative consequences.

At least a few years will have to pass before our work can become fully effective. It is possible, in the meantime, that setbacks will occur in the rhythm of our work because the effects of the last war will continue to disturb the maintenance of peace and the establishment of its bases. But the United Nations will overcome the errors of any nation or group of nations.

I do not fear for its future, but rather for the future of those who will not understand it and accept its dictates.

All idea of force is today obsolete and negative. The old order, based on political power, is trying to survive, but there is no longer room for predominance through force. The United Nations stands for the new order, based on peaceful accord, on understanding, on free discussion, and on the common and equal responsibility of peoples. It is the organ of world public opinion. This world to which we all aspire can only be constructed by the United Nations.

It is our duty not only to do away with all causes of war with all the means at our disposal, but also to lay the economic, political and social bases for peace.

This Assembly has shown an enlightened understanding of this task, and for this reason your decisions will go on record as a memorable contribution toward the peaceful and constructive solution of world problems.

Gentlemen, I thank each and all of you. The second session of the General Assembly is closed. I trust that the third session, in the coming year, will be a step as great as ours has been toward the maintenance of peace and international security.

Pierre Mendès-France

[1907-1982]

Pierre Mendès-France was Premier of France from June, 1954 to February, 1955. He has held several ministerial posts, and was French delegate to the United Nations Economic and Social Council, and executive director of the International Bank for Reconstruction and Development.

Steps were taken by the Western powers to rearm Germany, with provisions for the control of strength of armaments, and for the prohibition of isolated recourse to war on the part of any one of the powers. Following are parts of the address in which M. Mendès-France discussed the agreement, in addition to related topics, before the United Nations General Assembly, November 22, 1954.

THE SEARCH FOR INTERNATIONAL COOPERATION

I HAVE FOLLOWED your work with special interest in view of the fact that I myself, as you are aware, have long collaborated in the activities of this Organization—with an interest increased, moreover, by the fact that it seems to me that this session has enabled certain signs of an improvement in the situation to be happily manifested. It was the hope which several of us expressed last September. We have not been disappointed.

We may already assert that the atmosphere is more favorable and that certain agreements, which are limited in scope, it is true, but which we did not dare to hope for yesterday, enable us to envisage the future with a little more confidence. Once again, the pessimists were wrong.

It is our hope to see the stupendous resources of human genius, the discoveries of science and technical miracles, the consequences of which we can as yet hardly begin to gauge, utilized finally to ensure a decent life for all men instead of serving the cause of destruction. How could we forget here that the great majority of our fellow men are still deprived of those physical means of subsistence and social progress without which the words "freedom" and "democracy" remain mere abstractions?

For modern nations, over and above their present difficulties and divergencies, this is a challenge to which we must respond if we are to deserve the confidence of our peoples. The effort of the United Nations in the economic and social field must be added to the over-all efforts of all Governments to ensure a more rapid disappearance everywhere of hunger, disease and ignorance, those tenacious enemies of mankind.

Collective enterprise must remain concrete and realistic. It is useless to line up illusory projects, to pile up pious resolutions or to proclaim unattainable ideals.

The United Nations can and should cast aside dogmatism and exaggerated ambition, and act with patience and perseverance in analyzing the reasons for the insufficient economic development of our planet and the obstacles in the way of its advancement. They should seek together the means by which countries can help one another and concrete methods by which those who have already completed certain decisive stages may facilitate such a process for the others.

If the industrialization of the XIXth century was brilliant in its results, there is too great a tendency to forget that it was very often at the cost of a succession of painful adaptations, sufferings, and uprootings for the individual. The sole purpose of technical assistance programs is to enable countries now in the process of development to achieve the same results, though at a lesser cost.

This year again, the Assembly has devoted an important debate to the question of the economic development of underdeveloped countries. It is a matter of special concern to me; I participated in the first studies which the Economic and Social Council devoted to it, and I followed its development both in certain countries of Latin America and in the territories for which France is responsible.

It is my hope that the texts which you propose to adopt may encourage our Organization not to attack windmills but to deal with real difficulties which the harmonious solidarity of nations may effectively overcome.

There are, of course, so many needs and problems calling for the vigilance of the international community that the United Nations will constantly be seized of a very great number of matters at the same time. The confidence which the peoples will show in the Organization and the heed which Governments will pay to its opinions will depend to a great extent on its methods of work, and its resolve not to be overwhelmed by trying to do too much at one time. I have always found it an effective precept to deal with problems one by one, to devote oneself first to the most urgent among them, and not to abandon them before their solution has been defined, to know how to sacrifice those projects, among the mass of generous and useful ones, which do not aim at a priority objective on the importance of which agreement has been reached, and for which the Organization has the necessary means at its disposal.

The somewhat muddled haste of the initial years should be succeeded by more methodical construction. We have learned—at the expense of our fine dreams—what are the limits of the practical effectiveness of international cooperation. Those who wish gradually to widen these limits and extend the field of international competence should proceed with a maximum of vigilance and realism; otherwise the machinery will go wrong and the desire to pool techniques and to utilize resources for the welfare of all will be succeeded by another withdrawal of nations into their shells.

Mr. President, France's action in her recent initiatives has constantly stemmed from the spirit which animated the authors of the Charter nine years ago in San Francisco. Like them, we have wished to be guided by that great longing for peace which grips mankind. Like them, we have refused to admit the inevitability of wars, as we are convinced that mutual understanding and respect must enable States to establish lasting peaceful relations among themselves. We have therefore successively taken up the problems weighing on our future. We have examined them dispassionately, or rather with one single passion, that of finding solutions.

In July, we thus took an important step forward. The Far East found peace once more. The Geneva agreements hushed the roar of guns. Lengthy and difficult negotiations made it possible to remove the threat which weighed ever more heavily on the peace of Asia. At the same time three States, Cambodia, Laos and Vietnam, whose sovereignty and independence were once more solemnly recognized, saw their sufferings cease. Everywhere, this result was welcomed as a proof that men of goodwill can negotiate instead of fighting and that men can get together with a desire for understanding instead of rising up to destroy one another. That is how I conceive true fidelity to the spirit of the Charter.

In this spirit, I also attempted to broach a problem of particular concern to us: Tunisia. Here again, we refused to admit that there was no solution. Between two countries as closely linked as France and Tunisia, it could not be impossible to establish satisfactory relations, taking into account economic requirements and the wishes of all the inhabitants, with full respect for the aspirations and the civilization of all corncerned. In this field as in others, negotiations between parties animated with the same desire to succeed was to make it possible to lay down the foundations for a lasting agreement. On July 31, I went to Tunis. I wished to proclaim there my faith in the future of a liberal policy of mutual understanding and political, economic and social progress. As you know, negotiations were started shortly afterward between the French and Tunisian Governments, and we hope to see them successfully concluded very soon.

Finally, during this same period, the French Government had to deal with one of the most serious causes of conflict in our ancient and recent history: the centuries-old hostility between France and Germany. Insofar as the Paris agreements laid down the basis for equitable and open cooperation between the two countries, and insofar as they enable Germany to resume her place in the European community, we are conscious of having contributed to a step forward in the struggle for peace and security.

Our task is only beginning. The whole world will continue to suffer bitterly from its insecurity as long as there remains this tension between East and West which haunts all our minds. We must be prepared to reply to the concern and anxiety which so many men and women in every country feel today. If only to respect this concern and anxiety, we must in any case forego the diplomatic cleverness which is always tempting but most dangerous, and which has played too great a part in international affairs during this long period of tension.

Our duty is to seek and propose clear solutions, even if—as will inevitably be the case at first—they must be limited and modest.

The French Government would like to take part in this indispensable effort by sharing with you a few thoughts and suggestions on the problems which are at present our principal concern.

For the last several years the Soviet Union and the three Western powers have been exchanging notes. A few days ago the Soviet Union—after having proposed a four-power conference to be held some time this month—unexpectedly invited 20 or 25 countries to attend a meeting set for the 29th.

I shall be very frank in saying first that these proposals are neither realistic nor reasonable in their present form.

Without proper preparation—which is essential in such a venture—it is hard to see in such negotiations any concrete basis for success.

When negotiations do start—and we hope that that day will soon come—they should take place between parties whose positions are clearly defined, and do not lead to bargaining or intrigue. That is why there can be no objective and effective discussion within a four-power conference until the countries of Western Europe which are directly concerned have ratified the Paris treaty. To act otherwise would be a flight into the unknown and would spell certain failure. If we took the risk, what responsibilities would we not have placed on our shoulders?

We would have awakened immense hopes in the hearts of those peoples which yearn for peace and security; and at one fell blow these hopes would collapse. That is a course which we have no right to follow.

Does that mean that we must abandon the task of peace and the passionate search for an international detente? No, certainly not. The French Government hereby affirms that its will to act for peace has not faltered and will not falter.

We shall not let the idea gain credence that the West, that the Atlantic Community, rejects peace or that it brushes aside the opportunities of effecting a rapprochement and conciliation, that it despairs of ever seeing the establishment of a system of peaceful coexistence capable of restoring confidence. That is why we loudly proclaim that the door to negotiation is not closed. Quite the contrary.

We may expect that the signatories of the Paris agreements will have completed the ratification procedure at the beginning of next spring. Such will certainly be the case for France; the National Assembly will make its decision as early as December, and the second of our assemblies, the Council of the Republic, probably in February. In other countries, parliamentary procedure may be a little slower, but, according to information available, the countries most directly concerned will have taken their final decision around March or April.

Why then should we not decide that a four-power conference be held in May for instance? The French Government is prepared, for its part, to organize it in Paris, if that were convenient to the three other participants.

It has not been sufficiently pointed out that, for the first time in history, the London and Paris agreements organize a system of regulation, limitation, control and publication of armaments among a certain number of countries. This doubtless deserves a few moments of thought. Since generous-minded men have started to seek means to prevent war, their imagination has led them to conceive a machinery of guarantees, the setting up and implementation of which would permit the creation of that security which the peoples of the world yearn for. The limitation and control of armaments have been defined by them as two essential guarantees of this security. It has often been shown that without these foundations the structure of peace would always be precarious.

The system of limitation and control of armaments provided for in the Paris agreements constitutes, in my view, a useful example, a prefiguration of a more general system. In proposing this, and in ensuring its adoption, the French Government had in mind the application of the same principles and rules on a European scale, and perhaps sometime later on a world scale.

In its note of November 13, the Soviet Union states that, in reply to the Paris agreements, the countries of Eastern Europe consider themselves threatened and will take measures to safeguard their security. At the risk of surprising our colleagues representing those countries here, I affirm that, for my part, I would be quite happy to see the creation of an Eastern European Defense association modeled upon the Western European Union, as long as it adopts the medalities provided for by the West for the publication, limitation and control of armaments.

If, by similar arrangements, the Soviet Union and the States associated with it adopted symmetrical formulae to ours, and provided that they include a certain degree of publicity, an important step forward would have been taken toward our goal.

Later, exchanges of information and mutual assurances could take place between the two systems. Perhaps the limitations or the controls might take on a contractual form.

A flexible regional plan would thus gradually be set up, with the field of application of the limitations, reductions and control increasing progressively.

These are only a summary outline and suggestions which should be cautiously explored with a view to a gradual definition of a system of collective security applicable to the whole of Europe. The main task today is to show that such projects can develop, provided they are drawn up in complete good faith, with the single resolve to furnish all concerned with the essential guarantees for the development of a feeling of security of which the peoples of Europe have been deprived for so long.

Of course, it is not incumbent upon the United Nations to settle directly the regional problems to which I have just referred. Nevertheless, they concern all countries and all men. It is not the peace or security of a single continent that is at stake. It is the peace and security of the entire world.

I must also say to you that our immense task in Europe can only be fulfilled with the moral support of world opinion, of which this great Organization is the interpreter.

So many difficulties must be overcome, so much distrust dispelled and so much prejudice conquered that a great deal of courage and perseverance will be required by men of good will in order to complete their mission. Our Organization brings them the assistance of an institution of a universal nature and enables them to know and understand one another. That is why my Government has great hope in the future of the United Nations which remain for the French people the center from which radiate the ideals of justice and peace.

Dag Hammarskjold
[1905-1961]

Dag Hammarskjöld, Swedish statesman appointed Secretary-General of the United Nations in 1953, was before that time economic and financial adviser to the Swedish government. Following are parts of his address at the 1955 Commencement of Stanford University, California, on June 19.

VALUES OF NATIONALISM AND INTERNATIONALISM

NATIONALISM—internationalism. These abstract words, so often abused, so often misunderstood, cover high ideals and strong emotions, reflect modes of thought and action which shape our world.

We often see the word "nationalism" used in a derogatory sense. The same is true of the word "internationalism." When nationalism connotes, for example, a "go-it-alone" isolationism, and internationalism an outlook which belittles the significance of national life and of nations as centers of political action and spiritual tradition, the words become contradictory and the attitudes they describe irreconcilable. From such interpretations of the words comes the tendency to think of nationalism as in fundamental conflict with an internationalist attitude.

But other interpretations lead to a quite different result. Nationalism and internationalism, when understood as meaning recognition of the value and the rights of the nation, and of the dependence of the nation on the world, represent essential parts of the mental and spiritual equipment of all responsible men in our time. Everybody today, with part of his being, belongs to one country, with its specific traditions and problems, while with another part he has become a citizen of a world which no longer permits national isolation. Seen in this light there could not be any conflict between nationalism and internationalism, between the nation and the world.

The question is not *either* the nation *or* the world. It is, rather, how to serve the world by service to our nation, and how to serve the nation by service to the world.

The dilemma is as old as mankind. There has always been the problem of how to harmonize loyalty to the smaller group, inside which we are working, with loyalty to the larger unit to which this group belongs. However, in our time this problem has taken on new proportions and a new significance. It has also developed aspects unknown to previous generations.

For vast multitudes this is an era when, for the first time. they have fully sensed the rights and responsibilities of free peoples and sovereign nations. It is also the era when freedom and sovereignty for the first time have been actually within their reach. Parallel with great social and economic revolutions within many countries, we witness now a world revolution from which peoples long dependent on others, begin to emerge as strong, dynamic national states.

In the pride of self-realization natural to these new states we should welcome the constructive element—a self-assertion like that of a young man coming of age, conscious of his powers, eager to find his own way, to make his voice heard and to render his contribution to progress. We should meet this new enthusiasm with understanding, in full appreciation of the rich gifts it may bring to a world of many nations and peoples in friendly competition. In world affairs such an attitude, which is in line with the great traditions of this country, may be regarded as an expression of true democracy in international life.

I have spoken about the positive aspect of the nationalism of a young state. Let us not forget that these positive elements can be turned into an explosive force if repressed or unguided. It is a sign of true statesmanship, both in the new countries and in older nations, so to direct national policies as to avoid collisions developing out of unwise reactions to the new forces. History places a burden on our shoulders. The creative urges of the emergent nations are tinged with strong emotions from the past. It is for all of us, denying neither the good nor the ills of that past, to look ahead and not to permit old conflicts to envenom the spirit of the creative work before us.

We have to face also another kind of new nationalism, which is a strong force in every state. It is a commonplace that recent technological changes have created a new kind of interdependence among nations and brought all peoples much closer to each other. For reasons which lie outside the political sphere, practically all mankind today must be regarded as a unit in important economic, technical, and political respects. Economic changes tend to sweep over all the world. New inventions influence quickly the life of all peoples. Because it is more difficult to limit wars to a single area, all wars are of concern to all nations. Not only construction, but also destruction may today be global.

It is natural that this new situation should provoke a resistance, inspired by the fear that our own country and her own private world might find itself submerged in some global development. And so we find people trying to find ways to isolate themselves from general trends and to build up closed, protected units. We can understand, or even sympathize with such a reaction, but we must recognize that if it represents a resistance to change, it is doomed to failure. Such self-sought isolation may persevere for some time. It will not endure forever, and the longer the change is resisted and adjustment shirked, the more violent will be the final reaction when the walls collapse.

The reply to nationists who wish to remain aloof in such vain efforts at self-protection is that the way to safeguard what they rightly want to defend is not isolation. The way is a vigorous and self-confident development, in free contact with the world, of the special qualities and assets of their nation and their people—a development which should give them their just weight in the international balance. Giving thus to the world what is specifically ours, we could manifest and protect our national character, while accepting change and opening our minds to the influences of the world.

Discussion about international integration, world organization, and world government throws much light on the problem of the nation versus the world. I would not regard the wide-spread and often vocal resistance to anything which might be construed as tending to limit national sovereignty as a new upsurge of nationalism. It should rather be regarded as a symptom of how heavily faith in national self-determination weighs in the scales in every effort to reconcile the nation and the world. Such expression of national feelings is both an asset and a liability. It is an asset to the extent that it reflects the determination to shape one's own fate and to take the responsibility for it. It is an asset as a brake on immature experiments in international integration. But it is a liability when it blinds our eyes to the necessity of that degree of international organization which has become necessary to national life.

Whatever doubts history may cast, I believe that the hope for a world of peace and order, inspired by respect for man, has never ceased to agitate the minds of men. I believe that it accounts for the great and noble human spirit behind the ravaged exterior of a history whose self-inflicted wounds have become more and more atrocious. And I believe that at the point we have now reached in our technical development, our creed may gain new possibilities to shape history.

This week we will celebrate here on the West coast and all over the world the 10th anniversary of the signing of the United Nations Charter. It will be an occasion for fresh thinking about the problems and the challenge of our world. The United Nations is an expression of our will to find a synthesis between the nation and the world. It is an attempt to provide us with a framework inside which it is possible to serve the world by serving our nation, and to serve our nation by serving the world. Whatever may be the past shortcomings of this experiment in world organization, it gives sense and direction to the efforts of all men who are striving toward a better world.

Nickolai Aleksandrovich Bulganin

[1896-1975]

Nikolai A. Bulganin became Premier of Soviet Russia in February, 1955, replacing Malenkov who had succeeded Stalin. For his work in helping to establish a Communist regime in Poland, Bulganin had been rewarded by a place on the Politburo in 1946, and in 1947 he became Deputy Premier.

Here presented are parts of Premier Bulganin's speech at the opening of the Geneva Conference of the heads of government of the Big Four, July 18, 1955. Some of President Eisenhower's comments at the same meeting are included in the section on United States Government.

THE LESSENING OF INTERNATIONAL TENSION

ON BEHALF of the Soviet Government, I am happy to greet Mr. Dwight Eisenhower, the President of the United States, M. Edgar Faure, the Prime Minister of France, and Sir Anthony Eden, the Prime Minister of Great Britain, and also the members of their delegations and to express a sincere wish that the work of our conference be a fruitful one.

I would like to express my great satisfaction at the opportunity to establish at this conference personal contacts with the heads of the governments of the United States, France and Britain..

We were glad to hear President Eisenhower's statement namely: The American people want to be friends with the Soviet peoples.

There are no natural differences between our peoples or our nations. There are no territorial conflicts or commercial rivalries.

Historically, our two countries have always been at peace. Further, Mr. President pointed out the need to lift artificial barriers between the two peoples.

We are in complete agreement with that since the lifting of the said barriers would meet both the national interests of the Soviet and American peoples and the interests of universal peace.

The principal purpose of our conference is to find ways to achieve the necessary understanding on the problems to be settled. The delegation of the Soviet Union has come to this conference with the desire to find, through joint efforts by all the participants, solutions for the outstanding issues and for its part, is prepared to give careful consideration to the proposals advanced by the other participants.

There can be no doubt that this is exactly what is expected of us by the people whose eyes are focused at this conference in Geneva. It is not fortuitous that many statesmen, recognizing the unbending will of the peoples for peace, are coming out with ever growing determination in favor of having outstanding problems settled on the basis of an adequate recognition of the legitimate rights of all parties concerned.

We are not inclined to minimize the difficulties that stand in the way towards the settlement of such problems, including the outstanding problems of Europe and Asia. These difficulties do exist and they are not insignificant, but if we have all come to this conference with a desire to find ways to overcome them, then that would be guarantee of the success of this conference. The Soviet Government is of the opinion that this conference of the heads of the governments of the four powers who are meeting for the first time in the ten post-war years can play a historic part provided we all show a genuine desire to achieve a relaxation of international tension and bring about a feeling of confidence between nations.

In the opinion of the Soviet Government the purpose of this conference is not to indulge in recriminations but to find ways and means to ease international tension and create an atmosphere of confidence in relations between nations.

The Soviet Government for its part, is prepared to contribute together with the governments of the United States, Britain and France to the achievement of that noble purpose.

The Soviet Government believes that in endeavoring to ameliorate relations between countries the four-power conference should pay due attention to the problem of strengthening economic ties between them and, in particular, to the developments of trade.

The present state of affairs when artificial restrictions of various kinds have been introduced in a number of countries as a result of which the economic and trade ties between many countries developed over many years have been broken, is one of the serious obstacles on the way to the relaxation of international tension.

Such restrictions that are usually introduced when the economy of a state is subordinated to the interests of military preparations cannot be justified in any way if one is governed by the desire for a settlement of the outstanding international problems and for the termination of the "cold war."

We do not point this out for the reason the economy of the Soviet Union cannot do without the restoration of normal economic and trade relations with other countries that were broken through no fault of ours.

We mention this because in this field there are considerable possibilities for establishing normal and friendly relations between countries and this could lead to favorable results for the improvement of the well-being of peoples, relaxation of international tension and consolidation of confidence among nations.

Accordingly, we stand for a broad development of international contacts and cooperation in the field of culture and science, for the removal of obstacles impeding intercourse among nations.

These are the most important questions which, in the opinion of the Soviet delegation, should be examined at our conference and these are the considerations which it wanted to put forward on these matters at the outset of our work.

The Soviet Government, for its part, will do all it can, so that the conference might justify the hopes of peoples craving for a peaceful and tranquil life.

Frank Lloyd Wright
[1869–1959]

Frank Lloyd Wright, the most widely influential of contemporary American architects, developed a style which constitutes one of the chief movements in twentieth century architectural design. He termed it "organic architecture," emphasis being placed on the purposes of the building, the materials used, and the relation of the building to the surrounding landscape. The following excerpts are drawn partly from material in a speech made in 1938 to the Association of Federal Architects in Washington, D.C., and partly from one of Mr. Wright's Sir George Watson Chair Lectures in London, 1939. Frank Lloyd Wright was known for his plain-speaking and uncompromising stand on his principles.

ON ARCHITECTURE

COLONIAL WILLIAMSBURG. It is an admirable restoration, authentic replica of the setting of our early historic settler's life. As a museum piece it is invaluable to us because it places it where we can see it and see through it. We may read (as I read there) something of what really was the matter with our forefathers when they got here—the men who came here as rebels against oppression (later to become revolutionists) to find a new and better land. They came and lived within shooting distance of the Indians and brought that culture with them which we now see in detail at Williamsburg. We see that it is all just what they had there, back home. Of course, "back home" is what all Englishmen in foreign lands wish for. If you watch Englishmen conduct their lives as their lives run around the whole world you will find them doing just what was done and just as near as possible as it was done back home, whether they are doing it in India, Africa, Australia, or at the North Pole. Whatever they did at home, that same thing they do so far as they can do it—south, north, east, or west in the new land in which they find themselves.

There Williamsburg then ran true to form. We must say that the restoration is a fine museum piece and as such valuable to Americans if they would only let it be a museum piece and not an illusion, and would study it for what significance it has where our life is concerned, and not attempting to live in it still. As an object lesson to the Nation in architecture, it is valuable. Studying the exhibit at Williamsburg closely, from the inside, one may see why and how, now, this Nation was contrived by the moneyed man for the moneyed man by the money minded; see why property was the criterion by means of which this union was to survive, if it could survive at all. You can read in this persistent "search for the elegant solution" that the culture which the colonists had on them (or with them) when they arrived was French culture modified by a century or two of English "taste." England had little elegance of her own so turned to that of the French, imitated French culture and, inevitably, brought that imitation to these shores. That is plain truth concerning the culture of our colonists. Now, why not, indeed, have a fine restoration of that culture where we can look it in the face for what it is worth today, and see what the culture was that lay in behind as one element in the culture of a mixed Nation such as this one of ours?

GOVERNMENT VS. ORGANIC ARCHITECTURE. The cultural influences in our country are like the "floo floo" bird. I am referring to the peculiar and especial bird who always flew backward. To keep the wind out of its eyes? No. Just because it didn't give a darn where it was going, but just had to see where it had been. Now, in the "floo floo" bird you have the true symbol of our Government architecture—too, and in consequence, how discredited American culture stands in the present time. All the world knows it to be funny except America. What prevented us and still prevents us from knowing it? Armchair education, let's say. Now, all this has parallels in history. The Romans were just as incognizant as we of the things of the spirit. They, too, had no culture of their own. England had none of her own, and we, having none, got what we have as a substitute second, third, or fourth hand from them all. Roman culture, for instance, was Greek. The Romans, however, did have great engineers (you have all heard of the arch), but what did the Romans do with their greatest invention—the arch? You know well enough that for centuries they wasted it by pasting a travesty of Greek trabeation over it to conceal the truth of structure, until finally, some vulgar Roman, more "uncultured" than the rest, one day got up and said: "Hell! Take it all away! What's the matter with the arch? It's a genuine, beautiful and noble thing"; and finally they got it, got the common arch as indigenous architecture. We, the modern Romans, probably are going to get architecture something like that same way. We are going to have a true architecture of glass, steel, and the forms that gratify our new sense of space. We are going to have it. No Colonial Eden is able, long, to say us nay.

Culture, given time, will catch up and assert itself in spite of reaction. This thing which we call America, as I have said, goes around the world today. It is chiefly spirit but that spirit is reality. Not by way of Government can we find encouragement of any help. No, we can have nothing by way of official Government until the thing is at least ten years in the past. What can Government do with an advanced idea? If it is still a controversial idea, and any good idea must be so, can Government touch it without its eye on at least the next election? It cannot. I know of nothing more silly than to expect "Government" to solve our advanced problems for us. If we have no ideas, how can Government have any?

THE EXPERT, ON TAP OR ON TOP? There is no very great difficulty in creating an organism, and entity, in the way of a building in which all needed services are incorporated features of the building. But that type of building, call it creation, cannot be under any "specialistic" system. Such creation must occur by single-minded mastery on the part of the creator of the building, that is, if we mean *organic* building. We cannot in organic building have a group of specialists; we have to relegate the expert to the backyard of the building, or to oblivion.

CLIENTS. No man can build a building for another who does not believe in him, who does not believe in what he believes in, and who has not chosen him because of this faith, knowing what he can do. That is the nature of architect and client as I see it. When a man wants to build a building he seeks an interpreter, does he not? He seeks some man who has the technique to express that thing which he himself desires but cannot do. So should a man come to me for a building he would be ready for me. It would be what I could do that he wanted.

Albert Einstein

[1879-1955]

Albert Einstein was one of the greatest mathematical physicists of all time. In 1939, he sent a letter to President Roosevelt, explaining the possibility of releasing atomic energy in a weapon of unprecedented power, and this information provided the impetus for government atomic research. After the bombing of Hiroshima in 1945 and the terrible destruction which resulted, Dr. Einstein made known his advocacy of world government for the maintenance of peace between nations. This is the theme of his address, somewhat abridged here, which was broadcast on Mrs. Roosevelt's television program, February 12, 1950.

PEACE IN THE ATOMIC AGE

I AM GRATEFUL to you for the opportunity to express my conviction in this most important political question.

The idea of achieving security through national armament is, at the present state of military technique, a disastrous illusion. On the part of the United States this illusion has been particularly fostered by the fact that this country succeeded first in producing an atomic bomb. The belief seemed to prevail that in the end it were possible to achieve decisive military superiority.

In this way, any potential opponent would be intimidated, and security, so ardently desired by all of us, brought to us and all of humanity. The maxim which we have been following during these last five years has been, in short: security through superior military power, whatever the cost.

The armament race between the U.S.A. and the U.S.S.R., originally supposed to be a preventive measure, assumes hysterical character. On both sides, the means to mass destruction are perfected with feverish haste—behind the respective walls of secrecy. The H-bomb appears on the public horizon as a probably attainable goal.

If successful, radioactive poisoning of the atmosphere and hence annihilation of any life on earth has been brought within the range of technical possibilities. The ghostlike character of this development lies in its apparently compulsory trend. Every step appears as the unavoidable consequence of the preceding one. In the end, there beckons more and more clearly general annihilation.

Is there any way out of this impasse created by man himself? All of us, and particularly those who are responsible for the attitude of the U.S. and the U.S.S.R., should realize that we may have vanquished an external enemy, but have been incapable of getting rid of the mentality created by the war.

It is impossible to achieve peace as long as every single action is taken with a possible future conflict in view. The leading point of view of all political action should therefore be: What can we do to bring about a peaceful co-existence and even loyal cooperation of the nations?

The first problem is to do away with mutual fear and distrust. Solemn renunciation of violence (not only with respect to means of mass destruction) is undoubtedly necessary.

Such renunciation, however, can only be effective if at the same time a supra-national judicial and executive body is set up empowered to decide questions of immediate concern to the security of the nations. Even a declaration of the nations to collaborate loyally in the realization of such a "restricted world government" would considerably reduce the imminent danger of war.

In the last analysis, every kind of peaceful cooperation among men is primarily based on mutual trust and only secondly on institutions such as courts of justice and police. This holds for nations as well as for individuals. And the basis of trust is loyal give and take.

William Faulkner

[1897–1962]

William Faulkner, one of the major American novelists of the twentieth century, is perhaps most admired for his novels, The Sound and the Fury, *and* As I Lay Dying. *He was awarded the 1949 Nobel Prize for literature, and gave the following speech on his acceptance of the award, December 10, 1950, at Stockholm, Sweden.*

ACCEPTANCE OF THE NOBEL PRIZE

I FEEL THAT this award was not made to me as a man, but to my work— a life's work in the agony and sweat of the human spirit, not for glory and least of all for profit, but to create out of the materials of the human spirit something which did not exist before. So this award is only mine in trust. It will not be difficult to find a dedication for the money part of it commensurate with the purpose and significance of its origin. But I would like to do the same with the acclaim too, by using this moment as a pinnacle from which I might be listened to by the young men and women already dedicated to the same anguish and travail, among whom is already that one who will some day stand where I am standing.

Our tragedy today is a general and universal physical fear so long sustained by now that we can even bear it. There are no longer problems of the spirit. There is only the question: When will I be blown up? Because of this, the young man or woman writing today has forgotten the problems of the human heart in conflict with itself which alone can make good writing because only that is worth writing about, worth the agony and the sweat.

He must learn them again. He must teach himself that the basest of all things is to be afraid; and, teaching himself that, forget it forever, leaving no room in his workshop for anything but the old verities and truths of the heart, the universal truths lacking which any story is ephemeral and doomed—love and honor and pity and pride and compassion and sacrifice. Until he does so, he labors under a curse. He writes not of love but of lust, of defeats in which nobody loses anything of value, of victories without hope and, worst of all, without pity or compassion. His griefs grieve on no universal bones, leaving no scars. He writes not of the heart but of the glands.

Until he learns these things, he will write as though he stood among and watched the end of man. I decline to accept the end of man. It is easy enough to say that man is immortal simply because he will endure: that when the last ding-dong of doom has clanged and faded from the last worthless rock hanging tideless in the last red and dying evening, that even then there will still be one more sound: that of his puny inexhaustible voice, still talking. I refuse to accept this. I believe that man will not merely endure: he will prevail. He is immortal, not because he alone among creatures has an inexhaustible voice, but because he has a soul, a spirit capable of compassion and sacrifice and endurance. The poet's, the writer's, duty is to write about these things. It is his privilege to help man endure by lifting his heart, by reminding him of the courage and honor and hope and pride and compassion and pity and sacrifice which have been the glory of his past. The poet's voice need not merely be the record of man, it can be one of the props, the pillars to help him endure and prevail.

Dylan Thomas

[1914-1953]

Dylan Thomas who was born and lived in South Wales, was recognized as among the most gifted British poets of recent times. He was noted for his voice, his poetry readings, and his speeches. The following talk, given here in part, was recorded by him to be broadcast over the British Broadcasting Corporation station, March 30, 1954; the actual broadcast of the recording took place after his death.

A VISIT TO AMERICA

Across the United States of America, from New York to California and back, glazed, again, for many months of the year, there streams and sings for its heady supper a dazed and prejudiced procession of European lecturers, scholars, sociologists, economists, writers, authorities on this and that and even, in theory, on the United States of America. And, breathlessly between addresses and receptions, in planes, and trains and boiling hotel bedroom ovens, many of these attempt to keep journals and diaries. At first, confused and shocked by shameless profusion and almost shamed by generosity, unaccustomed to such importance as they are assumed, by their hosts, to possess, and up against the barrier of a common language, they write in their note-books like demons, generalizing away, on character and culture and the American political scene. But towards the middle of their middle-aged whisk through middle-western clubs and universities, the fury of the writing flags; their spirits are lowered by the spirit with which they are everywhere strongly greeted and which, in ever-increasing doses, they themselves lower; and they begin to mistrust themselves and their reputations—for they have found, too often, that an audience will receive a lantern lecture on, say, ceramics, with the same uninhibited enthusiasm that it accorded the very week before to a paper on the Modern Turkish novel. And, in their diaries, more and more do such entries appear as "No way of escape!" or "Buffalo!" or "I am beaten," until at last they cannot write a word. And twittering all over, old before their time, with eyes like rissoles in the sand, they are helped up the gangway of the home-bound liner by kind bosom friends (of all kinds and bosoms) who bolster them on the back, pick them up again, thrust bottles, sonnets, cigars, addresses into their pockets, have a farewell party in their cabin, pick them up again, and snickering and yelping, are gone: to wait at the dockside for another boat from Europe and another batch of fresh green lecturers.

There they go, every spring, from New York to Los Angeles: exhibitionists, polemicists, histrionic publicists, theological rhetoricians, historical hoddy-doddies, balletomanes, ulterior decorators, windbags and bigwigs and humbugs, men in love with stamps, men in love with steaks, men after millionaires' widows, men with elephantiasis of the reputation (huge trunks and teeny minds), authorities on gas, bishops, best-sellers, editors looking for writers, writers looking for publishers, publishers looking for dollars, existentialists, serious physicists with nuclear missions, men from the B.B.C. who speak as though they had the Elgin Marbles in their mouths, potboiling philosophers, professional Irishmen (very lepri-corny), and I am afraid, fat poets with slim volumes.

Did we pass one another *en route* all unknowing, I wonder, one of us spry-eyed, with clean, white lectures and a soul he could call his own, going buoyantly west to his remunerative doom in the great State University factories, another returning dog-eared as his clutch of poems and his carefully typed impromptu asides? I ache for us both. There one goes, unsullied as yet, in his Pullman pride, toying, oh boy, with a blunderbuss bourbon, being smoked by a large cigar, riding out to the wide open spaces of the faces of his waiting audience.

He is vigorously welcomed by an earnest crew-cut platoon of giant collegiates all chasing the butterfly culture with net, notebook, poison, and label, each with at least thirty-six terribly white teeth, and is nursed away, as heavily gently as though he were an imbecile rich aunt with a short prospect of life, into a motor car in which, for a mere fifty miles or so travelled at poet-breaking speed, he assures them of the correctness of their asumption that he is half-witted by stammering inconsequential answers in an over-British accent to the genial questions about what international conference Stephen Spender might be attending at the moment or the reaction of British poets to the work of a famous American whose name he did not know or catch. He is then taken to a small party of only a few hundred people, all of whom hold the belief that what a visiting lecturer needs before he trips onto the platform is just enough martinis so that he can trip *off* the platform as well.

Late at night, in his room, he fills a page of his journal with a confused, but scathing, acount of his first engagement; summarizes American advanced education in a paragraph that will be meaningless tomorrow, and falls to sleep, where he is immediately chased through long dark thickets by a Mrs. Mabel Frankincense Mehaffey with a tray of martinis and lyrics. And there goes another happy poet bedraggledly back to New York, which struck him all of a sheepish, never-sleeping heap at first but which seems to him now after the ulcerous rigor of a lecturer's spring, as a haven cosy as toast, cool as an ice-box, and safe as sky-scrapers.

Eleanor Roosevelt

[1884–1962]

(Anna) Eleanor Roosevelt, wife of President Franklin D. Roosevelt, was active in public affairs, strongly advocating many social welfare measures. In December, 1945, she was appointed United States representative to the United Nations General Assembly, continuing until 1952. After that, she maintained her interest in the United Nations and took part in many projects relating to its work, speaking about it before many and varied audiences. Presented here are parts of her speech at the opening of a series of United Nations seminars at Brandeis University, December 17, 1954.

THE UNITED NATIONS AS A BRIDGE

You HEAR people say, "Why hasn't the United Nations done this or that?" The United Nations functions just as well as the member nations make it function, and no better or worse. And so the first thing to look at is, I think, the kind of machinery that was set up, and what it was meant to do

Now we have to go back in our minds to the time when the Charter was first planned. At that time the war was not over, and this was a dream, and everybody accepted it as a dream—an idea to set up an organization , the object of that organization being to keep peace.

Great areas of the world knew what it was like to have war on their doorsteps. We did not know what it was like, either to be occupied or to be bombed. That experience has made such a difference to many nations. I think we need to use our imaginations, because we really have to understand what the nations felt, what they feel today—where they actually were occupied or had great destruction within their own lands.

They had co-operated during the war; they believed that they were going to go on co-operating after the war. That was one of the great myths of the centuries.

They also believed that this organization they were setting up was to be an organization to maintain peace, not to make peace. Peace was going to be made, and then this organization would help to maintain it. What happened, of course, was that peace has never been found. And so this organization, which was not set up to meet certain questions, has had questions brought to it that were not in mind at the beginning.

But talk can have great value; you have to think of it as a bridge. You have to think of the General Assembly as a place where bridges are built between peoples.

We in the United States are an impatient people. We want to see results tomorrow. I am not sure sometimes that it isn't the people who can out-wait the other people, who have the advantage. Frequently, moving too fast can set you back.

People are meeting in the United Nations that come from backgrounds where there have been certain customs and habits for generations. Some people grow impatient of these. We might think occasionally that other people find their way the best, and not our way. There are things we can learn from other people. You must have as a basis to all understanding, the willingness to learn and the willingness to listen.

Even though we have difficulties through having the Soviets as a part of the organization, just remember that it may be a very good thing. That is the bridge—if ever a time comes when there is a crack and we can perhaps meet people of another country, a Soviet or a satellite, it may be the one real way of increasing understanding. At the present time, they use the United Nations as a platform to boast about what they achieve. What they are told to say, they have to say, just exactly as they are told to say it. It must be hard to be that much of a slave. Their government wants to reach their own people; a speech made by a Soviet delegate is reported in full in the Soviet press. No answer is ever reported. These things are real difficulties.

When we look upon the failures in the United Nations, we should not be disheartened, because if we take the failure and learn, eventually we will use this machinery better and better. We will also learn one important thing, and that is, no machinery works unless people make it work.

And in a democracy like ours, it is the people who have to tell their representatives what they want them to do. And it is the acceptance of individual responsibility by each one of us that actually will make the United Nations machinery work. If we don't accept that, and if we don't do the job, we may well fail—but it lies in our hands. And I think that is the main thing for us to remember today.

We are the strongest nation in the world. We, whether we like it or not, are the leaders. And we lead not only in military and economic strength, but we lead in knowing what are our values, what are the things we believe in, and in being willing to live up to them, and being willing to accept the fact that living up to them here, we help ourselves, but we also help the world.

J. Robert Oppenheimer
[1904-1967]

J. Robert Oppenheimer, American physicist, was the director of the laboratories in Los Alamos, New Mexico, where the atomic bomb was perfected. He had been professor of physics at the University of California and the California Institute of Technology. Later he was director of the Institute for Advanced Studies, Princeton, New Jersey. In 1953, his suspension as consultant to the Atomic Energy Commission caused extensive debate. In 1954, he was reelected director of the Institute for Advanced Studies.

Following are parts of the speech delivered by Dr. Oppenheimer at the closing of the Columbia University Bicentennial Anniversary celebration, December 26, 1954.

PROSPECTS IN THE ARTS AND SCIENCES

IN THE NATURAL sciences these are, and have been, and are most surely likely to continue to be, heroic days. Discovery follows discovery, each both raising and answering questions, each ending a long search, and each providing the new instruments for new search.

There are radical ways of thinking unfamiliar to common sense, connected with it by decades or centuries of increasingly specialized and unfamiliar experience. There are lessons how limited, for all its variety, the common experience of man has been with regard to natural phenomenon, and hints and analogies as to how limited may be his experience with man.

Every new finding is a part of the instrument kit of the sciences for further investigation and for penetrating into new fields. Discoveries of knowledge fructify technology and the practical arts, and these in turn pay back refined techniques, new possibilities for observation and experiment.

In any science there is a harmony between practitioners. A man may work as an individual, learning of what his colleagues do through reading or conversation; or he may be working as a member of a group on problems whose technical equipment is too massive for individual effort. But whether he is part of a team or solitary in his own study, he, as a professional, is a member of a community.

His colleagues in his own branch of science will be grateful to him for the inventive or creative thoughts he has, will welcome his criticism. His world and work will be objectively communicable and he will be quite sure that, if there is error in it, that error will not be long undetected. In his own line of work he lives in a community where common understanding combines with common purpose and interest to bind men together both in freedom and in cooperation.

This experience will make him acutely aware of how limited, how precious is this condition of his life; for in his relations with a wider society there will be neither the sense of community nor of objective understanding. He will sometimes find, it is true, in returning to practical undertakings, some sense of community with men who are not expert in his science, with other scientists whose work is remote from his, and with men of action and men of art.

The frontiers of science are separated now by long years of study, by specialized vocabularies, arts, techniques and knowledge from the common heritage even of a most civilized society, and anyone working at the frontier of such science is in that sense a very long way from home and a long way, too, from the practical arts that were its matrix and origin, as indeed they were of what we today call art.

The specialization of science is an inevitable accompaniment of progress; yet it is full of dangers, and it is cruelly wasteful, since so much that is beautiful and enlightening is cut off from most of the world. Thus it is proper to the role of the scientist that he not merely find new truth and communicate it to his fellows, but that he teach, that he try to bring the most honest and intelligible account of new knowledge to all who will try to learn.

This is one reason—it is the decisive organic reason—why scientists belong in universities. It is one reason why the patronage of science by and through universities is its most proper form; for it is here, in teaching, in the association of scholars, and in the friendships of teachers and taught, of men who by profession must themselves be both teachers and taught, that the narrowness of scientific life can best be moderated and that the analogies, insights and harmonies of scientific discovery can find their way into the wider life of man.

In the situation of the artist today there are both analogies and differences to that of the scientist; but it is the differences which are the most striking and which raise the problems that touch most on the evil of our day.

For the artist it is not enough that he communicate with others who are expert in his own art. Their fellowship, their understanding and their appreciation may encourage him; but that is not the end of his work, nor its nature.

The artist depends on a common sensibility and culture, on a common meaning of symbols, on a community of experience and common ways of describing and interpreting it. He need not write for everyone or paint or play for everyone. But his audience must be man, and not a specialized set of experts among his fellows.

Today that is very difficult. Often the artist has an aching sense of great loneliness, for the community to which he addresses himself is largely not there; the traditions and the history, the myths and the common experience, which it is his function to illuminate and to harmonize and to portray, have been dissolved in a changing world.

There is, it is true, an artificial audience maintained to moderate between the artist and the world for which he works: the audience of the professional critics, popularizers and advertisers of art. But though, as does the popularizer and promoter of science, the critic fulfills a necessary present function, and introduces some order and some communication between the artist and the world, he cannot add to the intimacy and the directness and the depth with which the artist addresses his fellow men.

To the artist's loneliness there is a complementary great and terrible barrenness in the lives of men. They are deprived of the illumination, the light and the tenderness and insight of an intelligible interpretation, in contemporary terms, of the sorrows and wonders and gaities and follies of man's life.

This may be in part offset, and is, by the great growth of technical means for making the art of the past available. But these provide a record of past intimacies between art and life; even when they are applied to the writing and painting and composing of the day, they do not bridge the gulf between a society too vast and too disordered and the artist trying to give meaning and beauty to its parts.

In an important sense, this world of ours is a new world, in which the unity of knowledge, the nature of human communities, the order of society, the order of ideas, the very notions of society and culture have changed and will not return to what they have been in the past. What is new is new not because it has never been there before, but because it has changed in quality.

One thing that is new is the prevalence of newness, the changing scale and scope of change itself, so that the world alters as we walk in it, so that the years of man's life measure not some small growth or rearrangement or moderation of what he learned in childhood, but a great upheaval.

What is new is that in one generation our knowledge of the natural world engulfs, upsets and complements all knowledge of the natural world before. The techniques, among which and by which we live, multiply and ramify, so that the whole world is bound together by communication, blocked here and there by the immense synopses of political tyranny.

The global quality of the world is new: our knowledge of and sympathy with remote and diverse peoples, our involvement with them in practical terms and our commitment to them in terms of brotherhood. What is new in the world is the massive character of the dissolution and corruption of authority, in belief, in ritual and in temporal order.

Yet this is the world that we have come to live in. The very difficulties which it presents derive from growth in understanding, in skill, in power. To assail the changes that have unmoored us from the past is futile, and, in a deep sense, I think it is wicked. We need to recognize the change and learn what resources we have.

Again I will turn to the schools, and, as their end and as their center, the universities. For the problem of the scientist is in this respect not different from that of the artist, nor of the historian. He needs to be a part of the community, and the community can only, with loss and peril, be without him. Thus it is with a sense of interest and hope that we see a growing recognition that the creative artist is a proper charge on the university, and the university a proper home for him: that a composer or a poet or a playwright or painter needs the toleration, understanding, the rather local and parochial patronage that a university can give; and that this will protect him to some extent from the tyranny of man's communication and professional promotion.

For here there is an honest chance that what the artist has of insight and of beauty will take root in the community and that some intimacy and some human bonds can mark his relations with his patrons. For a university rightly and inherently is a place where the individual man can form new syntheses, where the accidents of friendship and association can open a man's eyes to a part of science or art which he had not known before, where parts of human life, remote and perhaps superficially incompatible one with the other, can find in men their harmony and their synthesis.

The truth is that this is indeed inevitably and increasingly an open, and inevitably and increasing an eclectic world. We know too much for one man to know much, we live too variously to live as one. Our histories and traditions—the very means of interpreting life—are both bonds and barriers among us. Our knowledge separates as well as it unites; our orders disintegrate as well as bind; our art brings us together and sets us apart. The artist's loneliness, the scholar's despairing, because no one will any longer trouble to learn what he can teach, the narrowness of the scientist, these are not unnatural insignia in this great time of change.

This is a world in which each of us, knowing his limitations, knowing the evils of superficiality and the terrors of fatigue, will have to cling to what is close to him, to what he knows, to what he can do, to his friends and his tradition and his love, lest he be dissolved in a universal confusion and know nothing and love nothing.

Both the man of science and the man of art live always at the edge of mystery, surrounded by it; both always, as the measure of their creation, have had to do with the harmonization of what is new and what is familiar, with the balance between novelty and synthesis, with the struggle to make partial order in total chaos.

This cannot be an easy life. We shall have a rugged time of it to keep our minds open and to keep them deep, to keep our sense of beauty and our ability to make it, and our occasional ability to see it, in places remote and strange and unfamiliar.

But this is, as I see it, the condition of man; and in this condition we can help, because we can love one another.

Walter Philip Reuther

[1907–1970]

Walter P. Reuther was one of America's most prominent labor leaders. Starting work at the age of 16 as a bench hand, he rose to be elected president of the United Auto Workers in 1946 at the age of 39. Six years later he became president of the Congress of Industrial Organizations, and when, largely through his efforts, that organization merged with the American Federation of Labor in 1955, he became vice-president of the combined unions.

Progressive and idealistic, Reuther went beyond the issue of higher wages to envision the part that labor should play in building a better world. His differences with George Meany, president of the A.F.L.-C.I.O., culminated in 1968, when Reuther's union, the United Auto Workers, withdrew from the A.F.L.-C.I.O.

Following are excerpts from Mr. Reuther's remarks at a news conference on June 6, 1955, at the end of negotiations between the U.A.W. and the Ford Motor Company which resulted in a contract providing for a guaranteed semiannual wage.

A HISTORICAL AGREEMENT

THIS IS ONE of the most historical agreements that we have written in the twenty years of our union. It is the largest economic package that we have ever negotiated. It is in excess of 20¢ an hour. It provides for wage increases from 6 cents an hour to 16 cents and 17 cents an hour.

It provides for the highest level of pensions that we have ever had. A thirty-year worker with his Social Security and his wife's benefits will get more than $230 a month and a worker with thirty-five years work will get more than $240 a month.

It provides for better hospital-medical care, greater insurance coverage, and, of course, it provides the principle upon which we are going to build the guaranteed annual wage.

There are many other things in this package. They are too numerous to list, but the working agreement has been improved. Seniority has been strengthened, and I am very happy to say that I believe that both the company and the union have made a great contribution to both the well-being of the company and the workers, and together we have made a greater contribution to the American public.

Well, gentlemen, this has been one of the roughest and one of the most complex bargaining sessions that I have ever engaged in, but it has been well worth it.

Adlai Ewing Stevenson
[1900–1965]

Adlai E. Stevenson, whose biography appears on page 597, delivered an address at Smith College commencement exercise, June 6, 1955. Following are parts of this speech.

TO THE GRADUATING CLASS AT SMITH

...I AM NOT unmindful of the appalling fact that countless middle-aged moralists like me are rising these days on countless platforms all over the world to tell thousands of helpless young captives the score—and I suspect that all of those commencement orators are almost as uncomfortable as I am!

I think those commencement speakers and I have something else in common; they are all telling the seniors how important they are—as citizens in a free society, as educated, rational, privileged participants in a great historic crisis. But for my part I want merely to tell you young ladies that I think there is much you can do about that crisis in the humble role of house-wife—which, statistically, is what most of you are going to be whether you like the idea or not just now—and you'll like it!

To explain what I mean I must ask you to step a long way back and recall with me that over vast periods of history and over most of the globe the view has prevailed that man is no more than a unit in the social calculus. Tribal life—the way of life pursued by man for by far the longest period of his history, of which there are remnants today in Africa—knows no individuals, only groups with disciplines and group sanctions. But then at a certain point in time and place there occurred the most momentous revolution yet achieved by mankind—a revolution compared with which such achievements as the discovery of fire or the invention of the wheel seem modest. In the origins of our Western civilization, among two small peoples of the Eastern Mediterranean, the Greeks and the Jews, the great Copernican revolution of politics began:—the discovery that the state exists for man, not man for the state, and that the individual human personality, spirit, soul—call it what you will—contains within itself the meaning and measure of existence and carries as a result the full range of responsibility and choice.

Once the Greek vision of reason and the Jewish concept of moral choice had sent man forth onto the stage of history in this new guise of self-determination and responsibility, clearly only one form of society would provide a framework for the new energies and capacities that could now be released. That form of society is the free society upon which the peoples of the West have been engaged for the last two thousand years, with disasters and setbacks, with triumphs and tragedies, with long sweeps of history's pendulum between the extremes of freedom and tyranny, of individualism and collectivism, of rationalism and spiritualism.

But, as always, history's pendulum swung too far, this time toward the extreme of social fragmentation, of individualism, of abstract intellectualism. And it seems to me that the very process which, in the name of individual liberty, disintegrated the old order—this very process has developed into a powerful drive toward the precise opposite of individualism, namely totalitarian collectivism.

Let me put it this way: individualism promoted technological advances, technology promoted increased specialization, and specialization promoted an ever-closer economic interdependence between specialties. The more intense the specialization, the more complete the interdependence of the specialties—and this necessity of interdependence constitutes a powerful economic drive toward that extreme of a machine state in which individual freedom is wholly submerged.

As the old order disintegrated into this confederation of narrow specialties, each pulling in the direction of *its particular* interest, the individual person tended to become absorbed—literally—by *his particular* function in society. Having sacrificed wholeness of mind and breadth of outlook to the demands of their specialties, individuals no longer responded to social stimuli as total human beings; rather they reacted in partial ways as members of an economic class, or industry, or profession whose concern was with some limited self-interest.

Thus this typical Western man—or typical Western husband!—operates well in the realm of means, as the Romans did before him. But outside his specialty, in the realm of ends, he is apt to operate poorly or not at all. And this neglect of the cultivation of more mature values can only mean that his life, and the life of the society he determines, will lack valid purpose, however busy and even profitable it may be.

And here's where you come in: to restore valid, meaningful purpose to life in your home: to beware of instinctive group reaction to the forces which play upon you and yours, to watch for and arrest the constant gravitational pulls to which we are all exposed, your workaday husband especially, is our specialized, fragmented society that tend to widen the breach between reason and emotion, between means and ends.

And let me also remind you that you will live, most of you, in an environment in which "facts," the data of the senses, are glorified, and value—judgments are assigned inferior status as mere "matters of opinion." It is an environment in which art is often regarded as an adornment of civilization rather than a vital element of it, while philosophy is not only neglected but deemed faintly disreputable because "it never gets you anywhere." Even religion, you will find, commands a lot of earnest allegiance that is more verbal than real, more formal than felt.

You may be hitched to one of these creatures we call "Western man" and I think part of your job is to keep him Western, to keep him truly purposeful, to keep him whole.

In this decisive century it seems to me that we need not just "well-adjusted," "well-balanced" personalities, not just better groupers and conformers (*to casually coin* a couple of fine words) but more idiosyncratic, unpredictable characters (that rugged frontier word, "ornery," occurs to me); people who take open eyes and open minds out with them into the society which they will share and help to transform.

But before any of you gallant girls swear any mighty oaths about fighting the shrivelling corruptions and conformations of mind and spirit, before you adopt any rebellious resolutions for the future, make no mistake about it—it is much easier to get yourself and yours adjusted and to accept the conditioning which so many social pressures will bring to bear upon you. After all, tribal conformity and archaic dictatorship could not have lasted so long if they did not accord

Now, as I have said, women, especially educated women such as you, have a unique opportunity to influence us, man and boy, and to play a direct part in the unfolding drama of our free society. But, I am told that nowadays the young wife or mother is short of time for the subtle arts, that things are not what they used to be; that once immersed in the very pressing and particular problems of domesticity many women feel frustrated and far apart from the great issues and stirring debates for which their education has given them understanding and relish. Once they read Baudelaire. Now it is the Consumers' Guide. Once they wrote poetry. Now it's the laundry list. Once they discussed art and philosophy until late in the night. Now they are so tired they fall asleep as soon as the dishes are finished. There is, often, a sense of contraction, of closing horizons and lost opportunities. They had hoped to play their part in the crisis of the age. But what they do is wash the diapers.

Now, I hope I have not painted too depressing a view of your future, for the fact is that Western marriage and motherhood are yet another instance of the emergence of individual freedom in our Western society. Their basis is the recognition in women as well as men of the primacy of personality and individuality.

In short, far from the vocation of marriage and motherhood leading you away from the great issues of our day, it brings you back to their very center and places upon you an infinitely deeper and more intimate responsibility than that borne by the majority of those who hit the headlines and make the news and live in such a turmoil of great issues that they end by being totally unable to distinguish which issues are really great.

I hope you'll keep everlastingly at the job of seeing life steady and seeing it whole. And you can help others—husbands, children, friends—to do so too. You may, indeed you must, help to integrate a world that has been falling into bloody pieces. History's pendulum has swung dangerously far away from the individual, and you may, indeed you must, help to restore it to the vital center of its arc.

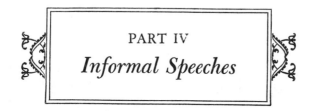

PART IV

Informal Speeches

Ralph Waldo Emerson
[1803–1882]

Following is the speech of Ralph Waldo Emerson, American philosopher and essayist, which he delivered at the Boston Burns Club, Boston, Massachusetts, on January 25, 1859, in commemoration of the hundredth anniversary of the birth of the Scottish poet.

THE MEMORY OF BURNS

MR. PRESIDENT AND GENTLEMEN:—I do not know by what untoward accident it has chanced—and I forbear to inquire—that, in this accomplished circle, it should fall to me, the worst Scotsman of all, to receive your commands, and at the latest hour, too, to respond to the sentiment just offered, and which, indeed, makes the occasion. But I am told there is no appeal, and I must trust to the inspiration of the theme to make a fitness which does not otherwise exist.

Yet, sir, I heartily feel the singular claims of the occasion. At the first announcement, from I know not whence, that the twenty-fifth of January was the hundredth anniversary of the birth of Robert Burns, a sudden consent warned the great English race, in all its kingdoms, colonies and states, all over the world, to keep the festival. We are here to hold our parliament with love and poesy, as men were wont to do in the Middle Ages. Those famous parliaments might or might not have had more stateliness, and better singers than we—though that is yet to be known—but they could not have better reason.

I can only explain this singular unanimity in a race which rarely acts together—but rather after their watchword, each for himself—by the fact that Robert Burns, the poet of the middle class, represents in the mind of men to-day that great uprising of the middle class against the armed and privileged minorities—that uprising which worked politically in the American and French Revolutions, and which, not in governments so much as in education and in social order, has changed the face of the world. In order for this destiny, his birth, breeding and fortune were low. His organic sentiment was absolute independence, and resting, as it should, on a life of labor. No man existed who could look down on him. They that looked into his eyes saw that they might look down on the sky as easily. His muse and teaching was common sense, joyful, aggressive, irresistible. Not Latimer, nor Luther, struck more telling blows against false theology than did this brave singer. The "Confession of Augsburg," the "Declaration of Independence," the French "Rights of man," and the "Marseillaise," are not more weighty documents in the history of freedom than the songs of Burns. His satire has lost none of its edge. His musical arrows yet sing through the air. He is so substantially a reformer, that I find his grand, plain sense in close chain with the greatest masters—Rabelais, Shakespeare in comedy, Cervantes, Butler, and Burns. If I should add another name, I find it only in a living countryman of Burns. He is an exceptional genius. The people who care nothing for literature and poetry care for Burns. It was indifferent—they thought who saw him—whether he wrote verse or not; he could have done anything else as well.

Yet how true a poet is he! And the poet, too, of poor men, of hodden-gray, and the Guernsey-coat, and the blouse. He has given voice to all the experiences of common life; he has endeared the farmhouse and cottages, patches and poverty, beans and barley; ale the poor man's wine; hardship, the fear of debt, the dear society of weans and wife, of brothers and sisters, proud of each other, knowing so few, and finding amends for want and obscurity in books and thought. What a love of nature! and—shall I say?—of middle-class nature. Not great, like Goethe, in the stars, or like Byron, on the ocean, or Moore, in the luxurious East, but in the homely landscape which the poor see around them—bleak leagues of pasture and stubble, ice, and sleet, and rain, and snow-choked brooks; birds, hares, field-mice, thistles, and heather, which he daily knew. How many "Bonny Doons," and "John Anderson my Joes," and "Auld Lang Synes," all around the earth, have his verses been applied to! And his love songs still woo and melt the youths and maids; the farm work, the country holiday, the fishing cobble, are still his debtors to-day.

And, as he was thus the poet of the poor, anxious, cheerful, working humanity, so had he the language of low life. He grew up in a rural district, speaking a patois unintelligible to all but natives, and he has made that Lowland Scotch a Doric dialect of fame. It is the only example in history of a language made classic by the genius of a single man. But more than this. He had that secret of genius to draw from the bottom of society the strength of its speech, and astonish the ears of the polite with these artless words, better than art, and filtered of all offense through his beauty. It seemed odious to Luther that the devil should have all the best tunes; he would bring them into the churches; and Burns knew how to take from fairs and gypsies, blacksmiths and drovers, the speech of the market and street, and clothe it with melody.

But I am detaining you too long. The memory of Burns—I am afraid heaven and earth have taken too good care of it to leave us anything to say. The west winds are murmuring it. Open the windows behind you, and hearken for the incoming tide, what the waves say of it. The doves, perching always on the eaves of the Stone Chapel [King's Chapel] opposite, may know something about it. Every home in broad Scotland keeps his fame bright. The memory of Burns—every man's and boy's, and girl's head carries snatches of his songs, and can say them by heart, and, what is strangest of all, never learned them from a book, but from mouth to mouth. The wind whispers them, the birds whistle them, the corn, barley, and bulrushes hoarsely rustle them; nay, the music boxes at Geneva are framed and toothed to play them; the hand organs of the Savoyards in all cities repeat them, and the chimes of bells ring them in the spires. They are the property and the solace of mankind. [Cheers.]

Charles Dickens
[1812–1870]

Charles Dickens, the English novelist, delivered the following speech at a farewell dinner given in his honor, in New York City, on April 18, 1868. Horace Greeley presided at the dinner.

ENGLISH FRIENDSHIP FOR AMERICA

GENTLEMEN:—I cannot do better than take my cue from your distinguished President, and refer in my first remarks to his remarks in connection with the old, natural, association between you and me. When I received an invitation from a private association of working members of the press of New York to dine with them to-day, I accepted that compliment in grateful remembrance of a calling that was once my own, and in loyal sympathy towards a brotherhood which, in the spirit, I have never quitted. To the wholesome training of severe newspaper work, when I was a very young man, I constantly refer my first successes; and my sons will hereafter testify to their father that he was always steadily proud of that ladder by which he rose. If it were otherwise, I should have but a very poor opinion of their father, which, perhaps, upon the whole, I have not. Hence, gentlemen, under any circumstances, this company would have been exceptionally interesting and gratifying to me. But whereas I supposed that like the fairies' pavilion in the "Arabian Nights," it would be but a mere handful, and I find it turn out, like the same elastic pavilion, capable of comprehending a multitude, so much the more proud am I of the honor of being your guest; for you will readily believe that the more widely representative of the press in America my entertainers are, the more I must feel the good-will and the kindly sentiments towards me of that vast institution.

Gentlemen, so much of my voice has lately been heard in the land, and I have for upwards of four hard winter months so contended against what I have been sometimes quite admiringly assured was "a true American catarrh"—a possession which I have throughout highly appreciated, though I might have preferred to be naturalized by any other outward and visible signs—I say, gentlemen, so much of my voice has lately been heard, that I might have been contented with troubling you no further, from my present standing-point, were it not a duty with which I henceforth charge myself, not only here but on every suitable occasion whatsoever and wheresoever, to express my high and grateful sense of my second reception in America, and to bear my honest testimony to the national generosity and magnanimity. Also, to declare how astounded I have been by the amazing changes that I have seen around me on every side— changes moral, changes physical, changes in the amount of land subdued and peopled, changes in the rise of vast new cities, changes in the growth of older cities almost out of recognition, changes in the graces and amenities of life, changes in the press, without whose advancement no advancement can be made anywhere. Nor am I, believe me, so arrogant as to suppose that in five-and-twenty years there have been no changes in me, and that I had nothing to learn and no extreme impressions to correct when I was here first.

And, gentlemen, this brings me to a point on which I have, ever since I landed here last November, observed a strict silence, though tempted sometimes to break it, but in reference to which I will, with your good leave, take you into my confidence now. Even the press, being human, may be sometimes mistaken or misinformed, and I rather think that I have in one or two rare instances known its information to be not perfectly accurate with reference to myself. Indeed, I have now and again been more surprised by printed news that I have read of myself than by any printed news that I have ever read in my present state of existence. Thus, the vigor and perseverance with which I have for some months past been collecting materials for and hammering away at a new book on America have much astonished me, seeing that all that time it has been perfectly well-known to my publishers on both sides of the Atlantic that I positively declared that no consideration on earth should induce me to write one. But what I have intended, what I have resolved upon (and this is the confidence I seek to place in you) is, on my return to England, in my own person, to bear, for the behoof of my countrymen, such testimony to the gigantic changes in this country as I have hinted at to-night. Also, to record that wherever I have been, in the smallest places equally with the largest, I have been received with unsurpassable politeness, delicacy, sweet temper, hospitality, consideration, and with unsurpassable respect for the privacy daily enforced upon me by the nature of my avocation here, and the state of my health. This testimony, so long as I live, and so long as my descendants have any legal right in my books, I shall cause to be re-published, as an appendix to every copy of those two books of mine in which I have referred to America. And this I will do and cause to be done, not in mere love and thankfulness, but because I regard it as an act of plain justice and honor.

Gentlemen, the transition from my own feelings towards and interest in America to those of the mass of my countrymen seems to be a natural one; but, whether or no, I make it with an express object. I was asked in this very city, about last Christmas time, whether an American was not at some disadvantage in England as a foreigner. The notion of an American being regarded in England as a foreigner at all, of his ever being thought of or spoken of in that character, was so uncommonly incongruous and absurd to me, that my gravity was, for the moment, quite overpowered. As soon as it was restored, I said that for years and years past I hoped

I had had as many American friends and had received as many American visitors as almost any Englishman living, and that my unvarying experience, fortified by theirs, was that it was enough in England to be an American to be received with the readiest respect and recognition anywhere. Hereupon, out of half-a-dozen people, suddenly spoke out two, one an American gentleman, with a cultivated taste for art, who, finding himself on a certain Sunday outside the walls of a certain historical English castle, famous for its pictures, was refused admission there, according to the strict rules of the establishment on that day, but who, on merely representing that he was an American gentleman, on his travels, had, not to say the picture gallery, but the whole castle, placed at his immediate disposal. The other was a lady, who, being in London, and having a great desire to see the famous reading-room of the British Museum, was assured by the English family with whom she stayed that it was unfortunately impossible, because the place was closed for a week, and she had only three days there. Upon that lady's going to the Museum, as she assured me, alone to the gate, self-introduced as an American lady, the gate flew open, as it were, magically. I am unwillingly bound to add that she certainly was young and exceedingly pretty. Still, the porter of that institution is of an obese habit, and, according to the best of my observation of him, not very impressible.

Now, gentlemen, I refer to these trifles as a collateral assurance to you that the Englishmen who shall humbly strive, as I hope to do, to be in England as faithful to America as to England herself, have no previous conceptions to contend against. Points of difference there have been, points of difference there are, points of difference there probably always will be between the two great peoples. But broadcast in England is sown the sentiment that those two peoples are essentially one, and that it rests with them jointly to uphold the great Anglo-Saxon race, to which our president has referred, and all its great achievements before the world. And if I know anything of my countrymen—and they give me credit for knowing something—if I know anything of my countrymen, gentlemen, the English heart is stirred by the fluttering of those Stars and Stripes, as it is stirred by no other flag that flies except its own. If I know my countrymen, in any and every relation towards America, they begin, not as Sir Anthony Absolute recommended that lovers should begin, with "a little aversion," but with a great liking and a profound respect; and whatever the little sensitiveness of the moment, or the little official passion, or the little official policy now, or then, or here, or there, may be, take my word for it, that the first enduring, great, popular consideration in England is a generous construction of justice.

Finally, gentlemen, and I say this subject to your correction, I do believe that from the great majority of honest minds on both sides, there cannot be absent the conviction that it would be better for this globe to be riven by an earthquake, fired by a comet, overrun by an iceberg, and abandoned to the Arctic fox and bear, than that it should present the spectacle of these two great nations, each of which has, in its own way and hour, striven so hard and so successfully for freedom, ever again being arrayed the one against the other. Gentlemen, I cannot thank your President enough or you enough for your kind reception of my health, and of my poor remarks, but, believe me, I do thank you with the utmost fervor of which my soul is capable. [Applause.]

Julia Ward Howe
[1819–1910]

Julia Ward Howe, American poet, delivered the following tribute to Oliver Wendell Holmes, famous American author, at a breakfast celebrating his seventieth birthday, in Boston, Massachusetts, December 3, 1870.

A TRIBUTE TO OLIVER WENDELL HOLMES

LADIES AND GENTLEMEN:—One word in courtesy I must say in replying to so kind a mention as that which is made, not only of me, but those of my sex who are so happy as to be present here to-day. I think, in looking on this scene, of a certain congress which took place in Paris more than a year ago, and it was called a congress of literary people, *gens de lettres*. When I heard that this was to take place I immediately bestirred myself to attend its sittings and went at once to the headquarters to find how I might do so. I then learned to my great astonishment that no women were to be included among these *gens de lettres,* that is, literary people. [Laughter.] Now, we have thought it a very modest phrase sometimes to plead that, whatever women may not be, they are people. [Laughter and applause.] And it would seem to-day that they are recognized as literary people, and I am very glad that you gentlemen have found room for the sisterhood to-day, and have found room to place them so numerously here, and I must say that to my eyes the banquet looks very much more cheerful than it would without them. [Applause.] It looks to me as though it had all blossomed out under a new social influence, and beside each dark stem I see a rose. [Laughter and applause.] But I must say at once that I came here entirely unprovided with a speech, and, not dreaming of one, yet I came provided with something. I considered myself invited as a sort of grandmother—indeed, I am, and I know a grandmother is usually expected to have something in her pocket. And I have a very modest tribute to the illustrious person whom we are met to-day to honor. With your leave I will read it.

> Thou metamorphic god!
> Who mak'st the straight Olympus thy abode,
>   Hermes to subtle laughter moving,
>   Apollo with serener loving,
> Thou demi-god also!

Who dost all the powers of healing know;
Thou hero who dost wield
The golden sword and shield,—
Shield of a comprehensive mind,
And sword to wound the foes of human kind;

Thou man of noble mold!
Whose metal grows not cold
Beneath the hammer of the hurrying years;
A fiery breath doth blow
Across its fervid glow,
And still its resonance delights our ears;

Loved of thy brilliant mates,
Relinquished to the fates,
Whose spirit music used to chime with thine,
Transfigured in our sight,
Not quenched in death's dark night,
They hold thee in companionship divine.

O autocratic muse!
Soul-rainbow of all hues,
Packed full of service are thy bygone years;
Thy wingèd steed doth fly
Across the starry sky,
Bearing the lowly burthens of thy tears.

I try this little leap,
Wishing that from the deep,
I might some pearl of song adventurous bring.
Despairing, here I stop,
And my poor offering drop,—
Why stammer I when thou art here to sing?

James Russell Lowell
[1819–1891]

James Russell Lowell, American poet, was Ambassador to the Court of St. James's from 1880 to 1885. Following is a speech delivered by Lowell at a dinner given in honor of Sir Henry Irving, in London, on July 4, 1883. Lord Chief Justice Coleridge presided. The toast was "Literature, Science, and Art," with speakers for each of the three subjects, Lowell's topic being Literature.

AFTER-DINNER ORATORY

MY LORD COLERIDGE, my lords, ladies and gentlemen:—I confess that my mind was a little relieved when I found that the toast to which I am to respond rolled three gentlemen, Cerberus-like, into one [laughter], and when I saw Science pulling impatiently at the leash on my left, and Art on my right, and that therefore the responsibility of only a third part of the acknowledgment has fallen on me. You, my lord, have alluded to the difficulties of after-dinner oratory. I must say that I am one of those who feel them more keenly the more after-dinner speeches I make. [Laughter.] There are a great many difficulties in the way, and there are three principal ones, I think. The first is the having too much to say, so that the words, hurrying to escape, bear down and trample out the life of each other. The second is when, having nothing to say, we are expected to fill a void in the minds of our hearers. And I think the third, the most formidable, is the necessity of following a speaker who is sure to say all the things you meant to say, and better than you, so that we are tempted to exclaim, with the old grammarian, "Hang these fellows, who have said all our good things before us!" [Laughter.]

Now the Fourth of July has several times been alluded to, and I believe it is generally thought that on that anniversary the spirit of a certain bird known to heraldic ornithologists—and I believe to them alone—as the spread eagle, enters into every American's breast, and compels him, whether he will or no, to pour forth a flood of national self-laudation. [Laughter and cheers.] This, I say, is the general superstition, and I hope that a few words of mine may serve in some sort to correct it. I ask you, if there is any other people who have confined their national self-laudation to one day in the year. [Laughter.] I may be allowed to make one remark as to a personal experience. Fortune has willed it that I should see as many —perhaps more—cities and manners of men as Ulysses; and I have observed one general fact, and that is, that the adjectival epithet which is prefixed to all the virtues is invariably the epithet which geographically describes the country that I am in. For instance, not to take any real name, if I am in the kingdom of Lilliput, I hear of the Lilliputian virtues. I hear courage, I hear common sense, and I hear political wisdom called by that name. If I cross to the neighboring Republic Blefusca—for since Swift's time it has become a Republic—I hear all these virtues suddenly qualified as Blefuscan. [Laughter.]

I am very glad to be able to thank Lord Coleridge for having, I believe for the first time, coupled the name of the President of the United States with that of her Majesty on an occasion like this. I was struck, both in what he said, and in what our distinguished guest of this evening said, with the frequent recurrence of an adjective which is comparatively new —I mean the word "English-speaking." We continually hear nowadays of the "English-speaking race," of the "English-speaking population." I think this implies, not that we are to forget, not that it would be well for us to forget, that national emulation and that national pride which are implied in the words "Englishman," and "American," but the word implies that there are certain perennial and abiding sympathies between all men of a common descent and a common language. [Cheers.] I am sure, my lord, that all you said with regard to the welcome which our distinguished guest will receive in America is true. His eminent talents as an actor, the dignified—I may say that illustrious—manner in which he has sustained the traditions of that succession of great actors who, from the time of Burbage to his own, have illustrated the English stage, will be as highly appreciated there as here. [Cheers.]

And I am sure that I may also say that the chief magistrate of England will be welcomed by the bar of the United States, of which I am an unworthy member, and perhaps will be all the more warmly welcomed that he does not come among them to practice. He will find American law administered—and I think he will agree with me in saying ably administered—by judges who, I am sorry to say, sit without the traditional wig of England. [Laughter.] I have heard since I came here friends of mine gravely lament this as something prophetic of the decay which was sure to follow so serious an innovation. I answered with a little story which I remember hearing from my father. He remembered the last clergyman in New England who still continued to wear the wig. At first it became a singularity and at last a monstrosity; and the good doctor concluded to leave it off. But there was one poor woman among his parishioners who lamented this sadly, and waylaying the clergyman as he came out of church she said, "Oh, dear doctor, I have always listened to your sermon with the greatest edification and comfort, but now that the wig is gone all is gone." [Laughter.] I have thought I have seen some signs of encouragement in the faces of my English friends after I have consoled them with this little story.

But I must not allow myself to indulge in any further remarks. There is one virtue, I am sure, in after-dinner oratory, and that is brevity; and as to that I am reminded of a story. [Laughter.] The Lord Chief Justice has told you what are the ingredients of after-dinner oratory. They are the joke, the quotation, and the platitude; and the successful platitude, in my judgment, requires a very high order of genius. I believe that I have not given you a quotation, but I am reminded of something which I heard when very young—the story of a Methodist clergyman in America. He was preaching at a camp meeting, and he was preaching upon the miracle of Joshua, and he began his sermon with this sentence: "My hearers, there are three motions of the sun. The first is the straightforward or direct motion of the sun; the second is the retrograde or backward motion of the sun; and the third is the motion mentioned in our text—'the sun stood still.' " [Laughter.]

Now, gentlemen, I don't know whether you see the application of the story—I hope you do. The after-dinner orator at first begins and goes straight forward—that is the straight-forward motion of the sun. Next he goes back and begins to repeat himself—that is the backward motion of the sun. At last he has the good sense to bring himself to the end, and that is the motion mentioned in our text, as the sun stood still. [Great laughter, in the midst of which Mr. Lowell resumed his seat.]

Oliver Wendell Holmes
[1809-1894]

A dinner in honor of Hon. John Lowell was given by the Boston Merchants Association, in Boston, on May 23, 1884. Oliver Wendell Holmes, famous American poet and author, delivered the following speech on this occasion.

DOROTHY Q.

MR. CHAIRMAN AND GENTLEMEN:—It was my intention, when I accepted the public invitation to be with you this evening, to excuse myself from saying a word. I am a professor emeritus, which means pretty nearly the same thing as a tired-out or a worn-out instructor. And I do seriously desire that, having during the last fifty years done my share of work at public entertainments, I may hereafter be permitted, as a post-prandial emeritus, to look on and listen in silence at the festivals to which I may have the honor of being invited—unless, indeed, I may happen to wish to be heard. [Applause.] In that case I trust I may be indulged, as an unspoken speech and an unread poem are apt to "strike in," as some complaints are said to, and cause inward commotions. [Applause.] Judge Lowell's eulogy will be on every one's lips this evening. His soundness, his fairness, his learning, his devotion to duty, his urbanity,—these are the qualities which have commended him to universal esteem and honor. [Applause.] I will not say more of the living; I wish to speak of the dead.

In respectfully proposing the memory of his great-great-grandmother [laughter], I am speaking of one whom few if any of you can remember. [Laughter.] Yet her face is as familiar to me as that of any member of my household. She looks upon me as I sit at my writing-table; she does not smile, she does not speak; even the green parrot on her hand has never opened his beak; but there she is, calm, unchanging, in her immortal youth, as when the untutored artist fixed her features on the canvas. To think that one little word from the lips of Dorothy Quincy, your great-great-grandmother, my great-grandmother, decided the question whether you and I should be here tonight [laughter], in fact whether we should be anywhere [laughter] at all, or remain two bodiless dreams of nature! But it was Dorothy Quincy's "Yes" or "No" to Edward Jackson which was to settle that important matter—important to both of us, certainly— yes, Your Honor; and I can say truly, as I look at you and remember your career, important to this and the whole American community. [Applause.]

The picture I referred to is but a rude one, and yet I was not ashamed of it when I wrote a copy of verses about it, three or four of which this audience will listen to for the sake of Dorothy's great-grandson. I must alter the pronouns a little, for this occasion only:—

Look not on her with eyes of scorn—
Dorothy Q. was a lady born;
Ay! since the galloping Normans came
England's annals have known her name;
And still to the three-hilled rebel town
Dear is that ancient name's renown,
For many a civic wreath they won,
The youthful sire and the gray-haired son.

O damsel Dorothy! Dorothy Q.!
Strange is the gift (we) owe to you!
Such a gift as never a king
Save to daughter or son might bring—
All (our) tenure of heart and hand,
All (our) title to house and land;
Mother and sister and child and wife
And joy and sorrow and death and life!

What if a hundred years ago
Those close-shut lips had answered "No!"
When forth the tremulous question came
That cost the maiden her Norman name,
And under the folds that look so still
The bodice swelled with the bosom's thrill—
Should (we) be (we), or could it be
One-tenth (two others) and nine-tenths (we)?

Soft is the breath of a maiden's Yes:
Not the light gossamer stirs with less;
But never a cable that holds so fast
Through all the battles of wave and blast,
And never an echo of speech or song
That lives in the babbling air so long!
There were tones in the voice that whispered then
You may hear to-day in a hundred men.

O lady and lover, now faint and far
Your images hover—and here we are,
Solid and stirring in flesh and bone—
Edwards and Dorothys—all their own—
A goodly record for time to show
Of a syllable whispered so long ago.

[Applause prolonged.]
I give you: "The memory of Dorothy Jackson, born Dorothy Quincy,
to whose choice of the right monosyllable we owe the presence of our
honored guest and all that his life has achieved for the welfare of the
community." [Great applause and cheers.]

Henry Morton Stanley
[1841–1904]

Henry M. Stanley, explorer of Africa, delivered the following speech at a dinner given in his honor by the Lotos Club, in New York City, on November 27, 1886.

THROUGH THE DARK CONTINENT

MR. CHAIRMAN and gentlemen of the Lotos Club:—One might start a great many principles and ideas which would require to be illustrated and drawn out in order to present a picture of my feelings at the present moment. I am conscious that in my immediate vicinity there are people who were great when I was little. I remember very well when I was unknown to anybody, how I was sent to report a lecture by my friend right opposite, Mr. George Alfred Townsend, and I remember the manner in which he said: "Galileo said: 'The world moves round,' and the world does move round," upon the platform of the Mercantile Hall in St. Louis—one of the grandest things out. [Laughter and applause.] The next great occasion that I had to come before the public was Mark Twain's lecture on the Sandwich Islands, which I was sent to report. And when I look to my left here I see Colonel Anderson, whose very face gives me an idea that Bennett has got some telegraphic dispatch and is just about to send me to some terrible region for some desperate commission. [Laughter.]

And, of course, you are aware that it was owing to the proprietor and editor of a newspaper that I dropped the pacific garb of a journalist and donned the costume of an African traveler. It was not for me, one of the least in the newspaper corps, to question the newspaper proprietor's motives. He was an able editor, very rich, desperately despotic. [Laughter.] He commanded a great army of roving writers, people of fame in the news-gathering world; men who had been everywhere and had seen everything from the bottom of the Atlantic to the top of the very highest mountain; men who were as ready to give their advice to National Cabinets [laughter] as they were ready to give it to the smallest police courts in the United States. [Laughter.] I belonged to this class of roving writers, and I can truly say that I did my best to be conspicuously great in it, by an untiring devotion to my duties, an untiring indefatigability, as though the ordinary rotation of the universe depended upon my single endeavors. [Laughter.] If, as some of you suspect, the enterprise of the able editor was only inspired with a view to obtain the largest circulation, my unyielding and guiding motive, if I remember rightly, was to win his favor by doing with all my might that duty to which according to the English State Church Catechism, "it had pleased God to call me." [Laughter and applause.]

He first dispatched me to Abyssinia—straight from Missouri to Abys-

sinia! What a stride, gentlemen! [Laughter.] People who lived west of
the Missouri River have scarcely, I think, much knowledge of Abyssinia,
and there are gentlemen here who can vouch for me in that, but it seemed
to Mr. Bennett a very ordinary thing, and it seemed to his agent in London
a very ordinary thing indeed, so I of course followed suit. I took it as a
very ordinary thing, and I went to Abyssinia, and somehow or other good
luck followed me and my telegrams reporting the fall of Magdala hap-
penèd to be a week ahead of the British Government's. The people said
I had done right well, though the London papers said I was an impostor.
[Laughter.]

The second thing I was aware of was that I was ordered to Crete to
run the blockade, describe the Cretan rebellion from the Cretan side, and
from the Turkish side; and then I was sent to Spain to report from the
Republican side and from the Carlist side, perfectly dispassionately.
[Laughter.] And then, all of a sudden, I was sent for to come to Paris.
Then Mr. Bennett, in that despotic way of his, said: "I want you to go
and find Livingstone." As I tell you, I was a mere newspaper reporter.
I dared not confess my soul as my own. Mr. Bennett merely said: "Go,"
and I went. He gave me a glass of champagne and I think that was superb.
[Laughter.] I confessed my duty to him, and I went. And as good luck
would have it, I found Livingstone. [Loud and continued cheering.] I
returned as a good citizen ought and as a good reporter ought and as a
good correspondent ought, to tell the tale, and arriving at Aden, I tele-
graphed a request that I might be permitted to visit civilization before I
went to China. [Laughter.] I came to civilization, and what do you think
was the result? Why, only to find that all the world disbelieved my story.
[Laughter.] Dear me! If I were proud of anything, it was that what I said
was a fact ["good!"]; that whatever I said I would do, I would endeavor
to do with all my might, or, as many a good man has done before, as my
predecessors had done, to lay my bones behind. That's all. [Loud cheering.] I was requested in an off-hand manner—just as any member of the
Lotos Club here present would say—"Would you mind giving us a little
résumé of your geographical work?" I said: "Not in the least, my dear
sir; I have not the slightest objection." And do you know that to make
it perfectly geographical and not in the least sensational, I took particular
pains and I wrote a paper out, and when it was printed. it was just about
so long [indicating an inch]. It contained about a hundred polysyllab ic
African words. [Laughter.] And yet "for a' that and a' that" the pundits
of the Geographical Society—Brighton Association—said that they hadn't
come to listen to any sensational stories, but that they had come to listen
to facts. [Laughter.] Well now, a little gentleman, very reverend, full of
years and honors, learned in Cufic inscriptions and cuneiform characters,
wrote to *The Times* stating that it was not Stanley who had discovered
Livingstone but that it was Livingstone who had discovered Stanley.
[Laughter.]

If it had not been for that unbelief, I don't believe I should ever have
visited Africa again; I should have become, or I should have endeavored
to become, with Mr. Reid's permission, a conservative member of the

Lotos Club. [Laughter.] I should have settled down and become as steady and as stolid as some of these patriots that you have around here, I should have said nothing offensive. I should have done some "treating." I should have offered a few cigars and on Saturday night, perhaps, I would have opened a bottle of champagne and distributed it among my friends. But that was not to be. I left New York for Spain and then the Ashantee War broke out and once more my good luck followed me and I got the treaty of peace ahead of everybody else, and as I was coming to England from the Ashantee War a telegraphic dispatch was put into my hands at the Island of St. Vincent, saying that Livingstone was dead. I said: "What does that mean to me? New Yorkers don't believe in me. How was I to prove that what I have said is true? By George! I will go and complete Livingstone's work. I will prove that the discovery of Livingstone was a mere fleabite. I will prove to them that I am a good man and true." That is all that I wanted. [Loud cheers.]

I accompanied Livingstone's remains to Westminster Abbey. I saw those remains buried which I had left sixteen months before enjoying full life and abundant hope. The *Daily Telegraph's* proprietor cabled over to Bennett: "Will you join us in sending Stanley over to complete Livingstone's explorations?" Bennett received the telegram in New York, read it, pondered a moment, snatched a blank and wrote: "Yes. Bennett." That was my commission, and I set out to Africa intending to complete Livingstone's explorations, also to settle the Nile problem, as to where the headwaters of the Nile were, as to whether Lake Victoria consisted of one lake, one body of water, or a number of shallow lakes; to throw some light on Sir Samuel Baker's Albert Nyanza, and also to discover the outlet of Lake Tanganyika, and then to find out what strange, mysterious river this was which had lured Livingstone on to his death —whether it was the Nile, the Niger, or the Congo. Edwin Arnold, the author of "The Light of Asia," said: "Do you think you can do all this?" "Don't ask me such a conundrum as that. Put down the funds and tell me to go. That is all." ["Hear! Hear!"] And he induced Lawson, the proprietor, to consent. The funds were put down, and I went.

First of all, we settled the problem of the Victoria that it was one body of water, that instead of being a cluster of shallow lakes or marshes, it was one body of water, 21,500 square miles in extent. While endeavoring to throw light upon Sir Samuel Baker's Albert Nyanza, we discovered a new lake, a much superior lake to Albert Nyanza—the dead Locust Lake —and at the same time Gordon Pasha sent his lieutenant to discover and circumnavigate the Albert Nyanza and he found it to be only a miserable 140 miles, because Baker, in a fit of enthusiasm had stood on the brow of a high plateau and looking down on the dark blue waters of Albert Nyanza, cried romantically: "I see it extending indefinitely toward the southwest!" Indefinitely is not a geographical expression, gentlemen. [Laughter.] We found that there was no outlet to the Tanganyika, although it was a sweet-water lake; we, settling that problem, day after day as we glided down the strange river that had lured Livingstone to his death, were as much in doubt as Livingstone had been, when he wrote his last letter and said: "I will never be made black man's meat for any-thing less than the classic Nile."

After traveling 400 miles we came to the Stanley Falls, and beyond them, we saw the river deflect from its Nileward course toward the north-west. Then it turned west, and then visions of towers and towns and strange tribes and strange nations broke upon our imagination, and we wondered what we were going to see, when the river suddenly took a decided turn toward the southwest and our dreams were put an end to. We saw then that it was aiming directly for the Congo, and when we had propitiated some natives whom we encountered by showing them crimson beads and polished wire, that had been polished for the occasion, we said: "This is for your answer. What river is this?" "Why, it is *the* river, of course." That was not an answer, and it required some persuasion before the chief, bit by bit digging into his brain, managed to roll out sonorously that, "It is the Ko-to-yah Congo." "It is the river of Congo-land." Alas for our classic dreams! Alas for Crophi and Mophi, the fabled fountains of Herodotus! Alas for the banks of the river where Moses was found by the daughter of Pharaoh! This is' the parvenu Congo! Then we glided on and on past strange nations and cannibals—not past those na-tions which have their heads under their arms—for 1,100 miles, until we arrived at the circular extension of the river and my last remaining com-panion called it the Stanley Pool, and then five months after that our journey ended.

After that I had a very good mind to come back to America, and say, like the Queen of Uganda: "There, what did I tell you?" But you know, the fates would not permit me to come over in 1878. The very day I landed in Europe the King of Italy gave me an express train to convey me to France, and the very moment I descended from it at Marseilles there were three ambassadors from the King of the Belgians who asked me to go back to Africa. "What! go back to Africa? Never! [Laughter.] I have come for civilization; I have come for enjoyment. I have come for love, for life, for pleasure. Not I. Go and ask some of those people you know who have never been to Africa before. I have had enough of it." "Well, perhaps, by and by?" "Ah, I don't know what will happen by and by, but, just now, never! never! Not for Rothschild's wealth!" [Laughter and applause.]

I was received by the Paris Geographical Society, and it was then I began to feel "Well, after all, I have done something, haven't I?" I felt superb [laughter], but you know I have always considered myself a Republican. I have those bullet-riddled flags, and those arrow-torn flags, the Stars and Stripes that I carried in Africa, for the discovery of Living-stone, and that crossed Africa, and I venerate those old flags. I have them in London now, jealously guarded in the secret recesses of my cabinet. I only allow my very best friends to look at them, and if any of you gentlemen ever happen in at my quarters, I will show them to you. [Ap-plause.]

After I had written my book, "Through the Dark Continent," I began to lecture, using these words: "I have passed through a land watered by the largest river of the African continent, and that land knows no owner. A word to the wise is sufficient. You have cloths and hardware and glassware and gunpowder and these millions of natives have ivory and gums and rubber and dyestuffs, and in barter there is good profit." [Applause.]

The King of the Belgians commissioned me to go to that country. My expedition when we started from the coast numbered 300 colored people and fourteen Europeans. We returned with 3,000 trained black men and 300 Europeans. The first sum allowed me was $50,000 a year, but it has ended at something like $700,000 a year. Thus, you see, the progress of civilization. We found the Congo, having only canoes. To-day there are eight steamers. It was said at first that King Leopold was a dreamer. He dreamed he could unite the barbarians of Africa into a confederacy and call it the Free State, but on February 25, 1885, the Powers of Europe and America also ratified an act, recognizing the territories acquired by us to be the free and independent State of the Congo. Perhaps when the members of the Lotos Club have reflected a little more upon the value of what Livingstone and Leopold have been doing, they will also agree that these men have done their duty in this world and in the age that they lived, and that their labor has not been in vain on account of the great sacrifices they have made to the benighted millions of dark Africa. [Loud and enthusiastic applause.]

Henry Ward Beecher
[1813–1887]

The following speech was delivered by Henry Ward Beecher, American clergyman and orator, at a dinner of the Chamber of Commerce of the State of New York, in New York City, on May 8, 1883.

MERCHANTS AND MINISTERS

MR. PRESIDENT and gentlemen merchants:—It may seem a little strange that, in one toast. two so very dissimilar professions should be associated. I suppose it is partly because one preaches and the other practises. [Laughter.] There are very many functions that are performed in common. Merchants are usually men forehanded; ministers are generally men empty-handed. [Laughter.] Merchants form important pillars in the structure of the Church. Ministers are appointed often to go forth to councils and associations, and a delegate is always sent with them. The object of the delegate is to keep the minister sober and to pay his expenses. [Laughter.] They are a very useful set of men in the Church. [Laughter.] But there are some moral functions that they have in common. It is the business of the minister to preach the truth. It is the interest of the merchant to practise it. I hold that not even the Church itself is more dependent upon fundamental moralities than is the whole commercial structure of the world. [Cries of "That's so!"]

There are three great elements that are fundamental elements. They are the same everywhere—among all people and in every business—truth, honesty and fidelity. [Applause.] And it is my mission to-night to say that, to a very large extent, I fear the pulpit has somewhat forgotten to make this the staple of preaching. It has been given too largely, recently, from the force of education and philosophical research, to discourse upon what are considered the "higher" topics—theology—against which I bring no charge. [Laughter.] But theology itself, that is not based on the profoundest morality, is an empty cloud that sails through the summer air, leaving as much drought as it found. I believe that there is a theology that pertains to the higher experiences of the human soul. As profoundly as any man, I believe in that.

To-day, I have been transplanting magnolia trees. I am speaking to-night as the farmer of Westchester County. [Laughter.] There is one that stands among the earliest I planted, twenty years ago, and now it is a vast ball of white. I suppose five hundred thousand magnificent cups are exhaling thanksgiving to God after the long winter has passed. Now, no man need tell me that the root that nestles in the ground is as handsome or smells as sweet as these vases in the air; but I should like to know what would become of all these white cups in the air, if the connection between those dirt-covered roots and the blossoms should be cut to-night. The root is the prime provider, and there can be no life and no blossom where there is no root connection.

Theology and all the rhetoric of preaching is well enough in its place, provided there is a clean and clear passage from all beauty, and all speculations, and all doctrine, down to fundamental, common, practical moralities without doubt. [Applause.] I hold, then, that it is the interest both of the Church and the Store to see to it that truth is spoken, and that honesty and equity prevail between man and man, nation and nation, people and people, and that men should be worthy of trust all over the world. [Applause.]

Speaking the truth is an artificial matter. [Laughter.] Men are no more born to speak the truth than they are to fire rifles, and, indeed, it is a good deal like that. It is only now and then that a man can hit the bull's-eye, and a great many can't hit the target at all. [Laughter.] Speaking the truth requires that a man should know a little about what is truth. It is not an easy thing to be a true man. We part with our fancies and call them truth. We part with our interests and call them truth. We part with our consciences, more often, and call that truth. [Laughter.]

The reason why these are fundamental moralities, and why they are so important to the commercial interests of men is this: commerce dies the moment, and is sick in the degree in which men cannot trust each other. [Applause.] That is the case in the smallest community, and it is more marked, the greater the magnitude of commercial enterprises. And it is one of the evidences that things are not so far gone as some would have us suppose, that men are willing to trust each other so largely in all parts of the earth. If a man can invest his hundreds of thousands of dollars on the ocean or in distant countries, where men cannot understand the documents we write, it shows that there is trust between man and man, buyers and sellers; and if there is trust between them it is because experience has created the probabilities of truthfulness in the actions of men and all the concordant circumstances. If men did not believe in the truth of men, they never would send to China, Japan or Mexico their great properties and interests, with no other guarantee than that the men are trustworthy. The shipmaster must be trustworthy, the officers of the government must be trustworthy, and that business goes on and increases the world over is a silent testimony that, bad as men do lie, they do not lie bad enough to separate man from man. [Laughter.]

Now, I wish to call your attention to one unpleasant state of affairs. It is not to me so very surprising that men intrusted with large interests are found to be so breakable. There is nothing in the make-up of a president that should cause him to make off with the funds committed to his management. There is nothing in being a cashier or director that ought to rot out a man so that he snaps under temptation. I admit that all men are breakable. Men are like timber. Oak will bear a stress that pine won't, but there never was a stick of timber on the earth that could not be broken at some pressure. There never was a man born on the earth that could not be broken at some pressure—not always the same nor put in the same place. There is many a man who cannot be broken by money pressure, but who can be by pressure of flattery. There is many a man impervious to flattery who is warped and biased by his social inclinations. There is many a man whom you cannot tempt with red gold, but you can with dinners and convivialities. One way or the other, every man is vincible. There is a great deal of meaning in that simple portion of the Lord's prayer, "Lead us not into temptation."

No man knows what he will do, according to the nature of the temptation as adapted to the peculiar weakness of his constitution. But this is that which is peculiar—that it requires piety to be a rascal. [Laughter.] It would almost seem as if a man had to serve as a superintendent of a Sunday School as a passport to Sing Sing. [Laughter.] How is it that pious men are defrauding their wards? That leading men in the Church are running off with one hundred thousand or two hundred thousand dollars? In other words, it would seem as if religion were simply a cloak for rascality and villainy. It is time for merchants and ministers to stand together and take counsel on that subject. I say the time has come when we have got to go back to old-fashioned, plain talk in our pulpits on the subject of common morality, until men shall think not so much about Adam as about his posterity [applause], not so much about the higher themes of theology, which are regarded too often as being the test of men's ability and the orthodoxy and salvability of churches.

Well, gentlemen, in regard to what men think in the vast realm of theology, where nobody knows anything about it, does not make any difference. [Laughter.] A man may speak and be lying, and not know it, when he had got up overhead in the clouds. But on the ground, where man meets man, where interests meet interests, where temptation pursues every man, where earthly considerations—greediness, selfishness, pride.

all influences are working together—we need to have every man, once a week at any rate, in the church, and every day at home, cautioned on the subject of the simple virtues of truth and honesty and fidelity; and a man that is, in these three respects, thoroughly educated, and education has trained him so that he is invincible to all the other temptations of life, has come not necessarily to be a perfect man, because he is ignorant of all theology; but I say that, over all the theories of theology, I think that education will lead more men to heaven than any high Church theology, or any other kind that leaves that out. [Applause.]

What, then, are we going to do? It seems to me there are three things that must be done. In the first place, the household must do its work. The things that we learn from our fathers and mothers we never forget, by whichever end they enter. [Laughter.] They become incorporated into our being, and become almost instincts, apparently. If we have learned at home to love and honor the truth, until we come to hate, as men hate filth, all lying, all double-tongued business—if we get that firmly ingrained, we shall probably carry that feeling to the end of life—and it is the most precious thread of life—provided we keep out of politics. [Laughter.]

Next, it seems to me that this doctrine of truth, equity and fidelity must form a much larger part and a much more instructive part of the ministrations of the Church than it does to-day. Wonder is a great many times expressed why the churches are so thin, why men do not go to meeting. The churches are always popular when people hear something there that they want to hear—when they receive that which gives them light, and food for thought, and incitement in all the legitimate ways of life. There they will go again and again. And if churches are supported on any other ground, they are illegitimate. The Church should feed the hungry soul. When men are hungry and get what they need, they go every day to get such food as that. [Applause.]

Next, there must be a public sentiment among all honorable merchants which shall frown, without fear or favor, upon all obliquity, upon everything in commerce, at home or abroad, that is violative of truth, equity and fidelity. [Applause.] These three qualities are indispensable to the prosperity of commerce. With them, with the stimulus, enterprise, opportunities and means that we have in our hands, America can carry the world. [Applause.] But without them, without these commercial understrata in the commerce of America, we shall do just as foolishly as other people have done, and shall come to the same disasters in the long run as they have come to. [Applause.]

So, then, gentlemen, this toast, "Ministers and Merchants," is not so strange a combination after all. You are the merchants and I am the minister, and I have preached to you and you have sat still and heard the whole of it; and with this simple testimony, with this foundation laid before you for your future prosperity, I have only to say, if you have been accustomed to do what the Mosaic law wisely forbids, you must not twine the hemp and the wool to make a thread under the Mosaic economy. You, merchants, must not twine lies and sagacity with your threads in weaving, for every lie that is told in business is a rotten thread in the fabric, and though it may look well when it first comes out of the loom, there will always be a hole there, first or last, when you come to wear it. [Applause.] No gloss in dressing, no finishing in bargain or goods, no lie, if it be an organic lie, no lie that runs through whole trades or whole departments, has any sanity, safety or salvation in it. A lie is bad from top to bottom, from beginning to end, and so is cheating— except in umbrellas, slate-pencils and such things. [Laughter.] There is a little line drawn before you come quite up to the dead line of actual transgression. [Laughter.] When a young man swears he will teach a whole system of doctrines faithfully, no one supposes he means it, but he is excused because everybody knows that he does not know what he is saying, and doesn't understand. Of course, there is the lying of permission, as when a lawyer says to a jury, in a bad case: "On my soul, gentlemen of the jury, I believe my client to be an injured man." We know he is lying; he knows it, and the jury know it, and so it is not lying at all, really. [Laughter.] And even when engineers make one estimate [glancing humorously in the direction of the gentleman who had eulogized the bridge management]—but we pay up another bill. [Prolonged laughter.] Leaving out these matters, lies of courtesy, lies of ignorance, professional lies, lawyers' lies, theologians' lies—and they are good men [laughter]—I come to common, vulgar lies, calico lies, broadcloth lies, cotton lies, silk lies, and those most verminous and multitudinous lies of grocers. [Roars of laughter.]

Gentlemen, I have been requested to say a word or two on monopoly. I wish, on my soul, there were a few men who had the monopoly of lying, and that they had it all to themselves. [Applause.] And now I go back to my first statement. The Church and the Store have a common business before them, to lay the foundation of sound morality, as a ground of temporal prosperity, to say nothing of any other direction. The minister and the merchant have a like interest. The minister for the sake of God and humanity, and the merchant for his own sake, to see to it that, more and more, in public sentiment, even in newspapers—which are perhaps as free as any other organs of life from bias and mistake [laughter]—lying shall be placed in the category of vermin. [Applause.] And so, with my benediction, gentlemen, I will leave you to meditate on this important topic. [Applause.]

Chauncey Mitchell Depew
[1834–1928]

Chauncey M. Depew, American lawyer and railroad executive, was one of the country's most noted after-dinner speakers. He delivered the following speech at a dinner of the New England Society held in New York City, on December 22, 1875.

WOMAN

MR. PRESIDENT:—I know of no act of my life which justifies your assertion that I am an expert on this question. I can very well understand why it is that the toast to "Woman" should follow the toast to "The Press." [Laughter.] I am called upon to respond to the best, the most suggestive, and the most important sentiment which has been delivered this evening, at this midnight hour, when the varied and ceaseless flow of eloquence has exhausted subjects and audience, when the chairs are mainly vacant, the bottles empty, and the oldest veteran and most valiant Roman of us all scarce dares meet the doom he knows awaits him at home. [Laughter.] Bishop Berkeley, when he wrote his beautiful verses upon our Western World, and penned the line "Time's noblest offspring is the last," described not so nearly our prophetic future as the last and best creation of the Almighty—woman—whom we both love and worship. [Applause.] We have here the President of the United States and the General of our Armies: around these tables is gathered a galaxy of intellect, genius, and achievement seldom presented on any occasion, but none of them would merit the applause we so enthusiastically bestow, or have won their high honors, had they not been guided or inspired by the woman they revered or loved.

I have noticed one peculiarity about the toasts this evening very remarkable in the New England Society: every one of them is a quotation from Shakespeare. If Elder Brewster and Carver and Cotton Mather, the early divines of Massachusetts, and the whole colony of Plymouth could have been collected together in general assembly, and have seen with prophetic vision the flower of their descendants celebrating the virtues of their ancestry in sentiments every one of which was couched in the language of a playwright, what would they have said? [Laughter.] The imagination cannot compass the emotions and the utterances of the occasion. But I can understand why this has been done. It is because the most versatile and distinguished actor upon our municipal stage is the president of the New England Society. We live in an age when from the highest offices of our city the incumbent seeks the stage to achieve his greatest honors. I see now our worthy president, Mr. Bailey, industriously thumbing his Shakespeare to select these toasts. He admires the airy grace and flitting beauty of Titania; he weeps over the misfortunes of Desdemona and Ophelia. Each individual hair stands on end as he contemplates the character of Lady Macbeth; but as he spends his nights with Juliet, he softly murmurs, "Parting is such sweet sorrow."

You know that it is a physiological fact that the boys take after their mothers, and reproduce the characteristics and intellectual qualities of the maternal, and not the paternal, side. Standing here in the presence of the most worthy representatives of Plymouth, and knowing as I do your moral and mental worth, the places you fill, and the commercial, financial, humane, and catholic impetus you give to our metropolitan life, how can I do otherwise than on bended knee reverence the New England mothers who gave you birth! [Applause.] Your worth, the places you fill, and the commercial, financial, humane president, in his speech to-night, spoke of himself as a descendant of John Alden. In my judgment, Priscilla uttered the sentiment which gave the Yankee the keynote of success, and condensed the primal elements of his character, when she said to John Alden, "Prythee, why don't you speak for yourself, John?" [Laughter.] That motto has been the spear in the rear and the star in the van of the New Englander's progress. It has made him the most audacious, self-reliant, irrepressible member of the human family; and for illustration we need look no farther than the present descent of Priscilla and John Alden.

The only way I can reciprocate your call at this late hour is to keep you here as long as I can. I think I see now the descendant of a *Mayflower* immortal who has been listening here to the glories of his ancestry, and learning that he is "the heir of all the ages," as puffed and swollen with pride of race and history, he stands solitary and alone upon his doorstep, reflects on his broken promise of an early return, and remembers that within "there is a divinity which shapes his end."

In all ages woman has been the source of all that is pure, unselfish, and heroic in the spirit and life of man. It was for love that Antony lost a world. It was for love that Jacob worked seven long years, and for seven more; and I have often wondered what must have been his emotions when on the morning of the eighth year he awoke and found the homely, scrawny, bony Leah instead of the lovely and beautiful presence of his beloved Rachel. A distinguished French philosopher answered the narrative of every event with the question, "Who was she?" Helen conquered Troy, plunged all the nations of antiquity into war, and gave the earliest, as it is still the grandest, epic which has come down through all time. Poetry and fiction are based upon woman's love, and the movements of history are mainly due to the sentiments or ambitions she has inspired. Semiramis, Zenobia, Queen Elizabeth, claim a cold and distant admiration; they do not touch the heart. But when Florence Nightingale, or Grace Darling, or Ida Lewis, unselfish and unheralded, perils all to succor and to save, the profoundest and holiest emotions of our nature render them tribute and homage. Mr. President, there is no aspiration which any man here to-night entertains, no achievement he seeks to accomplish, no great and honorable ambition he desires to gratify, which is not directly related to either or both a mother and a wife. From the hearthstone around which linger the recollections of our mother, from the fireside where our wife awaits us, come all the purity, all the hope, and all the courage with which we fight the battle of life. The man who is not thus inspired, who labors not so much to secure the applause of the world as the solid and more precious approval of his home, accomplishes little of good for others or of honor for himself. I close with the hope that each of us may always have near us

> A perfect woman, nobly planned,
> To warn, to comfort, and command.
> And yet a spirit still, and bright
> With something of an angel light.

Joseph Hodges Choate
[1832–1917]

Joseph H. Choate, great American lawyer and orator, was a nephew of Rufus Choate. Following are two of his speeches. The first he delivered in response to a toast, "The Bench and the Bar—Blessed are the peacemakers," at a dinner given by the Chamber of Commerce of the State of New York, in New York City, on May 13, 1879. The second, "The Pilgrim Mothers," he delivered at a dinner of the New England Society held in New York City, on December 22, 1880.

THE BENCH AND THE BAR

MR. PRESIDENT:—I rise with unprecedented embarrassment in this presence and at this hour to respond to this sentiment, so flattering to the feelings of all the members of the Bench and Bar [applause], to say nothing of that shrinking modesty inherent in the breast of every lawyer and which the longer he practices seems to grow stronger and stronger. [Laughter.] I have a specific trouble which overwhelms me at this moment, and that is that all the preparation I had made for this occasion is a complete miscarriage. [Laughter.]

I received this sentiment yesterday with an intimation that I was expected to respond to it. I had prepared a serious and sober essay on the relations of commerce to the law—the one great relation of client and counsel [laughter], but I have laid all that aside; I do not intend to have a single sober word tonight. [Laughter.] I do not know that I could. [Renewed laughter.] There is a reason, however, why nothing more of a sober sort should be uttered at this table; there is a danger that it would increase by however small a measure the specific gravity of the Chamber of Commerce of New York. Certainly nothing could be a greater calamity than that. [Laughter.] At an hour like this, sir, merchants like witnesses are to be weighed as well as counted; and when I compare your appearance at this moment with what it was when you entered this room, when I look around upon these swollen girths and these expanded countenances, when I see that each individual of the Chamber has increased his avoirdupois at least ten pounds since he took his seat at this table, why, the total weight of the aggregate body must be startling, indeed [laughter], and as I suppose you believe in a resurrection from this long session, as you undoubtedly hope to rise again from these chairs, to which you have been glued so long, I should be the last person to add a feather's weight to what has been so heavily heaped upon you. [Applause.]

I have forgotten, Mr. President, whether it was Josh Billings or Henry F. Spaulding, who gave utterance to the profound sentiment that there is no substitute for wisdom, and that the next best thing to wisdom is silence. [Laughter and applause.] And so, handing to the reporters the essay which I had prepared for your instruction, it would be my duty to sit down in peace. [Laughter.] But I cannot take my seat without repudiating some of the gloomy views which have fallen from the gentlemen who preceded me. My worthy pastor, the Rev. Dr. Bellows, has said, if I remember rightly his language, that there is a great distrust in the American heart of the permanence of our American institutions. [Laughter.]

Rev. Dr. Bellows: "I did not say anything of the kind." [Laughter and applause.]

Mr. Choate: Well, I leave it to your recollection, gentlemen of the jury, what he did say. [Laughter.]

I am perfectly willing that the doctor should speak for his own institution, but not for mine. I do not believe that a body of merchants of New York with their stomachs full have any growing skepticism or distrust of the permanence of the institution which I represent. [Laughter.] The poor, gentlemen, you have with you always, and so the lawyer will always be your sure and steadfast companion. [Applause.]

Mr. Blaine, freighted with wisdom from the floor of the Senate house and from long study of American institutions, has deplored the low condition of the carrying trade. Now, for our part, as representing one of the institutions which does its full share of the carrying trade, I repudiate the idea. We undoubtedly are still prepared to carry all that can be heaped upon us. [Laughter.] Lord Bacon, who was thought the greatest lawyer of his age, has said that every man owes a duty to his profession; but I think that can be amended by saying, in reference to the law, that every man in the community owes a duty to our profession [laughter]; and somewhere, at some time, somewhere between the cradle and the grave, he must acknowledge the liability and pay the debt. [Applause.] Why, gentlemen, you cannot live without the lawyers, and certainly you cannot die without them. [Laughter.] It was one of the brightest members of the profession, you remember, who had taken his passage for Europe to spend his summer vacation on the other side, and failed to go; and when called upon for an explanation, he said—why, yes; he had taken his passage, and had intended to go, but one of his rich clients had died, and he was afraid if he had gone across the Atlantic, the heirs would have got all of the property. [Applause and laughter.] .

Our celebrated Minister to Berlin [Andrew D. White] also has spoken a good many earnest words in behalf of the institutions he represents.

I did not observe any immediate response to the calls he made, but I could not help thinking as he was speaking, how such an appeal might be made, and probably would be made with effect, in behalf of the institution I represent, upon many of you in the course of the immediate future. When I look around me on this solid body of merchants, all this heaped-up and idle capital, all these great representatives of immense railroad, steamship and other interests under the face of the sun, I believe that the fortunes of the Bar are yet at their very beginning. [Applause.] Gentlemen, the future is all before us. We have no sympathy with Communism, but like Communists we have everything to gain and nothing to lose. [Laughter.]

But my attention must be called for a moment, before I sit down, to the rather remarkable phraseology of the toast. I have heard lawyers abused on many occasions. In the midst of strife we certainly are most active participants. But you apply the phrase to us: "Blessed are the peacemakers!" Well, now, I believe that is true. I believe that if you will devote yourself assiduously enough, and long enough, to our profession, it will result in perfect peace. [Laughter.] But you never knew—did you? —a lawsuit, if it was prosecuted vigorously enough and lasted long enough, where at the end there was anything left for the parties to quarrel over. [Continued laughter.]

Mr. President, I shall not weary your patience longer. This long program of toasts is not yet exhausted. The witching hour of midnight is not far off, and yet there are many statesmen, there are many lawyers, there are many merchants who are yet to be heard from, and so it is time I should take my seat, exhorting you to do justice always to the profession of the law. [Loud applause.]

George Graham Vest
[1830–1904]

George Graham Vest, United States Senator from Missouri from 1879 to 1903, was one of the leading orators and debaters of the Senate. As a young man practicing law in a small Missouri town, Vest represented a man who sued another for the killing of his dog. Vest displayed no interest in the testimony, but when his turn came to address the jury, he made the following speech—and won the case.

A TRIBUTE TO THE DOG

GENTLEMEN OF THE JURY: The best friend a man has in the world may turn against him and become his enemy. His son or daughter that he has reared with loving care may prove ungrateful. Those who are nearest and dearest to us, those whom we trust with our happiness and our good name may become traitors to their faith. The money that a man has, he may lose. It flies away from him, perhaps when he needs it most. A man's reputation may be sacrificed in a moment of ill-considered action. The people who are prone to fall on their knees to do us honor when success is with us, may be the first to throw the stone of malice when failure settles its cloud upon our heads.

The one absolutely unselfish friend that man can have in this selfish world, the one that never deserts him, the one that never proves ungrateful or treacherous is his dog. A man's dog stands by him in prosperity and in poverty, in health and in sickness. He will sleep on the cold ground, where the wintry winds blow and the snow drives fiercely, if only he may be near his master's side. He will kiss the hand that has no food to offer; he will lick the wounds and sores that come in encounter with the roughness of the world. He guards the sleep of his pauper master as if he were a prince. When all other friends desert, he remains. When riches take wings, and reputation falls to pieces, he is as constant in his love as the sun in its journey through the heavens.

If fortune drives the master forth an outcast in the world, friendless and homeless, the faithful dog asks no higher privilege than that of accompanying him, to guard him against danger, to fight against his enemies. And when the last scene of all comes, and death takes his master in its embrace and his body is laid away in the cold ground, no matter if all other friends pursue their way, there by the graveside will the noble dog be found, his head between his paws, his eyes sad, but open in alert watchfulness, faithful and true even in death.

Horace Porter
[1837–1921]

General Horace Porter, American diplomat, was widely known as a witty and eloquent after-dinner speaker. He delivered the following speech at a dinner of the New England Society, in New York City, on December 22, 1883. The toast was simply "Woman!"

WOMAN!

MR. PRESIDENT AND GENTLEMEN:—When this toast was proposed to me, I insisted that it ought to be responded to by a bachelor, by some one who is known as a ladies' man; but in these days of female proprietorship it is supposed that a married person is more essentially a ladies' man than anybody else, and it was thought that only one who had had the courage to address a lady could have the courage, under these circumstances, to address the New England Society. [Laughter.]

The toast, I see, is not in its usual order to-night. At public dinners this toast is habitually placed last on the list. It seems to be a benevolent provision of the Committee on Toasts in order to give man in replying to Woman one chance at least in life of having the last word. [Laughter.] At the New England dinners, unfortunately the most fruitful subject of remark regarding woman is not so much her appearance as her disappearance. I know that this was remedied a few years ago, when this grand annual gastronomic high carnival was held in the Metropolitan Concert Hall. There ladies were introduced into the galleries to grace the scene by their presence; and I am sure the experiment was sufficiently encouraging to warrant repetition, for it was beautiful to see the descendants of the Pilgrims sitting with eyes upturned in true Puritanic sanctity; it was encouraging to see the sons of those pious sires devoting themselves, at least for one night, to setting their affections upon "things above." [Laughter.]

Woman's first home was in the Garden of Eden. There man first married woman. Strange that the incident should have suggested to Milton the "Paradise Lost." [Laughter.] Man was placed in a profound sleep, a rib was taken from his side, a woman was created from it, and she became his wife. Evil-minded persons constantly tell us that thus man's first sleep became his last repose. But if woman be given at times to that contrariety of thought and perversity of mind which sometimes passeth our understanding, it must be recollected in her favor that she was created out of the crookedest part of man. [Laughter.]

The Rabbins have a different theory regarding creation. They go back to the time when we were all monkeys. They insist that man was originally created with a kind of Darwinian tail, and that in the process of evolution this caudal appendage was removed and created into woman. This might better account for those Caudle lectures which woman is in the habit of delivering, and some color is given to this theory, from the fact that husbands even down to the present day seem to inherit a general disposition to leave their wives behind. [Laughter.]

The first woman, finding no other man in that garden except her own husband, took to flirting even with the Devil. [Laughter.] The race might have been saved much tribulation if Eden had been located in some calm and tranquil land—like Ireland. There would at least have been no snakes there to get into the garden. Now woman in her thirst after knowledge showed her true female inquisitiveness in her cross-examination of the serpent, and, in commemoration of that circumstance, the serpent seems to have been curled up and used in nearly all languages as a sign of interrogation. Soon the domestic troubles of our first parents began. The first woman's favorite son was killed by a club, and married women even to this day seem to have an instinctive horror of clubs. The first woman learned that it was Cain that raised a club. The modern woman has learned it is a club that raises cain. Yet, I think, I recognize faces here to-night that I see behind the windows of Fifth Avenue clubs of an afternoon, with their noses pressed flat against the broad plate glass, and as woman trips along the sidewalk, I have observed that these gentlemen appear to be more assiduously engaged than ever was a government scientific commission in taking observations upon the transit of Venus. [Laughter.]

Before those windows passes many a face fairer than that of the Ludovician Juno or the Venus of Medici. There is the Saxon blonde with the deep blue eye, whose glances return love for love, whose silken tresses rest upon her shoulders like a wealth of golden fleece, each thread of which looks like a ray of the morning sunbeam. There is the Latin brunette with the deep, black, piercing eye, whose jetty lashes rest like silken fringe upon the pearly texture of her dainty cheek, looking like ravens' wings spread out upon new-fallen snow.

And yet the club man is not happy. As the ages roll on woman has materially elevated herself in the scale of being. Now she stops at nothing. She soars. She demands the co-education of the sexes. She thinks nothing of delving into the most abstruse problems of the higher branches of analytical science. She can cipher out the exact hour of the night when her husband ought to be home, either according to the old or the recently adopted method of calculating time. I never knew of but one married man who gained any decided domestic advantage by this change in our time. He was an *habitué* of a club situated next door to his house. His wife was always upbraiding him for coming home too late at night. Fortunately, when they made this change of time, they placed one of those meridians from which our time is calculated right between the club and his house. [Laughter.] Every time he stepped across that imaginary line it set him back a whole hour in time. He found that he could leave his club at one o'clock and get home to his wife at twelve; and for the first time in twenty years peace reigned around that hearthstone.

Woman now revels even in the more complicated problems of mathematical astronomy. Give a woman ten minutes and she will describe a heliocentric parallax of the heavens. Give her twenty minutes and she will find astronomically the longitude of a place by means of lunar culminations. Give that same woman an hour and a half, with the present fashions, and she cannot find the pocket in her dress.

And yet man's admiration for woman never flags. He will give her half his fortune; he will give her his whole heart; he seems always willing to give her everything that he possesses, except his seat in a horse car. [Laughter.]

Every nation has had its heroines as well as its heroes. England, in her wars, had a Florence Nightingale; and the soldiers in the expression of their adoration, used to stoop and kiss the hem of her garment as she passed. America, in her war, had a Dr. Mary Walker. Nobody ever stooped to kiss the hem of her garment—because that was not exactly the kind of garment she wore. [Laughter.] But why should man stand here and attempt to speak for woman, when she is so abundantly equipped to speak for herself? I know that is the case in New England; and I am reminded, by seeing General Grant here to-night, of an incident in proof of it which occurred when he was making that marvelous tour through New England, just after the war. The train stopped at a station in the State of Maine. The General was standing on the rear platform of the last car. At that time, as you know, he had a great reputation for silence—for it was before he had made his series of brilliant speeches before the New England Society. They spoke of his reticence—a quality which New Englanders admire so much—in others. [Laughter.] Suddenly there was a commotion in the crowd, and as it opened a large, tall, gaunt-looking woman came rushing toward the car, out of breath. Taking her spectacles off from the top of her head and putting them on her nose, she put her arms akimbo, and looking up, said: "Well, I've just come down here a runnin' nigh onto two mile, right on the clean jump, just to get a look at the man that lets the women do all the talkin'." [Laughter.]

The first regular speaker of the evening [William W. Evarts] touched upon woman, but only incidentally, only in reference to Mormonism and that sad land of Utah, where a single death may make a dozen widows. [Laughter.]

A speaker at the New England dinner in Brooklyn last night [Henry Ward Beecher] tried to prove that the Mormons came originally from New Hampshire and Vermont. I know that a New Englander sometimes in the course of his life marries several times; but he takes the precaution to take his wives in their proper order of legal succession. The difference is that he drives his team of wives tandem, while the Mormon insists upon driving his abreast. [Laughter.]

But even the least serious of us, Mr. President, have some serious moments in which to contemplate the true nobility of woman's character. If she were created from a rib, she was made from that part which lies nearest a man's heart.

It has been beautifully said that man was fashioned out of the dust of the earth while woman was created from God's own image. It is our pride in this land that woman's honor is her own best defense; that here female virtue is not measured by the vigilance of detective nurses; that here woman may walk throughout the length and the breadth of this land, through its highways and its byways, uninsulted, unmolested, clothed in the invulnerable panoply of her own woman's virtue; that even in places where crime lurks and vice prevails in the haunts of our great cities, and in the rude mining gulches of the West, owing to the noble efforts of our women, and the influence of their examples, there are raised up, even there, girls who are good daughters, loyal wives, and faithful mothers. They seem to rise in those rude surroundings as grows the pond lily, which is entangled by every species of rank growth, environed by poison, miasma and corruption, and yet which rises in the beauty of its purity and lifts its fair face unblushing to the sun.

No one who has witnessed the heroism of America's daughters in the field should fail to pay a passing tribute to their worth. I do not speak alone of those trained Sisters of Charity, who in scenes of misery and woe seem Heaven's chosen messengers on earth; but I would speak also of those fair daughters who came forth from the comfortable firesides of New England and other States, little trained to scenes of suffering, little used to the rudeness of a life in camp, who gave their all, their time, their health, and even life itself, as a willing sacrifice in that cause which then moved the nation's soul. As one of these, with her graceful form, was seen moving silently through the darkened aisles of an army hospital, as the motion of her passing dress wafted a breeze across the face of the wounded, they felt that their parched brows had been fanned by the wings of the angel of mercy.

Ah! Mr. President, woman is after all a mystery. It has been well said, that woman is the great conundrum of the nineteenth century; but if we cannot guess her, we will never give her up. [Applause.]

Thomas Henry Huxley
[1825-1895]

Thomas Henry Huxley, English biologist and essayist, delivered the following speech at the annual banquet of the Royal Academy, in London, on May 5, 1883.

SCIENCE AND ART

SIR FREDERIC LEIGHTON, your royal highnesses, my lords and gentlemen:— I beg leave to thank you for the extremely kind and appreciative manner in which you have received the toast of Science. It is the more grateful to me to hear that toast proposed in an assembly of this kind, because I have noticed of late years a great and growing tendency among those who were once jestingly said to have been born in a pre-scientific age to look upon science as an invading and aggressive force, which if it had its own way would oust from the universe all other pursuits. I think there are many persons who look upon this new birth of our times as a sort of monster rising out of the sea of modern thought with the purpose of devouring the Andromeda of art. And now and then a Perseus, equipped with the shoes of swiftness of the ready writer, with the cap of invisibility of the editorial article, and it may be with the Medusa-head of vituperation, shows himself ready to try conclusions with the scientific dragon. Sir, I hope that Perseus will think better of it [laughter]; first, for his own sake, because the creature is hard of head, strong of jaw, and for some time past has shown a great capacity for going over and through whatever comes in his way; and secondly, for the sake of justice, for I assure you, of my own personal knowledge that if left alone, the creature is a very debonair and gentle monster. [Laughter.] As for the Andromeda of art, he has the tenderest respect for that lady, and desires nothing more than to see her happily settled and annually producing a flock of such charming children as those we see about us. [Cheers.]

But putting parables aside, I am unable to understand how any one with a knowledge of mankind can imagine that the growth of science can threaten the development of art in any of its forms. If I understand the matter at all, science and art are the obverse and reverse of Nature's medal, the one expressing the eternal order of things, in terms of feeling, the other in terms of thought. When men no longer love nor hate; when suffering causes no pity, and the tale of great deeds ceases to thrill, when the lily of the field shall seem no longer more beautifully arrayed than Solomon in all his glory, and the awe has vanished from the snow-capped peak and deep ravine, then indeed science may have the world to itself, but it will not be because the monster has devoured art, but because one side of human nature is dead, and because men have lost the half of their ancient and present attributes. [Cheers.]

Carl Schurz
[1829–1906]

Carl Schurz, German-born American patriot and statesman, delivered the following speech at a dinner given by the Chamber of Commerce of the State of New York, in New York City, on November 5, 1881.

THE OLD WORLD AND THE NEW

MR. CHAIRMAN, and gentlemen of the Chamber of Commerce:—If you had been called upon to respond to the toast: "The Old World and the New" as frequently as I have, you would certainly find as much difficulty as I find in saying anything of the Old World that is new or of the New World that is not old. [Applause.]

And the embarrassment grows upon me as I grow older, and it would upon all of you, except perhaps my good friend, Mr. Evarts, who has determined never to grow old, and whose witty sayings are always as good as new. [Laughter.] Still, gentlemen, the scenes which we have been beholding during the last few weeks have had something of a fresh inspiration in them. We have been celebrating a great warlike event— not great in the number of men that were killed in it, but very great in the number of people it has made happy. It has made happy not only the people of this country who now count over fifty millions, but it has made happier than they were before the nations of the Old World, too; who, combined, count a great many more. [Applause.]

American Independence was declared at Philadelphia on July 4, 1776, by those who were born upon this soil, but American Independence was virtually accomplished by that very warlike event I speak of on the field of Yorktown, where the Old World lent a helping hand to the New. [Applause.] To be sure, there was a part of the Old World consisting of the British, and I am sorry to say, some German soldiers, who strove to keep down the aspirations of the New, but they were there in obedience to the command of a power which they were not able to resist, while that part of the Old World which fought upon the American side was here of its own free will as volunteers. [Cheers.]

It might be said that most of the regular soldiers of France were here also by the command of power, but it will not be forgotten that there was not only Lafayette, led here by his youthful enthusiasm for the American cause, but there was France herself, the great power of the Old World appearing as a volunteer on a great scale. [Cheers.] So were there as volunteers those who brought their individual swords to the service of the New World. There was the gallant Steuben, the great organizer who trained the American army to victory, a representative of that great nation whose monuments stand not only upon hundreds of battlefields of arms, but whose prouder monuments stand upon many more battlefields of thought. [Cheers.] There was Pulaski, the Pole, and De Kalb who died for American Independence before it was achieved. And there were many more Frenchmen, Germans, Swedes, Hollanders, Englishmen even, who did not obey the behests of power. [Cheers.] And so it may be said that the cause of the New World was the cause of volunteers of the Old. And it has remained the cause of volunteers in peace as well as in war, for since then we have received millions of them, and they are arriving now in a steady stream, thousands of them every week; I have the honor to say, gentlemen, that I am one of them. [Cheers.]

Nor is it probable that this volunteering in mass will ever stop, for it is in fact drawn over here by the excitement of war as much as by the victories of peace. It was, therefore, natural that the great celebration of that warlike event should have been turned or rather that it should have turned itself into a festival of peace on the old field of Yorktown— peace illustrated by the happy faces of a vast multitude, and by all the evidence of thrift and prosperity and well-being; peace illustrated by the very citizen soldiery who appeared there to ornament as a pageant, with their brilliant bayonets that peaceful festival; peace illustrated by the warmth of a grand popular welcome offered to the honored representatives of the Old World; peace illustrated, still more, by their friendly meeting upon American soil whatever their contentions at home may have been; peace glorified by what has already been so eloquently referred to by Dr. Storrs and Mr. Evarts; that solemn salute offered to the British flag, to the very emblem of the old antagonism of a hundred years ago; and that salute, echoing in every patriotic American heart, to be followed as the telegraph tells us now, by the carrying of the American flag in honor in the Lord Mayor's procession in London—all this a cosmopolitan peace festival, in which the Old World sent its representatives to join in rejoicing over the prosperity and progress of the New. [Cheers.]

There could hardly have been a happier expression of this spirit of harmony than was presented in the serenade offered to these gentlemen —representatives of the honored name of Steuben on the evening of their arrival in New York, the band playing first "The Watch on the Rhine," followed by the "Marseillaise" and "God Save the Queen," and then the martial airs of the Old World resolving themselves into the peaceful strains of the crowning glory of "Hail, Columbia!" and "Yankee Doodle." [Cheers.]

The cordiality of feeling which binds the Old and the New World together, and which found so touching, so tender, so wonderful an expression in the universal heartfelt sorrow of all civilized mankind at the great national bereavement, which recently has befallen us [the assassination of President Garfield], can hardly fail to be strengthened by this visit of the Old World guests whom we delight to honor. [Cheers.]

They have seen now something of our country, and our people; most of them, probably, for the first time, and I have no doubt they have arrived at the conclusion that the country for which Lafayette and Steuben and Rochambeau fought is a good country, inhabited by a good people [cheers]; a good country and a good people, worthy of being fought for by the noblest men of the earth; and I trust also when these gentlemen return to their own homes they will go back with the assurance that the names of their ancestors who drew their swords for American liberty stand in the heart of every true American side by side with the greatest American names, and that, although a century has elapsed since the surrender of Yorktown, still the gratitude of American hearts is as young and fresh and warm to-day as it was at the moment when Cornwallis hauled down his flag. [Applause.]

It seems to me also, gentlemen, that we have already given some practical evidence of that gratitude. The independence they helped to achieve has made the American nation so strong and active and prosperous that when the Old World runs short of provisions, the New stands always ready and eager even, to fill the gap, and by and by we may even send over some products of other industries for their accommodation. [Applause.]

In fact, we have been so very liberal and generous in that respect, that some of our friends on the other side of the sea are beginning to think that there may be a little too much of a good thing, and are talking of shutting it off by tricks of taxation. [Laughter.] However, we are not easily baffled. Not content with the contribution of our material products, we even send them from time to time, some of our wisdom, as, for instance, a few months ago, our friend, Mr. Evarts, went over there to tell them about the double standard—all that we knew and a good deal more. [Laughter.] We might even be willing to send them all the accumulated stock of our silver, if they will give us their gold for it. [Cheers.] It is to be apprehended that this kind of generosity will not be fittingly appreciated and in that respect they may prefer the wisdom of the Old World to that of the New. [Laughter.]

However, we shall not quarrel about that, for seriously speaking, the New and the Old World must and will, in the commercial point of view, be of infinite use one to another as mutual customers, and our commercial relations will grow more fruitful to both sides from year to year, and from day to day, as we remain true to the good old maxim: "Live and let live." [Cheers.] Nor is there the least speck of danger in the horizon threatening to disturb the friendliness of an international understanding between the Old World and the New. That cordial international understanding rests upon a very simple, natural, and solid basis. We rejoice with the nations of the Old World in all their successes, all their prosperity, and all their happiness, and we profoundly and earnestly sympathize with them whenever a misfortune overtakes them. But one thing we shall never think of doing, and that is, interfering in their affairs.

On the other hand they will give us always their sympathy in good and evil as they have done heretofore, and we expect that they will never think of interfering with our affairs on this side of the ocean. [Loud cheers.] Our limits are very distinctly drawn, and certainly no just or prudent power will ever think of upsetting them. The Old World and the New will ever live in harmonious accord as long as we do not try to jump over their fences and they do not try to jump over ours. [Cheers.]

This being our understanding, nothing will be more natural than friendship and good will between the nations of the two sides of the Atlantic. The only danger ahead of us might be that arising from altogether too sentimental a fondness for one another which may lead us into lovers' jealousies and quarrels. Already some of our honored guests may feel like complaining that we have come very near to killing them with kindness; at any rate, we are permitted to hope that a hundred years hence our descendants may assemble again to celebrate the memory of the feast of cordial friendship which we now enjoy, and when they do so, they will come to an American Republic of three hundred millions of people, a city of New York of ten million inhabitants, and to a Delmonico's ten stories high with a station for airships running between Europe and America on the top, and then our guests may even find comfortable hotels and decent accommodations at the deserted village of Yorktown.

But, in the meantime, I am sure our Old World guests who to-night delight us with their presence, will never cease to be proud of it that the great names of which they are the honored representatives are inscribed upon some of the most splendid pages of the New World's history, and will live forever in the grateful affection of the New World's heart. [Loud applause.]

William Schwenck Gilbert
[1836–1911]

On November 7, 1879, the Lotos Club of New York City gave a dinner in honor of William Schwenck Gilbert and Sir Arthur Sullivan, British collaborators, famous for their series of light operas, who were visiting the United States. Gilbert responded to the toast as follows.

"PINAFORE"

MR. CHAIRMAN AND GENTLEMEN:—As my friend Sullivan and I were driving to this Club this evening, both of us being very nervous and very sensitive, and both of us men who are highly conscious of our oratorical defects and deficiencies, and having before us vividly the ordeal awaiting us, we cast about for a comparison of our then condition. We likened ourselves to two authors driving down to a theater at which a play of theirs was to be played for the first time. The thought was somewhat harassing, but we dismissed it because we remembered that there was always an even chance of success [laughter], whereas in the performance in which we were about to take part there was no prospect of aught but humiliating failure.

We were rather in the position of prisoners surrendering to their bail, and we beg of you to extend to us your most merciful consideration. But it is expected of me, perhaps, that in replying to this toast with which your chairman has so kindly coupled my name, I shall do so in a tone of the lightest possible comedy. [Laughter.] I had almost said that I am sorry to say that I cannot do so; but in truth I am not sorry. A man who has been welcomed as we have been here by the leaders in literature and art in this city, a man who could look upon that welcome as a string on which to hang a series of small jokes would show that he was responding to an honor to which he was not entitled. For it is no light thing to come to a country which you have been taught to regard as a foreign country, and to find ourselves in the best sense of the word "at home" [applause] among a people whom we are taught to regard as strangers, but whom we are astonished to find are our intimate friends [applause]; and that proffered friendship is so dear to us that I am disposed, in behalf of my collaborator and myself, to stray somewhat from the beaten paths of after-dinner oratory, and to endeavor to justify ourselves in respect to a matter in which we have some reason to feel that we have been misrepresented.

I have seen in several London journals well-meant but injudicious paragraphs saying that we have a grievance against the New York managers because they have played our pieces and have offered us no share of the profits. [Laughter.] We have no grievance whatever. Our only complaint is that there is no international copyright act. [Applause.] The author of a play in which there is no copyright is very much in the position of an author or the descendants of an author whose copyright has expired. I am not aware that our London publishers are in the habit of seeking the descendants of Sir Walter Scott or Lord Byron, or Captain Marryat, and offering them a share of the profits of their publications. [Laughter.] I have yet to learn that our London managers seek out the living representatives of Oliver Goldsmith, or Richard Brinsley Sheridan or William Shakespeare, in order to pay them any share of the profits from the production of "She Stoops to Conquer," or "The Good-Natured Man," or "The Merchant of Venice." [Laughter.] If they do so, they do it on the principle that the right hand knows not what the left hand doeth [laughter], and as we have not heard of it, we presume, therefore, that they have not done so. And we believe that if those eminent men were to request a share of the profits, they would be met with the reply that the copyright on those works had expired.

And so if we should suggest it to the managers of this country, they would perhaps reply with at least equal justice: "Gentlemen, your copyright never existed." That it has never existed is due entirely to our own fault.

We consulted a New York lawyer, and were informed that, although an alien author has no right in his works, yet so long as they remained unpublished, we held the real title in them, and there was no process necessary to make them our own. We, therefore, thought we would keep it in unpublished form, and make more profit from the sale of the pianoforte score and the words of the songs at the theaters and at the music publishers.

We imagined that the allusions of the piece were so purely British in their character, so insular in fact, that they would be of no interest on this side; but events have shown that in that conclusion we were mistaken. At all events, we have also arrived at the conclusion that we have nobody to blame but ourselves. As it is, we have realized by the sale of the book and the piano score in London about $7,500 apiece, and under those circumstances I do not think we need to be pitied. [Laughter.] For myself, I certainly do not pose as an object of compassion. [Laughter.]

We propose to open here on the first of December at the Fifth Avenue Theater with a performance of "Pinafore." I will not add the prefixing initials, because I have no desire to offend your republican sympathies. [Laughter.] I may say, however, that I have read in some journals that we have come over here to show you how that piece should be played, but that I disclaim, both for myself and my collaborator. We came here to teach nothing—we have nothing to teach—and perhaps we should have no pupils if we did. [Laughter.] But apart from the fact that we have no copyright, and are not yet managers in the United States, we see no reason why we should be the only ones who are not to be permitted to play this piece here. [Laughter and applause.]

I think you will admit that we have a legitimate object in opening with it. We have no means of knowing how it has been played in this country, but we are informed that it has been played more broadly than in the old country—and you know that may be better or worse. [Laughter.]

Afterwards we propose to produce another piece, and in the fullness of time the longer it is delayed perhaps the better for us [laughter], and we propose to present it to an audience [laughter] in the same spirit in which we presented "Pinafore"—in a most serious spirit—not to permit the audience to see by anything that occurs on the stage that the actors are conscious of the really absurd things they are doing. Whether right or not, that is the way in which it was presented in London. We open with "Pinafore," not to show how that ought to be played, but to show how the piece that succeeds is about to be played, and to prepare the audiences for the reception of our new and highly preposterous story. [Applause.]

The kindness with which we have been received this evening emboldens me to believe that perhaps you will not consider this explanation altogether indecent or ill-timed. I have nothing more, gentlemen, to say, except to thank you most heartily for the complimentary manner in which you proposed our health, and to assure you that it is a compliment which is to me personally as delightful as it is undeserved. [Applause.]

Sir Arthur Sullivan

[1842–1900]

Sir Arthur Sullivan, English composer and collaborator with W. S. Gilbert in the creation of light operas, delivered the following speech at the annual dinner of the Royal Academy, in London, on May 2, 1891.

MUSIC

YOUR ROYAL HIGHNESS, my lords and gentlemen:—It is gratifying to find that at the great representative art-gathering of the year the sister arts are now receiving at the hands of the painters and sculptors of the United Kingdom that compliment to which their members are justly entitled. Art is a commonwealth in which all the component estates hold an equal position, and it has been reserved for you, sir, under your distinguished presidency, to give full and honorable recognition to this important fact. You have done so in those terms of delicate, subtle compliment, which whilst displaying the touch of the master, also bear the impress of genuine sympathy, by calling upon my friend Mr. Irving and myself, as representatives of the drama and of music, to return thanks for those branches of art to which our lives' efforts have been devoted.

I may add, speaking for my own art, that there is a singular appropriateness that this compliment to Music should be paid by the artist whose brain has conceived and whose hand depicted a most enchanting "Music Lesson." You, sir, have touched with eloquence and feeling upon some of the tenderer attributes of music; I would with your permission, call attention to another—namely, its power and influence on popular sentiment; for of all the arts I think Music has the most mighty, universal, and immediate effect. ["Hear! Hear!"] I know there are many educated and intelligent people who, absorbed in commerce, politics, and other pursuits, think that music is a mere family pastime—an ear-gratifying enjoyment. Great popularity has its drawbacks as well as its advantages, and there is no doubt that the widespread, instantaneous appreciation and popularity of melody has detracted somewhat from the proper recognition of the higher and graver attributes of music. But that music is a power and has influenced humanity with dynamic force in politics, religion, peace, and war, no one can gainsay. Who can deny the effect in great crises of the world's history of the Lutheran Chorale, "Ein' feste Burg," which roused the enthusiasm of whole towns and cities and caused them to embrace the reformed faith *en masse*—of the "Ça ira," with its ghastly association of tumbril and guillotine, and of the still more powerful "Marseillaise"? These three tunes alone have been largely instrumental in varying the course of history. [Cheers.]

Amongst our own people, no one who has visited the Greater Britain beyond the seas but must be alive to the depth of feeling stirred by the first bar of "God Save the Queen." It is not too much to say that this air has done more than any other single agency to consolidate the national sentiment which forms the basis of our world-wide Empire. [Cheers.] But, sir, my duty is not to deliver a dissertation on music, my duty is to thank you for the offering and the acceptation of this toast, which I do most sincerely.

With regard to the more than generous terms in which you, sir, have alluded to my humble individuality, I need not say how deeply I feel the spirit in which they were spoken. This much I would add—that highly as I value your kindly utterances, I count still more highly the fact that I should have been selected by you to respond for Music, whose dignity and whose progress in England are so near and dear to me at heart. [Cheers.]

Edward Everett Hale
[1822–1909]

The noted American author, Edward Everett Hale, responded to a toast, "Boston," at the first annual dinner of the New England Society of the city of Brooklyn, held on December 21, 1880.

BOSTON

Mr. chairman and gentlemen:—I am sure that there is not a Boston boy who hears me to-night who does not recollect that when he went out to his first Pilgrim dinner, or to see Fanny Kemble or to any other evening dissipation of fifty years ago, the last admonition of his mother was, "We will leave the candle burning for you, John, but you must be sure and be home before twelve o'clock!" I am sure that the memory of this admonition is lingering among our friends now that we are entering on the small hours, and that I must only acknowledge your courtesy and sit down. I feel, indeed, all along in your talk of hoar antiquity, that I owe my place here only to your extreme hospitality. In these aged cities you may well say to me, "You Bostonians are children. You are of yesterday," as the Egyptians said to the Greek traveler. For we are still stumbling along like little children, in the anniversaries of our quarter-millennium; but we understand perfectly well that the foundations of this city were laid in dim antiquity. I know that nobody knows when Brooklyn was founded. Your commerce began so long ago that nobody can remember it, but I know that there was a beaver trap on every brook in Kings County, while Boston was still a howling wilderness. These noble ancestors of yours had made themselves at home on Plymouth Rock before we had built a flatboat on any river in Massachusetts Bay. [Applause.]

It is only as the youngest daughter, quite as a Cinderella, that we of Boston have any claim on your matchless hospitality. But, as Cinderella should, we have done our best at home to make ready our sisters when they should go to the ball. When my brother Beecher, just now, closed his speech with a Latin quotation, I took some satisfaction in remembering that we taught him his Latin at the Boston Latin school. And I could not but remember when I listened with such delight to the address of Mr. Secretary Evarts, which you have just now been cheering, that the first time I heard this persuasive and convincing orator, was when he took the prize for elocution, a boy of thirteen, on the platform in the great hall in our old schoolhouse in School Street. Nay, I confess also, to a little feeling of local as well as national pride, when the President of the United States [Rutherford B. Hayes] was speaking. Just as he closes this remarkable administration, which is going to stand out in history, distinguished indeed among all administrations from the beginning, so pure has it been, so honorable and so successful—just as he closes this administration he makes here this statement of the principles on which are based the success of an American statesman, in a few fit words so epigrammatic that they will be cited as proverbs by our children and our children's children. As I heard that masterly definition of the laws which have governed the New Englander, I took pride in remembering that the President also was a graduate of our law school. These three are the little contributions which Cinderella has been preparing in the last half-century, for the first dinner-party of the Brooklyn Pilgrim Society.

I read in a New York newspaper in Washington the other day that something done in Boston lately was done with the "usual Boston intensity." I believe the remark was not intended to be a compliment, but we shall take it as one, and are quite willing to accept the phrase. I think it is true in the past, I hope it will be true in the future, that we go at the things which we have to do with a certain intensity, which I suppose we owe to these Puritan Fathers whom to-night we are celebrating. Certainly we have gone at this business of emigration with that intensity. It is perfectly true that there are in Brooklyn to-day more people than there are in Boston, who were born in Boston from the old New England blood. Not that Brooklyn has been any special favorite. When I met last year in Kansas a mass meeting of twenty-five thousand of the old settlers and their children, my daughter said to me: "Papa, I am glad to see so many of our own countrymen." She certainly had never seen so many before, without intermixture of people of foreign races. Now it is certainly our wish to carry that intensity into everything. If the thing is worth doing at all it is worth doing thoroughly. What we do we mean to do it for everybody. You have seen the result. We try, for instance, if we open a Latin school at all, to have it the best Latin school in the world. And then we throw it open to everybody, to native and heathen, to Jew and to Greek, to white and black and red, and we advise you to go and do likewise.

You recollect the old joke, I think it began with Preston of South Carolina, that Boston exported no articles of native growth but granite and ice. That was true then, but we have improved since, and to these exports we have added roses and cabbages. Mr. President, they are good roses, and good cabbages, and I assure you that the granite is excellent hard granite, and the ice is very cold ice. [Laughter and applause.]

Ulysses Simpson Grant
[1822-1885]

The New England Society of New York City held its seventy-fifth annual dinner on December 22, 1880, a day after its new rival in after-dinner oratory began banqueting in Brooklyn, on the other side of the East River. General Ulysses S. Grant, former President of the United States, was the speaker of the occasion.

THE NEW ENGLANDERS

Mr. president and gentlemen of the New England Society of the City of New York:—I suppose on an occasion of this sort you will expect me to say something about this Society and the people of New England and the Pilgrims who first landed on Plymouth Rock. It was my fortune last night to attend a banquet of this sort in the principal city on New York harbor. [Applause and laughter.] I did not know until I went there [Brooklyn] that it was the principal city [laughter]—the principal city of the harbor of New York, a city whose overflow has settled up Manhattan Island, which has built up fine houses, business streets, and shown many evidences of prosperity for a suburb, with a waste of people flowing across the North River that forms a third if not one-half the population of a neighboring state. [Applause.] As I say, it was my good fortune to attend a banquet of this sort of the parent society [laughter], and to which all the societies known, even including the one which is now celebrating its first anniversary in Las Vegas, New Mexico, owe their origin. [Laughter.] I made a few remarks there, in which I tried to say what I thought were the characteristics of the people who have descended from the Pilgrims. I thought they were a people of great frugality, great personal courage, great industry, and possessed within themselves of qualities which built up this New England population which has spread out over so much of this land and given so much character, prosperity, and success to us as a people and a nation. [Applause.] I retain yet some of the views I then expressed [peals of laughter], and should have remained convinced that my judgment was entirely right if it were not that some speakers came after me who have a better title to speak for the people of New England than myself, and who dispelled some of those views. [Renewed laughter.]

It is too many generations back for me to claim to be a New Englander. Those gentlemen who spoke are themselves New Englanders who have, since their manhood, emigrated to this great city that I speak of. They informed me that there was nothing at all in the Pilgrim Fathers to give them the distinguishing characteristics which we attribute to them [laughter], and that it was all entirely dependent upon the poverty of the soil and the inclemency of the climate where they landed. [Shouts of laughter.] They fell upon an ungenial climate, where there were nine months of winter and three months of cold weather [laughter], and that had called out the best energies of the men and of the women, too, to get a mere subsistence out of the soil, with such a climate. In their efforts to do that they cultivated industry and frugality at the same time, which is the real foundation of the greatness of the Pilgrims. [Laughter.] It was even suggested by some that if they had fallen upon a more genial climate and more fertile soil, they would have been there yet, in poverty and without industry. [Laughter.] I shall continue to believe better of them myself, and I believe the Rev. Dr. Storrs, who spoke here, will agree with me that my first judgment of them was probably nearly correct.

However, all jesting aside, we are proud in my section of the country of the New Englanders and of their descendants. We hope to see them spread over all this land, and carry with them the principles inculcated in their own sterile soil from·which they sprang. [Applause.] We want to see them take their independence of character, their self-reliance, their free schools, their learning, and their industry, and we want to see them prosper and teach others among whom they settle how to be prosperous. [Applause.] I am very much obliged to the gentlemen of the infant New England Society [laughter] for the reception which they have accorded to me and the other guests of this evening. I shall remember it with great pleasure, and hope that some day you will invite me again. [Long-continued applause.]

Samuel L. Clemens

[1835–1910]

Samuel Langhorne Clemens, the American humorist, world famous as "Mark Twain," was a gifted speaker as well as a writer. Three of his after-dinner speeches are presented here. "New England Weather" was the speech he delivered at a dinner of the New England Society, in New York City, on December 22, 1876. "The Babies" was the subject of the toast to which he responded at a dinner of the Army of Tennessee, in Chicago, on November 13, 1879. "Woman, God Bless Her!" was a speech also delivered at a dinner of the New England Society in New York City—on December 22, 1882.

NEW ENGLAND WEATHER

GENTLEMEN:—I reverently believe that the Maker who made us all, makes everything in New England—but the weather. [Laughter.] I don't know who makes that, but I think it must be raw apprentices in the Weather

Clerk's factory, who experiment and learn how in New England for board and clothes, and then are promoted to make weather for countries that require a good article and will take their custom elsewhere if they don't get it. [Laughter.] There is a sumptuous variety about the New England weather that compels the stranger's admiration—and regret. [Laughter.] The weather is always doing something there; always attending strictly to business; always getting up new designs and trying them on the people to see how they will go. [Laughter.] But it gets through more business in spring than in any other season. In the spring I have counted one hundred and thirty-six different kinds of weather inside of four and twenty hours. [Laughter.] It was I that made the fame and fortune of that man that had that marvelous collection of weather on exhibition at the Centennial that so astounded the foreigners. He was going to travel all over the world and get specimens from all the climes. I said: "Don't you do it; you come to New England on a favorable spring day." I told him what we could do, in the way of style, variety, and quantity. [Laughter.] Well, he came, and he made his collection in four days. [Laughter.] As to variety—why, he confessed that he got hundreds of kinds of weather that he had never heard of before. And as to quantity—well, after he had picked out and discarded all that was blemished in any way, he not only had weather enough, but weather to spare; weather to hire out; weather to sell; to deposit; weather to invest; weather to give to the poor. [Laughter and applause.]

The people of New England are by nature patient and forbearing; but there are some things which they will not stand. Every year they kill a lot of poets for writing about "Beautiful Spring." [Laughter.] These are generally casual visitors, who bring their notions of spring from somewhere else, and cannot, of course, know how the natives feel about spring. And so, the first thing they know, the opportunity to inquire how they feel has permanently gone by. [Laughter.]

Old Probabilities has a mighty reputation for accurate prophecy, and thoroughly well deserves it. You take up the papers and observe how crisply and confidently he checks off what to-day's weather is going to be on the Pacific, down South, in the Middle States, in the Wisconsin region; see him sail along in the joy and pride of his power till he gets to New England, and then—see his tail drop. [Laughter.] He doesn't know what the weather is going to be in New England. He can't any more tell than he can tell how many Presidents of the United States there's going to be next year. [Applause.] Well, he mulls over it, and by and by he gets out something about like this: Probable nor'-east to sou'-west winds, varying to the southard and westard and eastard and points between; high and low barometer, sweeping around from place to place; probable areas of rain, snow, hail, and drought, succeeded or preceded by earthquakes, with thunder and lightning. [Loud laughter and applause.] Then he jots down this postscript from his wandering mind to cover accidents: "But it is possible that the programme may be wholly changed in the mean time." [Loud laughter.]

Yes, one of the brightest gems in the New England weather is the dazzling uncertainty of it. There is only one thing certain about it, you are certain there is going to be plenty of weather [laughter]—a perfect grand review; but you never can tell which end of the procession is going to move first. You fix up for the drought; you leave your umbrella in the house and sally out with your sprinkling-pot, and ten to one you get drowned. [Applause.] You make up your mind that the earthquake is due; you stand from under and take hold of something to steady yourself, and the first thing you know, you get struck by lightning. [Laughter.] These are great disappointments. But they can't be helped. [Laughter.] The lightning there is peculiar; it is so convincing! When it strikes a thing, it doesn't leave enough of that thing behind for you to tell whether —well, you'd think it was something valuable, and a Congressman had been there. [Loud laughter and applause.]

And the thunder. When the thunder commences to merely tune up, and scrape, and saw, and key up the instruments for the performance, strangers say: "Why, what awful thunder you have here!" But when the baton is raised and the real concert begins you'll find that stranger down in the cellar, with his head in the ash-barrel. [Laughter.]

Now, as to the size of the weather in New England—lengthways, I mean. It is utterly disproportioned to the size of that little country. [Laughter.] Half the time, when it is packed as full as it can stick, you will see that New England weather sticking out beyond the edges and projecting around hundreds and hundreds of miles over the neighboring States. [Laughter.] She can't hold a tenth part of her weather. You can see cracks all about, where she has strained herself trying to do it. [Laughter.]

I could speak volumes about the inhuman perversity of the New England weather, but I will give but a single specimen. I like to hear rain on a tin roof, so I covered part of my roof with tin, with an eye to that luxury. Well, sir, do you think it ever rains on the tin? No, sir; skips it every time. [Laughter.]

Mind, in this speech I have been trying merely to do honor to the New England weather; no language could do it justice. [Laughter.] But after all, there are at least one or two things about that weather (or, if you please, effects produced by it) which we residents would not like to part with. [Applause.] If we had not our bewitching autumn foliage, we should still have to credit the weather with one feature which compensates for all its bullying vagaries—the ice-storm—when a leafless tree is clothed with ice from the bottom to the top—ice that is as bright and clear as crystal; every bough and twig is strung with ice-beads, frozen dewdrops, and the whole tree sparkles, cold and white, like the Shah of Persia's diamond plume. [Applause.] Then the wind waves the branches, and the sun comes out and turns all those myriads of beads and drops to prisms, that glow and hum and flash with all manner of colored fires, which change and change again, with inconceivable rapidity, from blue to red, from red to green, and green to gold; the tree becomes a sparkling fountain, a very explosion of dazzling jewels; and it stands there the acme, the climax, the supremest possibility in art or nature of bewildering, intoxicating, intolerable magnificence! One cannot make the words too strong. [Long-continued applause.]

Month after month I lay up hate and grudge against the New England weather; but when the ice-storm comes at last, I say: "There, I forgive you now; the books are square between us; you don't owe me a cent; go and sin some more; your little faults and foibles count for nothing; you are the most enchanting weather in the world!" [Applause and laughter.]

THE BABIES

MR. CHAIRMAN AND GENTLEMEN:—"The Babies!" Now, that's something like. We haven't all had the good fortune to be ladies; we have not all been generals, or poets, or statesmen; but when the toast works down to the babies, we stand on common ground—for we've all been babies. [Laughter.] It is a shame that for a thousand years the world's banquets have utterly ignored the baby, as if he didn't amount to anything! If you, gentlemen, will stop and think a minute—if you will go back fifty or a hundred years, to your early married life and recontemplate your first baby—you will remember that he amounted to a good deal—and even something over. [Laughter.]

You soldiers all know that when that little fellow arrived at family headquarters you had to hand in your resignation. He took entire command. You became his lackey, his mere bodyguard; and you had to stand around, too. He was not a commander who made allowances for the time, distance, weather, or anything else: you had to execute his order whether it was possible or not. And there was only one form of marching in his manual of tactics, and that was the double-quick. [Laughter.] He treated you with every sort of insolence and disrespect, and the bravest of you did not dare to say a word. You could face the death-storm of Donelson and Vicksburg, and give back blow for blow; but when he clawed your whiskers and pulled your hair, and twisted your nose you had to take it. [Laughter.] When the thunders of war sounded in your ears, you set your faces toward the batteries and advanced with steady tread; but when he turned on the terrors of his war-whoop [laughter], you advanced in—the other direction, and mighty glad of the chance, too. When he called for soothing sirup, did you venture to throw out any remarks about certain services unbecoming to an officer and a gentleman? No; you got up and got it! If he ordered his pap-bottle and it wasn't warm, did you talk back? Not you; you went to work and warmed it! You even descended so far in your menial office as to take a suck at that warm, insipid stuff yourself to see if it was right!—three parts water to one of milk, a touch of sugar to modify the colic, and a drop of peppermint to kill those immortal hiccoughs. I can taste that stuff yet! [Uproarious laughter.]

And how many things you learned as you went along! Sentimental young folks still take stock in that beautiful old saying, that when the baby smiles in his sleep it is because the angels are whispering to him. Very pretty, but "too thin"—simply wind on the stomach, my friends. [Laughter.] If the baby proposed to take a walk at his usual hour—half-past two in the morning—didn't you rise up promptly and remark (with a mental addition which wouldn't improve a Sunday-school much) that that was the very thing you were about to propose yourself? Oh, you were under good discipline. And as you went fluttering up and down the room in your "undress uniform" [laughter], you not only prattled undignified baby-talk, but even tuned up your martial voice, and tried to sing "Rock-a-bye-baby on the tree top," for instance. What a spectacle for an Army of the Tennessee! And what an affliction for the neighbors, too, for it isn't everybody within a mile around that likes military music at three o'clock in the morning. [Laughter.] And when you had been keeping that sort of thing up two or three hours, and your little velvet head intimated that nothing suited him like exercise and noise, and proposed to fight it out on that line if it took all night—Go on! What did you do? You simply went on till you dropped in the last ditch. [Laughter.]

I like the idea that a baby doesn't amount to anything! Why, one baby is just a house and a front yard full by itself; one baby can furnish more business than you and your whole interior department can attend to; he is enterprising, irrepressible, brimful of lawless activities; do what you please, you can't make him stay on the reservation. Sufficient unto the day is one baby. As long as you are in your right mind don't you ever pray for twins. Twins amount to a permanent riot; and there ain't any real difference between triplets and insurrection. [Great laughter.]

Among the three or four million cradles now rocking in the land, are some which this nation would preserve for ages as sacred things if we could know which ones they are. For in one of these cradles the unconscious Farragut of the future is at this moment teething. Think of it! and putting a word of dead earnest, unarticulated, but justifiable, profanity over it, too; in another, the future renowned astronomer is blinking at the shining Milky Way with but a languid interest, poor little chap, and wondering what has become of that other one they call the wet-nurse; in another, the future great historian is lying, and doubtless he will continue to lie until his earthly mission is ended; in another, the future President is busying himself with no profounder problem of State than what the mischief has become of his hair so early [laughter]; and in a mighty array of other cradles there are now some sixty thousand future office-seekers getting ready to furnish him occasion to grapple with the same old problem a second time! And in still one more cradle, somewhere under the flag, the future illustrious commander-in-chief of the American armies is so little burdened with his approaching grandeurs and responsibilities as to be giving his whole strategic mind, at this moment, to trying to find out some way to get his own big toe into his mouth, an achievement which (meaning no disrespect) the illustrious guest of this evening also turned his attention to some fifty-six years ago! And if the child is but the prophecy of the man there are mighty few will doubt that he succeeded. [Laughter and prolonged applause.]

WOMAN, GOD BLESS HER!

THE TOAST includes the sex, universally; it is to Woman comprehensively, wherever she may be found. Let us consider her ways. First comes the matter of dress. This is a most important consideration, and must be disposed of before we can intelligently proceed to examine the profounder depths of the theme. For text let us take the dress of two antipodal types —the savage woman of Central Africa and the cultivated daughter of our high modern civilization. Among the Fans, a great negro tribe, a woman when dressed for home, or to go out shopping or calling, doesn't wear anything at all but just her complexion. [Laughter.] That is all; it is her entire outfit. [Laughter.] It is the lightest costume in the world, but is made of the darkest material. [Laughter.] It has often been mistaken for mourning. [Laughter.] It is the trimmest, and neatest, and gracefulest costume that is now in fashion; it wears well, is fast colors, doesn't show dirt, you don't have to send it down-town to wash, and have some of it come back scorched with the flat-iron, and some of it with the buttons ironed off, and some of it petrified with starch, and some of it chewed by the calf, and some of it rotted with acids, and some of it exchanged for other customers' things that haven't any virtue but holiness, and ten-twelfths of the pieces overcharged for and the rest of the dozen "mislaid." [Laughter.] And it always fits; it is the perfection of a fit. [Laughter.] And it is the handiest dress in the whole realm of fashion. It is always ready, always "done up." When you call on a Fan lady and send up your card, the hired girl never says, "Please take a seat, madame is dressing; she'll be down in three-quarters of an hour." No, madame is always dressed, always ready to receive; and before you can get the door-mat before your eyes she is in your midst. [Laughter.] Then, again, the Fan ladies don't go to church to see what each other has got on; and they don't go back home and describe it and slander it. [Laughter.]

Such is the dark child of savagery, as to everyday toilet; and thus, curiously enough, she finds a point of contact with the fair daughter of civilization and high fashion—who often has "nothing to wear"; and thus these widely-separated types of the sex meet upon common ground. Yes, such is the Fan woman as she appears in her simple, unostentatious, everyday toilet; but on state occasions she is more dressy. At a banquet she wears bracelets; at a lecture she wears earrings and a belt; at a ball she wears stockings—and, with true feminine fondness for display, she wears them on her arms [laughter]; at a funeral she wears a jacket of tar and ashes [laughter]; at a wedding the bride who can afford it puts on pantaloons. [Laughter.] Thus the dark child of savagery and the fair daughter of civilization meet once more upon common ground, and these two touches of nature make their whole world kin.

Now we will consider the dress of our other type. A large part of the daughter of civilization is her dress—as it should be. Some civilized women would lose half their charm without dress; and some would lose all of it. [Laughter.] The daughter of modern civilization dressed at her utmost best, is a marvel of exquisite and beautiful art and expense. All the lands, all the climes, and all the arts are laid under tribute to furnish her forth. Her linen is from Belfast, her robe is from Paris, her lace is from Venice, or Spain, or France; her feathers are from the remote regions of Southern Africa, her furs from the remoter home of the iceberg and the aurora, her fan from Japan, her diamonds from Brazil, her bracelets from California, her pearls from Ceylon, her cameos from Rome; she has gems and trinkets from buried Pompeii, and others that graced comely Egyptian forms that have been dust and ashes now for forty centuries; her watch is from Geneva, her card-case is from China, her hair is from—from—I don't know where her hair is from; I never could find out. [Much laughter.] That is, her other hair—her public hair, her Sunday hair; I don't mean the hair she goes to bed with. [Laughter.] Why, you ought to know the hair I mean; it's that thing which she calls a switch, and which resembles a switch as much as it resembles a brickbat or a shotgun, or any other thing which you correct people with. It's that thing which she twists and then coils round and round her head, beehive fashion, and then tucks the end in under the hive and harpoons it with a hairpin. And that reminds me of a trifle: any time you want to, you can glance around the carpet of a Pullman car, and go and pick up a hairpin; but not to save your life can you get any woman in that car to acknowledge that hairpin. Now, isn't that strange? But it's true. The woman who has never swerved from cast-iron veracity and fidelity in her whole life will, when confronted with this crucial test, deny her hairpin. [Laughter.] She will deny that hairpin before a hundred witnesses. I have stupidly got into more trouble and more hot water trying to hunt up the owner of a hairpin in a Pullman car than by any other indiscretion of my life.

Well, you see what the daughter of civilization is when she is dressed, and you have seen what the daughter of savagery is when she isn't. Such is woman, as to costume. I come now to consider her in her higher and nobler aspects—as mother, wife, widow, grass-widow, mother-in-law, hired girl, telegraph operator, telephone helloer, queen, book-agent, wet-nurse, stepmother, boss, professional fat woman, professional double-headed woman, professional beauty, and so forth and so on. [Laughter.]

We will simply discuss these few—let the rest of the sex tarry in Jericho till we come again. First in the list of right, and first in our gratitude, comes a woman who—why, dear me, I've been talking three-quarters of an hour! I beg a thousand pardons. But you see, yourselves, that I had a large contract. I have accomplished something, anyway. I have introduced my subject. And if I had till next Forefathers' Day, I am satisfied that I could discuss it as adequately and appreciatively as so gracious and noble a theme deserves. But as the matter stands now, let us finish as we began —and say, without jesting, but with all sincerity, "Woman—God bless her!" [Applause.]

Charles William Eliot

[1834–1926]

Charles W. Eliot was president of Harvard University for forty years. The following speech was delivered by him at a dinner of the New England Society, in New York City, on December 22, 1877.

HARVARD AND YALE

Mr. PRESIDENT and gentlemen:—I am obliged to my friend Dr. Clarke [James Freeman Clarke, D.D.] for the complimentary terms in which he has presented me to you. But I must appeal to your commiseration. Harvard and Yale! Can any undergraduate of either institution, can any recent graduate of either institution, imagine a man responding to that toast? [Laughter.] However, I must make the best of the position, and speak of some points upon which the two institutions are clearly agreed. And here I am reminded of a story of a certain New England farmer, who said that he and 'Squire Jones had more cows between them than all the rest of the village; and his brag being disputed, he said he could prove it, for the 'Squire had forty-five cows and he had one, and the village altogether had not forty-six. [Laughter.]

We shall all agree that it is for the best interests of this country that it have sundry universities, of diverse tone, atmosphere, sphere, representing different opinions and different methods of study to some extent, and in different trainings, though with the same end. [Applause.] Holding this view, I have been somewhat concerned to see of late that the original differences between Harvard and Yale seem to be rapidly disappearing. For example, a good many years ago, Harvard set out on what is called the "elective" system, and now I read in the Yale catalogue a long list of studies called "optional," which strikes me as bearing a strong resemblance to our elective courses. [Laughter.] Again, my friend the Secretary of State has done me the honor of alluding to the reasons which induced his father, I suppose, rather than himself, to send him on that journey, which we Harvard men all deplore. [Laughter.]

Now, it is unquestioned, that about the year 1700 a certain number of Congregationalist clergymen, who belonged to the Established Church (for we are too apt to forget that Congregationalism was the "Established Church" of that time, and none other was allowed), thought that Harvard was getting altogether too latitudinarian, and though they were every one of them graduates of Harvard, they went off and set up another college in Connecticut, where a stricter doctrine should be taught. Harvard men have rather nursed the hope that this distinction between Harvard and Yale might be permanent. [Laughter.] But I regret to say that I have lately observed many strong indications that it is wholly likely to disappear. For example, to come at once to the foundations, I read in the papers the other day, and I am credibly informed it is true, that the head of Yale College voted to install a minister whose opinions upon the vital, pivotal, fundamental doctrine of eternal damnation are unsound. [Laughter.] Then, again, I look at the annual reports of the Bureau of Education on this department at Washington, and I read there for some years that Harvard College was unsectarian; and I knew that it was right, because I made the return myself. [Laughter.] I read also that Yale College was a Congregationalist College; and I had no doubt that that was right, because I supposed Dr. Porter had made the report. But now we read in that same report that Yale College is unsectarian. That is a great progress. The fact is, both these universities have found out that in a country which has no established church and no dominant sect you cannot build a university on a sect at all—you must build it upon the nation. [Applause.]

But, gentlemen, there are some other points, I think, of national education on which we shall find these two early founded universities to agree. For example, we have lately read, in the Message of the Chief Magistrate, that a national university would be a good thing. [Applause.] Harvard and Yale are of one mind upon that subject, but they want to have a national university defined. [Laughter.] If it means a university of national resort, we say amen. If it means a university where the youth of this land are taught to love their country and to serve her, we say amen [applause]; and we point, both of us, to our past in proof that we are national in that sense. [Applause.] But if it means that the national university is to be a university administered and managed by the wise Congress of the United States, then we should agree in taking some slight exceptions. [Laughter.] We should not question for a moment the capacity of Congress to pick out and appoint the professors of Latin and Greek, and the ancient languages, because we find that there is an astonishing number of classical orators in Congress, and there is manifested there a singular acquaintance with the legislation of all the Latin races. [Laughter.] But when it should come to some other humbler professorships we might perhaps entertain a doubt. For example, we have not entire faith in the trust that Congress has in the unchangeableness of the laws of arithmetic. [Laughter.] We might think that their competency to select a professor of history might be doubted. They seem to have an impression that there is such a thing as "American" political economy, which can no more be than "American" chemistry or "American" physics. [Applause.] Finally, gentlemen, we should a little distrust the selection by Congress of a professor of ethics. [Laughter.] Of course, we should feel no doubt in regard to the tenure of office of the professors being entirely suitable, it being the well-known practice of both branches of Congress to select men solely for fitness, without regard to locality, and to keep them in office as long as they are competent and faithful. [Laughter and applause.]

But, gentlemen, I think we ought to recur for a moment, perhaps, to the Pilgrim Fathers [laughter], and I desire to say that both Harvard and

Yale recognize the fact that there are some things before which universities "pale their ineffectual fires."

"Words are but breath; but where great deeds were done,
A power abides, transferred from sire to son."

Now, gentlemen, on that sandy, desolate spot of Plymouth great deeds were done, and we are here to commemorate them. Those were hard times. It was a terrible voyage, and they were hungry and cold and worn out with labor, and they took their guns to the church and the field, and the half of them died in the first winter. They were not prosperous times that we recall with this hour. Let us take some comfort from that in the present circumstances of our beloved country. She is in danger of a terrible disaster, but let us remember that the times which future generations delight to recall are not those of ease and prosperity, but those of adversity bravely borne. [Applause.]

Henry Watterson
[1840–1921]

Following is the speech of Henry Watterson, noted editor of the Louisville Courier-Journal, *which he delivered at the eighty-ninth anniversary dinner of the New England Society, in New York City, on December 22, 1894.*

THE PURITAN AND THE CAVALIER

Mr. president and gentlemen:—Eight years ago, to-night, there stood where I am standing now a young Georgian, who, not without reason, recognized the "significance" of his presence here—"the first southerner to speak at this board"—a circumstance, let me add, not very creditable to any of us—and in words whose eloquence I cannot hope to recall, appealed from the New South to New England for a united country.

He was my disciple, my protégé, my friend. He came to me from the southern schools, where he had perused the arts of oratory and letters, to get a few hints in journalism, as he said; needing so few, indeed, that, but a little later, I sent him to one of the foremost journalists of this foremost city, bearing a letter of introduction, which described him as "the greatest boy ever born in Dixie, or anywhere else."

He is gone now. But, short as his life was, its heaven-born mission was fulfilled; the dream of his childhood was realized; for he had been appointed by God to carry a message of peace on earth, good-will to men, and, this done, he vanished from the sight of mortal eyes, even as the dove from the ark.

I mean to take up the word where Grady left it off, but I shall continue the sentence with a somewhat larger confidence, and, perhaps, with a somewhat fuller meaning; because, notwithstanding the Puritan trappings, traditions, and associations which surround me—visible illustrations of the self-denying fortitude of the Puritan character and the sombre simplicity of the Puritan taste and habit—I never felt less out of place in all my life.

To tell you the truth, I am afraid that I have gained access here on false pretences; for I am no Cavalier at all; just plain Scotch-Irish; one of those Scotch-Irish southerners who ate no fire in the green leaf and has eaten no dirt in the brown, and who, accepting, for the moment, the terms Puritan and Cavalier in the sense an effete sectionalism once sought to ascribe to them—descriptive labels at once classifying and separating North and South—verbal redoubts along that mythical line called Mason and Dixon, over which there were supposed by the extremists of other days to be no bridges—I am much disposed to say, "A plague o' both your houses!"

Each was good enough and bad enough in its way, whilst they lasted; each in its turn filled the English-speaking world with mourning; and each, if either could have resisted the infection of the soil and climate they found here, would be to-day striving at the sword's point to square life by the iron rule of Theocracy, or to round it by the dizzy whirl of a petticoat! It is very pretty to read about the Maypole in Virginia and very edifying and inspiring to celebrate the deeds of the Pilgrim Fathers. But there is not Cavalier blood enough left in the Old Dominion to produce a single crop of first families, whilst out in Nebraska and Iowa they claim that they have so stripped New England of her Puritan stock as to spare her hardly enough for farm hands. This I do know, from personal experience, that it is impossible for the stranger-guest, sitting beneath a bower of roses in the Palmetto Club at Charleston, or by a mimic log-heap in the Algonquin Club at Boston, to tell the assembled company apart, particularly after ten o'clock in the evening! Why, in that great, final struggle between the Puritans and the Cavaliers—which we still hear sometimes casually mentioned—although it ended nearly thirty years ago, there had been such a mixing up of Puritan babies and Cavalier babies during the two or three generations preceding it, that the surviving grandmothers of the combatants could not, except for their uniforms, have picked out their own on any field of battle!

Turning to the Cyclopædia of American Biography, I find that Webster had all the vices that are supposed to have signalized the Cavalier, and Calhoun all the virtues that are claimed for the Puritan. During twenty years three statesmen of Puritan origin were the chosen party leaders of Cavalier Mississippi: Robert J. Walker, born and reared in Pennsylvania; John A. Quitman, born and reared in New York, and Sargent S. Prentiss, born and reared in the good old State of Maine. That sturdy Puritan, John Slidell, never saw Louisiana until he was old enough to vote and to fight; native here—an alumnus of Columbia College—but sprung from New England ancestors. Albert Sidney Johnston, the most resplendent of modern Cavaliers—from tip to toe a type of the species—the very rose and expectancy of the young Confederacy—did not have a drop of Southern blood in his veins; Yankee on both sides of the house, though born in Kentucky a little while after his father and mother arrived there from Connecticut. The Ambassador who serves our Government near the French Republic was a gallant Confederate soldier and is a representative southern statesman; but he owns the estate in Massachusetts where his father was born, and where his father's fathers lived through many generations.

And the Cavaliers, who missed their stirrups, somehow, and got into Yankee saddles? The woods were full of them. If Custer was not a Cavalier, Rupert was a Puritan. And Sherwood and Wadsworth and Kearny, and McPherson and their dashing companions and followers! The one typical Puritan soldier of the war—mark you!—was a Southern, and not a Northern, soldier; Stonewall Jackson, of the Virginia line. And, if we should care to pursue the subject farther back, what about Ethan Allen and John Stark and Mad Anthony Wayne—Cavaliers each and every one? Indeed, from Israel Putnam to "Buffalo Bill," it seems to me the Puritans have had rather the best of it in turning out Cavaliers. So the least said about the Puritan and the Cavalier—except as blessed memories or horrid examples—the better for historic accuracy.

If you wish to get at the bottom facts, I don't mind telling you—in confidence—that it was we Scotch-Irish who vanquished both of you—some of us in peace—others of us in war—supplying the missing link of adaptability—the needed ingredient of common sense—the conservative principle of creed and action, to which this generation of Americans owes its intellectual and moral emancipation from frivolity and pharisaism—its rescue from the Scarlet Woman and the mailed hand—and its crystallization into a national character and polity, ruling by force of brains and not by force of arms.

Gentlemen—Sir—I, too, have been to Boston. Strange as the admission may seem, it is true; and I live to tell the tale. I have been to Boston; and when I declare that I found there many things that suggested the Cavalier and did not suggest the Puritan, I shall not say I was sorry. But among other things, I found there a civilization perfect in its union of the art of living with the grace of life; an Americanism ideal in its simple strength. Grady told us, and told us truly, of that typical American who, in Dr. Talmage's mind's eye, was coming, but who, in Abraham Lincoln's actuality, had already come. In some recent studies into the career of that great man, I have encountered many startling confirmations of this judgment; and from that rugged trunk, drawing its sustenance from gnarled roots, interlocked with Cavalier sprays and Puritan branches deep beneath the soil, shall spring, is springing, a shapely tree—symmetric in all its parts—under whose sheltering boughs this nation shall have the new birth of freedom Lincoln promised it, and mankind the refuge which was sought by the forefathers when they fled from oppression. Thank God, the axe, the gibbet, and the stake have had their day. They have gone, let us hope, to keep company with the lost arts. It has been demonstrated that great wrongs may be redressed and great reforms be achieved without the shedding of one drop of human blood; that vengeance does not purify, but brutalizes; and that tolerance, which in private transactions is reckoned a virtue, becomes in public affairs a dogma of the most far-seeing statesmanship. Else how could this noble city have been redeemed from bondage? It was held like a castle of the Middle Ages by robber barons, who levied tribute right and left. Yet have the mounds and dykes of corruption been carried—from buttress to bell-tower the walls of crime have fallen—without a shot out of a gun, and still no fires of Smithfield to light the pathway of the victor, no bloody assizes to vindicate the justice of the cause; nor need of any.

So I appeal from the men in silken hose who danced to music made by slaves—and called it freedom—from the men in bell-crowned hats, who led Hester Prynne to her shame—and called it religion—to that Americanism which reaches forth its arms to smite wrong with reason and truth, secure in the power of both. I appeal from the patriarchs of New England to the poets of New England; from Endicott to Lowell; from Winthrop to Longfellow; from Norton to Holmes; and I appeal in the name and by the rights of that common citizenship—of that common origin—back both of the Puritan and the Cavalier—to which all of us owe our being. Let the dead past, consecrated by the blood of its martyrs, not by its savage hatreds—darkened alike by kingcraft and priest-craft—let the dead past bury its dead. Let the present and the future ring with the song of the singers. Blessed be the lessons they teach, the laws they make. Blessed be the eye to see, the light to reveal. Blessed be Tolerance, sitting ever on the right hand of God to guide the way with loving word, as blessed be all that brings us nearer the goal of true religion, true Republicanism and true patriotism, distrust of watchwords and labels, shams and heroes, belief in our country and ourselves. It was not Cotton Mather, but John Greenleaf Whittier, who cried:

> "Dear God and Father of us all,
> Forgive our faith in cruel lies,
> Forgive the blindness that denies.
>
> "Cast down our idols—overturn
> Our bloody altars—make us see
> Thyself in Thy humanity!"

John Hay
[1838–1905]

John Hay, statesman and author, was Ambassador to Great Britain in 1897. He delivered the following speech at a dinner of the Omar Khayyam Club, in London, on December 8, 1897.

OMAR KHAYYAM

GENTLEMEN:—I cannot sufficiently thank you for the high and unmerited honor you have done me to-night. I feel keenly that on such an occasion, with such company, my place is below the salt, but as you kindly invited me it was not in human nature for me to refuse. Although in knowledge and comprehension of the two great poets whom you are met to commemorate I am the least among them, there is no one who regards them with greater admiration, or reads them with more enjoyment than myself. I can never forget my emotions when I first saw Fitzgerald's translation of the Quatrains. Keats, in his sublime ode on Chapman's Homer, has described the sensation once for all:—

"Then felt I like some watcher of the skies,
When a new planet swims into his ken."

The exquisite beauty, the faultless form, the singular grace of those amazing stanzas, were not more wonderful than the depth and breadth of their profound philosophy, their knowledge of life, their dauntless courage, their serene facing of the ultimate problems of life and of death. Of course the doubt did not spare me, which has assailed many as ignorant as I was of the literature of the East, whether it was the poet or his translator to whom was due this splendid result. Was it, in fact, a reproduction of a new song, or a mystification of a great modern, careless of fame and scornful of his time? Could it be possible that in the eleventh century, so far away as Khorassan, so accomplished a man of letters lived, with such distinction, such breadth, such insight, such calm disillusion, such cheerful and jocund despair? Was this Weltschmerz, which we thought a malady of our day, endemic in Persia in 1100? My doubt lasted only till I came upon a literal translation of the Rubaiyat, and I saw that not the least remarkable quality of Fitzgerald's was its fidelity to the original. In short, Omar was a Fitzgerald before the latter, or Fitzgerald was a reincarnation of Omar. It is not to the disadvantage of the later poet that he followed so closely in the footsteps of the earlier. A man of extraordinary genius had appeared in the world; had sung a song of incomparable beauty and power in an environment no longer worthy of him, in a language of narrow range; for many generations the song was virtually lost; then by a miracle of creation, a poet, a twin-brother in the spirit to the first, was born, who took up the forgotten poem and sung it anew with all its original melody and force, and all the accumulated refinement of ages of art. [Cheers.]

It seems to me idle to ask which was the greater master; each seems greater than his work. The song is like an instrument of precious workmanship and marvellous tone, which is worthless in common hands, but when it falls, at long intervals, into the hands of the supreme master, it yields a melody of transcendent enchantment to all that have ears to hear. If we look at the sphere of influence of the two poets there is no longer any comparison. Omar sang to a half barbarous province; Fitzgerald to the world. Wherever the English speech is spoken or read, the Rubaiyat have taken their place as a classic. There is not a hill-post in India, nor a village in England, where there is not a coterie to whom Omar Khayyam is a familiar friend and a bond of union. In America he has an equal following, in many regions and conditions. In the Eastern States his adepts form an esoteric sect; the beautiful volume of drawings by Mr. Vedder is a centre of delight and suggestion wherever it exists. In the cities of the West you will find the Quatrains one of the most thoroughly read books in every Club Library. I heard Omar quoted once in one of the most lovely and desolate spots of the High Rockies. We had been camping on the Great Divide, our "roof of the world," where in the space of a few feet you may see two springs, one sending its water to the Polar solitudes, the other to the eternal Carib summer. One morning at sunrise as we were breaking camp, I was startled to hear one of our party, a frontiersman born, intoning these words of sombre majesty:—

> " 'Tis but a tent where takes his one day's rest
> A Sultan to the realm of death addressed.
> The Sultan rises and the dark Ferrash
> Strikes, and prepares it for another guest."

I thought that sublime setting of primeval forest and pouring cañon was worthy of the lines; I am sure the dewless, crystalline air never vibrated to strains of more solemn music.

Certainly our poet can never be numbered among the great popular writers of all times. He has told no story; he has never unpacked his heart in public; he has never thrown the reins on the neck of the winged horse, and let his imagination carry him where it listed. "Ah! the crowd must have emphatic warrant." Its suffrages are not for the cool, collected observer, whose eye no glitter can ever dazzle, no mist suffuse. The many cannot but resent that air of lofty intelligence, that pale and subtle smile. But he will hold a place forever among that limited number who, like Lucretius and Epicurus—without rage or defiance, even without unbecoming mirth—look deep into the tangled mysteries of things; refuse credence to the absurd, and allegiance to the arrogant authority, sufficiently conscious of fallibility to be tolerant of all opinions; with a faith too wide for doctrine and a benevolence untrammelled by creed, too wise to be wholly poets, and yet too surely poets to be implacably wise. [Loud cheers.]

Sir Henry Irving
[1838–1905]

Sir Henry Irving, noted English actor, delivered the following speech at the annual dinner of the Playgoer's Club, in London, on February 14, 1898.

THE DRAMA

MR. CHAIRMAN AND GENTLEMEN:—It is five years since I had the pleasure of sitting at your hospitable board and listening to that delightfully soothing and digestive eloquence with which we medicine one another after dinner. [Laughter.] In the course of those five years I daresay we have had many differences of opinion. The playgoer does not always agree with the player, still less with that unfortunate object, the poor actor-manager. But whatever you may have said of me in this interval, and in terms less dulcet, perhaps, than those which your chairman has so generously employed, it is a great satisfaction to me to feel that I still retain your esteem and good will. In a certain sense you are the manager's constituents. You cannot eject him from the office, perhaps, with that directness which distinguishes the Parliamentary operations. But you can stay away from the theater, and so eject his play. [Laughter.] On the whole that is a more disconcerting process than the fiercest criticism. One can always argue with the critics, though on the actor's part I know that is gross presumption. [Laughter.] But you cannot argue with the playgoer who stays away.

I am not making any specific accusations—only remarking that it is staying-power which impresses the importance of the Playgoer's Club upon the managerial mind. Moreover, to meet you like this has the effect of a useful tonic. I can strongly recommend it to some gentlemen who write to the newspapers. [Laughter.] In one journal there was a long correspondence—the sort of thing we generally get at one season of the year—about the condition of the stage, and a well-known writer who, I believe, combines the function of a dramatic critic with the responsibility of a watchdog to the Navy, informed his readers that the sad decadence of the British drama was due to the evils of party government. That is certainly an original idea; but I fancy that if the author were to unfold it to this company, he would be told that he had mistaken the Playgoer's Club for the War Office or the Admiralty. Still we ought to be grateful to the man who reveals a perfectly fresh reason for the eternal decline of the drama, though we may not, perhaps, anticipate any revolution in theatrical amusements even from the most thoroughgoing reform of the British Constitution.

In the public correspondence to which I have referred, a good deal was said about the need for a dramatic conservatoire. If such an institution could be rooted in this country, I have no doubt that it might yield many advantages. Years ago I ventured to suggest that the municipal system might be applied to the theater, as it is on the Continent, though I do not observe that this is yet a burning question in the county council politics, or that any reforming administrator has discovered that the drama ought to be laid on, like gas or water. [Laughter.] With all our genius for local government we have not yet found, like some Continental peoples, that the municipal theater is as much a part of the healthy life of the community as the municipal library or museum. ["Hear! hear!"] Whether that development is in store for us I do not know, but I can imagine certain social benefits that would accrue from the municipal incorporation of a dramatic conservatoire. It might check the rush of incompetent persons into the theatrical profession. Some persons who were intended by Nature to adorn an inviolable privacy are thrust upon us by paragraphers and interviewers, whose existence is a dubious blessing until it is assumed by censors of the stage that this business is part and parcel of theatrical advertisement.

Columns of this rubbish are printed every week, and many an actor is pestered to death for titbits about his ox and his ass and everything that is his. [Laughter.] Occasionally you may read solemn articles about the insatiable vanity of the actor, which must be gratified at any cost, as if vanity were peculiar to any section of humanity. But what this organized gossip really advertises is the industry of the gentlemen who collect it, and the smartness of the papers in which it is circulated. "We learn this," "We have reason to believe"—such forms of intolerable assurance give currency too often to scandalous and lying rumors which I am sure responsible journalism would wish to discourage. But this, I fear, is difficult, for contradiction makes another desirable paragraph, and it is all looked upon as desirable copy. [Laughter.]

Of course, gentlemen, the drama is declining—it always has been declining since the time of Roscius and beyond the palmy days when the famous Elephant Raja was "starred" over the head of W. C. Macready, and the real water tank in the Cataract of the Ganges helped to increase the attractions of John Kemble and Mrs. Siddons. But we ourselves are evidently in a parlous state at the present day, when actors vainly endeavor to struggle through twenty lines of blank verse—when we are told mechanical efforts and vast armies of supers make up the production of historical plays—when pathological details, we are told, are always well received—when the "psychonosological" (whatever that may be)— [laughter] is invariably successful—and when Pinero and Grundy's plays do not appeal to men of advanced thought, as I read the other day.

In all the lament about the decline of the drama there is one recurring note: the disastrous influence of long runs. If the manager were not a grossly material person, incapable of ideals, he would take off a successful piece at the height of its popularity and start a fresh experiment. [Laughter.] But he is sunk in the base commercialism of the age, and, sad to relate, he has the sympathies of the dramatic author, who wants to see his piece run say a hundred nights, instead of twenty. I don't know how this spirit of greed is to be subdued, though with the multiplication of playhouses, long runs may tend to become rare. A municipal subsidy or an obliging millionaire might enable a manager to vary his bill with comparative frequency, when he has persuaded the dramatic author that the run of a play till the crack of doom is incompatible with the interest of art. [Laughter.] I cannot help suspecting that the chief difficulty of a manager, under even the most artistic and least commercial conditions, will always be, not to check the inordinate proportions of success, but to secure plays which may succeed at all.

I hope you will not accuse me of taking a too despondent view of the drama, for believe me, I do not. To be sure, we sometimes hear that Shakespeare is to be annihilated, and that the poet's intellect has been overrated. And lately a reverend gentleman at Hampstead announced his intention of putting down the stage altogether. [Laughter.] The atmosphere of Hampstead seems to be intellectually intoxicating; at any rate it has a rather stimulating effect on a certain kind of dogmatic mind. This intolerance has been very eloquently rebuked by a distinguished man who is an ornament of the Church of England. It is Dean Farrar who says that these pharisaical attacks on the stage are inspired only by "concentrated malice." Well, the periodical misunderstanding to which the stage is exposed need cause but little disquiet. I have no doubt it will survive its many adventures, and that it will owe not a little of its tenacious vitality to your unflagging sympathy and hearty and generous encouragement. [Cheers.]

Robert Edwin Peary
[1856–1920]

Admiral Robert E. Peary, American Arctic explorer, delivered the following speech at a dinner given in his honor by the Lotos Club, in New York City, on February 2, 1907.

FARTHEST NORTH

IT IS UNNECESSARY for me, President Lawrence, to tell you how much and how deeply I appreciate your kindly words, how absolutely at home I feel by your side, and particularly in the precincts of the Lotos Club. I recall very distinctly several similar pleasant occasions here.

Many of you are aware of the fact that during the last eighteen months a new degree has been added, and the Stars and Stripes have been placed in the lead in the international race for the pole. But that is not the only result of the last eighteen months of work, for new lands have been discovered, and new and valuable scientific and geographic information and data have been obtained.

The point of view of Mr. Jesup and his associates in the Peary Arctic

Club has been that arctic work to-day is a simple business proposition, and should combine in intimate coördination two objects: the attainment of the pole as a matter of record and national *prestige,* and the securing of all possible geographic, hydrographic, and other scientific information from the unknown regions about the pole. And since the government has not considered it advisable to undertake the work, the club gladly assumed it, and shares the resulting honor, whatever there may be, and the scientific material, with the country and its museums.

The steamer *Roosevelt,* built especially for arctic work, sailed, in July, 1905, on her northern voyage. This ship was built from American timber from Maine, New Hampshire, and other States; built in an American shipyard and fitted with American machinery. The ship, one hundred and eight feet long and thirty-eight feet beam, was fundamentally better fitted for the work than any ship that had ever gone north, and was in reality a ship with auxiliary sail-power.

We followed the ordinary itinerary to Sydney, Cape Breton and then we beat our way up the west coast to Grantland, where we took on board the Eskimos. There is a little tribe of Eskimos who are the most northern people in the world, and they form one of the most important adjuncts in arctic work. I knew their capabilities, and so I was able to select the pick and flower of the entire tribe. These men, with their wives, their children, and their dogs and sledges—in fact, all their belongings—we took on board the ship, to act as drivers and carriers.

Off Cape Sabine we had eighteen days of incessant battle, a battle of a kind many of you cannot understand, using the ship as a huge battering-ram and driving it at the ice. Nobody at this dinner can imagine what that work was. After eighteen days we managed to reach Cape Sabine at last, five hundred miles from the pole itself.

Here I followed the routine of every arctic explorer, a routine which is compelled by the sequence of the arctic seasons. A ship goes north one summer in August or September, and goes into winter quarters before the months of darkness set in, when nothing can be done; and perhaps I can bring that home clearly to you when I say that the sun set for us on the 12th of October and rose again on the 6th of March. How many of you can really bring that home to yourselves? What would it be right here in New York if the sun were to set in October and not rise again until March? That winter night is really the only real source of trouble in arctic work. Ninety-nine out of a hundred people have the impression that the cold is the great trouble; but when you are up there, and dressed for it in fur clothing, and properly fed, the cold at seventy-seven degrees below zero is not nearly as disagreeable as is the damp, raw cold that we have in New York every winter.

And the last five hundred miles of that journey of only three thousand miles from New York to the pole must be accomplished with dogs and sledges; that is inevitable. The winter quarters of the *Roosevelt* were farther north than the winter quarters of any other arctic ship except one, the *Fram.*

We went along the coast, parallel with it for some sixty miles; we made some eighty miles when we came to a break or lead in the ice which was impassable. We sent two parties back for additional supplies, and sat down to wait for the lead to freeze or close over; and then, as we had some low temperatures, forty-five to sixty below zero, we put light loads on the sledges and crossed. Then from the northern side of the lead we made three good marches north, and were stopped by a blizzard which set the ice in motion. Here we built a hut for shelter, and one night we had to get out in the storm and build another. The ice-pack during this storm drifted eastward seventy miles, and you will naturally recognize that we were cut off from our supplies and the party was larger than we had supplies for, and that whatever was done had to be done by a quick dash if conditions proved favorable.

We therefore abandoned everything that was not absolutely necessary, and made a start. We put our best efforts to setting a pace, and the first march of thirty miles was made in ten hours; for the most part, I set the pace in the lead. On the second march we overtook one of the parties I had sent in advance, waiting beside a lead. They immediately hitched up and joined us, and we kept on with our small party of seven men and six teams until the 21st of April, when we halted in the middle of the day to take observations, which showed that we had reached latitude 87.6 north, which at present is the nearest approach to the North Pole. Nansen had previously reached 86.13, and Abruzzi reached 86.33, but both these points were practically at the opposite side of the pole from me. Perhaps it will bring home to you more clearly the narrowing of the record when I tell you that with the pole here [indicating], and my own point here, the distance is only 374 nautical miles. It is true that we had attained a record—we couldn't have come back without it—but the feeling that the record fell so far short of the splendid thing on which I had set my heart for years, and for which I had been almost literally straining my life out, was one of most intense disappointment. But you can possibly imagine where my heart was when I looked at the skeleton figures of the few remaining dogs, and remembered the drifting ice and big lead. I felt that I had cut the margin just as close as it could possibly be done, and from that point we turned back.

Before we turned, however, my flags were hoisted on the highest pinnacle near us, and a little beyond this I erected a cairn and in it I left a bottle containing a brief record and a piece of the silk flag—the flag that hangs over there, gentlemen, and which is the same one I have carried for six years. Had our provisions lasted, and had we been able to keep up a pace of twenty miles a day, in ten to twelve days we should have been at our goal.

The journey back to our last camp was one of exceeding difficulty, inasmuch as the drifting snow was constantly blowing in our faces, stinging like red-hot needles; and when we reached camp we were all nearly completely done up. There we slept one full sleep, and it was many days before we got another.

Finally we reached Storm Camp, and here we were detained twenty-four hours by a howling storm. The igloos here had been turned into ice grottoes, but they proved a welcome refuge. From here we picked our way with indescribable toil, and constantly using the pickax, to the big lead.

Five nights and days we spent by this lead, and on the fifth day my scouting party of Eskimos came in and reported that there was some young ice forming across the lead a few miles off, which might support us on our snowshoes over the rather more than two miles to the southern side. We wasted no time in getting to the place, and each man tied his snowshoes on carefully and we started across in skirmishing order, well extended. I had five-foot snowshoes and the others had four-foot ones. There was a distance of fifty feet between us as we walked across the tough young ice, which trembled and bent and yielded before us at every step. We couldn't stop, and we couldn't lift the snowshoes, they had to be carefully slid or pushed along. Never again do I care for any similar experience. At last we reached the southern side of the lead, and the sigh of relief of the two men nearest me was distinctly audible.

Well, we were safely over, so we camped for a while, and had a grand dinner—just of dog—and then we were ready again to keep on to the southward over ice that seemed almost impassable, and some of the pinnacles of which were the size of the dome of the Capitol in Washington, ranging from that down to a cobblestone. For the next three marches the going was frightful, and then it began to improve. I made out the summits of distant Greenland with my glass, and soon we were under the shelter of Cape Morris Jesup, and there was no longer any danger of drifting around it. On May 12 we came out on the ice-foot at Cape Neumeyer, for I was familiar with this coast, and I knew that we were likely to find game there. Within an hour we had four arctic hares, weighing from nine to ten pounds each, and the meat was more than delicious. Just before reaching the shore we crossed a fresh sledge-track, and for a moment I thought it was a party looking for me, but a closer inspection showed that it was a light sledge drawn by three weak dogs, and four weak men walking very slowly. As soon as we had slept a few hours I sent some of the Eskimos to find out, and the next day they came back with Clark and three Eskimos.

They had lost their way and were going away from the ship and would soon have perished. The addition of four men to my nearly starving party was an added burden, but we fortunately secured some ten more hares, and started for the ship.

During the march I had a scout out all the time looking for game—hares and musk oxen; and one day, just after we had killed a dog, a herd of musk oxen was seen some five miles distant. I footed it for five miles, and was lucky enough to kill the entire herd of seven. Then we camped there, and for two days and two nights we did nothing but eat and sleep. I did my share of it too. I simply hadn't the heart to make the others stop.

I need not speak of the voyage home, but may add a few remarks as to arctic work, on points not generally understood. The incentive of the earliest northern voyages was commercial, the desire of the northern

European nations to find a navigable northern route to the fabled wealth of the East. When the impracticability of such a route was proven, the adventurous spirit of Anglo-Saxon and Teuton found in the mystery, the danger, the excitement, which crystallized under the name "north pole," a worthy antagonist for their fearless blood. The result of their efforts has been to add millions to the world's wealth, to demonstrate some of the most important scientific propositions, and to develop some of the most splendid examples of manly courage and heroism that adorn the human record.

Let me call your attention to that flag, that tattered and torn and patched flag you see hanging over the mantel there. That is the flag from which I have taken pieces for deposit in the cairns I built. You will notice that three pieces are gone. One is in the cairn at the "farthest north," 87.6 degrees; a second piece I placed in a cairn I built on one of the twin peaks of Columbia, Cape Columbia; and the third in the cairn on the northern point of Jesup Land.

To the practical explorer, particularly those who will yet wrest their final secrets from the arctic and antarctic regions, the experience of the expedition, its freedom from sickness and death, especially the scurvy which has been the bane of so many expeditions, even up to some of the later antarctic ones; its methods and equipment, its rapidity of travel and its evolution of what I believe will be the true type of ship for arctic and antarctic work, able to fight, or drift, or sail equally well, as circumstances may demand, afford valuable lessons.

In view of the fact that the work has defined the most northern land in the world, and has fixed the northern limit of the world's largest island, was that work a useless expenditure of time, effort, and money? Neither the club nor I think so. The money was theirs, the time and effort mine.

But the scientific results are the immediate practical ones, and British and foreign commentators do not obscure or overlook them; and these results, together with the expedition's non-loss of a man, entire freedom from scurvy or sickness in any form, and return of the ship, have had their very friendly comments. No better illustration of the practical way in which the business men of the Peary Arctic Club have approached the work, and of our own practicality as a nation, could be afforded than the quiet way in which the club's expeditions have set forth, and particularly the recent return of the *Roosevelt,* as compared with the return of Nansen's *Fram.* The latter came into her home port with salvoes of artillery, a harbor covered with boats, and the shores lined with a cheering multitude, congratulations from king and parliament, and Nansen is to-day Norwegian ambassador to Great Britain. The *Roosevelt* steamed into New York harbor, lay at anchor for forty-eight hours, and went to her shipyard for repairs without a ripple.

The discovery not only of the north, but of the south pole as well, is not only our privilege, but our duty and destiny, as much as the building of the Panama Canal, and the control of the Pacific. The canal and the control of the Pacific mean wealth, commercial supremacy, and unassailable power; but the discovery of the poles spells just as strongly as the others, national *prestige,* with the moral strength that comes from the feeling that not even century-defying problems can withstand us.

Andrew Carnegie
[1835–1919]

Andrew Carnegie, American steel magnate and philanthropist, delivered the following speech at a dinner given by the Economic Club of New York in honor of General George W. Goethals, who had just completed the construction of the Panama Canal. The dinner was held in New York City, on March 5, 1914.

GENERAL GOETHALS AND THE PANAMA CANAL

Mr. president, ladies, and gentlemen:—I never suspected that I was to have so great an honor, so carefully given, as to become a follower of the distinguished speaker who has just taken his seat. [Applause.]

At long intervals a man appears who has done something of unique importance in the world. Long has he been in training for the task, and the world knew it not; but now the world can never cease to know that your guest of to-night has proved himself a genius who has changed world conditions. France had undertaken the difficult task of uniting the Atlantic and Pacific Oceans by a pass-way for ships upon the water. After years of labor the task was abandoned, and the long-cherished scheme seemed destined to fail. At this juncture our Government stepped forward, purchased the reversion, and renewed the seemingly hopeless attempt. Here was the critical moment. Where was there on earth, not *a* man but *the* man to whom this perilous task could safely be trusted? Nothing short of a genius for organization was needed. No man of that order seemed within reach. Geniuses are rare, but the choice fell upon your guest of to-night, and we began to examine his history. He was fortunate here. He was born in Brooklyn, and very fortunate for New York, for we claim partnership in everything good that Brooklyn has. [Applause and laughter.]

Studying the problems before him, our guest soon discovered that none of the conditions of success, as he has stated, had much to do at first with plans of construction. His enemy, sure to conquer him as it had conquered his predecessors, if not vanquished, was unsanitation, and here Providence had placed within his reach the one man of all the world—Brigadier-General Gorgas. [Applause.]

Now, ladies and gentlemen, note this. Genius always attracts genius. [Applause.] Though it cannot be said that those rare birds are so numerous as exactly to flock together. [Laughter.] In my experience I have not found them disposed to do that.

With such men coöperating, each marvelous in his domain, what problem could remain unsolved? Our country has long been remarkable for utilizing officers of the army and the navy in works of peace. I have seen the arduous tasks involved in the Fernandina breakwaters, for instance, in the rivers near Pittsburgh, upon the levees of the Mississippi, and the canals upon our Great Lakes, all under control of such army and navy officials. I believe that we are unique in this. I know of no other government that has the sense to use its commanders in the army and navy in work so profitable. [Applause.] This recalls one of Mr. Blaine's stories. I asked him what was one of the most attractive speeches he had ever heard in Congress—and he was there for many years. He could tell a good story himself. "Well," he said, "it was made by the Dutch ex-Governor of Pennsylvania who was subsequently elected to Congress. The debate in Congress was upon a bill which for the first time appropriated money to be used in improving fresh-water ponds. Many members held that Congress had no power under the Constitution to undertake improvement of fresh water. States must attend to this. National appropriations were confined to salt water. The Governor had never spoken a word in the House, and he had been there for two or three years, and the surprise was great when he was seen slowly to rise. The House was hushed into silence in a moment. What on earth was to come next? And then came the speech, short and to the point—'Mr. Speaker, I don't know "nutting" very much about the Constitution, but I know this: I wouldn't give a cent for a Constitution that didn't wash as well in fresh water as in salt.' " [Laughter.]

I said "cent" there. I understand the Governor used the more simplified spelling. [Laughter.] The House was convulsed, of course, and the appropriation was unanimously passed. Thus was our Constitution changed, not by law, but by laughter. It is astonishing what a good laugh sometimes can accomplish.

Your guest of the evening, gentlemen, had scores of difficulties to overcome, and many problems to solve, but he always solved them. Like the Governor, he rose to the occasion and swept the board, as the Dutch Governor did. The Governor changed the Constitution. You, guest of the evening, have changed world conditions; not only your country, but the whole world owes you an unpayable debt. [Applause.] Long may you live, Governor-that-is-to-be, and enjoy the world's prosperity. [Applause.]

Lord Cecil
[1864–1958]

Viscount Cecil of Chelwood, British statesman, was the guest of honor at a dinner given by the Pilgrims, in New York City, on January 2, 1925, shortly after he had completed a lecture tour in the United States. Following is the opening part of Lord Cecil's speech on this occasion.

ENGLISHMEN AND AMERICANS

MR. DEPEW, ladies and gentlemen:—My first duty is obviously to thank your Chairman for the very kind and flattering things that he has said of me. I was very grateful to him for everything that he said. I admit that there was one moment in which I felt a certain qualm of nervousness, when he began talking about lecturers from the other side of the Atlantic [laughter]; I didn't quite know how that was going to end. [Laughter.] But, fortunately, his courtesy got the better of his sincerity. [Laughter.]

Well, I thank you most heartily, and I am deeply grateful to you for being kind enough to entertain me to-night at dinner. The occasion, joyful, as it is, has an element of sadness for me, for it reminds me that this is my last evening in the United States. I deeply regret it. I deeply regret that my stay has been so short. I deeply regret it for many, many reasons, but among them because it has made it impossible for me to accept the invitations which I have received from other parts of your great country, and particularly because it has been impossible for me to visit the British Dominion of Canada, which I should have very dearly liked to have gone to, if I could have possibly managed it. I have the warmest possible feeling for my Canadian fellow subjects and for their great kindness to me on the last occasion when I visited them.

But it would be wrong for me in saying that, not to thank you once again, from the very bottom of my heart, for your marvelous courtesy and consideration to me—the courtesy and consideration which you always show to every guest who comes to your country.

You know as well as I do that American hospitality is proverbial throughout the world. Indeed, I was thinking to-day that if you followed the custom that prevails in some countries and an adjective were given to you; like you speak of "La Belle France" or "Merrie England," I think you would have to speak of "Hospitable America." It is only for one reason that I don't describe it as "princely," and that is for fear of unduly flattering princes. [Laughter.]

And really, if I may be allowed to say so without impertinence, it isn't only hospitality; it comes, if I may venture to say so, from the genuine kindness of your hearts. I like to think that that great quality is more easily displayed in the case of an Englishman than of any other guest. I remember last year, when I had the pleasure of being here, I had the honor of being received by your late President, Mr. Harding, and he received me with that cordial geniality which was well known in his case, and was good enough to ask me how I was getting on and how I had been received, and I told him that I couldn't exaggerate the kindness which I had met with on all hands; and he gave other reasons, but he said, "After all, one great reason for that is that you are an Englishman." And I must say that if he had searched the whole language for a compliment or a saying which would have pleased me, he could not have found one better than those few words.

I had the great honor this morning of being received by your present President, Mr. Coolidge, and in the course of conversation he too expressed his great gratification at the friendly relations which prevail between the two countries. In some mouths that would be a mere banality, a platitude. But if I may say so, England and America have one additional bond at the present moment. In the case of our Prime Minister and your President, we have a man of preëminent straightforwardness, a man whose every word we all know we can trust. [Applause.]

When Mr. Coolidge was good enough to say that to me this morning, I knew that he meant it from the bottom of his heart. And so the relations between our countries are very friendly.

I was very, very glad that you, sir, in the brilliant speech you have just delivered [referring to Mr. Depew] dated that friendliness from the time of the treaty of Ghent. I have always myself thought that the greatest title to fame that our minister, Lord Castlereagh, had, was in the signature of that treaty. It was a very remarkable performance and one which shows that it is possible to make a treaty of peace that will really lastingly give peace to the countries between whom it is made.

But I think it has many other reasons. Your Society is one; the greatly increased knowledge that prevails, both in England and America, of the national characteristics of the other people, is another.

I can remember a time—it was just dying out when I was young—when the typical Englishman, as seen through American spectacles, was a haughty and supercilious person of not any very great value to anyone except himself [laughter], and the typical American was a curious kind of caricature, a person of rude and rough manners, purse-proud and offensive and arrogant. I don't know whether any such prototype of the man ever existed; I doubt it very much. But certainly he is as extinct as the dodo at the present time. [Laughter.] But beyond all that, of course there is the racial bond; there is the fact that a very large proportion of us come from the same stock. I am profoundly grateful that it should be so. And more than that, there is, of course, what has often been alluded to, the great likeness in our ideals and aspirations, the great sources of which are in our literature and our history.

Shakespeare and the Bible count for a great deal in the good relations between England and America. The language, of course, is another bond. But much more than all that is the point of view. It is indeed that product of all the things that I have tried to describe.

It has been my good fortune—or evil fortune—to attend a great many international assemblies during the last few years, and whenever I have found an American colleague in those assemblies, whatever purpose we may have entered with, however divergent our apparent opinions originally were, in a quarter of an hour we always found ourselves pretty much agreed—not because we had talked one another over, but merely because in point of fact the same arguments appealed to both of us, the same point of view was that which was recommended to each of our minds. I believe that that essential sameness, identity of point of view, is the thing that is really responsible for the good relations between our countries more than any other single cause.

I believe, too—I am bound to believe—that among the causes of that very fortunate state of things has been something which isn't quite so often mentioned as it ought to be, and that is the law. Nothing was more striking than the great success which attended the visit of the American Bar Association to England during the last summer, with Mr. Secretary Hughes as one of the chief members of it. I believe that it brought the two countries together as much as anything that has happened for a long time past. The fact that we find constantly that we do appeal to the same principles in the law, that even the same names are great on both sides of the Atlantic, that Chief Justices Marshall and Story are just as great in England as I hope Mansfield and Blackburn are in this country, the fact that we appeal to the same authorities, that our principles go back to the same thing, that this great structure, one of the noblest structures that has ever been erected by the human intellect, the structure of the law that prevails in our two countries, comes from a common origin and appeals to common authorities—I believe these things have had an immense effect in bringing the two peoples in closer and closer relations.

Sir James Matthew Barrie
[1860–1937]

Sir James M. Barrie, British playwright and novelist, delivered the following speech in response to a toast, "Literature and the Press," proposed by Winston Churchill, then Chancellor of the Exchequer. The occasion was the annual dinner of the Printers' Pension Corporation, in London, in 1924.

LITERATURE AND THE PRESS

MAJOR ASTOR, Your Royal Highness, gentlemen—especially Mr. Churchill [laughter]:—What worries me is those two suspicious objects that have been put upon the table in front of me. [Laughter.] [Two microphones had been placed on the table to broadcast the speeches.] I do not know what they are, but I presume that one of them represents literature, and the other the press. [Laughter.] I think we should all feel very beholden to an eminent politician for coming here and talking to us so delightfully about literature and the press, especially at a moment when the country is on the eve of a general election [laughter]—I mean to vote this time. [Laughter.] But, though Mr. Churchill has been very nice about it, I know the real reason why I have been asked to reply for this toast. It is because I am the oldest person present. [Laughter.] Many years ago I saw, in an American "Whitaker," my name in a list headed "Interesting Octogenarians" [loud laughter], and I think therefore that the best thing I can do is to give you some literary recollections of far past days. [Laughter and cheers.] I dare say I may sometimes get a little muddled between past and present, between father and son, but then I notice that you have done that also to-night. [Laughter.] You have been congratulating Mr. Churchill on being Chancellor of the Exchequer. Of course, it was his father who was that. [Laughter.] I will tell you a secret—I know quite well what has been happening to Mr. Churchill, and I think that he is only wearing the laurels that he has so spendidly earned. [Cheers.] But let us couple with him to-night the father [cheers], who must be proud of his boy. ["Hear! Hear!"]

Those of you who are at present writing your reminiscences, and that must mean the greater number of you [laughter], I warn you that there is not much use having reminiscences nowadays unless you can remember Robert Louis Stevenson. [Laughter.] The only time I met Stevenson was in Edinburgh, and I had no idea who he was. It was in the winter of 1879; I well remember the wind was "blawin snell" when I set off that afternoon with my notebooks to the Humanities class of the University of Edinburgh. As I was crossing Princess Street—a blasty corner—I ran against another wayfarer. Looking up, I saw that he was a young man of an exceeding tenuity of body, his eyes, his hair, already beginning to go black, and that he was wearing a velvet jacket. He passed on, but he had bumped against me, and I stood in the middle of the street, regardless of the traffic, and glared contemptuously after him.

He must have grown conscious of this, because he turned around and looked at me. I continued to glare. He went on a little bit, and turned round again. I was still glaring, and he came back and said to me, quite nicely: "After all, God made me." [Loud laughter.] I said: "He is getting careless." [Renewed laughter and cheers.] He lifted his cane, and then, instead, he said: "Do I know you?" He said it with such extraordinary charm that I replied, wistfully: "No, but I wish you did." [Laughter.] He said, "Let's pretend I do," and we went off to a tavern at the foot of Leith Street, where we drank what he said was the favorite wine of the Three Musketeers. [Laughter.] Each of us wanted to pay [laughter], but it did not much matter, as neither of us had any money. [Laughter.]

We had to leave that tavern without the velvet coat and without my class books. When we got out it was snowing hard, and we quarreled—something about Mary Queen of Scots. [Laughter.] I remember how he chased me for hours that snowy night through the streets of Edinburgh, calling for my blood. [Laughter.] That is my only reminiscence of R. L. S., and I dare say that even that will get me into trouble. [Laughter.]

It may interest Major Astor to know that I was the man who bought the first copy of the *Times* containing the news of the victory of Waterloo. [Laughter.] I happened to be passing Printing House Square at the time, and I vividly remember the editor leaning far out of his window to watch the sales [laughter], and I heard him exclaim exultantly, "There goes one copy, at any rate." [Laughter.] Waterloo! I never knew Napoleon in his great days [laughter], but I chanced to be lodging in the same house that he came to, as you remember, as a stripling, just for a week, when he was trying to get a clerkship in the East India Company. [Laughter.] The old connection between France and Scotland brought us together. I remember well taking him one evening to Cremorne Gardens, then at the height of its popularity, and introducing him to a stout friend of mine, whom some of you may remember, Jos Sedley. What fun we had in the fog driving Jos home in his coach to Russell Square! Napoleon was singing gayly, and Jos was bulging out at both windows of the coach at once. [Loud laughter.] This is perhaps only interesting as being the first encounter between these two figures, who were afterwards to meet on the tented field. [Laughter.] Napoleon, as is now generally known, did not take up that clerkship in the East India Company. [Laughter.] I dissuaded him from it. [Loud laughter.] Looking back, I consider that this was one of my mistakes. [Laughter.]

Gentlemen, the unenviable shades of the great, who have to live on here after they have shed this mortal tenement! Not for them the dignity of dying and being forgotten, which is surely the right of proud man! Who knows that where they are fame is looked upon as a rather sordid achievement? The freer spirits may look upon those immortals with pity, because they have to go on dragging a chain here on earth. It may be that the Elysian Fields are not a place of honor, but of banishment!

"Literature and the press!" It is a noble toast, and never can it be drunk more fittingly than in honor of the best friend that literature and the press ever had—the printer. [Cheers.] All seems well with the press. We are gathered to-night around a Chairman not unconnected with a journal of which we can perhaps say, without vainglory, that it is a possession which all the nations envy us. [Loud cheers.] The press nowadays, as Mr. Churchill has said, takes all the world in its span. I cannot look at Mr. Churchill, because I have been told to look at these two things [the microphones] [laughter], but one who was very lately a Lord Chancellor, and now another, a Chancellor of the Exchequer, have both —I do not know whether Mr. Churchill is beginning to look a little nervous about what I am going to say next [laughter]—all I am going to say is in glorification of the press—when it is garbed in its Sunday best [laughter]—they are the two brightest jewels on its proud bosom.

Literature, when it can be heard at all above the sirens—Mr. Churchill has had a good deal to say about literature and the press, and has found that they are very much the same thing. He used an expression about there being no arbitrary dividing line between literature and the press.

I should like to give a definition of what I think is the arbitrary dividing line [laughter] just in half a dozen words. It is this—Literature used to be a quiet bird. All, I think, is very well with literature, especially with the young authors. From its looms comes much brave literature, devised by cunning hands, women's equally with men's. There is no question whether a woman is worthy of a place in our Cabinet. Those young authors! All hail to them! Happy they! Multitudinous seas incarnadine boil in their veins. They bear the thousand nightingales which we once thought we heard. They have a short way with the old hands, but in our pride in them we forgive them for that.

Irvin S. Cobb
[1876-1944]

The following speech was delivered by Irvin S. Cobb, American humorist and author, before the American Irish Historical Society, in New York City, on January 6, 1917.

THE LOST TRIBES OF THE IRISH IN THE SOUTH

MR. PRESIDENT, and ladies and gentlemen:—I am speaking but the plain truth when I tell you that I would rather be here to-night facing an assemblage of men and women of Irish blood and Irish breeding than to be in any other banquet hall on earth. For I am one who is Irish and didn't know it; but now that I do know it, I am prouder of that fact than of any one other thing on earth except that I am an American citizen.

I wonder if it ever occurred to you, what differences are to be found in many a country and in almost any country, between the temperaments and the spirits and the customs of those who live in the north of it, and those who live in the south of it? To the north, to Prussia, the German Empire has always looked for its great scientists and its great mathematicians and its propounders and expounders of a certain cool and analytical philosophy; but it was to the south, to Bavaria and to Saxony, that Germany had to turn for its poets and its story-tellers.

It was the north of France that produced and yet produces those men who have harnessed the forces of nature, who have made the earth tremble to the pulse-beat of their factories, who took the ore from the earth and the coal from the hillsides, and with them wrought out the great steel industries of that country; but it was out of the south of France that there came its marvelous fiction writers and minstrel bards, its greatest poets and its greatest dreamers; and out of that same south once upon a time there came, too, a fiery outpouring of shock-headed men and women who wore wooden shoes on their feet and red caps on their heads and who marched to the words of a song which has become the fighting song of every nation, craving liberty and daring to march and to die for it—the "Marseillaise Hymn." [Applause.]

The names of the Milanaise and the Lombards and the Venetians of modern Italy are synonymous with frugality in domestic affairs and energy in commercial pursuits, but it is down in the tip of the toe of the Latin boot that we find the Italian who loves the hardest and sings the loudest and fights for the very love of the fighting.

The north of Ireland, as we all know, has fathered the great business men of that little island, and the great manufacturers and the great theologians, many of them; and, regretful to say, it has also produced a spawn of human beings who, in the face of the fact that in every other land where men have equal opportunities, the Irishman has won his way to the front and has held his own with prince and potentate, yet cling to the theory that in Ireland, of all the spots of the world, the Irishman is not capable of governing himself. But always it was to the south of Ireland, and it is to the south of Ireland to-day, that one must turn to find the dreamer and the writer, the idealist and the poet. It is to the south of Ireland also that one must turn to seek for a people whose literature and whose traditions are saddened by the memory of the wrongs they have withstood and the persecutions they have endured and still endure, and yet whose spirits and whose characters are uplifted and sanctified by that happy optimism which seems everywhere on this footstool to be the heritage of the true Southerner. [Applause.]

In a measure these same things are true of our own country. The North excels in business, but the South leads in romance. The North opens wide the door of opportunity to every man who comes to its borders with willing hands and eager brain. The South opens a door, too, but it is the door of hospitality, and it bids the stranger enter in, not so much for what he can give, but for what he can take in the way of welcome. I think there is a reason, aside from topography and geography and climate and environment, for these differences between the common divisions of our great country. And I am going to come to that reason in a minute.

As a boy, down South, there were two songs that stirred me as no other songs could—one was a song that I loved and one a song that I hated, and one of these songs was the battle hymn of the South, "Dixieland," and the other was "Marching Through Georgia." But once upon a time when I was half-grown, a wandering piper came to the town where I lived, a man who spoke with a brogue and played with one. And he carried under his arm a weird contraption which to me seemed to be a compound of two fishing poles stuck in a hot-water bottle, and he snuggled it to his breast and·it squawked out its ecstasy, and then he played on it a tune called "Garryowen." And as he played it, I found that my toes tingled inside my shoes, and my heart throbbed as I thought it could only throb to the air of "Dixie." And I took counsel with myself and I said, "Why is it that I who call myself a pure Anglo-Saxon should be thrilled by an Irish air?" So I set out to determine the reason for it. And this is the kind of Anglo-Saxon I found out I was:

My mother was of the breed of Black Douglas of Scotland, as Scotch as haggis, and rebels, all of them, descendants of men who followed the fortunes of Bonnie Prince Charles, and her mother lived in a county in North Carolina, one of five counties where up to 1820, Gaelic was not only the language of the people in the street, but was the official language of the courts. It was in that selfsame part of North Carolina that there lived some of the men who, nearly a year before our Declaration of Independence was drawn up, wrote and signed the Mecklenburg Declaration, which was the first battle cry raised for American independence. On the other side, I found, by investigation, that my father's line ran back straight and unbroken to a thatched cottage on the green side of a hill in the Wicklow Mountains, and his people likewise had some kinsmen in Galway, and some in Dublin with whom, following the quaint custom of their land, they were accustomed to take tea and fight afterwards. [Applause and laughter.] I found I had a collateral ancestor who was out with the pikes in '98 and he was taken prisoner and tried for high crimes and misdemeanors against the British government, and was sentenced to be hanged by the neck until he was dead and might God have mercy on his soul! And he was hanged by the neck until he was dead, and I am sure God did have mercy on his soul, for that soul of his went marching on, transmitting to his people, of whom I am proud to be one, the desire to rebel against oppression and tyranny. [Applause.] I had three great-great-grandfathers, two of them Irish and one of them Scotch, who were Revolutionary soldiers, and I had a father who was a Confederate soldier. And of these facts, too, I am quite proud, for I find that my strain, being Irish, is always intent either on trying to run the government or trying to pull it down.

You Irish-descended people of the Northern States are proud of Shields, the son of an Irish emigrant, who, if my memory serves me aright, helped to direct the destinies of three American commonwealths and was United States Senator from all three. But I like to think of another Irishman, Matthew Lyon by name, the son of an humble Wicklow peasant, who was sold as a slave to the New England plantations because he, an Episcopalian, dared to raise his voice and his arm in defense of the rights of his Catholic neighbors and kinsmen in the County of Wicklow; and he bought his freedom with a black bull, which, according to family tradition, he first stole, and he became a United States Senator from Vermont, and cast the vote against the wishes of his constituents, which made Thomas Jefferson President of this country over Aaron Burr and by so doing altered the entire course of our country's history; and while he was in jail in a town in Vermont for his attacks on the odious Alien and Sedition Laws, he issued a challenge for a duel to the President of the United States, and being released, he moved down to Kentucky and became a Congressman; and later, having quarreled with all his neighbors there, he moved on to Arkansas and was named as Arkansas' first territorial delegate to Washington, and he might have moved still further west and might have filled still more offices had he not in the fullness of his maturity, when he was seventy years young, been thrown from a mule and had his spine injured so that he died. I like to think of Matthew Lyon and his career because he also was an ancestor of mine. [Applause and laughter.]

Well, as I said a bit ago, I set out to trace my Irish ancestry. In that undertaking I found a ready helper in a distant kinsman who was not carried away by the fetish that the South was all Anglo-Saxon, whatever that is; and he worked me early and late on family records. Indeed, he worked me so hard that sometimes I think I might have likened my position to that of a colored brother in a little town in my state who was the only member of his race at the local election who voted the Democratic ticket. It was felt that such loyalty should be rewarded, so the incoming administration created a Department of Street Cleaning —an institution hitherto unknown in that community—to consist of a boss or foreman, and a staff. Quite naturally the job of foreman went to a white man, but upon the worthy colored person was conferred the honor of being the staff. Now, he held to the theory, common even among those of the more enlightened races, that a political office meant much honor and much pay but mighty little work. Nevertheless, as a matter of form he carried a shovel with him on the morning when he reported for service. But the white man who was to serve over him had very different ideas regarding the obligation owing to the municipality. No sooner had the darkey cleaned up one pile of débris than the foreman would find another and yet another for him to wrestle with. It was four o'clock in the afternoon before the darkey so much as straightened his back or wiped the sweat off his brow or blew on the new-formed blisters in the palms of his hands. Finally he said: "Boss, ain't you got nuthin' to do but jes' to think up things fur me to do?"

"Yes," the white man said, "that's all my job—just to keep you busy."

The darkey said: "Well, suh, in that case you will be pleased to know you ain't goin' to be workin' to-morrow." [Laughter.]

But I kept on working and I discovered a lot of things about the lost tribes of the Irish in the South. The State of Kentucky from which I hail has been called the cradle of the Anglo-Saxon race in America, and it has been said that the mountaineers of that state, with their feuds and their Elizabethan, Chaucerian methods of speech represent the purest strains of English blood to be found to-day on this continent. Now, then, let us see if that is true. I have looked into that matter and I tell you that fifty per cent, at least, of the dwellers of the mountains of the South and notably of Kentucky and Virginia are the lineal descendants of runaway indenture men, Irish rebels mainly, from the Virginia plantations. I know a mountain county in Kentucky of which half of the population bear one of three names. They are either Mayos, or Patricks, or Powerses. And I once heard an orator stand up before an audience of those Mayos and Powerses and Patricks and congratulate them on their pure English descent, and they believed it! [Laughter.]

I wish you would pardon me once more for referring to my line of ancestry, for it is testimony to prove my claim. On my father's side I am descended from a group of men who went from New England to Kentucky and the names of these men were Lyon and Cobb, which is a Danish corruption of O'Connor, and Machen, and Clendenin, and O'Hara, and Glenn, which is a corruption of Glynn. What a hot bunch of Anglo-Saxons! [Laughter.]

The Congressional District in which I was born and where I used to live has thirteen counties in it. Listen to the names of these thirteen counties: Marshall, Calloway, Graves, McCracken, Lyon, Livingston, Caldwell, Trigg, Crittenden, Ballard, Hickman, Fulton, Carlisle—thirteen counties and all but two of them have Irish names.

What is true of my own section of Kentucky is true of the rest of the State. Daniel Boone has been called the first explorer of Kentucky and it has been said he was of English descent. Both of those statements are wrong. Daniel Boone was not the first explorer of Kentucky. The first man to explore Kentucky was an Irishman by the name of John Finley. But before him was still another Irishman by the name of McBride— James McBride. He lingers in state history as a shadowy figure, but I like to think of him as a red-haired chap with a rifle in one hand and possibly a demijohn in the other, coming out through the trackless wilderness alone and landing from his canoe on what was afterwards to be known as the Dark and Bloody ground. Aside from his name, it is proven that he was an Irishman by the legendary circumstances that immediately after coming ashore he carved his name in deep and enduring letters in the bark of the largest beech tree of the forest, and claimed all of the land that lay within his vision as his own, and shot an Indian or two and went on his way rejoicing. As for Daniel Boone, the great pathfinder, he really was descended from the line of Buhun, which is Norman-Irish, and his mother was a Morgan, and his wife was a Bryan, and his father was an Irish Catholic.

The records show that nearly three-fourths of that dauntless little band who under the leadership of George Rogers Clark, an Irishman, waded through the floods to take Vincennes and thereby won all the great Northwest Territory away from the British and gave to the American colonies what to-day is the richest part of the United States, were Irishmen— not Scotch-Irish, nor English-Irish, but plain Irish-Irish men who were rebels and patriots by instinct and born adventurers by reason of the blood which ran in their veins.

The first settlement of English-speaking Catholics beyond the Allegheny Mountains was not located in the North but in the South, and in my own State of Kentucky at that. It endures to-day, after having given to this country one of its greatest and most scholarly churchmen, Bishop Spaulding. [Applause.] The children of the pioneers of Kentucky, almost without exception, learned their first lessons in log cabins under the teachings of that strange but gifted race of men, the wandering Irish schoolmasters, who founded the old field schools of the South and to whom the South is largely indebted for the seeds of its culture.

Irishmen from Kentucky, Virginia, Pennsylvania and Maryland bore the brunt of the western campaigns in 1812 against the British. Irishmen from Kentucky fell thick at the disastrous battles of the Thames, and the Raisin, and their Irish bones to-day rest in that ground sanctifying it and making of it an American shrine of patriotism. It was the hand of a Kentucky Irishman, Colonel Richard Johnson, afterwards Vice President of the United States, that slew the great Tecumseh. A good share of the Kentucky and Tennessee riflemen who at New Orleans stood behind Andy Jackson's cotton bale breastworks, mowing down Packenham's Peninsular Veterans and making their red coats redder still with the life blood of those invaders, were Irishmen, real Irishmen. They proved their Irish lineage by the fact that they fell out and quarreled with Old Hickory, because he denied them all the credit for winning the fight, and he quarreled back, for he was by way of being an Irishman himself. [Laughter and applause.]

It was a Kentucky Irishman, Dr. Ephraim McDowell, who performed the first operation for ovariotomy—performed it on a kitchen table with a mad husband standing over him with a drawn revolver, threatening to shoot him if his wife died under the knife. But he went ahead and it was a successful operation, and it has brought relief and life and sanity to millions of women all over the world. It was a Kentucky Irishman and a soldier, Theodore O'Hara, who penned perhaps the most beautiful lyric poem, and certainly the sweetest tribute to the brave in our language, the immortal "Bivouac of the Dead." It was another Kentucky Irishman, the saintly poet-priest, Father Ryan, whose hand wrote those two fondest poems in memory of the Lost Cause, "The Conquered Banner" and "The Sword of Robert E. Lee."

In the Civil War it was a Kentuckian of Scotch and Irish descent who led the North—Abraham Lincoln—and it was another Kentuckian of mingled Irish and Scotch blood—Jefferson Davis—who was President of the Confederacy.

The historian Collins said the five greatest lawyers Kentucky ever produced were Barry, Rowan, Haggin, Breckenridge, and Bledsoe—four Irish names and one Indian name—and yet these five have been called Anglo-Saxons, too.

What is true of Kentucky is to a greater or less degree true of the rest of the South. It was an Irish Virginian, Patrick Henry, who sounded the first keynote of the American Revolution, and at the risk of his life, by his words paved the way for the Declaration of Independence. The South Carolina Irishman, John C. Calhoun, first raised the slogan of Nullification, and it was another Irishman, Andrew Jackson of Tennessee, who swore by the Eternal to hang him higher than Haman if he carried out his plan.

To-night you have heard a tribute, and a deserved one, to little Phil Sheridan of the North, but I want to couple his name with that of a Southern Irishman, the son of an Irish refugee, Pat Cleburne of Arkansas, one of the most gallant leaders that the Civil War produced. [Applause.] Pat Cleburne died on one of the bloodiest battlefields of Christendom in his stocking feet because as he rode into battle that morning he saw one of his Irish boys from Little Rock tramping barefooted over the frozen furrows of a wintry cornfield and leaving tracks of blood behind him. So he drew off his boots and bade the soldier put them on, and fifteen minutes later he went to his God in his stocking feet. Raleigh laid down his coat before Good Queen Bess, and has been immortalized for his chivalry, but I think a more courtly deed was that of the gallant Irishman, Pat Cleburne. For one was kowtowing before royalty and the other had in his heart only thoughtfulness and humanity for the common man afoot.

Sam Houston, the first president of the Lone Star State, was a Tennessee Irishman, Irish through and through, and the present President of the United States, a Southerner also, is half Irish. One of the most distinguished members of the Supreme Court in recent years was a Kentucky Irishman, John M. Harlan, and to-day two of the men who sit on that tribunal are Irishmen—White of Louisiana, the distinguished and honored Chief Justice, and McReynolds of Tennessee.

[Voice]: How about McKenna?

Mr. Cobb: He is not a Southerner, I regret to say. I suppose I could go on for hours, if your patience held out—and my throat—telling of the achievements of Irishmen, and of the imperishable records that Irishmen have left on the history of that part of the Union from which I came, but to call the roll of the great men who have done great things and won achievement and fame south of Mason and Dixon's line since there was such a line, would be almost like running through the parish registers of the counties of Ireland, both north and south. Indeed, in my opinion, it is not altogether topography or geography or climate that has made the South what it is, and given it those distinguishing characteristics which adorn it. The soft speech of the Southerner; his warm heart, and his hot head, his readiness to begin a fight, and to forgive his opponent afterwards; his veneration for women's chastity and his love for the ideals of his native land—all these are heritages of his Irish ancestry, transmitted to him through the generations. The North has put her heroes on a pension, but the South has put hers on a pedestal. There is not a Southern hamlet of any size to-day that has not reared a bronze or marble or granite monument to its own defenders in the Civil War, and there is scarce a Southern home where, at the knees of the mother, the children are not taught to revere the memories and remember the deeds of Lee and Jackson and Forrest, the Tennessee Irishman, and Morgan, the Kentucky Irishman, and Washington, and Light Horse Harry Lee, and Francis Marion, the Irish Swamp Fox of the Carolinas. I believe as firmly as I believe anything on earth that for that veneration, for that love of heroism and for that joying in the ideals of its soil, the South is indebted mainly to the Irish blood that courses through the veins of its sons and of its daughters.

No, ladies and gentlemen, the lost Irish tribes of the South are not lost; they are not lost any more than the "wild geese" that flew across the Channel from Ireland were lost. They are not lost any more than the McMahons who went to France, or the O'Donnells who went to Spain, or the Simon Bolivars and the O'Higginses who went to South America, or the O'Ferrells and the O'Briens who went to Cuba. For their Irish blood is of the strain that cannot be extinguished and it lives to-day, thank God, in the attributes and the habits and the customs and the traditions of the Southern people. Most of all it lives in one of their common characteristics, which, I think, in conclusion, may possibly be suggested by the telling of a story that I heard some time ago, of an Irishman in Mobile. As the story goes, this Irishman on Sunday heard a clergyman preach on the Judgment Day. The priest told of the hour when the trumpet shall blow and all peoples of all climes and all ages shall be gathered before the Seat of God to be judged according to their deeds done in the flesh. After the sermon he sought out the pastor and he said, "Father, I want to ask you a few questions touching on what you preached about to-day. Do you really think that on the Judgment Day everybody will be there?"

The priest said: "That is my understanding."

"Will Cain and Abel be there?"

"Undoubtedly."

"And David and Goliath—will they both be there?"

"That is my information and belief."

"And Brian Boru and Oliver Cromwell?"

"Assuredly they will be present."

"And the A. O. II.'s and the A. P. A.'s?"

"I am quite positive they will all be there together."

"Father," said the parishioner, "there'll be damn little judgin' done the first day."

[Applause and laughter.]

Will Rogers

[1879–1935]

The speeches of Will Rogers were extemporaneous as his humor was spontaneous. Here is one of the few recorded speeches of Rogers. It was delivered by him at a dinner given by the alumni of Columbia University, in New York City, in memory of Alexander Hamilton, on December 4, 1924.

WEALTH AND EDUCATION

PRESIDENT BUTLER paid me a compliment a while ago in mentioning my name in his introductory remarks, and he put me ahead of the Columbia graduates. I am glad he did that, because I got the worst of it last week. The Prince of Wales last week, in speaking of the sights of America, mentioned the Woolworth Building, the subway, the slaughterhouse, Will Rogers, and the Ford factory. He could at least put me ahead of the hogs.

Everything must be in contrast at an affair like this. You know to show anything off properly you must have the contrast. Now, I am here tonight representing poverty. We have enough wealth right here at this table, right here at the speaker's table alone—their conscience should hurt them, which I doubt if it does—so that we could liquidate our national debt. Every rich man reaches a time in his career when he comes to a turning point and starts to give it away. I have heard that of several of our guests here tonight, and that is one of the reasons that I am here. I would like to be here at the psychological moment.

We are here, not only to keep cool with Coolidge, but to do honor to Alexander Hamilton. Now, he was the first Secretary of the Treasury. The reason he was appointed that was because he and Washington were the only men in America at that time who knew how to put their names on a check. Signing a check has remained the principal qualification of a U. S. Secretary of the Treasury.

I am glad President Butler referred to it in this way. The principal reason, of course, was that the man he fought against wanted to be President. He was a Princeton man—or I believe it was Harvard,—anyway it was one of those primary schools. In fighting a duel, he forgot that in America our men over here could shoot. So unfortunately one of them was killed, which had never happened in the old country. So they did away with dueling. It was all right to protect your honor, but not to go as far as you like.

If you are speaking of finances here to-night, I do not believe that you could look further than President Butler. Butler is the word—to dig up the dough. Columbia was nothing twenty years ago. Now, he has gone around and got over a hundred buildings, and has annexed Grant's Tomb. He was the first man to go around to the graduates and explain to them that by giving money to Columbia it would help on the income tax and also perpetuate their names. We have an Alexander Hamilton Building. He landed these buildings and ran the place up to ninety millions or something like that. There are more students in the university than there are in any other in the world. It is the foremost university. There are thirty-two hundred courses. You spend your first two years in deciding what course to take, the next two years in finding the building that these courses are given in, and the rest of your life in wishing you had taken another course. And they have this wonderful society called the Alumni Association, a bunch of men who have gone to school and after they have come out formed a society to tell the school how to run it.

William Lyon Phelps
[1865–1943]

William Lyon Phelps, American educator and author, broadcast the following radio address on April 6, 1933.

OWNING BOOKS

The habit of reading is one of the greatest resources of mankind; and we enjoy reading books that belong to us much more than if they are borrowed. A borrowed book is like a guest in the house; it must be treated with punctiliousness, with a certain considerate formality. You must see that it sustains no damage; it must not suffer while under your roof. You cannot leave it carelessly, you cannot mark it, you cannot turn down the pages, you cannot use it familiarly. And then, some day, although this is seldom done, you really ought to return it.

But your own books belong to you; you treat them with that affectionate intimacy that annihilates formality. Books are for use, not for show; you should own no book that you are afraid to mark up, or afraid to place on the table, wide open and face down. A good reason for marking favorite passages in books is that this practice enables you to remember more easily the significant sayings, to refer to them quickly, and then in later years, it is like visiting a forest where you once blazed a trail. You have the pleasure of going over the old ground, and recalling both the intellectual scenery and your own earlier self.

Everyone should begin collecting a private library in youth; the instinct of private property, which is fundamental in human beings, can here be cultivated with every advantage and no evils. One should have one's own bookshelves, which should not have doors, glass windows, or keys; they should be free and accessible to the hand as well as to the eye. The best of mural decorations is books; they are more varied in colour and appearance than any wall-paper, they are more attractive in design, and they have the prime advantage of being separate personalities, so that if you sit alone in the room in the firelight, you are surrounded with intimate friends. The knowledge that they are there in plain view is both stimulating and refreshing. You do not have to read them all. Most of my indoor life is spent in a room containing six thousand books; and I have a stock answer to the invariable question that comes from strangers. "Have you read all of these books?" "Some of them twice." This reply is both true and unexpected.

There are of course no friends like living, breathing, corporeal men and women; my devotion to reading has never made me a recluse. How could it? Books are of the people, by the people, for the people. Literature is the immortal part of history; it is the best and most enduring part of personality. But book-friends have this advantage over living friends;

you can enjoy the most truly aristocratic society in the world whenever you want it. The great dead are beyond our physical reach, and the great living are usually almost as inaccessible; as for our personal friends and acquaintances, we cannot always see them. Perchance they are asleep, or away on a journey. But in a private library, you can at any moment converse with Socrates or Shakespeare or Carlyle or Dumas or Dickens or Shaw or Barrie or Galsworthy. And there is no doubt that in these books you see these men at their best. They wrote for *you*. They "laid themselves out," they did their ultimate best to entertain you, to make a favourable impression. You are necessary to them as an audience is to an actor; only instead of seeing them masked, you look into their inmost heart of heart.

Edward VIII
[1894–1972]

Here is the farewell address of former King Edward VIII of England, who abdicated his throne so that he could marry "the woman I love." This historic address was delivered by Edward, who became Duke of Windsor, over the radio to a world-wide alliance on December 11, 1936.

FAREWELL ADDRESS

At long last I am able to say a few words of my own. I have never wanted to withhold anything, but until now it has not been constitutionally possible for me to speak.

A few hours ago I discharged my last duty as King and Emperor, and now that I have been succeeded by my brother, the Duke of York, my first words must be to declare my allegiance to him. This I do with all my heart.

You all know the reasons which have impelled me to renounce the throne. But I want you to understand that in making up my mind I did not forget the country or the empire, which, as Prince of Wales and lately as King, I have for twenty-five years tried to serve.

But you must believe me when I tell you that I have found it impossible to carry the heavy burden of responsibility and to discharge my duties as King as I would wish to do without the help and support of the woman I love.

And I want you to know that the decision I have made has been mine and mine alone. This was a thing I had to judge entirely for myself. The other person most nearly concerned has tried up to the last to persuade me to take a different course.

I have made this, the most serious decision of my life, only upon the single thought of what would, in the end, be best for all.

This decision has been made less difficult to me by the sure knowledge that my brother, with his long training in the public affairs of this country and with his fine qualities, will be able to take my place forthwith without interruption or injury to the life and progress of the empire. And he has one matchless blessing, enjoyed by so many of you, and not bestowed on me—a happy home with his wife and children.

During these hard days I have been comforted by her majesty my mother and by my family. The ministers of the crown, and in particular, Mr. Baldwin, the Prime Minister, have always treated me with full consideration. There has never been any constitutional difference between me and them, and between me and Parliament. Bred in the constitutional tradition by my father, I should never have allowed any such issue to arise.

Ever since I was Prince of Wales, and later on when I occupied the throne, I have been treated with the greatest kindness by all classes of the people wherever I have lived or journeyed throughout the empire. For that I am very grateful.

I now quit altogether public affairs and I lay down my burden. It may be some time before I return to my native land, but I shall always follow the fortunes of the British race and empire with profound interest, and if at any time in the future I can be found of service to his majesty in a private station, I shall not fail.

And now, we all have a new King. I wish him and you, his people, happiness and prosperity with all my heart. God bless you all! God save the King!

Owen D. Young

[1874-1962]

Owen D. Young, chairman of General Electric Company, and expert on international finance, had a deep interest in the extension of education. Following are parts of an address which he delivered at Hendrix College, Arkansas, on November 20, 1934.

CULTURE

I DO NOT MEAN by culture the compression and concentration of the pedant, although frequently he has the raw material out of which culture can be made. In the sense that I am using it, culture represents a synthesis, a putting together of things, putting them together so completely that the combination has an individuality of its own. It may be only an amalgam; it is better if it be a chemical combination. Culture does not exist in the form of powder, a mere mass of incoherent particles.

The vital part of the incandescent electric lamp is the tungsten wire inside the bulb. The great invention in that lamp was the discovery of way to convert metallic tungsten into wire. It was well known that this metal would withstand the high heat required for incandescence over a long period without disintegration, but it was also known that tungsten was one of the most recalcitrant of the metals. Each particle was such a rugged individualist that it would have nothing to do with its neighbor. It seemed to have no social sense at all. The first tungsten lamps contained so-called "pressed" filaments. The metal was subjected to tremendous pressures in small grooves the size of a wire. It was found that if pressure enough could be applied, the particles would hold together in what appeared to be a wire, sufficiently to enable this fragile string to be placed into a lamp. The lamps were shipped to their destination in cushions and finally with the greatest care inserted in the sockets. They gave excellent light, but all of us older people can remember that if the children played tag once around the dining-room table all the lights went out. One day, courageous and daring men determined that that obstinate metal should be conquered, and it was. With high heats and extraordinarily ingenious methods, tungsten was so converted that it could be drawn into wire, and the wire became stronger than steel of equivalent size.

You must fuse at white heat the several particles of your learning into an element so ductible and so strong that nothing can destroy it without destroying you.

Let me be a little more specific. What is the use of studying Greek unless you can bring all the beauty of that language and literature into your thinking and your expression today? What is the use of studying Latin unless you can get through it a better understanding, a more complete feeling of the mighty activities in their heights and depths that made Rome both glorious and ignoble? What is the use of studying French unless through wider outlook and more varied contacts that language brings to you a better understanding of the world in which you live and an appreciation of that grace which is the basis of good manners? What is the use of studying history without co-relating it with the economics which for the most part has been its master? What is the use of studying economics or politics without relating them both to a knowledge of the physical sciences which shape their course? You have only to look beyond this campus today to see that the problems both of economics and of politics arise out of the machines which the research workers of the world have made.

My point is that it is not enough for you to study economics in an insulated compartment and history and government and the languages and the sciences. It is not enough to gather them up as separate particles into a powder which you carry out with your diploma. They must be fused and integrated.

John D. Rockefeller, Jr.
[1874-1960]

John D. Rockefeller, Jr., speaking on a radio program sponsored by the United Service Organizations, on July 8, 1941, listed "the things that make life most worth living."

OUR FAMILY CREED

THEY are the principles on which my wife and I have tried to bring up our family. They are the principles in which my father believed and by which he governed his life. They are the principles, many of them, which I learned at my mother's knee.

They point the way to usefulness and happiness in life, to courage and peace in death.

If they mean to you what they mean to me, they may perhaps be helpful also to our sons for their guidance and inspiration.

Let me state them:

I believe in the supreme worth of the individual and in his right to life, liberty and the pursuit of happiness.

I believe that every right implies a responsibility; every opportunity, an obligation; every possession, a duty.

I believe that the law was made for man and not man for the law; that government is the servant of the people and not their master.

I believe in the dignity of labor, whether with head or hand; that the world owes no man a living but that it owes every man an opportunity to make a living.

I believe that thrift is essential to well ordered living and that economy is a prime requisite of a sound financial structure, whether in government, business or personal affairs.

I believe that truth and justice are fundamental to an enduring social order.

I believe in the sacredness of a promise, that a man's word should be as good as his bond, that character—not wealth or power or position—is of supreme worth.

I believe that the rendering of useful service is the common duty of mankind and that only in the purifying fire of sacrifice is the dross of selfishness consumed and the greatness of the human soul set free.

I believe in an all-wise and all-loving God, named by whatever name, and that the individual's highest fulfillment, greatest happiness and widest usefulness are to be found in living in harmony with His will.

I believe that love is the greatest thing in the world; that it alone can overcome hate; that right can and will triumph over might.

These are the principles, however formulated, for which all good men and women throughout the world, irrespective of race or creed, education, social position or occupation, are standing, and for which many of them are suffering and dying.

These are the principles upon which alone a new world recognizing the brotherhood of man and the fatherhood of God can be established.

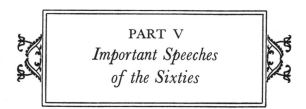

PART V

*Important Speeches
of the Sixties*

XIII. UNITED STATES

John Fitzgerald Kennedy
[1917–1963]

John Fitzgerald Kennedy, thirty-fifth President of the United States, developed the "New Frontier" approach to foreign and domestic problems which concerned our nation. Among the achievements of his term in office are the signing of the Nuclear Test Ban treaty, the creation of the Peace Corps, the ten-year plan for cooperation with Latin America (the Alliance for Progress), and the setting of specific goals for the space program with the allocation by Congress of the necessary funds. Much of the other legislation which he proposed, such as Medicare, was passed by Congress under later administrations. Kennedy served in the Navy in World War II. The Pulitzer Prize was awarded to him in 1957 for Profiles in Courage. *In Dallas, Texas, on November 22, 1963, President Kennedy was assassinated.*

Following is the text of President Kennedy's Inaugural Address in Washington on January 20, 1961. Kennedy was an eloquent spokesman and his Inaugural is a vital document. He expressed his thoughts and hopes in refreshing phrases, many of which are often referred to and quoted.

INAUGURAL ADDRESS

VICE PRESIDENT JOHNSON, Mr. Speaker, Mr. Chief Justice, President Eisenhower, Vice President Nixon, President Truman, Reverend Clergy, fellow citizens:

We observe today not a victory of party but a celebration of freedom—symbolizing an end as well as a beginning—signifying renewal as well as change. For I have sworn before you and Almighty God the same solemn oath our forebears prescribed nearly a century and three-quarters ago.

The world is very different now. For man holds in his mortal hands the power to abolish all forms of human poverty and all forms of human life. And yet the same revolutionary beliefs for which our forebears fought are still at issue around the globe—the belief that the rights of man come not from the generosity of the state but from the hand of God.

We dare not forget today that we are the heirs of that first revolution. Let the word go forth from this time and place, to friend and foe alike, that the torch has been passed to a new generation of Americans—born in this century, tempered by war, disciplined by a hard and bitter peace, proud of our ancient heritage—and unwilling to witness or permit the slow undoing of those human rights to which this nation has always been committed, and to which we are committed today at home and around the world.

Let every nation know, whether it wishes us well or ill, that we shall pay any price, bear any burden, meet any hardship, support any friend, oppose any foe to assure the survival and the success of liberty.

This much we pledge—and more.

To those old allies whose cultural and spiritual origins we share, we pledge the loyalty of faithful friends. United, there is little we cannot do in a host of new cooperative ventures. Divided, there is little we can do—for we dare not meet a powerful challenge at odds and split asunder.

To those new states whom we welcome to the ranks.of the free, we pledge our word that one form of colonial control shall not have passed away merely to be replaced by a far more iron tyranny. We shall not always expect to find them supporting our view. But we shall always hope to find them strongly supporting their own freedom—and to remember that, in the past, those who foolishly sought power by riding the back of the tiger ended up inside.

To those peoples in the huts and villages of half the globe struggling to break the bonds of mass misery, we pledge our best efforts to help them help themselves, for whatever period is required—not because the Communists may be doing it, not because we seek their votes, but because it is right. If a free society cannot help the many who are poor, it cannot save the few who are rich.

To our sister republics south of our border, we offer a special pledge—to convert our good words into good deeds—in a new alliance for progress—to assist free men and free governments in casting off the chains of poverty. But this peaceful revolution of hope cannot become the prey of hostile powers. Let all our neighbors know that we shall join with them to oppose aggression or subversion anywhere in the Americas. And let every other power know that this hemisphere intends to remain the master of its own house.

To that world assembly of sovereign states, the United Nations, our last best hope in an age where the instruments of war have far outpaced the instruments of peace, we renew our pledge of support—to prevent it from becoming merely a forum for invective—to strengthen its shield of the new and the weak—and to enlarge the area in which its writ may run.

Finally, to those nations who would make themselves our adversary, we offer not a pledge but a request: that both sides begin anew the quest for peace, before the dark powers of destruction unleashed by science engulf all humanity in planned or accidental self-destruction.

We dare not tempt them with weakness. For only when our arms are sufficient beyond doubt can we be certain beyond doubt that they will never be employed.

But neither can two great and powerful groups of nations take comfort from our present course—both sides overburdened by the cost of modern weapons, both rightly alarmed by the steady spread of the deadly atom, yet both racing to alter that uncertain balance of terror that stays the hand of mankind's final war.

So let us begin anew—remembering on both sides that civility is not a sign of weakness, and sincerity is always subject to proof. Let us never negotiate out of fear. But let us never fear to negotiate.

Let both sides explore what problems unite us instead of belaboring those problems which divide us.

Let both sides, for the first time, formulate serious and precise proposals for the inspection and control of arms—and bring the absolute power to destroy other nations under the absolute control of all nations.

Let both sides seek to invoke the wonders of science instead of its terrors. Together let us explore the stars, conquer the deserts, eradicate disease, tap the ocean depths and encourage the arts and commerce.

Let both sides unite to heed in all corners of the earth the command of Isaiah—to "undo the heavy burdens . . . [and] let the oppressed go free."

And if a beachhead of cooperation may push back the jungles of suspicion, let both sides join in creating a new endeavor—not a new balance of power, but a new world of law, where the strong are just and the weak secure and the peace preserved.

All this will not be finished in the first 100 days. Nor will it be finished in the first 1,000 days, nor in the life of this Administration, nor even perhaps in our lifetime on this planet. But let us begin.

In your hands, my fellow citizens, more than mine, will rest the final success or failure of our course. Since this country was founded, each generation of Americans has been summoned to give testimony to its national loyalty. The graves of young Americans who answered the call to service surround the globe.

Now the trumpet summons us again—not as a call to bear arms, though arms we need—not as a call to battle, though embattled we are—but a call to bear the burden of a long twilight struggle year in and year out, "rejoicing in hope, patient in tribulation"—a struggle against the common enemies of man: tyranny, poverty, disease and war itself.

Can we forge against these enemies a grand and global alliance, north and south, east and west, that can assure a more fruitful life for all mankind? Will you join in that historic effort?

In the long history of the world, only a few generations have been granted the role of defending freedom in its hour of maximum danger. I do not shrink from this responsibility—I welcome it. I do not believe that any of us would exchange places with any other people or any other generation. The energy, the faith, the devotion which we bring to this endeavor will light our country and all who serve it—and the glow from that fire can truly light the world.

And so, my fellow Americans: ask not what your country can do for you —ask what you can do for your country.

My fellow citizens of the world: ask not what America will do for you, but what together we can do for the freedom of man.

Finally, whether you are citizens of America or citizens of the world, ask of us here the same high standards of strength and sacrifice which we ask of you. With a good conscience our only sure reward, with history the final judge of our deeds, let us go forth to lead the land we love, asking His blessing and His help, but knowing that here on earth God's work must truly be our own.

On June 10, 1963, President Kennedy made a major statement on American foreign policy at the commencement exercises of American University, Washington, D.C. Dedicated to the theme that the time had arrived for a break in the cold war, and that the United States and the Soviet Union should re-examine their attitudes toward one another, this speech prepared the way for the signing of the Nuclear Test Ban treaty a month afterward.

In a later tribute to Kennedy, Nikita S. Khrushchev praised this speech as "courageous," and went on to say that here Kennedy "was outlining already more realistic principles of the relations between countries with different social systems."

This speech carries out with new force the theme of peace clearly begun in Kennedy's Inaugural speech and continued in his 1961 address to the United Nations. Near the end he announces his historic decisions to suspend nuclear testing in the atmosphere and to join with Moscow and London in an all-out effort to conclude a Nuclear Test Ban treaty. We give the speech in complete form except for a few very brief omissions.

THE STRATEGY OF PEACE

IT IS WITH great pride that I participate in this ceremony of the American University sponsored by the Methodist Church, founded by Bishop John Fletcher Hurst and first opened by President Woodrow Wilson in 1914.

This is a young and growing university, but it has already fulfilled Bishop Hurst's enlightened hope for the study of history and public affairs in a city devoted to the making of history and to the conduct of the public's business.

I have, therefore, chosen this time and place to discuss a topic on which ignorance too often abounds and the truth is too rarely perceived—and that is the most important topic on earth: world peace.

What kind of peace do I mean and what kind of peace do we seek? Not a Pax Americana enforced on the world by American weapons of war. Not the peace of the grave or the security of the slave. I am talking about genuine peace—the kind of peace that makes life on earth worth living—and the kind that enables men and nations to grow and to hope and build a better life for their children—not merely peace for Americans but peace for all men and women—not merely peace in our time but peace in all time.

I speak of peace because of the new face of war. Total war makes no sense in an age where great powers can maintain large and relatively invulnerable nuclear forces and refuse to surrender without resort to those forces. It makes no sense in an age when a single nuclear weapon contains almost ten times the explosive force delivered by all the Allied air forces in the second world war. It makes no sense in an age when the deadly poisons produced by a nuclear exchange would be carried by wind and water and soil and seed to the far corners of the globe and to generations yet unborn.

Today the expenditure of billions of dollars every year on weapons acquired for the purpose of making sure we never need them is essential to the keeping of peace. But surely the acquisition of such idle stockpiles—which can only destroy and can never create—is not the only, much less the most efficient, means of assuring peace.

I speak of peace, therefore, as the necessary rational end of rational men. I realize the pursuit of peace is not as dramatic as the pursuit of war—and frequently the words of the pursuer fall on deaf ears. But we have no more urgent task.

Some say that it is useless to speak of peace or world law or world disarmament—and that it will be useless until the leaders of the Soviet Union adopt a more enlightened attitude. I hope they do. I believe we can help them do it.

But I also believe that we must re-examine our own attitudes—as individuals and as a nation—for our attitude is as essential as theirs. And every graduate of this school, every thoughtful citizen who despairs of war and wishes to bring peace, should begin by looking inward—by examining his own attitude towards the course of the cold war and towards freedom and peace here at home.

First: Examine our attitude towards peace itself. Too many of us think it is impossible. Too many think it is unreal. But that is a dangerous, defeatist belief. It leads to the conclusion that war is inevitable—that mankind is doomed—that we are gripped by forces we cannot control.

We need not accept that view. Our problems are man-made. Therefore, they can be solved by man. And man can be as big as he wants. No problem of human destiny is beyond human beings. Man's reason and spirit have often solved the seemingly unsolvable—and we believe they can do it again.

I am not referring to the absolute, infinite concepts of universal peace and goodwill of which some fantasies and fanatics dream. I do not deny the value of hopes and dreams but we merely invite discouragement and incredulity by making that our only and immediate goal.

Let us focus instead on a more practical, more attainable peace—based not on a sudden revolution in human nature but on a gradual evolution in human institutions—on a series of concrete actions and effective agreements which are in the interests of all concerned.

There is no single, simple key to this peace—no grand or magic formula to be adopted by one or two powers. Genuine peace must be the product of many nations, the sum of many acts. It must be dynamic, not static, changing to meet the challenge of each new generation. For peace is a process—a way of solving problems.

With such a peace, there will still be quarrels and conflicting interests, as there are within families and nations. World peace, like community peace, does not require that each man love his neighbor—it requires only that they live together with mutual tolerance, submitting their disputes to a just and peaceful settlement. And history teaches us that enmities between nations, as between individuals, do not last forever. However fixed our likes and dislikes may seem, the tide of time and events will often bring surprising changes in the relations between nations and neighbors.

So let us persevere. Peace need not be impracticable—war need not be inevitable. By defining our goal more clearly—by making it seem more manageable and less remote—we can help all people to see it, to draw hope from it, and to move irresistibly towards it.

And second: let us re-examine our attitude towards the Soviet Union. It is discouraging to think that their leaders may actually believe what their propagandists write.

It is discouraging to read a recent authoritative Soviet text on military strategy and find, on page after page, wholly baseless and incredible claims —such as the allegation that "American imperialist circles are preparing to unleash different types of war . . . that there is a very real threat of a preventative war being unleashed by American imperialists against the Soviet Union . . . [and that] the political aims," and I quote, "of the American imperialists are to enslave economically and politically the European and other capitalist countries . . . [and] to achieve world domination . . . by means of aggressive wars."

Truly, as it was written long ago: "The wicked flee when no man pursueth." Yet it is sad to read these Soviet statements—to realize the extent of the gulf between us. But it is also a warning—a warning to the American people not to fall into the same trap as the Soviets, not to see only a distorted and desperate view of the other side, not to see conflict as inevitable, accommodation as impossible and communication as nothing more than an exchange of threats.

No government or social system is so evil that its people must be considered as lacking in virtue. As Americans, we find Communism profoundly repugnant as a negation of personal freedom and dignity. But we can still hail the Russian people for their many achievements—in science and space, in economic and industrial growth, in culture, in acts of courage.

Among the many traits the peoples of our two countries have in common, none is stronger than our mutual abhorrence of war. Almost unique among the major world powers, we have never been at war with each other. And no nation in the history of battle ever suffered more than the Soviet Union in the second world war. At least 20,000,000 lost their lives. Countless millions of homes and farms were burned or sacked. A third of the nation's territory, including two-thirds of its industrial base, was turned into a wasteland—a loss equivalent to the destruction of this country east of Chicago.

Today, should total war ever break out again—no matter how—our two countries will be the primary targets. It is an ironic but accurate fact that the two strongest powers are the two in the most danger of devastation. All we have built, all we have worked for, would be destroyed in the first 24 hours. And even in the cold war—which brings burdens and dangers to so many countries, including this nation's closest allies—our two countries bear the heaviest burdens. For we are both devoting massive sums of money to weapons that could be better devoted to combat ignorance, poverty and disease.

We are both caught up in a vicious and dangerous cycle with suspicion on one side breeding suspicion on the other, and new weapons begetting counter-weapons.

In short, both the United States and its allies, and the Soviet Union and its allies, have a mutually deep interest in a just and genuine peace and in halting the arms race. Agreements to this end are in the interests of the Soviet Union as well as ours—and even the most hostile nations can be relied upon to accept and keep those treaty obligations, and only those treaty obligations, which are in their own interest.

So, let us not be blind to our differences—but let us also direct attention to our common interests and the means by which those differences can be resolved. And if we cannot end now our differences, at least we can help make the world safe for diversity. For, in the final analysis, our most basic common link is that we all inhabit this small planet. We all breathe the same air. We all cherish our children's future. And we all are mortal.

Third: Let us re-examine our attitude towards the cold war, remembering we are not engaged in a debate, seeking to pile up debating points. We are not here distributing blame or pointing the finger of judgment. We must deal with the world as it is, and not as it might have been had the history of the last eighteen years been different.

We must, therefore, persevere in the search for peace in the hope that constructive changes within the Communist bloc might bring within reach solutions which now seem beyond us. We must conduct our affairs in such a way that it becomes in the Communists' interest to agree on a genuine peace. And above all, while defending our own vital interests, nuclear powers must avert those confrontations which bring an adversary to a choice of either a humiliating retreat or a nuclear war. To adopt that kind of course in the nuclear age would be evidence only of the bankruptcy of our policy—or of a collective death-wish for the world.

To secure these ends, America's weapons are non-provocative, carefully controlled, designed to deter and capable of selective use. Our military forces are committed to peace and disciplined in self-restraint. Our diplomats are instructed to avoid unnecessary irritants and purely rhetorical hostility.

For we can seek a relaxation of tensions without relaxing our guard. And, for our part, we do not need to use threats to prove that we are resolute. We do not need to jam foreign broadcasts out of fear our faith will be eroded. We are unwilling to impose our system on any unwilling people—but we are willing and able to engage in peaceful competition with any people on earth.

Meanwhile, we seek to strengthen the United Nations, to help solve its financial problems, to make it a more effective instrument for peace, to develop it into a genuine world security system—a system capable of resolving disputes on the basis of law, of insuring the security of the large and the small, and of creating conditions under which arms can finally be abolished.

At the same time we seek to keep peace inside the non-Communist world, where many nations, all of them our friends, are divided over issues which weaken Western unity, which invite Communist intervention or which threaten to erupt into war.

Our efforts in West New Guinea, in the Congo, in the Middle East and the Indian subcontinent have been persistent and patient despite criticism from both sides. We have also tried to set an example for others—by seeking to adjust small but significant differences with our closest neighbors in Mexico and Canada.

Speaking of other nations, I wish to make one point clear. We are bound to many nations by alliances. These alliances exist because our concern and theirs substantially overlap. Our commitment to defend Western Europe and West Berlin, for example, stands undiminished because of the identity of our vital interests. The United States will make no deal with the Soviet Union at the expense of other nations and other peoples, not merely because they are our partners, but also because their interests and ours converge.

Our interests converge, however, not only in defending the frontiers of freedom, but in pursuing the paths of peace.

It is our hope—and the purpose of allied policies—to convince the Soviet Union that she, too, should let each nation choose its own future, so long as that choice does not interfere with the choices of others. The Communist drive to impose their political and economic system on others is the primary cause of world tension today. For there can be no doubt that, if all nations could refrain from interfering in the self-determination of others, the peace would be much more assured.

This will require a new effort to achieve world law—a new context for world discussions. It will require increased understanding between the Soviets and ourselves. And increased understanding will require increased contact and communication.

One step in this direction is the proposed arrangement for a direct line between Moscow and Washington, to avoid on each side the dangerous delays, misunderstanding, and misreadings of the other's actions which might occur in a time of crisis.

We have also been talking in Geneva about other first-step measures of arms control, designed to limit the intensity of the arms race and reduce the risks of accidental war.

Our primary long-range interest in Geneva, however, is general and complete disarmament—designed to take place by stages, permitting parallel political developments to build the new institutions of peace which would take the place of arms. The pursuit of disarmament has been an effort of this Government since the 1920's. It has been urgently sought by the past three Administrations. And however dim the prospects are today, we intend to continue this effort—to continue it in order that all countries, including our own, can better grasp what the problems and the possibilities of disarmament are.

The only major area of these negotiations where the end is in sight—yet where a fresh start is badly needed—is in a treaty to outlaw nuclear tests. The conclusion of such a treaty—so near and yet so far—would check the spiraling arms race in one of its most dangerous areas. It would place the nuclear powers in a position to deal more effectively with one of the greatest hazards which man faces in 1963—the further spread of nuclear weapons. It would increase our security—it would decrease the prospects of war.

Surely this goal is sufficiently important to require our steady pursuit, yielding neither to the temptation to give up the whole effort nor the temptation to give up our insistence on vital and responsible safeguards.

I am taking this opportunity, therefore, to announce two important decisions in this regard:

First: Chairman Khrushchev, Prime Minister Macmillan and I have agreed that high-level discussions will shortly begin in Moscow towards early agreement on a comprehensive test ban treaty. Our hopes must be tempered with the caution of history—but with our hopes go the hopes of all mankind.

Second: To make clear our good faith and solemn convictions on the matter, I now declare that the United States does not propose to conduct nuclear tests in the atmosphere so long as other states do not do so. We will not be the first to resume. Such a declaration is no substitute for a formal, binding treaty—but I hope it will help us achieve one. Nor would such a treaty be a substitute for disarmament—but I hope it will help us achieve it.

Finally, my fellow Americans, let us examine our attitude towards peace and freedom here at home. The quality and spirit of our own society must justify and support our efforts abroad. We must show it in the dedication of our own lives—as many of you who are graduating today will have an opportunity to do, by serving without pay in the Peace Corps abroad or in the proposed National Service Corps here at home.

But wherever we are, we must all, in our daily lives, live up to the age-old faith that peace and freedom walk together. In too many of our cities today, the peace is not secure because freedom is incomplete.

It is the responsibility of the executive branch at all levels of government —local, state and national—to provide and protect that freedom for all of our citizens by all means within our authority. It is the responsibility of the legislative branch at all levels, wherever the authority is not now adequate, to make it adequate. And it is the responsibility of all citizens in all sections of this country to respect the rights of others and respect the law of the land.

All this is not unrelated to world peace. "When a man's ways please the Lord," the scriptures tell us, "he maketh even his enemies to be at peace with him." And is not peace, in the last analysis, basically a matter of human rights—the right to live out our lives without fear of devastation— the right to breathe air as nature provided it—the right of future generations to a healthy existence?

While we proceed to safeguard our national interests, let us also safeguard human interests. And the elimination of war and arms is clearly in the interest of both.

No treaty, however much it may be to the advantage of all, however tightly it may be worded, can provide absolute security against the risks of deception and evasion. But it can—if it is sufficiently effective in its enforcement and it is sufficiently in the interests of its signers—offer far more security and far fewer risks than an unabated, uncontrolled, unpredictable arms race.

The United States, as the world knows, will never start a war. We do not want a war. We do not now expect a war. This generation of Americans has already had enough—more than enough—of war and hate and oppression. We shall be prepared if others wish it. We shall be alert to try to stop it. But we shall also do our part to build a world of peace where the weak are safe and the strong are just.

We are not helpless before that task or hopeless of its success. Confident and unafraid, we labor on—not toward a strategy of annihilation but toward a strategy of peace. Thank you.

> *President Kennedy had long been an admirer of Robert Frost, and at Kennedy's request Frost read one of his poems as part of the inauguration ceremony. Amherst College invited President Kennedy to address an academic convocation on October 26, 1963, at which a new library was dedicated as a memorial to Robert Frost, who had died early in 1963. Kennedy's theme was the relationship between poetry and power; and he points out the importance of those who question power and in so doing serve their country equally with those who wield power. Kennedy in the course of the speech drew on some of Frost's most remembered poems. Following are major parts of the address.*

POETRY AND POWER

Mr. [John J.] McCloy, President [Calvin H.] Plimpton, Mr. [Archibald] MacLeish, distinguished guests, ladies and gentlemen:

I'm very honored to be here with you on this occasion, which means so much to this college and also means so much to art and the progress of the United States.

The library being constructed today—this college itself—all of this, of course, was not done merely to give this school's graduates an advantage—an economic advantage in the life struggle.

It does do that. But in return for that—in return for the great opportunity which society gives the graduates of this and related schools, it seems to me incumbent upon this and other schools' graduates to recognize their responsibility to the public interest.

And unless the graduates of this college and other colleges like it who are given a running start in life—unless they are willing to put back into our society those talents, the broad sympathy, the understanding, the compassion—unless they are willing to put those qualities back into the service of the great republic, then obviously the presuppositions upon which our democracy is based are bound to be fallible.

And therefore, I am proud to come to this college whose graduates have recognized this obligation and to say to those who are now here that the need is endless and I'm confident that you will respond.

Robert Frost said it:

> Two roads diverged in a wood and I—
> I took the one less traveled by,
> And that has made all the difference.

I hope that road will not be the less traveled by and I hope your commitment to the great public interest in the years to come will be worthy of your long inheritance since your beginning.

This day, devoted to the memory of Robert Frost, offers an opportunity for reflection which is prized by politicians as well as by others and even by poets. For Robert Frost was one of the granite figures of our time in America. He was supremely two things—an artist and an American.

A nation reveals itself not only by the men it produces but also by the men it honors, the men it remembers.

In America our heroes have customarily run to men of large accomplishments. But today this college and country honor a man whose contribution was not to our size but to our spirit; not to our political beliefs but to our insight; not to our self-esteem but to our self-comprehension.

In honoring Robert Frost we therefore can pay honor to the deepest sources of our national strength. That strength takes many forms and the most obvious forms are not always the most significant.

The men who create power make an indispensable contribution to the nation's greatness. But the men who question power make a contribution just as indispensable, especially when that question is disinterested.

For they determine whether we use power or power uses us. Our national strength matters; but the spirit which informs and controls our strength matters just as much. This was the special significance of Robert Frost.

He brought an unsparing instinct for reality to bear on the platitudes and pieties of society. His sense of the human tragedy fortified him against self-deception and easy consolation.

"I have been," he wrote, "one acquainted with the night."

And because he knew the midnight as well as the high noon, because he understood the ordeal as well as the triumph of the human spirit, he gave his age strength with which to overcome despair.

At bottom he held a deep faith in the spirit of man. And it's hardly an accident that Robert Frost coupled poetry and power. For he saw poetry as the means of saving power from itself.

When power leads man toward arrogance, poetry reminds him of his limitations. When power narrows the areas of man's concern, poetry reminds him of the richness and diversity of his existence. When power corrupts, poetry cleanses.

For art establishes the basic human truths which must serve as the touchstones of our judgment. The artist, however faithful to his personal vision of reality, becomes the last champion of the individual mind and sensibility against an intrusive society and an officious state.

The great artist is thus a solitary figure. He has, as Frost said, "a lover's quarrel with the world." In pursuing his perceptions of reality he must often sail against the currents of his time. This is not a popular role.

If Robert Frost was much honored during his lifetime, it was because a good many preferred to ignore his darker truths.

Yet in retrospect we see how the artist's fidelity has strengthened the fiber of our national life. If sometimes our great artists have been the most critical of our society it is because their sensitivity and their concern for justice, which must motivate any true artist, makes them aware that our nation falls short of its highest potential.

I see little of more importance to the future of our country and our civilization than full recognition of the place of the artist. If art is to nourish the roots of our culture, society must set the artist free to follow his vision wherever it takes him.

In a free society, art is not a weapon and it does not belong to the sphere of polemics and ideology. Artists are not engineers of the soul.

It may be different elsewhere. But democratic society—in it—the highest duty of the writer, the composer, the artist is to remain true to himself and to let the chips fall where they may.

I look forward to a great future for America—a future in which our country will match its military strength with our moral restraint, its wealth with our wisdom, its power with our purpose.

I look forward to an America which will not be afraid of grace and beauty, which will protect the beauty of our natural environment, which will preserve the great old American houses and squares and parks of our national past and which will build handsome and balanced cities for our future.

I look forward to an America which will reward achievement in the arts as we reward achievement in business or statecraft.

I look forward to an America which will steadily raise the standards of artistic accomplishment and which will steadily enlarge cultural opportunities for all of our citizens.

And I look forward to an America which commands respect throughout the world not only for its strength but for its civilization as well.

And I look forward to a world which will be safe not only for democracy and diversity but also for personal distinction.

Robert Frost was often skeptical about projects for human improvement. Yet I do not think he would disdain this hope.

As he wrote during the uncertain days of the Second War:

> Take human nature altogether since time began...
> And it must be a little more in favor of man.
> Say a fraction of one per cent at the very least...
> Our hold on the planet wouldn't have so increased.

Because of Mr. Frost's life and work, because of the life and work of this college, our hold on this planet has increased.

Martin Luther King, Jr.
[1929–1968]

The outstanding leader of the Negro's struggle for civil rights, Dr. Martin Luther King, Jr., was a firm advocate of non-violence as the means of achieving these rights. Minister of the Dexter Avenue Baptist Church in Montgomery, Alabama, Dr. King brought together the support of white and Negro clergymen, businessmen, professional men, and students in such actions as the Montgomery Bus Boycott. He received an A.B. degree from Morehouse College and a Ph.D. from Boston University. In 1964 he was awarded the Nobel Peace Prize. He was in Memphis, Tennessee, planning to march with members of the sanitation department in an appeal for better working conditions, when he was assassinated.

On August 28, 1963, Dr. King, as president of the Southern Christian Leadership Conference, was one of the principal speakers at the outdoor gathering of the Civil Rights March on Washington, D.C. The address was spoken from the steps of the Lincoln Memorial. (Copyright © 1963 by Martin Luther King, Jr.; reprinted by permission of Joan Daves.)

I HAVE A DREAM

I AM HAPPY to join with you today in what will go down in history as the greatest demonstration for freedom in the history of our nation.

Five score years ago, a great American, in whose symbolic shadow we stand, signed the Emancipation Proclamation. This momentous decree came as a great beacon light of hope to millions of Negro slaves who had been seared in the flames of withering injustice. It came as a joyous daybreak to end the long night of captivity.

But one hundred years later, we must face the tragic fact that the Negro is still not free. One hundred years later, the life of the Negro is still sadly crippled by the manacles of segregation and the chains of discrimination. One hundred years later, the Negro lives on a lonely island of poverty in the midst of a vast ocean of material prosperity. One hundred years later the Negro is still languishing in the corners of American society and finds himself an exile in his own land. So we have come here today to dramatize an appalling condition.

In a sense we have come to our nation's Capital to cash a check. When the architects of our republic wrote the magnificent words of the Constitution and the Declaration of Independence, they were signing a promissory note to which every American was to fall heir. This note was a promise that all men would be guaranteed the unalienable rights of life, liberty, and the pursuit of happiness.

It is obvious today that America has defaulted on this promissory note insofar as her citizens of color are concerned. Instead of honoring this sacred obligation, America has given the Negro people a bad check; a check which has come back marked "insufficient funds." But we refuse to believe that the bank of justice is bankrupt. We refuse to believe that there are insufficient funds in the great vaults of opportunity of this nation. So we have come to cash this check—a check that will give us upon demand the riches of freedom and the security of justice. We have also come to this hallowed spot to remind America of the fierce urgency of *now*. This is no time to engage in the luxury of cooling off or to take the tranquilizing drug of gradualism. *Now* is the time to make real the promises of Democracy. *Now* is the time to rise from the dark and desolate valley of segregation to the sunlit path of racial justice. *Now* is the time to open the doors of opportunity to all of God's children. *Now* is the time to lift our nation from the quicksands of racial injustice to the solid rock of brotherhood.

It would be fatal for the nation to overlook the urgency of the moment and to underestimate the determination of the Negro. This sweltering summer of the Negro's legitimate discontent will not pass until there is an invigorating autumn of freedom and equality. 1963 is not an end, but a beginning. Those who hope that the Negro needed to blow off steam and will now be content will have a rude awakening if the Nation returns to business as usual. There will be neither rest nor tranquility in America until the Negro is granted his citizenship rights. The whirlwinds of revolt will continue to shake the foundations of our Nation until the bright day of justice emerges.

But there is something that I must say to my people who stand on the warm threshold which leads into the palace of justice. In the process of gaining our rightful place we must not be guilty of wrongful deeds. Let us not seek to satisfy our thirst for freedom by drinking from the cup of bitterness and hatred. We must forever conduct our struggle on the high plane of dignity and discipline. We must not allow our creative protest to degenerate into physical violence. Again and again we must rise to the majestic heights of meeting physical force with soul force. The marvelous new militancy which has engulfed the Negro community must not lead us to a distrust of all white people, for many of our white brothers, as evidenced by their presence here today, have come to realize that their destiny is tied up with our destiny and their freedom is inextricably bound to our freedom. We cannot walk alone.

And as we walk, we must make the pledge that we shall march ahead. We cannot turn back. There are those who are asking the devotees of civil rights, "When will you be satisfied?" We can never be satisfied as long as the Negro is the victim of the unspeakable horrors of police brutality. We can never be satisfied as long as our bodies, heavy with the fatigue of travel, cannot gain lodging in the motels of the highways and the hotels of the cities. We cannot be satisfied as long as the Negro's basic mobility is from a smaller ghetto to a larger one. We can never be satisfied as long as a Negro in Mississippi cannot vote and a Negro in New York believes he has nothing for which to vote. No, no, we are not satisfied, and we will not be satisfied until justice rolls down like waters and righteousness like a mighty stream.

I am not unmindful that some of you have come here out of great trials and tribulations. Some of you have come fresh from narrow jail cells. Some of you have come from areas where your quest for freedom left you battered by the storms of persecution and staggered by the winds of police brutality. You have been the veterans of creative suffering. Continue to work with the faith that unearned suffering is redemptive.

Go back to Mississippi, go back to Alabama, go back to South Carolina, go back to Georgia, go back to Louisiana, go back to the slums and ghettos of our modern cities, knowing that somehow this situation can and will be changed. Let us not wallow in the valley of despair.

I say to you today, my friends, that in spite of the difficulties and frustrations of the moment I still have a dream. It is a dream deeply rooted in the American dream.

I have a dream that one day this nation will rise up and live out the true meaning of its creed: "We hold these truths to be self-evident; that all men are created equal."

I have a dream that one day on the red hills of Georgia the sons of former slaves and the sons of former slaveowners will be able to sit down together at the table of brotherhood.

I have a dream that one day even the state of Mississippi, a desert state sweltering with the heat of injustice and oppression, will be transformed into an oasis of freedom and justice.

I have a dream that my four little children will one day live in a nation where they will not be judged by the color of their skin but by the content of their character.

I have a dream today.

I have a dream that one day the state of Alabama, whose governor's lips are presently dripping with the words of interposition and nullification, will be transformed into a situation where little black boys and black girls will be able to join hand with little white boys and white girls and walk together as sisters and brothers.

I have a dream today.

I have a dream that one day every valley shall be exalted, every hill and mountain shall be made low, the rough places will be made plains, and the crooked places will be made straight, and the glory of the Lord shall be revealed, and all flesh shall see it together.

This is our hope. This is the faith with which I return to the South. With this faith we will be able to hew out of the mountain of despair a stone of hope. With this faith we will be able to transform the jangling discords of our nation into a beautiful symphony of brotherhood. With this faith we will be able to work together, to pray together, to struggle together, to go to jail together, to stand up for freedom together, knowing that we will be free one day.

This will be the day when all of God's children will be able to sing with new meaning "My country 'tis of thee, sweet land of liberty, of thee I sing. Land where my fathers died, land of the pilgrim's pride, from every mountainside, let freedom ring."

And if America is to be a great nation this must become true. So let freedom ring from the prodigious hilltops of New Hampshire. Let freedom ring from the mighty mountains of New York. Let freedom ring from the heightening Alleghenies of Pennsylvania!

Let freedom ring from the snowcapped Rockies of Colorado!

Let freedom ring from the curvaceous peaks of California!

But not only that; let freedom ring from Stone Mountain of Georgia!

Let freedom ring from Lookout Mountain of Tennessee!

Let freedom ring from every hill and mole hill of Mississippi. From every mountainside, let freedom ring.

When we let freedom ring, when we let it ring from every village and every hamlet, from every state and every city, we will be able to speed up that day when all of God's children, black men and white men, Jews and Gentiles, Protestants and Catholics, will be able to join hands and sing in the words of the old Negro spiritual, "Free at last! free at last! thank God almighty, we are free at last!"

Dwight David Eisenhower
[1890–1969]

President Eisenhower (see biographical sketch and other addresses, pp. 603–611) delivered his farewell address to the nation on January 17, 1961. The speech was broadcast over radio and television. Eisenhower here used the expression "military-industrial complex," warning of its possibly excessive influence. Emphasis is also placed on the danger of loss of individual initiative resulting from extensive government involvement in technology and research. Major portions of the speech are included here.

FAREWELL ADDRESS

THIS EVENING I come to you with a message of leave-taking and farewell, and to share a few final thoughts with you, my countrymen.

Our people expect their President and the Congress to find essential agreement on issues of great moment, the wise resolution of which will better shape the future of the nation.

My own relations with the Congress, which began on a remote and tenuous basis when, long ago, a member of the Senate appointed me to West Point, have since ranged to the intimate during the war and immediate post-war period, and finally to the mutually interdependent during these past eight years.

In this final relationship, the Congress and the Administration have, on most vital issues, cooperated well, to serve the national good rather than mere partisanship, and so have assured that the business of the nation should go forward. So my official relationship with the Congress ends in a feeling, on my part, of gratitude that we have been able to do so much together.

We now stand ten years past the midpoint of a century that has witnessed four major wars among great nations—three of these involved our own country.

Despite these holocausts America is today the strongest, the most influential and most productive nation in the world. Understandably proud of this pre-eminence, we yet realize that America's leadership and prestige depend, not merely upon our unmatched material progress, riches and military strength, but on how we use our power in the interests of world peace and human betterment.

A vital element in keeping the peace is our military establishment. Our arms must be mighty, ready for instant action, so that no potential aggressor may be tempted to risk his own destruction.

Our military organization today bears little relation to that known by any of my predecessors in peacetime—or, indeed, by the fighting men of World War II or Korea.

Until the latest of our world conflicts, the United States had no armaments industry. American makers of plowshares could, with time and as required, make swords as well.

But we can no longer risk emergency improvisation of national defense. We have been compelled to create a permanent armaments industry of vast proportions. Added to this, three and a half million men and women are directly engaged in the defense establishment. We annually spend on military security alone more than the net income of all United States corporations.

Now this conjunction of an immense military establishment and a large arms industry is new in the American experience. The total influence—economic, political, even spiritual—is felt in every city, every state house, every office of the Federal Government. We recognize the imperative need for this development. Yet we must not fail to comprehend its grave implications. Our toil, resources and livelihood are all involved; so is the very structure of our society.

In the councils of Government, we must guard against the acquisition of unwarranted influence, whether sought or unsought, by the military-industrial complex. The potential for the disastrous rise of misplaced power exists and will persist.

We must never let the weight of this combination endanger our liberties or democratic processes. We should take nothing for granted. Only an alert and knowledgeable citizenry can compel the proper meshing of the huge industrial and military machinery of defense with our peaceful methods and goals, so that security and liberty may prosper together.

Akin to and largely responsible for the sweeping changes in our industrial-military posture has been the technological revolution during recent decades.

In this revolution research has become central. It also becomes more formalized, complex and costly. A steadily increasing share is conducted for, by, or at the direction of the Federal Government.

Today the solitary inventor, tinkering in his shop, has been overshadowed by task forces of scientists, in laboratories and testing fields. In the same fashion, the free university, historically the fountainhead of free ideas and scientific discovery, has experienced a revolution in the conduct of research.

Partly because of the huge costs involved, a Government contract becomes virtually a substitute for intellectual curiosity.

For every old blackboard there are now hundreds of new electronic computers.

Another factor in maintaining balance involves the element of time. As we peer into society's future, we—you and I, and our Government—must avoid the impulse to live only for today, plundering, for our own ease and convenience, the precious resources of tomorrow.

We cannot mortgage the material assets of our grandchildren without risking the loss also of their political and spiritual heritage. We want democracy to survive for all generations to come, not to become the insolvent phantom of tomorrow.

Such a confederation must be one of equals. The weakest must come to the conference table with the same confidence as do we, protected as we are by our moral, economic and military strength. That table, though scarred by many past frustrations, cannot be abandoned for the certain agony of the battlefield.

Disarmament, with mutual honor and confidence, is a continuing imperative. Together we must learn how to compose differences—not with arms, but with intellect and decent purpose. Because this need is so sharp and apparent, I confess that I lay down my official responsibilities in this field with a definite sense of disappointment. As one who has witnessed the horror and the lingering sadness of war, as one who knows that another war could utterly destroy this civilization which has been so slowly and painfully built over thousands of years, I wish I could say tonight that a lasting peace is in sight.

Happily, I can say that war has been avoided. Steady progress toward our ultimate goal has been made. But so much remains to be done. As a private citizen, I shall never cease to do what little I can to help the world advance along that road.

So, in this, my last "good night" to you as your President, I thank you for the many opportunities you have given me for public service in war and in peace. I trust that, in that service, you find some things worthy. As for the rest of it, I know you will find ways to improve performance in the future.

To all the peoples of the world, I once more give expression to America's prayerful and continuing aspiration:

We pray that peoples of all faiths, all races, all nations, may have their great human needs satisfied; that those now denied opportunity shall come to enjoy it to the full; that all who yearn for freedom may experience its spiritual blessings; that those who have freedom will understand, also, its heavy responsibilities; that all who are insensitive to the needs of others will learn charity; that the scourges of poverty, disease and ignorance will be made to disappear from the earth; and that in the goodness of time, all peoples will come to live together in a peace guaranteed by the binding force of mutual respect and love.

Now, on Friday noon, I am to become a private citizen. I am proud to do so. I look forward to it.

Thank you, and, good night.

Robert S. McNamara
[1916-   ]

Robert S. McNamara was Secretary of Defense in the cabinet of President John F. Kennedy, and continued in that post under President Lyndon B. Johnson until 1968. Previously Mr. McNamara had been president of the Ford Motor Company. And more recently he has been president of the World Bank.

Following is an address given by him at a convention of the American Society of Newspaper Editors held in the Queen Elizabeth Hotel, Montreal, Canada, May 18, 1966. In addition to discussing the specific topics stated in the title of his address, Mr. McNamara indicates certain of his views about American foreign policy. Major parts of the speech are given here, with Mr. McNamara's approval.

WAR AND POVERTY

THERE is a special satisfaction for a Secretary of Defense to cross the longest border in the world—and realize that it is also the least armed border in the world. It prompts one to reflect how negative and narrow a notion of defense still clouds our century.

There is still among us an almost ineradicable tendency to think of our security problem as being exclusively a military problem—and to think of the military problem as being exclusively a weapons-system or hardware problem.

The plain, blunt truth is that contemporary man still conceives of war and peace in much the same stereotyped terms that his ancestors did. The fact that these ancestors—both recent and remote—were conspicuously unsuccessful at avoiding war, and enlarging peace, doesn't seem to dampen our capacity for clichés. We still tend to conceive of national security solely as a state of armed readiness: a vast, awesome arsenal of weaponry. We still tend to assume that it is primarily this purely military ingredient that creates security. We are still haunted by this concept of military hardware. But how limited a concept this actually is, becomes apparent when one ponders the kind of peace that exists between the United States and Canada.

It is a very cogent example. Here we are, two modern nations: highly developed technologically, each with immense territory, both enriched with great reserves of natural resources, each militarily sophisticated—and yet, we sit across from one another, divided by an unguarded frontier of thousands of miles . . . and there is not a remotest set of circumstances, in any imaginable time-frame of the future, in which our two nations would wage war on one another. . . .

We are at peace—truly at peace—because of the vast fund of compatible beliefs, common principles, and shared ideals. . . .

In the United States—over the past five years—we have achieved a considerably improved balance in our total military posture. That was the mandate I received from Presidents Kennedy and Johnson; and with their support, and that of the Congress, we have been able to create a strengthened force structure of land, sea, and air components—with a vast increase in mobility and matériel—and with a massive superiority in nuclear retaliatory power over any combination of potential adversaries.

Our capabilities for nuclear, conventional, and counter-subversive war have all been broadened and improved; and we have accomplished this through military budgets that were in fact lesser percentages of our gross national product than in the past.

From the point of view of combat readiness, the United States has never been militarily stronger. We intend to maintain that readiness.

But if we think profoundly about the matter, it is clear that this purely military posture is not the central element in our security. A nation can reach the point at which it does not buy more security for itself simply by buying more military hardware—we are at that point.

The decisive factor for a powerful nation—already adequately armed—is the character of its relationships with the world.

In this respect, there are three broad groups of nations: first, those that are struggling to develop; secondly, those free nations that have reached a level of strength and prosperity that enables them to contribute to the peace of the world; and finally, those nations who might be tempted to make themselves our adversaries.

For each of these groups, the United States—to preserve its own intrinsic security—has to have distinctive sets of relationships.

First, we have to help protect those developing countries which genuinely need and request our help, and which—as an essential precondition—are willing and able to help themselves.

Second, we have to encourage and achieve a more effective partnership with those nations who can and should share international peace-keeping responsibilities.

Third, we must do all we realistically can to reduce the risk of conflict with those who might be tempted to take up arms against us.

Let us examine these three sets of relationships in detail. First, the developing nations.

Roughly 100 countries today are caught up in the difficult transition from traditional to modern societies. There is no uniform rate of progress among them, and they range from primitive mosaic societies—fractured by tribalism and held feebly together by the slenderest of political sinews—to relatively sophisticated countries, well on the road to agricultural sufficiency and industrial competence.

This sweeping surge of development, particularly across the whole southern half of the globe, has no parallel in history. It has turned traditionally listless areas of the world into seething cauldrons of change. On the whole, it has not been a very peaceful process.

In the last eight years alone there have been no less than 164 internationally significant outbreaks of violence—each of them specifically designed as a serious challenge to the authority, or the very existence, of the government in question. Eighty-two different governments have been directly involved. What is striking is that only 15 of these 164 significant resorts to violence have been military conflicts between two states. And not a single one of the 164 conflicts has been a formally declared war.

Indeed, there has not been a formal declaration of war—anywhere in the world—since World War II.

The planet is becoming a more dangerous place to live on—not merely because of a potential nuclear holocaust—but also because of the large number of de facto conflicts and because the trend of such conflicts is growing rather than diminishing. . . .

There can, then, be no question but that there is an irrefutable relationship between violence and economic backwardness. And the trend of such violence is up, not down. The irreducible fact remains that our security is related directly to the security of the newly developing nations which genuinely need and request our help, and which demonstrably are willing and able to help themselves. The rub comes in this: we do not always grasp the meaning of the word *security* in this context. In a modernizing society, security means development. . . .

Development means economic, social, and political progress. It means a reasonable standard of living—and the word "reasonable" in this context requires continual redefinition. What is "reasonable" in an earlier stage of development will become "unreasonable" in a later stage.

As development progresses, security progresses; and when the people of a nation have organized their own human and natural resources to provide themselves with what they need and expect out of life, their resistance to disorder and violence will be enormously increased.

America has devoted a higher proportion of its gross national product to its military establishment than any other major free world nation. This was true even before our increased expenditures in Southeast Asia.

We have had, over the last few years, as many men in uniform as all the nations of Western Europe combined—even though they have a population half again greater than our own.

Now, the American people are not going to shirk their obligations in any part of the world, but they clearly cannot be expected to bear a disproportionate share of the common burden indefinitely. . . .

The plain truth is the day is coming when no single nation, however powerful, can undertake by itself to keep the peace outside its own borders. Regional and international organizations for peace-keeping purposes are as yet rudimentary; but they must grow in experience and be strengthened by deliberate and practical cooperative action.

In this matter, the example of Canada is a model for nations everywhere. As Prime Minister Pearson pointed out eloquently in New York just last week: Canada "is as deeply involved in the world's affairs as any country of its size. We accept this because we have learned over 50 years that isolation from the policies that determine war does not give us immunity from the bloody, sacrificial consequences of their failure. We learned that in 1914 and again in 1939. . . . That is why we have been proud to send our men to take part in every peace-keeping operation of the United Nations.". . .

The Organization of the American States in the Dominican Republic, the more than thirty nations contributing troops or supplies to assist the Government of South Vietnam, indeed even the parallel efforts of the United States and the Soviet Union in the Pakistan-India conflict—these efforts, together with those of the U.N., are the first attempts to substitute multi-national for unilateral policing of violence. They point to the peace-keeping patterns of the future. . . .

The conventional forces of NATO, for example, still require a nuclear backdrop far beyond the capability of any Western European nation to supply, and the United States is fully committed to provide that major nuclear deterrent.

However, the European members of the Alliance have a natural desire to participate more actively in nuclear planning. A central task of the Alliance today is, therefore, to work out the relationships and institutions through which shared nuclear planning can be effective. We have made a practical and promising start in the Special Committee of NATO Defense Ministers.

And even beyond the Alliance, we must find the means to prevent the proliferation of nuclear weapons. That is a clear imperative.

That brings me to the third and last set of relationships the United States must deal with: Those with nations who might be tempted to take up arms against us. These relationships call for realism. But realism is not a hardened, inflexible, unimaginative attitude. The realistic mind is a restlessly creative mind—free of naive delusions, but full of practical alternatives.

There are practical alternatives to our current relationships with both the Soviet Union and Communist China. A vast ideological chasm separates us from them—and to a degree, separates them from one another. There is nothing to be gained from our seeking an ideological rapprochement; but breaching the isolation of great nations like Red China, even when that isolation is largely of its own making, reduces the danger of potentially catastrophic misunderstandings, and increases the incentive on both sides to resolve disputes by reason rather than by force. . . .

There are many ways in which we can build bridges toward nations who would cut themselves off from meaningful contact with us. We can do so with properly balanced trade relations, diplomatic contacts, and in some cases even by exchanges of military observers.

There are no one-cliff bridges. If you are going to span a chasm, you have to rest the structure on both cliffs. . . .

President Johnson has put the matter squarely. By building bridges to those who make themselves our adversaries "we can help gradually to create a community of interest, a community of trust, and a community of effort."

Mutual interest—mutual trust—mutual effort; those are the goals. Can we achieve those goals with the Soviet Union, and with Communist China? Can they achieve them with one another? The answer to those questions lies in the answer to an even more fundamental question. Who is man? Is he a rational animal? If he is, then the goals can ultimately be achieved. If he is not, then there is little point in making the effort.

All the evidence of history suggests that man is indeed a rational animal —but with a near infinite capacity for folly. His history seems largely a halting, but persistent, effort to raise his reason above his animality. He draws blueprints for Utopia. But never quite gets it built. In the end, he plugs away obstinately with the only building material really ever at hand: his own part-comic, part-tragic, part-cussed, but part-glorious nature. I, for one, would not count a global free society out. Coercion, after all, merely captures man. Freedom captivates him.

Thank you very much.

Lyndon Baines Johnson
[1908–1973]

Lyndon Baines Johnson, thirty-sixth President of the United States, succeeded to the presidency on November 22, 1963, upon President Kennedy's death by assassination. Johnson started his career in public office in 1937 when he became a Representative in Congress from Texas. He served for several terms and in 1948 was elected Senator from Texas. He was elected Vice President in 1960. In 1964 he won election as President. During his administration Congress enacted important social welfare legislation; but the years were overshadowed by increased involvement in the Vietnam conflict.

On March 31, 1968, President Johnson addressed the nation, dealing with the problem of Vietnam. He called a halt to the bombing of most of North Vietnam. In a surprise statement at the end of the speech, he announced that he would not seek reelection in the 1968 campaign. We give major parts of the address.

ON VIETNAM AND ON THE DECISION
NOT TO SEEK REELECTION

GOOD EVENING, my fellow Americans.

Tonight I want to speak to you of peace in Vietnam and Southeast Asia.

No other question so preoccupies our people. No other dream so absorbs the 250 million human beings who live in that part of the world. No other goal motivates American policy in Southeast Asia.

For years, representatives of our Government and others have traveled the world seeking to find a basis for peace talks.

Since last September they have carried the offer that I made public at San Antonio. And that offer was this:

That the United States would stop its bombardment of North Vietnam when that would lead promptly to productive discussions—and that we would assume that North Vietnam would not take military advantage of our restraint.

Hanoi denounced this offer, both privately and publicly. Even while the search for peace was going on, North Vietnam rushed their preparations for a savage assault on the people, the Government and the allies of South Vietnam.

Their attack—during the Tet holidays—failed to achieve its principal objectives.

It did not collapse the elected Government of South Vietnam or shatter its army—as the Communists had hoped. It did not produce a "general uprising" among the people of the cities, as they had predicted.

The Communists were unable to maintain control of any of the more than 30 cities that they attacked, and they took very heavy casualties.

But they did compel the South Vietnamese and their allies to move certain forces from the countryside into the cities.

They caused widespread disruption and suffering. Their attacks, and the battles that followed, made refugees of half a million human beings.

The Communists may renew their attack any day. They are, it appears, trying to make 1968 the year of decision in South Vietnam—the year that brings, if not final victory or defeat, at least a turning point in the struggle.

This much is clear: If they do mount another round of heavy attacks, they will not succeed in destroying the fighting power of South Vietnam and its allies.

But tragically, this is also clear: Many men—on both sides of the struggle—will be lost. A nation that has already suffered 20 years of warfare will suffer once again. Armies on both sides will take new casualties. And the war will go on.

There is no need for this to be so. There is no need to delay the talks that could bring an end to this long and this bloody war.

Tonight, I renew the offer I made last August: to stop the bombardment of North Vietnam. We ask that talks begin promptly, that they be serious talks on the substance of peace. We assume that during those talks Hanoi will not take advantage of our restraint.

We are prepared to move immediately toward peace through negotiations. So tonight, in the hope that this action will lead to early talks, I am taking the first step to de-escalate the conflict. We are reducing—substantially reducing—the present level of hostilities, and we are doing so unilaterally and at once.

Tonight I have ordered our aircraft and our naval vessels to make no attacks on North Vietnam except in the area north of the demilitarized zone where the continuing enemy build-up directly threatens allied forward positions and where the movement of their troops and supplies are clearly related to that threat.

Even this very limited bombing of the North could come to an early end—if our restraint is matched by restraint in Hanoi. But I cannot in good conscience stop all bombing so long as to do so would immediately and directly endanger the lives of our men and our allies. Whether a complete bombing halt becomes possible in the future will be determined by events.

And tonight I call upon the United Kingdom and I call upon the Soviet Union—as co-chairman of the Geneva conferences and as permanent members of the United Nations Security Council—to do all they can to move from the unilateral act of de-escalation that I have just announced toward genuine peace in Southeast Asia.

The South Vietnamese know that further efforts are going to be required to expand their own armed forces; to move back into the countryside as quickly as possible; to increase their taxes; to select the very best men they have for civil and military responsibility; to achieve a new unity within their constitutional government, and to include in the national effort all those groups who wish to preserve South Vietnam's control over its own destiny.

President Thieu told his people last week, and I quote:

> We must make greater efforts, we must accept more sacrifices, because as I have said many times, this is our country. The existence of our nation is at stake, and this is mainly a Vietnamese responsibility.

On many occasions I have told the American people that we would send to Vietnam those forces that are required to accomplish our mission there. So with that as our guide we have previously authorized a force level of approximately 525,000.

In order that these forces may reach maximum combat effectiveness, the Joint Chiefs of Staff have recommended to me that we should prepare to send during the next five months the support troops totaling approximately 13,500 men.

A portion of these men will be made available from our active forces. The balance will come from reserve component units, which will be called up for service.

Now let me give you my estimate of the chances for peace—the peace that will one day stop the bloodshed in South Vietnam. That will—all the Vietnamese people will be permitted to rebuild and develop their land. That will permit us to turn more fully to our own tasks here at home.

I cannot promise that the initiative that I have announced tonight will be completely successful in achieving peace any more than the 30 others that we have undertaken and agreed to in recent years.

One day, my fellow citizens, there will be peace in Southeast Asia. It will come because the people of Southeast Asia want it—those whose armies are at war tonight; those who, though threatened, have thus far been spared.

Peace will come because Asians were willing to work for it and to sacrifice for it—and to die by the thousands for it.

But let it never be forgotten: peace will come also because America sent her sons to help secure it.

It has not been easy—far from it. During the past four and a half years, it has been my fate and my responsibility to be Commander in Chief. I have lived daily and nightly with the cost of this war. I know the pain that it has inflicted. I know perhaps better than anyone the misgivings it has aroused.

This I believe very deeply. Throughout my entire public career I have followed the personal philosophy that I am a free man, an American, a public servant and a member of my party—in that order—always and only.

For 37 years in the service of our nation, first as a Congressman, as a Senator and as Vice President, and now as your President, I have put the unity of the people first. I have put it ahead of any divisive partisanship. And in these times, as in times before, it is true that a house divided against itself by the spirit of faction, of party, of region, of religion, of race, is a house that cannot stand.

There is division in the American house now. There is divisiveness among us all tonight. And holding the trust that is mine, as President of all the people, I cannot disregard the peril of the progress of the American people and the hope and the prospect of peace for all peoples, so I would ask all Americans whatever their personal interest or concern to guard against divisiveness and all of its ugly consequences.

Fifty-two months and ten days ago, in a moment of tragedy and trauma, the duties of this office fell upon me.

I asked then for your help, and God's, that we might continue America on its course binding up our wounds, healing our history, moving forward in new unity, to clear the American agenda and to keep the American commitment for all of our people.

United we have kept that commitment. And united we have enlarged that commitment. And through all time to come I think America will be a stronger nation, a more just society, a land of greater opportunity and fulfillment because of what we have all done together in these years of unparalleled achievement.

Our reward will come in the life of freedom and peace and hope that our children will enjoy through ages ahead.

What we won when all of our people united just must not now be lost in suspicion and distrust and selfishness and politics among any of our people. And believing this as I do I have concluded that I should not permit the Presidency to become involved in the partisan divisions that are developing in this political year.

With American sons in the fields far away, with America's future under challenge right here at home, with our hopes and the world's hopes for peace in the balance every day, I do not believe that I should devote an hour or a day of my time to any personal partisan causes or to any duties other than the awesome duties of this office—the Presidency of your country.

Accordingly, I shall not seek, and I will not accept, the nomination of my party for another term as your President. But let men everywhere know, however, that a strong and a confident and a vigilant America stands ready tonight to seek an honorable peace; and stands ready tonight to defend an honored cause, whatever the price, whatever the burden, whatever the sacrifice that duty may require.

Thank you for listening. Good night and God bless all of you.

John William Gardner
[1912-   ]

Prominent as a social psychologist, John W. Gardner is widely known
for his book Excellence *(1961) with its challenging subtitle, "Can We*
be Equal and Excellent Too?"
      Mr. Gardner served as Secretary of Health, Education and Welfare
from 1965 to 1968, in the Johnson administration. In March, 1968, he
became chairman of the Urban Coalition, a privately endowed organiza-
tion concerned with the increasingly difficult problems of the cities;
and in September, 1970, he became chairman of Common Cause, an
organization which he founded to involve citizens in making needed
reforms in their government.
      Previously Mr. Gardner had taught for a number of years and had
been President of the Carnegie Corporation. He studied at Stanford
University (A.B., 1935) and at the University of California (Ph.D.,
1938).
      The address which follows was given at Cornell University on June 1,
1968, on the special occasion of Cornell's one hundredth commence-
ment. It is used here with Mr. Gardner's permission.

UNCRITICAL LOVERS, UNLOVING CRITICS

THIS one hundredth commencement is an occasion so rich in history that it
has administered a strong stimulus, perhaps too strong, to my sense of the
past and future. Had it been a milder stimulus, I could have contented
myself with the nostalgia, congratulations, and rosy prognosis traditional to
centennial celebrations. To look back reverently, to applaud present vitality,
to predict an upward path ahead would have been particularly easy in the
case of this great institution—so vital, so full of promise, so worthy of our
admiration.
      But this is not a year in the life of American universities, or in the life of
the nation, that invites such a traditional approach. So I am going to broaden
the focus beyond Cornell and beyond universities to human institutions
generally. I am going to take you on a 600-year tour of history, beginning
some three centuries ago and stretching three centuries into the future. Such
a tour might present some difficulties for a qualified historian, but it is a
mere finger exercise for the practiced commencement speaker.
      In the seventeenth and eighteenth centuries, increasing numbers of people
began to believe that men could determine their own fate, shape their own
institutions, and gain command of the social forces that buffeted them.
Before then, from the beginning, men had believed that all the major
features of their lives were determined by immemorial custom or fate or
the will of God. It was one of the Copernican turns of history that brought

man gradually over two or three centuries to the firm conviction that he could have a hand in shaping his institutions.

No one really knows all the ingredients that went into the change, but we can identify some major elements. One was the emergence with the scientific revolution of a way of thinking that sought objectively identifiable cause-and-effect relationships. People trained in that way of thinking about the physical world were bound to note that the social world, too, had its causes and effects. And with that discovery came, inevitably, the idea that one might manipulate the cause to alter the effect.

At the same time people became less and less inclined to explain their daily lives and institutions in terms of God's will. And that trend has continued to this day. Less and less do men suppose, even those who believe devoutly in a Supreme Being, that God busies himself with the day-to-day microadministration of the world.

While all of this was happening, new modes of transportation and communication were breaking down parochial attitudes all over the world. As men discovered that human institutions and customs varied enormously from one society to the next, it became increasingly difficult to think of one's own institutions as unalterable and increasingly easy to conceive of a society in which men consciously shaped their institutions and customs.

The result is that today any bright high school student can discourse on social forces and institutional change. A few centuries ago, even for learned men, such matters were "given," ordained, not subject to analysis, fixed in the great design of things.

Up to a point the new views were immensely exhilarating. In the writings of our founding fathers, for example, one encounters a mood approaching exaltation as they proceeded to shape a new nation. But more recently another consequence has become apparent: the new views place an enormous —in some instances, an unbearable—burden on the social structures that man has evolved over the centuries. Those structures have become the sole target and receptacle for all man's hope and hostility. He has replaced his fervent prayer to God with a shrill cry of anger against his own institutions. I claim no special insight into the unknowable Deity, but He must be chuckling.

Men can tolerate extraordinary hardship if they think it is an unalterable part of life's travail. But an administered frustration—unsanctioned by religion or custom or deeply rooted values—is more than the spirit can bear. So increasingly men rage at their institutions. All kinds of men rage at all kinds of institutions, here and around the world. Most of them have no clear vision of the kind of world they want to build; they only know they don't want the kind of world they have.

So much for the past and present.

I told you I would take you three centuries into the future. I am able to do this thanks to a Cornell scientist who recently discovered how man may step off the time dimension and visit the past or future at will. You may be surprised you haven't heard about this, but he's finding his capacity to know the future rather profitable. He doesn't want to publicize his findings until he has won a few more horse races.

At any rate he gave me a few pills, and since I'm not interested in horse races, I decided to find out what the future holds in the struggle between man and his institutions. I cannot guarantee the results. I do not offer what follows as a prediction. Perhaps the pill just gave me bad dreams.

The first thing I learned is that in the last third of the twentieth century the rage to demolish succeeded beyond the fondest dreams of the dismantlers. They brought everything tumbling down. Since the hostility to institutions was a product of modern minds, the demolition was most thorough in the most advanced nations.

You will be pleased to know that unlike the fall of Rome, this decline was not followed by hundreds of years of darkness. In fact, there followed less than a century of chaos and disorder. In the latter part of the twenty-first century the rebuilding began. Since chaos is always followed by authoritarianism, this was a period of iron rule, worldwide—a world society rigidly organized and controlled. I don't think I shall tell you what language was spoken.

But tyrannies tend to grow lax, even under futuristic methods of thought control. By the end of the twenty-second century, the sternly disciplined institutions of the world society had grown relatively tolerant, and the old human impulse to be free had begun to reassert itself.

In the new, more permissive atmosphere, men were again allowed to study history, which had been under a ban for two centuries. The effect was electric. To those austere and antiseptic minds, conditioned to the requirements of a technically advanced authoritarianism, the rediscovery of man's history was intoxicating. It generated an intellectual excitement that dominated the whole twenty-third century. Scholars were entranced by the variety of human experience, shocked by the violence and barbarism, saddened by the stupidities, and exalted by the achievements of their forebears. And as they searched that history, excitedly, sadly, lovingly, they returned increasingly to the twentieth century as a moment of curious and critical importance in the long pageant.

All the evidence available to them indicated that the preceding centuries had seen a vast and impressive movement in the direction of institutions that were responsive to the will of men. There were setbacks, to be sure, and trouble and hypocrisy and failures, but over the years the trend was unmistakable. Why then in the late twentieth century did men turn on their institutions and destroy them in a fit of impatience? As one twenty-third-century scholar put it, "Until we answer that question we shall never be sure that we are not preparing the same fate for ourselves."

As they studied the history of the twentieth century, they discovered that human expectations had risen sharply in the middle years of the century. They observed that men came to demand more and more of their institutions and to demand it with greater intransigence. And they noted that the demands for instant performance led to instant disillusionment, for while aspirations leapt ahead, human institutions remained sluggish—less sluggish, to be sure, than at any previous time in history, but still inadequately responsive to human need.

Twenty-third-century scholars agreed on these facts but they disagreed as to the implications. One school of thought said the big mistake had been to let aspirations loose in the first place. Human aspirations, they said, should be kept under tight control. The opposing school of thought argued that human aspirations were a dynamic force that held enormous potential for good. They insisted that the main requirement was to make human institutions less sluggish. The only errors of the mid-twentieth century, they said, was to release aspirations without designing institutions responsive enough to satisfy those aspirations.

After years of debate, the two schools of thought began to come together, and a common doctrine began to emerge. The first thing they agreed upon was that human aspirations *were* capable of contributing enormously to the dynamism of the society and therefore should not be tightly bottled up. But they also agreed that there must be procedural bounds within which the aspirations could express themselves.

Some were quick to point out that in the mid-twentieth century such procedural bounds did exist and functioned quite well, permitting extraordinary scope and variety of dissent until the last third of the century, when the bounds were increasingly rejected and the dissolution of the society began. Back of the rejection was the impatient hostility that late-twentieth-century man felt toward his institutions. Those who consciously sought the destruction of their society were never more than a small minority, but they found it easy to trigger the latent hostility of larger numbers of people. Many, of course, were ignorant of the long, painful evolution of procedures for the expression of dissent, for the protection of individual rights, for the maintenance of that framework of order without which freedom is impossible. Others were not ignorant but very angry. The result was the same.

The second thing twenty-third-century scholars came to agree upon was that if society is going to release aspirations for institutional change—which is precisely what many twentieth-century societies deliberately did—then it had better be sure its institutions are capable of such change. In this respect they found ·the twentieth century sadly deficient.

Most institutions were designed to obstruct change rather than facilitate it. And that is not really surprising. The institutions were, after all, designed by human beings, and most men most of the time do not want the institutions in which they themselves have a vested interest to change. Professors were often cited as an interesting example of this tendency, because they clearly favored innovation in other parts of the society but steadfastly refused to make universities into flexible, adaptive, self-renewing institutions.

There were, of course, a good many people in the twentieth century who did want change, but they were curiously indifferent to the task of redesigning their institutions so that change could be readily accomplished. Many of them were moral zealots who expended their total energy in headlong combat between themselves (whom they believed to be very, very good) and specified others (whom they believed to be very, very bad); and the object of the combat was to do in the bad ones, even if it meant doing in oneself. This led to endless hostilities, especially when those marked for assault had equally strong convictions about their *own* moral superiority. It was particularly difficult when the two groups spoke a different language or were separated by an ocean or thirty years in age.

There were other reformers who were considerably more discriminating and saw that to achieve their ends they *must* change human institutions. But even these often misconceived the fundamental task.

Each such reformer came to his task with a little bundle of desired changes. The society is intolerable, he would assert, because it has these specifiable defects: *a, b, c,* and so on. The implication was that if appropriate reforms *a', b'* and *c'* were carried through and the defects corrected, the society would be wholly satisfactory and the work of the reformer done.

That, as twenty-third-century scholars plainly saw, was a primitive way of viewing social change. The true task, they saw, was to design a society (and institutions) capable of continuous change, continuous renewal, continuous responsiveness. They understood that this was entirely feasible; indeed, they noted that the twentieth century had hit upon a number of partial solutions to the problem of designing self-renewing institutions but had never pursued the task with adequate vigor. (I might add that I, myself, wrote a book on this subject, back in the twentieth century. It was entitled *Self-Renewal.* I won't review its findings here, because I wouldn't want to spoil your enjoyment of the book.)

Because of their failure to design institutions capable of continuous renewal, twentieth-century societies showed astonishing sclerotic streaks. Even in the United States, which was then the most adaptable of all societies, the departments of the federal government were in grave need of renewal; state government was in most places an old attic full of outworn relics; in most cities municipal government was a waxwork of stiffly preserved anachronisms; the system of taxation was a tangle of dysfunctional measures; the courts were crippled by archaic organizational arrangements; the unions, the professions, the universities, the corporations—each had spun its own impenetrable web of vested interests.

Such a society could not respond to challenge. And it did not. But as one twenty-third-century scholar put it, "The reformers couldn't have been less interested in the basic adaptability of the society. That posed tough and complex tasks of institutional redesign that bored them to death. They preferred the joys of combat, of villain hunting. As for the rest of society, it was dozing off in front of the television set."

The twenty-third-century scholars made another exceptionally interesting observation. They pointed out that twentieth-century institutions were caught in a savage crossfire between uncritical lovers and unloving critics. On the one side, those who loved their institutions tended to smother them in an embrace of death, loving their rigidities more than their promise, shielding them from life-giving criticism. On the other side, there arose a breed of critics without love, skilled in demolition but untutored in the arts by which human institutions are nurtured and strengthened and made to flourish. Between the two, the institutions perished.

The twenty-third-century scholars understood that where human institutions were concerned, love without criticism brings stagnation, and criticism without love brings destruction. And they emphasized that the swifter the pace of change, the more lovingly men had to care for and criticize their institutions to keep them intact through the turbulent passages.

In short, men must be discriminating appraisers of their society, knowing coolly and precisely what it is about the society that thwarts or limits them and therefore needs modification. And so must they be discriminating protectors of their institutions, preserving those features that nourish and strengthen them and make them more free. To fit themselves for such tasks, they must be sufficiently serious to study their institutions, sufficiently dedicated to become expert in the art of modifying them.

Having arrived at these judgments, twenty-third-century leaders proceeded to redesign their own society for continuous renewal. Commenting on the debt they owed to the twentieth-century experience, one of them said: "It is not just that we have learned from twentieth-century mistakes. We have learned from twentieth-century insights. For in that troubled time there were men who were saying just what we are saying now. Had they been heeded, the solutions we have reached would have come 300 years earlier. But no one was listening."

Ladies and gentlemen, as I told you earlier, I cannot guarantee the glimpse of the future given me by my friend, the Cornell scientist. Come to think of it, he hasn't been winning his horse races consistently. So perhaps it's not too late to alter history's course.

President Perkins, I bow to this great institution on its hundredth anniversary. May it have from all members of the Cornell family the life-giving criticism and the nurturing, strengthening love that will insure its future.

George Wald
[1906–   ]

Harvard biologist George Wald spoke at the Kresge Auditorium of the Massachusetts Institute of Technology on March 4, 1969, before a group which included many students. The speech was part of the "March 4 Movement" protesting the misuse of science by the government. Dr. Wald is the 1967 Nobel prize winner in physiology and medicine. He discusses the major problems that confront today's generation: the draft, Vietnam, nuclear weapons, the population explosion. We give the address with Dr. Wald's permission in the somewhat shortened form approved by him for inclusion in the New Yorker. (Reprinted by permission; copyright © 1969, the New Yorker Magazine, Inc.)

A GENERATION IN SEARCH OF A FUTURE

ALL OF YOU know that in the last couple of years there has been student unrest, breaking at times into violence, in many parts of the world: in England, Germany, Italy, Spain, Mexico, Japan, and, needless to say, many parts of this country. There has been a great deal of discussion as to what it all means. Perfectly clearly, it means something different in Mexico from what it does in France, and something different in France from what it does in Tokyo, and something different in Tokyo from what it does in this country. Yet, unless we are to assume that students have gone crazy all over the world, or that they have just decided that it's the thing to do, it must have some common meaning.

I don't need to go so far afield to look for that meaning. I am a teacher, and at Harvard I have a class of about three hundred and fifty students— men and women—most of them freshmen and sophomores. Over these past few years, I have felt increasingly that something is terribly wrong—and this year ever so much more than last. Something has gone sour, in teaching and in learning. It's almost as though there were a widespread feeling that education has become irrelevant.

A lecture is much more of a dialogue than many of you probably realize. As you lecture, you keep watching the faces, and information keeps coming back to you all the time. I began to feel, particularly this year, that I was missing much of what was coming back. I tried asking the students, but they didn't or couldn't help me very much.

But I think I know what's the matter. I think that this whole generation of students is beset with a profound uneasiness, and I don't think that they have yet quite defined its source. I think I understand the reasons for their uneasiness even better than they do. What is more, I share their uneasiness.

What's bothering those students? Some of them tell you it's the Vietnam war. I think the Vietnam war is the most shameful episode in the whole of American history. The concept of war crimes is an American invention. We've committed many war crimes in Vietnam—but I'll tell you something interesting about that. We were committing war crimes in World War II, before the Nuremberg trials were held and the principle of war crimes was stated. The saturation bombing of German cities was a war crime. Dropping those atomic bombs on Hiroshima and Nagasaki was a war crime. If we had lost the war, it might have been *our* leaders who had to answer for such actions. I've gone through all that history lately, and I find that there's a gimmick in it. It isn't written out, but I think we established it by precedent. That gimmick is that if one can allege that one is repelling or retaliating for an aggression, after that everything goes.

And, you see, we are living in a world in which all wars are wars of defense. All War Departments are now Defense Departments. This is all part of the doubletalk of our time. The aggressor is always on the other side. I suppose this is why our ex-Secretary of State Dean Rusk went to such pains to insist, as he still insists, that in Vietnam we are repelling an aggression. And if that's what we are doing—so runs the doctrine—everything goes. If the concept of war crimes is ever to mean anything, they will have to be defined as categories of *acts*, regardless of alleged provocation. But that isn't so now.

I think we've lost that war, as a lot of other people think, too. The Vietnamese have a secret weapon. It's their willingness to die beyond our willingness to kill. In effect, they've been saying, You can kill us, but you'll have to kill a lot of us; you may have to kill all of us. And, thank heaven, we are not yet ready to do that.

Yet we have come a long way toward it—far enough to sicken many Americans, far enough to sicken even our fighting men. Far enough so that our national symbols have gone sour. How many of you can sing about "the rocket's red glare, the bombs bursting in air" without thinking, those are *our* bombs and *our* rockets, bursting over South Vietnamese villages? When those words were written, we were a people struggling for freedom against oppression. Now we are supporting open or thinly disguised military dictatorships all over the world, helping them to control and repress peoples struggling for their freedom.

But that Vietnam war, shameful and terrible as it is, seems to me only an immediate incident in a much larger and more stubborn situation.

Part of my trouble with students is that almost all the students I teach were born after World War II. Just after World War II, a series of new and abnormal procedures came into American life. We regarded them at the time as temporary aberrations. We thought we would get back to normal American life someday.

But those procedures have stayed with us now for more than twenty years, and those students of mine have never known anything else. They think those things are normal. They think that we've always had a Pentagon, that we have always had a big Army, and that we have always had a draft. But those are all new things in American life, and I think that they are incompatible with what America meant before.

How many of you realize that just before World War II the entire American Army, including the Air Corps, numbered a hundred and thirty-nine thousand men? Then World War II started, but we weren't yet in it, and, seeing that there was great trouble in the world, we doubled this Army to two hundred and sixty-eight thousand men. Then, in World War II, it got to be eight million. And then World War II came to an end and we prepared to go back to a peacetime Army, somewhat as the American Army had always been before. And, indeed, in 1950—you think about 1950, our international commitments, the Cold War, the Truman Doctrine, and all the rest of it—in 1950, we got down to six hundred thousand men.

Now we have three and a half million men under arms: about six hundred thousand in Vietnam, about three hundred thousand more in "support areas" elsewhere in the Pacific, about two hundred and fifty thousand in Germany. And there are a lot at home. Some months ago, we were told that three hundred thousand National Guardsmen and two hundred thousand reservists—so half a million men—had been specially trained for riot duty in the cities.

I say the Vietnam war is just an immediate incident because as long as we keep that big an Army, it will always find things to do. If the Vietnam war stopped tomorrow, the chances are that with that big a military establishment we would be in another such adventure, abroad or at home, before you knew it.

The thing to do about the draft is not to reform it but to get rid of it.

A peacetime draft is the most un-American thing I know. All the time I was growing up, I was told about oppressive Central European countries and Russia, where young men were forced into the Army, and I was told what they did about it. They chopped off a finger, or shot off a couple of toes, or, better still, if they could manage it, they came to this country. And we understood that, and sympathized, and were glad to welcome them.

Now, by present estimates, from four to six thousand Americans of draft age have left this country for Canada, two or three thousand more have gone to Europe, and it looks as though many more were preparing to emigrate.

A bill to stop the draft was recently introduced in the Senate (S. 503), sponsored by a group of senators that runs the gamut from McGovern and Hatfield to Barry Goldwater. I hope it goes through. But I think that when we get rid of the draft we must also drastically cut back the size of the armed forces.

Yet there is something ever so much bigger and more important than the draft. That bigger thing, of course, is the militarization of our country. Ex-President Eisenhower, in his farewell address, warned us of what he called the military-industrial complex. I am sad to say that we must begin to think of it now as the military-industrial-labor-union complex. What happened under the plea of the Cold War was not alone that we built up the first big peacetime Army in our history but that we institutionalized it. We built, I suppose, the biggest government building in our history to run it, and we institutionalized it.

I don't think we can live with the present military establishment, and its eighty-billion-dollar-a-year budget, and keep America anything like the America we have known in the past. It is corrupting the life of the whole country. It is buying up everything in sight: industries, banks, investors, scientists—and lately it seems also to have bought up the labor unions.

The Defense Department is always broke, but some of the things it does with that eighty billion dollars a year would make Buck Rogers envious. For example, the Rocky Mountain Arsenal, on the outskirts of Denver, was manufacturing a deadly nerve poison on such a scale that there was a problem of waste disposal. Nothing daunted, the people there dug a tunnel two miles deep under Denver, into which they have injected so much poisoned water that, beginning a couple of years ago, Denver has experienced a series of earth tremors of increasing severity. Now there is grave fear of a major earthquake. An interesting debate is in progress as to whether Denver will be safer if that lake of poisoned water is removed or is left in place.

Perhaps you have read also of those six thousand sheep that suddenly died in Skull Valley, Utah, killed by another nerve poison—a strange and, I believe, still unexplained accident, since the nearest testing seems to have been thirty miles away.

As for Vietnam, the expenditure of firepower there has been frightening. Some of you may still remember Khe Sanh, a hamlet just south of the Demilitarized Zone, where a force of United States Marines was beleaguered for a time. During that period, we dropped on the perimeter of Khe Sanh more explosives than fell on Japan throughout World War II, and more than fell on the whole of Europe during the years 1942 and 1943.

One of the officers there was quoted as having said afterwards, "It looks like the world caught smallpox and died."

The only point of government is to safeguard and foster life. Our government has become preoccupied with death, with the business of killing and being killed. So-called defense now absorbs sixty per cent of the national budget, and about twelve per cent of the Gross National Product.

A lively debate is beginning again on whether or not we should deploy antiballistic missiles, the ABM. I don't have to talk about them—everyone else here is doing that. But I should like to mention a curious circumstance. In September, 1967, or about a year and a half ago, we had a meeting of M.I.T. and Harvard people, including experts on these matters, to talk about whether anything could be done to block the Sentinel system—the deployment of ABMs. Everyone present thought them undesirable, but a few of the most knowledgeable persons took what seemed to be the practical view: "Why fight about a dead issue? It has been decided, the funds have been appropriated. Let's go on from there."

Well, fortunately, it's not a dead issue.

An ABM is a nuclear weapon. It takes a nuclear weapon to stop a nuclear weapon. And our concern must be with the whole issue of nuclear weapons.

There is an entire semantics ready to deal with the sort of thing I am about to say. It involves such phrases as "Those are the facts of life." No—these are the facts of death. I don't accept them, and I advise you not to accept them. We are under repeated pressure to accept things that are presented to us as settled—decisions that have been made. Always there is the thought: Let's go on from there. But this time we don't see how to go on. We will have to stick with these issues.

We are told that the United States and Russia, between them, by now have stockpiled nuclear weapons of approximately the explosive power of fifteen tons of TNT for every man, woman, and child on earth. And now it is suggested that we must make more. All very regrettable, of course, but "those are the facts of life." We really would like to disarm, but our new Secretary of Defense has made the ingenious proposal that now is the time to greatly increase our nuclear armaments, so that we can disarm from a position of strength.

I think all of you know there is no adequate defense against massive nuclear attack. It is both easier and cheaper to circumvent any known nuclear-defense system than to provide it. It's all pretty crazy. At the very moment we talk of deploying ABMs, we are also building the MIRV, the weapon to circumvent ABMs.

As far as I know, the most conservative estimates of the number of Americans who would be killed in a major nuclear attack, with everything working as well as can be hoped and all foreseeable precautions taken, run to about fifty million. We have become callous to gruesome statistics, and this seems at first to be only another gruesome statistic. You think, Bang! —and next morning, if you're still there, you read in the newspapers that fifty million people were killed.

But that isn't the way it happens. When we killed close to two hundred thousand people with those first, little, old-fashioned uranium bombs that we dropped on Hiroshima and Nagasaki, about the same number of persons were maimed, blinded, burned, poisoned, and otherwise doomed. A lot of them took a long time to die.

That's the way it would be. Not a bang and a certain number of corpses to bury but a nation filled with millions of helpless, maimed, tortured, and doomed persons, and the survivors huddled with their families in shelters, with guns ready to fight off their neighbours trying to get some uncontaminated food and water.

A few months ago, Senator Richard Russell, of Georgia, ended a speech in the Senate with the words "If we have to start over again with another Adam and Eve, I want them to be Americans; and I want them on this continent and not in Europe." That was a United States senator making a patriotic speech. Well, here is a Nobel laureate who thinks that those words are criminally insane.

How real is the threat of full-scale nuclear war? I have my own very inexpert idea, but, realizing how little I know, and fearful that I may be a little paranoid on this subject, I take every opportunity to ask reputed experts. I asked that question of a distinguished professor of government at Harvard about a month ago. I asked him what sort of odds he would lay on the possibility of full-scale nuclear war within the foreseeable future. "Oh," he said comfortably, "I think I can give you a pretty good answer to that question. I estimate the probability of full-scale nuclear war, provided that the situation remains about as it is now, at two per cent per year." Anybody can do the simple calculation that shows that two per cent per year means that the chance of having that full-scale nuclear war by 1990 is about one in three, and by 2000 it is about fifty-fifty.

I think I know what is bothering the students. I think that what we are up against is a generation that is by no means sure that it has a future.

I am growing old, and my future, so to speak, is already behind me. But there are those students of mine, who are in my mind always; and there are my children, the youngest of them now seven and nine, whose future is infinitely more precious to me than my own. So it isn't just their generation; it's mine, too. We're all in it together.

Are we to have a chance to live? We don't ask for prosperity, or security. Only for a reasonable chance to live, to work out our destiny in peace and decency. Not to go down in history as the apocalyptic generation.

And it isn't only nuclear war. Another overwhelming threat is in the population explosion. That has not yet even begun to come under control. There is every indication that the world population will double before the year 2000, and there is a widespread expectation of famine on an unprecedented scale in many parts of the world. The experts tend to differ only in their estimates of when those famines will begin. Some think by 1980; others think they can be staved off until 1990; very few expect that they will not occur by the year 2000.

That is the problem. Unless we can be surer than we now are that this generation has a future, nothing else matters. It's not good enough to give it tender, loving care, to supply it with breakfast foods, to buy it expensive educations. Those things don't mean anything unless this generation has a future. And we're not sure that it does.

I don't think that there are problems of youth, or student problems. All the real problems I know about are grown-up problems.

Perhaps you will think me altogether absurd, or "academic," or hopelessly innocent—that is, until you think of the alternatives—if I say, as I do to you now: We have to get rid of those nuclear weapons. There is nothing worth having that can be obtained by nuclear war—nothing material or ideological—no tradition that it can defend. It is utterly self-defeating. Those atomic bombs represent an unusable weapon. The only use for an atomic bomb is to keep somebody else from using one. It can give us no protection—only the doubtful satisfaction of retaliation. Nuclear weapons offer us nothing but a balance of terror, and a balance of terror is still terror.

We have to get rid of those atomic weapons, here and everywhere. We cannot live with them.

I think we've reached a point of great decision, not just for our nation, not only for all humanity, but for life upon the earth. I tell my students, with a feeling of pride that I hope they will share, that the carbon, nitrogen, and oxygen that make up ninety-nine per cent of our living substance were cooked in the deep interiors of earlier generations of dying stars. Gathered up from the ends of the universe, over billions of years, eventually they came to form, in part, the substance of our sun, its planets, and ourselves. Three billion years ago, life arose upon the earth. It is the only life in the solar system.

About two million years ago, man appeared. He has become the dominant species on the earth. All other living things, animal and plant, live by his sufferance. He is the custodian of life on earth, and in the solar system. It's a big responsibility.

The thought that we're in competition with Russians or with Chinese is all a mistake, and trivial. We are one species, with a world to win. There's life all over this universe, but the only life in the solar system is on earth, and in the whole universe we are the only men.

Our business is with life, not death. Our challenge is to give what account we can of what becomes of life in the solar system, this corner of the universe that is our home; and, most of all, what becomes of men—all men, of all nations, colors, and creeds. This has become one world, a world for all men. It is only such a world that can now offer us life, and the chance to go on.

Richard Milhous Nixon

[1913–   ]

Richard M. Nixon, thirty-seventh President of the United States, started his career as a lawyer, receiving his law degree from Duke University Law School. He entered the Navy in 1942, serving until the end of the war. Nixon was elected to the House of Representatives in 1946, and in 1950 to the Senate. When Eisenhower was campaigning for the presidency in 1952, he chose Nixon as his running mate. Nixon served as Vice President during the two Eisenhower administrations. In 1968 he was elected President; he was reelected in 1972.

On January 20, 1969, President Nixon gave his first inaugural address. Major portions of it are presented here.

FIRST INAUGURAL ADDRESS

SENATOR DIRKSEN, Mr. Chief Justice, Mr. Vice President, President Johnson, Vice President Humphrey, my fellow Americans and my fellow citizens of the world community:

I ask you to share with me today the majesty of this moment. In the orderly transfer of power, we celebrate the unity that keeps us free.

Each moment in history is a fleeting time, precious and unique. But some stand out as moments of beginning, in which courses are set that shape decades or centuries.

For the first time, because the people of the world want peace and the leaders of the world are afraid of war, the times are on the side of peace.

The greatest honor history can bestow is the title of peacemaker. This honor now beckons America—the chance to help lead the world at last out of the valley of turmoil and on to that high ground of peace that man has dreamed of since the dawn of civilization.

If we succeed, generations to come will say of us now living that we mastered our moment, that we helped make the world safe for mankind.

Standing in this same place a third of a century ago, Franklin Delano Roosevelt addressed the nation ravaged by depression, gripped in fear. He could say in surveying the nation's troubles: "They concern, thank God, only material things."

Our crisis today is in reverse.

We find ourselves rich in goods, but ragged in spirit; reaching with magnificent precision for the moon, but falling into raucous discord on earth.

We are caught in war, wanting peace. We're torn by division, wanting unity. We see around us empty lives, wanting fulfillment. We see tasks that need doing, waiting for hands to do them.

To a crisis of the spirit, we need an answer of the spirit.

And to find that answer, we need only look within ourselves.

As we measure what can be done, we shall promise only what we know we can produce; but as we chart our goals we shall be lifted by our dreams.

No man can be fully free while his neighbor is not. To go forward at all is to go forward together.

This means black and white together, as one nation, not two. The laws have caught up with our conscience. What remains is to give life to what is in the law: to insure at last that as all are born equal in dignity before God, all are born equal in dignity before man.

As we learn to go forward together at home, let us also seek to go forward together with all mankind.

I know that peace does not come through wishing for it—that there is no substitute for days and even years of patient and prolonged diplomacy.

I have taken an oath today in the presence of God and my countrymen: To uphold and defend the Constitution of the United States. And to that oath, I now add this sacred commitment: I shall consecrate my office, my energies and all the wisdom I can summon, to the cause of peace among nations.

Let this message be heard by strong and weak alike.

The peace we seek—the peace we seek to win—is not victory over any other people, but the peace that comes with healing in its wings; with compassion for those who have suffered; with understanding for those who have opposed us; with the opportunity for all the peoples of this earth to choose their own destiny.

Only a few short weeks ago, we shared the glory of man's first sight of the world as God sees it, as a single sphere reflecting light in the darkness.

As Apollo astronauts flew over the moon's gray surface on Christmas Eve, they spoke to us of the beauty of earth and in that voice so clear across the lunar distance we heard them invoke God's blessing on its goodness.

In that moment of surpassing technological triumph, men turned their thoughts toward home and humanity—seeing in that far perspective that man's destiny on earth is not divisible; telling us that however far we reach into the cosmos our destiny lies not in the stars but on earth itself, in our own hands, in our own hearts.

Our destiny offers not the cup of despair, but the chalice of opportunity. So let us seize it, not in fear, but in gladness—and "riders on the earth together," let us go forward, firm in our faith, steadfast in our purpose, cautious of the dangers; but sustained by our confidence in the will of God and the promise of man.

A dramatic event of the Nixon administration was the first landing of men on the moon. The astronauts who took part in this historic journey (the Apollo 11) were Neil Armstrong, Edwin Aldrin, Michael Collins. Neil Armstrong, the first of the astronauts to set foot on the moon, said as he touched its surface, "A small step for man, a giant step for mankind." Edwin Aldrin followed Armstrong. Michael Collins remained in orbit so that he could be rejoined by the other two and they could all make the return trip to earth. The Apollo 11 began its journey into space on July 16, 1969, and came back safely on July 24, 1969.

When the astronauts landed on the moon on July 21, 1969, President Nixon spoke to them over television. Following are his words:

TO THE ASTRONAUTS ON THE MOON

BECAUSE of what you have done, the heavens have become a part of man's world. And as you talk to us from the Sea of Tranquility it requires us to redouble our efforts to bring peace and tranquility to earth.

For one priceless moment in the whole history of man all the people on this earth are truly one—one in their pride in what you have done and one in our prayers that you will return safely to earth.

John Vliet Lindsay
[1921–]

John V. Lindsay was elected mayor of New York City in November, 1965, and reelected in 1969. He received both his B.A. degree and his LL.B. from Yale University. Starting his career as a lawyer, he was elected to Congress in 1957, serving until 1965.

Mayor Lindsay has worked tirelessly to give New York a progressive, vital, and constructive administration; and he has been a leading spokesman for the needs of the cities throughout the country.

Following is the text of Mayor Lindsay's Second Inaugural Address, delivered at City Hall, New York, December 31, 1969.

SECOND INAUGURAL ADDRESS AS MAYOR

JUSTICE [WILLIAM C.] HECHT, Governor Rockefeller, Controller [Abraham D.] Beame, City Council President [Sanford D.] Garelik, Controller [Mario A.] Procaccino, Council President [Francis X.] Smith, members of the City Council and of the Board of Estimate, reverend clergy, fellow New Yorkers.

This is the last day of the decade and we have, all of us, been through much hope and much sorrow. And if we have learned anything from these ten turbulent, unsettling years, we have learned not to assume too much, because assumptions have a way of falling before the merciless assault of facts.

So it is best not to plan on promises and dreams. If we do all we hope to do in the next four years, there will still be too much of crime and poverty, too much of slums and pollution. There will still be a city that often seems determined to frustrate those who love it most.

But this does not mean that we must surrender to the pressures afflicting New York. It means only an understanding that we are all human, we are all fallible. The test for this administration and for this city is whether we have learned, both from mistakes and from the real and vital beginnings that have been made.

We have, I think, all learned that the lifeblood of New York is something more than the grandeur of its skyline and the richness of its commerce and art. The life of the mind has always flourished in New York, and, properly nourished, it always will.

But the future of our city is bound up inseparably in its neighborhoods, in the dozens of communities where the quality of life is set. For, together, these communities set the quality of life for us as a city.

If the Bay Ridge home-owner is uncertain of his neighborhood's future, if the Harlem mother does not know if her child is learning at school, if the Forest Hills family fears to walk the streets at night, if the Morrisania office worker cannot travel home in comfort or even decency, then this city is not working for its citizens.

And it is in these conditions, in these neighborhoods, that this government must make its fights: in strengthening the work against crime, in cleaning the streets and the air and the water, in moving government out of the maze of offices and departments into the life of the neighborhood.

No one man can win these fights. They need the fusion of the city's talents: the dedication of men like the new Controller and the City Council President, Abe Beame and Sandy Garelik, the able men and women of the City Council and the Board of Estimate. Perhaps most important, we need the help of the men and women of our neighborhoods.

We intend to offer them the responsibility of charting the course of their communities. We ask their help. We offer our help.

We learned, too, that the hidden forces of change must be mastered by this government, for the sake of our future. We cannot stand by while the environment becomes a threat to our happiness, to our health and, ultimately, to life itself. We have begun the most committed fight of any City to save our environment. And in the next four years, that fight will be accelerated, because it is vital to our future and because it is right.

And we cannot stand by while men and women are victimized by deception in the marketplace. With inflation cutting into every family's economic strength, our citizens must be protected when they buy the necessities of life. And we are going to make that fight, because it is important to our people and because it is right.

And we will, despite all the setbacks and all of the obstacles, struggle against the vicious cycle of poverty and discrimination. To be condemned to suffering or powerlessness because you are the wrong color or speak the wrong language, or worship the wrong God, or come from the wrong country, is simply unjust. And the fight for justice must and will continue because *it* is right.

These goals cannot be won if we are drained of our own resources, if the energy of this nation is thrown into the work of death abroad instead of the work of life at home, if the city continues as a stepchild of the state. And so the fight for justice from Albany and Washington will continue, because *it* is right.

I know that we have been through a long—sometimes bitter—political campaign. And the differences among us will not disappear. Controversy is part of New York's vitality and none of us would have it any different. But we can at least recognize another loyalty beyond politics, and that is loyalty to this city and to its future—our future.

With that kind of new loyalty, we can accomplish much together, not out of some magic affection for each other, but out of a simple honest recognition that it is the only way to achieve what each of us wants.

It is not easy to live with turmoil and difficulty. At times it is barely endurable. We remain New Yorkers not simply because we live here, but because we know the kind of city this can be at its best.

This faith has strengthened us in times of danger. Today, as we approach a new decade with new uncertainties, that faith sustains us, and if we can work long enough and hard enough, we may yet redeem that faith and have the kind of city that speaks to the best within us.

This is a faith worthy of the greatest of all cities. With your help, we will be worthy of that faith, and of this city. Thank you.

Nikita Sergeyevich Khrushchev

[1894-1971]

Nikita Sergeyevich Khrushchev became Premier of the Union of Soviet Socialist Republics in March, 1958. Previously, from 1933, he had been First Secretary of the Communist Party of the Soviet Union. He had worked with Stalin, but in 1956 at an All Union Party Congress he denounced Stalin and "the cult of the individual" (referring to Stalin's assumption of dictatorial powers rather than continuing the collective leadership). As Premier, Khrushchev in his relations with the rest of the world followed a policy of "peaceful co-existence" in the Cold War. On April 24, 1962, Khrushchev was reelected Premier. However, dissatisfaction with the progress of the country in various parts of the economy, particularly in agriculture, led to his replacement on October 14, 1964, by Alexei Kosygin.

Following are major parts of the address Khrushchev gave on February 24-25, 1956, at a "secret meeting" of the party's Twentieth Congress in Moscow.

THE PERSONALITY CULT AND ITS CONSEQUENCES

COMRADES! In the report of the Central Committee of the party at the twentieth congress, in a number of speeches by delegates to the Congress, as also formerly during the plenary CC/CPSU [Central Committee of the Communist Party of the Soviet Union] sessions, quite a lot has been said about the cult of the individual and about its harmful consequences.

After Stalin's death the Central Committee of the party began to implement a policy of explaining concisely and consistently that it is impermissible and foreign to the spirit of Marxism-Leninism to elevate one person, to transform him into a superman possessing supernatural characteristics akin to those of a god. Such a man supposedly knows everything, sees everything, thinks for everyone, can do anything, is infallible in his behavior.

Such a belief about a man, and specifically about Stalin, was cultivated among us for many years.

At the present we are concerned with a question which has immense importance for the party now and for the future—[we are concerned] with how the cult of the person of Stalin has been gradually growing, the cult which became at a certain specific stage the source of a whole series of exceedingly serious and grave perversions of party principles, of party democracy, of revolutionary legality.

Because of the fact that not all as yet realize fully the practical consequences resulting from the cult of the individual, the great harm caused by the violation of the principle of collective direction of the party, and because of the accumulation of immense and limitless power in the hands of one person, the Central Committee of the party considers it absolutely necessary to make the material pertaining to this matter available to the twentieth congress of the Communist party of the Soviet Union.

In December, 1922, in a letter to the party congress Vladimir Ilyich wrote: "After taking over the position of Secretary General, Comrade Stalin accumulated in his hands immeasurable power and I am not certain whether he will be always able to use this power with the required care."

This letter, a political document of tremendous importance, known in the party history as Lenin's "testament," was distributed among the delegates to the twentieth party congress.

It was precisely during this period (1935–1937–1938) that the practice of mass repression through the Government apparatus was born, first against the enemies of Leninism—Trotskyites, Zinovievites, Bukharinites, long since politically defeated by the party, and subsequently also against many honest Communists, against those party cadres who had borne the heavy load of the Civil War, and the first and most difficult years of industrialization and collectivization, who actively fought against the Trotskyites and the rightists for the Leninist party line.

Stalin originated the concept "enemy of the people." This term automatically rendered it unnecessary that the ideological errors of a man or men engaged in a controversy be proven; this term made possible the use of the most cruel repression, violating all norms of revolutionary legality, against anyone who in any way disagreed with Stalin, against those who were only suspected of hostile intent, against those who had bad reputations in the main, and in actuality, the only proof of guilt used, against all norms of current legal science, was the "confession" of the accused himself; and, as subsequent probing proved, "confessions" were acquired through physical pressures against the accused.

It was determined that of the 139 members and candidates of the party's Central Committee who were elected at the seventeenth congress, ninety-eight persons, i.e., 70 per cent, were arrested and shot (mostly in 1937–38).

The same fate met not only the Central Committee members but also the majority of the delegates to the seventeenth party congress. Of 1,966 delegates with either voting or advisory rights, 1,108 persons were arrested on charges of antirevolutionary crimes, i.e., decidedly more than a majority. This very fact shows how absurd, wild and contrary to common sense were the charges of counter-revolutionary crimes made, as we now see, against a majority of participants at the seventeenth party congress.

After the criminal murder of Sergei M. Kirov, mass repressions and brutal acts of violation of Socialist legality began. On the evening of December 1, 1934, on Stalin's initiative (without the approval of the Political Bureau, which was passed two days later, casually) the secretary of the Presidium of the Central Executive Committee, Abel S. Yenukidze, signed the following directive:

1. Investigative agencies are directed to speed up the cases of those accused of the preparation or execution of acts of terror.

2. Judicial organs are directed not to hold up the execution of death sentences pertaining to crimes of this category in order to consider the possibility of pardon, because the Presidium of the Central Executive Committee of the U.S.S.R. does not consider as possible the receiving of petitions of this sort.

3. The organs of the Commissariat of Internal Affairs are directed to execute the death sentences against criminals of the above-mentioned category immediately after the passage of sentences.

This directive became the basis for mass acts of abuse against Socialist legality. During many of the fabricated court cases the accused were charged with "the preparation" of terroristic acts; this deprived them of any possibility that their cases might be re-examined, even when they stated before the court that their "confessions" were secured by force, and when, in a convincing manner, they disproved the accusations against them.

The majority of the Central Committee members and candidates elected at the seventeenth congress and arrested in 1937–1938 were expelled from the party illegally through the brutal abuse of the party statute, because the question of their expulsion was never studied at the Central Committee Plenum.

Now when the cases of some of these so-called "spies" and "saboteurs" were examined it was found that all their cases were fabricated. Confessions of guilt of many arrested and charged with enemy activity were gained with the help of cruel and inhuman tortures.

Comrade Eikhe was arrested April 29, 1938, on the basis of slanderous materials, without the sanction of the prosecutor of the U.S.S.R., which was finally received fifteen months after the arrest.

Eikhe was forced under torture to sign ahead of time a protocol of his confession prepared by the investigative judges in which he and several other eminent party workers were accused of anti-Soviet activity.

On October 1, 1939, Eikhe sent his declaration to Stalin in which he categorically denied his guilt and asked for an examination of his case. In the declaration he wrote:

There is no more bitter misery than to sit in the jail of a government for which I have always fought.

On February 4 Eikhe was shot. It has been definitely established now that Eikhe's case was fabricated; he has been posthumously rehabilitated.

A large part of these cases are being reviewed now and a great part of them are being voided because they were baseless and falsified. Suffice it to say that from 1954 to the present time the Military Collegium of the Supreme Court has rehabilitated 7,679 persons, many of whom were rehabilitated posthumously.

The power accumulated in the hands of one person, Stalin, led to serious consequences during the great patriotic war.

A cable from our London Embassy dated June 18, 1941, stated:

> As of now Cripps is deeply convinced of the inevitability of armed conflict between Germany and the U.S.S.R. which will begin not later than the middle of June. According to Cripps, the Germans have presently concentrated 147 divisions (including air force and service units) along the Soviet borders.

Despite these particularly grave warnings, the necessary steps were not taken to prepare the country properly for defense and to prevent it from being caught unawares.

When the Fascist armies had actually invaded Soviet territory and military operations began, Moscow issued the order that Stalin, despite evident facts, thought that the war had not yet started, that this was only a provocative action on the part of several undisciplined sections of the German army, and that our reaction might serve as a reason for the Germans to begin the war.

Stalin was very much interested in the assessment of Comrade Zhukov as a military leader. He asked me often for my opinion of Zhukov. I told him then, "I have known Zhukov for a long time; he is a good general and a good military leader."

After the war Stalin began to tell all kinds of nonsense about Zhukov, among others the following, "You praised Zhukov, but he does not deserve it. It is said that before each operation at the front Zhukov used to behave as follows: he used to take a handful of earth, smell it and say, 'We can begin the attack,' or the opposite, 'the planned operation cannot be carried out.'" I stated at that time, "Comrade Stalin, I do not know who invented this, but it is not true."

It is possible that Stalin himself invented these things for the purpose of minimizing the role and military talents of Marshal Zhukov.

All the more monstrous are the acts whose initiator was Stalin and which are rude violations of the basic Leninist principles of the nationality policy of the Soviet State. We refer to the mass deportations from their native places of whole nations, together with all Communists and Komsomols without any exception; this deportation action was not dictated by any military considerations.

The Ukrainians avoided meeting this fate only because there were too many of them and there was no place to which to deport them. Otherwise, he would have deported them also.

Let us also recall the "Affair of the Doctor Plotters." [Animation in the hall.] Actually there was no "affair" outside of the declaration of the woman doctor Timashuk, who was probably influenced or ordered by someone (after all, she was an unofficial collaborator of the organs of state security) to write Stalin a letter in which she declared that doctors were applying supposedly improper methods of medical treatment.

Such a letter was sufficient for Stalin to reach an immediate conclusion that there are doctor-plotters in the Soviet Union. He issued orders to arrest a group of eminent Soviet medical specialists. He personally issued advice on the conduct of the investigation and the method of interrogation of the arrested persons.

Stalin personally called the investigative judge, gave him instructions, advised him on which investigative methods should be used; these methods were simple—beat, beat and, once again, beat.

Comrades: The cult of the individual acquired such monstrous size chiefly because Stalin himself, using all conceivable methods, supported the glorification of his own person. This is supported by numerous facts. One of the most characteristic examples of Stalin's self-glorification and of his lack of even elementary modesty is the edition of his "Short Biography," which was published in 1948.

"Stalin is the worthy continuer of Lenin's work, or, as it is said in our party, Stalin is the Lenin of today." You see how well it is said; not by the nation but by Stalin himself.

Comrades: We must abolish the cult of the individual decisively, once and for all; we must draw the proper conclusions concerning both ideo-logical-theoretical and practical work.

It is necessary for this purpose:

First, in a Bolshevik manner to condemn and to eradicate the cult of the individual as alien to Marxism-Leninism and not consonant with the principles of party leadership and the norms of party life, and to fight inexorably all attempts at bringing back this practice in one form or another.

To return to and actually practice in all our ideological work the most important theses of Marxist-Leninist science about the people as the creator of history and as the creator of all material and spiritual good of humanity, about the decisive role of the Marxist party in the revolutionary fight for the transformation of society, about the victory of communism.

In this connection we will be forced to do much work to examine critically from the Marxist-Leninist viewpoint and to correct the widely spread erroneous views connected with the cult of the individual in the sphere of history, philosophy, economy and of the other sciences, as well as in the literature and the fine arts. It is especially necessary that in the immediate future we compile a serious textbook of the history of our party which will be edited in accordance with scientific Marxist objectivism, a textbook of the history of Soviet society, a book pertaining to the events of the civil war and the great patriotic war.

We are absolutely certain that our party, armed with the historical resolutions of the twentieth congress, will lead the Soviet people along the Leninist path to new successes, to new victories.

Long live the victorious banner of our party—Leninism!

Lord Snow
[1905–1980]

C. P. Snow, English author, is widely known as a novelist. But his training as a physicist gives him an unusual vantage point from which to assess the relationship between the humanities and the sciences. He has effectively expressed concern over the gap between these two cultural areas. Among Snow's chief novels are Strangers and Brothers *(1940),* The Masters *(1951),* The Conscience of the Rich *(1958),* The Affair *(1960), and, separate from the series of which the others are parts,* The Search *(1958). His full name is Charles Percy Snow. He is now Lord Snow.*

He delivered an oration at Birkbeck College, a division of the University of London, on December 12, 1961, in celebration of the college's 138th anniversary, dealing pleasantly and somewhat informally with the theme of the Two Cultures. With Lord Snow's permission and through the courtesy of Birkbeck College we give here major portions of the address.

RECENT THOUGHTS ON THE TWO CULTURES

My Lord and President, Mr. Vice-Chancellor, Master, Your Worships, Ladies and Gentlemen, I am delighted to be here this evening, partly because of my respect for this institution and for the Master, and partly for a more personal reason. In my chequered career I happen to have occupied a fairly large number of jobs, far too many, but I only once in my life applied for one. I did not get it. And that happened to be the job which the Master now occupies! So I thought it would be something of a pleasure, after 22 years, at last to have Birkbeck for a very short time at my mercy.

That, however, is the last good-natured remark I am going to make, for the moral of what I am going to say is, never give a public lecture, and, above all, never give a public lecture before a university audience. If you feel tempted to do so just pay a little attention to what has happened to me.

About three years ago I was invited to give a lecture called the Rede Lecture at my own University of Cambridge. The Rede Lecture has been going on a long time. It was started by a certain Sir Robert Rede about whom history, so far as I know, has nothing else to relate, which, since he died in 1531, is not all that surprising. The Lecture has been going on since 1525. The pay has been going on also at the same rate. Sir Robert Rede, bless his memory, endowed it quite handsomely by the standard of early Tudor lectureships; he endowed it to the extent of 9 gns. a year, which is what one still gets. But most of us are pleased to give it if we are asked, and I remember being quite flattered when the invitation arrived. I thought it was a chance to get rid of certain worries which were on my mind, and then have no more to do with them.

But it did not turn out that way. I remember the occasion moderately vividly. There was not such a large audience as here, because in Cambridge your old friends do not come to listen to you when you give a lecture. They look at you with icy disapproval in King's Parade outside. My chief memory of the evening is in fact that it was an infernally long time before the end of the lecture and the time I got a drink. I expected that that was the end of it, but in fact I have been pestered by this albatross which has been hanging round my neck ever since. Not only in this country, but in most other countries I have run into the subject head on. In America when I want to talk about anything else they always bring me back to this talk on the two cultures. I thought I would take a holiday from it, I went to Moscow, and within twelve hours I was rung up by their best literary critic asking if I would not like to go out to dinner to have a nice talk on—what do you think?—the two cultures. That is more or less the pattern in a great many places, far too many places in the world.

There is one simple lesson I must draw straight away, by the by. That is if you say anything which happens to touch a nerve like this you can be absolutely certain that you have said nothing original. The only possible explanation of saying something which gets excited interest in various different places is, of course, that large numbers of other people have been thinking exactly the same thing and you just happen to be the one character who has put the thought into words. I do impress that on you. There is absolutely nothing original in anything which gets more or less instantaneous interest. I say that with the more feeling, because I happen to have said two or three original things in my life and no one has paid any attention to them yet. But this, which I did happen to say, probably made its way because the time was exactly right.

I said this: it happened by pure chance that I have spent a lot of my life moving at very rapid intervals between scientists and literary persons. This was simply a chance, because I intended to be a writer and I happened to be trained professionally as a scientist and did some scientific reports. Soon it struck me that I was moving between two bodies of persons who represented in every way in which one can use the phrase, two cultures. They were different in a whole range of intellectual attitudes, and often in a whole range of moral attitudes. They were ceasing to communicate in intellectual terms across the gulf. They could, of course, communicate in the ordinary human terms. There is not much difficulty there. But neither of them had much feeling for what the other was doing, and neither had any really serious intellectual understanding of the other.

I pursued this train of thought for a while experimentally, as I happened, for my sins, to have had to interview—one of the jobs I am happy to say I have given up—a very large proportion of the scientists who are now between, I suppose, 25 and 45. During a period of years I interviewed something like 30,000 of these scientists, and of these 30,000 we found that except for the best the great bulk were effectively illiterate in terms of the literary culture. One would ask them—it was a thing I quoted in the original lecture—what do you read? Which seemed to us a fair enough question, but *they* did not think it was, they thought it was a remark in very bad taste. Then we pressed them a little, after all—you must read something sometime. They looked upon one with great resentment. Finally some of the bolder spirits said, "Well, I've tried a bit of Dickens," rather as though Dickens was an immensely esoteric writer, something like Joyce in the less lucid parts of *Finnegans Wake*.

On the other side the position is no better. Coming back discouraged from such interviews I used to tell the result to some of my literary friends, who would immediately assume a shining look of complacency. That would provoke me too. Then I would ask them various questions, one of which has become mildly notorious. I used to ask—"Can you tell me anything about the second law of thermodynamics?" There is no virtue in knowing the dictionary definition of the second law of thermodynamics, but if you know the train of thought which lies behind it then you have some possible hope of understanding the major structure of modern physics. One can go on multiplying examples of this gap, these lapses of communication, indefinitely.

But how do we cope with this problem? Is there any way of coping with the problem? Here I think the answers are quite clear. Yes, we can do something. There is no perfect solution. At the very best we shall only get a partial solution, but it seems to me there for us to try.

The answer to this entire problem, of course, is education. That is the only conceivable answer to making some bridge, some kind of common understanding, some kind of common culture. For people who are of what the Church of England call "mature years" the difficulties are much greater than for younger people, and the difficulties are not symmetrical. It is fairly easy for a member of the scientific culture, if he has got the will, and if we push him a bit, to get a certain acquaintance at least with the spirit, and to some extent with the practice, of the literary culture. That is, all scientists can read, even if they pretend they cannot.

The language of literature, and to a very large extent the language of much of art, is an accessible language which we have to speak because it is our own. But the language of science is more difficult. It is basically a conceptual language, and to pick up a conceptual language after about 20 is pretty hard. Nevertheless I believe with a determined effort a college such as this could teach people who have got scientific insight but not scientific education a great deal which would make them more comfortable and more comprehending in this world where we are now living.

Now to finish with. Some of my friends often say, "Why are you worried about all this? Isn't it in fact something which is inevitable, which is part of a divided, fractionated intellectual world, part of a process which is never going to stop and which is going to go on whatever any of us do?" My answer to that is, first, that I am not prepared to give up without a struggle, and I do not think any of us should be. Secondly, the cause is not as hopeless as they think. But also, and this is much more important, even if I thought it was perfectly hopeless I should go on as long as I could, because I believe for three different reasons that this existence of a division is desperately serious to us all.

First of all there is a harsh administrator's reason why the lack of communication between these cultures is going to be terribly dangerous for everyone. Most of the decisions of absolutely major importance all over the world in the next 20 years are going to have a large scientific content. If those decisions are taken by people without scientific insight, without any scientific experience, then the likelihood is they are going to be unwise and unimaginative decisions. They will be decisions taken simply on paper and on advice, and without any of the comprehension which you really need if you are going to make a decision about anything.

The second reason is that unless we can communicate then both these cultures are going to suffer, the literary one desperately because it needs some of the refreshment and the spring and the optimism and the confidence of science. And I believe too the scientific culture needs indirectly the human wisdom which still exists in parts of the literary culture, and possibly other things which the literary culture can give it. I believe certain parts of that strange connection between molecular biology, the central nervous system, communications, is going to be done better if the scientists have had certain literary training and experience.

But really I should be fooling you and less than honest if I thought that either of those were anything like my main reason. My main reason is nothing like so practical, and it is this: this divide seems to me a symbol of greater divides. I believe that the world is increasingly in danger of becoming split into groups which cannot communicate with each other, which no longer think of each other as members of the same species. These divides can be racial divides, they can be political divides, and here in our own world, our intellectual world, we are seeing the existence of an intellectual divide. If we allow these to happen our world will become a hell. We are members one of another, and anything which we can do, even of this kind, which is immediately to our hands, which allows people to begin to understand each other, is one of the contributions which we must make if we are to remain human.

Charles de Gaulle
[1890–1970]

Charles de Gaulle was President of the French Fifth Republic from 1959 until 1969. He served in World War I and as brigadier general in World War II. Following the occupation of France in 1940, de Gaulle organized the Free French forces in London, and was a leader in the French Resistance movement. In 1945, after the war, he was elected provisional President of the French Fourth Republic, but insufficient support led to his resignation and retirement in 1946. He returned to public office as Premier in 1958, and under a new constitution became President in 1959. On April 28, 1969, de Gaulle resigned as President because his program for constitutional reform was denied. Georges Pompidou was elected the new President.

One of de Gaulle's most notable accomplishments was in working out terms for ending the conflict in Algeria and bringing about Algerian independence on July 3, 1962. Before the signature of the Evian agreements, completing the plans for Algeria's independence, President Charles de Gaulle gave the following address, on June 8, 1962. The address was broadcast over French radio and television.

INDEPENDENCE FOR ALGERIA

In 23 days, the Algerian problem in its substance will be resolved for France. Algeria will determine its own future. Algeria and France will be able to cooperate organically and regularly with each other. The Algerians of European stock will have the necessary guarantees to participate, in full freedom, in full equality and in full brotherhood, in the life of the new Algeria. This is what France will have wanted and obtained.

Yes, in 23 days, the Algerian people, through the self-determination referendum, are going to ratify the Evian agreements, institute independence and sanction cooperation, just as the French people, through the referendum of last April 8, subscribed to it for their part. Thus, over and above all the crises and all the passions, it is through the free decision and reasoned agreement of two peoples that a new phase in their relationships and a new chapter of their history are about to open.

This being so, what role can and must the Frenchmen of Algeria—who have settled there, who love Algeria, who have done so much there already and of whom Algeria has so great a need—what role can and must these French people play in the Algeria of tomorrow? Once again I should like to express the hope that they will play their part fully, as soon as the last bloody mists with which some criminal madmen are still trying to blind them are dispelled. What role also can and must the leaders of the Moslem community play, for the good of their country—whether it be the leaders that are in office or the leaders that are about to take office, and who are certain before long to assume the capital responsibilities in the Algerian republic? What role, finally, must and can France play in the development of a nation to which she is attached by so many ties and which everything commands her to help become free and prosperous? After 132 years of the existence of the problem, which had tragic consequences on several occasions, and after seven years of senseless and grievous fighting, this result will bear the imprint of justice and reason. However, in order to attain this, France has had to overcome severe obstacles.

When, in 1958, we came to grips with the affair, we found—who has been able to forget it?—the powers of the Republic drowned in impotence, a plot of usurpation being formed in Algiers and drawn toward France by the collapse of the State, the nation suddenly finding itself on the brink of civil war. At the same time, the Moslem rebellion, having reached its climax and banking on our domestic crises, declared itself determined to triumph by arms, claimed to be sure of obtaining world support and offered the French community a single choice for its future: "the suitcase or the coffin." But, once the State was on its feet again and the catastrophe avoided—a recovery soon confirmed by the country's adoption of the necessary institutions by an 80 per cent majority of the voters—it was possible, step by step, to bring the affair to its end.

It was necessary that, in Algeria, our Army have control of the battlefield and the frontiers so that no failure could in any way jeopardize the will of France. It was necessary for us to squarely adopt self-determination and cooperation as political goals, while the implementation of the Constantine Plan was making all Algeria realize how essential France's aid was for its life. Thus the rebellion, renouncing its excesses and responding to the wish of the masses, came, little by little, to take the road to peace, to establish contact with us and, finally, to conclude agreements permitting Algeria to express its will with full knowledge of the facts. It was necessary that the international attempts at interference and pressure, which were multiplying endlessly, have no hold over our policy. It was necessary that the successive plots be shattered: the affair of the barricades, the insurrection of April, 1961, and, since then, the desperate acts of terrorist subversion, carried out, alas, by Frenchmen who resort to assassination, theft and blackmail—all uprisings aimed at forcing the hand of the Government, at shaking its foundations, toppling it and hurling France into the abyss.

What had to be done was done. But—as everyone saw—it is because the new institutions enable the State to act—whereas the old ones only hindered it—that the Government can make decisions instead of constantly equivocating and that it stands fast instead of forever tottering and stumbling. Above all, women and men of France, everyone has seen that the loyal confidence which you as a body have bestowed upon me has spurred and sustained me day after day and that this direct agreement between the people and the one who has the responsibility of leading it has become, in modern times, essential to the Republic.

To maintain, in this domain, what has just been tested—such must be our conclusion, once the Algerian question has been settled. In these times that are difficult and dangerous, but filled with hope, how many things, indeed, have to be done that govern our destiny. To pursue our development—in the fields of economy, welfare, population, education, science, technology; to practice cooperation with those States of the world—above all, those of Africa—with which we are linked by virtue of ideals, language, culture, economy and security; to contribute to the advancement of the two billion men who populate the underdeveloped countries; to equip ourselves with defense forces of such a kind that, for anyone, attacking France would mean certain death; to ensure together with our allies the integrity of the free world in the face of the Soviet threat; to help Western Europe build its unity, its prosperity, its strength and its independence; to hasten the day when, perhaps—the totalitarian regime having lost its virulence and lowered its barriers—all the peoples of our continent will meet in an atmosphere of equilibrium, common sense and friendship; in short, to accomplish the mission of France, we must, yes we must, be and freely remain a great and united people.

For the past four years, despite all the storms, this is fundamentally what we have been, as we then decided to be, overwhelmingly and solemnly, by means of universal suffrage. Justice and efficiency have thereby received their due. Women and men of France, we shall, by the same means, at the proper time, have to make sure that, in the future and above and beyond men who pass, the Republic may remain strong, well-ordered and continuous.

Vive la République! Vive la France!

Pope John XXIII
[1881–1963]

Pope John XXIII brought a liberal approach to the Papacy. His calling of an Ecumenical Council, the first in almost a hundred years, made possible the modernizing of many procedures in the Roman Catholic Church and also achieved greatly improved relations with other denominations and other religions.

Pope John XXIII had been born Angelo Giuseppe Roncalli. Becoming a priest in 1904, he later served as Vatican diplomatic representative in various European capitals in turn, acquiring a broad acquaintance with international affairs. He became a cardinal in 1953. In 1958 he was chosen Pope as successor to Pope Pius XII.

His views are most fully expressed in two major encyclicals. Mater et Magistra *(1961) is devoted to his social philosophy; and* Pacem in Terris *(1963) gives his views on the international scene.*

Pope John XXIII opened the Ecumenical Council (the twenty-first) on October 11, 1962. Following are major portions of his address on that occasion.

THE OPENING OF THE ECUMENICAL COUNCIL

THE MOTHER CHURCH rejoices that, by a singular gift of Divine Providence, the longed-for day has finally dawned when, under the auspices of the Virgin Mother of God, whose maternal dignity is commemorated on this feast, the Ecumenical Council Vatican II is being solemnly opened here beside St. Peter's tomb.

In calling this vast assembly of bishops, the latest and humble successor of the Prince of the Apostles who is addressing you intended to assert once again the church's magisterium [teaching power], which is unfailing and endures until the end of time: in order that this magisterium, taking into account the errors, the requirements and the opportunities of our time, might be presented in exceptional form to all men throughout the world.

Ecumenical Councils, whenever they are assembled, are a solemn celebration of the union of Christ and his church, and therefore they lead to the universal radiation of truth, to the proper guidance of individual, domestic and social life, to the strengthening of spiritual energies, in perennial uplift toward real and everlasting good.

There have elapsed three years of laborious preparation, during which a wide and profound examination was made regarding modern conditions of faith and religious practice, and of Christian and especially Catholic vitality. These years have seemed to us a first sign, an initial gift of celestial grace.

Illuminated by the light of this Council, the church, we confidently trust, will become greater in spiritual riches, and, gaining the strength of new energies therefrom, she will look to the future without fear. In fact, by bringing herself up to date where required, and by the wise organization of mutual cooperation, the church will make men, families and peoples really turn their minds to heavenly things.

The greatest concern of the Ecumenical Council is this: that the sacred deposit of Christian doctrine should be guarded and taught more efficaciously. That doctrine embraces the whole of man, composed as he is of body and soul, and, since he is a pilgrim on this earth, commands him to tend always toward heaven.

This demonstrates how our mortal life is to be ordered, in such a way as to fulfill our duties as citizens of earth and of heaven, and thus to attain the aim of life as established by God. That is, today all men, whether taken singly or as united in society, have the duty of tending ceaselessly, during their lifetimes, toward the attainment of heavenly things, and to use only for this purpose the earthly goods, the employment of which must not prejudice their eternal happiness.

The Lord has said: "Seek first the kingdom of God and his justice." The word "first" expresses the direction in which our thoughts and energies must move. We must not, however, neglect the other words of this exhortation of our Lord, namely: "And all these things shall be given you besides."

The salient point of this Council is not, therefore, a discussion of one article or another of the fundamental doctrine of the church, which has repeatedly been taught by the fathers and the ancient and modern theologians, and which is presumed to be well-known and familiar to all.

For this a Council was not necessary. But from the renewed, serene and tranquil adherence to all the teaching of the church in its entirety and preciseness, as it still stands resplendent in the acts of the Councils of Trent and Vatican I, the Christian, Catholic and apostolic spirit of the whole world expects a step forward toward a doctrinal penetration and a formation of consciences, in faithful and perfect conformity with the authentic doctrine, which, however, should be studied and expounded through the methods of research and through the literary forms of modern thought.

We might say that heaven and earth are united in the celebration of the Council: the saints of heaven, to protect our work, the faithful of the earth, continuing in prayer to the Lord, and you, seconding the inspiration of the Holy Spirit, in order that the work of all may correspond to the modern expectations and needs of the various peoples of the world. This requires of you serenity of mind, brotherly concord, moderation in proposals, dignity in discussion and wisdom of deliberation.

God grant that your labors and your work, to which look the eyes of all peoples and also the hopes of the entire world, may abundantly fulfill the aspirations of all.

Pope Paul VI
[1897–1978]

Pope Paul VI was elected Pope in 1963 succeeding Pope John XXIII. In many fields he strongly supports the liberal views of his predecessor. He continued the work of the Ecumenical Council, which achieved a large number of the goals that had been set for it. Pope Paul VI also broke precedent by making important plane trips from Rome to far places: to the Middle East, to India, and to the United States; and then later to each of the other continents of the world.

Pope Paul VI was born Giovanni Battista Montini. In 1920 he became a priest, engaging in scholarly work and in the Vatican diplomatic service. In 1958 he became a cardinal.

During Pope Paul VI's visit to New York in 1965, he addressed the United Nations, stating eloquently his conviction about world peace, using the phrase "No more war." We give major portions of this speech delivered on October 4, 1965.

NO MORE WAR

As WE BEGIN our address to this audience, which is unique in the world, we wish to express our profound gratitude to U Thant, your Secretary General, for the invitation which he extended to us to visit the United Nations, on the occasion of the twentieth anniversary of the foundation of this world institution for peace and for collaboration between the peoples of the entire earth.

In addition to our personal greetings, we bring you those of the Second Vatican Ecumenical Council now meeting in Rome and represented here by the eminent cardinals who accompany us.

In their name and in our own, to each and every one of you, honor and greeting.

This encounter, as you all understand, is of a twofold nature: It is marked both with simplicity and with greatness. With simplicity because you have before you a man like you, your brother, and even one of the smallest, among you who represent sovereign states, for he is vested, if you wish to think of him thus, with only a minuscule and almost symbolic temporal sovereignty, only as much as is necessary to leave him free to exercise his spiritual mission and to assure those who deal with him that he is independent of every other sovereignty of this world. He has no temporal power, nor any ambition to compete with you. In fact, we have nothing to ask for, no question to raise. We have at most a desire to express and a permission to request: namely, that of serving you in so far as lies within our competence, with disinterest, humility and love.

That is our first declaration. As you can see, it is so simple that it may seem insignificant to this Assembly, which is accustomed to deal with most important and most difficult matters.

Allow us to tell you that we have a message for you all, a happy message, to deliver to each one of you.

We might call our message, first of all, a solemn and moral ratification of this lofty institution. This message comes from our historical experience. As "an expert in humanity," we bring to this organization the suffrage of our recent predecessors, that of the entire Catholic episcopate and our own, convinced as we are that this organization represents the obligatory path of modern civilization and of world peace.

You mark a stage in the development of mankind: from now on retreat is impossible, progress essential.

To the plurality of states, which can no longer ignore one another, you offer an extremely simple and fruitful formula of coexistence.

This in itself is a great service to the cause of humanity, namely, to define clearly and to honor the national subjects of the world community, and to confirm their juridical status, which entitles them to be recognized and respected by all and from which there may derive an orderly and stable system of international life.

Your charter goes further than this, and our message advances with it. You exist and operate to unite the nations, to bind states together. Let us use this formula: To bring the one together with the other. You are an association. You are a bridge between peoples. You are a network of relations between states. We would almost say that your chief characteristic is a reflection, as it were, in the temporal field of what our Catholic church aspires to be in the spiritual field: unique and universal.

The logic of this wish, which might be considered to pertain to the very structure of your organization, leads us to complete it with other formulas. Thus, let no one, as a member of your union, be superior to the others: Never one above the other, this is the formula of equality.

And now our message reaches its highest point. Negatively, at first. You are expecting us to utter this sentence, and we are well aware of its gravity and solemnity: Never one against the other, never again, never more. Was it not principally for this purpose that the United Nations arose: Against war, in favor of peace? Listen to the lucid words of a great man, the late John Kennedy, who declared four years ago: "Mankind must put an end to war, or war will put an end to mankind." Many words are not needed to proclaim this loftiest aim of your institution. It suffices to remember that the blood of millions of men, that numberless and unheard-of sufferings, useless slaughter and frightful ruin, are the sanction of the pact which unites you, with an oath which must change the future history of the world: No more war, never again war. Peace, it is peace which must guide the destinies of peoples and of all mankind.

PART VI
SURVEY OF SPEECHES BY BLACK AMERICANS

Compiled by Philip S. Foner

Henry Highland Garnet
[1815–1881]

Born a slave in Maryland, Henry Highland Garnet escaped with his parents in 1824 and settled in the North. Educated as a teacher and minister, he became the pastor of a Presbyterian church in Troy, New York. In August, 1843, he attended the National Negro Convention in Buffalo, New York, and at that gathering delivered a militant speech entitled "An Address to the Slaves of the United States," which attracted national attention, and which failed by one vote of being adopted as the sentiment of the convention. Following is part of the speech.

AN ADDRESS TO THE SLAVES OF THE UNITED STATES OF AMERICA

BRETHREN AND FELLOW CITIZENS: Your brethren of the North, East, and West have been accustomed to meet together in National Conventions, to sympathize with each other, and to weep over your unhappy condition. In these meetings we have addressed all classes of the free, but we have never, until this time, sent a word of consolation and advice to you. We have been contented in sitting still and mourning over your sorrows, earnestly hoping that before this day your sacred liberties would have been restored. But, we have hoped in vain. Years have rolled on, and tens of thousands have been borne on streams of blood and tears to the shores of eternity. While you have been oppressed, we have also been partakers with you; nor can we be free while you are enslaved. We, therefore, write to you as being bound with you.

Many of you are bound to us, not only by the ties of a common humanity, but we are connected by the more tender relations of parents, wives, husbands, and sisters, and friends. As such we most affectionately address you.

Slavery has fixed a deep gulf between you and us, and while it shuts out from you the relief and consolation which your friends would willingly render, it afflicts and persecutes you with a fierceness which we might not expect to see in the fiends of hell. But still the Almighty Father of mercies has left us a glimmering ray of hope, which shines out like a lone star in a cloudy sky. Mankind are becoming wiser, and better—the oppressor's power is fading, and you, every day, are becoming better informed, and more numerous. Your grievances, brethren, are many. We shall not attempt, in this short address, to present to the world all the dark catalogue of the nation's sins, which have been committed upon an innocent people. Nor is it indeed necessary, for you feel them from day to day, and all the civilized world looks upon them with amazement.

Two hundred and twenty-seven years ago the first of our injured race were brought to the shores of America. They came not with glad spirits to select their homes in the New World. They came not with their own consent, to find an unmolested enjoyment of the blessings of this fruitful soil. The first dealings they had with men calling themselves Christians exhibited to them the worst features of corrupt and sordid hearts: and convinced them that no cruelty is too great, no villainy and no robbery too abhorrent for even enlightened men to perform, when influenced by avarice and lust. Neither did they come flying upon the wings of Liberty to a land of freedom. But they came with broken hearts, from their beloved native land, and were doomed to unrequited toil and deep degradation. Nor did the evil of their bondage end at their emancipation by death. Succeeding generations inherited their chains, and millions have come from eternity into time, and have returned again to the world of spirits, cursed and ruined by American slavery.

The propagators of the system, or their immediate successors, very soon discovered its growing evil, and its tremendous wickedness, and secret promises were made to destroy it. The gross inconsistency of a people holding slaves, who had themselves "ferried o'er the wave" for freedom's sake, was too apparent to be entirely overlooked. The voice of Freedom cried, "Emancipate your slaves." Humanity supplicated with tears for the deliverance of the children of Africa. Wisdom urged her solemn plea. The bleeding captive pled his innocence, and pointed to Christianity who stood weeping at the cross. Jehovah frowned upon the nefarious institution, and thunderbolts, red with vengeance, struggled to leap forth to blast the guilty wretches who maintained it. But all was vain. Slavery had stretched its dark wings of death over the land, the Church stood silently by—the priests prophesied falsely, and the people loved to have it so. Its throne is established, and now it reigns triumphant.

Nearly three millions of your fellow-citizens are prohibited by law and public opinion (which in this country is stronger than law) from reading the Book of Life. Your intellect has been destroyed as much as possible, and every ray of light they have attempted to shut out from your minds. The oppressors themselves have become involved in the ruin. They have become weak, sensual, and rapacious—they have cursed you—they have cursed themselves—they have cursed the earth which they have trod.

The colonies threw the blame upon England. They said that the mother country entailed the evil upon them, and they would rid themselves of it if they could. The world thought they were sincere, and the philanthropic pitied them. But time soon tested their sincerity. In a few years the colonists grew strong, and severed themselves from the British Government. Their independence was declared, and they took their station among the sovereign powers of the earth. The declaration was a glorious document. Sages admired it, and the patriotic of every nation reverenced the God-like sentiments which it contained. When the power of Government returned to their hands, did they emancipate the slaves? No; they rather added new links to our chains. Were they ignorant of the principles of liberty? Certainly they were not. The sentiments of their revolutionary orators fell in burning eloquence upon their hearts, and with one voice they cried, *Liberty or death*.

Oh, what a sentence was that! It ran from soul to soul like electric fire, and nerved the arms of thousands to fight in the holy cause of Freedom. Among the diversity of opinions that are entertained in regard to physical resistance, there are but a few found to gainsay the stern declaration. We are among those who do not.

Slavery! How much misery is comprehended in that single word. What mind is there that does not shrink from its direful effects? Unless the image of God be obliterated from the soul, all men cherish the love of liberty. The nice discerning political economist does not regard the sacred right more than the untutored African who roams in the wilds of Congo. Nor has the one more right to the full enjoyment of his freedom than the other. In every man's mind the good seeds of liberty are planted, and he who brings his fellow down so low, as to make him contented with a condition of slavery, commits the highest crime against God and man. Brethren, your oppressors aim to do this. They endeavor to make you as much like brutes as possible. When they have blinded the eyes of your mind—when they have embittered the sweet waters of life—when they have shut out the light which shines from the word of God—then, and not till then, has American slavery done its perfect work.

To such degradation it is sinful in the extreme for you to make voluntary submission. The divine commandments you are in duty bound to reverence and obey. If you do not obey them, you will surely meet with the displeasure of the Almighty. He requires you to love Him supremely, and your neighbor as yourself—to keep the Sabbath day holy—to search the Scriptures—and bring up your children with respect for His laws, and to worship no other God but Him. But slavery sets all these at nought, and hurls defiance in the face of Jehovah. The forlorn condition in which you are placed does not destroy your obligation to God. You are not certain of heaven, because you allow yourselves to remain in a state of slavery, where you cannot obey the commandments of the Sovereign of the universe. If the ignorance of slavery is a passport to heaven, then it is a blessing, and no curse, and you should rather desire its perpetuity than its abolition. God will not receive slavery, or ignorance, nor any other state of mind, for love and obedience to Him. Your condition does not absolve you from moral obligation. The diabolical injustice by which your liberties are cloven down, *neither God nor angels, or just men, command you to suffer for a single moment. Therefore it is your solemn and imperative duty to use every means, both moral, intellectual, and physical, that promises success.* If a band of heathen men should attempt to enslave a race of Christians, and to place their children under the influence of some false religion, surely Heaven would frown upon the men who would not resist such aggression, even to death. If, on the other hand, a band of Christians should attempt to enslave a race of heathen men, and to entail slavery upon them, and to keep them in heathenism in the midst of Christianity, the God of heaven would smile upon every effort which the injured might make to disenthrall themselves.

Brethren, it is as wrong for your lordly oppressors to keep you in slavery as it was for the man thief to steal our ancestors from the coast of Africa.

You should therefore now use the same manner of resistance as would have been just in our ancestors when the bloody footprints of the first remorseless soul-thief was placed upon the shores of our fatherland. The humblest peasant is as free in the sight of God as the proudest monarch that ever swayed a scepter. Liberty is a spirit sent out from God, and like its great Author, is no respecter of persons.

Brethren, the time has come when you must act for yourselves. It is an old and true saying that, "if hereditary bondmen would be free, they must themselves strike the blow." You can plead your own cause, and do the work of emancipation better than any others. The nations of the Old World are moving in the great cause of universal freedom, and some of them at least will, ere long, do you justice. The combined powers of Europe have placed their broad seal of disapprobation upon the African slave-trade. But in the slaveholding parts of the United States the trade is as brisk as ever. They buy and sell you as though you were brute beasts. The North has done much—her opinion of slavery in the abstract is known. But in regard to the South, we adopt the opinion of the *New York Evangelist*—"We have advanced so far, that the cause apparently waits for a more effectual door to be thrown open than has been yet." We are about to point you to that more effectual door. Look around you, and behold the bosoms of your loving wives heaving with untold agonies! Hear the cries of your poor children! Remember the stripes your father bore. Think of the torture and disgrace of your noble mothers. Think of your wretched sisters, loving virtue and purity, as they are driven into concubinage and are exposed to the unbridled lusts of incarnate devils. Think of the undying glory that hangs around the ancient name of Africa—and forget not that you are native-born citizens, and as such you are justly entitled to all the rights that are granted to the freest. Think how many tears you have poured out upon the soil which you have cultivated with unrequited toil and enriched with your blood; and then go to your lordly enslavers and tell them plainly, that you *are determined to be free*. Appeal to their sense of justice, and tell them that they have no more right to oppress you than you have to enslave them. Entreat them to remove the grievous burdens which they have imposed upon you, and to remunerate you for your labor. Promise them renewed diligence in the cultivation of the soil, if they will render to you an equivalent for your services. Point them to the increase of happiness and prosperity in the British West Indies since the Act of Emancipation. Tell them in language which they cannot misunderstand of the exceeding sinfulness of slavery, and of a future judgment, and of the righteous retributions of an indignant God. Inform them that all you desire is *Freedom*, and that nothing else will suffice. Do this, and forever after cease to toil for the heartless tyrants, who give you no other reward but stripes and abuse. If they then commence work of death, they, and not you, will be responsible for the consequences. You had far better all die—*die immediately*, than live slaves, and entail your wretchedness upon your posterity. If you would be free in this generation, here is your only hope. However much you and all of us may desire it, there is not much hope of redemption without the shedding of blood. If you must bleed, let it come at once—rather *die freemen than live to be the slaves.* It is impossible, like the children of Israel, to make a grand exodus from the land of bondage. The Pharaohs are on both sides of the blood-red waters! You cannot move *en masse* to the dominions of the British Queen —nor can you pass through Florida and overrun Texas, and at last find peace in Mexico. The propagators of American slavery are spending their blood and treasure that they may plant the black flag in the heart of Mexico and riot in the halls of the Montezumas. In language of the Reverend Robert Hall, when addressing the volunteers of Bristol, who were rushing forth to repel the invasion of Napoleon, who threatened to lay waste the fair homes of England, "Religion is too much interested in your behalf not to shed over you her most gracious influences."

Frederick Douglass
[1817–1895]

Frederick Douglass, the foremost Negro leader in nineteenth-century America, was born a slave on the Eastern Shore of Maryland. Upon his escape to the North in 1838, he dedicated his energies to the destruction of the system of slavery and rapidly became the outstanding Black Abolitionist. During and after the Civil War, he played a distinguished role as leader of and spokesman for his people. He ranks with the greatest of nineteenth-century orators. Below are parts of his most famous speeches.

In 1847, Douglass moved to Rochester, New York, where he began publication of his newspaper, The North Star. *He was requested to address the citizens of Rochester on the Fourth of July celebration in 1852. The speech was delivered under the title, "The Meaning of July Fourth for the Negro."*

THE MEANING OF JULY FOURTH FOR THE NEGRO

FELLOW CITIZENS: Pardon me, and allow me to ask, why am I called upon to speak here today? What have I or those I represent to do with your national independence? Are the great principles of political freedom and of natural justice, embodied in that Declaration of Independence, extended to us? And am I, therefore, called upon to bring our humble offering to the national altar, and to confess the benefits, and express devout gratitude for the blessings resulting from your independence to us?

Would to God, both for your sakes and ours, that an affirmative answer could be truthfully returned to these questions. Then would my task be light, and my burden easy and delightful. For who is there so cold that a nation's sympathy could not warm him? Who so obdurate and dead to the claims of gratitude, that would not thankfully acknowledge such priceless benefits? Who so stolid and selfish that would not give his voice to swell the hallelujahs of a nation's jubilee, when the chains of servitude had been torn from his limbs? I am not that man. In a case like that, the dumb might eloquently speak, and the "lame man leap as an hart."

But such is not the state of the case. I say it with a sad sense of disparity between us. I am not included within the pale of this glorious anniversary! Your high independence only reveals the immeasurable distance between us. The blessings in which you this day rejoice are not enjoyed in common. The rich inheritance of justice, liberty, prosperity, and independence bequeathed by your fathers is shared by you, not by me. The sunlight that brought life and healing to you has brought stripes and death to me. This Fourth of July is *yours*, not *mine*. *You* may rejoice, *I* must mourn. To drag a man in fetters into the grand illuminated temple of liberty, and call upon him to join you in joyous anthems, were inhuman mockery and sacrilegious irony. Do you mean, citizens, to mock me, by asking me to speak today? If so, there is a parallel to your conduct. And let me warn you, that it is dangerous to copy the example of a nation whose crimes, towering up to heaven, were thrown down by the breath of the Almighty, burying that nation in irrecoverable ruin. I can today take up the lament of a peeled and woe-smitten people.

"By the rivers of Babylon, there we sat down. Yes! We wept when we remembered Zion. We hanged our harps upon the willows in the midst thereof. For there they that carried us away captive, required of us a song; and they who wasted us, required of us mirth, saying, Sing us one of the songs of Zion. How can we sing the Lord's song in a strange land? If I forget thee, O Jerusalem, let my right hand forget her cunning. If I do not remember thee, let my tongue cleave to the roof of my mouth."

Fellow citizens, above your national, tumultuous joy, I hear the mournful wail of millions, whose chains, heavy and grievous yesterday, are today rendered more intolerable by the jubilant shouts that reach them. If I do forget, if I do not remember those bleeding children of sorrow this day, "may my right hand forget her cunning, and may my tongue cleave to the roof of my mouth!" To forget them, to pass lightly over their wrongs, and to chime in with the popular theme, would be treason most scandalous and shocking, and would make me a reproach before God and the world. My subject, then, fellow citizens, is "American Slavery." I shall see this day and its popular characteristics from the slave's point of view. Standing here, identified with the American bondman, making his wrongs mine, I do not hesitate to declare, with all my soul, that the character and conduct of this nation never looked blacker to me than on this Fourth of July. Whether we turn to the declarations of the past, or to the professions of the present, the conduct of the nation seems equally hideous and revolting. America is false to the past, false to the present, and solemnly binds herself to be false to the future. Standing with God and the crushed and bleeding slave on this occasion, I will, in the name of humanity, which is outraged, in the name of liberty, which is fettered, in the name of the Constitution and the Bible, which are disregarded and trampled upon, dare to call in question and to denounce, with all the emphasis I can command, everything that serves to perpetuate slavery—the great sin and shame of America! "I will not equivocate; I will not excuse"; I will use the severest language I can command, and yet not one word shall escape me that any man, whose judgment is not blinded by prejudice, or who is not at heart a slave-holder, shall not confess to be right and just.

But I fancy I hear some of my audience say it is just in this circumstance that you and your brother Abolitionists fail to make a favorable impression on the public mind. Would you argue more and denounce less, would you persuade more and rebuke less, your cause would be much more likely to succeed. But, I submit, where all is plain there is nothing to be argued. What point in the anti-slavery creed would you have me argue? On what branch of the subject do the people of this country need light? Must I undertake to prove that the slave is a man? That point is conceded already. Nobody doubts it. The slave-holders themselves acknowledge it in the enactment of laws for their government. They acknowledge it when they punish disobedience on the part of the slave. There are seventy-two crimes in the State of Virginia, which, if committed by a black man (no matter how ignorant he be), subject him to the punishment of death; while only two of these same crimes will subject a white man to like punishment. What is this but the acknowledgment that the slave is a moral, intellectual, and responsible being? The manhood of the slave is conceded. It is admitted in the fact that Southern statute-books are covered with enactments, forbidding, under severe fines and penalties, the teaching of the slave to read and write. When you can point to any such laws in reference to the beasts of the field, then I may consent to argue the manhood of the slave. When the dogs in your streets, when the fowls of the air, when the cattle on your hills, when the fish of the sea, and the reptiles that crawl, shall be unable to distinguish the slave from a brute, then I will argue with you that the slave is a man!

For the present it is enough to affirm the equal manhood of the Negro race. Is it not astonishing that, while we are plowing, planting, and reaping, using all kinds of mechanical tools, erecting houses, constructing bridges, building ships, working in metals of brass, iron, copper, silver, and gold; that while we are reading, writing, and cyphering, acting as clerks, merchants, and secretaries, having among us lawyers, doctors, ministers, poets, authors, editors, orators, and teachers; that while we are engaged in all the enterprises common to other men—digging gold in California, capturing the whale in the Pacific, feeding sheep and cattle on the hillside, living, moving, acting, thinking, planning, living in families as husbands, wives, and children, and above all, confessing and worshipping the Christian God, and looking hopefully for life and immortality beyond the grave—we are called upon to prove that we are men?

Would you have me argue that man is entitled to liberty? That he is the rightful owner of his own body? You have already declared it. Must I argue the wrongfulness of slavery? Is that a question for republicans? Is it to be settled by the rules of logic and argumentation, as a matter beset with great difficulty, involving a doubtful application of the principle of justice, hard to understand? How should I look today in the presence of Americans, dividing and subdividing a discourse, to show that men have a natural right to freedom, speaking of it relatively and positively, negatively and affirmatively? To do so would be to make myself ridiculous, and to offer an insult to your understanding. There is not a man beneath the canopy of heaven who does not know that slavery is wrong *for him*.

What! Am I to argue that it is wrong to make men brutes, to rob them of their liberty, to work them without wages, to keep them ignorant of their relations to their fellow men, to beat them with sticks, to flay their flesh with the lash, to load their limbs with irons, to hunt them with dogs, to sell them at auction, to sunder their families, to knock out their teeth, to burn their flesh, to starve them into obedience and submission to their masters? Must I argue that a system thus marked with blood and stained with pollution is wrong? No; I will not. I have better employment for my time and strength than such arguments would imply.

What, then, remains to be argued? Is it that slavery is not divine; that God did not establish it; that our doctors of divinity are mistaken? There is blasphemy in the thought. That which is inhuman cannot be divine. Who can reason on such a proposition? They that can, may; I cannot. The time for such argument is past.

At a time like this, scorching irony, not convincing argument, is needed. Oh! had I the ability, and could I reach the nation's ear, I would today pour out a fiery stream of biting ridicule, blasting reproach, withering sarcasm, and stern rebuke. For it is not light that is needed, but fire; it is not the gentle shower, but thunder. We need the storm, the whirlwind, and the earthquake. The feeling of the nation must be quickened; the conscience of the nation must be roused; the propriety of the nation must be startled; the hypocrisy of the nation must be exposed; and its crimes against God and man must be denounced.

What to the American slave is your Fourth of July? I answer, a day that reveals to him more than all other days of the year, the gross injustice and cruelty to which he is the constant victim. To him your celebration is a sham; your boasted liberty an unholy license; your national greatness, swelling vanity; your sounds of rejoicing are empty and heartless; your denunciation of tyrants, brass-fronted impudence; your shouts of liberty and equality, hollow mockery; your prayers and hymns, your sermons and thanksgivings, with all your religious parade and solemnity, are to him mere bombast, fraud, deception, impiety, and hypocrisy—a thin veil to cover up crimes which would disgrace a nation of savages. There is not a nation of the earth guilty of practices more shocking and bloody than are the people of these United States at this very hour.

Go where you may, search where you will, roam through all the monarchies and despotisms of the Old World, travel through South America, search out every abuse and when you have found the last, lay your facts by the side of the every-day practices of this nation, and you will say with me that, for revolting barbarity and shameless hypocrisy, America reigns without a rival.

*On April 14, 1876, the anniversary of Abraham Lincoln's assassina-
tion and of the emancipation of the slaves in the District of Columbia,
the freedmen's memorial monument to Lincoln was unveiled in Washington. By a joint resolution Congress had declared the day a holiday.
President Grant and his cabinet members, Supreme Court Justices, and
many Senators and Congressmen were present when Douglass delivered
the main address, "Oration in Memory of Abraham Lincoln."*

ORATION IN MEMORY OF ABRAHAM LINCOLN

Fellow-citizens, in what we have said and done today, and in what we may
say and do hereafter, we disclaim everything like arrogance and assumption.
We claim for ourselves no superior devotion to the character, history, and
memory of the illustrious name whose monument we have here dedicated
today. We fully comprehend the relation of Abraham Lincoln both to ourselves and to the white people of the United States. Truth is proper and
beautiful at all times and in all places, and it is never more proper and
beautiful in any case than when speaking of a great public man whose
example is likely to be commended for honor and imitation long after his
departure to the solemn shades, the silent continents of eternity. It must be
admitted, truth compels me to admit, even here in the presence of the monument we have erected to his memory, Abraham Lincoln was not, in the
fullest sense of the word, either our man or our model. In his interests, in
his associations, in his habits of thought, and in his prejudices, he was a
white man.

He was preëminently the white man's President, entirely devoted to
the welfare of white men. He was ready and willing at any time during
the first years of his administration to deny, postpone, and sacrifice the
rights of humanity in the colored people to promote the welfare of the
white people of this country. In all his education and feeling he was an
American of the Americans. He came into the Presidential chair upon
one principle alone, namely, opposition to the extension of slavery. His
arguments in furtherance of this policy had their motive and mainspring
in his patriotic devotion to the interests of his own race. To protect,
defend, and perpetuate slavery in the states where it existed Abraham
Lincoln was not less ready than any other President to draw the sword
of the nation. He was ready to execute all the supposed guarantees of
the United States Constitution in favor of the slave system anywhere inside the slave states. He was willing to pursue, recapture, and send back
the fugitive slave to his master, and to suppress a slave rising for liberty,
though his guilty master were already in arms against the Government.
The race to which we belong were not the special objects of his consideration. Knowing this, I concede to you, my white fellow-citizens, a
preëminence in this worship at once full and supreme. First, midst, and
last, you and yours were the objects of his deepest affection and his most
earnest solicitude. You are the children of Abraham Lincoln. We are at
best only his step-children; children by adoption, children by forces of
circumstances and necessity. To you it especially belongs to sound his

praises, to preserve and perpetuate his memory, to multiply his statues, to hang his pictures high upon your walls, and commend his example, for to you he was a great and glorious friend and benefactor. Instead of supplanting you at his altar, we would exhort you to build high his monuments; let them be of the most costly material, of the most cunning workmanship; let their forms be symmetrical, beautiful, and perfect; let their bases be upon solid rocks, and their summits lean against the unchanging blue, overhanging sky, and let them endure forever! But while in the abundance of your wealth, and in the fullness of your just and patriotic devotion, you do all this, we entreat you to despise not the humble offering we this day unveil to view; for while Abraham Lincoln saved for you a country, he delivered us from a bondage, according to Jefferson, one hour of which was worse than ages of the oppression your fathers rose in rebellion to oppose.

Fellow-citizens, ours is no new-born zeal and devotion—merely a thing of this moment. The name of Abraham Lincoln was near and dear to our hearts in the darkest and most perilous hours of the Republic. We were no more ashamed of him when shrouded in clouds of darkness, of doubt, and defeat than when we saw him crowned with victory, honor, and glory. Our faith in him was often taxed and strained to the uttermost, but it never failed. When he tarried long in the mountain; when he strangely told us that we were the cause of the war; when he still more strangely told us that we were to leave the land in which we were born; when he refused to employ our arms in defense of the Union; when, after accepting our service as colored soldiers, he refused to retaliate our murder and torture as colored prisoners; when he told us he would save the Union if he could with slavery; when he revoked the Proclamation of Emancipation of General Frémont; when he refused to remove the popular commander of the Army of the Potomac, in the days of its inaction and defeat, who was more zealous in his efforts to protect slavery than to suppress rebellion; when we saw all this, and more, we were at times grieved, stunned, and greatly bewildered; but our hearts believed while they ached and bled. Nor was this, even at that time, a blind and unreasoning superstition. Despite the mist and haze that surrounded him; despite the tumult, the hurry, and confusion of the hour, we were able to take a comprehensive view of Abraham Lincoln, and to make reasonable allowance for the circumstances of his position. We saw him, measured him, and estimated him; not by stray utterances to injudicious and tedious delegations, who often tried his patience; not by isolated facts torn from their connection; not by any partial and imperfect glimpses, caught at inopportune moments; but by a broad survey, in the light of the stern logic of great events, and in view of that divinity which shapes our ends, rough hew them how we will, we came to the conclusion that the hour and the man of our redemption had somehow met in the person of Abraham Lincoln. It mattered little to us what language he might employ on special occasions; it mattered little to us, when we fully knew him, whether he was swift or slow in his movements; it was enough for us that Abraham Lincoln was at the head of a great movement, and was in living and earnest sympathy with that movement, which, in the nature of things, must go on until slavery should be utterly and forever abolished in the United States.

When, therefore, it shall be asked what we have to do with the memory of Abraham Lincoln, or what Abraham Lincoln had to do with us, the answer is ready, full, and complete. Though he loved Cæsar less than Rome, though the Union was more to him than our freedom or our future, under his wise and beneficent rule we saw ourselves gradually lifted from the depths of slavery to the heights of liberty and manhood; under his wise and beneficent rule, and by measures approved and vigorously pressed by him, we saw that the handwriting of ages, in the form of prejudice and proscription, was rapidly fading away from the face of our whole country; under his rule, and in due time, about as soon after all as the country could tolerate the strange spectacle, we saw our brave sons and brothers laying off the rags of bondage, and being clothed all over in the blue uniforms of the soldiers of the United States; under his rule we saw two hundred thousand of our dark and dusky people responding to the call of Abraham Lincoln, and with muskets on their shoulders, and eagles on their buttons, timing their high footsteps to liberty and union under the national flag; under his rule we saw the independence of the black republic of Haiti, the special object of slaveholding aversion and horror, fully recognized, and her minister, a colored gentleman, duly received here in the city of Washington; under his rule we saw the internal slave-trade, which so long disgraced the nation, abolished, and slavery abolished in the District of Columbia; under his rule we saw for the first time the law enforced against the foreign slave trade, and the first slave-trader hanged like any other pirate or murderer; under his rule, assisted by the greatest captain of our age, and his inspiration, we saw the Confederate States, based upon the idea that our race must be slaves, and slaves forever, battered to pieces and scattered to the four winds; under his rule, and in the fullness of time, we saw Abraham Lincoln, after giving the slaveholders three months' grace in which to save their hateful slave system, penning the immortal paper, which, though special in its language, was general in its principles and effect, making slavery forever impossible in the United States. Though we waited long, we saw all this and more.

Can any colored man, or any white man friendly to the freedom of all men, ever forget the night which followed the first day of January, 1863, when the world was to see if Abraham Lincoln would prove to be as good as his word? I shall never forget that memorable night, when in a distant city I waited and watched at a public meeting, with three thousand others not less anxious than myself, for the word of deliverance which we have heard read today. Nor shall I ever forget the outburst of joy and thanksgiving that rent the air when the lightning brought to us the emancipation proclamation. In that happy hour we forgot all delay, and forgot all tardiness, forgot that the President had bribed the rebels to lay down their arms by a promise to withhold the bolt which would smite the slave-system with destruction; and we were thenceforward willing to allow the President all the latitude of time, phraseology, and every honorable device that statesmanship might require for the achievement of a great and beneficent measure of liberty and progress.

Fellow-citizens, there is little necessity on this occasion to speak at length and critically of this great and good man, and of his high mission in the world. That ground has been fully occupied and completely covered both here and elsewhere. The whole field of fact and fancy has been gleaned and garnered. Any man can say things that are true of Abraham Lincoln, but no man can say anything that is new of Abraham Lincoln. His personal traits and public acts are better known to the American people than are those of any other man of his age. He was a mystery to no man who saw him and heard him. Though high in position, the humblest could approach him and feel at home in his presence. Though deep, he was transparent; though strong, he was gentle; though decided and pronounced in his convictions, he was tolerant towards those who differed from him, and patient under reproaches. Even those who only knew him through his public utterance obtained a tolerably clear idea of his character and personality. The image of the man went out with his words, and those who read them knew him.

I have said that President Lincoln was a white man, and shared the prejudices common to his countrymen towards the colored race. Looking back to his times and to the condition of his country, we are compelled to admit that this unfriendly feeling on his part may be safely set down as one element of his wonderful success in organizing the loyal American people for the tremendous conflict before them, and bringing them safely through that conflict. His great mission was to accomplish two things: first, to save his country from dismemberment and ruin; and, second, to free his country from the great crime of slavery. To do one or the other, or both, he must have the earnest sympathy and the powerful coöperation of his loyal fellow-countrymen. Without this primary and essential condition to success his efforts must have been vain and utterly fruitless. Had he put the abolition of slavery before the salvation of the Union, he would have inevitably driven from him a powerful class of the American people and rendered resistance to rebellion impossible. Viewed from the genuine abolition ground, Mr. Lincoln seemed tardy, cold, dull, and indifferent; but measuring him by the sentiment of his country, a sentiment he was bound as a statesman to consult, he was swift, zealous, radical, and determined.

Though Mr. Lincoln shared the prejudices of his white fellow-countrymen against the Negro, it is hardly necessary to say that in his heart of hearts he loathed and hated slavery.... The man who could say, "Fondly do we hope, fervently do we pray, that this mighty scourge of war shall soon pass away, yet if God wills it continue till all the wealth piled by two hundred years of bondage shall have been wasted, and each drop of blood drawn by the lash shall have been paid for by one drawn by the sword, the judgments of the Lord are true and righteous altogether," gives all needed proof of his feeling on the subject of slavery. He was willing, while the South was loyal, that it should have its pound of flesh, because he thought that it was so nominated in the bond; but farther than this no earthly power could make him go.

Fellow-citizens, whatever else in this world may be partial, unjust, and uncertain, time, time! is impartial, just, and certain in its action. In the realm of mind, as well as in the realm of matter, it is a great worker, and often works wonders. The honest and comprehensive statesman, clearly discerning the needs of his country, and earnestly endeavoring to do his whole duty, though covered and blistered with reproaches, may safely leave his course to the silent judgment of time. Few great public men have ever been the victims of fiercer denunciation than Abraham Lincoln was during his administration. He was often wounded in the house of his friends. Reproaches came thick and fast upon him from within and from without, and from opposite quarters. He was assailed by Abolitionists; he was assailed by slaveholders; he was assailed by the men who were for peace at any price; he was assailed by those who were for a more vigorous prosecution of the war; he was assailed for not making the war an abolition war; and he was bitterly assailed for making the war an abolition war.

But now behold the change: the judgment of the present hour is, that taking him for all in all, measuring the tremendous magnitude of the work before him, considering the necessary means to ends, and surveying the end from the beginning, infinite wisdom has seldom sent any man into the world better fitted for his mission than Abraham Lincoln. His birth, his training, and his natural endowments, both mental and physical, were strongly in his favor. Born and reared among the lowly, a stranger to wealth and luxury, compelled to grapple single-handed with the flintiest hardships of life, from tender youth to sturdy manhood, he grew strong in the manly and heroic qualities demanded by the great mission to which he was called by the votes of his countrymen. The hard condition of his early life, which would have depressed and broken down weaker men, only gave greater life, vigor, and buoyancy to the heroic spirit of Abraham Lincoln. He was ready for any kind and any quality of work. What other young men dreaded in the shape of toil, he took hold of with the utmost cheerfulness.

> *A spade, a rake, a hoe,*
> *A pick-axe, or a bill;*
> *A hook to reap, a scythe to mow,*
> *A flail, or what you will.*

All day long he could split heavy rails in the woods, and half the night long he could study his English Grammar by the uncertain flare and glare of the light made by a pine-knot. He was at home on the land with his axe, with his maul, with gluts, and his wedges; and he was equally at home on water, with his oars, with his poles, with his planks, and with his boat-hooks. And whether in his flat-boat on the Mississippi River, or at the fireside of his frontier cabin, he was a man of work. A son of toil himself, he was linked in brotherly sympathy with the sons of toil in every loyal part of the Republic. This very fact gave him tremendous power with the American people, and materially contributed not only to selecting him to the Presidency, but in sustaining his administration of the Government.

Upon his inauguration as President of the United States, an office, even when assumed under the most favorable conditions, fitted to tax and strain the largest abilities, Abraham Lincoln was met by a tremendous crisis. He was called upon not merely to administer the Government, but to decide, in the face of terrible odds, the fate of the Republic.

A formidable rebellion rose in his path before him; the Union was already practically dissolved; his country was torn and rent asunder at the center. Hostile armies were already organized against the Republic, armed with the munitions of war which the Republic had provided for its own defence. The tremendous question for him to decide was whether his country should survive the crisis and flourish, or be dismembered and perish. His predecessor in office had already decided the question in favor of national dismemberment, by denying to it the right of self-defence and self-preservation—a right which belongs to the meanest insect.

Happily for the country, happily for you and for me, the judgment of James Buchanan, the patrician, was not the judgment of Abraham Lincoln, the plebeian. He brought his strong common sense, sharpened in the school of adversity, to bear upon the question. He did not hesitate, he did not doubt, he did not falter; but at once resolved that at whatever peril, at whatever cost, the union of the States should be preserved. A patriot himself, his faith was strong and unwavering in the patriotism of his countrymen. Timid men said before Mr. Lincoln's inauguration, that we had seen the last President of the United States. A voice in influential quarters said, "Let the Union slide." Some said that a Union maintained by the sword was worthless. Others said a rebellion of 8,000,000 cannot be suppressed; but in the midst of all this tumult and timidity, and against all this, Abraham Lincoln was clear in his duty, and had an oath in heaven. He calmly and bravely heard the voice of doubt and fear all around him; but he had an oath in heaven, and there was not power enough on earth to make this honest boatman, backwoodsman, and broad-handed splitter of rails evade or violate that sacred oath. He had not been schooled in the ethics of slavery; his plain life had favored his love of truth. He had not been taught that treason and perjury were the proof of honor and honesty. His moral training was against his saying one thing when he meant another. The trust that Abraham Lincoln had in himself and in the people was surprising and grand, but it was also enlightened and well founded. He knew the American people better than they knew themselves, and his truth was based upon this knowledge.

Fellow-citizens, the fourteenth day of April, 1865, of which this is the eleventh anniversary, is now and will ever remain a memorable day in the annals of this Republic. It was on the evening of this day, while a fierce and sanguinary rebellion was in the last stages of its desolating power; while its armies were broken and scattered before the invincible armies of Grant and Sherman; while a great nation, torn and rent by war, was already beginning to raise to the skies loud anthems of joy at the dawn of peace, it was startled, amazed, and overwhelmed by the crowning crime of slavery—the assassination of Abraham Lincoln. It was a new crime, a pure act of malice. No purpose of the rebellion was to be served by it. It was the simple gratification of a hell-black spirit of revenge. But it has done good after all. It has filled the country with a deeper abhorrence of slavery and a deeper love for the great liberator.

Had Abraham Lincoln died from any of the numerous ills to which flesh is heir; had he reached that good old age of which his vigorous constitution and his temperate habits gave promise; had he been permitted to see the end of his great work; had the solemn curtain of death come down but gradually—we should still have been smitten with a heavy grief, and treasured his name lovingly. But dying as he did die, by the red hand of violence, killed, assassinated, taken off without warning, not because of personal hate—for no man who knew Abraham Lincoln could hate him—but because of his fidelity to union and liberty, he is doubly dear to us, and his memory will be precious forever.

Fellow-citizens, I end, as I began, with congratulations. We have done a good work for our race today. In doing honor to the memory of our friend and liberator, we have been doing highest honors to ourselves and those who come after us; we have been fastening ourselves to a name and fame imperishable and immortal; we have also been defending ourselves from a blighting scandal. When now it shall be said that the colored man is soulless, that he has no appreciation of benefits or benefactors; when the foul reproach of ingratitude is hurled at us, and it is attempted to scourge us beyond the range of human brotherhood, we may calmly point to the monument we have this day erected to the memory of Abraham Lincoln.

Booker T. Washington
[1859?-1915]

Born in slavery, Booker T. Washington worked his way through Hampton Institute in Virginia, where he taught until 1881, when he was chosen to head a new school for Negroes in Tuskegee, Alabama. His Harvard University speech was included in Part I. The speech quoted below, delivered at the Atlanta Cotton Exposition, September 18, 1895, gained him acclaim in both the South and the North, and was hailed as an indication of the Negro's acceptance of the order of white supremacy which had been established in the South following the overthrow of Reconstruction. Following is the full text of the speech.

ATLANTA EXPOSITION ADDRESS

MR. PRESIDENT AND GENTLEMEN OF THE BOARD OF DIRECTORS AND CITIZENS:
One-third of the population of the South is of the Negro race. No enter-

prise seeking the material, civil, or moral welfare of this section can disregard this element of our population and reach the highest success. I but convey to you, Mr. President and Directors, the sentiment of the masses of my race when I say that in no way have the value and manhood of the American Negro been more fittingly and generously recognized than by the managers of this magnificent Exposition at every stage of its progress. It is a recognition that will do more to cement the friendship of the two races than any occurrence since the dawn of our freedom.

Not only this, but the opportunity here afforded will awaken among us a new era of industrial progress. Ignorant and inexperienced, it is not strange that in the first years of our new life we began at the top instead of at the bottom; that a seat in Congress or the state legislature was more sought than real estate or industrial skill; that the political convention or stump speaking had more attractions than starting a dairy farm or truck garden.

A ship lost at sea for many days suddenly sighted a friendly vessel. From the mast of the unfortunate vessel was seen a signal, "Water, water; we die of thirst!" The answer from the friendly vessel at once came back, "Cast down your bucket where you are." A second time the signal, "Water, water; send us water!" ran up from the distressed vessel, and was answered, "Cast down your bucket where you are." And a third and fourth signal for water was answered, "Cast down your bucket where you are." The captain of the distressed vessel, at last heeding the injunction, cast down his bucket, and it came up full of fresh, sparkling water from the mouth of the Amazon River. To those of my race who depend on bettering their condition in a foreign land or who underestimate the importance of cultivating friendly relations with the Southern white man, who is their next-door neighbor, I would say: "Cast down your bucket where you are"—cast it down in making friends in every manly way of the people of all races by whom we are surrounded.

Cast it down in agriculture, mechanics, in commerce, in domestic service, and in the professions. And in this connection it is well to bear in mind that whatever other sins the South may be called to bear, when it comes to business, pure and simple, it is in the South that the Negro is given a man's chance in the commercial world, and in nothing is this Exposition more eloquent than in emphasizing this chance. Our greatest danger is that in the great leap from slavery to freedom we may overlook the fact that the masses of us are to live by the productions of our hands, and fail to keep in mind that we shall prosper in proportion as we learn to dignify and glorify common labor and put brains and skill into the common occupations of life; shall prosper in proportion as we learn to draw the line between the superficial and the substantial, the ornamental gewgaws of life and the useful. No race can prosper till it learns that there is as much dignity in tilling a field as in writing a poem. It is at the bottom of life we must begin, and not at the top. Nor should we permit our grievances to overshadow our opportunities.

To those of the white race who look to the incoming of those of foreign birth and strange tongue and habits for the prosperity of the South, were

I permitted I would repeat what I say to my own race, "Cast down your bucket where you are." Cast it down among the eight millions of Negroes whose habits you know, whose fidelity and love you have tested in days when to have proved treacherous meant the ruin of your firesides. Cast down your bucket among these people who have, without strikes and labor wars, tilled your fields, cleared your forests, builded your railroads and cities, and brought forth treasures from the bowels of the earth, and helped make possible this magnificent representation of the progress of the South. Casting down your bucket among my people, helping and encouraging them as you are doing on these grounds, and, with education of head, hand, and heart, you will find that they will buy your surplus land, make blossom the waste places in your fields, and run your factories. While doing this, you can be sure in the future, as in the past, that you and your families will be surrounded by the most patient, faithful, law-abiding, and unresentful people that the world has seen. As we have proved our loyalty to you in the past, in nursing your children, watching by the sick-bed of your mothers and fathers, and often following them with tear-dimmed eyes to their graves, so in the future, in our humble way, we shall stand by you with a devotion that no foreigner can approach, ready to lay down our lives, if need be, in defense of yours, interlacing our industrial, commercial, civil, and religious life with yours in a way that shall make the interests of both races one. In all things that are purely social we can be as separate as the fingers, yet one as the hand in all things essential to mutual progress.

There is no defense or security for any of us except in the highest intelligence and development of all. If anywhere there are efforts tending to curtail the fullest growth of the Negro, let these efforts be turned into stimulating, encouraging, and making him the most useful and intelligent citizen. Effort or means so invested will pay a thousand per cent interest. These efforts will be twice blessed—"blessing him that gives and him that takes."

There is no escape through law of man or God from the inevitable:

> The law of changeless justice bind
>   Oppressor with oppressed;
> And close as sin and suffering joined
>   We march to fare abreast.

Nearly sixteen millions of hands will aid you in pulling the load upward, or they will pull, against you, the load downward. We shall constitute one-third and more of the ignorance and crime of the South, or one-third its intelligence and progress; we shall contribute one-third to the business and industrial prosperity of the South, or we shall prove a veritable body of death, stagnating, depressing, retarding every effort to advance the body politic.

Gentlemen of the Exposition, as we present to you our humble effort at an exhibition of our progress, you must not expect overmuch. Starting thirty years ago with ownership here and there in a few quilts and pumpkins and chickens (gathered from miscellaneous sources), remember the path that has led from these to the inventions and production of agricultural implements, buggies, steam-engines, newspapers, books, statuary, carving, paintings, the management of drug-stores and banks, has not been trodden without contact with thorns and thistles. While we take pride in what we exhibit as a result of our independent efforts, we do not for a moment forget that our part in this exhibition would fall far short of your expectations but for the constant help that has come to our educational life, not only from the Southern states, but especially from Northern philanthropists, who have made their gifts a constant stream of blessing and encouragement.

The wisest among my race understand that the agitation of questions of social equality is the extremest folly, and that progress in the enjoyment of all the privileges that will come to us must be the result of severe and constant struggle rather than of artificial forcing. No race that has anything to contribute to the markets of the world is long, in any degree, ostracized. It is important and right that all privileges of the law be ours, but it is vastly more important that we be prepared for the exercise of those privileges. The opportunity to earn a dollar in a factory just now is worth infinitely more than the opportunity to spend a dollar in an opera-house.

In conclusion, may I repeat that nothing in thirty years has given us more hope and encouragement, and drawn us so near to you of the white race, as this opportunity offered by the Exposition; and here bending, as it were, over the altar that represents the results of the struggles of your race and mine, both starting practically empty-handed three decades ago, I pledge that, in your effort to work out the great and intricate problem which God has laid at the doors of the South, you shall have at all times the patient, sympathetic help of my race; only let this be constantly in mind, that, while from representations in these buildings of the product of field, of forest, of mine, of factory, letters, and art, much good will come, yet far above and beyond material benefits will be that higher good, that, let us pray God, will come, in a blotting out of sectional differences and racial animosities and suspicions, in a determination to administer absolute justice, in a willing obedience among all classes to the mandates of law. This, this, coupled with our material prosperity, will bring into our beloved South a new heaven and a new earth.

W. E. B. Du Bois

[1868–1963]

Scholar and educator, one of the founders of the NAACP, and editor of its magazine Crisis *from 1910 to 1934, W. E. B. Du Bois was a dominant figure in the Negro struggle for equal rights in the twentieth century. In the early years of the century, Dr. Du Bois was the leading opponent of Booker T. Washington's ideology of accommodation.*

On October 20, 1946, Dr. Du Bois delivered the principal address at the closing session of the Southern Youth Legislature, sponsored by the Southern Negro Youth Congress. In slightly more than two thousand words, Dr. Du Bois brilliantly illuminated the basic nature of the social, political and economic life of the South. Following is the text of the speech.

BEHOLD THE LAND

THE FUTURE of American Negroes is in the South. Here three hundred and twenty-seven years ago, they began to enter what is now the United States of America; here they have made their greatest contribution to American culture; and here they have suffered the domination of slavery, the frustration of reconstruction and the lynching of emancipation. I trust then that an organization like yours is going to regard the South as the battle-ground of a great crusade. Here is the magnificent climate; here is the fruitful earth under the beauty of the southern sun; and here, if anywhere on earth, is the need of the thinker, the worker and the dreamer. This is the firing line not simply for the emancipation of the American Negro but for the emancipation of the African Negro and the Negroes of the West Indies; for the emancipation of the colored races; and for the emancipation of the white slaves of modern capitalistic monopoly.

Remember here, too, that you do not stand alone. It may seem like a failing fight when the newspapers ignore you; when every effort is made by white people in the South to count you out of citizenship and to act as though you did not exist as human beings while all the time they are profiting by your labor; gleaning wealth from your sacrifices and trying to build a nation and a civilization upon your degradation. You must remember that despite all this, you have allies and allies even in the white South. First and greatest of these possible allies are the white working classes about you. The poor whites whom you have been taught to despise and who in turn have learned to fear and hate you. This must not deter you from efforts to make them understand, because in the past in their ignorance and suffering they have been led foolishly to look upon you as the cause of most of their distress. You must remember that this attitude is hereditary from slavery and that it has been deliberately cultivated ever since emancipation.

Slowly but surely the working people of the South, white and black, must come to remember that their emancipation depends upon their mutual cooperation; upon their acquaintanceship with each other; upon their friendship; upon their social intermingling. Unless this happens each is going to be made the football to break the heads and hearts of the other.

White youth in the South is peculiarly frustrated. There is not a single great ideal which they can express or aspire to, that does not bring them into flat contradiction with the Negro problem. The more they try to escape it, the more they land into hypocrisy, lying and double-dealing; the more they become, what they least wish to become, the oppressors and despisers of human beings. Some of them, in larger and larger numbers, are bound to turn toward the truth and to recognize you as brothers and sisters, as fellow travelers toward the dawn.

There has always been in the South that intellectual elite who saw the Negro problem clearly. They have always lacked and some still lack the courage to stand up for what they know is right. Nevertheless they can be depended on in the long run to follow their own clear thinking and their own decent choice. Finally even the politicians must eventually recognize the trend in the world, in this country, and in the South. James Byrnes, that favorite son of this commonwealth, and Secretary of State of the United States, is today occupying an indefensible and impossible position; and if he survives in the memory of men, he must begin to help establish in his own South Carolina something of that democracy which he has been recently so loudly preaching to Russia. He is the end of a long series of men whose eternal damnation is the fact that they looked *truth* in the face and did not see it; John C. Calhoun, Wade Hampton, Ben Tillman are men whose names must ever be besmirched by the fact that they fought against freedom and democracy in a land which was founded upon democracy and freedom.

Eventually this class of men must yield to the writing in the stars. That great hypocrite, Jan Smuts, who today is talking of humanity and standing beside Byrnes for a United Nations, is at the same time oppressing the black people of Africa to an extent which makes their two countries, South Africa and the American South, the most reactionary peoples on earth. Peoples whose exploitation of the poor and helpless reaches the last degree of shame. They must in the long run yield to the forward march of civilization or die.

If now you young people, instead of running away from the battle here in Carolina, Georgia, Alabama, Louisiana and Mississippi, instead of seeking freedom and opportunity in Chicago and New York—which do spell opportunity—nevertheless grit your teeth and make up your minds to fight it out right here if it takes every day of your lives and the lives of your children's children; if you do this, you must in meetings like this ask yourselves what does the fight mean? How can it be carried on? What are the best tools, arms, and methods? And where does it lead?

I should be the last to insist that the uplift of mankind never calls for force and death. There are times, as both you and I know, when

Tho' love repine and reason chafe,
There came a voice without reply,
'Tis man's perdition to be safe
When for truth he ought to die.

At the same time and even more clearly in a day like this, after the millions of mass murders that have been done in the world since 1914, we ought to be the last to believe that force is ever the final word. We cannot escape the clear fact that what is going to win in this world is reason if this ever becomes a reasonable world. The careful reasoning of the human mind backed by the facts of science is the one salvation of man. The world, if it resumes its march toward civilization, cannot ignore reason. This has been the tragedy of the South in the past; it is still its awful and unforgivable sin that it has set its face against reason and against the fact. It tried to build slavery upon freedom; it tried to build tyranny upon democracy; it tried to build mob violence on law and law on lynching and in all that despicable endeavor, the state of South Carolina has led the South for a century. It began not the Civil War—not the War between the States—but the War to Preserve Slavery; it began mob violence and lynching and today it stands in the front rank of those defying the Supreme Court on disfranchisement.

Nevertheless reason can and will prevail; but of course it can only prevail with publicity—pitiless, blatant publicity. You have got to make the people of the United States and of the world know what is going on in the South. You have got to use every field of publicity to force the truth into their ears, and before their eyes. You have got to make it impossible for any human being to live in the South and not realize the barbarities that prevail here. You may be condemned for flamboyant methods; for calling a congress like this; for waving your grievances under the noses and in the faces of men. That makes no difference; it is your duty to do it. It is your duty to do more of this sort of thing than you have done in the past. As a result of this you are going to be called upon for sacrifice. It is no easy thing for a young black man or a young black woman to live in the South today and to plan to continue to live here; to marry and raise children; to establish a home. They are in the midst of legal caste and customary insults; they are in continuous danger of mob violence; they are mistreated by the officers of the law and they have no hearing before the courts and the churches and public opinion commensurate with the attention which they ought to receive. But that sacrifice is only the beginning of battle, you must re-build this South.

There are enormous opportunities here for a new nation, a new economy, a new culture in a South really new and not a mere renewal of an old South of slavery, monopoly and race hate. There is a chance for a new cooperative agriculture on renewed land owned by the state with capital furnished by the state, mechanized and coordinated with city life. There is chance for strong, virile trade unions without race discrimination, with high wage, closed shop and decent conditions of work, to beat back and hold in check the swarm of landlords, monopolists and profiteers who are today sucking the blood out of this land. There is chance for cooperative industry, built on the cheap power of T.V.A. and its future extensions. There is opportunity to organize and mechanize domestic service with decent hours, and high wage and dignified training.

There is a vast field for consumers cooperation, building business on public service and not on private profit as the main-spring of industry. There is chance for a broad, sunny, healthy home life, shorn of the fear of mobs and liquor, and rescued from lying, stealing politicians, who build their deviltry on race prejudice.

Here in this South is the gateway to the colored millions of the West Indies, Central and South America. Here is the straight path to Africa, the Indies, China and the South Seas. Here is the path to the greater, freer, truer world. It would be shame and cowardice to surrender this glorious land and its opportunities for civilization and humanity to the thugs and lynchers, the mobs and profiteers, the monopolists and gamblers who today choke its soul and steal its resources. The oil and sulphur; the coal and iron; the cotton and corn; the lumber and cattle belong to you the workers, black and white, and not to the thieves who hold them and use them to enslave you. They can be rescued and restored to the people if you have the guts to strive for the real right to vote, the right to real education, the right to happiness and health and the total abolition of the father of these scourges of mankind, *poverty*.

"Behold the beautiful land which the Lord thy God hath given thee." Behold the land, the rich and resourceful land, from which for a hundred years its best elements have been running away, its youth and hope, black and white, scurrying North because they are afraid of each other, and dare not face a future of equal, independent, upstanding human beings, in a real and not a sham democracy.

To rescue this land, in this way, calls for the *Great Sacrifice*. This is the thing that you are called upon to do because it is the right thing to do. Because you are embarked upon a great and holy crusade, the emancipation of mankind, black and white; the upbuilding of democracy; the breaking down, particularly here in the South, of forces of evil represented by race prejudice in South Carolina; by lynching in Georgia; by disfranchisement in Mississippi; by ignorance in Louisiana and by all these and monopoly of wealth in the whole South.

There could be no more splendid vocation beckoning to the youth of the twentieth century, after the flat failures of white civilization, after the flamboyant establishment of an industrial system which creates poverty and the children of poverty which are ignorance and disease and crime; after the crazy boasting of a white culture that finally ended in wars which ruined civilization in the whole world; in the midst of allied peoples who have yelled about democracy and never practiced it either in the British Empire or in the American Commonwealth or in South Carolina.

Here is the chance for young women and young men of devotion to lift again the banner of humanity and to walk toward a civilization which will be free and intelligent; which will be healthy and unafraid; and build in the world a culture led by black folk and joined by peoples of all colors and all races—without poverty, ignorance and disease!

Once, a great German poet cried: "Selig der den Er in Sieges Glanze findet."

"Happy man whom Death shall find in Victory's splendor."

But I know a happier one: he who fights in despair and in defeat still fights. Singing with Arna Bontemps the quiet, determined philosophy of undefeatable men:

> I thought I saw an angel flying low,
> I thought I saw the flicker of a wing
> Above the mulberry trees; but not again,
> Bethesda sleeps. This ancient pool that healed
> A Host of bearded Jews does not awake.
> This pool that once the angels troubled does not move.
> No angel stirs it now, no Saviour comes
> With healing in His hands to raise the sick
> And bid the lame man leap upon the ground.
>
> The golden days are gone. Why do we wait
> So long upon the marble steps, blood
> Falling from our open wounds? and why
> Do our black faces search the empty sky?
> Is there something we have forgotten? Some precious thing
> We have lost, wandering in strange lands?
>
> There was a day, I remember now,
> I beat my breast and cried, "Wash me God,"
> Wash me with a wave of wind upon
> The barley; O quiet one, draw near, draw near!
> Walk upon the hills with lovely feet
> And in the waterfall stand and speak!

Malcolm X
[1925–1965]

Malcolm Little was born in Omaha, Nebraska, on May 19, 1925. A dropout from school at fifteen, he was convicted of burglary and sent to prison in his twenty-first year. While in prison he was converted to the National of Islam (Black Muslims), and upon his release in 1952 adopted the name Malcolm X and became a leading figure in the movement. In 1963 he was suspended from his post as Minister of the New York Muslim temple. Following his suspension, he made two trips to Africa and the Middle East. Returning to the United States, Malcolm X began to organize a new movement called the Organization of Afro-American Unity. He dropped the Muslim religious ideology, but maintained the concept of black nationalism and rejected non-violence. On February 21, 1965, he was assassinated in the Audubon Ballroom in upper Harlem. At the time of his death, he was becoming the most dynamic leader of the Black Revolution. The following is part of a speech he delivered on "The Black Revolution" at a meeting sponsored by the Militant Labor Forum, a socialist organization, at Palm Gardens in New York City. (From Malcolm X Speaks, copyright © 1965 by Merit Publishers and Betty Shabazz. Reprinted by permission of Pathfinder Press, Inc.)

THE BLACK REVOLUTION

Just as we can see that all over the world one of the main problems facing the West is race, likewise here in America today, most of your Negro leaders as well as the whites agree that 1964 itself appears to be one of the most explosive years yet in the history of America on the racial front, on the racial scene. Not only is this racial explosion probably to take place in America, but all of the ingredients for this racial explosion in America to blossom into a world-wide racial explosion present themselves right here in front of us. America's racial powder keg, in short, can actually fuse or ignite a world-wide powder keg.

There are whites in this country who are still complacent when they see the possibilities of racial strife getting out of hand. You are complacent simply because you think you outnumber the racial minority in this country; what you have to bear in mind is wherein you might outnumber us in this country, you don't outnumber us all over the earth.

Any kind of racial explosion that takes place in this country today, in 1964, is not a racial explosion that can be confined to the shores of America. It is a racial explosion that can ignite the racial powder keg that exists all over the planet that we call earth. I think that nobody would disagree that the dark masses of Africa and Asia and Latin America are already seething with bitterness, animosity, hostility, unrest, and impatience with the racial intolerance that they themselves have experienced at the hands of the white West.

And just as they have the ingredients of hostility toward the West in general, here we also have 22 million African-Americans, black, brown, red, and yellow people, in this country who are also seething with bitterness and impatience and hostility and animosity at the racial intolerance not only of the white West but of white America in particular.

And by the hundreds of thousands today we find our own people have become impatient, turning away from your white nationalism, which you call democracy, toward the militant, uncompromising policy of black nationalism. I point out right here that as soon as we announced we were going to start a black nationalist party in this country, we received mail from coast to coast, especially from young people at the college level, the university level, who expressed complete sympathy and support and a desire to take an active part in any kind of political action based on black nationalism, designed to correct or eliminate immediately evils that our people have suffered here for 400 years.

The black nationalists to many of you may represent only a minority in the community. And therefore you might have a tendency to classify them as something insignificant. But just as the fuse is the smallest part or the smallest piece in the powder keg, it is yet that little fuse that ignites the entire powder keg. The black nationalists to you may represent a small minority in the so-called Negro community. But they just happen to be composed of the type of ingredient necessary to fuse or ignite the entire black community.

And this is one thing that whites—whether you call yourselves liberals or conservatives or racists or whatever else you might choose to be—one thing that you have to realize is, where the black community is concerned, although the large majority you come in contact with may impress you as being moderate and patient and loving and long-suffering and all that kind of stuff, the minority who you consider to be Muslims or nationalists happen to be made of the type of ingredient that can easily spark the black community. This should be understood. Because to me a powder keg is nothing without a fuse.

1964 will be America's hottest year; her hottest year yet; a year of much racial violence and much racial bloodshed. But it won't be blood that's going to flow only on one side. The new generation of black people that have grown up in this country during recent years are already forming the opinion, and it's a just opinion, that if there is to be bleeding, it should be reciprocal—bleeding on both sides.

It should also be understood that the racial sparks that are ignited here in America today could easily turn into a flaming fire abroad, which means it could engulf all the people of this earth into a giant race war. You cannot confine it to one little neighborhood, or one little community, or one little country. What happens to a black man in America today happens to the black man in Africa. What happens to a black man in America and Africa happens to the black man in Asia and to the man down in Latin America. What happens to one of us today happens to all of us. And when this is realized, I think that the whites—who are intelligent even if they aren't moral or aren't just or aren't impressed by legalities—those who are intelligent will realize that when they touch this one, they are touching all of them, and this in itself will have a tendency to be a checking factor.

The seriousness of this situation must be faced up to. I was in Cleveland last night, Cleveland, Ohio. In fact I was there Friday, Saturday and yesterday. Last Friday the warning was given that this is a year of bloodshed, that the black man has ceased to turn the other cheek, that he has ceased to be nonviolent, that he has ceased to feel that he must be confined by all these restraints that are put upon him by white society in struggling for what white society says he was supposed to have had a hundred years ago.

So today, when the black man starts reaching out for what America says are his rights, the black man feels that he is within his rights—when he becomes the victim of brutality by those who are depriving him of his rights —to do whatever is necessary to protect himself. An example of this was taking place last night at this same time in Cleveland, where the police were putting water hoses on our people there and also throwing tear gas at them—and they met a hail of stones, a hail of rocks, a hail of bricks. A couple of weeks ago in Jacksonville, Florida, a young teen-age Negro was throwing Molotov cocktails.

Well, Negroes didn't do this ten years ago. But what you should learn from this is that they are waking up. It was stones yesterday, Molotov cocktails today; it will be hand grenades tomorrow and whatever else is available the next day. The seriousness of this situation must be faced up to. You should not feel that I am inciting someone to violence. I'm only warning of a powder-keg situation. You can take it or leave it. If you take the warning, perhaps you can still save yourself. But if you ignore it or ridicule it, well, death is already at your doorstep. There are 22 million African-Americans who are ready to fight for independence right here. When I say fight for independence right here, I don't mean any non-violent fight, or turn-the-other-cheek fight. Those days are gone. Those days are over.

If George Washington didn't get independence for this country nonviolently, and if Patrick Henry didn't come up with a nonviolent statement, and you taught me to look upon them as patriots and heroes, then it's time for you to realize that I have studied your books well. . . .

1964 will see the Negro revolt evolve and merge into the world-wide black revolution that has been taking place on this earth since 1945. The so-called revolt will become a real black revolution. Now the black revolution has been taking place in Africa and Asia and Latin America; when I say black, I mean non-white—black, brown, red or yellow. Our brothers and sisters in Asia, who were colonized by the Europeans, our brothers and sisters in Africa, who were colonized by the Europeans, and in Latin America, the peasants, who were colonized by the Europeans, have been involved in a struggle since 1945 to get the colonialists, or the colonizing powers, the Europeans, off their land, out of their country.

This is a real revolution. Revolution is always based on land. Revolution is never based on begging somebody for an integrated cup of coffee. Revolutions are never fought by turning the other cheek. Revolutions are never based upon love-your-enemy and pray-for-those-who-spitefully-use-you. And revolutions are never waged singing "We Shall Overcome." Revolutions are based upon bloodshed. Revolutions are never compromising. Revolutions are never based upon negotiations. Revolutions are never based upon any kind of tokenism whatsoever. Revolutions are never even based upon that which is begging a corrupt society or a corrupt system to accept us into it. Revolutions overturn systems. And there is no system on this earth which has proven itself more corrupt, more criminal, than this system that in 1964 still colonizes 22 million African-Americans, still enslaves 22 million Afro-Americans.

There is no system more corrupt than a system that represents itself as the example of freedom, the example of democracy, and can go all over this earth telling other people how to straighten out their house, when you have citizens of this country who have to use bullets if they want to cast a ballot.

The greatest weapon the colonial powers have used in the past against our people has always been divide-and-conquer. America is a colonial power. She has colonized 22 million Afro-Americans by depriving us of first-class citizenship, by depriving us of civil rights, actually by depriving us of human rights. She has not only deprived us of the right to be a citizen, she has deprived us of the right to be human beings, the right to be recognized and respected as men and women. In this country the black can be fifty years old and he is still a "boy."

I grew up with white people. I was integrated before they even invented the word and I have never met white people yet—if you are around them long enough—who won't refer to you as a "boy" or a "gal," no matter how old you are or what school you come out of, no matter what your intellectual or professional level is. In this society we remain "boys."

So America's strategy is the same strategy as that which was used in the past by the colonial powers: divide and conquer. She plays one Negro leader against the other. She plays one Negro organization against the other. She makes us think we have different objectives, different goals. As soon as one Negro says something, she runs to this Negro and asks him, "What do you think about what he said?" Why, anybody can see through that today —except some of the Negro leaders.

All of our people have the same goals, the same objective. That objective is freedom, justice, equality. All of us want recognition and respect as human beings. We don't want to be integrationists. Nor do we want to be separationists. We want to be human beings. Integration is only a method that is used by some groups to obtain freedom, justice, equality and respect as human beings. Separation is only a method that is used by other groups to obtain freedom, justice, equality or human dignity.

Our people have made the mistake of confusing the methods with the objectives. As long as we agree on objectives, we should never fall out with each other just because we believe in different methods or tactics or strategy to reach a common objective.

We have to keep in mind at all times that we are not fighting for integration, nor are we fighting for separation. We are fighting for recognition as human beings. We are fighting for the right to live as free humans in this society. In fact, we are actually fighting for rights that are even greater than civil rights and that is human rights. . . .

PART VII
SUPPLEMENT:
IMPORTANT SPEECHES OF
1974–1997

Compiled by Stephen J. McKenna

INTRODUCTION

In the quarter century since the publication of the third edition of *World's Greatest Speeches*, the world in and about which people give public speeches has undergone some remarkable changes. With the pro-democracy movements in Eastern Europe in the late 1980s and the dissolution of the Soviet Union in 1991, the Cold War came to an end, and the superpower conflict ceased to be the defining fact of world politics. But far from marking "the end of history" as Francis Fukuyama famously speculated, the post-Cold War world has been beset by new (and sometimes very old) nationalistic and ethnic conflicts. In the midst of this "new world order," as former President George Bush called it, there have been other far-reaching events: the rise of a global market economy, the worldwide AIDS epidemic, a growing recognition of serious threats to the environmental stability of the planet, and the coming of an entirely new, digital mass medium.

For public speakers, probably the most significant development in recent years has been the vastly expanded reach and influence of the mass media, both old and new. Orators have come to realize, for example, that any speech may potentially find itself with a global audience. At the same time, speakers have increasingly responded to the mass media's own peculiar prerequisites. In an age when news moves at the speed of CNN, when speakers perpetually edit their words for the most favorable sound bite, when logical presentation is often eclipsed by the need for visual impact and instantaneous response, traditional assumptions about how public rhetoric functions have often come into question.

Nowhere has the influence of the mass media on public communication been more evident than in America. In tandem with television's rise to almost total dominance in domestic politics, a party system that had once been a boss-driven mechanism for leading large political constituencies, has sought to become more responsive to various smaller and even conflicting special interest groups. Accordingly, political rhetoric in America has often seemed less like a mode of civic deliberation than an exercise in mass marketing, with both political beliefs and politicians themselves packaged as so many consumer goods. There has followed a general hardening of partisan division and, by many accounts, a decline in the civility of public discourse.

Life in America has also been touched by (not to say converted to) a heterogeneous academic movement that broadly goes by the name "postmodernism." In its political guise, this philosophy (or anti-philosophy) would question the premises of this or any volume proposing to offer an anthology of works chosen according to the ideologically loaded criterion of "greatness." The postmodern perspective would oppose the idea stated in the introduction to the first edition that "history is primarily a record of important and dramatic events." Postmodernism unapologetically defends, even embraces sophistry, and so it would also find limiting (at best) the first edition's criterion of "logical presentation" as a standard for rhetorical achievement. It would take the third edition's inclusion of speeches by African-Americans as an admission of the general problem, but also as an insufficient remedy to a volume of 292 speeches in which a mere ten are by women.

The new selections included in this fourth edition of *World's Greatest Speeches* were chosen with an eye to these changes in the complexion of our rhetorical world. The reader will find fourteen new speeches by thirteen speakers and will encounter in them as many different answers to the question, "What makes a speech great?" These speeches are great because they seized the moment, or were delivered by historic persons, or succeeded at provoking strong responses or changes. Others achieve greatness because they captured the *zeitgeist*, voiced noble sentiments in a reasonable and eloquent way, or made new or silenced voices heard.

An attempt has been made to include speeches that span the time period since the third edition was published, while still encompassing many of the major events and cultural and philosophical concerns that evolved in that interim. There are four new speeches by women, two speeches from Africa, and two from Asia. It may strike some readers as an imbalance that among the relatively small number of speeches added, two should be by one controversial speaker, namely, Ronald Reagan. The reason for this is simply that both in terms of his rhetoric's direct influence on domestic and international affairs, and in terms of his indirect influence on the rhetorical style of other leaders, no other speaker of the last quarter century looms so large. Where possible, in order to preserve the spoken quality of the speeches, the texts have been taken from transcripts rather than from official published versions.

Despite the changes in our world and the different means by which orators have addressed those changes, one thing remains constant, and that is the simple fact of public speech as a powerful tool for dealing with problems of moment in human affairs. It is an appropriate accident then that this volume now begins and ends with funeral orations—one practically the essence of traditional oratory, the other a modern mass-media spectacle. It is a fitting emblem of the timelessness of great public speechmaking.

S. J. McK.

1999

Barbara Jordan
[1936–1996]

In 1966, Barbara Charline Jordan became the first African-American woman to be elected to the Texas state senate. Six years later, she became the first African-American woman from the South to win a seat in the United States House of Representatives. Her eloquence and judiciousness in the Nixon impeachment proceedings brought her wide national attention; nearly a quarter century later, she was frequently cited as a source of political wisdom during the impeachment of President Bill Clinton.

OPENING STATEMENT TO THE HOUSE
JUDICIARY COMMITTEE, PROCEEDINGS
IN THE IMPEACHMENT OF RICHARD NIXON
July 25, 1974

MR. CHAIRMAN, I join my colleague Mr. Rangel in thanking you for giving the junior members of this committee the glorious opportunity of sharing the pain of this inquiry. Mr. Chairman, you are a strong man, and it has not been easy but we have tried as best we can to give you as much assistance as possible.

Earlier today we heard the beginning of the Preamble to the Constitution of the United States, "We, the people." It is a very eloquent beginning. But when that document was completed, on the seventeenth of September in 1787, I was not included in that "We, the people." I felt somehow for many years that George Washington and Alexander Hamilton just left me out by mistake. But through the process of amendment, interpretation, and court decision I have finally been included in "We, the people."

Today I am an inquisitor. I believe hyperbole would not be fictional and would not overstate the solemnness that I feel right now. My faith in the Constitution is whole, it is complete, it is total. I am not going to sit here and be an idle spectator to the diminution, the subversion, the destruction of the Constitution.

"Who can so properly be the inquisitors for the nation as the representatives of the nation themselves?" (Federalist, no. 65). "The subject of its jurisdiction are those offenses which proceed from the misconduct of public men." That is what we are talking about. In other words, the jurisdiction comes from the abuse of violation of some public trust. It is wrong, I suggest—it is a misreading of the Constitution—for any member here to assert that for a member to vote for an article of impeachment means that that member must be convinced that the president should be removed from office. The Constitution doesn't say that. The powers relating to impeachment are an essential check in the hands of this body, the legislature, against and upon the encroachment of the executive. In establishing the division between the two branches of the legislature, the House and the Senate, assigning to the one the right to accuse and to the other the right to judge, the framers of this Constitution were very astute. They did not make the accusers and the judges the same person.

We know the nature of impeachment. We have been talking about it awhile now. "It is chiefly designed for the president and his high ministers" to somehow be called into account. It is designed to "bridle" the executive if he engages in excesses. "It is designed as a method of national inquest into the public men" (Hamilton, *Federalist*, no. 65). The framers confined in the congress the power if need be, to remove the president in order to strike a delicate balance between a president swollen with power and grown tyrannical, and preservation of the independence of the executive. The nature of impeachment is a narrowly channeled exception to the separation-of-powers maxim; the federal convention of 1787 said that. It limited impeachment to high crimes and misdemeanors and discounted and opposed the term "maladministration." "It is to be used only for great misdemeanors," so it was said in the North Carolina ratification convention. And in the Virginia ratification convention: "We do not trust our liberty to a particular branch. We need one branch to check the others." The North Carolina ratification convention: "No one need be afraid that officers who commit oppression will pass with immunity."

"Prosecutions of impeachments will seldom fail to agitate the passions of the whole community," said Hamilton in the *Federalist Papers*, no. 65. "And to divide it into parties more or less friendly or inimical to the accused." I do not mean political parties in that sense. The drawing of political lines goes to the motivation behind impeachment; but impeachment must proceed within the confines of the constitutional term "high crimes and misdemeanors."

Of the impeachment process, it was Woodrow Wilson who said that "nothing short of the grossest offenses against the plain law of the land will suffice to give them speed and effectiveness. Indignation so great as to overgrow party interest may secure a conviction; but nothing else can."

Common sense would be revolted if we engaged upon this process for insurance, campaign finance reform, housing, environmental protection, energy sufficiency, mass transportation. Pettiness cannot be allowed to stand in the face of such overwhelming problems. So today we are not being petty. We are trying to be big because the task we have before us is a big one.

This morning, in a discussion of the evidence, we were told that the evidence which purports to support the allegations of misuse of the CIA by the president is thin. We are told that that evidence is insufficient. What that recital of the evidence this morning did not include is what the president did know on June 23, 1972. The president did know that it was Republican money, that it was money from the Committee for the Re-Election of the President, which was found in the possession of one of the burglars arrested on June 17.

What the president did know on June 23 was the prior activities of E. Howard Hunt, which included his participation in the break-in of Daniel

Ellsberg's psychiatrist, which included Howard Hunt's participation in the Dita Beard ITT affair, which included Howard Hunt's fabrication of cables designed to discredit the Kennedy administration.

We were further cautioned today that perhaps these proceedings ought to be delayed because certainly there would be new evidence forthcoming from the president. The committee subpoena is outstanding, and if the president wants to supply that material, the committee sits here. The fact is that yesterday, the American people waited with great anxiety for eight hours, not knowing whether their president would obey an order of the Supreme Court of the United States.

At this point I would like to juxtapose a few of the impeachment criteria with some of the president's actions.

Impeachment criteria: James Madison, from the Virginia ratification convention. "If the president be connected in any suspicious manner with any person and there be grounds to believe that he will shelter him, he may be impeached."

We have heard time and time again that the evidence reflects payment to the defendants of money. The president had knowledge that these funds were being paid and that these were funds collected for the 1972 presidential campaign. We know that the president met with Mr. Henry Petersen twenty-seven times to discuss matters related to Watergate and immediately thereafter met with the very persons who were implicated in the information Mr. Petersen was receiving and transmitting to the president. The words are "if the president be connected in any suspicious manner with any person and there be grounds to believe that he will shelter that person, he may be impeached."

Justice Story: "Impeachment is intended for occasional and extraordinary cases where a superior power acting for the whole people is put into operation to protect their rights and rescue their liberties from violations."

We know about the Huston plan. We know about the break-in of the psychiatrist's office. We know that there was absolute complete direction in August 1971 when the president instructed Ehrlichman to "do whatever is necessary." This instruction led to a surreptitious entry into Dr. Fielding's office. "Protect their rights." "Rescue their liberties from violation."

The South Carolina ratification convention impeachment criteria: those are impeachable "who behave amiss or betray their public trust."

Beginning shortly after the Watergate break-in and continuing to the present time, the president has engaged in a series of public statements and actions designed to thwart the lawful investigation by government prosecutors. Moreover, the president has made public announcements and assertions bearing on the Watergate case which the evidence will show he knew to be false. These assertions, false assertions, impeachable, those who misbehave. Those who "behave amiss or betray their public trust."

James Madison again at the Constitutional Convention: "A president is impeachable if he attempts to subvert the Constitution."

The Constitution charges the president with the task of taking care that the laws be faithfully executed, and yet the president has counseled his aides to commit perjury, willfully disregarded the secrecy of grand jury proceedings, concealed surreptitious entry, attempted to compromise a federal judge while publicly displaying his cooperation with the processes of criminal justice. "A president is impeachable if he attempts to subvert the Constitution."

If the impeachment provision in the Constitution of the United States will not reach the offenses charged here, then perhaps that eighteenth-century Constitution should be abandoned to a twentieth-century paper shredder. Has the president committed offenses and planned and directed and acquiesced in a course of conduct which the Constitution will not tolerate? That is the question. We know that. We know the question. We should now forthwith proceed to answer the question. It is reason, and not passion, which must guide our deliberations, guide our debate, and guide our decision.

Alexander Solzhenitsyn
[1918–   ]

Nobel Prize-winning Russian novelist and Soviet dissident Alexander Solzhenitsyn delivered Harvard's commencement address four years into a forced exile from the Soviet Union. It was widely assumed that any dissenter from the Soviet system would warmly embrace the West, but with Solzhenitsyn it was otherwise. His stinging critique of materialism and democracy as they are practiced in later twentieth-century America provoked a wide response from the press, politicians, political scientists, and others, ranging from angry condemnation to puzzlement to nodding recognition. Though some of his predictions have fallen short of prophetic, Solzhenitsyn's words have acquired a new relevance in the post-Cold War era, when Russia is struggling to restructure herself in the image of Western political and economic models.

HARVARD COMMENCEMENT ADDRESS
June 8, 1978

I AM sincerely happy to be here with you on the occasion of the 327th commencement of this old and illustrious university. My congratulations and best wishes to all of today's graduates.

Harvard's motto is "Veritas." Many of you have already found out and others will find out in the course of their lives that truth eludes us as soon as our concentration begins to flag, all the while leaving the illusion that we are continuing to pursue it. This is the source of much discord. Also, truth seldom is sweet; it is almost invariably bitter. A measure of bitter truth is included in my speech today, but I offer it as a friend, not as an adversary. Three years ago in the United States I said certain things that were rejected and appeared unacceptable. Today, however, many people agree with what I then said.

The split in today's world is perceptible even to a hasty glance. Any of our contemporaries readily identifies two world powers, each of them already capable of utterly destroying the other. However, the understanding of the split too often is limited to this political conception: the illusion according to which danger may be abolished through successful diplomatic negotiations or by achieving a balance of armed forces. The truth is that the split is both more profound and more alienating, that the rifts are more numerous than one can see at first glance. The deep manifold splits bear the danger of equally manifold disaster for all of us, in accordance with the ancient truth that a kingdom—in this case, our Earth—divided against itself cannot stand.

There is the concept of the Third World: thus, we already have three worlds. Undoubtedly, however, the number is even greater; we are just too far away to see. Every ancient and deeply rooted self-contained culture, especially if it is spread over a wide part of the earth's surface, constitutes a self-contained world, full of riddles and surprises to Western thinking. As a minimum, we must include in this category China, India, the Muslim world, and Africa, if indeed we accept the approximation of viewing the latter two as uniform. For one thousand years Russia belonged to such a category, although Western thinking systematically committed the mistake of denying its special character and therefore never understood it, just as today the West does not understand Russia in Communist captivity. And while it may be that in past years Japan has increasingly become, in effect, a Far West, drawing ever closer to Western ways (I am no judge here), Israel, I think, should not be reckoned as part of the West, if only because of the decisive circumstance that its state system is fundamentally linked to religion.

How short a time ago, relatively, the small world of modern Europe was easily seizing colonies all over the globe, not only without anticipating any real resistance, but usually with contempt for any possible values in the conquered peoples' approach to life. It all seemed an overwhelming success, with no geographic limits. Western society expanded in a triumph of human independence and power. And all of a sudden the twentieth century brought the clear realization of this society's fragility. We now see that the conquests proved to be short-lived and precarious (and this, in turn, points to defects in the Western view of the world which led to these conquests). Relations with the former colonial world now have switched to the opposite extreme and the Western world often exhibits an excess of obsequiousness, but it is difficult yet to estimate the size of the bill which former colonial countries will present to the West and it is difficult to predict whether the surrender not only of its last colonies, but of everything it owns, will be sufficient for the West to clear this account.

But the persisting blindness of superiority continues to hold the belief that all the vast regions of our planet should develop and mature to the level of contemporary Western systems, the best in theory and the most attractive in practice; that all those other worlds are but temporarily prevented (by wicked leaders or by severe crises or by their own barbarity and incomprehension) from pursuing Western pluralistic democracy and adopting the Western way of life. Countries are judged on the merit of their progress in that direction. But in fact such a conception is a fruit of

Western incomprehension of the essence of other worlds, a result of mistakenly measuring them all with a Western yardstick. The real picture of our planet's development bears little resemblance to all this.

The anguish of a divided world gave birth to the theory of convergence between the leading Western countries and the Soviet Union. It is a soothing theory which overlooks the fact that these worlds are not at all evolving toward each other and that neither one can be transformed into the other without violence. Besides, convergence inevitably means acceptance of the other side's defects, too, and this can hardly suit anyone.

If I were today addressing an audience in my country, in my examination of the overall pattern of the world's rifts I would have concentrated on the calamities of the East. But since my forced exile in the West has now lasted four years and since my audience is a Western one, I think it may be of greater interest to concentrate on certain aspects of the contemporary West, such as I see them.

A decline in courage may be the most striking feature that an outside observer notices in the West today. The Western world has lost its civic courage, both as a whole and separately, in each country, in each government, in each political party, and of course, in the United Nations. Such a decline in courage is particularly noticeable among the ruling and intellectual elites, causing an impression of a loss of courage by the entire society. There remain many courageous individuals, but they have no determining influence on public life. Political and intellectual functionaries exhibit this depression, passivity, and perplexity in their actions and in their statements, and even more so in their self-serving rationales as to how realistic, reasonable, and intellectually and even morally justified it is to base state policies on weakness and cowardice. And the decline in courage, at times attaining what could be termed a lack of manhood, is ironically emphasized by occasional outbursts of boldness and inflexibility on the part of those same functionaries when dealing with weak governments and with countries that lack support, or with doomed currents which clearly cannot offer any resistance. But they get tongue-tied and paralyzed when they deal with powerful governments and threatening forces, with aggressors and international terrorists.

Must one point out that from ancient times a decline in courage has been considered the first symptom of the end?

When the modern Western states were being formed, it was reclaimed as a principle that governments are meant to serve man and that man lives in order to be free and pursue happiness. (See, for example, the American Declaration of Independence.) Now at last during past decades technical and social progress has permitted the realization of such aspirations: the welfare state. Every citizen has been granted the desired freedom and material goods in such quantity and of such quality as to guarantee in theory the achievement of happiness, in the debased sense of the word which has come into being during those same decades. (In the process, however, one psychological detail has been overlooked: the constant desire to have still more things and a still better life and the struggle to this end imprint many Western faces with worry and even depression, though it is customary to carefully conceal such feelings. This active and tense competition comes to dominate all human thought and does not in the least open a way to free spiritual development.) The individual's independence from many types of state pressure has been guaranteed, the majority of the people have been granted well-being to an extent their fathers and grandfathers could not even dream about; it has become possible to raise young people according to these ideals, preparing them for and summoning them toward physical bloom, happiness, the possession of material goods, money, and leisure, toward an almost unlimited freedom in the choice of pleasures. So who should now renounce all this, why and for the sake of what should one risk one's precious life in defense of the common good and particularly in the nebulous case when the security of one's nation must be defended in an as yet distant land?

Even biology tells us that a high degree of habitual well-being is not advantageous to a living organism. Today, well-being in the life of Western society has begun to take off its pernicious mask.

Western society has chosen for itself the organization best suited to its purposes and one I might call legalistic. The limits of human rights and rightness are determined by a system of laws; such limits are very broad. People in the West have acquired considerable skill in using, interpreting, and manipulating law (though laws tend to be too complicated for an average person to understand without the help of an expert). Every conflict is solved according to the letter of the law and this is considered to be the ultimate solution. If one is right from a legal point of view, nothing more is required, nobody may mention that one could still not be entirely right, and urge self-restraint or a renunciation of these rights, call for sacrifice and selfless risk: this would simply sound absurd. Voluntary self-restraint is almost unheard of. Everybody strives toward further expansion to the extreme limit of the legal frames. (An oil company is legally blameless when it buys up an invention of a new type of energy in order to prevent its use. A food product manufacturer is legally blameless when he poisons his produce to make it last longer: after all, people are free not to purchase it.)

I have spent all my life under a Communist regime and I will tell you that a society without any objective legal scale is a terrible one indeed. But a society with no other scale but the legal one is also less than worthy of man. A society based on the letter of the law and never reaching any higher fails to take advantage of the full range of human possibilities. The letter of the law is too cold and formal to have a beneficial influence on society. Whenever the tissue of life is woven of legalistic relationships, this creates an atmosphere of spiritual mediocrity that paralyzes man's noblest impulses.

And it will be simply impossible to bear up to the trials of this threatening century with nothing but the supports of a legalistic structure.

Today's Western society has revealed the inequality between the freedom for good deeds and the freedom for evil deeds. A statesman who wants to achieve something important and highly constructive for his country has to move cautiously and even timidly; thousands of hasty (and irresponsible) critics cling to him at all times; he is constantly rebuffed by parliament and the press. He has to prove that his every step is well-founded and absolutely flawless. Indeed, an outstanding, truly great person who has unusual and unexpected initiatives in mind does not get any chance to assert himself: dozens of traps will be set for him from the beginning. Thus mediocrity triumphs under the guise of democratic restraints.

It is feasible and easy everywhere to undermine administrative power and it has in fact been drastically weakened in all Western countries. The defense of individual rights has reached such extremes as to make society as a whole defenseless against certain individuals. It is time, in the West, to defend not so much human rights as human obligations.

On the other hand, destructive and irresponsible freedom has been granted boundless space. Society has turned out to have scarce defense against the abyss of human decadence, for example against the misuse of liberty for moral violence against young people, such as motion pictures full of pornography, crime, and horror. This is all considered to be part of freedom and to be counterbalanced, in theory, by the young people's right not to look and not to accept. Life organized legalistically has thus shown its inability to defend itself against the corrosion of evil.

And what shall we say about the dark realms of overt criminality? Legal limits (especially in the United States) are broad enough to encourage not only individual freedom but also some misuse of such freedom. The culprit can go unpunished or obtain undeserved leniency—all with the support of thousands of defenders in the society. When a government earnestly undertakes to root out terrorism, public opinion immediately accuses it of violating the terrorists' civil rights. There is quite a number of such cases.

This tilt of freedom toward evil has come about gradually, but it evidently stems from a humanistic and benevolent concept according to which man—the master of this world—does not bear any evil within himself, and all the defects of life are caused by misguided social systems, which must therefore be corrected. Yet strangely enough, though the best social conditions have been achieved in the West, there still remains a great deal of crime; there even is considerably more of it than in the destitute and lawless Soviet society. (There is a multitude of prisoners in our camps who are termed criminals, but most of them never committed any crime; they merely tried to defend themselves against a lawless state by resorting to means outside the legal framework.)

The press, too, of course, enjoys the widest freedom. (I shall be using the word "press" to include all the media.) But what use does it make of it?

Here again, the overriding concern is not to infringe the letter of the law. There is no true moral responsibility for distortion or disproportion. What sort of responsibility does a journalist or a newspaper have to the readership or to history? If they have misled public opinion by inaccurate information or wrong conclusions, even if they have contributed to mistakes on a state level, do we know of any case of open regret voiced by the same journalist or the same newspaper? No; this would damage sales. A nation may be the worse for such a mistake, but the journalist always gets away with it. It is most likely that he will start writing the exact opposite to his previous statements with renewed aplomb.

Because instant and credible information is required, it becomes necessary to resort to guesswork, rumors, and suppositions to fill in the voids, and none of them will ever be refuted; they settle into the readers' memory. How many hasty, immature, superficial, and misleading judgments are expressed every day, confusing readers, and are then left hanging? The press can act the role of public opinion or miseducate it. Thus we may see terrorists heroized, or secret matters pertaining to the nation's defense publicly revealed, or we may witness shameless intrusion into the privacy of well-known people according to the slogan "Everyone is entitled to know everything." (But this is a false slogan of a false era; far greater in value is the forfeited right of people not to know, not to have their divine souls stuffed with gossip, nonsense, vain talk. A person who works and leads a meaningful life has no need for this excessive and burdening flow of information.)

Hastiness and superficiality—these are the psychic diseases of the twentieth century and more than anywhere else this is manifested in the press. In-depth analysis of a problem is anathema to the press; it is contrary to its nature. The press merely picks out sensational formulas.

Such as it is, however, the press has become the greatest power within the Western countries, exceeding that of the legislature, the executive, and the judiciary. Yet one would like to ask: According to what law has it been elected and to whom is it responsible? In the Communist East, a journalist is frankly appointed as a state official. But who has voted Western journalists into their positions of power, for how long, and with what prerogatives?

There is yet another surprise for someone coming from the totalitarian East with its rigorously unified press: One discovers a common trend of preferences within the Western press as a whole (the spirit of the time), generally accepted patterns of judgment, and maybe common corporate interests, the sum effect being not competition but unification. Unrestrained freedom exists for the press, but not for the readership, because newspapers mostly transmit in a forceful and emphatic way those opinions which do not too openly contradict their own and that general trend.

Without any censorship in the West, fashionable trends of thought and ideas are fastidiously separated from those that are not fashionable, and the latter, without ever being forbidden, have little chance of finding their way into periodicals or books or being heard in colleges. Your scholars are free in the legal sense, but they are hemmed in by the idols of the prevailing fad. There is no open violence, as in the East; however, a selection dictated by fashion and the need to accommodate mass standards frequently prevents the most independent-minded persons from contributing to public life and gives rise to dangerous herd instincts that block successful development. In America, I have received letters from highly intelligent persons—maybe a teacher in a faraway small college who could do much for the renewal and salvation of his country, but the country cannot hear him because the media will not provide him with a forum. This gives birth to strong mass prejudices, to a blindness which is perilous in our dynamic era. An example is the self-deluding interpretation of the state of affairs in the contemporary world that functions as a sort of a petrified armor around people's minds, to such a degree that human voices from seventeen countries of Eastern Europe and Eastern Asia cannot pierce it. It will be broken only by the inexorable crowbar of events.

I have mentioned a few traits of Western life which surprise and shock a new arrival to this world. The purpose and scope of this speech will not allow me to continue such a survey, in particular to look into the impact of these characteristics on important aspects of a nation's life, such as elementary education, advanced education in the humanities, and art.

It is almost universally recognized that the West shows all the world the way to successful economic development, even though in past years it has been sharply offset by chaotic inflation. However, many people living in the West are dissatisfied with their own society. They despise it or accuse it of no longer being up to the level of maturity attained by mankind. And this causes many to sway toward socialism, which is a false and dangerous current.

I hope that no one present will suspect me of expressing my partial criticism of the Western system in order to suggest socialism as an alternative. No; with the experience of a country where socialism has been realized, I shall certainly not speak for such an alternative. The mathematician Igor Shafarevich, a member of the Soviet Academy of Science, has written a brilliantly argued book entitled *Socialism*; this is a penetrating historical analysis demonstrating that socialism of any type and shade leads to a total destruction of the human spirit and to a leveling of mankind into death. Shafarevich's book was published in France almost two years ago and so far no one has been found to refute it. It will shortly be published in English in the United States.

But should I be asked, instead, whether I would propose the West, such as it is today, as a model to my country, I would frankly have to answer negatively. No, I could not recommend your society as an ideal for the transformation of ours. Through deep suffering, people in our country have now achieved a spiritual development of such intensity that the Western system in its present state of spiritual exhaustion does not look attractive.

A fact which cannot be disputed is the weakening of human personality in the West while in the East it has become firmer and stronger. Six decades for our people and three decades for the people of Eastern Europe; during that time we have been through a spiritual training far in advance of Western experience. The complex and deadly crush of life has produced stronger, deeper, and more interesting personalities than those generated by standardized Western well-being. Therefore, if our society were to be transformed into yours, it would mean an improvement in certain aspects, but also a change for the worse on some particularly significant points. Of course, a society cannot remain in an abyss of lawlessness, as is the case in our country. But it is also demeaning for it to stay on such a soulless and smooth plane of legalism, as is the case in yours. After the suffering of decades of violence and oppression, the human soul longs for things higher, warmer, and purer than those offered by today's mass living habits, introduced as by a calling card by the revolting invasion of commercial advertising, by TV stupor, and by intolerable music.

All this is visible to numerous observers from all the worlds of our planet. The Western way of life is less and less likely to become the leading model.

There are telltale symptoms by which history gives warning to a threatened or perishing society. Such are, for instance, a decline of the arts or a lack of great statesmen. Indeed, sometimes the warnings are quite explicit and concrete. The center of your democracy and of your culture is left without electric power for a few hours only, and all of a sudden crowds of American citizens start looting and creating havoc. The smooth surface film must be very thin, then, the social system quite unstable and unhealthy.

But the fight for our planet, physical and spiritual, a fight of cosmic proportions, is not a vague matter of the future; it has already started. The forces of Evil have begun their decisive offensive. You can feel their pressure, yet your screens and publications are full of prescribed smiles and raised glasses. What is the joy about?

Very well known representatives of your society, such as George Kennan, say: "We cannot apply moral criteria to politics." Thus we mix good and evil, right and wrong, and make space for the absolute triumph of absolute evil in the world. Only moral criteria can help the West against communism's well-planned world strategy. There are no other criteria. Practical or occasional considerations of any kind will inevitably be swept away by strategy. After a certain level of the problem has been reached, legalistic thinking induces paralysis; it prevents one from seeing the scale and the meaning of events.

In spite of the abundance of information, or maybe partly because of it, the West has great difficulty in finding its bearings amid contemporary events. There have been naive predictions by some American experts who believed that Angola would become the Soviet Union's Vietnam or that the impudent Cuban expeditions in Africa would best be stopped by special U.S. courtesy to Cuba. Kennan's advice to his own country—to begin unilateral disarmament—belongs to the same category. If you only knew how the youngest of the officials in Moscow's Old Square roar with laughter at your political wizards! As to Fidel Castro, he openly scorns the United States, boldly sending his troops to distant adventures from his country right next to yours.

However, the most cruel mistake occurred with the failure to understand the Vietnam war. Some people sincerely wanted all wars to stop just as soon as possible; others believed that the way should be left open for national, or Communist, self-determination in Vietnam (or in Cambodia, as we see today with particular clarity). But in fact, members of the U.S. antiwar movement became accomplices in the betrayal of Far Eastern nations, in the genocide and the suffering today imposed on thirty million people there. Do these convinced pacifists now hear the moans coming from there? Do they understand their responsibility today? Or do they prefer not to hear? The American intelligentsia lost its nerve and as a consequence the danger has come much closer to the United States. But there is no awareness of this. Your short-sighted politician who signed the hasty Vietnam capitulation seemingly gave America a carefree breathing pause; however, a hundredfold Vietnam now looms over you. Small Vietnam had been a warning and an occasion to mobilize the nation's courage. But if the full might of America suffered a full-fledged defeat at the hands of a small Communist half-country, how can the West hope to stand firm in the future?

I have said on another occasion that in the twentieth century Western democracy has not won any major war by itself; each time it shielded itself with an ally possessing a powerful land army, whose philosophy it did not question. In World War II against Hitler, instead of winning the conflict with its own forces, which would certainly have been sufficient, Western democracy raised up another enemy, one that would prove worse and more powerful, since Hitler had neither the resources nor the people, nor the ideas with broad appeal, nor such a large number of supporters in the West—a fifth column—as the Soviet Union possessed. Some Western voices already have spoken of the need of a protective screen against hostile forces in the next world conflict; in this case, the shield would be China. But I would not wish such an outcome to any country in the world. First of all, it is again a doomed alliance with evil; it would grant the United States a respite, but when at a later date China with its billion people would turn around armed with American weapons, America itself would fall victim to a Cambodia-style genocide.

And yet, no weapons, no matter how powerful, can help the West until it overcomes its loss of will power. In a state of psychological weakness, weapons even become a burden for the capitulating side. To defend oneself, one must also be ready to die; there is little such readiness in a society raised in the cult of material well-being. Nothing is left, in this case, but concessions, attempts to gain time, and betrayal. Thus at the shameful Belgrade conference, free Western diplomats in their weakness surrendered the line of defense for which enslaved members of the Helsinki Watch Groups are sacrificing their lives.

Western thinking has become conservative: the world situation must stay as it is at any cost; there must be no changes. This debilitating dream of a status quo is the symptom of a society that has ceased to develop. But one must be blind in order not to see that the oceans no longer belong to the West, while the land under its domination keeps shrinking. The two so-called world wars (they were by far not on a world scale, not yet) constituted the internal self-destruction of the small progressive West which has thus prepared its own end. The next war (which does not have to be an atomic one; I do not believe it will be) may well bury Western civilization forever.

In the face of such danger, with such historical values in your past, with such a high level of attained freedom and, apparently, a devotion to it, how is it possible to lose to such an extent the will to defend oneself?

How has this unfavorable relation of forces come about? How did the West decline from its triumphal march to its present debility? Have there been fatal turns and losses of direction in its development? It does not seem so. The West kept advancing steadily in accordance with its proclaimed social intentions, hand in hand with a dazzling progress in technology. And all of a sudden it found itself in its present state of weakness.

This means that the mistake must be at the root, at the very foundation of thought in modern times. I refer to the prevailing Western view of the world which was born in the Renaissance and has found political expression since the Age of Enlightenment. It became the basis for political and social doctrine and could be called rationalistic humanism or humanistic autonomy: the proclaimed and practiced autonomy of man from any higher force above him. It could also be called anthropocentricity, with man seen as the center of all.

The turn introduced by the Renaissance was probably inevitable historically: the Middle Ages had come to a natural end by exhaustion, having become an intolerable despotic repression of man's physical nature in favor of the spiritual one. But then we recoiled from the spirit and embraced all that is material, excessively and incommensurately. The humanistic way of thinking, which has proclaimed itself our guide, did not admit the existence of intrinsic evil in man, nor did it see any task higher than the attainment of happiness on earth. It started modern Western civilization on the dangerous trend of worshipping man and his material needs. Everything beyond physical well-being and the accumulation of material goods, all other human requirements and characteristics of a subtler and higher nature, were left outside the area of attention of state and social systems, as if human life did not have any higher meaning. Thus gaps were left open for evil, and its drafts blow freely today. Mere freedom per se does not in the least solve all the problems of human life and even adds a number of new ones.

And yet in early democracies, as in American democracy at the time of its birth, all individual rights were granted on the ground that man is God's creature. That is, freedom was given to the individual conditionally, in the assumption of his constant religious responsibility. Such was the heritage of the receding one thousand years. Two hundred or even fifty years ago, it would have seemed quite impossible, in America, that an individual be granted boundless freedom with no purpose, simply for the satisfaction of his whims. Subsequently, however, all such limitations were eroded everywhere in the West; a total emancipation occurred from the moral heritage of Christian centuries with their great reserves of mercy and sacrifice. State systems were becoming ever more materialistic. The West has finally achieved the rights of man, and even to excess, but man's sense of responsibility to God and society has grown dimmer and dimmer. In the past decades, the legalistic selfishness of the Western approach to the world has reached its peak and the world has found itself in a harsh spiritual crisis and a political impasse. All the celebrated technological achievements of progress, including the conquest of outer space, do not redeem the twentieth century's moral poverty, which no one could have imagined even as late as the nineteenth century.

As humanism in its development was becoming more and more materialistic, it also increasingly allowed its concepts to be used first by socialism and then by communism. So that Karl Marx was able to say, in 1844, that "communism is naturalized humanism."

This statement has proved to be not entirely unreasonable. One does see the same stones in the foundations of an eroded humanism and of any type of socialism: boundless materialism; freedom from religion and religious responsibility (which under Communist regimes attains the stage of antireligious dictatorship); concentration on social structures with an allegedly scientific approach. (This last is typical of both the Age of Enlightenment and of Marxism.) It is no accident that all of communism's rhetorical vows revolve around Man (with a capital M) and his earthly happiness. At first glance it seems an ugly parallel: common traits in the thinking and way of life of today's West and today's East? But such is the logic of materialistic development.

The interrelationship is such, moreover, that the current of materialism which is farthest to the left, and is hence the most consistent, always proves to be stronger, more attractive, and victorious. Humanism which has lost its Christian heritage cannot prevail in this competition. Thus during the past centuries and especially in recent decades, as the process became more acute, the alignment of forces was as follows: Liberalism was inevitably pushed aside by radicalism, radicalism had to surrender to socialism, and socialism could not stand up to communism. The Communist regime in the East could endure and grow due to the enthusiastic support from an enormous number of Western intellectuals who (feeling the kinship!) refused to see communism's crimes, and when they no longer could do so, they tried to justify these crimes. The problem persists: In our Eastern countries, communism has suffered a complete ideological defeat; it is zero and less than zero. And yet Western intellectuals still look at it with considerable interest and empathy, and this is precisely what makes it so immensely difficult for the West to withstand the East.

I am not examining the case of a disaster brought on by a world war and the changes which it would produce in society. But as long as we wake up every morning under a peaceful sun, we must lead an everyday life. Yet there is a disaster which is already very much with us. I am referring to the calamity of an autonomous, irreligious humanistic consciousness.

It has made man the measure of all things on earth—imperfect man, who is never free of pride, self-interest, envy, vanity, and dozens of other defects. We are now paying for the mistakes which were not properly appraised at the beginning of the journey. On the way from the Renaissance to our days we have enriched our experience, but we have lost the concept of a Supreme Complete Entity which used to restrain our passions and our irresponsibility. We have placed too much hope in politics and social reforms, only to find out that we were being deprived of our most precious possession: our spiritual life. It is trampled by the party mob in the East, by the commercial one in the West. This is the essence of the crisis: the split in the world is less terrifying than the similarity of the disease afflicting its main sections.

If, as claimed by humanism, man were born only to be happy, he would not be born to die. Since his body is doomed to death, his task on earth evidently must be more spiritual: not a total engrossment in everyday life, not the search for the best ways to obtain material goods and then their carefree consumption. It has to be the fulfillment of a permanent, earnest duty so that one's life journey may become above all an experience of moral growth: to leave life a better human being than one started it. It is imperative to reappraise the scale of the usual human values; its present incorrectness is astounding. It is not possible that assessment of the President's performance should be reduced to the question of how much money one makes or to the availability of gasoline. Only by the voluntary nurturing in ourselves of freely accepted and serene self-restraint can mankind rise above the world stream of materialism.

Today it would be retrogressive to hold on to the ossified formulas of the Enlightenment. Such social dogmatism leaves us helpless before the trials of our times.

Even if we are spared destruction by war, life will have to change in order not to perish on its own. We cannot avoid reassessing the fundamental definitions of human life and human society. Is it true that man is above everything? Is there no Superior Spirit above him? Is it right that man's life and society's activities should be ruled by material expansion above all? Is it permissible to promote such expansion to the detriment of our integral spiritual life?

If the world has not approached its end, it has reached a major watershed in history, equal in importance to the turn from the Middle Ages to the Renaissance. It will demand from us a spiritual blaze; we shall have to rise to a new height of vision, to a new level of life, where our physical nature will not be cursed, as in the Middle Ages, but even more importantly, our spiritual being will not be trampled upon, as in the Modern Era.

This ascension is similar to climbing onto the next anthropological stage. No one on earth has any other way left but—upward.

Pope John Paul II
[1920–]

Archbishop of Krákow Karol Jozef Wojtyla was elected pope on October 16, 1978. His speech to the United Nations sounded many of the major themes which would guide his papacy over the next decades—the dignity of all human life, the values of spirituality, the urgent need for peace and social justice—and introduced him as an authoritative and energetic presence in world affairs.

ADDRESS TO THE UNITED NATIONS GENERAL ASSEMBLY
October 2, 1979

MR. PRESIDENT: my address today will be published in its entirety just as I wrote it. Because of its length, however, I shall now read it in a shortened form.

I desire to express my gratitude to the General Assembly of the United Nations, which I am permitted today to participate in and to address. My thanks go in the first place to the secretary general of the United Nations organization, Dr. Kurt Waldheim. Last autumn, soon after my election to the Chair of St. Peter, he invited me to make this visit, and he renewed his invitation in the course of our meeting in Rome last May. From the first moment I felt greatly honored and deeply obliged. And today, before this distinguished assembly, I also thank you, Mr. President, who have so kindly welcomed me and invited me to speak.

The formal reason for my intervention today is, without any question, the special bond of cooperation that links the Apostolic See with the United Nations organization, as is shown by the presence of the Holy See's permanent observer to this organization. The existence of this bond, which is held in high esteem by the Holy See, rests on the sovereignty with which the Apostolic See has been endowed for many centuries. The territorial extent of that sovereignty is limited to the small state of Vatican City, but the sovereignty itself is warranted by the need of the papacy to exercise its mission in full freedom and to be able to deal with any interlocutor, whether a government or an international organization, without dependence on other sovereignties. Of course the nature and aims of the spiritual mission of the Apostolic See and the Church make their participation in the tasks and activities of the United Nations very different from that of the states, which are communities in the political and temporal sense.

Besides attaching great importance to its collaboration with the United Nations organization, the Apostolic See has always since the foundation of your organization, expressed its esteem and its agreement with the historic significance of this supreme forum for the international life of humanity today. It also never ceases to support your organization's functions and initiatives, which are aimed at peaceful coexistence and collaboration between nations. There are many proofs of this. In the more than thirty years of the existence of the United Nations, it has received much attention in papal messages and encyclicals, in documents of the Catholic episcopate and likewise in the Second Vatican Council. Pope John XXIII and Pope Paul VI looked with confidence on your important institution as an eloquent and promising sign of our times. He who is now addressing you has, since the first months of his pontificate, several times expressed the same confidence and conviction as his predecessors.

This confidence and conviction on the part of the Apostolic See are the result, as I have said, not of merely political reasons but of the religious and moral character of the mission of the Roman Catholic Church. As a universal community embracing faithful belonging to almost all countries and continents, nations, peoples, races, languages and cultures, the Church is deeply interested in the existence and activity of the organization whose very name tells us that it unites and associates nations and states. It unites and associates, it does not divide and oppose. It seeks out the ways for understanding and peaceful collaboration, and endeavors with the means at its disposal and the methods in its power to exclude war, division and mutual destruction within the great family of humanity today.

This is the real reason, the essential reason, for my presence among you, and I wish to thank this distinguished assembly for giving consideration to this reason, which can make my presence among you in some way useful. Here, before the representatives of the states, I wish not only to thank you but also to offer you my special congratulations, since the invitation to the Pope to speak in your assembly shows that the United Nations organization accepts and respects the religious and moral dimension of those human problems that the church attends, in view of the message of troth and love that it is her duty to bring to the world.

The questions that concern your functions and receive your attention—as is indicated by the vast organic complex of institutions and activities that are part of or collaborate with the United Nations, especially in the fields of culture, health, food, labor and the peaceful uses of nuclear energy—certainly make it essential for us to meet in the name of man in his wholeness, in all the fullness and manifold riches of his spiritual and material existence, as I have stated in my encyclical *Redemptor Hominis*, the first of my pontificate.

Now, availing myself of the solemn occasion of my meeting with the representatives of the nations of the earth, I wish above all to send my greetings to all the men and women living on this planet. To every man and every woman, without any exception whatever, every human being living on earth is a member of a civil society, of a nation, many of them represented here.

Each one of you, distinguished ladies and gentlemen, represents a particular state, system and political structure, but what you represent above all are individual human beings. You are all representatives of men and women, of practically all the people of the world—individual men and women, communities and peoples who are living the present phase of their own history and who are also part of the history of humanity as a whole, each of them a subject endowed with dignity as a human person with his or her own culture, experiences and aspirations, tensions and sufferings, and legitimate expectations. This relationship is what provides the reason for all political activities, whether national or international, for in the final analysis this activity comes from man, is exercised by man and is for man. I would like to express the wish that in view of its universal character, the United Nations organization will never cease to be the forum, the high tribune from which all man's problems are appraised in truth and justice.

It was in the name of this inspiration, it was through this historic stimulus, that on June 26, 1945, toward the end of the terrible World War II, the charter of the United Nations was signed and on the following October 24, your organization began its life. Soon after, on December 10, 1948, came its fundamental document, the Universal Declaration of Human Rights, the rights of the human being as a concrete individual and of the human being in his universal value. This document is a milestone on the long and difficult path of the human race. The progress of humanity must be measured not only by the progress of science and technology, which shows man's uniqueness with regard to nature, but also and chiefly by the primacy given to spiritual values and by the progress of moral life.

Today, forty years after the outbreak of World War II, I wish to recall the whole of the experiences by individuals and nations that were sustained by a generation that is largely still alive. I had occasion not long ago to reflect again on some of those experiences, in one of the places that are most distressing and overflowing with contempt for man and his fundamental rights—the extermination camp of Auschwitz, which I visited during my pilgrimage to Poland last June. This infamous place is unfortunately only one of the many scattered over the continent of Europe. But the memory of even one should be a warning sign on the path of humanity today, in order that every kind of concentration camp anywhere on earth may once and for all be done away with. And everything that recalls those horrible experiences should also disappear forever from the lives of nations and states, everything that is a continuation of those experiences under different forms, namely the various kinds of torture and oppression, either physical or moral, carried out under any system, in any land. This phenomenon is all the more distressing if it occurs under the pretext of internal security or the need to preserve an apparent peace.

You will forgive me, ladies and gentlemen, for evoking this memory. But I would be untrue to the history of this century, I would be dishonest with regard to the great cause of man, which we all wish to serve, if I should keep silent, I who come from the country on whose living body Auschwitz was at one time constructed. But my purpose in invoking this memory is above all to show what painful experiences and sufferings by millions of people gave rise to the Universal Declaration of Human Rights, which has been placed as the basic inspiration and cornerstone of the United Nations organization.

This declaration was paid for by millions of our brothers and sisters at the cost of their suffering and sacrifice, brought about by the brutalization that darkened and made insensitive the human consciences of their oppressors and of those who carried out a real genocide. This price cannot have been paid in vain. If the truths and principles contained in this document were to be forgotten or ignored and were thus to lose the genuine self-evidence that distinguished them at the time they were brought painfully to birth, then the noble purpose of the United Nations could be faced with the threat of a new destruction. This is what would happen if the simple yet powerful eloquence of the Universal Declaration of Human Rights were decisively subjugated by what is wrongly called political interest, but often really means no more than one-sided gain and advantage to the detriment of others, or a thirst for power regardless of the needs of others—everything which by its nature is opposed to the spirit of the declaration. Political interest understood in this sense, if you will pardon me, ladies and gentlemen, dishonors the noble and difficult mission of your service for the good of your countries and of all humanity.

Fourteen years ago my great predecessor Pope Paul VI spoke from this podium. He spoke memorable words, which I desire to repeat today: "No more war, war never again. Never one against the other" or even one above the other, "but always," on every occasion, "with each other."

Paul VI was a tireless servant of the cause of peace. I wish to follow him with all my strength and continue his service. The Catholic Church in every place on earth proclaims a message of peace, prays for peace, educates for peace. This purpose is also shared by the representatives and followers of other churches and communities and of other religions of the world, and they have pledged themselves to it. In union with efforts by all people of good will, this work is certainly bearing fruit. Nevertheless we are continually troubled by the armed conflicts that break out from time to time. How grateful we are to the Lord when a direct intervention succeeds in avoiding such a conflict, as in the case of the tension that last year threatened Argentina and Chile.

It is my fervent hope that a solution also to the Middle East crises may draw nearer. While being prepared to recognize the value of any concrete step or attempt made to settle the conflict, I want to recall that it would have no value if it did not truly represent the first stone of a general over-all peace in the area, a peace that, being necessarily based on equitable recognition of the rights of all, cannot fail to include the consideration and just settlement of the Palestinian question. Connected with this question is that of the tranquillity, independence and territorial integrity of Lebanon within the formula that has made it an example of peaceful and mutually fruitful coexistence between distinct communities, a formula that I hope will, in the common interest, be maintained, with the adjustments required by the developments of the situation. I also hope for a special statute that, under international guarantees, as my predecessor Paul VI indicated, would respect the particular nature of Jerusalem, a heritage sacred to the veneration of millions of believers of the three great monotheistic religions, Judaism, Christianity and Islam.

We are troubled also by reports of the development of weaponry exceeding in quality and size the means of war and destruction ever known before. In this field also we applaud the decisions and agreements aimed at reducing the arms race. Nevertheless, the life of humanity today is seriously endangered by the threat of destruction and by the risk arising even from accepting certain tranquilizing reports. The continual preparations for war demonstrated by the production of ever more numerous, powerful and sophisticated weapons in various countries show that there is a desire to be ready for war, and being ready means being able to start it. It also means taking the risk that sometime, somewhere, somehow, someone can set in motion the terrible mechanism of general destruction.

It is therefore necessary to make a continuing and even more energetic effort to do away with the very possibility of provoking war, and to make such catastrophes impossible by influencing the attitudes and convictions, the very intentions and aspirations of governments and peoples. This duty, kept constantly in mind by the United Nations and each of its institutions, must also be a duty for every society, every regime, every government. This task is certainly served by initiatives aimed at international cooperation for the fostering of development. As Paul VI said at the end of his encyclical *Populorum Progressio*, "If the new name for peace is development, who would not wish to labor for it with all his powers?" However, this task must also be served by constant reflection and activity aimed at discovering the very roots of hatred, destructiveness and contempt—the roots of everything that produces the temptation to war, not so much in the hearts of the nations as in the inner determination of the systems that decide the history of whole societies.

The Universal Declaration of Human Rights has struck a real blow against the many deep roots of war, since the spirit of war, in its basic primordial meaning, springs up and grows to maturity where the inalienable rights of man are violated. This is a new and deeply relevant vision of the cause of peace, one that goes deeper and is more radical. It is a vision that sees the genesis, and in a sense the substance, of war in the more complex forms emanating from injustice viewed in all its various aspects. This injustice first attacks human rights and thereby destroys the organic unity of the social order, and it then affects the whole system of international relations. By applying this criterion we must diligently examine which principal tensions in connection with the inalienable rights of man can weaken the construction of this peace which we all desire so ardently and which is the essential goal of the efforts of the United Nations organization.

Man lives at the same time both in the world of material values and in that of spiritual values. For the individual living and hoping man, his needs, freedoms and relationships with others never concern one sphere of values alone, but belong to both. Material and spiritual realities may be viewed separately in order to understand better that in the concrete human being they are inseparable, and to see that any threat to human rights, whether in the field of material realities or in that of spiritual realities, is equally dangerous for peace, since in every instance it concerns man in his entirety.

Permit me, distinguished ladies and gentlemen, to recall a constant rule of the history of humanity, a rule that is implicitly contained in all that I have already stated with regard to integral development and human rights. The rule is based on the relationship between spiritual values and material or economic values. In this relationship, it is the spiritual values that are preeminent, both on account of the nature of these values and also for reasons concerning the good of man. It is easy to see that material goods do not have unlimited capacity for satisfying the needs of man: They are not in themselves easily distributed and, in the relationship between those who possess and enjoy them and those who are without them, they give rise to tension, dissension and division that will often even turn into open conflict. Spiritual goods, on the other hand, are open to unlimited enjoyment by many at the same time, without diminution of the goods themselves.

A critical analysis of our modern civilization shows that in the last hundred years it has contributed as never before to the development of material goods, but that it has also given rise, both in theory and still more in practice, to a series of attitudes in which sensitivity to the spiritual dimension of human existence is diminished to a greater or less extent, as a result of certain premises which reduce the meaning of human life chiefly to the many different material and economic factors—I mean to the demands of production, the market, consumption, the accumulation of riches or of the growing bureaucracy with which an attempt is made to regulate these very processes. Is this not the result of having subordinated man to one single conception and sphere of values?

What is the link between these reflections and the cause of peace and war? Since, as I have already stated, material goods by their very nature provoke conditionings and divisions, the struggle to obtain these goods becomes inevitable in the history of humanity. If we cultivate this one-sided subordination of man to material goods alone, we shall be incapable of overcoming this state of need. We shall be able to attenuate it and avoid it in particular cases, but we shall not succeed in eliminating it systematically and radically, unless we emphasize more and pay greater honor, before everyone's eyes, in the sight of every society, to the second dimension of the goods of man: the dimension that does not divide people but puts them into communication with each other, associates them and unites them.

I consider that the famous opening words of the Charter of the United Nations, in which the peoples of the United Nations, determined to save succeeding generations from the scourge of war, solemnly reaffirmed "faith in fundamental human rights, in the dignity and worth of the human person, in the equal rights of men and women and of nations large and small," are meant to stress this dimension. An analysis of the history of mankind, especially at its present stage, shows how important is the duty of revealing more fully the range of the goods that are linked with the spiritual dimension of human existence. It shows how important this task is for building peace and how serious is any threat to human rights. Any violation of them, even in a peace situation, is a form of warfare against humanity.

It seems that in the modern world there are two main threats. Both concern human rights in the field of international relations and human rights within the individual states or societies. The first of these systematic threats against human rights is linked in an overall sense with the distribution of material goods. This distribution is frequently unjust both within individual societies and on the planet as a whole. Everyone knows that these goods are given to man not only as nature's bounty; they are enjoyed by him chiefly as the fruit of his many activities, ranging from the simplest manual and physical labor to the most complicated forms of industrial production and highly qualified and specialized research and study. Various forms of inequality in the possession of material goods, and in the enjoyment of them, can often be explained by different historical and cultural causes and circumstances. But, while these circumstances can diminish the moral responsibility of people today, they do not prevent the situations of inequality from being marked by injustice and social injury.

People must become aware that economic tensions within countries and in the relationship between states and even between entire continents contain within themselves substantial elements that restrict or violate human rights. Such elements are the exploitation of labor and many other abuses that affect the dignity of the human person. It follows that the fundamental criterion for comparing social, economic and political systems is not, and cannot be, the criterion of hegemony and imperialism; it can be, and indeed it must be, the humanistic criterion, namely the measure in which each system is really capable of reducing, restraining and eliminating as far as possible the various forms of exploitation of man and of ensuring for him through work, not only the just distribution of the indispensable material goods, but also a participation, in keeping with his dignity, in the whole process of production and in the social life that grows up around that process.

Disturbing factors are frequently present in the form of the frightful disparities between excessively rich individuals and groups on the one hand, and on the other hand the majority made up of the poor or indeed of the destitute, who lack food and opportunities for work and education and are in great numbers condemned to hunger and disease. And concern is also caused at times by the radical separation of work from property, by man's indifference to the production enterprise to which he is linked only by a work obligation, without feeling that he is working for a good that will be his or for himself. It is no secret that the abyss separating the minority of the excessively rich from the multitude of the destitute is a very grave symptom in the life of any society. This must also be said with even greater insistence with regard to the abyss separating countries and regions of the earth. Surely the only way to overcome this serious disparity between areas of satiety and areas of hunger and depression is through coordinated cooperation by all countries. This requires above all else a unity inspired by an authentic perspective of peace. Everything will depend on whether these differences and contrasts in the sphere of the possession of goods will be systematically reduced through truly effective means, on whether the belts of hunger, malnutrition, destitution, underdevelopment, disease and illiteracy will disappear from the economic map of the earth, and on whether peaceful cooperation will avoid imposing conditions of exploitation and economic or political dependence, which would only be a form of neocolonialism.

I would now like to draw attention to a second systematic threat to man in his inalienable rights in the modern world, a threat which constitutes no less a danger than the first to the cause of peace. I refer to the various forms of injustice in the field of the spirit. Man can indeed be wounded in his inner relationship with truth, in his conscience, in his most personal belief, in his view of the world, in his religious faith, and in the sphere of what are known as civil liberties. Decisive for these last is equality of rights without discrimination on grounds of origin, race, sex, nationality, religion, political convictions and the like. For centuries the thrust of civilization has been in one direction: that of giving the life of individual political societies a form in which there can be fully safeguarded the objective rights of the spirit, of human conscience and of human creativity, including man's relationship with God. Yet, in spite of this, we still see in this field recurring threats and violations, often with no possibility of appealing to a higher authority or of obtaining an effective remedy.

Besides the acceptance of legal formulas safeguarding the principle of the freedom of the human spirit, such as freedom of thought and expression, religious freedom and freedom of conscience, structures of social life often exist in which the practical exercise of these freedoms condemns man, in fact if not formally, to become a second class or third class citizen, to see compromised his chances of social advancement, his professional career or his access to certain posts of responsibility, and to lose even the possibility of educating his children freely. It is a question of the highest importance that in internal social life, as well as in international life, all human beings in every nation and country should be able to enjoy effectively their full rights under any political regime or system. Only the safeguarding of this real completeness of rights for every human being without discrimination can ensure peace at its very roots.

With regard to religious freedom, which I as pope am bound to have particularly at heart, precisely with a view to safeguarding peace, I would like to repeat here, as a contribution to respect for man's spiritual dimension, some principles contained in the Second Vatican Council's declaration *Dignitatis Humanae*. "In accordance with their dignity, all human beings, because they are persons, that is, beings endowed with reason and free will and therefore bearing personal responsibility, are both impelled by their nature and bound by a moral obligation to seek the truth, especially religious truth. They are also bound to adhere to the truth once they come to know it and to direct their whole lives in accordance with its demands. The practice of religion of its very nature consists primarily of those voluntary and free internal acts by which a human being directly sets his course toward God. No merely human power can either command or prohibit acts of this kind. But man's social nature itself requires that he give external expression to his internal acts of religion, that he communicate with others in religious matters and that he profess his religion in community."

These words touch the very substance of the question. They also show how even the confrontation between the religious view of the world and the agnostic or even atheistic view, which is one of the signs of the times of the present age, could preserve honest and respectful human dimensions without violating the essential rights of conscience of any man or woman living on earth.

Respect for the dignity of the human person would seem to demand that, when the exact tenor of the exercise of religious freedom is being discussed or determined with a view to national laws or international conventions, the institutions that are by their nature at the service of religion should also be brought in. If this participation is omitted, there is a danger of imposing, in so intimate a field of man's life, rules or restrictions that are opposed to his true religious needs.

The United Nations has proclaimed 1979 the Year of the Child. In this perspective we must ask ourselves whether there will continue to accumulate over the heads of this new generation of children the threat of common extermination for which the means are in the hands of the modern states, especially the major world powers. Are the children to receive the arms race from us as a necessary inheritance? How are we to explain this unbridled race?

The ancients said: *"Si vis pacem, para bellum."* But can our age still really believe that the breathtaking spiral of armaments is at the service of world peace? In alleging the threat of a potential enemy, is it really not rather the intention to keep for oneself a means of threat, in order to get the upper hand with the aid of one's own arsenal of destruction? Here too it is the human dimension of peace that tends to vanish in favor of ever-new possible forms of imperialism.

It must be our solemn wish here for our children, for the children of all the nations on earth, that this point will never be reached. And for that reason I do not cease to pray to God each day so that in his mercy he may save us from so terrible a day.

At the close of this address, I wish to express once more before all the high representatives of the states who are present a word of esteem and deep love for all the peoples, all the nations of the earth, for all human communities. Each one has its own history and culture. I hope that they will live and grow in the freedom and truth of their own history. For that is the measure of the common good of each one of them. I hope that each person will live and grow strong with the moral force of the community that forms its members as citizens. I hope that the state authorities, while respecting the just rights of each citizen, will enjoy the confidence of all for the common good. I hope that all the nations, even the smallest, even those that do not yet enjoy full sovereignty and those that have been forcibly robbed of it, will meet in full equality with the others in the United Nations organization. I hope that the United Nations will ever remain the supreme forum of peace and justice, the authentic seat of freedom of peoples and individuals in their longing for a better future.

Ronald Reagan
[1911–   ]

An ex-Hollywood actor and, ex-corporate spokesman for General Electric named Ronald Reagan burst onto the American political scene in 1964 when he delivered a televised address supporting the presidential candidacy of Senator Barry Goldwater. As Governor of California, and then as President of the United States, Reagan gained a reputation as "The Great Communicator" for his ability to draw together his diverse constituencies of economic libertarians, social and religious conservatives, and cold war hawks by combining a uniquely informal, almost conversational delivery style with vivid, often sentimentalized imagery and a canny use of television. For his inauguration, the ceremony was for the first time held on the west steps of the Capitol instead of the east, so that TV cameras could be scripted to pan over the monuments in sync with his references to them in the speech. The drama was further heightened by an announcement made during the inauguration's opening prayer that American hostages held by Iranian revolutionaries in Tehran since November 1979 were to be released.

FIRST INAUGURAL ADDRESS
January 20, 1981

SENATOR HATFIELD, Mr. Chief Justice, Mr. President, Vice President Bush, Vice President Mondale, Senator Baker, Speaker O'Neill, Reverend Moomaw, and my fellow citizens: To a few of us here today, this is a solemn and most momentous occasion; and yet, in the history of our Nation, it is a commonplace occurrence. The orderly transfer of authority as called for in the Constitution routinely takes place as it has for almost two centuries and few of us stop to think how unique we really are. In the eyes of many in the world, this every-four-year ceremony we accept as normal is nothing less than a miracle.

Mr. President, I want our fellow citizens to know how much you did to carry on this tradition. By your gracious cooperation in the transition process, you have shown a watching world that we are a united people pledged to maintaining a political system which guarantees individual liberty to a greater degree than any other, and I thank you and your people for all your help in maintaining the continuity which is the bulwark of our Republic.

The business of our nation goes forward. These United States are confronted with an economic affliction of great proportions. We suffer from the longest and one of the worst sustained inflations in our national history. It distorts our economic decisions, penalizes thrift, and crushes the struggling young and the fixed-income elderly alike. It threatens to shatter the lives of millions of our people.

Idle industries have cast workers into unemployment, causing human misery and personal indignity. Those who do work are denied a fair return for their labor by a tax system which penalizes successful achievement and keeps us from maintaining full productivity.

But great as our tax burden is, it has not kept pace with public spending. For decades, we have piled deficit upon deficit, mortgaging our future and our children's future for the temporary convenience of the present. To continue this long trend is to guarantee tremendous social, cultural, political, and economic upheavals.

You and I, as individuals, can, by borrowing, live beyond our means, but for only a limited period of time. Why, then, should we think that collectively, as a nation, we are not bound by that same limitation?

We must act today in order to preserve tomorrow. And let there be no misunderstanding—we are going to begin to act, beginning today.

The economic ills we suffer have come upon us over several decades. They will not go away in days, weeks, or months, but they will go away. They will go away because we, as Americans, have the capacity now, as we have had in the past, to do whatever needs to be done to preserve this last and greatest bastion of freedom.

In this present crisis, government is not the solution to our problem. Government is the problem.

From time to time, we have been tempted to believe that society has become too complex to be managed by self-rule, that government by an elite group is superior to government for, by, and of the people. But if no one among us is capable of governing himself, then who among us has the capacity to govern someone else? All of us together, in and out of government, must bear the burden. The solutions we seek must be equitable, with no one group singled out to pay a higher price.

We hear much of special interest groups. Well, our concern must be for a special interest group that has been too long neglected. It knows no sectional boundaries or ethnic and racial divisions, and it crosses political party lines. It is made up of men and women who raise our food, patrol our streets, man our mines and our factories, teach our children, keep our homes, and heal us when we are sick—professionals, industrialists, shopkeepers, clerks, cabbies, and truck drivers. They are, in short, "We the people," this breed called Americans.

Well, this administration's objective will be a healthy, vigorous, growing economy that provides equal opportunity for all Americans, with no barriers born of bigotry or discrimination. Putting America back to work means putting all Americans back to work. Ending inflation means freeing all Americans from the terror of runaway living costs. All must share in the productive work of this "new beginning" and all must share in the bounty of a revived economy. With the idealism and fair play which are the core of our system and our strength, we can have a strong and prosperous America at peace with itself and the world.

So, as we begin, let us take inventory. We are a nation that has a government—not the other way around. And this makes us special among the nations of the Earth. Our Government has no power except that granted it by the people. It is time to check and reverse the growth of government which shows signs of having grown beyond the consent of the governed.

It is my intention to curb the size and influence of the Federal establishment and to demand recognition of the distinction between the powers granted to the Federal Government and those reserved to the States or to the people. All of us need to be reminded that the Federal Government did not create the States; the States created the Federal Government.

Now, so there will be no misunderstanding, it is not my intention to do away with government. It is, rather, to make it work—work with us, not over us; to stand by our side, not ride on our back. Government can and must provide opportunity, not smother it; foster productivity, not stifle it.

If we look to the answer as to why, for so many years, we achieved so much, prospered as no other people on Earth, it was because here, in this land, we unleashed the energy and individual genius of man to a greater extent than has ever been done before. Freedom and the dignity of the individual have been more available and assured here than in any other place on Earth. The price for this freedom at times has been high, but we have never been unwilling to pay that price.

It is no coincidence that our present troubles parallel and are proportionate to the intervention and intrusion in our lives that result from unnecessary and excessive growth of government. It is time for us to realize that we are too great a nation to limit ourselves to small dreams. We are not, as some would have us believe, doomed to an inevitable decline. I do not believe in a fate that will fall on us no matter what we do. I do believe in a fate that will fall on us if we do nothing. So, with all the creative energy at our command, let us begin an era of national renewal. Let us renew our determination, our courage, and our strength. And let us renew our faith and our hope.

We have every right to dream heroic dreams. Those who say that we are in a time when there are no heroes—they just don't know where to look. You can see heroes every day going in and out of factory gates. Others, a handful in number, produce enough food to feed all of us and then the world beyond. You meet heroes across a counter—and they are on both sides of that counter. There are entrepreneurs with faith in themselves and faith in an idea who create new jobs, new wealth and opportunity. There are individuals and families whose taxes support the Government and whose voluntary gifts support church, charity, culture, art, and education. Their patriotism is quiet but deep. Their values sustain our national life.

I have used the words "they" and "their" in speaking of these heroes. I could say "you" and "your" because I am addressing the heroes of whom I speak—you, the citizens of this blessed land. Your dreams, your hopes, your goals are going to be the dreams, the hopes, and the goals of this administration, so help me God.

We shall reflect the compassion that is so much a part of your makeup. How can we love our country and not love our countrymen, and loving them, reach out a hand when they fall, heal them when they are sick, and provide opportunities to make them self-sufficient so they will be equal in fact and not just in theory?

Can we solve the problems confronting us? Well, the answer is an unequivocal and emphatic "yes." To paraphrase Winston Churchill, I did not take the oath I have just taken with the intention of presiding over the dissolution of the world's strongest economy.

In the days ahead I will propose removing the roadblocks that have slowed our economy and reduced productivity. Steps will be taken aimed at restoring the balance between the various levels of government. Progress may be slow—measured in inches and feet, not miles—but we will progress. It is time to reawaken this industrial giant, to get government back within its means, and to lighten our punitive tax burden. And these will be our first priorities, and on these principles, there will be no compromise.

On the eve of our struggle for independence a man who might have been one of the greatest among the Founding Fathers, Dr. Joseph Warren, President of the Massachusetts Congress, said to his fellow Americans, "Our country is in danger, but not to be despaired of. . . . On you depend the fortunes of America. You are to decide the important questions upon which rests the happiness and the liberty of millions yet unborn. Act worthy of yourselves."

Well, I believe we, the Americans of today, are ready to act worthy of ourselves, ready to do what must be done to ensure happiness and liberty for ourselves, our children and our children's children.

And as we renew ourselves here in our own land, we will be seen as having greater strength throughout the world. We will again be the exemplar of freedom and a beacon of hope for those who do not now have freedom.

To those neighbors and allies who share our freedom, we will strengthen our historic ties and assure them of our support and firm commitment. We will match loyalty with loyalty. We will strive for mutually beneficial relations. We will not use our friendship to impose on their sovereignty, for our own sovereignty is not for sale.

As for the enemies of freedom, those who are potential adversaries, they will be reminded that peace is the highest aspiration of the American people. We will negotiate for it, sacrifice for it; we will not surrender for it—now or ever.

Our forbearance should never be misunderstood. Our reluctance for conflict should not be misjudged as a failure of will. When action is required to preserve our national security, we will act. We will maintain sufficient strength to prevail if need be, knowing that if we do so we have the best chance of never having to use that strength.

Above all, we must realize that no arsenal, or no weapon in the arsenals of the world, is so formidable as the will and moral courage of free men and women. It is a weapon our adversaries in today's world do not have. It is a weapon that we as Americans do have. Let that be understood by those who practice terrorism and prey upon their neighbors.

I am told that tens of thousands of prayer meetings are being held on this day, and for that I am deeply grateful. We are a nation under God, and I believe God intended for us to be free. It would be fitting and good, I think, if on each Inauguration Day in future years it should be declared a day of prayer.

This is the first time in history that this ceremony has been held, as you have been told, on this West Front of the Capitol. Standing here, one faces a magnificent vista, opening up on this city's special beauty and history. At the end of this open mall are those shrines to the giants on whose shoulders we stand.

Directly in front of me, the monument to a monumental man: George Washington, Father of our country. A man of humility who came to greatness reluctantly. He led America out of revolutionary victory into infant nationhood. Off to one side, the stately memorial to Thomas Jefferson. The Declaration of Independence flames with his eloquence.

And then beyond the Reflecting Pool the dignified columns of the Lincoln Memorial. Whoever would understand in his heart the meaning of America will find it in the life of Abraham Lincoln.

Beyond those monuments to heroism is the Potomac River, and on the far shore the sloping hills of Arlington National Cemetery with its row on row of simple white markers bearing crosses or Stars of David. They add up to only a tiny fraction of the price that has been paid for our freedom.

Each one of those markers is a monument to the kinds of hero I spoke of earlier. Their lives ended in places called Belleau Wood, The Argonne, Omaha Beach, Salerno and halfway around the world on Guadalcanal, Tarawa, Pork Chop Hill, the Chosin Reservoir, and in a hundred rice paddies and jungles of a place called Vietnam.

Under one such marker lies a young man—Martin Treptow—who left his job in a small town barber shop in 1917 to go to France with the famed Rainbow Division. There, on the western front, he was killed trying to carry a message between battalions under heavy artillery fire.

We are told that on his body was found a diary. On the flyleaf under the heading, "My Pledge," he had written these words: "America must win this war. Therefore, I will work, I will save, I will sacrifice, I will endure, I will fight cheerfully and do my utmost, as if the issue of the whole struggle depended on me alone."

The crisis we are facing today does not require of us the kind of sacrifice that Martin Treptow and so many thousands of others were called upon to make. It does require, however, our best effort, and our willingness to believe in ourselves and to believe in our capacity to perform great deeds; to believe that together, with God's help, we can and will resolve the problems which now confront us.

And, after all, why shouldn't we believe that? We are Americans. God bless you, and thank you.

SPEECH TO THE BRITISH PARLIAMENT
June 8, 1982

In this speech, Ronald Reagan made clear that his Cold War foreign policy would have at its core a persistent rhetorical demonization of the Soviet Union, juxtaposed with a vision of the West as the leader of a moral crusade against evil. (A year later, in another speech, he would borrow a Hollywood metaphor to refer to the Soviet Union as "an evil empire.") Tonally, the speech was almost anachronistic, echoing Cold War predecessors such as Eisenhower and Churchill. It was a diplomatically aggressive and therefore extremely daring—some said reckless—approach. While the speech thrilled anti-Soviet hawks, it was met with disdain by many others, including the British Labor Party (many of whose members refused to attend the speech), as well as continental Europeans who felt themselves more than ever caught in a frightening nuclear squeeze. But history suggests that the strategy worked.

THE JOURNEY of which this visit forms is part of a long one. Already it has taken me to two great cities of the West—Rome and Paris—and to the Economic Summit at Versailles. There, once again, our sister democracies have proved that, even in a time of severe economic strain, free peoples can work together freely and voluntarily to address problems as serious as inflation, unemployment, trade and economic development in a spirit of cooperation and solidarity.

Other milestones lie ahead later this week. In Germany, we and our NATO allies will discuss measures for our joint defense and America's latest measures for a more peaceful, secure world through arms reductions.

Each stop of this trip is important but, among them all, this moment occupies a special place in my heart and the hearts of my countrymen—a moment of kinship and homecoming in these hallowed halls.

Speaking for all Americans, I want to say how very much we feel at home in your house. Every American would because this is one of democracy's shrines. Here the rights of free people and the processes of representation have been debated and refined.

It has been said that an institution is the lengthening shadow of man. This institution is the lengthening shadow of all men and women who have sat here and all of those who have voted to send representatives here.

This is my second visit to Great Britain as President of the United States. My first opportunity to stand on British soil occurred almost a year and a half ago when your Prime Minister graciously hosted a diplomatic dinner at the British Embassy in Washington. Mrs. Thatcher said then that she hoped I was not distressed to find staring down at me from the grand staircase a portrait of His Royal Majesty, King George III. She suggested it was best to let bygones be bygones and—in view of our two countries' remarkable friendships in succeeding years—she added that most Englishmen today would agree with Thomas Jefferson that "a little rebellion now and then is a very good thing."

From here I will go to Bonn, and then Berlin, where there stands the grim symbol of power untamed. The Berlin Wall, that dreadful gash across the city, is in its third decade. It is the fitting signature of the regime that built it.

And a few hundred kilometers behind the Berlin Wall there is another symbol. In the center of Warsaw there is a sign that notes the distances to two capitals. In one direction it points towards Moscow. In the other it points towards Brussels, headquarters of Western Europe's tangible unity. The sign makes this point: Poland is not East or West. Poland is the center of European civilization. It has contributed mightily to that civilization. It is doing so today by being magnificently unreconciled to oppression.

Poland's struggle to be Poland and to secure the basic rights we often take for granted demonstrates why we dare not take those rights for granted. Gladstone, defending the Reform Bill of 1866, declared: "You cannot fight against the future. Time is on our side." It was easier to believe in the inevitable march of democracy in Gladstone's day—in that high noon of Victorian optimism.

We are approaching the end of a bloody century plagued by a terrible political invention—totalitarianism. Optimism comes less easily today, not because democracy is less vigorous, but because democracy's enemies have refined their instruments of repression. Yet optimism is in order because day by day democracy is proving itself to be a not at all fragile flower.

From Stettin on the Baltic to Varna on the Black Sea, the regimes planted by totalitarianism have had more than thirty years to establish their legitimacy. But none—not one regime—has yet been able to risk free elections. Regimes planted by bayonets do not take root.

The strength of the Solidarity movement in Poland demonstrates the truth told in an underground joke in the Soviet Union. It is that the Soviet Union would remain a one-party nation even if an opposition party were permitted, because everyone would join the opposition party.

America's time as a player on the stage of world history has been brief. I think understanding this fact has always made you patient with your younger cousins. Well, not always patient. I do recall that on one occasion Sir Winston Churchill said in exasperation about one of our most distinguished diplomats, "He is the only case I know of a bull who carries his china shop with him." Witty as Sir Winston was, he also had that special attribute of great statesman: the gift of vision, the willingness to see the future based on the experience of the past. It is this sense of history, this understanding of the past, that I want to talk with you about today, for it is in remembering what we share of the past that our two natures can make common cause for the future.

We have not inherited an easy world. If developments like the Industrial Revolution, which began here in England, and the gifts of science and technology have made life much easier for us, they have also made it more dangerous. There are threats now to our freedom, indeed, to our very existence, that other generations could never have imagined.

There is, first, the threat of global war. No President, no Congress, no Prime Minister, no Parliament, can spend a day entirely free of this threat. And I don't have to tell you that in today's world, the existence of nuclear weapons could mean, if not the extinction of mankind, then surely the end of civilization as we know it. That is why negotiations in intermediate range nuclear forces now underway in Europe and the START talks—Strategic Arms Reduction Talks—which will begin later this month, are not just critical to American or Western policy; they are critical to mankind. Our commitment to early success in these negotiations is firm and unshakable and our purpose is clear: reducing the risk of war by reducing the means of waging war on both sides.

At the same time, there is a threat posed to human freedom posed by the enormous power of modern states. History teaches the danger of government that overreaches: political control takes precedence over free economic growth; secret police, mindless bureaucracy—all combining to stifle individual excellence and personal freedom.

Now, I am aware that among us here and throughout Europe there is legitimate disagreement over the extent to which the public sector should play in a nation's economy and life. But on one point all of us are united: our abhorrence of dictatorship in all forms but most particularly totalitarianism and the terrible inhumanities it has caused in our time: the great purge, Auschwitz and Dachau, the Gulag and Cambodia.

Historians looking back at our time will note the consistent restraint and peaceful intentions of the West. They will note that it was the democracies who refused to use the threat of their nuclear monopoly in the forties and early fifties for territorial or imperial gain. Had that nuclear monopoly been in the hands of the Communist world, the map of Europe—indeed, the world—would look very different today. And certainly they will note it was not the democracies that invaded Afghanistan or suppressed Polish Solidarity or used chemical and toxin warfare in Afghanistan and Southeast Asia.

If history teaches anything, it teaches self-delusion in the face of unpleasant facts is folly. We see around us today the marks of our terrible dilemma—predictions of doomsday, antinuclear demonstrations, an arms race in which the West must, for its own protection, be an unwilling participant. At the same time we see totalitarian forces in the world who seek subversion and conflict around the globe to further their barbarous assault on the human spirit. What, then, is our course? Must civilization perish in a hail of fiery atoms? Must freedom wither in a quiet, deadening accommodation with totalitarian evil? Sir Winston Churchill refused to accept the inevitability of war or even that it was imminent. He said, "I do not believe that Soviet Russia desires war. What they desire is the fruits of war and the indefinite expansion of their power and doctrines. But what we

have to consider here today while time remains is the permanent prevention of war and the establishment of conditions of freedom and democracy as rapidly as possible in all countries."

Well, this is precisely our mission today: to preserve freedom as well as
peace. It may not be easy to see; but I believe we live now at a turning
point.

In an ironic sense Karl Marx was right. We are witnessing today a great
revolutionary crisis, a crisis where the demands of the economic order are
conflicting directly with those of the political order. But the crisis is happening not in the free, non-Marxist West but in the home of Marxism-
Leninism, the Soviet Union.

It is the Soviet Union that runs against the tide of history by denying
human freedom and human dignity to its citizens. It also is in deep economic difficulty. The rate of growth in the national product has been
steadily declining since the fifties and is less than half of what it was then.
The dimensions of this failure are astounding: a country which employs
one-fifth of its population in agriculture is unable to feed its own people.

Were it not for the private sector, the tiny private sector tolerated in
Soviet agriculture, the country might be on the brink of famine. These
private plots occupy a bare three percent of the arable land but account for
nearly one-quarter of Soviet farm output and nearly one-third of meat
products and vegetables. Overcentralized, with little or no incentives, year
after year the Soviet system pours its best resources into the making of
instruments of destruction. The constant shrinkage of economic growth
combined with the growth of military production is putting a heavy strain
on the Soviet people. What we see here is a political structure that no
longer corresponds to its economic base, a society where productive forces
are hampered by political ones.

The decay of the Soviet experiment should come as no surprise to us.
Wherever the comparisons have been made between free and closed societies—West Germany and East Germany, Austria and Czechoslovakia,
Malaysia and Vietnam—it is the democratic countries that are prosperous
and responsive to the needs of their people. And one of the simple but
overwhelming facts of our time is this: of all the millions of refugees we've
seen in the modern world, their flight is always away from, not toward the
Communist world. Today on the NATO line, our military forces face east
to prevent a possible invasion. On the other side of the line, the Soviet
forces also face east to prevent their people from leaving.

The hard evidence of totalitarian rule has caused in mankind an uprising of the intellect and will. Whether it is the growth of the new schools
of economics in America or England or the appearance of the so-called
new philosophers in France, there is one unifying thread running through
the intellectual work of these groups—rejection of the arbitrary power of
the state, the refusal to subordinate the rights of the individual to the
superstate, the realization that collectivism stifles all the best human
impulses.

Since the Exodus from Egypt, historians have written of those who sacrificed and struggled for freedom: the stand at Thermopylae, the revolt of
Spartacus, the storming of the Bastille, the Warsaw uprising in World War

II. More recently we have seen evidence of this same human impulse in one of the developing nations in Central America. For months and months the world news media covered the fighting in El Salvador. Day after day, we were treated to stories and film slanted toward the brave freedom fighters battling oppressive Government forces in behalf of the silent, suffering people of that country. Then one day those silent suffering people were offered a chance to vote to choose the kind of Government they wanted. Suddenly the freedom fighters in the hills were exposed for what they really are: Cuban-backed guerrillas who want power for themselves and their backers, not democracy for the people.

They threatened death to anyone who voted and destroyed hundreds of buses and trucks to keep people from getting to the polling places. But on election day the people of El Salvador, 1.4 million of them, braved ambush and gunfire, trudging miles to vote for freedom. They stood for hours in the hot sun waiting for their turn to vote. Members of our Congress who went there as observers told me of a woman hounded by rifle fire who refused to leave the line to have her wound treated until after she had voted. A grandmother, who had been told by the guerrillas that she would be killed when she returned from the polls told the guerrillas, "You can kill me, kill my family, kill my neighbors, but you can't kill us all." The real freedom fighters of El Salvador turned out to be the people of that country, the young, the old, and the in-between. Strange, but there has been little if any news coverage of that war since the election.

Perhaps they'll say it's because there are new struggles now. On distant islands in the South Atlantic, young men are fighting for Britain. And, yes, voices have been raised protesting their sacrifice for lumps of rock and earth so far away. But those young men aren't fighting for mere real estate. They fight for a cause, for the belief that armed aggression must not be allowed to succeed, and that people must participate in the decisions of government under the rule of law. If there had been firmer support for that principle some forty-five years ago, perhaps our generations wouldn't have suffered the bloodletting of World War II.

In the Middle East, the guns sound once more, this time in Lebanon, a country that for too long has had to endure the tragedy of civil war, terrorism, and foreign intervention and occupation. The fighting in Lebanon by all parties must stop and Israel must bring its forces home. But this is not enough. We must all work to stamp out the scourge of terrorism that in the Middle East makes war an ever-present threat.

But beyond the trouble spots lies a deeper, more positive pattern. Around the world today, the democratic revolution is gathering new strength. In India, a critical test has been passed with the peaceful change of governing political parties. In Africa, Nigeria is moving in remarkable and unmistakable ways to build and strengthen its democratic institutions. In the Caribbean and Central America sixteen of twenty-four countries have freely elected governments. And in the United Nations, eight of ten developing nations which have joined the body in the past five years are democracies.

In the Communist world as well, man's instinctive desire for freedom and self-determination surfaces again and again. To be sure, there are grim reminders of how brutally the police state attempts to snuff out this quest for self-rule: in 1953 in East Germany, 1956 in Hungary, 1968 in Czechoslovakia, 1981 in Poland. But the struggle continues in Poland, and we know there are even those who strive and suffer for freedom within the confines of the Soviet Union itself. How we conduct ourselves here in the Western democracies will determine whether this trend continues.

No, democracy is not a fragile flower; still, it needs cultivating. If the rest of this century is to witness the gradual growth of freedom and democratic ideals, we must take actions to assist the campaign for democracy.

Some argue that we should encourage democratic change in right-wing dictatorships, but not in Communist regimes. To accept this preposterous notion—some well-meaning people have—is to invite the argument that, once countries achieve a nuclear capability, they should be allowed an undisturbed reign of terror over their own citizens. We reject this course.

As for the Soviet Union, Chairman Brezhnev repeatedly has stressed that the competition of ideas and systems must continue and that this is entirely consistent with relaxation of tensions and peace. Well, we ask only that these systems begin by living up to their own constitutions, abiding by their own laws, and complying with the international obligations they have undertaken. We ask only for a process, a direction, a basic code of decency—not for an instant transformation.

We cannot ignore the fact that even without our encouragement there has been and will continue to be repeated explosion against repression and dictatorships. The Soviet Union itself is not immune to this reality. Any system is inherently unstable that has no peaceful means to legitimize its leaders. In such cases, the very repressiveness of the state ultimately drives people to resist it—if necessary, by force.

While we must be cautious about forcing the pace of change, we must not hesitate to declare our ultimate objectives and to take concrete actions to move toward them. We must be staunch in our conviction that freedom is not the sole prerogative of a lucky few but the inalienable and universal right of all human beings. So states the United Nations Universal Declaration of Human Rights, which, among other things, guarantees free elections.

The objective I propose is quite simple to state: to foster the infrastructure of democracy, the system of a free press, unions, political parties, universities, which allows a people to choose their own way to develop their own culture, to reconcile their own differences through peaceful means.

This is not cultural imperialism; it is providing the means for genuine self-determination and protection for diversity. Democracy already flourishes in countries with very different cultures and historical experiences. It would be cultural condescension, or worse, to say that any people prefer dictatorship to democracy. Who would voluntarily choose not to have the right to vote, decide to purchase government propaganda handouts instead of independent newspapers, prefer government to worker-controlled unions, opt for land to be owned by the state instead of those who till it, want government repression of religious liberty, a single political party instead of a free choice, a rigid cultural orthodoxy instead of democratic tolerance and diversity?

Since 1917, the Soviet Union has given covert political training and assistance to Marxist-Leninists in many countries. Of course, it also has promoted the use of violence and subversion by these same forces. Over the past several decades, West European and other social democrats, Christian democrats, and leaders have offered open assistance to fraternal, political, and social institutions to bring about peaceful and democratic progress. Appropriately, for a vigorous new democracy, the Federal Republic of Germany's political foundations have become a major force in this effort.

We in America now intend to take additional steps, as many of our allies have already done, toward realizing this same goal. The chairmen and other leaders of the national Republican and Democratic party organizations are initiating a study with the bipartisan American Political Foundation to determine how the United States can best contribute as a nation to the global campaign for democracy now gathering force. They will have the cooperation of congressional leaders of both parties, along with representatives of business, labor, and other major institutions in our society. I look forward to receiving their recommendations and to working with these institutions and the Congress in the common task of strengthening democracy throughout the world.

It is time that we committed ourselves as a nation—in both the public and private sectors—to assisting democratic development. We plan to consult with leaders of other nations as well. There is a proposal before the Council of Europe to invite parliamentarians from democratic countries to a meeting next year in Strasbourg. That prestigious gathering could consider ways to help democratic political movements. This November, in Washington, there will take place an international meeting on free elections, and next spring there will be a conference of world authorities on constitutionalism and self-government hosted by the Chief Justice of the U.S. Authorities from a number of developing countries—judges, philosophers and politicians with practical experience—have agreed to explore how to turn principle into practice and further the rule of law.

At the same time we invite the Soviet Union to consider with us how the competition of ideas and values—which it is committed to support—can be conducted on a peaceful and reciprocal basis. For example, I am prepared to offer President Brezhnev an opportunity to speak to the American people on our television if he will allow me the same opportunity with the Soviet people. We also suggest that panels of our newsmen periodically appear on each other's television to discuss major events.

I do not wish to sound overly optimistic, yet the Soviet Union is not immune from the reality of what is going on in the world. It has happened in the past: a small ruling elite either mistakenly attempts to ease domestic unrest through greater repression and foreign adventure, or it chooses a wiser course—it begins to allow its people a voice in their own destiny. Even if this latter process is not realized soon, I believe the renewed strength of the democratic movement, complemented by a global campaign for freedom, will strengthen the prospects for arms control and a world at peace.

I have discussed on other occasions, including my address on May 9, the elements of Western policies toward the Soviet Union to safeguard our interests and protect the peace. What I am describing now is a plan and a hope for the long term—the march of freedom and democracy which will leave Marxism-Leninism on the ash heap of history as it has left other tyrannies which stifle the freedom and muzzle the self-expression of the people. And that's why we must continue our efforts to strengthen NATO even as we move forward with our zero-option initiative in the negotiations on intermediate-range forces and our proposal for a one-third reduction in strategic ballistic missile warheads.

Our military strength is a prerequisite to peace, but let it be clear we maintain this strength in the hope it will never be used, for the ultimate determinant in the struggle that's now going on in the world will not be bombs and rockets but a test of wills and ideas, a trial of spiritual resolve: the values we hold, the beliefs we cherish, the ideals to which we are dedicated.

The British people know that, given strong leadership, time, and a little bit of hope, the forces of good ultimately rally and triumph over evil. Here among you is the cradle of self-government, the mother of Parliaments. Here is the enduring greatness of the British contribution to mankind, the great civilized ideas: individual liberty, representative government, and the rule of law under God.

I've often wondered about the shyness of some of us in the West about standing for these ideals that have done so much to ease the plight of man and the hardships of our imperfect world. This reluctance to use those vast resources at our command reminds me of the elderly lady whose home was bombed in the blitz. As the rescuers moved about, they found a bottle of brandy she'd stored behind the staircase, which was all that was left standing. And since she was barely conscious, one of the workers pulled the cork to give her a taste of it. She came around immediately and said, "Here now—there now, put it back. That's for emergencies."

Well, the emergency is upon us. Let us be shy no longer. Let us go to our strength. Let us offer hope. Let us tell the world that a new age is not only possible but probable.

During the dark days of the Second World War, when this island was incandescent with courage, Winston Churchill exclaimed about Britain's adversaries, "What kind of people do they think we are?" Well, Britain's adversaries found out what extraordinary people the British are. But all the democracies paid a terrible price for allowing the dictators to underestimate us. We dare not make that mistake again. So, let us ask ourselves, "What kind of people do we think we are?" And let us answer, "Free people, worthy of freedom and determined not only to remain so but to help others gain their freedom as well."

Sir Winston led his people to great victory in war and then lost an election just as the fruits of victory were about to be enjoyed. But he left office honorably and, as it turned out, temporarily, knowing that the liberty of his people was more important than the fate of any single leader. History recalls his greatness in ways no dictator will ever know. And he left us a message of hope for the future, as timely now as when he first uttered it, as opposition leader in the Commons nearly 27 years ago, when he said, "When we look back on all the perils through which we have passed and at the mighty foes that we have laid low and all the dark and deadly designs that we have frustrated, why should we fear for our future? We have," he said, "come safely through the worst."

Well, the task I've set forth will long outlive our own generation. But together, we too have come through the worst. Let us now begin a major effort to secure the best—a crusade for freedom that will engage the faith and fortitude of the next generation. For the sake of peace and justice, let us move toward a world in which all people are at last free to determine their own destiny.

Mario Cuomo
[1932–   ]

With this speech, Mario Cuomo, governor of New York from 1983 to 1990, earned a national reputation as perhaps the most eloquent and persuasive voice among dissenting Democrats during the Reagan era. President Reagan demurred from answering reporters when they asked for his response to Cuomo's criticisms, but Vice President George Bush conceded, "It was a good speech."

KEYNOTE ADDRESS,
1984 DEMOCRATIC NATIONAL CONVENTION
July 16, 1984

PLEASE ALLOW me to skip the stories and the poetry and the temptation to deal in nice but vague rhetoric. Let me instead use this valuable opportunity to deal immediately with the questions that should determine this election and that we all know are vital to the American people.

Ten days ago, President Reagan admitted that although some people in this country seem to be doing well nowadays, others were unhappy, even worried, about themselves, their families and their futures. The President said that he didn't understand that fear. He said, "Why, this country is a shining city on a hill." And the President is right. In many ways we are "a shining city on a hill." But the hard truth is that not everyone is sharing in this city's splendor and glory. A shining city is perhaps all the President sees from the portico of the White House and the verandah of his ranch, where everyone seems to be doing well.

But there's another city, there's another part to the shining city, the part where some people can't pay their mortgages and most young people can't afford one, where students can't afford the education they need and middle class parents watch the dreams they hold for their children evaporate. In this part of the city there are more poor than ever, more families in trouble. More and more people who need help but can't find it. Even worse:

there are elderly people who tremble in the basements of the houses there. And there are people who sleep in the city's streets, in the gutter, where the glitter doesn't show. There are ghettos where thousands of young people, without a job or an education, give their lives away to drug dealers every day.

There is despair, Mr. President, in the faces that you don't see, in the places that you don't visit in your shining city. In fact, Mr. President, this is a nation . . . Mr. President, you ought to know that this nation is more a "Tale of Two Cities" than it is just a "Shining City on a Hill." Maybe . . . maybe, Mr. President, if you visited some more places, maybe if you went to Appalachia where some people still live in sheds; maybe if you went to Lackawanna where thousands of unemployed steel workers wonder why we subsidize foreign steel; maybe, maybe, Mr. President, if you stopped in at a shelter in Chicago and spoke to the homeless there; maybe, Mr. President, if you asked a woman who had been denied the help she needed to feed her children because you said you needed the money for a tax break for a millionaire or for a missile we couldn't afford to use; maybe, maybe, Mr. President, but I'm afraid not.

Because, the truth is, ladies and gentlemen, that this is how we were warned it would be. President Reagan told us from the very beginning that he believed in a kind of social Darwinism—survival of the fittest. "Government can't do everything," we were told. "So it should settle for taking care of the strong and hope that economic ambition and charity will do the rest. Make the rich richer and what falls from the table will be enough for the middle class and those who are trying desperately to work their way into the middle class." You know the Republicans called it "trickle-down" when Hoover tried it. Now they call it "supply-side," but it's the same shining city for those relative few who are lucky enough to live in its good neighborhoods. But for the people who are excluded, for the people who are locked out—all they can do is stare from a distance at that city's glimmering towers.

It's an old story. It's as old as our history. The difference between Democrats and Republicans has always been measured in courage and confidence. The Republicans . . . the Republicans believe that the wagon train will not make it to the frontier unless some of the old, some of the young, some of the weak are left behind by the side of the trail. The strong, the strong they tell us will inherit the land! We Democrats believe in something else. We Democrats believe that we can make it all the way with the whole family intact. And we have, more than once, ever since Franklin Roosevelt lifted himself from his wheelchair to lift this nation from its knees. Wagon train after wagon train, to new frontiers of education, housing, peace; the whole family aboard; constantly reaching out to extend and enlarge that family; lifting them up into the wagon on the way; Blacks and Hispanics and people of every ethnic group, and Native Americans—all those struggling to build their families and claim some small share of America. For nearly fifty years we carried them all to new levels of comfort and security and dignity, even affluence; and remember this, some of us in this room today are here only because this nation had that kind of confidence. And it would be wrong to forget that.

So, here we are at this convention to remind ourselves where we come from and to claim the future for ourselves and for our children. Today, our great Democratic Party, which has saved this nation from depression, from fascism, from racism, from corruption, is called upon to do it again—this time to save the nation from confusion and division, from the threat of eventual fiscal disaster, and most of all from the fear of a nuclear holocaust—but that's not going to be easy. Mo Udall is exactly right, it won't be easy, and in order to succeed, we must answer our opponents polished and appealing rhetoric with a more telling reasonableness and rationality. We must win this case on the merits. We must get the American public to look past the glitter, beyond the showmanship, to the reality, the hard substance of things. And we'll do it, not so much with speeches that sound good as with speeches that are good and sound, not so much with speeches that will bring people to their feet as with speeches that will bring people to their senses. We must make . . . we must make the American people hear our "Tale of Two Cities." We must convince them that we don't have to settle for two city [sic] cities, that we can have one city, indivisible, shining for all of its people.

Now we will have no chance to do that if what comes out of this convention is a babble of arguing voices. If that's what's heard throughout the campaign—dissident sounds from all sides—we will have no chance to tell our message. To succeed we will have to surrender some small parts of our individual interests, to build a platform that we can all stand on, at once and comfortably. Proudly singing out, we need . . . we need a platform we can all agree to so that we can sing out the truth for the nation to hear, in chorus, its logic so clear and commanding that no slick Madison Avenue commercial, no amount of geniality, no martial music will be able to muffle the sound of the truth. And we Democrats must unite . . . we Democrats must unite so that the entire nation can unite, because surely the Republicans won't bring this country together. Their policies divide the nation into the lucky and the left out, into the royalty and the rabble. The Republicans are willing to treat that division as victory. They would cut this nation in half, into those temporarily better off and those worse off than before. And they would call that division recovery. Now we should not . . . now we should not be embarrassed or dismayed or chagrined if the process of unifying is difficult, even wrenching at times.

Remember that unlike any other party, we embrace men and women of every color, every creed, every orientation, every economic class. In our family are gathered everyone from the abject poor of Essex County in New York to the enlightened affluent of the gold coasts at both ends of the nation. And in between is the heart of our constituency: the middle class, the people not rich enough to be worry-free but not poor enough to be on welfare. The middle class—those people who work for a living because they have to, not because some psychiatrist told them it was a convenient way to fill the interval between birth and eternity—white collar and blue collar, young professionals—men and women in small business desperate for the capital and contracts that they need to prove their worth. We speak for the minorities who have not yet entered the mainstream. We speak for ethnics who want to add their culture to the magnificent mosaic that is America. We speak . . . we speak for women who are indignant that this nation refuses to etch into its governmental commandments the simple rule, "Thou shalt not sin against equality," a rule so simple—I was going to say, and I perhaps dare not, but I will—it's a commandment so simple it can be spelled in three letters: ERA! We speak . . . we speak for young people demanding an education and a future. We speak for senior citizens . . . we speak for senior citizens, who are terrorized by the idea that their only security, their Social Security, is being threatened. We speak for millions of reasoning people fighting to preserve our environment from greed and from stupidity. And we speak for reasonable people who are fighting to preserve our very existence from a macho intransigence that refuses to make intelligent attempts to discuss the possibility of nuclear holocaust with our enemy. They refuse . . . they refuse because they believe we can pile missiles so high that they will pierce the clouds and the sight of them will frighten our enemies into submission.

Now we're proud of this diversity. As Democrats we're grateful for it, we don't have to manufacture it the way the Republicans will next month in Dallas, by propping up mannequin delegates on the convention floor. But we—while we're proud of this diversity—we pay a price for it. The different people that we represent have different points of view. And sometimes they compete and even debate, and even argue. That's what our primaries were all about.

But now the primaries are over, and it is time when we pick our candidates and our platform here to lock arms and move into this campaign together. If you need any more inspiration to put some small part of your own difference aside to create this consensus then all you need to do is to reflect on what the Republican policy of "divide and cajole" has done to this land since 1980.

Now the President has asked the American people to judge him on whether or not he's fulfilled the promises he made four years ago. I believe as Democrats we ought to accept that challenge and just for a moment let us consider what he has said and what he's done. Inflation . . . inflation is down since 1980, but not because of the supply-side miracle promised to us by the President. Inflation was reduced the old-fashioned way, with a recession, the worse since 1932. Now how did we . . . we could have brought inflation down that way. How did he do it: 55,000 bankruptcies, two years of massive unemployment, 200,000 farmers and ranchers forced off the land, more homeless . . . more homeless than at any time since the Great Depression in 1932, more hungry—in this world of enormous affluence, the United States of America, more hungry, more poor—most of them women—and . . . and, he paid one other thing, a nearly $200 billion deficit threatening our future.

Now we must make the American people understand this deficit because they don't. The President's deficit is a direct and dramatic repudiation of his promise in 1990 to balance the budget by 1983. How large is it? The deficit is the largest in the history of the universe. President Carter's last budget had a deficit less than one third of this deficit. It is a deficit that, according to the President's own fiscal advisor, may grow to as much as $300 billion a year, for as far as the eye can see and ladies and gentlemen it is a debt so large that almost one half of the money we collect from the personal income tax each year goes just to pay the interest. It is a mortgage on our children's future that can be paid only in pain and that could bring this nation to its knees.

Now don't take my word for it, I'm a Democrat. Ask the Republican investment bankers on Wall Street what they think the chances of this recovery being permanent are. You see, if they're not too embarrassed to tell you the truth, they'll say that they're appalled and frightened by the President's deficit. Ask them what they think of our economy, now that it has been driven by the distorted value of the dollar back to its colonial condition: Now we're exporting agricultural products and importing manufactured ones. Ask those Republican investment bankers what they expect the rate of interest to be a year from now. And ask them, if they dare tell you the truth, you'll learn from them what they predict for the inflation rate a year from now because of the deficit.

Now how important is this question of the deficit? Think about it practically: What chance would the Republican candidate have had in 1980 if he had told the American people that he intended to pay for his so-called economic recovery with bankruptcies, unemployment, more homeless, more hungry and the largest Government debt known to human kind? If he had told the voters in 1990 that truth, would American voters have signed the loan certificate for him on Election Day? Of course not! That was an election won under false pretenses. It was won with smoke and mirrors and illusions. And that's the kind of recovery we have now as well.

And what about foreign policy? They said that they would make us and the whole world safer. They say they have by creating the largest defense budget in history—one that even they now admit is excessive—by escalating to a frenzy the nuclear arms race, by incendiary rhetoric, by refusing to discuss peace with our enemies, by the loss of 279 young Americans in Lebanon in pursuit of a plan and a policy that no one can find or describe. We give money to Latin American governments that murder nuns, and then we lie about it. We have been less than zealous in support of our only real friend, it seems to me, in the Middle East; the one democracy there, our flesh and blood ally, the State of Israel. Our . . . our policy . . . our foreign policy drifts with no real direction, other than an hysterical commitment to an arms race that leads nowhere, if we're lucky, and if we're not, it could lead us into bankruptcy or war.

Of course we must have a strong defense. Of course Democrats are for a strong defense. Of course Democrats believe that there are times that we must stand and fight, and we have. Thousands of us have paid for freedom with our lives, but always, when this country has been at its best, our purposes were clear. Now they're not. Now our allies are as confused as our enemies. Now we have no real commitment to our friends or to our ideals, not to human rights, not to the refuseniks, not to Sakharov, not to Bishop Tutu and the others struggling for freedom in South Africa. We . . . we have in the last few years spent more than we can afford. We have pounded our chests and made bold speeches, but we lost 279 young Americans in Lebanon and we live behind sandbags in Washington.

How can anyone say that we are safer, stronger or better? That . . . that is the Republican record. That its disastrous quality is not more fully understood by the American people I can only attribute to the President's amiability and the failure by some to separate the salesman from the product. But now . . . now . . . now it's up to us, now it's up to you and me to make the case to America. And to remind Americans that if they are not happy with all that the President has done so far, they should consider how much worse it will be if he is left to his radical proclivities for another four years unrestrained . . . unrestrained: If . . . if July . . . if July brings back Anne Gorsuch Burford, what can we expect of December? Where would . . . where would another four years take us? Where would four years more take us? How much larger will the deficit be? How much deeper the cuts in programs for the struggling middle class and the poor to limit that deficit? How high will the interest rates be? How much more acid rain killing our forests and fouling our lakes? And, ladies and gentlemen, please think of this, the nation must think of this: What kind of Supreme Court will we have? Please, we . . . we must ask ourselves what kind of Court and country will be fashioned by the man who believes in having government mandate people's religion and morality, the man who believes that trees pollute the environment, the man that believes that . . . that the laws against discrimination, against people go too far, a man who threatens Social Security and Medicaid and help for the disabled? How high will we pile the missiles? How much deeper will the gulf be between us and our enemies? And, ladies and gentlemen, will four years more make meaner the spirit of the American people?

This election will measure the record of the past four years. But more than that, it will answer the question of what kind of people we want to be. We Democrats still have a dream. We still believe in this nation's future. And this is our answer to the question. This is our credo: We believe in only the government we need. But we insist on all the government we need. We believe in a government that is characterized by fairness and reasonableness, a reasonableness that goes beyond labels. That doesn't distort or promise to do things that we know we can't do. We believe in a government strong enough to use words like "love" and "compassion" and smart enough to convert our noblest aspirations into practical realities. We believe in encouraging the talented, but we believe that while survival of the fittest may be a good working description of the process of evolution, a government of humans should elevate itself to a higher order. We . . . our . . . our government . . . our government should be able to rise to the level where it can fill the gaps that are left by chance or by a wisdom we don't fully understand. We would rather have laws written by the patron of this great city, the man called "the world's most sincere Democrat," St. Francis of Assisi, than laws written by Darwin. We believe . . . we believe, as Democrats, that a society as blessed as ours, the most affluent democracy in the world's history, one that can spend trillions on instruments of destruction, ought to be able to help the middle class in its struggle, ought to be able to find work for all who can do it, room at the table, shelter for the homeless, care for the elderly and infirm, and hope for the destitute. And we proclaim as loudly as we can the utter insanity of nuclear proliferation and the need for a nuclear freeze, if only to affirm the simple truth that peace is better than war because life is better than death. We believe in firm . . . we believe in firm but fair law and order. We believe proudly in the union movement. We believe . . . we believe in privacy for people, openness by government. We believe in civil rights and we believe in human rights. We believe in a single . . . we believe in a single fundamental idea that describes better than most textbooks and any speech that I could write what a proper government should be: the idea of family, mutuality; the sharing of benefits and burdens for the good of all; feeling one another's pain; sharing one another's blessings, reasonably, honestly, fairly without respect to race or sex or geography or political affiliation. We believe we must be the family of America, recognizing that at the heart of the matter we are bound one to another, that the problems of a retired school teacher in Duluth are our problems, that the future of the child . . . that the future of the child in Buffalo is our future, that the struggle of a disabled man in Boston to survive and live decently is our struggle, that the hunger of a woman in Little Rock is our hunger, that the failure anywhere to provide what reasonably we might, to avoid pain, is our failure.

For fifty years . . . for fifty years we Democrats created a better future for our children, using traditional Democratic principles as a fixed beacon, giving us direction and purpose, but constantly innovating, adapting to new realities: Roosevelt's alphabet programs; Truman's NATO and the GI Bill of Rights; Kennedy's intelligent tax incentives and the Alliance for Progress; Johnson's civil rights; Carter's human rights and the nearly miraculous Camp David peace accord. Democrats did it . . . Democrats did it and Democrats can do it again. We can build a future that deals with our deficit. Remember this: that fifty years of progress under our principles never cost us what the last four years of stagnation have. And we can deal with the deficit intelligently by shared sacrifice, with all parts of the nation's family contributing, building partnerships with the private sector, providing a sound defense without depriving ourselves of what we need to feed our children and care for our people.

We can have a future that provides for all the young of the present by marrying common sense and compassion. We know we can, because we did it for nearly fifty years before 1980. And we can do it again, if we do not forget . . . if we do not forget that this entire nation has profited by these progressive principles, that they helped lift up generations to the middle class and higher, that they gave us a chance to work, to go to college, to raise a family, to own a house, to be secure in our old age, and, before that, to reach heights that our own parents would not have dared dream of.

That struggle to live with dignity is the real story of the shining city. And it's a story, ladies and gentlemen, that I didn't read in a book or learn in a classroom. I saw it and lived it, like many of you. I watched a small man with thick calluses on both his hands work fifteen and sixteen hours a day. I saw him once literally bleed from the bottoms of his feet—a man who came here uneducated, alone, unable to speak the language, who taught me all I needed to know about faith and hard work by the simple eloquence of his example. I learned about our kind of democracy from my father. And I learned about our obligation to each other from him and my mother. They asked only for a chance to work and to make the world better for their children and they . . . they asked to be protected in those moments when they would not be able to protect themselves. This nation and this nation's government did that for them. And that they were able to build a family and live in dignity and see one of their children go from behind their little grocery store in South Jamaica on the other side of the tracks where he was born, to occupy the highest seat in the greatest state in the greatest nation in the only world we know is an ineffably beautiful tribute to the democratic process. And . . . and, ladies and gentlemen, on January 20, 1995 it will happen again, only on a much, much grander scale.

We will have a new President of the United States, a Democrat born not to the blood of kings but to the blood of pioneers and immigrants. And we will have America's first woman Vice President, the child of immigrants, and she . . . she . . . she will open with one magnificent stroke a whole new frontier for the United States. Now it will happen . . . it will happen; if we make it happen, if you and I make it happen. And I ask you now, ladies and gentlemen, brothers and sisters, for the good of all of us, for the love of this great nation, for the family of America, for the love of God: please make this nation remember how futures are built. Thank you and God bless you.

Bishop Desmond Tutu
[1931–   ]

The Norwegian Nobel Committee awarded the 1984 Nobel Peace Prize to Anglican clergyman Desmond Mpilo Tutu, Bishop of Lesotho and general secretary of the South African Council of Churches, in what it deemed "renewed recognition of the courage and heroism shown by black South Africans in their use of peaceful methods in the struggle against apartheid." The committee praised Tutu as "a unifying leader figure in the campaign to resolve the problem of apartheid in South Africa." The award and this speech came just as a new constitution granting limited representation to the country's 850,000 Indians and 2.8 million colored (mixed-race) persons, but none to some 23 million blacks, triggered a period of protest and violent crackdown.

NOBEL PEACE PRIZE ACCEPTANCE SPEECH
December 10, 1984

YOUR MAJESTY, members of the Royal Family, Mr. Chairman, Ladies and Gentlemen:

Before I left South Africa, a land I love passionately, we had an emergency meeting of the Executive Committee of the South African Council of Churches with the leaders of our member churches. We called the meeting because of the deepening crisis in our land, which has claimed nearly 200 lives this year alone. We visited some of the trouble spots on the Witwatersrand. I went with others to the East Rand. We visited the home of an old lady. She told us that she looked after her grandson and the children of neighbors while their parents were at work. One day the police chased some pupils who had been boycotting classes, but they disappeared between the township houses. The police drove down the old lady's street. She was sitting at the back of the house in her kitchen, whilst her charges were playing in the front of the house in the yard. Her daughter rushed into the house, calling out to her to come quickly. The old lady dashed out of the kitchen into the living room. Her grandson had fallen just inside the door, dead. He had been shot in the back by the police. He was six years old. A few weeks later, a white mother, trying to register her black servant for work, drove through a black township. Black rioters stoned her car and killed her baby of a few months old, the first white casualty of the current unrest in South Africa. Such deaths are two too many. These are part of the high cost of apartheid.

Every day in a squatter camp near Cape Town, called K.T.O., the authorities have been demolishing flimsy plastic shelters which black mothers have erected because they were taking their marriage vows seriously. They have been reduced to sitting on soaking mattresses, with their household effects strewn round their feet, and whimpering babies on their laps, in the cold Cape winter rain. Every day the authorities have carried out these callous demolitions. What heinous crime have these women committed, to be hounded like criminals in this manner? All they wanted is to be with their husbands, the fathers of their children. Everywhere else in the world they would be highly commended, but in South Africa, a land which claims to be Christian, and which boasts a public holiday called Family Day, these gallant women are treated so inhumanely, and yet all they want is to have a decent and stable family life. Unfortunately, in the land of their birth, it is a criminal offense for them to live happily with their husbands and the fathers of their children. Black family life is thus being undermined, not accidentally, but by deliberate Government policy. It is part of the price human beings, God's children, are called to pay for apartheid. An unacceptable price.

I come from a beautiful land, richly endowed by God with wonderful natural resources, wide expanses, rolling mountains, singing birds, bright shining stars out of blue skies, with radiant sunshine, golden sunshine. There is enough of the good things that come from God's bounty, there is enough for everyone, but apartheid has confirmed some in their selfishness, causing them to grasp greedily a disproportionate share, the lion's share, because of their power. They have taken eighty-seven percent of the land, though being only about twenty percent of our population. The rest have had to make do with the remaining thirteen percent. Apartheid has decreed the politics of exclusion. Seventy-three percent of the population is excluded from any meaningful participation in the political decision-making processes of the land of their birth. The new constitution, making provision for three chambers, for whites, coloreds, and Indians, mentions blacks only once, and thereafter ignores them completely. Thus this new constitution, lauded in parts of the West as a step in the right direction, entrenches racism and ethnicity. The constitutional committees are composed in the ratio of four whites to two coloreds and one Indian. Zero black. Two plus one can never equal, let alone be more than, four. Hence this constitution perpetuates by law and entrenches white minority rule. Blacks are expected to exercise their political ambitions in unviable, poverty-stricken, arid, Bantustan homelands, ghettoes of misery, inexhaustible reservoirs of cheap black labor, Bantustans into which South Africa is being balkanized. Blacks are systematically being stripped of their South African citizenship and being turned into aliens in the land of their birth. This is apartheid's final solution, just as Nazism had its final solution for the Jews in Hitler's Aryan madness. The South African Government is smart. Aliens can claim but very few rights, least of all political rights.

In pursuance of apartheid's ideological racist dream, over 3,000,000 of God's children have been uprooted from their homes, which have been demolished, whilst they have then been dumped in the Bantustan homeland resettlement camps. I say "dumped" advisedly; only things or rubbish is dumped, not human beings. Apartheid has, however, ensured that God's children, just because they are black, should be treated as if they were things, and not as of infinite value as being created in the image of God. These dumping grounds are far from where work and food can be procured easily. Children starve, suffer from the often irreversible consequences of malnutrition—this happens to them not accidentally, but by deliberate Government policy. They starve in a land that could be the breadbasket of Africa, a land that normally is a net exporter of food.

The father leaves his family in the Bantustan homeland, there eking out a miserable existence, whilst he, if he is lucky, goes to the so-called white man's town as a migrant, to live an unnatural life in a single sex hostel for eleven months of the year, being prey there to prostitution, drunkenness, and worse. This migratory labor policy is declared Government policy, and has been condemned, even by the white D.R.C. [Dutch Reformed Church], not noted for being quick to criticize the Government, as a cancer in our society. This cancer, eating away at the vitals of black family life, is deliberate Government policy. It is part of the cost of apartheid, exorbitant in terms of human suffering.

Apartheid has spawned discriminatory education, such as Bantu Education, education for serfdom, ensuring that the Government spends only about one-tenth on one black child per annum for education what it spends on a white child. It is education that is decidedly separate and unequal. It is to be wantonly wasteful of human resources, because so many of God's children are prevented, by deliberate Government policy, from attaining to their fullest potential. South Africa is paying a heavy price already for this iniquitous policy, because there is a desperate shortage of skilled manpower, a direct result of the short-sighted schemes of the racist regime. It is a moral universe that we inhabit, and good and right and equity matter in the universe of the God we worship. And so, in this matter, the South African Government and its supporters are being properly hoisted with their own petard.

Apartheid is upheld by a phalanx of iniquitous laws, such as the Population Registration Act, which decrees that all South Africans must be classified ethnically, and duly registered according to these race categories. Many times, in the same family one child has been classified white whilst another, with a slightly darker hue, has been classified colored, with all the horrible consequences for the latter of being shut out from membership of a greatly privileged caste. There have, as a result, been several child suicides. This is too high a price to pay for racial purity, for it is doubtful whether any end, however desirable, can justify such a means. There are laws, such as the Prohibition of Mixed Marriages Act, which regard marriages between a white and a person of another race as illegal. Race becomes an impediment to a valid marriage. Two persons who have fallen in love are prevented by race from consummating their love in the marriage bond. Something beautiful is made to be sordid and ugly. The Immorality Act decrees that fornication and adultery are illegal if they happen between a white and one of another race. The police are reduced to the level of peeping Toms to catch couples red-handed. Many whites have committed suicide rather than face the disastrous consequences that follow in the train of even just being charged under this law. The cost is too great and intolerable.

Such an evil system, totally indefensible by normally acceptable methods, relies on a whole phalanx of draconian laws such as the security legislation which is almost peculiar to South Africa. There are the laws which permit the indefinite detention of persons whom the Minister of Law and Order has decided are a threat to the security of the State. They are detained at his pleasure, in solitary confinement, without access to their family, their own doctor, or a lawyer. That is severe punishment when the evidence apparently available to the Minister has not been tested in an open court—perhaps it could stand up to such rigorous scrutiny, perhaps not; we are never to know. It is a far too convenient device for a repressive regime, and the minister would have to be extra special not to succumb to the temptation to circumvent the awkward process of testing his evidence in an open court, and thus he lets his power under the law to be open to the abuse where he is both judge and prosecutor. Many, too many, have died mysteriously in detention. All this is too costly in terms of human lives. The minister is able, too, to place people under banning orders without being subjected to the annoyance of the checks and balances of due process. A banned person for three or five years becomes a nonperson, who cannot be quoted during the period of her banning order. She cannot attend a gathering, which means more than one other person. Two persons together talking to a banned person are a gathering! She cannot attend the wedding or funeral of even her own child without special permission. She must be at home from 6:00 PM of one day to 6:00 AM of the next and on all public holidays, and from 6:00 PM on Fridays until 6:00 AM on Mondays for three years. She cannot go on holiday outside the magisterial area to which she has been confined. She cannot go to the cinema, nor to a picnic. That is severe punishment, inflicted without the evidence allegedly justifying it being made available to the banned person, nor having it scrutinized in a court of law. It is a serious erosion and violation of basic human rights, of which blacks have precious few in the land of their birth. They do not enjoy the rights of freedom of movement and association. They do not enjoy freedom of security of tenure, the right to participate in the making of decisions that affect their lives. In short, this land, richly endowed in so many ways, is sadly lacking in justice.

Once a Zambian and a South African, it is said, were talking. The Zambian then boasted about their Minister of Naval Affairs. The South African asked, "But you have no navy, no access to the sea. How then can you have a Minister of Naval Affairs?" The Zambian retorted, "Well, in South Africa you have a Minister of Justice, don't you?"

It is against this system that our people have sought to protest peacefully since 1912 at least, with the founding of the African National Congress. They have used the conventional methods of peaceful protest petitions, demonstrations, deputations, and even a passive resistance campaign. A tribute to our people's commitment to peaceful change is the fact that the only South Africans to win the Nobel Peace Prize are both black. Our people are peace-loving to a fault. The response of the authorities has been an escalating intransigence and violence, the violence of police dogs, tear gas, detention without trial, exile, and even death. Our people protested peacefully against the Pass Laws in 1960, and sixty-nine of them were killed on March 21, 1960, at Sharpeville, many shot in the back running away. Our children protested against inferior education, singing songs and displaying placards and marching peacefully. Many in 1976, on June 16th and subsequent times, were killed or imprisoned. Over 500 people died in that uprising. Many children went into exile. The whereabouts of many are unknown to their parents. At present, to protest that self-same discriminatory education, and the exclusion of blacks from the new constitutional dispensation, the sham local black government, rising unemployment, increased rents and General Sales Tax, our people have boycotted and demonstrated. They have staged a successful two-day stay away. Over 150 people have been killed. It is far too high a price to pay.

There has been little revulsion or outrage at this wanton destruction of human life in the West. In parenthesis, can somebody please explain to me something that has puzzled me? When a priest goes missing and is subsequently found dead, the media in the West carry his story in very extensive coverage. I am glad that the death of one person can cause so much concern. But in the self-same week when this priest is found dead, the South African Police kill twenty-four blacks who had been participating in the protest, and 6,000 blacks are sacked for being similarly involved, and you are lucky to get that much coverage. Are we being told something I do not want to believe, that we blacks are expendable and that blood is thicker than water, that when it comes to the crunch, you cannot trust whites, that they will club together against us? I don't want to believe that is the message being conveyed to us.

Be that as it may, we see before us a land bereft of much justice, and therefore without peace and security. Unrest is endemic, and will remain an unchanging feature of the South African scene until apartheid, the root cause of it all, is finally dismantled. At this time, the Army is being quartered on the civilian population. There is a civil war being waged. South

Africans are on either side. When the ANC [African National Congress] and the PAC [Pan-Africanist Congress] were banned in 1960, they declared that they had no option but to carry out the armed struggle. We in the SACC [South African Council of Churches] have said we are opposed to all forms of violence—that of a repressive and unjust system, and that of those who seek to overthrow that system. However, we have added that we understand those who say they have had to adopt what is a last resort for them. Violence is not being introduced into the South African situation de novo from outside by those who are called terrorists or freedom fighters, depending on whether you are an oppressed or an oppressor. The South African situation is violent already, and the primary violence is that of apartheid, the violence of forced population removals, of inferior education, of detention without trial, of the migratory labour systems, etc.

There is war on the border of our country. South African faces follow South African. South African soldiers are fighting against Namibians who oppose the illegal occupation of their country by South Africa, which has sought to extend its repressive systems of apartheid, unjust and exploitative.

There is no peace in Southern Africa. There is no peace because there is no justice. There can be no real peace and security until there be first justice enjoyed by all the inhabitants of that beautiful land. The Bible knows nothing about peace without justice, for that would be crying "Peace, peace," where there is no peace. God's Shalom, peace, involves inevitably righteousness, justice, wholeness, fullness of life, participation in decision making, goodness, laughter, joy, compassion, sharing and reconciliation.

I have spoken extensively about South Africa, first because it is the land I know best, but because it is also a microcosm of the world and an example of what is to be found in other lands in differing degree—when there is injustice, invariably peace becomes a casualty. In El Salvador, in Nicaragua, and elsewhere in Latin America, there have been repressive regimes which have aroused opposition in those countries. Fellow citizens are pitted against one another, sometimes attracting the unhelpful attention and interest of outside powers, who want to extend their spheres of influence. We see this in the Middle East, in Korea, in the Philippines, in Kampuchea, in Vietnam, in Ulster, in Afghanistan, in Mozambique, in Angola, in Zimbabwe, behind the Iron Curtain.

Because there is global insecurity, nations are engaged in a mad arms race, spending billions of dollars wastefully on instruments of destruction, when millions are starving. And yet, just a fraction of what is expended so obscenely on defense budgets would make the difference in enabling God's children to fill their stomachs, be educated, and given the chance to lead fulfilled and happy lives. We have the capacity to feed ourselves several times over, but we are daily haunted by the spectacle of the gaunt dregs of humanity shuffling along in endless queues, with bowls to collect what the charity of the world has provided, too little too late. When will we learn, when will the people of the world get up and say, "Enough is enough"? God created us for fellowship. God created us so that we should form the human family, existing together because we were made for one another. We are not made for an exclusive self-sufficiency but for interdependence, and we break the law of our being at our peril. When will we learn that an escalated arms race merely escalates global insecurity? We are now much closer to a nuclear holocaust than when our technology and our spending were less.

Unless we work assiduously so that all of God's children, our brothers and sisters, members of our one human family, all will enjoy basic human rights, the right to a fulfilled life, the right of movement, of work, the freedom to be fully human, within a humanity measured by nothing less than the humanity of Jesus Christ Himself, then we are on the road inexorably to self-destruction, we are not far from global suicide; and yet it could be so different.

When will we learn that human beings are of infinite value because they have been created in the image of God, and that it is a blasphemy to treat them as if they were less than this and to do so ultimately recoils on those who do this? In dehumanizing others, they are themselves dehumanized. Perhaps oppression dehumanizes the oppressor as much as, if not more than, the oppressed. They need each other to become truly free to become human. We can be human only in fellowship, in community, in *koinonia*, in peace.

Let us work to be peacemakers, those given a wonderful share in Our Lord's ministry of reconciliation. If we want peace, so we have been told, let us work for justice. Let us beat our swords into ploughshares.

God calls us to be fellow workers with Him, so that we can extend His Kingdom of Shalom, of justice, of goodness, of compassion, of caring, of sharing, of laughter, joy and reconciliation, so that the kingdoms of this world will become the Kingdom of our God and of His Christ, and He shall reign forever and ever. Amen. Then there will be a fulfillment of the wonderful vision in the Revelation of St. John the Divine [Rev 7:9-12]:

> After this I beheld, and lo, a great multitude, which no man could number, of all nations and kindreds and people and tongues, stood before the throne and before the Lamb, clothed with white robes, and palms in their hands, and cried with a loud voice, saying, "Salvation to our God, who sitteth upon the throne, and unto the Lamb." And all the angels stood round about the throne, and about the elders and the four beasts, and fell before the throne on their faces, and worshipped God, saying, "Amen; Blessing and glory and wisdom and thanksgiving and honor and power and might, be unto our God forever and ever. Amen."

---

500 Beijing University Faculty Members

In April of 1989, following the death of Hu Yaobang, a reform-minded Communist party official, Chinese university students held peaceful pro-democracy demonstrations in several Chinese cities. In Beijing, thousands of students and others inspired by them occupied Tiananmen Square, and the international media moved in. Tensions between the students and the government grew; three days after some 3,000 students had begun a hunger strike, and four days before the government would declare martial law, 500 Beijing Faculty signees issued this statement. On June 4, armored troops of the People's Liberation Army stormed the square, firing on the unarmed crowd. As a global audience watched on TV, hundreds of the demonstrators were killed and thousands were injured.

STATEMENT OF SUPPORT
FOR STUDENT PRO-DEMOCRACY MOVEMENT
May 16, 1989

THE "MAY 16 CIRCULAR" issued in 1966 is, in the minds of the Chinese people, nothing but a symbol of tyranny and darkness. Twenty-three years have passed, and today we are feeling the strong appeal of democracy and light. History has eventually come to a turning point.

Currently, a nationwide patriotic, democratic movement pioneered by young students is gaining momentum. In less than one month, large-scale mass demonstrations rose one after another in Beijing and other parts of the country, surging forward with great force. Several hundred thousand students took to the streets, protesting against corruption, calling for democracy and the rule of law, expressing the common opinions of workers, peasants, army men, cadres, intellectuals, and all other people in the working class.

This is the great awakening of the whole nation, which inherited and surpassed the "May 4th Movement" [that originated in 1919 with demonstrations for democracy and science]. This is an important juncture in history that will decide China's destiny.

Since the Third Plenary Session of the Eleventh Party Congress of the Central Committee held in December 1978, China has engaged in a modernization that promises national rejuvenation. Unfortunately, due to the slack development of political-system reform, the economic reform that has won its initial successes is suffering a serious setback, corruption becomes daily rampant, social conflicts have been sharply intensified, and the cause of reform is confronted with great crisis.

China is at a critical moment in history. At a time when the fate of the people, the country, and the party in power is to be decided, today, May 16, 1989, we—Chinese intellectuals at home and overseas who jointly signed this statement—solemnly declare in public our principled stand:

1) We hold that the Chinese Communist Party and the government have not adopted a wise attitude toward the current student movement, and signs show that not long ago they even intended to handle the student movement with high pressure and violence.

Lessons should be drawn from history: Such autocratic regimes as the Beijing government of 1919, the Kuomintang government in the 1930s and '40s, and the "Gang of Four" in the late 1970s all suppressed the student movements with violence, yet, without exception, they all ended up with humiliating failure.

History has proved that those who try to repress the student movement are destined to come to a disgraceful end. Recently, the Chinese Communist Party and the government began to take a praiseworthy, sensible stand, which has somewhat eased the tension. If they follow the laws of modern democratic politics, defer to the will of the people, [and] go along with world trends, then there will appear a democratic and stable China. Otherwise, a China with bright prospects will very possibly be led to the real abyss of turmoil.

2) To handle the present political crisis, the unavoidable prerequisite will be to recognize the legality of the autonomous student organization formed by democratic procedures. Denial of this prerequisite will contravene the freedom of association stipulated in China's constitution. The autonomous student organization was once labeled "illegal," which resulted in nothing but the aggravation of conflicts and the intensification of crisis.

3) It is government officials' corruption, strongly opposed by young students in the patriotic movement, that directly caused the current political crisis. The most serious error in the past ten years' reform was not made in education but in the negligence of political system reform.

The privileged bureaucratic system and feudalist prerogatives that remain basically intact in the reform have entered the economic situation. This is the genuine cause for pernicious corruption, which has not only devoured the fruits of economic reform, but also shaken the people's confidence in the Chinese Communist Party and the government. The Party and government should learn a profound lesson from this, [and] satisfy the people's demands in earnest by continuously carrying out the reform of the political system, abolishing prerogatives, eliminating "official profiteering," and clearing up corruption.

4) While the student movement was going on, news agencies such as the People's Daily and Xinhua News Agency withheld the true facts and deprived the citizens of their right to know. The Communist Party Committee of Shanghai City suspended Mr. Qin Benli, chief editor of the newspaper World Economic News, from his duties. The completely erroneous course of action mentioned above reflects an attitude of brazen neglect of the constitution.

Freedom of the press is an effective means to combat corruption, maintain national stability, and promote social development. Absolute power without any supervision or restriction will definitely lead to absolute corruption. If press freedom is not actually practiced, if any non-official newspaper is not allowed to exist, then all the aspirations and promises for reform and opening to the outside world will be nothing but hollow words.

5) It is wrong to define the student movement as anti-party, anti-socialist political turmoil. The basic meaning of freedom of speech is the recognition and protection of the citizens' right to voice their political dissidence. Every single political movement since the liberation of China in 1949 was waged to suppress disagreeing political opinions. A society with only one voice is by no means a stable society.

It is necessary for the Chinese Communist Party and the government to remind themselves of the historical lesson drawn from the bitter experience of the "Eliminating the Hu Feng Counterrevolutionary Clique" movement, the "Anti-Rightist Movement," the Great Cultural Revolution, the "Campaign to Clear Up Spiritual Contamination," and the "Anti-Bourgeois Liberalization" movement; to encourage the free airing of different views; to allow young students, intellectuals, and the whole people to discuss important state affairs. Only by doing so can true political stability and unity be realized.

6) It is wrong to propagate the "exposure and punishment" of the so-called "handful" of "bearded backstage manipulators behind the student movement." All citizens of the People's Republic of China, whether old or young, are politically equal in status, and have equal rights to participate in and comment on political affairs.

Liberty, democracy, and legality are never condescendingly bestowed gifts. All those who seek after truth and love freedom should make unremitting efforts to actually gain the rights our constitution promised to every citizen—namely, freedom of thought, freedom of speech, freedom of the press, freedom of publication, freedom of association, freedom of assembly, and freedom of demonstration.

We have come to a critical turning point in history.

The disaster-ridden Chinese nation should not miss its last opportunity, and there is no other way out.

Chinese intellectuals, who inherited the patriotic tradition and are constantly concerned about their country and people, should be aware of their unshirkable historical responsibility, step forward bravely to push forward the advance of democracy, and strive for the building of politically democratic and economically developed modern China!

Long live the People!

Long live the free and democratic motherland!

Nelson Mandela
[1918–   ]

Nelson Rolihlahla Mandela, the lifelong anti-apartheid activist, spent twenty-eight years in prison for his opposition to the white minority government of South Africa and its policies of racial discrimination. In 1990, President F. W. de Klerk, under domestic and international pressure, ordered Mandela's release and lifted the ban on his political organization, the African National Congress. After resuming leadership of the ANC, negotiations between Mandela and de Klerk led to the dismantling of apartheid and paved the way for major political reform. In 1993, Mandela and de Klerk were jointly awarded the Nobel Peace Prize; in 1996, Mandela was chosen president in South Africa's first open democratic elections.

ADDRESS TO A RALLY IN CAPE TOWN
ON HIS RELEASE FROM PRISON
February 11, 1990

FRIENDS, comrades and fellow South Africans.

I greet you all in the name of peace, democracy and freedom for all.

I stand here before you not as a prophet but as a humble servant of you, the people. Your tireless and heroic sacrifices have made it possible for me to be here today. I therefore place the remaining years of my life in your hands.

On this day of my release, I extend my sincere and warmest gratitude to the millions of my compatriots and those in every corner of the globe who have campaigned tirelessly for my release.

I send special greetings to the people of Cape Town, this city which has been my home for three decades. Your mass marches and other forms of struggle have served as a constant source of strength to all political prisoners.

I salute the African National Congress. It has fulfilled our every expectation in its role as leader of the great march to freedom.

I salute our President, Comrade Oliver Tambo, for leading the ANC even under the most difficult circumstances.

I salute the rank and file members of the ANC. You have sacrificed life and limb in the pursuit of the noble cause of our struggle.

I salute combatants of Umkhonto we Sizwe, like Solomon Mahlangu and Ashley Kriel who have paid the ultimate price for the freedom of all South Africans.

I salute the South African Communist Party for its sterling contribution to the struggle for democracy. You have survived forty years of unrelenting persecution. The memory of great communists like Moses Kotane, Yusuf Dadoo, Bram Fischer and Moses Mabhida will be cherished for generations to come.

I salute General Secretary Joe Slovo, one of our finest patriots. We are heartened by the fact that the alliance between ourselves and the Party remains as strong as it always was.

I salute the United Democratic Front, the National Education Crisis Committee, the South African Youth Congress, the Transvaal and Natal Indian Congresses and COSATU and the many other formations of the Mass Democratic Movement.

I also salute the Black Sash and the National Union of South African Students. We note with pride that you have acted as the conscience of white South Africa. Even during the darkest days in the history of our struggle you held the flag of liberty high. The large-scale mass mobilization of the past few years is one of the key factors which led to the opening of the final chapter of our struggle.

I extend my greetings to the working class of our country. Your organized strength is the pride of our movement. You remain the most dependable force in the struggle to end exploitation and oppression.

I pay tribute to the many religious communities who carried the campaign for justice forward when the organizations for our people were silenced.

I greet the traditional leaders of our country—many of you continue to walk in the footsteps of great heroes like Hintsa and Sekhukune.

I pay tribute to the endless heroism of youth, you, the young lions. You, the young lions, have energized our entire struggle.

I pay tribute to the mothers and wives and sisters of our nation. You are the rock-hard foundation of our struggle. Apartheid has inflicted more pain on you than on anyone else.

On this occasion, we thank the world community for their great contribution to the anti-apartheid struggle. Without your support our struggle would not have reached this advanced stage. The sacrifice of the frontline states will be remembered by South Africans forever.

My salutations would be incomplete without expressing my deep appreciation for the strength given to me during my long and lonely years in prison by my beloved wife and family. I am convinced that your pain and suffering was far greater than my own.

Before I go any further I wish to make the point that I intend making only a few preliminary comments at this stage. I will make a more complete statement only after I have had the opportunity to consult with my comrades.

Today the majority of South Africans, black and white, recognize that apartheid has no future. It has to be ended by our own decisive mass action in order to build peace and security. The mass campaign of defiance and other actions of our organization and people can only culminate in the establishment of democracy. The destruction caused by apartheid on our sub-continent is incalculable. The fabric of family life of millions of my people has been shattered. Millions are homeless and unemployed. Our economy lies in ruins and our people are embroiled in political strife. Our resort to the armed struggle in 1960 with the formation of the military wing of the ANC, Umkhonto we Sizwe, was a purely defensive action against the violence of apartheid. The factors which necessitated the armed struggle still exist today. We have no option but to continue. We express the hope that a climate conducive to a negotiated settlement will be created soon so that there may no longer be the need for the armed struggle.

I am a loyal and disciplined member of the African National Congress. I am therefore in full agreement with all of its objectives, strategies and tactics.

The need to unite the people of our country is as important a task now as it always has been. No individual leader is able to take on this enormous task on his own. It is our task as leaders to place our views before our organization and to allow the democratic structures to decide. On the question of democratic practice, I feel duty bound to make the point that a leader of the movement is a person who has been democratically elected at a national conference. This is a principle which must be upheld without any exceptions.

Today, I wish to report to you that my talks with the government have been aimed at normalizing the political situation in the country. We have not as yet begun discussing the basic demands of the struggle. I wish to stress that I myself have at no time entered into negotiations about the future of our country except to insist on a meeting between the ANC and the government.

Mr. de Klerk has gone further than any other Nationalist president in taking real steps to normalize the situation. However, there are further steps as outlined in the Harare Declaration that have to be met before negotiations on the basic demands of our people can begin. I reiterate our call for, inter alia, the immediate ending of the State of Emergency and the freeing of all, and not only some, political prisoners. Only such a normalized situation, which allows for free political activity, can allow us to consult our people in order to obtain a mandate.

The people need to be consulted on who will negotiate and on the content of such negotiations. Negotiations cannot take place above the heads or behind the backs of our people. It is our belief that the future of our country can only be determined by a body which is democratically elected on a non-racial basis. Negotiations on the dismantling of apartheid will have to address the overwhelming demand of our people for a democratic, non-racial and unitary South Africa. There must be an end to white monopoly on political power and a fundamental restructuring of our political and economic systems to ensure that the inequalities of apartheid are addressed and our society thoroughly democratized.

It must be added that Mr. de Klerk himself is a man of integrity who is acutely aware of the dangers of a public figure not honoring his undertakings. But as an organization we base our policy and strategy on the harsh reality we are faced with. And this reality is that we are still suffering under the policy of the Nationalist government.

Our struggle has reached a decisive moment. We call on our people to seize this moment so that the process towards democracy is rapid and uninterrupted. We have waited too long for our freedom. We can no longer wait. Now is the time to intensify the struggle on all fronts. To relax our efforts now would be a mistake which generations to come will not be able to forgive. The sight of freedom looming on the horizon should encourage us to redouble our efforts.

It is only through disciplined mass action that our victory can be assured. We call on our white compatriots to join us in the shaping of a new South Africa. The freedom movement is a political home for you too. We call on the international community to continue the campaign to isolate the apartheid regime. To lift sanctions now would be to run the risk of aborting the process towards the complete eradication of apartheid.

Our march to freedom is irreversible. We must not allow fear to stand in our way. Universal suffrage on a common voters' roll in a united democratic and non-racial South Africa is the only way to peace and racial harmony.

In conclusion I wish to quote my own words during my trial in 1964. They are as true today as they were then:

> I have fought against white domination and I have fought against black domination. I have cherished the ideal of a democratic and free society in which all persons live together in harmony and with equal opportunities. It is an ideal which I hope to live for and to achieve. But if needs be, it is an ideal for which I am prepared to die.

Václav Havel
[1936–   ]

Czech playwright Václav Havel spent a total of nearly five years in prison for his views and actions critical of his Czechoslovakia's communist-controlled government and its persistent human rights violations. In 1989, the peaceful "Velvet Revolution" involving mass demonstrations in part inspired by Havel and his writings, brought an end to the communist regime, and the newly installed parliament elected Havel president by an overwhelming margin. He travelled to Washington several months later and delivered this speech.

ADDRESS TO A JOINT SESSION OF CONGRESS
February 21, 1990

MY ADVISORS have advised me, on this important occasion, to speak in Czech. I don't know why. Perhaps they wanted you to enjoy the sweet sounds of my mother tongue.

The last time they arrested me, on October 27 of last year, I didn't know whether it was for two days or two years.

Exactly one month later, when the rock musician Michael Kocab told me that I would probably be proposed as a presidential candidate, I thought it was one of his usual jokes.

On the 10th of December 1989, when my actor friend Jiri Bartoska, in the name of the Civic Forum, nominated me as a candidate for the office of President of the Republic, I thought it was out of the question that the parliament we had inherited from the previous regime would elect me.

Twelve days later, when I was unanimously elected President of my country, I had no idea that in two months I would be speaking in front of this famous and powerful assembly, and that what I say would be heard by millions of people who have never heard of me and that hundreds of politicians and political scientists would study every word I say.

When they arrested me on October 27, 1 was living in a country ruled by the most conservative Communist government in Europe, and our society slumbered beneath the pall of a totalitarian system. Today, less than four months later, I am speaking to you as the representative of a country that has set out on the road to democracy, a country where there is complete freedom of speech, which is getting ready for free elections, and which wants to create a prosperous market economy and its own foreign policy.

It is all very strange indeed.

But I have not come here to speak of myself or my feelings, or merely to talk about my own country. I have used this small example of something I know well, to illustrate something general and important.

We are living in very odd times. The human face of the world is changing so rapidly that none of the familiar political speedometers are adequate.

We playwrights, who have to cram a whole human life or an entire historical era into a two-hour play, can scarcely understand this rapidity ourselves. And if it gives us trouble, think of the trouble it must give to political scientists, who spend their whole lives studying the realm of the probable.

Let me try to explain why I think the velocity of the changes in my country, in Central and Eastern Europe, and of course in the Soviet Union itself, has made such a significant impression on the face of the world today, and why it concerns the fate of us all, including you Americans. I would like to look at this, first from the political point of view, and then from a point of view that we might call philosophical.

Twice in this century, the world has been threatened by a catastrophe; twice this catastrophe was born in Europe, and twice you Americans, along with others, were called upon to save Europe, the whole world and yourselves. The first rescue mission—among other things—provided significant help to us Czechs and Slovaks.

Thanks to the great support of your President Wilson, our first president, Tomás Garrigue Masaryk, could found our modern independent state. He founded it, as you know, on the same principles on which the United States of America had been founded, as Masaryk's manuscripts held by the Library of Congress testify.

At the same time, the United States was making enormous strides. It became the most powerful nation on earth, and it understood the responsibility that flowed from this. Proof of this are the hundreds of thousands of your young citizens who gave their lives for the liberation of Europe, and the graves of American airmen and soldiers on Czechoslovak soil.

But something else was happening as well: the Soviet Union appeared, grew, and transformed the enormous sacrifices of its people suffering under totalitarian rule into a strength that, after World War Two, made it the second most powerful nation in the world. It was a country that nightly gave people nightmares, because no one knew what would occur to its rulers next and what country they would decide to conquer and drag into their sphere of influence, as it is called in political language.

All of this taught us to see the world in bipolar terms, as two enormous forces, one a defender of freedom, the other a source of nightmares. Europe became the point of friction between these two powers and thus it turned into a single enormous arsenal divided into two parts. In this process, one half of the arsenal became part of that nightmarish power, while the other—the free part—bordering on the ocean and having no wish to be driven into it, was compelled, together with you, to build a complicated security system, to which we probably owe the fact that we still exist.

So you may have contributed to the salvation of us Europeans, of the world and thus of yourselves for a third time: you have helped us to survive until today—without a hot war this time—but merely a cold one.

And now what is happening is happening: the totalitarian system in the Soviet Union and in most of its satellites is breaking down and our nations are looking for a way to democracy and independence. The first act in this remarkable drama began when Mr. Gorbachev and those around him, faced with the sad reality of their country, initiated their policy of *perestroika.* Obviously they had no idea either what they were setting in motion or how rapidly events would unfold. We knew a lot about the enormous number of growing problems that slumbered beneath the honeyed, unchanging mask of socialism. But I don't think any of us knew how little it would take for these problems to manifest themselves in all their enormity, and for the longings of these nations to emerge in all their strength. The mask fell away so rapidly that, in the flood of work, we have literally no time even to be astonished.

What does all this mean for the world in the long run? Obviously a number of things. This is, I am firmly convinced, an historically irreversible process, and as a result Europe will begin again to seek its own identity without being compelled to be a divided armory any longer. Perhaps this will create the hope that sooner or later your boys will no longer have to stand on guard for freedom in Europe, or come to our rescue, because Europe will at last be able to stand guard over itself. But that is still not the most important thing: the main thing is, it seems to me, that these revolutionary changes will enable us to escape from the rather antiquated straitjacket of this bipolar view of the world, and to enter at last into an era of multipolarity. That is, into an era in which all of us—large and small, former slaves and former masters—will be able to create what your great President Lincoln called "the family of man." Can you imagine what a relief this would be to that part of the world which for some reason is called the Third World, even though it is the largest?

I don't think it's appropriate simply to generalize, so let me be specific:

1) As you certainly know, most of the big wars and other conflagrations over the centuries have traditionally begun and ended on the territory of modern Czechoslovakia, or else they were somehow related to that area. Let the Second World War stand as the most recent example. This is understandable: whether we like it or not, we are located in the very heart of Europe, and thanks to this, we have no view of the sea, and no real navy. I mention this because political stability in our country has traditionally been important for the whole of Europe. This is still true today. Our government of national understanding, our present Federal Assembly, the other bodies of the state and I myself will personally guarantee this stability until we hold free elections, planned for June. We understand the terribly complex reasons, domestic political reasons above all, why the Soviet Union cannot withdraw its troops from our territory as quickly as they arrived in 1968. We understand that the arsenals built there over the past twenty years cannot be dismantled and removed overnight. Nevertheless, in our bilateral negotiations with the Soviet Union, we would like to have as many Soviet units as possible moved out of our country before the elections, in the interests of political stability. The more successful our negotiations, the more those who are elected in our places will be able to guarantee political stability in our country even after the elections.

2) I often hear the question: how can the United States of America help us today? My reply is as paradoxical as the whole of my life has been: you can help us most of all if you help the Soviet Union on its irreversible, but immensely complicated road to democracy. It is far more complicated than

the road possible to its former European satellites. You yourselves know best how to support, as rapidly as possible, the non-violent evolution of this enormous, multi-national body politic towards democracy and autonomy for all of its peoples. Therefore, it is not fitting for me to offer you any advice. I can only say that the sooner, the more quickly, and the more peacefully the Soviet Union begins to move along the road towards genuine political pluralism, respect for the rights of nations to their own integrity and to a working—that is a market—economy, the better it will be, not just for Czechs and Slovaks, but for the whole world. And the sooner you yourselves will be able to reduce the burden of the military budget borne by the American people. To put it metaphorically: the millions you give to the East today will soon return to you in the form of billions in savings.

3) It is not true that the Czech writer Václav Havel wishes to dissolve the Warsaw Pact tomorrow and then NATO [North Atlantic Treaty Organization] the day after that, as some eager nationalists have written. Václav Havel merely thinks what he has already said here, that for another hundred years, American soldiers shouldn't have to be separated from their mothers just because Europe is incapable of being a guarantee of world peace, which it ought to be, in order to make some amends, at least, for having given the world two world wars. Sooner or later Europe must recover and come into its own, and decide for itself how many of whose soldiers it needs so that its own security, and all the wider implications of that security, may radiate peace into the whole world. Václav Havel cannot make decisions about things it is not proper for him to decide. He is merely putting in a good word for genuine peace, and for achieving it quickly.

4) Czechoslovakia thinks that the planned summit conference of countries participating in the Helsinki process should take place soon, and that in addition to what it wants to accomplish, it should aim to hold the so-called Helsinki Two conference earlier than 1992, as originally planned. Above all, we feel it could be something far more significant than has so far seemed possible. We think that Helsinki Two should become something equivalent to the European peace conference, which has not yet been held; one that would finally put a formal end to the Second World War and all its unhappy consequences. Such a conference would officially bring a future democratic Germany, in the process of unifying itself, into a new pan-European structure which could decide about its own security system. This system would naturally require some connection with that part of the globe we might label the "Helsinki" part, stretching westward from Vladivostock all the way to Alaska. The borders of the European states, which by the way should become gradually less important, should finally be legally guaranteed by a common, regular treaty. It should be more than obvious that the basis for such a treaty would have to be general respect for human rights, genuine political pluralism and genuinely free elections.

5) Naturally we welcome the initiative of President Bush, which was essentially accepted by Mr. Gorbachev as well, according to which the number of American and Soviet troops in Europe should be radically

reduced. It is a magnificent shot in the arm for the Vienna disarmament talks and creates favorable conditions not only for our own efforts to achieve the quickest possible departure of Soviet troops from Czechoslovakia, but indirectly as well for our own intention to make considerable cuts in the Czechoslovak army, which is disproportionately large in relation to our population. If Czechoslovakia were forced to defend itself against anyone, which we hope will not happen, then it will be capable of doing so with a considerably smaller army, because this time its defense would be—not only after decades but even centuries—supported by the common and indivisible will of both its nations and its leadership. Our freedom, independence and our new-born democracy have been purchased at great cost, and we will not surrender them. For the sake of order, I should add that whatever steps we take are not intended to complicate the Vienna disarmament talks, but on the contrary to facilitate them.

6) Czechoslovakia is returning to Europe. In the general interest and in its own interest as well, it wants to coordinate this return—both politically and economically—with the other returnees, which means, above all, with its neighbors the Poles and the Hungarians. We are doing what we can to coordinate these returns. And at the same time, we are doing what we can so that Europe will be capable of really accepting us, its wayward children. Which means that it may open itself to us, and may begin to transform its structures—which are formally European but de facto Western European—in that direction, but in such a way that it will not be to its detriment, but rather to its advantage.

7) I have already said this in our parliament, and I would like to repeat it here, in this Congress, which is architecturally far more attractive: for many years, Czechoslovakia—as someone's meaningless satellite—has refused to face up honestly to its co-responsibility for the world. It has a lot to make up for. If I dwell on this and so many important things here, it is only because I feel—along with my fellow citizens—a sense of culpability for our former responsible passivity, and a rather ordinary sense of indebtedness.

8) Last but not least, we are of course delighted that your country is so readily lending its support to our fresh efforts to renew democracy. Both our peoples were deeply moved by the generous offers made a few days ago in Prague at the Charles University, one of the oldest in Europe, by your Secretary of State, Mr. James Baker. We are ready to sit down and talk about them.

Ladies and gentlemen, I've only been president for two months and I haven't attended any schools for presidents. My only school was life itself. Therefore I don't want to burden you any longer with my political thoughts, but instead I will move on to an area that is more familiar to me, to what I would call the philosophical aspect of those changes that still concern everyone, although they are taking place in our corner of the world.

As long as people are people, democracy in the full sense of the word will always be no more than an ideal; one may approach it as one would a horizon, in ways that may be better or worse, but it can never be fully attained. In this sense you too are merely approaching democracy. You have thousands of problems of all kinds, as other countries do. But you have one great advantage: you have been approaching democracy uninterruptedly for more than two hundred years, and your journey towards that horizon has never been disrupted by a totalitarian system. Czechs and Slovaks, despite their humanistic traditions that go back to the first millenium, have approached democracy for a mere twenty years, between the two world wars, and now for the three and a half months since the seventeenth of November of last year.

The advantage that you have over us is obvious at once.

The communist type of totalitarian system has left both our nations, Czechs and Slovaks—as it has all the nations of the Soviet Union and the other countries the Soviet Union subjugated in its time—a legacy of countless dead, an infinite spectrum of human suffering, profound economic decline, and above all enormous human humiliation. It has brought us horrors that fortunately you have not known.

At the same time, however—unintentionally, of course—it has given us something positive: a special capacity to look, from time to time, somewhat further than someone who has not undergone this bitter experience. A person who cannot move and live a somewhat normal life because he is pinned under a boulder has more time to think about his hopes than someone who is not trapped in this way.

What I am trying to say is this: we must all learn many things from you, from how to educate our offspring, how to elect our representatives, all the way to how to organize our economic life so that it will lead to prosperity and not to poverty. But it doesn't have to be merely assistance from the well-educated, the powerful and the wealthy to someone who has nothing and therefore has nothing to offer in return.

We too can offer something to you: our experience and the knowledge that has come from it.

This is a subject for books, many of which have already been written and many of which have yet to be written. I shall therefore limit myself to a single idea.

The specific experience I'm talking about has given me one great certainty: consciousness precedes Being, and not the other way around, as the Marxists claim.

For this reason, the salvation of this human world lies nowhere else than in the human heart, in the human power to reflect, in human meekness and in human responsibility.

Without a global revolution in the sphere of human consciousness, nothing will change for the better in the sphere of our Being as humans, and the catastrophe towards which this world is headed, whether it be ecological, social, demographic or a general breakdown of civilization, will be unavoidable. If we are no longer threatened by world war, or by the danger that the absurd mountains of accumulated nuclear weapons might blow up the world, this does not mean that we have definitively won. We are in fact far from definitive victory.

We are still a long way from that "family of man"; in fact, we seem to be receding from the ideal rather than drawing closer to it. Interests of all kinds: personal, selfish, state, national, group and, if you like, company interests still considerably outweigh genuinely common and global interests. We are still under the sway of the destructive and vain belief that man is the pinnacle of creation, and not just a part of it, and that therefore everything is permitted. There are still many who say they are concerned not for themselves, but for the cause, while they are demonstrably out for themselves and not for the cause at all. We are still destroying the planet that was entrusted to us, and its environment. We still close our eyes to the growing social, ethnic and cultural conflicts in the world. From time to time we say that the anonymous megamachinery we have created for ourselves no longer serves us, but rather has enslaved us, yet we still fail to do anything about it.

In other words, we still don't know how to put morality ahead of politics, science and economics. We are still incapable of understanding that the only genuine backbone of all our actions—if they are to be moral—is responsibility. Responsibility to something higher than my family, my country, my firm, my success. Responsibility to the order of Being, where all our authority is indelibly recorded and where, and only where, they will be properly judged.

The interpreter or mediator between us and this higher authority is what is traditionally referred to as human conscience.

If I subordinate my political behavior to this imperative mediated to me by my conscience, I can't go far wrong. If on the contrary I were not guided by this voice, not even ten presidential schools with two thousand of the best political scientists in the world could help me.

This is why I ultimately decided—after resisting for a long time—to accept the burden of political responsibility.

I'm not the first, nor will I be the last, intellectual to do this. On the contrary, my feeling is that there will be more and more of them all the time. If the hope of the world lies in human consciousness, then it is obvious that intellectuals cannot go on forever avoiding their share of responsibility for the world and hiding their distaste for politics under an alleged need to be independent.

It is easy to have independence in your program and then leave others to carry that program out. If everyone thought that way pretty soon no one would be independent.

I think that you Americans should understand this way of thinking. Wasn't it the best minds of your country, people you could call intellectuals, who wrote your famous Declaration of Independence, your Bill of Human Rights and your Constitution and who—above all—took upon themselves the practical responsibility for putting them into practice? The worker from Branik in Prague that your President referred to in his State of the Union message this year is far from being the only person in Czechoslovakia, let alone in the world, to be inspired by those great documents. They inspire us all. They inspire us despite the fact that they are over two hundred years old. They inspire us to be citizens.

[*Speaking English*] When Thomas Jefferson wrote that "Governments are instituted among Men, deriving their just Powers from the Consent of the Governed," it was a simple and important act of the human spirit.

What gave meaning to the act, however, was the fact that the author backed it up with his life. It was not just his words, it was his deeds as well.

I will end where I began: history has accelerated. I believe that once again, it will be the human mind that will notice this acceleration, give it a name, and transform those words into deeds.

Thank you.

1992 Political Convention Speeches by HIV-Infected Women

As late as 1992, many Americans still believed AIDS to be a disease affecting only gay men, minorities, and intravenous drug users. Both political party conventions that year featured speakers—white, heterosexual, upper class women—who did not fit these stereotyped categories. Their speeches increased awareness of a terrible epidemic, but they also demonstrated that the problem was as vexing politically as it was medically. Elizabeth Glaser was the wife of actor and Director Paul Glaser. She died in 1994. Mary Fisher is the daughter of a prominent donor to the Republican Party. Since her speech, she has published four books on the subject of AIDS.

DEMOCRATIC CONVENTION: ELIZABETH GLASER
July 14, 1992

I'M ELIZABETH GLASER. Eleven years ago, while giving birth to my first child, I hemorrhaged and was transfused with seven pints of blood. Four years later, I found out that I had been infected with the AIDS virus and had unknowingly passed it on to my daughter, Ariel, through my breast milk, and my son Jake, in utero.

Twenty years ago I wanted to be at the Democratic Convention because it was a way to participate in our country. Today I am here because it's a matter of life and death.

Exactly four years ago my daughter died of AIDS—she did not survive the Reagan administration. I am here because my son and I may not survive four more years of leaders who say they care, but do nothing. I am in a race with the clock. This is not about being a Republican or an Independent or a Democrat—it's about the future—for each and every one of us.

I started out just a mom—fighting for the life of her child. But along the way I learned how unfair America can be. Not just for people who have HIV, but for many, many people—gay people, people of color, children. A strange spokesperson for such a group—a well-to-do white woman—but I have learned my lessons the hard way—and I know that America has lost her path, and is at risk of losing her soul. America wake up—we are all in a struggle between life and death.

I understand the sense of frustration and despair in our country, because I know first hand about screaming for help and getting no answer. I went to Washington to tell Presidents Reagan and Bush we needed to do much, much more for AIDS research and care, and that children couldn't be forgotten. The first time, when nothing happened, I thought—oh, they just didn't hear. The second time, when nothing happened, I thought—maybe I didn't shout loud enough. But, now I realize that they don't hear because they don't want to listen. When you cry for help and no one listens, you start to lose hope.

I began to lose faith in America. I felt my country was letting me down. And it was.

This is not the America I was raised to be proud of. I was raised to believe that others' problems were my problems as well. But when I tell people about HIV, hoping they will care and try to help, I see the look in their eyes—it's not my problem, they're thinking. Well, it's everyone's problem, and we need a leader who will tell us that.

We need a visionary to guide us—to say it wasn't all right for Ryan White to be banned from school because he had HIV or a man or woman denied a job because they were infected with this virus. We need a leader who is truly committed to educating us.

I believe in America—but not with a leadership of selfishness and greed where the wealthy get health care and insurance and the poor don't. Do you know how much my AIDS care costs? Over $40,000 a year. Someone without insurance can't afford this. Even the drugs that I hope will keep me alive are out of reach for others. Is their life any less valuable? Of course not. This is not the America I was raised to be proud of—where the rich people get care and drugs that poor people can't. We need health care for all. We need a leader to say this, and do something about it.

I believe in America. But not with a leadership that talks about problems but is incapable of solving them. Two HIV commission reports with recommendations about what to do to solve this crisis sitting on shelves, gathering dust. We need a leader who will not only listen to these recommendations, but implement them.

I believe in America, but not with a leadership that doesn't hold government accountable. I go to Washington to the National Institutes of Health and say "Show me what you're doing on HIV." They hate it when I come because I try to tell them how to do it better. But that's why I love being a taxpayer: because it's my money and they must become accountable.

I believe in an America where our leaders talk straight. When anyone tells President Bush that the battle against AIDS is seriously underfunded, he juggles the numbers to mislead the public into thinking we're spending twice as much as we really are. While they play games with numbers, people are dying.

I believe in America, but an America where there is a light in every home—"a thousand points of light" just wasn't enough. My house has been dark for too long.

Once every generation, history brings us to an important crossroads.

Sometimes in life there is that moment when it's possible to make a change for the better. This is one of those moments.

For me, this is not politics. It's a crisis of caring.

In this hall is the future: women, men of all colors saying take America back. We are just real people wanting a more hopeful life. But words and ideas are not enough. Good thoughts won't save my family. What's the point of caring if we don't do something about it? We must have action. A President and a Congress that can work together so we can get out of this gridlock and move ahead. Because I don't win my war if the Congress cares and the President doesn't—or if the President cares and the Congress doesn't support the ideas.

The people in this hall—this week, the Democratic party—all of us can begin to deliver that partnership, and in November we can all bring it home.

My daughter lived seven years, and in her last year, when she couldn't walk or talk, her wisdom shone through. Who taught me to love when all I wanted to do was hate. She taught me to help others, when all I wanted to do was help myself. She taught me to be brave, when all I felt was fear.

My daughter and I loved each other with simplicity. America, we can do the same.

This was the country that offered hope. This was the place where dreams could come true. Not just economic dreams, but dreams of freedom, justice and equality. We all need to hope that our dreams can come true. I challenge you to make it happen, because all our lives, not just mine, depend on it.

REPUBLICAN CONVENTION: MARY FISHER
August 19, 1992

LESS THAN three months ago, at Platform Hearings in Salt Lake City, I asked the Republican Party to lift the shroud of silence which had been draped over the issue of HIV and AIDS. I have come tonight to bring our silence to an end.

I bear a message of challenge, not self-congratulations. I want your attention, not your applause. I would never have asked to be HIV-positive. But I believe that in all things there is a purpose, and I stand before you, and before the nation, gladly.

The reality of AIDS is brutally clear. Two hundred thousand Americans are dead or dying; a million more are infected. Worldwide, forty million, sixty million, or a hundred million infections will be counted in the coming few years. But despite science and research, White House meetings and congressional hearings, despite good intentions and bold initiatives, campaign slogans and hopeful promises—it is, despite it all, it's the epidemic which is winning tonight.

In the context of an election year, I ask you, here, in this great hall, or listening in the quiet of your home, to recognize that the AIDS virus is not a political creature. It does not care whether you are Democrat or Republican. It does not ask whether you are black or a white, male or female, gay or straight, young or old.

Tonight, I represent an AIDS community whose members have been reluctantly drafted from every segment of American society. Though I am white, and a mother, I am one with a black infant struggling with tubes in a Philadelphia hospital. Though I am female, and contracted this disease in marriage, and enjoy the warm support of my family, I am one with the lonely gay man sheltering a flickering candle from the cold wind of his family's rejection.

This is not a distant threat; it is a present danger. The rate of infection is increasing fastest among women and children. Largely unknown a decade ago, AIDS is the third leading killer of young-adult Americans today. But it won't be third for long, because, unlike other diseases, this one travels. Adolescents don't give each other cancer or heart disease because they believe they are in love. But HIV is different.

And we have helped it along. We have killed each other—with our ignorance, our prejudice, and our silence. We may take refuge in our stereotypes, but we cannot hide there long. Because HIV asks only one thing of those it attacks: Are you human? And this is the right question: Are you human?

Because people with HIV have not entered some alien state of being. They are human. They have not earned cruelty and they do not deserve meanness. They don't benefit from being isolated or treated as outcasts. Each of them is exactly what God made: a person. Not evil, deserving of our judgment; not victims, longing for our pity. People. Ready for support and worthy of compassion.

My call to you, my Party, is to take a public stand no less compassionate than that of the President and Mrs. Bush. They have embraced me and my family in memorable ways. In the place of judgment, they have shown affection. In difficult moments, they have raised our spirits. In the darkest hours, I have seen them reaching not only to me, but also to my parents, armed with that stunning grief and special grace that comes only to parents who have themselves leaned too long over the bedside of a dying child.

With the President's leadership, much good has been done. Much of the good has gone unheralded. As the President has insisted, "Much remains to be done." But we do the President's cause no good if we praise the American family but ignore a virus that destroys it. We must be consistent if we are to be believed. We cannot love justice and ignore prejudice, love our children and fear to teach them. Whatever our role, as parent or policy maker, we must act as eloquently as we speak, else we have no integrity.

My call to the nation is a plea for awareness. If you believe you are safe, you are in danger. Because I was not hemophiliac, I was not at risk. Because I was not gay, I was not at risk. Because I did not inject drugs, I was not at risk. My father has devoted much of his lifetime to guarding against another holocaust. He is part of the generation who heard Pastor Niemöller come out of the Nazi death camps to say, "They came after the Jews and I was not a Jew, so I did not protest. They came after the Trade Unionists, and I was not a Trade Unionist, so I did not protest. Then they came after the Roman Catholics, and I was not a Roman Catholic, so I did not protest. Then they came after me, and there was no one left to protest."

The lesson history teaches is this: If you believe you are safe, you are at risk. If you do not see this killer stalking your children, look again. There is no family or community, no race or religion, no place left in America that is safe. Until we genuinely embrace this message, we are a nation at risk.

Tonight, HIV marches resolutely toward AIDS in more than a million American homes, littering its pathway with the bodies of the young. Young men. Young women. Young parents. And young children. One of the families is mine. If it is true that HIV inevitably turns to AIDS, then my children will inevitably turn to orphans.

My family has been a rock of support. My eighty-four year old father, who has pursued the healing of the nations, will not accept the premise that he can't heal his daughter. My mother refuses to be broken. She still calls at midnight to tell wonderful jokes that make me laugh. Sisters and friends, and my brother Phillip (whose birthday is today) all have helped carry me over the hardest places. I am blessed, richly and deeply blessed, to have such a family.

But not all of you have been so blessed. You are HIV-positive but dare not say it. You have lost loved ones, but you dared not whisper the word AIDS. You weep silently. You grieve alone.

I have a message for you. It is not you who should feel shame, it is we. We who tolerate ignorance and practice prejudice, we who have taught you to fear. We must lift our shroud of silence, making it safe for you to reach out for compassion. It is our task to seek safety for our children, not in quiet denial but in effective action. Some day our children will be grown. My son Max, now four, will take the measure of his mother. My son Zachary, now two, will sort through his memories. I may not be here to hear their judgments, but I know already what I hope they are.

I want my children to know that their mother was not a victim. She was a messenger. I do not want them to think, as I once did, that courage is the absence of fear. I want them to know that courage is the strength to act wisely when most we are afraid. I want them to have the courage to step forward when called by their nation, or their Party, and give leadership, no matter what the personal cost. I ask no more of you than I ask of myself, or of my children.

To the millions of you who are grieving, who are frightened, who have suffered the ravages of AIDS firsthand: Have courage and you will find support. To the millions who are strong, I issue the plea: Set aside prejudice and politics to make room for compassion and sound policy.

To my children, I make this pledge: I will not give in, Zachary, because I draw my courage from you. Your silly giggle gives me hope. Your gentle prayers give me strength. And you, my child, give me the reason to say to America, "You are at risk." And I will not rest, Max, until I have done all I can do to make your world safe. I will seek a place where intimacy is not the prelude to suffering.

I will not hurry to leave you, my children. But when I go, I pray that you will not suffer shame on my account. To all within the sound of my voice,

I appeal: Learn with me the lessons of history and grace, so my children will not be afraid to say the word AIDS when I am gone. Then their children—and yours—may not need to whisper it at all.

God bless the children, God bless us all. Good night.

Daw Aung San Suu Kyi
[1945–   ]

As "one of the most extraordinary examples of civil courage in Asia in recent decades,"Burmese democratic opposition leader and non-violent human rights activist Daw Aung San Suu Kyi was awarded the Nobel Peace Prize in 1991. Held under house arrest since 1990 by the ruling military junta, Aung San Suu Kyi had just been released from detention when she delivered this speech as part of the largest gathering of women's interest groups in history, the United Nations-sponsored Fourth World Conference on Women in Beijing (of which the NGO Forum was part). The speech had to be given by videotape, for fear that if she left her country she would not be permitted to return. Some 4,000 women showed up to hear the address, but many were turned away because the movie theater in which it was shown seated only 1500. The speech was all the more remarkable for being heard in China, where the government had erected an intrusive security environment for the conference and had issued stern warnings that any criticism of Chinese policy or leaders would not be tolerated.

OPENING KEYNOTE ADDRESS,
NGO FORUM ON WOMEN, HUAIROU, CHINA
August 31, 1995

IT IS a wonderful but daunting task that has fallen on me to say a few words by way of opening this Forum, the greatest concourse of women—joined by a few brave men—that has ever gathered on our planet. I want to try and voice some of the common hopes which firmly unite us in our splendid diversity.

But first I would like to explain why I cannot be with you in person today. Last month I was released from almost six years of house arrest. The regaining of my freedom has in turn imposed a duty on me to work for the freedom of women and men in my country who have suffered far more—and who continue to suffer far more—than I have. It is this duty which prevents me from joining you today. Even sending this message to you has not been without difficulties. But the help of those who believe in international cooperation and freedom of expression has enabled me to overcome the obstacles. They have made it possible for me to make a small contribution to this great celebration of the struggle of women to mold their own destiny and to influence the fate of our global village.

The opening plenary of this Forum will be presenting an overview of the global forces affecting the quality of life of the human community and the challenges they pose for the global community as a whole and for women in particular as we approach the twenty-first century. However, with true womanly understanding, the convener of this forum suggested that among these global forces and challenges, I might wish to concentrate on those matters which occupy all my waking thoughts these days: peace, security, human rights and democracy. I would like to discuss these issues particularly in the context of the participation of women in politics and governance.

For millennia women have dedicated themselves almost exclusively to the task of nurturing, protecting and caring for the young and the old, striving for conditions of peace that favor life as a whole. To this can be added the fact that, to the best of my knowledge, no war was ever started by women. But it is women and children who have always suffered most in situations of conflict. Now that we are gaining control of the primary historical role imposed on us of sustaining life in the context of the home and family, it is time to apply in the arena of the world the wisdom and experience thus gained in activities of peace over so many thousands of years. The education and empowerment of women throughout the world cannot fail to result in a more caring, tolerant, just and peaceful life for all.

If to these universal benefits of the growing emancipation of women can be added the "peace dividend" for human development offered by the end of the Cold War, spending less on the war toys of grown men and much more on the urgent needs of humanity as a whole, then truly the next millennia will be an age the like of which has never been seen in human history. But there still remain many obstacles to be overcome before we can achieve this goal. And not least among those obstacles are intolerance and insecurity.

This year is the International Year for Tolerance. The United Nations has recognized that "tolerance, human rights, democracy and peace are closely related. Without tolerance, the foundations that form democracy and respect for human rights cannot be strengthened, and the achievement of peace will remain elusive." My own experience during the years I have been engaged in the democracy movement of Burma has convinced me of the need to emphasize the positive aspect of tolerance. It is not enough simply to "live and let live": genuine tolerance requires an active effort to try to understand the point of view of others; it implies broad-mindedness and vision, as well as confidence in one's own ability to meet new challenges without resorting to intransigence or violence. In societies where men are truly confident, women are not merely tolerated, they are valued. Their opinions are listened to with respect; they are given their rightful place in shaping the society in which they live.

There is an outmoded Burmese proverb still recited by men who wish to deny that women too can play a part in bringing necessary change and progress to their society: "The dawn rises only when the rooster crows." But Burmese people today are well aware of the scientific reasons behind the rising of dawn and the falling of dusk. And the intelligent rooster surely realizes that it is because dawn comes that it crows and not the other way 'round. It crows to welcome the light that has come to relieve the darkness of night. It is not the prerogative of men alone to bring light to this world: women with their capacity for compassion and self-sacrifice, their courage and perseverance, have done much to dissipate the darkness of intolerance and hate, suffering and despair.

Often the other side of the coin of intolerance is insecurity. Insecure people tend to be intolerant, and their intolerance unleashes forces that threaten the security of others. And where there is no security there can be no lasting peace. In its "Human Development Report" for this year the UNDP noted that human security "is not a concern with weapons—it is a concern with human life and dignity." The struggle for democracy and human rights in Burma is a struggle for life and dignity. It is a struggle that encompasses our political, social and economic aspirations. The people of my country want the two freedoms that spell security: freedom from want and freedom from fear. It is want that has driven so many of our young girls across our borders to a life of sexual slavery where they are subject to constant humiliation and ill-treatment. It is fear of persecution for their political beliefs that has made so many of our people feel that even in their own homes they cannot live in dignity and security.

Traditionally the home is the domain of the woman. But there has never been a guarantee that she can live out her life there safe and unmolested. There are countless women who are subjected to severe cruelty within the heart of the family which should be their haven. And in times of crisis when their menfolk are unable to give them protection, women have to face the harsh challenges of the world outside while continuing to discharge their duties within the home.

Many of my male colleagues who have suffered imprisonment for their part in the democracy movement have spoken of the great debt of gratitude they owe to their womenfolk, particularly to their wives who stood by them firmly, tender as mothers nursing their newly born, brave as lionesses defending their young. These magnificent human beings who have done so much to aid their men in the struggle for peace and justice—how much more could they not achieve if given the opportunity to work in their own right for the good of their country and of the world?

Our endeavors have also been sustained by the activities of strong and principled women all over the world who have campaigned not only for my release but, more importantly, for our cause. I cannot let this opportunity pass without speaking of the gratitude we feel towards our sisters everywhere, from heads of government to busy housewives. Their efforts have been a triumphant demonstration of female solidarity and of the power of an ideal to cross all frontiers.

In my country at present, women have no participation in the higher levels of government and none whatsoever in the judiciary. Even within the democratic movement only fourteen out of the 485 MPs elected in 1990 were women—all from my own party, the National League for Democracy. These fourteen women represent less than three percent of the total number of successful candidates. They, like their male colleagues, have not been permitted to take office since the outcome of those elections has been totally ignored. Yet the very high performance of women in our educational system and in the management of commercial enterprises proves their enormous potential to contribute to the betterment of society in general. Meanwhile our women have yet to achieve those fundamental rights of free expression, association and security of life denied also to their menfolk.

The adversities that we have had to face together have taught all of us involved in the struggle to build a truly democratic political system in Burma that there are no gender barriers that cannot be overcome. The relationship between men and women should, and can be, characterized not by patronizing behavior or exploitation, but by metta (that is to say loving kindness), partnership and trust. We need mutual respect and understanding between men and women, instead of patriarchal domination and degradation, which are expressions of violence and engender counter-violence. We can learn from each other and help one another to moderate the "gender weaknesses" imposed on us by traditional or biological factors.

There is an age-old prejudice the world over to the effect that women talk too much. But is this really a weakness? Could it not in fact be a strength? Recent scientific research on the human brain has revealed that women are better at verbal skills while men tend towards physical action. Psychological research has shown on the other hand that disinformation engendered by men has a far more damaging effect on its victims than feminine gossip. Surely these discoveries indicate that women have a most valuable contribution to make in situations of conflict, by leading the way to solutions based on dialogue rather than on viciousness and violence.

The Buddhist *Pavarana* ceremony at the end of the rainy season retreat was instituted by the Lord Buddha, who did not want human beings to live in silence, I quote, "like dumb animals." This ceremony, during which monks ask mutual forgiveness for any offense given during the retreat, can be said to be a council of truth and reconciliation. It might also be considered a forerunner of that most democratic of institutions, the parliament, a meeting of peoples gathered together to talk over their shared problems. All the world's great religions are dedicated to the generation of happiness and harmony. This demonstrates the fact that together with the combative instincts of man there exists a spiritual aspiration for mutual understanding and peace.

This forum of non-governmental organizations represents the belief in the ability of intelligent human beings to resolve conflicting interests through exchange and dialogue. It also represents the conviction that governments alone cannot resolve all the problems of their countries. The watchfulness and active cooperation of organizations outside the spheres of officialdom are necessary to ensure the four essential components of the human development paradigm as identified by the UNDP: productivity, equity, sustainability and empowerment. The last is particularly relevant: it requires that "development must be by people, not only for them. People must participate fully in the decisions and processes that shape their lives." In other words people must be allowed to play a significant role in the governance of their country. And "people" include women, who make up at least half the population of the world.

The last six years afforded me much time and food for thought. I came to the conclusion that the human race is not divided into two opposing camps of good and evil. It is made up of those who are capable of learning and those who are incapable of doing so. Here I am not talking of learning in the narrow sense of acquiring an academic education, but of learning as the process of absorbing those lessons of life that enable us to increase peace and happiness in our world. Women in their role as mothers have traditionally assumed the responsibility of teaching children values that will guide them throughout their lives. It is time we were given the full opportunity to use our natural teaching skills to contribute towards building a modern world that can withstand the tremendous challenges of the technological revolution which has in turn brought revolutionary changes in social values.

As we strive to teach others, we must have the humility to acknowledge that we too still have much to learn. And we must have the flexibility to adapt to the changing needs of the world around us. Women who have been taught that modesty and pliancy are among the prized virtues of our gender are marvelously equipped for the learning process. But they must be given the opportunity to turn these often merely passive virtues into positive assets for the society in which they live.

These, then, are our common hopes that unite us—that as the shackles of prejudice and intolerance fall from our own limbs we can together strive to identify and remove the impediments to human development everywhere. The mechanisms by which this great task is to be achieved provide the proper focus of this forum. I feel sure that women throughout the world who, like me, cannot be with you join me now in sending you all our prayers and good wishes for a joyful and productive meeting.

I thank you.

Earl of Spencer
[1964–   ]

On August 31, 1997, Diana, Princess of Wales was killed when the car in which she was riding crashed inside a Paris tunnel. The car was alleged to have been speeding in flight from press photographers. Her younger brother, Charles, delivered the eulogy at her funeral, which was held in Westminster Abbey and viewed by a global television audience numbering in the tens of millions. His attack on the tabloid media and his subtler criticisms of the British royal family were met with applause in the Abbey and in London's Hyde Park, where thousands of mourners watched on telescreens.

EULOGY: TRIBUTE TO DIANA, PRINCESS OF WALES
Sept. 6, 1997

I STAND before you today the representative of a family in grief, in a country in mourning, before a world in shock.

We are all united not only in our desire to pay our respects to Diana, but rather in our need to do so.

For such was her extraordinary appeal that the tens of millions of people taking part in this service all over the world via television and radio who never actually met her feel that they too lost someone close to them in the early hours of Sunday morning. It is a more remarkable tribute to Diana than I can ever hope to offer her today.

Diana was the very essence of compassion, of duty, of style, of beauty. All over the world she was a symbol of selfless humanity, a standard bearer for the rights of the truly downtrodden, a very British girl who transcended nationality, someone with a natural nobility who was classless and who proved in the last year that she needed no royal title to continue to generate her particular brand of magic.

Today is our chance to say thank you for the way you brightened our lives, even though God granted you but half a life. We will all feel cheated always that you were taken from us so young and yet we must learn to be grateful that you came along at all. Only now that you are gone do we truly appreciate what we are now without and we want you to know that life without you is very, very difficult.

We have all despaired at our loss over the past week, and only the strength of the message you gave us through your years of giving has afforded us the strength to move forward.

There is a temptation to rush to canonize your memory; there is no need to do so. You stand tall enough as a human being of unique qualities not to need to be seen as a saint. Indeed, to sanctify your memory would be to miss out on the very core of your being: your wonderfully mischievous sense of humor with a laugh that bent you double; your joy for life transmitted wherever you took your smile and the sparkle in those unforgettable eyes; your boundless energy which you could barely contain.

But your greatest gift was your intuition, and it was a gift you used wisely. This is what underpinned all your other wonderful attributes, and if we look to analyze what it was about you that had such a wide appeal, we find it in your instinctive feel for what was really important in all our lives.

Without your God-given sensitivity we would be immersed in greater ignorance at the anguish of AIDS and HIV sufferers, the plight of the homeless, the isolation of lepers, the random destruction of landmines. Diana explained to me once that it was her innermost feelings of suffering that made it possible for her to connect with her constituency of the rejected.

And here we come to another truth about her. For all the status, the glamour, the applause, Diana remained throughout a very insecure person at heart, almost childlike in her desire to do good for others so she could release herself from deep feelings of unworthiness, of which her eating disorders were merely a symptom. The world sensed this part of her character and cherished her for her vulnerability, whilst admiring her for her honesty.

The last time I saw Diana was on July 1, her birthday in London, when typically she was not taking time to celebrate her special day with friends but was guest of honor at a fundraising charity evening. She sparkled of course, but I would rather cherish the days I spent with her in March when she came to visit me and my children in our home in South Africa. I am proud of the fact that, apart from when she was on display meeting President Mandela, we managed to contrive to stop the ever-present paparazzi from getting a single picture of her. That meant a lot to her.

These were days I will always treasure. It was as if we had been transported back to our childhood when we spent such an enormous amount of time together—the two youngest in the family. Fundamentally she had not changed at all from the big sister who mothered me as a baby, fought with me at school and endured those long train journeys between our parents' homes with me at weekends.

It is a tribute to her level-headedness and strength that despite the most bizarre life imaginable after her childhood, she remained intact, true to herself.

There is no doubt that she was looking for a new direction in her life at this time. She talked endlessly of getting away from England, mainly because of the treatment that she received at the hands of the newspapers. I don't think she ever understood why her genuinely good intentions were sneered at by the media, why there appeared to be a permanent quest on their behalf to bring her down. It is baffling. My own and only explanation is that genuine goodness is threatening to those at the opposite end of the moral spectrum. It is a point to remember that of all the ironies about Diana, perhaps the greatest was this—a girl given the name of the ancient goddess of hunting was, in the end, the most hunted person of the modern age.

She would want us today to pledge ourselves to protecting her beloved boys William and Harry from a similar fate, and I do this here Diana on your behalf. We will not allow them to suffer the anguish that used regularly to drive you to tearful despair. And beyond that, on behalf of your mother and sisters, I pledge that we, your blood family, will do all we can to continue the imaginative way in which you were steering these two exceptional young men so that their souls are not simply immersed by duty and tradition but can sing openly as you planned.

We fully respect the heritage into which they have both been born and will always respect and encourage them in their royal role, but we, like you, recognize the need for them to experience as many different aspects of life as possible to arm them spiritually and emotionally for the years ahead. I know you would have expected nothing less from us.

William and Harry, we all care desperately for you today. We are all chewed up with sadness at the loss of a woman who was not even our mother. How great your suffering is, we cannot even imagine.

I would like to end by thanking God for the small mercies he has shown us at this dreadful time. For taking Diana at her most beautiful and radiant and when she had joy in her private life. Above all we give thanks for the life of a woman I am so proud to be able to call my sister, the unique, the complex, the extraordinary and irreplaceable Diana, whose beauty, both internal and external, will never be extinguished from our minds.

TOPICAL INDEX

*[A supplementary index of speeches added in the
third and fourth editions may be found on page 920.]*

* SEE ALSO *George Wald*, 770; *John Vliet Lindsay*, 779.
For Civil Rights, see *Booker T. Washington*, 331, 814; *Martin Luther King, Jr.*, 751; *Henry Highland Garnet*, 800; *Frederick Douglass*, 804, 808; *W. E. B. Du Bois*, 818; *Malcolm X*, 823.

INDEX BY NATIONS

INDEX OF SPEAKERS

[A supplementary index of speakers for the speeches added in the third and fourth editions may be found on page 920.]

SUPPLEMENTARY INDEX
FOR THE THIRD AND FOURTH EDITIONS

A CATALOG OF SELECTED
DOVER BOOKS
IN ALL FIELDS OF INTEREST

A CATALOG OF SELECTED DOVER
BOOKS IN ALL FIELDS OF INTEREST

CONCERNING THE SPIRITUAL IN ART, Wassily Kandinsky. Pioneering work by father of abstract art. Thoughts on color theory, nature of art. Analysis of earlier masters. 12 illustrations. 80pp. of text. 5⅜ x 8½.   23411-8 Pa. $4.95

ANIMALS: 1,419 Copyright-Free Illustrations of Mammals, Birds, Fish, Insects, etc., Jim Harter (ed.). Clear wood engravings present, in extremely lifelike poses, over 1,000 species of animals. One of the most extensive pictorial sourcebooks of its kind. Captions. Index. 284pp. 9 x 12.   23766-4 Pa. $14.95

CELTIC ART: The Methods of Construction, George Bain. Simple geometric techniques for making Celtic interlacements, spirals, Kells-type initials, animals, humans, etc. Over 500 illustrations. 160pp. 9 x 12. (USO)   22923-8 Pa. $9.95

AN ATLAS OF ANATOMY FOR ARTISTS, Fritz Schider. Most thorough reference work on art anatomy in the world. Hundreds of illustrations, including selections from works by Vesalius, Leonardo, Goya, Ingres, Michelangelo, others. 593 illustrations. 192pp. 7⅛ x 10¼.   20241-0 Pa. $9.95

CELTIC HAND STROKE-BY-STROKE (Irish Half-Uncial from "The Book of Kells"): An Arthur Baker Calligraphy Manual, Arthur Baker. Complete guide to creating each letter of the alphabet in distinctive Celtic manner. Covers hand position, strokes, pens, inks, paper, more. Illustrated. 48pp. 8¼ x 11.   24336-2 Pa. $3.95

EASY ORIGAMI, John Montroll. Charming collection of 32 projects (hat, cup, pelican, piano, swan, many more) specially designed for the novice origami hobbyist. Clearly illustrated easy-to-follow instructions insure that even beginning papercrafters will achieve successful results. 48pp. 8¼ x 11.   27298-2 Pa. $3.50

THE COMPLETE BOOK OF BIRDHOUSE CONSTRUCTION FOR WOODWORKERS, Scott D. Campbell. Detailed instructions, illustrations, tables. Also data on bird habitat and instinct patterns. Bibliography. 3 tables. 63 illustrations in 15 figures. 48pp. 5¼ x 8½.   24407-5 Pa. $2.50

BLOOMINGDALE'S ILLUSTRATED 1886 CATALOG: Fashions, Dry Goods and Housewares, Bloomingdale Brothers. Famed merchants' extremely rare catalog depicting about 1,700 products: clothing, housewares, firearms, dry goods, jewelry, more. Invaluable for dating, identifying vintage items. Also, copyright-free graphics for artists, designers. Co-published with Henry Ford Museum & Greenfield Village. 160pp. 8¼ x 11.   25780-0 Pa. $10.95

HISTORIC COSTUME IN PICTURES, Braun & Schneider. Over 1,450 costumed figures in clearly detailed engravings–from dawn of civilization to end of 19th century. Captions. Many folk costumes. 256pp. 8⅜ x 11¾.   23150-X Pa. $12.95

STICKLEY CRAFTSMAN FURNITURE CATALOGS, Gustav Stickley and L. & J. G. Stickley. Beautiful, functional furniture in two authentic catalogs from 1910. 594 illustrations, including 277 photos, show settles, rockers, armchairs, reclining chairs, bookcases, desks, tables. 183pp. 6½ x 9¼. 23838-5 Pa. $11.95

AMERICAN LOCOMOTIVES IN HISTORIC PHOTOGRAPHS: 1858 to 1949, Ron Ziel (ed.). A rare collection of 126 meticulously detailed official photographs, called "builder portraits," of American locomotives that majestically chronicle the rise of steam locomotive power in America. Introduction. Detailed captions. xi + 129pp. 9 x 12. 27393-8 Pa. $13.95

AMERICA'S LIGHTHOUSES: An Illustrated History, Francis Ross Holland, Jr. Delightfully written, profusely illustrated fact-filled survey of over 200 American lighthouses since 1716. History, anecdotes, technological advances, more. 240pp. 8 x 10¾. 25576-X Pa. $12.95

TOWARDS A NEW ARCHITECTURE, Le Corbusier. Pioneering manifesto by founder of "International School." Technical and aesthetic theories, views of industry, economics, relation of form to function, "mass-production split" and much more. Profusely illustrated. 320pp. 6⅛ x 9¼. (USO) 25023-7 Pa. $9.95

HOW THE OTHER HALF LIVES, Jacob Riis. Famous journalistic record, exposing poverty and degradation of New York slums around 1900, by major social reformer. 100 striking and influential photographs. 233pp. 10 x 7⅞. 22012-5 Pa. $11.95

FRUIT KEY AND TWIG KEY TO TREES AND SHRUBS, William M. Harlow. One of the handiest and most widely used identification aids. Fruit key covers 120 deciduous and evergreen species; twig key 160 deciduous species. Easily used. Over 300 photographs. 126pp. 5⅜ x 8½. 20511-8 Pa. $3.95

COMMON BIRD SONGS, Dr. Donald J. Borror. Songs of 60 most common U.S. birds: robins, sparrows, cardinals, bluejays, finches, more–arranged in order of increasing complexity. Up to 9 variations of songs of each species. Cassette and manual 99911-4 $8.95

ORCHIDS AS HOUSE PLANTS, Rebecca Tyson Northen. Grow cattleyas and many other kinds of orchids–in a window, in a case, or under artificial light. 63 illustrations. 148pp. 5⅜ x 8½. 23261-1 Pa. $5.95

MONSTER MAZES, Dave Phillips. Masterful mazes at four levels of difficulty. Avoid deadly perils and evil creatures to find magical treasures. Solutions for all 32 exciting illustrated puzzles. 48pp. 8¼ x 11. 26005-4 Pa. $2.95

MOZART'S DON GIOVANNI (DOVER OPERA LIBRETTO SERIES), Wolfgang Amadeus Mozart. Introduced and translated by Ellen H. Bleiler. Standard Italian libretto, with complete English translation. Convenient and thoroughly portable–an ideal companion for reading along with a recording or the performance itself. Introduction. List of characters. Plot summary. 121pp. 5¼ x 8½. 24944-1 Pa. $3.95

TECHNICAL MANUAL AND DICTIONARY OF CLASSICAL BALLET, Gail Grant. Defines, explains, comments on steps, movements, poses and concepts. 15-page pictorial section. Basic book for student, viewer. 127pp. 5⅜ x 8½. 21843-0 Pa. $4.95

BRASS INSTRUMENTS: Their History and Development, Anthony Baines. Authoritative, updated survey of the evolution of trumpets, trombones, bugles, cornets, French horns, tubas and other brass wind instruments. Over 140 illustrations and 48 music examples. Corrected and updated by author. New preface. Bibliography. 320pp. 5⅜ x 8½. 27574-4 Pa. $9.95

HOLLYWOOD GLAMOR PORTRAITS, John Kobal (ed.). 145 photos from 1926-49. Harlow, Gable, Bogart, Bacall; 94 stars in all. Full background on photographers, technical aspects. 160pp. 8⅜ x 11¼. 23352-9 Pa. $12.95

MAX AND MORITZ, Wilhelm Busch. Great humor classic in both German and English. Also 10 other works: "Cat and Mouse," "Plisch and Plumm," etc. 216pp. 5⅜ x 8½. 20181-3 Pa. $6.95

THE RAVEN AND OTHER FAVORITE POEMS, Edgar Allan Poe. Over 40 of the author's most memorable poems: "The Bells," "Ulalume," "Israfel," "To Helen," "The Conqueror Worm," "Eldorado," "Annabel Lee," many more. Alphabetic lists of titles and first lines. 64pp. 5$\frac{3}{16}$ x 8¼. 26685-0 Pa. $1.00

PERSONAL MEMOIRS OF U. S. GRANT, Ulysses Simpson Grant. Intelligent, deeply moving firsthand account of Civil War campaigns, considered by many the finest military memoirs ever written. Includes letters, historic photographs, maps and more. 528pp. 6⅛ x 9¼. 28587-1 Pa. $12.95

AMULETS AND SUPERSTITIONS, E. A. Wallis Budge. Comprehensive discourse on origin, powers of amulets in many ancient cultures: Arab, Persian Babylonian, Assyrian, Egyptian, Gnostic, Hebrew, Phoenician, Syriac, etc. Covers cross, swastika, crucifix, seals, rings, stones, etc. 584pp. 5⅜ x 8½. 23573-4 Pa. $12.95

RUSSIAN STORIES/PYCCKNE PACCKA3bl: A Dual-Language Book, edited by Gleb Struve. Twelve tales by such masters as Chekhov, Tolstoy, Dostoevsky, Pushkin, others. Excellent word-for-word English translations on facing pages, plus teaching and study aids, Russian/English vocabulary, biographical/critical introductions, more. 416pp. 5⅜ x 8½. 26244-8 Pa. $9.95

PHILADELPHIA THEN AND NOW: 60 Sites Photographed in the Past and Present, Kenneth Finkel and Susan Oyama. Rare photographs of City Hall, Logan Square, Independence Hall, Betsy Ross House, other landmarks juxtaposed with contemporary views. Captures changing face of historic city. Introduction. Captions. 128pp. 8¼ x 11. 25790-8 Pa. $9.95

AIA ARCHITECTURAL GUIDE TO NASSAU AND SUFFOLK COUNTIES, LONG ISLAND, The American Institute of Architects, Long Island Chapter, and the Society for the Preservation of Long Island Antiquities. Comprehensive, well-researched and generously illustrated volume brings to life over three centuries of Long Island's great architectural heritage. More than 240 photographs with authoritative, extensively detailed captions. 176pp. 8¼ x 11. 26946-9 Pa. $14.95

NORTH AMERICAN INDIAN LIFE: Customs and Traditions of 23 Tribes, Elsie Clews Parsons (ed.). 27 fictionalized essays by noted anthropologists examine religion, customs, government, additional facets of life among the Winnebago, Crow, Zuni, Eskimo, other tribes. 480pp. 6⅛ x 9¼. 27377-6 Pa. $10.95

FRANK LLOYD WRIGHT'S HOLLYHOCK HOUSE, Donald Hoffmann. Lavishly illustrated, carefully documented study of one of Wright's most controversial residential designs. Over 120 photographs, floor plans, elevations, etc. Detailed perceptive text by noted Wright scholar. Index. 128pp. 9¼ x 10¾. 27133-1 Pa. $11.95

THE MALE AND FEMALE FIGURE IN MOTION: 60 Classic Photographic Sequences, Eadweard Muybridge. 60 true-action photographs of men and women walking, running, climbing, bending, turning, etc., reproduced from rare 19th-century masterpiece. vi + 121pp. 9 x 12. 24745-7 Pa. $10.95

1001 QUESTIONS ANSWERED ABOUT THE SEASHORE, N. J. Berrill and Jacquelyn Berrill. Queries answered about dolphins, sea snails, sponges, starfish, fishes, shore birds, many others. Covers appearance, breeding, growth, feeding, much more. 305pp. 5¼ x 8¼. 23366-9 Pa. $8.95

GUIDE TO OWL WATCHING IN NORTH AMERICA, Donald S. Heintzelman. Superb guide offers complete data and descriptions of 19 species: barn owl, screech owl, snowy owl, many more. Expert coverage of owl-watching equipment, conservation, migrations and invasions, etc. Guide to observing sites. 84 illustrations. xiii + 193pp. 5⅜ x 8½. 27344-X Pa. $8.95

MEDICINAL AND OTHER USES OF NORTH AMERICAN PLANTS: A Historical Survey with Special Reference to the Eastern Indian Tribes, Charlotte Erichsen-Brown. Chronological historical citations document 500 years of usage of plants, trees, shrubs native to eastern Canada, northeastern U.S. Also complete identifying information. 343 illustrations. 544pp. 6½ x 9¼. 25951-X Pa. $12.95

STORYBOOK MAZES, Dave Phillips. 23 stories and mazes on two-page spreads: Wizard of Oz, Treasure Island, Robin Hood, etc. Solutions. 64pp. 8¼ x 11. 23628-5 Pa. $2.95

NEGRO FOLK MUSIC, U.S.A., Harold Courlander. Noted folklorist's scholarly yet readable analysis of rich and varied musical tradition. Includes authentic versions of over 40 folk songs. Valuable bibliography and discography. xi + 324pp. 5⅜ x 8½. 27350-4 Pa. $9.95

MOVIE-STAR PORTRAITS OF THE FORTIES, John Kobal (ed.). 163 glamor, studio photos of 106 stars of the 1940s: Rita Hayworth, Ava Gardner, Marlon Brando, Clark Gable, many more. 176pp. 8⅜ x 11¼. 23546-7 Pa. $12.95

BENCHLEY LOST AND FOUND, Robert Benchley. Finest humor from early 30s, about pet peeves, child psychologists, post office and others. Mostly unavailable elsewhere. 73 illustrations by Peter Arno and others. 183pp. 5⅜ x 8½. 22410-4 Pa. $6.95

YEKL and THE IMPORTED BRIDEGROOM AND OTHER STORIES OF YIDDISH NEW YORK, Abraham Cahan. Film Hester Street based on Yekl (1896). Novel, other stories among first about Jewish immigrants on N.Y.'s East Side. 240pp. 5⅜ x 8½. 22427-9 Pa. $6.95

SELECTED POEMS, Walt Whitman. Generous sampling from *Leaves of Grass.* Twenty-four poems include "I Hear America Singing," "Song of the Open Road," "I Sing the Body Electric," "When Lilacs Last in the Dooryard Bloom'd," "O Captain! My Captain!"—all reprinted from an authoritative edition. Lists of titles and first lines. 128pp. 5³⁄₁₆ x 8¼. 26878-0 Pa. $1.00

THE BEST TALES OF HOFFMANN, E. T. A. Hoffmann. 10 of Hoffmann's most important stories: "Nutcracker and the King of Mice," "The Golden Flowerpot," etc. 458pp. 5⅜ x 8½. 21793-0 Pa. $9.95

FROM FETISH TO GOD IN ANCIENT EGYPT, E. A. Wallis Budge. Rich detailed survey of Egyptian conception of "God" and gods, magic, cult of animals, Osiris, more. Also, superb English translations of hymns and legends. 240 illustrations. 545pp. 5⅜ x 8½. 25803-3 Pa. $13.95

FRENCH STORIES/CONTES FRANÇAIS: A Dual-Language Book, Wallace Fowlie. Ten stories by French masters, Voltaire to Camus: "Micromegas" by Voltaire; "The Atheist's Mass" by Balzac; "Minuet" by de Maupassant; "The Guest" by Camus, six more. Excellent English translations on facing pages. Also French-English vocabulary list, exercises, more. 352pp. 5⅜ x 8½. 26443-2 Pa. $9.95

CHICAGO AT THE TURN OF THE CENTURY IN PHOTOGRAPHS: 122 Historic Views from the Collections of the Chicago Historical Society, Larry A. Viskochil. Rare large-format prints offer detailed views of City Hall, State Street, the Loop, Hull House, Union Station, many other landmarks, circa 1904-1913. Introduction. Captions. Maps. 144pp. 9⅜ x 12¼. 24656-6 Pa. $12.95

OLD BROOKLYN IN EARLY PHOTOGRAPHS, 1865-1929, William Lee Younger. Luna Park, Gravesend race track, construction of Grand Army Plaza, moving of Hotel Brighton, etc. 157 previously unpublished photographs. 165pp. 8⅞ x 11¾. 23587-4 Pa. $13.95

THE MYTHS OF THE NORTH AMERICAN INDIANS, Lewis Spence. Rich anthology of the myths and legends of the Algonquins, Iroquois, Pawnees and Sioux, prefaced by an extensive historical and ethnological commentary. 36 illustrations. 480pp. 5⅜ x 8½. 25967-6 Pa. $10.95

AN ENCYCLOPEDIA OF BATTLES: Accounts of Over 1,560 Battles from 1479 B.C. to the Present, David Eggenberger. Essential details of every major battle in recorded history from the first battle of Megiddo in 1479 B.C. to Grenada in 1984. List of Battle Maps. New Appendix covering the years 1967-1984. Index. 99 illustrations. 544pp. 6½ x 9¼. 24913-1 Pa. $16.95

SAILING ALONE AROUND THE WORLD, Captain Joshua Slocum. First man to sail around the world, alone, in small boat. One of great feats of seamanship told in delightful manner. 67 illustrations. 294pp. 5⅜ x 8½. 20326-3 Pa. $6.95

ANARCHISM AND OTHER ESSAYS, Emma Goldman. Powerful, penetrating, prophetic essays on direct action, role of minorities, prison reform, puritan hypocrisy, violence, etc. 271pp. 5⅜ x 8½. 22484-8 Pa. $7.95

MYTHS OF THE HINDUS AND BUDDHISTS, Ananda K. Coomaraswamy and Sister Nivedita. Great stories of the epics; deeds of Krishna, Shiva, taken from puranas, Vedas, folk tales; etc. 32 illustrations. 400pp. 5⅜ x 8½. 21759-0 Pa. $12.95

BEYOND PSYCHOLOGY, Otto Rank. Fear of death, desire of immortality, nature of sexuality, social organization, creativity, according to Rankian system. 291pp. 5⅜ x 8½. 20485-5 Pa. $8.95

A THEOLOGICO-POLITICAL TREATISE, Benedict Spinoza. Also contains unfinished Political Treatise. Great classic on religious liberty, theory of government on common consent. R. Elwes translation. Total of 421pp. 5⅜ x 8½. 20249-6 Pa. $9.95

MY BONDAGE AND MY FREEDOM, Frederick Douglass. Born a slave, Douglass became outspoken force in antislavery movement. The best of Douglass' autobiographies. Graphic description of slave life. 464pp. 5⅜ x 8½. 22457-0 Pa. $8.95

FOLLOWING THE EQUATOR: A Journey Around the World, Mark Twain. Fascinating humorous account of 1897 voyage to Hawaii, Australia, India, New Zealand, etc. Ironic, bemused reports on peoples, customs, climate, flora and fauna, politics, much more. 197 illustrations. 720pp. 5⅜ x 8½. 26113-1 Pa. $15.95

THE PEOPLE CALLED SHAKERS, Edward D. Andrews. Definitive study of Shakers: origins, beliefs, practices, dances, social organization, furniture and crafts, etc. 33 illustrations. 351pp. 5⅜ x 8½. 21081-2 Pa. $8.95

THE MYTHS OF GREECE AND ROME, H. A. Guerber. A classic of mythology, generously illustrated, long prized for its simple, graphic, accurate retelling of the principal myths of Greece and Rome, and for its commentary on their origins and significance. With 64 illustrations by Michelangelo, Raphael, Titian, Rubens, Canova, Bernini and others. 480pp. 5⅜ x 8½. 27584-1 Pa. $9.95

PSYCHOLOGY OF MUSIC, Carl E. Seashore. Classic work discusses music as a medium from psychological viewpoint. Clear treatment of physical acoustics, auditory apparatus, sound perception, development of musical skills, nature of musical feeling, host of other topics. 88 figures. 408pp. 5⅜ x 8½. 21851-1 Pa. $11.95

THE PHILOSOPHY OF HISTORY, Georg W. Hegel. Great classic of Western thought develops concept that history is not chance but rational process, the evolution of freedom. 457pp. 5⅜ x 8½. 20112-0 Pa. $9.95

THE BOOK OF TEA, Kakuzo Okakura. Minor classic of the Orient: entertaining, charming explanation, interpretation of traditional Japanese culture in terms of tea ceremony. 94pp. 5⅜ x 8½. 20070-1 Pa. $3.95

LIFE IN ANCIENT EGYPT, Adolf Erman. Fullest, most thorough, detailed older account with much not in more recent books, domestic life, religion, magic, medicine, commerce, much more. Many illustrations reproduce tomb paintings, carvings, hieroglyphs, etc. 597pp. 5⅜ x 8½. 22632-8 Pa. $12.95

SUNDIALS, Their Theory and Construction, Albert Waugh. Far and away the best, most thorough coverage of ideas, mathematics concerned, types, construction, adjusting anywhere. Simple, nontechnical treatment allows even children to build several of these dials. Over 100 illustrations. 230pp. 5⅜ x 8½. 22947-5 Pa. $8.95

DYNAMICS OF FLUIDS IN POROUS MEDIA, Jacob Bear. For advanced students of ground water hydrology, soil mechanics and physics, drainage and irrigation engineering, and more. 335 illustrations. Exercises, with answers. 784pp. 6⅛ x 9¼. 65675-6 Pa. $19.95

SONGS OF EXPERIENCE: Facsimile Reproduction with 26 Plates in Full Color, William Blake. 26 full-color plates from a rare 1826 edition. Includes "TheTyger," "London," "Holy Thursday," and other poems. Printed text of poems. 48pp. 5¼ x 7. 24636-1 Pa. $4.95

OLD-TIME VIGNETTES IN FULL COLOR, Carol Belanger Grafton (ed.). Over 390 charming, often sentimental illustrations, selected from archives of Victorian graphics—pretty women posing, children playing, food, flowers, kittens and puppies, smiling cherubs, birds and butterflies, much more. All copyright-free. 48pp. 9¼ x 12¼. 27269-9 Pa. $7.95

PERSPECTIVE FOR ARTISTS, Rex Vicat Cole. Depth, perspective of sky and sea, shadows, much more, not usually covered. 391 diagrams, 81 reproductions of drawings and paintings. 279pp. 5⅜ x 8½. 22487-2 Pa. $7.95

DRAWING THE LIVING FIGURE, Joseph Sheppard. Innovative approach to artistic anatomy focuses on specifics of surface anatomy, rather than muscles and bones. Over 170 drawings of live models in front, back and side views, and in widely varying poses. Accompanying diagrams. 177 illustrations. Introduction. Index. 144pp. 8⅜ x11¼. 26723-7 Pa. $8.95

GOTHIC AND OLD ENGLISH ALPHABETS: 100 Complete Fonts, Dan X. Solo. Add power, elegance to posters, signs, other graphics with 100 stunning copyright-free alphabets: Blackstone, Dolbey, Germania, 97 more–including many lower-case, numerals, punctuation marks. 104pp. 8⅛ x 11. 24695-7 Pa. $8.95

HOW TO DO BEADWORK, Mary White. Fundamental book on craft from simple projects to five-bead chains and woven works. 106 illustrations. 142pp. 5⅜ x 8. 20697-1 Pa. $4.95

THE BOOK OF WOOD CARVING, Charles Marshall Sayers. Finest book for beginners discusses fundamentals and offers 34 designs. "Absolutely first rate . . . well thought out and well executed."–E. J. Tangerman. 118pp. 7¾ x 10⅝. 23654-4 Pa. $6.95

ILLUSTRATED CATALOG OF CIVIL WAR MILITARY GOODS: Union Army Weapons, Insignia, Uniform Accessories, and Other Equipment, Schuyler, Hartley, and Graham. Rare, profusely illustrated 1846 catalog includes Union Army uniform and dress regulations, arms and ammunition, coats, insignia, flags, swords, rifles, etc. 226 illustrations. 160pp. 9 x 12. 24939-5 Pa. $10.95

WOMEN'S FASHIONS OF THE EARLY 1900s: An Unabridged Republication of "New York Fashions, 1909," National Cloak & Suit Co. Rare catalog of mail-order fashions documents women's and children's clothing styles shortly after the turn of the century. Captions offer full descriptions, prices. Invaluable resource for fashion, costume historians. Approximately 725 illustrations. 128pp. 8⅜ x 11¼. 27276-1 Pa. $11.95

THE 1912 AND 1915 GUSTAV STICKLEY FURNITURE CATALOGS, Gustav Stickley. With over 200 detailed illustrations and descriptions, these two catalogs are essential reading and reference materials and identification guides for Stickley furniture. Captions cite materials, dimensions and prices. 112pp. 6½ x 9¼. 26676-1 Pa. $9.95

EARLY AMERICAN LOCOMOTIVES, John H. White, Jr. Finest locomotive engravings from early 19th century: historical (1804–74), main-line (after 1870), special, foreign, etc. 147 plates. 142pp. 11⅜ x 8¼. 22772-3 Pa. $10.95

THE TALL SHIPS OF TODAY IN PHOTOGRAPHS, Frank O. Braynard. Lavishly illustrated tribute to nearly 100 majestic contemporary sailing vessels: Amerigo Vespucci, Clearwater, Constitution, Eagle, Mayflower, Sea Cloud, Victory, many more. Authoritative captions provide statistics, background on each ship. 190 black-and-white photographs and illustrations. Introduction. 128pp. 8⅞ x 11¾. 27163-3 Pa. $14.95

EARLY NINETEENTH-CENTURY CRAFTS AND TRADES, Peter Stockham (ed.). Extremely rare 1807 volume describes to youngsters the crafts and trades of the day: brickmaker, weaver, dressmaker, bookbinder, ropemaker, saddler, many more. Quaint prose, charming illustrations for each craft. 20 black-and-white line illustrations. 192pp. 4⅝ x 6. 27293-1 Pa. $4.95

VICTORIAN FASHIONS AND COSTUMES FROM HARPER'S BAZAR, 1867–1898, Stella Blum (ed.). Day costumes, evening wear, sports clothes, shoes, hats, other accessories in over 1,000 detailed engravings. 320pp. 9⅜ x 12¼. 22990-4 Pa. $15.95

GUSTAV STICKLEY, THE CRAFTSMAN, Mary Ann Smith. Superb study surveys broad scope of Stickley's achievement, especially in architecture. Design philosophy, rise and fall of the Craftsman empire, descriptions and floor plans for many Craftsman houses, more. 86 black-and-white halftones. 31 line illustrations. Introduction 208pp. 6½ x 9¼. 27210-9 Pa. $9.95

THE LONG ISLAND RAIL ROAD IN EARLY PHOTOGRAPHS, Ron Ziel. Over 220 rare photos, informative text document origin (1844) and development of rail service on Long Island. Vintage views of early trains, locomotives, stations, passengers, crews, much more. Captions. 8⅞ x 11¾. 26301-0 Pa. $13.95

THE BOOK OF OLD SHIPS: From Egyptian Galleys to Clipper Ships, Henry B. Culver. Superb, authoritative history of sailing vessels, with 80 magnificent line illustrations. Galley, bark, caravel, longship, whaler, many more. Detailed, informative text on each vessel by noted naval historian. Introduction. 256pp. 5⅜ x 8½. 27332-6 Pa. $7.95

TEN BOOKS ON ARCHITECTURE, Vitruvius. The most important book ever written on architecture. Early Roman aesthetics, technology, classical orders, site selection, all other aspects. Morgan translation. 331pp. 5⅜ x 8½. 20645-9 Pa. $8.95

THE HUMAN FIGURE IN MOTION, Eadweard Muybridge. More than 4,500 stopped-action photos, in action series, showing undraped men, women, children jumping, lying down, throwing, sitting, wrestling, carrying, etc. 390pp. 7⅞ x 10⅝. 20204-6 Clothbd. $27.95

TREES OF THE EASTERN AND CENTRAL UNITED STATES AND CANADA, William M. Harlow. Best one-volume guide to 140 trees. Full descriptions, woodlore, range, etc. Over 600 illustrations. Handy size. 288pp. 4½ x 6⅜. 20395-6 Pa. $6.95

SONGS OF WESTERN BIRDS, Dr. Donald J. Borror. Complete song and call repertoire of 60 western species, including flycatchers, juncoes, cactus wrens, many more–includes fully illustrated booklet. Cassette and manual 99913-0 $8.95

GROWING AND USING HERBS AND SPICES, Milo Miloradovich. Versatile handbook provides all the information needed for cultivation and use of all the herbs and spices available in North America. 4 illustrations. Index. Glossary. 236pp. 5⅜ x 8½. 25058-X Pa. $7.95

BIG BOOK OF MAZES AND LABYRINTHS, Walter Shepherd. 50 mazes and labyrinths in all–classical, solid, ripple, and more–in one great volume. Perfect inexpensive puzzler for clever youngsters. Full solutions. 112pp. 8⅛ x 11. 22951-3 Pa. $4.95

PIANO TUNING, J. Cree Fischer. Clearest, best book for beginner, amateur. Simple repairs, raising dropped notes, tuning by easy method of flattened fifths. No previous skills needed. 4 illustrations. 201pp. 5⅜ x 8½. 23267-0 Pa. $6.95

A SOURCE BOOK IN THEATRICAL HISTORY, A. M. Nagler. Contemporary observers on acting, directing, make-up, costuming, stage props, machinery, scene design, from Ancient Greece to Chekhov. 611pp. 5⅜ x 8½. 20515-0 Pa. $12.95

THE COMPLETE NONSENSE OF EDWARD LEAR, Edward Lear. All nonsense limericks, zany alphabets, Owl and Pussycat, songs, nonsense botany, etc., illustrated by Lear. Total of 320pp. 5⅜ x 8½. (USO) 20167-8 Pa. $7.95

VICTORIAN PARLOUR POETRY: An Annotated Anthology, Michael R. Turner. 117 gems by Longfellow, Tennyson, Browning, many lesser-known poets. "The Village Blacksmith," "Curfew Must Not Ring Tonight," "Only a Baby Small," dozens more, often difficult to find elsewhere. Index of poets, titles, first lines. xxiii + 325pp. 5⅜ x 8¼. 27044-0 Pa. $8.95

DUBLINERS, James Joyce. Fifteen stories offer vivid, tightly focused observations of the lives of Dublin's poorer classes. At least one, "The Dead," is considered a masterpiece. Reprinted complete and unabridged from standard edition. 160pp. 5³⁄₁₆ x 8¼. 26870-5 Pa. $1.00

THE HAUNTED MONASTERY and THE CHINESE MAZE MURDERS, Robert van Gulik. Two full novels by van Gulik, set in 7th-century China, continue adventures of Judge Dee and his companions. An evil Taoist monastery, seemingly supernatural events; overgrown topiary maze hides strange crimes. 27 illustrations. 328pp. 5⅜ x 8½. 23502-5 Pa. $8.95

THE BOOK OF THE SACRED MAGIC OF ABRAMELIN THE MAGE, translated by S. MacGregor Mathers. Medieval manuscript of ceremonial magic. Basic document in Aleister Crowley, Golden Dawn groups. 268pp. 5⅜ x 8½. 23211-5 Pa. $9.95

NEW RUSSIAN-ENGLISH AND ENGLISH-RUSSIAN DICTIONARY, M. A. O'Brien. This is a remarkably handy Russian dictionary, containing a surprising amount of information, including over 70,000 entries. 366pp. 4½ x 6⅛. 20208-9 Pa. $9.95

HISTORIC HOMES OF THE AMERICAN PRESIDENTS, Second, Revised Edition, Irvin Haas. A traveler's guide to American Presidential homes, most open to the public, depicting and describing homes occupied by every American President from George Washington to George Bush. With visiting hours, admission charges, travel routes. 175 photographs. Index. 160pp. 8¼ x 11. 26751-2 Pa. $11.95

NEW YORK IN THE FORTIES, Andreas Feininger. 162 brilliant photographs by the well-known photographer, formerly with *Life* magazine. Commuters, shoppers, Times Square at night, much else from city at its peak. Captions by John von Hartz. 181pp. 9¼ x 10¾. 23585-8 Pa. $12.95

INDIAN SIGN LANGUAGE, William Tomkins. Over 525 signs developed by Sioux and other tribes. Written instructions and diagrams. Also 290 pictographs. 111pp. 6⅛ x 9¼. 22029-X Pa. $3.95

ANATOMY: A Complete Guide for Artists, Joseph Sheppard. A master of figure drawing shows artists how to render human anatomy convincingly. Over 460 illustrations. 224pp. 8⅜ x 11¼. 27279-6 Pa. $11.95

MEDIEVAL CALLIGRAPHY: Its History and Technique, Marc Drogin. Spirited history, comprehensive instruction manual covers 13 styles (ca. 4th century thru 15th). Excellent photographs; directions for duplicating medieval techniques with modern tools. 224pp. 8⅜ x 11¼. 26142-5 Pa. $12.95

DRIED FLOWERS: How to Prepare Them, Sarah Whitlock and Martha Rankin. Complete instructions on how to use silica gel, meal and borax, perlite aggregate, sand and borax, glycerine and water to create attractive permanent flower arrangements. 12 illustrations. 32pp. 5⅜ x 8½. 21802-3 Pa. $1.00

EASY-TO-MAKE BIRD FEEDERS FOR WOODWORKERS, Scott D. Campbell. Detailed, simple-to-use guide for designing, constructing, caring for and using feeders. Text, illustrations for 12 classic and contemporary designs. 96pp. 5⅜ x 8½. 25847-5 Pa. $3.95

SCOTTISH WONDER TALES FROM MYTH AND LEGEND, Donald A. Mackenzie. 16 lively tales tell of giants rumbling down mountainsides, of a magic wand that turns stone pillars into warriors, of gods and goddesses, evil hags, powerful forces and more. 240pp. 5⅜ x 8½. 29677-6 Pa. $6.95

THE HISTORY OF UNDERCLOTHES, C. Willett Cunnington and Phyllis Cunnington. Fascinating, well-documented survey covering six centuries of English undergarments, enhanced with over 100 illustrations: 12th-century laced-up bodice, footed long drawers (1795), 19th-century bustles, 19th-century corsets for men, Victorian "bust improvers," much more. 272pp. 5⅜ x 8¼. 27124-2 Pa. $9.95

ARTS AND CRAFTS FURNITURE: The Complete Brooks Catalog of 1912, Brooks Manufacturing Co. Photos and detailed descriptions of more than 150 now very collectible furniture designs from the Arts and Crafts movement depict davenports, settees, buffets, desks, tables, chairs, bedsteads, dressers and more, all built of solid, quarter-sawed oak. Invaluable for students and enthusiasts of antiques, Americana and the decorative arts. 80pp. 6½ x 9¼. 27471-3 Pa. $8.95

HOW WE INVENTED THE AIRPLANE: An Illustrated History, Orville Wright. Fascinating firsthand account covers early experiments, construction of planes and motors, first flights, much more. Introduction and commentary by Fred C. Kelly. 76 photographs. 96pp. 8¼ x 11. 25662-6 Pa. $8.95

THE ARTS OF THE SAILOR: Knotting, Splicing and Ropework, Hervey Garrett Smith. Indispensable shipboard reference covers tools, basic knots and useful hitches; handsewing and canvas work, more. Over 100 illustrations. Delightful reading for sea lovers. 256pp. 5⅜ x 8½. 26440-8 Pa. $7.95

FRANK LLOYD WRIGHT'S FALLINGWATER: The House and Its History, Second, Revised Edition, Donald Hoffmann. A total revision—both in text and illustrations—of the standard document on Fallingwater, the boldest, most personal architectural statement of Wright's mature years, updated with valuable new material from the recently opened Frank Lloyd Wright Archives. "Fascinating"–*The New York Times*. 116 illustrations. 128pp. 9¼ x 10¾. 27430-6 Pa. $12.95

PHOTOGRAPHIC SKETCHBOOK OF THE CIVIL WAR, Alexander Gardner. 100 photos taken on field during the Civil War. Famous shots of Manassas Harper's Ferry, Lincoln, Richmond, slave pens, etc. 244pp. 10⅝ x 8¼.   22731-6 Pa. $9.95

FIVE ACRES AND INDEPENDENCE, Maurice G. Kains. Great back-to-the-land classic explains basics of self-sufficient farming. The one book to get. 95 illustrations. 397pp. 5⅜ x 8½.   20974-1 Pa. $7.95

SONGS OF EASTERN BIRDS, Dr. Donald J. Borror. Songs and calls of 60 species most common to eastern U.S.: warblers, woodpeckers, flycatchers, thrushes, larks, many more in high-quality recording.   Cassette and manual 99912-2 $9.95

A MODERN HERBAL, Margaret Grieve. Much the fullest, most exact, most useful compilation of herbal material. Gigantic alphabetical encyclopedia, from aconite to zedoary, gives botanical information, medical properties, folklore, economic uses, much else. Indispensable to serious reader. 161 illustrations. 888pp. 6½ x 9¼. 2-vol. set. (USO)   Vol. I: 22798-7 Pa. $9.95
Vol. II: 22799-5 Pa. $9.95

HIDDEN TREASURE MAZE BOOK, Dave Phillips. Solve 34 challenging mazes accompanied by heroic tales of adventure. Evil dragons, people-eating plants, blood-thirsty giants, many more dangerous adversaries lurk at every twist and turn. 34 mazes, stories, solutions. 48pp. 8¼ x 11.   24566-7 Pa. $2.95

LETTERS OF W. A. MOZART, Wolfgang A. Mozart. Remarkable letters show bawdy wit, humor, imagination, musical insights, contemporary musical world; includes some letters from Leopold Mozart. 276pp. 5⅜ x 8½.   22859-2 Pa. $7.95

BASIC PRINCIPLES OF CLASSICAL BALLET, Agrippina Vaganova. Great Russian theoretician, teacher explains methods for teaching classical ballet. 118 illustrations. 175pp. 5⅜ x 8½.   22036-2 Pa. $5.95

THE JUMPING FROG, Mark Twain. Revenge edition. The original story of The Celebrated Jumping Frog of Calaveras County, a hapless French translation, and Twain's hilarious "retranslation" from the French. 12 illustrations. 66pp. 5⅜ x 8½.   22686-7 Pa. $3.95

BEST REMEMBERED POEMS, Martin Gardner (ed.). The 126 poems in this superb collection of 19th- and 20th-century British and American verse range from Shelley's "To a Skylark" to the impassioned "Renascence" of Edna St. Vincent Millay and to Edward Lear's whimsical "The Owl and the Pussycat." 224pp. 5⅜ x 8½.   27165-X Pa. $5.95

COMPLETE SONNETS, William Shakespeare. Over 150 exquisite poems deal with love, friendship, the tyranny of time, beauty's evanescence, death and other themes in language of remarkable power, precision and beauty. Glossary of archaic terms. 80pp. 5³⁄₁₆ x 8¼.   26686-9 Pa. $1.00

BODIES IN A BOOKSHOP, R. T. Campbell. Challenging mystery of blackmail and murder with ingenious plot and superbly drawn characters. In the best tradition of British suspense fiction. 192pp. 5⅜ x 8½.   24720-1 Pa. $6.95

THE WIT AND HUMOR OF OSCAR WILDE, Alvin Redman (ed.). More than 1,000 ripostes, paradoxes, wisecracks: Work is the curse of the drinking classes; I can resist everything except temptation; etc. 258pp. 5⅜ x 8½. 20602-5 Pa. $5.95

SHAKESPEARE LEXICON AND QUOTATION DICTIONARY, Alexander Schmidt. Full definitions, locations, shades of meaning in every word in plays and poems. More than 50,000 exact quotations. 1,485pp. 6½ x 9¼. 2-vol. set.
Vol. 1: 22726-X Pa. $17.95
Vol. 2: 22727-8 Pa. $17.95

SELECTED POEMS, Emily Dickinson. Over 100 best-known, best-loved poems by one of America's foremost poets, reprinted from authoritative early editions. No comparable edition at this price. Index of first lines. 64pp. 5³⁄₁₆ x 8¼.
26466-1 Pa. $1.00

CELEBRATED CASES OF JUDGE DEE (DEE GOONG AN), translated by Robert van Gulik. Authentic 18th-century Chinese detective novel; Dee and associates solve three interlocked cases. Led to van Gulik's own stories with same characters. Extensive introduction. 9 illustrations. 237pp. 5⅜ x 8½. 23337-5 Pa. $7.95

THE MALLEUS MALEFICARUM OF KRAMER AND SPRENGER, translated by Montague Summers. Full text of most important witchhunter's "bible," used by both Catholics and Protestants. 278pp. 6⅝ x 10. 22802-9 Pa. $12.95

SPANISH STORIES/CUENTOS ESPAÑOLES: A Dual-Language Book, Angel Flores (ed.). Unique format offers 13 great stories in Spanish by Cervantes, Borges, others. Faithful English translations on facing pages. 352pp. 5⅜ x 8½.
25399-6 Pa. $8.95

THE CHICAGO WORLD'S FAIR OF 1893: A Photographic Record, Stanley Appelbaum (ed.). 128 rare photos show 200 buildings, Beaux-Arts architecture, Midway, original Ferris Wheel, Edison's kinetoscope, more. Architectural emphasis; full text. 116pp. 8¼ x 11. 23990-X Pa. $9.95

OLD QUEENS, N.Y., IN EARLY PHOTOGRAPHS, Vincent F. Seyfried and William Asadorian. Over 160 rare photographs of Maspeth, Jamaica, Jackson Heights, and other areas. Vintage views of DeWitt Clinton mansion, 1939 World's Fair and more. Captions. 192pp. 8⅞ x 11. 26358-4 Pa. $12.95

CAPTURED BY THE INDIANS: 15 Firsthand Accounts, 1750-1870, Frederick Drimmer. Astounding true historical accounts of grisly torture, bloody conflicts, relentless pursuits, miraculous escapes and more, by people who lived to tell the tale. 384pp. 5⅜ x 8½. 24901-8 Pa. $8.95

THE WORLD'S GREAT SPEECHES, Lewis Copeland and Lawrence W. Lamm (eds.). Vast collection of 278 speeches of Greeks to 1970. Powerful and effective models; unique look at history. 842pp. 5⅜ x 8½. 20468-5 Pa. $14.95

THE BOOK OF THE SWORD, Sir Richard F. Burton. Great Victorian scholar/adventurer's eloquent, erudite history of the "queen of weapons"–from prehistory to early Roman Empire. Evolution and development of early swords, variations (sabre, broadsword, cutlass, scimitar, etc.), much more. 336pp. 6⅛ x 9¼.
25434-8 Pa. $9.95

AUTOBIOGRAPHY: The Story of My Experiments with Truth, Mohandas K. Gandhi. Boyhood, legal studies, purification, the growth of the Satyagraha (nonviolent protest) movement. Critical, inspiring work of the man responsible for the freedom of India. 480pp. 5⅜ x 8½. (USO)   24593-4 Pa. $8.95

CELTIC MYTHS AND LEGENDS, T. W. Rolleston. Masterful retelling of Irish and Welsh stories and tales. Cuchulain, King Arthur, Deirdre, the Grail, many more. First paperback edition. 58 full-page illustrations. 512pp. 5⅜ x 8½.   26507-2 Pa. $9.95

THE PRINCIPLES OF PSYCHOLOGY, William James. Famous long course complete, unabridged. Stream of thought, time perception, memory, experimental methods; great work decades ahead of its time. 94 figures. 1,391pp. 5⅜ x 8½. 2-vol. set.
Vol. I: 20381-6 Pa. $13.95
Vol. II: 20382-4 Pa. $14.95

THE WORLD AS WILL AND REPRESENTATION, Arthur Schopenhauer. Definitive English translation of Schopenhauer's life work, correcting more than 1,000 errors, omissions in earlier translations. Translated by E. F. J. Payne. Total of 1,269pp. 5⅜ x 8½. 2-vol. set.
Vol. 1: 21761-2 Pa. $12.95
Vol. 2: 21762-0 Pa. $12.95

MAGIC AND MYSTERY IN TIBET, Madame Alexandra David-Neel. Experiences among lamas, magicians, sages, sorcerers, Bonpa wizards. A true psychic discovery. 32 illustrations. 321pp. 5⅜ x 8½. (USO)   22682-4 Pa. $9.95

THE EGYPTIAN BOOK OF THE DEAD, E. A. Wallis Budge. Complete reproduction of Ani's papyrus, finest ever found. Full hieroglyphic text, interlinear transliteration, word-for-word translation, smooth translation. 533pp. 6½ x 9¼.
21866-X Pa. $11.95

MATHEMATICS FOR THE NONMATHEMATICIAN, Morris Kline. Detailed, college-level treatment of mathematics in cultural and historical context, with numerous exercises. Recommended Reading Lists. Tables. Numerous figures. 641pp. 5⅜ x 8½.
24823-2 Pa. $11.95

THEORY OF WING SECTIONS: Including a Summary of Airfoil Data, Ira H. Abbott and A. E. von Doenhoff. Concise compilation of subsonic aerodynamic characteristics of NACA wing sections, plus description of theory. 350pp. of tables. 693pp. 5⅜ x 8½.   60586-8 Pa. $14.95

THE RIME OF THE ANCIENT MARINER, Gustave Doré, S. T. Coleridge. Doré's finest work; 34 plates capture moods, subtleties of poem. Flawless full-size reproductions printed on facing pages with authoritative text of poem. "Beautiful. Simply beautiful."–Publisher's Weekly. 77pp. 9¼ x 12.   22305-1 Pa. $7.95

NORTH AMERICAN INDIAN DESIGNS FOR ARTISTS AND CRAFTSPEOPLE, Eva Wilson. Over 360 authentic copyright-free designs adapted from Navajo blankets, Hopi pottery, Sioux buffalo hides, more. Geometrics, symbolic figures, plant and animal motifs, etc. 128pp. 8⅜ x 11. (EUK)   25341-4 Pa. $8.95

SCULPTURE: Principles and Practice, Louis Slobodkin. Step-by-step approach to clay, plaster, metals, stone; classical and modern. 253 drawings, photos. 255pp. 8⅛ x 11.
22960-2 Pa. $11.95

THE INFLUENCE OF SEA POWER UPON HISTORY, 1660–1783, A. T. Mahan. Influential classic of naval history and tactics still used as text in war colleges. First paperback edition. 4 maps. 24 battle plans. 640pp. 5⅜ x 8½. 25509-3 Pa. $14.95

THE STORY OF THE TITANIC AS TOLD BY ITS SURVIVORS, Jack Winocour (ed.). What it was really like. Panic, despair, shocking inefficiency, and a little heroism. More thrilling than any fictional account. 26 illustrations. 320pp. 5⅜ x 8½. 20610-6 Pa. $8.95

FAIRY AND FOLK TALES OF THE IRISH PEASANTRY, William Butler Yeats (ed.). Treasury of 64 tales from the twilight world of Celtic myth and legend: "The Soul Cages," "The Kildare Pooka," "King O'Toole and his Goose," many more. Introduction and Notes by W. B. Yeats. 352pp. 5⅜ x 8½. 26941-8 Pa. $8.95

BUDDHIST MAHAYANA TEXTS, E. B. Cowell and Others (eds.). Superb, accurate translations of basic documents in Mahayana Buddhism, highly important in history of religions. The Buddha-karita of Asvaghosha, Larger Sukhavativyuha, more. 448pp. 5⅜ x 8½. 25552-2 Pa. $12.95

ONE TWO THREE . . . INFINITY: Facts and Speculations of Science, George Gamow. Great physicist's fascinating, readable overview of contemporary science: number theory, relativity, fourth dimension, entropy, genes, atomic structure, much more. 128 illustrations. Index. 352pp. 5⅜ x 8½. 25664-2 Pa. $8.95

ENGINEERING IN HISTORY, Richard Shelton Kirby, et al. Broad, nontechnical survey of history's major technological advances: birth of Greek science, industrial revolution, electricity and applied science, 20th-century automation, much more. 181 illustrations. ". . . excellent . . ."–*Isis.* Bibliography. vii + 530pp. 5⅝ x 8¼. 26412-2 Pa. $14.95

DALÍ ON MODERN ART: The Cuckolds of Antiquated Modern Art, Salvador Dalí. Influential painter skewers modern art and its practitioners. Outrageous evaluations of Picasso, Cézanne, Turner, more. 15 renderings of paintings discussed. 44 calligraphic decorations by Dalí. 96pp. 5⅜ x 8½. (USO) 29220-7 Pa. $4.95

ANTIQUE PLAYING CARDS: A Pictorial History, Henry René D'Allemagne. Over 900 elaborate, decorative images from rare playing cards (14th–20th centuries): Bacchus, death, dancing dogs, hunting scenes, royal coats of arms, players cheating, much more. 96pp. 9¼ x 12¼. 29265-7 Pa. $12.95

MAKING FURNITURE MASTERPIECES: 30 Projects with Measured Drawings, Franklin H. Gottshall. Step-by-step instructions, illustrations for constructing handsome, useful pieces, among them a Sheraton desk, Chippendale chair, Spanish desk, Queen Anne table and a William and Mary dressing mirror. 224pp. 8⅛ x 11¼. 29338-6 Pa. $13.95

THE FOSSIL BOOK: A Record of Prehistoric Life, Patricia V. Rich et al. Profusely illustrated definitive guide covers everything from single-celled organisms and dinosaurs to birds and mammals and the interplay between climate and man. Over 1,500 illustrations. 760pp. 7½ x 10⅛. 29371-8 Pa. $29.95

Prices subject to change without notice.

Available at your book dealer or write for free catalog to Dept. GI, Dover Publications, Inc., 31 East 2nd St., Mineola, N.Y. 11501. Dover publishes more than 500 books each year on science, elementary and advanced mathematics, biology, music, art, literary history, social sciences and other areas.